HUMAN RESOURCE MANAGEMENT

AN EXPERIENTIAL APPROACH

McGRAW-HILL SERIES IN MANAGEMENT

Consulting Editors
Fred Luthans
Keith Davis

Also Available from McGraw-Hill

SCHAUM'S OUTLINE SERIES IN ACCOUNTING, BUSINESS, & ECONOMICS

Most outlines include basic theory, definitions, and hundreds of solved problems and supplementary problems with answers.

Titles on the Current List Include:

Accounting I, 3d edition
Accounting II, 3d edition
Advanced Accounting
Advanced Business Law
Bookkeeping & Accounting, 2d edition
Business Law
Business Mathematics
Business Statistics, 2d edition
College Business Law
Contemporary Mathematics of Finance
Cost Accounting I, 2d edition
Cost Accounting II
Development Economics
Financial Accounting
Intermediate Accounting I, 2d edition
Intermediate Accounting II
International Economics, 3d edition
Introduction to Mathematical Economics, 2d edition
Investments
Macroeconomic Theory, 2d edition
Managerial Accounting
Managerial Economics
Managerial Finance
Mathematical Methods for Business & Economics
Mathematics of Finance
Microeconomic Theory, 3d edition
Money and Banking
Operations Management
Personal Finance
Principles of Economics
Statistics and Econometrics

Available at your College Bookstore. A complete listing of Schaum titles may be obtained by writing to:
Schaum Division, McGraw-Hill, Inc., Princeton Road, S-1, Hightstown, NJ 08520.

HUMAN RESOURCE MANAGEMENT

AN EXPERIENTIAL APPROACH

H. JOHN BERNARDIN

Department of Management and International Business
Florida Atlantic University

JOYCE E. A. RUSSELL

Department of Management
The University of Tennessee

McGraw-Hill, Inc.
New York   St. Louis   San Francisco   Auckland   Bogotá   Caracas
Lisbon   London   Madrid   Mexico   Milan   Montreal   New Delhi
Paris   San Juan   Singapore   Sydney   Tokyo   Toronto

HUMAN RESOURCE MANAGEMENT
An Experiential Approach

6 7 8 9 0 SEM SEM 9 0 9 8 7 6

ISBN 0-07-004916-5

This book was set in Times Roman by Beacon Graphics
Corporation.
The editors were Lynn Richardson and Dan Alpert;
the designer was Karen K. Quigley;
the production supervisor was Louise Karam.
Project supervision was done by The Total Book.
Semline, Inc., was printer and binder.

Library of Congress Cataloging-in-Publication Data

Bernardin, H. John.
    Human resource management: an experiential approach / H. John
Bernardin, Joyce E. A. Russell.
        p.   cm.—(McGraw-Hill series in management.)
    Includes bibliographical references and index.
    ISBN 0-07-004916-5
    1. Personnel management—United States.   I. Russell, Joyce E. A.
II. Title.   III. Series
HF5549.2.U5B456   1993
658.3—dc20   92-28999

ABOUT
THE
AUTHORS

H. John Bernardin is University Professor of Research in the College of Business at Florida Atlantic University. He earned his Ph.D. in Industrial and Organizational Psychology from Bowling Green State University in 1975. Professor Bernardin is the coeditor of the *Human Resource Management Review* and has had editorial board appointments on the *Academy of Management Review, Human Resource Planning,* and *Human Resources Management.* He has authored or edited four books and published over 100 articles. He has consulted for numerous organizations and served as an expert witness in many employment discrimination cases. Dr. Bernardin is the former chair of the Division of Personnel/Human Resources of the National Academy of Management.

Joyce E. A. Russell is an Associate Professor of Management at The University of Tennessee. She earned her Ph.D. in Industrial and Organizational Psychology from The University of Akron in 1982. Dr. Russell serves on the editorial board of the *Journal of Vocational Behavior* and the Executive Committee of the Academy of Management's Women in Management Division. She has served as Co-Chair of the Southeastern Industrial & Organizational Psychology Association, and on the Board of Directors of the American Society of Training and Development, Smoky Mountain Chapter. She has published over 30 articles, book chapters, or reviews. She has provided human resource management consulting to a number of public and private sector organizations.

JB dedicates the book to Kathleen who has (and will) overcome all obstacles and whose lurf and inspiration saw me through the rough spots.

JEAR dedicates the book to Michael who brightens up my every day and helps us experience the really important things—he is truly cherished.

CONTENTS

PREFACE

This text differs from other human resource management (HRM) texts in providing theoretical and experiential approaches to the study of HRM while focusing on the enhancement of student personal competencies. Students are given the conceptual background and content necessary to understand the relevant issues in HRM. In addition, they will participate in individual and group exercises which require the application of chapter content to specific problems designed to develop critical personal competencies.

Our book is the first attempt to directly link student learning experiences in HRM with assessed competencies judged by experts to be essential for graduating business students. As we discuss in Chapter 1, recent studies have been critical of the readiness of business graduates for work, noting deficiencies in a number of areas, including communication skills, analytical thinking, decision-making ability, and leadership potential. While other experiential texts are available, this is the first to attempt to provide adequate coverage of the subject matter in each of the vital areas of HRM while preparing the student to "learn by doing." This is also the first attempt among HRM texts to provide a research-based methodology for the assessment of the critical competencies and to provide a process by which students may evaluate the extent to which they have improved their competencies as they progress through the course.

All the experiential exercises in this book were designed to enhance some or all of the critical personal competencies in the context of HRM subject matter. We introduce the student to these competencies in the first chapter and attempt to develop them all the way through the text. To do so, we use participation in experiential exercises requiring the application of the HRM knowledge expected of practicing managers. The experiential exercises were developed so as to facilitate greater learning through class interaction and projects. There is usually an individual writing component to the exercise followed by group interaction and consensus building. A 1991 study by Dr. Richard Light at Harvard University found that this approach to undergraduate education is superior to the standard straight lecture approach.

Successful completion of these field-tested exercises, combined with the assessment processes described in Appendix B, should foster student development in all the areas experts believe to be critical in preparing business students for their first "real jobs."

Studies show that the majority of business graduates will ultimately manage or supervise employees. Research in this area shows that the two areas which prove to be the most troublesome and crucial for managers are performance management and dealing with an increasingly diverse workforce (e.g., equal employment opportunity). Our objective with this book is to emphasize knowledge and direct experience in these areas without compromising treatment of the other domains of HRM. Procedures are available in this text to require students to evaluate their own performance and that of peer group members after completion of most of the experiential exercises. Research also shows that the more experience a person has had with the performance management process, the more effective that individual is in fulfilling this important managerial responsibility.

We have incorporated exercises and discussion questions throughout the text which require the student to consider equal employment opportunity laws in particular HRM contexts. So, unlike the standard HRM text which covers EEO in one chapter, this book compels the student to weigh the EEO implications of HRM activities such as job analysis (Chapter 4), downsizing programs (Chapter 5), personnel selection processes (Chapters 6 and 7), employee training and development (Chapter 8), performance appraisal (Chapter 10), compensation (Chapters 11 and 12), and other major HRM activities. We have devoted considerable discussion to the implications of the new Civil Rights Act of 1991 and the Americans with Disabilities Act of 1990, two laws which will have a profound influence on personnel practices.

We do not shy away from any of the significant, yet controversial issues of the day. For example, among the controversial topics we cover and for which we have experiential exercises are ethnic score differences on employee screening devices, affirmative action programs, sexual harassment, employment-at-will, random drug testing with no probable cause, smoking in the workplace, executive compensation, employee assistance programs, and equal pay for work of comparable worth.

Another distinctive feature of this book is our enlisting the assistance of a number of experts in the HRM field for contributions to particular areas of HRM. This was done to ensure that the material was current, and focused on the most important, up-to-date issues. The book is carefully integrated: we worked hard to establish theme and reading continuity across the chapters. Our experts were selected on the basis of their experience, knowledge, and research accomplishments in a particular area of HRM and/or their experience with well-tested, experiential exercises which foster learning in a critical HRM content area. Since HRM is strongly influenced by a number of disciplines (e.g., law, economics, psychology, sociology, strategic management), we sought out expertise to represent these varied orientations. We believe the finished product represents a broader perspective than a book prepared by authors from only one of those disciplines.

A few other distinguishing features of this text should also be noted. First, international issues are discussed in most chapters to illustrate both the special and common characteristics of international HRM. Given today's competitive global marketplace, HR professionals need increasingly to understand international strategies if they are to provide meaningful assistance to their firms. We have also devoted separate chapters to the issues of "quality" and competitive HRM advantage. Interwoven in each chapter of the book is an underlying theme of improving quality and increasing competitive advantage with more effective HRM practices.

We have also included an appendix devoted to measurement issues related to HRM. Appendix A is available to those instructors who wish to emphasize quantitative assessments of HRM practices and estimating the financial value (i.e., utility) of various HRM activities. The appendix also includes two exercises designed to enhance understanding of critical measurement issues related to HRM.

ACKNOWLEDGMENTS

A number of people have made valuable contributions to this book. First, we would like to thank the various editors and staff members with whom we have worked at McGraw-Hill, including Kathy Loy, Eileen Gualberto, Dan Alpert, Alan Sachs, Lynn Richardson, and Kate Scheinman. We would also like to acknowledge the many reviewers from various universities and colleges who provided helpful comments and suggestions: Debra A. Arvanites, Villanova University; Dan Braunstein, Oakland University; Robert L. Cardy, Arizona State University; Herschel N. Chait, Indiana State University; Joan G. Dahl, California State University, Northridge; Randy L. DeSimone, Rhode Island College; William L. Eslin, Glassboro State College; Nancy Johnson, University of Kentucky; Katherine Karl, Western Michigan University; John F. P. Konarski, Florida International University; Jacqueline Landau, Suffolk University; Robert M. Madigan, Virginia Polytechnic Institute; Herff L. Moore, University of Central Arkansas; James S. Russell, Lewis

and Clark College; Janet Stern Solomon, Towson State University; Lee Stepina, Florida State University, Charles M. Vance, Loyola Marymount University; Richard A. Wald, Eastern Washington University; Elizabeth C. Wesman, Syracuse University; Kenneth M. York, Oakland University; and Mary D. Zalesny, University of Missouri–St. Louis.

Contributors of chapters or portions of chapters were: David O. Ulrich, Barbara A. Lee, Scott A. Snell, Monica Favia, Michael M. Harris, Barbara K. Brown, Joan E. Pynes, P. Christopher Earley, Diana Deadrick, Philip J. Decker, Barry R. Nathan, Jeffrey S. Kane, Kimberly F. Kane, Lee P. Stepina, James R. Harris, Alan Cabelly, E. Brian Peach, M. Ronald Buckley, Nancy Brown Johnson, Roger L. Cole, Harriette S. McCaul, Fred E. Schuster, Marion Schubinski, Thomas Becker, and Marcia Avedon. Contributors of experiential exercises were: Sue A. Dahmus, Jeffrey D. Kudisch, Marilyn A. Perkins, Jarold Abbott, Gregory Redmon, Joan E. Pynes, Peter Villanova, M. Ronald Buckley, Robert W. Eder, J. R. Biddle, Patrick Wright, James A. Breaugh, Barbara Hassell, Lee P. Stepina, James R. Harris, Jeffrey S. Kane, Kimberly F. Kane, Roger L. Cole, Scott A. Snell, Ann M. Herd, Larry A. Pace, Caroline C. Wilhelm, Sheila Kennelly-McGinnis, Stephanie D. Myers, Paul Guglielmino, Lucy Guglielmino, Fred E. Schuster, E. Brian Peach, and Nancy Brown Johnson.

Many colleagues provided enormous assistance—by contributing their comments on earlier drafts, reviewing exercises, or furnishing extensive reference materials. We truly appreciate the efforts of Lynn B. Curtis, Laura A. Davenport, Aaron T. Fausz, Jeffrey D. Kudisch, Ann Rigell, Michael C. Rush, Kimberly Frank, Kathy Schmidt, Tammy A. Sitver, Peggy Kennedy, Robert Guthman, Gregory Redmon, and Liesa Bernardin. We would also like to thank our departments for their assistance during these difficult budget times. Special thanks go to Oscar S. Fowler and to the staff (Carolyn, June, Jackie, Maggie) at the Management Department at The University of Tennessee and to Dean Stanley Hille and Fred Schuster, College of Business at Florida Atlantic University. Isabel Miller, Carol Annunziato, Connie Brown, and Sherry Rosenstein provided impeccable clerical assistance on Professor Bernardin's behalf.

We would also like to express our deepest appreciation to our families for their support, encouragement, and patience throughout this entire process. Thanks to Michael, Gerri, Bruce, Colleen, Kathy, Chuck, Suzanne, Brian, Kitty, Manny, Rosie, Kathleen, Liesa, Maxine, and Loudie. Special thanks to Liesa Bernardin for her fine work on the indexes.

H. John Bernardin
Joyce E. A. Russell

C H A P T E R

HUMAN RESOURCE MANAGEMENT IN A CHANGING ENVIRONMENT

OVERVIEW

Human resource management (HRM) concerns the recruitment, selection, development, compensation, retention, evaluation, and promotion of personnel within an organization. The human resources (HR) of an organization consist of all people who perform its activities. In a sense, all decisions which affect the workforce concern the organization's HRM function. Regardless of the size (or existence) of a formal HRM or personnel department, the activities involved in HRM are pervasive throughout the organization.

A goal of this book will be to provide information and experiences to be used in ultimately improving the effectiveness of HRM activities in which the student will be involved in the future. Our thesis is that the most effective HRM programs, policies, and practices are those which are established, maintained, and improved with the organization's mission and strategic plan in mind, and in particular, with total customer satisfaction as the ultimate goal.

It is also our view that this is not how HRM is typically carried out in U.S. organizations. HRM activities are sometimes faddish and disjointed, with little consideration of the organization's mission or goals. Many HRM activities are directed at correcting a problem rather than anticipating and planning to avoid problems in the future. Programs are often initiated as a result of a serious personnel problem such as a lawsuit or to keep up with what a competitor is doing. For example, Southeast Bank in Florida implemented an expensive computer-based managerial training program simply because a major competitor used the program. No attempt was made either to assess the actual need for the training or to assess the effects of the training in terms of service quality or customer satisfaction. Often, there is limited integration among the various HRM activities such as personnel selection, training, and performance appraisal. IBM is often cited as a paragon of HRM effectiveness. One division, however, installed personal computers in its Burlington, Vermont, factories only to discover that the factory workers required training in high school algebra in order to run them.[1] Most organizations do not assess the long-term consequences of their HRM programs or activities. One large department store chain used the same psychological test to hire sales personnel for over 8 years. At no time was an attempt made to assess whether the test actually worked (it didn't). Many U.S. companies now use graphology, or handwriting analysis, to assess personnel potential, despite the fact that no study has ever determined the method to be predictive of anything important. In a year in which the company lost $3 billion, its stock price dropped to a four-year low, unit sales per salaried employee plummeted, and more market share was lost to the Japanese, GM awarded 80 percent of its managers a performance bonus and dismissed fewer than 100 (of over 100,000) salaried workers for poor performance.

Some organizations, however, look at the HRM function as a major contributor to the accomplishment of the organization's mission and a source of competitive advantage. We believe this new conceptualization is essential for American business as we head toward the twenty-first century. In *Megatrends 2000*, John Naisbitt and Patricia Aburdene place heavy emphasis on the role of HRM in preparing America for the millennium. "It will require a tremendous human resource effort to transform corporate America into the decentralized, customer-oriented model of the information society. Yet that is what is needed for the United States to fully participate in the blooming global economy. With new markets, with a single-market Europe, and with new competitors from Asian countries, corporations need people who can think critically, plan strategically, and adapt to change."[2]

OBJECTIVES

After studying this chapter, you should be able to:

1. Describe the field of HRM and the increasing importance of HRM.
2. Explain the trends relevant to the growing importance of HRM, including the U.S. productivity crisis, greater global competition, the increasing role of regulations and lawsuits, and the changing demographics of the workforce.
3. Describe the major activities performed by HRM professionals in the context of six domains.
4. Discuss the role of employee involvement in designing and implementing effective HRM programs in the context of the critical HRM constituencies.

The chief executive officer (CEO) of a medium-sized manufacturing company once confided that, not too long ago, the major responsibility of the personnel director was to organize the annual company picnic. The executive claimed that the personnel officer always carried the watermelon. While this is obviously an exaggeration, it is certainly true that personnel officers, in the words of Rodney Dangerfield, "got no respect." One personnel manager even referred to the personnel department as "the dumping ground for people who couldn't hack it in operations...people basically failed their way into personnel." Essentially, the role was viewed as clerical in nature, with the personnel department overseeing basic tasks such as record keeping, compliance with a myriad of regulations, and payroll.

The good news, however, is that the status of HRM activities is improving in the United States. One 1989 survey found that HR programs are now much more closely tied to business plans than they were in 1983.[3] The HRM function is becoming more professional, due to the higher educational and skill levels of HRM practitioners. In addition, the personnel function has been given a new name, "human resources," and bigger budgets have been allocated for HRM activities. Responsibilities have also been expanded, and greater prestige has been associated with the position. A 1988 survey of corporate CEOs found that the majority of top HRM executives now report *directly* to the CEO and that 43 percent of Fortune 500 firms assigned the top HR professional to a vice-president position.[4]

In general, senior management is slowly coming to realize that, like the financial and operations side of the company, employees should be viewed as a "resource" or "social capital." Although there is an initial investment in the form of employee recruiting and training costs, it is apparent that the investment can ultimately yield a positive return over time, with the proper care and maintenance. In fact, there is a growing realization that HRM activities have a great deal to do with productivity and related product and service quality. Companies are now more fully recognizing that their workforce can be their greatest strength. Merck, the pharmaceutical giant, earned the top spot among 307 companies in *Fortune* magazine's 1992 Corporate Reputations survey of over 8000 senior executives, the sixth year in a row for the honor. Merck credits their remarkable record to "attracting, developing, and keeping good people."[5] Many of the other most-admired companies, such as Liz Claiborne, Wal-Mart, Levi Strauss, and Johnson & Johnson, attribute their success to their human resources.

Training and preparation for HRM professionals have improved dramatically in recent years. Salaries for jobs in the HRM area have increased and are now competitive with those in accounting, finance, and marketing. The profession is also attracting more innovative, creative, and career-oriented professionals. An increasing percentage of business undergraduates are selecting HR as a major, and HRM is a popular M.B.A. specialization. Most important, a growing portion of senior management now recognizes that HRM is critical for organizational effectiveness and can provide advantages in an increasingly competitive environment. Greater demands are being made on HRM professionals. Today, the HRM function must be conceptualized in a business capacity which is constantly focused on the strategy of the organization. That is, HR professionals must increasingly illustrate how they can make a difference in the company's bottom line. As suggested by James G. Parkel, director of personnel for IBM, "Today, HRM professionals are much more concerned with business management functions, government relations and international issues—issues beyond human resources. . . . HR professionals will be judged on their ability to be innovative and cost-effective, along with their ability to get the job done in conjunction with line management."[6]

TRENDS RELATED TO THE INCREASED IMPORTANCE OF HRM

There are a number of reasons for the increased attention being given to HR by senior-level management. Most experts cite declining U.S. productivity and an increasingly competitive work environment as the two most significant trends that have expanded the role and importance of the HRM function in organizations. Other contributors to the increased attention to HRM have been increased laws and regulations; the proliferation of lawsuits related to HR; changes in workforce characteristics; and a poor fit between workforce knowledge, skills, and abilities and job requirements. We will discuss each of these trends below.

The U.S. Productivity Crisis

The most important reason for the increased interest in HRM is the perceived connection between HRM activities and claims of a productivity crisis in the United States and the related indictment of the quality of U.S. products and services. A sizable portion of corporate America has come to the realization that the United States has a serious productivity and quality problem which requires immediate attention. A smaller but growing percentage of managers recognizes the importance of HR in dealing with the problem.

One review on the subject of American productivity and what we can do about it concludes that "U.S. competitiveness has seriously eroded, the international competitive challenges are far stronger than most people realize, the U.S. response is inadequate to meet the challenges, and not only can the United States lose its world leadership, but at the moment it is losing."[7] While there are others who are less pessimistic, there is no expert on the subject who considers the productivity levels of the United States in recent years to be superior to or even on a par with those of its major international competitive rivals (Japan, Korea, Germany, and France). The prospects for the future are rather bleak. After an exhaustive 1992 examination of U.S. competitiveness in 13 industries, *Fortune* magazine concluded that "the pain endured by American industry in the 1980's has yet to translate into major gains, either in market share or in relative competitiveness. . . . American companies continue to lose ground in many markets that promise the fastest growth—and biggest profits—over the next decade."[8] The United States gets "A" grades in only two industries (pharmaceuticals and forest products) and "C" grades or worse in five industries, including computers, motor vehicles, and electronics.

A team of leading scientists, engineers, and economists from the Massachusetts Institute of Technology (MIT) concluded their comprehensive review of American productivity with the following ominous statement: "Relative to other nations and relative to its own history, America does indeed have a serious productivity problem.... It is manifested by sluggish productivity growth and by shortcomings in the quality and innovativeness of the national products.[9] The productivity figures are hard to dispute. Based on a trend analysis begun in 1973, one projection has the United States ranked behind Japan, Belgium, Germany, Norway, France, and Canada in productivity by the year 2000.[10] Figure 1.1 summarizes a number of facts which do not bode well for twenty-first century America. While the United States is still No. 1 on most statistical indicators of productivity, our lead is quickly evaporating.

Experts maintain that the best measure of where a country is going is the productivity growth rate which measures the change in productivity. For example, for the years 1973–1990, the U.S. growth rate was 1.5 percent. During the same period, Germany's rate of growth was 3.1 percent. While there has been improvement in the most recent years, particularly in manufacturing, even the most optimistic growth rates for the United States do not compare favorably with those of most nations that provided comparable data. One of the most startling statistics is that U.S. productivity trends are below average, as compared to our 10 most significant foreign competitors. In fact, the most recent data comparing U.S. manufacturing productivity to Japan's places the United States at only 55 percent of the Japanese rate.[11]

Even more troubling are productivity data from the service economy. In the United States, services represent 75 percent of the workforce and close to 70 percent of the gross national product.[12] Nine out of every ten new jobs are predicted to be in the services sector in the next 20 years. Yet the productivity figures are very disturbing since they reflect a stagnant or even decreasing rate of productivity for the services industry. In addition, there is little indication that the trend can be reversed. While the U.S. productivity level is still the highest in the world, the lead is diminishing.

THE IMPORTANCE OF PRODUCTIVITY DATA.

But why are productivity figures so important? Aren't other measures related to the economy more important?

FIGURE 1.1
SOME DISTURBING FACTS ABOUT THE UNITED STATES

The United States is the world's largest debtor nation.

Total U.S. debt exceeds $7 trillion.

Foreign debt will exceed $700 billion by 1995.

The world's seven largest banks are all Japanese.

Productivity in U.S. services industry is about zero since 1980.

By the year 2000, the United States will rank No. 6 in productivity level for developed nations.

The United States ranks last in productivity growth for the last 10 years.

Median incomes in the United States were 8 percent lower in 1986 than they were in 1973.

Hourly earnings per worker in 1986 were equivalent to 1969 figures.

Seven out of ten high-technology U.S. industries have lost market share since 1965.

Japan graduates (per capita) twice as many engineers as does the United States.

Non-U.S. citizens hold nearly 50 percent of U.S. patents.

The United States holds the world record for trade deficits.

The United States consistently finishes near the bottom in student international competition in math and science.

The U.S. high school dropout rate is 25 percent and climbing.

Some studies put the U.S. functional illiteracy rate at 30 percent and climbing.

Japan's trade surplus with the United States was $41 billion in 1990.

Source: Adapted with the permission of The Free Press, a Division of Macmillan, Inc. From *American business: A two-minute warning* by C. Jackson Grayson and Carla O'Dell. Copyright © 1987 by The Free Press.

According to historian Angus Maddison, the rise and fall of nations throughout history can be traced to levels of productivity. He likens current trends in U.S. productivity to those of nineteenth-century England.[13] Another historian describes "the U.S. as an aging economy, increasingly arteriosclerotic, slower to adapt, to respond, to innovate, fits the broad picture.... In this process the country is following the path of many others, of which Britain is only the most recent.... Productivity is the major correlate of a nation's standard of living and the best measure of economic performance.... History shows that the nation that is the productivity leader eventually becomes the dominant world leader—economically, militarily, and politically."[14]

EXPLANATIONS FOR THE U.S. PRODUCTIV-ITY RATE. So how did the United States get into the shape it is in? There have been a host of theories offered, ranging from macroeconomic perspectives dealing with the economy, industry, governmental regulations, and labor force characteristics to microeconomic perspectives dealing with issues facing organizations, management, unions, and employees. Figure 1.2 presents a summary of the possible causes.

Without question, macroeconomic variables such as the cost of capital, energy costs, or inflation can affect productivity. Some experts contend that the federal government has fostered inflation through policies that allow large deficits and cost-of-living adjustments to contracts and entitlements. The inflation has affected capital investment in new plants, equipment, and research and development. The fact is that many U.S. plants in heavy industry (e.g., autos, steel) are now simply inferior to European and Japanese plants. Others maintain that compliance with regulations and the epidemic of lawsuits are main culprits. Related to this is the social state of the nation. As one bad statistician recently put it, "There are now more lawyers in the United States than people." Some decry employee theft and the increased crime and violence in this country. One of the most popular theories to explain the productivity decline is the failure to

FIGURE 1.2
POSSIBLE CAUSES OF U.S. PRODUCTIVITY PROBLEMS

MACRO ISSUES	MICRO ISSUES
Economical	**Organizational**
High tax rates	Obsolete plants
Low savings and investment	Obsolete machines
Excessive regulation	Insufficient plants/machines
Inflation	Inadequate R&D
Fluctuating economy	
Excessive defense spending	**Management**
Energy prices	Short-term focus
Materials shortages	Inattention to operations
Protection, quotas	Inattention to quality
Subsidies to inefficiency	Overstaffing
Government too high a percentage of GNP	Excessive analytic management
	Excessive specialization of workers
	Inattention to human factors
Industry	Excessive attention to legal issues
Insufficient research and development (R&D)	Insufficient attention to mergers
Restrictive antitrust regulations	Insufficient personnel training
	Excessive executive pay
	Resistance to change
Governmental regulations	Decline in risk taking
Bureaucratic delays	Adversarial attitude toward unions
Government paperwork	
Government waste	
Low government productivity	**Unions**
	Excessive work restrictions
Labor force characteristics	Featherbedding (getting paid for special
Low education standards	services not performed)
Illiteracy rate	Rigid job classifications
Adversial relations with private sector	Adversarial attitudes to management
Poor work ethic	Pay greater than productivity
Shifts to service sector	Output deliberately kept low
High crime rates	
Shifts in worker values and attitudes	**Employees**
Focus on self	Preference for leisure time
Psychology of entitlement	Resistance to change
Litigious society	No pride in workmanship
High employee theft	Abuse of alcohol and drugs
	Inexperience
	Poor work ethic

Source: Modified from R.H. Hayes and S.C. Wheelwright. *Restoring our competitive edge.* New York: John Wiley & Sons, 1984, p. 393. Copyright © 1984 by John Wiley & Sons. Reprinted by permission of John Wiley & Sons, Inc.

recognize the role of people in the productivity ratio. The business world and management have been preoccupied with short-term variables such as "return on investment," "cost per unit," and "earnings per share." Only a few companies carefully weigh the role of workers and their potentiality for providing more and higher-quality products and services. This failure to perceive a strong connection between the "human dimension" and productivity is changing, albeit slowly. There are now many examples of how a new management team took over a business in a sorry state and in a short time, and with the same and perhaps fewer line personnel, turned the company around. Unfortunately, many of these stories involve Japanese management taking over a U.S. company.

THE ROLE OF HRM IN IMPROVING PRODUCTIVITY AND PRODUCT AND SERVICE QUALITY. Many notable commentators on the state of U.S. productivity urge American managers to look closely at the role HR can play in reviving the stagnant productivity levels. C. Jackson Grayson, head of the American Productivity Center in Houston, Texas, proposes an "agenda for adjustment" in which companies have "a constant improvement mind-set, automating, simplifying their structures, increasing employee involvement in real business issues, tying pay to performance, and improving quality." Grayson is quick to point out that, unfortunately, only a small number of firms are implementing the changes which are necessary. "The majority of American firms are not responding at all, doing very little, or engaging in a flurry of activity, much of it short-term cost reduction, layoffs, slam-bang automation, and closings of inefficient operations. . . . such efforts give the appearance of adjustment but have not changed the core way firms do business." Regarding the role of human resources in productivity, the study concludes that "human resources get a little more notice from senior management, but compared to the attention given to financial, legal, and marketing strategies, people strategies—including employee involvement, man-machine operating systems, and rewards—are still hind dog."[15]

This perception of the role of HRM appears to be changing rapidly. One illustration of the increased importance being placed on HR is the weight given to HR activities in the process of evaluating companies for quality products and service. Florida Power & Light was the first U.S. company to be given the Deming Award, a prestigious recognition of quality improvement presented in Japan annually since 1951 and named after W. Edwards Deming, an American consultant to industry. Many of the criteria for this award focus on HR activities directed at quality improvement. Florida Power & Light stressed employee involvement and performance management systems as critical to its quality improvement. Employee involvement programs and performance management systems are two important components of HRM.

The Malcolm Baldrige National Quality Awards, U.S. presidential citations given to companies that show the greatest progress in improving the quality of their products, service, and customer satisfaction, also place substantial weight on the role of HR activities in achieving quality and consumer satisfaction.[16] Figure 1.3 describes the purposes and objectives of the award. Although the award was established by Congress only in 1987, experts in product and service quality maintain that its growing prestige and recognition are already having an impact upon U.S. businesses that goes far beyond the relatively small number of companies which have actually applied for or won the award. The director of the program, for example, reported that over 210,000 copies of the very detailed application forms were mailed out in 1991 alone.

The application form presents a process through which companies can conduct a thorough self-examination in seven general categories: leadership, information and analysis, strategic quality planning, HR utilization, quality assurance of products and services, quality results, and customer satisfaction. Most of the companies which requested an application did not actually apply for the award but rather wanted to use the application as a means of self-assessment and an outline for change. The seven categories are further broken down into 33 subcategories, each weighted with a number of points totaling 1000. For example, a maximum of 40 points is given to a subcategory dealing with employee involvement which asks the applicants to describe the means available for all employees to contribute effectively to the company's quality objectives. Several other of the 33 subcategories deal directly with HRM activities (e.g., performance management, compensation, recognition programs, training and development). Federal Express, a 1990 winner for quality service, received maximum points for the clear linkage it has established between its primary measure of quality service and its performance management and compensation systems. Its Baldrige citation noted that management bonuses are directly tied to performance of the whole organization in meeting performance goals. Bonuses are suspended if employees do not rate management leadership at least as high as the previous year in an annual survey. The Zytec Corporation, a Minnesota electronics manufacturer which won the award in 1991, was also cited for its worker involvement processes, which included a formal employee survey system.

Cadillac Motor Division, a 1990 Baldrige winner in the manufacturing class, cited a number of HRM activities directed at warranty-related costs, the company's primary quality measure. The 29 percent decrease in warranty costs was linked to numerous HRM activities.

FIGURE 1.3
PURPOSES AND OBJECTIVES OF THE MALCOLM BALDRIGE AWARD

THE MALCOLM BALDRIGE NATIONAL QUALITY IMPROVEMENT ACT OF 1987 – PUBLIC LAW 100-107

The Malcolm Baldrige National Quality Award was created by Public Law 100-107, signed into law on August 20, 1987. The Award Program, responsive to the purposes of Public Law 100-107, led to the creation of a new public-private partnership. Principal support for the program comes from the Foundation for the Malcolm Baldrige National Quality Award, established in 1988.

The Award is named for Malcolm Baldrige, who served as Secretary of Commerce from 1981 until his tragic death in a rodeo accident in 1987. His managerial excellence contributed to long-term improvement in efficiency and effectiveness of government.

The Findings and Purposes Section of Public Law 100-107 states that:

"1. the leadership of the United States in product and process quality has been challenged strongly (and sometimes successfully) by foreign competition, and our Nation's productivity growth has improved less than our competitors over the last two decades.

2. American business and industry are beginning to understand that poor quality costs companies as much as 20 percent of sales revenues nationally, and that improved quality of goods and services goes hand in hand with improved productivity, lower costs, and increased profitability.

3. strategic planning for quality and quality improvement programs, through a commitment to excellence in manufacturing and services, are becoming more and more essential to the well-being of our Nation's economy and our ability to compete effectively in the global marketplace.

4. improved management understanding of the factory floor, worker involvement in quality, and greater emphasis on statistical process control can lead to dramatic improvements in the cost and quality of manufactured products.

5. the concept of quality improvement is directly applicable to small companies as well as large, to service industries as well as manufacturing, and to the public sector as well as private enterprise.

6. in order to be successful, quality improvement programs must be management-led and customer-oriented and this may require fundamental changes in the way companies and agencies do business.

7. several major industrial nations have successfully coupled rigorous private sector quality audits with national awards giving special recognition to those enterprises the audits identify as the very best; and

8. a national quality award program of this kind in the United States would help improve quality and productivity by:

   A. helping to stimulate American companies to improve quality and productivity for the pride of recognition while obtaining a competitive edge through increased profits;

   B. recognizing the achievements of those companies which improve the quality of their goods and services and providing an example to others;

   C. establishing guidelines and criteria that can be used by business, industrial, governmental, and other organizations in evaluating their own quality improvement efforts, and

   D. providing specific guidance for other American organizations that wish to learn how to manage for high quality by making available detailed information on how winning organizations were able to change their cultures and achieve eminence."

At IBM-Rochester, manufacturer of a mid-range computer, changes were made in employee involvement and training programs as a result of the company's 1989 Baldrige application. The changes were among the major variables IBM linked to a 50 percent time reduction in the development of a new computer and were mentioned in the 1990 citation for the company.

We will refer to the Baldrige criteria again when we discuss particular HR activities in the chapters to follow. While too much can be made of a national award for quality products and services and increased productivity, there can be no question that the Baldrige Award has had an impact and that HRM activities are receiving more attention in the quest for improved products and services and increased productivity. A 1990 survey, for example, found an increasing number of companies using innovative HRM activities as part of quality management programs. Among the most common approaches are employee involvement programs, pay-for-performance systems, workforce planning, organizational restructuring, and sociotechnical systems (work teams).[17]

A recurring theme throughout this book is that HR policies and practices can enhance productivity, product, and service quality, and can create and sustain a competitive advantage. We will focus on those efforts which have proved most successful in meeting these goals. You will note that HR activities and practices typically focus on a small number of outcomes or criteria. The most important of these criteria are measures of individual or unit performance, productivity, or product/service quality; employee absenteeism, turnover, and accidents; aberrant employee behavior such as theft or substance abuse; and employee attitudes toward work. Research has established that the results of HRM programs which are measured in terms of these criteria can be directly linked to substantial cost savings, financial performance, and increased productivity. Let us turn to some illustrations of recent HRM activities directed at these criteria.

Frito-Lay recently instituted a training program through its HRM division to cross-train workers for several jobs in an effort to reduce downtime from employee vacancies. AMC Theatres developed a battery of applicant tests in order to identify individuals most likely to perform more effectively and to stay with the company longer. Blockbuster Video tried an applicant test which purported to help reduce employee theft, and developed a new performance management system for all employees. Owens-Corning Fiberglass trained all its managers in statistical quality analysis as a part of its Total Quality Management program. John Hancock Insurance installed a new managerial pay-for-performance system in order to increase regional sales and decrease employee turnover. J. Walter Thompson recently developed a new incentive system to promote creative advertising ideas from its consumer research and accounting units. RJR Nabisco replaced a fixed rate commission with a new compensation system for its advertisers which linked ad agency compensation to the success of the campaign.

In the past, these types of HRM interventions were rarely linked to macro productivity or cost figures in order to show a reliable financial benefit. The inability to link such HRM practices to the "bottom line" may explain why personnel departments in the past have had so little clout. While marketing departments were reporting the bottom-line impact of a new marketing strategy in terms of market share or sales volume, personnel could only show that absenteeism or turnover was reduced by some percentage. The relationship between these reductions and a specific financial benefit was rarely assessed. As Peter Drucker once said, "the constant worry of all personnel administrators is their inability to prove that they are making a contribution to the enterprise."[18]

Research in the last few years, however, has established a strong connection between many HRM programs and activities and the critical bottom-line figure. For example, specific HRM activities have been shown to be directly linked to corporate performance indicators such as return on investment and return on equity. HR researchers have developed a number of useful statistical tools which can yield reliable dollar values for virtually all HRM activities.

For example, one study of the effects of preemployment drug testing for the U.S. Postal Service showed not only a 59 percent higher rate of absenteeism for applicants who tested positive and a 47 percent higher rate of involuntary turnover, but a cost-savings estimate in excess of $4 million per year if applicants were screened using the test.[19] Another study showed a net return to a bank of more than $148,000 (over 5 years) as a function of a training program for only 65 supervisors.[20] We will present numerous other examples in subsequent chapters.

A number of popular books in management have also contributed to the increased perceived connection between HRM activities and productivity figures. For example, you will find numerous references to the importance of HRM in best-sellers such as *In Search of Excellence, A Passion for Excellence,* and *Megatrends 2000.*[21] Many schools now require a course in HRM in their degree programs. For example, Harvard University requires a course in HRM to fulfill requirements for its prestigious M.B.A. degree. Many of our nation's finest schools routinely bring business leaders from labor and management to their campuses to interact with faculty and students. These leaders invariably stress the importance of HRM activities for American competitiveness. The MIT Commission on Productivity urges the incorporation of HRM into the core curriculum of business education.[22]

Increasing International Competition and the Expanding Global Economy

While U.S. productivity figures are probably the most important reason for the increased interest in HRM, there are other important trends or environmental characteristics which may also be correlated with the greater emphasis on HRM activity. One of these trends is the increasing international competition for U.S. products and services and the expanding global economy. With the incredible international political events in recent years, the global economy and competition are expanding rapidly both in terms of new countries and new markets.

As one expert put it, "There is nothing that any American organization does that is not directly affected by developments throughout the world. The emerging technologies, the competition and the opportunities are global... All organizations, regardless of locales, soon must evaluate work force skills, costs and availability on a global basis."[23] The chances are now better than ever that you may work for a foreign corporation in your own community. For example, the majority of 1991 Hondas driven in the United States were actually manufactured in the United States. There is also a much higher probability than 10 years ago that you will work for a large American company but have an overseas assignment or that your company will have some type of joint venture with a foreign corporation. Businessland, for example, the biggest U.S. dealer in personal computers, recently moved into Japan with the help of four of Japan's biggest electronics firms.[24] All of these scenarios obviously place a heavy burden on HRM professionals since the unique features of those situations are often related to HRM activities, potential difficulties, and, of course, problems.

Figure 1.4 presents a summary of HRM activities related to international joint ventures.

Another response to the increasing global competition is organizational restructuring, often in the form of downsizing, "right sizing," or reductions in workforce. More than half of the Fortune 1000 firms went through a major reorganization in 1987 alone.[25] Apple Computers, Sears, AT&T, ARCO, CBS, Du Pont, GM, Kodak, and IBM are among the many corporate giants which have reduced their workforces by over 10 percent in the last 5 years. HRM departments are often required to assist in organizational restructuring, make layoff decisions, conduct counseling for those who are displaced, and assist in developing new staffing plans as a result of the corporate downsizing. As we will describe in more detail below and in Chapter 3, HR managers are also asked to help in the development of a legal defense against allegations of discrimination related to corporate downsizing. Unfortunately, this HR involvement with corporate downsizing often occurs only after decisions and possible discrimination have occurred.

The effects of increases in international competition cannot be separated from the productivity we alluded to earlier. As the MIT group put it, the combined problem "will impoverish America relative to other nations that have adapted more quickly and effectively to pervasive changes in technology and markets."[26]

Increased Government Regulation and Litigation

Another important trend affecting the status of HRM is the proliferation of regulations and lawsuits related to HR. In general, these laws and regulations reflect societal

FIGURE 1.4
UNIQUE HRM CHALLENGES IN INTERNATIONAL JOINT VENTURES

HR ACTIVITY	HRM CHALLENGES
Staffing	Host country may demand staffing policies contrary to maximizing profits.
Decision making	Conflicts among diverse constituent groups; complexity of decision processes.
Communication	Interpersonal problems due to geographical dispersion and cultural differences.
Compensation	Perceived and real compensation differences.
Career planning	Perceptions regarding value of overseas assignments; difficulties in reentry.
Performance management	Differences in standards; difficulties in measuring performance across countries.
Training	Special training for functioning in international joint venture (IJV) structure.

Source: Adapted from O. Shenkar and Y. Zeira. Human resource management in international joint ventures: Directions for research. *Academy of Management Review, 12,* 1987, 546–557. Reprinted with permission.

responses to economic, social, or political issues. For example, the Civil Rights Act of 1964 (and amended in 1991), which prohibits job discrimination on the basis of race, sex, religion, or national origin, was passed primarily in response to the tremendous differences in economic outcomes of blacks versus whites. The 1990 Americans with Disabilities Act (ADA) was passed to promote equal opportunity for people with disabilities. Another example is the proliferation of state laws regarding corporate acquisitions and mergers, laws protecting AIDS victims and homosexuals from employment discrimination, and even regulations regarding family leave benefits and video display terminals. Organizations are bound by a plethora of federal, state, and local laws, regulations, executive orders, and rules which have an impact on virtually every type of personnel decision. There are health and safety regulations; laws regarding employee pensions and other compensation programs, plant closures, and mergers and acquisitions; new immigration laws; and a growing number of equal opportunity laws and guidelines. ADEA, OFCCP, OSHA, EEOC, ADA, and ERISA are but a few of the acronyms with which HRM professionals and practicing managers must be familiar. Each represents a major regulatory effort. The Civil Rights Act of 1991 and the ADA will undoubtedly increase costly litigation related to HRM.

Organizations spend considerable time and expense in order to comply with these laws and regulations or to defend against allegations regarding violations. For example, State Farm Insurance settled a sex discrimination lawsuit in 1992 brought by the Equal Employment Opportunity Commission (EEOC) for $180 million. The EEOC recently settled a similar suit with Honda of America for $6 million. A jury in a California case granted a female manager from Texaco over $17 million after she claimed she was twice passed over for promotion because she is a woman. Westinghouse Electric Corporation agreed to a $35 million settlement in an age discrimination suit involving 4000 employees affected by their reorganization. A judge in California returned a $5.3 million judgment against Shell Oil for dismissing an executive solely because he was a homosexual, a violation of California state law. An accounting firm recently lost a $43 million case involving an "unlawful discharge," an increasingly common type of lawsuit which challenges the long-held principle of employment-at-will—the rule that an employer could terminate employees *at will* as long as it did not violate some other law, regulation, or collective bargaining agreement. The 1980s have seen a growing number of exceptions allowed to the "at-will" doctrine. One of the most heavily publicized cases involved Safeway Stores, which went through a leveraged buyout (LBO) in 1985 and immediately terminated 300 people in California. The result was

a class action, wrongful discharge suit, and a settlement of more than $8 million.

One of the most common lawsuits today is brought under the Age Discrimination in Employment Act (ADEA), which prohibits job discrimination against people over the age of 39. Many such individuals are claiming violations of this law when they are terminated under a corporate downsizing effort. Pratt and Whitney, a division of United Technology, was sued by 50 people under ADEA who claimed they were terminated due to their age and salary as part of a downsizing program. Pratt maintained that the terminations were based on company needs and employee performance. The National Football League (NFL) was sued by a former referee who claimed he was terminated because of his age and not his performance, as the NFL claims. Such individual claims of age discrimination are increasing in number due to the aging of the U.S. workforce.

Organizations must constantly monitor their HRM programs to ensure compliance with EEO laws and the volatile interpretations of those laws. The proliferation of lawsuits and laws related to personnel decisions and policy has undoubtedly contributed greatly to the increased importance given to HRM by senior management.

Changing Characteristics of the Workforce

EDUCATIONAL AND SKILL LEVELS. By the year 2000, 25 percent of the workforce will have college degrees. These employees have a lot to offer in terms of their capacity to contribute to the improvement of organizational effectiveness. The more educated workers are also demanding more involvement in corporate decision making. They seek a greater voice in corporate affairs and due process issues. The shift from manual work to knowledge work in this country means that we can no longer rely on people for their physical horsepower alone but, rather, will be relying upon them for their intellectual "horsepower."[27] Consequently, greater demands are placed on the HR function to meet more demanding employee needs for innovative programs in training, compensation, performance management, and career development.

ATTITUDES. Attitudes of American workers are also changing. Employees now demand better coordination between lifestyle needs (family, leisure) and employment needs. In fact, in recent years leisure pursuits have become more highly valued than work and family goals.[28] Du Pont Corporation recently reported the results of a survey suggesting that family obligations now play a greater role in career choices for both men and women. American workers are more interested in possessing jobs with more meaningful work that allows for self-fulfillment and work satisfaction. They want jobs which provide greater challenges and enable them to use more skills and knowledges. These changes in employee attitudes and values require the use of different HR strategies in organizations. No longer can organizations simply use pay and promotion as the primary motivators for performance. Instead, they must develop new staffing plans and restructure jobs to offer opportunities for employees to seek personal fulfillment in their work. They must further recognize the impact that plant closings and reductions in force have on employees' commitment to their jobs and the organization.[29]

DIVERSITY OF WORKERS.   Another trend affecting HRM policies and practices is the increasing diversity of the workforce. Today, a greater number of women and minorities have entered the workforce and are beginning to move into previously white, male-dominated positions (e.g., managers). According to the Hudson Institute, over the next 10 years only 15 percent of people entering the U.S. workforce will be native-born white males.[30] In addition, greater percentages of dual-career couples compose the labor force. In the past, the "typical" worker was a male (often white) who was a member of a single-earner household. Today, fewer than 20 percent of the employees fit this description. There is also an increasing number of workers with disabilities entering the workforce for the first time due to the passage of the Americans with Disabilities Act. As a result of these changes in workforce composition, organizations are starting to develop more flexible work schedules, as well as better training programs, travel plans, child-care arrangements, and career development strategies, so that work and non-work responsibilities can be more easily integrated. Building and sustaining a quality workforce from this diversity may be one of the greatest challenges of all for HRM and practicing managers. Such diversity may also prove to be an important asset in international business.

LABOR SHORTAGES AND AGING OF THE WORKFORCE.   The shortage of young workers in the United States is already a major problem in the fast-food, retail, and lodging industries and is beginning to hurt small business in general. The U.S. workforce is aging. By the year 2000, the median age in the United States will be over 35[31] and over 40 percent of the workforce will be over 40 years of age. As we discussed earlier, the age of 40 is critical in that people 40 and over are covered by the ADEA, which prohibits age discrimination in the workplace. It is projected that the number of lawsuits brought under ADEA will increase substantially in the next decade as the huge "baby-boomer" cohort becomes

eligible and because older employees are becoming more aware of their rights. As a result, HR professionals will need to become more actively involved in dealing with potential age discrimination issues. Another issue created by the aging of the workforce, particularly the greater proportion of baby-boomers (now aged 25 to 44), may be the increased incidence of "plateauing" in middle career. Workers may be stuck in the same jobs with little prospect for promotion. Plateauing may promote feelings of stagnation, alienation, and boredom. HR professionals and management will need to design alternative methods of career development and to build more satisfaction and achievement into the jobs themselves, to assist these employees.

The U.S. supply of young workers will continue to fall until about 1996, when it will start to increase again. Until then, HRM professionals and managers will continue to find it difficult to recruit qualified workers for entry-level jobs. As a result, employers will need to expand their labor markets. McDonald's and Burger King, for example, now actively recruit senior citizens as counter personnel. The Marriott Corporation employs many people with mental disabilities for a variety of hard-to-fill positions. Companies are now recruiting in inner-city minority and immigrant neighborhoods and providing transportation to jobs in the suburbs. More part-time workers are being hired, and a variety of enticements are being offered to attract workers.

JOB SKILLS GAP.   David Kearns, former CEO of Xerox, calls it "the making of a national disaster." Brad Butler, former CEO of Procter & Gamble, fears the development of a "third world within our own country." James Burke, CEO of Johnson & Johnson, referred to it as "the American dream turned nightmare." These executives are referring to the growing problem of structural unemployment in the United States.[32] *Structural unemployment* refers to the inability of the labor market to match workers with the jobs which are available. There are projections of an increased demand for technological skills at a time when scores on standardized tests in math and science are going down. Most entry-level positions now require some computer skills, and assembly-line work now calls for a more sophisticated understanding of mathematics. Over 50 percent of jobs in the year 2000 will require some college or technical training beyond high school, while projections for illiteracy exceed 70 million by the same year. Unfortunately, the percentage of the potential working population which is adequately prepared for technological training is on the decrease. According to one report, as many as 90 percent of all jobs in American organizations will be altered by a form of expert, technological system or another form of artificial intelligence by the year 2005. With increases in automation and information technology, there is likely to be a growing percentage of the population which reflects a nearly irreversible status of structural unemployment. American business has become more involved in education in recent years, in an attempt to reverse this ominous trend. The Secretary of Labor established a commission in 1990 to study the skill requirements for American workers in the twenty-first century and to coordinate HR policy on a continuing basis. Many companies have taken matters into their own hands. Polaroid, Hewlett-Packard, Motorola, and Unisys are among the many companies which now provide in-house training in basic math, reading, and writing.

The report card on college-educated workers is not particularly flattering either. A 1988 survey of business leaders' attitudes toward the skills of business school graduates indicated a need for greater development of personal competencies such as written and oral communication skills, leadership, and analytic thinking.[33] Another report from a panel of business school deans and senior business executives concluded that too many business school graduates are ill prepared to manage in this global economy.[34] The report stressed the need to enhance managerial competencies with a more practical focus on business education. This position was echoed by the MIT Commission on Productivity, which called for greater student participation in the learning process and the development of basic competencies which will prepare the graduating business student for any challenge.

One international researcher concluded that these personal competencies enable workers to make larger contributions to the productivity of the firm and prepare them better for lifelong learning. The idea is to provide skills as a "generalized polyvalent resource that can be put to many different and, most importantly, as yet unknown future uses."[35] He argues that the experiential educational processes of Japan and Germany are more compatible with this philosophy.

All of the trends we have reviewed are having a profound effect on HRM in U.S. corporations. The changing demographics and cultural diversity, the increased number of lawsuits and regulations, and the growing demands on American workers in the context of a paramount need to improve U.S. productivity and establish a competitive edge create a situation that will challenge HRM professionals and line management into the twenty-first century. These trends place greater demands and increased attention on HRM. Through better coordination with organizational planning and strategy, HR can be used to create and sustain an organization's advantage in an increasingly competitive world. There is no doubt that the intense and growing competition has placed greater pressure on organizations to carefully examine their costs. Edward Lawler, a prominent management author, states that "particularly in corporations that are facing international competition, all staff departments are being asked to justify their cost structures on a competitive basis.... Head-count comparisons are being made by corporations to check the ratio of employees to members of the HR department." There is a great opportunity for HRM to meet new and old challenges as a business partner. Lawler sees the most pressing need in the area of corporate strategy. "The HR function must become a partner in developing an organization's strategic plan, for human resources are a key consideration in determining strategies that are both practical and feasible."[36]

This HR partnership must evolve out of the major activities of the HR function. The next section will introduce you to these major activities and discuss how they relate to one another and to the desired outcomes we described earlier.

THE ACTIVITIES OF HRM

There are many diverse activities involved in HRM. Figure 1.5 presents a list of the most common activities performed by HRM professionals. We can classify these diverse HRM activities under six HR policy domains: (1) organizational design; (2) staffing; (3) reward systems, benefits, and compliance; (4) performance management; (5) employee and organizational development; and (6) communications and public relations.

Organizational design involves the arrangement of work tasks based on the interaction of people, technology, and the tasks to be performed in the context of the mission, goals, and strategic plan of the organization. HRM activities such as HR planning, job analysis, organizational restructuring, job design, computerization, and worker-machine interfaces are subsumed under this policy area. Corporate downsizing efforts often begin with a critical analysis of how the work is performed and how jobs and work units relate to one another.

After the organization is structured and jobs are clearly defined in terms of the necessary knowledge, skills, and abilities, positions must be staffed. *Staffing* has to do with the flow of people into, through, and out of the organization. Recruitment, employee orientation, personnel selection, promotion, and outplacement (assistance for terminated employees) are among the functions which fit into this domain. Of the six HR domains, staffing is probably the one most likely to be affected by litigation.

Reward systems, benefits, and compliance have to do with any type of reward or benefit which may be available to employees, such as compensation, merit pay,

FIGURE 1.5
MAJOR ACTIVITIES OF HRM PROFESSIONALS

Organizational Design
HR planning
Job analysis
Job design
Work teams (Sociotechnical systems)
Information systems

Staffing
Recruiting/interviewing/hiring
Affirmative action
Promotion/transfer/separation
Outplacement services
Induction/orientation
Employee selection methods

**Communications and
public relations**
Personnel records/reports/information systems
Employee communications/publications
Suggestion systems
Personnel research

Performance management
Management appraisal/management
  by objectives
Productivity/enhancement programs
Customer-focused performance appraisal

**Reward systems, benefits
and compliance**
Safety programs/OSHA compliance
Health/medical services
Complaint/disciplinary procedures
Compensation administration
EEOC compliance
Wage/salary administration
Insurance benefits administration
Unemployment compensation administration
Pension/profit sharing plans
Labor relations/collective bargaining

**Employee and organizational
development**
Management/supervisory development
Career planning/development
Employee assistance/counseling programs
Skill training, nonmanagement
Retirement preparation programs
Attitude surveys

Source: Adapted from D. Ulrich and D. Lake. *Organizational capability competing from the inside out.* New York: John Wiley & Sons, 1987. Copyright © 1987 by John Wiley & Sons. Reprinted by permission of John Wiley & Sons, Inc.

profit sharing, health care, parental leave programs, vacation leave, and pensions. The activities also include the myriad of compliance requirements facing organizations from local, state, and federal agencies. Health and safety issues and unemployment policy are two of the major areas within this domain.

Managerial decisions with regard to work systems can have a profound effect on productivity and the quality of working life. *Employee and organizational development* programs are concerned with fostering and maintaining employee skills based on organizational and employee needs. Developmental activities may include training, career development plans, and retirement programs. *Performance management* activities include assessments of individual, unit, or other aggregated levels of performance to measure (and improve) work performance. Obviously, merit pay systems require accurate measures of employee performance. *Communication and public relations* activities are concerned with the sharing of information among employees, management, customers, and outside constituents. Information systems, personnel research, attitude surveys, and company publications are all included here. We will examine each of these HRM domains in the chapters to follow.

Employee Involvement in HRM Activities

Underlying all the HRM activities presented in Figure 1.5 is the extent of employee involvement or influence. According to Harvard professor Michael Beer and colleagues, the essential question in this area is, "How much responsibility, authority, and power should the organization voluntarily delegate and to whom?"[37] Will management seek to minimize the power and influence of employees, or will influence be shared in critical areas related to employee welfare, such as reward systems, appraisal, and staffing? The critical task for management is to determine the extent to which employees will be involved in organizational decision making. Senior management, by virtue of its actions, can adopt either an implicit policy of little or no employee influence or a participatory culture with high levels of employee involvement. Attitude surveys, open-door policies, ombudsmen, quality-of-work-life programs, and self-managing teams are examples of high-participatory HRM practices. As mentioned above, a 1990 survey found an increase in such activities in American corporations.[38] The Baldrige criteria discussed earlier place great emphasis on employee involvement in the assessment of processes related to organizational effectiveness. Many of the most admired U.S. corporations (Wal-Mart, Liz Claiborne, Merck, Levi Strauss, Coca-Cola, 3M) have high levels of employee involvement.

The policy regarding degree of employee influence is related to the general philosophy management has about the quality of working life for its employees. Some organizations set an objective of establishing and maintaining a high quality of working life for their employees regardless of the effects of this objective on corporate performance or productivity. These organizations are more likely to adopt programs and policies which facilitate employee influence. Merck, Hewlett-Packard, Procter & Gamble, Westinghouse, Federal Express, Disney World, and Johnson's Wax, for example, have corporate mission statements which reflect a high quality of working life for their employees. Other organizations consider a higher quality of working life as a means to a desired end-state. These companies have determined or hypothesized that programs such as quality circles, team building, attitude surveys, and other forms of employee involvement have an impact on product and service quality and customer satisfaction, and thus should be maintained. With this perspective, such programs are sustained only when it is believed that they have a positive effect upon important indicators of organizational performance. Still other organizations allow employee participation only to the extent that it is legislated or mandated as, for example, through collective bargaining. With this philosophy, management often considers stockholders to be the only major constituency to which it is responsible.

There obviously organizations which do not clearly fit into one of these three philosophical categories. Some may have had either positive or negative experiences with employee involvement programs and may have changed philosophies accordingly. Many U.S. companies are unsure about the effects of such programs yet are willing to try them out in order to assess their impact empirically. Based on the 1990 survey discussed above, the number of such companies is increasing steadily as they seek a "competitive edge" in an increasingly competitive world.

The management philosophy regarding employee influence will have a great deal to do with the activities pursued within all six HRM domains we described above. For example, the process by which personnel are promoted could be the traditional "top-down" assessment, or input could be gathered from peers, subordinates, or the work team. At GM's Saturn plant in Tennessee, for example, workers participate in the selection of team members and the promotion of team leaders. The same thing is true for the extent of participation in the allocation of rewards. Management may assume complete control over the design and administration of these programs. They

may be compelled to negotiate these procedures through collective bargaining, or they can choose to involve employees to a lesser or greater extent.

It is the position of this book that management must recognize employees as an important constituency group who have legitimate interests in organizational functioning and whose performance clearly is ultimately related to customer satisfaction and competitive advantage. Management must attempt to integrate employee interests with the interests of the stockholders, customers, suppliers, and the community at large. A company's competitiveness depends upon its long-term financial relationship with all major stakeholders. Customers require high-quality products and services at a competitive price. Workers require competitive compensation and a high quality of working life. Suppliers have financial claims. And of course shareholders want higher stock prices and bigger dividends. It is our view that long-term financial success depends on the ability of senior management to enhance the organization's competitive position by focusing on customer requirements. Success in this endeavor will depend to a large extent on whether management can convince all employees of the virtues of this philosophy. The ultimate goal should be to foster the long-term interest of all constituent groups. HRM professionals will be increasingly called upon to assist in this critical endeavor. HRM programs and activities should be developed, sustained, and evaluated in the context of their relationship to the ultimate criterion of total customer satisfaction.

Effectiveness Criteria for HRM Activities

Developing the specific criteria which define effectiveness for HRM activities is one of the most difficult problems which must be addressed by HRM professionals and practicing managers. Effective performance at the individual or aggregated level can be defined according to six criteria.[39] The most effective employees or work units are those providing the highest possible *quantity* and *quality* of work at the lowest *cost* and in the most *timely* fashion, with a minimum of *supervision* and with a maximum of *positive impact* on coworkers, organizational units, and the client/customer population. Another conceptualization breaks these six down into simply effectiveness and efficiency, with *effectiveness* defined as meeting or exceeding customer requirements and *efficiency* defined as meeting those requirements at the lowest cost possible. HRM professionals and practicing managers spend considerable time in developing, administering, and maintaining performance management systems which attempt to measure and improve effectiveness and efficiency.

While the relative weights to be applied to the six criteria should be directly linked to organizational objectives such as increased sales, reduced costs, and of course customer satisfaction, they rarely are. Most organizations have difficulty even measuring overall performance in a reliable manner, and few systematically relate individual performance to performance aggregated to the unit or corporate level. Organizations rarely get down to specifics about all six criteria and, most important, about their relationship to the objectives of the organization or measures of either internal or external customer satisfaction. When reliable and valid measurements of these criteria are taken, they are rarely related to either internal or external customer satisfaction except at the most superficial level. As stated above, there is a growing realization that such linkage is vital to competitive advantage. For the Baldrige Awards, for example, maximum points for HRM activities such as worker involvement and training and development can only be gained if the company clearly links these processes with improved product or service quality and customer satisfaction.

HRM professionals must possess up-to-date knowledge on activities such as HR planning, compensation, performance management, personnel staffing, information systems, equal employment opportunity (EEO), recruitment, and training. Perhaps more important, HRM professionals must be able to convince line managers of the value of these activities for meeting organizational goals and for creating and sustaining a competitive edge. This means instilling in line managers and employees a sense of ownership in the HRM practices. To the extent that management, in general, is motivated by an agenda incompatible with the agenda of the HRM function, the effectiveness of the HRM system is in serious jeopardy. It is not enough that the HRM departmental staff possesses state-of-the-art knowledge of HRM practices. Line management must also recognize the importance of these activities and behave accordingly. HRM personnel must also realize that their function is important only to the extent that their processes ultimately affect the competitive position of the organization and total customer satisfaction. We should look at the HRM function as a strategic supplier of staff, training, programs, etc., with many internal customers and a myriad of requirements. Theoretically at least, these internal customer requirements should be linked to measures of product and service quality as defined by external customers and ultimately their total satisfaction.[40] The most effective HRM departments work closely with line managers to identify critical performance requirements of the personnel function necessary for meeting specific organizational business needs.[41] In the chapters to follow, we will present numerous examples of HRM professionals working in concert with line management to meet the strategic goals of the organization and ultimately to improve customer satisfaction.

SUMMARY

HRM is to some extent concerned with any organizational decision which has an impact on the workforce or the potential workforce. While there is typically an HR or personnel department in middle to large corporations, general management is still primarily responsible for the application of HRM policies and practices. There are critical competencies for general management and HRM professionals. An organization needs both competent personnel trained in HRM and motivated managers who recognize the importance of HRM activities and apply optimal procedures in the context of the ultimate goal of total customer satisfaction. Ideally, HR managers should be placed in line management positions rather than staff positions so that they can enforce decisions rather than simply serve as advisers. Currently, this doesn't occur in most American businesses. Unfortunately, personnel functions are often perceived by line managers to be out of step with and at times in opposition to the real mission and objectives of the organization. The most effective HR departments are those in which HRM policy and activities are established in congruence with the mission and specific objectives of the organization in terms of customer requirements. HRM should assist management in the difficult task of integrating and coordinating the interests of the various organizational constituencies, with the ultimate criterion being to enhance the organization's competitive position through higher productivity and higher-quality products and services which enhance customer satisfaction. The key to competitive advantage is to increase output with fewer inputs while at the same time improving product or service quality and customer satisfaction. The focus should be on customer requirements. We believe HRM can and should play a significant role in this endeavor.

Chapter 2 will explore the critical competencies required of general management and HRM professionals in order to create and sustain a competitive advantage and increase customer satisfaction. These competencies include knowing the business, keeping aware of current HR developments, managing the process of change, and integrating these roles.

DISCUSSION QUESTIONS

1. Why is the increased diversity of the U.S. workforce a greater challenge for HRM? What specific HRM activities are most affected?
2. How do productivity concerns influence organizational policies and procedures regarding HRM activities?

3. Think of an HRM function that you consider to be most related to customer satisfaction. Does it matter whether you're thinking of a product or a service?

4. Why is the personnel/HRM function not very respected among line management? How could this be changed?

5. Why is the support of line management critical to the effective functioning of HRM practices in an organization? Provide some suggestions for ensuring that this support is maintained.

6. Some writers and researchers maintain that U.S. youth today is not prepared for the increased global competition. Do you agree or disagree? Explain.

7. Are the criticisms regarding the personal competencies of college graduates well founded? If so, to what extent is the university system to blame?

NOTES

1. Nussbaum, B. (Sept. 19, 1988). Needed: Human capital. *Business Week,* pp. 100–103.

2. Naisbitt, J., and Aburdene, P. (1990). *Megatrends 2000.* New York: William Morrow, p. 48.

3. Sirota, A., Alper, S., and Peau, R. (1989). Report to respondents: Survey of views toward human resources policies and practices. Boston, MA: Unpublished manuscript. See also: Ferris, G. R., and Judge, T. A. (1991). Personnel/human resources management: A political influence perspective. *Journal of Management, 17*(2), 447–488.

4. Langer, S. (1988). *The Abbott, Langer and Associates compensation report.* Crete, IL: Abbott, Langer & Associates.

5. Ballen, K. (Feb. 10, 1992). America's most admired corporations. *Fortune,* p. 43.

6. Finney, M. I. (1988). Leading the way into HR's new age. *Personnel Administrator, 33,* 42–49.

7. Grayson, C. J., and O'Dell, C. O. (1988). *American business: A two-minute warning.* New York: The Free Press, p. 4.

8. Kupfer, A. (Mar. 9, 1992). How American industry stacks up. *Fortune,* p. 30.

9. Dertouzos, M. L., Lester, R. K., and Solow, R. M. (1989). *Made in America: Regaining the competitive edge.* Cambridge, MA: The MIT Press, p. 166.

10. Bureau of Labor Statistics (August 1991). Washington: U.S. Department of Labor.

11. See note 7.

12. LeBeouf, M. (1988). *The productivity challenge.* New York: Macmillan, pp. 10–11.

13. Maddison, A. (1982). *Phases of capitalist development.* Oxford, England: Oxford University Press.

14. Kindelberger, C. (1980). Historical perspective on the decline in U.S. productivity. In C. Grayson (ed.), *Dimensions of productivity research.* Houston, TX: American Productivity Center, p. 724.

15. See note 7, p. 13.

16. Holusha, J. (Oct. 21, 1990). The Baldrige badge of courage—and quality. *The New York Times,* p. F12. See also: Hill, R. C., and Freedman, S. M. (1992). Managing the quality process: Lesson from a Baldrige Award winner. A conversation with CEO John W. Wallace. *The Executive, 6,* 76–88.

17. Drucker, P. (May 22, 1986). Goodbye to the old personnel department. *The Wall Street Journal,* p. F1.

18. See note 17.

19. Normand, J., Salyard, S. D., and Mahoney, J. J. (1990). An evaluation of pre-employment drug testing. *Journal of Applied Psychology, 75,* 629–639.

20. Mathieu, J. E., and Leonard, R. L. (June 1987). Applying utility concepts to a training program in supervisory skills: A time-based approach. *Academy of Management Journal,* pp. 316–335. See also: Schuster, F. E. (1986). *The Schuster report: The proven connection between people and profits.* New York: John Wiley & Sons.

21. Peters, T. J., and Austin, N. (1985). *A passion for excellence: The leadership difference.* New York: Random House. Peters, T. J., and Waterman, R. H., Jr. (1982). *In search of excellence: Lessons from America's best-run companies.* New York: Warner Books. See also: note 2.

22. See note 9.

23. Hallett, J. J. (1987). *Worklife visions.* Alexandria, VA: American Society for Personnel Administration, pp. 45, 46.

24. Zachary, G. P. (June 6, 1990). Businessland enters Japan, aided by 4 big local firms. *The Wall Street Journal,* p. B1.

25. Cameron, K., Freeman, S. J., and Mishra, A. K. (1991). Best practices in white collar downsizing: Managing contradictions. *The Executive, 5,* 57–73.

26. See note 22, p. 166.

27. See note 23, pp. 45, 46.

28. Yankelovich, D. (1986). *New rules.* New York: Random House.

29. Nussbaum, B. (Aug. 4, 1986). The end of corporate loyalty. *Business Week,* pp. 42–49.

30. Goddard, R. W. (February 1989). Workforce 2000. *Personnel Journal,* pp. 65–71. See also: Jamieson, D., and O'Mara, J. (1991). *Managing Workforce 2000: Gaining the diversity advantage.* San Francisco, CA: Jossey-Bass.

31. Hall, D. T., and Goodale, J. G. (1986). *Human resource management: Strategy, design, and implementation.* Glenview, IL: Scott, Foresman.

32. Fiske, C. (Sept. 25, 1989). Impending U.S. jobs disaster: Work force unqualified to work. *The New York Times,* p. 1. See also: Kantrowitz, B., and Wingert, P. (Feb. 17, 1992). An "F" in world competition. *Newsweek,* p. 57.

33. Porter, L., and McKibbin, L. E. (1988). *Management education and development.* New York: McGraw-Hill. See also: Penley, L. E., Alexander, E. R., Jernigan, I. E., and Henwood, C. I. (1991). Communication abilities of managers: The relationship to performance. *Journal of Management, 17*(1), 57–76.

34. Fuchsberg, G. (June 6, 1990). Business schools get bad grades. *The Wall Street Journal,* pp. B1, B2.

35. Streeck, W. (1987). *Skills and the limits of neo-liberalism: The enterprise of the future as a place of learning.* Paper presented at the Congress on Changes in Work and Social Transformation. Universitario di Studi Europei, Turin, Italy, Nov. 27–29, p. 21.

36. Lawler, E. E. (Jan. 22–27, 1988). HRM: Meeting the new challenges. *Personnel,* p. 24.

37. Beer, M., Spector, B., Lawrence, P. R., Mills, D. Q., and Walton, R. E. (1985). *Human resource management.* New York: The Free Press, p. 8.

38. American Productivity and Quality Center (1990). *Putting strategy to work: Tools for cost and quality management.* Palo Alto, CA: Electric Power Research Institute.

39. Bernardin, H. J., and Kane, J. S. (1993). *Performance appraisal: A contingency approach to system development and evaluation.* Boston, MA: PWS-Kent.

40. Bernardin, H. J. (1992). An "analytic" framework for customer-based performance content development and appraisal. *Human Resource Management Review, 2,* 81–102.

41. Taylor, M. (1988). Changing the personnel function to meet changing business needs. *Personnel Management, 20*(9), 28–32.

EXERCISE 1.1 AN INTERVIEW WITH AN HRM SPECIALIST

OVERVIEW

Chapter 1 presents an overview of the major activities of HR professionals today. As noted, HRM practitioners serve a variety of roles in organizations and are often classified as personnel directors, personnel managers, or HRM staff members. Individuals specializing in specific HRM job activities may be working in departments of training, labor relations, equal employment opportunity or affirmative action, compensation, or personnel research.

LEARNING OBJECTIVES

After completing this exercise, you should be able to:

1. Describe some of the major HRM responsibilities and activities of HRM professionals.
2. Explain some of the contemporary problems or difficulties encountered in HRM work.
3. Derive a list of major job activities useful for understanding the six HRM domains.

PROCEDURE

Part A: Individual Analysis

Step 1. Read Chapter 1, paying particular attention to the discussion of HRM activities.

Step 2. Identify a practicing HRM or personnel professional and conduct a short interview with that person for purposes of gathering information about the person's job and background, the organization, and the major job-related problems confronting the individual. An at-tempt should be made to interview the most senior-level HR employee of the organization (e.g., the vice president of human resources or the personnel director) either by phone or in person. Form 1.1.1 should be used as a format for conducting the interview and recording responses.

Part B: Group Analysis

Step 1. Students should assemble in class in groups of about six and review each individual report. The group should then identify common problems mentioned by the HR professionals. The characteristics of the organization should be considered in the context of the problems. For example, are there any clear differences in problems confronting HRM professionals from service versus manufacturing organizations, or public- versus private-sector organizations? Students should have a clear understanding of the HRM professional's position and reporting relationships within the organization. The group should also attempt to identify the HRM activities listed in Figure 1.5 which are most related to the problems discussed. The problems should be assessed in the context of the trends discussed in Chapter 1. The group should also discuss the professional's views of how line management views the personnel function (cooperative, adversarial).

Step 2. A spokesperson will be designated to report each group's findings. After all spokespersons have presented their list of activities and difficulties, the class should suggest HRM strategies and programs which could address the most common problems raised. Trends related to the relationship between line management and HRM professionals should also be discussed.

FORM 1.1.1
INTERVIEW FORMAT FOR HRM PROFESSIONALS

Interviewer's Name _____ Interview Date _____

HRM Professional's Name _____ Company _____

1. How would you describe the organization (e.g., public/private, size, service/manufacturing, union/nonunion, major competitors, international business, growing, stagnant, downsizing)?

2. What is your position title?

3. a. How many years have you occupied this position?

   b. How many years have you been employed by this organization?

4. a. Briefly, describe your background (education, previous experience).

   b. Which aspects of your background are most directly related to your current job duties?

5. a. How many employees do you directly supervise?

   b. To whom do you report? What is his or her job title?

6. Describe the organization's Human Resource or personnel department. How many employees are there in the department?

7. What do you regard as your three most significant job responsibilities? Be as specific as possible. (The student may use Figure 1.5 if the HRM professional needs some suggestions.)

8. What do you regard as the three most significant and specific challenges or difficulties you face in your current job responsibilities? For each, briefly describe the steps you have taken (or are planning to take) to deal with each of the problems.

   Challenges   **Action Strategies**

9. Describe your relationship with line management. In general, how would you characterize the relationship (supportive, adversarial, cooperative)? Explain your answer.

EXERCISE 1.2
AN ASSESSMENT OF CUSTOMER SATISFACTION AND THE RELATIONSHIP TO HRM ACTIVITIES

OVERVIEW

Chapter 1 describes a variety of new challenges confronting organizations today, including problems of productivity, product quality and service, and customer satisfaction. A host of theories have been offered to explain our productivity problems, ranging from macroeconomic perspectives dealing with the economy, industry, governmental regulations, and labor force characteristics to microeconomic perspectives dealing with management, unions, and employees.

As a practicing manager or an HRM specialist, you will be asked to meet the HR challenges related to particular problems of productivity or customer satisfaction. Nine out of every ten jobs are predicted to be in the services sector in the next 20 years. Yet the productivity figures are very disturbing since they reflect a stagnant or even decreasing rate of productivity for the services industry. Assessments of product and service quality are also unfavorable to the United States, and customer service indexes are also woefully low in most of the services sector. Research shows that HR policies and practices have the potential to enhance customer satisfaction, increase productivity, and improve product and service quality. As we maintain in Chapter 1, the most effective HRM programs are those in which the focus is always on the ultimate criterion of customer satisfaction. This exercise focuses on those HRM efforts which are customer-oriented and serves to generate discussion about steps which can be taken to improve customer satisfaction.

LEARNING OBJECTIVES

After completing this exercise, you should be able to:

1. Identify some examples of how HRM can affect customer satisfaction.
2. View customer satisfaction from an HRM perspective on such matters as the impact of employee attitudes, the diversity of worker characteristics, the job skills gap, and how you as a manager or HRM specialist could improve customer satisfaction through HRM activities.
3. Identify HRM activities that may be useful for tackling problems related to customer satisfaction.

PROCEDURE

Part A: Individual Analysis

Visit several local businesses (a bank, a campus bookstore, a fast-food restaurant, a department store, or a local mall are possibilities). Evaluate each on the extent to which it has provided customer satisfaction. As an alternative, think back over recent visits to such establishments, or reflect on recent experiences you have had at your university or college. On Form 1.2.1, write two examples of what you regard as poor customer service. On Form 1.2.2, write two examples of what you regard as excellent customer service. After describing each experience, review the HRM activities listed in Figure 1.5 and form hypotheses about what categories of HRM activities may have been primarily responsible for the excellent or poor customer service. Generate a list of the possible causes. Be creative in your hypotheses, and attempt to go beyond simple theories, such as citing a "training" problem as the cause. Bring the completed forms to class for discussion.

Part B: Group Analysis

Approximately six students should be designated to discuss responses on Form 1.2.1, with another six designated as observers of the group. If possible, each observer should be assigned to observe the group performance of only one group participant. The observer should review the participant's Form 1.2.1 prior to group discussion. Each observer should use Form 1.2.4 as the context for observing group participation of the participant to whom he or she has been assigned.

All members of the first discussion group should also read each others' 1.2.1 forms and attempt to discern trends in the incidents. For example, was the dissatisfaction mainly caused by poor product quality or by poor service quality? Was the product or service representative incompetent or not sufficiently knowledgeable about the product or service? After identifying trends, each group should identify the HRM activities most related to the poor customer service. Generate a list of the most important HRM activities the group believes to be directly or indirectly responsible for the customer service problems. The group should attempt to reach consensus on the top three HRM activities which could be directed at correcting the customer service problems.

After about 15 minutes of discussion, each observer should evaluate the assigned participant's performance in the group, using Form 1.2.4, and each participant should complete the self-assessment on Form 1.2.3. The pairs should then switch roles, and the new discussion group should discuss the responses on Form 1.2.2, also attempting to identify the major HRM activities thought to be the causes of the excellent customer services which were provided and the extent to which HRM was responsible relative to other organizational functions. The second group can use the first group's analysis as a starting point. Again, the group should attempt to reach consensus on the top three HRM activities thought to be responsible for the positive customer satisfaction.

Part C: Self-Assessment, Peer Assessment, and Feedback Session (Optional)

After completion of the second group exercise, discussion participants should make a self-assessment using the rating scale on Form 1.2.3, while the observer is completing Form 1.2.4 (extra forms may be copied). After Forms 1.2.3 and 1.2.4 are completed, students should pair off and take turns reviewing their respective self-assessments and peer assessments. Discussion should then center on each individual's performance in the group, written responses, and areas of personal strength or weakness, as well as the rationales of the students' respective positions regarding HRM activities. Each student should then answer the Assessment Questions for Exercise 1.2 (page 33).

FORM 1.2.1

Name _____ Group _____

Write about two situations in which you felt very dissatisfied with the customer service you received. Describe each circumstance in some detail, and consider the causes of the service in terms of possible HRM activities. What were you expecting, and what did you receive? Answer the questions below.

1. Describe the organization (e.g., fast-food, department store, university setting).

Situation 1   **Situation 2**

2. Describe the incident and the poor service in some detail. What did you expect, and what did you get?

Situation 1   **Situation 2**

3. What do you regard as the major causes of your dissatisfaction? To what extent do you believe HRM activities were related to your dissatisfaction? Specifically, which activities are most related to the customer service problem, and how could HRM improve the service?

Situation 1   **Situation 2**

FORM 1.2.2

Name _____ Group _____

Write about two situations in which you felt very satisfied with the customer service you received. Describe each circumstance in some detail, and consider the causes of the service in terms of possible HRM activities. What were you expecting, and what did you receive? Answer the questions below.

1. Describe the organization (e.g., fast-food, department store, university setting).

Situation 1   **Situation 2**

2. Describe the incident and the good service in some detail. What did you expect, and what did you get?

Situation 1   **Situation 2**

3. What do you regard as the major causes of your satisfaction? To what extent do you believe HRM activities were related to your satisfaction? Specifically, which activities do you believe to be most related to the customer service you received?

Situation 1   **Situation 2**

FORM 1.2.3
SELF-ASSESSMENT

Name _____ Group _____

With respect to only your performance on this exercise (both the written and group discussion parts), rate the extent to which you exhibited the behaviors described below, and mark your ratings in the spaces provided. Use the following scale:

x. Does not apply

1. Not at all

2. To a small extent

3. To some extent

4. To a great extent

5. To a very great extent

To what extent did you:

_____ 1. Help to establish a clear course of action needed to complete the work?

_____ 2. Speak effectively in the group?

_____ 3. Argue persuasively for a point of view?

_____ 4. Present your point of view concisely?

_____ 5. Write clearly and concisely?

_____ 6. Show sensitivity to other group members?

_____ 7. Stimulate and guide group members toward resolution of the assignment?

_____ 8. Listen carefully to other opinions and suggestions?

_____ 9. Analyze all pertinent information carefully before taking a position?

_____ 10. Display a willingness to state a position in a complex situation?

FORM 1.2.4
PEER ASSESSMENT

Peer/Observer Name_____ Discussant's Name_____ Group_____

Directions for observation: Become familiar with the 10 behaviors or activities listed below. Observe your designated discussant on the extent to which he or she exhibited these behaviors with respect to the exercise. Be prepared to explain your observations and the basis for your assessments. Please note that assessments of "5" on all behaviors would represent clearly outstanding and *rare* performance in the exercise. A more likely profile would be a spread of assessments across the 10 behaviors, with some assessments reflecting excellent performance while others reflect a need to improve in an area. *Rate the extent to which the participant exhibited the behaviors described below and mark your ratings in the spaces provided. Use the following scale:*

x. Does not apply

1. Not at all

2. To a small extent

3. To some extent

4. To a great extent

5. To a very great extent

To what extent did the participant:

_____ 1. Help to establish a clear course of action needed to complete the work?

_____ 2. Speak effectively in the group?

_____ 3. Argue persuasively for a point of view?

_____ 4. Present a point of view concisely?

_____ 5. Write clearly and concisely?

_____ 6. Show sensitivity to other group members?

_____ 7. Stimulate and guide group members toward resolution of the assignment?

_____ 8. Listen carefully to other opinions and suggestions?

_____ 9. Analyze all pertinent information carefully before taking a position?

_____ 10. Display a willingness to state a position in a complex situation?

Exercise 1.2
Assessment Questions

Name _____ Group _____

1. Describe the experience you had in providing feedback on your designated discussant's performance. To what extent did you feel comfortable in that role? How might that role be improved with better directions, better assessment devices, etc.?

2. How did you feel about receiving feedback on your group performance? To what extent did you find the feedback helpful? How might that process be improved? To what extent did your self-assessment match the peer assessment?

3. Did this exercise give you a better understanding of the relationship between HRM-related activities and customer satisfaction? Explain your answer.

CHAPTER

COMPETITIVE ADVANTAGE THROUGH HUMAN RESOURCES*

*Contributed by David O. Ulrich.

OVERVIEW

As noted in Chapter 1, because organizations face increasing competition, managers have been confronted with greater demands to ensure organizational survival and competitive advantage. Consequently, they have sought strategies and practices that may assist them to meet outside pressures. Mergers, acquisitions, strategic alliances, downsizing, and restructuring are common responses to the new challenges facing organizations. The more effective use of human resources (HR) should be an integral part of these and other responses to these challenges.[1]

This chapter will discuss how the effective utilization of human resources can assist organizations in achieving a competitive advantage. We will describe several organizations which have pursued a competitive advantage through their HR. We will also identify the skills needed by managers and HR professionals if they are to assist organizations to become more competitive through the six HR policy domains introduced in Chapter 1.

OBJECTIVES

After studying this chapter, you should be able to:

1. Understand what is meant by competitive advantage, and why it is important for organizations to maintain it.
2. Describe how HR activities may provide businesses with a competitive advantage.
3. Identify the skills that general managers and human resource management (HRM) professionals will need if they are to assist organizations in becoming competitive.

Borg-Warner was a successful, diversified company with four major businesses: automotive parts, chemicals, protective services, and credit reporting. These businesses had been brought together to balance diverse business cycles; when one industry was flat, the other industries would be successful. In early 1987, Borg-Warner executives faced a serious challenge. The stock of the company was selling for approximately $35 per share. Analysts felt that the "breakup" value of Borg-Warner was closer to $55 per share. The breakup value is the sum of the amounts each of the four businesses could be independently sold for to separate buyers. This gap between actual and breakup value meant that a number of major investors and takeover artists began to buy Borg-Warner stock.

To avoid being taken over and broken up by investors, Borg-Warner managers decided to work with Merrill Lynch to buy back their own stock for a leveraged buy-out (LBO). With Merrill Lynch support, Borg-Warner borrowed approximately $4 billion and purchased all its stock, making it a private firm not traded on Wall Street. Unfortunately, by borrowing $4 billion, the business incurred an enormous debt payment (approximately $400 million per year) that actually exceeded annual profits of about $240 million. This meant that managers had to find ways of earning an additional $160 million in profits in 1988 and in each subsequent year to make payments on the debt. One short-term solution was to sell some of the businesses. In 1988, Borg-Warner sold the credit reporting business to TRW and the chemicals business to General Electric. The remaining protective service and automotive businesses still had to earn enormous cash to cover their debt.

The executives of Borg-Warner concluded that the key to success was to change the mind-set of the managers. That is, they wanted to change the way managers thought about their work in the business. If managers could begin to think as if they were owners, they might begin making decisions to emphasize savings. To help managers think like owners, the company asked managers throughout the organization to invest in the new company. Managers were required to invest from $50,000 to $1 million in the private company. This meant that managers tapped into their personal savings or pension plans. In addition, all managers in the company were offered training to help them understand the implications of the LBO. With such personal investments at stake, and because of training efforts, Borg-Warner managers began to change their mind-set, and the company was able to make payments on its debt.[2]

In competitive environments that firms such as Borg-Warner face, managers are rightfully concerned about how they can continue to be successful.[3] One major agenda for most firms facing technological, social, and competitor changes is to create a sustainable competitive advantage.[4]

COMPETITIVE ADVANTAGE

Competitive advantage refers to the ability of an organization to formulate strategies to exploit profitable opportunities, thereby maximizing its return on investment.[5] Two major principles, perceived customer value and uniqueness, describe the extent to which a business has a competitive advantage.

Customer Value

Competitive advantage occurs if customers perceive that they receive value from their transaction with an organization. Ensuring that customers receive value from transactions with a business requires that all employees focus on understanding customer needs and expectations. This can occur if customers are involved in designing products or service processes or are encouraged to assist companies in the design of HRM systems which would foster the delivery of desired goods and services.

Maintaining Uniqueness

The second principle of competitive advantage derives from offering a product or service that your competitor cannot easily imitate or copy. For example, you open a restaurant and serve hamburgers, and a competitor moves in next to you and also serves hamburgers that taste, cost, and are prepared just like yours. You may lose a large part of your business to your competitor unless you quickly offer something unique in your restaurant. Your restaurant needs to have something that is unique to continue to attract customers. Competitive advantage comes to a business when it adds value to customers through some form of uniqueness.

SOURCES OF UNIQUENESS. The key to any business's competitive advantage is to ensure that its uniqueness lasts over time. Three traditional avenues exist to offer customers uniqueness. These include having capabilities in finances or economics, strategy or product, and technology or operations. In addition to these sources, businesses may offer customers uniqueness through a nontraditional capability, namely, organizational processes. The four mechanisms for offering uniqueness are described below.

First, a business needs a *financial or economic capability.* This form of uniqueness occurs when a business receives special access to financial funding or is able to produce a good or service cheaper than someone else. If, for example, you had received a financial gift from family or friends to build your hamburger restaurant, without repayment of the gift, you might be able to charge less for your product than a competitor who borrowed money from a bank or financial institution. Your cheaper price for a hamburger would then become a source of uniqueness that customers would value.

The second source of uniqueness is *strategic or product capability.* That is, a business needs to offer a product or service that differentiates it from other products or services. In the hamburger wars, each restaurant has attempted to offer unique products and services to attract customers. Salad bars, taco bars, breakfasts, kids' meals, and games or prizes are examples of ways restaurants have attempted to make their products unique and appealing to customers.

A third source of uniqueness for a business is *technological or operational capability.* That is, a business should have a distinctive way of building or delivering its product or service. In the hamburger restaurant business, the different types of ovens used to prepare the hamburgers (broiled versus flame-grilled) may distinguish restaurants from each other. Customers may prefer one technological (cooking) process over another. In more complex businesses, technological capability may include research and development (R&D), engineering, computer systems, and manufacturing facilities.

A fourth source of uniqueness for a company that is seeking competitive advantage may be *organizational capability.* Organizational capability represents the business's ability to manage the organizational systems and people in order to match customer and strategic needs.[6] In a complex, dynamic, uncertain, and turbulent environment (e.g., changing customers, technology, suppliers, relevant laws and regulations), organizational capability derives from the organization's flexibility, adaptiveness, and responsiveness. In less dynamic environments, organizational capability derives from maintaining continuity and stability of organization practices. In a restaurant, organizational capability may be derived from having employees who ensure that when customers enter the restaurant, their needs are better met than when the customers go to a competitor's restaurant. That is, employees will want to ensure that customers are served promptly and pleasantly, and that the food is well prepared.

To better meet customer needs through people, organizational systems need to be put in place. These organizational systems help to determine how people are hired, trained, motivated, and treated, and how they become committed to the business. As discussed in Chapter 1, the primary organization systems that affect employees are a business's HRM practices.[7]

HRM practices are the set of organizational activities that directly affect how employees perceive their jobs. As noted in Chapter 1, six domains of HRM activities have been identified. These are: organizational design, staffing; employee and organizational development; performance management; reward systems, benefits, and compliance; and communications and public relations. In Figure 2.1, some of the critical issues and activities that should be considered and choices that should be made in each of these domains are listed. As these activities are adapted to conditions confronting organizations, businesses should gain (and maintain) competitive advantage. In fact, at companies such as 3M, Procter & Gamble, and Donnelly Mirrors, research has shown that the use of innovative HRM programs, especially employee-centered management practices, were the primary reasons for the firms' financial successes.[8]

At Borg-Warner, organizational capability has been a critical source of sustained competitiveness. Borg-Warner's challenge has been to create a new mind-set among managers so that they would think like owners. The change in the reward system and the training and communication programs informing employees about the

FIGURE 2.1
SAMPLE OF ISSUES AND CHOICES FOR HRM PRACTICES

ORGANIZATIONAL DESIGN
- The extent to which the organization should formalize how work is to be accomplished through a set of standardized operating procedures, formal chains of command, extensive rules and regulations, and detailed job descriptions.
- The extent to which different organizational units maintain their independence and responsiveness to their unique market niches while integrating their work with other organizational units through liaison teams, matrix organizations, etc.
- The design of jobs so that individuals within the organization work on tasks which are rewarding and self-reinforcing.
- The processes used to shape the organizational structure (e.g., how decisions are made, how widely accountability is distributed, how clearly roles and responsibilities are defined).

STAFFING
- The type of criteria to set for bringing in new employees (e.g., short-term versus long-term, full-time versus part-time, contract versus leased employees, job-focused versus career-focused, customer perspective).
- Procedures for recruiting and socializing new employees into the organization (e.g., orientation, socialization, and mentoring programs).
- Design of career paths and ladders in the organization (e.g., within one function versus across different functions).
- Processes for succession planning (e.g., formalized systems, involvement of senior managers, integration with strategic planning, link to developmental programs, emphasis on internal versus external candidates).
- Types of programs for terminated employees (e.g., during layoffs, downsizing, early retirements).

EMPLOYEE AND ORGANIZATIONAL DEVELOPMENT
- Desired outcomes of development (e.g., conceptual understanding, skill building, attitude change, team building, problem solving).
- Types of participants in developmental programs (e.g., new employees, first-line supervisors, middle-level managers, top executives).
- The nature of the content built into developmental programs, and how programs are integrated with the strategic direction of firms.

- Delivery of training programs (e.g., internal versus external faculty and facilities, use of line managers).
- Evaluation of programs to assess changes in employee or organizational performance.
- Alternatives to development used to create organizational competencies (e.g., cross-functional career moves, special assignments).

PERFORMANCE MANAGEMENT
- Types of standards set for employees or units (e.g., behavior-focused versus outcome-focused, short-term versus long-term, explicit versus implicit, linked to individual versus strategic performance or plans).
- Types of performance review feedback sessions offered (e.g., frequency, nature of feedback, monitoring of feedback sessions, forms used, formal reporting systems in existence, managerial accountability).
- Processes used to ensure that feedback occurs continually (e.g., quarterly reviews).
- Sources of data for measurement and criterion development (e.g., clients, customers, peers, subordinates).

REWARD SYSTEMS, BENEFITS, AND COMPLIANCE
- Types of financial incentives existing (e.g., short-term versus long-term, base versus incentive pay, pay for performance versus pay for seniority).
- The extent to which reward systems are linked to strategic plans and encourage employees to work toward accomplishing business needs and meeting customer requirements.
- The extent to which rewards are based on individual versus group or corporate performance.
- Structure of nonfinancial rewards (e.g., recognition programs, titles, informal status symbols).

COMMUNICATIONS AND PUBLIC RELATIONS
- Types of information presented to employees, manner of presentation (e.g., confidential versus public).
- Types of communication channels; dissemination of information inside and outside the organization; opinion surveys; open-door policies.
- Design of communication programs (e.g., public meetings, management forums for discussion, videos, written communications, bulletins).

LBO were used to build this new mind-set among employees. Employee pay was directly linked to paying down the debt, and a monthly communication briefing reported progress toward this strategic goal.[9]

HRM AS A COMPETITIVE ADVANTAGE

The previous discussion provides a basis for thinking about HR as a competitive advantage. Below, we review three specific ways that HRM activities can build organizational capability and sustain a business's competitive advantage: implementing a strategy, dealing with change, and building strategic unity.

HRM and Strategy Implementation

Any business that wants to remain successful must continually assess and formulate new strategies to meet the needs of its customers in more effective ways. It is important that employees be informed about the organization's strategic mission. For example, at Motorola, employees are kept apprised of their company's strategic plan, goals, and subsequent performance.[10] Employees receive corporate performance data relative to goals on a quarterly basis. HRM practices should be the mechanisms used to focus people's attention on the major strategic issues in the organization. In general, by addressing the choices and issues raised in Figure 2.1, organizations can determine how they should alter their HRM practices to meet their strategic goals. For example, if the organization is emphasizing cost or differentiation strategies, several changes in HRM activities can enable those strategies to become a major focus in the organization. A cost-oriented strategy, for example, calls for multiskilled employees; smaller, less experienced staffs; broad and deep delegation and accountability; and a focus on performance-based pay with a great emphasis on efficiency and financial impact. A differentiation strategy calls for specialists in product design and development, higher budgets for research and development, rewards for innovative ideas related to quality, and customer-based performance appraisal.

Unfortunately, many businesses fail to carefully and seriously consider the HRM issues described previously in Figure 2.1 as part of their strategic planning efforts. These businesses often end up with Strategic Plans on Top Shelf (SPOTS). These SPOTS are elegantly drafted, documented, and detailed descriptions of what the business strategy should be, but they fail to include the means for accomplishing the strategy.

One organization which did successfully modify existing HRM practices to meet strategic goals was Borg-Warner. After the LBO at Borg-Warner, the ability to generate cash to cover the large debt was critical. Numerous activities were undertaken to ensure that more cash came into the organization quickly. For example, in one division, the receivables, or the amount due from customers, were averaging payment in 90 days. This meant that for 90 days, customers had use of money due to Borg-Warner. In addition, sales commissions were paid on the point of sale, so the sales force had no incentive to collect money, only to make sales. Thus, to meet its cash needs, Borg-Warner changed the terms of sales and modified the HR reward system so that half of the commission was received on the point of sale and half on collection of receivables. As a result, receivables were reduced from 90 to 30 days. Clearly, changing the incentive system facilitated the accomplishment of the organization's strategic goal of generating cash.

HR and the Capacity for Change

In a constantly changing business world, organizations must be able to adapt to changes or risk failure, and yet the first reaction that most people have to change is resistance. Typically, individuals express concern over changing habits, norms, and ways of doing things. In organizations, the capacity for change may be increased by using HRM tools correctly. For example, organizations

interested in becoming more adaptable to environmental pressures and changes should hire people who are flexible, and should develop people in such a way that they will realize that change is an important part of growth. Further, the company should set performance standards to encourage flexibility and diversity, and should reward employees for being innovative. J. Walter Thompson (JWT) was troubled by the quality and quantity of proposed advertising campaigns. Its executives came up with an innovative solution: let their research and account management departments generate ideas along with the creative department. Executives at JWT credit the new system for winning new accounts with Goodyear Tire and Nuprin. Organizations need to comunicate to employees the types of changes that are needed and why they are critical for the company's survival and success.

In an increasingly competitive environment, organizations with a greater capacity for change are more likely to satisfy, retain, and attract customers. In the automotive industry, in the 1970s, the "lead time" for new cars was about 7 years. That is, it took about 7 years to go from a new concept to a prototype to production. In the early 1980s, Ford introduced the Taurus/Sable cars in about 3½ years, cutting the lead time by half. This reduction in lead time came, in part, from extensive training of all employees involved in the Taurus/Sable project. The lead time was further reduced by creating a product team of suppliers, engineers, manufacturers, distributors, assembly workers, and customers who all worked together offering input into the design and building of the new cars. This novel group effort of involving all important parties, coupled with the other HRM changes (e.g., training, staffing, communication, rewards), allowed Ford to increase its capacity for change and to significantly reduce its lead time. Consequently, the increased capacity for change had an impact on Ford's profits and performance.[11] Unfortunately, the U.S. automakers still have a way to go in improving "lead time" and several other key efficiency indicators.

Human Resources and Strategic Unity

The third way that organizations can develop organizational capability and sustain competitive advantage is by building strategic unity. Strategic unity represents the extent to which stakeholders inside (e.g., employees) and outside a business (e.g., customers) share a core set of values and assumptions about the business. For example, if the stakeholders believe that customer service is of central importance to corporate performance, this core value can be developed and nurtured among employees, suppliers, and customers of the business.

Nordstrom, a retail chain that started in Seattle and expanded throughout the United States, includes high commitment to customer service as part of its organizational mission. Training programs, incentive programs, and communication programs consistently focus on the importance of customer service. For Nordstrom, internal strategic unity exists since employees at all levels and in all departments share a similar commitment. This commitment is achieved despite the fact that a high percentage of Nordstrom employees are unionized. The benefit of the internal unity is that it channels employees' attention toward an important organizational goal. Also, in this case, the unity helps the company to provide a unique service to customers that cannot easily be copied by competitors. As a result, when customers link Nordstrom with extraordinary service, Nordstrom enhances its competitive position.[12]

SKILLS REQUIRED FOR HRM COMPETITIVENESS

For HRM practices to be used to gain competitive advantage, both general managers and HRM professionals must have a set of skills or competencies that build competitiveness. As noted in Chapter 1, competencies represent an individual's knowledge, skills, abilities, and activities performed. That is, these individuals should know the business, keep aware of current HR developments, manage the process of change, and integrate all these roles in the context of the organization's mission. To refine these broad skills, general managers and HRM professionals alike should become proficient in oral and written communication, decision making, leadership, innovative thinking, planning and organizing, and objectivity about themselves.

General Manager Skills

General managers have primary responsibility for ensuring that businesses have a competitive advantage. To do this, they must integrate financial, strategic, technological, and organizational capabilities. Most important, they must assist businesses in developing stronger organizational capabilities so that they are able to effectively use HRM activities to build competitiveness. To strengthen existing organizational capabilities, general managers need to develop at least four broad skills or competencies: creating a need for HRM changes, creating a vision of the importance of HRM practices, generating support for HRM activities, and becoming proficient in the delivery of HRM practices.

CREATE A NEED FOR HRM CHANGES. Individuals must be convinced that they need to change before they will be committed to any program for change. Until employees feel a need to pay attention to certain

activities, they are unlikely to do so. Since HRM practices are central to business competitiveness, general managers must encourage employees to be aware of existing HRM practices in the organization. General managers should share data about the organization to help employees recognize how important HRM practices are to the overall success of the company. Typically, they share results of organizational effectiveness criteria (e.g., absenteeism records, grievances filed, productivity indexes) and HRM programs (e.g., staffing, training) that may be related to these criteria. For example, at the Marriott Corporation, data for each facility on turnover and retention rates are shared with employees to indicate how successful the current reward programs or staffing systems are.

CREATE A VISION OF THE IMPORTANCE OF HRM PRACTICES. Most successful businesses have identified the direction in which they are headed. This direction reflects not only short-term goals (meeting this quarter's profit plan), but a longer-term vision (e.g., a 5- or 10-year plan) as well. The long-range vision reflects the organization's goals and core principles and values.

General managers who want to use HRM practices for competitiveness need to relate the company's strategic vision to its HRM practices. That is, general managers must emphasize the important role that employees play in the company's ability to meet its long-term business plans. This was done at the Marriott Corporation when general managers identified the HRM activities that were needed (e.g., staffing, retention, and incentive programs) to assist the corporation in meeting its long-range goal of being the employer of choice. Similarly, at Borg-Warner, the relationship between the business goals (e.g., generating cash to cover debt) and HRM practices (e.g., rewards, development, performance appraisal, communication practices) was made explicit by general managers.

GENERATE COMMITMENT TO USING HRM ACTIVITIES. General managers need to demonstrate their personal support for HRM activities. They can do this, for example, by participating in staffing activities (e.g., succession planning) or by serving as trainers or trainees in management development programs. They can also use effective performance appraisal practices (e.g., providing timely feedback to subordinates) and encourage their supervisory subordinates to do the same. In addition, general managers need to build commitment among employees to use recommended HRM practices. They may do this by sharing information throughout the organization about the importance of HRM practices, through speeches, training programs, orientation programs, newsletters, and slogans. For example, at Marriott Corporation, general managers spoke extensively about the importance of being the employer of choice, and used this theme in all the corporation's newsletters, videos, training programs, and annual meetings.

General managers can enhance commitment to HRM practices by encouraging employees to participate in the various HRM programs. For example, individuals can be appointed to HRM task forces or they can be requested to prepare and deliver presentations on the importance of HRM to employees or external groups. At one computer firm, turnover of high-performing engineers was high (about 20 percent) after 3 years with the company. In an effort to reduce the turnover, the highest-rated engineers were assigned to spend 3 months recruiting. As recruiters, the engineers had to present the value of working at the company to students on college campuses. After 3 months and many sales pitches for working with the company, the engineers expressed greater personal commitment to the firm, and turnover was reduced.

LEARN AND BECOME PROFICIENT IN THE DELIVERY OF HRM PRACTICES. General managers who develop competence in HRM practices need to be current on the delivery of alternative HRM tools. That is, they need to know when to use career development programs, assist in downsizing efforts, or adapt staffing systems to address organizational issues. Such proficiency may derive from continued education through attending seminars, reading, or meeting with experts. As discussed in Chapter 3, underlying this competency in HRM practices is a knowledge of the legal and regulatory implications of HRM activities. As general managers become more knowledgeable about HRM practices, they should make more informed choices about the appropriate activities to use. As a result, the organization's competitive advantage should improve.

HRM Professional Skills

HRM professionals share responsibility with general managers for using HRM practices to build organizational competitiveness. As HRM professionals link their work with business needs, they become strategic business partners and build competitiveness through HRM practices.[13] Three cases illustrate how HRM professionals became business partners and enhanced corporate performance.

BAXTER HEALTHCARE AND AMERICAN HOSPITAL SUPPLY. When Baxter Healthcare and American Hospital Supply merged in 1985 to form the largest hospital supply firm in the world, HRM professionals at all levels of the organization displayed leadership roles. The greatest challenge to this merger was the ability to integrate diverse cultures, mind-sets, and individuals into a commonly focused and rationally organized

business that added value to investors and customers. HRM professionals identified a series of processes that would define jobs, identify and create a shared vision, and enable the new company to be competitive in the marketplace.[14] Jobs were redesigned to enhance understanding of customer needs, training programs were established to develop a unified value structure, and performance management and pay-for-performance systems were installed which directed the focus of operations toward increasing perceived customer value.

FEDERAL AVIATION ADMINISTRATION. After the controller strike in 1981, executives at the Federal Aviation Administration (FAA) realized that they had to improve working conditions and morale throughout the agency. To begin this implementation effort, the HRM professionals designed training programs for the top 1000 managers. These programs were designed on the assumption that managers should use the HRM tools to improve morale within the agency. HRM professionals worked as strategic business partners to help create a vision for the agency and to institute the process to share the vision. Employee opinion surveys were instituted, along with subordinate appraisals of supervisors and managers, to assess the extent to which management was helping the controllers do the best possible job.

WHIRLPOOL. As the appliance industry became increasingly competitive through mergers and increased global competition, executives at Whirlpool knew they had to become even more aggressive to remain competitive. Working with the vice president of human resources, the chairperson at Whirlpool established a vision for the company through the year 2000. With the goal of institutionalizing and building commitment to the vision, a 1-week executive program was designed to enable the top 50 officers and managers in the company to discuss the organization's vision and prepare action plans. This executive development program became a major tool for creating unity and making change happen at Whirlpool.

In each of these cases, HRM professionals played a significant role as business partners to develop strategic plans for the organization and to design HRM activities that would add value to the business operations.[15] To serve in this partnership role, the HRM professionals demonstrated mastery in three broad skill areas and were able to integrate their knowledge of these areas. The three skill domains were knowing the business, designing and delivering appropriate HRM programs, and managing the process of change. These are illustrated in Figure 2.2.

KNOW THE BUSINESS. HRM professionals as business partners need to know the business or understand

FIGURE 2.2
HR COMPETENCIES NEEDED FOR STRATEGIC BUSINESS PARTNERS

BUSINESS COMPETENCIES
- **Financial or economic.** Know the organization's capabilities in finance, strategy, and technology.
- **Strategic or product capabilities.** Know customer requirements and how to measure them.
- **Technological.** Know the most important R&D and technological operations as related to the products or service.

HRM DESIGN AND DELIVERY COMPETENCIES
- **Organizational design.**
- **Staffing.**
- **Employee and organizational development.**
- **Performance management.**
- **Reward systems, benefits, and compliance.**
- **Comunications and public relations.**

MANAGEMENT-OF-CHANGE COMPETENCIES
- **Contracting** to establish relationships with clients, customers, outside experts.
- **Diagnosing** problems from the perspective of all constituents.
- **Intervening** as a change agent to lay groundwork for implementation.
- **Implementing** changes to facilitate competitive advantage.
- **Evaluating** changes to assess effects and make alterations.
- **Influencing** to make adjustments in interventions based on the data.

the organization's capabilities in finance, strategy, and technology. Knowing the firm's *economic* or financial capability means knowing how the firm gains access to capital, how the firm manages cost of capital, how financial systems are used within the firm to measure performance, and how resources are allocated according to financial criteria. Being aware of *strategic* or product capabilities means understanding customer buying criteria, identifying differentiated product features, and dealing with issues of market segmentation. Knowing the organization's *technological* capability requires that HRM professionals understand the research and development (R&D), engineering, and manufacturing processes of product development. Learning about the business requires that HRM professionals spend time with customers, line managers, R&D technicians, and others who are central to business operations. Reading business plans, asking questions about specific technical operations, and subscribing to technical publications exemplify ways to gain this competency. At Baxter Healthcare, the FAA, and Whirlpool, HRM professionals understood the financial, product, and technological components so that they were able to devise HRM programs that directly contributed to business success.

DESIGN AND DELIVER HRM PROGRAMS. In order to design and deliver timely and effective HRM programs, HRM professionals need to be experts in behavioral science. They need to continually update their knowledge and skills in the areas of organizational design, staffing, employee and organizational development, performance management, reward systems, benefits and compliance, and communication and public relations. They can accomplish this by attending conferences, reading current literature, conducting research, and talking with colleagues in companies and academic settings. HRM professionals should also monitor the organization's HRM programs in order to make any necessary additions and revisions, and to ensure that the programs reflect state-of-the-art practices in consonance with the mission and strategic goals of the organization and legal guidelines.

MANAGE THE PROCESS OF CHANGE. HRM professionals need to be able to manage change processes so that business needs merge with HRM activities. They can do this by contracting relationships with clients, customers, and outside experts; gaining influence within the organization; diagnosing problems; implementing changes; intervening with ideas; and evaluating program results. Merely knowing the contents of a new compensation or performance appraisal program does not guarantee that the program will be useful to the organization, even if such programs appear to be consistent with the business strategy. HRM professionals also need to be able to manage the change process by identifying any potential resistance to the changes and building commitment to the new programs.

INTEGRATION. The ability to integrate business knowledge, HRM design and delivery skills, and change process competencies is essential if HRM practitioners are to be successful. For example, the HRM professionals at Baxter were able to bring together two diverse organizations into a new, stronger organization because they knew the business, designed and delivered timely HRM programs, and knew how to institute and manage change effectively. Likewise, in the FAA, the senior HR executives who succeeded were those who understood the operations of the agency, were current in how the agency's HRM practices could be modified to build morale and commitment, and involved the appropriate operations managers in building commitment to change.

SUMMARY

Competitive advantage has become and will continue to be a major driving force for most businesses. To attain competitive advantage, businesses need to add value to customers and offer uniqueness. Four capabilities provide a business's uniqueness: financial, strategic or product, technological or operational, and organizational. To create and sustain competitive advantage, organizational capability should be emphasized. Organizational capability derives from a business's HRM practices.

HRM practices build competitiveness because they allow for strategic implementation, create a capacity for change, and instill strategic unity. To accomplish these three outcomes, HRM activities from all six domains need to be used. These domains are organizational design; staffing; employee training and organizational development; performance management; reward systems, benefits and compliance; and communications and public relations. To use HRM practices for competitiveness, general managers and HRM professionals need to acquire and maintain business competencies, HRM design and delivery competencies, and management-of-change competencies.

In general, the view of HRM outlined in this chapter provides a foundation for integrating HRM activities into the organization's mission and goals. We have emphasized that HRM professionals should be actively involved in building more competitive organizations through the six HRM domains. One necessary competency for both line managers and HRM professionals is a knowledge of the legal implications of all HRM activities. Among the most important elements of this competency are the many equal employment opportunity (EEO) laws and regulations which affect all six of the HRM domains. We will explore this critical area in Chapter 3.

DISCUSSION QUESTIONS

1. What is meant by the term "competitive advantage"? Why is it important for an organization?
2. How can HRM activities be used to assist organizations in becoming more competitive?
3. What skills are needed by general managers and HRM professionals if they are to help organizations to attain a competitive advantage?
4. Provide some recommendations for how general managers and HRM professionals can acquire the skills they need to utilize HRM programs effectively.
5. Provide two examples of companies you are familiar with which are not using their HRM programs to maintain or create a competitive advantage. What specific suggestions would you offer to them?

NOTES

1. Ulrich, D. (1989). Tie the corporate knot: Gaining complete customer commitment. *Sloan Management Review, 30*(4), 19–27.
2. See note 1.
3. Porter, M. E. (1980). *Competitive strategy: Techniques for analyzing industries and competitors.* New York: The Free Press. See also: Vesey, J. T. (1991). The new competitors: They think in terms of 'speed-to-market.' *Academy of Management Executive, 5*(2), 23–33.
4. Porter, M. E. (1985). *Competitive advantage: Creating and sustaining superior performance.* New York: The Free Press. See also: Hitt, M. A., Hoskisson, R. E., and Harrison, J. S. (1991). Strategic competitiveness in the 1990s: Challenges and opportunities for U.S. executives. *Academy of Management Executive, 5*(2), 7–22.
5. Hill, C. W. L., and Jones, G. R. (1989). *Strategic management: An integrated approach.* Boston, MA: Houghton Mifflin. See also: Fiol, C. M. (1991). Managing culture as a competitive resource: An identity-based view of sustainable competitive advantage. *Journal of Management, 17*(1), 191–212.
6. Ulrich, D. (1987). Organizational capability as a competitive advantage: Human resource professionals as strategic partners. *Human Resource Planning, 10*(4), 169–184.
7. See note 1. See also: Ulrich, D., and Lake, D. (1991). Organizational capability: Creating competitive advantage. *Academy of Management Executive, 5*(1), 77–92.
8. Schuster, F. E. (1988). Reviving productivity in America. *Personnel Administrator, 33*(7), 65–68. See also: McCann, J. E. (1991). Design principles for an innovating company. *Academy of Management Executive, 5*(2), 76–93.
9. See note 1.
10. See note 8.
11. See note 1.
12. See note 1.
13. See note 6. See also: Burack, E. H. (1985). Linking corporate business and human resource planning: Strategic issues and concerns. *Human Resource Planning, 8*(3), 133–145.
14. Ulrich, D., Cody, T., LaFasto, F., and Rucci, T. (1990). Human resources at Baxter Health Care Corporation merger: A strategic partner role. *Human Resource Planning, 12*, 87–102.
15. See note 1. See also: Dyer, L. (1984). Studying human resource strategy: An approach and an agenda. *Industrial Relations, 23*, 156–169; Niehaus, R. J., and Price, R. (1987). *Strategic human resource planning applications.* New York: Plenum Publishers; Schuler, R. S., and Jackson, S. E. (1987). Linking competitive advantage with human resource management practices. *Academy of Management Executive, 1*(3), 207–219.

EXERCISE 2.1
HR ISSUES AT VALLEY
NATIONAL BANK*

OVERVIEW

In Chapter 2, you were introduced to the HR issues that HRM professionals and general managers must deal with if they are to assist the organization in becoming competitive and in meeting its goals. This exercise enables you to further develop your analytical skills as you assess the HR issues affecting competitiveness at Valley National Bank.

LEARNING OBJECTIVES

After completing this exercise, you should be able to:

1. Identify HR issues that may affect organizational effectiveness and competitiveness.
2. Develop strategies for dealing with HR concerns.
3. Appreciate the difficulties in resolving HR problems.

PROCEDURE

Part A: Individual Analysis

Step 1. Read Chapter 2, paying particular attention to the HR issues and concerns outlined in Fig-

---

*Contributed by David O. Ulrich.

ure 2.1 in the context of the discussion on competitive advantage.

Step 2. Read the background information on Valley National Bank provided in Exhibits 2.1.1 and 2.1.2. In the context of what you consider to be the bank's competitive advantage, identify the major HR issues facing the vice president's department. Outline some strategies for dealing with these issues. Develop a rank-ordered priority list of the first three issues which require your attention. Provide a written justification for your recommendations. Enter your rank orderings and justifications in the space provided on Form 2.1.1. Provide your opinions of the recommendations from Mr. Sterrett as well, and answer the assessment questions at the end of the exercise.

Part B: Group Analysis

Step 1. In groups of about six, identify what you believe to be the competitive advantage of the accounting department. Review all individual 2.1.1 forms and assessment question answers and determine the HR issues of greatest concern to the accounting department. Reach a consensus on the top three issues which can affect the competitive advantage. Discuss why these issues must be resolved if the department is to assist the bank in becoming more competitive in the 1990s. Identify the benefits and drawbacks to each recommendation.

Step 2. A representative from each group should present the consensus recommendations and rationale to the rest of the class.

EXHIBIT 2.1.1
BACKGROUND INFORMATION FOR VALLEY NATIONAL BANK

RECENT BANK HISTORY

Valley National Bank (VNB) is a relatively young financial institution with close to $10 billion in assets, although it will shortly have about $12 billion in assets. As a whole, there is a wealth of technical talent in the company, yet most of the experiences have been developed within the confines of $1 and $2 billion institutions. The managers and employees have not had much collective experience in managing a $12 billion company. In addition, members of senior management currently recognize that they must make some critical strategic decisions regarding the future if the bank is to remain competitive in the 1990s.

ACCOUNTING DEPARTMENT

The vice president of accounting reports directly to the senior vice president of management accounting, who in turn reports to the controller of the company (see the condensed organizational chart in Exhibit 2.1.2.). The vice president, Suzanne Roberts, was promoted to her current position to manage the Accounting Department, which the previous manager had let get out of control. Her job is to provide computer software to line and staff management throughout the organization so that managers may be able to make better decisions in the daily operations of their respective departments. The tools, although difficult to implement, have proved to be very useful in institutions with postures of high growth. The information is financial in nature and, for the most part, is not the type of information that VNB bankers are used to receiving. Therefore, Ms. Roberts' current charge is twofold: (1) to educate the company in the use of the information so that the bank will ultimately benefit in terms of bottom-line results and (2) to identify those sectors of business in which the bank does exceptionally well so that better and more focused strategic decisions can be made.

As challenging as her stated primary job responsibilities are, Ms. Roberts believes that another issue she currently faces is getting the right people in the right places in her department so that they can accomplish their goals. When she came into the department, she quickly concluded that some of the best contributors in the department were also the lowest-paid employees.

Bob Phillips was the former manager of the department. Through a merger, he came to VNB to manage the department, having had experience in supervising two people at his previous position. In his role as vice president of accounting, he was asked to supervise about 10 people. Over the course of 2 years, things got so out of hand that his employees did not know what they were supposed to do, except in emergency situations which seemed to be happening every day. Performance reviews of employees were late by up to 6 months. Naturally, employee morale was very low and attitudes toward the company became hardened. Good people quit the bank or transferred to other departments. The job of finding replacements for these individuals was poorly done, with the result that, often, the first person who walked in for an interview was hired. Today, there are several people working for the department who probably should never have been hired in the first place. Unfortunately, their options are such that it probably pays them to stay rather than voluntarily leave.

Bob clearly lacked the organizational and planning skills needed to effectively manage his people for the tasks at hand. In addition, his weak interpersonal skills have created hard feelings among employees in the department. He can usually arrive at a very good financial or accounting solution to a problem, and he has an extensive knowledge of the information tools. However, he has a very difficult time working with other people in a practical way to implement his solutions.

Needless to say, there is resentment left over among some employees because Bob is still paid a very good salary and has a good title to go with his general incompetence and reduced responsibilities. Ms. Roberts expresses her belief that the company should sever its ties with Bob, but other external factors make this choice difficult. For example, Bob has faced some very severe personal and health problems since transferring to VNB.

Carla Goodman is an employee who previously worked for Bob for about 15 years. When the Accounting Department at VNB was established, she was placed in charge of several people and given a promotion of two pay grade levels. This decision proved to be disastrous, because it became apparent that she could not (or would not) accept the responsibility of supervising and reviewing people. She was quickly relieved of these duties, but her salary grade level remained intact, so that today she is overpaid for her overall responsibilities. Her title is such that it implies a lower pay level in the company, but it fools no one. She is somewhat above average as a technical worker and understands the flow of transactions quite well. Currently, Ms. Roberts often has Carla working by herself since she doesn't make a very good impression upon other people. She has the tendency to openly criticize the company, which arouses the concerns of other employees. In fact, on occasion, she and Bob resort to shouting matches to get their respective points across to each other.

Greg Williams has been with the company about 8 years and has worked for Ms. Roberts for about 2½ years in various capacities. He has progressed in a very normal fashion in the bank. However, he has seen younger people like Ms. Roberts move ahead of him on the organizational ladder. He expresses concern that his career may be leveling off unless something dramatic happens. He is not the quickest person to "catch onto things" in a technical sense and has a difficult time interacting effectively with people. These factors reduce his chances for a promotion. In general, he is a conscientious, mild-mannered employee who doesn't normally complain about things. He is good at taking orders but not very good at handing them out.

Kathy Lewis is the most promising employee in the department today in terms of future potential within the company. She is technically sharp, with considerable knowledge of the new information systems, and has shown some promise in the effective management of people. She has been an employee of the company for a number of years, and she worked for Bob at the previous bank before the merger. She understands his odd nature. Her skills allow her to get more done than most people can do, and she is willing to put in extra hours of work. She did announce her resignation from the company at one time because of the mounting problems of the department, but a senior vice president talked her into staying by implying that changes would be made sometime. Kathy is probably worth more to the bank than her current salary indicates, especially in light of the salaries that Bob and Carla get. The normal guidelines should allow her to catch up in the next 1 to 2 years. She could probably also gain from receiving experiences in other departments, but Ms. Roberts recognizes that she could not afford to let Kathy go due to the lack of depth of the other employees.

Overall, things are probably not as bad as they may appear to be. Ms. Roberts does, however, get concerned from time to time about the general lack of depth in the department, as the rest of the bank looks to accounting for help in becoming more competitive. Ms. Roberts has met with Mr. Sterrett of the HRM Department, who has recommended that Mr. Phillips be terminated immediately but that Ms. Goodman be retained because of a possible sex discrimination lawsuit.

EXHIBIT 2.1.2
ORGANIZATIONAL CHART FOR VALLEY NATIONAL BANK

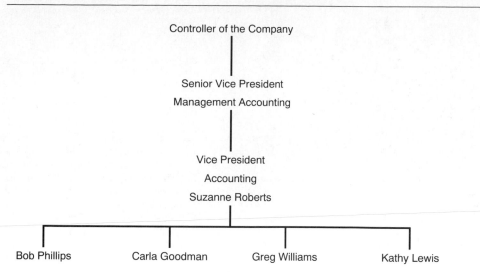

FORM 2.1.1
PRIORITY LIST OF HRM ISSUES

Name _____ Group _____

First HRM area in need of attention:

      Justification:

      Action to be taken:

Second area in need of attention:

      Justification:

      Action to be taken:

Third area in need of attention:

      Justification:

      Action to be taken:

Do you agree or disagree with Mr. Sterrett's recommendations? Explain your position. How would you respond to these recommendations?

Exercise 2.1
Assessment Questions

Name _____ Group _____

1. Where do the problems facing Ms. Roberts fit in terms of the six HRM domains?

2. What other information would be helpful to you in preparing the actions you recommend?

3. What steps would you take to determine the legality of your action?

4. What is "unique" about VNB? How could this "uniqueness" give the bank a competitive advantage?

EXERCISE 2.2
THE COMPETITIVE ADVANTAGE OF
MARRIOTT CORPORATION*

OVERVIEW

In 1987, Marriott Corporation employed approximately 220,000 employees. From 1964 through 1987, Marriott had been one of the most successful firms in the United States, with 20 percent compounded growth in both sales and return on equity. It had established a strong presence in a variety of service-related industries: hotels, airline food service, business food service, family dining, and contract services. A key to Marriott's success in each of these lines of business came from its deserved reputation for providing outstanding service to guests and customers. As a result of excellent service, the Marriott Corporation was considered by customers as the "preferred provider," or the provider customers thought of first when making lodging or food choices.

In 1988, at their management planning meeting, Marriott executives decided that a second major emphasis was necessary for continued success in the 1990s. Along with being the "provider of choice," Marriott decided to become the "employer of choice." It was felt that if Marriott could not continue to attract, retain, and manage employees, then the corporation's rapid growth would slow down. As Marriott Corporation enters the more competitive decade of the 1990s, managing employees and becoming the employer of choice is not an option; it is seen as central to business success and should be directly linked to the "provider of choice" emphasis. For example, one of Marriott Corporation's central challenges has been to ensure that qualified employees join and stay in the business. Hiring more mature employees, allowing for part-time work schedules, and busing employees from some distance to the work setting have become staffing practices designed to help meet Marriott's organizational capability.

LEARNING OBJECTIVES

After completing this exercise, you should be able to:

1. Identify a number of specific HRM practices which can be pursued by Marriott to create and sustain its goal to be the "employer of choice."

---

*Contributed by David O. Ulrich.

2. Understand the connection between the goals of being the "employer of choice" and the "provider of choice."

PROCEDURE

In the context of this discussion on competitive advantage, what specific steps should Marriott take to create and sustain its image as the "employer of choice"?

Part A: Individual Analysis

Before class, generate a list of three actions the organization can take which will directly contribute to this goal and fit within the framework of competitive advantage. Bear in mind that because competitive advantage does entail labor costs, your recommendations must be made in the context of estimated relative costs for the various actions the organization could take. Try to think of organizational characteristics and policies to which you would be attracted as a recent college graduate. In other words, to what characteristics of an employer and a job are you most attracted? How could Marriott use this information to meet its objectives in the context of cost control, the "provider of choice" emphasis, competitive advantage, and total customer satisfaction? Prepare your priority list on Form 2.2.1, with a concise written justification for your rank ordering of actions. Also, complete the assessment questions for the exercise.

Part B: Group Analysis

Step 1. In groups of about six people, exchange your priority lists so that all group members have had an opportunity to review each one. Attempt to reach consensus on a rank-ordered list of three specific actions the Marriott Corporation should take to contribute to its goal of becoming the "employer of choice" in the context of one or more principles of competitive advantage, and in terms of the "provider of choice" emphasis. How could the HRM systems contribute to the "employer of choice" while at the same time developing the HR competencies summarized in Figure 2.2?

Step 2. A group leader will be designated who will present the consensus view of the group. Discussion should focus on the extent to which the various groups agree on the priority list of Marriott activities.

FORM 2.2.1
PRIORITY LIST FOR MARRIOTT

Name _____ Group _____

Competitive Advantage Principle

Priority 1:

Justification:

Priority 2:

Justification:

Priority 3:

Justification:

Exercise 2.2
Assessment Questions

Name _____ Group _____

1. To what extent do your recommendations generalize to organizations other than Marriott? If they do not generalize, why not?

2. What competitive advantage principle did you consider in compiling your priority list?

3. What other preparation could you have made for class discussion on the Marriott Corporation?

3

C H A P T E R

EQUAL EMPLOYMENT OPPORTUNITY*

*Contributed by H. John Bernardin and Barbara A. Lee.

OVERVIEW

Chapter 1 summarized the regulatory environment in which human resource management (HRM) is practiced today. Many experts in the field have noted that the legal environment is the most important component of the external environment for HRM, and that legal considerations are the primary constraint on personnel decisions and the primary force shaping personnel policy. For example, there is a plethora of federal and state laws and regulations related to workers' compensation, unemployment compensation, employee wages, health and safety in the workplace, retirement, employee benefits, rights of privacy, and employee protection against unjust dismissal. While all these laws are important and will be considered in appropriate chapters of this book, no other area of the regulatory environment has had such a profound effect on HRM as equal employment opportunity (EEO). For example, in the last few years, two major pieces of federal legislation, the Americans with Disabilities Act (ADA) of 1990 and the Civil Rights Act of 1991, have become law. We are devoting this entire chapter to EEO, to emphasize its importance and its impact on all six of the HRM domains reviewed in Chapters 1 and 2. In fact, every major activity of HRM is affected by the EEO laws and regulations we will discuss in this chapter. The processes by which employers recruit, hire, place, promote, compensate, lay off, and terminate employees can fall under the close scrutiny of the courts and regulatory agencies on the basis of some form of EEO legislation.

The purpose of this chapter is to provide an overview of EEO laws and regulations. We will begin with descriptions of the most important laws in EEO and the legal interpretations of those laws. We will conclude with a discussion of the implications of these laws for personnel practice. Our major objective for this chapter is to provide a framework which will help you evaluate the legality of specific HRM practices.

OBJECTIVES

After studying this chapter, you should be able to:

1. Understand the various laws related to EEO and their implications for HRM.
2. Identify potential problems in personnel policy and practice as related to EEO.
3. Understand the importance of judicial interpretation for EEO law.

Prior to the civil rights movement of the early 1960s, employment decisions were made routinely on the basis of an applicant's or a worker's race, gender, religion, or other characteristics unrelated to job qualifications or performance. In 1962, for example, nonwhites represented 11 percent of the civilian labor force but 22 percent of the unemployed. Nonwhites were twice as likely as whites to hold semiskilled or unskilled jobs. Median annual income for nonwhite males in 1960 was 60 percent of the median income of white males; nonwhite women earned 50 percent of their white female counterparts' wages.[1] And across racial groups, women earned less than men, even in identical jobs.

The laws we will discuss in this chapter were designed to prohibit employers from using such criteria as race, gender, disability, or age to exclude certain persons from employment or from certain employment benefits. They were also designed to restore the unfairly treated worker to the position she or he would have held absent the discrimination. Our focus will be on preventing unfair treatment and the subsequent potential legal vulnerability of managers under the civil rights laws.

Employment discrimination occurs in a variety of ways, and there are a number of methods for seeking redress through the courts. While the legal definition of "discrimination" differs depending on the specific law, it can be broadly defined as employment decision making or working conditions which are advantageous (or disadvantageous) to members of one group compared to members of another group. The decision making can apply to personnel selection, admission to training programs, promotions, work assignments, transfers, compensation, layoffs, punishments, and dismissals. The conditions can also pertain to the work atmosphere itself. For example, a common lawsuit today concerns allegations of sexually harassing behaviors at work which cause an individual's work environment to be offensive or intimidating.

Figure 3.1 presents a list of the possible bases for suits involving allegations of employment discrimination. Of the many sources of redress which are available, the most frequently used sources are Title VII of the 1964 U.S. Civil Rights Act, the Age Discrimination in Employment Act of 1967, Presidential Executive Order No. 11246, and state fair employment laws. The Americans with Disabilities Act extends the protections of the civil rights laws to persons with physical or mental disabilities. This new law is certain to generate a great deal of litigation, as employers attempt to provide "reasonable accommodations" for individuals with disabilities. Although the 1973 Rehabilitation Act also prohibits discrimination against individuals with disabilities, it applies only to companies with federal contracts.

Under the version of Title VII of the Civil Rights Act of 1964 in effect through late 1991, discrimination lawsuits were difficult to win and plaintiffs could receive up to 2 years of back pay and other "make-whole" remedies, but no compensatory or punitive damages (compensatory

FIGURE 3.1
BASES AND SOURCES OF REDRESS FOR ALLEGED EMPLOYMENT DISCRIMINATION

SOURCE	PURPOSE	ADMINISTRATION
Fifth Amendment, U.S. Constitution	To protect against federal violation of "due process"	Federal courts
Thirteenth Amendment, U.S. Constitution	To abolish slavery	Federal courts
Fourteenth Amendment, U.S. Constitution	To protect against state violations of "due process" and to afford equal protection for all	Federal courts
Civil Rights Act, 1866	To establish the right of all citizens to make and enforce contracts	Federal courts
Civil Rights Act, 1871	To make citizens liable for suits	Federal courts
Equal Pay Act, 1963	To prohibit sex discrimination in wages and salary: equal pay for equal work	EEOC and federal courts
Civil Rights Act, 1964 (Title VII), as amended in 1991	In 703(a) and (b), to declare all discriminatory employment practices unlawful	EEOC and federal courts
Age Discrimination in Employment Act (ADEA), 1967, as amended in 1978 and 1986	To prohibit discrimination against persons age 40 and older	EEOC and federal courts
Equal Employment Opportunity Act, 1972	To extend coverage of the 1964 Civil Rights Act to include both public and private sectors, educational institutions, labor organizations, and employment agencies	EEOC and federal courts
Rehabilitation Act, 1973	To protect persons with disabilities against discrimination (public sector)	Department of Labor
Americans with Disabilities Act (ADA), 1990	To prohibit discrimination against persons with disabilities	EEOC and federal courts
Executive Orders 11246 and 11375	To prohibit discrimination by contractors or subcontractors of federal agencies	OFCCP
Executive Order 11478	To prescribe merit as a basis for federal personnel policy, to prohibit discrimination, and to mandate equal opportunity programs	Office of Personnel Management
State laws	To prohibit discrimination and to establish fair employment practices commissions	Fair Employment Practices Commission
Local laws	To prohibit discrimination	Municipal courts

Source: H. J. Bernardin and J. S. Kane. *Performance appraisal: A contingency approach to system development and evaluation.* Boston: PWS-Kent, 1993 (projected publication date).

damages include those for pain and suffering, medical expenses, etc., while punitive damages are intended to "punish" the defendant and may bear no relationship to the plaintiff's actual loss). In addition, the U.S. Supreme Court issued several rulings in 1989 that reinterpreted Title VII and made it even more difficult for plaintiffs to prevail. In response to the Court's actions, Congress amended Title VII in late 1991 and not only overturned the Court's rulings, but added other measures designed to increase employees' protections under this law. Compensatory and punitive damages are now available. And Title VII now covers U.S. citizens working abroad for U.S. companies.

Many of the 1991 changes to Title VII were also applied to the Americans with Disabilities Act, so it is likely that lawsuits alleging disability discrimination will increase as well. Furthermore, equal employment laws similar to Title VII exist in 41 states, as well as Washington, D.C., and Puerto Rico. There are also state and local laws which vary on the legality of certain personnel practices. For example, five states, the District of Columbia, and over 80 municipalities have laws prohibiting employment discrimination against homosexuals and persons infected with HIV or persons having AIDS.

Employers are now well aware of how costly violations of EEO laws can be. Because millions of dollars are now at stake in many cases, organizations are more careful about their personnel practices, with the establishment of monitoring systems, EEO offices, and training programs in EEO for personnel decision makers and supervisors. These activities are paying off, as employers are now winning a higher percentage of discrimination cases than they were in the 1970s. One component of this orientation is simply making personnel decision makers aware of EEO laws. Let us follow this approach by introducing you to the major laws which account for most of the regulation and litigation in EEO.

TITLE VII OF THE CIVIL RIGHTS ACT OF 1964

The Civil Rights Act was signed by President Johnson in 1964, and was amended by the *Equal Employment Opportunity Act* in 1972 and the *Civil Rights Act* of 1991. Title VII deals specifically with discrimination in employment, and prohibits discrimination based on race, color, religion, sex, or national origin. Figure 3.2 provides major excerpts from Title VII. The act covers all employers having more than 15 employees except private clubs, religious organizations, and places of employment connected to an Indian reservation. The U.S. Equal Employment Opportunity Commission (EEOC) was created to monitor and enforce compliance with Title VII. Originally, the major functions of the EEOC were to investigate complaints and to try to resolve disputes through conciliation. The 1972 amendments increased the authority of the EEOC to bring action against organizations in the courts.

The EEOC also issues interpretive regulations regarding employment practices. Among the most important regulatory interpretations issued by the EEOC are the *Uniform Guidelines on Employee Selection Procedures,* adopted in 1978, which provide recommendations for employment staffing, and the *Interpretative Guidelines on Sexual Harassment,* issued in 1980. While these guidelines are not law, the courts often use them to evaluate whether an alleged behavior violates the law. The EEOC also requires that most organizations submit an annual EEO-1 form, shown in Figure 3.3. Data from these forms are used to identify possible patterns of discrimination in particular organizations or segments of the workforce. The EEOC may then take legal action against an organization, based on these data.

Title VII does not prohibit discrimination based on seniority systems, veterans' preference rights, national security reasons, or job qualifications based on test scores, backgrounds, or experience, even when the use of such practices may be correlated with race, sex, color, religion, or national origin. Title VII also does not prohibit "bona fide occupational qualifications" (BFOQs) or discriminatory practices whenever these practices are "reasonably necessary to the normal operation of the organization." For example, a BFOQ which excludes one group (e.g., males or females) from an employment opportunity is permissible if the employer can argue that the "essence of the business" requires the exclusion, that is, when business would be significantly affected by not employ-

ing members of one group exclusively. Pan American Airways tried this argument in *Diaz v. Pan American World Airways.*[2] Pan Am presented data which showed that a majority of its customers preferred female flight attendants, stating that not hiring males was done for important business reasons. In this case, a federal appellate court ruled that customer preference was not a legally defensible reason for discrimination. Further, the court stated that discrimination based on sex is valid only when the essence of the business would be undermined by not hiring members of one sex exclusively. A recent case involved Johnson Controls, Inc., a car battery manufacturer that excluded women of child-bearing years from jobs where there was high exposure to lead and possible harm to the unborn fetus. The company argued that this policy falls within the BFOQ exception to Title VII because it is essential to a safe workplace. In its 1991 decision in *United Automobile Workers v. Johnson Controls, Inc.*[3] the Supreme Court disagreed. The Court found that such fetal protection policies, used at one time by over a dozen large companies employing 10,000 workers, are a form of sex discrimination in violation of Title VII. The High Court emphasized that the BFOQ exception applies only to a policy which involves the "essence of the business," such as worker or customer safety, not the safety of an unborn fetus. "Women who are as capable of doing their jobs as their male counterparts may not be forced to choose between having a child and having a job," the Court said in its majority opinion against Johnson Controls.

In general, the position of the courts regarding BFOQs clearly favors judgments about the performance, abilities, or potential of specific individuals rather than discrimination by class or categories. The Court has said that the BFOQ exception to Title VII is a narrow one, limited to policies that are directly related to a worker's ability to do the job.

Filing a Title VII Lawsuit

If an individual believes that he or she has been a victim of illegal discrimination and wishes to pursue a claim through the legal system, the complaint must first be filed with an office of the EEOC. An illustration of this process is provided in Figure 3.4. This complaint must be filed within 6 months of the alleged discriminatory practice. The EEOC will investigate the complaint or refer it to a local or state EEO human rights agency (called a "deferral" agency). Through interviews, on-site visits, and evaluation of records, the investigating agency will then determine whether there is probable cause to believe that a violation of Title VII exists. If the agency determines no probable cause, the complainant is so notified and informed that a private lawsuit may still be filed

FIGURE 3.2
EXCERPTS FROM TITLE VII OF THE CIVIL RIGHTS ACT OF 1964

SECTION 703

(a) It shall be an unlawful practice for an employer
(1) to fail to hire or to discharge any individual, or otherwise to discriminate against any individual with respect to compensation, terms, conditions, or privileges of employment, because of such individual's race, color, religion, sex, or national origin; or (2) to limit, segregate, or classify employees or applicants for employment in any way which would deprive or tend to deprive any individual of employment opportunities or otherwise adversely affect status as an employee, because of such individual's race, color, religion, sex, or national origin.

(e) Notwithstanding any other provision of this title,
(1) it shall not be an unlawful employment practice for an employer to hire and employ those employees . . . on the basis of religion, sex, or national origin in those certain instances where religion, sex, or national origin is a bona fide occupational qualification reasonably necessary to the normal operation of that particular business or enterprise. . . .

(h) Notwithstanding any other provision of this title, it shall not be an unlawful employment practice for an employer to apply different standards of compensation, or different terms, conditions, or privileges of employment pursuant to a bona fide seniority or merit system, or a system which measures earnings by quantity or quality of production or to employees who work in different locations, provided that such differences are not the result of an intention to discriminate because of race, color, religion, sex, or national origin, nor shall it be unlawful employment practice for an employer to give and act upon the results of any professionally developed ability test provided that such test, its administration or action upon the results is not designed, intended, or used to discriminate because of race, color, religion, sex, or national origin. . . .

(j) Nothing contained in this title shall be interpreted to require any employer . . . to grant preferential treatment to any individual or to any group because of the race, color, religion, sex, or national origin of such individual or group on account of an imbalance which may exist with respect to the total number or percentage of persons of any race, color, religion, sex, or national origin employed by any employer . . . in comparison with the total number or percentage of persons of such race, color, religion, sex, or national origin in any community, State, section, or other area, or in the available work force in any community, State, section, or other area.

SECTION 704

(a) It shall be an unlawful employment practice for an employer to discriminate against any employees or applicants for employment . . . because the employee or applicant has opposed any practice made an unlawful employment practice by this title, or because he or she has made a charge, testified, assisted, or participated in any matter in an investigation, proceeding, or hearing under this title.

FIGURE 3.3
EEO-1 FORM

Standard Form 100
(Rev. 12-76)
Approved GAO 8-180541 (R0077)
Expires 12-31-78

EQUAL EMPLOYMENT OPPORTUNITY
EMPLOYER INFORMATION REPORT EEO-1

Joint Reporting
Committee
• Equal Employment
Opportunity Commission
• Office of Federal Contract
Compliance Programs

SECTION A—TYPE OF REPORT
Refer to instructions for number and types of reports to be filled

1. Indicate by marking in the appropriate box the type of reporting unit for which this copy of the form is submitted (MARK ONLY ONE BOX)

(1) ❑   Single-establishment Employer Report

Multi-establishment Employer
(2) ❑ Consolidated Report
(3) ❑ Headquarters Unit Report
(4) ❑ Individual Establishment Report (submit one for each establishment with 25 or more employees)
(5) ❑ Special Report

2. Total number of reports being filed by this Company (Answer on Consolidated Report only)

Section B—COMPANY IDENTIFICATION (To be answered by all employers)

OFFICE USE ONLY

1. Parent Company

a. Name of parent company (owns or controls establishment in item 2) omit if same as label

a.

Name of receiving office | Address (Number and street)

b.

City or town | County | State | ZIP Code | b. Employer Identification No.

2. Establishment for which this report is filed (Omit if same as label)

a. Name of establishment

c.

Address (Number and street) | City or town | County | State | ZIP code

d.

b. Employer Identification No. | (If same as label skip)

3. Parent company affiliation (Multi-establishment Employers Answer on Consolidated Report only)

a. Name of parent—affiliated company | b. Employer Identification No.

Address (Number and street | City or town | County | State | ZIP code

---

Section C—EMPLOYERS WHO ARE REQUIRED TO FILE (To be answered by all employers)

❑ Yes ❑ No 1 Does the entire company have at least 100 employees in the payroll period for which you are reporting?

❑ Yes ❑ No 2 Is you company affiliated through common ownership and/or centralized management with other entities in an enterprise with a total employment of 100 or more?

❑ Yes ❑ No 3 Does the company or any of its establishments (a) have 50 or more employees AND (b) is not exempt as provided by 41 CFR 60-1.5. AND either (1) is a prime government contractor or first-tier subcontractor, and has a contract, subcontract, or purchase order amounting to $50,000 or more, or (2) serves as a depository of Government funds in any amount or is a financial institution which is an issuing and paying agent for U.S. Savings Bonds and Savings Notes?

NOTE: If the answer is yes to ANY of these questions, complete the entire form, otherwise skip to Section G.

FIGURE 3.3 *(Continued)*

Section D—EMPLOYMENT DATA

Employment at the establishment–Report all permanent, temporary, or part-time employees including apprentices and on-the-job trainees unless specifically excluded as set forth in the instruction. Enter the appropriate figures on all lines and in all columns. Blank spaces will be considered as zeros.

JOB CATEGORIES	OVERALL TOTALS (SUM OF COL. B THRU K)	MALE WHITE (NOT OF HISPANIC ORIGIN)	MALE BLACK (NOT OF HISPANIC ORIGIN)	MALE HISPANIC	MALE ASIAN OR PACIFIC ISLANDER	MALE AMERICAN INDIAN OR ALASKAN NATIVE	FEMALE WHITE (NOT OF HISPANIC ORIGIN)	FEMALE BLACK (NOT OF HISPANIC ORIGIN)	FEMALE HISPANIC	FEMALE ASIAN OR PACIFIC ISLANDER	FEMALE AMERICAN INDIAN OR ALASKAN NATIVE
	A	B	C	D	E	F	G	H	I	J	K
Officials and Managers											
Professionals											
Technicians											
Sales Workers											
Office and Clerical											
Craft Workers (Skilled)											
Operatives (Semi-Skilled)											
Laborers (Unskilled)											
Service Workers											
TOTAL											
Total employment reported in previous EEO-1 report											

(The trainees below should also be included in the figures for the appropriate occupational categories above)

Formal On-the-job trainees												
	White											
	Production											

1 NOTE: On consolidated report, skip questions 2–5 and Section E.

2 How was the information as to race or ethnic group in Section D obtained.
   1 ☐ Visual Survey 3 ☐ Other—Specify ....
   2 ☐ Employment Record ....
3 Dates of payroll period used–

4 Pay period of last report submitted for this establishment

5. Does this establishment employ apprentices?
   This year? 1 ☐ Yes 2 ☐ No
   Last year? 1 ☐ Yes 2 ☐ No

Section E—ESTABLISHMENT INFORMATION

1. Is the location of the establishment the same as that reported last year?

1. ☐ Yes   2. ☐ No   3 ☐ Did not last year   4 ☐ Reported on combined basis

2. Is the major business activity at this establishment the same as that reported last year?

1 ☐ Yes   2 ☐ No   3 ☐ No report last year   4 ☐ Reported on combined

OFFICE USE ONLY

3. What is the major activity of this establishment? (Be specific, i.e., manufacturing steel castings, retail grocer, wholesale plumbing supplies, title insurance, etc. Include the specific type of product or type of service provided, as well as the principal business or industrial activity.

a.

Section F—REMARKS

Use this item to give any identification data appearing on last report which differs from that given above, explain major changes in composition or reporting units, and other pertinent information.

Section G—CERTIFICATION (See instructions G)

Check one
1. ☐ All reports are accurate and were prepared in accordance with the instructions (check on consolidated only)
2. ☐ This report is accurate and was prepared in accordance with the instructions.

Name of Certifying Official	Title	Signature	Date
Name of person to contact regarding this report (Type or print)	Address (Number and street)		
Title	City and State	ZIP Code	Telephone Area Code / Number / Extension

FIGURE 3.4
THE PROCESS OF FILING DISCRIMINATION COMPLAINTS

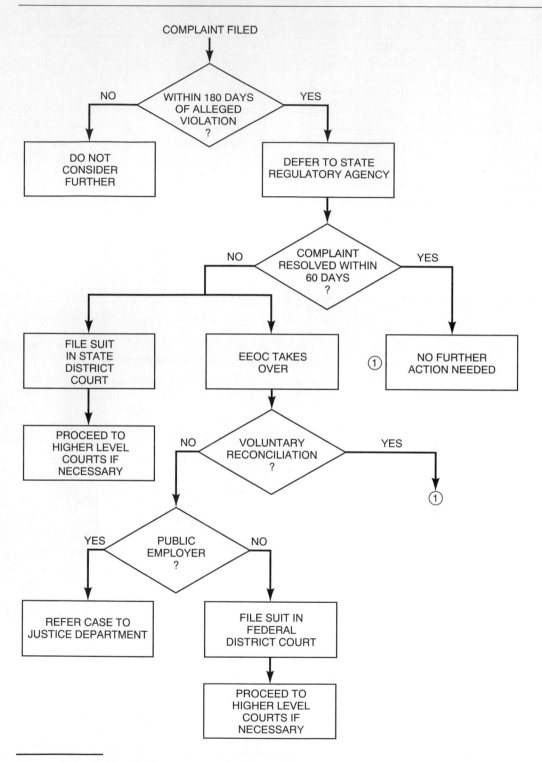

Source: W. F. Cascio. *Managing human resources: Productivity, quality of work life, profits.* New York: McGraw-Hill, 1992, p. 75. Reprinted with permission.

in federal court. The complainant is given a "right-to-sue" letter, which signifies that the EEOC no longer has exclusive jurisdiction over the case. A complaining party may obtain a right-to-sue letter before the EEOC has ruled in the case as long as at least 180 days have elapsed since the individual filed with the EEOC. If probable cause is determined, the EEOC will attempt to settle the matter through a process known as *conciliation*. The objective of conciliation is to gain an agreement by all parties while avoiding litigation. If conciliation fails, the EEOC may file suit in federal district court if the employer is private, or may refer the case to the U.S. Justice Department if the employer is a public agency.

The Supreme Court has established the legal steps to be followed in a Title VII action. Although the plaintiff retains the "burden of proof," a model is used such that the burden of producing evidence shifts from the plaintiff to the defendant and back to the plaintiff. Initially the complainant or plaintiff has the burden to show that a *prima facie* case of discrimination exists. This means he or she must show that there is a high likelihood that a violation of EEO law has occurred. After the plaintiff produces sufficient evidence to establish a prima facie case, the burden of producing evidence shifts to the employer or defendant, who must provide some proof of a legitimate, nondiscriminatory reason for the employment decision. Finally, the burden of producing evidence shifts back to the plaintiff to show either that the reason given was a pretext for discrimination or that an alternate practice, less discriminatory in its effect, would achieve the employer's purpose equally well. Title VII cases can be brought under one of two theories: disparate impact and disparate treatment. The steps to follow for each are illustrated in Figure 3.5.

DISPARATE TREATMENT. Plaintiffs can demonstrate a prima facie case of discrimination by showing *disparate treatment,* the most frequently used theory. According to the procedures established in the 1973 *McDonnell Douglas v. Green* Supreme Court case, plaintiffs must show that an employer treats one or more members of a protected group differently.[4] For example, the use of different criteria for promotion depending on the candidate's sex would constitute disparate treatment. Female applicants who were not hired by a firm might show that the employer asked them questions about their marital status or child-care arrangements which were not asked of male applicants.

In disparate treatment cases, the Supreme Court established that the burden is on the plaintiff to prove that the employer *intended* to discriminate because of race, sex, color, religion, or national origin. For example, Alice Burdine claimed that she was a victim of sex discrimination by the Texas Department of Community Affairs.

Her employer was not required, said the U.S. Supreme Court, to prove that it did not discriminate against her, but needed only to "articulate some legitimate nondiscriminatory reason" for the negative decision. The Court indicated that the plaintiff has the ultimate burden of proving that an employer intentionally discriminated against the plaintiff.[5]

DISPARATE IMPACT. According to procedures established in the 1971 *Griggs v. Duke Power Company* case, plaintiffs can show that an employer's practices had a *disparate impact* on members of a protected group by showing that the employment procedures (e.g., hiring, promotions, entry into training) had a disproportionately negative effect on members of a protected group.[6] Such impact is illegal if the employment practice is not "job-related" or related to the employment in question. For example, if an organization hires 50 whites and 10 blacks, from 100 white and 100 black applicants, then disparate impact has occurred. Whether or not the employer had good intentions or didn't mean to discriminate is unnecessary to the courts in this type of lawsuit. After the plaintiff shows evidence of disparate impact, the employer must carry the burden of producing evidence of business necessity or "job relatedness" for the employment practice. Finally, the burden shifts back to the plaintiff, who must show that an alternative procedure is available that is equal to or better than the employer's practice and has a less discriminatory effect.

Figure 3.6 presents a list of employment practices having potential disparate impact against minorities or females. The most common examples are employment tests, educational requirements, and physical characteristics (e.g., a height requirement). Of course, whether the use of such practices constitutes illegal discrimination depends on the employment situation. Most experts on EEO law contend that recent Supreme Court rulings make it easier for employers to defend the use of such practices when they can be shown to be closely related to the job.

DETERMINING DISPARATE OR ADVERSE IMPACT. The yardstick recommended by the EEOC in the *Uniform Guidelines* and adopted in numerous cases for determining disparate or adverse impact is the "four-fifths" rule. This means that a selection rate (number selected/number applied) for a protected group cannot be less than four-fifths or 80 percent of the rate for the group with the highest selection rate. For example, the City of Columbus, Ohio, used a paper-and-pencil, multiple-choice examination to screen applicants for its firefighter positions. While 84 percent of the whites passed the examination, only 27 percent of the blacks did. Using the four-fifths rule, 80 percent of the highest selection rate (84 percent) is 67 percent. The 27 percent selection rate

FIGURE 3.5
EVIDENCE AND PROOF IN TITLE VII CASES

EVIDENCE BURDEN	DISPARATE TREATMENT	DISPARATE IMPACT
Plaintiff's initial burden (prima facie case)	He or she belongs to the discriminated-against group He or she applied and was qualified He or she was rejected The position remained open to applicants with equal or fewer qualifications	Unequal impact of the practice(s) in question on different groups
Defendant's rebuttal burden	Articulate a "legitimate nondiscriminatory reason for the rejection"	Demonstrate that the challenged practice is job-related for the position in question and consistent with business necessity
Plaintiff's burden in response	Show that the stated reason is a pretext by demonstrating, e.g.: —the employer doesn't apply that reason equally to all —the employer has treated the plaintiff unfairly before —The employer engages in other unfair employment practices OR Show the plaintiff's group membership was a factor in the rejection decision	Show that a less discriminatory alternative practice does exist
Defendant's burden in response	Show that the decision would have been the same even if it had not taken plaintiff's group membership into account	

Source: Adapted from J. Ledvinka and V. G. Scarpello, *Federal regulation of personnel in human resource management.* Boston, MA: PWS-Kent, 1991, p. 54. Reprinted with permission.

for the other group (blacks) is less than 67 percent, so the test was determined to have an adverse impact on blacks.

The disparate impact theory was used in a great many cases involving "neutral employment practices" such as tests, entrance requirements, and physical requirements. In *Watson v. Fort Worth Bank & Trust,* the Supreme Court extended use of the theory in cases involving "subjective" employment practices such as interviews, performance appraisals, and job recommendations. Thus, statistical data such as the four-fifths rule can be used in a disparate impact case to establish prima facie evidence of discrimination when decisions are based on subjective employment practices.[7]

Despite the Court's extension of disparate impact to subjective employment practices, there is little agreement on precisely how a plaintiff can demonstrate disparate impact, or how an employer can defend against such a charge. Although the U.S. Supreme Court ruled in 1989 that the employer need not prove that the challenged practice was a valid measure of the job requirements, Congress overturned that ruling in the Civil Rights Act of 1991. The new law, however, is unclear as to precisely what an employer must demonstrate; it simply says that the employer must demonstrate "that the challenged practice is job related for the position in question and consistent with business necessity." Open to interpretation, as well, is the new law's requirement that plaintiffs "demonstrate that each particular challenged employment practice causes a disparate impact, except that if the [plaintiff] can demonstrate to the court that the elements of [an em-

FIGURE 3.6
EMPLOYEE SCREENING DEVICES WITH POTENTIAL DISPARATE IMPACT

Educational requirements	Preferences for relatives of present employees
Tests	Use of walk-in or word-of-mouth recruiting
Experience requirements	
Height and weight requirements	Reference checks
Physical agility tests	Promoting from within
Excluding applicants with arrest-conviction records	Promotion based on supervisor recommendations
Excluding unwed parents	Excluding applicants with less than honorable discharges
Preferences for applicants with honorable discharges	

Source: Bureau of National Affairs, *Fair employment practices manual.* Washington: Bureau of National Affairs, 1983, pp. 401ff., 421.

ployer's] decision-making process are not capable of separation for analysis, the decision-making process may be analyzed as one employment practice." Since most employers use multiple criteria to make selection, promotion, or similar decisions, disentangling the contribution of each criterion to the disparate impact will be extremely difficult, if it is possible at all. We can expect much litigation, then, over just what both employees and the companies they sue must demonstrate under this new law.

Some organizations sought to retain the use of tests while avoiding disparate impact violations by interpreting test scores as a function of the ethnicity of the test taker. For example, the exact raw score would be interpreted differently depending on whether the test taker was white, Hispanic, or African-American. Employers could rank-order each individual within his or her own racial group and then choose the top candidates from each. The 1991 Civil Rights Act prohibits this type of race or sex norming.

Proving Job Relatedness

There is a large body of case law which provides legal definitions of the term "job-related." The major case in this area is *Griggs v. Duke Power,* in which the Supreme Court struck down the use of an employment test and a high school educational requirement for entry-level personnel selection. Such practices were judged to be discriminatory because they excluded a disproportionate number of blacks from employment, and because the employer could not show that the hiring requirements were related to performance on the job. As the Court noted, if an employment practice cannot be shown to be related to job performance, and that practice operates to exclude protected classes, then the practice is prohibited.

Since the Griggs decision was rendered in 1971, there have been many cases which have focused on job-relatedness issues. In *Albemarle Paper Company v. Moody,*[8] the Supreme Court clarified the job-relatedness defense, requiring a careful job analysis to identify the specific knowledge, skills, and abilities necessary to perform the job. They also required the employer to use specific criteria on which to evaluate job performance in showing the job relatedness of a test.

In *Connecticut v. Teal,* the Supreme Court declared that the "job-relatedness" argument must be applied to all steps of a multiple-hurdle selection procedure. Winnie Teal had been denied promotion to a supervisory position because of a low score on a written exam which was the first hurdle of the promotion process.[9] When the final promotion decisions were made, however, there was no disproportionate impact on blacks. In fact, the bottom line actually favored blacks. Of the 48 black candidates, 22.9 percent were promoted, while of the 259 white candidates, only 13.5 percent were promoted. Of course this outcome didn't help Ms. Teal, who had been eliminated at the first step in the selection process. She claimed a Title VII violation because the written exam itself had a disproportionate impact against blacks and was not job-related. The Supreme Court agreed with Ms. Teal. If one part of the selection procedure has adverse impact upon a group covered under Title VII, it must be shown to be job-related since it denies an employment opportunity to a disproportionate number of minorities and prevents them from proceeding to the next step in the selection process. This is necessary despite the fact that the bottom-line outcome of the employment decisions may be favorable to the same group.

While proving job relatedness seems like a fairly simple task for an organization, it has proved to be quite cumbersome in court. In fact, of the cases dealing specifically with job relatedness, after a prima facie case was established, the majority of the cases were lost by the employer. This may have been because some courts have required employers to adhere to the *Uniform Guidelines on Employee Selection Procedures.* These guidelines describe very specific, detailed procedures for proving job relatedness. Chapter 6 and Appendix A discuss these requirements in greater detail.

Sexual, Ethnic, and Racial Harassment

You may recall the 1991 U.S. Senate hearings on the nomination of Judge Clarence Thomas to the Supreme Court. University of Oklahoma professor Anita Hill alleged that she was sexually harassed by Judge Thomas while he was the director of the EEOC, the government agency in charge of investigating such charges. It is estimated that between 50 and 70 percent of the female workforce has been subjected to some form of sexual harassment. Over 10,000 such charges were filed with the EEOC in 1991 alone. Under Title VII, sexual harassment is illegal since it constitutes discrimination with respect to a person's conditions of employment. These conditions can refer to psychological and emotional workplace conditions that are coercive or insulting to an individual. The EEOC has published guidelines for employers dealing with sexual harassment issues. According to the guidelines, sexual harassment is defined as follows:

> Unwelcome sexual advances, requests for sexual favors, and other verbal or physical conduct of a sexual nature constitute sexual harassment when (1) submission to such conduct is made either explicitly or implicitly a term or condition of an individual's employment, (2) submission to or rejection of such conduct by an individual is used as the basis for employment decisions affecting such individual, or (3) such conduct has the purpose or effect of unreasonably interfering with an individual's work performance or creating an intimidating, hostile, or offensive working environment.

Recent decisions having to do with the last part of the definition have led to a substantial increase in the number of suits filed (and won) that alleged sexual harassment under Title VII. In *Bundy v. Jackson*[10] the Court stated that it was not necessary for the plaintiff to establish a causal relationship between the rejection of sexual advances and a specific personnel action such as a dismissal or a layoff. Rather, it was only necessary for the plaintiff to establish that the harassment created unfavorable or hostile working conditions for him or her. The Supreme Court supported this theory in 1986 in *Meritor Savings Bank v. Vinson*.[11] Any workplace conduct that is "sufficiently severe or pervasive to alter the conditions of employment and create an abusive working environment" constitutes illegal sexual harassment.

Research on the judicial outcomes of sexual harassment claims identified the following correlates of favorable legal outcomes for the claimant: (1) when the harassment involved physical contact of a sexual nature, (2) when sexual propositions were linked to threats or promises of a change in the conditions of employment, (3) when the claimant notified management of the problem before filing charges, and (4) when the organization had no formal policy toward sexual harassment which had been communicated to its employees.[12] However, under *Meritor,* if the harasser is the victim's supervisor,

the harassment need not be reported to the company in order for the plaintiff to prevail. In some cases, such as *Morris v. American National Can,* when a claimant wins, she or he is entitled to back pay, retroactive seniority, and compensation for workdays missed for trial preparation.[13]

The Civil Rights Act of 1991 provides for compensatory and punitive damages (in addition to back pay) of up to $300,000 for companies with over 500 employees. Some states also allow sexual harassment lawsuits under tort theories. With punitive damages allowed and no caps, some awards have been in the millions.

EMPLOYER LIABILITY. To what extent is the employer liable for sexual harassment committed by its employees? Employers are generally liable for the acts of their supervisors and managers regardless of whether the employer is aware of the acts. Regarding coworkers, if the employer knew or should have known of the harassment and did nothing to stop it, it will be liable. The courts are generally clear that this rule applies to any kind of harassment: racial, ethnic, or religious. Employers may also be liable for behaviors committed by nonemployees, clients, or outside contractors in the workplace if they knew or should have known about the acts and didn't take appropriate action. Essentially, the courts have made it clear that an organization is liable for harassment when management is aware of the activity yet does not take immediate and appropriate corrective action.

An employer is not, however, always liable for sexual harassment. For example, a company is less likely to be found liable under the following conditions: (1) there is a specific policy on harassment which an employee violated, (2) there is a company grievance procedure which the complainant did not follow, and (3) the grievance procedure allows the complainant to bypass the alleged harasser in filing the violation.

A recent legal development may make it somewhat easier for female plaintiffs to recover in sexual harassment cases. In *Ellison v. Brady,* a federal appellate court created a "reasonable woman" standard that it applied to the issue of whether the sexually oriented conduct constituted a hostile or offensive environment.[14] Since research demonstrates that women and men differ in their responses to sexually oriented behavior, the court in *Ellison* was convinced that it was inappropriate to use the viewpoint of a man (or men in general) to determine whether a reasonable woman would have found the conduct to be unwelcome, a requirement that the woman must meet in order to prevail. *Ellison* will very likely result in an increase in the use of expert witnesses who will testify how a reasonable woman would respond to whatever behavior is being challenged, and since the data demonstrate that women are more likely than men to find sexually oriented conduct offensive, this standard may lead to more victories for employees.

MANAGEMENT STRATEGIES.   Due to the steady increase in Title VII litigation regarding sexual harassment, the following strategies have been recommended for organizations:

1. Develop a written policy against sexual harassment, including a definition of sexual harassment and a strong statement by the CEO that it will not be tolerated.
2. Conduct training to make managers aware of the definition and issues involved.
3. Inform employees that they should expect a workplace free from harassment, and what actions they can take under Title VII if their rights are violated.
4. Detail the sanctions for violators and protection for those who make any charges.
5. Establish a grievance procedure for alleged victims of harassment.
6. Investigate claims made by victims.
7. Discipline violators of the policy.

Seniority Systems

Title VII permits bona fide seniority systems if they are established without an intent to discriminate, even if such systems restrict employment opportunities for certain classes of individuals. Thus, a promotional system which awards "points" toward promotion for past service is not illegal under Title VII. Nor is a "last-hired, first-fired" policy which adversely affects blacks or females who were recently hired as part of an affirmative action program. For example, the courts state that you cannot deny white employees the benefits of their seniority in order to provide remedies for minorities. This rationale has applied to cases involving organizations facing layoffs and operating under consent decrees imposed by the courts for a past history of discrimination such as *Firefighters Local Union No. 1784 v. Stotts.*[15] It has also applied to firms with voluntary affirmative action programs. For example, in *Wygant v. Jackson Board of Education,*[16] the Court struck down a Michigan school district plan which sought to protect minority hiring gains by laying off white teachers ahead of blacks with less seniority.

The Supreme Court has mandated retroactive seniority to give the "rightful place" to individuals who were denied employment opportunities because of illegal discrimination under Title VII. For example, in *Franks v. Bowman Transportation Co.,*[17] individuals denied employment opportunities due to illegal discrimination in 1968 would be awarded "retroactive seniority" back to this date to allow them to regain their "rightful place."

EXECUTIVE ORDER 11246, AS AMENDED BY EXECUTIVE ORDER 11375

In 1965, President Johnson signed Executive Order 11246, which prohibits discimination in *federal* employment on the basis of race, creed, color, or national origin. In 1968, it was amended by Executive Order 11375 to change the word "creed" to "religion" and to add sex discrimination to the other prohibited items. The executive order applies to all federal agencies, contractors, and subcontractors, including all the facilities of the company holding the contract regardless of which plant the work is conducted at. Contractors and subcontractors with more than $50,000 in government business and 50 or more employees are not only prohibited from discriminating, but also must take *affirmative action* to ensure that applicants and employees are not treated differently as a function of their sex, religion, race, color, or national origin. According to the Department of Labor, more than 95,000 companies employing 27 million workers and having contracts worth a total of $184 billion are covered by the federal program.

Although there is no one generally recognized definition, affirmative action has to do with the extent to which employers make an effort through their personnel practices to attract, retain, and upgrade members of the protected classes of the 1964 Civil Rights Act. Affirmative action may refer to several strategies including: actively recruiting underrepresented groups in a firm, changing management and employee attitudes about various protected groups, eliminating irrelevant employment practices that bar protected groups from employment, and granting preferential treatment to protected groups.[18]

The executive order is enforced by the Department of Labor through the Office of Federal Contract Compliance Programs (OFCCP). The OFCCP is charged with processing complaints as well as compliance review. This means that in addition to reviewing complaints, the OFCCP can visit a company's facilities and review the affirmative action plans for compliance with the law. The OFCCP has issued "guidelines" for compliance which include "targets or goals" to bring the number of minority and female workers up to their percentages in the available labor pool. Such "goals" are to be "affirmatively pursued." While these goals are not meant to be hard-and-fast quotas for personnel practices, there is no doubt that goals are interpreted as quotas by some OFCCP compliance officers, and pressure is exerted and action is taken against federal contractors according to this interpretation.

If noncompliance is found, the OFCCP generally first tries to reach a conciliation agreement with the firm through special hiring or recruitment programs, seniority credit, or back pay. For example, Prudential Insurance Company recently signed a conciliation agreement in which it agreed to provide training to over 8000 minorities and women who were rejected for jobs over a 5-year period. The company also agreed to offer jobs to a percentage of those who were trained. Prudential was never formally charged with discrimination before the company entered into the conciliation agreement. If an agreement cannot be reached, the firm is scheduled to have a hearing with a judge. If an agreement is still not reached during this time, employers may lose their government contracts or have their payments withheld. They may also lose the right to bid on future government contracts or be debarred from all subsequent contract work until affirmative action programs are judged to be more effective. Needless to say, contractors and subcontractors pay careful attention to the OFCCP. For example, over 400,000 employers have affirmative action programs which are reviewed by the OFCCP.

Although the executive order applies only to organizations receiving federal funds, many other organizations, both public and private, have decided to implement voluntary affirmative action programs, either to redress previous discriminatory employment practices or because they wish to make their workforces more culturally diverse and representative of the labor market. Such voluntary affirmative action plans involve race- or gender-conscious employment decisions. As a result, they have sometimes been challenged as "reverse discrimination," which is illegal under Title VII. In the first affirmative action case to reach the U.S. Supreme Court, *United Steelworkers of America v. Weber,* the justices approved Kaiser Aluminum's voluntary affirmative action plan because it did not unnecessarily trammel the interests of majority employees and because it was a temporary measure that would cease when blacks reached parity with their representation in the labor market.[19] Courts reviewing subsequent challenges to voluntary affirmative action programs have used the *Weber* test to ascertain their legality.

It has been argued that affirmative action is appropriate only as a remedy for past discrimination against specific individuals. In its recent decisions, however, the Supreme Court has clearly opposed this narrow application. In the majority opinion in *Wygant v. Jackson Board of Education,* the court stated that "a carefully constructed affirmative action program need not be limited to the remedying of specific instances of identified discrimination." Justice Lewis Powell stated that "in order to

remedy the effects of prior discrimination, it may be necessary to take race into account...innocent persons may be called upon to bear some of the burden of the remedy."[20]

Federal courts can order involuntary affirmative action programs, and organizations can implement voluntary affirmative action programs without court mandate. The courts have clarified criteria for voluntary and involuntary affirmative action plans. It has been suggested that voluntary plans (1) be designed to eradicate old patterns of discrimination, (2) not impose an "absolute bar" to white advancement, (3) be temporary, (4) not "trammel the interests of white employees," and (5) be designed to eliminate racial imbalance. For involuntary affirmative action programs, it has been suggested that preferential treatment is legal when it (1) is necessary to remedy "pervasive and egregious discrimination"; (2) is used as a flexible benchmark for court monitoring, rather than as a quota; (3) is temporary; and (4) does not "unnecessarily trammel the interests of white employees."[21]

Despite the apparent legal protection for voluntary affirmative action plans, managers must tread carefully to avoid reverse discrimination lawsuits. Race- or gender-conscious employment decisions made in the absence of an affirmative action plan may result in a successful claim of reverse discrimination by a rejected majority applicant or employee.[22] Managers must ensure that all individuals meet the stated job requirements (although they need not be the "best" qualified), and that affirmative action plans are carefully drafted and followed.

The Current Status of Affirmative Action

The 1987 Supreme Court ruling in *Johnson v. Santa Clara Transportation Agency* provided further clarity to the remedies which have been pursued under affirmative action and EEO.[23] According to the Court, organizations may adopt voluntary programs to hire and promote qualified minorities and women to correct a "manifest imbalance" in their representation in various job categories, even when there is no evidence of past discrimination. This was the first time that the Supreme Court explicitly ruled that women as well as blacks and other minorities can receive preferential treatment. The decision also affects the most common employment situation in the United States today: work situations in which it is difficult or impossible to prove past discrimination, but a statistical disparity exists in the number of females and minorities in certain occupations relative to population statistics.

While the majority of the Supreme Court decisions favor affirmative action and preferential personnel practices, there now appear to be some important qualifiers on the appropriateness of these practices, including: (1) Affirmative action plans should be "narrowly tailored" to achieve their ends with a timetable for ending the preferential practice. (2) Class-based firing or layoff schemes are too harsh on the innocent and inappropriate in most circumstances. (3) Preferential personnel practices of any kind are appropriate only in employment situations in which there is a prior history of discrimination. One interpretation is that this last qualifier invalidates Executive Order 11246 because the "goals" required for compliance automatically necessitate preferential hiring and promotion practices in contractors with no such prior history of discrimination. Unfortunately, there is no clear message from the Supreme Court on this interpretation of its latest findings. Also unclear is the literal meaning of "prior discrimination." In its earlier decision in *United Steelworkers of America v. Weber,* the Supreme Court said it was acceptable to use affirmative action programs to remedy "manifest racial imbalance" regardless of whether an employer had been guilty of discriminatory job practices in the past.[24] With its latest decisions, it appears that preferential treatment for groups covered under Title VII may be more restrictive.

Two Supreme Court rulings in 1989 and actions in 1991 cast doubt on the future of affirmative action programs. In fact, some experts now believe that judicial commitment to EEO and affirmative action that began with the Griggs case in 1971 may be over and that Congress may be pressured into a more active role on civil rights issues.[25] In *Martin v. Wilks*[26] the Court ruled that white firefighters who were denied promotions because of an out-of-court affirmative action settlement favoring blacks could challenge the settlement. The court-approved affirmative action settlement was reopened because white employees charged reverse discrimination. Had it not been nullified by the Civil Rights Act of 1991, the ruling would have reduced the number of out-of-court settlements in EEO cases.

The second case, *City of Richmond v. J. A. Croson Co.*[27] showed that courts will apply stringent standards to preferential treatment by public agencies. In this case, the Supreme Court threw out a policy by the City of Richmond to require that 30 percent of the dollar amount of business contracts be given to minority firms. The Court stated that the city's plan was not compelling since there was no showing of prior discrimination by the city. This case did not involve employment, so its meaning is unclear for managers. The new civil rights legislation does not change the *Croson* precedent.

Recent changes in the composition of the U.S. Supreme Court may signal a diminution or elimination of judicial support for affirmative action. Three justices who upheld affirmative action in earlier cases have retired and have been replaced by conservative justices. The result in the *Croson* case, and earlier statements by three justices that Title VII prohibits affirmative action because it uses sex or race as a criterion for employment decisions, suggest that affirmative action may not survive the nineties. Until the Supreme Court changes its rulings, however, managers should continue to comply with affirmative action plans, particularly if the organization receives federal funds.

THE EQUAL PAY ACT OF 1963

The Equal Pay Act (EPA) prohibits unequal pay for men and women who are performing equal work on jobs in the same establishment requiring equal skill, effort, and responsibility and performed under similar working conditions. Pay differences between equal jobs can, however, be justified when that differential is based on (1) a seniority system, (2) a merit system, (3) a piece-rate payment system which measures earnings by quality or quantity of production, or (4) any factor other than sex (e.g., different work shifts, different experience). For example, the Goebel Insurance Company was able to successfully defend a policy of lower pay for Ms. Betty Benninger because it was shown that her quantity of work productivity was less than that of her fellow male employees.

In the 1970s and early 1980s, EPA lawsuits were common and several settlements were very costly to large employers. For example, AT&T has spent over $500 million correcting pay inequities as the result of a consent decree signed in 1973.[28] In addition to legal liability for paying women less than men who did the same work, companies claiming to have a merit-pay system but unable to show a rational, fairly administered performance evaluation system did not fare well either.

A great deal of the litigation in EPA suits has focused on defining what is meant by "equal work" and determining possible exemptions to the law. In general, the courts have determined that jobs need not be identical but rather must be *substantially* equal for the EPA to apply. Thus, the courts have generally embraced an "equal pay for substantially equal work" interpretation of the EPA. The amount of litigation brought under the EPA fell sharply in the late 1980s since most companies are now in compliance.

Comparable Worth/Pay Equity

There is no question that the EPA has provided some help to equalize pay for women who are performing essentially the same work as men. Yet, with 4 years of college, women in 1991 averaged over $27,000 a year. Men with only a high school diploma earned almost the same.

Over 80 percent of the women in the U.S. workforce work in occupations that are dominated by women. For example, 96 percent of registered nurses and 99 percent of secretaries are women. Thus, the EPA has had virtually no impact on the wages of workers in female-dominated jobs and, in general, on the wage disparities between men and women across jobs. There can be little arguing the fact that the wages of female-dominated jobs (e.g., clerical) are depressed relative to the wages of male-dominated jobs (e.g., plumbing, construction). The remedy for such disparities is very controversial. There are many who maintain that wage disparities constitute illegal discrimination. A 1981 study by the National Academy of Sciences, for example, found that while there are many factors related to the wage gap between men and women, sex discrimination may account for over half of these differences.[29] The advocates of *comparable worth* or "pay equity" legislation call for the determination of wages based on the worth or value of a given job for an organization, and not the "market value" of the job (e.g., what other organizations pay for the job).

Numerous suits have been filed on behalf of women using the comparable worth theory to attack wage and salary discrimination under Title VII. Comparable worth cases cannot be brought under the Equal Pay Act because the jobs being compared in such cases are not similar. For example, some celebrated comparable worth cases have compared nurses and tree trimmers.[30]

In a comparable worth case, evidence is often presented which shows that female-dominated jobs of the same comparable value or worth to an organization as male-dominated jobs are nonetheless paid substantially less. The "worth" of a job, under the comparable worth theory, is determined by performing a job evaluation. Points are given according to the difficulty of the job, the amount of independence it gives the worker, the consequence of errors, the amount of education and/or experience it requires, etc. Job evaluations have not been viewed by the courts as reliable indicators of the worth of a job, and the courts have been reluctant to require employers to ignore the market and set salaries solely on the basis of job evaluation scores.[31] Federal judges have not been willing to extend Title VII to cover comparable worth claims.

While the courts have not accepted the argument that "comparable worth is required by Title VII," several states and localities have now passed legislation requiring that public jobs be paid according to their "worth" to the organization. For example, Washington State agreed to provide supplemental pay increases from 1986 to 1992 to affected employees, and the bill is estimated at $482 million.[32] At this time, at least 20 states have passed some form of comparable worth legislation to raise the pay of employees in jobs filled predominately by women.[33] We will discuss the issue of "comparable worth" in more detail in Chapter 11.

THE AGE DISCRIMINATION IN EMPLOYMENT ACT OF 1967, AMENDED IN 1978 AND 1986

The Age Discrimination in Employment Act (ADEA) was designed to prohibit discrimination due to age in employment decisions (e.g., hiring, job retention, compensation, and other terms and conditions). The ADEA was initially applied to workers aged 40 to 65 years, but it was later amended to include workers up to age 70 (1978), and still later to include all those over age 39 (1986). Another result of the amendments was the lifting of the mandatory retirement age of 70 for federal employees. This means that, with a few exceptions to be discussed below, mandatory or forced retirement for reasons of age is illegal. The ADEA applies to employers with 20 or more employees; unions of 25 or more members; employment agencies; and federal, state, and local governments.

As we discussed in Chapter 1, due to the aging of the workforce, the number of ADEA cases has increased every year since 1978. Many ADEA lawsuits have also been filed related to an organization's downsizing efforts, where people terminated as part of a downsizing or restructuring claim to be victims of age discrimination. The EEOC possesses the authority to administer the act, and can review compliance in organizations even when no formal charge has been filed. For example, in 1992 the EEOC gave Catholic University one year to work out a settlement with a philosophy professor who had been terminated. If the university fails to comply, the EEOC says it will sue on behalf of Professor Paul Weiss, who is 90. The ADEA provides for a trial by jury, which may be important if jurors are sympathetic to older workers. The ADEA also permits employees to recover double damages if the employer's conduct is found to have been "willful," which means that plaintiffs may win more than simply lost wages if intentional discrimination is proved.

Similar to Title VII cases, there are certain requirements for establishing a prima facie case of age discrimination. These include showing that (1) the employee is a member of the protected age group (40 or older); (2) the employee has the ability to perform satisfactorily at some absolute or relative level (e.g., relative to other employees involved in the decision process or at an absolute standard of acceptability); (3) the employee was not hired, promoted, or compensated, or was discharged, laid off, or forced to retire; and (4) the position was filled or maintained by a younger person.[34] Once a prima facie case has been established by the court, the defendant must present evidence that "reasonable factors" other than age were the basis of the personnel decision.

One of the most common scenarios for litigation under ADEA concerns the termination of an employee due to alleged poor performance. For example, in *Mastie v. Great Lakes Steel Corp.,*[35] the employer maintained that Mr. Mastie had been discharged in a reduction in force due to his poorer performance relative to other employees. Mr. Mastie presented personnel records reflecting an exemplary performance record and a history of merit-based salary increases. However, the court found for the employer and said that the controlling issue should be whether age was a *determinative* factor in the personnel decision, *not* the "absolute accuracy" or correctness of the personnel decision. Several other courts have established that it is not the role of the court to "second-guess" employers in their personnel decisions, i.e., did they really discharge the poorest performer or hire the very best person? The critical question in ADEA litigation is simply whether age was a "determinative factor" in a personnel decision. It is the plaintiff's responsibility to establish this as fact, which makes it difficult for plaintiffs to win such cases.

There is likely to be an increase in ADEA litigation not only because of the increased proportion of workers who are covered by the law (due to the aging of the workforce) but because so many companies are attempting to reduce their labor costs in increasingly competitive markets. Older workers tend to make more money than younger workers and use more health benefits. These workers at least perceive that they were victims of age discrimination during a downsizing. Their perceptions are sometimes accurate.

The ADEA and Bona Fide Occupational Qualifications

There are occasions on which age discrimination is legal, although they apply to a limited number of employers. For example, Greyhound Bus Lines survived a court challenge to their rule that they would accept no applicants over 40 years of age to drive their buses. The company successfully contended that age was a bona fide occupational qualification (BFOQ) since it was related to the safe conduct of the bus line.[36] Other cases have supported the use of age as a BFOQ. In general, if public safety is relevant and the employee must be in good physical condition, the courts have supported the use of age requirements, in terms of both entry-level positions and, more commonly, mandatory retirement for certain jobs. Congress specifically exempted public safety personnel in the 1986 amendments, allowing mandatory retirement

for police officers and firefighters (usually 55 years of age). The courts have generally recognized these age ceilings as legal BFOQs, but only when the employer can demonstrate that (1) physical fitness, and especially good aerobic fitness, is important to the job and (2) the employer applies the same physical fitness standards to employees under age 40 as to older employees. The EEOC provides the following rules for the imposition of BFOQs: (1) The age limit is reasonably necessary for the business. (2) All or almost all individuals over the age are unable to perform adequately. (3) Some people over the age have a disqualifying characteristic (e.g., health) that cannot be determined independently of age. Regarding the public safety exemption imposed by Congress, the 1986 amendment also required the EEOC to conduct a study to determine whether age can be replaced by some other criterion in making retirement decisions in public safety departments. The study commenced in 1991.

THE REHABILITATION ACT OF 1973

The Rehabilitation Act prohibits discrimination on the basis of physical or mental disability. A person with a disability is defined as one who (1) has an impairment which affects a major life activity, (2) has a history of such an impairment, or (3) is considered to have one. Major life activities refer to functions such as seeing, speaking, walking, caring for oneself, and working. Individuals with disabilities also include those with mental handicaps and may include those with illnesses making them unfit for employment (e.g., heart disease, cancer, diabetes, drug dependency, or alcoholism). Most states have similar laws protecting workers with disabilities from discrimination.

All federal agencies and federal contractors or subcontractors of over $2500 are required by the Rehabilitation Act to take affirmative action for the employment of qualified persons with disabilities. Enforcement is carried out by the Department of Labor's Employment Standards Administration. In recent years, increasingly more cases have been filed charging bias against workers with disabilities. For example, of the more than 7000 discrimination complaints filed against the U.S. Postal Service in 1989, nearly 20 percent involved disability bias claims.[37] The legal requirements entail job accommodations (physical modification of the work setting), accessibility changes (e.g., access ramps), interviewing restrictions (focus on essential functions of the job), and special training programs for nondisabled employees on disabilities and how to deal with them. Under the Rehabilitation Act, a person with a disability is considered qualified for a job if an individual analysis determines that he or she can, with "reasonable accommodations," perform the essential functions of the job. Employers must make such accommodations unless it can be shown that the accommodations would impose an "undue hardship" upon the firm.

The Rehabilitation Act and state laws protecting individuals with disabilities have received recent attention because of judgments that people with AIDS suffer a disability and thus are entitled to protection under the act. Since it is illegal under the act to discriminate against people with disabilities who are "otherwise qualified" for a particular job, service, or benefit, AIDS victims may now file suit for discrimination. This legal position has serious implications for employers, schools, and other organizations. Since AIDS first received national attention, victims have been fired from jobs, barred from schools, and denied medical attention. As stated in a Justice Department memorandum, "the treatment of persons with AIDS, grounded in irrational public prejudices, is precisely one of the kinds of behaviors that led to the enactment of the Rehabilitation Act." The memo noted that while there may certainly be situations in which this is no violation of the law because a person may pose a genuine threat to the health of others, such situations should be rare because "AIDS is not readily communicable, and not spread by casual contact."[38]

THE AMERICANS WITH DISABILITIES ACT OF 1990

It is estimated that the government now spends $60 billion a year to support people with disabilities, including over 8 million who would like to work but cannot find employment. In 1990, Congress passed the *Americans with Disabilities Act* (ADA), which extends the rights and privileges of federal contractors' employees with disabilities to virtually all employees. Figure 3.7 presents excerpts from the ADA. The ADA provides that qualified individuals with disabilities may not be discriminated against by a private-sector organization or a department or agency of a state or local government employing 15 or more employees, and must provide individuals with disabilities with "reasonable accommodations" which don't place an undue hardship on the business. It is not yet clear what "reasonable accommodations" refer to, although they may be determined on a case-by-case basis and may include reassignment, part-time work, and flexible schedules. They may also include providing readers, interpreters, assistants, or attendants.

The ADA also specifies requirements for accommodations for public transportation provided by public transit authorities. For example, all new fixed-route buses must have lifts to make them accessible to individuals

with disabilities unless it can be shown that none are available from the manufacturers. In addition, public facilities such as restaurants, doctors' offices, pharmacies, grocery stores, shopping centers, and hotels must be made accessible to individuals with disabilities unless undue hardship would occur for the business. It is not clear, however, exactly how organizations will show "undue hardship," although the law suggests that a reviewing court compare the cost of the accommodation with the employer's operating budget.[39] This issue will certainly provide much grist for the litigation mill as employers, employees, and judges begin to apply this new law.

PREGNANCY DISCRIMINATION ACT OF 1978

The Pregnancy Discrimination Act prohibits employment practices which discriminate on the basis of pregnancy, childbirth, or related medical conditions (e.g., abortion). This means that a woman is protected from being fired, or refused a job or promotion, simply because she is pregnant or has had an abortion. She also cannot be forced to take a leave of absence as long as she is able to work.

Under the law, women are not guaranteed the same job or, indeed, any job when they return from pregnancy leave. However, a percentage of U.S. companies have adopted either a "same job," "comparable job," or "some job" policy for women who wish to return to work[40] (38 percent, 43 percent, and 6 percent, respectively). The employer must adopt such a policy with consideration to the *disparate treatment* theory of Title VII, and pregnancy should be treated like any other disability. In other words, if other employees on disability leave are entitled to return to their jobs when they are able to work again, then women who have been unable to work due to pregnancy should also be entitled to return.

The act also requires that employers must provide benefits coverage for pregnancy as fully as for other medical conditions. In other words, a woman unable to work for pregnancy-related reasons is entitled to disability benefits or sick leave on the same basis as other employees unable to work for medical reasons.

The Pregnancy Discrimination Act does not prohibit states from requiring additional benefits for pregnant employees. The Supreme Court, for example, upheld a California law which required employees to provide up to 4 months of unpaid pregnancy disability leave with guaranteed reinstatement, even though males with disabilities were not entitled to the same benefit.[41] Several other states have adopted family leave legislation which guarantees employees the right to several weeks of unpaid leave to care for a newborn, adopted child, or family

FIGURE 3.7
EXCERPTS FROM THE AMERICANS WITH DISABILITIES ACT OF 1990

SECTION 102. Discrimination

(a)   General Rule. No covered entity shall discriminate against a qualified individual with a disability because of the disability of such individual.

(b)   Construction. As used in subsection (a), the term "discrimination" includes:

(1) limiting, segregating, or classifying a job applicant or employee in a way that adversely affects the opportunities or status of such applicant or employee because of . . . disability . . .

(2) participating in a contractual or other arrangement or relationship that has the effect of subjecting a qualified applicant or employee with a disability to the discrimination prohibited by this title . . .

(5) not making reasonable accommodations to the known physical or mental limitations of a qualified individual who is an applicant or employee, unless such covered entity can demonstrate that the accommodation would impose an undue hardship on the operation of the business of such covered entity, and;

(7) using employment tests or other selection criteria that screen out or tend to screen out an individual with a disability or a class of individuals with disabilities unless the test or other selection criteria, as used by the covered entity, is shown to be job-related for the position in question and is consistent with business necessity.

(c)   Medical Examinations and Inquiries.

(1) In general. The prohibition against discrimination as referred to in subsection (a) shall include medical examinations and inquires.

Section 3. Definitions

(2)   Disability. The term "disability" means, with respect to an individual:

(A) a physical or mental impairment that substantially limits one or more of the major life activities of such individual;

(B) a record of such an impairment, or;

(C) being regarded as having such an impairment.

Section 101. Definitions

(7)   Qualified Individual with a Disability. The term "qualified individual with a disability" means an individual with a disability who, with or without reasonable accommodation, can perform the essential functions of the employment position that such individual holds or desires.

(8)   Reasonable Accommodation. The term "reasonable accommodation" may include:

(A) making existing facilities used by employees readily accessible to and usable by individuals with disabilities, and;

(B) job restructuring, part-time or modified work schedules, reassignment to a vacant position, acquisition or modification of equipment or devices, appropriate adjustment or modifications of examinations, training materials or policies, the provision of qualified readers or interpreters, and other similar accommodations for individuals with disabilities.

(9)   (A) In general. The term "undue hardship" means an action requiring significant difficulty or expense.

FIGURE 3.7 *(Continued)*

(B) Determination. In determining whether an accommodation would impose an undue hardship on a covered entity, factors to be considered include:

    (i) the overall size of the business;

    (ii) the type of operation, and;

    (iii) the nature and cost of the accommodation.

Section 103. Defenses

(b) Qualification Standards. The term "qualification standards" may include a requirement that an individual with a currently contagious disease or infection shall not pose a direct threat to the health or safety of other individuals in the workplace.

Section 104. Illegal Drugs and Alcohol

(a) Qualified Individual with a Disability. For purposes of this title, the term "qualified individual with a disability" shall not include any employee or applicant who is a current user of illegal drugs. . . .

(b) Authority of Covered Entity. A covered entity:

(1) may prohibit the use of alcohol or illegal drugs at the workplace by all employees:

(2) may require that employees shall not be under the influence of alcohol or illegal drugs at the workplace;

(3) may require that employees behave in conformance with the requirements established under the "The Drug-Free Workplace of 1988" (41 U.S.C. 701 et seq.) [See Chapter 16.]

(4) may hold an employee who is a drug user or alcoholic to the same qualification standards for employment or job performance and behavior that such entity holds other employees. . . .

(c) Drug Testing.

(1) In general. For purposes of this title, a test to determine the use of illegal drugs shall not be considered a medical examination.

member who is ill. The U.S. Congress passed the Family and Medical Leave Act, which would have extended similar benefits to most workers, but the bill was vetoed by President Bush. It is likely that this issue will be raised in future years on the federal level, and more states are likely to pass family leave laws in the interim.

EEO AND INTERNATIONAL HRM

The increased emphasis being placed on overseas duty as a necessary condition for upper management positions raises an important issue related to what might be considered "customer relations" or customer preference. We've all heard of the oppression of women in many parts of the world. In some Middle Eastern countries, for example, women could not even attain a work visa to enter the country. Even female U.S. soldiers fighting to free Kuwait were subjected to a myriad of discriminatory practices which are the norm in Saudi Arabia and other Middle Eastern countries. Sexist legislation is commonplace in many countries, including India, Pakistan, and almost all of the Middle Eastern countries. Sexism is endemic to most of Latin America and Japan, where women are expected to quit their employment at about age 25 and raise a family.[42] Although this general attitude is slowly changing in Japan, the percentage of women who are managers in Japan is still very low. There is also evidence of racism in Japan, as well as evidence that Japanese managers prefer to work with white Americans rather than minorities.

Given the pervasive sexism and racism, can a company make an argument of "business necessity" when it purposely denies women or minorities the opportunity for overseas assignments? Could the company claim a BFOQ, for example, by collecting survey data indicating that the host country nationals preferred white males and use these data as a basis for denying overseas assignments to females and minorities? Probably not. Although there is no clear mandate from the courts on this as yet, the few related cases seem to indicate, much like *Pan American v. Diaz,* that customer/client preferences do not justify discrimination against classes covered by Title VII. The same principle probably also holds for age discrimination and discrimination against persons with disabilities.

Lawrence Abrams was denied a lucrative opportunity to work at a hospital in Saudi Arabia because he was a Jew. The Baylor College of Medicine, which had arranged the 3-month assignment, stated that a visa would be very difficult to obtain for him. In fact, Baylor had not even bothered to check on the visa policy. A jury was not persuaded by Baylor's argument and found the college guilty of discrimination under Title VII.[43] But what if Baylor had asked and the Saudi government had refused to grant a work visa? Would this result have constituted discrimination?

Could a company use an economic business necessity argument, claiming that sending women to Japan, for example, would result in less revenue for the company? If a company made such a claim, it might end up in court trying to explain why the few studies on this subject indicate that the women who do get assignments overseas do just fine. For example, one study in Asia found that 97 percent of the women viewed their assignment as successful and 42 percent said that the fact that they were female actually helped them in their jobs.[44] There is little research supporting the contention that women would be less effective in foreign assignments than males.

Many multinational companies have policies for their expatriates regarding EEO. The employment manual of Bechtel, for example, states that U.S. citizens are protected by all relevant U.S. federal EEO laws while they are on foreign soil. Many other major multinational U.S. corporations have similar policies. But are expatriates really covered by federal EEO laws when they are assigned to countries other than the United States? While the Supreme Court said no in 1991, the Civil Rights Act of 1991 extends Title VII and ADA coverage to American citizens who work overseas for U.S. companies.[45]

Many U.S. companies have branches, subsidiaries, or joint venture partners in Western Europe (and, increasingly, in Eastern Europe as well). Many U.S. multinationals have considerable experience with the various regulatory systems of Western European countries, some of which require national-level collective bargaining and others of which have relatively little labor regulation.

The aim of the 12 member nations of the European Community is to harmonize regulatory systems (in HRM as well as in other aspects of business) as a mechanism for achieving a single market. Although a more uniform approach to employment relations in these 12 countries might appear to simplify HRM, changing to a more uniform system might be difficult. Furthermore, the European Community's social agenda provides considerable protection to workers and unions—protection that is contrary to the philosophy of a number of the leaders of multinationals.

The European Community has issued several directives that bind each member nation. For example, three directives require equal treatment by sex, equal pay, and the European version of comparable worth (called "equal value"). One proposed directive would require Europe-wide employee works councils for any company that operates in two or more member nations of the European Community and has at least 100 employees at each location. Another proposed directive would require prorated benefits, such as pensions, vacation pay, and sick leave, for part-time and temporary employees. A third would require companies that incorporate as "European companies" to allow employees to serve on their supervisory boards, and would give the employees a veto power over the selection of the HR manager!

These directives are significant because, under the Treaty of Paris (the document that governs the European Community), national courts must reinterpret national laws in light of these directives. This means, for example, that even if the United Kingdom's Parliament does not amend British legislation to conform with European Community law, the British courts are obliged to rewrite British law if an issue arises that must be resolved under European law.

The emergence of Eastern Europe from communist influence and the reluctance of some member nations of the European Community may slow the progress toward a single European market, but changes are already beginning to take place in the HRM function in these countries. HR managers with international responsibilities can expect slow but significant change in European Community labor regulation during this decade.[46]

SUMMARY

Despite the confusing array of laws and regulations on EEO, the underlying principle is clear. EEO simply means that individuals should be given an *equal opportunity* in employment decisions. EEO does not mean preferential treatment for one individual over another because of race, color, sex, religion, national origin, age, or disability. For instance, white males have won racial and sex discrimination suits against organizations which have violated Title VII by hiring less qualified minorities or women.[47] The EEO laws clearly state that treatment at work and opportunity for work should be unrelated to the race, sex, and other personal characteristics of individual workers. The implications of the most recent Supreme Court rulings related to EEO are still unclear with regard to affirmative action, but appear to impose tighter restrictions regarding race- or gender-conscious employment practices.

While the implications of EEO litigation may be confusing, it is clear that managers will be on relatively safer ground if they adhere to the following strategy with regard to employment practices: (1) Monitor personnel decisions to ensure that there is no evidence of disparate treatment or a disproportionate impact caused by particular personnel practices. (2) If there are disparities, determine whether the practices causing the disparity are essential for the business or are "job-related." (3) Eliminate the practices if they are not "job-related." Not only will such a strategy protect managers from EEO claims, it will also lead to better personnel decisions overall.

In general, most would agree that EEO legislation has had positive effects on the occupational status of minorities and females. An additional benefit is that EEO laws and the threat of EEO litigation have forced managers to "clean up their act" with regard to personnel policy and practice. While the paperwork may be voluminous and the compliance requirements may seem ominous, there can be little doubt that EEO laws and regulations have fostered a fairer system of employment opportunity and a more systematic and valid process for personnel decisions. The efforts of managers in this regard are critical to organizational effectiveness, and their mistakes can be extremely costly. Personnel practices may be the most heavily regulated area of organizational life today. HR professionals and practicing managers cannot learn too much about this vital area, especially given the increasing diversity of the workforce.

In the following chapters, we will have more to say about legislation and employment practices. The importance of EEO issues for virtually all HRM activities cannot be overstated. Students should consider the implications of the Civil Rights Act, the ADEA, the ADA, and other federal, state, and local laws when we discuss topics such as job analysis and design, HR planning, recruitment, personnel selection, training and development, performance appraisal, and compensation. As we cover these topics in the pages to follow, we will often test your ability to apply knowledge of EEO to particular HRM activities and action. Competence in EEO issues is critical for line managers making decisions about people and jobs and HRM professionals establishing policies and procedures. We also emphasize that the content of this chapter is more likely to go out of date faster than any other area of HRM. In the volatile area of EEO, current, state-of-the-art knowledge gives an organization a competitive advantage.

DISCUSSION QUESTIONS

1. In terms of EEO, how can customer requirements or preferences be used in the process of hiring people?
2. What are the roles of the EEOC and the OFCCP? What is the value of the guidelines published by the EEOC for HR professionals and managers?
3. Describe the procedures required to file a discrimination lawsuit under the disparate impact and disparate treatment theories. How is adverse impact determined? Provide a scenario illustrating evidence of adverse impact in an employment decision.
4. Based on your reading of the major EEO laws, what information should an employer include in a personnel policies and procedures manual given to all employees?
5. What steps would you take to ensure compliance with the ADA?
6. What steps would you take to prevent ADEA cases after a major restructuring or reduction in force?
7. Should homosexuality be added as a characteristic covered under Title VII of the Civil Rights Act? Explain your answer.
8. What impact will punitive damages and jury trials (now available through the Civil Rights Act of 1991) have on EEO litigation?

NOTES

1. Ledvinka, J., and Scarpello, V. (1991). *Federal regulation of personnel and human resource management.* Boston, MA: PWS-Kent.
2. *Diaz v. Pan American Airways* (1971). 422 F.2d 385 (5th Cir.). *EEOC Sex Discrimination Guidelines* (Nov. 10, 1980). Section 1604.11. Employment agencies, promotion plans targeted by EEOC, OFCCP (Mar. 29, 1990).
3. Wemiel, S. (Mar. 21, 1991). Justices bar "fetal protection" policies. *The Wall Street Journal,* pp. B1, B8.
4. *McDonnell Douglas v. Green* (1973). 411 U.S. 972 (U.S. Supreme Court).
5. *Texas Department of Community Affairs v. Burdine* (1981). 450 U.S. 248 (U.S. Supreme Court).
6. *Griggs v. Duke Power Company* (1971). 401 U.S. 424 (U.S. Supreme Court).
7. *Watson v. Fort Worth Bank & Trust* (1988). 487 U.S. 977 (U.S. Supreme Court).
8. *Albemarle Paper Company v. Moody* (1975). 422 U.S. 405 (U.S. Supreme Court).
9. *Connecticut v. Teal* (1982). 457 U.S. 440 (U.S. Supreme Court).
10. *Bundy v. Jackson* (1981). 641 F.2d 934, 24 FEP 1155 (D.C. Cir.).

11. *Meritor Savings Bank v. Vinson* (1986). 40 FEP Cases 1822 (U.S. Supreme Court). See also: Bradshaw, D. S. (1987). Sexual harassment: Confronting the troublesome issues. *Personnel Administrator, 32*(1), 51–53. Thacker, R. A., and Ferris, G. R. (1991). Understanding sexual harassment in the workplace: The influence of power and politics within dyadic interaction of harasser and target. *Human Resource Management Review, 1,* 23–38. Hoyman, M., and Robinson, R. (1980). Interpreting the new sexual harassment guidelines. *Personnel Journal 59*(12), 996. Thornton, T. (1986). Sexual harassment: Discouraging it in the work place. *Personnel, 63*(8), 18–26.

12. Terpstra, D. E., and Baker, D. D. (1988). Outcomes of sexual harassment charges. *Academy of Management Journal, 31*(1), 185–194. See also: Terpstra, D. E., and Baker, D. D. (1992). Outcomes of Federal court decisions on sexual harassment. *Academy of Management Journal, 35,* 181–190.

13. *Morris v. American National Can* (1989). 52 FEP Cases 210 (USDC, Eastern Missouri).

14. *Ellison v. Brady* (1991). 924, F2nd, 872 (9th Cir.).

15. *Firefighters Local Union No. 1784 v. Stotts* (1984). 34 FEP Cases 1702 (U.S. Supreme Court).

16. *Wygant v. Jackson Board of Education* (1986). 106 U.S. 1842 (U.S. Supreme Court).

17. *Franks v. Bowman Transportation Co.* (1976). 483 U.S. 814 (U.S. Supreme Court).

18. Scarpello, V. G., and Ledvinka, J. (1988). *Personnel/ human resource management: Environments and functions.* Boston, MA: PWS-Kent.

19. *United Steelworkers of America v. Weber* (1979). 443 U.S. 193 (U.S. Supreme Court).

20. See note 16.

21. *Johnson v. Santa Clara Transportation Agency* (Mar. 26, 1987). *Daily Labor Report,* pp. A1, D1–D19.

22. See note 1.

23. See note 21.

24. See note 19.

25. See note 1.

26. *Martin v. Wilks* (1989). 109 S. Ct. 2180 (U.S. Supreme Court).

27. *City of Richmond v. J. A. Croson Co.* (1989). 109 S. Ct. 706 (U.S. Supreme Court).

28. Loomis, C. F. (Jan. 15, 1979). AT&T in the throes of "equal employment." *Fortune,* pp. 45–57.

29. Trieman, D., and Hartmen, H. (eds.) (1981). *Women, work, and wages.* Washington: National Academy of Sciences. See also: Haberfeld, Y. (1992). Employment discrimination: An organizational model. *Academy of Management Journal, 35,* 161–180.

30. Beatty, R.W., and Beatty, J. (1982). Job evaluation and discrimination. In H. J. Bernardin (ed.), *Women in the workforce.* Lexington, MA: Praeger, pp. 205–234.

31. *AFSCME v. Washington* (1985). FEPR (5th Cir.).

32. Kilborn, P. T. (May 31, 1990). Wage gap between sexes is cut, but at a price. *New York Times,* A1, D22.

33. Seligman, D. (May 1984). Pay equity is a bad idea. *Fortune,* pp. 136–137.

34. *Schwager v. Sun Oil Company of PA* (1979). 591 F.2d. 58 (10th Cir.).

35. *Mastie v. Great Lakes Steel Corp.* (1976). 424 F. Supp. 1299 (U.S. District Court, Michigan).

36. *Hodgson v. Greyhound Lines, Inc.* (1975). 419 U.S. 1122.

37. *Fair Employment Practices* (1990). Washington: Bureau of National Affairs, p. 40.

38. Department of Justice memo (1990). Washington: U.S. Department of Justice.

39. Carey, J. H. (Aug. 15, 1990). Americans with Disabilities Act of 1990. *Employment Testing, 4*(3), 629–633. See also: Shaller, E. H. (1991). "Reasonable accommodation" under the Americans with Disabilities Act: What does it mean? *Employee Relations Law Journal, 16,* 431–451.

40. *Pregnancy and employment: The complete handbook on discrimination, maternity leave, and health and safety* (1987). Washington: Bureau of National Affairs.

41. *California Federal Savings & Loan Association v. Guerra* (1987). 42 FEP Cases 1073.

42. Tung, R. (1984). *Key to Japan's strength: Human power.* Lexington, MA: Lexington Books. See also: Adler, N. J., and Israeli, D. N. (eds.) (1988). *Women in management worldwide.* Armonk, N.Y.: M. E. Sharpe, Inc.

43. *Abrams, L. A. v. Baylor College of Medicine* (1990). Civ. A. Nos. H-81-1433, H-82-3253.

44. Adler, N. J. (Summer 1984). Women in international business: Where are they? *California Management Review,* pp. 78–89. See also: Adler, N. J. (1983). Cross cultural management research: The ostrich and the trend. *Academy of Management Review, 8,* 226–232.

45. *EEOC v. Arabian Oil Co.* (1991). 55 EDD, 111 S. Ct. 1227 (U.S. Supreme Court).

46. Collins, Lawrence (1990). *European Community Law in the United Kingdom.* London, England: Butterworth's. See also: Blanpain, R. (1991). *Labour law and industrial relations of the European Community.* Deventer, Netherlands: Kluwer.

47. See note 1.

EXERCISE 3.1
ZIMPFER V. PALM BEACH COUNTY

OVERVIEW

In Chapter 3, you were presented with a variety of laws affecting HRM activity. One of those laws was the ADEA. The following case requires you to apply your understanding of the ADEA to provide some suggestions for Palm Beach County.

LEARNING OBJECTIVES

After completing this exercise, you should be able to:

1. Identify the critical issues associated with age discrimination cases.
2. Provide recommendations for a plaintiff filing an age discrimination case, and for the employer in defending EEO practices.
3. Outline policies that organizations should adopt to prevent charges of age discrimination among their employees.

PROCEDURE

Part A: Individual Analysis

Step 1. Read the background material on Palm Beach County provided in Exhibit 3.1.1.

Step 2. Assume the role of the HR director and answer all of the questions on Form 3.1.1.

Part B: Group Analysis

Step 1. In groups of about six people, students should attempt to reach consensus on the four questions. Each student should review the Form 3.1.1 filled out by every other student prior to the discussion.

Step 2. The instructor will designate one (or more) representatives to present each group's consensus positions.

EXHIBIT 3.1.1
BACKGROUND MATERIAL FOR PALM BEACH COUNTY: ADEA CHARGE, POSITION DESCRIPTION, AND NATURE OF WORK FOR EMPLOYEE RELATIONS MANAGER

Palm Beach County has requested your opinon regarding an alleged violation of the Age Discrimination in Employment Act. Mr. Bryce Zimpfer, age 52, has been an employee of the county for 16 years in the employee relations area. The Department of Human Resources posted a job vacancy for Employee Relations Manager (see below), and Mr. Zimpfer applied for the position. The department filled the position with Mr. Brad Merriman, age 33, an outside applicant with less experience in employee relations than Mr. Zimpfer.

After filing a timely complaint with the EEOC, Mr. Zimpfer retained Ms. Lynn Szymoniak, an attorney who is now attempting to reach a settlement with the division's legal staff. In preparation for these negotiations, the attorney asked an industrial psychologist, Dr. Kimberly Frank, to examine the résumés of the job applicants and submit a report as to whether Mr. Zimpfer was more qualified for the position than Mr. Merriman (see Exhibit 3.1.2). Dr. Frank submitted a report and concluded that on the basis of her résumé analysis, Mr. Zimpfer was more qualified for the position than Mr. Merriman (see Exhibit 3.1.3).

JOB VACANCY ANNOUNCEMENT
POSITION DESCRIPTION

This is professional personnel and labor relations work developing and managing programs and activities to enhance relationships between management and employees; to promote employee satisfaction, well-being, and quality of work life; to develop greater productivity in the workforce; and to achieve sound labor-management working relationships. The work is of a highly responsible nature, requiring considerable independent judgment and decision making. The work is performed under the direction of the director, employee relations and personnel, and is reviewed through conferences, reports, and results achieved.

EXAMPLES OF WORK

Initiates and manages programs which aim to improve communication and participation. These may be employee orientation meetings, committees, attitude surveys, suggestion boxes, awards programs, newsletters, newspapers, handbooks, benefits brochures, and other media such as posters or payroll stuffers which communicate policies and practices to employees.

Develops programs which monitor and detect employees' dissatisfactions with policies or working conditions. These include adequate complaint and grievance procedures, communication of these to employees, and adequate follow-up with management to resolve problems.

Initiates procedures for reviewing adverse actions taken by supervisors to ensure that such actions are fair. Investigates the facts of the case and determines whether any disciplinary action is appropriate. Directs and trains supervisors in discipline and discharge procedures.

Develops and monitors performance review systems, employee assistance programs, incentive and award programs, quality circles, and other programs with the purpose of motivating workers toward greater productivity.

Initiates programs to improve the quality of supervision, primarily training programs to improve knowledge of effective supervisory practices. May develop and present training programs for supervisors. May write and disseminate supervisors' handbooks or manuals.

Assists the director in interpreting the provisions of labor contracts to supervisors. May conduct supervisory training sessions in contract administration.

Reviews and recommends policy and benefit changes to the director which are needed to enhance employee-management relations.

Audits and approves personnel actions when applicable to ensure compliance with policies.

May supervise counselors or specialists in carrying out these employee relations activities.

Performs related work as required.

REQUIRED KNOWLEDGE, SKILLS, AND ABILITIES

Thorough working knowledge of federal and state laws affecting public personnel administration and labor relations.

Thorough knowledge of merit system principles and policies.

Knowledge of organization and functions.

Knowledge of the principles of management and supervision.

Ability to organize work and supervise professional staff.

Ability to write and interpret correspondence and reports.

Ability to speak to a wide variety of groups and present ideas effectively.

Ability to deal tactfully and persuasively with staff, employees, supervisors, administrators, and union officials.

Ability to conduct personal and investigative interviews.

Ability to interpret complex legal cases and documents.

Ability to conduct independent research and analysis.

MINIMUM ENTRANCE REQUIREMENTS

Graduation from an accredited college or university with major course work in HRM, industrial relations, labor relations, or a closely related field; considerable progressively responsible experience in employee or labor relations; or any equivalent combination of related training and experience.

EXHIBIT 3.1.2
LETTER OF INQUIRY FROM CULLEN & SZYMONIAK, P. A.

CULLEN & SZYMONIAK, P.A.

ATTORNEYS-AT-LAW

1030 Lake Avenue

Lake Worth, Florida 33460

(407) 585-4666

MARK A. CULLEN   October 25   **LYNN E. SZYMONIAK**

Kimberly Frank, Ph.D.
10475 Northwest Michigan Avenue
Birmingham, Michigan 48275

Dear Dr. Frank:

I am very pleased that you are available to assist us with the Bryce Zimpfer case. Please find enclosed the following documents:

1. The job announcement, announcing the position of Employee Relations Manager;

2. A job description for the position of Employee Relations Manager;

3. Copies of the newspaper ads announcing this position;

4. A Referral List of the candidates chosen for an interview for the position of Employee Relations Manager;

5. The résumés, cover letters, and applications of the applicants listed on the referral list; and

6. The application and résumé of Bryce Zimpfer.

Based on your review of the above documents, please advise me:

1. Whether Mr. Zimpfer's qualifications equalled or exceeded the qualifications of the applicants selected for an interview; and

2. In particular, whether Bryce Zimpfer's qualifications equalled or exceeded the qualifications of J. Brad Merriman—the candidate ultimately selected for the position.

The experts' reports are to be exchanged on this case on November 15. Thank you again for your assistance.

Yours truly,

Lynn E Szymoniak

LYNN E. SZYMONIAK, ESQ.

Enclosures

85

EXHIBIT 3.1.3
RESPONSE TO CULLEN & SZYMONIAK, P. A., BY KIMBERLY FRANK, PH.D.

KIMBERLY FRANK, PH.D.
INDUSTRIAL PSYCHOLOGIST
10475 NORTHWEST MICHIGAN AVENUE
BIRMINGHAM, MICHIGAN 48275

November 13

Lynn E. Szymoniak, Esq.
Cullen & Szymoniak, P.A.
1030 Lake Avenue
Lake Worth, FL 33460

Dear Ms. Szymoniak:

The purpose of this letter is to respond to your request for expert opinion in matters related to Bryce Zimpfer. In your letter of October 25, you requested that I render an opinion regarding the following:
1. Whether Mr. Zimpfer's qualifications equalled or exceeded the qualifications of the applicants selected for an interview; and
2. In particular, whether Bryce Zimpfer's qualifications equalled or exceeded the qualifications of J. Brad Merriman—the candidate ultimately selected for the position.

In rendering my opinion, I have reviewed the following documents:
1. The job announcement from Palm Beach County announcing the position of Employee Relations Manager;
2. A job description for the position of Employee Relations Manager;
3. Copies of the newspaper ads announcing this position;
4. A Referral List of the candidates chosen for an interview for the position of Employee Relations Manager;
5. The résumés, cover letters, and applications of the applicants listed on the referral list; and
6. The application and résumé of Bryce Zimpfer.

Based on my review of the aforementioned documents, I have the following opinions:
1. Mr. Zimpfer's qualifications equalled or exceeded the qualifications of several of the applicants selected for an interview; and
2. Mr. Zimpfer's qualifications exceeded the qualifications of Mr. J. Brad Merriman.

EXHIBIT 3.1.3 *(Continued)*

The following is a description of the procedure which I followed to arrive at these opinions:

1. Based on a reading of the job announcement, the job description and the newspaper ad, I constructed three applicant/work requirement matrices for purposes of assessing applicant qualifications with regard to program/activities, work examples, and required knowledge, skills, and abilities, and other characteristics (KASOCs). See Figures 1, 2, and 3. The first column of each matrix represents the critical work requirements of the job as reflected in the job announcement, etc.

2. I read each résumé and recorded those work requirements with which each applicant had experience or a requisite KASOC. I performed this task on three occasions (for the three matrices), each time evaluating the résumés in random order.

3. I performed the identical task described in Step 2 five days later with no reference to the completed matrices from Step 2. Thus, I made two independent evaluations of each of the three work requirement matrices.

4. I examined the discrepancies in the applicant/requirement cells of each matrix from the Step 2 and Step 3 evaluations and reviewed the résumés for purposes of reconciling the disagreements. The totals in the last row of Figures 1, 2, and 3 reflect the final evaluations I have made of each candidate after reconciling the few discrepancies between the Step 2 and Step 3 evaluations.

5. The opinions rendered above with regard to Mr. Zimpfer are based on the final evaluations of the three matrices.

The matrix analysis on which I have based my opinions represents a "job-related" and objective approach to the evaluation of applicant résumés. It is far superior in terms of validity and reliability to a non-quantitative evaluation procedure which calls for a global evaluation of the applicants in terms of suitability for a multi-faceted job.

Sincerely,

Kimberly Frank

Kimberly Frank, Ph.D.

MMJ:im

EXHIBIT 3.1.3 *(Continued)*

Figure 1

PROGRAMS AND ACTIVITIES ANALYSIS

Programs/Activities	Zimpfer	Atkinson	Bender	Bledsoe	Merriman	Schwab
Performance appraisals	X	X		X	X	
Employee assistance	X		X			X
Employee benefits	X	X	X	X	X	
Employee publications	X		X		X	
Counseling and discipline	X				X	
Grievance procedures	X		X	X		X
Attendance and leave policy	X			X		
Lay-off policy	X				X	
Unemployment compensation						
Contract administration	X	X	X	X	X	
TOTALS	9	3	5	5	6	2

EXHIBIT 3.1.3 *(Continued)*

Figure 2

WORK SAMPLE ANALYSIS

Examples of Work	Zimpfer	Atkinson	Bender	Bledsoe	Merriman	Schwab
Employee orientation	X		X			X
Attitude surveys	X		X			
Suggestion boxes						
Awards program			X			
Newsletters	X		X			
Handbooks	X					
Benefits brochure	X	X				
Grievance procedures	X		X	X		
Disciplinary action			X	X		X
Supervisory training	X	X	X	X		X
Interpreting labor contracts		X	X		X	X
Policy and benefits	X	X	X	X	X	X
Audits and approves personal actions				X		
TOTALS	8	4	9	5	2	5

EXHIBIT 3.1.3 *(Continued)*

Figure 3

KASOC ANALYSIS

	Zimpfer	Atkinson	Bender	Bledsoe	Merriman	Schwab
State and federal law	X	X	X	X	X	X
Ability to speak to variety of groups	X		X	X		X
Conduct interviews	X	X	X		X	X
Interpret complex legal cases and documents						X
Conduct independent research	X		X			X
TOTALS	4	2	4	2	2	5

FORM 3.1.1

Name _____ Group _____

1. Does the evidence indicate that Mr. Zimpfer was a victim of age discrimination according to ADEA? Why or why not?

2. What (if any) further evidence should be ascertained before the county fully understands the legal implications of its actions?

3. What action do you recommend that the county take in this matter?

4. What policies should the company adopt to reduce the possibility of age discrimination suits in the future?

EXERCISE 3.2
GOEBEL ET AL. V. JAYJOE CLOTHIERS

OVERVIEW

Many Title VII cases involve the presentation of statistical evidence which is alleged to indicate illegal discrimination. The purpose of this exercise is to review the statistical evidence presented and to assess the implications of the data for the organization.

LEARNING OBJECTIVES

After completing this exercise, you should be able to:

1. Calculate adverse impact for a selection procedure.
2. Provide recommendations for a plaintiff filing a race discrimination case, and for the employer in defending EEO practices.
3. Outline the selection procedure the organization should adopt to prevent charges of race discrimination among their employees.

PROCEDURE

Part A: Individual Analysis

Step 1. Read the background material on *Goebel et al. v. Jayjoe Clothiers* provided in Exhibit 3.2.1.

Step 2. Assume the role of the HR director and study the case described below. Please prepare concise, written responses for the legal division of Jayjoe Clothiers. Provide these responses on Form 3.2.1.

Part B: Group Analysis

Step 1. In groups of six, members should attempt to reach consensus on question 1 of Form 3.2.1.

A rationale for the position should be developed which includes relevant court citations.

Step 2. The instructor will designate one member from each group to present the group position and rationale.

EXHIBIT 3.2.1
GOEBEL ET AL. V. JAYJOE CLOTHIERS

A division of Jayjoe Clothiers had 16 openings for assistant store manager last year and, as part of the company's affirmative action program, filled the vacancies with 10 blacks and 6 whites. The selection process used a multiple-hurdle approach which began with an application form and an intelligence test. Applicants who scored 60 (out of 100) or higher on the intelligence test were then given an interview by the store managers. Based on the interview performances, the 16 vacancies were filled.

The numbers of blacks and whites who passed the intelligence test were as follows:

	Test scores	
	BLACK APPLICANTS	WHITE APPLICANTS
Number scoring 60 or higher	25	74
Number scoring lower than 60	26	29
Total	51	103

Dennis Goebel, a black applicant who scored 39 on the test, filed suit on behalf of all black applicants who failed the exam. Mr. Goebel claimed race discrimination based on Title VII of the Civil Rights Act of 1964.

Jayjoe Clothiers has argued that over 62 percent of the actual supervisory vacancies were filled with blacks (i.e., 10 out of 16) and that, thus, there was obviously no racial discrimination in the selection process.

FORM 3.2.1

Name _____ Group _____

1. Were Mr. Goebel and other black applicants victims of racial discrimination because of the hiring policies of the defendant? Explain your position, citing specific cases to support your position.

2. Is there evidence of disparate impact against blacks in the decisions which were made? On what basis did you arrive at this position?

Name _____ Group _____

3. If disparate impact is evident, what steps should the defendant take next? Provide specific recommendations.

4. An associate of the Personnel Department is arguing that Jayjoe should continue to use the examination but that the test scores should be interpreted by the ethnic classification of the test taker. For example, raw scores on the exam would be converted to percentages *within ethnic classifications*. With such a procedure, African-Americans taking the test who received the same raw score as whites would receive a higher percentage score on the exam because of the ethnic interpretation. He argues that this procedure would enable Jayjoe to continue using a valid and useful test while avoiding adverse impact. Take a position on this recommendation and provide the rationale.

EXERCISE 3.3
COMPLAINT OF MS. SMITH

OVERVIEW

In recent years, the number of lawsuits filed for sexual harassment has steadily increased. As a result, it is becoming more and more important for employers to be familiar with how sexual harassment is defined and what they should do to prevent such instances from occurring in the workplace. This exercise challenges you to think about some of these issues.

LEARNING OBJECTIVES

After completing this exercise, you should be able to:

1. Define what is meant by sexual harassment.
2. Provide recommendations for a plaintiff filing a case charging sexual harassment, and for the employer in defending the company's practices.
3. Outline the policies the organization should adopt to prevent charges of sexual harassment in the future.

PROCEDURE

Part A: Individual Analysis

Step 1. Read the background material on the complaint of Ms. Smith provided in Exhibit 3.3.1.

Step 2. As a member of the grievance committee, you have been asked to consider the questions presented on Form 3.3.1. Please prepare concise written responses to each of the questions presented on Form 3.3.1.

Part B: Group Analysis

Step 1. In groups of about six people, students should attempt to reach consensus on the questions on Form 3.3.1. Prior to discussion, each student should read all other group members' responses.

Step 2. The instructor will designate one student to present each group's position on the questions on Form 3.3.1.

EXHIBIT 3.3.1
COMPLAINT OF MS. SMITH

Ms. Kathleen Smith has filed a complaint with the internal grievance committee claiming sexual harassment on the job. She has threatened to file a formal complaint with the EEOC if nothing is done about the situation.

A cashier at one of the retail stores, Ms. Smith claims that Mr. Edward Jayjo, assistant store manager, has propositioned her on numerous occasions over the last 12 months. These sexual advances have been made in Mr. Jayjo's office while they were alone and, on several other occasions, in front of other cashiers, who corroborate her story. There is also no evidence that Ms. Smith provoked Mr. Jayjo with her dress or personal manner. Ms. Smith complained to Mr. Joseph Garcia, the store manager, who agreed to look into the matter.

In the 12 months in which the alleged sexual harassment took place, the following personnel actions were taken at the store:

PERCENT OF SALARY INCREASES FOR THE YEAR
All cashiers, 5.8% (average)
Ms. Smith, 7.5%

CHRISTMAS BONUSES
All cashiers, $250 (average)
Ms. Smith, $500

PROMOTIONS TO HEAD CASHIER
Total: 4 (including Ms. Smith)

In his response to the complaint, Mr. Garcia stated, "There is clearly no evidence that refusal to submit to sexual advances is related to any negative action against Ms. Smith. She is a good employee and is recognized as such through merit increases, bonuses, and promotions. There is also no evidence of physical contact."

Name _____ Group _____

1. Based on the above information, does the sexual harassment constitute a violation of the law? Explain your position, citing any relevant cases.

2. If you responded yes to question 1, is the company legally liable for the violation? Why or why not?

Name_____ Group _____

3. What (if any) action do you recommend that the company take in this matter?

4. What policies and procedures should be established to prevent such charges in the future? Prepare a detailed outline of your recommendations.

EXERCISE 3.4
A CASE OF REVERSE
DISCRIMINATION?

OVERVIEW

Chapter 3 presents considerable detail on Title VII of the Civil Rights Act and the evolution of affirmative action programs. The purpose of this exercise is to introduce some of the complexities and ramifications of these programs. A real case is described which involves allegations of reverse discrimination.

LEARNING OBJECTIVES

After completing the exercise, you should be able to:

1. Understand the variables which must be considered when determining the legality of affirmative action programs.
2. Know the conditions under which the sex (or race) of an employee may be taken into consideration for personnel decisions.

PROCEDURE

Part A: Individual Analysis

Step   1.   Each student should study the case presented in Exhibit 3.4.1 and take either position A or position B. On Form 3.4.1, write a concise paragraph (no more than 150 words) which provides the basis for your position on the case (cite specific cases or material to support your position).

Step   2.   Complete the remaining assessment questions on Form 3.4.1.

Part B: Group Analysis

Step   1.   In groups of no more than six, students should review each student's individual report and assessment questions and then attempt to reach consensus on a position. Once the consensus is reached, each group should adopt a group position paragraph (no more than 75 words).

Step   2.   One group member will be asked to present the group's position to the rest of the class.

EXHIBIT 3.4.1

After 4 tough years of working on the road for the Santa Ana County transportation agency, Diane Harrison applied for a less strenuous desk job as a road dispatcher. At that time not one of the California agency's 238 skilled positions was held by a woman. Harrison knew, however, that 2 years earlier, the county had enacted a voluntary affirmative action policy designed to correct that imbalance.

Harrison has 18 years of clerical experience and almost 5 years as a road maintenance worker. Another candidate for the position, Edward Jones, had 11 years as a road yard clerk (a clerical positon) and 4 years as a road maintenance worker. He also had previous experience as a dispatcher in private employment.

The position of road dispatcher required 4 years of dispatcher or road maintenance work experience with the county. Twelve employees applied for the job. Nine were judged to be qualified and interviewed by a two-person board. Seven of the applicants scored about 70 and were certified as eligible for selection. Jones tied for second at 75, and Harrison ranked next with 70. At a second interview, three agency supervisors recommended that Jones be promoted. At the second interview, one male panel member described Harrison as a rabble-rousing, "skirt-wearing" troublemaker.

The local supervisor picked Jones, but the county's affirmative action coordinator recommended Harrison. When Harrison got the job, Jones got a lawyer. Like Allen Bakke and Brian Weber and countless other white males since the advent of affirmative action programs some 20 years ago, Jones claimed he was a victim of reverse discrimination and filed suit under Title VII of the 1964 Civil Rights Act.

Positions

A. The Santa Ana plan is consistent with Title VII's purpose of eliminating the effects of past employment discrimination. Given the obvious imbalance in the skilled craft division and given the agency's commitment to eliminating such imbalances, it was appropriate to consider as one fact the sex of Ms. Harrison in making its decision. Thus, the court should decide in favor of Santa Ana County.

B. To decide against Mr. Jones is to complete the process of converting Title VII from a guarantee that race or sex will not be the basis for employment determinations to a guarantee that it often will. Ever so subtly, we effectively replace the goal of a discrimination-free society with the quite incompatible goal of proportionate representation by race and by sex in the workplace. Thus, the court should decide in favor of Mr. Jones.

FORM 3.4.1

Name _____ Group _____

1. What position do you support (A or B)? Write an opinion based on your understanding of Title VII and relevant case law.

2. What conditions are necessary in order for an organization to show preference for one group over another?

3. Given the actual wording in Title VII (see Figure 3.2), how can an organization show preference to women as in this case?

4. To what extent did you take into consideration the great disparity in the number of male and female dispatchers? Does this disparity document sex discrimination?

EXERCISE 3.5
JOSEPH GARCIA V. HOOTERS
CAMERON V. LA VIEILLE MAISON

OVERVIEW

What is allowable as a BFOQ? The Supreme Court has said that BFOQs are allowable if they are "reasonably necessary to the normal operation of that particular business." What if a business has a competitive strategy that appeals to a particular segment of the population which has certain strong preferences for services to be provided by the establishment? (Recall the discussion of the *Pan Am v. Diaz* Supreme Court case.) The 1991 decision in *UAW v. Johnson Controls* stated that the exception to Title VII in the form of BFOQs applies only to policies that involve the "essence of the business." The purpose of this exercise is to present two real cases with characteristics that are hardly unique in an industry. We will ask you to take a position on the legality of a company policy which the company claims falls under the "business essence" BFOQ exception to Title VII.

LEARNING OBJECTIVES

After completing this exercise, you should be able to:

1. Understand the conditions under which a BFOQ is allowable.
2. Know the role of customer preference in Title VII cases.
3. Consider the implications of the case for other similar policies in the industry.

PROCEDURE

Part A: Individual Analysis

Prior to class, read the case histories in Exhibit 3.5.1 and answer the questions on Form 3.5.1.

Part B: Group Analysis

Step 1. In groups of about six people, each student should review the other group members' responses. Then the group should attempt to reach a consensus view on each of the questions.

Step 2. One person should be designated as the group spokesperson, and the group position should be presented to the class.

EXHIBIT 3.5.1

JOSEPH GARCIA V. HOOTERS

Hooters Restaurants had a competitive strategy of appealing to the young, affluent male population through a number of features. Large-screen television for sports events, happy hours, sports celebrity events, and very attractive waitresses were part of their strategy. Joseph Garcia was a waiter from Chicago who had worked at similar restaurants for over 10 years. He heard from a friend that Hooters was hiring. However, he was told he would have to apply in person. When he showed up at one of the 25 franchise establishments, he was told that they were not in fact hiring. He learned a few weeks later that an attractive female had been hired at the same restaurant. He filed a timely claim with the EEOC.

CAROL CAMERON V. LA VIEILLE MAISON

La Vieille Maison is a five-star restaurant in East Cupcake, Florida. Carol Cameron, a waitress with over 10 years of experience in "upscale" restaurants and an esoteric knowledge of wine, applied for a job at La Vieille Maison in a period when the restaurant was hiring waiters in preparation for the heavy winter season. She was not hired. The restaurant employs only waiters and makes the argument that five-star French restaurants traditionally employ only waiters. After learning that La Vieille Maison had hired three new waiters, Ms. Cameron filed a timely Title VII lawsuit against the restaurant.

Name _____ Group _____

1. Was Mr. Garcia a victim of sex discrimination? Explain your answer in some detail based on your understanding of BFOQs.

2. Was Ms. Cameron a victim of sex discrimination? Explain your answer.

3. In principle, do you see these cases as the same in terms of your interpretation of legal BFOQs? Explain your answer.

4. When can customer preference be used as a basis for making decisions about people you hire or retain?

4

C H A P T E R

JOB ANALYSIS

OVERVIEW

Job analysis is considered to be the foundation or building block for most human resource (HR) systems in organizations. Corporate restructuring, quality improvement programs, HR planning, job design, recruitment, selection, training, career development, performance appraisal, and compensation are among the systems which are typically based on information derived from job analysis. As we discussed in Chapter 3, the legal environment affecting virtually all personnel decisions has had a great deal to do with the importance attached to job analysis and explains why there is much greater emphasis placed on job analysis in the United States than in other countries.

Consider the following scenarios:

Nationsbank was interested in the development of an employee screening test for 40 different jobs ranging from teller to loan officer. They wanted to be certain that the test was legally defensible and "job-related" in the context of the new Civil Rights Act and the ADA. A consultant recommended a job analysis of each job.

The State of Virginia passed a law mandating state employee pay to be based on performance. However, there was a need for the development of a performance appraisal system. The first step in the development of the appraisal system was a job analysis to identify the critical behaviors or outcomes to be evaluated.

Two laboratory technicians have similar job experience and education, but are employed at different local hospitals. One technician makes $5000 more per year than the other. The lower-paid employee asks her HR Department to review her pay based on the external compensation market. A job description was needed to do the wage survey.

The Monsanto Corporation has many jobs which stipulate specific physical requirements (e.g., "must be able to lift 75 pounds"). The company is concerned that some of the requirements are unnecessary and may be in violation of the 1991 Civil Rights Act or the "reasonable accommodations" provisions of the Americans with Disabilities Act (ADA).

An assembly plant of Chrysler Corporation adopts a team-based approach to factory work by assigning specific tasks to a team rather than to individuals. The team will divide up the work, which is as clearly defined and standardized as in typical American factories, but all team members are expected to be able to perform any of the work tasks. What information will the HR department at Chrysler need in order to redesign the jobs for work teams and to determine qualifications for team membership?

Pratt and Whitney, the jet engine division of United Technologies, seeks to improve its competitiveness through the elimination of activities no longer essential to the business, a reduction in overhead of 30 percent, and the improvement of existing job functions in the context of customer requirements. The modification, addition, and elimination of some jobs are anticipated.

IBM adopted a process management approach to the evaluation and restructuring of each unit. All job tasks and outcomes were assessed in the context of critical internal customers and how their requirements related to the requirements of external customers.

Job analysis information is needed for each of these situations to assist the employees and the organizations in their efforts. Job descriptions and job specifications are needed to attract and select employees, to evaluate the compensation system, and to make particular compensation decisions. Job standards are used to evaluate employees; job factors are needed to group jobs to develop wage and salary systems; and job duties and context factors are examined to redesign and evaluate jobs and restructure organizations. As one expert in human resource management (HRM) put it, "job analysis may be viewed as the hub of virtually all human resources administration and management activities necessary for the successful functioning of organizations. Hardly a program of interest to human resource specialists and other practitioners whose work pertains to organizational personnel does not depend on or cannot benefit from job analysis results."[1] This chapter subscribes to this view in describing the importance of job analysis for the field of HRM. Discussion centers on the purposes for job analysis as well as the major approaches for collecting job analysis data.

OBJECTIVES

After studying this chapter, you should be able to:

1. Understand what a job analysis is and what the major products are.
2. Explain the purposes and uses for job analysis data.
3. Compare and contrast methods for collecting job analysis data.
4. Describe commonly used and newer methods for conducting a job analysis.
5. Explain how job analysis information is applied to job design efforts.
6. Prepare a job analysis report.

DEFINING JOB ANALYSIS

Job analysis is the process of gathering information about a job. It is an attempt to "reduce to words the things that people do in human work."[2] There are several major steps in conducting a job analysis. First, the major tasks, activities, behaviors, or duties to be performed on the job must be determined. This can be done by one or more task-oriented methods, which are described in a later section. Once the tasks and activities have been identified, the relative importance or relative frequency with which the various tasks are performed are assessed. Next, the critical *knowledges, abilities, skills, and other characteristics (KASOCs)* necessary to perform the tasks must be identified. *Knowledge* refers to an organized body of information, usually of a factual or procedural nature applied directly to the performance of a function. An *ability* refers to a demonstrated competence to perform an observable behavior or a behavior that results in an observable product. A *skill* is a competence to perform a learned psychomotor act, and may include a manual, verbal, or mental manipulation of data, people, or things. Finally, *other characteristics* include personality factors, attitudes, aptitudes, or physical or mental traits needed to perform the job. The job analysis report of a patrol officer, for example, might indicate that the job requires knowledge of laws, oral communication skills, driving ability, and dependability to do the job adequately.

Depending on the particular method of job analysis, there are numerous products which can be derived from the effort. The most frequent and commonly used products of job analysis include job descriptions and job specifications. *Job descriptions* define the job in terms of its content and scope. Although the format can vary, the job description may include information on job duties and responsibilities, an identification of critical internal and external customers, equipment to be used on the job, working conditions, relationships with coworkers, and the extent of supervision required. Figure 4.1 presents an example of a job or position description for a compensation manager.

Job specifications consist of the KASOCs needed to carry out the job tasks and duties. Specific educational requirements (e.g., Ph.D., M.B.A., Ed.D., M.S.W.), certifications or licenses (e.g., CPA, certified financial planner), or other credentials are often listed in job specifications. Figure 4.2 presents an example of the job specifications for a compensation manager. You will note that a college degree in personnel, HR, industrial psychology, or a related field is required for the compensation manager job. A job analysis should be the basis of this specification. Specifications should be derived from the KASOC.

As we discussed in Chapter 3, job specifications are often contested in court because they may have adverse impact upon groups protected by equal employment opportunity (EEO) laws. Certainly job specifications which result in adverse impact upon such groups must be derived from thorough job analyses if they are to be upheld in court. Also, analysts should consider the incremental compensation which may be required by a job specification that may not be essential for performance on the job. Many business schools now stipulate that a Ph.D. is required for any faculty position, although it is conceivable that a candidate with an M.B.A. would be less costly and perhaps more effective as an instructor.

The stipulations of specific tasks to be performed and specifications for the job are not without critics. In Japan, for example, new employees are typically hired without job descriptions or specifications. Japan places much reliance on in-house training and job rotation to foster versatility in the skills of each new employee. Japanese managers think that job descriptions can be harmful to their team-building approach to management. Many experts in job design and organizational restructuring embrace this view and believe that job descriptions should be written for units or teams, with all team members responsible for (or at least qualified to perform) all unit functions or activities. Individual job descriptions are thought to be detrimental to work group effectiveness. However, particularly in these litigious times, job descriptions are needed and can be written in such a way as to facilitate a team-oriented approach to work processes. Highly detailed job descriptions are very common in Europe, where they are frequently required by regulation or collective bargaining agreement. Every employee at the Volvo plant in Sweden, for example, has a detailed job description based on a quantitative job analysis even though the assembly process at Volvo is based on teamwork rather than on the traditional assembly line. Daimler-Benz and Siemens, two giant German companies, also use detailed job descriptions for each position in their firms.

PURPOSES FOR JOB ANALYSIS

Despite the criticism, job analysis is used for a variety of purposes in both the private and the public sector, particularly in larger organizations (see Figure 4.3). Smaller businesses are less likely to use formal approaches for conducting job analyses and may instead rely on less structured methods for writing job descriptions and setting job specifications. In larger organizations, however, such as state and federal government agencies, personnel may be hired and trained as job analysts. In these positions, their primary duty is to perform job analyses and related activities.

FIGURE 4.1
PD FOR A COMPENSATION MANAGER

Job Title: Compensation Manager   DOT Code: 166.167-022

Reports to: _____

General Summary:

Responsible for the design and administration of employee compensation programs. Insures proper consideration of the relationship of salary to performance of each employee and provides consultation on salary administration to managers and supervisors.

Principal Duties and Responsibilities:

1. Insures the preparation and maintenance of job descriptions for each current and projected position. Prepares all job descriptions, authorizing final drafts. Coordinates periodic review of all job descriptions, making revisions as necessary. Educates employees and supervisors on job description use and their intent by participation in formal training programs and by responding to their questions. Maintains accurate file of all current job descriptions. Distributes revised job descriptions to appropriate individuals.

2. Insures the proper evaluation of job descriptions. Serves as chair of Job Evaluation Committee, coordinating its activities. Resolves disputes over proper evaluation of jobs. Assigns jobs to pay ranges and reevaluates jobs periodically through the Committee process. Conducts initial evaluation of new positions prior to hiring. Insures integrity of job evaluation process.

3. Insures that Company compensation rates are in accordance with the Company philosophy. Maintains current information concerning applicable salary movements taking place in comparable organizations. Obtains or conducts salary surveys as necessary. Conducts analysis of salary changes among competitors and presents recommendations on salary movements on an annual basis.

4. Insures proper consideration of the relationship of salary to the performance of each employee. Inspects all performance appraisals and salary reviews, authorizing all pay adjustments.

5. Develops and administers the performance appraisal program. Develops and updates performance appraisal instruments. Assists in the development of training programs to educate supervisors on using the performance appraisal system. Monitors the use of the performance appraisal instruments to insure the integrity of the system and proper use.

FIGURE 4.1 *(Continued)*

6. Assists in the development and oversees the administration of all bonus payments up through the Officer level.

7. Researches and provides recommendations on executive compensation issues.

8. Coordinates the development of an integrated HR information system. Assists in identifying needs; interfaces with the Management Information Systems Department to achieve departmental goals for information needs.

9. Performs related duties as assigned or as the situation dictates.

FIGURE 4.2
JOB SPECIFICATIONS FOR A COMPENSATION MANAGER

REQUIRED KNOWLEDGES, SKILLS, AND ABILITIES
1. Knowledge of compensation and HRM practices and principles
2. Knowledge of job analysis procedures
3. Knowledge of survey development and interpretation practices
4. Knowledge of current performance appraisal issues for designing, implementing, and maintaining systems
5. Skill in conducting job analysis interviews
6. Skill in writing job descriptions, memorandums, letters, and proposals
7. Skill in making group presentations, conducting job analysis interviews, and explaining policies and practices to employees and supervisors
8. Skill in performing statistical computations including regression, correlation, and basic descriptive statistics
9. Ability to conduct meetings
10. Ability to plan and prioritize work

EDUCATION AND EXPERIENCE REQUIREMENTS
This position requires the equivalent of a college degree in personnel, human resources, or industrial psychology, or a related degree, plus 3 to 5 years' experience in personnel, 2 to 3 of which should include compensation adminstration experience. An advanced degree in industrial psychology, business administration, or personnel management is preferred.

WORK ORIENTATION FACTORS
This position may require up to 15 percent travel.

Job analysis data has been collected for recruitment and selection purposes in a large number of companies. For example, Tenneco Oil Company developed recruiting techniques for their customer service representatives based on the results of a standardized job analysis instrument. Exxon Corporation and AT&T employ a standardized questionnaire to analyze their jobs in order to develop or identify personnel selection tests for entry-level employees. The state of New York also used a job analysis method to establish job specifications for highway patrol officers.

The *Fort Lauderdale News and Sun Sentinel* used a quantitative job analysis method to develop a test to select customer service representatives and redesign the job. Information compiled from job analyses has also been used for developing performance appraisal systems. Palm Beach County, Florida, for example, used the critical incident technique (CIT) to derive performance rating scales for county teachers. The Federal Aviation Administration (FAA), the Digital Equipment Corporation, and the states of Virginia and Tennessee relied on interviewing results from their job analyses to develop performance appraisal systems for managers. Job analysis data have also been used for job redesign purposes. Motorola Corporation used a standardized, task-based instrument to collect the necessary information to develop work teams. Numerous organizations also use job analysis information to develop training curricula.

While job analysis is typically used to derive specific information about particular jobs, as we stated above, job analysis data can be aggregated to the unit or function level so that the end products such as job description or job specifications are defined at the team level rather than for particular positions.

Legal Significance of Job Analysis Data

There has been strong interest in job analysis since passage of the Civil Rights Act in 1964 and subsequent court rulings.[3] In particular, the U.S. Supreme Court decisions in *Griggs v. Duke Power Company* and *Albemarle Paper Company v. Moody* emphasized the importance of demonstrating the job relatedness of employee selection systems. One way to demonstrate job relatedness is by conducting a thorough job analysis to justify personnel job specifications.

The legal importance of job analysis has not waned in the slightest since 1964. There are still a great number of court cases which focus on the results of (or the

FIGURE 4.3
PURPOSES OF JOB ANALYSIS INFORMATION

Job description. A complete job description should contain job identification information, a job summary, the job duties and accountabilities, and job specification or employment standards information.

Job classification. Job classification is the arrangement of jobs into classes, groups, or families according to some systematic scheme. Traditional classification schemes have been based on organizational lines of authority, technology-based job/task content, and human behavior-based job content.

Job evaluation. Job evaluation is a procedure for classifying jobs in terms of their relative worth both within an organization and within the related external labor market.

Job design restructuring. Job design deals with the allocation and arrangement of organizational work activities and tasks into sets in which a singular set of activities constitutes a "job" and is performed by the job incumbent. Job restructuring or redesign consists of reallocation or rearrangement of the work activities into different sets.

Personnel requirements/specifications. Personnel requirements and specifications for a particular job are the personal knowledge, skills, aptitudes, attributes, and traits that are related to successful performance of that job. Job specifications may be identified as minimum qualifications, as essential characteristics, or as desirable specifications.

Performance appraisal. Performance appraisal is a *systematic* evaluation of employees' job performance by their supervisors or others who are familiar with their performance. The principal purpose of performance appraisal is to influence performance through administrative decisions (e.g., promotions, layoffs, transfers, or salary increases) and developmental feedback given to an employee (e.g., informing an individual about his or her job-related strengths and weaknesses).

Worker training. Training is a systematic, intentional process of developing specific skills and influencing behavior of organizational members such that their resultant behavior contributes to organizational effectiveness. Here, the term *behavior* includes any aspect of human activity, cognition, or feeling directed toward the accomplishment of work tasks.

Worker mobility. Worker mobility (career development and pathing) is the movement of individuals into and out of positions, jobs, and occupations. From the perspective of the individual, both self-concepts and social situations change, making the process of job/occupational choice continuous due to growth, exploration, establishment, maintenance, and decline. Organizations often find it advantageous to promote the worker mobility process (the interaction of personal factors and opportunities) through the establishment of formal career counseling/development programs, based on carefully delineated job information.

Efficiency. Improving efficiency in jobs involves both the development of optimal work processes and the design of equipment and other physical facilities with particular reference to people's work activities, including work procedures, work layout, and work standards.

Safety. Similar to efficiency, improving safety in jobs involves the development of optimal work processes and safe design of equipment and physical facilities. However, the focus is on identifying and eliminating unsafe work behaviors, physical conditions, and environmental conditions.

HR planning. HR planning consists of anticipatory and reactive activities by which an organization ensures that it has and will continue to have the right number and kind of people at the right places, at the right times, performing jobs that maximize both the service objectives and/or profit of the organization. It includes the activities by which an organization enhances the self-actualization and growth needs of its people and allows for the maximum utilization of their skills and talents.

Legal/quasi-legal requirements. Laws, regulations, and guidelines established by government agencies [e.g., CRA, ADA, EEOC, Office of Federal Contract Compliance Programs (OFCCP), OSHA] have set forth requirements related to one or more of the 12 job analysis uses listed above that adequate job analysis data would help an organization meet.

Source: Adapted from R. A. Ash, Job analysis in the world of work. In S. Gael (ed.), *The job analysis handbook for business, industry, and government,* Vol. I. New York: John Wiley & Sons, 1988, pp. 5, 8. Reprinted with permission.

nonexistence of) a job analysis. For example, many women have filed lawsuits contesting the physical agility tests (e.g., push-ups, sit-ups) mandated for entry into police or firefighters' academies. They often claim adverse impact since a greater proportion of women than men are disqualified as a result of such tests. United Airlines recently settled a lawsuit brought by female flight attendants contesting weight limits for the position. There have also been a number of lawsuits filed on behalf of older workers who lost their jobs because of a mandatory retirement age. For example, an Indianapolis bus driver used the Age Discrimination in Employment Act (ADEA) to challenge the mandatory retirement age of 55. In this case, job analysis data were introduced at trial to support the age limit.

As discussed in Chapter 3, statistics can be used to establish prima facie evidence of discrimination under the disparate impact theory. The burden of proof then rests upon the employer, who must show that the selection device or job specification (e.g., the test, test score, educational requirement) is job-related or a business necessity. In one case involving physical abilities, firefighter candidates were required to scale a fence 6 feet in height in a prescribed amount of time. Since a higher percentage of women were unable to scale the fence than men, the court asked the city to show how scaling a fence 6 feet in height was job-related. The city presented job analysis data which demonstrated that the average fence in the jurisdiction was 6 feet in height and that scaling fences was an activity which must be performed frequently by competent firefighters. Legal challenges to job specifications involving physical attributes (e.g., strength, speed) and mental attributes are likely to increase in light of the new *Americans with Disabilities Act* (ADA). The ADA specifies that employers must make "reasonable accommodations" that would allow qualified people with disabilities to per-

form a given job. According to the Equal Employment Opportunity Commission (EEOC), such accommodations may include physical renovations of the job.

METHODS OF COLLECTING JOB ANALYSIS DATA

A variety of methods are used to collect information about jobs, including observation, performing the job, interviews, critical incidents, diaries, records, and questionnaires. Figure 4.4 presents a list of the various data

FIGURE 4.4
COMMON JOB ANALYSIS DATA COLLECTION METHODS

Observation: Direct observation of job duties, work sampling or observation of segments of job performance, and indirect recording of activities (e.g., on film).
Advantages: Allows for a deeper understanding of job duties than relying on incumbents' descriptions.
Disadvantages: Unable to observe mental aspects of jobs (e.g., decision making of managers, creativity of scientists). May not sample all important aspects of the job, especially important yet infrequently performed activities (e.g., use of weapons by police).

Performing the job: Actual performance of job duties by the analyst.
Advantages: Analyst receives firsthand experience of contextual factors on the job including physical hazards, social demands, emotional stressors, and mental requirements. Useful for jobs that can be easily learned.
Disadvantages: May be dangerous for hazardous jobs (e.g., firefighters, patrol officers) or unethical/illegal for jobs requiring licensing or extensive training (e.g., medical doctor, psychologist, pharmacist). Analyst may be exposed only to frequently performed activities.

Interviews: Individual and group interviews with job incumbents, supervisors, subordinates, clients, or other knowledgeable sources.
Advantages: Information on infrequently performed activities and physical and mental activities can be collected. The use of multiple sources instead of one source can provide a more comprehensive, unbiased view of the job.
Disadvantages: Value of the data is dependent on the interviewers' skills and may be faulty if they ask ambiguous questions. Interviewees may be suspicious about the motives for the job analysis (e.g., fearful it will alter their compensation) and may distort the information they provide.

Critical incidents: Descriptions of behavioral examples of exceptionally poor or good performance, and the context and consequences in which they occur.
Advantages: Since observable and measurable behaviors are described, the information can be readily used for performance appraisal and training purposes. May provide insights into job expectations as defined by incumbents.

Disadvantages: Descriptions of average or typical behavior are not collected, and so the data may be less than inclusive of the entire job domain. Gathering the incidents may be time-consuming.

Diaries: Descriptions of daily work activities by incumbents.
Advantages: Written in terms familiar to incumbents and supervisors so the data may be easier to use (e.g., in developing performance appraisal measures). May provide insights into the reasons for job activities.
Disadvantages: Time-consuming to document. Accounts may be biased. May not include mental activities (e.g., innovativeness) or a representative account of all activities.

Background records: Review of relevant materials, including: organizational charts, DOT, company training manuals, organizational policies and procedures manuals, or existing job descriptions.
Advantages: Provides analyst with preliminary job information which assists in developing interview questions or questionnaires. Provides useful contextual information for the job. Is relatively easy to collect.
Disadvantages: May not provide complete information and generally needs to be supplemented with data collected using other methods. Materials may be outdated. Usually provides limited information on specific KASOCs required as well as importance ratings of tasks.

Questionnaires: Structured forms and activity checklists (PAQ, FJA, MPDQ, TI-CODAP) as well as open-ended or unstructured questions.
Advantages: Generally less expensive and quicker to use than other methods. Can reach a large sample of incumbents or sources, which allows for a greater coverage of informed individuals. Responses can often be quantified and analyzed in a variety of meaningful ways (e.g., comparisons can be made across jobs or departments for compensation or selection purposes).
Disadvantages: Questions may be interpreted incorrectly. How respondents interpret questions is difficult to assess. Response rate may be low, making the results less generalizable. Often expensive and time-consuming to develop, score, or analyze. Open-ended questions are difficult to quantify and require content analysis which is time-consuming.

collection methods available, along with some of their relative advantages and disadvantages.[4] As noted, an analyst, most often the supervisor for the position under study, can simply observe the job and record his or her observations. The analyst can also actually perform the job. Many corporations now require high-level managers to spend time performing jobs in which there is personal contact with the customer. Blockbuster Video, for example, has its managers work the cash register on weekends, and Xerox Corporation sends its top managers on sales calls. The basic idea is to better understand the customer's perspective on the business. Individual or group interviews can be conducted with incumbents, supervisors, or subordinates for the position under study. Incumbents or observers can be asked to maintain a diary or to record critical incidents regarding their performance or behavior on the job.[5] Available records of work activities or other relevant information, such as job descriptions, an organizational chart, and policies and procedures manuals, can be reviewed by the analyst to have background data on the job. Relevant job descriptions listed in the *Dictionary of Occupational Titles (DOT)* can also be reviewed. The DOT, which includes standardized, comprehensive descriptions of job duties for over 200,000 occupations, is described in a later section.[6]

Questionnaires or checklists can be completed by incumbents, supervisors, clients, or subordinates. Respondents can be asked to list the major tasks they perform as well as to rate the importance or frequency of performance of each task, or the time spent on it. Also, respondents can indicate how important a specific knowledge, skill, or ability is for completing the tasks. Methods are available for determining the importance of job tasks. For example, in the method known as the "content validity ratio," job experts are asked to rate the importance of each task and the ratio is determined by the extent to which experts agree on the importance rating.[7] A variety of standardized questionnaires exist for conducting job analyses and some of the more commonly used ones are described in a later section.

Dimensions on Which Job Analysis Methods Can Vary

Job analysis methods can vary along several dimensions, including (1) the types of job analysis information provided, (2) the forms in which job information is illustrated, (3) the standardization of the job analysis content, and (4) the sources of job information.[8] Each of these dimensions is described below.

TYPES OF JOB ANALYSIS INFORMATION. Job analysis methods can solicit a variety of types of information. Approaches, such as the Task Inventory Comprehen-

sive Occupational Data Analysis Program (TI-CODAP), are called *task- or job-oriented* methods since they indicate the tasks or duties required to perform the job. For example, "performing cardiopulmonary resuscitation" is considered an important task for a nurse. Other methods such as the Position Analysis Questionnaire (PAQ) are considered *person- or worker-oriented* approaches since information is collected on the KASOCs or behaviors (e.g., decision making, communicating) needed to perform the tasks satisfactorily. In the nurse example, a person-oriented job analysis may determine that "knowledge of disorders of the circulatory system" is critical for competent nursing. The PAQ and other job analysis methods also collect data on the machines, tools, and work aids used. Still other methods record contextual factors of the job (e.g., physical working conditions, environmental hazards, contact with coworkers). Some job analysis methods also provide information on work performance standards (e.g., quality and quantity standards, error analysis) and specific customer requirements.

THE FORM OF JOB INFORMATION. Job analysis information can be presented in qualitative or quantitative form, depending on the job analysis method used. Most job analysis methods are *qualitative* in the sense that the job is described in a narrative, nonnumerical manner, resulting in verbal or narrative descriptions of job information. The CIT, discussed later, is an example of a qualitative method. Other methods, such as the PAQ and TI-CODAP, are *quantitative* and provide descriptive information in numerical form. Common examples include a list of tasks along with ratings of the relative frequency or importance with which they are performed and descriptions of the production or error rates per time period. In most cases, job analysis approaches include both quantitative and qualitative information.

THE STANDARDIZATION OF THE JOB ANALYSIS CONTENT. Many HRM professionals have created a uniform or consistent method for obtaining job analysis information. Some job analysis methods, for example, have a set number of questions or items to which responses are required. The job analyst may be asked to write the major objectives of the position, the most important tasks to be performed, what KASOCs an occupant should have for the position, what the work products or outcomes are, and who the critical customers for the products or services are. The quantitative approaches are more standardized. The PAQ, for example, has standard content for all the jobs that are under study. Other methods have a standardized content (listing of tasks) for a group of similar jobs, but another list may be used for a different set of jobs.

SOURCES OF JOB INFORMATION. There are a number of potential sources of information about a job. Devices such as cameras can be used to observe tasks, and physiological recording devices can be used to assess employees' reactions. Perhaps most common is the use of individuals, such as job incumbents and supervisors for the job under study, as sources. Other possibilities include job analysts or specialists trained to conduct job analyses, outside observers or consultants, subordinates to the job under study, clients or customers, or persons simply in a good position to observe the job as it is performed. For example, sources able to provide information on the job of a professor may include professors themselves, their supervisors or department heads, students, administrators, and other colleagues.

COMMONLY USED JOB ANALYSIS APPROACHES

There are a great number of job analysis approaches available today. One of the best current sources of information on job analysis approaches is the two-volume *Job Analysis Handbook for Business, Industry, and Government* published in 1988. The *Handbook* describes 18 different job analysis approaches in use today.[9] We will concentrate our discussion on those methods which have been used most often and briefly describe some of the new and promising methods.

PAQ

The PAQ is a standardized questionnaire which assesses activities using 187 items in six categories.[10] These are:

1. **Information input.** Where and how does the worker obtain the information needed to perform the job (e.g., use of visual or sensory input)?
2. **Mental processes.** What reasoning, planning, decision-making, or information-processing activities are necessary to perform the activities?
3. **Work output.** What physical activities are performed, and what tools are used?
4. **Relationships with other persons.** What relationships with other people are required to perform the job (e.g., negotiating, performing supervisory activities)?
5. **Job context.** In what physical and social contexts is the work performed (e.g., hazards, stress)?
6. **Other job characteristics.** What other activities or characteristics are relevant to the job (e.g., apparel required, work schedule, salary basis)?

Sample items for the six categories of the PAQ are presented in Figure 4.5.

Items on the PAQ are rated using one of several different scales, including importance, amount of time required, extent of use, possibility of occurrence, applicability, and difficulty.[11] The PAQ can be completed in about 2½ hours. The completed questionnaires are then shipped to PAQ services headquarters for computerized scoring. Each job is scored on 32 dimensions, and a profile is constructed for the job. Norms are provided so that the job profile can be compared to profiles of "benchmark" jobs. Usually, a computer printout is prepared for each job which illustrates the job dimension scores and profile, and also provides estimates of aptitude test data (e.g., the average scores expected for incumbents on standardized tests) and job evaluation points for compensation purposes.[12]

The extensive research which has been conducted with the PAQ makes it one of the most useful of the standardized job analysis instruments, particularly for selection and compensation purposes. With the passage of the 1991 Civil Rights Act, the use of the PAQ to justify the use of certain tests which result in disparate impact is likely to be even more important. The approach is also excellent for small businesses with little or no expertise in HR and organizations seeking job specifications and possible selection procedures to fill a small number of jobs. PAQ results can help to set a wage for a new job and to identify the most valid tests for selecting personnel for the job. For example, Progressive Industries, a toolmaker for the automotive industry, used the PAQ to identify the most valid tests for selecting trainees to become lathe operators. PAQ analysis identified particular abilities and specific tests which tapped those abilities.

Considerable research supports the use of the PAQ. However, the PAQ must usually be completed by trained job analysts rather than incumbents or supervisors since the language in the questionnaire is difficult and at a fairly high reading level.[13] The instrument also lacks the specificity which can be gained by a questionnaire developed within the company for one or more particular positions. For example, job descriptions derived from a PAQ analysis are less detailed than descriptions derived from a qualitative approach to job analysis.

TI-CODAP

The TI-CODAP was developed by the U.S. Air Force in order to describe and cluster jobs.[14] Detailed task statements (sometimes as many as 500 per job) are written to describe the work. Each task statement consists of an action, an object of the action, and essential modifiers. For example, a task statement for the job of *medical technician* might be "performs spinal fluid cell counts" or "examines bacteriological specimens microscopically."

FIGURE 4.5
SAMPLE ITEMS FROM THE PAQ

POSITION ANALYSIS QUESTIONNAIRE (PAQ)

1 INFORMATION INPUT

1.1 Sources of Job Information

Rate each of the following items in terms of the extent to which it is used by the worker as a source of information in performing the job.

Code	Extent of Use (U)
N	Does not apply
1	Nominal very infrequent
2	Occasional
3	Moderate
4	Considerable
5	Very substantial

1.1.1 Visual Sources of Job Information

1 | U | Written materials (books, reports, office notes, articles, job instructions, signs, etc.)

2 | U | Quantitative materials (materials which deal with quantities or amounts, such as graphs, accounts, specifications, tables of numbers, etc.)

3 | U | Pictorial materials (pictures or picturelike materials used as *sources* of information, for example, drawings, blueprints, diagrams, maps, tracings, photographic films, x-ray films, TV pictures, etc.)

----

2 MENTAL PROCESSES

2.2 Information Processing Activities

In this section are various human operations involving the "processing" of information or data. Rate each of the following items in terms of how *important* the activity is to the completion of the job.

Code	Importance to This Job (I)
N	Does not apply
1	Very minor
2	Low
3	Average
4	High
5	Extreme

39 | I | Combining information (*combining*, synthesizing, or integrating information or data from two or more sources to establish new facts, hypotheses, theories, or a more complete body of *related* information, for example, an economist using information from various sources to predict future economic conditions, a pilot flying aircraft, a judge trying a case, etc.)

40 | I | Analyzing information or data (for the purpose of identifying *underlying* principles or facts by *breaking down* information into component parts, for example, interpreting financial reports, diagnosing mechanical disorders or medical symptoms, etc.)

49 | S | Using mathematics (indicate, using the code below, the highest level of mathematics that the individual must understand as required by the job)

Code | Level of Mathematics
N | Does not apply.
1 | Simple basic (counting, addition and subtraction of 2-digit numbers or less).
2 | Basic (addition and subtraction of numbers of 3 digits or more, multiplication, division, etc.)
3 | Intermediate (calculations and concepts involving fractions, decimals, percentages, etc.)
4 | Advanced (algebraic, geometric, trigonometric, and statistical concepts, techniques, and procedures usually applied in standard practical situations).
5 | Very advanced (advanced mathematical and statistical theory, concepts, and techniques, for example, calculus, topology, vector analysis, factor analysis, probability theory, etc.)

----

3 WORK OUTPUT

3.6 Manipulation/Coordination Activities

Rate the following items in terms of how important the activity is to completion of the job

Code	Importance to This Job (I)
N	Does not apply
1	Very minor
2	Low
3	Average
4	High
5	Extreme

93 | I | Finger manipulation (making careful finger movements in various types of activities, for example, fine assembly, use of precision tools, repairing watches, use of writing and drawing instruments, hand painting of china, etc., usually the hand and arm are *not* involved to any great extent).

94 | I | Hand-arm manipulation (the manual control or manipulation of objects through hand and/or arm movements, which may or may not require continuous visual control, for example, repairing automobiles, packaging products, etc.)

FIGURE 4.5 *(Continued)*

RELATIONSHIPS WITH OTHER PERSONS

4 RELATIONSHIPS WITH OTHER PERSONS

This section deals with different aspects of interaction between people involved in various kinds of work.

Code	Importance to This Job (*I*)
N	Does not apply
1	Very minor
2	Low
3	Average
4	High
5	Extreme

4.1 Communications

Rate the following in terms of how *important* the activity is to the completion of the job. Some jobs may involve several or all of the items in this section.

4.1.1 Oral (communicating by speaking)

99 | I | Advising (dealing with individuals in order to counsel and/or guide them with regard to problems that may be resolved by legal, financial, scientific, technical, clinical, spiritual, and/or other professional principles).

100 | I | Negotiating (dealing with others in order to reach an agreement or solution, for example, labor bargaining, diplomatic relations, etc.)

4.3 Amount of Job-required Personal Contact

112 | S | Job-required personal contact (indicate, using the code below, the extent of job-required contact with others, individually or in groups, for example, contact with customers, patients, students, the public, superiors, subordinates, fellow employees, official visitors, etc.; consider *only* personal contact which is definitely *part* of the job).

Code *Extent of Required Personal Contact*

1 Very infrequent (almost no contact with others is required)
2 Infrequent (limited contact with others is required)
3 Occasional (moderate contact with others is required)
4 Frequent (considerable contact with others is required)
5 Very frequent (almost continual contact with others is required)

---

5 JOB CONTEXT

5.1 Physical Working Conditions

This section lists various working conditions. Rate the average amount of time the worker is exposed to each condition during a *typical* work period.

Code	Amount of Time (*T*)
N	Does not apply (or is very incidental)
1	Under 1/10 of the time
2	Between 1/10 and 1/3 of the time
3	Between 1/3 and 2/3 of the time
4	Over 2/3 of the time
5	Almost continually

5.1.1 Outdoor environment

135 | T | Out-of-door environment (subject to changing weather conditions).

---

6 OTHER JOB CHARACTERISTICS

6.4 Job Demands (cont.)

172 | | Following set procedures (need to follow specific set procedures or routines in order to obtain satisfactory outcomes, for example, following check-out lists to inspect equipment or vehicles, following procedures for changing a tire, performing specified laboratory tests, etc.)

173 | | Time pressure of situation (rush hours in a restaurant, urgent time deadlines, rush jobs, etc.)

Source: E. J. McCormick and P. R. Jeanneret, Position Analysis Questionnaire (PAQ). In S. Gael (ed.), *The job analysis handbook for business, industry, and government,* Vol. II. New York: John Wiley & Sons, 1988, pp. 826–827. Reprinted with permission.

JOB-TASK INVENTORY ANALYSIS

	CHECK	TIME SPENT Present Job

1. Check tasks you perform now (3).
2. If you don't do it – Don't check it.
3. In the "Time Spent" column, rate all checked (3) tasks

CHECK

3 IF DONE NOW

Keep 3 Within Block

AFS 981X0

#2 PENCIL ONLY–PLEASE

NOTE: If any task you perform under this duty is not listed, please specify on blank pages at end of booklet.

TIME SPENT
Present Job

RATE

1. Very small amount.
2. Much below avg.
3. Below avg.
4. Slightly below avg.
5. About avg.
6. Slightly above avg.
7. Above avg.
8. Much above avg.
9. Very large amount.

#	Task	CHECK	TIME SPENT (1-9)
188.	Clean treatment areas to maintain aseptic conditions		1 2 3 4 5 6 7 8 9
189.	Flush oral evacuator systems		1 2 3 4 5 6 7 8 9
190.	Lubricate dental equipment or appliances		1 2 3 4 5 6 7 8 9
191.	Lubricate hand pieces		1 2 3 4 5 6 7 8 9
192.	Maintain asepsis of instrument storage areas		1 2 3 4 5 6 7 8 9
193.	Maintain dental supply cabinets		1 2 3 4 5 6 7 8 9
194.	Prepare work order or maintenance requests		1 2 3 4 5 6 7 8 9
195.	Remove or replace components of dental lights		1 2 3 4 5 6 7 8 9
196.	Remove or replace components of dental units		1 2 3 4 5 6 7 8 9
197.	Remove or replace components of hand pieces		1 2 3 4 5 6 7 8 9
198.	Remove or replace components of surgical aspirators		1 2 3 4 5 6 7 8 9
199.	Service test new or repaired equipment prior to use		1 2 3 4 5 6 7 8 9
	G. PERFORMING GENERAL SUPPORT FUNCTIONS		
200.	Apply prescribed topical medications		1 2 3 4 5 6 7 8 9
201.	Assist in emergency procedures, such as managing syncope or providing oxygen to patients		1 2 3 4 5 6 7 8 9
202.	Assist with intravenous (IV) sedations		1 2 3 4 5 6 7 8 9
203.	Clean dental instruments		1 2 3 4 5 6 7 8 9
204.	Disinfect dental equipment		1 2 3 4 5 6 7 8 9
205.	Disinfect dental instruments		1 2 3 4 5 6 7 8 9
			1 2 3 4 5 6 7 8 9

Source: R.E. Christal and J.J. Weissmuller, Job-task inventory analysis. In S. Gael (ed.), *The job analysis handbook for business, industry, and government,* Vol. II. New York: John Wiley & Sons, 1988. p. 1037. Reprinted with permission.

After task statements are written and edited, job incumbents are asked to indicate the relative amount of time they spend on each task. Figure 4.6 presents an example of a task-rating page. Responses are then clustered via computer analysis into occupational groupings so that jobs having similar tasks and the same relative time-spent values are organized together. Considerable time is required to write the task statements for TI-CODAP, and a large number of incumbents are needed in order to derive stable job clusters. Once the task statements are written, however, the method can yield data for a number of important job analysis purposes, such as setting job specifications, designing training courses, studying the tasks performed by minorities and women, identifying potential job hazards, and establishing individual experience records for succession planning.[15]

The TI-CODAP system is completely computerized and adaptable for most automated systems. Most jobs are adequately sampled with the method, and employees also perceive TI-CODAP to be a fair approach to job analysis. TI-CODAP task statements may be outdated if the instrument is used "off the shelf." In addition, because TI-CODAP is a task-oriented approach, KASOCs are not directly assessed and can only be inferred from the task statements.

Management Position Description Questionnaire

Although the PAQ and TI-CODAP have been used for managerial positions, the Management Position Description Questionnaire (MPDQ) is a standardized instrument designed specifically for use in analyzing managerial jobs. The 274-item questionnaire contains 15 sections, one of which is presented in Figure 4.7.[16]

Completing the MPDQ takes 2½ hours. In most sections, respondents are asked to indicate how significant each item is to the position. For example, they may state that "contact with clerical staff" is of substantial significance to the position. Responses to the questionnaire are sent to Control Data Business Advisors, Inc., where computer software generates eight reports, including a management position description (PD), a position-tailored performance appraisal form, and a group comparison report.[17] A sample portion of MPDQ report is provided in Figure 4.8.

Functional Job Analysis

Functional job analysis (FJA) is a worker-oriented job analytic approach which attempts to describe the whole person on the job. This includes the functional, specific content, and adaptive skills needed by an individual to perform a job satisfactorily.[18] FJA actually emerged as a

result of work in the development and extension of the *DOT* in 1939 and 1949.

DOT. The DOT classifies jobs based on a nine-digit code. Figure 4.9 presents the DOT description for a manager of a personnel department. The first three digits (166) specify the occupational code, the title of the job, and the industry. The next three digits (117) indicate the extent to which the job incumbent has responsibility and judgment over the data (coordinating), people (negotiating), and things (handling). The last three digits (018) are used to classify the job alphabetically within the occupational group with the same level of complexity. For the middle three digits in the nine-digit DOT code, jobs are classified in a predefined hierarchical order according to their complexity (where 0 represents the highest level). These classifications are concerned with the relationships between people, data, and things. The analyst's job is to arrange these relationships according to their complexity. An analyst preparing a FJA, for example, would rate *mentoring* in a job as the most complex relationship involving people. Figure 4.10 presents the hierarchy of people, data, and things which must be assessed for each job by the job analyst. The people scale refers to interactions between people, communication, and interpersonal actions. The data scale measures facts, ideas, mental operations, and knowledge of conditions. The things scale assesses interaction with and response to tangibles and images visualized spatially.

FJA PROCEDURE. FJA is a comprehensive job analysis approach that involves five steps. The first involves the *identification of the organization's purpose, goals, and objectives* for the FJA analysis. This analysis describes what should be as well as what is. The second step is the *identification and description of tasks*, in which tasks are defined as actions, or as action sequences designed to contribute a specified end result to the accomplishment of an objective.[19] The task actions or action sequences may be physical (e.g., operating an electric typewriter), mental (e.g., analyzing data), or interpersonal (e.g., consulting with another person). The task statements which are developed using FJA must conform to a specific written format consisting of an action verb, the immediate result to be accomplished, the equipment which is required, and the nature of the instructions to be received. A sample task statement is illustrated in Figure 4.11.

The third step in FJA involves an *analysis of tasks*. Each task is analyzed using seven scales. These include the three worker function scales (data, people, things), a worker instruction scale (degree of supervision imposed), and the three General Education Development Scales of reasoning, mathematics, and language.[20] Following this step, the analyst next *develops performance*

FIGURE 4.7
THE SUPERVISING SECTION OF THE MPDQ

Part 6
Supervising

These activities are directed toward the supervision of subordinates and units in your organization, or units for which you provide a human resource staff service. Many of these activities may not be a significant part of a position with few subordinates.

Directions:

Step 1 – Significance

Indicate how significant each activity is to your position by entering a number between 0 and 4 in the column next to it. Remember to consider both its **importance** in light of all the other position activities and **frequency** of occurrence.

> *0 – **Definitely not** a part of the position.*
> *1 – **Minor significance** to the position.*
> *2 – **Moderate significance** to the position.*
> *3 – **Substantial significance** to the position.*
> *4 – **Crucial significance** to the position.*

Step 2 – Comments

Use this space to clarify or comment on any aspects of **Supervising** that you feel are not adequately covered by the questions.

_____
_____
_____
_____
_____
_____
_____
_____
_____
_____
_____

The following response scale is used:

0 – *Definitely not* a part of the position.
1 – *A minor* part of the position.
2 – *A moderate* part of the position.
3 – *A substantial* part of the position.
4 – *A crucial and most significant* part of the position.

FIGURE 4.7 *(Continued)*

Significance

The Duties Of This Position Require You To:

_____ 1. Define areas of responsibility for supervisory/managerial personnel.

_____ 2. Schedule activities of subordinates on a day-to-day basis to maintain steady work flow.

_____ 3. Interact face-to-face with subordinates on an almost daily basis.

_____ 4. Delegate work and assign responsibility to subordinates.

_____ 5. Facilitate the completion of assignments when subordinates are unable to meet commitments.

_____ 6. Provide detailed instructions to subordinates when making assignments.

_____ 7. Coach subordinates on technical aspects of the job.

_____ 8. Provide on-the-job training for employees.

_____ 9. Frequently review and provide feedback concerning the accuracy and efficiency of subordinates' work.

_____ 10. Motivate employees through interpersonal interactions rather than through external incentives (e.g., pay, promotion, status, etc.).

_____ 11. Motivate subordinates to improve performance through a process of goal setting and positive reinforcement (i.e., incentives).

_____ 12. Work with subordinates to identify and correct weaknesses in performance.

_____ 13. Conduct formal performance appraisals with subordinates.

_____ 14. Develop executive-level management talent.

_____ 15. Establish formal career development plans with employees.

_____ 16. Implement career development and management succession plans.

_____ 17. Identify the training needed for employees to acquire the skills/knowledge necessary for advancement and ensure that the appropriate training is obtained.

_____ 18. Work with employees in highly emotional situations concerning personal or career problems.

_____ 19. Arbitrate conflicts between supervisors and employees.

_____ 20. Investigate and/or settle employee grievances/complaints.

_____ 21. Take necessary action to prevent and/or resolve alleged discriminatory practices.

_____ 22. Interpret, administer, and enforce personnel policies and practices (e.g., employee benefits, training or education reimbursement, affirmative action).

_____ 23. Interpret and administer union contract agreements in the supervision of subordinates.

_____ 24. Interview and hire individuals for approved positions.

FIGURE 4.8
SAMPLE PORTION OF MPDQ

MANAGEMENT
POSITION DESCRIPTION

NAME:	B. B. BARKER	ORGANIZATION:	CDBA
EMPLOYEE I.D.:	222	SUPERVISOR:	D.D. DUNCAN
POSITION TITLE:	MANAGER	SUPERVISOR'S TITLE:	MANAGER
FUNCTIONAL AREA:	HUMAN RESOURCES	% OF JOB DESCRIBED:	90%
SUPERVISORY LEVEL:	SUPERVISOR	DATE COMPLETED:	9/11/84

I. GENERAL INFORMATION

A. HUMAN RESOURCE RESPONSIBILITIES

– Management responsibility for **7** employees:

   5 (71%) Full Time–Salaried Exempt
   2 (28%) Part Time–Salaried Nonexempt

– **7** report directly and **0** report on a dotted line basis.
   –Highest direct subordinate: **SR. PROGRAMMER**

– **No** geographically separate facilities managed directly.

B. FINANCIAL RESPONSIBILITIES

– No annual operating budget.

– Sales for last fiscal year:	**$ 78,000.**
– Sales objective for current fiscal year:	**$ 220,000.**
– Revenue for last fiscal year:	**$ 275,000.**
– Revenue objective for current fiscal year:	**$ 230,000.**

II. POSITION ACTIVITIES

A. DECISION MAKING

Decision Making: **5%** of jobholder's time is spent on this function and it is **VERY IMPORTANT** to this position.

– Related activities and their significance:

Significance	Item No.	Activity
CRUCIAL	5	Consider the long-range implications of decisions.
CRUCIAL	8	Make decisions in new/unusual situations without clear guidelines on basis of precedent/experience.
CRUCIAL	11	Make critical decisions under time pressure.
CRUCIAL	18	Process and evaluate a variety of information before making a decision.
CRUCIAL	21	Make decisions that significantly affect customers/clients.
SUBSTANTIAL	4	Make decisions concerning the future direction of operations.
SUBSTANTIAL	7	Consider legal or ethical constraints, as well as company policy or goals, when making decisions.
SUBSTANTIAL	12	Make major product/program/technology/marketing decisions in implementing strategic business plan.
SUBSTANTIAL	14	Make decisions without hesitation when required.
MODERATE	1	Evaluate the costs/benefits of alternative solutions to problems before making decisions.

Source: The Management Position Description Report. Copyright © 1984 Control Data Business Advisors, Inc. All rights reserved. Reprinted with permission.

**FIGURE 4.9
MANAGER, PERSONNEL 166.117.018**

Plans and carries out policies relating to all phases of personnel activity. Recruits, interviews, and selects employees to fill vacant positions. Plans and conducts new employee orientation to foster positive attitudes toward company goals. Keeps record of insurance coverage, pension plan, and personnel transactions, such as hires, promotions, transfers, and terminations. Investigates accidents and prepares reports for insurance carrier. Conducts wage survey within labor market to determine competitive wage rate. Prepares budget of personnel operations. Meets with shop stewards and supervisors to resolve grievances. Writes separation notices for employees separating with cause and conducts exit interviews to determine reasons behind separations. Prepares reports and recommends procedures to reduce absenteeism and turnover. Contracts with outside suppliers to provide employee services, such as canteen, transportation, or relocation service. May keep records of hired employee characteristics for governmental reporting purposes. May negotiate collective bargaining agreement.

Source: U.S. Department of Labor, *Dictionary of occupational titles,* 4th ed. Washington: Government Printing Office, 1977, p. 98.

standards to assess the results of a worker's tasks. The fifth and final step is the *development of training content* required for an occupant of the job.

FJA is used frequently for government jobs, the main purposes of which are to prepare job descriptions and to derive job specifications. Like the PAQ, FJA reveals a quantitative assessment of each job under study. Because the FJA and the resultant DOT job description provide a quantitative score on each job as a function of its complexity in relationship with people, data, and things, the results are particularly useful in setting wage rates and in developing employee succession plans. One problem with the FJA, however, is that training in its use takes considerable time, which makes it costly and inaccessible for most organizations.

CIT

The CIT is a qualitative approach to job analysis used to obtain specific, behaviorally focused descriptions of work or other activities. The technique was originally developed as a training needs assessment and performance appraisal tool.[21] Individuals recalled and reported specific behavioral examples of incidents that reflected exceptionally good or exceptionally poor performance. A critical incident should possess four characteristics. It should be *specific,* focus on *observable* behaviors that have been exhibited on the job, describe the *context* in which the behavior occurred, and indicate the *consequences* or outcomes of the behavior. A critical incident must also be sufficiently detailed so that knowledgeable people will be able to picture the incident as it was experienced by the individual.[22] One vivid example of a critical incident characterizing extremely poor performance was provided by a police officer in describing an ex-partner. He wrote, "While on duty, this officer went out of his assigned duty area, went into a bar, got drunk and had his gun stolen."

A critical incident report references actual behavior in a specific situation with no mention of traits or judgmental inferences. The following is an example of a well-written critical incident: "I observed an employee looking through the scrap tub. Shortly later, she came to me stating that someone had thrown a large piece of cast iron piston into the scrap tub. We salvaged this piston and, a short time later, used this piece to make a pulley for a very urgently needed job." The following example does *not* qualify as a well-written critical incident: "The employee completely lacked initiative in getting the job done. While there was plenty of opportunity, I couldn't count on her to deliver." This incident mentions a trait (initiative), does not describe either the situation or the employee's behavior in any detail, and is judgmental in nature.

**FIGURE 4.10
FJA WORKER FUNCTION SCALES**

DATA FUNCTION SCALE FOURTH DIGIT	PEOPLE FUNCTION SCALE FIFTH DIGIT	THINGS FUNCTION SCALE SIXTH DIGIT
0 Synthesizing	0 Mentoring	0 Operating/controlling II
1 Coordinating	1 Negotiating	1 Setting up
2 Innovating	2 Supervising	2 Precision working
3 Analyzing	3 Instructing	3 Starting up
4 Compiling	4 Consulting	4 Driving/controlling
5 Computing	5 Persuading	5 Operating/controlling
6 Copying	6 Coaching	6 Manipulating
7 Comparing	7 Exchanging information	7 Tending
8 Handling	8 Taking instructions/helping	8 Feeding/offbearing

Source: Modified from U.S. Department of Labor, *Dictionary of occupational titles,* 4th ed. Washington: Government Printing Office, 1977, p. xviii.

FIGURE 4.11
FJA TASK STATEMENTS

Data	People	Things	Data	People	Things		Reas.	Math	Lang.	
W.F.–LEVEL			W.F.–ORIENTATION			INSTR.	G.E.D.			TASK NO.
3B	1A	2B	70%	5%	25%	2	3	1	4	
Goal: (To be completed by individual user.)						OBJECTIVE: (To be completed by individual user.)				

TASK: Types/transcribes standard form letter, including specified information from records provided, following S.O.P. for form letter, but adjusting standard form as required for clarity and smoothness, etc., in order to prepare letter for mailing.

TO DO THIS TASK

PERFORMANCE STANDARDS

Descriptive:
- Types with reasonable speed and accuracy.
- Format of letter is correct.
- Any changes/adjustments are made correctly.

Numerical:
- Completes letter in X period of time.
- No uncorrected typing, mechanical, or adjustment errors per letter.
- Fewer than X omissions of information per X no. letters typed.

TO THESE STANDARDS

TRAINING CONTENT

Functional:
- How to type: letters.
- How to transcribe material, correcting mechanical errors.
- How to combine two written sets of data into one.

Specific:
- How to obtain records and find information in them.
- Knowledge of S.O.P. for standard letter format: how/where to include information.
- Knowledge of information required in letter.
- How to use particular typewriter provided.

THE WORKER NEEDS THIS TRAINING

Source: S. A. Fine, Functional job analysis. In. S. Gael (ed.), *The job analysis handbook for business, industry, and government,* Vol. II. New York: John Wiley & Sons, 1988, p. 1023. Reprinted with permission.

The CIT has been used to study a variety of jobs, such as those of airline pilots, air traffic controllers, research scientists, dentists, industrial foremen, life insurance agents, salesclerks, and college professors. The major purpose of the use of CIT is to develop performance appraisal systems. CIT is also an excellent approach to the development of customer satisfaction instruments. Customers provide the examples of effective and ineffective customer service, which are then used to develop a standardized customer service evaluation instrument.

Burger King, Continental Bank, and the Chicago Police Department are among the many organizations which have used the CIT to develop performance appraisal instruments for employees and to derive training content for personnel.

NEWER METHODS OF JOB ANALYSIS

There are many other methods for job analyses. The interested reader should consult the *Job Analysis Handbook* for a summary and analysis of each of the major approaches. We will, however, introduce the reader to some of the more innovative approaches which have been developed in the last few years.[23]

The Combination Job Analysis Method

The Combination Job Analysis Method (C-JAM)[24] was introduced to serve as both a task-oriented and a worker-oriented job analysis method. The method borrows from the FJA and TI-CODAP methods to derive both task attributes and worker attributes.

The task-oriented aspect is conducted using the following steps: (1) Subject matter experts (SMEs) write enough task statements to adequately cover the main dimensions of the job. (2) Task statements are edited. (3) Each task statement is rated on scales for relative time spent, difficulty, and criticality. (4) A task importance value is then derived for each task using the following formula:

$$\text{Task importance value} = \text{difficulty} \times \text{criticality} + \text{time spent}$$

(5) Task statements are then ranked according to their importance value.

Following this, SMEs use a worker-oriented approach by generating a list of KASOCs based on the task statements and their importance value. SMEs are then asked to rate whether (yes or no) each KASOC is "necessary for new workers" and is "practical to expect." They are also instructed to rate the degree to which each KASOC "distinguishes the superior worker from the average worker." The importance rating for each KASOC is then derived using responses from these four rating scales.

The C-JAM method requires considerable time and effort on the part of SMEs. For those who cannot afford the time necessary to conduct the full C-JAM method, a shortened version known as the Brief Job Analysis Method (B-JAM) is also offered. There has been little research on either of these approaches, but both appear to have great potential for providing data for more of the purposes of job analysis.

Multimethod Job Design Questionnaire

The Multimethod Job Design Questionnaire (MJDQ) was developed as a tool to be used in designing jobs.[25] MJDQ uses a scale composed of items designed to measure the principles of job design from the motivational, mechanistic, biological, and perceptual/motor perspectives. Among the motivational items measured are the extent of autonomy on the job and the level of social interaction required. Mechanistic items include the specialization of the materials and procedures and the extent of repetition required. Biological items include tool design, level of effort, and endurance. Perceptual/motor items concern workplace lighting, control and display identification, and display visibility.

The results of limited research with the MJDQ have been positive with blue-collar workers and professionals.[26] That is, it has been shown that jobs with design characteristics conducive to high employee motivation result in workers with greater job satisfaction, efficiency, comfort, and reliability. There is no evidence to date, however, that the MJDQ is useful for other purposes beyond job design.

Job Compatibility Questionnaire

The Job Compatibility Questionnaire (JCQ) was designed as a job analysis method to be used primarily in the development of personnel selection instruments.[27] The method is also useful as a diagnostic tool to determine particular HRM intervention strategies in addition to personnel selection. Unlike other job analysis methods, the JCQ gathers information on all aspects of a job which are hypothesized to be related to employee performance, absences, turnover, and job satisfaction. Thus, the term "job analysis" is interpreted in the broadest sense to encompass all major factors related to important personal worker outcomes. The underlying assumption of the JCQ is that the greater the compatibility between a job applicant's preferences for job characteristics and the characteristics of a job as perceived by job incumbents, the greater the probability of employee effectiveness and longer tenure. The goal of the methodology is to derive reliable measures of perceived job characteristics and to derive personnel selection instruments capable of assessing the extent to which job applicants' preferences are compatible with these characteristics. The selection instrument derived from the JCQ is designed to predict and ultimately increase the level of employee effectiveness. In addition, the instrument can be used to identify job characteristics which can be altered to increase group effectiveness.

The JCQ is a 400-item instrument that measures job factors which have been shown by previous research to be related to one or more effectiveness criteria (e.g., performance, turnover, absenteeism, job satisfaction). Items cover the following job factors: task requirements, physical environment, customer characteristics, coworker characteristics, leader characteristics, compensation preferences, task variety, job autonomy, physical demands, and work schedule.

The JCQ is administered to job incumbents who are very familiar with either a specific position to be filled and/or a target job under study. Respondents are asked to indicate the extent to which each JCQ item is descriptive of the job or position under study. A sample list of characteristics is presented below:

Working alone all day

Having different projects which challenge the intellect

Staying physically active all day

Working at my own pace

Being able to choose the order of my work tasks

Working under the constant threat of danger

Having to copy or post numerical data all day

Having to make public speeches

Working under extreme time pressure

Having an opportunity to be creative at work

The average time required to complete the JCQ is 30 minutes and can be reduced by removing items from the instrument that do not apply to the job (e.g., customer characteristics). There is also a provision for adding important characteristics that are not covered on the JCQ. Responses on the JCQ are used to derive a selection instrument with a scoring key. The details of this process are discussed in Chapter 6. Research indicates that the JCQ has potential in predicting employee effectiveness for customer service representatives, theatre personnel, and security guards.[28] Research is under way to determine to what extent the methodology may be generalized to other jobs and its usefulness for redesigning job characteristics when JCQ data indicate a greater opportunity to improve effectiveness by redesigning the job.[29] At Tenneco Corporation, for example, responses to the JCQ indicated strong preferences for a pay-for-performance system and a more reliable work schedule. These work characteristics, shown to be related to employee turnover, could be changed at relatively little cost. At AMC The-

atres, for example, JCQ data indicated that incumbents were dissatisfied with the extent of feedback on their performance from supervisors.[30] AMC developed a supervisory training program to correct this problem. Other recommendations were made to redesign the job to increase effectiveness. Let us turn now to a discussion of job analysis used exclusively for job design.

JOB ANALYSIS AND JOB DESIGN

One of the direct applications of job analysis data has been in job design and redesign efforts. This has been particularly true in recent years with the increasing interest in the quality of employees' work life. In general, most of these efforts have focused on redesigning jobs by enriching them, which entails providing more meaningful work, greater responsibility, a sense of empowerment, and greater worker autonomy.[31] One of the most well known and researched job enrichment approaches is the *Job Characteristics Model*.[32] Over 200 studies have investigated the validity and utility of this approach.[33] We will discuss this approach to job enrichment in greater detail in Chapter 13. The *Job Diagnostic Survey (JDS)* is used to assess employees' perceptions of the degree to which each of the five core dimensions is present in their job.[34] Figure 4.12 presents a sample of questions from the JDS.

The Job Characteristics Model emphasizes enhancing the intrinsic aspects of an employee's work and the interaction of the individual with the job itself. Essentially, the model states that workers will be better motivated and more satisfied, will produce better-quality work, and will have less absenteeism and turnover to the extent that they experience three psychological states. These states are the beliefs that: (1) their work is meaningful, (2) they have responsibility for the outcomes of their work, and (3) they receive feedback on the results of their work. The JDS is used to diagnose the perceived extent of five core dimensions—skill variety, task identity, task significance, autonomy, and feedback—that exists on a job.

Skill variety refers to the extent to which a job requires the use of a variety of skills, activities, and abilities in order to complete the work.

Task identity is the extent to which job incumbents can complete a whole and identifiable task (e.g., doing a job from beginning to end with a visible outcome).

Task significance is the extent to which a job has a substantial impact on the lives or work of other people.

FIGURE 4.12
SAMPLE QUESTIONS FROM THE JDS, AN INSTRUMENT DESIGNED TO MEASURE THE KEY ELEMENTS OF THE JOB CHARACTERISTICS THEORY

1 ----------2----------3----------4----------5----------6----------7

Very little   Moderately   Very much

1. To what extent do managers or coworkers let you know how well you are doing on your job?

2. In general, how significant or important is your job? That is, are the results of your work likely to significantly affect the lives or well-being of other people?

3. How much autonomy is there in your job?

4. To what extent does your job involve doing a "whole" and identifiable piece of work?

5. How much variety is there in your job? That is, to what extent does the job require you to do many different things at work using a variety of your skills and talents?

6. To what extent does your job require you to work closely with other people (either clients or people in related jobs in your organization)?

7. To what extent does doing the job itself provide you with information about your work performance? That is, does the actual work itself provide clues about how well you are doing—aside from the feedback coworkers or managers may provide?

Source: J.R. Hackman and G.R. Oldham, The Job Characteristics Survey: An instrument for the diagnosis of jobs and the evaluation of job design projects. *JSAS Catalogue of Selected Documents in Psychology, 4,* Ms. No. 810. Components of job characteristics model.

Autonomy is the extent to which the job gives incumbents discretion, independence, and freedom in scheduling and planning work procedures.

Feedback from the job itself is the extent to which carrying out the work activities results in incumbents receiving clear and direct knowledge about how well they are performing.

The most comprehensive review of the Job Characteristics Model found that it is generally valid and that JDS responses are more highly related to employee job satisfaction than to measures of productivity or employee job turnover.[35]

The work team concept at the Chrysler plant in New Castle, Indiana, was created with the Job Characteristics Model in mind. Workers (all members of the UAW) are now called "technicians" and their line supervisors are called "team advisors." The 77 teams at the plant assign tasks, talk with customers, order repairs, and even do the hiring for their teams. Absenteeism is under 3% (from over 7%) and defects are down to 20 (per million) from 300 prior to the team concept. Needless to say, Chrysler is happy with this new approach to job design.

Any job design effort must be done in the context of other personnel systems such as the compensation and performance appraisal systems. Workers who receive greater responsibility may initially be enthusiastic, yet if the pay structure is not changed and they aren't given opportunities for advancement in the firm, they may lose some of their excitement. We will deal with the important issue of job design as it relates to productivity and employee motivation in more detail in Chapter 13.

BIAS IN JOB ANALYSIS DATA

There has been considerable research on the extent to which job analysis data is subject to some form of bias. Most of this research has focused on the potential sex biases in job evaluation for setting pay rates.[36] Chapter 11 will explore this issue in greater detail. Briefly, the research to date indicates that job analysis data are generally free of gender or racial bias.[37] However, courts have often been critical of the racial/sexual composition of committees responsible for conducting job analyses and deriving job specifications. A job specification stipulated by an all-white-male panel of job experts which ultimately resulted in adverse impact could be subject to more of a legal challenge because of the composition of the panel.

There has also been some research investigating whether the source of the job information influences the nature of the data collected. In general, the source (e.g., incumbents, supervisors, trained observers) does not appear to greatly influence the type of data collected. There is some evidence, however, that incumbents and supervisors agree more about the tasks performed than they do about the attributes which are required to perform the job well.[38] Surprisingly, there is no research comparing customer perspectives with those of incumbents or supervisors. Job incumbents and supervisors also tend to inflate job importance ratings relative to professional job analysts. There is evidence that those who know more about the job tend to make more reliable and accurate judgments.[39] Naive raters do not seem to provide job analysis information equivalent to the information provided by experts of the job.[40] There is not, however, support for the view that incumbents who are more effective at their jobs provide different information about their jobs than do low performers.[41]

More research is needed to explore possible sources of bias in job analysis data and the processes involved in deriving job analysis data. Such research may reveal better methods for gathering and integrating job analysis data to enhance its accuracy and usefulness.

CHOOSING THE BEST JOB ANALYSIS METHOD FOR A SPECIFIC PURPOSE

A number of studies have examined the relative effectiveness of various job analysis methods.[42] For example, one study asked experienced job analysts to indicate the extent to which four methods accomplished the various purposes for job analysis.[43] In addition, they were asked to evaluate the amount of training required to use the method, the sample sizes required for deriving reliable results, and the costs to administer and score the job analysis method. Figure 4.13 presents a summary of the results.

The results indicated that, of the methods evaluated, if the purpose is to generate a job description or to do job classification or job design, the best job analysis methods are TI-CODAP and FJA. CIT is probably not as good for job classification purposes. The best methods for job evaluation are FJA, TI-CODAP, and the PAQ. If the purpose of the job analysis is to develop a performance appraisal instrument, the recommended method is CIT. It must be pointed out that the newer approaches have not yet been evaluated in these comparison studies, so future research may lead to other recommendations.

All experts agree that the choice of job analysis method depends upon the purposes to be served by the data. There is no one best way to conduct a job analysis. The purposes for the data and the practicality of the various methods for particular organizations must be considered. The most definitive finding from the research on the relative effectiveness of the various methods is that multiple methods of job analysis should be used whenever possible. For example, a quantitative approach such as the PAQ should probably be augmented by a qualitative approach such as the CIT, which can provide more specific information about jobs than what can typically be derived from the quantitative methods.

SUMMARY

Job analysis is considered one of the most important tools of HR professionals. The data collected is used as a

FIGURE 4.13
EVALUATION OF JOB ANALYSIS METHODS BY EXPERIENCED JOB ANALYSTS

	METHODS WITH HIGHEST EFFECTIVENESS RATINGS			
	PAQ	TI-CODAP	FJA	CIT
Organizational Purpose				
Job description		X	X	
Job classification	X	X	X	
Job evaluation	X	X	X	
Job design restructuring		X	X	
Personnel requirements/specifications	X		X	
Performance appraisal		X	X	X
Worker training		X	X	X
Worker mobility	X	X	X	
Efficiency/safety	X	X	X	X
Human resource planning	X	X	X	
Legal/quasi-legal requirements	X	X	X	

Source: Modified from E. L. Levine, R. A. Ash, H. Hall, and F. Sistrunk, Evaluation of job analysis methods by experienced job analysts. *Academy of Management Journal, 26,* 339–348, 1983. Reprinted with permission.

starting point in the design of most HR systems including restructuring, HR planning, recruitment strategies, selection processes, training and career development programs, performance appraisal systems, job design/restructuring efforts, compensation plans, and health and safety requirements. We will explore all these activities in the chapters to follow. A job analysis helps to ensure that HR systems will be professionally sound and will meet legal requirements. As noted in Chapter 3, HR systems which involve personnel decisions such as selection, pay, promotion, and terminations should be based on a determination of the important job duties and KASOCs necessary for successful job performance. Even if the legal mandate did not exist, effective HR practice dictates the linkage between HR practices and job analysis information.

While many contemporary management gurus preach that job descriptions promote individualism to the detriment of unit effectiveness, we believe that job analysis and job descriptions can actually facilitate more effective group and unit effectiveness through clearer definitions of responsibilities and of the relative importance of tasks and working relationships between positions and individuals. Job descriptions do not have to say that the incumbent will perform only those specific tasks defined in the description regardless of circumstances. To the extent that job descriptions foster an "It's not my job" philosophy of work and a deviation in attention from customer requirements as related to the work products, the gurus are right. The trick is to develop and use job analysis information with customer requirements as the context for its use.

There are a variety of approaches available to collect job analysis data. These include performing the job, observation, and interviews with incumbents or other knowledgeable sources such as customers. Critical incidents, examining worker diaries, reviewing organizational records, and using standardized questionnaires are some of the most common methods. The PAQ, TICODAP, FJA, and the MDPQ are a few of the most popular quantitative methods. Since researchers continue to develop additional job analysis methods, HR professionals should keep current with respect to changes in this area. We will address in more detail how job analysis is used for some of the HRM purposes in the chapters to follow.

DISCUSSION QUESTIONS

1. The Civil Rights Act of 1991 will increase the significance of job analysis. True or false? Explain your answer.
2. Some scholars argue that having highly detailed job descriptions for every position can interfere with group effectiveness. If so, is there anything which can be done to prevent such interference?

3. For each of the following HR systems, what information from a job analysis is needed to develop a professional and legally defensible system?
   a. Training program for new employees
   b. Selection system
   c. Performance appraisal system
   d. Compensation system
   e. Job design
4. Describe the advantages and disadvantages of using interviews, observation, and questionnaires for collecting job analysis data.
5. How might you involve customers in the development of job descriptions and job specifications? Are there any constraints on what customers can stipulate in job specifications?
6. On the basis of your understanding of ADA, how could job analysis be used to conform with the law? Could job analysis be used to assess "reasonable accommodation"?

NOTES

1. Gael, S. (ed.) (1988). *The job analysis handbook for business, industry, and government*, Vols. I, II. New York: John Wiley & Sons, p. xv.
2. Ash, R. A. (1988). Job analysis in the world of work. In S. Gael (ed.), *The job analysis handbook for business, industry, and government*, Vol. I. New York: John Wiley & Sons, pp. 3–13.
3. Thompson, D. E., and Thompson, T. A. (1982). Court standards for job analysis in test validation. *Personnel Psychology, 35*, 865–874.
4. See note 2.
5. Cascio, W. F. (1992). *Managing human resources: Productivity, quality of work life, profits.* New York: McGraw-Hill.
6. U.S. Department of Labor (1977). *Dictionary of occupational titles*, 4th ed. Washington: U.S. Government Printing Office.
7. Lawshe, C. H. (1975). A quantitative approach to content validity. *Personnel Psychology, 28*, 563–575.
8. McCormick, E. J. (1976). Job and task analysis. In M. D. Dunnette (ed.), *Handbook of industrial and organizational psychology.* Chicago, IL: Rand McNally, pp. 651–696.
9. See note 1. See also: Spector, P. E., Brannick, M. T., and Coovert, M. D. (1989). Job analysis. In C. L. Cooper and I. T. Robertson (eds.). *International Review of Industrial and Organizational Psychology.* New York: John Wiley & Sons, pp. 281–328.
10. McCormick, E. J., and Jeanneret, P. R. (1988). Position analysis questionnaire. In S. Gael (ed.), *The job analysis handbook for business, industry, and government*, Vol. II. New York: John Wiley & Sons, pp. 825–842.
11. McCormick, E. J., Jeanneret, P. R., and Mecham, R. C. (1972). A study of job characteristics and job dimensions as based on the Position Analysis Questionnaire (PAQ). *Journal of Applied Psychology, 56*, 347–368.

12. See note 11.

13. See note 11.

14. Christal, R. F. (1974). The United States Air Force occupational research project (AFHRL-TR-73-75). Lockland Air Force Base, TX: Air Force Human Resources Laboratory. *JSAS Catalog of Selected Documents in Psychology, 4,* 61 (Ms. No. 651). Springfield, VA: National Technical Information Service.

15. Christal, R. E., and Weismuller, J. J. (1988). Job-task inventory analysis. In S. Gael (ed.), *The job analysis handbook for business, industry, and government,* Vol. II. New York: John Wiley & Sons, pp. 1036–1050.

16. Page, R. C. (1988). Management position description questionnaire. In S. Gael (ed.), *The job analysis handbook for business, industry, and government,* Vol. II. New York: John Wiley & Sons, pp. 860–879.

17. Tornow, W.W., and Pinto, P. R. (1976). The development of a managerial job taxonomy: A system for describing, classifying, and evaluating executive positions. *Journal of Applied Psychology, 61,* 410–418.

18. Fine, S. A. (1988). Functional job analysis. In S. Gael (ed.), *The job analysis handbook for business, industry, and government,* Vol. II. New York: John Wiley & Sons, pp. 1019–1035.

19. Fine, S. A., and Wiley, W.W. (1971). *An introduction to functional job analysis: A scaling of selected tasks from the social welfare field.* Kalamazoo, MI: W. E. Upjohn Institute for Employment Research.

20. Bemas, S. E., Belenky, A. H., and Soder, D. A. (1983). *Job analysis: An effective management tool.* Washington: Bureau of National Affairs.

21. Flanagan, J. C. (1954). The critical incident technique. *Psychological Bulletin, 51,* 327–358.

22. Bownas, D., and Bernardin, H. J. (1988). The critical incident method. In S. Gael (ed.), *The job analysis handbook for business, industry and government,* Vol. II. New York: John Wiley & Sons, pp. 1120–1137.

23. See notes 1 and 9.

24. Levine, E. L. (1983). *Everything you always wanted to know about job analysis.* Tampa, FL: Mariner Publishing.

25. Campion, M. A., and Thayer, P.W. (1985). Development and field evaluation of an interdisciplinary measure of job design. *Journal of Applied Psychology, 70,* 29–43.

26. See note 25.

27. Bernardin, H. J. (1989). Innovative approaches to personnel selection and performance appraisal. *Journal of Management Systems, 1,* 25–76. See also: Bernardin, H. J. (1987). Development and validation of a forced-choice scale to measure job-related discomfort among customer service representatives. *Academy of Management Journal, 30,* 162–173; Villanova, P., and Bernardin, H. J. (1990). Work behavior correlates of interviewer job compatibility. *Journal of Business and Psychology, 5,* 179–195.

28. See note 27.

29. See notes 1 and 9.

30. Levine, E. L., Ash, R. A., Hall, H., and Sistrunk, F. (1983). Evaluation of job analysis methods by experienced job analysts. *Academy of Management Journal, 26,* 339–348.

31. Hackman, J. R., and Oldham, G. R. (1976). Motivation through the design of work: Test of a theory. *Organizational Behavior and Human Performance, 16,* 250–279.

32. Hackman, J. R., and Oldham, G. R. (1980). *Work redesign.* Reading, MA: Addison-Wesley.

33. Fried, Y., and Ferris, G. R. (1987). The validity of the Job Characteristics Model: A review and meta-analysis. *Personnel Psychology, 40,* 287–322. Fried, Y. (1991). Meta-analytic comparison of the job diagnostic survey and job characteristics inventory as correlates of work satisfaction and performance. *Journal of Applied Psychology, 76,* 690–697.

34. Hackman, J. R., and Oldham, G. R. (1975). Development of the Job Diagnostic Survey. *Journal of Applied Psychology, 60,* 159–170. See also: Lublin, J. S. (Feb. 13, 1992). Trying to increase worker productivity, more employers alter management style. *The Wall Street Journal,* pp. B1, B3.

35. See note 33.

36. Treiman, D. J., and Hartmann, H. J. (eds.) (1981). *Women, work, and wages: Equal pay for jobs of equal value.* Washington: National Academy Press.

37. See notes 1 and 9.

38. Cornelius, E. T. (1988). Practical findings from job analysis research. In S. Gael (ed.), *The job analysis handbook for business, industry, and government,* Vol. I. New York: John Wiley & Sons, pp. 48–68.

39. DeNisi, A. S., Cornelius, E. T., and Blencoe, A. G. (1987). Further investigation of common knowledge effects on job analysis ratings. *Journal of Applied Psychology, 72,* 262–268.

40. Friedman, L., and Harvey, R. J. (1986). Can raters with reduced job descriptive information provide accurate Position Analysis Questionnaire (PAQ) ratings? *Personnel Psychology, 39,* 779–789.

41. Conley, P. R., and Sackett, P. R. (1987). Effects of using high- versus low-performing job incumbents as sources of job analysis information. *Journal of Applied Psychology, 72,* 434–437.

42. See note 23. See also: Landy, F. J., and Vasey, J. (1991). Job analysis: The composition of SME samples. *Personnel Psychology, 44,* 27–50.

43. Levine, E. L., Thomas, J. N., and Sistrunk, F. (1988). Selecting a job analysis approach. In S. Gael (ed.), *The job analysis handbook for business, industry, and government,* Vol. I. New York: John Wiley & Sons, pp. 339–352. See also: Ash, R. A., and Levine, E. L. (1980). A framework for evaluating job analysis methods. *Personnel, 57,* 53–59. Ash, R. A., Levine, E. L., and Sistrunk, F. (1983). The role of job-based methods in personnel and human resources management. In K. M. Rowland and G. D. Ferris, (eds.), *Research in personnel and human resources management,* Vol. 1. Greenwich, CT: JAI Press, pp. 45–84.

OVERVIEW

The purpose of this exercise is to show you how to write a PD that describes either a job you have now or have had in the past or, if you have never worked, the job of someone else. As stated in Chapter 4, job descriptions or PDs are used for a number of personnel decisions. For example, many organizations start with job descriptions when they do restructuring and job design. Job descriptions are routinely used to set and adjust wage rates. The information can also be used to assist in recruitment efforts or to develop selection devices, work teams, or performance appraisal systems. To serve HR purposes most effectively, the PD must be current and accurate and it must be consistent with the goals and objectives of the organization, particularly in terms of customer requirements.

LEARNING OBJECTIVES

After completing this exercise, you should be able to:

1. Identify the key components of job descriptions.
2. Prepare a PD report, including data on position objectives, tasks and duties, supervision and guidance, contacts, services and products provided to critical customers, and job qualifications or specifications.
3. Understand the purposes to be served by the PD.

PROCEDURE

Part A: Individual Assignment: Completion of the Position Description

Prior to class, read the general guidelines for completing the PD (Exhibit 4.1.1). Then complete Form 4.1.1, the PD.

Part B: Peer Review

Students should bring their completed Form 4.1.1 to class. Students should be paired off and review their respective PDs. Each student should serve as an examiner to try to interpret the PD of the other person. The examiner should try to sum up what is involved in the job and whether clear task statements have been written. The evaluation should involve an assessment of the extent to which the job description could serve the purposes for job analysis described in Figure 4.3. The incumbent should clear up any confusion about job duties, requirements, and job specifications. Any needed changes to the PD should be made directly on Form 4.1.1. The discussion should focus on any job specifications for the job, particularly those which may serve to disqualify people on the basis of characteristics such as race, sex, age, or disability. Also, the examiner should focus on the identification of the customers with whom the incumbent has contact for products or services, and should determine whether certain tasks on which the incumbent spends considerable time may be unnecessary in terms of the needs of the internal and external customers. The examiner should continue to seek clarification until he or she is confident that the PD is as good as it can be. The examiner should then sign Form 4.1.1 in the space provided.

Part C: Assessment

Students should complete the assessment questions for the exercise.

EXHIBIT 4.1.1
GENERAL GUIDELINES FOR COMPLETING THE PD

The PD should be written in your own words, not in technical or "classified" language. Basically the PD should be a collection of the tasks that add up to the total work assignment. All major work activities that are performed in the job should be described. The tools and equipment should be mentioned. Also include the decisions made in performing the job: the outcomes, products, or services; and the relevant customers.

Samples of completed PDs for the jobs of public health nurse and mechanic helper are provided in Exhibits 4.1.2 and 4.1.3. Review these samples as you read these instructions. Note the various sections of the PD (see Form 4.1.1).

PART I: COMPILING ORGANIZATIONAL INFORMATION

Step 1. Following the items in Part I (Organizational Information) of Form 4.1.1, state the name of the incumbent, the date, and the official job title. In item 5, you should state the working title if it is different from the "official" job title. Employees are often given working titles. For example, a supervisor on a road crew may officially be called a highway maintenance engineer.

Step 2. If possible, ask a supervisor or a personnel officer to complete the information requested in the other items listed in Part I of Form 4.1.1.

Step 3. After reviewing the instructions, complete the items in Part II (Position Information) of Form 4.1.1. This is the most important part of the PD, since it provides information on the duties of the position.

PART II. POSITION INFORMATION

Item 11. Objective

Item 11 asks you to state the chief objective of the position. This statement should be no more than two to three sentences. It should state why it is important that the tasks and duties that make up the job are performed. In writing item 11, it may help if you think of this statement as a definition of the position, or perhaps as the essential aspect of the job. For example, the objective of a *child welfare supervisor* may be: "To orientate new case workers located in local courts, detention homes, and children's institutions by planning and teaching classes and seminars on social casework principles." This example of a position's main objective was used because: (1) It is *brief* (has no more than several lines). (2) It is *descriptive* (states the main tasks and duties of the position without giving detailed information). (3) It gives the reader an *overview* (what to expect in the more detailed listing of tasks). (4) It states the *main purpose* for which the position exists.

Item 12. Tasks and Duties

In this section, you are to identify the tasks and duties that are performed in the job. Read the instructions for item 12 on Form 4.1.1, and write down the tasks on a separate sheet of paper. Then arrange the tasks in order of importance, with the most important first and the least important last. Next decide on the percentage of the total working time that each task requires. Be sure the percentages total to 100 percent.

Writing all the tasks and duties of the position is difficult. Outlined below are some guidelines that should help. Following these are some examples of "good" and "poor" task statements.

1. Use an action verb to start each task statement, such as "compile," "enter," "total," "balance," "write," "answer," "telephone," or "interview." Avoid nondescriptive verbs such as "prepare," "conduct," "coordinate," "process," and "assist." These verbs do not tell the reader what you are really doing.

2. Use task statements to explain: What is done? What actions are you performing? To what or to whom? What is the purpose of this task? What references, resources, tools, equipment, or work aids are you using? Do you write reports? Do you train and supervise employees?

3. Try to group closely related tasks together. Grouping tasks will help you more clearly define and explain to the reader what you are responsible for in your position.

4. It is important to include all the major tasks and duties of your position. It is not necessary to include minor things such as "sit in chair, pull open drawer, take out a pen from desk, begin to write."

EXAMPLES OF GOOD AND POOR TASK STATEMENTS

POOR	GOOD
Ensure that all daily cash is accounted for.	Balance cash in register by comparing it with the total on the register tape. Locate and correct errors in order to account for all cash receipts. Write totals on cash report for approval by head cashier.
Assist with the inspection of construction projects.	Inspect construction operations (erosion control, asphaltic concrete paving, painting, fencing, sign placement). Compare visual observations with the construction specifications and plans.
Train subordinate employees.	Instruct employees under his or her supervision in company policies, office procedures, applicable state and federal laws, and firm report preparation to facilitate improved job performance. Distribute company reading materials, schedule work assignments, and lead staff meetings.

Item 13. Supervision and Guidance

Item 13 asks you to state what work actions and/or decisions are made without first getting a supervisor's approval. This decision making is an important element in the evaluation of the job. In answering this question, consider the following examples.

1. If you are a clerk typist, you may edit a memorandum that was drafted by your supervisor, in order to make it more grammatically correct.

EXHIBIT 4.1.1 *(Continued)*

2. If you are a clerk, you may set up your own filing procedures and reorganize your section's files.

You may also want to list any procedural manuals, laws, and/or standards that are used as guides in the work.

Item 14. Contacts

In many positions, contact with other people is a necessary part of the job. Item 14 requests that you list any required contacts you have with individuals, customers, or organizations. Also state the purpose of these contacts, how often they occur (e.g., daily, weekly) and whether they are inside or outside the organization.

Item 15. Most Important Service or Product; Internal and External Customers

Item 15 requests a list of the most important services or products that are expected from this position and an identification of the internal and external customers who receive them (not by name, just by category). Note that managers or supervisors should not always be considered customers and their demands may in fact require tasks to be performed which detract from your attention to more important customers (e.g., external customers). Demands from managers should be linked to demands from internal or external customers.

Item 16. Entry Requirements/Job Specifications

Item 16 asks for information on the KASOCs that an employee must possess on the *first* day of the job. This information will be used in recruiting new employees. There are four sections to be answered.

1. **KASOCs.** State the qualities that a new employee must bring to the position. Use the definitions provided in Chapter 4.
2. **Special licenses, registration, or certification.** Identify occupational certifications or licenses, if any, that an applicant must hold in order to comply with laws or regulations.
3. **Education or training.** State the educational background or area of study that would provide the knowledge required for entry into the position.
4. **Experience.** State the level and type of experience an applicant should have to be qualified to fill the position. Examples include "journey level carpentry with experience in remodeling interiors" and "supervisory experience."

EXHIBIT 4.1.2
PUBLIC HEALTH NURSE PD

PART I: ORGANIZATIONAL INFORMATION

1. Name (last, first, middle):

    Black, Sandy C.

2. Date:

    Nov. 12,

3. Job title:

    Public health nurse

4. Position number:

    123456

5. Working title (if different):

6. Agency:

    DHRS

7. Work location (county or city) and location code:

    Montgomery County—4226

8. Agency code:

9. Title and position number of immediate supervisor:

    Head Nurse—921433

10. Organizational unit:

    Dzaidzo Hospital

PART II: POSITION INFORMATION

11. Objective of the position:

    To ensure that state employees are in good health by providing public health services.

12. Tasks and duties:

Percent of Total Working Time	Work Tasks and Duties
25	Evaluates employees' or potential employees' physical condition by taking medical histories, examining the employee using diagnostic tools such as stethoscope and otoscope, and interprets the results of the laboratory tests.
25	Treats work-related injuries to reduce absenteeism by administering medication and vaccines under the clinical guidance of a physician.
15	Meets routinely with staff to review existing clinical services in order to improve them.
20	Reviews accident reports to identify health and safety hazards. Analyzes causes of accidents and makes recommendations to management for eliminating hazards.
5	Develops programs to educate employees on health-related issues. Uses self-prepared or programmed lesson plans, films, and other audiovisual materials.
5	Orders supplies to maintain an adequate inventory. Completes requisition forms and sends them to the planning or supply room.
5	Answers requests for medical status of employees from insurance companies or personnel staff by discussing results of examinations and current medical status over the telephone or by completing medical forms.
———
100	

13. Describe work actions and/or decisions you make *without* prior approval and the extent of advice and guidance received from your supervisor.

    I decide how to treat minor injuries—giving first aid. I determine whether a laboratory test is within acceptable limits. I plan educational programs.

EXHIBIT 4.1.2 (Continued)

14. Contacts:

Inside/Outside Contacts	Purpose	How Often	Organization
Employees	Perform physicals, treat injuries, and obtain information on the workplace	Daily	Inside
Insurance companies	Provide medical claim information	Weekly	Outside
Benefits staff (DPT)	Provide information for worker's compensation claims	Monthly	Inside

15. The most important service or product provided:

Contact with and treatment of employees.

16. Qualifications for entry into the position:

a. KASOCs:
Ability to obtain personal information from people and to determine whether they are being truthful. Knowledge of nursing services in the employment setting.

b. Special licenses, registration, or certification:
RN

c. Education or training (cite major area of study):
Nursing

d. Level and type of experience:
Experience in providing nursing services to a wide variety of people.

17. I understand the above statements, and they are complete to the best of my knowledge.

Sandy C. Black   _Nov. 12_
Employee's signature   Date

Connie Brown   _November 13_
Reviewer's signature   Date

EXHIBIT 4.1.3
MECHANIC HELPER PD

PART I: ORGANIZATIONAL INFORMATION

1. Name (last, first, middle):

    Green, Chris M.

2. Date:

    April 19

3. Job title:

    Mechanic helper

4. Position number:

5. Working title (if different):

6. Agency:

7. Work location (county or city) and location code:

    Detroit

8. Agency code:

9. Title and position number of immediate supervisor:

    Chief Mechanic

10. Organizational unit:

PART II: POSITION INFORMATION

11. Objective of the position:

    To maintain highway construction equipment in good operating condition by inspecting and repairing equipment, when necessary.

12. Tasks and duties:

Percent of Total Working Time	Work Tasks and Duties
25	Inspects highway equipment to identify any operating problems by visually checking and listening to the equipment.
25	Repairs highway equipment, cars, dump trucks, and small engines needed to perform road maintenance work by overhauling motor transmissions and differentials, replacing axles, springs, and wheel bearings using small motorized shop equipment, hand tools, and shop repair manuals.
20	Maintains equipment to prevent breakdowns by installing spark plugs, starters, and distributor caps; changing oil; and greasing equipment using standard mechanic tools.
15	Tunes up and analyzes gasoline engines in order to locate minor problems and provide for optimum engine performance by using the Peerless Engine Analyzer.
15	Helps other mechanics by gathering tools and parts, purchasing, and picking up parts at local suppliers and moving equipment from one place to another as directed by the foreman.
100	

13. Describe work actions and/or decisions you make *without* prior approval and the extent of advice and guidance you received from your supervisor.

    I decide how to repair the equipment. If the work is going to take more hours than planned, I tell my supervisor.

EXHIBIT 4.1.3 *(Continued)*

14. Contacts:

Inside/Outside Contacts	Purpose	How often	Organization
Supply stores	Pick-up parts or supplies	Weekly	Outside

15. The most important service or products provided and the customers:

Perform repair work as assigned. Customer is car owner.

16. Qualifications for entry into the position:

a. KASOCs:
Knowledge of gasoline powered engines.
Ability to drive equipment.
Ability to read and follow instructions in repair manual.

b. Special licenses, registration, or certification:
Apprentice license for mechanic

c. Education or training (cite major area of study):
Heavy equipment mechanics

d. Level and type of experience:

17. I understand the above statements, and they are complete to the best of my knowledge.

Chris M. Green
Employee's signature

April 19
Date

Bobby Diangelo
Supervisor's signature

4-20
Date

FORM 4.1.1
THE PD

PART I: ORGANIZATIONAL INFORMATION

1. Name (last, first, middle):

2. Date:

3. Job title:

4. How many people in the organization have this title?

5. Working title (if different):

6. Organization:

7. Work location (county or city):

8. Division within organization:

9. Title of immediate supervisor:

10. Organizational unit:

PART II: POSITION INFORMATION

11. State the chief *objective* of the position in a brief statement:

12. Prior to filling out the next section, think about the *tasks and duties* performed in the position. Consider the time spent on the tasks and duties, how important they are to achievement of the objective of the position, and the processes or ways in which they are performed. After considering these aspects of the position, state the tasks and duties that are performed in the position.

   * State the *most important* duty first and finish with the *least important* duty.

   * Calculate the percentage that each duty requires of the total working time. Be sure these percentages total 100 percent.

   * Include *all* tasks, duties and functions that are performed except those that occupy 2 percent or less time, unless they are considered very important.

Percent of Total Working Time	Work Tasks and Duties

100   (Add additional pages if needed.)

13. What work actions and/or decisions are made *without* prior approval? To what extent is advice and guidance from a supervisor received? State examples of the type of supervisory advice and guidance that are received as well as actions or decisions made without prior approval.

14. List and explain the *contacts*, if any, both within and outside the organization, that are a routine function of the work. Do not list contacts with supervisors, coworkers, and subordinates.

Inside/Outside Contacts	Purpose	How Often	Organization

15. What are the *most important* services or products expected from an incumbent in the position described? Who are the customers (internal or external) of these products or services?

Most important service/product: Customer:

Second most important:

Third most important:

Fourth most important:

FORM 4.1.1 *(Continued)*

16. What are the *qualifications for entry* into the position:

    a. What KASOCs should a new employee bring to this position?

    b. Special licenses, registration, or certification:

    c. Education or training (cite major area of study):

    d. Level and type of experience:

17. I understand the above statements, and they are complete to the best of my knowledge.

_____   _____
Employee's signature   Date

_____   _____
Supervisor's signature (optional)   Date

_____   _____
Examiner's signature   Date

Exercise 4.1
Assessment Questions

Name _____

1. What are the advantages and disadvantages to using this approach compared to the PAQ?

2. When preparing the job description, why is it important to list the critical customers for the products or services and the major tasks and duties of the job? Are there tasks which could be excluded with little or no effect on critical customers?

3. How often should a position description form be updated? Explain your response.

4. Explain how your job description could be used to evaluate your performance, to redesign the job, or to develop methods for hiring people for the position.

5. Do you think having a highly detailed job description is actually counterproductive for this job? Explain your answer.

*EXERCISE 4.2 DEVELOPING A TASK ANALYSIS QUESTIONNAIRE (TAQ)**

OVERVIEW

Although Chapter 4 discusses many standardized, off-the-shelf methods for gathering job-related information (e.g., PAQ, TI-CODAP, MPDQ), job analysts can develop their own standardized inventories. While the development of such instruments can be time-consuming and expensive, they are intuitively appealing because they are tailor-made to match a particular job or group of jobs. Moreover, individuals who are surveyed will likely perceive this approach to be fair since the specificity of the information is greater than with most other methods. The focus of this exercise will be on collecting job-related information, developing and distributing a task analysis questionnaire (TAQ), and determining critical (or essential) job tasks.

LEARNING OBJECTIVES

After completing this exercise, you should be able to:

1. Understand the process of gathering job-related information from a variety of sources (e.g., background information, interviews, questionnaires).
2. Compile and synthesize data in order to develop and implement a TAQ.
3. Differentiate between essential tasks and other less critical tasks that are not necessary for successful job performance.
4. Describe and design a quantitative, task-oriented approach to analyzing jobs.

PROCEDURE

Part A: Individual Assignment: Preparation for the TAQ

Step   1.   Before beginning the exercise, review the most common methods for collecting job-related data (see Figure 4.4).

Step   2.   For the purposes of this exercise, the position of *restaurant manager* will be examined. Familiarize yourself with the job, its duties and tasks, and its job specifications by at least reviewing the DOT and the condensed sample job description in Exhibit 4.2.1. (Hint: See job code 187.167-106.) Feel free to use other methods for collecting additional information regarding this job.

Step   3.   Once you are familiar with this particular job, set up an interview with a restaurant manager in your local community. Use the structured interview form (Form 4.2.1) for the interview. Take notes on the interview or, if allowed, tape-record the interview. Notice that the CIT is couched within the questionnaire. The questionnaire can be useful in identifying tasks, knowledge, skills, and abilities associated with the job of restaurant manager.

Part B: Individual Assignment: Development of the TAQ

Step   1.   After the interview is complete, combine that data with the information gathered from the DOT and the job description. Next, use the information to write task statements describing the job. Review the criteria for good task statements, as described in Exhibit 4.2.3.

Step   2.   Following the format in Form 4.2.2, write your task statements in the column labeled "Task." Include as many task statements as possible in order to adequately cover the task domain associated with the job of restaurant manager. Be sure to leave space at the end of the inventory for comments from respondents (this is important because you may have omitted important job tasks). Answer the assessment questions for the exercise.

Part C: Peer Review

Step   1.   In groups of about six, discuss and compare your draft TAQs. Determine (a) whether additional information is needed, (b) whether information should be deleted, (c) whether any changes should be made to the TAQs, (e.g., regarding redundant items, poorly written task statements, etc.), and (d) the extent to which differences are a function of the unique characteristics of the various managerial positions.

Step   2.   After the discussion is completed, make any necessary revisions to the TAQs so that each group has a standard form.

Part D: Individual Assignment: Distribution of the TAQ

Step   1.   Distribute your completed TAQ to at least two local restaurant managers so that they can rate

---

*Contributed by Jeffrey D. Kudisch.

the job tasks by importance and frequency. If possible, try to avoid using the same manager you interviewed.

Step 2. Each group should collect the TAQs and use Lawshe's (see note 7) Content Validity Ratio (CVR) to determine the tasks that are "essential" to a restaurant manager's job success. For this exercise, essential tasks will be denoted by *importance ratings* of 3, 4, or 5. A CVR for each item/task is computed by using the following formula:

$$CVR = (n_e - N/2)/(N/2)$$

where n_e is the number of subject matter experts (SMEs) indicating a task as "essential" and N is the total number of SMEs. In short, the CVR is a quantitative estimate of the agreement among job experts (who in this case are the restaurant managers and their supervisors). Let's say, for example, that the following six responses were obtained for task statement 1:

RESPONDENT	IMPORTANCE RATING	FREQUENCY RATING
Restaurant manager 1	4	5
Restaurant manager 2	2	4
Restaurant manager 3	3	4
Restaurant manager 4	5	4
General manager 1	3	4
General manager 2	4	4

Using Lawshe's (1975) formula, the CVR for task statement 1 would be as follows:

$$CVR = (5 - 6/2)/6/2 = 0.667$$

According to the table in Exhibit 4.2.2, .667 fails to meet the minimum value for statistical significance (.99) required when using six SMEs (panelists). Hence, this task would be eliminated from any job analysis product using essential tasks (e.g., a job description).

Part E: Group Presentation and Discussion

Step 1. Each group should compile its TAQ results, review the answers to the assessment questions, and prepare a group summary report and short presentation. The presentation should include (a) the relationship among ratings by the managers, (b) a summary of the essential tasks identified as well as possible explanations of why certain tasks were not considered to be essential across positions, (c) problems encountered during the entire process, (d) limitations associated with the findings, (e) recommendations for changes in the process, and (f) specific uses for the data.

Step 2. After all presentations are completed, discuss the similarities and differences among the group members' reports. Also, refer back to Chapter 4 to discuss how the final information obtained from the TAQ can be used to facilitate HR issues (e.g., revising or creating job descriptions, determining essential tasks for training and development, developing a method for selecting managers). In particular, attempt to reach consensus on the methods which might be useful for selecting restaurant managers.

EXHIBIT 4.2.1
SAMPLE JOB DESCRIPTION FOR A RESTAURANT MANAGER

Job title:	Restaurant manager
Job code:	187.167-106
Status:	Exempt
Store:	Knoxville location
Reports to:	General manager and area supervisor
Supervises:	Waiters/waitresses, kitchen, utility, bartending, and host/hostess staff
Written by:	I. M. Dining
Date:	November 25, 1991

JOB SUMMARY

Coordinates and directs food service activitites of the restaurant. Examines materials (e.g., inventory, facility, sales reports) to determine needs and to facilitate food preparation. Confers with other personnel and outside individuals in order to handle issues and coordinate activities for efficient dining room, kitchen, utility, and bar operations. Directs hiring, training, assignment, and counseling of personnel. Interacts with guests in order to enhance dining experiences and to investigate and resolve food and/or service complaints. Performs miscellaneous duties as needed.

DUTIES AND RESPONSIBILITIES

1. Inventory/facility maintenance

   Conducts routine maintenance checks on equipment and facility.

   Reviews food stock/products in order to count, verify, and record inventory.

   Summarizes inventory findings in order to forecast daily food preparation.

   Receives, inspects, and verifies deliveries from vendors.
   Submits requisitions to vendors in order to restock items
   (e.g., food, linens) as necessary.

2. Administrative duties

   Communicates with other managers by reading and adding comments to daily log.

   Reviews store figures in order to assess sales, labor costs, waste, etc.

   Reads relevant company mail (e.g., memos, letters, reports).

   Prepares bank deposits.

   Attends off-site meetings, training sessions, and/or seminars as needed.

EXHIBIT 4.2.1 *(Continued)*

3. Scheduling and staffing

>   Reviews employee work schedules for shift.
>
>   Makes changes in work schedules as needed.
>
>   Calls in, reassigns, or sends employees home in order to meet budget, sales, or needs.
>
>   Determines staffing needs for each shift.
>
>   Approves requests for schedule changes, days off, vacation, shift trades, etc.

4. Employee relations

>   Discusses unsatisfactory/satisfactory performance with employees.
>
>   Disciplines (e.g., by oral or written warning) employees for poor performance.
>
>   Terminates employees who demonstrate unsatisfactory performance.
>
>   Conducts performance appraisal reviews with employees.
>
>   Conducts crew and staff meeting as needed.

5. Guest and customer relations

>   Greets and seats guests when necessary (e.g., during lunch or dinner rushes).
>
>   Questions guests while they are dining in order to assess the quality of food and/or service.
>
>   Responds to dissatisfied guests in order to listen to and resolve complaints.
>
>   Authorizes complementary meals and/or beverages when necessary.
>
>   Reviews comment cards left by guests in order to determine restaurant effectiveness.

6. Product preparation and service

>   Expedites food in order to facilitate meal service.
>
>   Instructs employees regarding portion sizes, product quality, etc.
>
>   Prepares and cooks food products as needed (e.g., during dinner rushes).
>
>   Prepares, mixes, and serves alcoholic beverages as needed.
>
>   Prepares food products for guests to take out.

EXHIBIT 4.2.1 *(Continued)*

KNOWLEDGE, SKILLS, AND ABILITIES

Knowledge of relevant policies and procedures

Knowledge of equipment operation, assembly, and maintenance (e.g., fryers, mixers).

Knowledge of company food products (including recipes, portions, presentation).

Knowledge of measurement scales (e.g., cups, ounces, pounds).

Knowledge of local, state, and federal sanitation and health codes.

Knowledge of EEO rules, regulations, and laws.

Knowledge of dining room operations.

Knowledge of safety procedures (e.g., for grease, gas and electric fires, burns).

Knowledge of computer or register operations (including keyboard maintenance, reports, changeovers).

Knowledge of local and state liquor laws and ordinances.

Knowledge of bartending (including mixes, garnishes).

Knowledge of financial management principles in the areas of budgeting, purchasing, and forecasting.

Ability to add, subtract, divide, and multiply numbers with speed and accuracy (e.g., knowledge of arithmetic needed to handle monetary transactions).

Ability to effectively and clearly present and express information orally to individuals and/or groups.

Ability to effectively and clearly present and express written information to others.

Ability to work rapidly during rush periods.

Ability to refrain from overreacting to excessive levels of stress.

Ability to organize and plan activities, and to set priorities.

Ability to delegate authority.

Ability to secure relevant information and solve problems.

Ability to make decisions, render judgments, and take appropriate actions.

Ability to work with others (teamwork).

Ability to take charge and to direct, develop, and coordinate activities.

Ability to modify behavior according to changing conditions and situations.

Ability to prepare and cook food products.

Ability to prepare and make beverage products.

EXHIBIT 4.2.2
MINIMUM VALUES OF CVR FOR TASK TO
BE "ESSENTIAL"

NO. OF PANELISTS	MIN. VALUE*
5	.99
6	.99
7	.99
8	.75
9	.78
10	.62
11	.59
12	.56
13	.54
14	.51
15	.49
20	.42
25	.37
30	.33
35	.31
40	.29

Source: C.H. Lawshe (1975). A quantitative approach to content validity. *Personnel Psychology, 28,* 568.
*When all say "essential," the CVR is computed to be 1.00. (It is adjusted to .99 for ease of manipulation.) When the number saying "essential" is more than half, but less than all, the CVR is somewhere between zero and .99.

EXHIBIT 4.2.3
CRITERIA FOR GOOD TASK STATEMENTS

Each task statement should:
- Refer to a single job function
- Refer to a whole task which makes logical sense
- Describe tasks while avoiding task modifiers
- Avoid ambiguous phrases
- Use recognizable terminology
- Avoid the use of abbreviations
- Represent the appropriate spectrum of difficulty
- Use specific rather than general statements
- Avoid redundant information
- Start with a present-tense, action verb
- Avoid multiple-action verbs unless they are invariably performed together
- Demonstrate brevity and conciseness

Source: W. Wooten, Essentials of job analysis. Unpublished manuscript, 1981.

Section 1: General Information

How long have you worked in the food industry? _____

How long have you been with (*company name*)? _____

What is your present position in the company? _____

How long have you occupied your present position? _____

Section 2: Working Relationships

Who are some of the people that a restaurant manager would come in contact with during any particular workweek? Note: Ask the following questions for *each* type of contact. Be sure to probe for additional persons (e.g., vendors, district supervisor, customers, etc.).

Who typically instigates such interactions and how often are they instigated?
(e.g., manager 80 percent, employee 20 percent of the time).

What (if any) are the critical products or services you must provide to these contacts?

Section 3: Duties and Tasks Associated with a Typical Workday

Think about a typical day at work and some of the duties associated with the job of restaurant manager (e.g., opening the restaurant). In general, what is the first thing (you do/a manager does) when (you get/he or she gets) to the restaurant. The second thing? etc. (Probe for general duties and functions.)

(Based on previous question.) Please take a minute and list each of the individual tasks that must be done to successfully accomplish that job duty. (Probe for specifics. Be sure to ask "What is it about the task that is most difficult?" and "What abilities seem most required to perform this task?")

Carefully think about tasks (you do/a manager does) that might only be performed once in a while or infrequently. Please describe these tasks.

Section 4: Critical Incidents

What makes the difference between an effective and an ineffective restaurant manager?
Think back over specific incidents that you yourself have witnessed during the past 6 to 12 months which indicate either effective or ineffective performance. For each incident that you recall, answer the following three questions:

1. What were the circumstances surrounding the incident? In other words, what was the background? What was the situation?

2. What exactly did the individual do that was either effective or ineffective? (Try to cite effective behavior or outcomes first, and probe for observable behavior.)

3. How is the incident you described an example of effective or ineffective behavior? In other words, how did this behavior affect the task or tasks the individual was performing? What were the specific consequences or outcomes that resulted from the behavior?

Section 5: Requisite Knowledge, Skills and Abilities

Do you think that a person being hired for such a position would need previous restaurant experience? If so, how much?

What type of educational background is necessary for successful performance on this job? Explain your answer.

Now think about those skills and abilities *essential* for a restaurant manager's successful job performance. Do you think any of the following apply? Add others if you desire. (Check only if *essential*.)

_____ Oral communication	_____ Cooperative
_____ Written communication	_____ Outgoing/sociable
_____ Delegation	_____ Flexibility
_____ Dependability, carefulness	_____ Stress tolerance/emotional stability
_____ Leadership	_____ Creativity, experimenting
_____ Perception/problem solving	_____ Other (please specify)
_____ Decision making	_____
_____ Initiative (e.g., ability to be a self-starter)	_____

Please list the specific knowledge essential to a restaurant manager's job performance (e.g., knowledge of bartending, health regulations).

FORM 4.2.2
SAMPLE TASK ANALYSIS QUESTIONNAIRE

Student Name: _____

IMPORTANCE RATING SCALE:

5 = Of critical importance to this job

4 = Very important to this job

3 = Important to this job

2 = Of minor importance to this job

1 = Unimportant to this job

0 = Not performed

FREQUENCY RATING SCALE:

5 = Perform very often

4 = Perform often/regularly

3 = Perform sometimes

2 = Perform occasionally

1 = Perform rarely

0 = Not performed

TASK	IMPORTANCE	FREQUENCY
1. Reviews store figures in order to assess sales, labor costs, waste, etc.		
2. Conducts routine maintenance checks on equipment and facility.		
3. Communicates with other managers by reading and adding to daily log.		
4. Inspects areas (e.g., kitchen, rest rooms, dining room) for compliance with safety and health codes.		
5. Counts cash in both vault and register drawers.		
6. Prepares registers (changes dates, codes, etc.) for daily use (e.g., reports, hourly).		
7.		
8.		
9.		
10.		
11.		
12.		
13.		
14.		
15.		
16.		

Exercise 4.2
Assessment Questions

Name: _____

1. How might the information you gathered be used to develop or choose methods for selecting managers?

2. What do you think would happen if the managers you involved in the study were aware that you were doing the job analysis as part of a compensation study? How could you control for this potential source of bias?

3. What advantages do you see in this approach as compared to a standardized job analysis method such as the PAQ or FJA?

4. Could this methodology be used to conform to the requirements of the ADA? Why or why not?

EXERCISE 4.3
USE OF THE CRITICAL INCIDENT
TECHNIQUE TO ANALYZE THE JOB OF
UNIVERSITY PROFESSOR

OVERVIEW

The CIT is heralded as one of the best job analysis methods for the development of performance appraisal systems and training programs. You will recall from the chapter discussion that experts in job analysis rated the CIT as one of the best methods for these purposes. The purpose of this exercise is to write and critique critical incidents representing the performance of college instructors. The incidents will ultimately be used to develop an appraisal system for professors.

LEARNING OBJECTIVES

After completing this exercise, you should be able to:

1. Know the difference between a good and a bad critical incident.
2. Evaluate incidents and revise them for purposes of appraisal development.
3. Understand the procedures to be followed in developing work functions from the CIT.

PROCEDURE

Part A: Individual Analysis (Prior to Class)

Step 1. Review the section in the chapter on the criteria for useful critical incidents. Make four copies of Form 4.3.1, write five critical incidents (one per form) based on observations and experiences you have had with college instructors. Write at least two examples of effective performance and two of ineffective performance. Students should also answer the assessment questions for the exercise.

Part B: Group Analysis

Step 1. Working in pairs, students should read and evaluate incidents written by one another, using the criteria for usefulness presented in the text. Incidents which fail to meet the criteria should be rewritten after the consultation.

Make sure all the incidents are written in the same format (i.e., describing a specific incident or single behavior, using active voice and behavioral verbs, citing a visible incident, describing the context and the results or outcomes of the action; being specific on the results or outcomes).

Step 2. In groups of about six people, the incidents written by group members should be subjected to a "content analysis." The purpose of the content analysis is to identify common themes, or functions of behavior. The term "function" implies a category of events or incidents which fit together conceptually. For example, one such function for university professors might be "grading and testing procedures." Students will write many incidents pertaining to the way in which grades are assigned and tests are administered and scored. These incidents might all fit into the function "grading and testing procedures." Another example of a function might be "communication skills," in which examples of effective and ineffective communication skills are presented. Positive and negative incidents can fit into the same function; the only requirement is that they describe something pertaining to that function. Each group member should read through all the incidents, looking for consistencies or common themes running through the ways in which professors perform well or poorly. The group should first develop a methodology for sorting incidents into piles representing functions. After the initial sorting process, group members should go back through the remaining unsorted examples and try to identify new and different functions underlying them. Continue this process until as many functions are identified as are needed to represent all incidents. Label each of the functions with a short phrase. The group should also agree on what function each incident belongs in and record that function on Form 4.3.1 in the space entitled "Possible function label." One group member should then write the function titles on the blackboard and indicate the number of critical incidents which represent each function.

Step 3. The overlap of the functions developed by each group should be determined through class discussion. The class should attempt to finish with 7 to 15 functions which represent all the functions generated for all groups. Function titles should be merged or rewritten to accommodate all perspectives, and short definitions of each functions should be written.

Step 4. Students should be regrouped and given sets of critical incident forms (Form 4.3.1). Each incident should be linked to one of the class functions identified in step 3. After group discussion and consensus is reached, the function title should be written on each form in the section entitled "Final function label." Students should then review their responses to assessment questions 2 and 4.

FORM 4.3.1
CRITICAL INCIDENT FORM

Think back over your observations of various college professors. Try to recall noteworthy examples of things professors did that illustrate either unusually effective or unusually ineffective performance. Write one example on each form.

1. What were the circumstances leading up to this example?

2. Describe exactly what was done that qualifies the example as either effective or ineffective.

3. What were the results or outcomes of the actions? (Be specific.)

Possible function label _____

Final function label _____

Your name _____

Incident number _____

Group number _____

Exercise 4.3
Assessment Questions

Name _____ Group _____

1. How could the CIT be used to prepare professors for teaching in the classroom?

2. The book describes the CIT as one of the best methods for developing performance appraisal systems. How do you propose to use the incidents and job functions to develop an actual performance appraisal system?

3. To what extent would different types of incidents and different functions result if professors wrote incidents and derived functions?

4. Every CIT is supposed to include a specific outcome or consequence of the exhibited behavior. What purpose could be served by this collection of outcomes?

C H A P T E R

HUMAN RESOURCE PLANNING AND RECRUITMENT*

---

*Contributed by Scott A. Snell and Monica Favia.

OVERVIEW

Chapter 2 proposed organizational capability as a possible source of competitive advantage for organizations. This capability is derived from the human resource (HR) practices of the company. Organizational capability becomes a competitive advantage when the HR practices allow for strategic implementation, create a capacity for change, and instill strategic unity. The staffing function of human resource management (HRM) is critical for accomplishing these three components of organizational capability. Two of the most important aspects of staffing are planning and recruitment. Planning is the forecasting of HR needs in the context of strategic business planning. As we discussed in Chapter 1, the human resource planning (HRP) process of the past was typically reactive in nature, with business needs defining personnel needs. However, with major changes and increasing uncertainty in the business environment, many organizations are adopting a longer-term perspective and integrating HRP with business planning.[1] For example, Kathryn Connors, the vice president of HR at Liz Claiborne, states that "human resources is part of the strategic planning process. It's part of policy development, line extension planning and the merger and acquisition process. Little is done in the company that doesn't involve us in the planning, policy or finalization stages of any deal."[2] Unfortunately, the extent of involvement of HR in strategic planning as practiced by Liz Claiborne is still rather unusual. The more typical practice is for an HRM unit to receive personnel forecasting plans to implement. In terms of competitive advantage, however, the good news is that most foreign competitors also conduct their planning and recruitment in a reactive manner rather than as a fully integrated system. There is thus opportunity for competitive advantage in terms of organizational capability for U.S. companies.

Recruitment is the process of attracting applicants for current and future needs. Merck, the giant pharmaceutical company, was rated as the most admired company for the sixth straight year in *Fortune* magazine's 1992 survey of over 8,000 senior executives. Richard Markham, head of worldwide marketing for the company, credits its success to attracting, developing, and keeping good people. Promotions and salary increases for executives are affected by how many people are recruited and trained. "We look at recruiting with the same kind of intensity as we do discovering new molecules in the lab."[3] The Merck recruiting process is fully integrated with the HR planning process. However, this integration too is not how recruitment is typically conducted in U.S. companies. The Merck emphasis on recruitment is certainly the exception to the rule.

The purpose of this chapter is to provide an overview of the planning and recruitment process. We will discuss the relationship between planning, recruitment, and the other HRM functions; the process of downsizing; the various sources available for recruiting and their relative effectiveness; the advantages and disadvantages of internal and external recruiting; and the role of equal employment opportunity (EEO) in the planning and recruitment process.

OBJECTIVES

After studying this chapter, you should be able to:

1. Understand the importance of HRP to the organization.
2. Identify the six steps in the HRP process.
3. Identify the methods by which an organization can develop forecasts of anticipated personnel demand and understand labor markets.
4. Understand how an organization can stay apprised of and can evaluate its personnel supply and, if necessary, implement a downsizing program.
5. Determine which recruitment methods are best for given situations.
6. Understand the pros and cons of internal versus external recruiting.
7. Know the most important features of recruitment advertising.
8. Know the EEO implications of recruitment and planning.

Pratt and Whitney (P&W), a jet engine division of United Technologies, had a big problem. Its marketing projections for the 1990s predicted lower demand due primarily to decreases in defense spending and increased competitiveness from General Electric (GE) and Rolls Royce. P&W's administrative or overhead expenses had increased faster in the previous 5 years than had expenses in other areas of operations. A reduction in administrative costs was considered to be strategically vital in order to make the company more competitive and to prepare it for the twenty-first century. Based on a detailed study of the major competitors, P&W concluded that a 30 percent reduction in costs could facilitate the company's competitive advantage. HRP was a critical component of the strategic planning process since labor costs were considered a primary area in which cuts could be made.

Strategy is defined as "a process through which the basic mission and objectives of the organization are set and a process through which the organization uses its resources to achieve its objectives."[4] As we discussed in Chapter 2, one source of competitive advantage for an organization is its personnel. The most effective organizations today have fully integrated their HRP process with their business strategies. Planning is a multifaceted process that requires future thinking, integrated decision making, formalized procedures, and programming. HRP incorporates each of these components, but at its root, HRP is best conceived as a problem-solving process. While we typically focus on the particular techniques used by HR planners, these techniques are simply tools for solving underlying employment problems. "Problems," in this case, are defined as the difference between what is and what might be.[5] These also include opportunities and threats. The identification of problems, threats, and opportunities is also central to the strategic planning process. Therefore, for purposes of HRP we refer to these collectively as PTOs (i.e., problems, threats, opportunities). Effective HRP closes the gap between a current and a desired state of affairs. Consequently, to understand the appropriateness of HRP, we must first examine the underlying characteristics of PTOs.

PTOs

Routine PTOs: Bureaucratic Solutions

Some PTOs are extremely simple and routine. For example, every morning when the general manager of Spring Hill Greenhouses, Inc., in Lodi, Ohio, arrives at work, the doors are locked, the lights are off, the cash register is empty, flowers and plant materials are in the back storage cooler, incoming orders are on the facsimile machine or AFS/FTD/Teleflora computer system, and messages are with the local answering service. These routine PTOs are easily addressed through a set of assigned standardized operating procedures (i.e., each employee has an assigned duty). In fact, these solutions are so well programmed that most of us probably would not view these situations as problematic at all. Yet such regularly occurring nuisances, if not eliminated, would constitute an insurmountable set of obstacles that literally would make the business stop. A great deal of HRP operates this way—what can be referred to as the *bureaucratic role* of HRP. In order to resolve routine PTOs, HR plans spell out standardized operating procedures, responsibilities, rules, regulations, and decision criteria in advance. Interestingly, many of these bureaucratic solutions become so well ingrained that the PTOs themselves are forgotten and yet the practices become institutionalized. The results of job analysis in the form of job descriptions and specifications reflect this institutionalization.

Uncertain PTOs: Adaptive Solutions

Other problems in HRP are much less routine or simple. That is, some issues arise infrequently and involve multiple aspects of the organization. The sheer variation among individuals in organizations makes HRP a complicated endeavor. These types of PTOs are, therefore, characterized by uncertainty. Solutions to uncertain PTOs

require forethought and flexibility—what can be referred to as the *adaptive role* of HRP. For example, around certain holidays, business at Spring Hill Greenhouses leaps dramatically. In fact, almost 40 percent of 1991 revenues came during the 3 weeks in which Valentine's Day, Mother's Day, and Christmas occurred. To take advantage of these business fluctuations, Spring Hill recruits part-time employees who take up the slack in making deliveries as well as designing corsages, bouquets, and fresh arrangements. Some of these recruits are former employees who have left the business for one reason or another (e.g., retirement, education, or to raise families). These solutions derive from an HR plan that anticipates and adapts to change before it occurs.

Some uncertainty can be quite positive. Grumman Industries, for example, had undergone a substantial downsizing due primarily to a lack of orders for its F-14 aircraft. With peace breaking out all over Eastern Europe in 1990 and a burgeoning U.S. deficit, the 1990s did not look like a good decade for F-14 sales. Then Operation Desert Storm created certain immediate demand for the aircraft, as well as uncertain future demand. While planning for the 1990s is obviously difficult for Grumman, HR plans are being adapted in anticipation of several demand scenarios.

Ambiguous PTOs: Strategic Solutions

Finally, in addition to routine and uncertain PTOs, some issues in HRP are characterized by ambiguity. That is, multiple interpretations or points of view may exist surrounding any PTO. When events or problems are equivocal, the appropriate solution is the one that influences or legitimizes a particular point of view—what can be referred to as the *strategic role* of HRP. Extending from the adaptive role, the strategic role assumes that one not only reacts and adjusts to the environment but proactively creates that environment as well. That is, companies make their own futures. At Spring Hill Greenhouses, the recruiting plan builds on a strategic alignment with the Medina County Joint Vocational School (MCJVS). In particular, since 1973 the president of Spring Hill has held a concurrent position in horticulture at MCJVS in which he has the opportunity to identify and train potential recruits, and to provide them with part-time internships. Other firms in other industries institute similar recruiting strategies to foster strategic alignments with external parties worldwide. These strategic solutions include job fairs, company-funded educational programs with schools and universities, internships, and cooperative assignments. These strategies help to create a particular perspective among involved parties and reduce ambiguity about the employment picture with the organization.

The critical issue in managing the bureaucratic, adaptive, or strategic roles of HRP is to match the appropriate solution types to particular PTO types. The process for determining this match is outlined in Figure 5.1. In each case, HRP includes (1) environmental scanning, (2) labor demand analysis, (3) labor supply analysis, (4) gap analysis, (5) action programming, and (6) control and evaluation. Let us examine each of these factors.

HRP: MATCHING SOLUTIONS TO PTOs

Step One: Environmental Scanning

Environmental scanning helps planners to identify and anticipate sources of PTOs. This process provides a better understanding of the context in which HR decisions are or will be made. On the one hand, environmental scanning is used to *analyze*, or tease apart, the individual sources of PTOs. At first glance the environment is a muddled array of positive events (opportunities) and negative events (threats). Whether a problem is viewed positively (e.g., as an opportunity) or negatively (e.g., as a threat) has a great deal to do with the solution adopted. Some of the best planners are those who can turn a threat into an opportunity. For example, while most companies in "smokestack" industries view unions as a serious threat to performance, the executives at National Intergroup, Inc. (formerly National Steel), work side by side with their unions to improve quality and productivity. In this case, a potential threat became an opportunity available to the company. The environmental scan of future markets and competitor positions by P&W provided relatively clear opportunities and threats for the future.

On the other hand, environmental analysis is also used to *synthesize* the wide variety of PTOs into an integrated whole. The sheer variety of demands placed on the organization requires some method for tying them to-

gether to assess their joint effects. At Quaker Oats, for example, HR planners were able to synthesize over 50 personnel programs into a list of 10 that were of top priority to the firm in the context of its strategic plan.[6] In addition to their variety, some of these PTOs place competing demands on the firm. For example, the need for efficiency and the need for innovation sometimes lead to inconsistent HR policies. Environmental scanning helps HR planners to set priorities, find synergies among programs, and create future occurrences. Some other examples are discussed below.

EXTERNAL ENVIRONMENT. The external environment is denoted by PTOs arising outside the organization. Industry *competition* has a profound impact on HR planning. P&W, for example, was driven to take action due to the cost-reduction programs of their chief competitors, Rolls Royce and GE. They knew they would be at a competitive disadvantage in contract bids. As argued in Chapter 1, businesses must utilize their HR as effectively as their material, financial, and technological resources. Given the importance of managing for competitive advantage, organizations are increasingly aware that talented employees are vital to their success. This is clearly illustrated in the history of the National Aeronautics and Space Administration (NASA) in recent years. Many aerospace leaders and former NASA officials conclude that the decline in the agency is a direct result of the decline in the quality and competence of its technical staff. Many of the best technical people have been lost to the private sector, and experts say the agency is short of its personnel goals by thousands of workers.

Labor market conditions influence HR planning in terms of both the number and the types of available employees. In a loose *labor market,* qualified recruits are abundant. However, many labor markets are extremely tight. For example, there are current shortages in cutting-edge technologies (e.g., optics, laser technology, electromagnetics, composites technology), medicine and medical support, electrical engineering, manufacturing engineering, plastics, languages, statistics, and certain areas of academia. Tight markets limit the availability of labor, drive up the price of those employees who are selected, and even limit the extent to which an organization can be selective in its hiring procedures. For example, many hospitals hesitate to administer valid selection tests to applicants for physical therapist jobs because qualified applicants for these jobs are in such short supply.

The relevant labor market for an employer is defined by occupation, geography, and employer competition. Obviously, the job and the skills or job specifications play the greatest role in the definition of the relevant labor market and the ease (or difficulty) with which positions can be filled. The labor market can also be greatly affected by geography. Bechtel, the giant international

FIGURE 5.1

1. **Environmental scanning.** Identify and anticipate sources of PTOs; scanning the external environment (competitors, regulation) and the internal environment (strategy, technology, culture)
2. **Labor demand forecast.** Project how business needs will affect HR needs, using qualitative methods (e.g., Delphi, nominal) and quantitative methods (trend analysis, simple and multiple linear regression analysis)
3. **Labor supply forecast.** Project resource availability from internal and external sources
4. **Gap analysis.** Reconcile the forecast of labor supply and demand
5. **Action programming.** Implement the recommended solution from step 4
6. **Control and evaluation.** Monitor the effects of the HRP by defining and measuring critical criteria (e.g., turnover costs, breakeven costs of new hires, recruitment costs, performance outcomes)

construction company, received several million dollars in contracts with Kuwait to rebuild the country after the war with Iraq. However, the company had great difficulty in recruiting civil engineers and other specialists to go to Kuwait, which had been ravaged in the 1991 war. Even high wages did not attract the necessary number of qualified professionals. Competing employers are the third factor defining the labor market. The number and type of employees seeking similarly qualified personnel or offering similar compensation in the same geographical location can serve to define the labor market. Bechtel was at a disdavantage not only because of the geographical location of the work but also because it was competing with several other construction companies which had received contracts from Kuwait. Similar problems developed for companies doing business in what used to be East Germany. Siemens, the German electronics company, for example, had considerable difficulty in hiring engineers and scientists for jobs in East German ventures because a high percentage of these skilled workers had relocated to what used to be West Germany and to other European countries. Due to economic conditions and living standards in the area that was East Germany, American companies such as Woolworth, Coca-Cola, and McDonald's report difficulty in recruiting expatriates for these overseas assignments. Similar problems are now being realized by U.S. companies venturing into most of the nations making up what used to be the Soviet Union. Other overseas assignments are highly valued by U.S. managers, and incentives for the expatriate assignments are being reduced. *The Wall Street Journal,* for example, eliminated a housing allowance and other benefits for employees assigned to its European bureaus.

Figure 5.2 presents a summary of the relevant labor market as defined by occupation and geography. Since labor can constitute as much as 80 percent (or more) of operating expenses, and since most businesses compete at least partly on a price/cost basis, managing the labor market is a crucial HR activity. To complicate this issue further, there are relatively fewer workers for entry-level jobs (the "baby bust" generation). Accommodations also need to be made for dual-career families, single-parent employees, and part-time workers. Fortunately, the increasing participation rates of women and minorities expand the possibilities for qualified labor.[7]

As we discussed in Chapter 3, *government regulations* also influence HR planning. EEO legislation, such as Title VII of the Civil Rights Act, the 1991 Civil Rights Act, the Age Discrimination in Employment Act (ADEA), the 1990 Americans with Disabilities Act (ADA), and Executive Order 11246, requires that companies pay close attention to the manner in which they treat individuals. (Recall our discussion earlier about the so-called glass ceiling and glass walls.) A myriad of state and local laws regulating personnel practice must also be closely monitored. For example, most states now have laws which govern the way in which employees are treated in mergers and acquisitions. P&W developed an extensive training program on government regulations with an emphasis on age discrimination. This was done as part of the cost-reduction efforts which their executives knew would involve employee transfers and terminations.

Another important federal law for HR planners is the Workers Adjustment Retraining Notification Act (WARN) of 1988. WARN requires employers to give 60-day advance notice of plant closings and mass layoffs that result in employment losses. It applies to any business employing 100 or more full-time employees who work a total of at least 4000 hours, not counting overtime. No employment loss is considered to have occurred if the closing or layoff is the result of relocation or consolidation and the employer provides employees with particular reemployment opportunities. Employers violating WARN are subject to several penalties. Ways to avoid adverse effects of WARN include providing: (1) 60 days of wages and benefits in lieu of notice, (2) voluntary and unconditional payment to employees, and (3) continuing notice of possible layoffs.[8] These constraints must be managed concurrently with other employment problems (e.g., availability of labor, qualifications of those who apply).

The most extensive revision of U.S. immigration laws in over 50 years will surely affect HR planning as well. The 1990 Immigration Act will expand opportunities for companies to transfer multinational executives and managers while at the same time restricting the ability of U.S. corporations to hire foreign national professionals. In addition, employees with a master's or a Ph.D. degree will be given immigration preferences. HR professionals in planning and recruiting should be fully apprised of the new regulations prior to the development of an international search for skilled personnel. Many hospitals, for example, now recruit nurses outside the United States for U.S. assignments. As of 1991, however, in order to do such recruiting, a hospital has to apply for a "temporary professional worker" visa and file a labor-condition application. This application requires the organization to attest to a "prevailing-wage" (or higher) rate for foreign employees, the absence of a strike at the place of employment, proper working conditions, a public posting of the requests for visas, and an indication of the number of workers sought. Provisions are available for formal complaints to be filed in opposition to the request for visas.[9]

INTERNAL ENVIRONMENT. In contrast to the external environment, the internal environment is comprised of PTOs arising from within the organization. As stated above, some HR planners have begun to blend HR planning with *strategic planning* in order to ensure that

FIGURE 5.2
RELEVANT LABOR MARKETS, BY GEOGRAPHIC AND EMPLOYEE GROUPS

RELEVANT LABOR MARKET

GEOGRAPHIC SCOPE	EMPLOYEE GROUPS/OCCUPATIONS					
	PRODUCTION	OFFICE AND CLERICAL	TECHNICIANS	SCIENTISTS AND ENGINEERS	MANAGERIAL PROFESSIONAL	EXECUTIVE
Local: Within relatively small areas, such as cities or metropolitan statistical areas—MSAs (e.g., Dallas metropolitan area)	Most likely	Most likely	Most likely	—	—	—
Regional: Within a particular area of the state or county or several states (e.g., Greater Boston area)	Only if in short supply or critical	Only if in short supply or critical	Most likely	Likely	Likely	—
National: Across the country	—	—	—	Most likely	Most likely	Most likely
International: Across several countries	—	—	—	Only for critical skills or those in very short supply	Only for critical skills or those in very short supply	Likely

Source: G. T. Milkovich and J.W. Boudreau. *Human Resource Management,* 6th ed., Homewood, IL: Richard D. Irwin, 1991, p. 36. Reprinted with permission.

the goals and resource deployments of HR work in concert with those of the organization as a whole. For example, in the mid-1970s, Corning Glass and Chase Manhattan Bank were each undertaking turnaround strategies.[10] In order to meet the requirements of these strategies, HR planning was designed to select and place executives who had entrepreneurial and managerial skills. Similarly, in order to reposition itself (postdivestiture), American Telephone and Telegraph (AT&T) had to recruit and select salespeople with extensive marketing experience rather than engineering experience.[11] Other corporate and business strategies suggest different HR requirements. For example, mergers and acquisitions require redesign of structures and jobs.[12] Geographic expansion or consolidation requires managerial succession planning and development and an assessment of labor markets in the areas planned for expansion. International expansion represents an extreme case of this type of business growth. But expansion does not always mean concurrent growth in employment. For example, during the 1980s many firms had aggressive plans for business growth, while either reducing head count or holding it constant. Instead of requiring new employees, this type of strategy required job redesign, retraining, and reassignment of human resources. In contrast to growth, some competitive strategies required considerable employee downsizing or redeployment; these types of HR activities are evident in a host of companies such as IBM, GM, HRB Singer, Honeywell, Control Data, and Ford Motor Company.[13] In addition to strategy, *technology* evokes an important set of PTOs for HR planning. For example, industry investment in automation has nearly quadrupled since 1980, to almost $40 billion. Researchers have shown that technological change may affect both the number and the kind of jobs in a firm.[14] Other HR changes may emanate from technology as well. For example, the Saturn Division of General Motors (GM) reflects a different paradigm for manufacturing (i.e., teamwork). Likewise, Saturn requires a markedly different way of managing HR, including staffing, training, compensation, and labor relations practices.[15]

Finally, organizational *culture* poses a unique set of PTOs for HR planners. For example, as discussed in Chapter 2, during the 1985 merger of Baxter Travenol and American Hospital Supply, HR planners were concerned about blending two very different corporate cultures. American executives ran their own divisions without interference, whereas Baxter was centrally managed. Also, American's philosophy involved working very closely with its customers. Baxter, on the other hand, stressed technology development and managing its own people. This represented a potential threat. However, the executives from both companies worked diligently with the HR staff to integrate employees from both companies into a unified corporate culture which defined the new organization (Baxter Healthcare Corporation). The new hybrid culture provided an opportunity to facilitate the merger process.[16]

These examples provide only a glimpse of the different forces inside and outside the organization that influence HR planning. The purpose of environmental scanning is to *identify* PTOs, *understand* how the mix of these forces interact with each other and the firm, *predict* their future effects, and provide a means to *control* their impact.

Step Two: Labor Demand Forecast

A forecast of labor demand derives from a projection of how business needs will effect HR. Each of the environmental forces discussed above is likely to exert pressure on HR demand—both in terms of the number and types of employees required and in terms of the number and types of jobs utilized. The HR planner must anticipate these needs, add focus to an otherwise confusing array of possibilities, and set priorities for conflicting goals. Labor demand forecasting methods fall into two categories: qualitative and quantitative. As each category embraces certain assumptions, a combination of the two is preferred.

QUALITATIVE METHODS. The simplest method for projecting labor demand is a *centralized* approach in which the HR department examines the current business situation and determines staffing requirements for the rest of the firm. While this approach is simple, it is generally not accurate. A top-down approach assumes that the central HR office has an accurate understanding of the business as well as the needs of each unit or function. In large, complex firms, these assumptions typically do not hold. A more preferred method involves a *decentralized* process[17] wherein each unit or functional manager subjectively derives his or her own staffing needs. These projections are aggregated to create an overall composite forecast for the company.

At P&W, for example, top management set a goal of 30 percent cost reduction for each functional unit. Unit managers were asked to conduct a job analysis of each job under their jurisdiction and, after analysis, to submit proposals for workload reduction and other cost reduction options. A procedure was established to present the various reduction options including a method for the presentation of a rationale if the manager failed to make the 30 percent target reduction.

Other firms have experimented with formalized problem-solving methods, such as the *Delphi technique,* for minimizing interpersonal and jurisdictional conflicts.[18] The Delphi technique avoids face-to-face group discussion by the use of an intermediary. Experts take turns at presenting a forecast statement and assumptions. The intermediary passes on the forecasts and assumptions to the others. Revisions are then made independently and anonymously by the experts. The intermediary then pools and summarizes the judgments and gives them to the experts. This process is continued until a consensus forecast emerges or until the intermediary concludes that more than one perspective must be presented. In comparison with linear regression analysis (discussed below), the Delphi technique has been shown to produce better 1-year forecasts, but there can be difficulties in reaching consensus on complex problems.[19]

The full Delphi process can take considerable time. For example, the Gap, a clothing retailer, took over 4 months to forecast the number of buyers needed for the next year using a Delphi method. The use of "networked" computers can do much to reduce the time for Delphi forecasting.

The *nominal group technique* is similar to the Delphi method. However, experts join at a conference table and independently list their ideas in writing.[20] The experts then share their ideas with the group in turn. As the ideas are presented, a master list of the ideas is compiled so that everyone can refer back to them. The ideas are discussed and ranked by member vote.[21]

QUANTITATIVE METHODS. Quantitative methods are based on the assumption that the future is an extrapolation from the past. *Trend analysis* incorporates certain business factors (e.g., units produced, revenues) and a productivity ratio (e.g., employees per units produced). To illustrate, P&W calculated 16 jet engines per factory worker and almost 20 support, marketing, and management personnel for every 100 factory workers. Their external environmental scanning data indicated more favorable ratios for GE, which, as previously mentioned, was one of P&W's chief competitors. By projecting changes in the business factor and/or the productivity ratio, we can forecast changes in the labor demand. There are six steps in trend analysis:

1. Find the appropriate business factor that relates to the size of the workforce.
2. Plot the historical record of that factor in relation to the size of the workforce.
3. Compute the productivity ratio (average output per worker per year).
4. Determine the trend.
5. Make necessary adjustments in the trend, past and future.
6. Project to the target year.[22]

The use of the appropriate business factor is critical to the success of trend analysis.[23] Learning curves assume that the average number of units produced per employee will increase as more units are produced. Such an increase is expected because workers learn to perform their tasks more efficiently over time. Learning curves are evident in virtually all industries. For example, in the automotive industry, learning curves for new models improve by more than 50 percent through the life of the model. At P&W, the learning curve for one particular engine exceeded 60 percent from start-up to the final production year. The business factor should of course be directly related to the essential purpose for the business. Typically, universities use student enrollment by discipline, hospitals use patient-days, manufacturers use output needs, and retailers use sales adjusted by inventory.

Simple and multiple linear regression are the most commonly used statistical procedures for forecasting labor demands. Simple linear regression uses information from the past relationship between the organization's employment level and some criterion known to be related to employment. For example, most companies can establish a statistical relationship between sales or work output and level of employment. Such a relationship, however, is also influenced by the learning curve. Learning curves can be studied and used to make more accurate projections of future employment levels. More complicated quantitative methods involving *multiple regression* and *linear programming* further this process by incorporating operational constraints (e.g., budgets, mix of labor) into the mathematical models. Through this elaboration, it is possible to forecast demand under varying business scenarios. Multiple regression may use several factors which correlate with labor needs. For example, in preparation for its collective bargaining negotiations, GM used several different sales figures, GNP, gross domestic profit, capital investments, and other factors to forecast labor needs for the next 6 years. GM used historical data which statistically related each factor to labor demands. Future demand was then forecast based on current data on each of the factors.

While our discussion of labor demand may suggest that planners attempt to establish a singular forecast, the outcome of this process is typically a set of potential scenarios. A scenario is a multifaceted portrayal of the mix of business factors in conjunction with the array of HR needs. As such, each scenario or forecast is an elaborate set of "if-then" statements; that is, "if" the business context presented us with scenario A, "then" our labor demand forecast would be B. Ideally, HR planning is as comprehensive as possible to provide leeway for a wide variety of business activities.

Step Three: Labor Supply Forecast

Labor supply forecasts reveal some of the constraints placed on business planning. Whereas the labor demand forecast projects HR needs, the labor supply forecast projects resource availability. This step of HR planning is vital in that it conveys an inventory of the firm's current and projected competencies. This skill base sets an upper limit on the commitments and challenges the firm can undertake (all else being equal). From a problem-solving perspective, labor supply represents the "raw materials" available to address PTOs. Supply forecasts are typically broken down into two categories: *external supply* and *internal supply*.

INTERNAL SUPPLY.   Internal labor supply consists of the individuals and jobs currently available within the firm. Data from *personnel or skills inventories* are used to make projections into the future based on current trends. These trends include not only the number and kinds of individuals in each job but also the flow of employees in, through, and out of the organization. Specifically, a skills inventory includes an assessment of the knowledge, skills, abilities, experience, and career aspirations of each of the present workers. This record should be updated at least every 2 years and should include changes such as new skills, degree completions, and changed job duties. These inventories aid in the internal recruitment process. If skills inventories are not updated, present employees may be overlooked for job openings within the organization.[24] This may result in increased search costs in addition to dissatisfaction among employees who were overlooked. Accordingly, internal supply forecasts must take into account the company's current practices pertaining to hiring, firing, transfer, promotion, development, and attrition. Succession planning and replacement charts are used to identify individuals who might fill a given slot if the incumbent leaves. These techniques are most useful for individual-level problems with short-term planning-time horizons. There are over 300 computerized human resource information systems (HRIS) now available, many of which include skills inventories. GE and Dun & Bradstreet, for example, have used electronic data files on its employees for years as an aid for internal promotions and for required EEO reports. P&W used an HRIS to project successions, early retirements, future openings, and overstaffing problems. Figure 5.3 presents an example of a skills inventory.

Two of the most important concerns regarding the use of electronic data bases for personnel are privacy rights and security problems. Security problems can be handled with the right systems and software provisions. Privacy issues are much more difficult. Many states and the federal government have privacy laws which may pertain to the use, content, and access of an HRIS.

More complicated transition models such as Markov analysis are used for long-range forecasts in large companies. Markov analysis uses historical information from personnel movements of the internal labor supply to predict what will happen in the future. Using data collected over a number of years, an estimate is made of the likelihood that persons in a particular job will remain in that job or be transferred, promoted, demoted, terminated, or retired. Probabilities are used to represent the historical flow of personnel through the oranization, a "transition matrix" is formed from these probabilities, and future personnel flows are estimated from this matrix.[25] Figure 5.4 presents Markov data from a division of Progressive Tool and Industries, one of the largest tool companies serving the domestic automotive industry (Progressive designs and manufactures the tooling for assembly lines). The transition probability matrix presents percentages or probabilities of employee movement through four positions within the division. The data are retrieved from personnel records and averaged over a 5-year period. The matrix shows that 70 percent of assemblers remain in the position after 1 year with a turnover (quit or fired) rate of 20 percent. The matrix also shows that 80 percent of workers who do the more skilled machinist job are retained after 1 year, with only 5 percent turnover rate. These data were used by Progressive to plan a recruiting strategy based on projected contracts. The data indicated a strong need to evaluate the assembler job to determine the causes of the high turnover rate and the need to concentrate recruiting at that level in anticipation of shortages of assemblers in the coming year when contracts were expected to expand.

Both Eaton Corporation[26] and Weyerhaeuser[27] have used Markov analysis successfully in their forecasts. However, two experiences at Corning Glass proved unsuccessful because the transition probabilities were unreliable.[28] A minimum of 50 people in each job of the transition matrix is recommended to ensure adequate reliability in forecasting. At Progressive, for example, projections for oversupplies of foremen were based on small numbers and proved to be relatively inaccurate. More research is needed on Markov analysis to determine the key variables affecting its accuracy. Variables such as unemployment rate, changes in competitor status, causes of turnover, changes in HR policies, and business plans or customer demand, which may differ significantly from the situation in which the probabilities were established, will have a profound effect on the usefulness of Markov projections in the future.

EXTERNAL SUPPLY.   External supply consists of individuals in the labor force who are potential recruits of the firm (including those working for other firms). The skill levels being sought determine the relevant labor market. The entire country (or the world) may be the relevant labor market for highly skilled jobs (e.g., physicians, chemists, biologists, physicists), whereas the relevant labor market for unskilled jobs is usually the local community. Determining the relevant labor market also

FIGURE 5.3
AN EXAMPLE OF A SKILLS INVENTORY

SKILLS INVENTORY

Employee name: I. M. Nameless   Date printed: 1–1–78
Employee number: 28036   Department: 319

KEY WORDS

WORD	DESCRIPTION	ACTIVITY
1. Accounting	Tax accounting	Supervising and analyzing
2. Bookkeeping	General ledger	Supervising
3. Auditing	Computer records	Analyzing

WORK EXPERIENCE

FROM	TO	DESCRIPTION
1. 1973	1978	Chief Tax Accountant at XYZ Stores
2. 1965	1973	Bookkeeper at XYZ Manufacturing
3. 1964	1965	Auditing Training at XYZ Bank

EDUCATION

DEGREE	MAJOR	YEAR
1. MBA	Business administration	1964
2. BS	Accounting	1962

SPECIAL COURSES

COURSE	DATE
1. Management theory	1974
2. Business planning	1971
3. Computer audits	1965

MEMBERSHIPS

1. American Accounting Society
2. American Management Association

LICENSES

NAME	DATE
1. CPA	1965

LANGUAGES

NAME	FLUENCY
1. Spanish	Fluent
2. French	Read

POSITION PREFERENCE

1. Accounting
2. Auditing

LOCATION PREFERENCE

1. San Francisco
2. San Diego

HOBBIES

1. Bridge
2. Amateur radio
3. Boating

Employee signature: _____   Personnel Department: _____
              Date: _____   Date: _____

Source: R. A. Kaumeyer, *Planning and using skills inventory systems.* New York: Van Nostrand Reinhold, 1979. Reprinted with permission.

FIGURE 5.4
MARKOV ANALYSIS AT PROGRESSIVE INDUSTRIES

	A	M	F	S	Exit
Assemblers (A)	.70	.10			.20
Machinists (M)	.05	.80	.10		.05
Foreman (F)		.10	.75	.05	.10
Supervision (S)			.05	.90	.05

	Staffing Levels	A	M	F	S	Exit
Assemblers (A)	250	175	25			50
Machinists (M)	120	6	96	12		6
Foremen (F)	40		4	30	2	4
Supervision (S)	20			1	18	1
Forecast		181	125	43	20	61

means determining what type of recruiting approach should be used. Several governmental and industrial reports (e.g., Bureau of Labor Statistics, Public Health Service, Northwestern Endicott Lindquist Report) regularly forecast the supply of labor and make estimates of available workers in general job and demographic categories. These forecasts are extrapolations into the future based on current trends. Many companies have taken advantage of the cheap, unskilled labor supply which is available outside the United States. As we will discuss at greater length in Chapter 11, many companies have basic assembly work done at a fraction of the cost in Mexico, South Korea, Taiwan, and Hong Kong. There are over 1600 maquiladoras, or "twin plants," in Mexico which pay about 10 percent of what unskilled labor in the United States commands.

COMPUTER MODELING.   Computers are used in the most sophisticated forecasting approaches. Various mathematical formulas are used in computer models that simultaneously use extrapolation, indexation, survey results, and estimates of employment changes to compute future HR needs. Over time the computer's formulas are refined according to actual changes in HR demand. Computer modeling for the most part is found only in large organizations with years of experience in HRP.[29] The U.S. armed forces probably have the most sophisticated computer modeling approaches to planning and recruitment in employment today. AT&T uses computer modeling as part of its HRP in order to forecast employment needs and develop different scenarios for meeting the needs. Its package of incentives for early retirement, along with plant closing and other actions, was derived from a careful analysis of various options via computer modeling. Some federal agencies also use computer modeling. The Internal Revenue Service (IRS), plagued for years by shortages of auditors and accountants, relies on a computer model to develop college recruiting plans.

Step Four: Gap Analysis

Gap analysis is used to reconcile the forecasts of labor demand and supply. At a minimum, this process identifies potential shortages or surpluses of employees, skills, and jobs. In addition, however, planners can juxtapose several environmental forecasts with alternative supply and demand forecasts in order to determine a firm's preparedness for different business scenarios. From a problem-solving perspective, gap analysis is used to pair up potential PTOs and solutions in order to evaluate how a firm might attack the future. This decision-making process involves (1) a search for alternative solutions, (2) evaluation of alternatives, and (3) choice of solutions.

Gap analysis has revealed a need for employee downsizing in a majority of Fortune 1000 companies in recent years. The approaches to downsizing are many and varied. Some companies adopt a last-in, first-out policy, in which layoffs are based strictly on employee seniority. Of course, many organizations are constrained by collective bargaining agreements which require such a policy. For example, the latest contract between GM and the United Auto Workers (UAW) includes specific provisions for methods of reductions in force. Other companies have

adopted policies based strictly on company needs and employee performance. One survey found that 25 percent of companies used employee performance as one basis for layoffs. Digital Equipment Corporation, for example, imposed such a decision strategy on its managers in its downsizing efforts (the workforce was reduced by over 5000). Still other companies have offered a variety of options for achieving certain employment levels, including early retirement programs, retraining, and redeployment efforts. International Business Machines (IBM), AT&T, Ford, Xerox, Bank of America, and many other of the largest U.S. firms have used various forms of early retirement programs. Over 10,000 IBM employees took early retirement in 1988. While the program helped IBM to minimize layoffs of full-time employees, the company lost some of its best employees, who opted for one of the attractive termination programs. The 1991–1992 downsizing program focused on offering early retirement only to noncritical employees, terminating marginal employees for cause, and offering less attractive transfer options to those who were not needed in their current jobs. One of IBM's biggest problems in achieving its downsizing goals, however, is that its performance appraisal system has not provided enough useful data to make performance-based actions. Since 1984, AT&T has reduced its staff by 100,000 through a variety of programs, working in cooperation with two unions. Each of the 19 operating units must submit detailed workforce reduction plans, which must be approved at corporate headquarters before action is taken. P&W conducted job analysis and redesign, determined labor shortages and excesses, and conducted special performance assessments to identify the most qualified incumbents for newly structured jobs. More than 85 percent of Fortune 1000 firms implemented downsizing of their white-collar staff between 1987 and 1991 (more than 50 percent downsized in 1990 alone).

One recent empirical study of the U.S. auto industry identified the processes used in effective white-collar downsizing.[30] Six general strategies were identified as most predictive of effective downsizing. Figure 5.5 presents a summary of the findings. Effective downsizing in the study was defined as improvements in productivity, quality, and employee morale following the downsizing effort. Most of the companies had implemented downsizing as a reaction to loss of market share or lower productivity. Most firms looked at downsizing as simply a workforce reduction process rather than as a restructuring or redesign of jobs in the context of corporate strategy or planning. The most effective firms, however, looked at downsizing as an opportunity to create or improve the company's competitive advantage through restructuring, overhead reduction, and performance management. The process created a frame of mind that would be sustained after the major downsizing effort was complete. The idea

FIGURE 5.5
STRATEGIES FOR EFFECTIVE DOWNSIZING

The most effective downsizing:

1. Was implemented by comand from the top down but initiated from the bottom up.
2. Was short-term and across-the-board but also long-term and focused.
3. Paid special attention to terminated employees and those who survived.
4. Was targeted inside the firm but also included the external network (e.g., contractors, subcontractors).
5. Resulted in small semi-autonomous units within larger organizations as well as strong centralized functions.
6. Emphasized downsizing as a means to an end but also as the targeted end.

Source: K. S. Cameron, S. J. Freeman, and A. K. Mishra, Best practices in white collar downsizing: Managing contradictions. *Academy of Management Executive, 5,* 57–63, 1991. Reprinted with permission.

was to create and maintain a "lean-and-mean" mentality in management that would be sustained long after the specific downsizing goals were met. The most effective firms looked at downsizing, or "rightsizing," as one approach to creating competitive advantage. Ford, for example, set a goal of 21 employee-hours per vehicle for 1990, a figure lower than those of GM and Chrysler but still a few hours higher than those of Honda, Nissan, and Toyota (and 3 hours lower than Ford's 1988 figure). Downsizing was just one of several programs aimed at the employee-hour reduction goal. The 21-hour goal was met through these efforts, and a 19-hour goal was set for 1992.

As indicated in Figure 5.5, some of the problems associated with downsizing can be minimized with good planning and strategy. In addition to examining performance data and redeployment options, such planning may include *outplacement* services for employees which involve job coaching, résumé preparation, placement services, and interview training. Outplacement services are becoming available in Japan as well, where companies are now faced with a need to downsize.

SEARCH FOR ALTERNATIVE SOLUTIONS. As discussed above, in HRP there are likely to be multiple scenarios that are worthy of consideration. Environmental scanning and labor forecasts identify a range of possible PTOs—some of which are routine, others uncertain, still others ambiguous. HR planners must exercise their ingenuity to create a range of possible solutions to the PTOs they identify. At this stage, the range of possibilities can be increased by seeking input from executives, line managers, employees, customers, and consultants in a "brainstorming" process. A qualitative approach such as Delphi can be used at this point as well.

As part of their HR planning process, the Upjohn Corporation asks line managers to answer four basic questions: (1) How does each job relate to the strategic plan of the work unit? (2) Are there alternatives to full-time jobs that should be considered to accomplish the same objectives (e.g., temporary workers, part-time employees, consultants, subcontractors, overtime)? (3) What are the projected costs of each job? (4) What specific impact will the job have on critical and clearly defined effectiveness criteria?

More and more companies have been asking similar questions regarding their workplaces and coming up with rather unique answers. For example, employee leasing gained in popularity with small companies after passage of the 1986 Tax Equity and Fiscal Responsibility Act (TEFRA), which formally recognized this employment arrangement. With employee leasing, a leasing company assumes complete responsibility for the employee, including pay and benefits. Omnistaff, Inc., the largest U.S. leasing company with over 1400 corporate clients and 12,000 employees, has had a 20 percent growth rate since 1985. The major advantages of employee leasing are a savings in pension benefits due to the provisions of TEFRA, sizable tax breaks, and of course, reduced administrative costs. Employees can actually benefit as well, since the leasing company can offer a better package due to group discounts for insurance. The major disadvantage for the employer is some loss of control over the employee.[31]

A more significant trend in creative HR planning is permanent part-time employees. We already discussed the IBM policy of maintaining a part-time workforce at about 10 percent of its total workforce. The program enables the company to maintain a labor pool in line with the business cycle and to minimize layoffs. Many other companies, particularly in services, are now following suit. Digital Equipment Corporation, Ryder Truck, United Parcel Service (UPS), and NCR are among the major companies now maintaining a sizable percentage of their workforce on part-time status. According to the Bureau of Labor Statistics, 20 percent of the U.S. workforce worked part-time in 1990. Two-thirds of this group were women. While working parents consider part-time employment a good thing, women's groups such as the National Organization for Women (NOW) decry the trend as fostering a "marginal" employment policy characterized by low wages and no benefits. Companies which have adopted policies of maintaining permanent part-time staff for many job classifications report substantial cost savings and relatively little difficulty in recruiting and retaining capable staffs.

Another alternative solution in HRP for dealing with the increasing diversity of the workforce is job sharing. Job sharing divides a single job between two or more workers. American Express has adopted this policy for its customer service representatives and has reduced its employee turnover rate and recruitment costs significantly.

More employees are also hiring temporary help, called "temps," particularly in clerical data processing industrial jobs. The National Association of Temporary Services reported a growth rate in temporary employment in excess of 20 percent through the 1980s. While employers generally report that temporaries are typically hired for "emergencies," an increasing number report considerable cost savings as well, with temps judged to be as productive as permanent employees.[32]

EVALUATION OF ALTERNATIVES.   After a host of alternative solutions are raised, HR planners must evaluate these alternatives based on the characteristics of the PTOs they purport to solve. Recall that routine PTOs call for bureaucratic solutions (e.g., job assignments, work procedures), uncertain PTOs require adaptive solutions (e.g., hiring new employees, using part-time or temporary employees, retraining old employees, early retirements), and ambiguous PTOs require strategic solutions (e.g., head-hunting among competitors, lobbying at agencies, negotiating with unions). Other considerations may also come into play, such as current practices (and resistance to change); resource constraints (e.g., time, money); and personal values of owners, executives, labor, etc. The outcome of this phase should be a clear understanding of the viability and practicality of alternative solutions.

CHOICE OF SOLUTIONS.   Effective HRP closes the gap between the current and a desired state of affairs. Consequently, the choice of any solution or set of solutions should be made relative to the characteristics of employment problems. However, since there are likely to be several solutions that are equally viable or desirable, the choice process is likely to be heavily influenced by the values of the decision makers (e.g., executives, HR planners, line managers). Some of these decision makers may differ in their attitudes regarding resource constraints (time and money spent), employee morale, financial performance, customer satisfaction, etc. These differences may result in a political debate. In general, it is advisable to choose a solution that takes advantage of opportunities, minimizes threats, capitalizes on strengths, and ameliorates weaknesses. This approach balances the many and varied demands placed on the organization and on the HR function, and maximizes degrees of freedom for future action. Of course, the various solutions should be considered in the context of external environment constraints such as the legal or regulatory environment. For example, many companies have faced class action lawsuits based on allegations of age discrimination in down-

sizing efforts. Despite careful efforts to avoid litigation in its cost-reduction program, P&W, for example, was sued by more than 50 former employees who claimed age discrimination.

Step Five: Action Programming

Most problem solving fails due to lack of action, and most plans fail due to poor implementation. Action programming is the final step of HRP—the step that takes the adopted solution and lays out the sequence of events that need to be executed to realize the plan. As Will Rogers once said, "It does very little good to be on the right track if you are not going anywhere." In the previous four steps of HRP, the task was to derive the solution that would best address the PTOs raised through environmental scanning and labor forecasts. The purpose of action programming is to make certain that those decisions become reality. In general, there are two aspects of programming: internal and external.

Internal programming. Many of the solutions in HRP rest on actions inside the firm with the current workforce. For routine PTOs, in particular, bureaucratic adjustments in HR practices can be easily programmed internally (e.g., through job design or assignments). In addition, for some uncertain PTOs, adaptive adjustments such as training, career planning, promotions, and compensation design can be made internally.

External programming. Other solutions in HRP require going outside the firm to interact with constituencies in the environment (e.g., labor unions, competitors). In particular, when HR plans require drastically different skills from what employees currently possess and/or when the time frame for change is quite short, the firm will likely need to recruit from the outside labor market.

Step Six: Control and Evaluation

In order to show how firms make the transition from HRP to action programming, as well as how they make the choice between internal and external action programming, this section outlines various approaches to recruitment. In addition, the philosophy and processes underlying the recruitment function are discussed.

Control and evaluation monitor the effectiveness of HR plans over time. Deviations from a plan are identified and actions are taken. The extent to which HR objectives have been met is identified by the feedback resulting from the outcomes of HRP. Essentially, it has been suggested that long-range planning activities require the attainment of short-run objectives. Examples include turnover costs, workforce reduction effects from early retirement programs, breakeven costs of new hires, and analysis of costs of recruits as compared with the training and development costs of existing employees. Obviously, actual staffing levels compared to projected levels should be evaluated for accuracy. Doing evaluations such as cost-benefit analysis make it easier to determine whether long-run planning objectives will be met.

THE RECRUITMENT FUNCTION: PUTTING HRP INTO ACTION

Moving from HRP to recruitment is essentially a process of translating broad strategies into operational tasks. The major responsibility for this process typically rests with the HRM department, although most tasks are shared with line managers. HR managers are responsible for determining recruitment policy, ensuring EEO compliance, and training and evaluating the recruiters. In addition, many organizations such as Merck, Coca-Cola, Xerox, IBM, and Procter & Gamble actively involve line managers and employees as recruiters. As mentioned above, conflict between HR and line managers can occur when their priorities diverge. For example, line managers may be more concerned about filling a position quickly, while HR managers may be more concerned about affirmative action guidelines and hiring goals or complying with EEO regulations.

Based on the HR plan (more specifically, gap analysis), the organization has a fairly good idea of its overall recruitment or downsizing needs. However, this information must be operationalized and communicated to others who will be taking the action. Three essential steps for translating future needs into specific operational terms are (1) job analysis, (2) time-lapse data, and (3) yield ratio.

Job Analysis

Recruiters and HR planners rely on two aspects of job analysis information to identify the critical skills for which they will recruit. First, job descriptions provide an outline of the responsibilities, duties, and tasks to be performed by the potential employee. Second, the job specifications outline the knowledge, skills, and abilities and other characteristics required of the applicant. In general, the more specific the recruitment design, the more efficient and effective it is. Poorly designed recruiting is more expensive and takes longer.[33] Job analysis information which accurately reflects the requirements needed for the job can have a direct impact on the effectiveness of any recruitment and planning effort. Job analysis information can also be used in a downsizing effort, as jobs are restructured based on the new organizational structure. As we discussed in Chapter 4, specific job analysis strategies are available for writing job descriptions and specifications based on an organization's competitive strategy. P&W followed this process as part of its downsizing and cost-reduction methods.

While HRP gives information on the number of jobs needed and job analysis describes the requirements of the jobs, management must know when to start a recruiting process and how extensive the search should be. This is where time-lapse data (TLD) and yield ratios come in.

TLD

TLD provides the average time that elapses between points of decision making in recruiting. For example, if a recruitment plan calls for using newspaper advertisements, past records may reflect that the job is ultimately filled an average of 2 months after the publication of an ad. Thus, the ad should be placed at least 2 months before the job has to be filled. Data may also be available on the time lapses between interviews and offers, and between offers and acceptances. When combined with yield ratios, the TLD can provide useful information for planning a recruitment effort.[34]

Yield Ratios

A yield ratio for any recruiting source is simply the ratio of applicants to hires at each step in the selection process. For example, a series of newspaper ads may result in 1000 applications for employment. Of these 1000 applications, 100 are judged to meet some "minimum qualifications" (yield at this step is thus 20 to 1: 100 who are "minimally qualified," 5 of whom were ultimately hired). Of the group of 100 candidates, 50 may accept invitations to be interviewed; of the 50, 10 may be given job offers. Of the 10 people who are given job offers, 5 may accept positions. Thus, the overall yield is 200:1 (i.e., 1000 applications to 5 people hired). Assuming that the labor market has not changed dramatically from when the yield ratios were derived and that similar methods of recruiting are to be used (e.g., advertising in the same papers), this ratio can be used as the basis for planning future recruitment efforts. By going backward from the yield ratio, the recruiter can estimate how many applicants will be necessary in order to fill a certain number of positions. The recruiter can then adjust the recruiting effort accordingly, with more (or less) advertising, more (or fewer) trips to college campuses, etc. Yield ratios can also be calculated using some other criterion (e.g., new hires who work for 1 year or more).

Recruitment is a never-ending process for many jobs in which there are critical shortages of highly specialized skills. As we discussed above, there are tight labor markets for many occupations today and strong indications that markets will get even tighter, particularly for knowledge-intensive jobs. Most hospitals recruit for nurses on a continuous basis because they are constantly understaffed. Often, advertisements for nurses today promise not only high pay but more involvement in their jobs and hospital management, bonuses of $3000 or more for signing up, bonuses for staying on the job a certain length of time, flexible work schedules, child care, and free tuition for advanced courses. Some employers even offer maid service and free housing for nurses who are willing to work at various locations based on demand. Many high-tech manufacturing firms recruit for engineers and computer programmers year round as well. Several U.S. computer companies recruit heavily in foreign countries—in particular, India, Taiwan, Russia, and South Africa. Computer Consulting Services Corporation of Montvale, New Jersey, has a technical staff that is 90 percent imported. Some companies have difficulty filling even the unskilled positions. The fast-food industry, for example, beset by turnover rates in excess of 300 percent (three incumbents for every job in 1 year), often advertises and takes applications for counter personnel throughout the year for many locations. Many companies have mobile recruiting units which visit high schools and shopping malls to solicit applications. McDonald's cooperates with the American Association of Retired Persons (AARP) to attract senior citizens for hard-to-fill counter-personnel positions. AMC Theatres also concentrates its recruiting on senior citizens. Chemical Bank in New York must interview 50 applicants to find 1 who can be successfully trained as a teller. In general, the changing demographics of the U.S. workforce and the changing nature of the demands of work indicate that recruitment will be more challenging in the years to come. As one expert put it, "Until the economy stabilizes, salaries are raised in many areas of health care and education, and our school systems improve, human resource professionals will continue to be faced with the current crisis in employee recruitment."[35]

Internal Recruitment Sources

There are two general sources of recruiting: internal and external. Internal recruiting seeks applicants for positions from among the ranks of those currently employed. With the exception of entry-level positions, most organizations try to fill positions with current employees (one survey indicated 96 percent of companies use internal recruiting beyond entry-level positions).[36]

There are three major advantages to internal recruiting. First, it is considerably less costly than external recruiting. Second, organizations typically have a better knowledge of internal applicants' skills and abilities than that which can be acquired of candidates in an external recruiting effort. Through performance appraisal and other sources of information about current personnel, decision makers typically have much more extensive knowledge of internal candidates and thus make more valid selection decisions. Third, an organizational policy of promoting from within can enhance employees' morale, organizational commitment, and job satisfaction. These variables have been shown to be correlated with lower employee turnover rates and higher productivity.

There are disadvantages to internal recruiting as well. One theory is that the approach simply perpetuates the old ways of doing things—that creative problem solving may be hindered by the lack of "new blood." Some organizations complain of unit raiding, in which divisions compete for the same people. For example, raiding for clerical positions is quite common in universities, where position descriptions (PDs) can be written in such a way that a secretary may move to a new position in another department for a higher salary. A third possible disadvantage is that politics probably has a greater impact on internal recruiting and selection than does external recruiting. Thus, while more job-related information may be known about internal candidates, personnel decisions involving internal candidates are more likely to be affected by the political agendas of the decision makers.

Internal recruiting programs must be carefully integrated with other HR functions. Effective HR succession planning, job analysis, personnel selection, and performance appraisal are all important for an effective system which can fill required positions with the most qualified personnel in the shortest amount of time. Administrators of such programs should be knowledgeable about EEO legislation and litigation, as numerous lawsuits have been filed related to internal recruiting and placement decisions. The Civil Rights Act of 1991 mandated a study of the "glass ceiling" effect in U.S. business, a theory that most women and minorities are blocked from high-level executive positions. A 1992 study proposes a "glass wall" effect as well which deprives women of lateral movement into critical positions such as marketing, production, and sales management. Experience in these jobs is often viewed as essential for advancement to senior-level positions.[37]

While most large companies have formal succession plans at the managerial level, a much lower percentage of small to medium-size firms have formal systems. A job posting system can enhance the effectiveness of internal recruiting. Job posting is a process in which announcements of positions are made available to all current employees through company newsletters, bulletin boards, etc. Surprisingly, only a small percentage of organizations have formal systems of job posting for vacant positions within the organization. When properly implemented, job posting systems can substantially improve the quality of the job placements which are made within an organization and protect the organization from EEO complaints. Figure 5.6 presents guidelines for effective job posting systems.

External Recruitment Sources

External recruiting concerns recruitment from outside the organization. One of the biggest advantages of external recruiting is that the approach can facilitate the introduction of new ideas and thinking into corporate decision making. A major disadvantage is that the introduction of new personnel may have a negative impact on work group cohesion and morale. Also, new personnel from outside the organization typically take longer to learn the ropes of the job. Another possible disadvantage is that external recruiting can be very costly. For example, companies have paid in excess of $50,000 to executive search firms for locating a single high-level manager. The Employment Management Association estimates that the average cost per hire for external recruiting is about $5000.[38] Several methods of external recruitment are discussed below.

WALK-INS. The most common and least expensive approach for candidates is direct applications, in which job seekers submit unsolicited material (e.g., a résumé) or simply show up in person seeking employment. Direct applications can also provide a pool of potential employees to meet future needs. While direct applications are particularly effective in filling entry-level and unskilled positions, some organizations, because of their reputations or geographical locations, compile excellent pools of potential employees from direct applications for skilled positions.

REFERRALS. A second source of recruiting is current employee referrals. Some organizations have formal systems of employee referral for occupations with great demand. P&W, for example, pays current employees a $500 bonus if engineers whom they refer are ultimately

FIGURE 5.6

Plan

    Outline the details of the system

    Involve the employees in planning

Determine Eligibility Requirements

    Tenure with company

    Time in recent position

    Allowable number of annual bids

    Allowable number of simultaneous bids

    Lateral transfer

    Status with company

Outline Job Requirements and Content

    Job title and department

    List of specific tasks, duties, responsibilities

    List of job specifications (e.g., training, experience, education)

    Salary ranges

    Application process

    Deadlines

    Work schedule

    Format

    Affirmative action statements

Establish Employee Awareness

    Maximize employee awareness of positions

Establish Time Frames

    Time between posting and application deadline

    Time to notify applicants of hiring decisions

    Time given the superior prior to his or her subordinate's switching jobs

Determine Policies for Notifying Present Supervisor

    Informed prior to bidding?

    Informed only if subordinate seriously considered?

    Informed only if employee selected?

Determine Applicant Review Procedures

Provide Applicant Feedback

    Notification of decision in writing

    If not hired, outline reasons

Establish an Appeals Procedure

Source: L. S. Kleiman and K. J. Clark, Recruitment: An effective job posting system. *Personnel Journal, 63,* 20, 22, 25, February 1984. Reprinted with permission.

hired and work for the company for at least 1 year. While formal systems of referral are more effective in attracting interested applicants, there is also some evidence that the quality of the applicants is lower than that which results from informal referrals.[39]

The extensive use of employee referrals can also cause EEO problems. In *EEOC v. Detroit Edison*, the court concluded that "the practice of relying on referrals by a predominantly white workforce rather than seeking new employees in the marketplace for jobs was discriminatory."[40]

ADVERTISING.   A third common method of recruiting is advertising. Advertising can range from a simple classified ad to an elaborate media campaign on radio or television. The approach can be quite versatile in its ability to provide information about job opportunities while targeting specific labor markets in particular geographical areas. While the majority of advertising is in newspapers, many organizations go beyond the typical newspaper ads for tight labor markets. You have undoubtedly seen TV commercials extolling the virtues of starting a career in the armed forces (Operation Desert Storm had a profound effect on armed forces recruiting). Xerox, Merrill Lynch, General Telephone and Electronics (GTE), and Dow Chemical are among the companies which use television to attract applicants for hard-to-fill positions.[41] One survey found that 88 percent of surveyed companies used newspaper ads to fill positions, and 40 percent of the firms advertised in trade or professional journals.[42]

Most experts agree that the advertising must contain the following information: (1) the job content (primary tasks and responsibilities); (2) a realistic description of working conditions, particularly if they are unusual; (3) the location of the job; (4) the compensation, including the fringe benefits; (5) job specifications (e.g., education, experience); and (6) to whom one applies.[43]

Since advertising can be very expensive, record keeping on the successes of the various media sources can help to identify the approaches with the biggest potential payoff for future recruiting. Figure 5.7 presents a summary of some of the advantages and disadvantages of the various media options.

EEO considerations are also critical for advertising.[44] A men's clothing retailer decided to target younger men with its new fall line. As part of that effort, they advertised for "young, energetic" assistant managers at the same time that they were firing a 48-year-old man who had been with the company for 10 years. An ADEA lawsuit resulted in an out-of-court settlement in excess of $100,000. If the organization is using an advertising agency to prepare its ads, a person knowledgeable about EEO laws should review all materials for potential problems.

EMPLOYMENT AGENCIES.   Employment agencies are used by many companies for identifying potential workers. There are publicly funded agencies which provide free placement services and private agencies which charge either the employee or the employer for a placement or referral. The major functions of these agencies are to increase the pool of possible applicants and to do preliminary screening. Private agencies are most effective when: (1) the organization has had difficulty in building a pool of qualified applicants, (2) the organization is not equipped to develop a sophisticated recruitment effort, (3) there is a need to fill a position quickly, (4) the organization is explicitly recruiting minorities or females, and (5) the organization is attempting to recruit individuals who are not actively seeking employment.[45]

There are about 2400 federally funded but state-run employment agencies under the U.S. Training and Employment Service (USTES). All persons drawing unemployment compensation must apply through one of these agencies. The most recent approach to job placement under USTES is to attempt to match applicants' aptitudes and interests with the requirements of the job. In general, neither employers nor employees are satisfied with the service which is offered, but efforts are being made to improve the service.[46]

SEARCH FIRMS.   In selecting a search firm, experts recommend the following criteria: (1) The firm has restricted its recruiting to specific industries. (2) The firm pays its sales personnel based on the completion of an assignment. (3) The firm uses primary data sources rather than secondary sources such as computerized lists of potential candidates and association directories. (4) Firms which also do outplacement services should be avoided. (Outplacement is a professional service for terminated employees, which may include placement in another job.)

Many recruiting firms now specialize in "targeted" recruiting for middle-management jobs. One of the largest firms is DHR International, which, for one fee, provides a list of candidates whose credentials match job specifications and, for an additional fee, completes the search process.

The fees for search firms can be very high, with estimates ranging from 20 to 50 percent of the first-year salaries of the individuals placed. Reviews on the effectiveness of search firms are rather mixed. According to one review, 50 percent of the filled job searches take twice as long to fill as promised. Fewer than 50 percent of contracts to fill positions are actually filled.[47] More search firms are now charging a flat rate rather than a percentage of salary. Says one recruiter, "By charging a flat rate, we are able to remain objective in presenting candidates to the client. We do not show only the high-priced

FIGURE 5.7

Type of Medium	Advantages	Disadvantages	When to Use
Newspapers	Short deadlines. Ad size flexibility. Circulation concentrated in specific geographic areas. Classified sections are well organized for easy access by active job seekers.	Easy for prospects to ignore. Considerable competitive clutter. Circulation not specialized; you must pay for a great number of unwanted readers. Poor printing quality.	When you want to limit recruiting to a specific area. When sufficient numbers of prospects are clustered in a specific area. When enough prospects are reading help-wanted ads to fill hiring needs.
Magazines	Specialized magazines reach pinpointed occupation categories. Ad size flexibility. High-quality printing. Prestigious environment. Long life; prospects keep and reread magazines.	Wide geographic circulation—usually cannot be used to limit recruiting to a specific area. Long lead time for ad placement.	When job is specialized. When time and geographic limitations are not of utmost importance. When involved in ongoing recruiting programs.
Directories	Specialized audiences. Long life.	Not timely. Often have competitive clutter.	Appropriate only for ongoing recruiting programs.
Direct mail	Most personal form of advertising. Unlimited number of formats and amount of space. By selecting names by zip code, mailing can be pinpointed to precise geographic area.	Difficult to find mailing list of prospects by occupation at home addresses. Cost for reaching each prospect is high.	If the right mailing list can be found, this is potentially the most effective medium; no other medium gives the prospect as much a feeling of being specially selected. Particularly valuable in competitive situations.
Radio and television	Difficult to ignore. Can reach prospects who are not actively looking for a job better than newspapers and magazines. Can be limited to specific geographic areas. Creatively flexible. Can dramatize employment story more effectively than printed ads. Little competitive recruitment clutter.	Only brief, uncomplicated messages are possible. Lack of performance; prospect cannot refer back to ad. (Repeated airings are necessary to make an impression.) Creation and production of commercials—particularly TV—can be time-consuming and costly. Lack of special interest selectivity; paying for waste circulation.	In competitive situations when not enough prospects are reading your printed ads. When there are multiple job openings and there are enough prospects in a specific geographic area. When a large impact is needed quickly, a "blitz" campaign can saturate an area in 2 weeks or less. Useful to call attention to printed ads.

Source: "Planning for recruitment advertising: Part II," by B. S. Hodes, copyright June 1983. Reprinted with the permission of *Personnel Journal,* Costa Mesa, CA.

candidates; we show the most qualified." Many companies have begun to demand the flat-fee approach because of the tendency of percentage-based recruiters to recommend high-priced candidates.[48]

CAMPUS VISITS. One major source of recruiting for professional and managerial positions is the college campus. Numerous organizations, and in particular the larger organizations, send recruiters to campuses several times a year to inform graduates and future graduates about career opportunities. One survey found that 50 percent of all managers and professionals with less than 3 years of experience were hired through college recruiting.[49] There is no question that college recruiting is successful at filling vacancies. There is a question, however, about the extent to which vacancies are filled with the most qualified people.

The cost of college recruiting can be enormous. One conservative estimate of the cost is almost $2000 per hired graduate.[50] Despite this substantial cost, program evaluation is rarely done and little attention is given to recruiting processes.[51] When evaluation is done, the criterion for evaluation is simply filled vacancies or number of offers accepted rather than a measure of the quality of those who are recruited. Recruiters also receive little guidance on interviewing procedures, despite evidence that the interviewing format is important for the accuracy of the predictions which are made.

The recruiting process should commence long before there are any recruiting visits to the campus. Recruiters should become familiar with the university and its personnel before the recruiting visit. Job descriptions and specifications should be mailed to the campus before the recruiter arrives. Another good strategy is to set up internship programs through the university.[52] In general, the most effective college recruiting efforts are those which facilitate a long-term relationship with the college through a variety of cooperative programs between the school and the organization. Again, record keeping on past experience will be very helpful in planning future campus recruiting. NCR, for example, uses a computer to centralize its entire college recruiting operation. Résumés are entered on the computer upon receipt, along with applicant preferences for certain job characteristics. Also, recruiters can instantly retrieve extensive information about a particular school, as well as status reports on particular candidates.[53] Due to the expense of college recruiting, reliable yield ratios are even more important. Computerized systems like NCR's are ideal for future planning.

One of the largest recruiters of college graduates is the federal government. Recent research on the ability of the government to attract the most qualified graduates is not encouraging. One survey found that only 38 percent of graduates were interested in careers with the federal government. The private sector was viewed as offering more prestige and power than the public sector.[54] The research also indicated that the government could do a much better job of recruiting graduates through more on-campus visits and a concerted effort to dissolve its less favorable public image.

OTHER SOURCES. Two other recruiting sources which should be mentioned are professional associations and computerized services. The first is professional societies or associations within specialized areas. College faculty in business, for example, are often recruited through the Academy of Management and other academic associations. A burgeoning new area of recruiting is computerized job listings. Connexions of Cambridge, Massachusetts, for example, charges an employer over $600 for an eight-paragraph ad. Job applicants pay $15 to look at the complete listings. Connexions has the system set up in such a way that a candidate can log on and apply for a job immediately through the computer. Several other computerized services are now available, and the preliminary evaluations are positive. Sears, Roebuck and Company, for example, filled six mid-level technical jobs in 1989 using a computerized service. The staffing manager concluded that compared to normal advertising, "the computerized data base won hands over fist."[55] Intel Corporation recently filled 19 jobs through University Pronet, a data base of graduates from several universities. Philip Morris uses the services of the Career Placement Registry, which has 125,000 résumés in a data base. Electronic job descriptions and résumés may become commonplace in the near future.

Recruiting, Affirmative Action, and Illegal Hiring

As discussed in Chapter 3, Executive Order 11246 requires that contractors and subcontractors with more than $50,000 in federal government business must take affirmative action to ensure that applicants and employees are recruited for vacant positions. The Office of Federal Contract Compliance Programs (OFCCP) requires submission of a formal affirmative action plan which should include "targets or goals" to bring the number of minority and female workers to the approximate levels in the available labor pool. According to the OFCCP, such goals should be "affirmatively pursued."

The OFCCP conducts compliance reviews, which often end in a conciliation agreement that the company will make special recruitment efforts and other adjustments in HRM staffing policy. Failure to comply can ultimately lead to debarment, where the OFCCP renders a company ineligible for government contract work. (Over 50 companies have been debarred.)

Recruitment with affirmative action should follow a policy similar to the following: 1. Conduct an evaluation of the workforce to identify underrepresentation at entry level and beyond; 2. Identify the target labor markets after evaluating the job relatedness and business need of all job specifications; 3. Develop a recruitment, training, and career development strategy; 4. Prepare all job announcements; and 5. Start the recruitment campaign. Organizations are probably on the safest legal ground, and certainly the most advantageous competitively, if they adhere to a pure affirmative action policy in which they make a concerted effort to expand the pool of candidates to include culturally diverse representation from all minority groups and women. The decision to hire or promote, however, is based solely on qualifications.

As Robert E. Allen, CEO of AT&T, puts it: "Affirmative action is not just the right thing to do, it's a business necessity." The Council on Career Development for Minorities, Inc., based in Dallas, Texas, is an excellent source for recruiters and students. In addition, there are several excellent computerized sources of information on minority candidates.

Employers must abide by the Immigration Reform and Control Act (IRCA), which went into effect in 1988. The IRCA holds employers responsible for screening applicants' eligibility for lawful employment, the goal of which is to stop the flow of illegal immigrants. The employer's duty is not to recruit, hire, or continue to employ "unauthorized aliens," and to verify the identity of each new employee. One negative aspect of the IRCA is that there have been numerous complaints of discrimination against Hispanic Americans who claim employers will not hire them because they fear IRCA violations. Employers must require documentation of each applicant's status.

What Method of Recruiting Is Most Effective?

There have been few studies comparing the effects of different methods for recruitment. The criteria which have been used in these studies also differ; they include cost per hire, number of résumés, time lapse from recruiting to filling the vacancy, interview/invitation ratio, applicant performance on the job, and job tenure or turnover. A recent emphasis has also been placed on minority hiring patterns as a function of the recruiting effort and relative to population statistics and census data on potential employees. These comparisons may be critical if EEO litigation is pending.

In general, the comparative studies on recruitment methods suggest that the more informal methods (e.g., walk-ins, referrals) are more likely to lead to longer job tenure than the more formal sources, such as newspaper ads.[56] Newspaper ads typically generate the greatest number of applicants for a position, as compared to the other methods. Another study found that people who had previously worked for the organization had superior performance records, longer job tenure, and better attendance.[57]

Many of the problems in recruiting may be a consequence of the way in which recruiters are rewarded. Recent research has shown that criteria pertaining to the organization's direct costs of recruiting are the ones on which recruiters are typically evaluated.[58] For example, recruiters for a large manufacturing company in the South are compensated in relation to a cost-per-hire measure, or what one staff member refers to as the "warm-body" phenomenon. This emphasis on cost figures may explain the general lack of systematic research relating recruiting methods to higher-level criteria such as work quality. In the context of affirmative action, persons assigned to meet specific EEO goals or timetables are often evaluated on the extent to which they meet the goals or timetables rather than on the extent to which the positions have been filled with qualified personnel. The conflicting incentives of recruiters and line management can cause problems when the time comes to make job offers.

The effectiveness of the various methods of recruiting has also been shown to vary as a function of particular method characteristics. For example, college recruiting is apparently enhanced when the recruiter is between the ages of 30 and 55, is perceived to have stature in the company (line managers are preferred to professional recruiters), is verbally fluent with good interpersonal skills, and has an extensive knowledge of the company and the particular job.[59] The success of any recruiting effort, however, is more dependent on the job characteristics themselves. College students, for example, place the greatest weight on pay, fringe benefits, and the type of work. Recruiters often underestimate the importance of such factors relative to others.[60]

Philosophies of Recruiting

The traditional philosophy of recruiting has been to get as many people to apply for a job as possible. The idea is to obtain the lowest possible selection ratio (SR) given a fixed recruiting cost. A *selection ratio* is the proportion of job openings to applicants. An SR of 0.10 means there are 10 applicants for every job opening. A lower SR is more desirable to a firm because it enables an organization to be more selective in the people actually hired. This assumption holds true as long as the cost of recruiting from that larger pool is not exorbitant.

A persuasive argument can be made that matching the needs of the organization to the needs of the applicant will enhance the effectiveness of the recruitment process.[61] The result will be a workforce which is likely to stay with the organization longer and to perform at a higher level of effectiveness. In the context of this matching philosophy, a process of realistic recruitment is recommended. An important component of realistic recruiting is a "realistic job preview" (RJP). RJPs provide the characteristics of the job to applicants so that they can evaluate the compatibility of this realistic presentation of the job with their own work preferences. Applicants for bank teller jobs at Sun Bank are told that they will spend most of the workday on their feet, that some customers will be rude and demanding, that some work periods will be particularly stressful, and that they will be expected to work on alternate Saturdays. RJPs can result in a self-selection process which screens out people who are most likely to have difficulty on the job. The Marine Corps shows a video of what boot camp is like at Parris Island. The video dissuades a lot of visitors to Marine recruiting stations. Applicants who are hired after being exposed to an RJP are also better able to cope because they have more realistic expectations about the job.[62] Many companies doing international work provide extensive RJPs for potential expatriates and their families. Bechtel, the giant construction company, provides a 60-minute video of life in Saudi Arabia which engineers and their spouses view before they make a commitment for a 1-year assignment.

Research on realistic recruiting shows lower rates of employee turnover for employees recruited with RJPs, particularly for more complex jobs, and higher levels of job satisfaction and performance at the initial stages of employment. RJPs are more beneficial for organizations hiring at the entry level, when there are low selection ratios (i.e., many applicants per position), and under conditions of relatively low unemployment (i.e., where people have more job options). Otherwise, the approach may increase the cost of recruiting by increasing the average time it takes to fill each position.[63]

Another approach to staffing which fits into the matching philosophy is the use of the Job Compatibility Questionnaire (JCQ) discussed in Chapter 4 and illustrated in Chapter 6.[64] The JCQ provides a quantitative match between job applicant preferences and the actual characteristics of a job, including compensation, benefits, work schedule, customer interactions, and the work to be performed. Data from the JCQ can also be used to construct a realistic job preview.

Understanding the Recruits

Effective recruiting requires that the organization know what potential applicants are thinking—what their needs and desires are regarding all major characteristics of the job. For example, how important are the various elements of the fringe benefit package? Are applicants interested in special work schedules, child care, particular work locations? Organizations also need to be keenly aware of how candidates search for jobs. What outlets do they rely on for job information? To what extent do they rely on outside referral agencies for job placement? Should recruitment be restricted to specific geographical areas based on the search behavior of potential candidates? At least some answers to these questions can be gathered over time based on the past recruiting successes and failures of the organization. Recruitment is one area of HRM in which a computerized system of detailed record keeping would be most beneficial for recruiting efforts in the future. Unfortunately, most organizations rely on recruiters' "hunches" to make decisions. They do little to organize their past recruiting efforts in such a way that systematic research could help to determine their future strategies. Research indicates that these hunches are not particularly accurate. Several computerized data processing systems are now available for maintaining critical information related to past recruiting efforts.

HRP AND RECRUITMENT FOR MULTINATIONAL CORPORATIONS

The majority of Fortune 500 companies are now multinational in nature in that some portion of their business (and profits) are derived from overseas operations. Some of the largest, most prestigious U.S. companies (e.g., Merck, Pepsico, IBM, Exxon, Shell, Coca-Cola) derive close to 50 percent of their revenues from overseas business. Given the immense market potential of the Eastern bloc and the level of interest and activity in the new Soviet Commonwealth, this figure is likely to get even higher for many U.S. corporations. Approximately 25,000 U.S. firms have offices overseas, with over 33 percent of business profits from overseas functions. Unfortunately, the relationship between HRP and strategic planning for international ventures is even weaker than for U.S. operations, despite the fact that many experts regard HR issues as more important to the success of an overseas operation than domestic operations.

All agree that international HRM is more complicated than domestic HRM. All six of the HRM domains we discussed in Chapters 1 and 2 are more complicated with regard to international HRM. Planning and design are more unpredictable because of the importance of volatile environmental and political issues in the host country which can affect the overseas operations. For example, after considerable success penetrating the Japanese market, Milwaukee-based Harley-Davidson has had to respond to considerable Japanese political pressure directed at restricting their growth. The pressure is affecting their forecasts of market penetration in Japan. If anything, an increase in the 60 percent market share Harley now has in the United States is encouraged by local politics.

Terrorism is taken very seriously with regard to overseas assignments and operations, and it seriously disrupts planning and recruitment. Needless to say (and unfortunately), the level and extent of terrorist activity are unpredictable. The implications of the 1992 European Community are still unclear in terms of HRM activities. Of course, the current state of virtually all former Eastern bloc nations makes planning and market forecasting for these new potential markets extremely tenuous. The skilled labor pool in the Asia Pacific Region (i.e., Malaysia, Phillippines, Singapore, Taiwan, Indonesia) is not very favorable. There is a shortage of skilled workers and professionals.

All of the other five major activity domains (i.e., staffing, communications and public relations, performance management, reward systems and compliance, and employee development) are more difficult and more unpredictable in overseas operations not only because of environmental volatility but also because many of the methods which have proved effective in U.S. settings do not necessarily work for international staffing, performance management, and the other domains. The insurance industry, for example, puts considerable weight on biographical information in the selection of insurance agents. The validity of methods for predicting sales success, which we will discuss in Chapter 6, has never been studied for overseas sales and thus may not apply in the hiring of expatriate Americans, in-country nationals, or third-country nationals.

Within the rewards/compliance domain of HRM activities, issues related to family, housing, dependent care and schooling, spouse employment, taxation, and health care tend to complicate the international HRM function. These issues also make the economic and psychological implications of errors in international HRM relatively greater than in domestic assignments.

One recent study identified the critical issues affecting planning and recruitment aspects of international HRM for the 1990s.[65] The major challenges were: (1) identifying top managerial talent early in the process, (2) identifying criteria for success in overseas assignments, (3) motivating employees to take overseas assignments, and (4) establishing a stronger connection between the strategic plan of the company and HRP. Few experts would argue with the contention that these challenges are more onerous with international planning and recruitment. The third challenge, motivating employees to take overseas assignments, may prove to be a problem for a while. One 1989 survey, for example, found that 56 percent of personnel managers working for 56 multinational corporations indicated that a foreign assignment is either detrimental to or immaterial for one's career. Only 20 percent consider their companies' repatriation policies adequate to meet the needs of returning expatriates.[66] Lawrence Buckley, personnel manager for GE, for example, says the "re-entry process isn't as smooth as you'd like it to be." He states that GE is making progress in this area but that it is "still a problem for us and U.S. industry in general."[67] Whereas many managers still perceive an overseas assignment as a banishment of sorts, corporations now place more and considerable weight on overseas experience as a requirement for high-level executive assignments. For example, Honeywell, Allied-Signal, and Rohm & Haas all virtually require overseas assignments prior to senior management placement. Robert Eaton, the

head of GM's European operations, was certainly not a forgotten man. Chrysler named him to succeed Lee Iacocca in 1993. With the increased sophistication of international communications and the growing importance of international operations for corporate strategy, studies showing managers perceiving a loss of visibility at headquarters due to overseas assignments probably apply less today than only a few years ago.

Underlying all HRM challenges is the strategic position of the multinational corporation regarding the relationship of the overseas operation to the parent company. The recruitment strategy for overseas assignments is directly tied to this strategic position. U.S. companies may recruit and select from one (or more) of three sources: (1) the pool of U.S. personnel who would be expatriated to the foreign assignment, (2) the pool of candidates from the country of the overseas operations, and (3) candidates from all nationalities. Ethnocentrism, the policy of using only home-country executives for overseas assignments, really makes sense either financially or strategically only when the company is just starting the operation. Otherwise, the disadvantages of this approach far outweigh the advantages. Japanese companies using this philosophy in their U.S. operations have encountered a number of problems, including a proliferation of EEO lawsuits and, in particular, age discrimination cases as Japanese companies replace American managers over the age of 40 with sometimes younger, Japanese managers. The use of nationals in overseas operations can reduce language and cultural problems, the need for expensive training programs, and of course the tremendous cost of placing expatriates and their families in overseas assignments. Japanese women may be one major pool of highly skilled workers which American companies could tap for penetration into Japanese markets. As we discussed in Chapter 3, Japanese females are still subjected to considerable employment discrimination in their own country and are very attracted to U.S. corporations for this reason. As we said earlier, however, there is a shortage of skilled workers in almost all of the Asia Pacific region. The geocentric policy of hiring the best person regardless of nationality is the formal policy of choice for most large U.S. corporations but is certainly not without its problems. Such a management team may have more difficulties than usual in communicating with each other and in understanding the subtle implications of cultural differences.

For a U.S. corporation that maintains a close strategic relationship with its overseas division (as opposed to a philosophy of autonomous operations), the most common strategy for managerial recruitment and job placement is a balance between expatriates and nationals. Sales and production personnel are typically recruited from the national pool. Companies which have a "hands-off" managerial philosophy about autonomous foreign operations they may have acquired or developed typically use expatriates in coordination with nationals until the parent company is comfortable with the operation and until the profits of the foreign division are acceptable. Most of the expatriates may then be recalled, to reduce the overhead of the operation. At least this was the trend in 1989 when one survey found that about 150,000 employees now work abroad, down almost 25 percent from 1986 figures.[68]

SUMMARY

HRP seeks to place the right employees in the right jobs at the right time, thereby providing the means for an organization to pursue its competitive strategy and fulfill its mission. Planning improves an organization's ability to create and sustain competitive advantage and to cope with PTOs arising from change—technological, social, political, and environmental. HRP systematically attempts to forecast personnel demand, assess supply, and reconcile the two. Personnel demand can be assessed by using qualitative methods such as the Delphi technique and quantitative methods. Internal supply may be forecast by using HRIS, replacement charts, and Markov analysis. Internal shortages are resolved through training and/or recruitment. The information gathered is used in action planning to develop an HR strategy. HRP is an ongoing process in which control and evaluation procedures are necessary to guide activities. Deviations from the plan and their causes must be identified in order to assess whether the plan should be revised.

Recruitment is the process of finding and attracting applicants who are interested in and qualified for position vacancies. Recruitment should encompass both the attraction and the selection of the most qualified personnel. The ideal recruitment program is one in which a sufficient number of qualified applicants are attracted to and ultimately accept positions in an efficient manner. Unfortunately, the typical assessment of recruitment policies, programs, and personnel in the past has focused simply on whether positions were filled and on the cost and speed of filling positions, rather than evaluating the quality of the personnel who were hired and placed. The most recent writing on recruitment, however, has placed a greater emphasis on the quality dimension of the recruiting effort. There is increasing evidence that the various approaches to recruiting result in different outcomes for the organization. The evaluation of recruiting programs in the future is thus more likely to focus on the quality dimension of the people who are hired in addition to the "body-count" criteria which are typically used. We have emphasized the quality criterion in this chapter, and advocate the "matching" philosophy for personnel recruiting. This philosophy can also shape the personnel selection process which we will address in Chapter 6.

DISCUSSION QUESTIONS

1. How should HRP involve a comparison with competitors? What critical data are required in order to assess competitive advantage?
2. Why is planning an important activity? What are some of the advantages of effective planning?
3. Some organizations do a thorough job analysis first and then HRP as part of a restructuring process. Others do HRP first and then job analysis. What makes more sense to you and why?
4. Discuss the possible pros and cons of the two qualitative methods of forecasting labor demand.
5. If actual performance of the HR plan differs from desired performance, what remedial steps might you use?
6. Employee referral is a popular method of recruiting candidates. What are its advantages and disadvantages?
7. What are the advantages and disadvantages of the various external recruitment sources?
8. What are the effects of the "glass ceiling" and "glass wall"? What are the causes of these barriers and how can they be prevented?
9. Suppose a key employee has just resigned and you are the department manager. After you have sent your request to personnel for a replacement, how could you help the recruiter to find the best replacement?

NOTES

1. Jackson, S. E., and Schuler, R. S. (February 1990). Human resource planning. *American Psychologist*, pp. 223–239. See also: Dyer, L. (ed.) (1986) *Human resource planning: Tested practices in five U.S. and Canadian companies.* New York: Random House. Schuler, R. S., and Jackson, S. E. (August 1987). Linking human resource practices with competitive strategies. *Academy of Management Executive*, 1(3), 207–219. Cascio, W. F., and Zammuto, R. F. (1989). "Societal trends and staffing policies." In W. F. Cascio (ed.), *Human resource planning employment and placement,* ASPA/BNA Series. Washington: Bureau of National Affairs.
2. Lawrence, S. (April 1989). Voice of HR experience. *Personnel Journal*, p. 70.
3. Ballen, K. (Feb. 10, 1992). America's most admired corporations. *Fortune*, p. 43.
4. Tichy, N., Fombrun, C., and Devanna, M. (1982). Strategic human resource management. *Sloan Management Review*, 23, 47.

5. Pounds, W. F. (1969). The process of problem finding. *Industrial Management Review, 11,* 1–19.

6. Baytos, L. M. (1984). A "no-frills" approach to human resource planning. *Human Resource Planning, 7,* 39–46. See also: Olian, J. D., and Rynes, S. L. (1984). Organizational staffing: Integrating practice with strategy. *Industrial Relations, 23,* 170–183. Burack, E. J. (1988). A strategic planning and operational agenda for human resources. *Human Resource Planning, 11,* 63–68. Dyer, L. (1982). Human resource planning. In K. M. Rowland and G. R. Ferris (eds.), *Personnel Management,* Boston, MA: Allyn & Bacon, pp. 31–47.

7. Bureau of Labor Statistics, U.S. Department of Labor, 1991.

8. Rydzel, J. A. (1988–1989). Plant-closing legislation—living with prenotification. *Employment Relations Today, 15,* 271–277. See also: Nowlin, W. A., and Sullivan, P. (1989). The plant closing law: Worker protection or government interference? *Industrial Management, 31,* 16–19.

9. See note 8.

10. Hall, D. T., and Goodale, J. G. (1986). *Human resource management: Strategy, design, and implementation.* Glenview, IL: Scott, Foresman. See also: Coates, J. F. (1987). An environmental scan: Projecting human resource trends. *Human Resource Planning, 10,* 209–210.

11. See note 10.

12. Burack, E. H. (1988). *Creative human resource planning and applications: A strategic approach.* Englewood Cliffs, NJ: Prentice-Hall. See also: Milliman, J., Von Glinow, M. A., and Nathan, M. (1991). Organizational life cycles and strategic international human resource management in MNCs: Implications for congruence theory. *Academy of Management Review, 16,* 318–339.

13. Hanson, G. B. (June 1985). Innovative approach to plant closings: The UAW-Ford experience at San Jose. *Monthly Labor Review,* pp. 34–37.

14. Ettlie, J. E. (1988). *Taking charge of manufacturing.* San Francisco: Jossey-Bass. See also: Majchrzak, A. (1988). *The human side of factory automation.* San Francisco: Jossey-Bass.

15. *Business Week* (Apr. 9, 1990). Here comes Saturn. pp. 56–61. See also: Larson, C. E., and Lafasto, F. M. J. (1989). *Teamwork: What must go right, what can go wrong.* Newbury Park, CA: Sage Publications.

16. Rucci, A. J., Lafasto, F. M. J., and Ulrich, D. (1990). Managing organizational change: A merger case study. Unpublished manuscript. See also: Page, R. C., and Van De Vort, D. M. (1989). Job analysis and HR planning. In W. F. Cascio (ed.), *Human resource planning employment and placement,* ASPA/BNA Series. Washington: Bureau of National Affairs.

17. Golden, K. A., and Ramanujam, V. (Winter 1985). Between a dream and a nightmare: On the integration of human resource management and strategic business planning processes. *Human Resource Management,* pp. 429–452.

18. Delbecq, A. L., Van de Ven, A. H., and Gustafson, D. H. (1975). *Group techniques for progress planning: A guide to nominal and Delphi processes.* Glenview, IL: Scott, Foresman.

19. Gannon, M. J. (1979). *Organizational behavior.* Boston, MA: Little Brown.

20. See note 18.

21. See note 18.

22. Wikstrom, W. S. (1971). *Manpower planning: Evolving systems.* New York: The Conference Board. See also: Piskor, W. G., and Dudding, R. C. (1978). A computer-assisted manpower planning model. In D. T. Bryant and R. J. Niehaus (eds.), *Manpower planning and organization design,* New York: Plenum Press, pp. 145–154. DeLuca, J. R. (1988). Strategic career management in nongrowing, volatile business environments. *Human Resource Planning, 11,* 49–62.

23. Greenlaw, P. S., and Kohl, J. P. (1986). *Personnel management: Managing human resources.* New York: Harper & Row.

24. Werther, W. B., Jr., and Davis, K. (1989). *Human resources and personnel management.* New York: McGraw-Hill.

25. Heneman, H. G., III, and Sandver, M. G. (October 1977). Markov analysis in human resource administration: Applications and limitations. *Academy of Management Review, 2*(4), 535–542. See also: Hooper, J. A., and Catelanello, R. E. (1981). Markov analysis applied to forecasting technical personnel, *Human Resource Planning, 4*(2), 41–47.

26. See note 25.

27. Buller, P. F., and Maki, W. R. (1981). A case history of a manpower planning model, *Human Resource Planning, 4,* 129–138.

28. Dyer, L. (1982). Human resource planning. In K. M. Rowland and G. R. Ferris (eds.), *Personnel management.* Boston: Allyn & Bacon, 31–47.

29. Walker, J. W. (1974). Evaluating the practical effectiveness of human resource planning applications. *Human Resource Management, 32,* 21–28. See also: Werther, W. B., Jr., and Davis, K. (1989). *Human resources and personnel management.* New York: McGraw-Hill.

30. Cameron, K. S., Freeman, S. J., and Mishra, A. K. (1991). Best practices in white collar downsizing: Managing contradictions. *Academy of Management Executive, 5,* 57–63. See also: McKinley, W. Decreasing organizational size: To untangle or not to untangle? *The Academy of Management Review, 17,* 112–123; Sutton, R. I., and D'Aunno, T. (1992). Building a model of work force reduction that is grounded in pertinent theory and data: Reply to McKinley. *Academy of Management Review, 17,* 124–137. Francis, G. J., Mohr, J., and Andersen, K. (1992). HR balancing: Alternative downsizing. *Personnel Journal, 71,* 71–80.

31. Munchus, G. (1988). Employee leasing: Benefits and threats, *Personnel, 65,* 59–61. See also: Simonetti, J. L., Nykodym, N., and Sell, L. M. (1988). Temporary employees: A permanent boom? *Personnel, 65,* 50–56.

32. See note 31.

33. Brocklyn, P. L. (May 1988). Employer recruitment practices. *Personnel,* pp. 63–65.

34. See note 33.

35. See note 33, p. 65.

36. HRM Update (January 1985). *Personnel Administrator*, p. 16.

37. Lopez, J. A. (Mar. 3, 1992). Study says women face glass walls as well as ceilings. *The Wall Street Journal*, pp. B1, B2.

38. Meyers, M. (1987). Is your recruitment all it can be? *Personnel Journal, 66*, 56.

39. Brocklyn, P. L. (May 1988). Employer recruitment practices. *Personnel*, 63–65. See also: Laabs, J. J. (May 1991). Affirmative outreach. *Personnel Journal*, 86–93.

40. *EEOC v. Detroit Edison* (1975). 515 F.2d 301 (6th Cir.). See also: Schenkel-Savitt, S., and Seltzer, S. P. (1987–1988). Recruitment as a successful means of affirmative action. *Employee Relations Law Journal, 13*(3), 465–470.

41. Hodes, B. S. (1982). *The principles and practice of recruitment advertising. A guide for personnel professionals.* New York: Frederick Fell. See also: Bucalo, J. P. (1983). Good advertising can be more effective than other recruitment tools. *Personnel Administrator*, pp. 73–79. Caldwell, D. F., and Spivey, W. A. (1983). The relationship between recruiting source and employee success: An analysis by race. *Personnel Psychology, 36*, 67–72. Decker, P. J., and Cornelius, E. T. (1979). A note on recruiting sources and job survival rates. *Journal of Applied Psychology, 64*, 463–464.

42. Rubenfeld, S., and Crino, M. (1981). Are employment agencies jeopardizing your selection process? *Personnel, 58*, 71.

43. Hodes, B. S. (1982). *The principles and practice of recruitment advertising: A guide for personnel professionals.* New York: Frederick Fell.

44. National Research Council (1989). *Fairness in employment testing.* Washington: National Academy Press.

45. Dee, W. (1983). Evaluating a search firm. *Personnel Administrator, 28*, 41–43, 99–100.

46. Fowler, E. M. (Nov. 14, 1989). Recruiters focusing techniques. *The New York Times*, p. Y35.

47. Dee, W. (1983). Evaluating a search firm. *Personnel Administrator, 28*, 41–43, 99–100.

48. See note 46.

49. Lindquist, V. R., and Endicott, F. S. (1989). *Trends in the employment of college and university graduates in business and industry.* Evanston, IL: Northwestern University.

50. Rynes, S. L., and Boudreau, J. W. (1986). College recruiting in large organizations: Practice, evaluation, and research implications. *Personnel Psychology, 39*, 729–757.

51. See note 50.

52. Hanigan, M. (1987). Campus recruiters upgrade their pitch. *Personnel Administrator, 32*, 56.

53. Lubbock, J. E. (August 1983). A look at centralized college recruiting. *Personnel Administrator*, 28–30.

54. U.S. Merit Systems Protection Board (1988). *Attracting quality graduates to the federal government: A view of college recruiting.* Washington: U.S. Merit Systems Protection Board.

55. Deutsch, C. H. (May 6, 1990). Headhunting from a data base. *The New York Times*, p. F25.

56. Kleiman, L. S., and Clark, K. J. (1984). Recruitment: An effective job posting system. *Personnel Journal, 63*, 20, 22, 25. See also: Taylor, M. S., and Schmidt, D. W. (1983). A process oriented investigation of recruitment source effectiveness. *Personnel Psychology, 36*, 343–354. Breaugh, J. A. (1981). Relationships between recruiting sources and employee performance, absenteeism, and work attitudes. *Academy of Management Journal, 24*, 142–147. Rynes, S. L., Heneman, H. G., III, and Schwab, D. P. (1980). Individual reactions to organizational recruiting: A review. *Personnel Psychology, 33*, 529–542. Rynes, S. L., and Miller, H. E. (1983). Recruiter and job influences on candidates for employment. *Journal of Applied Psychology, 68*, 147–154.

57. Gannon, M. J. (1971). Source of referral and employee turnover. *Journal of Applied Psychology, 55*, 226–228.

58. Rynes, S. L. (1990). Recruitment, organizational entry, and early work adjustment. In M. D. Dunnette (ed.), *Handbook of industrial and organizational psychology*, 2d ed. Chicago, IL: Rand-McNally.

59. Bartol, K. M., and Martin, D. C. (1988). *Recruitment source as a resource: The value of pay-related information to part-time job applicants.* Paper presented at the annual meeting of the Academy of Management. See also: Taylor, M. S., and Bergmann, T. J. (1987). Organizational recruitment activities and applicants' reactions at different stages of the recruitment process. *Personnel Psychology, 40*(2), 261–285. Taylor, M. S., and Sniezek, J. A. (1984). The college recruitment interview: Topical content and applicant reactions. *Journal of Occupational Psychology, 57*, 47–56.

60. Giles, W. F., and Feild, H. S., Jr. (1982). Accuracy of interviewers' perceptions of the importance of intrinsic and extrinsic job characteristics to male and female applicants. *Academy of Management Journal, 24*, 148–157.

61. Wanous, J. P. (1980). *Organizational entry: Recruitment, selection and socialization of newcomers.* Reading, MA: Addison-Wesley. See also: Rynes, S. L., Bretz, R. D. Jr., and Gerhart, B. (1991). The importance of recruitment in job choice: A different way of looking. *Personnel Psychology, 44*, 487–522.

62. Premack, S. L., and Wanous, J. P. (1985). A meta-analysis of realistic job preview experiments. *Journal of Applied Psychology, 70*, 706–719. See also: Popovich, P., and Wanous, J. P. (1982). The realistic job preview as a persuasive communication. *Academy of Management Review, 7*, 570–579. Dean, R. A., and Wanous, J. P. (1984). The effects of realistic job previews on hiring bank tellers. *Journal of Applied Psychology, 69*, 61–68. Vandenberg, R. J., and Scarpello, V. (1990). The matching model: An examination of the processes underlying realistic job previews. *Journal of Applied Psychology, 75*, 60.

63. McEvoy, G. M., and Cascio, W. F. (1985). Strategies for reducing employee turnover: A meta-analysis. *Journal of Applied Psychology, 70*, 342–353.

64. Bernardin, H. J. (1989). Innovative approaches to personnel selection and performance appraisal. *Journal of Management Systems, 1,* 25–36.

65. Dowling, P. J. (1989). Hot issues overseas. *Personnel Administrator, 34,* 68–72. See also: Dowling, P. J., and Schuler, R. S. (1990). *International dimensions of human resource management.* Boston, MA: PWS-Kent. See note 12, Milliman, J., Von Glinow, M., and Nathan, M. (1991).

66. Moran, J. M., Stahl, W., and Boyer, R. (1989). Survey of personnel managers at 56 international companies. Cited in O'Boyle, T. (Dec. 11, 1989). Grappling with the expatriate issue. *The Wall Street Journal,* pp. B1, B4.

67. Organization Resource Counselors, Inc. (1989). The price of an expatriate. Cited in O'Boyle, T. (Dec. 11, 1989). Grappling with the expatriate issue. *The Wall Street Journal,* pp. B1, B4.

68. See note 67.

EXERCISE 5.1
A TURNOVER PROBLEM AT THE FORT LAUDERDALE HERALD*

OVERVIEW

This chapter discusses the importance of using data for better HRP and recruitment. The employee matching model is described. This exercise presents some data from a newspaper which documents the problems the company is having in recruiting and retaining employees. Your job is to use the data as a basis for recommendations for improving the process and reducing the turnover problem.

OBJECTIVES

After completing this exercise, you should be able to:

1. Know how to calculate and use yield ratios for planning.
2. Know how an HR problem (e.g., turnover) can be solved efficiently and effectively using HRP and recruitment.

PROCEDURE

Part A: Individual Analysis

Prior to class, read the following background data on the *Fort Lauderdale Herald*. Using the information which is provided, think about the implications of this information for future recruitment at the newspaper. Then answer the questions on Form 5.1.1.

The *Fort Lauderdale Herald* is located in one of the fastest-growing regions in the United States. As the migration of new residents from the Northeast and the Midwest has increased the population of south Florida, subscriptions to the paper have risen sharply. The newspaper's increased circulation has generated the need for more customer service representatives. There is also an increase in competition in the area, with two new papers and the expansion of a Miami paper into the metropolitan area.

---

*Contributed by Joan E. Pynes.

The advertisement for customer service representative states the following qualifications: typing 35 WPM, filing, experience in customer contact. The job involves answering the telephone, referring customer calls to a supervisor, and some selling of additional services. The starting salary is $5.65 an hour for a 30-hour workweek. Customer service "reps," as they are called, work 6 days of 5-hour shifts per week. They do not receive any fringe benefits.

The majority of the workday is spent talking with subscribers on the telephone regarding account or delivery problems with the newspaper. Billing errors consume about 50 percent of the reps' time. Most of the remaining time is spent responding to customer complaints such as late or improper delivery, or nondelivery. Examples of the complaints are: "The newspaper was supposed to be delivered at seven a.m. but it did not arrive until nine o'clock." "The paper was thrown into a puddle and can't be read." "The paper was thrown into my neighbor's yard." Most of the subscribers who call to register complaints are not friendly.

While the newspaper has been able to successfully recruit new customer service reps, turnover in the position is very high. The director of human resources has prepared recruitment data (shown in Form 5.1.1). The data show that 200 applicants from all recruiting sources had to be screened to produce 78 who accepted a job offer. Within 6 months of hiring, over half of the new hires had resigned from the newspaper. Exit interviews with departing customer service reps revealed many reasons for their dissatisfaction with the job (see Exhibit 5.1.1).

The director of human resources has asked you to analyze the recruitment and selection process and the related data, and to make specific recommendations. Enter the yield ratios for each step in the recruitment and selection process on Form 5.1.1 based on the data presented. Think about the implications of these data for future recruitment at the newspaper, and answer the questions on the form. Bring the completed form to class.

Part B: Group Analysis

In groups, members should review each other's forms and then attempt to reach consensus on the questions. Analyze the recommendations in the context of the turnover problem, the potential effects on other HR programs, and the costs of implementation. Justify specific recommendations with relevant research. A group spokesperson will then be designated to present the group consensus recommendations.

EXHIBIT 5.1.1
MOST FREQUENTLY GIVEN EXPLANATIONS FOR
CUSTOMER SERVICE REPRESENTATIVE
TURNOVER, LAST 3 YEARS

All customer service reps are required to work on Saturdays and Sundays from seven a.m. to one p.m.

Seventy-five percent of calling customers are irate about things over which the customer service reps have no control.

Customer service reps must sit for long periods of time, talking with customers on the phone. Physical movement is restricted.

Customer service reps have little contact with coworkers.

The work environment is noisy and hectic.

Customer service reps have not been trained to respond to billing complaints.

Supervisors monitor a sample of calls taken each day and often contradict what the customer service reps say to customers.

FORM 5.1.1

Name _____ Group _____

DATA ON RECRUITMENT SOURCES FOR CUSTOMER SERVICE REPRESENTATIVES, LAST 3 YEARS

RECRUITMENT SOURCE	NUMBER OF APPLICANTS	POTENTIALLY QUALIFIED	INTERVIEWED	QUALIFIED AND OFFERED JOB	ACCEPTED JOB	TOTAL 6-MONTH SURVIVAL	RECRUITMENT COST
Newspaper ads	122	98	74	66	60	28	$ 465
Walk-in applicants	41	22	14	10	7	3	295
Public employment agency	37	29	17	14	11	7	250
Total	200 [a]	149 [b]	105	90 [c]	78 [d]	38 [e]	$1010
Yield ratio	___	___	___	___	___		

a. 115 whites, 60 blacks, and 25 Hispanics
b. 91 whites, 43 blacks, and 15 Hispanics
c. 65 whites, 20 blacks, and 5 Hispanics

d. 60 whites, 15 blacks, and 3 Hispanics
e. 31 whites, 5 blacks, and 2 Hispanics

1. What conclusions can you draw from the recruiting data?

2. What strategies should the *Herald* consider to reduce the high turnover rate?

3. What recommendations would you make for improving working conditions at the *Herald* ?

4. What additional studies should be done based on the data in the exhibit?

EXERCISE 5.2
HRP AT SIGNATURE FORMS, INC.*

OVERVIEW

The chapter presents a number of strategies for forecasting HR supply and demand in the context of the organization's competitive strategy. Among the most popular of the quantitative methods is Markov analysis. The method can be used to assess internal labor supply and to identify labor shortages. Results can then be interpreted in the context of other company data. Recruiting sources can be evaluated on the basis of labor supply and needs.

OBJECTIVES

After completing this exercise, you should be able to:

1. Use Markov analysis in HR planning.
2. Understand the advantages and pitfalls of the Markov approach.
3. Understand the advantages and disadvantages of the various recruiting options.

PROCEDURE

Part A: Individual Analysis

Prior to class, each student should review the scenario for Signature Forms, Inc. (SFI), presented below, complete the exhibits, and answer all the questions on Form 5.2.1. Bring your completed exhibits and Form 5.2.1 to class.

Part B: Group Analysis

In groups of about six people, students should review all completed forms and exhibits and reach consensus answers for questions designated by the instructor.

SCENARIO

Kelly Davies has recently been hired as office and HR manager, a new position at SFI. SFI, a small regional printer of custom business forms, is located in Indianapolis, Indiana. The majority of SFI's clients are insurance companies, physicians and medical clinics, real estate companies, retailers, and other medium-sized businesses. SFI's products are blank multipart business forms such as order forms, invoices, vouchers, and claim forms, which are used to process various business transactions. These forms are custom-printed, with corporate logos and layouts formatted to clients' specific needs.

Kelly was hired as part of a major strategy change at SFI. Royce Henderson founded SFI in 1963, and the firm slowly but steadily grew, building a reputation for high quality and service. James Henderson replaced his father as CEO in 1986 and has redirected the firm's strategy. SFI has purchased a vacant supermarket as part of its plan to aggressively expand operations over the next 2 years. This building will provide increased pressroom and warehouse space. Two key changes, which Kelly is responsible for planning and implementing, will affect SFI's HR plan. These key changes are as follows:

1. Renovation of the supermarket will be completed in 6 months. SFI's new building will house equipment that will double its current plant capacity.
2. The new facility will run two regular shifts and one half-capacity shift. Two shifts are currently run in SFI's original site.

Kelly has retained you as consultant to assist in the development of an organized approach to HRP at SFI. She is interested in your response to each of the questions on Form 5.2.1.

Since SFI has not had a formal HR office in the past, Kelly starts by compiling information on staffing and turnover activities at SFI in the past year, in order to estimate the internal demand and expected internal labor supply. These data are summarized in Exhibit 5.2.1.

One obvious step in HRP at SFI is to estimate the internal demand for press workers as a result of increasing plant capacity and adding a third shift. The new facility will have the same number of presses as the current plant, doubling the present capacity. In addition, a third shift will be added to work nights in the new facility. However, the third shift will operate at only half the capacity of the first or second shift (i.e., only half the equipment will be staffed and operated during the night shift).

Using the information in Exhibit 5.2.1, estimate the number of press workers that will be needed, taking into account both the plant expansion and the addition of a third shift. Enter your estimates in Exhibit 5.2.2 (Form 5.2.1).

You recommend that Kelly assess the available internal supply of press workers at the plant this year using a Markov analysis (a technique for estimating staff transitions or changes within and outside the firm), as described below.

The first step in a Markov analysis is to determine the percentage of all employees in each job category who are promoted (or demoted), the percentage who are termi-

---

*Contributed by Scott A. Snell and Sheila Kennelly-McGinnis.

**EXHIBIT 5.2.1
STAFFING AND TURNOVER, LAST YEAR**

POSITION CATEGORY	TOTAL POSITIONS	REASON FOR VACANCY		TOTAL HIRES	SOURCES
		PROMOTION	EXIT		INTERNAL PROMOTION OR EXTERNAL RECRUIT
Administrators: CEO, sales, plant, & accounting managers	4		1	1	Sales representative promoted
Professionals: Sales representatives	10	1	2	3	Campus recruit
Technicians: Graphics technicians	6		2	2	Tech school recruit
Administrative support:					
Manager, office, & HR	1		1	1	Executive search firm
Telemarketing	6		2	2	1 promoted, 1 recruit
Office	12	2	3	5	2 promoted, 3 recruit
Production, skilled:					
Journey-level press operators	20		6	6	Apprentices promoted
Press apprentices	20	6	12	18	Assistants promoted
Production, unskilled:					
Press assistants	32	18	14	32	Advertisements
Shipping & warehouse	15	—	6	6	Advertisements
Totals:	126	27	49	76	

nated, and the percentage who stay in their job class. For example, the second row of Exhibit 5.2.3 on Form 5.2.1 would be completed by recording the total number of press apprentice positions at SFI (N in time 1). Using the staff analysis, Kelly counts how many were subsequently (in time 2) promoted to operator, how many stayed as apprentices, how many were demoted (if any), and how many terminated employment at SFI (for any reason). The transition probabilities are simply the number of workers making a specific type of change divided by the total in that category. Examine the pattern in Exhibit 5.2.3.: the percentage of employees who do not change positions lies on the diagonal; the percentage of employees who are promoted is below the diagonal; the percentage of employees who are demoted is above the diagonal; the percentage of employees who terminate in each category is in the last column. Each percentage is the overall probability of occurrence of that change during the year.

CALCULATING MARKOV TRANSITION PROBABILITIES.
Based on the staffing and turnover information in Exhibit 5.2.1, compute the transition percentages (in decimals) for SFI's press operator, press apprentice, and press assistant positions. For example, of the total of 20 press apprentice positions at SFI (time 1), 6 were promoted during the year (time 2), and so the probability of promotion is 0.30. Complete the probabilities of change or transition for the rest of the positions. Enter your data in Exhibit 5.2.4 (Form 5.2.1).

The transition probability matrix is a tool that can be used to project SFI's staffing dynamics under the planned expansion. Use the forecasted demand from Exhibit 5.2.2 and the expected probabilities from Exhibit 5.2.3 to complete the Markov analysis for SFI.

1. Record the total forecasted demand for operators, apprentices, and assistants as calculated in Exhibit 5.2.2 in the projected total "Demand" column in Exhibit 5.2.5 (Form 5.2.1).

2. Multiply the demand for a position category by the transition probability to compute the numbers of employees promoting, remaining, and terminating for each job class. Record your numbers in Exhibit 5.2.5.

3. Add each column to determine the projected available internal supply of workers for each job class. Comparing the projected demand totals (in the first column) with the total supply available internally (in the row) indicates whether internal staffing levels are adequate to meet demand.

Using Exhibit 5.2.5, subtract the demand (in the first column) from the total supply for each position type—operator, apprentice, and assistant. A negative result indicates insufficient internal supply to meet the demand, which may require recruitment and training to solve the shortage.

After completing and reviewing your work, study Exhibit 5.2.6 and answer all remaining questions on Form 5.2.1.

Name _____   Group _____

1. What problems should Kelly consider in developing an HR plan for SFI?

2. What information should Kelly collect to help in the planning process?

3. Where does SFI appear to use a "career ladder" and promote from within the firm?

4. Describe SFI's hiring pattern for jobs in plant operations.

5. What might be some reasons for this hiring pattern?

FORM 5.2.1 *(Continued)*

Name _____ Group _____

Exhibit 5.2.2

POSITION	CURRENT FIRST AND SECOND SHIFTS	NEW PLANT FIRST AND SECOND SHIFTS	NEW PLANT THIRD SHIFT	TOTAL
Operators:				
Apprentices:				
Assistants:				

Exhibit 5.2.3

PERCENTAGES OF STAFF IN TRANSITION (TIME 2)

POSITION	TOTAL TIME 1	OPERATOR	APPRENTICE	ASSISTANT	EXIT
Operator:	N	Not changed	Demoted	Demoted	Exit
Apprentice:	N	Promoted	Not changed	Demoted	Exit
Assistant:	N	Promoted	Promoted	Not changed	Exit

Exhibit 5.2.4

PERCENTAGES OF STAFF IN TRANSITION (TIME 2)

POSITION	TOTAL TIME 1	OPERATOR	APPRENTICE	ASSISTANT	EXIT
Operator:					
Apprentice:	20	6/20 = 0.30			
Assistant:					

Exhibit 5.2.5

POSITION	DEMAND TOTAL	PROJECTED INTERNAL TRANSITIONS			
		OPERATOR	APPRENTICE	ASSISTANT	EXIT
Operator					
Apprentice					
Assistant					
Available supply					

Name _____ Group _____

6. What benefits and problems might occur as a result of SFI's hiring pattern?

7. What is SFI's overall turnover rate (i.e., number of terminations as compared to number of positions)? What is SFI's turnover rate in production?

8. What assumptions are necessary for the Markov analysis used by SFI?

9. What would increase Kelly's confidence in the accuracy of the Markov estimates?

10. Where does your analysis project a labor shortage for SFI?

Name _____   Group _____

11. What suggestions for meeting these shortages do you have for Kelly?

12. What positions does SFI typically fill from external recruiting sources?

13. What are the advantages of using external recruiting sources?

14. What are the disadvantages of using external recruiting sources?

15. What positions does SFI typically fill from internal recruiting sources?

FORM 5.2.1 *(Continued)*

Name _____   Group _____

16. What are the advantages of using internal recruiting sources?

17. What are the disadvantages of using internal recruiting sources?

18. What external recruiting sources do you suggest for filling the following positions at the new plant? Explain your answers.

  a. Sales representative:

  b. Graphics technician:

  c. Press operators:

  d. Press apprentices:

  e. Press assistants:

  f. Shpping and warehouse:

EXHIBIT 5.2.6
SFI'S OFFICE AND PRODUCTION POSITIONS

JOB CATEGORY	DUTIES AND QUALIFICATIONS
Office support:	
Accounting	Accounts payable, accounts receivable, payroll, clerk: deposits, ledgers. *Requires:* Associate degree or 2 years accounting education.
Secretary	Word processing (correspondence, reports); organize and prioritize work; administrative follow-up. *Requires:* High school plus 2 years; 60 WPM typing.
Customer service rep	Order processing, pricing, shipping, questions, service records. *Requires:* High school plus 1 year office work; 50 WPM, phone skills.
Receptionist	Receive visitors, route calls, sort mail. *Requires:* High school; 40 WPM typing; phone and people skills.
Data entry operator	Enter and print invoices and orders on computer. *Requires:* 6 months data-entry experience; mathematical skills.

PLANT OPERATIONS POSITIONS	
Skilled press operators:	
Journeyman level	Press setups and specification changes; inking, cleaning, maintenance checks and servicing. *Requires:* High school or general equivalency diploma; 12 months apprentice experience.
Apprentice level	Assist on press setup and operations. *Requires:* High school or general equivalency diploma; 6 months pressroom experience.
Unskilled factory positions:	
Press assistants	Load and unload paper; box and move finished goods; operate and adjust machinery; do pressroom cleanup *Requires:* High school or general equivalency diploma; mechanical skills; ability to lift 50 pounds.
Shipping and warehouse workers	Pull and process orders; stack and load orders; process order records. *Requires:* High school or general equivalency diploma; record keeping; ability to lift 50 pounds.
Graphic design positions:	
Senior graphics technician	Consult with clients and sales staff; design graphics and visuals; prepare pasteups and camera-ready art; prepare mattes, plates; operate camera and equipment. *Requires:* Associate degree, graphic arts; 2 years production work.
Graphics technician	Assist clients and sales staff; design graphics and visuals; prepare layouts; do detail work for pasteups and camera-ready art; produce mattes, plates; operate camera and equipment. *Requires:* Associate degree, graphic arts.

EXERCISE 5.3
AN APPROACH TO DOWNSIZING

OVERVIEW

Chapter 5 discusses the extent of corporate restructuring and downsizing which has occurred in the United States in recent years. Many management experts maintain that overhead reduction and downsizing is required in order for U.S. corporations to remain competitive. The purpose of this exercise is to assess the effectiveness of a downsizing strategy on the part of a phosphate company.

OBJECTIVES

After completion of this exercise, you should have:

1. A better understanding of different approaches to downsizing and the advantages and disadvantages of each.
2. Knowledge of the potential problems which can develop with downsizing programs.

PROCEDURE

Part A: Individual Analysis

Prior to class, review the notes on the management meeting in which the company president announces the need to downsize (Exhibit 5.3.1). Answer the questions on Form 5.3.1.

Part B: Group Analysis

In groups of about six people, attempt to reach consensus on the Form 5.3.1 answers. Organize a group response to items 2 and 3. The instructor will designate one presenter.

**EXHIBIT 5.3.1
NOTES FROM DOWNSIZING MEETING**

CONFIDENTIAL

STAFF MEETING NOTES

Meeting called by company president Jarold Abbott. All unit managers attended.

The purpose of the meeting is to make preparations for a unit manpower review (UMR) and a "show and tell," with the goal of reducing the company's personnel by about one-half. We will use UMR, a performance appraisal of each employee, to clean house. New organization charts are to be drawn up as if we were going all out—taking every bit of the "fat" out. "Show and tell" will be a reduction in force from ½ rate to ⅓ rate. (In preparing the organization charts for the UMR and the "show and tell," early retirement may be an area to look at. I will distribute a list of employees who would be eligible for a program we are considering.)

We have some 30 people in the hourly ranks between ages 60 and 65 and some 22 people on salary aged 55 and up. We want to reduce hourly staff by 200 people and salaried staff by 60. This includes both the UMR phase and the "show-and-tell" phase.

Administrative

Presently there are three people in the traffic area. Smith states that at present rates, this is one person too many. This department can function with the supervisor and one clerk, with possibly ½ person from another area in accounting assisting when the workload is high.

The purchasing supervisor's position is a training slot. He handles most of the contracts and fills in as a buyer to provide vacation relief for purchasing agents and the storekeeper. He spends a great deal of time supervising the warehouse to improve purchasing and warehousing. Abbott stated that the warehouse is where we should "stash" maintenance supervisors as storekeepers and storage superintendents. Three people could be used here, assuming no warehouse coverage on third shift.

Cost accounting.   The messenger can go. Records retention could possibly be handled by the inventory clerk, the data processing clerk, or the property control clerk.

Laboratory.   Will be reorganized, with a reduction of seven people.

Projects.   Herz supervises project engineers and handles special projects. He, with Andrews, will head up the wet rock grinding study. There are three senior project engineers: Valk is handling the absorbing tower and pump tank project. Naberhaus is working on the rock wetting project and on special projects for production. Wischmeyer is an electrical engineer.

Plant engineering.   Konopnicki is supervising plant engineers, with heavy emphasis on vibration analysis and mechanical failures.

There is one senior plant engineer (Lamb).

There are two plant engineers I (Broussard and Martin). Martin is learning vibration analysis and working with Konopnicki. Broussard is an expert on rubber lining materials.

There are three development engineers (Stanton, Neff, and Chamberlin). Neff will be transferred to projects group and Stanton reassigned to maintenance. Consider eliminating chief plant engineer position and returning Konopnicki to senior plant engineer.

Process.   Andrews supervises process engineers and makes sure that government environmental regulations are in force. Andrews will also be working on wet rock grinding study.

There is one chemist I (Riddle), who does all forms on governmental regulations, pond water balances, and any special DAP projects.

There are two process engineers I (Marrone and Katzaras). Marrone will temporarily fill in for Andrews. Katzaras is working on the cogeneration project.

There is one engineer II (Stone), who is working on DAP projects.

Environmental engineering.   One supervisor and three technicians keep track of governmental sampling.

Gayle is to draw up an organization chart reflecting the number of people she needs with no capital projects and operating at ⅓ rate (interface with production and maintenance). Possibly eliminate chief plant engineer and move to maintenance. Project can cover both areas.

Production

Presently the production department is structured with four production superintendents and four area superintendents. At ⅓ rate, Abbott would like to restructure to combine areas I and IV and areas II and III. This would eliminate two superintendents and keep four area superintendents. Possibly eliminate area superintendent in area IV (Price), who will be interviewing for position at Hardee County. Four shift supervisors can be eliminated at ⅓ rate; these people will become guards under industrial relations. Some early retirement will be offered.

Maintenance

The department is now staffed by two general superintendents and one superintendent of planning and coordination. The area superintendent position in area III could be eliminated (Garcia is retirement age), and the planner (Card) could be moved over to pick up contractors. One maintenance clerk can also be eliminated. At ⅓ rate, No. 2 and No. 3 shifts in area I could be eliminated. Eliminate No. 3 shift in area II, and possibly also eliminate shift 1. McDuffie will draw up an organization chart as if Goebel, Garcia, and Lopata were to retire.

FORM 5.3.1

Name_____ Group_____

1. How do you evaluate this approach to workforce reduction? What did the president do right and what did he do wrong?

2. Three months after this meeting, Garcia (age 58) and Lopata (age 55) were discharged. Based on the information you have reviewed, were Garcia and Lopata victims of age discrimination? Explain your answer.

   If necessary, what additional information do you require?

3. How would you have done the downsizing differently? Provide a chronology of steps.

C H A P T E R

PERSONNEL SELECTION*

*Contributed by Michael M. Harris and Barbara K. Brown.

OVERVIEW

The matching model of employee recruitment discussed in Chapter 5 requires methods of personnel selection which successfully predict employee effectiveness. As discussed in Chapter 2, competitive advantage is enhanced by hiring applicants with the capacity for high performance, based on the definition of performance effectiveness for the particular competitive situation. The key to competitive advantage is to increase output with fewer inputs while at the same time improving product or service quality. A company is also interested in selecting employees who will not only be effective but also will work for the company as long as it wants them and will not engage in counterproductive behavior, such as substance abuse, avoidable accidents, and employee theft. Companies use a variety of selection methods to make these predictions and ultimately enhance competitive advantage. Standardized tests, performance testing, reference checks, application blanks, and interviews are the most common methods. We will discuss all these methods in Chapters 6 and 7. An increasing number of companies are now using some form of testing to assess the potential of job applicants. The use of paper-and-pencil tests to assess work aptitude and personality traits, in addition to the use of drug testing to screen for substance abuse, are becoming increasingly common in industry today.

This chapter will introduce you to personnel selection, describe some of the most popular types of tests, review the research evidence on their use, and discuss the social and legal implications of selection methods. First, we will provide an overview of personnel selection and the typical steps used in the process. Then we will review the various forms of standardized tests which purport to assess applicants' aptitudes, skills, or personalities. The chapter will conclude with a discussion of the use of performance testing, application blanks, biographical data, reference checks, and drug tests in the preemployment selection process.

OBJECTIVES

After studying this chapter, you should be able to:

1. Define the various types of personnel tests.
2. Identify some of the most popular forms of performance testing.
3. Understand the validity evidence for testing and potential problems with its use.
4. Discuss approaches to more effectively use application blanks, reference checks, and biographical data in order to increase their validity and legal defensibility.
5. Discuss the available approaches to drug testing.

The Hartford Insurance Group had a serious problem. While its recruitment efforts were successful in attracting a large number of applicants for entry-level insurance agent positions, profits were sluggish, the rate of new insurance policies was flat, and the turnover rate approached 100 percent (the quit rate in a year almost equaled the number of agent positions). The company contracted with the Life Insurance Marketing Research Association (LIMRA), a consulting firm from Hartford, Connecticut, which specializes in personnel selection. The Hartford Group asked LIMRA to evaluate the personnel selection system, to determine the validity and potential legal liability of the processes, and to make recommendations for improvements. Of course, underlying this evaluation was a need for Hartford to improve its competitive position in the industry by increasing sales and decreasing costs. The company estimated that the cost of training a new agent was over $4000. With many agents quitting in less than a year, the company often did not even recover its training costs. Hartford needed new selection methods which could increase sales and identify the applicants most likely to stay with the company.

Personnel selection is the process of gathering and assessing information about job candidates. The process applies both to entry-level personnel decisions and to internal decisions regarding job candidates for promotions, transfers, and even job retention as part of corporate downsizing efforts.

You will recall from Chapter 4 that job analysis should identify the knowledge, abilities, skills, and other characteristics (KASOCs) which are necessary for successful performance on the job. The first thing LIMRA did in the Hartford project was to conduct a new and more thorough job analysis of the agent job to get better information on the KASOCs required for the job. After the critical KASOCs are identified, the appropriate recruitment methods are pursued, and a pool of qualified applicants is established, the organization must embark on a process of selecting the applicants for the positions to be filled. This process of personnel selection varies substantially from company to company. While the Hartford Group, for example, used only a college degree requirement, an application blank, and an interview, other insurance companies use far more complex methods to select their people. Prudential, for example, uses a battery of psychological and aptitude tests followed by a biographical inventory and a detailed and structured interview with candidates. Another insurance company uses an assessment center which involves an entire day of testing in simulated work situations.

As with the job analysis and the recruitment process, personnel selection should be directly linked to the human resource planning (HRP) function and the strategic objectives of the company. For example, you may recall from the discussion in Chapter 2 that Marriott sought to be the hotel chain of choice by frequent travelers. As part of this strategy, the company developed a selection system designed to identify people who could be particularly attentive to customer demands. Hartford had a major marketing strategy aimed at selling insurance to working women. They needed a *legal* selection system which could identify people most likely to sell to this targeted segment.

Figure 6.1 presents a chronology of events in the staffing process and the major options available for personnel selection. The previous chapters on job analysis, planning, and recruitment have gotten us to the point of selecting job candidates based on information from one or more of the selection methods listed in Figure 6.1. We will review each of these methods in this and the next chapter.

We will include a summary of the *validity* of each selection method. A great deal of research has been conducted on the extent to which the various selection methods successfully predict some important criterion such as performance on the job or employee turnover. This is the essence of the term "validity." Empirical or criterion-related validity, discussed in detail in Appendix A, involves the statistical relationship between performance on some predictor or selection method (e.g., a test or an interview) and performance or some other measure of on-the-job effectiveness (e.g., sales, supervisory ratings, job turnover, employee theft). The statistical relationship is usually reported as a *correlation coefficient,* which is a summary index of the degree of relationship between the predictor and the criterion. Correlations can range from −1 to +1, with the sign (positive or negative) indicating the direction of a relationship and the magnitude indicating the strength of a relationship. In general, correlations

between useful selection methods and important job criteria are in the range of .2 to .6. As discussed in Appendix A, higher correlations usually result in greater utility (or economic payoff) for a selection method. Utility formulas are available for converting correlations into dollar savings or profits that are attributable to a particular selection method (see Appendix A).

Another form of validity (discussed later in this chapter and in Chapter 4) is content validity. Content validity is an expert assessment of the extent to which the content of a selection method is representative of the content of the job. For example, a typing test using WordPerfect software could be considered to have content validity for a clerical job in which typing on WordPerfect is required. We will have more to say on the subject of content validity in the pages to follow.

LIMRA investigated the Hartford Group's selection methods using both criterion-related and content validation procedures. The resulting study strongly suggested that new methods of personnel selection should be used if the company hoped to increase sales and decrease employee turnover. The methods LIMRA considered and recommended in lieu of the old procedures are discussed in the balance of this chapter. The first method it considered was a standardized testing program.

PERSONNEL TESTING

According to a recent survey, the use of testing is on the increase in corporate America, with 84 percent of surveyed companies indicating the use of some form of test for personnel selection.[1] Personnel testing has been around for a long time. The Paris Transportation Society, for example, used a battery of tests to screen for streetcar operators in 1908.[2] World Wars I and II provided the major impetus for the testing industry when U.S. armed forces needed efficient and valid screening devices. The tests which were developed in this effort resulted in the screening of over a million military recruits. The end of World War II saw a dramatic increase in the development and use of tests, as thousands of veterans applied for industrial jobs. However, the increase in the use of mental ability tests in industry stopped suddenly with the proliferation of court cases challenging their use under Title VII of the Civil Rights Act of 1964, the most important of which was the 1971 Supreme Court ruling in *Griggs v. Duke Power Company* (see the discussion in Chapter 3).

The 1980s saw a revival of interest in the use of mental or cognitive ability tests, bolstered by recent research which indicates that aptitude or cognitive ability tests are valid for virtually all jobs in the U.S. economy. Many industrial psychologists and other testing experts subscribe to the notion that such tests have "generalizable validity,"

FIGURE 6.1
STEPS IN THE DEVELOPMENT AND EVALUATION OF A SELECTION PROCEDURE

1. **Perform job analysis and HR planning.** Identify KASOCs.
2. **Develop recruitment strategy.**
3. **Select or develop selection procedures.** Review options for assessing applicants on KASOCs:
   a. Application blanks, biographical data, preliminary interview
   b. Standardized tests (cognitive, personality, motivational, psychomotor)
   c. Background, reference checks, drug tests
   d. Performance tests, assessment centers
   e. Interviews
4. **Determine validity of selection methods:**
   a. Criterion-related validation
   b. Expert judgment (content validity)
   c. Validity generalization
5. **Determine weighting system for selection methods and resultant data.**

that is, that these particular types of tests are valid across a great variety of jobs and settings and that the tests can have significantly positive economic consequences for a company which uses them. The dilemma facing organizations is that while mental or cognitive ability tests have been shown to be valid predictors of job performance, their use nonetheless can create legal problems because minorities tend to score lower.[3]

There has also been an increase in the use of various forms of personality testing, in part due to the growing concern over employee theft and other counterproductive behavior, the outlawing of the polygraph test, and potential corporate liability for the behavior of their employees. As discussed in Chapter 1, lawsuits for "negligent hiring" and "negligent retention" attempt to hold an organization responsible for the behavior of employees when there is little or no attempt to assess critical characteristics of those who are hired or retained. For example, one pizza delivery service recently settled a lawsuit in which one of its delivery personnel was involved in a fatal accident. The driver had a long and disturbing psychiatric history.

Cognitive ability tests are the most frequently used paper-and-pencil tests employed today. Cognitive ability tests attempt to measure mental, clerical, mechanical, or sensory capabilities in job applicants. The Scholastic Aptitude Test (SAT), the American College Test (ACT), and the General Mental Ability Test (GMAT) are examples of cognitive ability tests with which you may be familiar. Most cognitive ability tests are administered in a paper-and-pencil format under standardized conditions of test administration.

Cognitive ability tests are controversial. On the average, blacks and Hispanics tend to score lower than whites on virtually all these tests. Thus, use of these tests can affect employment and other opportunities for minorities. Under the controversial rules of the NCAA, low scores can also bar athletes from competing at the collegiate level. We will address the critical issue of test score differences as a function of ethnicity later in the chapter. Let us begin our discussion with a definition of cognitive ability testing and brief descriptions of some of the most popular tests. Then we will review the validity evidence for these tests. We will conclude with a focus on the legal aspects of cognitive ability testing in the context of the latest research, ethnic score differences, and case law.

What Is a Cognitive Ability Test?

Cognitive ability tests measure one's aptitude or mental capacity to acquire knowledge based on the accumulation of learning from all possible sources. They are also known as intelligence tests or mental ability tests. Such tests are often distinguished from achievement tests,

which attempt to measure the effects of knowledge obtained in a standardized environment (e.g., your final exam in this course could be considered a form of achievement test). Cognitive ability or aptitude tests are typically used to predict future performance. For example, the SAT and the ACT were developed to measure ability to master college-level material. Having made this distinction between achievement tests and ability tests, however, we hasten to point out that in practice there is no clear distinction between these two classes of tests. Achievement tests can be used to predict future behavior, and all tests measure some degree of accumulated knowledge.

There are hundreds of mental ability tests available. Some of the most frequently used and highly regarded tests are the Wechsler Adult Intelligence Scale, the Wonderlic Personnel Test, the Flanagan Industrial Test, the General Aptitude Test Battery, and the Armed Services Vocational Aptitude Battery. In addition, many of the largest U.S. companies have developed their own battery of cognitive ability tests. American Telephone and Telegraph (AT&T), for example, evaluates applicants for its nonsupervisory positions on the basis of scores on one or more of its 16 mental ability subtests. Knight-Ridder, a large communications firm, has a battery of 10 aptitude tests, some of which are even used to select newspaper carriers. Let us examine three of the best-known cognitive ability tests.

One of the most widely used mental ability tests is the *Wonderlic Personnel Test*. In fact, the publisher of this test has data from over 1 million applicants. First copyrighted in 1938, the Wonderlic consists of nine versions of a 50-item test covering a variety of areas, including mathematics, vocabulary, spatial relations, perceptual speed, and analogies. An example of a mathematics question is: "A watch lost 1 minute 18 seconds in 39 days. How many seconds did it lose per day?" A typical vocabulary question is: "Usual is the opposite of: (a) rare, (b) habitual, (c) regular, (d) simultaneous, (e) always." An item which assesses ability in spatial relations requires the test taker to choose which of five figures would form two depicted shapes. Applicants have 12 minutes to complete the 50 items.

You may remember the Wonderlic from our discussion of the Supreme Court rulings in *Griggs v. Duke Power Company* and *Albemarle v. Moody.* As discussed in Chapter 3, in *Griggs,* scores on the Wonderlic had an adverse impact upon blacks (a greater proportion of blacks flunked the test than did whites) and Duke Power was unable to show that the test was "job-related." Despite early courtroom setbacks and a decrease in use following the *Griggs* decision, the use of the Wonderlic has increased in recent years. Because of its long history and extensive use, normative data are available on the Wonderlic, with scores broken down by ethnicity, gender, geographical region, position applied for, education, and age.

The *General Aptitude Test Battery* (GATB) was developed by the U.S. Employment Service for career counseling and job placement. The GATB consists of 12 separately timed subtests, eight of which are paper-and-pencil tests and four of which involve manipulation of objects. The paper-and-pencil subtests include vocabulary, arithmetic reasoning, computation, name comparison, spatial relations, form matching, tool matching, and mark making. Primarily due to controversy regarding the scoring methods used for the GATB, in July 1990, the U.S. Department of Labor suspended use of the GATB by state and local employment service offices for a 2-year period. During this 2-year period, the GATB is to undergo modifications to improve its effectiveness.

The *Armed Services Vocational Aptitude Battery* (ASVAB) was designed for selection and classification of enlistees in the armed forces. The ASVAB was recently reviewed and revised. Scores on the ASVAB are used to place all recruits in military occupational specialties (e.g., computer technician, infantry, mechanic). The ASVAB consists of 12 subtests, such as numerical operations, attention to detail, word knowledge, mechanical comprehension, and automotive information. These subtests are combined to form six subscores: verbal, math, perceptual speed, mechanical, trade technical, and academic ability.

Tests of Specific Ability

A variety of tests have also been developed to measure specific abilities, such as clerical ability, physical ability, or psychomotor ability. These tests assess factors such as eye-hand coordination, sensory skills, and mechanical ability. The most widely used mechanical ability test is the *Bennett Mechanical Comprehension Test* (BMCT). First developed in the 1940s, the BMCT consists mainly of pictures depicting mechanical situations with questions pertaining to the situations. The respondent's job is to understand and describe relationships between physical forces and mechanical issues.

While there are several tests available for the assessment of clerical ability, the most popular is the *Minnesota Clerical Test* (MCT).[4] The MCT requires test takers to quickly compare either names or numbers and to indicate when a pair are the same. The name comparison part of the test has been shown to be related to reading speed and spelling accuracy, and number comparison is related to arithmetic ability.

As we discussed in Chapter 4, the validity of physical ability tests has come under close scrutiny lately, particularly with regard to their use for public safety jobs. Many lawsuits have been filed on behalf of female applicants for police and firefighter jobs who do not pass some type of physical ability test such as push-ups, sit-ups, or chin-ups. In fact, there is a high probability of adverse impact on women when a physical ability test is used to make selection decisions. A series of studies has identified 11 physical abilities, such as equilibrium, flexibility, upper-body static strength, coordination, and trunk strength.[5] Physical abilities analysis and rating forms are available to assess the physical requirements of the job under study. Sensory ability testing concentrates on the measurement of hearing and sight acuity, reaction time, and psychomotor skills such as eye-hand coordination. Such tests have been shown to be related to quantity and quality of work output and accident rates.[6]

Racial Differences in Test Performance

Many organizations discontinued the use of cognitive ability tests because of the Supreme Court ruling in *Griggs*. Despite fairly strong evidence that the tests are valid, and their increased use by U.S. business, the details of the *Griggs* case illustrate the continuing problem with the use of such tests. The Duke Power Company required new employees either to have a high school diploma or to pass the Wonderlic Personnel Test and the Bennett Mechanical Comprehension Test. While 58 percent of whites who took the tests passed, only 6 percent of blacks passed. According to the U.S. Supreme Court, the Duke Power Company was unable to provide sufficient evidence to support the job relatedness of the tests or the "business necessity" for their use. Accordingly, the Supreme Court ruled that the company had discriminated against blacks under Title VII of the 1964 Civil Rights Act. As we discussed in Chapter 3, the rationale for the Court's decision gave rise to the theory of disparate impact. This theory was incorporated into the Civil Rights Act of 1991.

The statistical data presented in the *Griggs* case are not unusual. Blacks, on average, score significantly lower than whites on cognitive ability tests, and Hispanics, on average, fall about midway between average black and white scores. Thus, under the disparate impact theory of discrimination, plaintiffs are likely to establish adverse impact based on the proportion of blacks versus whites who pass such tests. If the *Griggs* case weren't enough, the 1975 U.S. Supreme Court ruling in *Albemarle Paper Company v. Moody* probably convinced many organizations that the use of cognitive ability tests was too risky. In *Albemarle*, the Court applied specific and difficult guidelines to which the defendant had to conform in order to establish the job relatedness of the particular test. The *Uniform Guidelines in Employee Selection Procedures*, as issued by the Equal Employment Opportunity Commission (EEOC), also established rigorous and potentially costly guidelines to be followed by an organization in order to support the job relatedness of the test if adverse impact should result from its use. Current interest in cognitive ability tests was spurred by the research on "validity generalization," which strongly supported the validity of cognitive ability tests for virtually all jobs. This research projected substantial increases in productivity and cost savings for organizations which use the tests to make decisions.[7] Let us now examine the validity evidence for cognitive ability tests in more detail.

The Validity of Cognitive Ability Tests

Research has shown that the validity of cognitive ability tests is much higher than previously thought and that validity is generalizable across jobs and settings. One study funded by the federal government, however, found relatively lower validities for the GATB compared to those reported in the validity generalization research.[8] One criticism of the research on cognitive ability tests in general and the conclusions regarding validity generalization is that most of the studies used supervisor ratings as the performance criterion. In the typical study, blacks tend to score lower on the test and to be rated as less effective for actual job performance by white supervisors. Thus, it is argued that much of what cognitive ability tests may be predicting is simply supervisor liking or bias, perhaps related to ethnicity or social class. One study indirectly examined this important issue by comparing the validities based on the type of criteria used in studies involving clerical personnel.[9] The authors found that the average validities for cognitive ability tests were nearly identical in the prediction of supervisory ratings and actual production quantity, a criterion not as likely to be affected by the proposed class or ethnic bias. Thus, regardless of whether a subjective measure (i.e., supervisor ratings) or an objective measure (i.e., production quantity) was used as the criterion, cognitive ability tests showed the same validity generalization results in the prediction of job performance.

A major question that still remains regarding the validity generalization results for cognitive ability tests is whether these tests are the most valid method of personnel selection across all job situations or whether other methods such as biographical data and personality tests are more valid in certain situations and for some jobs. Are there procedures which can make more accurate predictions than mental ability tests for some job situations? Are cognitive ability tests the best predictors of sales success, for example? Another issue concerns the extent to which other measures can enhance predictions beyond what cognitive ability tests can predict. Human performance is generally thought to be a function of a person's

ability and motivation. Would a combination of methods (e.g., a cognitive ability test and a personality or motivational test) result in significantly better prediction than the cognitive ability test alone? Research indicates that even small improvements in selection method validity may lead to significant gains in productivity. Accordingly, the use of other tests that address the motivational components of human performance in addition to a cognitive ability test may increase the competitive advantage of the company.

Why Do Minorities Score Lower than Whites on Cognitive Ability Tests?

This question has interested researchers for years, and there appears to be no clear answer. Most HRM experts now generally take the view that these differences are "*not* created by these tests, but are preexisting, and thus the problem is not a defect or deficiency in the tests."[10] Thus, the issue for HRM experts is not how to modify the test itself, but how to *use* the test in the most effective way. A panel of the National Academy of Sciences concluded that cognitive ability tests have limited but real ability to predict how well job applicants will perform and that these tests predict minority group performance as well as they predict the future performance of nonminorities. In other words, the tests themselves are not to blame for differences in scores.

How Do Organizations Deal with Race Differences on Ability Tests?

In order to maximize the utility of a test, the most effective way to use a valid cognitive ability test would be to select "top-down," using the raw scores. That is, all things being equal, if an organization needed to hire 10 people, the individuals with the 10 highest scores on the test would be selected. However, as described above, this strategy is likely to result in adverse impact and thus create legal problems.

One approach to solving the problem is to set an arbitrary cutoff score on the test and then to ignore score differences above the cutoff score and make hiring decisions on some other basis. For example, many U.S. cities set a minimum cutoff score for entrance exams for police and firefighters at the point where there would be no violation of the 80 percent (or four-fifths) adverse impact rule. Test score differences above this minimum cutoff score are not taken into account in the ultimate selection decision. The major disadvantage of this approach is that it will cause a significant decline in the utility of a valid test, because people could be hired who are at the lower end of the scoring continuum and hence less qualified than people at the upper end of the continuum who may not be selected. Virtually all the research on cognitive ability test validity indicates that the relationship between test scores and job performance is linear; that is, higher test scores go with higher performance and lower scores go with lower performance. Thus, setting a low cutoff score and ignoring score differences above this point can result in the hiring of many people who are only minimally qualified. Hence, while use of a low cutoff score may enable an organization to comply with the 80 percent adverse impact rule, the test will lose considerable utility.[11] Another approach to the problem, known as "race norming," is the interpretation of raw scores in the context of the test taker's race. A test taker thus gets a percentile score which has been converted based on the person's performance relative to others of the same race only. Race norming was used by many organizations prior to the passage of the Civil Rights Act of 1991, which explicitly bars the practice.

The use of cognitive ability tests obviously presents a dilemma for organizations. The evidence supports the argument that such tests are valid predictors of job performance across a wide array of jobs. Use of such tests has been shown to have economic utility and to result in greater productivity and considerable cost savings to employers. It is also clear that selection decisions which are based solely on the scores of such tests will result in adverse impact upon blacks and Hispanics. Such adverse impact can, of course, entangle an organization in costly litigation. If the organization chooses to avoid adverse impact, the question becomes whether to throw out a test which has been shown to be useful in predicting job performance or to keep the test and reduce or eliminate the level of adverse impact by placing less emphasis on the raw score of a test. Does such a policy then leave a company open to reverse discrimination lawsuits by whites who were not selected for employment although their raw scores on the test were higher than scores obtained by some minorities who were hired? Many organizations, particularly in the public sector, have abandoned the use of cognitive ability tests in favor of other methods, such as interviews, which result in less adverse impact but lower validity.

PERSONALITY AND MOTIVATIONAL TESTING

While research supports the use of cognitive ability tests for personnel selection, virtually all HRM professionals regard performance as a function of both ability and motivation. Scores on ability tests say little or nothing about a person's motivation to do the job. We can all think of examples of individuals who have a great deal of ability or intelligence but have been unsuccessful in many situations. Most of us, for example, can remember a classmate in school who was very bright but received poor grades due to low motivation. In general, the validity of cognitive ability tests for predicting sales success is rather low, and much could be done to improve prediction.

Most personnel selection programs attempt an informal or formal assessment of an applicant's motivation through psychological testing or a job interview. Some of these assessments are based on scores from standardized tests or performance testing such as job simulations or assessment centers, while others are more informal and derived from an interviewer's "gut reaction" or intuition. This section will review the abundant literature on the measurement and prediction of motivation and personality using paper-and-pencil testing. We will then introduce you to performance testing. We have reserved Chapter 7 for the employment interview, which is still the most frequently used method of personnel selection.

Motivational testing has always intrigued people. In most instances, a personality test is used. Although personality tests are not used as often as cognitive ability tests, their use is on the increase. A 1988 survey indicated that 32 percent of responding companies indicated use of personality tests, up from 22 percent in 1985.[12] Some organizations place great weight on personality testing for employment decisions. Examples of companies that have used personality testing for years as a tool for employee selection and placement, and even promotion decisions, are Sears, Roebuck and Company; Standard Oil of New Jersey; and AT&T. More companies are now using some form of personality test to screen applicants for "risk factors" related to possible counterproductive behavior. A national jeweler, for example, screens all employees using the sixteen Personality Factors Questionnaire (16PF) test, a standardized test we will describe below. Many companies use personality tests to assess an applicant's orientation toward customers. Knight-Ridder, the newspaper company, puts considerable weight on such a test in the selection of journalists.

We will begin this section with a definition of personality and provide brief descriptions of some of the more popular personality tests. We will review the validity of these tests and provide an overview of relevant legal and ethical issues. We will conclude with a description of four relatively new personality tests which have shown potential as selection and placement devices.

What Is Personality?

While *personality* has been defined in many ways, the most widely accepted definition is that it refers to an individual's consistent pattern of behavior. This consistent pattern is composed of "psychological traits." A recent review notes that an "impressive body of literature has accumulated which provides compelling evidence for the robustness of the five-factor model" of personality.[13] These five factors are: 1. Introversion/extroversion (outgoing, sociable); 2. Emotional stability; 3. Agreeableness/likability (friendliness, cooperative); 4. Conscientious (dependability, carefulness); and 5. Intellect (imaginative, curious, experimenting). The so-called Big Five model is not without its critics who suggest that more than five traits are necessary. Others criticize the trait approach and prefer a "situationist" perspective, maintaining that behavior is inconsistent, particularly across situations and measurement methods. A popular approach today is the "interactionist" perspective, which maintains that an individual's behavior is a function of personality, the situation, and the interaction between the two.[14] While most measures of personal characteristics have adopted the pure trait approach, some of the more recent efforts have attempted to enhance prediction with the interactionist approach. Trait-based personality tests have been developed to predict behavior in a variety of contexts, including the workplace. There are literally thousands of personality tests available that purport to measure hundreds of different traits or characteristics.[15] We will review the basic categories of personality testing next. Figure 6.2 presents a summary of some of the most popular tests.

Projective Personality Measures

Personality tests can be sorted into two broad categories: projective tests and self-report inventories. Projective tests have several common characteristics, the most significant of which is that the purpose and scoring procedure of the test are disguised from the test taker. Unlike self-report inventories, projective techniques are purposely ambiguous and provide the respondent with great discretion in responding. The response is then interpreted as a manifestation of personality or motivation. The most famous projective test is probably the *Rorschach inkblot test,* which presents a series of inkblots to the respondents and asks them to report what they see in each inkblot.

While numerous projective tests exist, the *Miner Sentence Completion Scale* (MSCS) is one of the few that was specifically designed for use in the employment setting. The aim of this test is to measure managers' motivation to manage others. The test consists of 40 incomplete sentences, such as "My family doctor...," "Playing golf...," and "Dictating letters...." The test taker is instructed to complete each sentence. According to the developer of these tests, the way in which an applicant completes the sentences reflects his or her motivation along seven areas. These areas are: capacity to deal with authority figures, dealing with competitive games, handling competitive situations, assertiveness, motivation to direct others, motivation to stand out in a group,

FIGURE 6.2
EXAMPLES OF PERSONALITY AND MOTIVATIONAL TESTS

TEST	PURPOSE
Projective Techniques:	
Thematic Apperception Test (TAT)	Measures need for achievement, power, and affiliation
Miner Sentence Completion Scale	Measures motivation to manage others
Graphology	Measures numerous personal attributes, including intelligence, creativity, and emotional stability
Self-Report Inventories:	
Gordon Personal Profile Inventory	Measures 8 factors (e.g., leadership, vigor)
Guilford-Zimmerman Temperament	Measures 10 traits (e.g., objectivity, stability)
Minnesota Multiphasic Personality Inventory (MMPI)	Screens for aberrant or deviant behavior (e.g., depression, anxiety, mania)
Kuder Preference Record	Measures occupational interests
Sixteen Personality Factors Questionnaire (16PF)	Measures 16 factors (e.g., assertiveness, trusting, group-oriented, anxiety, emotional stability, conscientiousness)
Job Compatibility Questionnaire (JCQ)	Measures job-person compatibility (e.g., customer orientation, type of work, structure, work hours, working conditions, autonomy)

and desire to perform day-to-day administrative tasks. Research with the instrument supports the view that profit-making organizations attract people with higher motivation to manage as measured by the MSCS because such organizations offer higher pay than do non-profit-making organizations. A recent study found predictive utility for the MSCS in China.[16]

Another projective test that has been used occasionally for employment purposes is the *Thematic Apperception Test* (TAT). The TAT typically consists of a series of pictures that depict one or more persons in different situations. Test takers are asked to describe who the people are, what is happening in the situation (the picture is somewhat ambiguous and open to interpretation), and what the outcome of the situation will be. Although a variety of scoring systems have been developed for interpreting a test taker's responses, one of the most popular approaches involves rating the responses with regard to the test taker's need for power (i.e., need to control and influence others), need for achievement (i.e., need for task success), and need for affiliation (i.e., need for social relationships). Like the MSCS, the TAT has been used primarily for managerial selection.

One form of projective test which has received considerable attention recently is graphology, or handwriting analysis. With this approach, a sample of a person's handwriting is mailed to a graphologist who (for anywhere from $10 to $50) provides an assessment of the person's intelligence, creativity, emotional stability, negotiation skills, problem-solving skills, and numerous other personal attributes. According to some writers, graphology is used extensively in Europe as a hiring tool. *The Wall Street Journal* recently reported an increase in the use of the method in the United States: "With the government pulling the plug on the polygraph, employers clamming up on job references and liabilities from "negligent hiring . . . it is one alternative managers are exploring in an effort to know whom they are hiring."[17] Unfortunately, while the use of the method may be increasing, there is no evidence that the method does anything but provide an assessment of penmanship. The only published studies on the validity of graphology have found no validity in the approach.

Self-Report Personality Inventories

Self-report inventories which purport to measure personality or motivation are much more popular today than projective techniques. Some instruments screen applicants for aberrant or deviant behavior [e.g., the Minnesota Multiphasic Personality Inventory (MMPI), the 16PF]; others attempt to identify potentially high performers;

and others, particularly more recently developed tests, are directed at specific criteria such as employee theft, job tenure/turnover, or accident proneness.

Self-report personality inventories typically consist of a series of short statements concerning one's behaviors, thoughts, emotions, attitudes, past experiences, preferences, or characteristics. The test taker responds to each statement using a standardized rating scale. For example, respondents may be asked to indicate the extent to which they are "happy" or "sad," or "like to work in groups" or "prefer working alone." See Figure 6.2 for a summary of some of the most popular self-report inventories and what they purport to measure.

One well-known inventory is the *Gordon Personal Profile-Inventory* (GPPI), which contains eight scales: ascendancy (the tendency to assume leadership roles), responsibility, emotional stability, sociability, cautiousness, original thinking, personal relations, and vigor. Items on the GPPI are organized into groups of four. For each group of four items, the respondent is instructed to mark the item that is most like him or her, and the item that is least like him or her. An example of a group of items is: "(a) prefers to get up early in the morning; (b) doesn't care for popular music; (c) has an excellent command of English; (d) maintains a poorly balanced diet."

Another popular instrument is the *Guilford-Zimmerman Temperament Survey* (GZTS), which provides scores on 10 psychological traits: general activity, restraint, ascendance, sociability, emotional stability, objectivity, friendliness, thoughtfulness, personal relations, and masculinity. Respondents are instructed to answer "yes," "no," or "uncertain." Sample items are "You are often in low spirits" and "You start work on a new project with a great deal of enthusiasm."

One of the most respected personality tests is the *Minnesota Multiphasic Personality Inventory,* (MMPI). The MMPI has been used extensively for jobs that concern the public safety or welfare (e.g., law enforcement, security, nuclear power plants). The test is designed to identify pathological problems in respondents, not to predict job effectiveness.

The recently revised version of the MMPI consists of over 566 statements, such as "I am fearful of going crazy," "I am shy," "Sometimes evil spirits control my actions," "In walking, I am very careful to step over sidewalk cracks," and "Much of the time, my head seems to hurt all over." For each statement, respondents indicate "true," "false," or "cannot say." The MMPI reveals scores on 10 clinical scales (e.g., depression, hysteria, paranoia, schizophrenia) plus four "validity" scales which enable the interpreter to assess the credibility or truthfulness of the answers. Millions of people from at least 46 different countries, ranging from psychotics to Soviet cosmonauts have struggled through the strange questions. Litigation related to negligent hiring often focuses on whether an organization properly screened job applicants. Failure to use the MMPI in filling sensitive jobs is often cited in legal arguments as an indication of "negligent hiring" (although not always persuasively).

One instrument, mentioned earlier, that is used by many organizations for selection and promotions is the 16PF, which provides scores on 16 psychological traits such as conscientiousness, stability, anxiety, and independence. The so-called Big Five we discussed earlier are all assessed on the 16PF. The test is also used to screen applicants for counterproductive behavior, such as potential substance abuse or employee theft. The U.S. Department of State uses the 16PF as part of its assessment package for overseas assignments.

A different type of self-report questionnaire that has been used in industry is the occupational interest inventory. Occupational interest inventories are designed to assess career choice or preference; however, they have also been used on occasion for preemployment hiring and placement. The U.S. armed forces, for example, use an interest inventory for assignments to military occupational training. One popular occupational inventory is the *Kuder Preference Record,* which consists of groups of three items describing different activities. For example, one group of items is: "(a) Go for a long hike in the woods; (b) go to a symphony concert; (c) go to an exhibit of new inventions." For each group of items, the test taker is instructed to indicate which activity he or she would most like to engage in and which activity he or she would least like to participate in. Another popular occupational interest inventory is the *Strong-Campbell Interest Inventory.* In this test, a respondent's preferences for over 300 different activities are compared to ratings of these activities by job occupants in over 150 different occupations. Respondents then receive feedback which indicates the compatibility of their preferences with the responses of incumbents in those positions.

The Validity of Personality Tests

There are some potentially useful personality tests, and there are a great number of really bad ones. Thus, unlike the evidence on cognitive ability tests we cannot make "generalizable" comments regarding their validity. Some instruments have shown adequate validity, others no validity at all. For example, a review of 26 studies involving the MSCS found an average validity coefficient of .35.[18] On the other hand, graphology has not been shown to have any validity at all in the prediction of job performance. A 1991 review of the literature indicated that if

personality traits are selected through a job analysis, the average validities of the traits (.38) in predicting job performance is considerably better than what we had previously thought.[19] However, a much wider variance in validities was obtained with personality tests than was obtained with cognitive ability tests. The researchers concluded that "the full potential of personality traits in personnel selection will be realized only when confirmatory research strategies employing personality-oriented job analysis become the standard practice for determining which traits are relevant to predicting performance on a given job."[20]

WHY DO PERSONALITY TESTS HAVE MIXED VALIDITY?   A number of explanations have been given for the inconsistent validity of personality tests in the employment context. First, applicants can "fake" personality tests so that their personalities will be reflected on the tests as compatible with the requirement of the job. Second, some proponents of personality testing have asserted that most of the validity studies involving personality tests are poorly designed and have very small sample sizes. These experts contend that more carefully designed research would demonstrate higher validity for personality tests.

The third possible explanation is that behavior is situationally determined to a great extent and that personality traits alone do not predict criteria such as job performance or employee turnover. Recall some of the examples of items from personality tests listed earlier in this chapter. Note that most of the examples are not specific to the workplace; in fact, most of them are quite general. Research has found that behavior is very dependent on the situation.[21] Thus, a person may be friendly in some settings (e.g., outside work) and less sociable in other settings (e.g., at work). Hence, it is possible that in order to enhance predictability, personality tests must be made more specific to the workplace. Let us examine next some newer approaches to measuring personality and motivation.

New Approaches to the Assessment of Motivation and Personality

Some of the newer forms of personality or motivation assessment focus on particular problems or characteristics of the workplace. For example, honesty or integrity tests attempt to predict the growing problem of employee theft. Another new test attempts to predict accident proneness. Other new instruments are designed for particular employment situations and problems.

HONESTY/INTEGRITY TESTS. It is estimated that over 5 million job applicants will take some form of honesty test in 1991. These tests are commonly used for jobs in which workers have access to money, such as retail stores, fast-food chains, and banks. Paper-and-pencil honesty tests have become more popular since the polygraph, or lie detector, test was banned in 1988 by the Employee Polygraph Protection Act. This federal law prohibits the use of the polygraph for selection and greatly restricts the use of the test for other employment situations. There are some employment exemptions to the law (e.g., security services, businesses involving controlled substances, and government employers).

Most honesty tests contain items concerning an applicant's attitudes toward theft. Sample items typically assess an individual's beliefs about the amount of theft that takes place (e.g., "What percentage of people take more than $1 per week from their employer?"), punitiveness toward theft (e.g., "Should a person be fired if caught stealing $5?"), and thoughts about stealing (e.g., "Have you ever thought about taking company merchandise without actually taking any?"). Other honesty tests include items that have been found to correlate with theft. For example, the following items appear on one such instrument: "You freely admit your mistakes," "You like to do things that shock people," and "You have had a lot of disagreements with your parents." Many banks and retail establishments use honesty tests for employee screening.

The validity evidence for paper-and-pencil honesty tests is fairly strong, and there is no evidence of adverse impact. However, critics point to a number of problems with the validity studies. First, practically all the validity studies have been conducted by the test publishers themselves; there have been very few independent validation studies. Second, few criteria-related validity studies use employee theft as the criterion. While a report by the American Psychological Association concluded that evidence supports the validity of some of the more carefully developed honesty tests, a recent federal government study concluded that the "existing research is insufficient as a basis for supporting the assertion that these tests can reliably predict dishonest behavior in the workplace."[22] Honesty tests cannot be used as the sole basis for an employment decision in Massachusetts. Similar legislation is pending in other states.

THE PREDICTION OF ACCIDENT PRONENESS. Accidents are a major problem in the workplace, causing deaths, injuries, and a great deal of expense for companies. Preemployment testing is one strategy some companies have turned to, in an effort to lower accident rates.

One new test developed for this purpose is the *Safety Locus of Control* (SLC), which is a paper-and-pencil test containing 17 items assessing attitudes toward safety.[23] A sample item is "Avoiding accidents is a matter of luck." Although the SLC is a rather new measure, initial validity studies have been encouraging. Such studies have been conducted in several different industries, including transportation, hotel, and manufacturing. In addition, these investigations indicate no adverse impact upon minorities and women.

CUSTOMER SERVICE ORIENTATION. Given the increase in service-related industries in the United States and global competition, more firms have become interested in ensuring quality service to customers. The *Service Orientation Index* (SOI) was initially developed as a means of predicting the helpfulness of nurses' aides in a large, inner-city hospital.[24] The test items were selected from a longer scale and were chosen on the basis of a study which examined the correlations of the items with performance by the aides on three dimensions: patient service, assisting other personnel, and communication. Examples of items on the SOI are "I always notice when people are upset" and "I never resent it when I don't get my way." Several other studies of the SOI involving clerical employees and truck drivers have reported positive results as well.

THE PREDICTION OF JOB COMPATIBILITY. Another new motivational instrument designed to predict employee performance and turnover is the *Job Compatibility Questionnaire* (JCQ).[25] The JCQ was developed to determine whether an applicant's preferences for work characteristics match the characteristics of the job. Test takers are presented with groups of items and are instructed to indicate which item is most desirable and which is least desirable. As we discussed in Chapter 4, the items are grouped based on a job analysis that identifies those characteristics which are common to the job or jobs to be filled. A sample group is: "(a) being able to choose the order of my work tasks; (b) having different and challenging projects; (c) staying physically active on the job; (d) clearly seeing the effects of my hard work." The items are grouped in such a way that the scoring key is hidden from the respondent and faking is thus reduced or eliminated.

Studies involving customer service representatives working for a newspaper, counter personnel employed by a fast-food chain, and personnel at AMC Theatres indicate that the JCQ can successfully predict employee turnover and job performance.[26] Also, no evidence of adverse impact has been found.

ESTABLISHING A TESTING PROGRAM

Establishing a psychological testing program is a difficult undertaking. The advice of an industrial psychologist is invaluable. At a minimum, the following strategy should be followed before using psychological tests:

1. Most reputable testing publishers provide a test manual. Study the manual carefully, particularly the adverse impact and validity evidence. Has the test been shown to predict success in jobs similar to the jobs you're trying to fill? Have adverse impact studies been performed? What have been the findings? Have positive studies conducted by independent researchers been published in scholarly journals? Have qualified experts with advanced degrees in psychology or related fields been involved in the research? Are there directions with regard to administering and interpreting the instrument for individuals with disabilities?

2. Check to see whether the test has been reviewed in the *Mental Measurements Yearbook* (available in most university libraries). The *Yearbook* publishes scholarly reviews of the test by qualified impartial academics.

3. Ask the test publishers for the names of several companies that have used the test. Call a sample of them and determine whether they have conducted adverse impact and validity studies. Determine whether legal actions have been taken related to the test. If so, what are the implications for your situation?

4. Obtain a copy of the test from the publisher and carefully examine all the test items. Consider each item in the context of ethical, legal, and privacy ramifications. Keep in mind that organizations have lost court cases because of specific items on a test.

The main point is to proceed cautiously in the selection and adoption of psychological tests. If you are impressed with a slick test brochure, take a step back and evaluate the product in the same manner you would evaluate any product before buying it. In general, it is always advisable to contact someone who can give you an objective, expert appraisal.

APPLICATION BLANKS, BIOGRAPHICAL DATA, AND REFERENCES

We have included application blanks and reference checks in this chapter because they are most effective when used like paper-and-pencil tests. For example, when the scoring keys for application blanks are empiri-

cally derived, the data can be used in the same manner as the scores from a paper-and-pencil test. The same principle applies to the proper use of reference material. Unfortunately, this is not how application blanks and references are typically used. Rather, these tools are usually used in an informal, intuitive manner.

Application Blanks

One of the most common sources of information for personnel selection is the application blank. Recall from the previous discussion that some selection tools assess ability, while others assess motivation. It is less clear that responses on an application blank measure ability. Most likely, the approach, like references, measures both ability and motivation to varying degrees. Often used as an initial screening method, the application blank can provide much more than a first cut. As in employment testing or any other selection procedure, when information on the application blank is used as a basis for screening people, the process falls under the scrutiny of the courts for possible equal employment opportunity (EEO) violations. Human resource (HR) managers should be cautious about using information on an application blank which disproportionately screens out minorities, women, or individuals with disabilities. In addition, HR managers must be careful not to ask illegal questions. For example, with passage of the 1990 Americans with Disabilities Act (ADA), application blanks should *not* include questions about an applicant's state of health or disabilities unless the issues are directly related to job performance.

While application blanks can obviously yield information relevant to an employment decision, the weight (or lack of weight) assigned to particular information by decision makers can often seriously undermine their usefulness. Decision makers often disagree on the relative importance of certain information on an application blank. For example, they may disagree on the amount of education or experience required. Recall that the Hartford Group required a bachelor's degree in business for the sales representative position. Did management within the Hartford Group believe that new applicants should be required to have an M.B.A.? Should 5 years' experience as a CPA be required? Is the person overeducated for the position? Does the fact that an applicant lives 50 miles from the office indicate he or she is likely to quit as soon as another job comes along which is closer to home? People who use application blanks typically assign subjective weights to the information, which may or may not be related to an important criterion such as performance or job tenure. The best way to use and interpret information on an application blank is to derive an objective weighting system based on an empirical research study.

An *empirical study* is one in which the responses on the application blanks are statistically related to one or more important criteria in such a way that critical predictive relationships can be identified. For example, the data could indicate whether M.B.A. employees are in fact more effective than employees who don't have an M.B.A. The process of statistically weighting the information on an application blank may enhance the use of the information on an application blank and improve the validity of the whole process. Below, we will briefly describe the process of deriving a *weighted application blank* (WAB). The WAB is simply an application blank that may be scored like a paper-and-pencil test. The WAB provides a score for each job candidate—a score which is comparable across all the candidates.

WABs have been used in a variety of settings and for a variety of jobs. WABs are used extensively in the insurance industry in the selection of agents, for clerical and sales jobs, and even for high-level jobs such as production supervisors and research scientists. In order to conduct the study to derive the weights for WABs, application and criterion data (e.g., job tenure and performance) are needed on a large representative sample (at least 150) of the employees in the position under study. Although there are many variations, the basic steps in the process of deriving weights for WABs are as follows:

1. **Select the criterion measure.** The first decision is what aspect of employee effectiveness is to be predicted. Research has shown that WABs are particularly useful in predicting turnover or job tenure.

2. **Determine the criterion groups.** Effectiveness must be defined in such a way that people can be classified as either effective or ineffective. A minimum of 50 employees is needed for each of the two groups.

3. **Code the existing application blanks.** A coding system must be developed for the responses on the application blank, and the system must be applied to the 100 application blanks of the people who were utilized in step 2. The response coding system should, of course, be uniform across the 100 applications. For example, "education" might be coded as follows: "1, not a high school graduate; 2, high school graduate; 3, some college; 4, college graduate; 5, some graduate work; 6, graduate degree."

4. **Derive the item response weights.** The item response weights and the relative weights for the responses are determined by comparing the responses of effective and ineffective employees, using various formulas.

5. **Cross-validate the weighting system.** The weighting system is cross-validated by using a "hold out" sample of employees who were not a part of the original study. A minimum of 50 new employees is needed for this step. The purpose of the cross-validation is to apply the scoring system to the application blanks of the holdout group to see whether the scores on the application blanks can successfully predict the criterion status of these employees. Thus, a total score on each application blank is derived based on the weighting system. The total score is then statistically related to the criterion status of each person.

6. **Derive a cutoff score.** The cutoff score is set in such a way that applicants who score at that level (or higher) are hired (or at least pass the first hurdle) and those who do not score at this level are not employed. Specific formulas are available for determining an optimal cutoff score.

A great deal of research supports the use of WABs in personnel selection. While the development of the scoring system obviously requires considerable work, the resultant decisions are often superior to those based on a subjective interpretation of the information on an application blank. Nevertheless, given the need for a large sample size, the WAB technique will probably only be useful for jobs with many incumbents.

Biographical Information Blanks

Biographical information blanks (BIBs) are a lot like WABs, except that the items on a BIB tend to be more personal and experiential (based on personal background and life experiences). Often presented in a multiple-choice format, BIBs are developed in much the same manner as WABs. Figure 6.3 presents some examples of items from a BIB for the U.S. Navy. Research with BIBs has shown the method can be an effective tool in the prediction of job turnover, job choice, and job performance. In one study conducted at the U.S. Naval Academy, biographical information derived from life-history essays of accomplishments was written in multiple-choice format and used on a BIB (see Figure 6.3).[27] Recent research suggests that BIBs may have validity that is generalizable across occupations and companies.[28]

Reference Checks

Over 95 percent of companies do reference checking. References are checked in an attempt to gather information from people who have had previous experience with the applicant. One purpose is to simply verify the information provided by the applicant regarding previous employment and experience. This is important because research indicates that between 20 and 25 percent of job applications include at least one major fabrication.[29] A second

**FIGURE 6.3
EXAMPLES OF BIB ITEMS**

How often have you made speeches in front of a group of adults?

How often have you set long-term goals or objectives for yourself?

How often have other students come to you for advice?

How often have you had to persuade someone to do what you wanted?

How often have you felt that you were an unimportant member of a group?

How often have you felt awkward about asking for help on something?

How often do you work in study groups with other students?

How often have you had difficulties in maintaining your priorities?

How often have you felt "burnt out" after working hard on a task?

How often have you felt pressured to do something when you thought it was wrong?

Source: C. J. Russell, J. Matson, S. E. Devlin, and D. Atwater, Predictive validity of biodata items generated from retrospective life experience essays. *Journal of Applied Psychology, 75,* 569–580, 1990. Copyright 1990 by the American Psychological Association. Reprinted by permission.

purpose is to assess the potential success of the person for the new job. Unfortunately, a proliferation of lawsuits has engendered a great reluctance on the part of evaluators to provide anything other than a statement about when a person was employed and in what capacity. These lawsuits have been directed at previous employers for defamation of character, fraud, and intentional infliction of emotional distress. Many organizations will not allow employees to provide any information on a former employee other than dates of employment and job title.

It is possible to construct a format for outside information on job candidates which provides for performance-based data on specific, job-related areas.[30] A performance rating form can be constructed which asks the evaluator to indicate the extent to which the candidate was effective in performing a list of job tasks. The tasks to be evaluated are those which are most important for the position to be filled. An alternative approach asks the evaluator to rate the extent of job-related knowledge, skill, ability, or other characteristics of a candidate. These ratings can then be weighted on the basis of the relative importance of the knowledges, abilities, skills, and other characteristics (KASOCs) for the position to be filled.

Despite the difficulty with and problems of obtaining accurate reference information, employers are encouraged to do their utmost to obtain this information. If, for no other reason, a "good-faith" effort to obtain

verification of employment history may enable a company to successfully win a negligent hiring lawsuit.[31]

DRUG TESTING

Drug abuse is generally regarded as one of the most serious problems confronting the United States today. The cost to productivity is thought to be in the billions and on the increase. Drug abuse in the workplace has been linked to employee theft, accidents, absences, and other counterproductive behavior. One survey found almost 25 percent of employees from the retail sector of the U.S. economy tested positively for drugs. To combat this problem, many organizations are turning to drug testing for job applicants and incumbents. While some of the tests are in the form of paper-and-pencil examinations, the vast majority are clinical tests of urine samples or urinalysis. Hair analysis is also gaining in popularity. Blockbuster Video requires a 3-inch hair sample to use in tracing drug use back 3 months. Needless to say, this testing is controversial. According to the American Management Association (AMA), 63 percent of firms now use some form of drug testing. About one-third of companies with testing programs said they fire workers who test positive. Ninety-six percent of firms refuse to hire applicants who test positive. The most common practice is to test job applicants, but drug testing of job incumbents either through a randomized procedure or based on probable cause is also on the increase.[32]

The most common form of urinalysis testing is the immunoassay test, which applies an enzyme solution to a urine sample and measures change in the density of the sample. The major difficulty with immunoassay tests is that they are sensitive to some legal drugs as well as illegal drugs. Due to this problem, it is recommended that a positive immunoassay test be followed by a more reliable "confirmatory" test such as gas chromatography. The only errors in testing that can occur with the confirmatory tests are due to positive results from passive inhalation (e.g., marijuana), which is rare, and laboratory blunders, such as mixing urine samples.

Of course, positive drug test results say little regarding the individual's ability to perform the job. Most testing gives little or no information about the amount of the drug which was used, when it was used, how frequently it was used, and whether the applicant or candidate will be (or is) less effective on the job.

The legal implications of drug testing may have changed significantly since this chapter was written. As of the present, drug testing is generally legal for both pre-employment screening and on-the-job assessment. However, some dismissals of incumbents based on a random drug test (despite no evidence of performance decrements) have been challenged successfully by employees. Also, collective bargaining units have strongly opposed such programs. For those employment situations in which the collective bargaining agreement has allowed drug testing, the punitive action based on the results is subject to arbitration. One study found that a majority of dismissals based on drug tests were overturned by arbitrators.[33] Among the arguments against drug testing are that it is an invasion of privacy, it is an "unreasonable search and seizure," and it violates the right of due process. Most experts agree that all three of these arguments may apply to public employers (e.g., governments) but do not apply to private industry. However, California has laws that extend the right of privacy to private-sector employees, and drug testing programs have been challenged under these laws. Even with regard to public employment, however, the U.S. Supreme Court has ruled that drug testing is legal when the public safety is relevant (e.g., in transportation). We will explore drug testing in more detail in Chapter 16.

Ethical Issues in Testing

Some critics have expressed concern over the widespread use of employment tests on the grounds that these procedures may be an invasion of individuals' privacy, may produce information that will affect an individual's employment opportunities, and may compel people to falsify information.[34] Some types of employment tests seem particularly prone to these concerns. Among the selection devices reviewed in this chapter that seem most likely to face these problems are drug tests, reference checks, application blanks, honesty tests, and personality tests.[35] For example, one survey revealed that over 60 percent of respondents felt that questions regarding arrest records, memberships in community organizations, and the like were inappropriate. Court cases at the state level have also challenged particular items on standardized personality tests as violations of privacy provisions.

Experts in the field of employment testing who support the use of these types of selection procedures have responded to these challenges in a number of ways. First, various professional standards and guidelines have been devised to protect the confidentiality of test results. There are also some legal avenues employees and applicants can pursue that prevent organizations from carelessly releasing information (e.g., libel, defamation, and antidiscrimination laws). Second, almost any interpersonal interaction, whether it be in the context of an interview or an informal discussion with an employer over a lunch, involves the exchange of information. Thus, advocates of employment testing contend that every selection procedure comprises some invasion of the applicant's privacy. Finally, in the interests of high productivity and staying within the law,

organizations may need to violate an individual's privacy.[36] Companies that have government contracts, for example, are obliged to maintain a safe work environment, which in turn may require drug testing of employees.

Concern over the confidentiality and ethics of employment testing will continue to be voiced, particularly as computer data bases expand in scope and availability to organizations. At the same time, it is likely that there will be increasing calls for more legislation at federal, state, and local levels to restrict company access to and use of employment-related information.

PERFORMANCE TESTING*

Despite their valuable contribution to employee selection, paper-and-pencil tests have problems and limitations. While the validity of cognitive ability tests is clear, the potential legal implications which stem from their use is considerable. In addition, the validity of paper-and-pencil measures of applicant motivation or personality is not nearly as impressive. Many experts suggest that the prediction of job performance can be enhanced through performance or situational testing which involves "samples" of actual or simulated job behaviors or tasks required for the job. Performance testing is more complex than paper-and-pencil testing in that behavioral responses are required by test takers which are similar to the responses required on the job.[37]

A work sample consists of tasks which represent the type, complexities, and difficulty level of activities that are actually required on the job. Applicants must demonstrate that they possess the necessary skills needed for successful job performance. The most obvious example of a work sample is a word processing test for clerical personnel. More complex examples attempt to simulate what managers must do on the job. Assessment centers, for example, often use several work samples or simulations of on-the-job behaviors typically exhibited by managers.

The objective of performance testing is to assess a candidate's ability to do the job. Thus, applicants for clerical positions may be required to take tests on word processors, or to demonstrate their proficiency in shorthand or their ability to file documents. These exercises are work samples because word processing, filing, and shorthand are representative of the tasks someone in a clerical position might be asked to do. The applicants are expected to possess these skills at the time of the interview. Performance tests are active in that they measure dynamic behavior, in contrast to psychological measurements of qualities such as aptitude, achievement, or

*This section contributed by Joan E. Pynes.

interest. A performance test is relatively more effective to the degree that there is an overlap between the tasks or activities required in the test situation and the tasks required for the actual job. For example, requesting that clerical applicants demonstrate shorthand skills is effective only if shorthand skills are required for the position. To ensure that performance tests are tailored to match the important activities of the job, the performance test should be developed from the tasks, behaviors, and responsibilities identified in a job analysis (see Chapter 4).

The performance testing process should be as standardized as possible, with consistent and precise instructions, testing material, conditions, and equipment. For example, it would not be fair to have some clerical applicants take a test with word processing software compatible with the software to be used on the job while others took the exam with different, incompatible software. All candidates must also have the same time allotment to complete the test. There must be a specific standard of performance with which to compare applicants' efforts. For example, a minimum passing score for the exam should be set and applied to all the applicants (e.g., 40 WPM with 2 errors).

Many organizations use various forms of work samples or performance tests. AT&T, for example, uses a telephone simulation as a major step in its process for the selection of operators. The city of Miami uses a number of work sample tests for mechanical and electronic jobs. The U.S. Navy conducts extensive work sample testing for many of its skill-based positions. Digital Equipment Corporation uses a debugging work sample in the selection process for computer programmers. Nationsbank gives prospective tellers a short training course on cashing checks and then presents a series of videotapes showing different check-cashing situations. The National Board of Medical Examiners, which administers a battery of tests doctors must pass before practicing, plans to include a performance test which assesses "bedside manner."

The Assessment Center Method

An *assessment center* has been defined as a method which enables "standardized evaluation of behavior on multiple inputs. Multiple trained observers and techniques are used. Judgements [sic] about behavior are made, in part, from specially developed assessment simulations."[38] Job candidates at assessment centers are typically tested with performance tests or work samples which simulate the work environment. Some centers also use paper-and-pencil tests as part of the assessment process. At the Center for Creative Leadership in Greensboro, North Carolina, high-level managers complete an extensive battery of cognitive and personality tests and receive subor-

dinate, peer, and superior assessments prior to their participation in a week-long assessment procedure.

Private-sector organizations, educational institutions, military organizations, and public safety and other governmental agencies have used the assessment center method to identify candidates for selection, placement, and promotion. Assessment centers are used most frequently for supervisory or managerial positions in both the private and the public sectors. However, there have been many applications of the method to nonadministrative positions, as in the selection of sales personnel, vocational rehabilitation counselors, planning analysts, social workers, personnel specialists, research analysts, firefighters, and police officers. Assessment centers are also used for training and development. For example, thousands of executives have participated in the assessment center developed by the Center for Creative Leadership. Among the numerous organizations which use the assessment center method for selection or employee development are TVA, AT&T, International Business Machines (IBM), Ford, Xerox, Procter & Gamble, the U.S. Department of Defense, the Central Intelligence Agency (CIA), and the Federal Aviation Administration (FAA). The assessment center method is expensive, with costs ranging from a low of about $125 per candidate to as much as $3000 for upper-level managerial candidates.

With the typical assessment center method, information about an employee's strengths and weaknesses is acquired through a combination of assessment exercises. These exercises are designed to simulate the type of work which the candidate will be expected to do. Performance in the situational exercises is observed and evaluated by a team of trained assessors. The assessors' judgments on each exercise are compiled and integrated to form a summary rating for each candidate being assessed.

Many variations exist in the actual operation of assessment centers. Some primary variations among assessment center programs are: differences in their purpose and use (viz., selection, promotion, training and development), the length of the assessment process (from 1 day to 1 week), the ratio of assessors to assessees, the extent of assessor training, the size of the group assessed, and the number and type of assessment instruments and exercises.[39]

All assessment centers call for an assessment of job dimensions or competencies. For example, United Technology evaluates managers on the following competencies: oral presentation, initiative, leadership, planning and organizing, written communication, decision making, and interpersonal skills.

Dimensions have been defined as clusters of behaviors that are specific, observable, and verifiable, and that can be reliably and logically classified together.[40] For example, the dimension *written communication* was defined by United Technology as the "clear expression of ideas in writing and in good grammatical form." Behavioral examples of written communication were further broken down as follows: "Exchanges information/reports with superior regarding the day's activities, . . . completes all written reports and required forms in a manner that ensures the inclusion of all data necessary to meet the needs of the personnel using the information, . . . uses appropriate vocabulary and avoids excessive technical jargon in required correspondence." Figure 6.4 presents a set of dimensions and their definitions as used in an assessment center for selecting supervisors. These dimensions have been shown to be critical for success in both supervisory and managerial positions.

The assessment dimensions and exercises are developed from the results of a job analysis. The exercises allow trained assessors to observe, record, classify, and evaluate job-relevant behaviors. Some of the most common assessment exercises are in-baskets, leaderless group discussions, oral presentations, and role plays. We will review each of these next. Figure 6.5 presents summary descriptions of four exercises used in an assessment center to select first-line supervisors for a high-tech organization.

IN-BASKET. The in-basket consists of a variety of materials of varying importance and priority which would typically be handled by an incumbent. A set of instructions usually asks candidates to imagine that they are placed in an administrative position and must deal with a number of memos and items accumulated in their in-basket. They are given background information about the unit they are managing, and they must deal with the in-basket materials in a limited amount of time. Written responses are required on each memo. The candidates are then interviewed by trained assessors who review the out-baskets and question the actions taken. In-baskets are typically designed to measure oral and written communication skills, planning, decisiveness, initiative, and organization skills.

LEADERLESS GROUP DISCUSSION. Candidates are assembled in groups of three to six people, after they have individually considered an issue or problem. Their instructions are to make specific recommendations and decisions. A leader is not designated for the group, but one usually emerges in the course of the group interaction. Two or more assessors typically observe the interaction as the group attempts to reach consensus on the issue. The leaderless group discussion has been used to assess dimensions such as oral communication, tolerance for stress, adaptability, leadership, and persuasiveness. Some graduate schools now use the leaderless group discussion to select students for graduate programs, or to provide feedback to students.

FIGURE 6.4
ASSESSMENT CENTER DIMENSIONS

Leadership: Direct, coordinate, and guide the activities of others; monitor, instruct, and motivate others in the performance of their tasks; assign duties and responsibilities, and follow up on assignments; utilize available human and technical resources in accomplishing tasks and in achieving solutions to problems; follow through within organizational guidelines.

Interpersonal: Be sensitive to the needs and feelings of others; respond empathetically; consistently display courtesy in interpersonal contacts; develop rapport with others; be cognizant of and respect the need in others for self-esteem.

Organizing and planning: Create strategies to enable self and others to accomplish specific results; utilize prescribed strategies; fix schedules and priorities so as to meet objectivities; coordinate personnel and other resources; establish and utilize follow-up procedures.

Perception and analysis: Identify, assimilate, and comprehend the critical elements of a situation; identify alternative courses of action; be aware of situational or data discrepancies; evaluate salient factors and elements essential to resolution of problems.

Decision making: Exercise logical and sound judgment in use of resources; adequately assess a situation and make a sound and logical determination of an appropriate course of action based on the facts available, including established procedures and guidelines; select solutions to problems by weighing the ramifications of alternative courses of action.

Oral and nonverbal communication: Present information to others concisely and without ambiguity; articulate clearly; use appropriate voice inflection, grammar, and vocabulary; maintain appropriate eye contact; display congruent nonverbal behavior.

Adaptability: Modify courses of action to accommodate situational changes; vary behavior in accordance with changes in human and interpersonal factors; withstand stress.

Decisiveness: Make appropriate decisions; make decisions spanning many different areas; render judgments, take action, and make commitments; react quickly to situational changes; make determinations based on available evidence; defend actions when challenged by others.

Written communications: Present and express information in writing, employing unambiguous, concise, and effective language; use correct grammar, punctuation, and sentence structure; adjust writing style to the demands of the communication.

ORAL PRESENTATION. Candidates are allowed a brief time to plan, organize, and prepare a presentation on an assigned topic. An assessment center developed by IBM, for example, requires candidates for sales management positions to prepare and deliver a 5-minute oral presentation in which they present one of their hypothetical staff members for promotion and then defend the staff member in a group discussion. IBM uses this exercise to

**FIGURE 6.5
DESCRIPTION OF ASSESSMENT
CENTER EXERCISES**

Customer situation: A large equipment user (a selected national account) has recently been experiencing problems involving a particular piece of equipment, culminating in a systems-down situation. Problems with the equipment could include software, and parts received to fix the equipment are damaged.

The participant will be required to review information about the problem for 30 minutes and generate potential courses of action. Participants will then meet in groups to devise a consensus strategy for dealing with the problem. Assessors should expect a plan of action from the participants and may probe the participants for additional contingency plans. The participants will have 45 minutes to discuss the customer problem and develop a strategy.

Employee discussion: In this exercise, the participant must develop a strategy for counseling a subordinate (a senior customer service engineer) who has recently been experiencing performance problems. The participant will have 30 minutes to review information regarding the technician's declining performance over the last few months.

The participant will then have 15 minutes to prepare a brief report on the individual with recommendations for submission to the district manager. The participant will then meet with two assessors to discuss the strategy.

In-basket: In this exercise, the participant will assume the role of a newly transferred branch manager. The participant will have 90 minutes to review information related to various issues (technical developments, equipment maintenance specifications, customer information, etc.). The participant will be instructed to spend this time identifying priorities and grouping related issues, as well as indicating courses of action to be taken. The participant will then take part in a 15-minute interview with an assessor to clarify the actions taken and the logic behind the decisions that were made.

Problem analysis: In this exercise the participant will be required to review information on three candidates and provide a recommendation on which of the three should be promoted to a branch manager position. The participant will have 90 minutes to review information and prepare a written recommendation. The participants will then meet in groups to derive a consensus recommendation for the district manager.

evaluate aggressiveness, selling ability, self-confidence, resistance to stress, and interpersonal contact.[41]

ROLE-PLAY EXERCISE. For this common assessment center exercise, candidates assume the role of the incumbent in the position and deal with a subordinate about a performance problem. (The subordinate is a trained role player.) Another possibility is to have candidates interact with "clients" or individuals external to the organization, requiring them to obtain information or alleviate a problem. For example, a candidate for the position of vocational rehabilitation counselor, who is applying

for a job with the Massachusetts Rehabilitation Commission, assumes the role of a counselor who is meeting a client for the first time. The candidate is responsible for gaining information on the client's case and establishing rapport with the client.[42]

The Assessment Process

All the candidates in an assessment center (usually 6 to 12 people) perform the same tasks and are evaluated by assessors who have received extensive training on assessment center methodology. The behavioral dimensions which are assessed in each activity are clearly defined, and the assessors are given instructions and practice in how to recognize the designated behaviors.

Often, assessors are representatives from the organization who are at least two levels above the position for which the candidates are being assessed. This is done to diminish the potential for contamination, which may result from an assessor allowing prior association with a candidate to interfere with making an objective evaluation. Some assessment centers use outside consultants and psychologists as assessors.

The assessment center candidates are observed by different assessors in each exercise. The assessors are responsible for observing the actual behavior of the candidate during each exercise and documenting how each candidate performed. Figure 6.6 presents an example of an assessor rating form for the "leadership" dimension, used in the selection of supervisors at the Bendix Corporation.

After the participants complete all the exercises, the assessors typically assemble for a team meeting to pool their impressions and arrive at an overall consensus rating for each candidate on each dimension. An overall assessment rating for selection or promotion purposes is also derived.

Validity and Adverse Impact of Assessment Centers and Other Performance Tests

The research evidence supports the validity of assessment centers. However, with few exceptions, assessment center validity studies have focused on administrative positions such as managers and supervisors.[43] The methodology has also proved to be valid for law enforcement personnel.[44] One review of the validity literature found that assessment centers correlated .53 with promotion within the organization, but only .36 with rated job behavior.[45]

The validity evidence of work samples and performance testing is also strong. One review found an average validity of .54 for work samples.[46] While the validities reported for assessment centers are no higher than those reported for most cognitive ability tests, decisions made

FIGURE 6.6
EXAMPLE OF ASSESSOR RATING FORM

Leadership   Rating _____

Direct, coordinate, and guide the activities of others; monitor, instruct, and motivate others in the performance of their tasks; assign duties and responsibilities, and follow up on assignments; utilize available human and technical resources in accomplishing tasks and in achieving solutions to problems; follow through within organizational guidelines.

Key points:*

• Requested technical support when necessary.

• Provided specific guidance to others through written means.

• Took initiative to reallocate Branch I workforce personnel.

• Assigned tasks to others.

Positive   Negative

* These are general points; specific behaviors need to be listed by the assessor.

in assessment centers appear to be much more defensible in court and to result in less adverse impact than cognitive ability testing.

COMBINING PROCEDURES AND DATA FOR PERSONNEL DECISIONS

A number of selection procedures have been proposed in this chapter, and an underlying theme is that more than one approach should be used. For example, LIMRA's re-search led to a recommendation of a standardized biographical instrument, a battery of four cognitive ability tests, a sales aptitude test, and a detailed structured interview. But how should the data from the different tests be combined so that a final decision can be made regarding the applicant(s) to be selected?

One approach is to weight scores from each approach equally after standardizing the data. Each applicant receives a standard score on each predictor, the standard scores are summed, and the candidates are rank-ordered according to the summed scores. Another approach is to weight scores based on their empirical validity (i.e., the extent to which each is correlated with the criterion of interest). Multiple regression analysis can be used, in which scores on the criterion of interest are regressed onto all the scores on the predictors. The resultant regression weights are then used to weight scores on the instruments in the future. Research shows that equal or unit weighting does as well or better than empirically derived weighting for most situations (there are a few exceptions).

LIMRA recommended unit weights for all valid instruments except an expensive team-based interview. They recommended rank-ordering candidates based on all criteria except the interview and then interviewing the top candidates based on the number of positions they had to fill. This multiple-step process saved time and money. Most companies which use a variety of different instruments follow a similar procedure with the least expensive procedure (e.g., paper-and-pencil tests, gathering biographical data) used initially and a second set of procedures (e.g., performance tests) used next for candidates who perform well in the first phase of testing. After screening based on the second set of instruments, interviews are conducted with the top scorers from the second phase of testing. The CIA, the Federal Bureau of Investigation (FBI), numerous insurance companies, and a number of the most prestigious graduate business schools follow a similar procedure. For example, the Wharton School at the University of Pennsylvania does initial screening on the basis of the GMAT and undergraduate performance, then requests answers to lengthy essay questions. Students who survive these hurdles are interviewed on the campus by several faculty members.

What are the legal implications of this multiple-step process? Do you remember the U.S. Supreme Court ruling in *Connecticut v. Teal,* which we discussed in Chapter 3? Mr. Teal was eliminated from further consideration at the first step of a multiple-step selection process. He claimed that he was a victim of Title VII discrimination. The Supreme Court said that even if the company actually hired a disproportionately greater number of minorities after the entire selection process, the job relatedness of the first step must be determined because that was the step in which Mr. Teal was eliminated.

Another issue is where to set the cutoff score in a multiple cutoff system such as that recommended by LIMRA. Where, for example, do you set the cutoff score for the paper-and-pencil tests in order to identify candidates who are eligible for further testing? Unfortunately, there is no clear answer to this important question. In general, if data are available, cutoff scores for any step in the process should be set so as to ensure that a minimum predicted standard of job performance is met. If data are not available, cutoff scores should be based upon a consideration of the cost of subsequent selection procedures

per candidate, the legal defensibility of each step in the process (i.e., its job relatedness), and the adverse impact of possible scores at each step.

PERSONNEL SELECTION FOR OVERSEAS ASSIGNMENTS*

One expert on expatriate assignments tells the story of a major U.S. food manufacturer who selected the new head of the marketing division in Japan. The assumption made in the selection process was that the management skills required for successful performance in the United States were identical to the requirements for an overseas assignment. The new director was selected primarily because of his superior marketing skills. Within 18 months his company lost 89 percent of its existing market share.[47]

What went wrong? The problem may have been the criteria which were used in the selection process. The selection criteria used to hire a manager for an overseas position must focus on more facets of a manager than the selection of someone for a domestic position. The weight given to the various criteria may also be different for overseas assignments. Besides succeeding in a job, an effective expatriate must adjust to a variety of factors, including: differing job responsibilities even though the same job title is used; language and cultural barriers that make the training of local personnel difficult; family matters such as spouse employment and family readjustment; simple routine activities which are frustrating in the new culture; and the lack of traditional support systems, such as religious institutions or social clubs. The marketing head in Japan, for example, spent considerable time during the first 6 months of his assignment simply trying to deal with family problems and to adjust to the new environment. This experience is hardly unique. One survey of 80 U.S. multinational corporations found that over 50 percent of the companies had expatriate failure rates of 20 percent or higher.[48] The reasons cited for the high failure rate were as follows (presented in order of importance): (1) inability of the manager's spouse to adjust to the new environment, (2) the manager's inability to adapt to a new culture and environment, (3) the manager's personality or emotional immaturity, (4) the manager's inability to cope with new overseas responsibilities, (5) the manager's lack of technical competence, and (6) the manager's lack of motivation to work overseas. Obviously, some of these problems have to do with training and career issues. One international recruiter writes that "American executives are hesitant to take on overseas as-

---

*This section contributed by P. Christopher Earley.

signments because of a loss of visibility at headquarters" and the fear of losing status when repatriated.[49]

Several of the factors listed above concern the process of selecting personnel for such assignments. The food manufacturer placed almost all the decision weight on the technical competence of the individual, apparently figuring that he and his family could adjust or adapt to almost anything. In fact, we now know that adjustment can be predicted to some extent and that personnel selection systems should place emphasis on adaptability along with the ability to interact well with clients, customers, and business associates who are of a different culture. Surprisingly, few organizations place emphasis on so-called relational abilities in the selection of expatriates. In fact, a recent review of expatriate selection cites the "domestic equals overseas performance equation" as one of the major problems in expatriate selection. The result is an overemphasis on technical skills and previous accomplishments in a domestic setting.[50] The study concluded that the selection of expatriates should focus on four key dimensions: (1) self-orientation, (2) other-directedness, (3) perceptual factors, and (4) cultural toughness. The self-orientation dimension is concerned with activities which serve to enhance self-esteem through reinforcement substitution, stress reduction, and technical competence. Stress levels can be measured with personality instruments. The other-directed dimension has to do with the ability to interact with host-country nationals. The perceptual dimension reflects an ability to understand how foreigners behave and can also be measured with standardized personality instruments. The cultural toughness dimension has to do with the extent to which the culture and environment of the host country are different from those in the United States. To the extent that the difference is great, more weight should be given to the other three dimensions.

Of course, one critical question which must first be addressed is whether a corporation would be better off hiring someone from within the host country. Figure 6.7 presents a decision model which begins with the question whether the position could be filled from within the host country. If the answer to this question is no, the model provides a chronology of the questions to be answered in the selection of an expatriate. If the answer is yes, the decision makers must be aware of any applicable host laws regarding personnel selection. In Poland and Sweden, for example, prospective employees must have prior knowledge of any testing and can prohibit the release of testing data to the company. Many European countries require union participation in all selection decisions for host nationals. Thus, companies may find that hiring host nationals is more problematic than going the expatriate route. Assuming that the host option is rejected, what steps should be followed to make better staffing deci-

sions about expatriates? Let us examine some organizations which select large numbers of expatriates, and do it quite successfully.[51]

The Peace Corps has only a 12 percent turnover rate (i.e., people who prematurely end their assignments). Of the 12 percent, only 3 to 4 percent are attributed to selection errors. The Peace Corps receives an average of 5000 applications a month. The initial screening is based on five sources of information. The selection process begins with an elaborate application and biographical data form which provides information on background, education, vocational preferences, and volunteer activity in the past. Second, the applicant must take a placement test to assess general intelligence and language aptitude. Third, college or high school transcripts are used for placement rather than screening. The fourth step requires up to 15 references from a variety of sources. Although the general tendency among references is to provide positive views of candidates, one study found that for sensitive positions such as Peace Corps volunteer, references often provide candid comments about applicants. The final step is an interview with several Peace Corp representatives. During the interview process the candidate is asked about preferred site locations and specific skills, as well as how he or she would deal with hypothetical problems that might occur overseas. An ideal candidate must be flexible and tolerant of others and must indicate a capacity to get work done under adverse conditions. The interviews also provide the Peace Corps staff with details concerning the candidate's background and preferences so that appropriate work assignments may be determined.

Based on these four sources of information, the screeners assess a candidate using the following questions: (1) Does the applicant have a skill that is needed overseas, or a background that indicates he or she may be able to develop such a skill within a 3-month training period? This question is designed to match the candidate with a job required by a foreign government, such as botanist, small business consultant, or medical worker. (2) Is the applicant personally suited for the assignment? This question focuses on personality traits such as flexibility, maturity, and emotional stability.

Another expert on expatriate selection suggests focusing the process on environmental, task, and individual factors.[52] The environmental factors concern the specific national setting to which an expatriate may be assigned. Task factors deal with the specific job to be performed. Individual factors concern the makeup and situation of the person being considered for the assignment. Candidates should be selected on the basis of all these dimensions rather than solely on job competence.

The weight to be given to these factors differs as a function of the position to be filled. For example, a position which has an operational element requiring an in-

FIGURE 6.7
MODEL OF THE SELECTION PROCESS FOR OVERSEAS ASSIGNMENTS

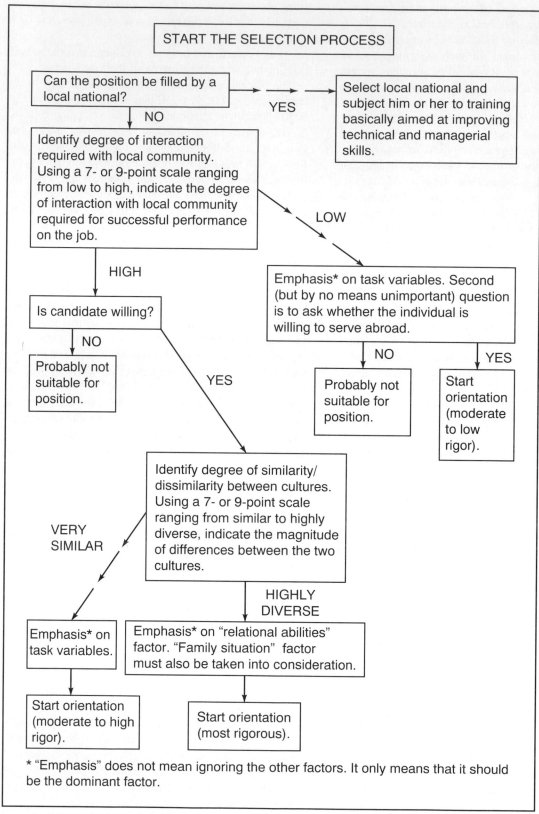

Source: R.L. Tung, Selection and training for overseas assignments. *California Journal of World Business, 16*, 68–78, 1981. Reprinted with the permission of the Columbia Journal of World Business, copyright 1981.

dividual to perform in a preexisting structure does not require strong interpersonal skills. A "structure reproducer," however—an individual who builds a structure in a foreign locale similar to his or her domestic structure—does need strong interpersonal skills. Thus, the selection system should focus on the cultural environment, job elements, and individual talents, and the weights given to the various criteria should be determined by the individual job. A job analysis would be helpful in this regard. This system is exemplified by Texas Instruments (TI), a manufacturer of electronics and high-technology equipment based in Dallas. TI has a variety of foreign investments and subsidiaries including several located in the Pacific-Asian basin. In seeking expatriates for start-up ventures, the company focuses on such issues as an individual's familiarity with the region and culture (environment), specific job knowledge for the venture (job elements), knowledge of the language spoken in the region, and interpersonal skills. TI uses several methods to make assessments on these dimensions, including paper-and-pencil personality tests.

Many companies emphasize the "manager as ambassador" approach since the expatriate may act as the sole representative of the home office. IBM and GE, for example, select people who best symbolize the esprit de corps of the company and who recognize the importance of overseas assignments for the company.

Our review of the most successful systems for selecting expatriates provides a set of recommendations for a selection system. First, potential expatriates are identified through posted announcements, peer and/or superior nominations, or performance appraisal data. Second, promising candidates are contacted and presented with an overview of the work assignment. A realistic job preview would be ideal at this stage. Third, applicants are examined using a number of selection methods, including paper-and-pencil tests and performance tests. A growing number of companies now use standardized instruments to assess personality traits. The 16PF, for example, has been used for years to select overseas personnel for the U.S. Department of State and is now used by a small number of large U.S. companies and executive search companies which specialize in expatriate assignments. However, despite the fact that relational ability is considered to be a major predictor of success as an expatriate, the one available survey of the subject found that only 5 percent of companies were assessing this ability through a formal process (e.g., paper-and-pencil tests, performance appraisals).

After a small pool of qualified candidates is identified, candidates are interviewed and the best matches are selected for the assignment. Successful expatriates are ideal as interviewers. Chapter 7 provides recommendations for enhancing the validity of interview decisions. Do the more rigorous selection systems result in a higher rate of expatriate success? One study found a strong relationship between the rigor of the selection process and the success of the expatriate.[53]

PERSONNEL SELECTION IN OTHER COUNTRIES

The use of employment tests in other countries of the world varies widely. Turning first to Asian countries, Korean employers use employment tests extensively; one survey indicated that more than 85 percent of Korea's largest conglomerates selected new employees solely on the basis of tests.[54] These tests tended to be written examinations covering English language skills, common sense, and knowledge of specific disciplines. Most other major Asian countries appear to make far less use of employment tests.

A much smaller percentage of Japanese companies use employment tests for selection in Japan.[55] This may be due to the fact that most people are hired directly from the universities, and the prestige of the university attended is a major criterion for selection purposes. While the use of intelligence and personality tests for staffing decisions is far less common in Japan than in the United States, some translations of English versions are available in Japan. For example, the Wechsler Intelligence Scale for Adults, the Wonderlic, the 16PF, the MMPI, the Guilford personality instruments, and the Rorschach inkblot test are all available in Japan and are used by a small number of companies.[56]

Some Japanese companies make extensive use of paper-and-pencil and performance testing to hire U.S. workers for some of the more than 1400 Japanese plants throughout the United States. Mazda, Mitsubishi, and Isuzu are among the companies that do considerable testing. Entry-level tests cover basic math and verbal aptitude, psychomotor skills such as manual dexterity, and technical knowledge for the skilled trades. Mazda uses a "job-fitness" test which assesses applicants' attitudes toward the Japanese style and philosophy of work. The contents look similar to a test that would screen out people who would be receptive to a unionization drive. Toyota uses an assessment center in which candidates discuss a manufacturing problem on a hypothetical assembly line. Candidates also actually participate in an assembly task for circuit boards, while assessors evaluate their ability to do tedious work and to maintain a fast pace. The selection process concludes with a drug test and an interview in which representatives from several departments participate.

Other Japanese companies with plants in the United States rely on other methods for personnel selection. The Nissan plant in Tennessee has a 1-week probationary or tryout period; a high percentage of new people are not asked to return after the tryout. Nippondenso utilizes the assessment center to select managers. Many other companies make extensive use of employment interviews in which all or most team members participate in the selection process and provide critical input for the final decision.

A survey of companies in Hong Kong and Singapore revealed little use of employment tests.[57] Although some clerical and office tests (e.g., typing) were used, only two companies from these countries indicated use of personality, cognitive ability, or related tests. Finally, China also makes little use of employment testing, although this is not surprising given that employees are usually assigned to companies, rather than being chosen by the organizations.[58]

European countries, including England, have had a variety of experiences with the use of employment tests. Although systematic reports on the use of tests in these countries are generally not available,[59] some general conclusions can be drawn. For example, a wide variety of employment tests appear to be used in Switzerland, including graphology and astrology.[60] In Italy, however, selection tests are forbidden by law![61]

There have been several surveys regarding selection methods in England. One survey found that over 80 percent of companies in England do some type of reference check,[62] and another found that almost 40 percent of firms in England had used personality tests and 25 percent used cognitive ability tests to assess managers. Interestingly, as compared with the United States, the use of graphology was relatively high; about 8 percent of surveyed firms in England reported use of this procedure on some occasions.

Unions in Europe are much more involved in the development and selection of hiring procedures than are unions in the United States. The "right of determination" for German Work Councils, for example, has established an obligation for companies to confer with the union on matters related to personnel. It is likely that the European Community will adopt standards for testing which will apply to all 12 EC nations.

In sum, there is wide variation in the use of employment tests outside the United States. While some countries have severe restrictions on the use of personnel selection tests (e.g., Italy), test use is far more extensive in others (e.g., Korea). The United States and England appear to be major centers for research and development of employment tests. Japanese companies make extensive use of testing for their U.S. plants.[63]

SUMMARY

Due to the need to increase productivity and provide insulation from lawsuits, the importance of effective preemployment testing is increasing. In this chapter we have reviewed a number of commonly used tests, which have varying reliability, validity, and legal implications. While cognitive ability tests are among the most valid measures, they also frequently result in adverse impact upon minority groups. Conversely, many personality tests are safe from legal problems because they have no adverse impact, but their validity is more questionable. A majority of U.S. companies now use preemployment drug tests. While these tests are generally legal to use, their legality differs from state to state. There is recent evidence that drug tests will screen out less effective employees. Reference checks may not be a particularly "valid" selection device, but court decisions regarding negligent hiring lawsuits indicate that employers should do their best to check applicant references. Finally, paper-and-pencil honesty tests are being used by a growing number of companies, given restrictions on polygraph testing. Despite some political activity to amend the polygraph law to include a federal ban on these tests as well, the limited research on these tests seems to support their use. Tests which assess job compatibility appear to have potential in predicting performance and turnover.

Assessment center and performance testing results tend to be more accurate than the results of some other sources of data, such as performance appraisals or interview performance, because the behaviors exhibited in multiple exercises provide a more comprehensive picture of candidates' ability to perform a given job, reflecting both aptitude and motivation to do the work. However, assessment center testing and other performance tests are typically more expensive than other methods of personnel selection. Most companies use a variety of selection procedures, typically proceeding through the process in the chronology presented in Figure 6.1, but unfortunately stopping at Step 3 before implementing the process. While some organizations combine the information from the various sources by using a statistical model which enhances the accuracy of decision making, most companies apply a subjective weighting system to determine the rank-ordering of candidates for the positions to be filled.

Almost all companies use an employment interview at some point in the selection process. We will discuss this important method of selection next. Employers must carefully monitor their selection methods with regard to relevant local, state, and federal legislation (U.S. and other countries) and, in particular, in the context of the recently enacted Civil Rights Act of 1991 and the ADA. Particular attention should be paid to the "reasonable accommodation" requirement of ADA, which stipulates that selection procedures must be altered when necessary to accommodate people with disabilities. Employers may be required to devise special arrangements when testing people with disabilities.

DISCUSSION QUESTIONS

1. Given that cognitive ability tests are likely to cause adverse impact, would you still recommend their use? Explain your answer.
2. Will the Civil Rights Act of 1991 make it easier or harder to defend the use of tests for personnel decisions?
3. What (if any) impact will the 1990 ADA (discussed in Chapter 3) have on the use of psychological testing for personnel decisions?
4. If you were given a personality test as part of an employment application process, would you answer the questions honestly, or would you attempt to answer them based on your image of the "correct" way to answer? What implications does your response have for the validity of personality testing?
5. The use of drug testing as a basis for hiring is an invasion of privacy and should be outlawed for most jobs. Do you agree or disagree?
6. Given that the validity of assessment centers and work samples is not significantly greater than that reported for mental ability tests, why would an organization choose the far more costly approach?
7. It has been proposed that students be asked to do work simulations similar to those used in managerial assessment centers. Assessments would then be made on students' competencies in decision making, leadership, oral communication, planning and organizing, written communication, and self-objectivity. What other methods could be used to assess student competencies in these areas?
8. Many of the exercises in this book are forms of performance tests which are designed to assess and develop competencies found to be critical for students' success after graduation. How could the assessment and feedback processes be improved to achieve these objectives?

NOTES

1. Human Resource Management News (1989). Test use on the increase. Washington: Bureau of National Affairs.
2. Gatewood, R. D., and Feild, H. S. (1990). *Human resource selection.* Chicago, IL: Dryden.
3. Aiken, L. (1988). *Psychological testing and assessment.* Boston: Allyn & Bacon.
4. See note 2. See also: Douglas, J. A., Feld, D. E., and Asquith, N. (1989). *Employment testing manual.* Boston, MA: Warren, Gorham, Lamont.
5. See note 2. See also: Fleishman, E. A. (1988). Some new frontiers in personnel selection research. *Personnel Psychology, 42,* 679–701.
6. Ghiselli, E. E. (1966). *The validity of occupational aptitude tests.* New York: John Wiley & Sons.
7. Schmidt, F. L. (1988). The problem of group differences in ability test scores in employment selection. *Journal of Vocational Behavior, 33,* 272–292. See also: Betz, N. E. (1988). Fairness in employment testing. *Journal of Vocational Behavior, 33*(3), 225–477. Schmidt, F. L., and Hunter, J. (1980). Employment testing: Old theories and new research findings. *American Psychologist, 36,* 1128–1137. Glaser, R., and Bond, L. (eds.) (1980). Testing: Concepts, policy, practice, and research. *American Psychologist, 36*(10), 997–1189.
8. Hartigan, J. A., and Wigdor, A. K. (eds.) (1989). *Fairness in employment testing.* Washington: National Academy Press.
9. Nathan, B., and Alexander, R. (1988). A comparison of criteria for test validation: A meta-analytic investigation. *Personnel Psychology, 41,* 517–535.
10. See note 7.
11. See note 8.
12. *Human Resource Management News* (June 8, 1988). Washington: Bureau of Business Publications.
13. Digman, J. M. (1990). Personality structure: Emergence of the five-factor model. *Annual Review of Psychology, 41,* 417–440. See also: Cortina, J. M., Doherty, M. L., and Schmitt, N. (1992). The "big five" personality factor in the IPI and MMPI: Predictors of police performance. *Personnel Psychology, 45,* 119–140. Barrick, M. R., and Mount, M. K. (1991). The big five personality dimensions and job performance: A meta-analysis. *Personnel Psychology, 44,* 1–26.
14. Patsfall, M. R., and Feimer, N. (1985). The role of person-environment fit in job performance and satisfaction. In H. J. Bernardin and D. Bownas (eds.), *Personality assessment in organizations.* New York: Praeger, pp. 53–81. See also: Trevino, L. K. (1986). Ethical decision making in organizations: A person-situation interactionist model. *Academy of Management Review, 11,* 601–617; O'Reilly III, C. A., Chatman, J., and Caldwell, D. F. (1991). People and organizational culture: A profile comparison approach to assessing person-organization fit. *The Academy of Management Review, 34,* 487–516.
15. Bernardin, H. J., and Bownas, D. (1985). *Personality assessment in organizations.* New York: Praeger.
16. Miner, J. B. (1985). Sentence completion measures in personnel research: The development and validation of the Miner Sentence Completion Scales. In H. J. Bernardin and D. Bownas (eds.), *Personality testing in organizations.* New York: Praeger, pp. 145–176. See also: Miner, J. B., Chen, C. C., and Yu, K. C. (1991). Testing theory under adverse conditions: Motivation to manage in the people's republic of China. *Journal of Applied Psychology, 76,* 343–349.
17. McCarthy, M. J. (Aug. 25, 1988). Handwriting analysis as a personnel tool. *The Wall Street Journal,* p. B1.
18. See note 16.
19. Tett, R. P., Jackson, D. N., and Rothstein, M. (1991). Personality measures as predictors of job performance: A meta-analytic review. *Personnel Psychology, 44,*

703–742. See also: Hough, L. M., Eaton, N. K., Dunnette, M. D., Kamp, J. D., and McCloy, R. A. (1990). Criterion related validities of personality constructs and the effect of response distortion on those validities. *Journal of Applied Psychology, 75,* 581–595.

20. See note 19, p. 732.

21. See note 14.

22. U.S. Congress, Office of Technology Assessment (1990). *The use of integrity tests for preemployment screening.* OTA-SET-442. Washington: Government Printing Office. p. ii. See also: American Psychological Association (1991). *Questionnaires used in the prediction of trustworthiness in pre-employment selection decisions: An APA task force report.* Washington: APA; Sackett, P. R., Burris, L. R., and Callahan, C. (1989). Integrity testing for personnel selection: An update. *Personnel Psychology, 42,* 491–530.

23. Jones, J. W., and Wuebker, L. J. (1988). Accident prevention through personnel selection. *Journal of Business and Psychology, 3,* 187–198.

24. Hogan, J., Hogan, R., and Busch, C. M. (1984). How to measure service orientation. *Journal of Applied Psychology, 69,* 167–173.

25. Bernardin, H. J. (1989). Innovative approaches to personnel selection and performance appraisal. *Journal of Management Systems, 1,* 25–36.

26. See note 25.

27. Russell, C. J., Mattson, J., Devlin, S. E., and Atwater, D. (1990). Predictive validity of biodata items generated from retrospective life experience essays. *Journal of Applied Psychology, 75,* 569–580. See also: Kluger, A., Reilly, R. R., and Russell, C. J. (1991). Faking biodata tests: Are option-keyed instruments more resistant? *Journal of Applied Psychology, 76,* 889–896. Mael, F. A. (1991). A conceptual rationale for the domain and attributes of biodata items. *Personnel Psychology, 44,* 763–792.

28. Schmidt, F. L., Ones, D. S., and Hunter, J. E. (1992). Personnel selection. In L. Porter and M. Rosensweig (eds.), *Annual Review of Psychology, 43,* 627–670. See also: Rothstein, H. R., Schmidt, F. L., Erwin, F. W., Owens, W. A., and Sparks, C. P. (1990). Biographical data in employment selection: Can validities be made generalizable? *Journal of Applied Psychology, 75,* 175–184.

29. LoPresto, R., Micham, D. E., and Ripley, D. E. (1986). *Reference checking handbook.* Alexandria, VA: American Society of Personnel Administration.

30. Bernardin, H. J., and Beatty, R. W. (1984). *Performance appraisal: Assessing human behavior at work.* Boston: Kent-PWS.

31. Fenton, J. W. (April 1990). Negligent hiring/retention adds to human resources woes. *Personnel Journal,* 62–73.

32. U.S. Department of Labor, Bureau of Labor Statistics (1989). *Survey of Employer Anti-Drug Programs.* Washington: Department of Labor.

33. Geidt, T. (1985). Drug and alcohol abuse in the work place: Balancing employer and employee rights. *Employer Relations Law Journal, 11,* 181–205. See also: Faley, R. H., Kleiman, L. S., and Wall, J. (1988) Drug

testing in public and private-sector workplace: Technical and legal issues. *Journal of Business and Psychology, 3,* 154–186. See also: Murphy, K. R., Thornton III, G. C., and Reynolds, D. H. (1990). College students' attitudes toward employee drug testing programs. *Personnel Psychology, 43,* 615–632; Crant, J. M., and Bateman, T. S. (1990). An experimental test of the impact of drug testing programs on potential job applicants' attitudes and intentions. *Journal of Applied Psychology, 75,* 127–131.

34. Cherrington, D. J. (1987). *Personnel management: The management of human resources.* Dubuque, IA: William C. Brown.

35. Stone, E. and Stone, D. (1987). Effects of missing application-blank information on personnel selection decisions: Do privacy protection strategies bias the outcome? *Journal of Applied Psychology, 72,* 452–456.

36. See note 35.

37. Wernimont, P. F., and Campbell, J. P. (1968). Signs, samples, and criteria. *Journal of Applied Psychology, 52,* 372–376.

38. Task Force Assessment Center Standards (1980). Standards and ethical considerations for assessment center operations. *Personnel Administrator, 25,* 35–38.

39. Thornton, G. C., III, and Byham, W. C. (1982). *Assessment centers and managerial performance.* New York: Academic Press. See also: Fitzgerald, L. F., and Quaintance, M. K. (1982). Survey of assessment center in state and local government. *Journal of Assessment Center Technology, 5,* 9–19. See also: Schneider, J. R., and Schmitt, N. (1992). An exercise design approach to understanding assessment center dimension and exercise constructs. *Journal of Applied Psychology, 77,* 32–41. See also: Schmitt, N., Schneider, J. R., and Cohen, S. A. (1990). Factors affecting validity of a regionally administered assessment center. *Personnel Psychology, 43,* 1–12; Gaugler, B. B., and Rudolph, A. S. (1992). The influence of assessee performance variation on assessors' judgements. *Personnel Psychology, 45,* 77–98; Reilly, R. R., Henry, S., and Smither, J. W. (1990). An examination of the effects of using behavior checklists on the construct validity of assessment center dimensions. *Personnel Psychology, 43,* 71–84.

40. See note 39. See also: Shore, T. H., Shore, L., and Thornton, G. C., III (1992). Construct validity of self- and peer evaluations of performance dimensions in an assessment center. *Journal of Applied Psychology, 77,* 42–54.

41. Kraut, A. I., and Scott, G. J. (1972). Validity of an operational management assessment program. *Journal of Applied Psychology, 56,* 124–129.

42. Goldberg, R. T., Costello, K., Wiesen, J. P., and Popp, A. (1980). Use of the assessment center method for external hires: The case of the rehabilitation counselor. *Assessment and Development, 7,* 4–7.

43. Bray, D. W., and Campbell, R. J., (1968). Selection of salesmen by means of an assessment center. *Journal of Applied Psychology, 52,* 36–41. See also: McEvoy, G. M., Beatty, R. W., and Bernardin, H. J. (1987). Unan-

swered questions in assessment center research. *Journal of Business and Psychology, 2,* 97–111.

44. Pynes, J. E., and Bernardin, H. J. (1989). Predictive validity of an entry-level police officer assessment center. *Journal of Applied Psychology, 74,* 831–833.

45. Gaugler, B. B., Rosenthal, D. B., Thornton, G. C., III, and Benton, C. (1987). Meta-analysis of assessment center validity. *Journal of Applied Psychology, 72,* 493–511. Schippmann, J. S., Prien, E. P., and Katz, J. A. (1990). Reliability and validity of in-basket performance measures. *Personnel Psychology, 43,* 837–860.

46. Hunter, J. E., and Hunter, R. F. (1984). Validity and utility of alternative predictors of job performance. *Psychological Bulletin, 96,* 72–98.

47. Tung, R. L. (May 1987). Expatriate assignments: Enhancing success and minimizing failure. *The Academy of Management Executive,* pp. 118–125.

48. See note 47.

49. Labor Letter (Jan. 16, 1991). *Wall Street Journal,* p. 1.

50. Mendenhall, M., and Oddou, G. (1985). The dimensions of expatriate acculturation: A review. *Academy of Management Review, 19,* 39–47.

51. Henry, E. R. (1951). What business can learn from Peace Corps selection and training. *Personnel, 42,* 17–25. See also: Dowling, P. J., and Schuler, R. S. (1990). *International dimensions of human resource management.* Boston: PWS-Kent.

52. Hays, R. D. (1971). Ascribed behavioral determinants of success-failure among U.S. expatriate managers. *Journal of International Business Studies, 2,* 40–46.

53. Tung, R. L. (1981). Selection and training of personnel for overseas assignments. *Columbia Journal of World Business, 16,* 68–78.

54. Von Glinow, M. A., and Chung, B. J. (1990). Comparative human resource management practices in the United States, Japan, Korea, and the People's Republic of China. In A. Nedd, G. R. Ferris, and K. M. Rowland (eds.), *Research in personnel and human resources management: International human resources management* (suppl. 1, pp. 153–171). Greenwich, CT: JAI Press.

55. See note 37.

56. Tsujioka, B. (1989). Psychological assessment in Japan in these decades. *Applied Psychology: An International Review, 38,* 353–372.

57. Koenig, R. (Dec. 1, 1987). Exacting employer: Toyota takes pains and time, filling jobs at its Kentucky plant. *The Wall Street Journal,* pp. 1, 31.

58. Latham, G. P., and Napier, N. K. (1990). Chinese human resource management practices in Hong Kong and Singapore: An exploratory study. In A. Nedd, G. R. Ferris, and K. M. Rowland (eds.), *Research in personnel and human resources management: International human resources management.* (suppl. 1, pp. 173–199.). Greenwich, CT: JAI Press.

59. See note 37.

60. Shimmin, S. (1989). Selection in a European context. In P. Harriot (ed.), *Assessment and selection in organizations.* Chichester, England: John Wiley & Sons, pp. 109–118.

61. See note 60.

62. See note 60.

63. Shackleton, V. J., and Newell, S. (1989). Selection procedures in practice. In P. Herriot (ed.), *Assessment and selection in organizations,* Chichester, England: John Wiley & Sons, pp. 257–271.

EXERCISE 6.1
SHOULD TENNECO USE THE
WONDERLIC TEST?

OVERVIEW

Although mental ability tests have been shown to be valid, they are likely to result in adverse impact upon minorities because of average test score differences. Recall the chapter discussion of the Wonderlic Personnel Test. The purpose of this exercise is to consider the options available for dealing with the problem of a valid test which will probably cause adverse impact.

LEARNING OBJECTIVES

After completing this exercise, you should:

1. Have a better understanding of the implications of the use of cognitive ability tests.
2. Be capable of developing and articulating a rationale for the use of a cognitive ability test under specific circumstances.

PROCEDURE

Part A: Individual Analysis

Prior to class, read the scenario presented below regarding the Tenneco Corporation and answer the questions on Form 6.1.1. Be prepared to defend your position in group discussion.

Part B: Group Analysis

In groups of from 4 to 6 people, each student should review the written responses of other members to the questions on Form 6.1.1. The group should then attempt to reach consensus on each of the questions. Written group responses should be developed for each of the questions, and a group spokesperson should be designated to present the group's position on the use of the test.

SCENARIO

Tenneco Corporation is considering the use of the Wonderlic Personnel Test as part of its selection process for assistant store managers. Each assistant store manager has management responsibilities for one convenience store. Responsibilities include complete supervision of at least 15 employees, including hiring, firing, and scheduling; budgetary matters; inventory; vendor deliveries; and customer complaints and inquiries. Because Tenneco hopes to maintain a promotion-from-within policy, it administered the Wonderlic to 300 store employees. The average scores of minorities and whites who took the 100-point exam were as follows: blacks, 63; Hispanics, 70; and whites, 75 (the standard deviation was 10). The 5-week training program at Tenneco headquarters has room for only 20 managerial trainees. The training is required for promotion to assistant store manager. As an HRM personnel specialist, you have been asked to recommend a specific policy for the use of the Wonderlic. Answer each of the questions on Form 6.1.1.

FORM 6.1.1

Name _____ Group number _____

1. Assuming that only 20 candidates are to be selected for the training program and that the Wonderlic Personnel Test is to be used as the sole basis for entry into the training, is adverse impact against minorities likely?

   Explain your answer.

2. Given your response to question 1, what are the policy options for this situation? What policy do you recommend that Tenneco adopt for the use of the Wonderlic? Defend your response by considering the job situation, the need for further research, legal and social implications, and alternative methods of selection. Provide a detailed policy recommendation and a rationale for action.

EXERCISE 6.2
*THE IN-BASKET**

OVERVIEW

As discussed in Chapter 6, one of the most popular performance tests is the in-basket. The in-basket is used in assessment centers and as a "stand-alone" performance test. The purpose of this exercise is to give the student an experience with an in-basket and with the process of assessment.

LEARNING OBJECTIVES

After completing this exercise, you should be able to:

1. Understand the features of an in-basket exercise.
2. Explain the process of evaluating in-basket performance.
3. Discuss methods of improving the exercise as an assessment or development tool.

PROCEDURE

Part A. Individual Analysis

Step 1. Out of class, follow the instructions for completion of the in-basket exercise.

Step 2. Using Form 6.2.1 and the dimension definitions which are provided, do a preliminary self-assessment on how well you completed the in-basket. Keep Form 6.2.1 for discussion.

Part B. Group Analysis

Step 1. Each student will be given an out-basket which was completed by another student. Review the out-basket, and make notes on the actions which were taken.

Step 2. Students are then paired up and take turns discussing their in-basket responses. The focus of the conversation should be on the response to each of the memos.

Step 3. After both in-baskets are discussed, students should first review their self-assessments on Form 6.2.1 and make whatever changes are thought to be justified. Then, each student should evaluate the other student's performance using Form 6.2.2. Student pairs should then reconvene and exchange Forms 6.2.2. Conversation should then focus on the ratings on each dimension, and discrepancies in self-assessments versus peer assessments on each dimension. The pair should also identify the steps which could be taken to increase agreement between the self-assessment and peer assessment ratings.

Step 4. Class discussion will focus on the validity of the in-basket and the feedback session.

Step 5. Students should complete the exercise assessment questions.

EXHIBIT 6.2.1
THE IN-BASKET

For the next 75 minutes you are D. Graham, supervisor in the sales department for Textron at its corporate office in Triville. The company has offices throughout the United States. A few words about Textron...

Textron sells and services telephone equipment. The company doesn't make telephones, but it sells telephone equipment made by some of the largest manufacturers. Textron sells and services three main items: (1) home telephones, (2) answering machines, and (3) telephone systems for small businesses. The company has built a reputation for excellent customer relations, responsive service, and a professional selling style that focuses upon meeting customers' needs. The company is known for selling the highest-quality products and servicing problems in a timely fashion. Treating employees fairly is emphasized, and Textron is active in community affairs. As the newest member of the Textron management team, you are expected to help the company achieve these objectives.

Here's the situation:

Allen Duval has been a sales supervisor in the Small Business Phone Systems Department for 6 years. This department is responsible for soliciting new customers and taking orders from existing customers. All its employees deal with customers over the phone. Yesterday morning you were called in and told that Allen was seriously injured in an automobile accident and will be out for 6 to 8 months. You have been chosen to replace him, effective today. Having worked as a sales representative for several years at Textron, you are quite familiar with how things work. Your employees will arrive at 8:30 a.m. Since it's your first day, you decided to arrive early to check out any mail that had accumulated in his in-basket. It is 7:00 a.m. on November 3, and you are in Allen Duval's office (your new office). At 8:15 you will have a brief meeting with your boss, Bob Morris, to get ready for the start of the day. For the next 75 minutes you are going to go through Allen Duval's in-basket and complete as much of it as you possibly can. You want to impress your boss with your ability to handle your new supervisory responsibilities, including the administrative duties. In completing the in-basket, be sure you make complete notes about what you intend to do with each item. When appropriate, write memos and/or instructions. Everything you do or plan to do should be in writing.

Remember that it is 7:00 a.m. on November 3. You must leave in 75 minutes for a brief meeting with your boss before your employees arrive. Your out-basket should be completed by then.

---

*Contributed by Sue A. Dahmus.

EXHIBIT 6.2.2

TEXTRON

MEMORANDUM

To: D. Graham

From: Susie Wise

Re: Information

Date: November 2

Congratulations on your promotion. As your secretary, I have enclosed a few things that might be helpful as you deal with Mr. Duval's in-basket. Attached you will find:

1. Organization charts to tell who's who
2. Mr. Duval's calendar
3. A list of employees with a review of their performance
4. This week's order and service records

If there's anything I can help you with, please let me know. By the way, may I have this afternoon off to visit Mr. Duval in the hospital? I've worked for him for the last 10 years. Also, Varner left work rather upset today.

EXHIBIT 6.2.3
ORGANIZATION CHART

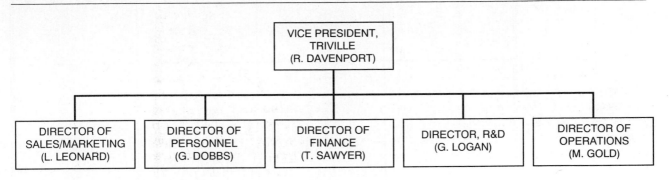

EXHIBIT 6.2.4
SALES/MARKETING ORGANIZATION CHART

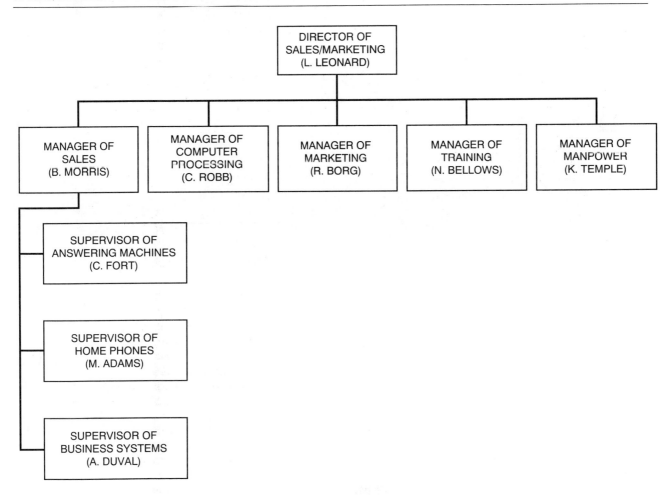

EXHIBIT 6.2.5

NOVEMBER

SUN.	MON.	TUES.	WED.	THURS.	FRI.	SAT.
1	2	3 Meeting with R. Borg, one p.m.	4	5 Supervisors' meeting, ten a.m.	6	7 Speech judging
8	9	10	11	12	13 Seminar— Chicago	14
15	16 Productivity report due to Norris	17	18	19	20	21
22 / 29	23 / 30	24	25 M. Wells— vacation	26 THANKSGIVING	27	28

EXHIBIT 6.2.6

TEXTRON

MEMORANDUM

To: All supervisors

From: B. Morris

Re: Workforce reduction

Date: 10/28

We may be faced with having to reduce our workforce in the next few months. To assist in this effort, please provide a list of employees who might be eligible for early retirement.

EXHIBIT 6.2.7

TEXTRON

MEMORANDUM

To: D. Graham

From: Supervisors

Re: Welcome!

Date: 11/2

Welcome aboard! The other supervisors are anxious to meet you. How about you and your spouse dropping by Charlie Fort's place Saturday night (11/7) for dinner. We'll all be there.

See you then.

EXHIBIT 6.2.8

TEXTRON

MEMORANDUM

To: All supervisors

From: B. Morris

Re: Summary reports

Date: 11/2

Effective today, sales and new order summaries for the preceding week are due in my office by no later than noon on Tuesday.

EXHIBIT 6.2.9

TEXTRON

MEMORANDUM

To: A. Duval

From: L. Leonard

Re: Job reassignments

Date: 11/1

I've thought about your request to grant Halpern a reassignment because of an ongoing medical problem and must decide against the idea. It would be setting a dangerous precedent. Please explain our decision to Halpern.

EXHIBIT 6.2.10

TEXTRON

MEMORANDUM

To: All supervisors

From: B. Morris

Re: EEO complaint

Date: 11/1

A black female who was not hired for our sales representative job has filed a complaint with the EEOC alleging sex and race discrimination. An EEO representative wants us to explain the job relatedness of the Wonderlic Personnel Test and the college degree requirement. I would appreciate your help on this.

EXHIBIT 6.2.11

TEXTRON

MEMORANDUM

To: A. Duval

From: R. Borg

Re: Customer complaints

Date: 10/30

Yesterday I received a letter from a customer complaining about the way she was treated by one of your employees, Mike Wells. This is the third complaint letter I have received in 2 months on Mr. Wells.

EXHIBIT 6.2.12

TEXTRON

MEMORANDUM

To: All supervisors

From: B. Morris

Re: Meeting

Date: 10/30

There will be a marketing meeting in the West Conference Room at two p.m. on November 9. All sales supervisors are required to attend.

EXHIBIT 6.2.13

TEXTRON

MEMORANDUM

To: A. Duval

From: B. Morris

Re: Harassment complaint

Date: 9/3

Varner has complained of sexual harassment. Please look into it ASAP.

EXHIBIT 6.2.14

TEXTRON

MEMORANDUM

To: All supervisors

From: L. Leonard

Re: Dates/phone calls

Date: 10/29

On several occasions it has been brought to my attention that our sales employees are receiving far too many phone calls while on the job. Whenever they take personal phone calls, it ties up phone lines and slows down ordering.

Also, the number of employees showing up late has increased in recent weeks. Even though they may be only a few minutes late, remember: time is money!

Please draft an announcement stating your policy on these issues right away.

EXHIBIT 6.2.15
LIST OF EMPLOYEES

NAME	POSITION	COMPANY ID	REMARKS
A. Green	Sales representative	32215	New employee
M. Wells	Sales representative	29675	Very good rep; good technical knowledge
C. Halpern	Technical consultant	45367	Solid, consistent performer
A. Smith	Sales representative	22349	Very assertive and vocal about her areas; reliable performer
S. Biggs	Technical consultant	88721	August hire; still needs more technical knowledge
F. Varner	Records clerk	12947	Super! Top performer with computer; keeps paperwork straight
R. Donazzi	Technical consultant	66378	Problem getting to work on time; a good performer, though
G. Jones	Sales representative	20903	Dedicated, tries hard; needs more technical knowledge
S. Arnold	Sales representative	39883	Real problem; late, lazy, and arrogant
P. Larson	Records clerk	55467	Reliable; a bit slow on the computer

EXHIBIT 6.2.16
SALES/SERVICE SUMMARIES

NAME	DATE					TOTALS FOR WEEK
	10/26	10/27	10/28	10/29	10/30	
	TOTAL ORDERS/NEW ORDERS					
A. Smith	118/27	99/16	79/20	106/29	135/40	537/132
M. Wells	151/34	144/40	102/20	111/19	100/25	608/138
S. Arnold	66/12	77/10	69/11	88/14	80/6	380/53
A. Green	89/14	99/19	103/24	114/24	130/38	535/119
G. Jones	111/34	101/30	99/20	99/16	117/29	527/129

FORM 6.2.1
SELF-ASSESSMENT ON PERFORMANCE DIMENSIONS

Your name _____

Your rating:

_____   Decision making: Choosing among alternative courses of action that are based on logical assumptions and available factual information. This includes a basic willingness to form judgments, make decisions, take action, and/or commit oneself in complex situations.

_____   Leadership: Utilization of appropriate interpersonal styles to stimulate and guide individuals or groups toward goal and/or task accomplishment.

_____   Oral communication: Presentation skills, effective expression of ideas or viewpoints to others in individual or group situations (includes gestures, nonverbal communications, and the use of visual aids).

_____   Perception of threshold cues: Perception of cues in the behavior of others, which includes social sensitivity, sensing reactions of others, and ability to read nonverbal cues.

_____   Personal impact: Creating a good early impression and maintaining that impression, commanding attention and respect, and *showing an air of confidence through verbal and nonverbal presentation.*

_____   Planning and organizing: Establishing a course of action that will enable oneself and/or others to accomplish specific goals; planning proper assignments of personnel and appropriate allocations of resources.

_____   Self-objectivity: Realistic evaluation of one's own assets and liabilities; this includes insight into personal motives, skills, and abilities as applied to the job.

_____   Written communication: Clear expression of ideas in writing and in appropriate grammatical form.

Use the following scale to make your ratings:

1 Very ineffective

2 Ineffective

3 Somewhat effective

4 Effective

5 Very effective

X Cannot rate, does not apply

FORM 6.2.2
PEER ASSESSMENT ON PERFORMANCE DIMENSIONS

Your name _____ The other student's name _____

Your rating:

_____   <u>Decision making:</u> Choosing among alternative courses of action that are based on logical assumptions and available factual information. This includes a basic willingness to form judgments, make decisions, take action, and/or commit oneself in complex situations.

_____   <u>Leadership:</u> Utilization of appropriate interpersonal styles to stimulate and guide individuals or groups toward goal and/or task accomplishment.

_____   <u>Oral communication:</u> Presentation skills, effective expression of ideas or viewpoints to others in individual or group situations (includes gestures, nonverbal communications, and the use of visual aids).

_____   <u>Perception of threshold cues:</u> Perception of cues in the behavior of others, which includes social sensitivity, sensing reactions of others, and ability to read nonverbal cues.

_____   <u>Personal impact:</u> Creating a good early impression and maintaining that impression, commanding attention and respect, and *showing an air of confidence through verbal and nonverbal presentation.*

_____   <u>Planning and organizing:</u> Establishing a course of action that will enable oneself and/or others to accomplish specific goals; planning proper assignments of personnel and appropriate allocations of resources.

_____   <u>Self-objectivity:</u> Realistic evaluation of one's own assets and liabilities; this includes insight into personal motives, skills, and abilities as applied to the job.

_____   <u>Written communication:</u> Clear expression of ideas in writing and in appropriate grammatical form.

Use the following scale to make your ratings:

1 Very ineffective

2 Ineffective

3 Somewhat effective

4 Effective

5 Very effective

X Cannot rate, does not apply

Exercise 6.2
Assessment Questions

Name _____

1. To what extent did your self-assessment agree with the evaluation made by the peer assessor? How do you account for the differences?

2. What changes would you make with this in-basket in order to improve its validity?

3. What structure (if any) would you add to the in-basket interview process to enhance the learning experience?

EXERCISE 6.3
HIRING A PLANT MANAGER AT DYNAMO INDUSTRIES*

OVERVIEW

Personnel selection decisions are typically based on a collection of information from several sources. An organization may have test scores, previous performance appraisals, interview ratings, biographical information, and other data on the candidates. The purpose of this exercise is to give you a feel for the process of making a final recommendation based on such a collection of data. In addition, through the group interaction, you should gain an understanding of the process involved in a leaderless group discussion.

Your assignment is to review candidate credentials for the plant manager (PM) position at Dynamo Industries in Pittsburgh.

LEARNING OBJECTIVES

After completing this exercise, you should be able to:

1. Distinguish between candidate information which is valuable and should be considered in the decision and information which should be ignored.
2. Articulate your rationale for decisions.
3. Suggest ways in which the selection process could be improved.
4. Understand the dynamics of a leaderless group discussion.

PROCEDURE

Part A: Individual Analysis

Out of class, review the material presented below. Assume the following:
You are the vice president of HR. You are to write a report (a 1-page executive summary followed by *no more* than 3 double-spaced pages of supporting information) which includes the following:

a. A rank-ordering of your top four choices for the Pittsburgh job.
b. An *in-depth* discussion of how this rank-ordering was reached (a rationale for why some candidates are

ranked higher than others and others are not ranked at all).
c. A discussion of how the selection process for hiring a PM should be changed in the future (e.g., additional selection devices to use, additional information to gather, sources to drop or change). This report will be sent to the vice president of production and to the president of Dynamo Industries.

Part B: Group Analysis

Step 1. Bring your report to class. Students will be designated as either observers or discussants for round 1 and then reverse roles for round 2. Prior to group discussion, all observers should review all discussants' written reports, and all discussants should review all observers' reports.

Step 2. After all the reports are read, ratings should be made on the "written communications" competency of the assessment form (Appendix B; no other ratings should be done at this point).

Step 3. After the papers are returned to their authors, the discussants should commence discussion in an attempt to reach consensus on the top four candidates and the rationale for the position. Observers should pay careful attention to the way in which each group member participates in the exercise.

Step 4. After about 15 minutes, discussants should complete the self-assessment form (Appendix B) to assess their own performance in the group and on the exercise, and observers should complete the assessment forms for all participants (peer assessments).

Step 5. After the ratings are completed, observers and participants should reverse roles. The new discussants should attempt to reach consensus on the changes to be made in the hiring practices of Dynamo, by drawing up a priority list of three changes.

Step 6. After about 15 minutes, discussants and observers should again complete the assessment forms.

Step 7. (Optional) Students may be paired off from rounds 1 and 2, and comparisons may be made of the self-assessments versus the peer assessments. Discussion should center on specific observations of how each student performed in the group and on the extent of agreement (or disagreement) on the assessment forms.

Step 8. Students should answer the assessment questions for the exercise.

*Contributed by James A. Breaugh.

SCENARIO

Dynamo Industries is a medium-sized manufacturer of small electrical motors. It has its headquarters in St. Paul, Minnesota. The firm employs 9800 persons. Dynamo has plants in St. Paul; Columbus, Ohio; Atlanta, Georgia; San Diego, California; Pittsburgh, Pennsylvania; Providence, Rhode Island; and Little Rock, Arkansas. All the plants are unionized, although the power of the unions varies greatly from plant to plant.

Recently, the company has been trying to hire a new PM (see the job description in Exhibit 6.3.1) for the Pittsburgh plant (PMs report directly to the vice president of production). Although Dynamo Industries has experienced slightly above average growth and profit compared to its competitors, the Pittsburgh plant has been a trouble spot. Over the last 3 years, production costs have been extremely high and there has been a good deal of labor strife (e.g., numerous work slowdowns, an excessive number of grievances filed). The most recent Pittsburgh PM was terminated, although by mutual agreement the company stated that she left for a better job with another company.

Because of the importance of the PM position, Dynamo Industries has used several expensive selection devices. The information obtained through these devices is detailed in Exhibits 6.3.3 to 6.3.6. After a thorough recruitment effort (both within and outside the company) and some initial screening, the list of job candidates has been reduced to eight names. You will find background information on each of the eight candidates in Exhibit 6.3.2.

EXHIBIT 6.3.1
JOB DESCRIPTION (WRITTEN BY THE VICE PRESIDENT OF PRODUCTION)

The PM is ultimately responsible for the operating efficiency of the entire plant. In fulfilling his or her responsibilities, the PM regularly consults with subordinate supervisory personnel (the PM frequently delegates duties). A PM must be somewhat knowledgeable about production methods and the capabilities of equipment. Some of the activities the PM is directly or indirectly involved in include: (1) material procurement; (2) plant maintenance; (3) quality control; (4) manpower utilization; (5) establishing budgets; (6) revising production schedules because of equipment failure or operation problems; (7) consulting with engineering personnel concerning the modification of machinery in order to improve production quantity, the quality of products, and employee safety; (8) conducting hearings to resolve employee grievances, (9) participating in union-management contract negotiations; (10) safety management; and (11) community relations.

EXHIBIT 6.3.2
BACKGROUND INFORMATION ON THE CANDIDATES

1. **George Martin.** Age 44. Education: B.A, University of Wisconsin; M.A. (industrial relations) Cornell University. Martin is a PM of a relatively small plant for one of Dynamo's competitors (the plant has 580 nonunion employees and is located in Cleveland, Ohio). Martin has held the PM job for the past 6 years and has been with the competitor for 14 years. No reference information was gathered because Martin is concerned about his present employer's reaction.

2. **Tony Caciopo.** Age: 59. Education: high school graduate. Caciopo is an assistant PM in Dynamo's Providence plant. He has been with Dynamo for 24 years. He has been assistant PM in Providence for the last 10 years. He had a severe heart attack 4 years ago but appears to have recovered. Ten years ago, he was offered a job as PM by Dynamo but turned it down because of health problems his wife was having.

3. **Kathy Joyce.** Age: 36. Education: B.A., Indiana University. Joyce is currently PM of Dynamo's Little Rock plant. She desires a lateral transfer because it would enhance job opportunities for her husband. She has been with Dynamo for 5 years and PM at Little Rock for 2 years.

4. **Barry Fein.** Age: 49. Education: Associate Degree (2 years), from Morehead State University. Up until 2 months ago, Fein was plant manager at a large, unionized textile plant. Two months ago, the company Fein worked for discontinued the product line made by his plant, and he was let go. Fein had been with this company for 20 years and PM for 5 years. His letters of reference are excellent.

5. **Ron Jackson.** Age: 33. Education: B.A., Howard University; M.B.A., Northwestern. Jackson is currently an assistant PM at Dynamo's Pittsburgh plant. He has been with the company for 4 years and assistant PM for 2 years. He has served as acting PM at Pittsburgh for the last 2 months.

6. **Jay Davis.** Age: 46. Education: B.A., Harvard; M.B.A., Harvard. Davis is currently assistant PM at Dynamo's Atlanta plant. He has been with Dynamo for 10 years; for the last 7 years he has been an assistant PM (6 years in St. Paul, the last year in Atlanta).

7. **Frank Hall.** Age: 58. Education: B.S. (chemistry), Duke University. Hall is currently vice president of production at one of Dynamo's major competitors. He says he seeks a demotion so that he will be required to travel less. He has been vice president of production for 6 years. Prior to that, he was a PM for 12 years. The plant was organized. No reference information is available, but he has received outstanding reviews in trade publications for his performance as vice president.

8. **Tom Doyle.** Age: 36. Education: B.A., Williams College, M.B.A., University of Chicago. For the last 2 years, Doyle has worked as special assistant to Dynamo's vice president of production. Prior to this, he was an assistant PM for 2 years and PM (at the Little Rock plant) for 3 years. Tom was the youngest PM ever appointed at Dynamo. He was very ineffective as a PM and after 3 years was removed from the position.

Dynamo Industries does not really have an established philosophy for filling job openings. In the past, it has favored promotion from within the company. However, the vice president of production was hired externally. Dynamo has no policy whatsoever on lateral transfers. In the recent past, such transfers have been a somewhat rare occurrence. The key issue seems to be whether the company benefits from the transfer.

EXHIBIT 6.3.3
PERSONALITY PROFILES

Each of the 8 candidates was examined by a psychologist, who utilized personality tests [i.e., the 16PF and the Thematic Apperception Test (TAT)] in drawing the conclusions listed below.

	CANDIDATE'S RATING		
	HIGH	MEDIUM	LOW
Ability to handle stress	Martin Caciopo Davis	Joyce Fein Doyle	Hall Jackson
Ability to resolve conflict	Martin Davis Caciopo	Joyce Doyle Hall	Fein Jackson
Interpersonal skills	Martin Joyce	Hall Jackson Caciopo	Davis Fein Doyle
Most likely to succeed as a PM	Martin Caciopo Davis	Joyce Doyle Hall	Fein Jackson

EXHIBIT 6.3.4
INTERVIEW RATINGS

Each of the inverviewers went through a 1-day interview training program. The vice president of production's interviews averaged 3 hours in length. The other interviews averaged 60 minutes. Interview ratings were made on a 7-point scale (from 1 for "poor candidate" to 7 for "excellent candidate"). All interviews were semistructured.

	VICE-PRESIDENT, PRODUCTION	VICE-PRESIDENT, HUMAN RESOURCES	COLUMBUS PLANT MANAGER	ATLANTA PLANT MANAGER
George Martin	6.5	7	5.5	4
Tony Caciopo	5	5.5	4.5	6
Kathy Joyce	6	6.5	5	5.5
Barry Fein	4	4	3	4
Ron Jackson	5	5.5	4.5	5
Jay Davis	4.5	5	3.5	6.5
Frank Hall	6.5	7	*	4
Tom Doyle	5.5	6	4.5	6

*The interviewer was on vacation the day of the interview.

EXHIBIT 6.3.5
INTELLIGENCE TESTS AND HANDWRITING ANALYSES

The intelligence test given by Dynamo Industries is commonly used for selecting candidates for management. Individuals scoring below 115 tend not to do well in managerial jobs. Standard error equals 3.5.

The handwriting analyst (graphologist) rated the plant manager candidates in terms of their likelihood of success as the Pittsburgh PM (from −3 for "very poor prospect" to +3 for "very strong prospect").

CANDIDATE	INTELLIGENCE TEST	HANDWRITING RATING
George Martin	119	1
Tony Caciopo	116	+1
Kathy Joyce	141	+1
Barry Fein	122	0
Ron Jackson	114	+2
Jay Davis	148	+2
Frank Hall	112	+3
Tom Doyle	125	+3

EXHIBIT 6.3.6
PROMOTABILITY RATINGS, PERFORMANCE RATINGS, AND WORK SAMPLE SCORES

A promotability rating was made as part of the annual performance review (the scale ranges from 7 for "ready for immediate promotion" to 1 for "should not be promoted"). The performance rating ranges from 1 for "poor performance" to 7 for "exceptional performance" (in the candidate's current job). As part of the selection process, all applicants went through a series of work sample tests (i.e., in-basket, leaderless group discussion, and production planning exercise). Scoring was done by trained raters from the personnel department (20 was the highest possible score).

CANDIDATE	PROMOTABILITY	PERFORMANCE	WORK SAMPLE SCORE
George Martin	NA	NA	19.5
Tony Caciopo	6	5	15.5
Kathy Joyce	5	6	17.5
Barry Fein	NA	NA	18.5
Ron Jackson	5.5	5	18
Jay Davis	7	7	16.5
Frank Hall	NA	NA	19
Tom Doyle	5.5	6	17.5

Exercise 6.3
Assessment Questions

Name _____

1. To what extent did you agree with the peer assessments which were made on your group performance? What steps could be taken to increase the level of agreement between your self assessment and the peer assessment?

2. Do you think that the leaderless group discussion is a useful tool for personnel assessment? What changes in the exercise should be made in order to increase its validity as a personnel assessment method?

3. Could Dynamo successfully defend a lawsuit brought by one of the candidates not selected under the Civil Rights Act of 1991 or the ADEA? Explain your answer.

C H A P T E R

EMPLOYMENT
INTERVIEWS*

*Contributed by Diana Deadrick.

OVERVIEW

While the use of paper-and-pencil tests and performance tests has increased in recent years, the most common personnel selection tool is still the employment interview. Primarily due to its expense, the interview is typically one of the last of the selection hurdles used after other methods have shortened the list of potential candidates. Often, the manner in which interviews are conducted is not conducive to high validity. For example, the typical job interview involves a single interviewer who asks no predetermined set of questions with no specific basis for evaluating the applicants interviewed. By the way, this unstructured approach is definitely not the best way to conduct an interview—only the most common.

There are three key features of the employment interview. First, the interview is a *subjective evaluation* of applicant suitability that relies on human judgment. Perceptual factors underlying this decision-making process play a critical, and possibly contaminating, role in the interview. For instance, stereotypes, first impressions, and attitudes of the interviewers have been found to influence not only the conduct of the interview but the resultant decisions as well. Therefore, it is important to examine the decision-making process as a means of understanding how interviewer decisions are reached, the effectiveness of those decisions, and the usefulness of the interview as a selection aid.

Second, the interview is used to make decisions about the degree of fit between people and jobs. As a selection tool, the interview is used to screen applicants and/or predict which applicants will be successful on the job and in the organization. The screening function focuses on applicants' qualifications to perform the job, whereas the predictive function focuses on their potential ability to succeed in the job and the organization. In both cases, selection decisions can be improved if the interview contributes relevant, reliable, and valid information about job applicants that is not available through other means, such as the methods we discussed in the previous chapter. Because of the subjective nature of this decision tool, the potential for discriminatory bias is apparent. The legal implications of using employment interviews concern the validity of interview decisions as prescribed by equal employment opportunity (EEO) laws and guidelines.

Last, the matching process described above involves *information* both about the individual applicants and about the specific job and organization. The major purpose of the interview is to obtain and synthesize information about the abilities of an individual and the requirements of the job. Therefore, up-to-date job information plays an important role in the ability of an interviewer to evaluate a job candidate. Without adequate knowledge about the job specifications, the interviewer is likely to rely on implicit stereotypes of an "ideal" job candidate and possibly increase the bias in the interview. Thus, up-to-date job analysis information goes hand in hand with good interviewing. Corporate planning and corporate culture are also relevant to the predictive equation and should affect the content of the interview and the weight given to the various responses.

This chapter will examine the three aspects of the employment interview. First, the decision-making process is examined in order to understand how interview decisions are determined. Second, the decision-making outcomes are described, thus examining the "effectiveness" of interview decisions and the legal implications of those decisions. Last, selection interview guidelines will be suggested for improving the effectiveness of the interview.

OBJECTIVES

After studying this chapter, you should be able to:

1. Explain how both individual and situational factors can distort the interview process.
2. Review the validity of different approaches to interviewing.
3. Describe how a structured approach to interviewing can affect decision outcomes.
4. Summarize the discriminatory biases that might affect interview decisions.
5. Explain the different purposes of the employment interview.
6. Summarize the different types of interview formats, and explain how each one can improve decision outcomes.

If they haven't done so already, almost every student will eventually take part in a job interview. Nearly 100 percent of organizations use the employment interview as one basis for the selection of personnel. Some universities now use interviews to select students for graduate programs. Dartmouth, Carnegie-Mellon, the University of Tennessee, and the Wharton School, for example, routinely interview applicants for their M.B.A. programs. Many companies now provide extensive training programs and specific guidelines for interviewers. As Tom Newman, director of training at S. C. Johnson & Sons, Inc., puts it, interviewing is now "much more of a science." And the "science" pays off, as research clearly shows greater validity for more systematic interviewing. Mobil Oil, Radisson Hotels International, the Marriott Corporation, and Sun Bank are among many of the companies that conduct extensive programs to prepare their interviewers. We will review some of these methods in this chapter. Let us begin with the basics and examine the underlying perceptual processes that characterize interviewers' evaluations.

DECISION-MAKING PROCESS

Consider the amount of stimuli that surrounds you everyday. If you recognized, processed, analyzed, stored, and recalled every piece of incoming information, chances are you would never get anything done! Instead, people use a perceptual process that enables them to screen, select, categorize, and interpret relevant information. This "filtering" process allows people to selectively receive and interpret information for decision-making purposes, resulting in the following "benefits": (1) A *coping mechanism,* which enables people to initially select and screen information. This process of selectivity reduces the amount of stimuli that a person must process and thus reduces the amount of uncertainty in the environment. (2) An *efficiency mechanism,* which enables people to subsequently categorize and interpret information. This process of organization increases the meaning attached to the selected information, and thus increases the degree of understanding about the environment.

The result is that individuals selectively receive and process only that information which is relevant for their own decision-making purposes. An example of selective perception is impression formation in which only certain pieces of information are used for making judgments. Impressions are based on information cues that are important to an individual at a certain point in time. Because these information cues are often unique to the perceiver, impressions about a person (e.g., a job applicant) can differ from person to person. Though a variety of factors influence the perceptual process, they can be categorized under three general headings of influence factors or cues affecting the job interview[1]:

1. **Attributes of the applicant.** The intensity, motives, and physical characteristics of the job applicant.
2. **Attributes of the interviewer or interviewers.** The motives, previous learning, personality, and physical characteristics of the interviewer or interviewers.
3. **Attributes of the situation.** Environmental conditions such as time, noise, light, and heat.

Attributes of the Job Applicant

In the context of the interview, the attributes of the applicant refer to characteristics which influence an interviewer's attention and impression of the applicant. For example, voice modulation, body language, posture, and visible characteristics such as sex, weight, ethnicity, and physical attractiveness are factors that might influence the interviewer's judgments about a job applicant.[2] A common phenomenon is *stereotyping* in which an impression about an individual is formed on the basis of his or her group membership (e.g., race) rather than individual attributes. Stereotyping involves categorizing groups according to general traits and then attributing those traits to a particular individual once his or her group membership is known.[3] Although stereotypes are a common and convenient means of efficiently processing information, they can be a source of error (bias) when people mistakenly attribute traits they *believe* to be true for an entire group to one member, without considering that person as an individual. Figure 7.1 lists some of the more common applicant attributes that have been shown to lead to rating bias.[4]

Attributes of the Interviewer

The attributes of the interviewer refer to personal characteristics of the interviewer that might influence his/her ability to make decisions. For example, personal values and previously learned associations between certain information cues and decision responses might influence the decision-making process.[5] One type of perceptual influence due to the interviewer's personal characteristics is a "similar-to-me" attribution in which an impression is formed by the interviewer on the basis of a perceived similarity between applicant and interviewer. This perceived similarity might be based on the interviewer's attitudes, interests, or group membership, thus causing certain information, or individuals, to be placed in a more favorable light than others. The danger is that judgments of similarity can cause rating errors; the areas of similarity may not be relevant to the particular job for which the interview is being conducted. A list of interviewer attributes that have been shown to distort the interview process is shown in Figure 7.2.[6]

In response to the problems of interviewer bias and the high cost of face-to-face interviews, many companies conduct computer interviews to screen applicants. Telecomputing Interviewing Services in San Francisco, for example, lists over 1000 clients which conduct computer interviews for mostly entry-level jobs. Bloomingdale's hired all its personnel for its Miami store using computer interviewing to question applicants about work attitudes, substance abuse, and employee theft. As Ellen Pollin, personnel manager at Bloomingdale's puts it, the "machine never forgets to ask a question and asks each question in the same way." Other companies are using videoconferencing to interview employees, particularly managerial prospects. Merrill Lynch and Texas Instruments claim considerable cost savings with no loss in validity using videoconferences.

FIGURE 7.1
APPLICANT ATTRIBUTES THAT AFFECT RATING BIAS

ATTRIBUTES	EXAMPLES OF RESEARCH FINDINGS
Gender bias	Influenced by type of job (role-congruent jobs) and competence. Female interviewers gave higher ratings than male interviewers.
First-impression effect	Early impressions were more important than factual information for interviewer judgments. Hire decisions were related to the interviewer's causal interpretation (attribution) of an applicant's past outcomes.
Contrast effect	Interviewers' evaluations of job candidates were influenced by the quality and characteristics of the previous candidates.
Nonverbal communication	Applicants who looked straight ahead, as opposed to downward, were rated as being more alert, assertive, and dependable; they were also more likely to be hired. Applicants who demonstrated a greater amount of eye contact, head moving, and smiling received higher evaluations.
Physical attractiveness	More attractive applicants received higher evaluations.

Sources: See note 2.

FIGURE 7.2
INTERVIEWER ATTRIBUTES THAT AFFECT RATING BIAS

ATTRIBUTES	EXAMPLES OF RESEARCH FINDINGS
Similarity effect	Interviewers gave more positive ratings to applicants perceived to be similar to themselves. Interviewers resisted using additional information to evaluate applicants once they perceived the applicants to be similar to themselves.
"Likability"	Interviewers gave more positive ratings to candidates they liked. Interpersonal attraction was found to influence interviewers' perceptions of applicant qualifications.
"Ideal stereotype"	Interviewers judged applicants against their own stereotype of an "ideal" job candidate. These stereotypes may be unique to each interviewer, or they may be a common stereotype shared by a group of raters.
Information favorability	Interviewers weighted negative information more heavily than positive information. Interviewers spent more time talking when they had already formed a favorable decision.
Information utilization	Interviewers placed different importance (weights) on the information content of the interview, resulting in idiosyncratic information-weighting strategies. Discrepancies often arose between interviewers' intended (nominal) information weights and the actual information weights they used to arrive at a decision.

Sources: See note 5.

Citizens Bank of Maryland has sharply reduced interviewer involvement by combining a short, structured interview with one video developed especially for tellers and another for customer service representatives. The video provides a realistic job preview that describes the positive and negative features of the job and then tests applicants on job-related verbal, quantitative, and interpersonal skills. The test, which costs Citizens Bank $27 per applicant, is completed and scored on a computer. Citizens Bank reports a significant drop in turnover with this method, compared to turnover rates when hiring decisions were based on an unstructured interview in which interviewers had no formal set of questions to ask.

Attributes of the Situation

Factors such as stress, background noise, interruptions, time pressures, and other conditions surrounding the interview can influence interviewers' attention to information.[7] The amount of information available to the interviewer prior to the actual interview session is an important factor. If little background information about the job is available, the decision-making process may be distorted due to irrelevant or erroneous assumptions about job requirements. The lack of job information causes the interviewer to rely on his or her assumptions about what the job requires, which may not be consistent across different interviewers or across different interview sessions. Rating errors occur because non-job-related information is collected and used in the decision-making process. Figure 7.3 contains a list of some of the situation attributes that have been found to distort the interview process.[8]

Summary

In summary, applicant, interviewer, and situation attributes are factors that can potentially bias the decision-making process and result in erroneous evaluations during the interview. There are two facets to this bias: a general rating bias and a more specific discriminatory bias. The *rating bias* refers to unfair, but not necessarily illegal, distortions that are attributable to the underlying impressions and stereotypes associated with job applicants. The *discriminatory bias* refers to unfair and illegal distortions based on an applicant's sex, race, age, disabilities, or other characteristics. The factors shown in Figures 7.1 and 7.2 are some of the general perceptual influences that affect rating bias and contribute to discriminatory bias as well. Discriminatory bias will be examined more fully in the discussion on decision-making outcomes.

Applicant Behaviors

While the discussion so far has focused on interviewer reactions to the interview process, applicant's reactions also have an impact on that process. For example, an applicant's communication skills (verbal and nonverbal) will affect the interviewer's impression and evaluation. In fact, applicants' verbal communication skills sometimes receive too much weight in an interviewer's overall judgment of applicants for jobs which do not require high levels of verbal skills. Additional characteristics of applicants, such as their own motives and expectations, can influence both their perceived and their actual interview performance. Self-perceptions influence applicants' behaviors which, in turn, influence the interviewer's judgments. In addition to self-perceptions, an applicant's perception of the interviewer also influences the decision-making process. The interviewer's behavior—verbal and nonverbal—causes applicants to form impressions about both the individual interviewer and the company as a whole. Just as impressions influence the interviewer's decision to hire, impressions also influence the applicant's decision to accept or reject a job offer. Although research in this area is limited, Figure 7.4 lists some of the factors that have been shown to influence impression formation from the applicant's perspective.[9] This figure also contains suggestions for how an applicant might make a favorable impression on interviewers.

DECISION-MAKING OUTCOMES

The information obtained in an interview provides a basis for subsequent selection (and placement) decisions. Of particular interest is the overall quality of employment decisions based on interviews: How reliable is the

FIGURE 7.3
SITUATIONAL ATTRIBUTES THAT AFFECT RATING BIAS

ATTRIBUTES	EXAMPLES OF RESEARCH FINDINGS
Job information	Interviewers who received more information about the job used it for evaluation decisions. Increased job information reduced the effect of irrelevant attributes and increased reliability between raters.
Applicant information	Interviewers' preinterview impressions of applicant qualifications had a strong influence on postinterview impressions and recommendations to hire. Interviewers with favorable preinterview impressions of applicants evaluated those applicants as having done a better job of answering the interview questions.
Decision time	Interviewers reached a final decision early in the interview process; some studies have indicated the decision is made after an average of 4 minutes. Hire decisions were made sooner than no-hire decisions.

Sources: See note 7.

FIGURE 7.4
APPLICANT EVALUATIONS AND SKILLS

SELF-PERCEPTIONS
* Applicants with a high motivation to succeed were more confident of success after the interview, yet those with an intermediate motivation to succeed received higher interviewer evaluations.
* Applicants with high self-esteem had higher expectations for interview success, but they overestimated how well they performed in the interview.

COMMUNICATION
* Applicants who maintained direct eye contact, a smile, good posture, interpersonal distance, voice modulation, and fluency of speech were more likely to be hired.
* Verbal content generally influences interviewer evaluations more than the nonverbal communication.

IMPRESSIONS OF INTERVIEWER
* Applicants' impressions of the interview were better when interviewers used nonverbal approval.
* Applicants' evaluations of the interviewer and the job were influenced by their perceptions of the interviewer's personality, manner of delivery, and adequacy of information.

"IMPRESSION MANAGEMENT"
* Applicants' effectiveness can be increased by training procedures such as modeling, role playing, and directive feedback.
* Job offer probability can be increased if the applicant emphasizes "motivators," such as responsibility and opportunity for advancement, rather than "hygiene factors," such as salary and job security.
* Interviewers' impressions and evaluations can be enhanced if the interviewee has memberships in groups such as fraternities, sororities, and professional societies.

Sources: See notes 2 and 3.

interview information? How valid is that information for predictive purposes? That is, to what extent do interview judgments predict subsequent job performance?[10] In general, the validity of the employment interview has been hampered by perceptual factors such as first impressions, stereotypes, and lack of adequate job information.[11] The influences listed previously in Figures 7.1 to 7.3 help to explain these findings. The validity of the interview procedure has also been impaired by underlying personal perceptual bias, which affects factors such as different information utilization and different questioning content. However, recent efforts to improve interview effectiveness indicate that certain types of interviews are more reliable and valid than the typical, unstructured format. For instance, interview questions based on job analysis (see Chapter 4), as opposed to psychological or trait information, increase the validity of the interview procedure. In addition, structured interviews, which represent a standardized approach to systematically collecting and rating applicant information, have yielded substantially higher

reliability and validity results than unstructured interviews. Recent research findings suggest that the effectiveness of interview decisions can be improved by carefully defining what information is to be evaluated during the interview and by systematically evaluating that information using consistent rating standards. The most recent reviews of the subject concluded that structured interviews are more valid than unstructured interviews and, in general, that the selection interview has at least modest validity (overall validity about 0.30).[12]

Discriminatory Bias

The potential for litigation involving employment interviews is high, given the potentially biasing nature of the process.[13] Many cases have involved the questions which are asked at the interviews. The employment interview is in essence a "test" and is thus subject to the same laws and guidelines that prohibit discrimination on the basis of age, race, sex, religion, national origin, or disability. Some states and municipalities also have laws protecting smokers and homosexuals. Furthermore, the interview process is similar to the subjective nature of the performance appraisal process; hence, many of the court decisions concerning the use of performance appraisals apply to the interview as well.[14] In general, the courts have not been kind to employers that used vague, inadequate hiring standards; subjective, idiosyncratic interview evaluation criteria; or biased questions that were not job-related.[15] The courts have also criticized employers for inadequate interviewer training and the use of irrelevant interview questions. In essence, the courts have focused on two basic issues for determining interview discrimination: the content of the interview and the impact of the decisions.[16]

The first issue involves discriminatory intent: Do certain questions convey an impression of underlying discriminatory attitudes? Discriminatory intent (and discriminatory treatment) is most likely to occur when non-job-related questions are asked of only one protected group of job candidates and not others. For example, women applying for work as truck drivers at Spokane Concrete Products were questioned about child-care options and other issues not included in the interviews of male applicants. The court found disparate treatment of females and a violation of Title VII. In another example, a female applicant to a bank was questioned extensively by an interviewer about what she would do if her 6-year-old child was sick, while no such questions were directed at male applicants. She didn't get the job but did get a lawyer. The court concluded that the child-care questions constituted sex discrimination.

Some state and local laws prohibit certain types of questions. For example, over 170 complaints were filed against Delta Airlines in 1992 by job applicants who claimed they were asked questions about marital status and sexual habits. Such questions are prohibited by New York State's human rights statute.

The second issue pertains to discriminatory impact: Does the interview inquiry result in a differential, or adverse, impact on protected groups? If so, are the interview questions valid and job-related? Discriminatory impact occurs when the questions asked of all candidates implicitly screen out a majority of the members of a protected group. Questions about arrests, for example, can have a discriminating impact on minorities. For example, questions about arrests were used by some interviewers of the Detroit Edison Company, which provided no training, job analysis information, or specific questions for its all-white staff of interviewers. The process could not be defended in light of the adverse impact which resulted from interview decisions based on answers to questions which were not job-related (including arrest record).

In summary, the inherent bias in the interview and the relatively poor validity reported for unstructured interview decisions make this selection tool vulnerable to charges of discrimination. Employers need to quantify, standardize, and document interview judgments. Furthermore, employers should train interviewers, continuously evaluate the reliability and validity of interview decisions, and monitor interviewer decisions for any discriminatory effects such as adverse impact. As mentioned earlier, many companies such as S. C. Johnson, Radisson Hotels, and Mobil Oil now have extensive training programs for interviewers, which include interviewing procedures, potential discriminatory areas, rating procedures, and role plays.

The research evidence regarding the discriminatory effects of the interview is based on the stereotyping processes that affect female and minority job applicants. The evidence, which is generally inconclusive, is summarized below.[17]

SEX DISCRIMINATION. Although early research studies indicated that female applicants generally receive lower interview evaluations than male applicants, more detailed analyses suggest that this effect is largely dependent upon the type of job in question, the amount of job information available to the interviewer, and/or the qualifications of the candidate. In some studies, research suggests that females have received higher ratings than male applicants.

RACE DISCRIMINATION. There is mixed evidence for racial bias in interviewer evaluations. Relatively few studies have investigated race discrimination, with some studies indicating a negative bias and others a positive bias. There is some indication that black interviewers rate black applicants higher while white interviewers rate white applicants higher.

AGE DISCRIMINATION. Although the research indicates that older applicants generally receive lower evaluations than younger applicants, this effect is influenced by the type of job in question, interviewer characteristics, and the content of the interview questions (i.e., traits versus qualifications). The evidence for age bias is mixed and suggests that, like sex bias, age bias might be largely determined by the type of job under study and the particular interviewer.

DISABILITY DISCRIMINATION. Few research studies have examined bias against applicants with disabilities. The evidence that does exist suggests that applicants with disabilities receive lower hiring evaluations but higher ratings for personal factors such as motivation. Before any conclusions about such bias can be made, more research needs to be conducted which examines the nature of the disability and the impact of situational factors, such as the nature of the job. Because persons with disabilities are now protected by the 1990 Americans with Disabilities Act (ADA), and because individuals with legal drug dependencies and illnesses such as cancer, multiple sclerosis (MS), and acquired immune deficiency syndrome (AIDS) are included in the protection provided by the act, this form of discrimination is likely to become much more controversial than it has been in the past and litigation in this area is likely to increase substantially. Interviewers must be aware of the "reasonable accommodation" provisions of the law which apply to methods of testings and assessment. (See Chapter 3 for a discussion of the ADA.)

Overall, the research evidence on discriminatory bias is insufficient to support firm general conclusions. Nonetheless, employers should examine their interview process for discriminatory bias, train interviewers in ways to prevent biased inquiries, provide interviewers with thorough and specific job specifications, structure the interview around a thorough and up-to-date job analysis, and monitor the activities and assessments of individual interviewers.[18] Without question, certain interviewers can be found guilty of one or more of the discriminatory biases described above.

SELECTION INTERVIEW GUIDELINES

The interview appears to be an institutionalized activity in the selection process. Therefore, guidelines for developing and using an interview procedure are necessary for both practical and legal reasons. The suggestions that follow are based on over 70 years of research that has examined the process and outcomes of selection interviews. The administrative guidelines describe planning and evaluation activities, and the procedural guidelines focus on design and implementation activities. These suggestions are summarized in Figure 7.5.

Administrative Guidelines

The issues listed at the top of Figure 7.5 focus on interview development and evaluation.[19] These activities are divided into four general categories: purpose, situation, training, and evaluation.

PURPOSE. The first step in developing, or redesigning, the employment interview is to establish the purpose of the procedure. Employers must decide whether the information collected from the interview is to be used as a screening mechanism or as a predictive measurement device. The difference between these two uses has to do with the *placement* of the interview in the selection process (a rough, initial screening tool versus a probing, specific ability assessment) and the *information* to be collected (past achievements versus potential aptitudes). An additional, often implicit purpose is that the interview is a public relations tool in which the applicants' assessments of the company are as important as the company's assessment of them. The point is that each of these objectives entails different interview procedures and methods of evaluations. For example, a selection interview should evaluate the job-related characteristics of applicants; an assessment of effectiveness should focus on reliability and validity assessments. In contrast, a public relations interview is not used for selection purposes but rather for "image" purposes; an effectiveness evaluation should focus on the interviewer's credibility and public image, and should evaluate the applicant's reaction. Interviewers must be careful in what they say in a recruiting interview of this nature. An interviewer for Blue Cross and Blue Shield of Michigan discussed permanent employment with an applicant. Several years later, the applicant, who had become an employee and had later been terminated, won a judgment for contract violation because Blue Cross had discharged him in violation of the promise made by the recruiter.

SITUATION. The situational factors that surround the interview include both the job and the physical environment. With regard to the *job,* thorough and up-to-date job information should be collected, reviewed, and disseminated to all interviewers prior to the interview sessions. This information includes the job analysis, the job description, and/or job specifications (see Chapter 4). Based on this information, it will be possible for interviewers to identify and document the requirements of the job in question. Furthermore, a clear statement of job requirements will enable follow-up evaluations to ensure that the information collected by interviewers is in fact required for effective job performance.

Many multinational corporations use successful expatriate managers to develop and conduct interviews for the selection of managers for overseas assignments. These interviewers tend to have a better understanding of the major requirements of these jobs than do managers with no overseas experience. Many companies, including Ford, Nestlé, Procter & Gamble, Texaco, and Philip Morris, credit improvements in their expatriate placements to their interviewing processes, which involve experienced and successful expatriates who have had experience in the overseas jobs to be filled.

The *physical environment* for interviews should be maintained consistently, providing a standardized setting for the interviews. The conditions surrounding the interview might influence the decision-making process; therefore, extraneous factors such as noise, temperature, and interruptions should be controlled. As we discussed earlier, in one effort to standardize the interview process and reduce costs as well, some companies use computer interviewing. Using either a voice system or a keyboard format, companies such as Bloomingdale's use computer interviews to question applicants about work attitudes, employee theft, and other issues.

TRAINING. The need for interviewer training cannot be overemphasized. Our previous discussion of the decision-making process indicated that interviewers need to be trained regarding how to evaluate job candidates, the

FIGURE 7.5
INTERVIEW PROCEDURE GUIDELINES

Administrative Issues

Purpose	Screening versus selection
	Selection versus nonselection
Situation	Job information
	Physical environment
Training	Process training
	Instrument training
Evaluation	Overall decision effectiveness
	Individual decision effectiveness

Procedural Issues

Content	"What" information is collected:
	Motivational and interpersonal factors
	Job-related content
Format	"How" information is collected:
	Types of interviews
	Rating forms

criteria to be used in the evaluation, how to use evaluation instruments, and how to avoid common biases and potentially illegal questions. First, *process training* should sensitize raters to inherent biases and help them to develop more effective strategies for categorizing and analyzing information. Johnson's Wax, for example, found that most interviewers made their decision about an applicant after only 5 minutes. They trained their people to withhold judgment and gather information free of the first-impression bias. Workshops and group discussions should be used to train interviewers in how to:

1. **Use job information.** Understand job requirements, and relate these requirements to their questioning content and strategy.
2. **Reduce rating bias.** Practice interviewing, and provide feedback and group discussion about rating errors and potential legal problems.
3. **Communicate effectively.** Develop rapport with applicants, "actively listen," and recognize differences in semantics.

In addition, *instrument training* should focus on using a standardized (structured) approach for conducting the information exchange. This training should focus on how to:

1. **Use interview guides or outlines.** Structure the interview content, and quantitatively rate applicant responses.
2. **Exchange information.** Focus on relevant applicant information, and provide applicants with adequate and timely information about both the job and the company.

EVALUATION. Once implemented, the interview procedure should be evaluated in terms of the effectiveness of the overall interview outcomes and the effectiveness of individual interviewer decisions. These outcome evaluations should include determinations of:

1. **Reliability.** The extent to which interviewers agree in their evaluations of applicants.
2. **Content validity.** The scope and job relatedness of questions.
3. **Predictive validity.** The relationship between interview decisions (predictions) and actual on-the-job performance.
4. **Interviewer validation.** Individualized validity evidence on each interviewer.
5. **Interviewer feedback.** Follow-up information about the overall validity of interviews, each interviewer's validity and applicant success patterns, and any changes in job requirements.

Procedural Guidelines

Figure 7.5 also contains a list of issues for use in conducting an interview, focusing on content and format issues.[20]

The following are general suggestions based on legal and practical concerns; more specific content guidelines should be based on the specific organization and the relevant state and local laws.

1. Exclude traits that can be measured by more valid employment tests—for example, intelligence, job aptitude or ability, job skills, and knowledge.
2. Include motivational and interpersonal factors that are required for effective job performance. These two areas seem to have the most potential for both overall and interviewer validity. Interviewers should assess only those factors which are specifically exhibited in the behavior of the applicant during the interview and which are critical for performance in the job to be filled (based on a job analysis).
3. "Match" interview questions (content areas) with the job analysis data of the position to be filled and the strategic goals of the organization.
4. Avoid biased language, jokes which may detract from the formality of the interview, and inquiries that are not relevant to the job in question.
5. Limit the amount of preinterview information to complete information about applicants' qualifications and ambiguous data in need of clarification. Knowledge of test results, letters of reference, and other sources of information tends to bias the interview.
6. Word interview questions in a manner that permits the applicant to fully respond. Avoid leading (answer implied in question), argumentative, and rhetorical questions (only one answer is obvious).

The format suggestions deal with how the interview content is structured and evaluated. These suggestions describe different types of interview procedures and rating forms for standardizing and documenting interviewer evaluations.[21]

TYPES OF INTERVIEWS. There are a variety of interview formats in use. In fact, the lack of standardization has contributed to poor reliability and validity of both overall interview decisions and the decisions of individual interviewers. However, improvements in the effectiveness of the procedure have been made, based on the following types of interview formats.

Structured interviews range from highly structured procedures to semistructured inquiries. In a highly structured interview, interviewers ask the same questions of all candidates in the same order. These questions are based on a job analysis and are reviewed for relevance, accuracy, completion, ambiguity, and bias. A semistructured interview provides general guidelines, such as an outline of either mandatory or suggested questions, and recording forms for note taking and summary ratings. In contrast, the traditional, unstructured interview is typically characterized by open-ended questions that are not necessarily based on or related to the job to be filled. The use of either a structured or semistructured interview procedure standardizes the content and process of the interview, and thus improves the reliability and validity of the subsequent judgments.

In *group/panel interviews,* multiple interviewers independently record and rate applicants' responses during the interview session. The panel typically includes the job supervisor and a personnel representative or other job expert who helped to develop the interview questions. As part of the interview process, the panel reviews job specifications, interview guides, and ways to avoid rating errors prior to each interview session. Procter & Gamble, for example, uses a minimum of four interviews for each position to be filled. The Central Intelligence Agency (CIA) uses a minimum of three interviews for each job candidate. The use of a panel interview reduces the impact of idiosyncratic biases that single interviewers might introduce and appears to increase both the reliability and the validity of the procedure. Many team-based production operations now use team interviews to add new members and select team leaders. The Saturn plant of General Motors (GM), in Spring Hill, Tennessee, is one example. In general, more than one interviewer per applicant will result in higher validity for the interview.

Situational or behavioral interviews require applicants to describe how they would behave in specific situations. The interview questions are based on the critical incident technique (CIT) of job analysis, which calls for examples of unusually effective or ineffective job behaviors for a particular job (see Chapter 4). These incidents are converted into interview questions which describe a situation and then require the job applicants to tell how they would handle that situation. Each question is accompanied by a rating scale, and interviewers evaluate applicants in terms of how effective or ineffective their responses are. For example, Palm Beach County, Florida, asked the following question of all applicants for the job of high school principal: "Members of the PTA have complained about what they regard as overly harsh punishment imposed by one teacher regarding cheating on an exam. How would you handle the entire matter?" Another question had to do with a teacher who was not complying with regulations regarding the administration of standardized tests. The candidate was asked to provide a chronology of actions to be taken regarding the situation. The situational approach may be highly structured and

may include an interview panel. For example, three Palm Beach County principals trained in situational interviewing listened to applicants' responses, asked questions if necessary, and then made independent evaluations of each response. The underlying assumption is that applicants' responses to the hypothetical job situations are predictive of what they would actually do on the job. This technique improves interviewers' reliability and validity. Behavioral interviewing may involve probing beyond the initial answer. For example, at GM's Saturn plant, employees are first asked to describe a project in which they have participated as group or team members. Probing may involve work assignments, examples of good and bad teamwork, difficulties in completing the project, and other related projects.

RATING FORMS.   Interview questions are intended to elicit evaluation information; therefore, rating forms are recommended in order to provide a systematic scoring system for interpreting and evaluating information obtained from applicants. Based on the job analysis, the specified content of the interview, and the degree of structure for the procedure, ratings forms should be constructed with the following features. First, the ratings should be behaviorally specific, based on possible applicant responses exhibited during the interview. Second, the ratings should reflect the relevant dimensions of job success, providing a focused evaluation of only the factors required for job performance. Third, the ratings should be based on quantitative rating scales that provide a continuum of possible applicant responses, ordered in terms of desirability. Ideally, the rating scales should provide response anchors (descriptions) at multiple points along the continuum of possible responses. These anchors provide examples of good, average, and poor applicant responses for each interview question. The use of anchored rating forms reduces rater error and increases rater accuracy. This approach, using specific, multiple ratings for each content area of the interview, is preferred to using an overall, subjective suitability rating that is not explicitly job-relevant. Figure 7.6 presents two examples of a behavior rating scale for use in interviewing.

SUMMARY

The accuracy of interview decisions is limited by the information-processing capabilities of interviewers. As one review of the research concluded, "the typical unstructured selection interview is invalid. The interviewer operates as a poor information processor. He collects unsystematic and incomplete data and weighs it according to an invalid stereotype. He then combines it into an of-

FIGURE 7.6
EXAMPLES OF QUESTIONS FROM SITUATIONAL INTERVIEWS

A. A customer comes into the store to pick up a watch he left for repair. The repair was supposed to have been completed a week ago, but the watch is not back yet from the repair shop. The customer is very angry. How would you handle the situation?

1	(Low)	Tell the customer the watch is not back yet and ask him to check back with you later.
3	(Average)	Apologize. Tell the customer that you will check into the problem and call him or her back later.
5	(High)	Put the customer at ease and call the repair shop while the customer waits.

B. For the past week you have been consistently getting the jobs that are the most time-consuming (e.g., poor handwriting, complex statistical work). You know it's nobody's fault because you have been taking the jobs in priority order. You have just picked your fourth job of the day and it's another "loser." What would you do?

1	(Low)	Thumb through the pile and take another job.
2	(Average)	Complain to the coordinator, but do the job.
3	(High)	Take the job without complaining and do it.

Sources: Adapted from J. A. Weekley and J. A. Gier, Reliability and validity of the situational interview for a sales position. *Journal of Applied Psychology, 3,* 1987, 484–487. G. P. Latham and L. M. Saari, Do people do what they say? Further studies on the situational interview. *Journal of Applied Psychology, 4,* 1984, 569–573. Copyrights 1987, 1984 by the American Psychological Association. Adapted by permission.

ten invalid prediction."[22] Factors such as characteristics of the applicant, the interviewer, and the situation can influence and distort the decision-making process, resulting in less than optimal interview decisions. Because employment interviews entail complex decision-making activities, interviewers often try to simplify the process and, in doing so, bias their decisions. This inherent bias poses both legal and practical implications for management.[23] Because interviewer bias reduces the probability of selecting the highest performing candidates, overall organization performance can be affected.

The reliability and validity of the decision-making outcomes indicate how effective the interview is as a selection tool. Like any other selection tool, the interview procedure is a means of making inferences about the fit between the applicant's ability to do the job and the organization's requirements for it. The informal, unstructured nature of most interviews, typically conducted by only one interviewer, coupled with the biased decision-making process, reduces the likelihood of a systematic analysis of applicant qualifications and jeopardizes the quality of performance predictions. Although the reliability and validity of interview decisions can be improved by using a structured approach, the incremental validity of these interviews needs to be determined.

Incremental validity refers to the improvement in predictive efficiency attributable to the interview as compared with other selection procedures such as those discussed in Chapter 6. As to the degree that the content of a structured interview overlaps other selection procedures, such as ability tests, work samples, assessment centers, personality measures, or biographical data, the question arises whether the interview adds any additional information that is not available through more objective and/or economical selection tools. As a general rule, the interview tends to have relatively *lower* validity for jobs in which specific knowledge is strongly related to success on the job (e.g., knowledge related to science, computers, engineering, or mathematics).[24] Organizations must analyze their current selection procedures and determine to what extent the interview improves overall validity in the context of cost considerations.

The administrative guidelines described in this chapter are intended to ensure that the validity of the interview is maximized while interviewer bias is minimized. In turn, the procedural guidelines define both the content and the method of the interview inquiry, therefore providing a means of improving the overall effectiveness of the interview procedure. However, a final dilemma facing organizations that use the interview as a selection tool is the issue of *functional utility.*[25] What is the unique contribution of the interview in the employment decision? This is a practical assessment of the usefulness of the interview based on a determination of which information is best collected through the interview process and whether interviewers' decisions based on that information are consistent and accurate. In order to achieve functional utility from the interview, organizations must evaluate their overall selection procedures and determine: (1) what factors are best and most consistently evaluated during the interview and (2) whether other selection procedures can measure those identified factors as well as or better than the interview, with consideration given to the cost of the selection options as well. Organizations should also focus on the purpose of the selection interview. Interviews which attempt to assess a candidate's fit while simultaneously recruiting the candidate usually fail at both.

The most effective personnel selection systems place a great emphasis on the interaction between the person and the organization in the prediction of effectiveness.[26]

The matching model we presented in Chapter 5, for example, calls for an assessment of the applicant in the context of both job and organizational characteristics and a realistic assessment of the organization and the job by the applicant. This matching model is particularly effective in high-involvement organizations in which employees have considerable latitude in the workplace. Interviewing, particularly in this context, is perhaps the most important of the selection options for assessing the person-organization fit. At Sun Microsystems, one of the fastest-growing U.S. companies, job applicants are interviewed several times by as many as 20 interviewers. The interview data is considered in the context of the results of an extensive battery of psychological tests. Toyota (USA) conducts a formal interview for all positions at its Georgetown, Kentucky, facility. The interview results are combined with assessment center data, a work sample, and an aptitude test. The most effective selection systems integrate data from the interview with other sources and weigh the information in the context of the matching or person-organization fit model.[27]

DISCUSSION QUESTIONS

1. What is stereotyping? Give examples of legal and illegal stereotypes.
2. How can you prevent interviewers from discriminating against people with disabilities?
3. Describe how an organization might improve the reliability and validity of interviews.
4. Contrast an unstructured interview with a situational or behavioral interview.
5. "The most efficient solution to the problem of interview validity is to do away with the interview and substitute paper-and-pencil measures." Do you agree or disagree? Explain.
6. Why do you suppose differences in interview performance between ethnic groups are less than differences on cognitive ability tests, as we discussed in Chapter 6?

NOTES

1. Szilagyi, A. D., Jr., and Wallace, M. J., Jr. (1987). *Organizational behavior and performance,* 4th ed. Glenview, IL: Scott, Foresman, pp. 61–63. See also: Dipboye, R. L. (1992). *Selection interviews: Process perspectives.* Cincinnati, OH: South-Western. Anderson, N. H., and Shackleton, V. J. (1990). Decision making in the graduate selection interview. *Journal of Applied Psychology, 44,* 267–268.

2. Schmitt, N. (1976). Social and situational determinants of interview decisions: Implications for the employment interview, *Personnel Psychology,* pp. 79–101. See also: Arvey, R. D. (1979a). Unfair discrimination in the employment interview: Legal and psychometric aspects, *Psychological Bulletin,* pp. 736–765. Arvey, R. D. (1979b). *Fairness in selecting employees.* Reading, MA: Addison-Wesley, pp. 155–181. Arvey, R. D., and Campion, J. E. (1982). The employment interview: A summary and review of recent research, *Personnel Psychology,* pp. 281–322. Raza, S. M., and Carpenter, B. N. (1987). A model of hiring decisions in real employment interviews, *Journal of Applied Psychology,* pp. 596–603. Graves, L. M., and Powell, G. N. (1988). An investigation of sex discrimination in recruiters' evaluations of actual applicants, *Journal of Applied Psychology,* pp. 20–29. Binning, J. F., Goldstein, M. A., Garcia, M. F., and Scattaregia, J. H. (1988). Effects of preinterview impressions on questioning strategies in same- and opposite-sex employment interviews, *Journal of Applied Psychology,* pp. 30–37.

3. See note 2 (1979b), pp. 156–163. See also: note 1, Dipboye (1992).

4. See note 2.

5. See note 2. See also: Webster, E. C. (1964). *Decision making in the employment interview.* Montreal: Eagle.

6. See note 5.

7. See note 2. See also: note 5; Dipboye, R. L. (1989). Threats to the incremental validity of interviewer judgments. In R. W. Eder and G. R. Ferris (eds.), *The employment interview.* Newbury Park, CA: Sage Publications, pp. 45–60. Cronshaw, S. F., and Wiesner, W. H. (1989). The validity of the employment interview: Models for research and practice. In Eder and Ferris (eds.), *The Employment Interview,* pp. 269–281.

8. See note 7.

9. See note 2, Arvey and Campion (1982). See also: note 7, Eder and Ferris (eds.) (1989), pp. 193–203 (Politics) and pp. 204–215 (Impression management); Powell, G. N. (1991). Applicant reactions to the initial employment interview: Exploring theoretical and methodological issues. *Personnel Psychology, 44*(1), 67–84.

10. Cascio, W. F. (1987). *Applied psychology in personnel management,* 3d ed. Englewood Cliffs, NJ: Prentice-Hall, pp. 121–162. See also: note 2, Arvey (1979b), pp. 9–38.

11. Schneider, B., and Schmitt, N. (1986). *Staffing organizations,* 2d ed. Glenview, IL: Scott, Foresman, p. 385. See also: Bowen, D. E., Ledford, G. E., and Nathan, B. R. (1991). Hiring for the organization, not the job. *Academy of Management Executive, 5*(4), 35–51. Macon, T. H., and Dipboye, R. L. (1990). The relationship of interviewers' preinterview impressions to selection and recruitment outcomes. *Personnel Psychology, 43,* 745–768. Kinicki, A. J., Lockwood, C. A., Hom, P. W., and Griffeth, R. W. (1990). Interviewer predictions of applicant qualifications and interviewer validity: Aggregate and individual analyses. *Journal of Applied Psychology, 75,* 477–486.

12. The more recent, optimistic findings for improved reliability and validity results are based on cumulative reviews of validity studies: Harris, M. M. (1989). Reconsidering the employment interview: A review of recent literature and suggestions for future research. *Personnel Psychology,* pp. 691–726. McDaniel, M. A., Whetzel, L. L., Schmidt, F. L., Hunter, J. E., and Maurer, S. (1991). The validity of employment interviews: A review and meta-analysis, Unpublished manuscript. Wiesner, W. H., and Cronshaw, S. F. (1988). A meta-analytic investigation of the impact of interview format and degree of structure on the validity of the employment interview, *Journal of Occupational Psychology,* pp. 275–290.

13. See note 2, Arvey (1979b), p. 155; Arvey (1979a).

14. See note 2, Arvey (1979b), pp. 164–165. See also: *Stamps v. Detroit Edison,* 6 Feb 612. *EEOC v. Spokane Concrete Products,* 534 F. Supp. 518 (1982).

15. See note 2, Arvey (1979a); Arvey (1979b), pp. 164–168. See also: Campion, J. E., and Arvey, R. D. (1989). Unfair discrimination in the employment interview. In R.W. Eder and G. R. Ferris (eds.), *The employment interview.* Newbury Park, CA: Sage Publications, pp. 61–72.

16. See note 2, Arvey (1979a).

17. The summary in the text is based on the following sources: note 2, Arvey (1979a). Arvey, R. D., Miller, H. E., Gould, R., and Burch, P. Interview validity for selecting sales clerks, *Personnel Psychology,* 1987, pp. 1–12. Note 2, Arvey (1979b), pp. 168–179. Note 15, Campion and Arvey (1989). Note 12, Harris (1989).

18. See note 2, Arvey and Campion (1982), pp. 314–316.

19. These suggestions are based mainly on critiques and recommendations from the following sources: Wagner, R. (1949). The employment interview: A critical summary. *Personnel Psychology,* pp. 17–46. Wright, O. R., Jr. (1969). Summary of research on the selection interview since 1964. *Personnel Psychology,* pp. 391–413. Note 2, Schmitt (1976); Arvey and Campion (1982); Arvey (1979). Campion, M. A., Pursell, E. D., and Brown, B.

(1988). Structured interviewing: Raising the psychometric properties of the employment interview. *Personnel Psychology,* pp. 25–42. Note 7, Cronshaw and Wiesner (1989).

20. See note 2, Arvey (1979b), pp. 180–212; Arvey and Campion (1982). See also: note 2, Schmitt (1976). Note 19, Wagner (1949); note 12, McDaniel et al. (1991); and note 7, Dipboye (1989).

21. See note 2, Schmitt (1976); Arvey and Campion (1982). See also: Weekly, J. A., and Gier, J. A. (1987). Reliability and validity of the situational interview for a sales position. *Journal of Applied Psychology,* pp. 484–487. Note 11, Schneider and Schmitt (1986), pp. 389–393. Note 19, Campion, Pursell, and Brown (1988).

22. Porter, L., Lawler, E. E., and Hackman, J. R. (1975). *Behavior in organizations.* New York: McGraw-Hill, p. 145.

23. *Watson v. Fort Worth Bank & Trust,* 108 S.Ct. 2777 (1988). *Price Waterhouse v. Hopkins,* 57 L.W. 4469 (1989). See also: Ryan, A. M., and Lasek, M. (1991). Negligent hiring and defamation: Areas of liability related to preemployment inquiries. *Personnel Psychology, 44,* 293–320.

24. See note 7, Dipboye (1989).

25. Ulrich, L., and Trumbo, D. (1965). The selection interview since 1949, *Psychological Bulletin,* pp. 100–116. See also: note 2, Schmitt (1976), pp. 93–94.

26. See note 11, Bowen, Ledford, and Nathan (1991).

27. Rynes, S., and Gerhart, B. (1990). Interviewer assessments of applicant "fit": An exploratory investigation. *Personnel Psychology, 43,* 13–36. Singer, M. S., and Bruhns, C. (1991). Relative effect of applicant work experience and academic qualification on selection interview decisions: A study of between-sample generalizability. *Journal of Applied Psychology, 76,* 550–559. Fear, R. D., and Chiron, R. J. (1990). *The evaluation interview.* New York: McGraw-Hill.

EXERCISE 7.1
WHAT QUESTIONS SHOULD YOU ASK
IN AN INTERVIEW?*

OVERVIEW

Chapter 7 describes the potential legal liability inherent in the employment interview. Given the subjective nature of the process and the discretion which interviewers typically exercise in the interview, there is great opportunity for biases which could be interpreted as violations of any number of state, federal, or local laws on equal opportunity. Other issues to consider are "negligent hiring" and "employment-at-will." The purpose of this exercise is to explore the potential legal implications of a number of questions often posed by interviewers. The student may want to review Chapter 3 before attempting this exercise.

LEARNING OBJECTIVES

After completing this exercise, you should:

1. Be able to identify interview questions which are of questionable legality or potentially problematic.
2. Know the major laws and legal implications which may affect the interview process.

---

*Contributed by Robert W. Eder and M. Ronald Buckley.

PROCEDURE

Part A: Individual Analysis

Step 1. Prior to class, check whether each question on Form 7.1.1 is potentially illegal (should probably be avoided during an employment interview). For those questions which you consider to be illegal or potentially illegal, provide a justification for your position and cite the law.

Step 2. Complete the Assessment Questions.

Part B: Group Analysis

In groups of about six, students should compare responses on each item of Form 7.1.1 and decide on a group response and justification for each. The items should then be divided up among the students so that each group member is prepared to present the group position on a portion of the 22 items. Also, the group should compose a response to each of the assessment questions for this exercise. Class discussion will focus on group responses to each item and possible discrepancies in the correct answers.

FORM 7.1.1

Name _____ Group _____

LAWFUL   UNLAWFUL

_____ _____   1. Would you mind if I called you by your first name?

_____ _____   2. Are you a citizen of the United States?

_____ _____   3. Are you married or do you live with someone?

_____ _____   4. Have you ever been arrested?

_____ _____   5. What professional societies do you belong to?

_____ _____   6. What kinds of people do you enjoy working with the most?

_____ _____   7. Are you planning to start a family soon?

_____ _____   8. How long do you expect your husband will remain here before changing jobs?

_____ _____   9. I can't help but notice the great shape you've kept yourself in. How do you do it?

_____ _____   10. We're looking for someone who can relate effectively to college students; you're 52?

_____ _____   11. Have you ever been convicted of a crime (beyond traffic violations)?

_____ _____   12. Will your family or personal obligations interfere with your ability to keep the hours of this job?

_____ _____   13. How does your military experience relate to this job?

_____ _____   14. What are your religious beliefs?

_____ _____   15. How do you feel about getting personally involved with someone at work?

_____ _____   16. Would you be willing to work on Yom Kippur?

_____ _____   17. How long have you lived around here?

_____ _____   18. Are you a smoker or a nonsmoker?

_____ _____   19. Are you a homosexual?

_____ _____   20. What plans do you have for taking care of the children if you get this job?

_____ _____   21. Do you consider yourself handicapped in any way?

_____ _____   22. Is there any history of chronic illness in your family?

Exercise 7.1
Assessment Questions

Name _____

1. How would you design a training program so that future interviewers would understand what can and cannot be asked in an employment interview?

2. If your organizational research had clearly determined that employees with children under the age of 5 are much more likely to be absent from work than others, could the company then ask situational questions about what the applicant would do if his or her children were sick?

3. How would you design a structured interview and a testing program for an overseas assignment?

4. Discuss the ethical and legal implications of asking applicants for the health histories of family members. Setting aside the possible legal issues, should a company take family health into consideration when evaluating an applicant?

EXERCISE 7.2
AN EVALUATION OF INTERVIEW QUESTIONS*

OVERVIEW

Chapter 7 describes the kinds of questions which are most useful for a valid employment interview. Situational or behavioral interviewing was described as a method for enhancing the validity of interview judgments. The purpose of this exercise is to evaluate a number of questions which were asked during hiring interviews to determine the extent to which each follows the guidelines for good interviews provided in the chapter. Students will also be asked to rewrite those questions which are judged to be defective.

LEARNING OBJECTIVES

After completing this exercise, you should be able to:

1. Distinguish between ineffective and effective interview questions.
2. Rewrite interview questions so as to make them more job-related.

PROCEDURE

Part A: Individual Analysis

Step 1. Prior to class, review each of the questions presented in Form 7.2.1 to determine whether you consider it to be an effective question for an employment interview. Rewrite (or delete) any questions which you feel could be improved or are unnecessary. Do your revisions directly below the items on Form 7.2.1. If you feel that a question should be dropped altogether, explain your position directly below the question. Add other questions which you think would be useful (see the job description in Exhibit 7.2.1). The position you are trying to fill is "computer systems analyst III." Assume

as the interviewer you have a completed application form and a résumé for each applicant.

Step 2. Also prior to class, complete the Assessment Questions for the exercise.

Part B: Group Analysis

Step 1. In groups of about six, students should compare responses to each of the questions and attempt to resolve any disagreements. The group should then devise a complete plan for conducting the interview and a chronology for the entire interview process. The interview process should include a method for compiling the interview data and using the data in conjunction with other information regarding the job applicants.

Step 2. Each group should prepare a written outline of the events, and one spokesperson should be designated to present the group's complete interview process.

EXHIBIT 7.2.1
JOB DESCRIPTION FOR COMPUTER SYSTEMS ANALYST III

CRITICAL KASOCs

Systems design: Ability to design systems that can be implemented as recommended.

Program coding: Ability to code systems so that they can be easily debugged.

Understanding program specifications: Ability to identify errors.

Knowledge of existing software and its applications.

Documentation: Ability to write easily interpretable documentation.

Debugging: Ability to discern debugging strategies and document the solutions.

Knowledge of job control language (JCL): Applicants should know most JCL statements.

Working with customers: Ability to listen to and evaluate customers' complaints.

JOB SPECIFICATIONS

Minimum qualifications: Bachelor's degree in computer science or a related discipline; at least 2 years of experience as systems analyst; knowledge of Fortran, PLI, and at least one other language.

*Contributed by Robert W. Eder and M. Ronald Buckley.

FORM 7.2.1

Name _____ Group number _____

1. Do you like programming?

2. Where did you go to school?

3. Why did you leave your last job?

4. I assume you would prefer minimal supervision?

5. Have you thought about your future in this field?

6. Well, we were looking for someone with a little more experience. (Brief pause.) Tell me about your last job.

7. Why should we hire you?

8. We believe in giving people a great deal of responsibility; what do you think?

9. You don't mind traveling, do you?

10. Have you ever been fired or asked to resign?

11. What interests you the most about this job?

12. You seem highly qualified for the position. Are you interested in a long career with us?

Exercise 7.2
Assessment Questions

Name _____

1. For this type of job, to what extent would you weight interview information relative to other sources of data about the applicants? What factors would you consider in this decision?

2. After discussing the various questions and their relative effectiveness, what do you consider to be the underlying factors which determine the effectiveness or ineffectiveness of interview questions?

EXERCISE 7.3
AN INTERVIEW ROLE PLAY*

OVERVIEW

Chapter 7 makes recommendations for the development and administration of valid employment interviews. This exercise provides an opportunity for students to follow these recommendations as they develop job-related interviews for two jobs. They will conduct mock interviews and serve in the roles of observer, interviewer, and job applicant.

LEARNING OBJECTIVES

After completing this exercise, you should:

1. Be able to write job-related, behavioral interview questions.
2. Know a procedure for deriving a summary score for the applicant.
3. Understand how the validity and reliability of interview ratings can be enhanced.

PROCEDURE

Part A: Individual Analysis

Prior to class, each student should review the description of Edbuck, Inc. (EBI), in Exhibit 7.3.1, as well as the job description for an EBI administrative officer (Exhibit 7.3.2). Read also the job description for a campus residence adviser (Exhibit 7.3.3). Write a format for a 6-minute interview which includes three behavioral questions for each job, and devise a method for rating the responses and deriving a summary rating of potentiality for each job candidate. Think of these three questions as starting points from which a variety of follow-up questions are possible.

Part B: Group Analysis

Step 1. In groups of three, one member should be designated as the observer, one the interviewer, and one the job applicant. The first interviewer should select one of the two jobs and conduct a 6-minute interview with the job applicant. The observer's job is to review the interviewer's questions and then take notes on the performance of both the interviewer and the applicant.

Step 2. After completion of the interview, the observer reviews the interviewer's questions again, the response format, and the scoring procedure.

Step 3. Group members should then switch roles, and the second job should be the focus of the next 6-minute interview.

Step 4. The final round may involve either of the two jobs; the third interviewer should make the choice.

Step 5. Each group member should provide feedback to the other members regarding the way in which the interviews were conducted, the scoring methods, the rating scales used, and the behavioral questions which were written and asked. Form 7.3.1 should be used for this purpose. Job applicants should also be briefed on their responses to the questions. In general, each person should brief the others on the extent to which they followed the recommendations presented in Chapter 7 for enhancing rating validity.

EXHIBIT 7.3.1
DESCRIPTION OF THE COMPANY

Edbuck, Inc. (EBI) is a mid-size organization whose primary objectives are the following: (1) the manufacture of sporting equipment, including running shoes, baseball and football equipment, and equipment necessary for most racquet sports; (2) the manufacture of balls for use in professional sporting activities; (3) research and development (R&D) where necessary (e.g., running shoes, baseball bats, gloves). EBI is located in Philadelphia. It is only 10 years old and has grown rapidly since its founding by five people: an engineer, a former professional athlete, a former designer of computer hardware, a lawyer, and a D.B.A. in management. These five founders still own over 90 percent of the stock in this closed corporation, although not in equal shares.

EBI had about $6 million in gross sales last year. EBI has finally gotten to the point where the five founders no longer take part in daily operations. Their expertise is better spent on other duties. They hired an administrative vice president a year ago to oversee the operations, but soon realized that this person was overburdened as well. Thus they decided to look for an administrative officer who would be responsible for the clerical aspects and some technical aspects of the operations, while the administrative vice president, to whom the officer would report, would still oversee the major functional areas. The five principals of EBI are actually board members, but they still do take part in some operating-level decisions in their areas of expertise.

The administrative vice president is a middle-aged white male who has a bachelor's degree from Auburn University in management. When hired, he had 20 years of administrative experience and was considered a "good catch" by the directors of EBI. He is a native of the Northeast, is married, has no children, and is an avid outdoorsman. He is knowledgeable and competent and has the respect of those who work for him. His leadership style is very structured and authoritarian, and he finds it difficult to delegate work without checking it over closely.

---

*Contributed by Robert W. Eder and M. Ronald Buckley.

EXHIBIT 7.3.2
ADMINISTRATIVE OFFICER'S JOB—EDBUCK, INC.

The administrative officer will be in charge of such activities as contract administration, personnel record keeping, training and development, wage and salary administration, and coordinating efforts of the scientific/technical and manufacturing personnel. Report writing, planning, and policy-making are additional duties. Selection and staffing are currently handled by each individual division of EBI, as are performance appraisal, wage and salary administration, and motivation programs. There is currently no union in EBI. Operating-level persons are highly skilled.

DESCRIPTION OF WORK

General statement of duties: Supervises and coordinates responsible administrative work, which is complex in nature and involves program responsibility; does related work as required.

Supervision received: Receives policy guidance from the administrative vice president or board members.

Supervision exercised: Plans, organizes, develops, coordinates, and directs a staff of administrative and clerical personnel. Total at all levels exceeds 20 individuals.

EXAMPLES OF DUTIES

Administers, coordinates, and directs a complex administrative management program involving program responsibility for a department or equivalent; organizes and directs the day-to-day work of personnel and engages in long-range planning.

Establishes methods of work and develops departmental procedures and policies for administrative functions.

Directs budgeting, training, record keeping, and personnel and general administrative functions.

Directs or performs studies of work pertaining to efficiency, work flow, procedures, work standards, and research and planning.

Develops reports for various areas.

Develops and implements immediate and long-range plans for administrative areas of the organization.

Performs related work as required.

REQUIRED KASOCs

Extensive and broad knowledge of complex administrative management programs. Skill and ability in administering, planning, and directing personnel in day-to-day programs appropriate to the position to be filled. Ability to interpret and apply laws, rules, regulations, and industry practices. Ability to relate to and coordinate department activities with employees, other departments, and the general public.

QUALIFICATIONS FOR APPOINTMENT

Education: Graduation from a college or university, with major course work in business (or public) administration or related field.

Experience: Two years of progressively responsible experience in a supervisory, technical, or professional area related to management or administration. Familiarity with computer software is a plus.

Or a combination of education and experience. Equivalent to the above.

EXHIBIT 7.3.3
JOB TITLE: UNIVERSITY RESIDENCE ADVISER

DESCRIPTION OF WORK

General statement of duties: In-house official of the Department of Residence Living, responsible for offering advice and referral, enforcing university residence hall policies, administering the physical environment of a specific unit, programming events, facilitating communication flow, participating in staff development, and handling administrative details. The residence adviser (RA) will have a residential unit of approximately 50 students and will be required to account for 15 hours of work per week in one or more of the above areas.

Supervision received: The RA is immediately responsible to the head residence hall director of the hall in which he or she works. The RA is afforded a high degree of autonomy as long as he or she remains within the university guidelines. Direct supervision may be forthcoming if a special task or action is mandated by the director of residence living or by an area director.

Supervision exercised: Limited supervision of the residents assigned to the RA's unit.

MAJOR DUTIES AND THEIR DEFINITIONS (In Order of Importance)

1. Advises and counsels an assigned group of approximately 50 student residents on a single floor of a dormitory. Available for a minimum of 2 hours a day, 7 days a week, to listen to and help resolve students' personal and academic problems through: active listening techniques, mediation techniques, conducting floor meetings, and programming educational seminars.

2. Refers residents to services and organizations on campus and in the local area, to resolve problems that cannot be resolved through RA advising and counseling, and/or to satisfy residents' personal goals and interests. Posts information on bulletin boards, engages in one-to-one conversations, and holds group meetings.

3. Enforces federal, state, local, and university regulations that pertain to residence hall living: inspects common living areas for cleanliness in accordance with university standards; confronts (and/or reports to area director on) violators of drugs, noise, alcohol, fire, and maintenance regulations to maintain the health and/or safety of the dormitory residents, the university community, and the physical plant.

4. Communicates to residents information which may be issued by Department of Residence Living staff members or other sources, including health services, public safety, campus security, and intramural athletics, to keep residents informed of policies, organizations, and upcoming events. Communicates by posting signs and literature, drafting memos, and conducting meetings. Occasionally required to gather information requested by other Department of Residence Living staff.

5. Designs and implements activities and programs for floor residents to foster a community atmosphere, by assessing residents' needs through administering interest surveys and interfacing with residents; and planning and scheduling parties, study breaks, and other events.

6. Attends weekly meetings with other Department of Residence Living staff to receive information and to discuss common problems and goals.

7. Performs duties in accordance with Department of Residence Living requirements. Tasks include inspecting rooms, reporting damage to area directors, filing time cards, and processing room changes.

FORM 7.3.1
INTERVIEW SUMMARY SHEET

Your name _____

Interviewer's name _____

In your role as observer, evaluate all aspects of the interviewer's performance (including the quality of the questions). Write a short narrative regarding the interviewer's performance. What did he or she do well? Where is there a need for improvement? Comment on the behavioral questions, the scoring procedure proposed, and the rating scales.

What other selection procedures do you recommend for this job? How much weight would you give to the interview as it was conducted? Explain your answer.

How effective was the interviewer in gathering job-related information? Circle one response below and explain your rating.

7	6	5	4	3	2	1
(Highly effective)						(Not very effective)

C H A P T E R

ORGANIZATIONAL TRAINING*

*Written by Phillip J. Decker and Joyce E. A. Russell.

OVERVIEW

The selection methods discussed in Chapters 6 and 7 attempt to assess the match between an applicant's ability and the requirements of the job. Some of the methods are clearly designed to predict ability to learn the requirements of the jobs through some form of training program (e.g., cognitive ability tests), while other methods attempt to measure knowledge, skills, or abilities that are a necessary condition for acceptable performance at the outset of employment (e.g., performance testing). While some of these methods have proved to be good predictors of subsequent performance on the job, the reported validities of all methods underscore the need for good training. In addition, in the context of growing international competition and the need for more adaptive work design to create and sustain competitive advantage, continuous training is essential. As we discussed in Chapter 1, U.S. firms face greater challenges than ever to maintain their position among the top economic powers. American businesses are painfully realizing that their place at the top is not guaranteed, and that they must find solutions to the lagging productivity, competitiveness, motivation, and creativity of the workforce.[1] In addition to more valid selection methods, more companies seek competitive advantage through the training and retraining of American workers. Given the more intense pressures to compete, improve quality and customer service, and lower costs, American companies have come to view training as a function critical to organizational survival and success.

Among companies which have moved training to the top of the corporate agenda are Motorola, Inc.; Corning Glass Works; International Business Machines (IBM); Saturn Corporation; Ford Motor Company; and Johnson & Johnson. IBM alone spends over $1 billion yearly on the education of its employees.[2] Chapter 1 discussed some of the strongest trends affecting American business today. Increased competition, rapid changes in technology, the growing diversity of the workforce, and occupational obsolescence are among the most important challenges for the next decades. Some of these forces are summarized in Figure 8.1. Training is one of the most important responses to these challenges.

The purpose of this chapter is to provide an overview of employee training. We will discuss the importance of training in the context of the organization's competitive strategy and the need to link training needs with the mission and goals of the organization. You will learn how to design and evaluate a training program and to tailor the training to particular situations.

FIGURE 8.1
MAJOR FORCES AFFECTING CORPORATIONS AND THEIR IMPLICATIONS FOR TRAINING

FORCES	TRAINING IMPLICATIONS
Increased global and domestic competition	Greater need for competitive strategies. Employees need to be skilled in the technical aspects of their jobs. Managers need to be trained in management techniques that maximize employee productivity.
Rapid changes in technology and computerization	Employees need to be trained to have higher technological skills (e.g., computers, engineering) and to be able to adapt to changes in operations, job design, and work flow.
Changes in the workforce	The workforce is increasingly being made up of more minorities, women, people with disabilities, older workers, and better-educated people who value self-development and personal growth. Managers need to be able to relate to issues facing diverse employees and to work in a cooperative manner with employees. Also, they need to ensure that employees are capable of participating more in organizational decisions.
Greater demands on management time	Managers need to be trained to be able to make quick and accurate decisions.
Widespread mergers, acquisitions, and divestitures	Long-term training plans are needed which are linked to corporate business plans and strategies.
Occupational obsolescence and the emergence of new occupations	Greater changes in occupations (due to the changing nature of the economy; the shift from manufacturing to service industries; and the impact of research, development, and new technology) require flexible training policies to prevent lower productivity and increased turnover.

Sources: Modified from R. R. Camp, P. N. Blanchard, and G. E. Huszczo, *Toward a more organizationally effective training strategy and practice.* Englewood Cliffs, NJ: Prentice-Hall, © 1986, p. 26. Adapted by permission of Prentice-Hall, Inc. J. Casner-Lotto and associates, *Successful training strategies: Twenty-six innovative corporate models.* San Francisco, CA: Jossey-Bass, 1988. p. 2. Used with permission.

OBJECTIVES

After studying this chapter, you should be able to:

1. Define what is meant by training, and describe why it is a critical function for corporations today.
2. Explain how to conduct a needs assessment, including performing organizational, task, and person analyses, and how to derive instructional objectives for a training program.
3. Know how to design a training program to facilitate learning, particularly among adult learners.
4. Identify the critical elements related to transfer of training.
5. Compare and contrast the various techniques available for training, including their relative advantages and disadvantages.
6. Identify and distinguish between the four types of evaluation criteria.
7. Compare and contrast the different experimental designs available for evaluating training programs.
8. Understand the components of training programs for employee orientation and international assignments.

DEFINING TRAINING AND DEVELOPMENT

Training is defined as any attempt to improve employee performance on a currently held job or one related to it. To be effective, training should involve a learning experience, be a planned organizational activity, and be designed in response to identified needs. Ideally, training should be designed to meet the goals of the organization while simultaneously meeting the goals of individual employees.[3] The term "training" is often confused with the term "development." *Development* refers to learning opportunities designed to help employees grow. Such opportunities do not have to be limited to improving employees' performance on their current jobs. At Ford Motor Company, for example, a new systems analyst is required to take a course on Ford standards for user manuals. The content of this training is needed to perform the systems analyst job at Ford. The systems analyst may also, however, enroll in a course entitled "Self-Awareness," the content of which is not required on the current job. This situation illustrates the difference between "training" and "development."[4]

POPULARITY OF TRAINING

The costs of organizational training often exceed $40 billion per year, including staff salaries, seminars, training conferences, training facilities, equipment, training materials, and services purchased from consultants and vendors.[5] *Training* magazine indicated that over 36 million employees of 2500 surveyed firms received formal training in 1986 alone.[6] Clearly, training activities are big business in terms of the amount of money spent and the number of employees involved.

While top managers recognize the value of training to help their firms gain a competitive edge, so too do employees. Employees understand that opportunities for training enable them to grow and advance in their careers. In fact, in a recent review of the 100 best sales companies to work for, training was rated by job candidates as the most important variable to consider in job selection. Twenty-nine companies in the "best 100" were given perfect ratings for their training for sales employees. Among the most highly rated for training were Aetna Life & Casualty, American Telephone and Telegraph (AT&T), Black & Decker, Eastman Kodak Company, General Electric Company (GE), IBM, Procter & Gamble, Westinghouse Electric Corp., and Eli Lilly & Co.[7]

The jobs most likely to receive training in corporations include: management (including executives, senior managers, middle managers, first-line supervisors) professionals, administrative employees, and office/clerical staff. Primarily because of changes in technology and lack of skills at the entry level, there has also been an increase in the training provided for customer service employees, salespeople, and production workers.[8] Corporations are offering a variety of training programs to meet their organizational needs. Figure 8.2 lists some of the more commonly used training programs and the percentages of firms using them. A growing number of companies have recently initiated productivity and quality improvement programs in the context of the Deming Prize and the Baldrige Awards we discussed in Chapter 1. Many companies have also recently provided training and awareness programs in sexual harassment.

A SYSTEMS VIEW OF TRAINING

Wherever training activities are planned, the basic process of training remains the same. Figure 8.3 illustrates this process by showing the three major steps involved in training efforts. These include needs assessment, development, and evaluation. Briefly, the goal of the *assessment* phase is to collect information to determine whether training is needed in the organization. If it is needed, what becomes important is to determine where in the organization training is needed; what kind of training is needed; and what specific knowledges, abilities, skills, and other characteristics (KASOCs) should be taught.

FIGURE 8.2
COMMONLY USED TRAINING PROGRAMS

TYPES OF TRAINING	PERCENTAGE* PROVIDING
New-employee orientation	80.7
Performance appraisals	66.2
Word processing	63.5
Time management	63.3
Leadership	62.0
New-equipment operation	60.9
Hiring/selection	59.6
Product knowledge	56.9
Stress management	54.8
Train-the-trainer	52.6
Listening skills	52.4
Team building	51.2
Safety	51.0
Motivation	48.7
Problem solving	48.0
Delegation skills	46.8
Public speaking/presentation	45.3
Interpersonal skills	45.1
Goal setting	44.9
Decision making	43.2
Computer applications	42.8
Planning	42.3
Writing skills	41.4
Computer programming	40.6
Managing change	40.0
Data processing	39.5
Management information systems (MIS)	39.5
Conducting meetings	38.4
Negotiating skills	35.9
Substance abuse	35.0
Smoking cessation	34.4
Strategic planning	34.2
Quality control	34.1
Finance	28.4
Purchasing	24.9
Outplacement/retirement planning	24.0
Creativity	21.6
Ethics	19.7
Reading skills	19.3
Foreign language	10.9
Other (topics not listed)	4.9

*Of organizations with 100 or more employees.
Source: J. Gordon, Who is being trained to do what? Reprinted with permission from the October 1988 issue of *Training* Magazine. Copyright 1988, Lakewood Publications, Inc., Minneapolis. All rights reserved.

This information is collected by conducting three types of analyses—at the organizational, job, and person levels. After the information is compiled, objectives for the training program can be derived.

The goal of the *development* phase of training is to design the training environment necessary to achieve the objectives. This means that human resource (HR) professionals must review relevant learning issues, including characteristics of adult learners and learning principles as they apply to the particular training situation and poten-

tial trainees under consideration. Also, HR professionals must identify or develop training materials and techniques to use in the program. Finally, after the appropriate learning environment is designed or selected, the training is conducted.

The goal of the *evaluation* phase is to examine whether the training program has been effective in meeting the stated objectives. The evaluation phase requires the identification and development of criteria, which should include participants' reactions to the training, assessments of what they learned in the training program, measures of their behavior after the training, and indicators of organizational results (e.g., changes in productivity data, sales figures, employee turnover, accident rates). The evaluation phase necessitates choosing an experimental evaluation design to assess the effectiveness of training. The choice of the criteria and the design are both made *before* training is actually conducted in order to ensure that training will be properly evaluated. After the training is completed, the program is then evaluated using the criteria and design selected.

NEEDS ASSESSMENT

The first step in training is to determine whether a need for training actually exists. An organization should commit its resources to a training activity only if the training can be expected to achieve some organizational goal. The decision to conduct training must be based on the best available data, which is collected by conducting a needs assessment. This needs analysis should ideally be conducted in the context of a human resource planning (HRP) program, as outlined in Chapter 5. Organizations that implement training programs without conducting needs assessments may be making errors. For example, a needs assessment might reveal that less costly interventions (e.g., personnel selection, a new compensation system, job redesign) could be used in lieu of training.[9]

A *needs assessment* is a systematic, objective determination of training needs, which involves conducting three primary types of analyses. These analyses are used to derive objectives for the training program. The three analyses consist of an organizational analysis, a job analysis, and a person analysis.[10] After compiling the results from these analyses, the HR professional is ready to derive objectives for the training program.

Many trainers suggest that a training need is any discrepancy between what is desired and what exists. Thus, one of the goals of the needs assessment is to note any discrepancies. For example, the World Bank recently determined through a needs assessment that many of its constituents from eastern Europe required training in

FIGURE 8.3
A SYSTEMS MODEL OF TRAINING

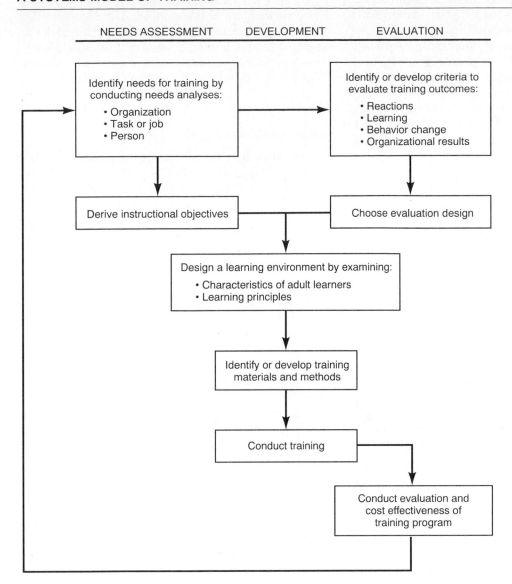

transforming state-owned businesses into self-sustaining businesses. The organization contracted with a number of universities to develop and provide the necessary training.

Comparisons between the expected level of performance specified (from the job analysis) and the current level of performance exhibited (evident in the person analysis) may indicate performance discrepancies. The Sheraton Corporation, for example, specified that all hotel managers must be familiar with the implications of the 1990 Americans with Disabilities Act (ADA) for hotel operations (see Chapter 3). A test of the law was administered, and scores on the test were used as a basis for identifying managers who needed training on the implications of the law. Performance discrepancies should not,

however, be automatically interpreted as a need for training.[11] The analyst must determine whether the discrepancy is a skill or knowledge deficiency, thus requiring training. If, however, the required skill is present and performance is still lacking, then the problem may be motivational in nature and thus require some other type of organizational intervention (e.g., pay for performance, discipline). Let us next examine the three levels of analysis in more detail.

Organizational Analysis

An organizational analysis tries to answer the question of *where* the training emphasis should be placed in the company, and what factors may affect training. To do this, the HR professional should examine organizational goals, personnel inventories, and climate and efficiency indexes. This examination should ideally be conducted in the context of the labor supply forecast and gap analysis discussed in Chapter 5 as a part of the HRP effort. Organization system constraints that may adversely affect the training process should also be explored. Many companies rely on very detailed surveys of the workforce to determine training needs as part of the planning effort. Motorola and IBM, for example, conduct annual surveys which assess particular training needs in the context of the company's short- and long-term goals.

The review of short- and long-term goals of the organization and any trends that may affect these goals is done to channel the training toward specific issues of importance to the firm (e.g., improved customer satisfaction or employee quality of work life, increased productivity). For example, after Merrill Lynch pleaded guilty to a number of fraudulent business practices, the new chief executive officer (CEO) ordered training in business ethics for all employees. In order to minimize layoffs, IBM retrained hundreds of employees to be sales representatives. Not only were they able to reduce layoffs, but the larger sales staff was able to attack another corporate goal—to improve customer satisfaction.

As we discussed in Chapter 5, an HRS inventory can reveal projected employee mobility, retirements, and turnover. The more sophisticated personnel inventories can also indicate the number of employees in each knowledge and skill group, which can then be compared to the skills needed based on the gap analysis of the HR planning process. For example, Ford's Manufacturing Systems Division decided to change to a new programming language for future support work based on internal customer needs. The first step was to determine the extent to which the current staff was sufficiently skilled in the new language. A computerized personnel inventory quickly revealed how many of the staff had at least basic knowledge of and experience with the new language.

A review of climate and efficiency indexes is important to identify problems that could be alleviated with training.[12] Climate indexes are quality of work life indicators and include records on turnover, grievances, absenteeism, productivity, accidents, attitude surveys, employee suggestions, and labor-management data (e.g., strikes, lockouts). Efficiency indexes consist of costs of labor, materials, and distribution, the quality of the product, downtime, waste, late deliveries, repairs, and equipment utilization. These data are examined to find any discrepancies between desired and actual performance.

It is important to identify any organizational system constraints on training efforts. For example, if the benefits of training are not clear to members of top manage-

ment, they may not plan and budget appropriately for training. Consequently, the training program may not be properly designed or implemented. Top managers might also not evaluate and reward managers and employees for using behaviors learned in training. This would send a message to trainees that training is not important and would seriously undermine the effectiveness of the training efforts.[13]

Job Analysis

A job analysis tries to answer the question of *what* should be taught in training so that the trainee can perform the job satisfactorily. As we discussed in Chapter 4, a job analysis should document the tasks or duties involved in the job as well as the KASOCs and other characteristics needed to carry out the duties. When conducting a job analysis to determine training needs, both a *worker-oriented* approach, which focuses on identifying behaviors and KASOCs, and a *task-oriented* approach, which describes the work activities performed, should be used. A worker-oriented method, such as the critical incident technique (CIT), is valuable because it specifies the skills and abilities that should be developed in training. A task-oriented approach, such as the Task Inventory Comprehensive Occupational Data Analysis (TI-CODAP), is beneficial in identifying specific training objectives which are used in curriculum development and program evaluation. As discussed in Chapter 4, ideally more than one method of job analysis should be used to determine training needs. If interviews or questionnaires are used and discrepancies exist between what a supervisor says is an important job duty and what an employee states, these discrepancies should be resolved before any training programs are designed.[14] You may recall from the discussion in Chapter 4 that some experts rated CIT, TI-CODAP, and functional job analysis as highly effective methods for identifying training needs.

Person Analysis

A person analysis attempts to answer the question of *who* needs training in the firm and the specific types of training needed. To do this, the performance of individuals, groups, or units on major job duties (taken from the performance appraisal data) is compared to the expected performance standards (as identified in the job analysis). Given these data, one should be able to determine which job incumbents (or groups of incumbents) are successful at completing the tasks required. Many companies use self-assessments in this process. For example, Ford determined the training needs for a new computer language based on a self-assessment questionnaire distributed to the staff. At the managerial level, many organizations [e.g.,

Continental Bank, IBM, Radio Corporation of America (RCA), Federal Express, the World Bank, and the Federal Aviation Administration (FAA)] use peers and subordinates to provide performance information about their managers. At Ford, each supervisor is responsible for completing an individual training plan for each subordinate. The plan is developed jointly by the supervisor and the subordinate. The two decide on the courses which should be taken and the time frame for completion. The goal is for each employee to reach a certain level of proficiency considered necessary for current and future tasks. Many organizations in the service sector rely on customers for information about sales personnel. Bloomingdale's, for example, uses "paid" customers to assess the sales techniques of probationary employees. The data are then used to determine the appropriate managerial intervention to take with the employee (e.g., training, discipline, new compensation). We will discuss some of these interventions in greater detail in Chapter 10.

Performance discrepancies are used to indicate areas needing attention. It is important to determine whether any discrepancies are due to a lack of KASOCs, which KASOCs are missing, and whether they can be developed in employees through training. Individuals may lack the necessary skills, or may perceive themselves as lacking the skills (i.e., they may lack confidence in their abilities). In these cases, training may be needed. In other situations, employees may have the skills yet lack the needed motivation to perform, and other action may be called upon (e.g., changes in the reward system, discipline). Employees can also be tested on the desired be-

haviors by using a performance test like those discussed in Chapter 6. If they can perform the duties satisfactorily, the organization will know that skills training is not required. The U.S. Navy, for example, uses miniature training and testing in order to determine skill level prior to comprehensive training. Pratt and Whitney (P&W) uses an assessment center to measure supervisory skills judged to be critical based on its goals.

Techniques for Collecting Needs Assessment Data

A variety of techniques have been suggested for conducting a needs assessment and for collecting data to use in the organizational, job, and person analyses. A list of these techniques is provided in Figure 8.4. It should be noted that some of the techniques (e.g., work sampling) can be used for more than one type of analysis. Thus, efforts to coordinate and integrate results are recommended.

Deriving Instructional Objectives

After completing the three types of analyses in the needs assessment, the HR professional should begin to develop instructional or learning objectives for the performance discrepancies identified. Instructional objectives describe the performance you want trainees to be able to exhibit before you consider them competent.[15] Well-written learning objectives should contain observable actions (e.g., time on target; error rate for things that can be identified, ordered, or charted), measurable criteria (e.g.,

FIGURE 8.4
DATA SOURCES USED IN TRAINING NEEDS ASSESSMENT

ORGANIZATIONAL ANALYSIS	JOB ANALYSIS	PERSON ANALYSIS
Organizational goals and objectives	Job descriptions	Performance data or appraisals
Personnel inventories	Job specifications	Work sampling
Skills inventories	Performance standards	Interviews
Organizational climate indexes	Performing the job	Questionnaires
Efficiency indexes	Work sampling	Tests (KASOCs)
Changes in systems or subsystems (e.g., equipment)	Reviewing literature on the job	Customer/employee attitude surveys
Management requests	Asking questions about the job	Training progress
Exit interviews	Training committees	Rating scales
MBO or work planning systems	Analysis of operating problems	CIT
Customer survey/satisfaction data		Diaries
		Devised situations (e.g., role play)
		Assessment centers
		MBO or work planning systems

Source: Modified from M. L. Moore and P. Dutton, Training needs analysis: Review and critique. *Academy of Management Review, 3,* 1978, pp. 534–535, 537–538, 539–540. Used with permission.

percentage correct), and the conditions of performance (e.g., specification as to when the behavior should occur).[16] Figure 8.5 provides examples of the effective characteristics of learning objectives.

ADVANTAGES TO LEARNING OBJECTIVES.

Although HR professionals can develop training programs without deriving learning objectives, there are several advantages to developing them. First, the process of defining learning objectives helps HR professionals identify criteria for *evaluating* training programs. For example, specifying an instructional objective of a 20 percent reduction in waste reveals that measures of waste may be important indicators of program effectiveness. Second, learning objectives direct trainers to the specific issues and content to focus on. This ensures that trainers are addressing important topics and goals that have been

identified through strategic HR planning. Also, learning objectives guide trainees by specifying what is expected of them at the end of training. Finally, specifying objectives makes the HR department more accountable and more clearly linked to HR planning and other HR activities, which may make the training program easier to sell to line managers.

DEVELOPMENT OF THE TRAINING PROGRAM

After a needs analysis has been conducted and the HR professional is confident that training is needed to address the performance problem or to advance the firm's mission, the training program is developed. This can be done by an in-house training staff or by outside consul-

FIGURE 8.5
STANDARDS FOR LEARNING (BEHAVIORAL) OBJECTIVES

	The Observable Action May Be Expressed as:		Measurable Criteria Answer Questions as: How often? How well? How many? How much? How will we know it is okay?	Conditions of Performance	
	Verb or action	Object		What's given?	What are the variables?
After training, the worker will be able to	add	6% sales tax	exactly 6% on *all* sales	by checking a chart on the cash register.	
	identify	corporate officers	18 of the top 20	by looking at a photo or by hearing the title.	
	activate	the turn signal	for *all* turns	by using the automatic signal in the car.	
After training, drivers will	1. raise 2. extend 3. give	left arm right arm proper signal	upward at elbow for straight left for ⅛ mile before turning *or* ¼ block before turning	right turn ⎫ left turn ⎭ when driving when driving	if no automatic signal. in the country. in the city.
After training, the worker will be able to	smile		at *all* customers	even when exhausted or ill	unless customer is irate.
	express	concern about the fact that the customer is unhappy	with *all* irate people by brief (fewer than ten words) apology only after customer has stopped talking		no matter how upset, or abusive, or profane the customer becomes!
	ask	open questions	which cannot be answered *yes* or *no* or with *facts*	whenever probing for feelings.	
	relieve	tension in subordinates	by asking open questions	when employee seems angry, frustrated, confused, or tense.	

Source: D. Laird, *Approaches to training and development,* 2d ed. Reading, MA: Addison-Wesley, 1985, p. 106. Used with permission.

tants. Many firms now even design and manage their own corporate training centers. Some of them include Ford, GE, Union Carbide, IBM, Xerox, Ecolab, Black & Decker, Aetna Life & Casualty, Kodak, and Goodyear Tire & Rubber.[17] To develop the program, the HR professional should design a training environment conducive to learning. This can be done by setting up preconditions for learning and by arranging the training environment to ensure learning. Following this, the HR professional should examine various training methods and techniques, and choose the combination most beneficial for accomplishment of the instructional objectives of the training program.

Designing a Learning Environment for Training

To design a training program in which learning will be facilitated, HR professionals should review the basic principles of how individuals learn. This is done in order to set up effective preconditions for learning so that trainees will be prepared for the training program.[18] Learning principles should be reviewed and integrated into the design of the training program and materials. Also, issues of how to maximize transfer of new behaviors to the job should be addressed. Finally, trainers should design the programs to meet the needs of adults as learners, which means understanding how adults best learn.

Preconditions of Learning

Trainees must be ready to learn before they are placed in any training program. To ensure this, HR professionals should determine whether trainees are *trainable* (i.e., whether they have the ability to learn and are motivated to learn). In addition, HR professionals should try to gain the *support* of trainees and their supervisors prior to actually implementing the training program.

TRAINABILITY.   Before a learner can benefit from formal training, he or she must be trainable or ready to learn. This means that the trainee must have both the ability and the motivation to learn. To have the *ability,* the trainee must possess the skills and knowledge prerequisite to mastery of the material. One way to determine this is to give trainees a work sample (i.e., an example of the types of skills to be performed on the job) and measure how quickly they are able to learn the material or how well they are able to perform the skills.

Assessing trainees' ability to learn is of increasing concern to corporate America. The CEO of Johnson & Johnson describes the need for readiness as "the American dream turned nightmare" simply because individuals do not have the ability to learn.[19] In view of the increasing technological knowledge required in most jobs, many Americans are not being educated at a level compatible with the requirements of most entry-level jobs. The chair of the board of Bell South stated that "in 1987, fewer than 10% of employment candidates met our skill and ability requirements for sales, services, and technical jobs."[20] This situation appears to be getting worse in the United States since the entry-level jobs of the future are being "upskilled" while the pool of qualified workers is shrinking.

It's not enough for trainees to have the ability to learn the skills; they must also have the desire or *motivation* to learn. One way to assess their motivation to learn is to examine how involved they are in their own jobs and career planning efforts. The assumption is that the individuals who are more highly involved will have higher motivation to learn.[21] Some companies also link successful completion of training programs with compensation. At Ford, for example, employees must select 40 hours of training from a list of options. An employee must fulfill the 40 hours in order to qualify for merit pay.

GAINING THE SUPPORT OF TRAINEES AND OTHERS.   If trainees do not see the value of training, they will be unlikely to learn new behaviors or use them on their jobs. Trainees should be informed in advance about the benefits that will result from training. If they see some incentives for training, it may strengthen their motivation to learn the behaviors, practice them, and remember them. To gain the support of trainees for the training program, the trainer must point out the intrinsic (e.g., personal growth) and extrinsic (e.g., promotion) benefits of attending training. At Saturn Corporation, employees are strongly encouraged to receive skills training. In fact, 5 percent of their yearly compensation is based on the amount of training they receive.

In addition to garnering the support of trainees for training, the support of their supervisors, coworkers, and subordinates should be sought. For example, if the trainees' supervisors are not supportive of training, then they may not facilitate the learning process (e.g., allow employees time off for training, reward them for using new skills). Likewise, if their peers or subordinates ridicule them for attending training, they may not be motivated to attend training programs or to learn in them. This would mean that the training would not be effective in changing behaviors and would not be very cost-effective for the firm. HR professionals can improve the likelihood of acquiring others' support for training by getting their opinions on the content of training, the location, and the times. For example, a training program conducted during a department's slow times might meet with greater acceptance than the same program offered during the busiest times.

Conditions of the Learning Environment

After ensuring that the preconditions for learning are met, trainers should build a training environment in which learning is maximized. To do this, trainers need to make decisions about how best to arrange the training environment. That is, should they use whole versus part learning? Massed versus spaced practice? Overlearning? Should they provide knowledge of results, or feedback? They also need to determine how to maximize attention and retention. Learning principles should be built into the training environment as well into the training materials used. Each of these issues is briefly described below.

WHOLE VERSUS PART LEARNING. Research has shown that when a complex task is to be learned, it should be broken down into its parts. Learners should learn each part separately, starting with the simplest and going on to the most difficult. However, part learning should be combined with whole learning; that is, trainees should be shown the whole performance so that they will know what their final goal is. The training content should be broken down into integrated parts, and each part should be learned until it can be performed accurately. Then a trainee should be allowed to put all the parts together and practice the whole task.

MASSED VERSUS SPACED PRACTICE. It has been shown that spaced practice (i.e., practicing the new behavior and taking rest periods in between) is more effective than massed practice (practicing the new behavior without breaks), especially for motor skills. If a learner has to concentrate for long periods of time without rest, learning and retention may suffer. It's a little like cramming for an examination: rapid forgetting sets in very soon. Consequently, spaced practice seems to be more productive for long-term retention and for transfer of learning to the work setting.

OVERLEARNING. Overlearning (i.e., practicing beyond the point of first accurate recall), can be critical in both the acquisition and transfer of knowledge and skills. Overlearning is desirable when the task to be learned in a program is not likely to be immediately practiced in the work situation and when performance must be maintained during periods of emergency and stress. For example, overlearning skills for driving or flying may be important so that in a crisis situation the individual will be able to quickly remember what actions should be taken.

KNOWLEDGE OF RESULTS. For trainees to improve training performance, they need to receive timely and specific feedback or knowledge of results. This is because feedback serves informational and motivational purposes. It tells trainees how discrepant their performance is from the desired performance, and what particular skills or behaviors they need to correct. Also, it can motivate them to meet their performance goals once they see that they are coming close to accomplishing them. Trainers should build into the training environment opportunities for providing feedback to trainees.

ATTENTION. Trainers should try to design training programs and materials to ensure that trainees devote attention to them. They can do this by choosing a training environment that is comfortable for trainees (e.g., that has good temperature, lighting, and seats) and free from distractions (e.g., phone calls, interruptions from colleagues). Also, they should make sure that trainees are familiar with and have accepted the instructional objectives. They can do this by asking trainees to describe how accomplishing the objectives will resolve problems on the job. If trainees are able to translate learning objectives into relevant job issues, they may pay more attention to the training sessions.[22]

RETENTION. The ability to retain what is learned is obviously relevant to the effectiveness of a training program. Many factors have been found to increase retention. If the material presented to trainees is *meaningful* to them, they should have an easier time understanding and remembering it. Trainers can make the content meaningful by: (1) presenting trainees with an overview of what is to be learned so that they will be able to see the overall picture; (2) using examples and terms familiar to the trainees; and (3) organizing the material from simple to complex. Retention can also be enhanced by *rehearsal* or requiring trainees to periodically recall what they have learned (e.g., by testing them).

Using Learning Principles to Develop Training Materials

The learning principles described above should be considered not only when designing the training environment but also when developing training materials. Any materials used with trainees should be capable of stimulating them into learning and remembering the information. To ensure that this occurs, trainers need to make sure that the learning principles are built into their training materials. For example, the materials should provide illustrations and relevant examples to stimulate trainees. In addition, the objectives of the material should be clearly stated and a summary should be provided.[23]

Transfer of Training

The ultimate goal of any organizational training program is that the learning that occurs during training be transferred back to the job. To maximize transfer, the following suggestions have been offered:[24]

1. Maximize the similarity between the training context and the job context. That is, the training should resemble the job as closely as possible.
2. Require practice of the new behaviors, and even overlearning.
3. Include a variety of stimulus situations in the practice so that trainees will learn to generalize their knowledge and skills.
4. Label or identify the important features of the content to be learned in order to distinguish the major steps involved.
5. Make sure that the general principles underlying the specific content are understood.
6. Ensure that there is a supportive climate for learning and for transferring new behaviors. This can be done by building managerial support (emotional and financial) for training, by providing trainees with the freedom to set personal performance goals, and by encouraging trainees to take risks.

RELAPSE PREVENTION. Sometimes, despite trainers' best efforts to get individuals to transfer what they have learned back to the job, it is difficult for trainees to maintain new behaviors or skills over a long period. They may revert to their old habits. What is needed to assist trainees is what has been labeled as *relapse prevention*.[25] A model of the relapse prevention process used to increase the long-term maintenance of newly acquired behaviors is presented in Figure 8.6. It emphasizes the learning of a set of self-control and coping strategies.

Employees should be made aware of the relapse process itself by informing them that there are some situations that make it difficult for trainees to use their new behaviors. They should learn to identify and anticipate high-risk situations. Also, they should be instructed on how to use coping strategies to avoid such situations. Teaching these issues should increase trainees' self-efficacy or perception that they have control over the situation and can effectively use their new behaviors.

Characteristics of Adult Learners

In the past, the only educational concepts and techniques available for training programs were those developed for the education of children. In recent years, however, varying techniques for helping adults to learn have been developed. One of the primary discoveries is that adults as learners are very different from children. These differences must be considered in the design of training programs. Four basic concepts have been suggested for use in distinguishing between adult and child education.[26] These are self-concept, experience, readiness to learn, and time perspective. These characteristics and their implications for training are described below and in Figure 8.7.

SELF-CONCEPT. One difference between children's and adults' learning is affected by the individual's self-concept. While children see themselves as dependent persons, adults tend to resent being in situations in which they are treated with a lack of respect, talked down to, judged, or otherwise treated like children. Thus, educators should be facilitators rather than dominant teachers and adult trainees should be able to give some input into what is taught.

EXPERIENCE. Adults have accumulated vast quantities of experience whereas children have not. Experience can lead adults to make choices about what should be taught and in what format. In adult education, this experience should be valued and elaborated upon in class discussion. In educating children, the emphasis is on one-way communication and assigned readings. The education of adults, in contrast, should include experiential learning, two-way communication, group discussions, role playing, and skill practice sessions. This way, the experience of all participants can be brought to the issues at hand.

READINESS TO LEARN. In child education, the teacher decides on both the content and the sequence of learning. In adult education, the learners themselves can identify what they wish to learn and the sequence of learning. In this way, the trainer serves primarily as a resource person to help the adult learners diagnose their own learning needs.

TIME PERSPECTIVE. In child education, students are expected to store up information for use on some far-off day, and they readily accept this format. Adults, on the other hand, are interested in being able to immediately apply what they have learned to solve pressing problems. Thus, trainers need to be able to show the immediate relevance of issues to adult learners.

FIGURE 8.6
A MODEL OF THE RELAPSE PREVENTION PROCESS

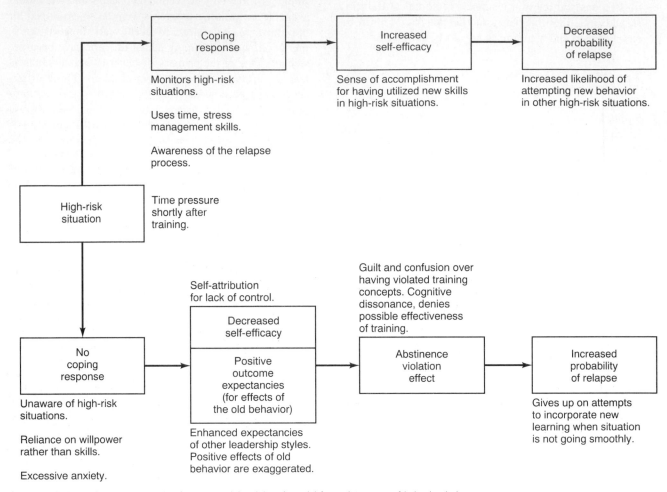

Source: R. D. Marx, Relapse prevention for managerial training: A model for maintenance of behavioral change. *Academy of Management Review, 7,* 1982, 434. Used with permission.

CHOOSING METHODS FOR THE TRAINING PROGRAM

Training methods can be divided into two categories: (1) Methods that are primarily informational or transmittal in nature. That is, they use primarily one-way communication in which information is transmitted to the learners, and (2) Methods that are experiential in nature. That is, the learner interacts with either the instructor, a computer/simulator, or other trainees to practice the skill. Some of the major methods, including their uses, benefits, and limitations, are described below and in Figures 8.8 and 8.9

Generally, most training programs utilize several training techniques, since no one approach is best suited for every purpose. For example, IBM's sales training program includes both classroom and on-the-job training (OJT), both of which are given over a 1-year period.[27]

AMC Theatres uses videotapes, detailed training manuals, and OJT programs to train ushers and concession personnel. To determine which combination of methods to select for a particular training program, a developer should first clearly define the purpose of and (through needs assessment) the audience for the training. In addition, an assessment of the resources available to conduct the training is necessary. This will mean examining the staff, materials, and budget capable of handling the training demands.

At a minimum, the training methods selected should (1) motivate the trainee to learn the new skill, (2) illustrate the desired skills to be learned, (3) be consistent with the content (e.g., use an interactive approach to teach interpersonal skills), (4) allow for active participation by trainees to fit with the adult learning model, (5) provide opportunities for practice and overlearning, (6) provide feedback on performance during training, (7) encourage

FIGURE 8.7
CHARACTERISTICS OF ADULT LEARNERS AND IMPLICATIONS FOR TRAINING

CHARACTERISTICS OF ADULT LEARNERS	IMPLICATIONS FOR TRAINING
Self-Concept The adult learner sees himself or herself as capable of self-direction and desires others to see him or her the same way. The person has the capacity to be self-directing.	A climate of openness and respect is helpful in identifying what the learners want and need to learn. Adults enjoy planning and carrying out their own learning experiences. Adults need to be able to evaluate their own progress towards self-chosen goals.
Experience Adults bring a lifetime of experience to the learning situation. Youths tend to see experience as something that has happened to them, while to adults, their experiences define who they are.	Less use is made of conventional informational techniques, more of experiential techniques or self-directed learning. Discovery of how to learn from experience is the key to self-actualization. Mistakes are seen as opportunities for learning.
Readiness to Learn Adult developmental tasks move toward social and occupational role competence and away from the physical developmental tasks of childhood.	Adults need opportunities to identify the competency requirements of their social and occupational roles. Adult readiness to learn and teachable moments peak at those points at which learning opportunity is coordinated with a recognition of the need to know.
Problem-Centered Time Perspective Youths think of education as the accumulation of knowledge for use in the future. Adults tend to think of learning as a way to be more effective in problem solving today.	Adult education needs to be problem-centered rather than theory-oriented. Formal curriculum development is less valuable than finding out what the learners need to learn. Adults need the opportunity to apply and try out their learning.

Source: E. Sullivan and P. Decker, *Effective management in nursing,* 2d ed. Reading, MA: Addison-Wesley, 1988, p. 338. Used with permission.

positive transfer from the training to the job, and (8) be cost-effective.[28]

Informational Methods

Informational methods are used primarily to teach factual material, skills, or attitudes. Generally, they do not require trainees to actually experience or practice the material taught during the training session.[29] Some of the more commonly used informational techniques include lectures, audiovisual presentations, and self-directed learning (SDL) methods [e.g., independent study and programmed instruction (PI)].

LECTURES. The lecture method is the most commonly used technique for training employees and teaching students. The method is often supplemented by audiovisual aids, motion pictures, or television. The approach can also vary in the degree to which discussion is permitted, since some lectures involve all one-way communication while others may allow trainees to participate by asking questions or providing comments. Many companies employ motivational speakers who provide lectures to employees on product and service quality, competitive advantage, and higher productivity. Among the most popular speakers are Tom Peters, author of *In Search of Excellence,* John Naisbitt, author of *Megatrends,* and H. Ross Perot.

AUDIOVISUALS. A variety of audiovisuals are available to trainers, including films, videos, slides, overheads, audiotapes, flip charts, and chalkboards. Often, audiovisuals are used to supplement other training techniques, including lectures and self-directed learning methods. They can address a variety of topics such as motivational techniques, performance appraisal interviews, and teamwork. Generally, many of these aids are inexpensive. They are also useful because of their versatility, and they typically allow for replays to help trainees grasp difficult points. A number of videos are now available on cultural diversity, sexual harassment, and workplace safety.

SDL METHODS. Several informational methods for training are considered to be SDL approaches because

FIGURE 8.8
INFORMATIONAL TRAINING METHODS

USES	BENEFITS	LIMITATIONS
Lecture		
Gaining new knowledge	Equally as good as PI and television.	Learners are passive.
To present introductory material	Low cost. Reaches a large audience at one time. Audience is often comfortable with it.	Poor transfer. Depends on the lecturer's ability. Is not tailored to individual trainees.
Audiovisuals		
Gaining new knowledge	Can reach a large audience at one time.	Is not tailored to individual trainees.
Gaining attention	Allows for replays. Versatility.	Must be updated. Passive learners.
Independent Study		
Gaining new knowledge	Allows trainees to go at their own pace.	Expensive to develop a library of materials.
Completing degree requirements	Minimizes trainers' time.	Materials must be designed to adjust to varying reading levels.
Continuous education	Minimizes costs of development.	Performance depends on trainee's motivation. Is not applicable to all jobs.
Programmed Instruction		
Gaining new knowledge	Allows trainees to go at their own pace.	Expensive to develop.
Pretraining preparation to ensure that all trainees have similar backgrounds	Can guarantee mastery at a specified level.	Is not applicable to all tasks (e.g., cognitive tasks).
	Encourages active trainee involvement.	Does not lead to higher performance than lectures.
	Provides immediate feedback to trainees.	

the trainee takes responsibility for learning the necessary knowledges and skills at his or her own pace. A wide range of decisions can be given to the trainee, including the topic of study, objectives, resources, schedule, learning strategy, type and sequence of activities, and media.[30] In most cases, trainees work without direct supervision; set their own pace; and are allowed to choose their own activities, resources, and learning environments. Generally, the training department's role is to provide assistance by establishing learning centers with available materials and by having trained facilitators on hand for questions. Larger companies, such as IBM, Sunoco, and P&W, have been successful in setting up such centers and in encouraging SDL by employees.[31]

The advantages of SDL include: (1) reduced training time, as compared to more conventional methods (e.g., lecture); (2) more favorable attitudes by trainees, as compared to conventional techniques; (3) minimal reliance on instructors or trainers; (4) mobility (i.e., a variety of places can be used for training); (5) flexibility (i.e., trainees can learn at their own pace); (6) consistency of the information taught to all trainees; and (7) cost savings. There are also several disadvantages, including: (1) high developmental time for course materials and extensive planning requirements, (2) difficulties in revising and updating materials, and (3) limited interactions with peers and trainers.[32]

Research indicates that employees with higher levels of readiness for SDL as measured by the Self-Directed Learning Readiness Scale (SDLRS) were likely to be higher-level managers,[33] to be satisfactory or outstanding performers,[34] to possess greater creativity,[35] and to have a higher degree of life satisfaction.[36] Also, employees who were outstanding performers in jobs requiring high levels of creativity or problem solving or involving high levels of change were likely to have high SDLRS scores. In addition, employees with high SDLRS scores[37] were successful in relatively unstructured learning situations in which much responsibility rests on the learners.[38]

A variety of SDL approaches are available. Two of the more commonly used techniques include independent study and PI. *Independent study* requires a trainee to synthesize and remember the contents of written material, audio or videotapes, or other sources of information. The training or personnel department can develop a library of materials for trainees to use in teaching themselves at their own pace about various skills or knowledges. Companies such as Coors, Digital Equipment Corporation, Kraft, and U.S. Gypsum utilize extensive self-study materials for their sales employees. Trainees can also design their own training curriculum by opting for correspondence courses or enrolling in independent study courses at local schools. Generally, in

FIGURE 8.9
EXPERIENTIAL TRAINING METHODS

USES	BENEFITS	LIMITATIONS
OJT		
Learning job skills	Good transfer.	Depends on the trainer's skills and willingness.
Apprenticeship training	Limited trainer costs.	May be costly due to lost production and mistakes.
Job rotation	High trainee motivation since training is relevant.	May have frequent interruptions due to job demands.
		Often is haphazardly done.
		Trainees may learn bad habits.
CBT		
Gaining new knowledge	Self-paced.	Costly.
Drill and practice	Standardization of training over time.	Trainees may fear using computers.
Individualized training	Feedback given.	Limited opportunities for trainee interaction.
	Good retention.	Less useful for training interpersonal skills.
Equipment Simulators		
To reproduce real-world conditions	Effective for learning and transfer.	Costly to develop.
For physical and cognitive skills	Can practice most of the job skills.	Sickness can occur.
For team training		Requires good fidelity.
Games and Simulations		
Decision-making skills	Resembles the job tasks.	Highly competitive.
Management training	Provides feedback.	Time-consuming.
Interpersonal skills	Presents realistic challenges.	May stifle creativity.
Case Study or Analysis		
Decision-making skills	Decision-making practice.	Must be updated.
Analytical skills	Real-world training materials.	Criticized as being unable to teach general management skills.
Communication skills	Active learning.	Trainers often dominate discussions.
To illustrate diversity of solutions	Good for developing problem-solving skills.	
Role Play		
For changing attitudes	Gain experience of other roles.	Initial resistance of trainees.
To practice skills	Active learning.	Trainees do not take it seriously.
To analyze interpersonal problems	Close to reality.	
Behavior Modeling		
To teach interpersonal skills	Allows practice.	Time-consuming.
To teach cognitive skills	Provides feedback.	May be costly to develop.
	Retention is improved.	
Sensitivity Training		
To enhance self-awareness	Can improve self-concept.	May be threatening.
To allow trainees to see how others see them	Can reduce prejudice.	May have limited generalizability to job situations.
To improve insights into differences	Can change interpersonal behaviors.	

these programs, trainees are required to master the content on their own without direct supervision.

Programmed instruction is an individual learning method that allows self-paced study of books and written materials on a variety of technical and nontechnical topics. For example, Dean Witter uses a 3-month PI program to train new stockbrokers. Most PI programs build in the important learning principles by (1) specifying what is to be learned (i.e., the behavioral objectives); (2) breaking the learning topic down into small, discrete steps; (3) presenting each step to the trainee and requiring him or her to respond to each step of the learning process (i.e., by reading each part); (4) testing the trainees' learning at each step (i.e., by responding to questions); (5) providing immediate feedback to the trainee on whether his or her response was correct or incorrect; and (6) testing the level of skill or knowledge acquired at the end of the training module.

Experiential Methods

Experiential methods are used primarily to teach physical and cognitive skills and abilities. These techniques include OJT, computer-based training (CBT), equipment simulations, games and other simulations, case analyses, role playing, behavior modeling, and sensitivity training. Let us briefly review each of these techniques.

OJT. Approximately 90 percent of all industrial training is conducted on the job.[39] OJT is conducted at the work site and in the context of the job. Often, it is informal, as when an experienced worker shows a trainee how to perform the job tasks. Also, the trainer may watch over the trainee to provide guidance during practice or learning. In some recent cases, the trainer may be a retired employee. For instance, at Corning Glass Works, new employees are paired with retirees for a brief on-the-job introduction to the company culture and market data. Following this, they are exposed to formal classroom and field training.[40] Many companies combine OJT with formal classroom training. For example, Dow Chemical alternates sales employees between classroom training at corporate headquarters and OJT experiences in the field for a year. Similarly, Wang Laboratories spends up to 9 months alternating salespeople from company headquarters and field offices.[41]

Apprenticeship programs are often considered OJT programs because they involve a substantial amount of OJT, even though they do consist of some off-the-job training. Typically, the trainee follows a prescribed order of course work and hands-on experience. For example, most professions or trades (e.g., medicine, teaching, carpentry, plumbing) require some type of apprenticeship program, which may last anywhere from 2 to 5 years. A large part of these programs involves OJT in addition to formal course work.

Another commonly used technique for OJT is *job rotation,* which involves moving employees from one job to another to broaden their experience.[42] Many companies are interested in having their employees be able to perform several job functions so that their workforce is more flexible and interchangeable. For example, in the automobile industry today, it is fairly common to see employees being trained on two or more tasks (e.g., painting and welding). This is done at GM's Saturn plant in order to relieve employees' boredom as well as to make the company less dependent on specialized workers. GE requires all managerial trainees to participate in an extensive job rotation program in which the trainees must perform all jobs they will eventually supervise. We will discuss job rotation in more detail in Chapter 13.

CBT and CAI. Use of computers to train employees is becoming increasingly more common among organizations, especially for training technical skills. One 1986 survey found that 50 percent of companies used some form of CBT.[43] The figure is undoubtedly much higher today. A 1987 study found that 81 percent of Fortune 500 firms indicated that they planned on incorporating CBT into their training programs in the future.[44] The most popular word processing software packages (e.g., Word-Perfect, Word Star) use CBT to introduce learners to the use of the software. The U.S. Armed Forces use CBT extensively for training many of their technicians. In some CBT programs, trainees can interact directly with computers to actually learn and practice new skills. This approach is similar to the PI system, and is called *computer-assisted instruction* (CAI). In addition, CBT systems can have computers on hand for trainees to use periodically to solve problems. In most cases, computers are used to teach computer skills such as programming, word processing, data processing, and how to use applications software (e.g., Lotus 1-2-3; D base). However, computer software is available in many other areas as well. For example, a program entitled "Keep Your Hands to Yourself" simulates a tense sexual harassment scenario.

EQUIPMENT SIMULATIONS. Some training may involve machines or equipment systems designed to reproduce physiological and psychological conditions of the real world that are necessary in order for learning and transfer to occur. For example, driving simulators or flight simulators are often used to train employees in driving or flying skills. Also, equipment simulators are relied on a great deal in training for space missions (e.g., astronaut training).

GAMES AND OTHER SIMULATIONS. Many training programs rely on the use of a variety of games or nonequipment simulations. In fact, simulation games appear to be gaining in popularity, with hundreds of different types of games available for teaching technical, managerial, professional, or other business-related skills. Some of the more common games include in-baskets and business games.

Generally, most games are used to teach skills such as decision making, as well as analytical, strategic, or interpersonal skills. For example, *business games* require trainees to assume various roles in a company (e.g., president, marketing vice president). The trainees are usually given several years' worth of information on the company's products, technology, and HRs, and are asked to deal with the information in a compressed period of time (several weeks or months). They make decisions regarding production volumes, inventory levels, and prices in an environment in which other trainees are running competitor companies. "Looking Glass" is an example of one managerial business game developed by the Center for Creative Leadership to train managers.

In-baskets are used to train managerial candidates in decision-making skills by requiring them to act on a variety of memos, reports, and other correspondence that are typically found in a manager's in-basket. As we discussed in Chapter 6, participants must prioritize items and respond to them in a limited time period. In-baskets are often included in assessment centers. For example, the method is used as one component of a week-long executive development program at the Center for Creative Leadership in Greensboro, North Carolina.

CASE ANALYSES. Most business students are very familiar with case analysis, a training method often used in management training to improve analytical skills. Trainees are asked to read a case report which describes the organizational, social, and technical aspects of an organizational problem (e.g., poor leadership, intergroup conflict). Each trainee prepares a report in which he or she describes the problems and offers solutions (including potential risks and benefits). Working in a group, trainees may then be asked to justify the problems they have identified and their recommendations. The trainer's role is to facilitate the group's learning and to help the trainees to see the underlying management concepts in the case.

ROLE PLAYING. In a role-playing exercise, trainees act out roles and attempt to perform the behaviors required in those roles. This method is often used to teach skills such as oral communication, interpersonal skills, leadership styles, performance feedback reviews, and interviewing techniques. For example, one trainee may be assigned the role of a supervisor giving performance appraisal feedback to a subordinate, while another trainee plays the role of the subordinate. The other trainees in the group observe the role play and offer feedback on the effective and ineffective behaviors used. Xerox uses role plays in some of its training programs to teach managers how to develop a culturally diverse workforce. At Digital Equipment Corporation, two training center employees act out a scene in which a woman fails to express her displeasure with the sexual advances of a colleague. The trainees analyze the role play and recommend an appropriate response. One expert estimates that 90 percent of Fortune 500 companies offer special training about sexual harassment.[45]

BEHAVIOR MODELING. Behavior modeling is quickly growing as a training technique for use with managers. Many large companies such as Exxon, Westinghouse, and Union Carbide use this approach.[46] The method consists of five consecutive components: (1) modeling (watching someone perform a behavior, usually on videotape), (2) retention (processes to help the trainee retain what was observed), (3) behavioral rehearsal (using role plays to practice new behaviors), (4) feedback or reinforcement (receiving observers' impressions of the behaviors performed), and (5) transfer of learning.

SENSITIVITY OR LABORATORY TRAINING. In this training method, which was very popular for management training in previous decades, a small group of about 8 to 14 individuals work together to develop interpersonal or team-building skills. In an unstructured setting, trainees focus on the "here and now" to describe issues of interest or concern to them. The trainer generally does not structure the discussion yet may intercede if the comments become harmful to participants. In the discussions, trainees provide feedback to one another about interpersonal styles or skills in order to help each other grow as individuals. The purposes may be to help trainees develop as individuals, to improve listening skills, to gain insights into why individuals behave as they do, or to try out new ways of behaving in an environment where feedback and practice are allowed.

EVALUATION*

Evaluation involves the collection of information on whether trainees were satisfied with the program, learned the material, and were able to apply the skills back on the job. In addition, evaluation ensures that programs are accountable and are meeting the particular needs of employees in a cost-effective manner. This is especially important today, as organizations attempt to cut costs and improve quality in their firms. Without evaluation, it is very difficult to show that training was the reason for any improvements. As a result, management may reduce training budgets or staffs in times of financial hardship. For example, 10 percent of respondents to a training survey indicated budget reductions in 1988 after the stock market crash.[47]

While most companies recognize the importance of evaluation, few actually evaluate their training

---

*Contributed by Phillip J. Decker, Barry R. Nathan, and Joyce E. A. Russell.

programs.[48] A review of Fortune 500 companies found that only a small number conduct evaluations of their programs.[49] Another study found that fewer than 12 percent of 285 companies evaluate their supervisory training programs.[50] Evaluations are conducted routinely by progressive companies such as Motorola, Xerox, Merck, and Federal Express. These firms recognize that training programs must be evaluated in order to ensure that employees are being prepared for the future and possible skill obsolescence.[51]

Most training evaluations assess only the reactions of training participants. One survey found that 77 percent of companies collected only *reaction* data to evaluate their training programs.[52] While trainee reactions are important and are useful for making future changes in programs, these data alone do not indicate whether the trainees have actually learned the material or are capable of performing the behaviors on the job. For example, the University of Texas at Austin initially used only reactions or "happiness questions" to evaluate the effectiveness of a business communications skills course for its staff. Dissatisfied with the data, the university later added learning and behavioral measures to supplement the reactions and provide for a more thorough evaluation of the program.[53]

For an evaluation to be complete, several types of criteria should be collected. In addition, an experimental design should be utilized to show that any changes detected in trainees' performance before and after training were due to the training program and not to some other factor (e.g., changes in top management, equipment, or compensation packages).

Types of Criteria

HR professionals should try to collect four types of data when evaluating training programs: measures of reactions, learning, behavior change, and organizational results.[54]

REACTIONS. Reaction measures are designed to assess trainees' opinions regarding the training program. Using a questionnaire, trainees are asked at the end of training to indicate the degree to which they were satisfied with the trainer, the subject matter and content, the materials (books, pamphlets, handouts), and the environment (room, breaks, meals, temperature). Also, they may be asked to indicate the aspects of the program they considered most valuable and least useful. You have undoubtedly been asked to complete a course evaluation instrument for some of your classes. This is a *reaction* measure.

Favorable reactions to a program do not guarantee that learning has taken place nor that appropriate behaviors have been adopted. However, it is important to col-

lect reaction data for several reasons: (1) to find out how satisfied trainees were with the program, (2) to make any needed revisions in the program, and (3) and to ensure that other trainees will be receptive to attending the program. Trainees should be given ample time at the end of the session to complete the reaction form. Also, HR professionals should assess trainees' reactions several months after the program to determine how relevant trainees felt the training was to their jobs. An example of a reaction form is presented in Figure 8.10.

LEARNING. Learning measures assess the degree to which trainees have mastered the concepts, knowledges, and skills of the training. Typically, learning is measured by paper-and-pencil tests (e.g., essay-type questions, multiple choice), performance tests, and simulation exercises.[55] These measures should be designed to sample the content of the training program. Trainees should be tested on their levels of understanding before and after training, to determine the effect of training on their knowledge. Figure 8.11 presents two examples of performance tests used to assess learning.

BEHAVIORS. Behaviors of trainees before and after training should be compared to assess the degree to which training has changed their performance. This is important because one of the goals of training is to modify the on-the-job behavior or performance of trainees. Behaviors can be measured by relying on the performance evaluation system to collect ratings of trainees both before and after training. For example, supervisors of the FAA must submit subordinate evaluations of their supervisory behavior prior to attending the national training center in Florida. Subordinates also submit evaluations of the same supervisors 6 months after the training. To determine whether or not the supervisors' skills have improved due to training, the performance evaluations they received from their subordinates before and after completion of training are compared. A variety of performance appraisal measures can be used to assess behavioral changes of trainees. These are described in more detail in Chapter 10.

ORGANIZATIONAL RESULTS. The purpose of collecting organizational results is to examine the impact of training on the work group or the entire company. Data may be collected before and after training on criteria such as productivity, turnover, absenteeism, accidents, grievances, quality improvements, scrap, sales, and customer satisfaction. The HR professional will try to show that the training program was responsible for any changes noted in these criteria. This may be difficult to do without a careful design and data collection strategy, since many other factors could explain the changes detected.

FIGURE 8.10
AN EXAMPLE OF A TRAINEE REACTION QUESTIONNAIRE

Evaluation Questionnaire

(Please return this form *unsigned* to the Training and Development Group)

1. Considering everything, how would you rate this program? (Check one)
   Unsatisfactory _____ Satisfactory _____ Good _____ Outstanding _____

   Please explain briefly the reasons for the rating you have given:

2. Were your expectations: exceeded _____ matched _____ fallen below _____? (Check one)

3. Are you going to recommend this training program to other members of your department?
   Yes _____ No _____ If you checked "yes," please describe the job titles held by the people to whom you would recommend this program?

   _____

4. Please rate the relative value (1 = very valuable; 2 = worthwhile; 3 = negligible) of the following components of the training program to you:

   Videocassettes _____   Role-playing exercises _____
   Workbooks _____   Small group discussions _____
   Small group discussions _____ Lectures _____
   Cases _____   Readings, Articles _____

5. Please rate the main lecturer's presentation (1 = not effective; 2 = somewhat effective; 3 = very effective) in terms of:

   Ability to Communicate _____
   Emphasis on Key Points _____
   Visual Aids _____
   Handout Materials _____

6. Please rate the following cases, readings, and videocassettes by placing a checkmark in the appropriate column:

	Excell.	Good	Fair	Poor
Overcoming Resistance to Change				
Reviewing Performance Goals				
Setting Performance Goals				
Handling Employee Complaints				
Improving Employee Performance				
Slade Co.				
Superior Slate Quarry				
McGregor's Theory X and Y				
Henry Manufacturing				
First Federal Savings				
Claremont Industries				

7. Was the ratio of lectures to cases (check one): High _____ OK _____ Low _____?

8. Were the videocassettes pertinent to your work? (check one)
   To most of my work? _____
   To some of my work? _____
   To none of my work? _____

9. To help the training director and the staff provide further improvements in future programs, please give us your frank opinion of each case discussion leader's contribution to your learning. (Place your checkmarks in the appropriate boxes.)

	Excellent	Above Average	Average	Below Average	Poor
DAVIS					
GLEASON					
LAIRD					
MARTIN					
PONTELLO					
SHALL					
SOMMERS					
WILSON					
ZIMMER					

10. How would you evaluate your participation in the program? (check)

Overall workload:	Too heavy _____	Just right _____	Too light _____
Case preparation:	Too heavy _____	Just right _____	Too light _____
Homework assignments:	Too heavy _____	Just right _____	Too light _____

11. What suggestions do you have for improving the program?

   _____
   _____
   _____

Source: K. N. Wexley and G. P. Latham, *Developing and training human resources in organizations.* Glenview, IL: Scott, Foresman, 1991, pp. 110–111. Reprinted with permission.

FIGURE 8.11
EXAMPLES OF LEARNING PERFORMANCE TESTS

MECHANICS

"You have in front of you a gear reducer, a line shaft, bearings, and coupling. I want you to assemble and adjust the proper alignment so that the finished assembly is a right-hand-driven (or left-hand-driven) assembly. Set the coupling gaps 1/8 inch apart. You do not have to put the grind member in place or fasten the coupling covers. After you are finished, I will ask you where and how the grind member should go in. You will have 45 minutes to complete this job."

PAINTERS

"I want you to boost yourself up about 10 feet off the floor using this boatsman chair, and then tie yourself so that you won't fall. After that, I would like you to hook this spray gun to the air supply, set the regulator to the correct pressure, and spray this wall."

Source: K.N. Wexley and G.P. Latham, *Developing and training human resources in organizations,* Glenview, IL: Scott, Foresman, 1991, p. 117. Reprinted with permission.

For example, changes in dollar sales could be due to a new incentive system rather than to a sales training program. Some of the experimental designs which can help evaluate the effects of the training are described below.

Designs for Evaluating Training

After deciding on the criteria to use in evaluating a training program, the HR professional should choose an experimental design. The design is used to answer two primary questions: (1) whether or not a change has occurred in the criteria (e.g., learning, behavior, organizational results) and (2) whether or not the change can be attributed to the training program.[56]

Designs employ two possible strategies to answer these questions. The first is to compare trainees' performance before and after participation in training. This is done to determine what changes may have occurred in learning, behavior, or organizational results. While this is important for answering the question of whether a change has taken place, it is deficient in answering the question of whether the change can be attributed to the training program, since the criteria may have changed for any number of reasons. What is needed to answer the second question is a design comparing the changes which took place in the trainees with changes that occurred in another group of employees who did not receive the training (e.g., a control group), yet who are similar to the training group in important ways (e.g., in that they have similar job titles and ranks and are in the same geographical location). The most effective experimental designs use both strategies (i.e., before-after measures and

a control group) and are thus able to answer both questions.[57] Some of the more commonly used designs for training evaluation are described below.[58]

ONE-SHOT POSTTEST-ONLY DESIGN. In many organizations, training is designed and conducted with no prior thought given to evaluation. For example, a sales manager may decide to put all his or her sales personnel through a course entitled "Effective Customer Relations." After the course is completed, the sales manager decides to evaluate it. This design looks like the one shown here.

TRAINING———————————————MEASURE

Any of the four types of criteria (e.g., reactions, learning, behavior, and organizational results) could be used as the "after" measures. It would be difficult, however, to know what, if any, changes occurred since no "before" measure (e.g., no pretest) was made. In addition, since the results may not be compared with those of another group who did not receive training, it would not be possible to say whether any change was due to the training. As a result, this design is not recommended.

ONE-GROUP PRETEST-POSTTEST DESIGN. Another design for evaluating the training group on the criteria of interest is to measure the group before and after the training. This design is as follows:

MEASURE————TRAINING————MEASURE

This design is able to assess whether a change has occurred for the training group in the criteria (e.g., learning, behavior). Unfortunately, it is not able to tell whether or not the change is due to training, since there is no control group. A change that is detected could have been caused by the introduction of new equipment or a new manager, or by any number of other reasons. Thus, this design is not extremely useful and is not recommended.

POSTTEST-ONLY CONTROL GROUP DESIGN. A much stronger design for assessing the effectiveness of a training program is shown here.

GROUP 1—R: TRAINING———————   MEASURE

GROUP 2—R: NO TRAINING—————MEASURE

In this design, two groups are used and individuals are *randomly assigned* (R) to either group (i.e., an individual has an equal chance of being put in either group 1, the training group, or group 2, the control group). The use of random assignment helps to initially equalize the two groups. This is important to ensure that any differences between the two groups after training are not simply caused by differences in ability, motivation, or experience. The posttest-only control group design is useful when it is difficult to collect criteria measures on individuals prior to offering them the training. (For example, an HR professional may believe that giving individuals a pretest, such as a learning test, might overly influence their scores on the posttest, which might be the same learning measure. Another HR professional may not have time to give tests.) Individuals are randomly assigned to the two groups, and their scores on the posttest are compared. Any differences on the posttest can be attributed to the training program, since it is assumed that the two groups were somewhat equal prior to training. From the organization's standpoint, it would be beneficial to make sure the employees from the control group are placed in a training program at a later time.

PRETEST-POSTTEST CONTROL-GROUP DESIGN.
Another powerful design that is recommended for use in training evaluation is as follows:

GROUP 1—R: MEASURE———TRAINING———MEASURE

GROUP 2—R: MEASURE——NO TRAINING——MEASURE

Individuals are randomly assigned to the two groups. Criteria measures are collected on both groups before and after the training program is offered, yet only one group actually receives the training. Comparisons are made of the changes detected in both groups. If the change in group 1 is significantly different from the change in group 2, we can be somewhat certain that it was caused by the training. Since many organizations will want all the employees in both groups to receive the training, the training can be offered to group 2 at a later time.

MULTIPLE TIME-SERIES DESIGN.
Another design recommended for use in training evaluation is shown below.

GROUP 1—R: MEASURE – MEASURE – MEASURE —
                         TRAINING — MEASURE – MEASURE –
                         MEASURE

GROUP 2—R: MEASURE – MEASURE – MEASURE —
                         NO TRAINING — MEASURE – MEASURE –
                         MEASURE

In this design, individuals are randomly assigned to two groups, and the criteria measures are collected at several times before and after the training has been offered. This design allows the HR professional to observe any changes between the two groups over time. If the effects of training held up over several months, this design would offer stronger support for the program.

Assessing the Costs and Benefits of Training

To conduct a thorough evaluation of a training program, it is important to assess the costs and benefits associated with the program. This is difficult to do but may be important for showing top management the value of training for the organization. For example, in one case, the net return of a training program for bank supervisors was calculated to be $148,400 over a 5-year period.[59] Generally, a utility model would be used to estimate the value of training (benefits minus costs). (See Appendix A for a discussion of the estimation of utility.)

Some of the costs that should be measured for a training program include needs assessment costs, salaries of training designers, purchase of equipment (computers, videos, handouts), program development costs, evaluation costs, trainers' costs (e.g., salaries, travel, lodging, meals), facilities rental, trainee wages during training, and other trainee costs (e.g., travel, lodging, meals).[60] An example of the costs calculated for an off-site management meeting is shown in Figure 8.12.

It is important to compare the benefits of the training program with its costs. One benefit that should be estimated is the dollar payback associated with the improvement in trainees' performance after receiving training. Since the results of the experimental design will indicate any differences in behavior between those trained and those untrained, the HR professional can estimate for that particular group of employees (e.g., managers, engineers) what this difference is worth in terms of the salaries of those employees. Another factor that should be considered when estimating the benefits of training is the duration of the training's impact—that is, the length of time during which the improved performance will be maintained. While probably no programs will show benefits forever, those that do incur longer-term improved performance will have greater value to the organization.

SPECIAL TRAINING PROGRAMS

Employee Orientation Programs

In a 1986 survey by *Training* magazine, the most prevalent type of formal training in U.S. companies was new-employee orientation. At least 80 percent of U.S. firms with more than 50 employees provide some type of orientation.[61] The trend seems to be continuing, as more firms have been placing their new employees in orientation programs to familiarize them with their supervisors and coworkers, the company policies and procedures, the requirements of their jobs, and the organizational culture.

FIGURE 8.12
COST BREAKDOWN FOR AN OFF-SITE MANAGEMENT MEETING

	TOTAL COSTS	COST PER PARTICIPANT PER DAY
Development of Programs (Figured on an Annual Basis)		
1. Training department overhead		
2. Training staff salaries		
3. Use of outside consultants		
4. Equipment and materials for meetings (films, supplies, workbooks)		
	$100,000	100.00*
Participant Cost (Figured on an Annual Basis)		
1. Salaries and benefits of participants (figured for average participant)	$ 20,000	
2. Capital investment in participants (based on an average of various industries from *Fortune* magazine)	25,000	
	$ 45,000	190.68†
Delivery of One Meeting of 20 Persons		
1. Facility costs		
a. Hotel rooms	$ 1,000	
b. Three meals daily	800	
c. Refreshment breaks	60	
d. Miscellaneous tips, telephone	200	
e. Reception	200	
	$ 2,260	$ 56.50‡
2. Meeting charges		
a. Room rentals		
b. Audiovisual rentals		
c. Secretarial services		
3. Transportation to the meeting	$ 2,500	62.50§
		$119.00
Cost per Day per Person		
Development of programs	$ 100	
Participant cost	190	
Delivery of one meeting (hotel and transportation)	119	
Total	$ 409	

*To determine cost per day, divide $100,000 by the number of meeting days held per year (10). Then divide the answer ($10,000) by the total number of management people attending (100) all programs. The result is $100 per day, per manager, per meeting.
†To determine cost per day, divide the total of $45,000 by 236 (average number of working days in a year). The result is $190.68 per day of a work year.
‡To determine cost per day per person, divide the group total ($2,260) by the number of participants (20). Then divide the resulting figure ($133) by the number of meeting days (2). The result is $56.50 per day.
§To determine cost per day per person, divide the group total ($2,500) by the number of people (20). Then divide the resulting figure ($125) by the number of meeting days (2). The result is $62.50 per day.
Note: Meeting duration: 2 days. Number of attendees: 20 people. These costs do not reflect a figure for the productive time lost of the people in the program. If that cost were added, the above cost would increase dramatically.
Source: Modified from W. J. McKeon, How to determine off-site meeting costs, *Training and Development Journal,* 35(5), 1981, p. 117. Used with permission.

Unfortunately, most of these programs are not properly planned, implemented, or evaluated. All too often, new employees are given a brief introduction to the company and are then left to learn the ropes by themselves. Such an approach may lead to feelings of confusion, frustration, stress, and uncertainty among new employees.[62]

Generally, the objectives of an employee orientation program are threefold: (1) to assist the new employee in adjusting to the organization; (2) to clarify the job requirements, demands, and performance expectations; and (3) to get the employee to understand the organization's culture and quickly adopt the organization's goals, values, and behaviors.[63] For example, Corning Glass Works developed an orientation program for all its new employees to help them make the transition to the company, their specific jobs, and the community.[64]

Most orientation programs consist of three stages: (1) a general introduction to the organization, often given by the HR department; (2) a specific orientation to the department and the job, typically given by the employee's immediate supervisor; and (3) a follow-up meeting to verify that the important issues have been addressed and employee questions have been answered.[65] This follow-up meeting usually takes place between a new employee and his or her supervisor a week or so after the employee has begun working.

The orientation program used by the Disney Corporation for employees of Walt Disney World in Orlando, Florida, follows this multiple-stage format in most respects. Individuals begin their employment by attending a 1-day program entitled "Disney Traditions II," which describes the history of the organization and the values of the culture. On this first day, employees are also taken on a tour of the facilities. On the second day, they are provided with descriptions of the policies and procedures. On the third day, OJT begins, and the new employee works with an assigned buddy who is an experienced co-worker. Buddies spend anywhere from 2 days to 2 weeks showing new employees their job duties and providing feedback as they attempt to perform the tasks. As a result of participating in the orientation program, employees express less confusion about their new jobs.[66]

The issues and topics that should be addressed throughout the three stages are presented in Figure 8.13. The HR department should be actively involved in planning, conducting, and evaluating orientation programs. It should also enlist the support of senior employees to serve as mentors to new employees. Also, supervisors should be called upon to help orient new employees to the workforce and should receive training on how to do this. Supervisors should be required to complete a checklist in the follow-up meeting, indicating that they have discussed with new employees the major issues of concern. Employees should sign the checklist to confirm that they have received the orientation information. Evaluation of the orientation program is a responsibility of the HR department. To assess the effectiveness of the program, HR professionals should examine whether the program is appropriate, easy to understand, interesting, flexible for diverse types of employees, and economical or cost-effective.[67]

Training for International Assignments

U.S. firms have begun to realize that to be successful in their overseas projects, they need to better prepare individuals to work in international assignments. As we discussed in Chapter 6, studies document a high rate of expatriate failures, ranging from 25 to 50 percent.[68] These early returns can be costly for firms with respect to goodwill, reputation, and finances.[69] In fact, costs have been estimated between $55,000 and $150,000 per expatriate failure, for a total of about $2 billion a year.[70] In many cases, the difficulties encountered by expatriates have been blamed on inadequate training programs. For example, Honeywell, Inc., surveyed 347 managers who lived abroad or traveled regularly and found that increased training was cited as critical for executives and employees assigned overseas.

Despite the importance of training individuals for international assignments, training does not seem to be a high priority for most firms. A 1985 survey revealed that fewer than 25 percent of U.S. companies offered any type of training for international assignees, and those that did offer training provided only brief introductory training.[71] Other countries, such as Japan, are more committed to the importance of training for international assignments. Honda of America sent 42 U.S. supervisors to the parent company in Tokyo after preparing them with language lessons, cultural training, and lifestyle orientation. Such practices explain the low (less than 10 percent) failure rate cited for most of Japan's multinational corporations. In Japanese firms, overseas training is typically conducted over a 1-year period, during which international assignees are taught about the culture, customs, and business techniques of the host country.[72]

A growing number of U.S. firms have shown a commitment to international training and "globalization." Moog, Inc., a manufacturer of precision systems for the aerospace industry, relied on training in 1984 when it opened a new manufacturing plant in the Phillipines. Within 6 months, the company had to train its employees to take on a variety of manufacturing duties in an overseas operation. Moog expressed satisfaction with the training because by 1988, all the employees who had been trained were still employed.[73] Other U.S. companies that have invested in training for international assignees include Bechtel, Amoco, GE, IBM, 3M Company, Xerox, Hospital Corporation of America, and Chase Manhattan Bank.[74] American Express provides U.S. business school students summer jobs in a foreign location. Colgate-Palmolive trains about 15 recent graduates for multiple overseas assignments.

SKILLS NEEDED BY INTERNATIONAL ASSIGNEES. In order to design effective training programs to better prepare U.S. managers and employees for assignments overseas, it is important to understand the kinds of skills they will need for international assignments. As we discussed in Chapter 6, in addition to good technical skills, individuals who will be working overseas need skills in languages and an understanding of social customs, cultural values, codes of conduct, and motiva-

FIGURE 8.13
TOPICS COVERED IN AN EMPLOYEE ORIENTATION PROGRAM

GENERAL ORIENTATION TO THE ORGANIZATION CONDUCTED BY THE HR DEPARTMENT

Organization Overview

Overview of the company

History

Products

Goals and mission

Long-range plans

Organization structure

Organizational chart

Facts on the key managers

Culture and values

Ethical principles and codes

Policies and Procedures

Employee handbook

Working conditions

Work hours

Vacation and leave

ID card

Provision of pay and benefits

Discipline system

Appeal system

Suggestions system

Promotion and assignments

Probationary period

Career development system

Training plans

Supervision

Performance appraisal system

Retirement information

Termination of employment

Communication channels

Personnel records

Union-Management Issues

Grievance procedures

Safety equipment

Employee rights and responsibilities

Management rights and responsibilities

Copy of the union contract

Shop steward relations

Safety

First aid stations

Emergency procedures

Fire prevention guidelines

Accident procedures

Use of alcohol and drugs on the job

OSHA regulations

Salary

Pay period

Overtime pay

Supplemental pay periods

Tax shelter options

Holiday pay

Deductions

Longevity pay

Credit union

Benefits

Insurance (information and copies of
medical, dental, group health, disability, life,
workers' compensation forms)

Leave (personal illness, family illness or
death, jury duty, military duty, maternity or
paternity leave)

List of holidays

Vacations

Physical Facilities

Map and tour of facilities

Career resource center

Library or resources

Lounges and cafeteria

Parking

Restricted areas

Rest rooms

Equipment and supplies

Facilities for people with disabilities

FIGURE 8.13 *(Continued)*

SPECIFIC ORIENTATION TO THE DEPARTMENT AND JOB CONDUCTED BY THE SUPERVISOR

Department Overview

Relationship to other departments

Goals and mission

Long-range plans

Procedures

Copies of required forms (e.g., expense reimbursement

Work flow

Facilities

Tour of the department (e.g., water fountains, smoking areas, fire alarms, supervisor's office, staffs' area, supplies)

Telephone numbers of key personnel

Safety

Emergency procedures

Security system

Accident reports

Job Information

Copy of job description

Duties and responsibilities

Performance goals

Performance standards and expectations

Performance appraisal procedures and dates for reviews

Working conditions (hours of work, dress, lunch hours, breaks, personal calls, overtime)

Copies of performance appraisal forms

List of training opportunities

Career paths for positions

Introduction to Coworkers and Staff

Staff support

Assigned mentors or advisors

Individual or group meetings with coworkers

Sources: Modified from G. Dessler, *Personnel management.* Reston, VA: Reston Publishing, 1984, pp. 223–227 W. D. St. John, The complete employee orientation program, *Personnel Journal, 59,* 1980, pp. 373–378. Used with permission.

---

tion and reward systems in the host country. For Middle Eastern assignments, for example, Bechtel places great emphasis on the importance of religion in the culture. Also, expatriates need assistance in the practical aspects of foreign assignments (e.g., housing, schools, currency, health issues). Further, their families need to be willing to live abroad and should be adaptive and supportive.

Prior to presenting several specific examples of cross-cultural training programs, it will be useful to discuss how cultural training differs from traditional training. Cultural training[75] focuses on several goals: (1) *Communication.* Expatriates will need to understand and communicate directly and through nonverbal means in order to listen to the concerns and motives of others. (2) *Decision making.* They will have to develop conclusions and take actions on the basis of inadequate, unreliable, and conflicting information, and to trust their feelings, impressions, and facts. (3) *Commitment.* They will need to become involved in relationships and to inspire confidence in others. (4) *Ideals.* They will have to value the causes and objectives of others from a radically different social environment. (5) *Problem solving.* They will have to make decisions needed to achieve common goals. From this description, it is apparent that intercul-

tural training focuses heavily on influencing interpersonal skills and perceptions.

There are numerous examples of cross-cultural training programs used by organizations. For instance, ARAMCO, a Saudi-Arabian corporation, uses an extensive orientation program for employees and their families. The program includes practical housekeeping information such as local transportation, shopping, day-to-day finances, and comparisons of the beliefs and customs of the Saudi and American peoples. The International Development Agency's predeparture program for overseas volunteers has several objectives, including the following: communicate respect, be nonjudgmental, display empathy, practice role flexibility, and tolerate ambiguity.

TRAINING TECHNIQUES. To acquire the skills necessary to be successful in an international assignment, a variety of training techniques can be utilized.[76] These are presented in Figure 8.14. In any program developed, it is recommended that the international assignee and his or her family be actively involved in the training in order to ease the transition and build a supportive environment. Most firms that offer international training

FIGURE 8.14
TECHNIQUES FOR INTERNATIONAL TRAINING

METHOD	TECHNIQUE	PURPOSE
Informational training	Lectures Reading material Videotapes Movies/television	Area studies, company operation, parent-country institutions
Experiential workshops	Simulations Role playing Cultural assimilators	Culture-general and culture-specific negotiation skills; reduction of ethnocentrism
Sensitivity training	Communication workshops T-groups Outward Bound trips	Self-awareness, communication styles, empathy, listening skills, nonjudgmentalism
Field experiences	Meeting with ex-international assignees Minicultures Host-family surrogate	Customs, values, beliefs, nonverbal behavior, religion
Language skills	Classes Cassettes	Interpersonal communication, job requirements

Source: S. Ronan, Training the international assignee. In I. L. Goldstein and associates (eds.), *Training and development in organizations,* San Francisco, CA: Jossey-Bass, 1989, p. 438. Used with permission.

utilize many of these approaches. For example, Procter & Gamble uses several methods to refine language skills and to improve intercultural awareness among international assignees.[77] Their new "P&G College" for new and mid-level managers places heavy emphasis on "globalization" issues.

To teach employees about area studies or the host country's environment (e.g., its geography, climate, political system, customs, religion, labor force, and economy) and the company's international operations, *informational* approaches such as lectures, reading material, videotapes, and movies can be effectively used. To teach trainees about the host country's norms, values and interpersonal styles so that they will be able to understand and negotiate with host individuals, *experiential* approaches may be beneficial. These might include role playing, simulations, and cultural assimilators (simulations specific to the culture).

Field experiences are recommended to provide a more in-depth view of the host country's customs, values, and behaviors. These experiences can take a variety of forms, including: (1) short family trips to the host country; (2) informal meetings with other American families that have lived in the host country; (3) minicultures (i.e., the family visits a multicultural environment in the United States, such as an ethnic neighborhood); and (4) host-family surrogates (i.e., a U.S. family from a background similar to the host country has the expatriate family stay with them for a period of time so that they can observe the customs). Finally, *language skill* classes and cassettes are recommended for use in developing skills in interpersonal communication and in the kinds of day-to-day conversations that the family will encounter in the host country.

SUMMARY

Over the years, training has become increasingly popular as an HR tool for improving employee and managerial performance in organizations. It has been estimated that the majority of organizations provide some type of formal training, and spend millions of dollars doing so. The U.S. government itself spends over $500 million each year to train new employees and to retrain current employees.[78]

Successful training in organizations depends upon a systematic approach involving careful needs assessment, solid program design, and thorough evaluation of results. Training programs should not be designed as quick fixes for organizational problems, nor should they rely on faddish techniques just because they are popular at the present time. Instead, training should be designed to meet the particular needs of the organization and its employees. It should be viewed as a *continuous learning* endeavor which is designed to help employees and managers to stay current and to anticipate future needs. As greater demands are placed on organizations to remain competitive, firms must ensure that their workforces are motivated and able to take on these challenges. An emphasis on continual training and education is one way this can be done. For example, it has been predicted that by the year 2000 managers in the United States will spend 82 hours per year on educational activities.[79]

Many of the most successful U.S. companies have integrated their training programs with their employee career development programs. In the past, training programs and departments have emphasized employer needs for training in the context of the firm's strategic plan. Career development programs tend to emphasize the employee's perspective. Ideally, training and career planning should be well integrated into an HRM system, with a focus on the strategic plan of the organization and customer requirements. We will discuss these matters in Chapter 9.

DISCUSSION QUESTIONS

1. Many companies spend considerable money on providing training in interpersonal skills. Do you think such training really works? Explain your answer.

2. What would be the major features of a training program designed to make workers aware of sexual harassment in the workplace? Whom would you select to attend such a training program? How would you evaluate the effects of the training? Would such training be effective? Explain your answers.

3. Suppose that you are instructed to determine whether a training curriculum is needed to train managers on dealing with a diverse workforce (e.g., minorities, women, older workers, people with disabilities). How would you proceed in conducting the needs assessment?

4. Describe several characteristics of adult learners. Why is it important to consider these factors when designing training for employees?

5. Suppose that you are the professor for this class. Write several instructional objectives for the class. Why is it important to prepare objectives *prior* to developing and conducting training?

6. Suppose that you are going to design a training program for newly hired first-line sales managers. Results from the needs assessment indicate that they will need training on company policies and procedures, handling customer complaints, and motivating sales personnel. What learning principles will you build into the program? What training methods will you choose? Explain your choices.

7. Describe what you would say to convince top management of the importance of *evaluating* a company training program. Explain what criteria you would use and what design you would recommend. Provide a rationale.

8. How would you evaluate the effectiveness of this experiential text relative to other approaches and texts in HRM?

NOTES

1. Rosenberg, M. J. (1990). Performance technology: Working the system. *Training, 27*(2), 43–48. See also: Forward, G. E., Beach, D. E., Gray, D. A., and Quick, J. C. (1991). Mentofacturing: A vision for American industrial excellence. *Academy of Management Executive, 5*(3), 32–44.

2. Schaaf, D. (1990). Lessons from the "100 best." *Training 27*(2), 18–20. See also: Cox, T. (1991). The multicultural organization. *Academy of Management Executive, 5*(2), 34–47.

3. Camp, R. R., Blanchard, P. N., and Huszczo, G. E. (1986). *Toward a more organizationally effective training strategy and practice.* Englewood Cliffs, NJ: Prentice-Hall.

4. Nadler, L. (1984). Human resource development. In L. Nadler (ed.), *The handbook of human resource development.* New York: John Wiley & Sons, pp. 1–47. See also: Cox, T., and Blake, S. (1991). Managing cultural diversity: Implications for organizational competitiveness. *Academy of Management Executive, 5*(3), 45–56.

5. Lee, C. (1988). Training budgets: Neither boom nor bust. *Training 25*(10), 41–46. See also: Godkewitsch, M. (1987). The dollars and sense of corporate training. *Training, 24*(5), 79–81. Note 1.

6. Gordon, J. (1986a). *Training* magazine's industry report 1986. *Training, 23*(10), 26–28. See also: Goldstein, I. L., and Gilliam, P. (1990). Training system issues in the year 2000. *American Psychologist, 45,* 134–143.

7. See note 2.

8. Gordon, J. (1986b). Where the training goes. *Training, 23*(10), 49–50, 52–54, 57–60, 62–63.

9. Rossett, A. (1990). Overcoming obstacles to needs assessment. *Training, 27*(3), 36, 38–41.

10. Moore, M. L., and Dutton, P. (1978). Training needs analysis: Review and critique. *Academy of Management Review, 3,* 532–545. See also: McAfee, R. B., and Champagne, P. J. (1988). Employee development: Discovering who needs what. *Personnel Administrator, 33*(2), 92–98.

11. Mager, R. F., and Pipe, P. (1984). *Analyzing performance problems or "You really oughta wanna,"* 2d ed. Belmont, CA: David Lake Publishing.

12. See note 3.

13. Salinger, R. D. (1973). Disincentives to effective employee training and development. Washington: U.S. Civil Service Commission Bureau of Training.

14. Goldstein, I. L. (1986). *Training in organizations: Needs assessment, development, and evaluation,* 2d ed. Monterey, CA: Brooks-Cole.

15. Mager, R. F. (1975). *Preparing instructional objectives.* Belmont, CA: Pitman Learning, Inc.

16. Laird, D. (1985). *Approaches to training and development,* 2d ed. Reading, MA: Addison-Wesley.

17. See note 2.

18. See note 14.

19. Fiske, E. B. (Sept. 25, 1989). Impending U.S. jobs "disaster": Work forces unqualified to work. *The New York Times,* pp. 1, 12.

20. See note 19, p. 12.

21. Noe, R. A., and Schmitt, N. (1986). The influence of trainee attitudes on training effectiveness: Test of a model. *Personnel Psychology, 39,* 497–523. See also: Baldwin, T. T., Magjuka, R. J., and Loher, B. T. (1991). The perils of participation: Effects of choice of training on trainee motivation and learning. *Personnel Psychology, 44*(1), 51–66.

22. See note 3.

23. Silber, K. H., and Stelnicki, M. B. (1987). Writing training materials. In R. L. Craig (ed.), *Training and development handbook,* 3d ed. New York: McGraw-Hill, pp. 263–285.

24. Ellis, H. C. (1965). *The transfer of leraning.* New York: Macmillan. See also: Stark, C. (1986). Ensuring skills transfer: A sensitive approach. *Training and Development Journal, 10*(3), 50–51. Note 14.

25. Marx, R. D. (1982). Relapse prevention for managerial training: A model of maintenance of behavior change. *Academy of Management Review, 7,* 433–441.

26. Knowles, M. S. (1978). *The modern practice of adult education.* New York: Associated Press.

27. See note 2.

28. Cascio, W. F. (1992). *Managing human resources: Productivity, quality of work life, profits,* 3d ed. New York: McGraw-Hill. See also: Carroll, S. J., Jr., Paine, F. T., and Ivancevich, J. M. (1972). The relative effectiveness of training methods: Expert opinion and research. *Personnel Psychology, 25,* 495–510. Fisher, C. D., Schoenfeldt, L. F., and Shaw, J. B. (1990). *Human resource management.* Boston, MA: Houghton Mifflin.

29. Scarpello, V. G., and Ledvinka, J. (1988). *Personnel/ human resource management: Environments and functions.* Boston, MA: PWS-Kent.

30. Budd, M. L. (1987). Self-instruction. In R. L. Craig (ed.), *Training and development handbook: A guide to human resource development,* 3d ed. New York: McGraw-Hill, pp. 488–499.

31. Guglielmino, L. M., and Guglielmino, P. J. (1988). Self-directed learning in business and industry: An information age imperative. In H. Long and associates (eds.), *Adult self-directed learning: Application and theory.* Athens: Adult Education Office, University of Georgia.

32. See note 30.

33. Roberts, D. G. (1986). *A study of the use of the self-directed learning readiness scale as related to selected organization variables.* Doctoral dissertation. Washington, DC: George Washington University.

34. Guglielmino, L. M., and Guglielmino, P. J. (1991). Expanding your readiness for self-directed learning. King of Prussia, PA: *Organization design and development.* See also note 33.

35. Torrance, E. P., and Mourad, S. (1978). Some creativity and style of learning and thinking correlates of Guglielmino's Self-Directed Learning Readiness Scale. *Psychological Reports, 43,* 1167–1171.

36. Sabbaghian, Z. (1979). *Adult self-directedness and self-concept: An exploration of relationship.* Doctoral dissertation. Ames: Iowa State University.

37. See note 31. See also: Durr, R. E. (1992). *An examination of readiness for self-directed learning and selected personnel variables at a large midwestern electronics development and manufacturing corporation.* Unpublished doctoral dissertation. Florida Atlantic University.

38. Savoie, M. (1979). *Continuing education for nurses: Predictors of success courses requiring a degree of learner self-direction.* Doctoral dissertation. Toronto, Canada: University of Canada.

39. Bureau of National Affairs (1990). Training facts and figures. In *Bulletin to Management.* Washington: Bureau of National Affairs.

40. See note 2.

41. See note 2.

42. Mondy, R.W., and Noe, R. M. (1990). *Human resource management,* 4th ed. Boston, MA: Allyn & Bacon.

43. See note 8.

44. Madlin, N. (1987). Computer-based training comes of age. *Personnel, 64*(11), 64–65.

45. Lublin, J. S. (Dec. 2, 1991). Sexual harassment is tipping agenda in many executive education programs. *The Wall Street Journal,* B1.

46. See note 8. See also: Baldwin, T. T. (1992). Effects of alternative modeling strategies on outcomes of interpersonal skill training. *Journal of Applied Psychology, 77*(2), 147–154.

47. Gordon, J. (1988). Who is being trained to do what? *Training, 25*(10), 51–60.

48. Latham, G. P. (1988). Human resource training and development. *Annual Review of Psychology, 39,* 545–582.

49. Clegg, W. H. (1987). Management training evaluation: An update. *Training and Development Journal, 41*(2), 65–71.

50. Smeltzer, L. R. (1979). Do you really evaluate, or just talk about it? *Training,* (8), 6–8.

51. Bushnell, D. S. (1990). Input, process, output: A model for evaluating training. *Training and Development Journal, 44*(4), 41–43.

52. Catalanello, R. L., and Kirkpatrick, D. L. (1968). Evaluating training programs: The state of the art. *Training and Development Journal, 22*(5), 2–9. See also: Arvey, R. D., Maxwell, S. E., Salas, E. (1992). The relative power of training evaluation designs under different cost configurations. *Journal of Applied Psychology, 77*(2), 155–160.

53. Bell, J. D., and Kerr, D. L. (1987). Measuring training results: Key to managerial commitment. *Training and Development Journal,* (1), 70–73. See also: Note 30.

54. Kirkpatrick, D. (1983). Four steps to measuring training effectiveness. *Personnel Administrator, 28*(11), 19–25. See also: Trost, A. (1985). "They may love it but will they use it?" *Training and Development Journal, 39*(1), 66–68. Ostroff, C. (1991). Training effectiveness measures and scoring schemes: A comparison. *Personnel Psychology, 44,* 353–374.

55. Phillips, J. J. (1983). *Handbook of training evaluation and measurement methods.* San Diego, CA: University Associates.

56. See note 28, Fisher et al. (1990). See also: Gist, M. E., Stevens, C. K., and Bavetta, A. G. (1991). Effects of self-efficacy and post-training intervention on the acquisition and maintenance of complex interpersonal skills. *Personnel Psychology, 44*(4), 837–862.

57. See note 56.

58. Campbell, D. T., and Stanley, J. C. (1963). *Experimental and quasi-experimental designs for research.* Boston, MA: Houghton Mifflin.

59. Mathieu, J. E., and Leonard, R. L. (1987). Applying utility concepts to a training program in supervisory skills:

A time-based approach. *Academy of Management Journal, 30,* 316–335.

60. See note 56.

61. See note 8.

62. Feldman, D. C., and Brett, J. M. (1983). Coping with new jobs: A comparative study of new hires and job changers. *Academy of Management Journal, 26,* 258–272. See also: Fisher, C. D. (1986). Organizational socialization: An integrative review. In K. M. Rowland and G. R. Ferris (eds.), *Research in Personnel and Human Resources Management, 4,* 101–145.

63. See note 56. See also: Meyer, J. P., Bobocel, R., and Allen, N. J. (1991). Development of organizational commitment during the first year of employment: A longitudinal study of pre- and post-entry influences. *Journal of Management, 17*(4), 717–734.

64. See note 28, Cascio (1989).

65. Reed-Mendenhall, D., and Millard, C.W. (1980). Orientation: A training and development tool. *Personnel Administrator, 25*(8), 42–44.

66. London, M. (1989). *Managing the training enterprise: High-quality, cost-effective employee training in organizations.* San Francisco, CA: Jossey-Bass. See also: Caffarella, R. S. (1985). A checklist for planning successful training programs. *Training and Development Journal, 39*(3), 81–83.

67. See note 28, Cascio (1992).

68. Hogan, G.W., and Goodson, J. R. (1990). The key to expatriate success. *Training and Development Journal 44*(1), 50, 52. See also: McEnery, J., and DesHarnais, G. (1990). Culture shock. *Training and Development Journal, 44*(4), 43–47. Dowling, P. J., and Schuler, R. S. (1990). *International dimensions of human resource management.* Boston, MA: PWS-Kent.

69. Ronen, S. (1989). Training the international assignee. In I. L. Goldstein and associates (eds.), *Training and development in organizations.* San Francisco, CA: Jossey-Bass, pp. 417–453.

70. See note 68, McEnery and DesHarnais (1990).

71. See note 68, McEnery and DesHarnais (1990). See also: Milliman, J., Von Glinow, M. A., and Nathan, M. (1991). Organizational life cycles and strategic international human resource management in multinational companies: Implications for congruence theory. *Academy of Management Review, 16*(2), 318–339.

72. See note 68, Hogan and Goodson (1990).

73. French, W. (1990). *Human resources management,* 2d ed. Boston, MA: Houghton Mifflin.

74. Copeland, L. (1988). Learning to manage a multicultural work force. *Training, 25*(5), 48–49, 51, 55–56. See also: Copeland, L. (1985). Cross-cultural training: The competitive edge. *Training, 22*(7), 49–53; Lubin, J. S. (Mar. 31, 1992). Younger managers learn global skills. *The Wall Street Journal,* B1.

75. Gudykunst, W. B., and Hammer, M. R. (1983). Basic training and design: An approach to intercultural training. In D. Landis and R.W. Brislin (eds.), *Handbook of intercultural training,* Vol. 1. Elmsford, NY: Pergamon, pp. 118–154.

76. Copeland, M. J. (1987). International training. In R. L. Craig (ed.). *Training and development handbook.* New York: McGraw-Hill, pp. 717–725. See also: Note 69.

77. See note 76.

78. See note 14.

79. Fulmer, R. M. (1986). Educating managers for the future. *Personnel, (2),* 70–73. See also: The new shape of global business (July 31, 1989). *Fortune,* pp. 280–323.

EXERCISE 8.1
*CONDUCTING A NEEDS ASSESSMENT**

OVERVIEW

In order to determine whether training is needed to address a particular area of concern in an organization (e.g., performance problem), it is first necessary to conduct a needs assessment. As stated in Chapter 8, a thorough needs assessment consists of an organizational analysis, a job or task analysis, and a person analysis. The purpose of this exercise is to give you some practice in conducting a needs assessment.

LEARNING OBJECTIVES

After completing this exercise, you should be able to:

1. Understand the various components of a needs assessment.
2. Be able to develop items for conducting an organizational analysis, a task analysis, and a person analysis.
3. Be able to interpret the results of a needs assessment and describe the implications for designing a training program.

---

*Contributed by Jeffrey D. Kudisch, Stephanie D. Myers, and Joyce E. A. Russell.

PROCEDURE

Part A: Group Analysis

Step 1. Prior to coming to class, each person should review Chapter 8, paying particular attention to the section on needs assessment. Divide up into groups of two to three individuals.

Step 2. Choose a job with which you are very familiar. Collect and review job analysis data (see Chapter 4 for data collection options). From this material, generate a list of possible training topics for an individual in that job (i.e., What are the different types of training that might be beneficial for performing that job?). For example, if the job is a patrol officer, some of the possible training topics might include: handling firearms, dealing with domestic issues, arrest procedures, teamwork, stress management, legal issues, and investigation. You should generate as long a list as possible (e.g., around 40 to 50 topics).

Step 3. Using Form 8.1.1, interview several employees (at least two) in the job you have chosen. Try to choose a representative sample of employees for the interviews. You may interview them individually or in a group.

Step 4. Summarize your findings from the needs assessment in a report to the vice president of HR. Offer specific recommendations regarding training for the job.

FORM 8.1.1

Job _____ Organization _____

Interviewer (s) _____ Date _____

Part A: Background Information on Interviewee

Years in the job _____ Years in the company _____

Highest level of education completed:

Part B: Organizational Analysis (Attitudes and Climate for Training)

From your perspective, what are the purposes of training?

How successful are current training programs in your firm for achieving these purposes?

If you asked a fellow worker to give his or her opinion regarding training in this firm, what would the response likely be?

FORM 8.1.1 *(Continued)*

Do you think trainees are motivated to attend training? Explain your response.

Do you think employees in your organization experience any resistance to training? Do you have any suggestions for minimizing this resistance?

What positive consequences are associated with successful completion of training (e.g., increased pay, greater promotional opportunities, recognition)? Are there any negative consequences associated with training (e.g., loss of production, loss of status among coworkers)?

Do you think it is difficult for trainees to apply the skills they learned in training once they return to the job? Why or why not?

For training programs you have attended, are you asked to provide your *reactions* to the programs? Are you given *learning* tests before and after training to assess a change in your learning? If so, describe the types of measures that are used to assess your reactions and learning.

FORM 8.1.1 *(Continued)*

Part C: Task and Person Analysis

Describe the major duties of your job. Rank them in terms of importance (1 = most important).

Take a moment to think about an individual who is especially *effective* at your job. What knowledges, skills, or abilities does this person possess? Can these skills be enhanced through training? If yes, explain the type of training that might be useful.

Looking ahead over the *next 5 years*, do you foresee any additional job demands being added to the current responsibilities in your job? If so, what additional skills or abilities will be needed to meet these demands?

Note to the interviewer: Hand the list of possible training topics to the interviewees. Give them the following instructions:

Step 1. After looking over the list, *circle* the *10 areas* that are most *critical* to successful performance in your job.

Step 2. Of the 10 items you circled, check those areas in which *training would be beneficial* to your job performance.

329

EXERCISE 8.2
DEVELOPMENT AND EVALUATION OF A TRAINING PROGRAM FOR GRADUATE STUDENT INSTRUCTORS

OVERVIEW

A common practice in many universities is to give graduate students complete responsibility for teaching an undergraduate class. While graduate students may possess adequate knowledge to cover the subject matter, many have not had training or any prior experiences to be able to organize a class, prepare lectures or tests, grade papers, etc. The purpose of this exercise is to develop a training program for graduate students and to propose a design for evaluating the training.

LEARNING OBJECTIVES

After completing this exercise, you should be able to:

1. Outline the steps to be followed in the conceptualization, development, and evaluation of a training program.
2. Discuss the advantages and disadvantages of the various training techniques and the evaluation design options.
3. Develop an approach to determining who should receive the training.

PROCEDURE

Part A: Individual Analysis

Step 1. Prior to class, review the memo in Exhibit 8.2.1 from the university provost. As a member of the task force to develop and evaluate a new training program, your first assignment is to develop an outline of the steps to be followed in order to develop the most effective (and practical) training program for graduate student instructors.

Step 2. On Form 8.2.1, write a chronology of the steps you will follow to complete the assignment. Pay close attention to what the provost has requested in the memo.

Part B: Group Analysis

Step 1. In groups of four to six students, each member should review the others' responses on Form 8.2.1.

Step 2. The group should attempt to reach consensus on the chronology of events and the position to be taken on the issues raised by the provost. One group member should take careful notes to represent the consensus of opinion and all aspects of the training program, the design of evaluation, and the criteria to be used as a part of the evaluation process.

Part C: Class Discussion

One member of each group should present the group's recommendations for the steps to be followed for the training program. Class discussion will follow on the areas where the groups agree and disagree. An attempt should be made to reach consensus on all major points which must be addressed by the task force.

EXHIBIT 8.2.1
THE PROVOST'S MEMO REQUESTING YOUR RECOMMENDATIONS

To: Students

From: Stephanie Sterrett, University Provost

Subject: Charge to the training task force

Congratulations on your appointment to the task force on graduate
student teaching. As you may know, there have been a number of concerns
raised about the quality of teaching at our university. While the
graduate students are highly motivated to teach, most of the students
have received very little training or preparation prior to teaching
their undergraduate classes. Your job as part of the task force is as
follows: (1) to determine whether there really is a need for such
training; (2) if there is a need, to outline the objectives and the
content of the training; (3) to state which graduate students should
receive the training (i.e., all students or only those who fail to meet
some imposed standard); (4) to identify the specific techniques that are
recommended to be used (e.g., lecture, role plays); and (5) to provide a
plan for ensuring that the training will be effective (i.e., specifying
the criteria and experimental design that should be used in evaluation.

Prior to the group meeting, take a position on each of the issues I
have raised (and any others you can think of) and provide a detailed
chronology using Form 8.2.1.

I look forward to our meeting.

FORM 8.2.1
CHRONOLOGY OF STEPS FOR TRAINING PROGRAM DEVELOPMENT AND EVALUATION

Name_____ Group_____

ASSIGNMENT   DETAILED DESCRIPTION OF ACTION TO BE TAKEN

Step 1.

Step 2.

Step 3.

Step 4.

Step 5.

Step 6.

Step 7.

Step 8.

EXERCISE 8.3
LEARNING PREFERENCE
ASSESSMENT*

OVERVIEW

Chapter 8 discussed the increasing importance of continued learning as a training technique for use with employees bombarded with technological advances. More companies are holding employees responsible for knowledge of these advances, and employees are realizing that they must continue to learn on their own if they are to avoid obsolescence. For example, in one study employees in the aerospace industry reported spending twice as much time on SDL projects as did other employees. In the following exercise, you will learn more about the impact of learning preferences in the workplace. You will complete a questionnaire which assesses your own learning preferences.

LEARNING OBJECTIVES

After completing this exercise, you should be able to:

1. Estimate your own learning preferences.
2. Describe ways of incorporating SDL into the training process.

PROCEDURE

Part A: Individual Analysis

Prior to class, read Chapter 8, and complete the questionnaire in Form 8.3.1. Bring Form 8.3.1 to class.

*Contributed by Paul Guglielmino and Lucy Guglielmino.

Part B: Group Analysis

Step 1. After your instructor has provided the scoring key and norms for the questionnaire, work in groups of five or six to share your scores with one another and discuss your views on the validity and usefulness of the measure. How could a company use this instrument as part of its training program?

Step 2. Provide some ideas for increasing the level of readiness among employees for SDL. Assume that you are a manager and you want to encourage SDL among your employees. Describe several strategies you might use to get them to manage their own learning.

Part C: Class Discussion

As a class, discuss the importance of using SDL approaches to the continuing training of employees. Explain the relative advantages and disadvantages of these approaches over other, more conventional training techniques (e.g., lecture, films).

FORM 8.3.1
LEARNING PREFERENCE ASSESSMENT

Name _____ Group _____

<u>Instructions:</u> The following items are sample items taken from the SDLRS. The measure is designed to assess your learning preferences and your attitudes toward learning. Using the scale below, write in one number for each item on the blank to the left of the item. Answer as candidly as possible. There are no right or wrong answers.

1 = Almost never true of me. I hardly ever feel this way.
2 = Not often true of me. I feel this way less than half of the time.
3 = Sometimes true of me. I feel this way about half of the time.
4 = Usually true of me. I feel this way more than half of the time.
5 = Almost always true of me. There are very few times when I don't feel this way.

_____ 1.   I know what I want to learn.

_____ 2.   When I see something that I don't understand, I stay away from it.

_____ 3.   If there is something I want to learn, I can figure out a way to learn it.

_____ 4.   If I discover a need for information that I don't have, I know where to go to get it.

_____ 5.   In a classroom situation, I expect the instructor to tell all class members exactly what to do at all times.

_____ 6.   I can learn things on my own better than most people.

_____ 7.   Even if I have a great idea, I can't seem to develop a plan for making it work.

_____ 8.   In a learning experience, I prefer to take part in deciding what will be learned and how.

_____ 9.   Difficult study doesn't bother me if I'm interested in something.

_____ 10.   If there is something I have decided to learn, I can find time for it, no matter how busy I am.

_____ 11.   If I can understand something well enough to get by, it doesn't bother me if I still have questions about it.

_____ 12.   The people I admire most are always learning new things.

_____ 13.   I don't like it when people who really know what they're doing point out mistakes that I am making.

_____ 14.   I try to relate what I am learning to my long-term goals.

_____ 15.   I am capable of learning for myself almost anything I might need to know.

_____ 16.   I'm better than most people at trying to find out things I need to know.

_____ 17.   I become a leader in group learning situations.

_____ 18.   I don't like challenging learning situations.

_____ 19.   It's better to stick to the learning methods that we know will work instead of always trying new ones.

_____ 20.   I want to learn more so that I can keep growing as a person.

C H A P T E R

CAREER DEVELOPMENT

OVERVIEW

> The landscape of the job market is changing . . . advancing technology, increasing demand for services and an aging population are just some of the forces burying some occupations and creating high ground for others. . . . Because of changing economics and technology, count on acquiring new skills and training throughout your career if you want to succeed. Not long ago you could get out of school without acquiring additional formal training, but now learning is a life-long situation. The Bureau of Labor Statistics estimates that the average worker will have six employers in the course of a lifetime. . . . A growing number of professionals are looking for new employers, making lateral shifts into new departments within their companies, and going off on their own. . . . Negotiating your own route to professional success, whether with one company or by moving on, calls for keeping an eye on the big picture, seeing the opportunities, and having the agility to grab them.[1]

The sentiments expressed above reflect the fact that the workplace has changed and that individuals are altering some of their career-related attitudes and behaviors. Not long ago, individuals believed that there was *only one* occupation for which each person was best suited, that the best career decision would be made when a person was *young*, and that once a field was chosen the choice was *irreversible*. They also believed that *interests* were more important in determining career choices than were skills and aptitudes, and that individuals who were successful in a career only moved *upward*.[2] Today, fewer people subscribe to these assumptions about careers.

Now more than ever before, it is apparent that individuals must develop new and better personal skills of self-assessment and career planning, especially since organizations do not have the resources to completely plan individuals' careers.[3] Organizations have, however, become more active in implementing career development programs. In fact, the workplace has recently emerged as a legitimate and appropriate setting for supporting career programs through training and development programs. Companies are designing career programs in efforts to increase employee productivity, prevent job "burnout" and obsolescence, and improve the quality of employees' work lives.[4] Human resource (HR) departments of large companies have taken a greater interest in career development, and the HR manager has never before faced so many challenges in meeting the needs of individual employees and organizations for well-designed career systems.[5]

The purpose of this chapter is to describe some of the career-related issues of relevance to HR professionals and practicing managers. We will begin by defining some key career concepts and models, and will then describe some of the issues involved in designing career development systems in organizations. Also, we will describe the various components of career systems and how career systems can be coordinated with training and development programs.

OBJECTIVES

After studying this chapter, you should be able to:

1. Understand the important concepts and models of organizational career development, reasons for understanding career development, and current concerns in this field.
2. Be able to distinguish life and career stages that individuals face and the implications of these stages for designing career programs.
3. Be able to identify the steps involved in designing career development systems.
4. Be able to describe the components of career development systems.
5. Understand the importance of integrating career development programs with other organizational HR systems, particularly training programs and performance appraisal.

DEFINITIONS

While most people think the term "career" means "advancement" in an organization, a broader view defines *career* as an "individually perceived sequence of attitudes and behaviors associated with work-related activities and experiences over the span of a person's life."[6] In other words, the term "career" has an *internal* focus and refers to the way an individual views his or her career, as well as an *external* focus that refers to the actual series of job positions held by the individual.[7] Understanding career development in an organization requires an examination of two processes: how individuals plan and implement their own career goals (career planning), and how organizations design and implement their career development programs (career management). These processes are illustrated in Figure 9.1. As noted, *career planning* is a deliberate attempt by an individual to become more aware of his or her own skills, interests, values, opportunities, constraints, choices, and consequences. It involves identifying career-related goals and establishing plans for achieving those goals.[8] *Career management* is considered to be an organizational process which involves preparing, implementing, and monitoring career plans undertaken by an individual alone or within the organization's career systems.[9]

A *career development system* is a formal, organized, planned effort to achieve a balance between individual

FIGURE 9.1
A MODEL OF ORGANIZATIONAL CAREER DEVELOPMENT

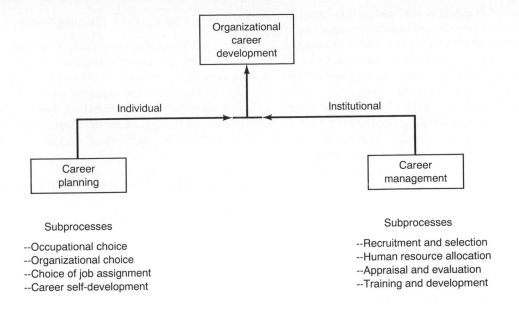

Career: The sequence of a person's work-related activities and behaviors and associated attitudes, values, and aspirations over the span of one's life.

Organizational career development: The outcomes emanating from the interaction of individual career planning and institutional career management processes.

Career planning: A deliberate process for (1) becoming aware of self, opportunities, constraints, choices, and consequences, (2) identifying career-related goals, and (3) programming of work, education, and related developmental experiences to provide the direction, timing, and sequence of steps to attain a specific career goal.

Career management: An ongoing process of preparing, implementing, and monitoring career plans undertaken by the individual alone or in concert with the organization's career system.

Source: T. G. Gutteridge, Organizational career development systems: The state of the practice. In D.T. Hall and associates, *Career development in organizations.* San Francisco, CA: Jossey-Bass, 1986, p. 54. Used with permission.

career needs and organizational workforce requirements.[10] It is a mechanism for meeting the present and future HR needs of an organization.[11] For example, Coca-Cola implemented a career development system so that it would be better able to develop its own employees to meet future staffing needs and to promote employees internally.[12] Basically, career development practices are designed to enhance the career satisfaction of employees and to improve organizational effectiveness.[13] It may, however, be difficult to completely integrate individual and organizational career efforts because the rate at which an individual grows and develops may not parallel an organization's needs. For example, a recent survey conducted by Tenneco Oil found that 48 percent of surveyed employees felt ready to assume supervisory responsibilities. Unfortunately, the company was in a downsizing mode and had no plans to promote anyone in the next 2 years.[14]

This chapter emphasizes the importance of understanding career development in organizations by examining the interaction of individual and organizational career processes. Of particular value is an understanding of career processes within an HR system, and the role that managers must play in designing career development systems. One model focuses on a dynamic interaction of the individual and the organization over time through the "matching" process we described in Chapters 5 and 6. If the matching process works well, the organization and the individual will benefit. The organization may experience increased productivity, higher organizational commitment, and long-range effectiveness, and the employee may have greater satisfaction, security, and personal development.[15]

IMPORTANCE OF UNDERSTANDING CAREER DEVELOPMENT

Today's competitive business environment has forced organizations to restructure and downsize, resulting in fewer hierarchical levels and fewer promotional opportunities for employees.[16] At the same time, companies are under increased pressure to either improve productivity or risk falling prey to larger corporations. The creation of new technologies has required that individuals update their skills to avoid becoming outdated or obsolete. One internal study at Ford, for example, found that there was only a 19 percent overlap between the knowledge acquired to earn a computer science degree in 1980 and the knowledge required to be a practicing computer scientist in 1990.

Current workforce changes have included a greater proportion of older workers, minority employees, people with disabilities, working mothers, and members of the baby-boomer generation competing for a limited number of jobs. As we discussed in Chapter 1, employees themselves have changed their values; they want more self-fulfillment in work, and they want to be in charge of their own career planning. They want opportunities for growth in their careers, and they want to expand their knowledges and skills.[17] Also, they demand well-balanced lives in which comparable value is placed on work, family, and leisure.[18]

Finally, social changes have included increased societal pressures on organizations to be more responsible. For example, corporations are now more likely to offer child-care programs, flexible work scheduling, and parental leave time. In addition, as discussed in Chapter 3, the increasing rate of litigation concerning employment opportunity through laws such as the Age Discrimination in Employment Act (ADEA), the Americans with Disabilities Act (ADA), the 1991 Civil Rights Act, and the Equal Pay Act has placed more responsibility on companies to avoid discrimination in their career development programs.[19]

In the future, a greater emphasis will be placed on designing and implementing relevant career systems in organizations. Organizations will have to find more creative ways for people to develop, since employees will not be able to rely on organizational growth to provide career opportunities (e.g., promotions). The line manager may experience greater pressure to provide career counseling to employees, and the HR department may be called upon to offer training for managers in career coaching skills.[20] For example, the Coca-Cola and Ford Motor Company career systems require training for all managers in how to conduct career development discussions with employees in the context of the annual performance appraisal interview. The intent is to make managers more accountable for the development of their employees.[21]

Concerns in Career Development

Figure 9.2 illustrates some current concerns for career management and career planning. These issues reflect the growing importance of mutual career development between employees and organizations. Also, they reveal that individuals and organizations will have to become more active in their career development efforts in order to meet the changing needs of workers and companies.

LIFE AND CAREER DEVELOPMENT

Life and Career Stages

To design career development systems in organizations, HR managers must have an appreciation of the kinds of decisions and issues that individuals face throughout their careers.[22] An understanding of these issues requires a study of career development theories, life development

FIGURE 9.2
CURRENT CONCERNS IN CAREER MANAGEMENT AND CAREER PLANNING

CURRENT CONCERNS IN CAREER MANAGEMENT
1. Strategic HR planning
2. Succession planning
3. Assessment and development of management potential
4. Training managers in career coaching or counseling skills
5. Alternative or nontraditional career paths
6. Leave policies
7. Legitimation of exit, downward movement
8. Issues for dual-career couples
9. Linking of career management systems with career planning systems

CURRENT CONCERNS IN CAREER PLANNING
1. More concern for self-directed careers
2. Mid-career coming earlier
3. More questioning and rejection of job moves (including promotions)
4. More honest self-assessment
5. More career plateauing by choice
6. More two-career planning; more family inputs to career decisions
7. Desire for more mutual career planning with company
8. Need for more information on company career opportunities
9. Desire for more company assistance in implementing career plans (link to corporate career management system)

Source: D.T. Hall, An overview of current career development theory, research, and practice. In D.T. Hall and associates, *Career development in organizations.* San Francisco, CA: Jossey-Bass, 1986, p. 6. Used with permission.

theories, and the interrelationships among career stages and life stages. In Figure 9.3, a model of the career and life stages and psychological issues individuals confront is presented. Since most of the research for the model was based on studies involving primarily men, the information may be less generalizable to women. The career experiences of women and men have been shown to differ to some degree.[23] For example, marital and parental roles have a different impact on the career progress of women versus men (e.g., women more often make career choices to accommodate their spouse's careers). Women and men experience differences in the career preparation they receive, societal opportunities and constraints, and child-care concerns.

Career and life stage models are closely related because both are linked to age and cultural norms. That is, both reveal a repeating pattern of *growth*, or developing new and challenging skills as one enters a stage;

FIGURE 9.3
LIFE AND CAREER STAGES

AGE	LIFE STAGE/ CAREER STAGE	FAMILY ROLE/ CAREER TASKS	PSYCHOLOGICAL ISSUES
15–22	Adolescence	Single adult	Developing a self-identity Balancing independence with emotional support
	Precareer: exploration	Finding a career Getting an education	Discovering own needs and interests Developing a realistic self-assessment of abilities
22–30	Young adult transition	Married adult	Balancing personal needs with an intimate relationship
	Early career: trial	Getting a viable first job	Developing self-confidence Working with others
30–38	Young adulthood	Parent of young children	Adjusting to parenthood Maintaining an intimate relationship
	Early career: establishment	Choosing an area of competence Becoming a contributor	Deciding on a level of professional and organizational commitment Dealing with failure on first projects
38–45	Mid-life transition	Parent of adolescents	Reassessing values Dealing with ambivalent feelings toward children
	Middle career: transition	Reassessing career abilities Preparing to be a mentor	Reassessing progress toward ambitions Resolving work life/personal conflicts
45–55	Middle adulthood	Parent of grown children	Building a deeper marital relationship Dealing with feelings of loss
	Middle career: growth	Being a mentor	Dealing with younger fast-trackers Using wisdom-based experience
55–62	Late-life adult transition	Grandparent of young children	Developing new hobbies and activities Helping children financially and emotionally with their families
	Late career: maintenance	Making strategic organizational decisions Concern for the broader organizational role	Concern for the company's welfare Handling political or important decisions without getting upset
62–70	Late adulthood	Grandparent of adolescents Widow or widower	Dealing with increased awareness of death Coming to terms with life choices
	Late career: withdrawal	Developing leaders Accepting less power	Finding new sources of life satisfaction outside job Maintaining self-esteem without a job

Source: Modified from D.C. Feldman, *Managing careers in organizations.* Glenview, IL: Scott, Foresman, 1988, pp. 14–15, 18–19. Used with permission.

stabilization, or demonstrating highly productive performance during a stage; and *transition,* or making changes from the demands of the present stage to the anticipated demands of the next stage.[24] To be effective, career programs need to be tailored to meet the unique needs of individuals at varying stages in their lives and careers.[25] Described below are the needs of individuals at each career period and some strategies that can be used by individuals and organizations to meet those needs.

Early-Career Issues

The early-career period poses two major tasks for employees—establishment and achievement. New employees must adapt to being workers, get established in their work, and achieve some initial successes. Also, they must develop sound relationships between their careers and the nonwork aspects of their lives (e.g., family, recreational pursuits). During this period, it is important for individuals to maintain effective performance on the job and attain sponsorship or support from key members of the organization. Also, early-career employees must develop more insight into their career orientations, set realistic career goals, and understand how different career paths may affect their goal accomplishments.[26]

Organizations can help new employees to engage in career exploration and establish their careers during the early-career phase by developing effective recruitment, orientation, and mentoring practices; providing job challenges and responsibilities; and offering constructive performance feedback. In addition, companies should encourage employees to participate in self-assessment exercises, and should work with them to help them determine realistic and flexible career paths and formulate career plans. Also, employers should assist employees in developing supportive relationships with their supervisors and other key people in the organization.[27] Some companies, such as Bank of America, assign mentors to young managers to help them "learn the ropes."[28] Some companies use assessment centers for career development. American Telephone and Telegraph (AT&T), for example, has a program for early identification of managerial talent which provides feedback to employees for career planning.

Middle-Career Issues

The middle-career period is often defined as the halfway point in a career. The major tasks facing employees in the middle-career period are to confront and reappraise their early career decisions, make changes in their dreams, and remain productive at work.[29] Also, employees may need to determine how to use their experiences beyond the technical, specialist skills (i.e., they may need to

learn how to be generalists), and they may need to learn how to cope with becoming "plateaued." A *plateau* is the point in a career at which the chance of future promotions is low. Mid-career employees may also face obsolescence when they discover that their knowledges and skills are no longer up-to-date enough to enable them to perform their jobs effectively. In fact, they may even lose their jobs and have to deal with the financial and emotional consequences of being terminated.[30] During mid-career, individuals are often confronted with mid-life psychological problems including the recognition of mortality, physical problems, and changed relationships with family members.[31] Sometimes these difficulties may result in a period of crisis for individuals. To effectively manage the mid-career period, it is important that individuals reassess how they are doing relative to their ambitions, and decide how important their careers are going to be in their total lives. For example, will their careers have priority over their families, leisure pursuits, community activities, etc.? Individuals should keep "positive, growth-oriented attitudes toward life" and recognize that they may experience ambivalence and anxiety during this stage.[32] Having realistic expectations about potential crises may actually help individuals to cope with changes or stress.[33] Mid-career employees should also try to develop insight into their values and motives, reevaluate their current career prospects, and define career goals that can be achieved in a variety of jobs.[34]

There are a number of things that organizations can do to promote effective career management among mid-career employees. To help employees understand their mid-career experiences, employers can provide a variety of mobility opportunities, including lateral transfers and project assignments. Some companies (e.g., Equitable Life Assurance Society, Digital Equipment Corporation) have institutionalized corporate policies regarding the use of lateral transfers.[35] Also, employers should offer sufficient challenges and responsibilities on current jobs to maintain employees' involvement and productivity. For instance, General Foods Corporation provides challenging assignments to employees in its professional development program, which is designed to build employee competence.[36] Prudential Life Insurance Company and General Electric Company (GE) rotate their managers into different positions to improve their performance by giving them new perspectives on their work.[37] Organizations should also facilitate frequent skills assessments and career counseling with mid-career employees. To prevent obsolescence, employers should encourage mid-career employees to participate in training programs, cross-training opportunities, and continuing education programs. Also, employers should offer opportunities for sabbaticals.[38] For example, as we discussed in Chapter 8, Ford Motor Company provides extensive training and development options for mid-career employees. Xerox and IBM are among the growing number of companies offering sabbaticals for employees to assume temporary academic positions, and Burger King offers "renewal" seminars for its managers.

Late-Career Issues

For a small number of employees, the major task of the late-career period is to prepare themselves to move up into senior leadership roles according to the executive succession plan in the company. These key individuals will have the job of shaping the direction of the organization and may exercise considerable power in these roles.[39] For the majority of employees, however, the primary tasks of the late-career period are to remain productive and to prepare for effective retirement.[40] During late career, most employees have to deal with the aftermath of mid-career obsolescence or "plateauing," as well as with negative age biases on the job.[41] Also, late-career employees have to cope with downward job moves they may receive in the organization.[42]

In order to adjust successfully to late careers, individuals should maintain positive, forward-thinking attitudes and receive social support from colleagues and spouses.[43] Late-career employees should engage in long-term planning of their finances and leisure pursuits with their spouses, and should plan their retirements with care and attention.[44]

Organizations can assist late-career employees by understanding the unique problems they encounter and by helping them to retire with minimal difficulty. Companies should develop and enforce nondiscriminatory policies regarding older workers. Also, employers should provide job challenges and continual training for late-career employees, to maintain their motivation. In addition, employers should create positive incentives for early retirement and participation in preretirement programs, and should establish flexible work patterns for employees nearing retirement ages.[45] For example, IBM, AT&T, and Johnson's Wax have innovative programs for early retirement and part-time work for older employees. These programs have not only been beneficial for improving the outlook of the older workers and retirees but have also saved the companies considerable money.[46]

Implications of Life or Career Models for Understanding Career Development

An appreciation of the nature of career stages and life stages may help HR professionals to manage the transitions of employees more smoothly.[47] Models of career and life stages can illustrate how home and work lives are interrelated, what difficulties may be encountered by individuals in nontraditional career paths, how life and career stages influence life and job satisfaction, and what the critical points are in adult development.[48] Knowing the problems that individuals must solve during different stages of their adult development may be valuable for identifying their needs at different stages of career development. These may consist of both task and emotional needs, as illustrated in Figure 9.4. For example, an understanding of the issues confronting mid-career employees might suggest that technical skills updating would be a useful strategy for meeting their task needs, while counseling might help to meet their emotional needs.

DESIGNING CAREER DEVELOPMENT SYSTEMS

An effective career development system attempts to integrate a series of individual career planning and organizational career management activities that involve the employee, management, and the organization. For example, most career programs (e.g., those at IBM, Bell Atlantic, Xerox) involve career assessment by the employee, with the manager serving as a facilitator and the organization providing a supportive environment.[49]

Some of the benefits of a career development system for employees, managers, and the organization are presented in Figure 9.5. As shown, managers can benefit from career development programs by being better able to communicate with and develop their staff. As one example, the Federal National Mortgage Association reduced turnover of its sales force by 50 percent after instituting a supervisory training program on career planning. Also, employees may benefit from a career development system by acquiring a deepened appreciation for their own skills and career possibilities and assuming a greater responsibility for managing their own careers. The organization may gain from a career development system by increased employee loyalty, improved communication throughout the organization, and strengthened HR systems.

Roles and Responsibilities in Career Development Activities

A career development program requires specific responsibilities for HR professionals, employees, managers, and the organization. For example, Digital Equipment Corporation has a full-time career development counselor who works closely with the director of training and development for the organization. Such counselors are usually responsible for developing new career programs, training line managers as career coaches, and evaluating the successes or failures of the career development programs.

FIGURE 9.4
TRAINING NEEDS WITHIN CAREER STAGES

STAGE	TASK NEEDS	EMOTIONAL NEEDS
Trial	Varied job activities Self-exploration	Making preliminary job choices Settling down
Establishment/advancement	Job challenge Developing competence in a specialty area Developing creativity and innovation Rotating into a new area after 3 to 5 years	Dealing with rivalry and competition; facing failures Dealing with work-family conflicts Support Autonomy
Mid-career	Technical updating Developing skills in coaching others Rotating into a new job requiring new skills Developing a broader view of work and role in firm	Expressing feelings about mid-life Reorganizing thinking about self in relation to work and family Reducing self-indulgence and competitiveness
Late career	Planning for retirement Shifting from a power role to one of consultation Identifying and developing successors Beginning activities outside the organization	Support and counseling for seeing one's work as a platform for others Developing a sense of identity through extraorganizational activities

Source: D.T. Hall and M. A. Morgan, Career development and planning. In K. Pearlman, F. L. Schmidt, and W.C. Hamner (eds.), *Contemporary problems in personnel,* 3d ed. New York: John Wiley & Sons, 1983, p. 229. Used with permission.

FIGURE 9.5
BENEFITS OF A CAREER DEVELOPMENT SYSTEM

MANAGERS/SUPERVISORS	EMPLOYEES	ORGANIZATION
Increased skill in managing own careers	Helpful assistance with career decisions	Better use of employee skills
Greater retention of valued employees	Enrichment of present job and increased job satisfaction	Dissemination of information at all organization levels
Better communication between manager and employee	Better communication between employee and manager	Better communication within the organization as a whole
More realistic staff and development planning	More realistic goals and expectations	Greater retention of valued employees
Productive performance appraisal discussions	Better feedback on performance	Expanded public image as a people developer
Greater understanding of the organization	Current information on the firm and the future	Increased effectiveness of personnel systems
Enhanced reputation as a people developer	Greater personal responsibility for career	Greater clarification of goals of the organization

Source: Z. B. Leibowitz, C. Farren, and B.L. Kaye, *Designing career development systems.* San Francisco, CA: Jossey-Bass, 1986, p. 7. Used with permission.

They may also set up career development activities for members of certain groups in the organization (e.g., fast-track employees, minorities, female managers, dual-career couples).[50] Figure 9.6 presents a summary of the responsibilities of the employee, the manager, and the organization in a career development program.

In career planning activities, employees must determine job and career preferences and initiate discussions with their supervisors about job expectations and career options.[51] In career management activities, employees are primarily responsible for submitting any necessary career-related information to management and the organization.

Managers play an integral role in career development by serving as the link between employees' needs and those of the firm. In career planning activities, managers are assumed to be career counselors or coaches with employees. You may recall our earlier discussion of Ford's

FIGURE 9.6
RESPONSIBILITIES FOR CAREER DEVELOPMENT IN ORGANIZATIONS

CAREER PLANNING ACTIVITIES

Employee's Responsibilities

Self-assess abilities, interests, and values.

Analyze career options.

Decide on development objectives and needs.

Communicate development preferences to manager.

Map out mutually agreeable action plans with manager.

Pursue agreed-upon action plan.

Manager's Responsibilities

Act as catalyst; sensitize employee to the development planning process.

Assess realism of employee's expressed objectives and perceived needs.

Counsel employee and develop a mutually agreeable plan.

Follow up and update employee's plans as appropriate.

Organization's Responsibilities

Provide career-planning model, resources, counseling, and information needed for individualized career planning.

Provide training in career development planning to managers and employees and career counseling to managers.

Provide skills training programs and on-the-job developmental opportunities.

CAREER MANAGEMENT ACTIVITIES

Employee's Responsibilities

Provide accurate information to management regarding skills, work experiences, interests, and career aspirations.

Manager's Responsibilities

Validate information provided by employee.

Provide information about vacant job positions for which the manager is responsible.

Use all information provided by the process to: (1) identify all viable candidates for a vacant position and make a selection and (2) identify career development opportunities (job openings, training programs, rotation assignments) for an employee and place him or her accordingly.

Organization's Responsibilities

Provide information system and process to accommodate management's decision-making needs.

Organize and update all information.

Ensure effective usage of information by: (1) designing convenient methods for collecting, analyzing, interpreting, and using the information and (2) monitoring and evaluating the effectiveness of the process.

Source: F. J. Minor, Computer applications in career development planning. In D.T. Hall and associates, *Career development in organizations.* San Francisco, CA: Jossey-Bass, 1986, pp. 205–206. Used with permission.

training and development program, which requires managers and supervisors to serve as coaches in the completion of an education and training plan for each employee. Coaches review courses which have been taken, assignments, and the strategic plan of the organization. Through performance appraisal discussions, managers assist employees in developing realistic pictures of themselves for career planning.[52] In career management activities, managers primarily play information-provider roles by informing employees about possible career opportunities.

For career planning activities, the organization primarily offers support to the career efforts of its employees and managers, and furnishes any necessary information and training. For career management functions, it is actively involved in seeking out career-related information for use in the company. For example, there are a number of consulting firms which specialize in providing career counseling, assessment, and outplacement.

Steps Involved in Establishing a Career Development System

Career development programs are not really a new idea. For example, Western Electric Corp. and GE have sponsored programs since 1920.[53] What is new, however, is the development of guidelines for designing a career system.[54] First, an organization should start small and expand gradually, initially using a pilot study to test the new career system. The career program should be built to complement other HR systems in the company and, in particular, training and performance appraisal. Built into the HR system should be a balanced mix of individual exercises (e.g., self-assessment) and organizational interventions (e.g., succession charts, training needs analysis). For instance, Du Pont Corporation's Pioneering Research Laboratory uses a variety of career components (e.g., psychological tests, courses, a library, seminars) to allow for differences among participants in personal prefer-ences.[55] Success indicators (i.e., indicators of program effectiveness) should be established so that program evaluators can measure the results of the program and publicize its successes.[56]

One planning model which emphasizes an organizational change perspective in its recommendations for designing career systems is presented in Figure 9.7. According to this model, an organization must perceive a need or problem, have a picture or vision of how the change will affect the organization, determine an action plan or steps for intervention, and maintain the change or ensure results. These steps are briefly described below.

STEP 1. NEEDS.   Just as with training, the first step in designing a career development system is to conduct a needs assessment. This involves examining the present state of the organization to identify the most critical needs or problem areas. At this step, it is necessary to review the organization's culture to assess its readiness for change and to review its current HR systems or structures (e.g., performance appraisal, training and development, compensation) to see how a career development program might be able to build on them. Potential groups for career development may include plateaued managers, new employees, high-potential employees on the fast track, dual-career couples, preretirement employees, and disadvantaged employees (e.g., minorities, women, people with disabilities).

To collect the necessary information in the needs stage, a variety of data collection strategies should be used, and existing data on the organization (e.g., survey results, personnel records, exit interviews) should also be reviewed.[57] An evaluation of any prior attempts at career planning would also be helpful. HR professionals may be able to learn from these prior attempts, and to recruit the assistance of advisory groups to provide council and support. For example, Mobil Oil was concerned that the company was losing too many young female employees. They sent out over 2000 questionnaires and conducted over 400 exit interviews and 100 interviews with spouses of current employees. Their research indicated that both men and women, but particularly women, feared they would be relocated often and were dissatisfied with career development opportunities in the company.

At the end of the needs analysis step, the HR manager should be able to describe *what the current situation is* in the organization, *what the situation should be,* and *what should be done* to remedy any discrepancies.[58] At Mobil, for instance, task forces were set up to plan formal career development programs. Also, steps were taken to reduce the probability of relocation.

FIGURE 9.7
STEPS AND TASKS IN ESTABLISHING A CAREER DEVELOPMENT SYSTEM

STEP 1.   NEEDS: DEFINING THE PRESENT SYSTEM
Establish roles and responsibilities of employees, managers, and the organization.

Identify needs; establish target groups.

Establish cultural parameters; determine organizational receptivity, support, and commitment to career development.

Assess existing HR programs or structures; consider possible links to a career development program.

Determine prior attempts at solving the problem or need.

Establish the mission or philosophy of the program.

Design and implement needs assessment to confirm the data or collect more data.

Establish indicators or criteria of success.

STEP 2.   VISION: DETERMINING NEW DIRECTIONS AND POSSIBILITIES
Create a long-term philosophy.

Establish the vision or objectives of the program.

Design interventions for employees, managers, and the organization.

Organize and make available career information needed to support the program.

STEP 3:   ACTION PLAN: DECIDING ON PRACTICAL FIRST STEPS
Assess the plan and obtain support from top management.

Create a pilot program.

Assess resources and competencies.

Establish an advisory group.

Involve advisory group in data gathering, program design, implementation, evaluation, and monitoring.

STEP 4:   RESULTS: MAINTAINING THE CHANGE
Create long-term formalized approaches.

Publicize the program.

Evaluate and redesign the program and its components.

Consider future trends and directions for the program.

Source: Z. B. Leibowitz, C. Farren, and B. L. Kaye, *Designing career development systems.* San Francisco, CA: Jossey-Bass, 1986, p. 273. Used with permission.

STEP 2. VISION.   To link the needs of the career system with later interventions, there must be a description of the ideal career development system (i.e., the vision). This vision or strategic plan is developed by thinking about new directions and possibilities for the organization and using the results as a guide in figuring out the objectives of the career program and the interventions that will be most effective. At this step, models of life and career development might be helpful as a conceptual framework. In addition, familiarity with career development components (i.e., activities and programs) is necessary. These components are described in a later section.

Managers should be actively involved in the development of the vision in order to develop a sense of ownership in the program, especially since many of them will serve as career counselors to their subordinates. Also, it is important for managers to be educated about the benefits and realities of career development and to be involved in the data collection and implementation steps. Further, they should participate in training programs to improve their career coaching skills. At the end of the vision step, the company should have a plan for what the solution to any career development problems might look like.

STEP 3. ACTION PLAN. To ensure that the vision will be put into effect, it is important to decide on an action plan. The support of top management must be obtained early on, and an advisory group should be created to get realistic input from a variety of sources in the firm and to build a broader base of support for the program. The advisory group will work with HR professionals to outline an action plan and set up a pilot program to initially try out the career program. The career management programs at AT&T, 3M Company, and Frito-Lay utilized pilot programs to reduce resistance to career systems and to build support.[59]

Any career development system requires top-management support. "Networks" should be provided so that managers can share their enthusiasm and reinforce one another. Also, top management should be informed regarding the costs and benefits of the career program.[60] Sears Roebuck & Company, IBM, Ford, and General Motors (GM) are among the firms known for their strong top-level support for career programs.[61] Many companies include career development activities as major managerial functions which are evaluated annually. IBM, Continental Bank, Wells Fargo Bank, and Ford are among the companies which ask subordinates to evaluate the extent to which managers are successful in career development activities. These subordinate evaluations are an important component of making overall evaluations of managers.

STEP 4. RESULTS. To maintain a career development program, it is essential to integrate the program into the organization's ongoing employee training and development strategy. Also, the program should be evaluated to determine revisions and to win the continued support of top management. Figure 9.8 illustrates some of the criteria that may be used to evaluate the program or indicate success. As noted above, success can be measured by individual and organizational goal attainment, the actions that are completed (e.g., use of career tools), and any changes in performance measures and attitudes.

Research on the effectiveness of career development programs is sparse, yet promising. One study found that 44 percent of administrators of career development programs for Fortune 500 companies regarded them as "very helpful."[62] IBM evaluated the effectiveness of its career development workshop, and found improvements in the participants' abilities and in their responsibilities for their own career planning. They also discovered that employees' perceptions of better job opportunities (defined as opportunities to use new and different skills) had increased substantially.[63] Du Pont found that after participating in a career program, employees had clearer career objectives, were more familiar with possible career options, and felt that management had shown a greater concern for career development.[64] Pratt and Whitney (P&W) also reported that its turnover rate for new engineers had decreased by 25 percent after it instituted a career development program.

Of course, measures of program success may vary depending on *whom* you are asking in the organization. That is, employees, managers, organizations, and the HR staff may differ in the specific factors they view as indicative of program success. For example, employees may say that a career program is effective if it organizes a way for them to plan and manage their career interests or offers them opportunities to discuss their career decisions with their supervisors. Managers may view a career program as successful if it offers them staffing flexibility or helps them to identify pools of qualified employees to meet forecasted openings. Organizations may find a program to be useful if it increases the attractiveness of the organization to potential employees (recruits) or raises the motivation and productivity of current employees. Finally, the HR staff may determine that a program is successful if it has credibility or enhances the reputation of the HR department with line managers.[65]

COMPONENTS OF CAREER DEVELOPMENT SYSTEMS

A variety of career components (i.e., activities and tools) exist for use in organizations. HR managers who serve as internal consultants responsible for designing the career development system should be familiar with these components. Some of the activities described are *individual career planning* tools, and others are commonly used for *organizational career management*.[66] In general, the

FIGURE 9.8
INDICATORS OF CAREER PROGRAM EFFECTIVENESS

GOAL ATTAINMENT

Achievement of prespecified individual and organizational objectives on qualitative as well as quantitative dimensions.

INDIVIDUAL	ORGANIZATION
Exercise greater self-determination.	Improve career communications between employees and supervisors.
Achieve greater self-awareness.	Improve individual/organizational career match.
Acquire necessary organizational career information.	Enhance organization's image.
Enhance personal growth and development.	Respond to EEO and AA pressures.
Improve goal-setting capability.	Identify pool of management talent.

ACTIONS OR EVENTS COMPLETED
1. Employee use of career tools (participation in career workshops, enrollment in training courses)
2. Career decisions conducted
3. Employee career plans implemented
4. Career actions taken (promotions, cross-functional moves)
5. Management successors identified

CHANGES IN PERFORMANCE INDEXES
1. Reduced turnover rates
2. Lower employee absenteeism
3. Improved employee morale
4. Improved employee performance ratings
5. Reduced time to fill job openings
6. Increased promotion from within

ATTITUDES OR PERCEPTIONS
1. Evaluation of career tools and practices (participant's reaction to career workshop, supervisor's evaluation of job posting system)
2. Perceived benefits of career system
3. Employees express career feelings (responses to career attitude survey)
4. Evaluation of employee career planning skills
5. Adequacy of organizational career information

Source: T. G. Gutteridge, Organizational career development systems: The state of the practice. In D.T. Hall and associates, *Career development in organizations.* San Francisco, CA: Jossey-Bass, 1986, p. 76. Used with permission.

most effective career development programs will use both types of activities.

Figure 9.9 illustrates some of the career development activities available for use. Some of the more popular ones include: (1) self-assessment tools (e.g., career planning workshops, career workbooks), (2) individual counseling, (3) information services (e.g., job posting systems, skills inventories, career ladders or career paths, career resource centers, and other communication formats), (4) initial employment programs (e.g., anticipatory socialization programs, realistic recruitment, employee orientation programs), (5) organizational assessment programs (e.g., assessment centers, psychological testing, promotability forecasts, succession planning), and (6) developmental programs (e.g., assessment centers, job rotation programs, in-house training, tuition-refund plans, mentoring).

Self-Assessment Tools

Self-assessments are usually among the first techniques implemented by organizations in their career development efforts.[67] Thus, it is important for managers to become familiar with the different self-assessment and career exploration instruments available. Typically, individuals who complete self-assessment exercises for career planning purposes go through a process in which they think through their life roles, interests, skills, and work attitudes and preferences. They try to plan their short- and long-term goals, develop action plans to meet

**FIGURE 9.9
ORGANIZATIONAL CAREER DEVELOPMENT
INTERVENTIONS**

Self-assessment tools
   Career planning workshops
   Career workbooks

Individual counseling

Information services
   Job posting systems
   Skills inventories
   Career ladders and paths
   Career resource centers

Organizational assessment programs
   Assessment centers
   Psychological testing
   Promotability forecasts
   Succession planning

Developmental programs
   Assessment centers
   Job rotation programs
   Tuition refund plans
   Internal training programs
   Mentoring programs

Programs to address issues confronting employees at various career stages
   Early-career issues
      Anticipatory socialization programs
      Realistic recruitment
      Employee orientation programs
   Mid-career issues
      Job rotation
      Downward moves
      Developmental programs
   Late-career issues
      Workshops on older worker issues
      Preretirement programs
      Incentives for early retirement
      Flexible work patterns

Career programs for special target groups
   Fast-track or high-potential employees
   Terminated employees (outplacement programs)
   Supervisors
   Women, minorities, and employees with disabilities
   Programs to assist employed spouses and parents
      Policies on hiring couples
      Work-family programs
      Job-sharing programs
      Relaxed policies on transfers and travel
      Flexible work arrangements
      Paid and unpaid leave (maternity, paternity)
      Child-care services

Source: J. E. A. Russell, Career development interventions in organizations, *Journal of Vocational Behavior, 38,* 1991, p. 244. Used with permission.

those goals, and identify any obstacles and opportunities that might be associated with them.[68] Hewlett-Packard employees complete a variety of self-assessment exercises, including vocational interest tests and diaries, before meeting with their managers for career counseling.[69] Two tools often used to assist individuals in their self-assessments include career planning workshops and career workbooks.

CAREER PLANNING WORKSHOPS. After individuals complete their self-assessments, they may share their findings with other individuals in career workshops.[70] For example, GE provides career training to its engineering staff, followed by periodic meetings to share results.[71] In general, most workshops use experiential exercises in a structured, participative group format to educate individuals on how to prepare and follow through on their career strategies. A group format is often valuable to help participants receive feedback from others so that they can check the reality of their plans and consider other alternatives. In addition, workshops are beneficial in helping employees to gain greater self-awareness and insight and to learn more about career opportunities in the organization.[72]

CAREER WORKBOOKS. Career workbooks consist of questions and exercises designed to guide individuals as they figure out their strengths and weaknesses, job and career opportunities, and the necessary steps for reaching their goals.[73] One popular example of a generic career workbook is the annual book *What Color Is Your Parachute?*[74] Individuals use this manual to learn about their career possibilities. It provides suggestions for job hunting and making career changes. Many workbooks are tailor-made for a particular company and can be completed in several sessions.[75] If such "home-grown" workbooks are used, they should contain a statement of the organization's career policy, a description of the relevant career options in the organization, and a description of the strategies available for obtaining career information. The workbooks should also illustrate the organization's structure, career paths, and job qualifications for jobs along the career ladders.[76]

Individual Counseling

One of the most common career development activities used in organizations is career counseling.[77] The purpose of individual career counseling is to help employees discuss their career goals in one-on-one counseling sessions using workbooks and other self-assessment exercises. Discussions of the employees' interests, goals, current job activities and performance, and career objectives often occur. Because the counseling sessions are often conducted on a one-on-one basis, they may be very time-consuming and not as cost-effective as other career development methods.[78]

Generally, career counseling is provided by the HR department, although some organizations hire professional counselors and others use line managers as career counselors. If supervisors are used in career counseling sessions, they should be given clearly defined roles and training.[79] Also, supervisors should be rewarded for their efforts as career coaches, to encourage them to devote the necessary time to this role.[80] For example, at Federal National Mortgage Association and Baxter Health Care Corporation, managers' bonuses are directly linked to the career development programs established for women and minorities. Both companies identify key females and minorities early in their careers and develop specific plans for helping them to acquire the necessary skills for advancement.

Information Services

Internal communication systems are often used by organizations to alert employees to employment opportunities at all levels, including upward, downward, and lateral moves. Also, they may be used to keep ongoing records of employees' skills, knowledges, and work experiences and preferences. These records are valuable for pointing out possible candidates for job openings in the company.[81] Several systems commonly used for compiling and communicating career-related information include job posting systems, skills inventories, career ladders and paths, and career resource centers.

JOB POSTING SYSTEMS. As discussed in Chapter 5, job posting systems are used by companies to inform employees about openings in the organization through bulletin boards, newsletters, and other company publications. While it obviously serves an informational purpose, posting may also be useful as a motivational tool if it implies that the organization is more interested in selecting employees from within the company than from outside the organization. Some guidelines for effective job posting systems include posting all permanent promotion and transfer opportunities for at least 1 week before recruiting outside the organization, outlining minimum requirements for the position (including specific training courses), describing decision rules that will be used, making application forms available, and informing all applicants about how the job was filled.[82] At Ford, a training matrix is available for each job family in which specific courses are identified as recommended for a particular job classification.

SKILLS INVENTORY. Skills inventories, which are files of data on employees' skills, abilities, experiences, and education, are often computerized. They may contain comprehensive records of employees' work histories,

qualifications, education degrees and major fields of study, accomplishments, training completed, skill and knowledge ratings, career objectives, geographical preferences, and anticipated retirement dates. Skills inventories are created to help organizations learn the characteristics of their workforces so that they can effectively utilize the skills of their employees. Also, they reveal shortages of critical skills among employees, which is useful for indicating training needs.

CAREER LADDERS AND CAREER PATHS. Organizations usually map out steps (job positions) that employees might follow over time. These steps are used to document possible patterns of job movement, including vertical or upward moves and lateral or cross-functional moves. Illustrations of career paths and ladders are helpful for answering employees' questions about career progression and future job opportunities in the organization. For example, GM groups jobs by job families—such as HR, engineering, clerical, and systems professional—to show employees the career possibilities in each of the various job fields. Typically, the description of a career path or ladder illustrates a career plan complete with the final goal, intermediate steps, and timetables for reaching the goal.[83] Common in many organizations is the development of career paths for fast-track employees which outline the series of career moves that will prepare them for upper management.

CAREER RESOURCE CENTER AND OTHER COMMUNICATION FORMATS. One increasingly popular approach for providing career information is a career resource center.[84] A center consists of a small library in the organization established to distribute career development materials such as reference books, learning guides, and self-study tapes. For example, Mountain Bell Telephone Company operates three centers which contain a variety of services to help employees assess their own skills and plan careers.[85] Other methods for communicating organizational career information and programs may include the use of flyers, brochures, newsletters, and career manuals.

Initial Employment Programs in Organizations

As discussed in Chapter 5, when an employee first starts working in a company, he or she generally has been exposed to some type of recruitment effort and company orientation. Or if the employee has worked part-time for a company or served in an internship program, he or she has been socialized regarding the unique characteristics of the job and organization. These initial employment programs may be valuable mechanisms to familiarize the employee with the career policies and procedures of the organization.[86]

ANTICIPATORY SOCIALIZATION PROGRAMS. Socialization programs (e.g., internships, cooperative education programs) are beneficial for individuals to develop accurate, realistic expectations about their chosen career fields and about the world of work. By working for an organization part-time or for several months, individuals may learn how well they are suited to the particular job or organization. This knowledge may help them to gain a better sense of responsibility, maturity, and self-confidence about work.

REALISTIC RECRUITMENT. As discussed in Chapter 5, when job applicants are given a realistic, balanced, accurate view of the organization and the job (i.e., when they are provided with positive and negative information), they experience less reality shock, dissatisfaction, and turnover.[87] This is true for new employees as well as current employees who are transferring to new jobs in the organization.[88] To meet career development needs, job applicants should be informed in realistic job previews about the skills required in various positions in the organization and about their own readiness and aptitude for those positions. This information should assist them in developing their future career goals and action plans.

EMPLOYEE ORIENTATION PROGRAMS. As stated in Chapter 8, orientation programs for new employees are beneficial for reducing anxieties since they provide information on organizational policies, procedures, rules, work requirements, and sources of information. Also, orientation programs may be used to educate employees about any career programs, career paths, and opportunities for advancement within the company.[89] For example, Texas Instruments, Inc., has developed an orientation program to address the unique concerns of new employees regarding career options.[90] The program includes a realistic job preview, an introduction to the formal mentoring program, a bibliography of readings relevant to career planning, and guidelines for career planning based on a study of Texas Instrument employees.

Organizational Assessment Programs

Assessment programs consist of methods for evaluating employees' potential for growth and development in the organization. They include assessment centers, psychological testing, promotability forecasts, and succession planning.

ASSESSMENT CENTERS. In addition to their use as decision-making tools, assessment centers are popular as developmental tools. AT&T, J. C. Penney, Sears, IBM, GE, Bendix, and P&W are among the companies that use assessment centers for development as well as employee decision making.[91] As described in Chapter 6, participants in the program of an assessment center engage in a variety of situational exercises, including tests, interviews, in-baskets, leaderless group discussions, and business games. Their performance on these exercises is evaluated by a panel of trained raters (usually middle- to upper-level managers), and they are given in-depth developmental feedback on their strengths and weaknesses. This feedback is often very useful for improving participants' own insights into their skills and for helping them to outline future career goals and plans.[92]

PSYCHOLOGICAL TESTING. Diagnostic tests and inventories may be used for self-assessment or with career counseling. Written tests are used to help individuals determine their vocational interests, personality types, work attitudes, and other personal characteristics that may reveal their career needs and preferences.[93] Among the useful tests are the Strong Interest Inventory, the Self-Directed Search, and the Kuder Preference Record, which assess preferences for certain jobs and job characteristics.

PROMOTABILITY FORECASTS. Forecasts are used by the organization to make early identifications of individuals with exceptionally high career potential. Once individuals are identified, they are given relevant developmental experiences to groom them for higher positions. Several companies including Xerox now have such programs for women and minorities in an effort to get greater female and minority representation at higher managerial levels.

SUCCESSION PLANNING. Succession planning involves having senior executives periodically review their top executives and those in the next-lower level to determine several backups for each senior position. Succession planning is usually restricted to senior-level management positions and can be informal or formal.[94] In informal succession planning, the individual manager identifies and grooms his or her own replacement. Formal succession planning involves an examination of strategic (long-range) plans, HR forecasts, and the data on all potential candidates. In addition, it includes the determination and clarification of the managerial position requirements and the development of plans for meeting future managerial requirements.

Developmental Programs

Developmental programs consist of skills assessment and training programs that organizations may use to develop their employees for future positions. Development programs may be internal and run by the HR staff, or may be offered externally in the form of seminars and workshops. Du Pont offers in-house seminars on various job functions. Lists of employee contacts are handed out to enable individuals to find out more about various job functions discussed in the seminars.[95] Other corporations offer 3- to 4-year training programs at lower levels to groom employees for subsequent managerial positions.[96] A recent survey of 12 leading companies found that they agreed on the criteria for a successful executive development process: (1) extensive chief executive officer (CEO) involvement, (2) a clearly stated development policy, (3) CEO development linked to the business strategy, (4) an annual succession planning process and on-the-job developmental assignments, and (5) line management responsibility for the program.[97]

Some commonly used programs for development include assessment centers, job rotation programs, in-house training programs, and tuition-refund plans.[98] Assessment centers are useful for helping employees to better understand their strengths and weaknesses for managerial jobs, although they can be quite expensive, with costs ranging from $125 to over $3000 per candidate. Many companies use job rotation programs which enable employees to develop a broader base of skills as part of a managerial training program. Most Fortune 500 companies cover expenses for job-related and career-oriented courses taken at colleges. Also, they offer internal programs on a variety of topics including technical training and interpersonal skills.[99]

Another developmental program that is gaining in popularity is mentoring. Mentoring consists of establishing formal relationships between junior and senior colleagues or peers that contribute to career functions (e.g., sponsorship, coaching, and protection of the colleague, exposure to important contacts and resources, assignment of challenging work) and to psychosocial functions (e.g., role modeling, counseling, acceptance and confirmation of the colleague, friendship).[100] Having a mentor is an important aid in the development of the protégé and may also be valuable for improving the job involvement and satisfaction of the mentor.[101] Some companies with formal mentoring programs are Federal Express, Xerox, Merrill Lynch, and The Jewel Companies.[102]

CAREER PROGRAMS FOR SPECIAL GROUPS

Career development programs are often put into effect to meet the unique needs of particular employees. Although many different groups and issues may be targeted for career development, the more common programs focus on work-family issues, outplacement, late-career programs and preretirement workshops, disadvantaged employees, fast-track employees, supervisors, and repatriates.

Work-Family Programs

Because of the increasing numbers of working mothers and two-income households,[103] organizations have become more interested in assisting individuals to deal with conflicting demands between their work and family roles. Employers are beginning to realize that individuals may experience role conflict and difficulties in dealing with travel, child care, household tasks, and job transfers, and may have trouble in setting priorities for their various roles and responsibilities.[104] This may be especially true for dual-career couples because of their high levels of career commitment.

Organizations are becoming more involved in designing programs to help employees manage their role conflict by providing a place and a procedure for discussing conflicts and coping strategies. For example, Continental Bank offers work-family seminars given half during company time and half during employees' personal time.[105] Also, organizations are changing their practices with regard to recruitment, travel, transfers, promotions, scheduling hours, and benefits to meet the needs of the larger numbers of dual-career couples.[106] For example, GE and Procter & Gamble require fewer geographic moves in order to advance.[107] Du Pont has developed more flexible employment plans to accommodate the family demands of both male and female employees. Du Pont also trains its supervisors to be more sensitive to family issues, allows longer parental leave for fathers and mothers, and has instituted adjustable work schedules.[108] Mobil Oil provides more flexible work schedules, a proposed part-time option, childbirth and other leaves, and a national network of child-care information. We will explore work-family programs further later in the chapter.

Outplacement Programs

Outplacement is designed to assist terminated employees, particularly those laid off by reduction-in-force (RIF) efforts, in making the transition to new employment. Generally, external counselors are used in outplacement programs; individuals are able to share their feelings about being let go in a supportive environment during individual counseling sessions. Workshops may also be used to show individuals how to become successful job seekers by teaching them how to identify their skills and abilities, develop résumés, and interview with prospective employers. For example, when Tennessee Valley Authority (TVA) had to reduce its workforce, the HR department assisted employees by providing counseling and helped them to find jobs with other firms. Outplacement programs stressing the importance of self-confidence and individual career planning may be particularly beneficial for middle- or late-career employees who have been laid off.

Late-Career Employee Programs and Preretirement Workshops

Given the increasing numbers of older workers, some organizations are offering programs to help supervisors increase their awareness of issues facing late-career employees. Many young people have misconceptions about aging which can affect the way in which they interact with older workers. Generally, supervisors are instructed on the changing demographics of the workforce, laws regarding older employees, stereotypes and realities of the aging process, and differences in values and attitudes between younger and older workers. Also, they may be taught to develop action plans for enhancing the performance of their older workers. These plans may consist of giving older workers more concrete feedback, allowing them to serve as mentors, and providing them with training and cross-training opportunities.[109]

The focus of preretirement workshops is to help preretirees understand the life and career concerns they may face as they prepare for retirement.[110] The topics that may be discussed include health, finances, making the transition from work to retirement status, safety, housing and location, legal affairs, time utilization, Social Security, second careers, use of leisure time, and problems of aging. Often, individual counseling and group workshops are used, and efforts are made to tailor the programs to the needs of the participants and their spouses. Another type of assistance given to preretirees may be education, as in the Retirement Education Assistance Plan available to potential retirees at IBM.[111]

Special Programs for Women, Minorities, and Employees with Disabilities

To adhere to equal employment opportunity (EEO) or affirmative action (AA) guidelines, some organizations are supporting minority recruitment, selection, and training efforts. In addition, they are beginning to provide additional feedback, educational opportunities, counseling, and career management seminars to meet the unique needs of women and minority employees. These practices are designed to help such employees compete for management positions.[112] For example, top managers at Xerox encourage the development of networks and support groups for women and minority groups (e.g., African-Americans, Hispanics). Aluminum Company of America (ALCOA) uses computer simulation games to make managers more sensitive to overt and subtle forms of discrimination against women. At Merck and at Mead Corporation, male executives participate in workshops to change their attitudes toward women and to sensitize supervisors to the needs for balancing work and family.[113] These types of programs seem to be particularly needed since the progress of women and minorities into upper management positions has been slow.[114] U.S. West, for example, found that 1 out of 21 white males reached middle management or higher positions at the Denver Communications Company, but only 1 out of 138 white women and 1 out of 289 nonwhite women attained this status. The company started a leadership development program for women. Over one-half of the female participants were ultimately promoted. Other firms (e.g., Corning, Merck, Gannett Company) have started tying managers' bonuses to their success at meeting EEO or upward mobility goals for women's progress.[115] To assist in the placement and advancement of employees with disabilities, the Department of Justice offers written material and a video on hiring and developing individuals with disabilities. Other firms (e.g., Xerox, American Express, Disney) have begun offering diversity training programs to reduce discrimination due to disability, race, gender, and age.

For women in particular, some of the larger, more progressive firms have developed programs to help women fit into the prevalent corporate cultures. In other cases, the organizations have attempted to change their own structures to better accommodate the needs of women employees and managers. Many believe that organizations will have to become more flexible in addressing issues of concern to women, especially since 67 percent of the future workforce growth is expected to come from women. Some strategies that organizations have used to assist women have included offering career planning services (e.g., personal counseling, workshops, coaching, job postings) and developmental programs (e.g., assessment centers, job rotation, additional training opportunities, formal mentoring programs). For example, Gulf Oil's program includes individual assessment, advising, and a career planning workshop. Work-family issues have been addressed through workshops which focus on work-family conflicts and through offering leave for childcare, flexible work arrangements, relaxed organizational policies on travel and transfers, childcare support, and childcare referral systems. Companies including Hewlett-Packard, Eastman Kodak, General Motors, Mellon Bank, and Aetna Life and Casualty offer flexible work arrangements such as job sharing, part-time employment, and flexitime to assist dual-career couples. At Touche Ross, mothers who want to stay on the partnership track are able to alter their workweek to 4 days to allow them time with their children. Individuals are able to negotiate the issue with their respective superiors. It takes these women 10 to 12 years to reach the partner level compared to 8 to 10 years for individuals working full time. Similarly, at Peat Marwick Mitchell, managers are allowed to take a lighter client load and less than a 40-hour workweek for up to 2 to 3 years. Pacific Bell and Mountain Bell have programs where managers can work at home on computer terminals, and at Mutual Life Insurance Company, individuals are able to work some of their hours at home. Other companies offer relaxed job transfer and travel plans or paternity and maternity leaves (e.g., Procter & Gamble, Lotus Development, General Foods, Gannett). A few firms, such as Johnson & Johnson, offer support for elder care.

One recently proposed strategy for addressing work-family conflict for women managers has been called the "mommy track." It has been argued that women managers who primarily want careers should be differentiated in organizations from women managers who want both careers and families. It has been suggested that career-primary women (i.e., women who are willing to set aside family considerations) should be treated like their male counterparts. As high-potential candidates, they should be identified early and provided with developmental opportunities to help them advance into the highest levels in the organization. Career-and-family women, on the other hand, should receive a different type of assistance so that they can eventually work in middle management positions. It has been advocated that they be helped in planning for and managing their maternity leaves, allowed flexibility in their careers (e.g., part-time work, job sharing), and helped to find high-quality childcare. Organizations would provide alternative career paths, extended leaves of absence, flexible scheduling, flexitime, job sharing, and telecommuting as options to women who select the "mommy track." In this way, organizations would be able to retain effective managers, while at the same time reducing the conflict experienced by working mothers.

Since the discussion of the "mommy track" began in 1989, it has generated considerable controversy. Some opponents contend that these views reinforce prejudices of male executives that women are not really committed to careers. They fear that male executives will have a ready excuse for denying women promotional opportunities, and will continue to believe that it is a bad investment to groom working mothers for top management jobs. In addition, they argue that the "mommy track" perpetuates the existing masculine culture where women are required to "fit in" rather than forcing the firm's culture to change. Also, the "mommy track" continues to place the burden of childcare on women, rather than on both

parents, and assumes that no women in senior management will want to have children. Opponents further argue that managerial women should not have to choose between having a career and a family, especially since men are not typically faced with that choice, and women should not have to make the decision early and then have to stay in one track for the duration of a career.[116]

Fast-Track Employees

Organizations often identify "stars" or "water-walkers," individuals with high career potential, and place them on a fast track for upward moves in the company. AT&T, for example, uses assessment centers for the early identification of managerial talent. Especially recruited and selected employees are given rapid and intensive developmental opportunities in the company.[117] The identification and development of such employees require organizations to exert extra recruitment efforts and to monitor the employees' career progress frequently. Organizations provide considerable feedback, training, and counseling, as well as offer quicker job changes and more challenging job assignments to these employees, particularly during their first few years on the job. Southland Corporation, for example, has a computerized career development program for fast-track employees that helps them to establish their career plans.[118]

Managers who are responsible for identifying and developing fast-track employees should be recognized for their efforts if they are to take their responsibilities seriously. For example, Baxter Health Care links managers' bonuses to the early identification and development of promising female employees.

Supervisors

Supervisors serve four roles with their subordinates: coach, adviser, performance appraiser, and referral agent.[119] As such, they should be taught how to help subordinates develop and implement their career plans in one-on-one counseling sessions, and should be instructed on how to integrate counseling into their performance appraisal and selection activities. AT&T has one such program in place for training supervisors in career counseling, performance appraisal skills, and mutual goal setting with subordinates.[120]

Repatriates

As we discussed in Chapter 8, an increasing number of organizations have been offering training to expatriates to prepare them for their overseas assignments. While this is important, it is also critical to offer some developmental opportunities for repatriates to prepare them for returning to the home firm after an overseas assignment. Such repatriation training is fairly commonplace in Japanese and European firms, but in most American firms it is not done. In fact, one survey revealed that only 31 percent of American companies reported any type of repatriation program for managers reentering the domestic organization.[121] This may explain why American managers who are repatriates have more difficulties in adjusting than do their Japanese and European counterparts.[122]

Most American repatriates experience considerable adjustment problems and "reentry shock" upon their return to their firm. They report having difficulty in getting back to high levels of productivity.[123] They also report feeling disoriented in relation to their communities and coworkers, and they are frustrated by their organizations' limited attempts to place them back in permanent assignments.[124] In fact, many of them complain that they have been penalized for taking international assignments since they are placed in lower-level positions than their peers when they return. This is changing dramatically as more companies now require international experience for upper management positions and greater emphasis is placed on "globalization." Most organizations still do not fully utilize the new skills and experiences that repatriates bring back to their firms. As a result, many current international assignments are not being used in as cost-effective a manner as they could be.

For a repatriate transition to be successful, several career development practices are recommended.[125] Once back at the firm, repatriates should be given opportunities to use the experiences and skills they gained from the international assignments. They should be given definite assignments, and these assignments should be clearly linked to their career paths. Mentors should be provided to help repatriates cope with the transition. If necessary, retraining and reorientation should be provided to help them learn about changes in their jobs, the department, or the organization. Finally, assistance in housing and compensation should be provided, to ease the transition. Taken together, these practices should reduce the amount of stress and disorientation experienced by repatriates as well as improve the quality and quantity of their performance. In addition, such practices may cause repatriates to become more committed and less likely to leave the firm.[126]

SUMMARY

Career development programs must be integrated with and supported by the existing HR programs in the organization if they are to be successful.[127] Career programs and HR programs are linked to the degree that they help each other meet individual and organizational needs.[128] In Figure 9.10, the interface between career development and HR planning is depicted. While these two systems are not identical, they are related to the degree that they use some of the same techniques to meet individuals' growth needs and organizations' staffing needs. The linkage with training and development programs is particularly important.

Career development programs should be supported by other HR systems in addition to HR planning. For example, individuals should refer to performance appraisal information and illustrations of organizational career paths to help them in career planning. This information may help employees to evaluate their strengths and weaknesses and to set goals based on possible career alternatives. Supervisors should also be able to use performance appraisal data to assist employees in developing realistic career plans. In Coca-Cola's career program, managers are given training to provide such guidance.[129] We will discuss the performance appraisal process in Chapter 10.

Career or job changes by employees should be based on an understanding of organizations' job descriptions, job posting systems, and selection policies. The continued development of employees and rewards for their performances should be founded on organizational training and development systems and compensation plans. Finally, organizational career information and planning systems should be developed to be consistent with organizations' strategic plans and existing forecasting systems, skills inventories, and succession plans.[130]

Coordinated, integrated efforts of the HR staff, employees, managers, and organizations are the key to success in career development. Career development programs must be concerned with organizational and individual effectiveness over the short and long run.[131] It is the responsibility of the HR staff to work with management to ensure that career programs are integrated with the HR functions and are routinely evaluated. It is, however, the responsibility of management to view career development as necessary to an effective HR system. Managers must be willing to work with HR professionals to formulate new strategies for career development and to provide support to them as they design and implement new career development programs.[132]

DISCUSSION QUESTIONS

1. Can corporations really afford to have formal career development policies and programs, given the need to be flexible in terms of staffing?

FIGURE 9.10
RELATIONSHIP BETWEEN CAREER DEVELOPMENT AND HR PLANNING

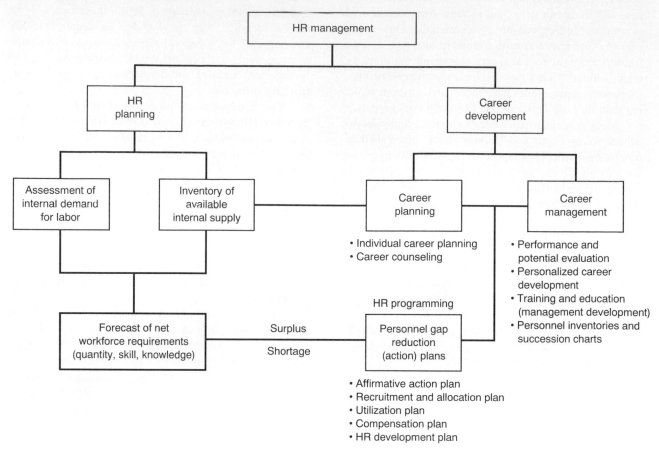

Source: T. G. Gutteridge, Organizational career development systems: The state of the practice. In D. T. Hall and associates, *Career development in organizations.* San Francisco, CA: Jossey-Bass, 1986, p. 57. Used with permission.

2. Should women be placed in special "mommy" career tracks or "managerial career" tracks depending on their work-family priorities and their career aspirations? Should similar dual-track ladders be available to male employees?

3. What is the role of EEO in career development?

4. What is the role of the HR staff in designing and implementing career development programs?

5. Describe several kinds of career development programs that are available for career planning and career management.

6. What is the value of self-assessment for individual career planning and organizational career management? Why should employees seek feedback from others regarding their self-assessment?

7. Why is it important to integrate career development programs with other HR programs (e.g., performance appraisal, training, selection, compensation)? Offer some suggestions for how this can be done.

8. Should organizations make special efforts to deal with career-family problems through part-time work, job sharing, flexitime, and other programs?

NOTES

1. Deigh, R., Rachlin, J., and Saltzman, A. (Apr. 25, 1988). How to keep from getting mired. *U.S. News and World Report,* pp. 76–77, 79–80. See also: Rachlin, J. (Apr. 25, 1988). Best jobs for the future. *U.S. News and World Report,* pp. 60–62. London, M., and Stumpf, S. A. (1986). Individual and organizational career development in changing times. In D. T. Hall and associates (eds.), *Career development in organizations.* San Francisco, CA: Jossey-Bass, pp. 21–49.

2. Osipow, S. H. (1986). Career issues through the life span. In M. S. Pallak and R. Perloff (eds.), *Psychology and work: Productivity, change, and employment.* Washington, DC: American Psychological Association,

pp. 137–168. See also: Dalton, G.W., and Thompson, P. H. (1985). *Novations: Strategies for career management.* Glenview, IL: Scott, Foresman. Mirabile, R. J. (1987). New directions for career development. *Training and Development Journal,* *41*(12), 30–33.

3. Hall, D.T. (1987). Careers and socialization. *Journal of Management, 13,* 301–321. See also: Slaney, R. B., and Russell, J. E. A. (1987). Perspectives on vocational behavior, 1986: A review. *Journal of Vocational Behavior, 31,* 111–173.

4. Leibowitz, Z. B., and Schlossberg, N. (1981). Designing career development programs in organizations. In D. H. Montross and C. J. Shinkman (eds.), *Career development in the 1980's: Theory and practice.* Springfield, IL: Charles C. Thomas, pp. 277–291. See also: Brown, D., Brooks, L., and associates (1984). *Career choice and development: Applying contemporary theories to practice.* San Francisco: Jossey-Bass. Von Glinow, M. A., Driver, M. J., Brousseau, K., and Prince, J. B. (1983). The design of a career oriented human resource system. *Academy of Management Journal, 8,* 23–32. Mirabile, R. J. (1988). Using action research to design career development programs. *Personnel, 65*(11), 4, 6, 10–11.

5. Walker, J.W., and Gutteridge, T. G. (1979). *Career planning practices: An AMA survey report.* New York: AMACOM.

6. Hall, D.T. (1976). *Careers in organizations.* Glenview, IL: Scott, Foresman.

7. See note 3.

8. Hall, D.T. (1986). Dilemmas in linking succession planning to individual executive learning. *Human Resource Management, 25,* 235–265. See also: Carnazza, J. (1982). *Succession/replacement planning: Programs and practices.* New York: Center for Research in Career Development, Columbia University Graduate School of Business.

9. See note 8.

10. Leibowitz, Z. B., Farren, C., and Kaye, B. L. (1986). *Designing career development systems.* San Francisco: Jossey-Bass. See also: Farren, C., and Kaye, B. (1984). The principles of program design: A successful career development model. *Personnel Administrator, 29,* 109–118. Granrose, C. S., and Portwood, J. D. (1987). Matching individual career plans and organizational career management. *Academy of Management Journal, 30,* 699–720.

11. Bolyard, C.W. (1981). Career development: Who's responsible in the organization. In D. H. Montross and C. J. Shinkman (eds.), *Career development in the 1980s: Theory and practice,* Springfield, IL: Charles C. Thomas, pp. 292–299.

12. Slavenski, L. (1987). Career development: A systems approach. *Training and Development Journal, 41*(2), 56–60.

13. Pazy, A. (1987). Sex differences in responsiveness to organizational career management. *Human Resource Management, 26,* 243–256.

14. See note 4, Leibowitz and Schlossberg (1981). See also: Feldman, D. C. (1988). *Managing careers in organizations.* Glenview, IL: Scott, Foresman.

15. Schein, E. H. (1978). *Career dynamics: Matching individual and organizational needs.* Reading, MA: Addison-Wesley.

16. Tichy, N., Fombrun, C., and Devanna, M. (1984). Strategic human resources management. In J. A. Sonnenfeld (ed.), *Managing career systems: Channeling the flow of executive careers.* Homewood, IL: Richard D. Irwin, pp. 303–318.

17. Gooding, G. J. (1988). Career moves—for the employee, for the organization. *Personnel, 65*(4), 112, 114, 116.

18. London, M., and Mone, E. M. (1987). *Career management and survival in the workplace.* San Francisco: Jossey-Bass. See also: Derr, C. B. (1986). *Managing the new careerists.* San Francisco: Jossey-Boss.

19. Minor, F. J. (1986). Computer applications in career development planning. In D.T. Hall and associates (eds.), *Career development in organizations.* San Francisco: Jossey-Bass, pp. 202–235.

20. Hall, D. T., and Goodale, J. G. (1986). *Human resource management: Strategy, design, and implementation.* Glenview, IL: Scott, Foresman. See also: Souerwine, A. H. (1981). The manager as career counselor: Some issues and approaches. In D. H. Montross and C. J. Shinkman (eds.), *Career development in the 1980's: Theory and practice.* Springfield, IL: Charles C. Thomas, pp. 363–378.

21. See note 12.

22. Greenhaus, J. H. (1987). *Career management.* New York: Dryden Press. See also: Brooks, J. L., and Seers, A. (1991). Predictors of organizational commitment: Variations across career stages. *Journal of Vocational Behavior, 38,* 53–64.

23. Betz, N. E., and Fitzgerald, L. F. (1987). *The career psychology of women.* Orlando, FL: Academic Press. See also: Gutek, B. A., and Larwood, L. (eds.) (1987). *Women's career development.* Newbury Park, CA: Sage. Larwood, L., Stromberg, A. H., and Gutek, B. A. (eds.) (1985). *Women and work: An annual review,* vol. 1. Beverly Hills, CA: Sage. Russell, J. E. A. (in press). Career counseling for women in management. In W. B. Walsh and S. H. Osipow (eds.), *Career counseling for women.* Hillsdale, NJ: Lawrence Erlbaum.

24. Levinson, D. J. (1986). A conception of adult development. *American Psychologist, 41,* 3–13. See also: Vondracek, F.W., Lerner, R. M., and Schulenberg, J. E. (1986). *Career development: A life-span developmental approach.* Hillsdale, NJ: Lawrence Erlbaum.

25. Hall, D.T., and associates (1986). *Career development in organizations.* San Francisco, CA: Jossey-Bass.

26. See note 22, Greenhaus (1987).

27. See note 22, Greenhaus (1987).

28. Cascio, W. F. (1992). *Managing human resources: Productivity, quality of work life, profits.* (3d ed.) New York: McGraw-Hill. See also: Whitely, W., Dougherty, T.W., and Drcher, G. F. (1991). Relationship of career

mentoring and socioeconomic origin to managers' and professionals' early career progress. *Academy of Management Journal, 34*(2), 331–351.

29. See note 22, Greenhaus (1987).
30. See note 14, Feldman (1988).
31. Kotter, J. P., Faux, V. A., and McArthur, C. (1978). *Self-assessment and career development.* Englewood Cliffs, NJ: Prentice-Hall. See also: note 15, Schein (1978).
32. See notes 15, 31.
33. See note 6.
34. See note 14, Feldman (1988).
35. McCaffrey, W. T. (1981). Career growth versus upward mobility. *Personnel Administrator, 26*(5), 81–87. See also: Hall, D. T., and Isabella, L. (1985). Downward moves and career development. *Organizational Dynamics, 14*, 5–23. Kaye, B. (1982). *Up is not the only way: A guide for career development practitioners.* Englewood Cliffs, NJ: Prentice-Hall.
36. Courtney, R. S. (1986). A human resources program that helps management and employees prepare for the future. *Personnel, 63*(5), 32–40.
37. Gottschalk, E. C., Jr. (Oct. 22, 1981). Blocked paths: Promotions grow few as "baby boom" group eyes managers' jobs. *The Wall Street Journal,* pp. 1, 16.
38. Leana, C. R., and Feldman, D. C. (1986). *Job loss: Perception, reactions, and coping behaviors.* Paper presented at the national meeting of the Academy of Management, Chicago, IL. See also: note 14, Feldman (1988).
39. Dalton, G. W., Thompson, P. H., and Price, R. L. (1977). The four stages of professional careers: A new look at performance by professionals. *Organizational Dynamics, 6*, 19–42.
40. See note 22, Greenhaus (1987).
41. Bird, C. P., and Fisher, T. D. (1986). Thirty years later: Attitudes toward the employment of older workers. *Journal of Applied Psychology, 71*, 515–517. See also: Rosen, B., and Jerdee, T. H. (1985). *Older employees: New roles for valued resources.* Homewood, IL: Dow Jones-Irwin. Doering, M., Rhodes, S. R., and Schuster, M. (1983). *The aging worker.* Beverly Hills, CA: Sage Publications. Kite, M. E., Deaux, K., and Miele, M. (1991). Stereotypes of young and old: Does age outweigh gender? *Psychology and Aging, 6*(1), 19–27.
42. See note 14, Feldman (1988).
43. See note 15.
44. See note 22. See also: Fletcher, W. L., and Hansson, R. O. (1991). Assessing the social components of retirement anxiety. *Psychology and Aging, 6*(1),. 76–85.
45. See note 22, Greenhaus (1987); note 14, Feldman (1988). See also: Herzog, A. R., House, J. S., and Morgan, J. N. (1991). Relations of work and retirement to health and well-being in older age. *Psychology and Aging, 6*(2), 202–211.
46. See note 28, Cascio (1989).
47. See note 14, Feldman (1988).
48. See note 15.
49. See note 17.
50. See note 14, Feldman (1988).
51. See notes 18, 22, Greenhaus (1987).
52. Nusbaum, H. J. (1986). The career development program at Du Pont's Pioneering Research Laboratory. *Personnel, 63*(9), 68–75.
53. See note 17.
54. Gutteridge, T. G. (1986). Organizational career development systems: The state of the practice. In D. T. Hall and associates (eds.), *Career development in organizations.* San Francisco, CA: Jossey-Bass, pp. 50–94. See also: note 10, Leibowitz, Farren, and Kaye (1986).
55. See note 10, Leibowitz, Farren, and Kaye (1986).
56. See note 10, Leibowitz, Farren, and Kaye (1986).
57. See note 8, Hall (1986).
58. See note 10, Leibowitz, Farren, and Kaye (1986). See also: Williamson, B. A., and Otte, F. L. (1986). Assessing the need for career development. *Training and Development Journal, 40*(3), 59–61.
59. See note 14, Feldman (1988).
60. See note 10, Leibowitz, Farren, and Kaye (1986). See also: Leibowitz, Z. B., Kaye, B., and Farren, C. (1986). Overcoming management resistance to career development programs. *Training and Development Journal, 40*(10), 77–81.
61. See note 14, Feldman (1988). See also: Souerwine, A. H. (1981). Career planning: Getting started with top management support. In D. H. Montross and C. J. Shinkman (eds.), *Career development in the 1980's: Theory and practice.* Springfield, IL: Charles C. Thomas, pp. 300–311.
62. Keller, J., and Piotrowski, C. (1987). Career development programs in Fortune 500 firms. *Psychological Reports, 61*(3), 920–922.
63. Bardsley, C. A. (1987). Improving employee awareness of opportunity at IBM. *Personnel, 64*(4), 58–63.
64. See note 52.
65. See note 10, Leibowitz, Farren, and Kaye (1986).
66. Russell, J. E. A. (1991). Career development interventions in organizations. *Journal of Vocational Behavior, 38*, 237–287. See also: note 54, Gutteridge (1986). Meier, S. T. (1991). Vocational behavior 1988–1990: Vocational choice, decision-making, career development interventions, and assessment. *Journal of Vocational Behavior, 39*, 131–181.
67. Gutteridge, T. G., and Otte, F. L. (1983). *Organizational career development: State of the practice.* Washington, DC: ASTD press.
68. See note 22, Greenhaus (1987); note 10, Leibowitz, Farren, and Kaye (1986); note 14, Feldman (1988).
69. Wilhelm, W. R. (1983). Helping workers to self-manage their careers. *Personnel Administrator, 28*(8), 83–89.
70. Scarpello, V. G., and Ledvinka, J. (1988). *Personnel/ human resource management: Environments and functions.* Boston, MA: PWS-Kent.
71. Jackson, T., and Vitberg, A. (1987). Career development, part 2: Challenges for the organization. *Personnel, 64*(3), 68–72.
72. See note 20, Hall and Goodale (1986).

73. See note 70.

74. Bolles, R. N. (1988). *What color is your parachute?* Berkeley, CA: Ten Speed.

75. See note 20, Hall and Goodale (1986).

76. Burack, E. H., and Mathys, N. J. (1980). *Career management in organizations: A practical human resource planning approach.* Lake Forest, IL: Brace-Park.

77. See note 5, Walker and Gutteridge (1979).

78. See note 20, Hall and Goodale (1986).

79. See notes 18, 5.

80. Phillips, J. J. (1986). Four practical approaches to supervisors' career development. *Personnel, 63*(3), 13–15.

81. Milkovich, G. T., and Boudreau, J. W. (1988). *Personnel/human resource management.* Plano, TX: Business Publications.

82. Sherman, A. W., Bohlander, G. W., and Chruden, H. J. (1988). *Managing human resources.* Cincinnati, OH: South-Western Publishing. See also: note 81.

83. Dowd, J. J., and Sonnenfeld, J. A. (1984). A note on career programs in industry. In J. A. Sonnenfeld (ed.), *Managing career systems: Channeling the flow of executive careers.* Homewood, IL: Richard D. Irwin, pp. 318–328.

84. See note 80.

85. See note 71.

86. See note 22, Greenhaus (1987).

87. Wanous, J. P. (1980). *Organizational entry: Recruitment, selection, and socialization of newcomers.* Reading, MA: Addison-Wesley.

88. See note 18, London and Mone (1987).

89. See note 83.

90. See note 14, Feldman (1988).

91. See note 81.

92. See note 70.

93. See note 70.

94. See note 8, Hall (1986). See also: Smith, M., and White, M. C. (1987). Strategy, CEO specialization, and succession. *Administrative Science Quarterly, 32,* 263–280. Sorcher, M. (1985). *Predicting executive success: What it takes to make it into senior management.* New York: John Wiley & Sons. Friedman, S. D., and Saul, K. (1991). A leader's wake: Organization member reactions to CEO succession. *Journal of Management, 17*(3), 619–642.

95. See note 52.

96. Gaertner, K. N. (1988). Managers' careers and organizational change. *Academy of Management Executive, 11,* 311–318.

97. Fenwick-Magrath, J. A. (1988). Executive development: Key factors for success. *Personnel, 65*(7), 68–72. See also: Friedman, S. D. (1986). Succession systems in large corporations: Characteristics and correlates of performance. *Human Resource Management, 25,* 191–213. Mahler, W. R. (1987). Executive development. In R. L. Craig (ed.), *Training and development handbook: A guide to human resource development,* 3d ed. New York: McGraw-Hill, pp. 564–579. Mahler, W. R., and Gaines, F. (1983). *Succession planning in leading companies.* Midland Park, NJ: Mahler Publishing.

98. See note 8, Hall (1986).

99. See note 17.

100. Kram, K. E. (1986). Mentoring in the workplace. In D. T. Hall (ed.), *Career development in organizations,* San Francisco, Jossey-Bass, pp. 160–201. See also: Kram, K. E. (1985). *Mentoring at work.* Glenwood: IL: Scott, Foresman. Kram, K. E., and Isabella, L. (1985). Mentoring alternatives: The role of peer relationships in career development. *Academy of Management Journal, 28,* 110–132.

101. See note 3, Hall (1987).

102. Odiorne, G. S. (1985). Mentoring—An American management innovation. *Personnel Administrator, 30*(5), 63–70.

103. Cook, M. F. (1987). *New directions in human resources: A handbook.* Englewood Cliffs, NJ: Prentice-Hall. See also: Hall, D. T., and Richter, J. (1988). Balancing work life and home life: What can organizations do to help? *Academy of Management Executive, 11,* 213–223.

104. See note 22, Greenhaus (1987). See also: Lobel, S. A. (1991). Allocation of investment in work and family roles: Alternative theories and implications for research. *Academy of Management Review, 16*(3), 507–521.

105. See note 103, Hall and Richter (1988). See also: Latack, J. C. (1984). Career transitions within organizations: An exploratory study of work, nonwork, and coping strategies. *Organizational Behavior and Human Performance, 34,* 296–322.

106. Sekaran, U. (1986). *Dual-career families.* San Francisco, CA: Jossey-Bass. See also: note 8, Hall (1986).

107. Mathis, R. L., and Jackson, J. H. (1988). *Personnel/human resource management.* St. Paul, MN: West.

108. See note 107.

109. See note 22, Greenhaus (1987).

110. See note 103, Cook (1987).

111. See note 17.

112. See note 11, Bolyard (1981); note 14, Feldman (1988); note 5. See also: Ragins, B. R., and Cotton, J. L. (1991). Easier said than done: Gender differences in perceived barriers to gaining a mentor. *Academy of Management Journal, 34*(14), 939–951. Swanson, J. L., and Tokar, D. M. (1991). Development and initial validation of the career barriers inventory. *Journal of Vocational Behavior, 39,* 344–361.

113. Hymowitz, C. (Nov. 15, 1983). Tradition-bound ALCOA develops training to challenge concerns of old-boy network. *The Wall Street Journal,* p. 37. See also: Kanter, R. M. (1977). *Men and women of the corporation.* New York: Basic Books. See note 23, Russell (in press).

114. See note 3, Hall (1987). Cox, T. H., and Harquail, C. V. (1991). Career paths and career success in the early career stages of male and female MBAs. *Journal of Vocational Behavior, 39,* 54–75.

115. Trost (Nov. 22, 1989). New approach forced by shifts in population. *Wall Street Journal,* pp. B1, B4. See also: Pave, I. (June 23, 1986). A woman's place is at GE, Federal Express, P&G . . . *Business Week,* pp. 75–76.

116. See note 23, Russell (in press). See also: Schwartz, F. N. (1989). Management women and the new facts of life. *Harvard Business Review, 67*(1), 65–76. Taylor, A. (Aug. 18, 1986). Why women managers are bailing out. *Fortune,* pp. 16–23. Zeitz, B., and Dusky, L. (1988). *The best companies for women.* New York, NY: Simon & Schuster, Williams, M. J. (Sept. 12, 1988). Women beat the corporate game. *Fortune,* pp. 128–138. Deutsch, C. H. (Jan. 28, 1990). Saying no to the mommy track. *The New York Times,* F29.

117. See note 83. See also: Thompson, P., Kirkham, K., and Dixon, J. (1985). Warning: The fast track may be hazardous to organizational health. *Organizational Dynamics, 13,* 21–33.

118. See note 14, Feldman (1988).

119. See note 10.

120. Miller, D. B. (1978). Career planning and management in organizations. In M. Jelinek (ed.), *Career management for the individual and the organization,* Chicago: St. Clair Press, pp. 353–360.

121. Harvey, M. G. (1989). Repatriation of corporate executives: An empirical study. *Journal of International Business Studies, 20,* 131–144.

122. Tung, R. L. (1988). The new expatriate. Cambridge, MA: Ballinger. See also: Murray, F. T., and Murray, A. H. (1986). SMR Forum: Global managers for global businesses. *Sloan Management Review, 27,* 75–80.

123. Feldman, D. C. (1991). Repatriate moves as career transitions. *Human Resource Management Review, 1*(3), 163–178.

124. See note 121.

125. See note 123.

126. See note 123. See also: Gregersen, H. B. (1992). Commitments to a parent company and a local work unit during repatriation. *Personnel Psychology, 45*(1), 29–54.

127. See note 4, Glinow, Driver, Brousseau, and Prince (1983).

128. See note 22, Greenhaus (1987).

129. See note 12.

130. See note 10, Leibowitz, Farren, and Kaye (1986).

131. See note 15.

132. See note 3, Hall (1987); note 8, Hall (1986).

EXERCISE 9.1
*ATTITUDES ABOUT OLDER PEOPLE**

OVERVIEW

As noted throughout this book, the workforce is aging. This is due primarily to three factors: (1) the increasing life expectancy of individuals; (2) the aging of the large number of baby-boomers; and (3) the decline in birth rates over the past two decades. The aging of the workforce raises the issue of how individuals view older adults and older employees. That is, what stereotypes do they have about older adults, and what are the consequences of these views for older workers? The purpose of this exercise is to assist you in understanding your own views about older workers.

LEARNING OBJECTIVES

After completing this exercise, you should be able to:

1. Be aware of the facts of aging.
2. Understand your own views and perceptions of older individuals.

---

*Contributed by Barbara Hassell.

3. Understand how stereotypes about older individuals may influence individuals' behavior toward them in the workplace.

PROCEDURE

Part A: Individual Analysis

Step 1. Complete Form 9.1.1. Bring your responses to class to be scored.

Step 2. Score your responses in class.

Part B: Group Analysis

Step 1. As a class, address the issues associated with each item on the questionnaire.

Step 2. Address the following questions:
  a. To what extent did the class possess erroneous facts about aging workers?
  b. Why did they possess these inaccurate pictures about older adults?
  c. What are the consequences of stereotypes of older adults for the workplace?
  d. What recommendations would you make for correcting these stereotypes in the workplace? What type of training programs do you recommend and how would you evaluate them?

Name _____ Group _____

Directions: For each item, respond by answering **true** or **false** in the space provided on the left. Be candid in choosing the response that best tells what you believe.

_____ 1. The majority of older people (past age 65) are senile (i.e., have defective memories, are disoriented or demented).

_____ 2. All five senses tend to decline in old age.

_____ 3. Most older people have no interest in, or capacity for, sexual relations.

_____ 4. Lung capacity tends to decline in old age.

_____ 5. The majority of older people feel miserable most of the time.

_____ 6. Physical strength tends to decline in old age.

_____ 7. At least one-tenth of the aged are living in long-stay institutions (i.e., nursing homes, mental hospitals).

_____ 8. Aged drivers have fewer accidents per person than drivers under 65.

_____ 9. Most older workers cannot work as effectively as younger workers.

_____ 10. About 80 percent of the aged are healthy enough to carry out their normal activities.

_____ 11. Most older people are set in their ways and unable to change.

_____ 12. Older people usually take longer to learn something new.

_____ 13. It is almost impossible for most older people to learn new things.

_____ 14. The reaction time of most older people tends to be slower than the reaction time of younger people.

_____ 15. In general, most older people are pretty much alike.

_____ 16. The majority of older people are seldom bored.

_____ 17. The majority of older people are socially isolated and lonely.

_____ 18. Older workers have fewer accidents than younger workers.

_____ 19. Over 20 percent of the U.S. population are now age 65 or over.

_____ 20. Most medical practitioners tend to give low priority to the aged.

_____ 21. The majority of older people have incomes below the poverty level (as defined by the federal government).

_____ 22. The majority of older people are working or would like to have some kind of work to do (including housework and volunteer work).

_____ 23. People tend to become more religious as they age.

_____ 24. The majority of older people are seldom irritated or angry.

_____ 25. The health and socioeconomic status of older people (compared to younger people) in the year 2000 will probably be the same as now.

Source: E. Palmore (1977). Facts on aging. *The Gerontologist, 17,* p. 315. Used with permission.

EXERCISE 9.2
CAREER DEVELOPMENT
SELF-ASSESSMENT EXERCISE

OVERVIEW

Most career development programs in organizations use self-assessment exercises. In fact, these exercises may be the first activities employees participate in that help them to better understand their personal career interests and goals. Self-appraisal is important for enhancing self-awareness. It generally requires the collection of data about yourself, such as your values, interests, and skills, and the determination of goals and action plans for life and career planning. As an employee you might want to engage in a self-assessment exercise for career planning purposes. As a HR professional, you might be asked to develop a self-assessment exercise to use with employees for career planning purposes. Examples of some of the possible activities that may be included in a self-assessment exercise are included in this exercise.

LEARNING OBJECTIVES

After completing this exercise, you should be able to:

1. Understand your own values, skills, interests, experiences, and life and career preferences.
2. Be able to describe your immediate goals, the associated benefits and risks, and the skills you may need to develop to meet your goals.
3. Understand some of your own work attitudes and preferences and the issues associated with making career decisions and changes.
4. Be able to describe some of the activities used in a self-assessment exercise.

PROCEDURE

Part A: Individual Analysis

Step 1. Complete the self-assessment exercise in Form 9.2.1 prior to coming to class. Be as candid as possible in your responses.

Step 2. Each individual should answer the assessment questions listed in Form 9.2.2.

Part B: Group Analysis

As a class, address the following issues:

1. Discuss the importance of using a self-assessment as a career planning tool. Describe how a self-assessment may be beneficial for individual growth and development as well as for organizational HR purposes (e.g., staffing, training).
2. Explain how you might use a self-assessment tool as part of a career development system you design for an organization.

FORM 9.2.1
CAREER SELF-ASSESSMENT INSTRUMENT

Name_____

Part A: Values and Experiences

1. Describe the roles in your life that are important to you. Examples might include your work or career, family life, leisure, religious life, community life, and volunteer activities. Explain why these roles are important to you. Indicate how important each role is to your total life satisfaction. Assign a percent to each role (0 to 100 percent) so that the total adds up to 100 percent.

2. Describe your background and experiences, including:

    a. <u>Education</u>. List the names of technical schools or colleges you have attended. List degrees earned or to be earned, and your major or minor.

    b. <u>Work experience</u>. List any jobs you have held, including part- and full-time jobs, voluntary jobs, internships, and cooperative education (co-ops).

    c. <u>Skills</u>. Describe any skills that you possess that you feel would be valued in the workplace.

    d. <u>Extracurricular activities.</u> Describe any nonwork activities that you engage in for personal development or recreational pursuits.

    e. <u>Accomplishments.</u> Summarize any recognition you have received that is related to your education, work experience, skills, or extracurricular activities.

3. Read the following list of skills. Put a + next to those you feel you are particularly strong in, and circle those you would like to develop more thoroughly in the future.

    Communication (written or oral communication, listening skills)

    Management skills (supervising, persuading others, planning, organizing, delegating, motivating others)

    Interpersonal skills (working effectively with others)

    Team building (working effectively with groups or teams)

    Creativity (innovativeness, generating ideas)

    Training skills (ability to teach skills and knowledges to others)

    Mathematical skills (computation ability, budgeting, accounting proficiency)

    Sales/promotion (ability to persuade, negotiate, influence)

    Scientific skills (investigative abilities, researching, analyzing)

    Service skills (handling complaints, customer relations)

    Office skills (word processing, filing, bookkeeping, record keeping)

4. Rate yourself on each of the following personal qualities or work characteristics. Write one response for each characteristic, using the following scale: 1, very low; 2, low; 3, average; 4, high; 5, very high.

    _____ Emotional maturity   _____ Dependability in completing work

    _____ Initiative/independence   _____ Flexibility and open-mindedness

    _____ Punctuality   _____ Perseverance/willingness to work

    _____ Ability to handle conflict   _____ Ability to set and achieve goals

    _____ Ability to plan, organize, and determine work priorities

FORM 9.2.1 *(Continued)*

Part B: Work Attitudes and Preferences

1. Describe an ideal job for you. What would it be like? Describe the activities, people, rewards, and other features that would be a part of your job experience.

2. Think about the ideal job you described above. Rank the following values in terms of how important they are for you in your work (1, most important; 11, least important).

Values or Conditions	Rank
Independence or autonomy	_____
Financial reward or affluence	_____
Sense of achievement or accomplishment	_____
Helping others	_____
Creating something	_____
Equality, fairness	_____
Loyalty	_____
Job security	_____
Pleasant working conditions	_____
Friendships at work	_____
Variety of tasks	_____

3. What talents do you wish to use in your work?

4. What type of working relationships with other people do you prefer? That is, do you prefer working alone or with other people? Do you enjoy working with a few people you know well, or helping people you don't know?

5. What type of physical work setting is desirable to you (e.g., office, outdoors, plant)?

6. How much freedom and independence do you want in your work? For example, do you want to set your own hours? Determine your own projects to work on?

7. Think of one time when you felt like a real professional. What were you doing or what had you just done? Why was this achievement meaningful?

Part C: Goals and Action Planning

1. Describe your career goals for the next several years.

2. What specific things will you need to do to meet your goals?

3. What internal and external obstacles might you encounter along the way toward achievement of your goals?

4. Describe any skills or assistance you will need to meet your goals.

5. How much commitment do you have to your goals? Explain.

Form 9.2.2
Assessment Questions

1. What did you learn about yourself that you did not realize before?

2. How important is your career and work in your total life? Why is this important to realize?

3. How can completing a self-assessment assist you in preparing a résumé or interviewing for a job?

4. What will you do to follow up on this self-assessment?

10

C H A P T E R

PERFORMANCE APPRAISAL*

*Contributed by Jeffrey S. Kane and Kimberly F. Kane.

OVERVIEW

While we have discussed the importance of performance appraisal in several previous chapters, appraisal is nonetheless regarded as one of the most troubling areas of human resource management (HRM).[1] More than 95 percent of organizations report the use of formal systems of appraisal,[2] but the majority of those involved in this activity express considerable dissatisfaction with it. This includes not only the people who conduct appraisals but the people who are evaluated and the administrators of the programs as well. As one manager from Digital Equipment Corporation put it, "I'd rather kick bricks with my bare feet than do appraisals!" Appraisal systems are rarely able to deliver all their intended benefits to employers or employees.[3] In fact, several surveys have revealed widespread dissatisfaction in relatively large organizations (e.g., Fortune 500 companies) which presumably have the resources to acquire the best appraisal technology available.[4] For example, one survey found that a majority of respondents—51 percent—reported that their systems were only slightly effective and that they had numerous problems with appraisals (e.g., inadequate performance standards, weak linkage between the appraisal systems and personnel decisions, intentional rating inflation to avoid confrontations with poorly performing employees).[5] Surveys of small and medium-sized companies report even more dissatisfaction.

Organizations are constantly searching for better ways to appraise performance. Pratt and Whitney (P&W), the jet engine division of United Technologies, made significant changes in its appraisal system in 2 consecutive years only to abandon the system for a completely different approach the very next year. Blockbuster Video has revised its appraisal system for 3 consecutive years. The state of Florida installed a teacher evaluation system in 1984 and abandoned it in 1986 due to widespread discontent. Even International Business Machines (IBM) had to install a new system as part of a major downsizing effort because its old, highly regarded performance appraisal system resulted in such lenient ratings that few performance distinctions could be made among the workers and little evidence indicated that there were any unproductive workers. Ten percent of Big Blue's workforce received "below satisfactory" appraisals under the new system in 1992—the first step to termination.

Dissatisfaction with performance appraisal systems has existed for many years, but organizations can no longer afford to live with poor appraisal systems. The reasons why the needed improvements in performance appraisal effectiveness cannot be put off any longer can be found in three of the trends we first discussed in Chapter 1. Let us briefly review them here. First, there is a continued lack of growth in U.S. productivity, while the growth of many of the country's international competitors continues to increase.[6] The reversal of this trend can be at least partly achieved by focusing on improvements in employee productivity. One of the primary strategies for enhancing human productivity is performance management, and the very foundation of performance management is performance appraisal. In the previous chapters, we discussed the role of performance measurement in the evaluation and improvement of personnel selection systems, training systems, and career development programs. The identification and measurement of critical performance criteria are vital for improving an organization's competitive advantage through better products and services and greater responsiveness to customer requirements.

A second trend is the increasing role that performance plays in litigation today. In fact, performance appraisal is the most heavily litigated personnel practice today.[7] As we discussed in Chapter 3, legal grounds for challenging appraisal systems are expanding, and litigation can thus be expected to increase. Two recently enacted laws, the Civil Rights Act of 1991 and the 1990 Americans with Disabilities Act (ADA), are examples of federal laws which will surely generate a plethora of litigation related to performance appraisal. There has also been a dramatic increase in the number of lawsuits claiming "unlawful termination," the focus of which is often on the process of performance appraisal.

The third major trend is the growing diversity of the workforce. With greater proportions of women, members of minority groups, and older workers in the labor force, unfairness and biases already present in appraisal systems, either real or perceived, may be magnified by greater diversity and differences between raters and ratees. Consequently, organizations will need to be increasingly scrupulous in encouraging fairness and objectivity in appraisal practices and personnel decisions.[8]

The overall objective of this chapter is to provide recommendations for improving the effectiveness of performance appraisals in organizations. This includes enhancing the development, implementation, and evaluation of appraisal systems.

OBJECTIVES

After reading this chapter, you should be able to:

1. Understand the value and uses of performance appraisals in organizations.
2. Be able to describe legal issues associated with performance appraisals.
3. Be able to describe the decisions necessary in designing an appraisal system (e.g., content, process, raters, ratees, administrative issues).

4. Be able to explain the steps to follow in developing an appraisal system.
5. Be able to describe the necessary steps for implementing an appraisal system.
6. Understand how to evaluate the effectiveness of an appraisal system.

DEFINING PERFORMANCE

Despite the importance of performance appraisal, few organizations clearly define what they are trying to measure. In order to design a system for appraising performance, it is important to first define what is meant by the term "work performance." Although a person's job performance depends on some combination of ability, effort, and opportunity, it can be measured in terms of outcomes or results produced. *Performance* is defined as the *record of outcomes* produced on a *specified job function* or activity during a *specified time period*. For example, a trainer working for the World Bank was evaluated on her "organization of presentations," which was defined as "the presentation of training material in a logical and methodical order." The extent to which she was able to make such "orderly" presentations would be one measure of outcomes related to that function. Obviously a sales representative would have some measure of sales as an outcome for a primary function of that job. Customer service is a likely candidate as another important function which would have very different outcome measures for defining "performance." College professors are typically evaluated on three general work functions: teaching, research, and service. Performance in each of these three areas is defined by one or more different outcome measures.

Performance on a job as a whole is equal to the sum (or average) of performances on the job functions or activities. For example, the World Bank identified eight job functions for its trainers (e.g., use of relevant examples, participant involvement, evaluation procedures). The functions have to do with the work which is performed and *not* with the characteristics of the person performing. Unfortunately, many performance appraisal systems confuse measures of performance with measures of the person. We emphasize that the definition of performance refers to a set of outcomes produced during a certain period of time, and does not refer to traits or personal characteristics of the performer.[9]

USES OF PERFORMANCE APPRAISAL

The information collected from performance appraisals is most often used for compensation, performance improvement or management, feedback, and documentation. Figure 10.1 illustrates the primary uses of performance appraisal according to a 1987 survey taken in small and large organizations.[10] As we discussed in previous chapters, appraisal data are also used for staffing decisions (e.g., promotion, transfer, discharge, layoffs), training needs analysis, employee development, and research and evaluation. Several of these uses are described below.

Performance Management and Compensation

Performance appraisal information may be used by supervisors to manage the performance of their employees. Appraisal data can reveal employees' performance weaknesses, which managers can refer to when setting goals or target levels for improvements. Performance management programs may be focused on one or more of the following organizational levels: individual performers, work groups or organizational subunits, or the entire organization.

To motivate employees to improve their performance and achieve their target goals, supervisors can use incentives such as pay-for-performance programs (e.g., merit pay, incentives, bonus awards). As we mentioned in Chapter 1, one of the strongest HRM trends in this country is toward some form of pay-for-performance system. Many firms, including Westinghouse Electric Corp., Amoco, and Reading & Bates, have recently installed appraisal systems which link performance with pay.[11] Obviously, effective performance measurement is necessary for these systems to work. Under IBM's new appraisal system, those identified as "superstars" can earn up to $50,000 bonuses for their performance. The trend toward pay for performance is so significant that we have devoted an entire chapter to it (Chapter 12).

Internal Staffing

Performance appraisal information is also used to make staffing decisions. These decisions involve finding employees to fill positions in the organization or reducing the numbers of employees in certain positions. Many organizations rely on performance appraisal data to decide which employees to move upward (promote) to fill openings and which employees to retain as a part of a downsizing effort.

One problem with relying on performance appraisal information in making decisions about job movements is that employee performance is measured only for the *current* job. If the job at the higher, lateral, or lower level is different from the employee's current job, it may be difficult to estimate how the employee will perform on the new job. Consequently, organizations have resorted to using assessment procedures in addition to appraisal data

FIGURE 10.1
PRIMARY USES OF PERFORMANCE APPRAISAL DATA

USE	SMALL FIRMS	LARGE FIRMS	TOTAL
Compensation	80.2	66.7	74.9
Performance improvement	46.3	53.3	48.4
Feedback	40.3	40.6	40.4
Documentation	29.0	32.2	30.2
Promotion*	26.1	22.8	24.8
Training	5.1	9.4	7.3
Transfer*	8.1	6.1	7.3
Discharge*	4.9	6.7	5.6
Layoffs*	2.1	2.8	2.4
Personnel research	1.8	2.8	2.2
Manpower planning*	0.7	2.8	1.5

*Staffing decision.
Source: A. H. Locher and K. S. Teel, Assessment: Appraisal trends. *Personnel Journal, 67*(9), 1988, p. 140. Reprinted with permission.

to make staffing decisions. These assessment methods include those described in Chapters 6 and 7, such as assessment centers, work samples, and structured interviews. Unfortunately, assessment methods have the drawback of indicating only how employees will perform when peak performance is demanded and not how they will perform on a typical basis.[12] As we discussed in Chapter 5, most companies focus on internal recruiting for placement at supervisory and managerial levels. Despite problems, performance appraisal still plays a major role in the process of moving people through the organization.

Many companies use performance appraisal data in making decisions about reducing the workforce. In most private-sector firms, appraisal information and job needs are the only data used to determine which employees to lay off or terminate, while in unionized companies, seniority is the primary basis for making reduction-in-force (RIF) decisions. In agencies of the federal government, RIF decisions must be made by applying equal weight to performance and length of employment (i.e., seniority).

At least 23 states now have provisions which may require terminations to be based on "just cause." Montana now requires that there be a "just reason" to fire a worker.[13] If an appraisal system can be shown to be biased, unreliable, or inaccurate, RIF decisions based on it may not be defensible in several states. Moreover, when RIFs are based on comparisons of appraisal scores for people in different jobs, the organization must be prepared to defend the comparability of scores across jobs.

Training Needs Analysis

In one survey, nearly 90 percent of respondents indicated that their firms use appraisal data to determine employees' needs for training. For example, Northern Telecom, Inc., uses appraisal data with exempt employees to de-

termine training needs and career paths for individual employees.[14] RCA, 3M Company, Honeywell, IBM, Continental Bank, and the Federal Aviation Administration (FAA) are among a growing number of organizations which ask subordinates to evaluate their supervisors or managers. The results are revealed to each manager with suggestions for specific remedial action (if needed). Honeywell, for example, has specific training modules based on appraisal ratings for several job functions. Carnival Cruise Lines monitors customer service representative calls to determine specific training needs related to customer requirements.

Research and Evaluation

Appraisal data can also be used to determine whether various human resource (HR) programs (e.g., selection, training) are effective. For example, when Weyerhauser wanted to assess the effects of its managerial training program, it gathered on-the-job performance data on the specific areas which had been the objectives of the training. When Toledo, Ohio, wanted to know whether its police officer selection test was valid, it collected performance appraisal data on officers who had taken the test when they were hired so that test scores could be correlated with their job performance. When London House, the Chicago-based test publisher, attempted to establish the validity of its employee integrity test, it developed a specially designed appraisal form to assess counterproductive behavior in services.

LEGAL ISSUES ASSOCIATED WITH PERFORMANCE APPRAISALS

Since performance appraisal data is used to make many important personnel decisions (e.g., pay, promotion, selection, termination), it is understandable that it is a major target of legal disputes involving employee charges of unfairness and bias.[15] There are several legal avenues a person may pursue to obtain relief from discriminatory performance appraisals. As discussed in Chapter 3, the most widely used federal laws are Title VII of the 1964 Civil Rights Act and the Age Discrimination in Employment Act (ADEA). Exceptions to the employment-at-will doctrine often involve performance appraisals as well. One theory accepted in some states as an exception to employment-at-will is known as "implied covenant of good faith." This theory essentially states that termination without cause is unacceptable after an employee has established a long record of acceptable (or better) performance with an organization. Betty Benninger worked for the AAA Motor Club for over 15 years, and in each of those years, her performance was judged to be at a very high level. After she was dismissed, she filed a wrongful termination suit, espousing the implied covenant of good faith theory. In the state of Michigan, this theory was accepted and Ms. Benninger prevailed. Obviously, performance appraisal data played a vital role in this litigation.

"Termination for cause only" is the most common policy on the international scene. Thus, decisions to terminate either employees who have overseas assignments or employees who are from the host country or another country must usually be based on performance and not on employment at will. The "termination for cause only" policy puts even greater pressure on multinational corporations to have effective performance appraisal systems.

Below are several recommendations to assist employers in conducting fair performance appraisals and avoiding legal suits. Gleaned from case law, these recommendations are intended as prescriptive measures that employers should take to develop fair and legally defensible performance appraisal systems.[16] Since case law and court rulings are continually updated, this is not a guaranteed "defense-proof" list, but rather constitutes sound personnel practices that protect the rights of both employers and employees.

1. Legally defensible appraisal *procedures:*
   a. Personnel decisions should be based on a formal, standardized performance appraisal system.
   b. Performance appraisal processes should be uniform for all employees within a job group, and decisions based on those performance appraisals should be monitored for differences according to the race, sex, national origin, religion, disability, or age of employees. While obtained differences as a function of any of these variables are not necessarily illegal, an organization will have more difficulty in defending an appraisal system with ratings related to these variables.
   c. Specific performance standards should be formally communicated to employees.
   d. Employees should be able to formally review the appraisal results.
   e. There should be a formal appeal process through which ratees can rebut raters' judgments.
   f. Raters should be provided with written instructions or training on how to conduct appraisals properly to facilitate systematic, unbiased appraisals.
   g. Personnel decision makers should be informed of antidiscrimination laws and made aware of legal and illegal activity regarding decisions based on appraisals.

2. Legally defensible appraisal *content:*
   a. Performance appraisal content should be based on a job analysis.
   b. Appraisals based on ratee traits should be avoided.
   c. Objective, verifiable performance data (e.g., sales, productivity, not ratings) should be used whenever possible.
   d. Constraints on employee performance which are beyond the employee's control should be prevented from contaminating the appraisal, to ensure that employees have equal opportunities to achieve a given appraisal score.
   e. Specific job-related performance dimensions should be used rather than global measures or single overall measures.
   f. Performance dimensions should be assigned weights that reflect their relative importance in calculating the composite performance score.

3. Legally defensible *documentation* of appraisal results:
   a. A thorough written record of evidence leading to termination decisions should be maintained (e.g., performance appraisals and performance counseling to advise employees of performance deficits and to assist poor performers in making needed improvements).
   b. Written documentation (e.g., specific behavioral examples) for extreme ratings should be required and must be consistent with the numerical ratings.
   c. Documentation requirements should be consistent among raters.

4. Legally defensible *raters:*
   a. Raters should be trained in how to use the appraisal system.
   b. Raters must have the opportunity to observe the ratee firsthand or to review important ratee performance products.
   c. Use of more than one rater is desirable in order to lessen the amount of influence of any one

rater and to reduce the effects of biases. Peers, subordinates, clients, and customers are possible sources in addition to the supervisor.

DESIGNING AN APPRAISAL SYSTEM

The process of designing an appraisal system should involve managers, employees, and HR professionals[17] in making decisions about each of the following issues:

*   Measurement content
*   Measurement process
*   Defining the rater (i.e., who should rate performance)
*   Defining the ratee (i.e., the level of performance to be rated)
*   Administrative characteristics

It is a challenge to make the correct decisions since no single set of choices is optimal in all situations. The starting point should be the strategic plan of the organization. The details of the plan should be reviewed in order to design an appraisal system consistent with the overall goals of the firm. For example, Key Bank designed a performance management system to meet specific corporate, department, and individual strategies and goals.[18] National Car Rental developed a new appraisal system so that it would be directly compatible with the objectives of the organization. One of those objectives was to increase repeat corporate business. Thus, greater weight was placed on behaviors and results related to this objective. Customers played a key role in the development of the system.

The choice of each element of an appraisal system is dependent, or *contingent,* upon the nature of the situation in which the system is to be used. The approach advocated here is to systematically assess the contingencies present in a situation, which we call a *contingency model for appraisal system design.* In the rest of this section we shall examine the choices that must be made for each issue.

Measurement Content

In the course of designing an appraisal system, there are three choices that concern the content on which performance is to be measured:

*   The focus of the appraisal
*   Types of criteria
*   Performance level descriptors (PLDs)

THE FOCUS OF THE APPRAISAL. Appraisal can be either person-oriented (focusing on the person

who performed the behavior) or work-oriented (focusing on the *record of outcomes* that the person achieved on the job). Effective performance appraisal focuses on the record of outcomes and, in particular, on outcomes directly linked to an organization's mission, objectives, and customer requirements. Some Sheraton hotels offer 25-minute room service or the meal is free. Sheraton employees who are directly related to room service are appraised on the record of outcomes specifically related to this service guarantee. Lenscrafters guarantees new glasses in 60 minutes or they're free. Individual and unit performance is measured by the average time taken to get the new glasses into the customer's hands. These are outcomes. In general, personal traits (e.g., dependability, integrity, perseverance, loyalty) should not be used in evaluating performance since they tend to foster stereotyping and other biases, and are difficult to defend should litigation result. In addition, people who are evaluated on traits perceive little value in the feedback and are often less motivated to perform well after the appraisal than before. In general, outcomes defined by critical internal or external customers are the most compatible with business objectives.

TYPES OF CRITERIA. Most conventional appraisal systems require raters to make a single overall judgment of performance on each project or job function. For example, determining an overall rating for a manager's performance on "planning and organizing" would be characteristic of this approach. Making an overall rating of the extent to which your instructor presented "organized lectures" is another example. There are, however, six criteria by which the value of performance for any work function may be assessed.[19] For example, raters could evaluate either the "timeliness" or the "quality" of a manager's "planning and organizing" skill. You could assess either the "quantity" or the "quality" of "organized lectures." The six criteria are listed and defined in Figure 10.2. Although not all these criteria may be relevant to every job function, a subset of them will be.

The HR professional has the task of determining whether raters should assess employees' performance on each job function as a whole (i.e., considering all relevant criteria simultaneously) or should assess each relevant criterion of performance for each job activity separately. For example, a very common appraisal form is the narrative or essay; the rater simply writes an unstructured evaluation of the employee, which may or may not break the evaluation down in terms of specific work functions or criteria. The overall rating approach is faster than making assessments on separate criteria but has the major drawback of requiring raters to simultaneously consider as many as six different criteria and to mentally compute their average. The probable result of all this sub-

FIGURE 10.2
THE SIX PRIMARY CRITERIA ON WHICH THE VALUE OF PERFORMANCE MAY BE ASSESSED

1. **Quality:** The degree to which the process or result of carrying out an activity approaches perfection, in terms of either conforming to some ideal way of performing the activity or fulfilling the activity's intended purpose.
2. **Quantity:** The amount produced, expressed in such terms as dollar value, number of units, or number of completed activity cycles.
3. **Timeliness:** The degree to which an activity is completed, or a result produced, at the earliest time desirable from the standpoints of both coordinating with the outputs of others and maximizing the time available for other activities.
4. **Cost effectiveness:** The degree to which the use of the organization's resources (e.g., human, monetary, technological, material) is maximized in the sense of getting the highest gain or reduction in loss from each unit or instance of use of a resource.
5. **Need for supervision:** The degree to which a performer can carry out a job function without either having to request supervisory assistance or requiring supervisory intervention to prevent an adverse outcome.
6. **Interpersonal impact:** The degree to which a performer promotes feelings of self-esteem, goodwill, and cooperation among coworkers and subordinates.

Source: H. J. Bernardin and J. S. Kane, *Performance appraisal: A contingency approach to system development and evaluation,* 2d ed. Boston, MA: PWS-Kent, 1993. Reprinted with permission.

jective reasoning may be less accurate ratings than those done on each relevant criterion for each job activity. In addition, less specific feedback will be provided to the performer. In general, the greater the specificity in the content of the appraisal, the more effective the appraisal system.

PERFORMANCE LEVEL DESCRIPTORS. Work-oriented appraisal systems typically require raters to compare performance on each job function with a set of benchmarks. These benchmarks are brief descriptions of levels of performance, and are referred to as "anchors" or *performance level descriptors* (PLDs). PLDs or anchors may take three different forms: adjectives or adjectival phrases, behavioral descriptions or critical incidents, and outcomes or results produced.

Adjectival benchmarks (e.g., "satisfactory," "very low," "below standard," "rarely") are highly subjective because their interpretation can mean different things to different raters. For example, one manager's definition of "below standard" may be quite different from another manager's definition. Behavioral PLDs or anchors consist of descriptions of the actions or behaviors taken by the person being appraised. For example, if the job function is "scheduling meetings," the behavioral anchors may be "sends notices about meetings," "visits employees to remind them about meetings," and "posts notices about

meetings in key locations." Behavioral anchors are very useful for developmental purposes since raters are able to give specific behavioral feedback to employees (e.g., by identifying skill areas that need improvement). Results-oriented PLDs are based on outcomes produced and may be, for example, "number of customer complaints," "number of units produced," "number of units rejected by quality control," or "number of days absent." Generally, results-oriented PLDs are preferable to either adjectival or behavioral PLDs when performance outcomes are important and identifiable and when the person's contribution to the results can be clearly distinguished. Behavioral PLDs should be used if outcomes cannot be linked to a particular person or group of persons. At Sheraton, for example, the "timeliness" of room service was assessed for the work unit (i.e., all persons related to room service for specified work shifts). At Blockbuster Video, paid "customers" evaluate the quality of service they receive from individual stores.

Measurement Process

The second set of issues to be considered in designing an appraisal system is the system's measurement process. Among the choices which must be made are the type of measurement scale, the types of rating instruments, control of rating errors, accounting for situational constraints on performance, and the overall score computation method.

TYPE OF MEASUREMENT SCALE. Certain types of personnel decisions need higher levels of precision than others. For example, if an organization wants to be able to single out the highest (or lowest) performers in a group for special recognition (or for discipline), measurements at the *ordinal* level will suffice. That is, employees need to be ranked only from best to worst. Other personnel decisions (e.g., selection decisions and identification of developmental needs) require the use of a more precise measurement scale (e.g., an interval level). For example, at Digital Equipment Corporation, managers determine promotions based on appraisal data across units. The extent to which one employee is judged to be superior to another is thus needed. An interval level scale will be able to indicate this, since it reveals the ranking of employees' performance as well as the actual difference in their scores (i.e., how much better one employee is than others). An appraisal system must be designed using a measurement scale at the needed level of precision.

TYPES OF RATING INSTRUMENTS. There are three basic ways in which raters can make performance assessments: (1) they can make comparisons among ratees' performances; (2) they can make comparisons *among* anchors or PLDs and select the one most descriptive of the person being appraised; and (3) they can compare individuals *to* anchors or PLDs. These approaches are shown in simplified form in Figure 10.3.[20] Some of the most popular rating instruments representing each of these three ways are described in the next section. The essay or narrative method we discussed above does not fit into any of these categories since this approach involves no measurement process. If numbers must be derived from an essay appraisal, the numbering system would then fit into one of the above three categories.

RATING INSTRUMENTS: COMPARISONS AMONG RATEES' PERFORMANCES.

Paired comparisons, straight ranking, and forced distribution are appraisal systems which require raters to make comparisons among ratees according to some measure of effectiveness. *Paired comparisons* require the rater to compare all possible pairs of ratees on "overall performance" or some other standard. This task can become cumbersome for the rater as the number of employees increases and more comparisons are needed. The formula for the number of possible pairs of employees is $n(n - 1)/2$, where $n =$ the number of employees. For example, if a rater had to do paired comparisons of 20 employees, 190 comparisons would be required. *Straight ranking*, or rank-ordering, asks the rater to simply identify the "best" employee, the "second best," etc., until the rater has identified the worst employee. For example, the National Collegiate Athletic Association (NCAA) rankings in football and basketball are based on a rank-ordering of the teams by coaches and the press. When Safeway Foods had to downsize its workforce, managers were required to derive a rank-ordering of all line supervisors within their units for purposes of terminating the lowest-ranked 30 percent.

Forced distribution usually presents the rater with a limited number of categories (usually five to seven) and requires (or "forces") the rater to place a designated portion of the ratees into each category. A forced distribution usually places the majority of employees in the middle category (i.e., with average ratings or raises), while fewer employees are placed in higher and lower categories. Some organizations use forced distributions to assign pay increases, while others use them to assign performance ratings to ensure that raters do not assign all their employees the most extreme (e.g., highest) possible ratings. Forced distributions have been used by Merck & Company, Inc., which requires divisions to place employees in five categories relative to their peers. Each supervisor must place 5 percent of employees in the top category, "exceptional"; 15 percent in the next highest, "with distinction"; 70 percent in the middle, "high Merck standard"; 8 percent in the next lowest, "room for improvement"; and 2 percent in the lowest performance category, "not acceptable" relative to their peers.[21] Merck began using the system when it found that the previous rating scale was unable to make distinctions among employees for merit purposes (almost everyone was rated at the highest level). IBM adopted a similar approach in 1992, requiring bosses to put 10 percent of rated employees in the highest category and 10 percent in the lowest. Figure 10.4 presents an example of a general forced-distribution rating format.

RATING INSTRUMENTS: COMPARISONS AMONG PLDs.

The *forced-choice* technique is a rating method which requires the rater to make comparisons among anchors or PLDs for a job activity. The method is specifically designed to reduce (or eliminate) intentional rating bias in which the rater deliberately attempts to rate

---

FIGURE 10.3
RATING FORMAT OPTIONS

1. **Comparisons among performances:** Compare the performances of all ratees to each PLD for each job activity, function, or overall performance. Rater judgments may be made in one of the following ways:

   a. Indicate which ratee in each possible *pair* of ratees performed closest to the performance level described by the PLD or attained the highest level of overall performance.
   - Illustrative method: paired comparison

   b. Indicate how the ratees ranked in terms of closeness to the performance level described by the PLD.
   - Illustrative method: straight ranking

   c. Indicate what percentage of the ratees performed in a manner closest to the performance level described by the PLD. (*Note:* The percentages have to add up to 100 percent for all the PLDs within each job activity or function.)
   - Illustrative method: forced distribution

2. **Comparisons among PLDs:** Compare all the PLDs for each job activity or function and select the one (or more) that best describes the ratee's performance level. Rater judgments are made in the following way:

   Indicate which of the PLDs fit the ratee's performance best (and/or worst).
   - Illustrative method: forced choice

3. **Comparisons to descriptors (PLDs):** Compare each ratee's performance to each PLD for each job activity or function. Raters' judgments are made in one of the following ways:

   a. Whether or not the ratee's performance matches the PLD.
   - Illustrative methods: graphic rating scales such as BARS; MBO

   b. The degree to which the ratee's performance matches the PLD.
   - Illustrative methods: all summated rating scales such as BOS and PDA methods

   c. Whether the ratee's performance was better than, equal to, or worse than that described by the PLD.
   - Illustrative method: mixed standard scales

FIGURE 10.4
A FORCED DISTRIBUTION SCALE

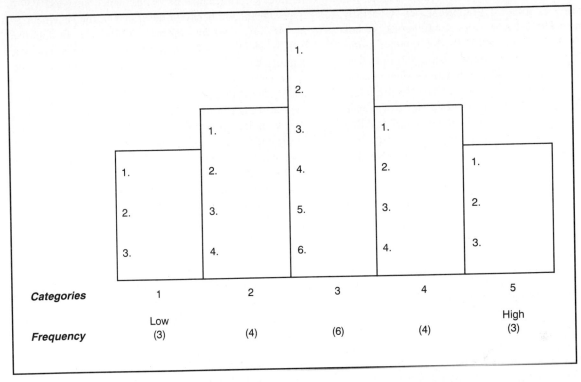

Categories	1	2	3	4	5
	Low				High
Frequency	(3)	(4)	(6)	(4)	(3)

Note: In this example, 20 persons must be rated in five categories based on their overall performance. The numbers in parentheses indicate the number of persons who must be placed in each category. Rank orderings within categories are not usually required.

Source: H. J. Bernardin and R.W. Beatty, *Performance appraisal: Assessing human behavior at work.* Boston, MA: PWS-Kent, 1984, p. 112. Reprinted with permission.

individuals high (or low) irrespective of their performance. The rationale underlying the approach is that statements are grouped in such a way that the scoring key is not known to the rater (i.e., the way to rate higher or lower is not apparent). The most common format is a group of four statements from which the rater must select two as "most descriptive" of the person being rated. The rater is unaware of which statements (if selected) will result in higher (or lower) ratings for the ratee because all four statements appear equally desirable or undesirable. There are usually at least 20 groups of four statements. As an example, if you were asked to select the two statements which are most descriptive of your instructor for this class, which two would you select?

1. Is patient with slow learners.
2. Lectures with confidence.
3. Keeps the interest and attention of the class.
4. Acquaints the class with objectives for each lesson in advance.

The statements are chosen to be equal in desirability to make it more difficult for the rater to pick out the ones that can give the ratee the highest or lowest ratings. However, only two of the items are characteristic of highly effective performers. In this example, items 1 and 3 have been shown to discriminate between the most effective and the least effective professors. Items 2 and 4 do not generally discriminate between effective and ineffective performers. If you selected statements 1 and 3 as most descriptive of your instructor, then he or she would be awarded 2 points. This procedure would be used with each of the groups of statements to determine the total score for each ratee. Raters are not given the scoring scheme so that they will be unable to intentionally give performers high or low ratings.

RATING INSTRUMENTS: COMPARISONS TO PLDs. Methods which require the rater to compare the employee's performance with specified anchors or descriptors include graphic rating scales, behaviorally anchored rating scales (BARS), management by objectives (MBO), summated scales [e.g., behavioral observation scales (BOS) and mixed standard scales (MSS)], and performance distribution assessment. *Graphic rating scales* are the most widely used type of rating format. In fact, a recent survey of organizations reported that they were used in 57 percent of the firms surveyed.[22] Figure 10.5 presents some examples of graphic scales. Generally, graphic rating scales use adjectives or numbers as anchors or descriptors. The system used at Textron requires ratings of "problem area," "meets expectation," "significant strength," or "not applicable" for functions such as meeting deadlines, team building, and safety effectiveness.[23]

One of the most heavily researched types of graphic scales is *behaviorally anchored rating scales* (BARS). As shown in Figure 10.6, BARS are graphic scales with specific behavioral descriptions defining various points along the scale for each dimension. One rating method for BARS asks raters to record specific observations of the employee's performance relevant to the dimension on the scale. For example, in Figure 10.6, the rater has written in "Stuck to the course outline..." and then selected a point on the scale which best represents the ratee's performance on that function. That point should be selected by comparing the ratee's actual observed performance with the behavioral expectations which are provided as "anchors" on the scale. The rationale behind writing observations on the scale prior to selecting an anchor is to ensure that raters are basing their ratings of expectations on actual observations of performance. In addition, the observations can be given to ratees as feedback on their performance.

The method of *summated scales* is one of the oldest formats and remains one of the most popular for the appraisal of job performance. The most recent version of summated scales is *behavioral observation scales* (BOS). An example of a summated scale is presented in Figure 10.7. For BOS, the rater is asked to indicate how frequently the ratee has performed each of the listed behaviors.

Performance distribution assessment (PDA) is the only rating method that formally corrects appraisals to hold ratees accountable for only that level of performance which was feasible and under the control of the performer.[24] PDA calls for ratings of relative frequency in the context of feasible outcomes.

Mixed standard scales (MSS) are rating instruments which, like the forced-choice approach, attempt to control deliberate response bias by raters. MSS usually consist of sets of three statements that describe high, medium, and low levels of performance on a job activity or dimension. For example, in a validation study, the Toledo, Ohio, Police Department developed a dimension called "crime prevention" for its patrol officers. The high-performance item for crime prevention was "Takes numerous steps both to prevent and to control crime." The average performance item was "Makes some effort to emphasize crime prevention," and the low-performance item was "Has very little or no contact with citizens to inform them of crime-

prevention methods." Statements are then randomized on the rating form, and the rater is asked to indicate whether the ratee's performance is "better than," "as good as," or "worse than" the behavior described in the statement.

Management by objectives (MBO) is an appraisal system which calls for a comparison between specific, quantifiable target goals and the actual results achieved by an employee. The measurable, quantitative goals are usually mutually agreed upon by the employee and supervisor at the beginning of an appraisal period. During the review period, progress toward the goals is monitored. At the end of the review period, the employee and supervisor meet to evaluate whether the goals were achieved and to decide on new goals. The goals or objectives are usually set for individual employees or work units and usually differ across employees or units depending on the circumstances of the job. For this reason, MBO has been shown to be useful for defining "individual" or unit performance in the context of strategic plans. As a motivational technique, as long as the goals or objectives set are specific in nature and attainable as perceived by the performer while still being difficult, MBO is an effective approach to improving performance and motivating employees. MBO is not recommended as a method for comparing people or units since goals usually vary across individuals and work units and those which are set are not equally attainable in the context of potential situational constraints on performance (we discuss this topic in the next section). While MBO has not been used in organizations as frequently as graphic rating scales, its use is very common at the managerial level.

Generally, the choice of rating instrument has a negligible effect on rating accuracy, with the critical exception being that the greater the precision in the definition of "performance," the more effective the appraisal for any of the purposes we described above.[25] Thus, the main basis for selecting a rating instrument for use should be other factors, such as how well the instrument fits with the level of precision needed and the purposes to be served by the data. If only ordinal levels of measurement are needed and if performance is carefully defined as the basis for the comparisons, formats using comparisons among ratee performance (e.g., ranking) are adequate. At the higher levels of precision (e.g., interval level), the rating instruments based on "comparison to descriptors" offer the most direct approaches to eliciting the needed rater responses. Ease of use and acceptability to raters and ratees should also be considered in choosing a rating instrument. Forced distribution methods are not popular among raters.

Some organizations use a combination of rating instruments. For example, state employees in the Governor's Job Training Office in Colorado use a system which combines the attributes of MBO, essay appraisal, and forced choice.[26] AMOCO uses an essay, forced

FIGURE 10.5
EXAMPLES OF GRAPHIC RATING SCALES

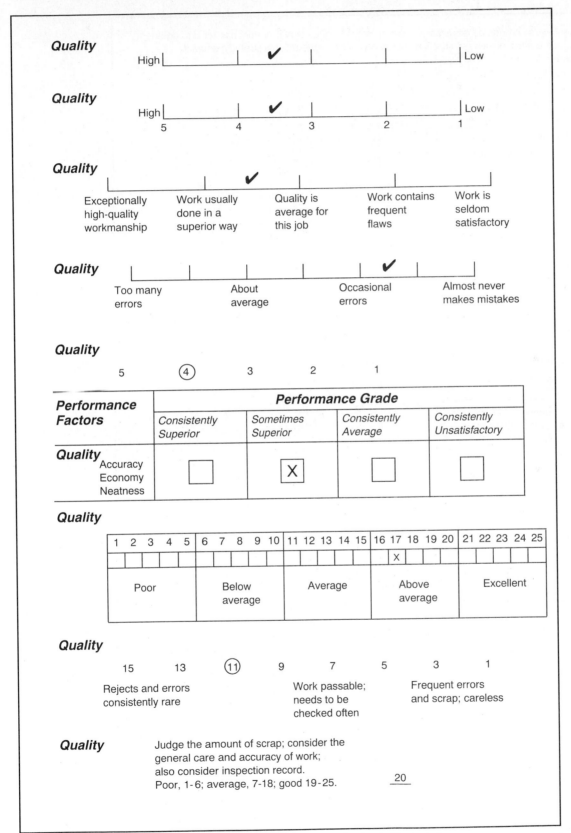

Source: R. M. Guion. *Personnel Testing.* New York: McGraw-Hill, 1984, p. 98. Reprinted with permission.

FIGURE 10.6
AN EXAMPLE OF A BEHAVIORALLY ANCHORED RATING SCALE

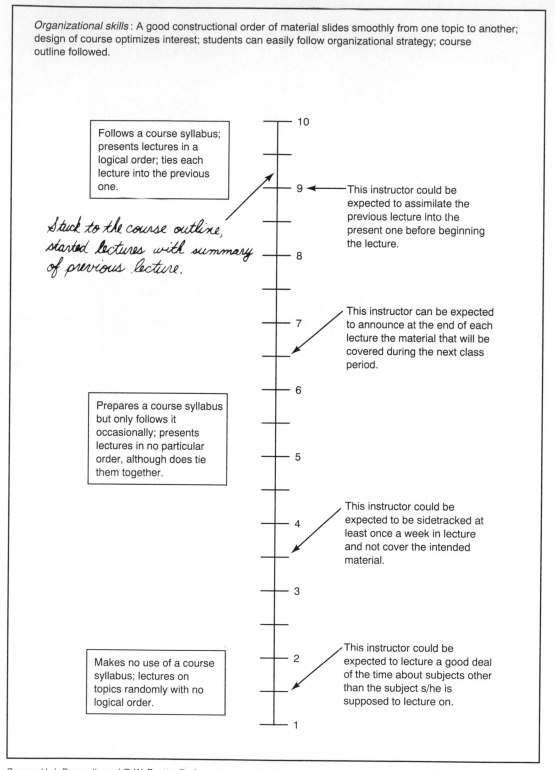

Organizational skills: A good constructional order of material slides smoothly from one topic to another; design of course optimizes interest; students can easily follow organizational strategy; course outline followed.

Follows a course syllabus; presents lectures in a logical order; ties each lecture into the previous one.

Stuck to the course outline, started lectures with summary of previous lecture.

This instructor could be expected to assimilate the previous lecture into the present one before beginning the lecture.

This instructor can be expected to announce at the end of each lecture the material that will be covered during the next class period.

Prepares a course syllabus but only follows it occasionally; presents lectures in no particular order, although does tie them together.

This instructor could be expected to be sidetracked at least once a week in lecture and not cover the intended material.

Makes no use of a course syllabus; lectures on topics randomly with no logical order.

This instructor could be expected to lecture a good deal of the time about subjects other than the subject s/he is supposed to lecture on.

Source: H. J. Bernardin and R.W. Beatty, *Performance appraisal: Assessing human behavior at work.* Boston, MA: PWS-Kent, 1984, p. 84. Reprinted with permission.

FIGURE 10.7
A SUMMATED RATING SCALE

Directions: Rate your manager on the way he or she has conducted performance appraisal interviews. Use the following scale to make your ratings:

1 = Always
2 = Often
3 = Occasionally
4 = Seldom
5 = Never

1. Effectively used information about the subordinate in the discussion.
2. Skillfully guided the discussion through the problem areas.
3. Maintained control over the interview.
4. Appeared to be prepared for the interview.
5. Let the subordinate control the interview.
6. Adhered to a discussion about the subordinate's problems.
7. Seemed concerned about the subordinate's perspective on the problems.
8. Probed deeply into sensitive areas in order to gain sufficient knowledge.
9. Made the subordinate feel comfortable during discussions of sensitive topics.
10. Projected sincerity during the interview.
11. Maintained the appropriate climate for an appraisal interview.
12. Displayed insensitivity to the subordinate's problems.
13. Displayed an organized approach to the interview.
14. Asked the appropriate questions.
15. Failed to follow up with questions when they appeared to be necessary.
16. Asked general questions about the subordinate's problems.
17. Asked only superficial questions that failed to confront the issues.
18. Displayed considerable interest in the subordinate's professional growth.
19. Provided general suggestions to aid in the subordinate's professional growth.
20. Provided poor advice regarding the subordinate's growth.
21. Made specific suggestions for helping the subordinate develop professionally.
22. Remained calm during the subordinate's outbursts.
23. Responded to the subordinate's outbursts in a rational manner.
24. Appeared to be defensive in reaction to the subordinate's complaints.
25. Backed down inappropriately when confronted.
26. Made realistic commitments to help the subordinate get along better with others.
27. Seemed unconcerned about the subordinate's problems.
28. Provided poor advice about the subordinate's relationships with others.
29. Provided good advice about resolving conflict.
30. When discussing the subordinate's future with the company, encouraged him or her to stay on.
31. Used appropriate compliments regarding the subordinate's technical expertise.
32. Motivated the subordinate to perform the job well.
33. Seemed to ignore the subordinate's excellent performance record.
34. Made inappropriate ultimatums to the subordinate about improving performance.

distribution, and graphic scales to evaluate managers. P&W used a ranking and a BARS format to conduct a special appraisal as part of its downsizing program. IBM's new seven-page annual evaluation calls for the forced distribution of 10 percent of subordinates in the top and bottom of a four-category system, plus a rank-ordering of each employee for contributions to the business.

Some organizations (60 percent of those surveyed) use different appraisal systems for different levels of employees. For example, at Electro-Biology, Inc., nonexempt employees are rated on simple graphic rating scales and exempt employees are rated on a combination of MBO and forced-distribution ranking.[27] Digital uses both MBO and summated scales to evaluate managers while using a graphic approach for nonmanagerial personnel.

CONTROL OF RATING ERRORS. Performance ratings are subject to a wide variety of inaccuracies and biases referred to as "rating errors." These errors occur in rater observations, judgment, and information processing,[28] and can seriously affect performance appraisal results. Among the most commonly cited rating errors are the following:

Leniency: Ratings for employees are generally at the high end of the scale regardless of their actual performances. Surveys have identified leniency as the most serious problem with appraisals whenever they are linked to important administrative decisions like compensation or promotions.[29]

Central tendency: Ratings for employees tend to be toward the center of the scale regardless of the actual performance of ratees.

Halo effect: The rater allows a rating on one dimension (or an overall impression) for an employee to influence the ratings he or she assigns to other dimensions for that employee. That is, the rater inappropriately assesses ratee performance similarly across different job functions, projects, or performance dimensions.

Rater affect: Includes favoritism, stereotyping, and hostility. Excessively high or low scores are given only to certain individuals or groups based on rater attitudes toward the ratee, not on actual behaviors or outcomes. Sex, race, age, and friendship biases are examples of this type of error, which is the most common basis for lawsuits involving performance appraisals. The Civil Rights Act of 1991 establishes Title VIII-covered biases as illegal if established.

Primacy and recency effects: The rater's ratings are heavily influenced either by behaviors exhibited by the ratee during the early stages of the review period (primacy) or by behaviors or outcomes exhibited by the ratee near the end of the review period (recency).

Perceptual set: The tendency for raters to see what they want to see or expect to see. For example, expectations of a given level of performance often affect judgments of actual performance. Expecting low levels of performance, for example, can lead to higher judgments of performance than deserved by the ratee's actual performance. The opposite is true for an expectation of high levels of performance.

All these errors can arise in either of two different ways: as the result of *unintentional* errors in the way people observe, store, recall, and report events, or as the result of *intentional* efforts to assign inaccurate ratings.[30] If rating errors are *unintentional,* raters may commit them because they do not have the necessary skills to make accurate ratings or the content of the appraisal is not carefully defined. Attempts to control unconscious, unintentional errors most often focus on rater training. Training to improve raters' observational and categorization skills (called "frame-of-reference training") have been shown to increase accuracy and consistency.[31] This training consists of creating a common frame of reference among raters in the observation process. Raters are familiarized and tested on the performance dimensions and the rating scale content, and then given opportunities to practice making ratings. Following this, they are given feedback on their practice ratings. They are also given descriptions of critical incidents of performance which illustrate outstanding, average, and unsatisfactory levels of performance on each dimension, so that they will know what behaviors or outcomes to consider when making their ratings. Southeast Hospital combined this approach with supervisory training on the whole appraisal process. AT&T and AMC Theatres have used the approach in validation studies.

A second strategy for controlling unintentional rating errors is to reduce the number of performance judgments a rater is required to make in order to try to avoid biases and errors. For example, a rating instrument using this strategy might pose rating questions which require objective responses, such as "On what percent of all the times that Sue organized a meeting did she fail to contact everyone to attend the meeting?" or "On what percent of all the times that Sue organized a meeting did it begin and end on time?" The responses to these questions would be mathematically converted into appraisal scores.

Raters may commit rating errors *intentionally* for political reasons or to provide certain outcomes to their employees or themselves.[32] One of the most common

intentional rating errors in organizations is leniency. Managers may assign higher ratings than an employee deserves to avoid a confrontation with the employee, to protect an employee suffering from personal problems, to acquire more recognition for the department or themselves, or to be able to reward the employee with a bonus or promotion. Although less common, managers may also intentionally assign more severe ratings than an employee deserves, with a goal such as (1) motivating the employee to work harder, (2) teaching the employee a lesson, or (3) building a case for firing the employee. Attempts to control intentional rating errors include: developing more specific and verifiable dimensions, hiding scoring keys by using rating instruments such as forced-choice or mixed standard scales requiring cross-checks, additional raters, or reviews of ratings by other people; training raters on how to provide negative feedback to employees; and reducing the rater's motivation to assign inaccurate ratings. For example, the state of Virginia has reduced raters' motivation to rate leniently by rewarding them for the extent to which they (1) carefully define "performance" for their employees and (2) conform to the regulations of the rating system regarding documentation for extreme ratings.[33]

ACCOUNTING FOR SITUATIONAL CONSTRAINTS ON PERFORMANCE. One of the major factors that causes inaccurate and unfair performance appraisals is the practice of blaming employees for poor performance that was caused by factors completely beyond their control.[34] Any student who has been graded on a group project may have experienced a problem where team members did not carry their share of the workload and your performance was affected. Many conditions present in the job situation or work assignment can hold a person back from performing as well as he or she could. Examples of such constraints are inadequate tools, lack of supplies, not enough money, too little time, lack of information, poor libraries, breakdowns in equipment, and not enough help from others. For example, truck inspectors may be limited in the number of trucks they can check for defects if they must spend considerable portions of some workdays in court presenting testimony against offenders. They may, however, still be held accountable for inspecting a certain number of trucks despite these other job duties. If, in a group project, one of your team members fails to retrieve vital information, the constraint could seriously hamper your ability to do your tasks. Situational factors which hinder an employee's job performance are called *situational constraints* and are described in Figure 10.8.[35] An appraisal system design should consider the effects of situational constraints so that ratees will not be unfairly downgraded for these uncontrollable factors. PDA is one rating method which

**FIGURE 10.8
POSSIBLE SITUATIONAL CONSTRAINTS ON
PERFORMANCE**

1. Absenteeism or turnover of key personnel
2. Slowness of procedures for action approval
3. Inadequate clerical support
4. Shortages of supplies and/or raw materials
5. Excessive restrictions on operating expenses
6. Inadequate physical working conditions
7. Inability to hire needed staff
8. Inadequate performance of coworkers or personnel in other work units on whom an individual's work depends
9. Inadequate performance of subordinates
10. Inadequate performance of managers
11. Inefficient or unclear organizational structure or reporting relationships
12. Excessive reporting requirements and administrative paperwork
13. Unpredictable workloads
14. Excessive workloads
15. Changes in administrative policies, procedures, and/or regulations
16. Pressures from coworkers to limit an individual's performance
17. Unpredictable changes or additions to the types of work assigned
18. Lack of proper equipment
19. Inadequate communication within the organization
20. The quality of raw materials
21. Economic conditions (e.g., interest rates, labor availability, and costs of basic goods and services)
22. Inadequate training

incorporates assessments of the effects of situational constraints directly into the rating process.

A common source of error, known as "actor/observer bias," is for the observer or rater to discount the role of situational factors in an employee's performance, while the performer tends to place relatively greater emphasis on the effects of the situational constraints in hindering performance. Rater training programs should focus on making raters more aware of potential constraints on employee performance. Research shows that this approach to training results in more effective appraisals and greater agreement between self and supervisory appraisals.[36]

OVERALL SCORE COMPUTATION.   Once performance has been assessed on each of the job's important functions, products, or services, it is usually necessary to produce an overall score reflecting the level of performance on the job as a whole. There are two primary ways to produce an overall score:

- **Judgmental:**   The rater forms a subjective judgment of overall performance, usually after completing the ratings of performance on each of the job's separate functions or dimensions (e.g., oral communication, negotiation, service to the profession).

- **Mathematical:**   The rater or some other scorer mathematically computes the weighted or unweighted mean of the ratings of performance on each of the job's activities or functions.

The judgmental approach to determining an overall score is commonly used in organizations, although it can lead to overall performance ratings that bear little relation to performance on the specific dimensions of the job. The mathematical approach is more likely to accurately reflect overall performance based on all job functions. The question for the rater using the mathematical approach is whether to compute the overall score (1) by giving equal weight to the ratings on the various job activities or functions or (2) by assigning them different weights based on their relative importance. Assuming that it is possible to derive reliable measures of importance, the latter approach is superior, particularly when the importance weights are derived in the context of the unit's or organization's strategic goals or of customer preferences.

Defining the "Rater"

Ratings can be provided by ratees, supervisors, peers, clients or customers, or high-level managers. In 92 percent of organizations surveyed, appraisals are made by an employee's immediate supervisor, and in most cases the supervisor has sole responsibility for the appraisal.[37] In McLean Home, managers receive evaluations from their directors and also provide self-appraisals.[38] At Nuffield Hospitals, employees evaluate their own performance and present the evaluations to supervisors. The purpose is to encourage employees to take an active role in their own development.[39] State of Virginia employees use a formal self-appraisal process as well. In general, however, formal self-appraisals are rare. One survey found that only 6.7 percent of firms allow for a formal self-appraisal, despite the fact that employees want to add their input to the appraisal process.[40]

With increasing frequency, organizations are concluding that multiple rater types are beneficial to use in their appraisal systems. Ratings collected from several raters are more accurate, have fewer biases, are perceived to be more fair, and are less often the targets of lawsuits and grievances.[41] Also, many of the rater types used (e.g., customers, peers) have direct and unique knowledge of at least some aspects of the ratee's job performance, and provide reliable and valid performance information on some job activities. In fact, the use of raters who represent all critical internal and external customers contributes to the accuracy and relevance of the appraisal system.[42]

Many organizations have found that it is not very difficult to set up a system using more than one source for ratings.[43] IBM, for example, has been using a multiple rating system for its managers since 1964. Subordinate appraisal plays a critical role in the process. In addition, in many organizations (e.g., Xerox; IBM; Motorola, Inc.), with the advent of matrix structures, project teams, and leaderless work groups, multiple rater types are being used because there is no longer a traditional supervisor in existence or the supervisor is no longer directly observing the employees' performance. For example, in high-technology firms [e.g., IBM; Texas Instruments, Inc. (TI); Intel Corporation] or "think tanks" (e.g., Lawrence Livermore Laboratories, GA Technologies, Inc.), employees work on tasks and projects apart from their supervisor's direct guidance.[44] Other firms [e.g., Federal Express, Tennessee Valley Authority (TVA), Domino's Pizza] use multiple rater types (e.g., subordinates, customers, supervisors) to determine how effectively managers are meeting goals for improved quality of services.[45] Many organizations use self-, subordinate, peer, and superior ratings as a comprehensive appraisal prior to a training program. The FAA, for example, provides feedback from superiors, subordinates, and peers to each participant prior to the start of the mandatory supervisory training program. The data are contrasted with the participant's self-appraisal on the same performance factors. The Center for Creative Leadership in Greensboro, North Carolina, requires all participants in its 1-week assessment center program to first submit evaluations from superiors, peers, and subordinates. These data are tabulated by the center, and the feedback is reported to participants on the first day of the assessment center program. Participants consider this feedback to be among the most valuable feedback they receive. The Powertrain Division of GM uses peers, subordinates, and superiors to evaluate its managers. A recent company survey found that 90 percent of managers prefer the new system to the old ranking system.

Many companies now use external customers as an important source of information about employee performance related to service. At Avis Rent a Car, for example, customers can evaluate employees on customer-care balance sheets. The Britannia Building Society in the United Kingdom has developed criteria for assessing both internal and external customer service for purposes of individual appraisal. The Marriott Corporation places considerable weight on its customer survey data in the evaluation of each hotel as well as work units within the hotels. In addition to Blockbuster Video, which we mentioned earlier, Burger King, McDonald's, Domino's Pizza, and Taco Bell are among the companies which hire professional "customers" or "mystery shoppers" to visit specific installations and provide detailed appraisals of several performance functions.

The number of rater types that should be used in rating the performance of an employee depends on the number of rater types that can furnish unique perspectives on the performance of the ratee. By *unique perspectives* we mean people in a position to furnish not only different information but also information processed through less severe biases. To decide how many different rater types should be used, cost-benefit ratings and logistic feasibility should be considered. For example, do the payoffs of using multiple rater types offset the costs entailed (e.g., for development of additional forms, rater training, allocation of additional time to administrative activity)? Also, can ratings by multiple raters be coordinated to ensure the timely completion of all ratings without disrupting regular operations? Another consideration is the symbolic significance of participation in the appraisal process. Do Marriott customers perceive better customer service simply because they have been asked to participate in the process? Are subordinates more satisfied with their jobs or with management in general because they participated in the evaluation of their managers? Conceptualizing all possible raters as all possible customers (internal and external) is a good approach to setting up a multiple rater system. The approach is also consistent with the recent emphasis on "total quality management," which is discussed in Chapter 13. If only a supervisor or manager is to be used, that rater should seek performance information from all critical internal and external customers in preparation for the formal appraisal. To the extent to which ratees look at the evaluator (e.g., the supervisor or manager) as their only important customer, the system can easily operate to the detriment of the organization. The focus for both raters and ratees should be on actual internal and external customer requirements. Just as the measurement of the performance dimensions should have this focus, so should the identification of the sources of rating.

Defining the "Ratee"

Many people assume that appraisals always focus on an *individual* level of performance. There are alternatives to using the individual as the ratee, which are becoming more common in organizations as more and more firms [e.g., General Foods Corporation, Rohm & Haas, Alcoa, General Motors (GM) and its Saturn Corporation, Westinghouse Electric Corp.] shift to using more self-managing teams, autonomous work groups, teamwork (e.g., Exxon), and participative management (e.g., Motorola, Inc.) to get work done.[46] Specifically, the ratee may be defined at the individual, work group, division, or organizationwide level. It is also possible to define the ratee at multiple levels. For example, under some conditions it may be desirable to appraise performance both at the work group level for merit pay purposes and at the individual level to identify developmental needs. Burger King, for example, awards cash bonuses to branch stores by using a customer-based evaluation process, while also maintaining an individual appraisal system within each store. Delta Airlines assesses customer service at the group level only, while other job activities are assessed at the individual employee level. Similarly, Sheraton Corporation derives a group-level evaluation for room service while evaluating other functions at the individual level.

Two conditions which make it desirable to assess performance at a higher level of aggregation than the individual level are high work group cohesiveness and difficulty in identifying individual contributions. *High work group cohesiveness* refers to the shared feeling among work group members that they form a team. Such an orientation promotes high degrees of cooperation among group members for highly interdependent tasks.[47] Appraisals focused on individual performance may undermine the cooperative orientation needed to maintain this cohesiveness and tend to promote individualistic or even competitive orientations. *The difficulty in identifying individual contributions* is also important to consider. In some cases, workers are so interdependent, or their individual performance is so difficult to observe, that there is no choice but to focus appraisals on the performance of the higher aggregate of which they are a part. For example, team members at the Saturn plant have received cross training and may engage in all aspects of the job. In most cases, their individual performance is difficult to separate from that of the team's. This was also the case at Delta Airlines. To the extent that such conditions exist, it is advisable to consider using a higher level than the individual when evaluating performance. Evaluations may be made of the group's performance, the department's, or the organization's as a whole. Eastman Kodak, for example, abandoned its old top-down system and now employs a peer rating system to assess team members.

Administrative Characteristics

In any appraisal system, a variety of administrative decisions must be made. These decisions include the frequency and timing of appraisals, the rating medium, and the method of feedback.

FREQUENCY AND TIMING OF APPRAISALS. This refers to the number of times per year each employee is to be formally appraised and the time period (e.g., months) between formal appraisals. Usually, appraisals are conducted once or twice per year, with equal intervals between them (e.g., every 12 months or 6 months). For example, 69 percent of firms surveyed reported that appraisals were conducted annually, 22 percent reported that they were done semiannually, and 9 percent stated that they were done at varying intervals.[48] In another survey, 90 percent of the respondents indicated that appraisals were conducted annually.[49] In some organizations (e.g., the Minnesota Department of Transportation), employees reported that appraisals conducted once a year "were enough."[50] Other organizations are finding that it may be desirable to have more frequent (e.g., quarterly) formal appraisals, if blocks of work are regularly completed or adequate samples of behaviors and outcomes can be obtained by the end of each quarter. For example, the TVA requires quarterly performance reviews for every employee.

Many organizations conduct appraisals as frequently as every 30 or 60 days during the first 6 months to 1 year of employment, in order to monitor the performance of new employees during a probationary or orientation period.[51] These firms find that more frequent appraisals are desirable because they provide more feedback to employees and also because they avoid the surprises that employees report about their ratings during annual performance reviews.[52] These firms also find that one formal appraisal a year cannot provide the timely or specific feedback needed to accomplish significant improvements in performance.[53]

Intervals between appraisals may be fixed (e.g., every 6 months, on the employee's anniversary date, or during the last month of the fiscal year). One survey found that half the respondents used anniversary dates and half used a common review date.[54] Intervals also may be variable, based on such factors as very poor or very high performance, consideration for a promotion, and project completion dates. College instructors, for example, are typically evaluated at the completion of each class, with ratings from all classes then averaged to derive a semester or academic year average. Many organizations use both types of intervals: fixed for regularly occurring personnel decisions (e.g., merit pay) and variable for appraisals triggered by unusual events (e.g., needs for reduction in force). P&W, for example, conducted annual appraisals at the end of the year but developed and used a new appraisal system for purposes of a major downsizing. This approach can cause problems, however. A class action suit was brought by terminated P&W employees over the age of 40 under the ADEA. The plaintiffs maintained that their performance was judged to be superior to many of the younger employees under the annual appraisal system but was rated lower in a special appraisal by managers who were faced with the need to reduce overhead.

RATING/DATA COLLECTION MEDIUM. The widespread use of computer terminals in the workplace has made viable the option of having raters record performance appraisal ratings directly on computers. There are several advantages to using computers for rating. The results can immediately be integrated into the computerized central personnel record systems that most organizations are now keeping, thereby eliminating the need for clerks to enter the data. The amount of paper that has to be generated, distributed, and filed is drastically reduced. Of the many computer programs now available, some can monitor rater responses for logic and completeness during the rating process. The choice of a rating medium depends, however, on the sophistication of the raters and the availability of computers in the workplace. If computers or terminals are readily available, computerized systems certainly make a great deal of sense.

Computers and other high-tech tools are now used routinely to monitor the performance of workers in customer service, telecommunications, and travel. Supervisors also surreptitiously monitor employees' calls with customers. Employers claim that performance has increased as a direct consequence of these monitoring systems. Employee advocacy groups argue that such monitoring creates great stress and that turnover rates and productivity ultimately suffer. The National Association of Working Women (NAWW), for example, reports having received thousands of complaints about electronic eavesdropping since the establishment of a hotline for such complaints. As a result of the controversy, federal legislation which would curb the practice is pending. Among the provisions of the bill is a restriction on the use of computer-generated data as the sole means of performance appraisal.[55]

METHOD OF FEEDBACK. Raters should communicate appraisal results to ratees in a formal feedback meeting between the supervisor and the employee. The formal feedback session should *not* serve as the only time the supervisor gives feedback to employees on their performance. Feedback serves an important role both for motivational and informational purposes and for the sake of improved rater-ratee communications.[56] For example, supportive feedback can lead to greater motivation, and feedback discussions about pay and advancement can lead to greater employee satisfaction with the process.[57] Specific feedback is more likely to increase an individual's performance[58] and is therefore recommended over general feedback.

The biggest hazard for the rater in providing performance feedback may be ratees' reactions to the feedback. Generally, ratees believe that they have performed at higher levels than do observers of their performance.[59] This is especially true at the lower performance levels where there is more room for disagreement and a greater motive among ratees to engage in ego-defensive behavior (recall our discussion of the actor/observer bias). It is no wonder that raters are often hesitant about confronting poor performers with negative appraisal feedback and may be lenient when they do.[60] Although pressure on managers to give accurate feedback may override their reluctance to give negative feedback,[61] the pressure doesn't make the experience any more pleasant or any less likely to evoke a leniency bias. Feedback to inform poor performers of performance deficiencies and to encourage improvement doesn't always lead to performance improvements.[62] Many employees view their supervisors less favorably after the feedback[63] and feel less motivated after the appraisal.[64] The fear or discomfort experienced in providing negative feedback tends to differ across managers. One survey, the Performance Appraisal Self-Efficacy Scale (PASES), showed that the level of discomfort felt by a rater was correlated with leniency, that is, the greater the discomfort, the greater the leniency. Rater training, designed to reduce ratees' level of discomfort in giving negative information has been shown to be effective in reducing leniency.[65]

To create a supportive atmosphere for the feedback meeting between the employee and supervisor, here are several recommendations: The rater should remove distractions, avoid being disturbed, and allow sufficient time for the meeting. Raters seem to have trouble adhering to these guidelines. For example, employees of the Minnesota Department of Transportation reported that their supervisors generally spent less than 15 minutes in feedback meetings, which is substantially less than the 60 minutes often recommended.[66] Raters should be informal and relaxed and allow the employee the opportunity to share his or her insights. Topics that should be addressed include praise for special assignments; the employee's own assessment of his or her performance; the supervisor's response to the employee's assessment; action plans to improve the subordinate's performance; perceived constraints on performance which require subordinate or supervisory attention; and the employee's career aspirations, ambitions, and developmental goals. Nuffield Hospitals is one organization which incorporates many of these ideas into its appraisal feedback meetings. In sum, raters should provide feedback which is clear, descriptive, job-related, constructive, frequent, timely, and realistic. Research clearly shows, however, that if the annual appraisal meeting is the only time the subordinate gets feedback on performance, the supervisor is doing a poor job of supervising.[67]

DEVELOPING AN APPRAISAL SYSTEM

After planning the design of an appraisal system by making decisions about the measurement content and process, determining who raters should be, and making necessary administrative decisions, it is time to actually develop the appraisal system. The development of an effective appraisal system consists of following seven basic steps, as described below.

1. *Start with job analyses.* Any effort to develop an appraisal system must begin with complete information about the jobs to be appraised. This information is generated through job analyses which describe the job requirements [e.g., knowledges, abilities, skills, and other characteristics (KASOCs)], job content (e.g., major tasks, activities, or duties), and job context features (e.g., responsibilities, physical surroundings)].[68] Reading & Bates recognized the importance of relying on job descriptions as the basis for the development of the appraisal context. This approach enabled supervisors to focus on employee behaviors and outcomes rather than traits, and to develop better documentation as a basis for administrative decisions.[69] (See Chapter 4 for a more thorough discussion of the importance of conducting job analyses for performance appraisal purposes.) As we discussed in Chapter 4, the critical incident technique (CIT) is ideal for the development of highly detailed appraisal content. The job analysis should involve all possible rater groups as well.

2. *Specify performance dimensions and develop PLDs.* Using as much involvement by incumbents, supervisors, and other critical internal and external customers as possible, specify the job functions, and the criteria (e.g., quality, quantity, timeliness) relevant to each, on which employee performance is to be appraised (see Figure 10.2). These job activity or function-by-criterion combinations will make up the system's performance dimensions. Following this, compose the necessary number of PLDs for each performance dimension. These descriptors should be defined as specifically as possible and in the context of the unit or organization's strategic goals. Wherever possible, these descriptors should include countable results or outcomes which are important for the strategic goals of the unit or organization, ideally as defined by critical customers. Even in the case of a ranking or forced distribution, one PLD per dimension should be used (usually called a "ranking factor") which describes the standard or ideal performance on the basis of which employees are compared or ranked.

3. *Scale the PLDs.* This is the process of determining the values to attach to each PLD. At this time you can also have raters determine the weights to be assigned to each performance dimension when computing an overall performance score. For example, raters may decide that answering phones makes up 30 percent of a clerical person's job. This factor would be assigned a weight of 0.30. The information necessary for computing scale values and weights is typically collected through a scaling survey questionnaire administered to critical customers. The survey asks for opinions about the value of PLDs and the relative value of the functions.

4. *Develop a rating form or program.* The actual device used to collect ratings or reports of performance is usually a form to be completed by the rater. Figure 10.9 presents a very common, although generally ineffective, format for rating. A growing number of organizations now use computers to record ratings. A goal to strive for in developing either manual forms or computer-based systems is ease of use. That is, the process should be easy to understand and the time required to rate each performance dimension should be no more than 1 or 2 minutes.

5. *Develop a scoring procedure.* In simple systems, the score on each performance dimension is simply the rating that was entered, and the overall score is just the average of the dimension scores. More sophisticated systems require a more involved process of hand or computer scoring. These may require development of scoring formulas, scoring sheets, procedures for submitting raw ratings for scoring, and procedures for recording the scores and preparing score reports for raters and ratees.

6. *Develop an appeal process.* In one survey, 79 percent of respondents indicated that their companies' appraisal systems allow employees an opportunity to provide comments on appraisal forms. In 32 percent of firms, formal appeal or grievance systems existed to enable employees to appeal "unfair" appraisals.[70] Another survey reported that 94 percent of firms gave ratees the opportunity to rebut ratings.[71] Recall our discussion earlier in the chapter on the importance of appeal processes with regard to litigation concerning appraisal. Specific appeal procedures should be developed for dealing with disputed appraisal results. Disputed appraisal results may include cases in which ratees disagree with their

FIGURE 10.9
A TYPICAL PERFORMANCE APPRAISAL FORM

1. Employee's Name—Last, First, Middle Brown, Mary Eloise	2. Department Institutions	3. Division or Agency State Home and Training School	
4. Social Security No. 123-45-6789	5. Class Title, Grade, and Step Personnel Officer	6. Period of Report From: To: 3/1/92 3/1/93	7. Reason for Report Annual

8. **GENERAL INSTRUCTIONS**

THIS FORM IS TO BE COMPLETED IN DUPLICATE, AND ALL ENTRIES SHOULD BE TYPE-WRITTEN OR PRINTED IN INK. AFTER THE EMPLOYEE'S PERFORMANCE HAS BEEN EVALUATED BY THE SUPERVISOR AND REVIEWED BY HIGHER-LEVEL SUPERVISION, THE EMPLOYEE WILL BE COUNSELED CONCERNING HIS OR HER PERFORMANCE AND WILL SIGN ALL COPIES OF THIS FORM. THE EMPLOYEE'S SIGNATURE INDICATES THAT PERFORMANCE HAS BEEN REVIEWED AND DISCUSSED. EMPLOYEES WHO DO NOT CONCUR WITH THE EVALUATION MAY INDICATE THEIR DISAGREEMENT NEXT TO THEIR SIGNATURE. THE ORIGINAL WILL BE FILED IN THE INDIVIDUAL'S DEPARTMENT PERSONNEL FOLDER. THE SECOND COPY WILL BE GIVEN TO THE EMPLOYEE AT THE TIME OF THE EVALUATION. IF THE RATING IS "OUTSTANDING", "BELOW STANDARD", OR "UNSATISFACTORY", A THIRD COPY SHOULD BE COMPLETED AND FORWARDED WITH SUPPORTING NARRATIVE TO THE DEPARTMENT OF PERSONNEL. DETAILED INFORMATION ON HOW TO FILL OUT THIS FORM CAN BE FOUND IN THE "SUPERVISOR'S PERFORMANCE PLANNING AND REVIEW MANUAL."

9. Overall Employee Evaluation:

Total of Performance Values 28.0

☐ Outstanding*   ☐ Below Standard*

☒ Above Standard   ☐ Unsatisfactory*

☐ Standard

Refer to the "Supervisor's Performance Planning and Review Manual" to determine overall evaluation.

*Attach narrative explanation describing specific areas of Outstanding, Below Standard, or Unsatisfactory performance.

10. ___*Sherman L. Studley*___   *Feb 8, 1993*
    Supervisor's Signature   Date

11. ___*Betty Lincoln*___   *Feb 10, 1993*
    Higher-Level Supervisor's Signature   Date

12. _____   _____
    *Principal Department Head's Signature   Date

    *Required for Outstanding, Below Standard, or Unsatisfactory Reviews.

13. The performance plan and review have been discussed with my supervisor.

    ___*Mary Eloise Brown*___   *Feb. 15, 1993*
    Employee's Signature   Date

FIGURE 10.9 *(Continued)*

PERFORMANCE VALUE DEFINITIONS

4 CONSISTENTLY EXCEEDS WHAT IS EXPECTED	3 FREQUENTLY EXCEEDS WHAT IS EXPECTED	2 CONSISTENTLY ACHIEVES WHAT IS EXPECTED	1 OCCASIONALLY FAILS TO ACHIEVE WHAT IS EXPECTED	0 CONSISTENTLY FAILS TO ACHIEVE WHAT IS EXPECTED

Performance Factors — Performance Values: 4 3 2 1 0

1. Quality of Work
[4.2] Consider the extent to which completed work is accurate, neat, well-organized, thorough, and applicable

Researches and compiles data for reports. Takes dictation, transcribes, and types correspondence, reports, and minutes of meetings. Prepares and maintains monthly reports of training activities.

2. Quantity of Work
[2.5] Consider the extent to which the amount of work completed compares to quantity standards for the job or compares to quantity produced by other employees.

Maintains internal suspense system to ensure replies to correspondence within 4 working days. Reduces processing time of applications within the unit by 2 weeks.

3. Taking Action Independently
[ ] Consider the extent to which the employee shows initiative in making work improvements, identifies and corrects errors, develops new work tasks, or solves problems.

4. Relationship with People
[1.3] Consider the extent to which the employee works cooperatively with others, recognizes the needs and desires of other people, treats others with respect and courtesy, and inspires their respect and confidence.

Answers phone, makes appointments and reservations for division chief. Answers routine inquiries by visitors to the division. The department will receive no more than 1 complaint because of discourteous service.

5. Work Habits
[2.0] Consider how well the employee organizes and uses work tools and time, cares for equipment, is reliable and punctual, and observes established safety standards.

Prepares and maintains monthly report in accordance with established procedures. Ensures that clerical equipment is in good operating condition. Cleans and covers each piece of equipment daily per established procedures.

6. Effectiveness of Supervision
[ ] Consider how well the supervisor leads, directs, and utilizes subordinates; conducts performance reviews and employee development reviews on schedule; and administers personnel policies and procedures effectively and fairly among subordinates.

7. Pertinent Performance Factors Not Shown Above
[ ]

Sub-total

Grand Total

appraisals as well as cases in which appraisals are challenged by a higher-level manager. For any appeal, procedures should be specified for the number of appeal stages, the composition of an arbitration panel or panels, the rules of evidence, and the criteria for reaching judgments.

7. *Develop rater and ratee training programs and manuals.* Every appraisal system needs to clearly describe the duties of the raters and ratees who will be using the system. These may be described in written instructions on the appraisal forms, in training manuals, or through rater training programs. The rater's duties include observing performance, preparing for the appraisal, considering possible constraints on performance, performing the actual rating, scoring the rating, processing the completed rating, and providing the results to ratees. The degree to which the rater's ratings will be reviewed by higher-level management should also be covered, since in 74 percent of firms surveyed, appraisals are indeed reviewed by higher-level managers.[72] Finally, the appeal and adjudication process should be fully described. All this information is necessary to ensure that the appraisal system is effectively used and legally defensible. One of the prescriptions for a more legally defensible system is that raters be given instructions for or training in the use of the system. Generally, most organizations do provide written instructions for raters (82 percent of firms surveyed) or rater training (60 percent of firms surveyed).[73]

Ratees should be made fully aware of the appraisal process through publication of a ratee manual, training, or some other communication. Ratees should be given a description of how the appraisal system was developed, how they can get copies of the standards they will be appraised against, how to interpret the feedback report, what the ratings will be used for in the organization, how to appeal their appraisal scores and the standards by which an appeal will be evaluated and finally judged, and the protection they have against retaliation for challenging their appraisals. The FAA provides ratees with all this information, plus a guideline for specific remedial steps the ratee can take if ratings are not at an optimal level on certain performance dimensions.

IMPLEMENTING AN APPRAISAL SYSTEM

After an appraisal system has been designed and developed, it must be implemented. The process of actually putting the system into operation consists of the following steps: training, integration with the organiza-

tion's human resource information system (HRIS), and a pilot test.

Training

This is the most important component of a system's implementation. Separate training sessions should be held for at least three groups: raters, ratees, and decision makers and analysts. The training should focus on clarification of the information provided in the manuals for raters and ratees, and should "sell" the benefits of the program to all system users including top management. For example, at Reading & Bates, half-day rater training workshops are provided to all supervisors, and top-management support is generated for the appraisal system.[74] In Nuffield Hospitals, no hospital is allowed to use the appraisal system until all involved parties have received formal training. The training covers interviewing techniques, performance coaching, and mentoring, and uses videos, role plays, and other exercises.[75] Likewise, at Westinghouse, all raters in a new appraisal system are required to receive training in coaching and counseling, documentation, and conducting formal appraisals. Employees are also taught to document performance observations and are informed about the details of performance review sessions.[76]

Integration with HRIS

Ideally, the results of appraisals (whether manual or computer-based) of every employee should ideally be entered into a computerized data base. This is necessary to handle the data administration and scoring and to evaluate ratings for errors (e.g., leniency, halo, central tendency).[77] For example, at Hilton International, appraisal data are entered into an HRIS computer data base and combined with other information about individuals, career development programs, work units, and specific hotels.[78] The computerized appraisal system at E-Systems, Inc., is tied to a mainframe and linked with the personnel and payroll systems. Using graphics software, the distribution of appraisal ratings is analyzed to show the types of rating errors that may exist in the entire organization and in specific departments.[79] At the Defense Communications Agency, a division of the U.S. Department of Defense, all appraisal data are linked with the career ladders program as an important component of the succession planning system. Wells Fargo Bank and Continental Bank integrated their managerial appraisal systems with their employee surveys to provide more comprehensive information to managers about the quality of work life of their employees.

Pilot Test

A final, critical step in the implementation process is a tryout of the system, or a pilot test. Given all the details involved in the design, development, and implementation of an appraisal system, it is unrealistic to expect that everything is going to run smoothly the first time the system is used. Any system will have problems that can't be foreseen, and the only way to find and resolve them without having to suffer minor or major disasters is to try out the system. The pilot test should be made as realistic as possible, even including the detail of having some employees file mock appeals. Questionnaires should be distributed to raters and ratees after the tryout process to get their reactions and to identify trouble spots.

It is vital that a new appraisal system get off on the right foot. The first time it is used "for real" should leave people with a favorable impression. If not, the system may never achieve the level of cooperation necessary to make it work effectively. The FAA and the U.S. Postal Service, for example, conducted extensive pilot testing for their systems for subordinate appraisal of managers. Several important changes were based on the results of the pilot studies. For example, the FAA needed to better coordinate its subordinate appraisal system with its annual employee opinion survey so that contradictory information would not flow to management. (The pilot data had indicated that managers reported confusion over the seemingly contradictory results from the two sources of information.)

EVALUATING APPRAISAL SYSTEM EFFECTIVENESS

After an appraisal system is implemented in an organization, it should be evaluated to ensure that it meets its intended purposes effectively. For example, Marriott's installation of a new appraisal system was part of a renewed emphasis on customer service. The critical measure of the appraisal system's effectiveness was thus the extent to which it improved customer service. Few organizations evaluate appraisal systems at this level, however. As with many other HR systems (e.g., training), evaluations are often not conducted at all. A comprehensive evaluation of a performance appraisal system requires the collection of several types of data, including user reactions, inferential validity, discriminating power, and possible adverse impact. We shall review each of these measures of effectiveness below.

User Reactions

It is vital to learn the attitudes and reactions of raters and ratees to an appraisal system because any system ultimately depends on them for its effectiveness. Attitudes of employees can be assessed prior to the implementation of a new system to see how receptive they may be to a pending system. A survey of state government employees found that employees who believed that their supervisors could rate them fairly and thought that they could measure quality were comparatively receptive and less resistant to a pending appraisal system.[80] Reactions should also be assessed after implementation of a new system. No matter how sophisticated an appraisal system may be, if employees and managers are resistant to using it, the appraisal system will not be effective. At Westinghouse, both raters and ratees are asked to evaluate the appraisal system in terms of the coaching and counseling sessions, the practicality of the forms, and the quality of performance standards. A task force works with the HR staff each year to formally review the appraisal system to ensure that it is working.[81] Employees at the Minnesota Department of Transportation are surveyed to assess their opinions regarding the frequency of appraisals, the use of informal appraisal methods, and the opportunity for self-appraisals.[82] At American Cyanamid Company, surveys were administered to managers both before and after installation of a new system, to compare their reactions to the previous system with their reactions to the new system. Those using a system which did not require forced distribution ratings were found to be more likely to report that the system was fair, showed logical links between the appraisals and pay and promotions, and was based on the major aspects of the job.[83]

It is important to assess raters' reactions to find out whether they perceive the system as easy to use and its content as representative of the important job content.[84] Also, raters should be asked whether they feel they have been adequately trained to use the system and have been given enough time to complete appraisals. Furthermore, they should be asked to indicate their commitment to making the system work. One survey found that the extent to which a rater perceives that other raters are using the system fairly predicts the extent of leniency bias committed by that rater.[85]

It is also important to collect ratees' reactions to an appraisal system, because ratees exert powerful influences on the tendency of raters to appraise accurately. If ratees feel unfairly appraised and resent raters, they will probably react in a defensive or hostile fashion. The raters may then assign more lenient ratings to the employees for the next appraisal session in order to avoid conflict and confrontations. This inflation will damage the accuracy of the appraisals. Generally, ratees want a system that they perceive as being fair, informative, useful, and free of bias. Their opinions on these issues should be assessed after the system has been implemented. One study found that ratees perceived a system which incorporated assessments of possible constraints on employee performance as fairer than another system which did not take such constraints into account.[86]

Inferential Validity

When considering how effectively an appraisal system operates, the issue of validity refers to accuracy—that is, the extent to which its scores correspond to the *true* levels and standings of the performances being appraised (e.g., to what degree an employee who is rated as "average" really is exhibiting average performance). The problem is that often we have no idea of what the true level of performance is.[87] We can rely only on subjective ratings or records of performance. If we had a method of assessing true performance, we would be using that method as our appraisal measure.

In the absence of any way to assess a system's internal validity directly, the best approach seems to be to infer validity by determining whether the appraisal system is reliable, free from bias, and relevant, and whether it has discriminant validity.[88] The most important measure of reliability for appraisal is the extent to which independent raters agree on an evaluation. (Appendix A presents a detailed discussion of reliability.) Freedom from bias is the degree to which the ratings are free from evidence of errors (e.g., leniency, central tendency, halo, sexual stereotyping). An appraisal system's relevance is the degree to which it encompasses all of a job's critical functions as defined by internal and external customers and their applicable criteria, and excludes irrelevant activities or functions. Appraisals that are relevant also weight the functions in proportion to their relationship to effective performance as defined by customers and, more important, to the goals of the organization or work unit. Discriminant validity, related to halo effect, is the degree to which ratees are ordered differently on each performance dimension—in other words, it determines the extent to which ratings on one dimension are related to ratings on other dimensions. Low correlations are desirable because each performance dimension should measure a separate work function.

Discriminating Power

If an appraisal system is successful at differentiating ratee performances in the job or jobs for which it is being used, it is said to have discriminating power. The difficulty in assessing appraisal systems on this criterion lies in defining what constitutes successful differentiation. How much differentiation is optimal? Can we expect the distribution of ratees' scores to form a normal curve over the possible range of scores? In many cases, this expectation may be unreasonable if employees have been carefully recruited, selected, and trained. The question of how much differentiation is desirable must be answered clearly before a system's discriminating power can be evaluated. After one organization recently installed a pay-for-performance system, the very first round of appraisals under the new system found that 98 percent of rated employees were eligible for the highest merit raise. Management, concluding that the system had insufficient discriminating power, contracted with the consulting firm of Booz, Allen and Hamilton to gain more discrimination in the appraisal system. As we said earlier, IBM had the same problem with its performance appraisal system and instituted a forced-distribution method because of the lack of differentiation. Employees are rated on a 4-point scale with 10 percent receiving the top and bottom grades, and the rest getting the middle ratings. Many IBM employees strongly oppose the imposition of the 10 percent requirement for effective and ineffective employees, given the thorough HRM processes in employee selection, training, and development.

Adverse or Disparate Impact

This criterion focuses on whether the appraisal scores of members of groups protected by laws (e.g., laws concerning race, gender, age, disabilities, and veterans) are significantly different from others. For example, if the performance of minority employees is evaluated as being significantly lower than the performance of white employees, then adverse or disparate impact may be evident if personnel decisions are made based on the appraisals. (See the related discussion in Chapter 3.)

If adverse impact is found, the organization will need to do some additional checks on the appraisal system. For example, the organization should determine whether the group of employees adversely affected was likely to be given assignments that were more difficult, more aversive, or subject to more situational constraints than those of other employees, or whether they received lower appraisals than they deserved based on other data. If so, then it would be unwise to continue to use the appraisal system. Maxine Liesa was terminated by Lopata Furniture for poor sales performance. Maintaining that there were constraints on her ability to achieve sales quotas, she was able to show that the company had failed to provide adequate samples of the products she was supposed to sell, as compared to the samples provided to other sales personnel. The court regarded this problem as a serious (and unfair) constraint on her ability to achieve her sales quotas. In a case brought under ADEA, P&W had difficulty in defending the fact that many older workers received lower ratings than younger employees who were doing the same work only after the company embarked on a substantial cost-cutting program in which managers were evaluated on the extent to which they could achieve a 40 percent reduction in overhead. A disproportionate number of older workers were terminated because of the appraisal results.

If no problems are found with the appraisal system, it can be used even if there are differences in appraisal results as a function of race, gender, age, or disabilities. In general, however, personnel decisions based on appraisal systems which result in adverse impact are difficult to defend, particularly if the prescriptions we presented earlier in this chapter are not characteristic of the system.

SUMMARY

Performance appraisals have become increasingly important tools for organizations to use in managing and improving the performance of employees, in making timely and accurate staffing decisions, and in enhancing the overall quality of the firm's services and products. The design, development, and implementation of appraisal systems are not endeavors which can be effectively handled by following the latest fad or even by copying other organizations' systems. Instead, a new appraisal system must be considered a major organizational change effort which should be pursued in the context of improving the organization's competitive advantage. As with any such change effort, individuals who wish to preserve the status quo will be resistant to change, no matter how beneficial it may be for the organization. These sources of resistance to change have to be identified and managed so as to build incentives for using a new appraisal system.

Even after a well-designed system has been implemented, the work is still not done. An appraisal system has to be maintained by monitoring its operation through periodic evaluations. Only an appraisal system that is kept finely tuned in the context of customer expectations will enable managers to have a rational basis for making sound personnel decisions and for contributing to the kinds of gains in U.S. productivity that are so critically needed in today's times.

Among HRM decisions and activities, some of the most important concern the organization's compensation system. Effective performance appraisal must also be carefully integrated with an organization's compensation system, particularly when the organization is seeking a close connection between performance and pay. We will turn our attention to the HRM activities related to compensation in Chapters 11 and 12.

DISCUSSION QUESTIONS

1. Why has performance appraisal taken on increased significance in recent years?
2. As the workforce becomes more diverse, why does performance appraisal become a more difficult process?
3. How would you determine whether an organization's appraisal system was legally defensible?
4. Many managers describe performance appraisal as the responsibility which they like the least. Why is this so? What could be done to improve the situation?
5. Describe several advantages and disadvantages to using rating instruments which are based on comparisons among ratees' performance, comparisons among PLDs (descriptors), and comparisons to PLDs (descriptors).
6. What steps would you take if your performance appraisal system resulted in disparate or adverse impact?
7. Under what circumstances would you use customer or client evaluations as a basis for appraising employees?
8. Why should managers provide ongoing and frequent feedback to employees about their performance?
9. Some of the leaders of the "total quality movement" such as Deming say performance appraisal is counterproductive. Do you agree or disagree?
10. Do you think managers should be evaluated by their subordinates? If so, how should the information be used and what procedures should be followed?

NOTES

1. Bernardin, H. J., and Kane, J. S. (1993). *Performance appraisal: A contingency approach to system development and evaluation.* 2d ed. Boston, MA: PWS-Kent. See also: A. K. Wigdor and B. F. Green (eds.) (1992). *Performance assessment for the workplace,* vols. I and II: *The technical issues.* Washington, DC: National Academy Press.
2. Bretz, R. D., Milkovich, G. T., and Read, W. (1990). *Comparing the performance appraisal practices in large firms with the directions in research literature: Learning more and more about less and less.* Working paper 89-17. Ithaca, NY: Cornell University, Industrial Labor Relations School. See also: Levine, H. Z. (1986). Performance appraisals at work. *Personnel, 63*(6), 63–71.
3. Lwumeyer, J., and Beebe, T. (1988). Employees and their appraisal: How do workers feel about the company grading scale? *Personnel Administrator, 33*(12), 76–80.
4. Kane, J. S., and Kane, K. F. (1988). *A survey of performance appraisal effectiveness in Fortune 500 firms: A report of the findings.* Unpublished report. See also: Laud, R. L. (1984). Performance appraisal practices in the Fortune 300. In C. J. Fombrun, N. M. Tichy, and M. A. Devanna (eds.), *Strategic human resource management.* New York: John Wiley and Sons, pp. 111–126. Locher, A. H., and Teel, K. S. (1977). Performance appraisal: A survey of current practices. *Personnel Journal, 56,* 245–255.

5. See note 4, Kane and Kanc (1988).

6. Lawler, E. E., III (1987). Paying for performance: Future directions. In D. B. Balkin and L. R. Gomez-Mejia (eds.), *New perspectives on compensation.* Englewood Cliffs, NJ: Prentice-Hall.

7. See note 1.

8. Ghorpade, J. V. (1988). *Job analysis: A handbook for the human resource director.* Englewood Cliffs, NJ: Prentice-Hall.

9. Romanoff, K. E. (1989). The ten commandments of performance management. *Personnel, 66*(1), 24–28.

10. See note 4, Locher and Teel (1977).

11. Cowfer, D. B., and Sujansky, J. (1987). Appraisal development at Westinghouse. *Training and Development Journal, 41*(7), 40–43. See also: Hall, T. C. (1987). Starting over. *Training and Development Journal, 41*(12), 60–62. Wagel, W. H. (1988). A software link between performance appraisals and merit increases. *Personnel, 65*(3), 9–14. Woods, J. G., and Dillion, T. (1985). The performance review approach to improving productivity. *Personnel, 62*(3), 20–27.

12. Kane, J. S. (1986). Performance distribution assessment. In R. A. Berk (ed.), *Performance assessment: Methods and applications.* Baltimore: Johns Hopkins University Press, pp. 237–273. See also: Sackett, P. R., Zedeck, S., and Fogli, L. (1988). Relations between measures of typical and maximum job performance. *Journal of Applied Psychology, 73,* 482–486.

13. Holley, W. H., and Walters, R. S. (1987). An employment at will vulnerability audit. *Personnel Journal, 66*(4), 130–139. See also: Krueger, A. B. (1991). The evolution of unjust-dismissal legislation in the United States. *Industrial and Labor Relations Review, 44,* 644–660.

14. See note 2, Levine (1986).

15. Barrett, G. V., and Kernan, M. C. (1987). Performance appraisal and terminations: A review of court decisions since *Brito v. Zia* with implications for personnel practices. *Personnel Psychology, 40*(3), 489–503. See also: Note 1. Koys, D. J., Briggs, S., and Grenig, J. (1986). Individual states' judicial decisions on the challenges to employment-at-will. *Proceedings of the Academy of Management, 46,* 255–259.

16. See note 1.

17. See note 9.

18. Addams, H. L., and Embley, K. (1988). Performance management systems: From strategic planning to employee productivity. *Personnel, 65*(4), 55–60.

19. See note 12, Kane (1986).

20. Coombs, C. H. (1964). *A theory of data.* New York: John Wiley and Sons. See also: Kane, J. S., and Lawler, E. E., III (1978). Methods of peer assessment. *Psychological Bulletin, 85,* 555–586.

21. Wagel, W. H. (1987). Performance appraisal with a difference. *Personnel, 64*(2), 4–6.

22. See note 10.

23. Levy, M. (1989). Almost-perfect performance appraisals. *Personnel Journal, 68*(4), 76, 78, 80, 83.

24. Kane, J. S., and Kane, K. F. (1992). The analytic frame-work: The most promising approach for the advancement of performance appraisal. *Human Resource Management Review, 2*(1), 37–40.

25. Bernardin, H. J. (1992). An "analytic" framework for customer-based performance content development and appraisal. *Human Resource Management Review, 2*(1), 81–102. See also: Landy, F. J., and Farr, J. (1983). *The measurement of work performance.* New York: Academic Press. Landy, F. J., and Farr, J. (1980). Performance rating. *Psychological Bulletin, 87,* 72–97.

26. See note 11, Hall (1987).

27. See note 14.

28. Feldman, J. (1992). The case for nonanalytic performance appraisal. *Human Resource Management Review, 2*(1). See also: Note 25, Landy and Farr (1983). Feldman, J. M. (1981). Beyond attribution theory: Cognitive processes in performance ratings. *Journal of Applied Psychology, 66,* 127–148. Murphy, K. R., and Cleveland, J. N. (1991). *Performance appraisal: An organizational perspective.* Boston, MA: Allyn & Bacon.

29. Milkovich, G. T., and Wigdor, A. K. (eds.) (1991). *Pay for performance: Evaluating performance appraisal and merit pay.* Washington, DC: National Research Council.

30. Banks, C. G., and Murphy, K. R. (1985). Toward narrowing the research-practice gap in performance appraisal. *Personnel Psychology, 38*(2), 335–345. See also: Hogan, E. A. (1987). Effects of prior expectations on performance ratings: A longitudinal study. *Academy of Management Journal, 30,* 354–368. Kane, J. S., and Lawler, E. E., III (1979). Performance appraisal effectiveness: Its assessment and determinants. In B. Staw (ed.), *Research in organizational behavior,* vol. 1. Greenwich, CT: JAI Press. Note 28, Murphy and Cleveland (1991).

31. Athey, T. R., and McIntyre, R. M. (1987). Effect of rater training on rater accuracy: Level-of-processing theory and social facilitation theory perspectives. *Journal of Applied Psychology, 72,* 239–244. See also: Bernardin, H. J., and Buckley, M. R. (1981). A consideration of strategies in rater training. *Academy of Management Review, 6,* 205–212. Bernardin, H. J., and Pence, E. C. (1980). Rater training: Creating new response sets and decreasing accuracy. *Journal of Applied Psychology, 65,* 60–66. McIntyre, R. M., Smith, D. E., and Hassett, C. E. (1984). Accuracy of performance ratings as affected by rater training and perceived purpose of rating. *Journal of Applied Psychology, 69,* 147–156. Pulakos, E. D. (1984). A comparison of rater training programs: Error training and accuracy training. *Journal of Applied Psychology, 69,* 581–588. Pulakos, E. D. (1986). The development of training programs to increase accuracy with different rating tasks. *Organizational Behavior and Human Decision Processes, 38,* 76–91.

32. Longenecker, C. O., Gioia, D. A., and Sims, H. P., Jr. (1987). Behind the mask: The politics of employee appraisal. *The Academy of Management Executive, 1,* 183–193. See also: Note 28, Murphy and Cleveland (1991). Wilson, M. C. (1990). *Factors related to*

distortion of performance appraisal ratings, Unpublished doctoral dissertation. Knoxville: The University of Tennessee.

33. See note 15, Barrett and Kernan (1987). See also: Fox, S., and Dinur, Y. (1988). Validity of self-assessment: A field evaluation. *Personnel Psychology, 41,* 581–592. Farh, J. L., and Werbel, J. D. (1986). Effects of purpose of the appraisal and expectations of validation on self-appraisal leniency. *Journal of Applied Psychology, 71,* 527–529. Note 12, Kane (1986). Note 30, Kane and Lawler (1979). Note 28, Murphy and Cleveland (1991).

34. Bernardin, H. J., and Villanova, P. J. (1986). Performance appraisal. In E. A. Locke (ed.), *Generalizing from laboratory to field settings:* Lexington, MA: Lexington Books, pp. 43–62.

35. Peters, L. H., and O'Connor, E. J. (1980). Situational constraints and work outcomes: The influence of a frequently overlooked construct. *Academy of Management Review, 5,* 391–397.

36. Bernardin, H. J. (1989). Increasing the accuracy of performance measurement: A proposed solution to erroneous attributions. *Human Resource Planning, 12,* 239–250.

37. See note 10.

38. See note 14.

39. Wilson, J., and Cole, G. (1990). A healthy approach to performance appraisal. *Personnel Management, 22*(6), 46–49.

40. See note 3. See also: Farh, J., Dobbins, G. H., and Cheng, B. (1991). Cultural relativity in action: A comparison of self-ratings made by Chinese and U.S. workers. *Personnel Psychology, 44*(1), 129–148. London, M., and Wohlers, A. J. (1991). Agreement between subordinate and self-ratings in upward feedback. *Personnel Psychology, 44*(2), 375–390.

41. Bernardin, H. J. (1986). Subordinate appraisal: A valuable source of information about managers. *Human Resource Management, 25,* 421–439. See also: Harris, M. M., and Schaubroeck, J. (1988). A meta-analysis of self-supervisor, self-peer, and peer-supervisor ratings. *Personnel Psychology, 41,* 43–62. Note 25, Landy and Farr (1983). Tsui, A. S., and Barry, B. (1986). Interpersonal affect and rating errors. *Academy of Management Journal, 29,* 586–598. Wohlers, A. J., and London, M. (1989). Ratings of managerial characteristics: Evaluation difficulty, co-worker agreement, and self-awareness. *Personnel Psychology, 42,* 235–261.

42. See note 41, Bernardin (1986). See also: Bernardin, H. J., and Beatty, R.W. (1984). *Performance appraisal: Assessing human behavior at work.* Boston, MA: PWS-Kent. Fiske, D.W., and Cox, J. A. (1960). The consistency of ratings by peers. *Journal of Applied Psychology, 44,* 11–17. Note 41, Harris, and Schaubroeck (1988). Note 20, Kane and Lawler (1978). Mabe, P. A., III, and West, S. G. (1982). Validity of self-evaluation of ability: A review and meta-analysis. *Journal of Applied Psychology, 67,* 280–296.

43. Edwards, M. R. (1990). Implementation strategies for multiple rater systems. *Personnel Journal, 69*(9), 130, 132, 134, 137, 139.

44. Edwards, M. R. (1990). A joint effort leads to accurate appraisals. *Personnel Journal, 69*(6), 122, 124, 126, 128.

45. Schuler, R. S., and Huber, V. L. (1990). *Personnel and human resource management,* 4th ed. St. Paul, MN: West Publishing. See also: Hoffman, C. C., Nathan, B. R., and Holden, L. M. (1991). A comparison of validation criteria: Objective versus subjective performance measures and self-versus-supervisor ratings. *Personnel Psychology, 44,* 601–619.

46. See note 44. See also: Gabor, A. (Jan. 26, 1992). Take this job and love it. *The New York Times,* F1, F6.

47. Lanza, P. (1985). Team appraisals. *Personnel Journal, 64*(3), 47–51.

48. See note 10.

49. See note 14.

50. See note 3.

51. See note 3.

52. See note 1.

53. Lawrie, J.W. (1989). Your performance: Appraise it yourself. *Personnel, 66*(1), 21–23.

54. See note 14.

55. Allen, M. (Sept. 24, 1991). Legislation could restrict bosses from snooping on their workers. *The Wall Street Journal,* pp. B1, B7.

56. Ashford, S. J., and Cummings, L. L. (1983). Feedback as an individual resource: Personal strategies of creating information. *Organizational Behavior and Human Performance, 32,* 370–398. See also: Locke, E. A., Cartledge, N., and Koeppel, J. (1968). Motivational effects of knowledge of results: A goal-setting phenomenon. *Psychological Bulletin, 70,* 474–485. Note 28, Murphy and Cleveland (1991). Northcraft, G. B., and Earley, P. C. (1989). Technology, credibility, and feedback use. *Organizational Behavior and Human Decision Processes, 44,* 83–96.

57. Dorfman, P.W., Stephan, W. G., and Loveland, J. (1986). Performance appraisal behaviors: Supervisor perceptions and subordinate reactions. *Personnel Psychology, 39,* 579–597. See also: Note 40, Farh, Dobbins, and Cheng, (1991). Note 40, London and Wohlers (1991). Nathan, B. R., Mohrman, A. M., Jr., and Milliman, J. (1991). Interpersonal relations as a context for the effects of appraisal interviews on performance and satisfaction: A longitudinal study. *Academy of Management Journal, 34,* 352–369.

58. Earley, P. C. (1988). Computer-generated performance feedback in the magazine-subscription industry: *Organizational Behavior and Human Decision Processes, 41,* 50–64.

59. Fiske, S. T., and Taylor, S. E. (1984). *Social cognition.* Reading, MA: Addison-Wesley. See also: Jones, E. E., and Davis, K. E. (1965). From acts to dispositions: The attribution process in person perception. In L. Berkowitz (ed.), *Advances in experimental social psychology,* vol. 2. New York: Academic Press, pp. 220–266. Ross,

L. (1977). The intuitive psychologist and his shortcomings: Distortions in the attribution process. In L. Berkowitz (ed.), *Advances in experimental social psychology,* vol. 9. New York: Academic Press, pp. 174–226.

60. Fisher, C. D. (1979). Transmission of positive and negative feedback to subordinates: A laboratory investigation. *Journal of Applied Psychology, 64,* 533–540. See also: Ilgen, D. R., and Knowlton, W. A. (1980). Performance attributional effects of feedback from superiors. *Organizational Behavior and Human Performance, 25,* 441–456.

61. Larson, J. R. (1986). Supervisors' performance feedback to subordinates: The impact of subordinate performance valence and outcome dependence. *Organizational Behavior and Human Decision Processes, 37,* 391–408.

62. See note 57.

63. Cederblom, D. (1982). The performance appraisal interview: A review, implications, and suggestions. *Academy of Management Review, 7,* 219–227.

64. Becker, T. E., and Klimoski, R. J. (1989). A field study of the relationship between the organizational feedback environment and performance. *Personnel Psychology, 42,* 343–358.

65. Kirkpatrick, D. L. (1986). Performance appraisals: Your questions answered. *Training and Development Journal, 40*(5), 68–71.

66. See note 1. See also: Meyer, H. H. (1991). A solution to the performance appraisal feedback enigma. *Academy of Management Executive, 5*(1), 68–76.

67. Day, D. (1989). Performance management year-round. *Personnel, 66*(8), 43–45. See also: Romanoff, K. E. (1989). The ten commandments of performance management. *Personnel, 66*(1), 24–28.

68. Bemis, S. E., Belenky, A. H., and Soder, D. A. (1983). Job analysis: *An effective management tool.* Washington: The Bureau of National Affairs.

69. Woods, J. G., and Dillion, T. (1985). The performance review approach to improving productivity. *Personnel, 62*(3), 20–27.

70. See note 10.

71. See note 14.

72. See note 10.

73. See note 10.

74. See note 69.

75. See note 39.

76. See note 11.

77. See note 44.

78. See note 14.

79. See note 21.

80. Rush, M. C., Facteau, J. D., Russell, J. E. A., and Dobbins, G. H. (April 1991). *Contextual factors related to perceptions of a pending appraisal system.* Paper presented at the annual meeting of the Society for Industrial and Organizational Psychology, St. Louis, MO.

81. See note 11.

82. See note 3.

83. Gellerman, S. W., and Hodgson, W. G. (1988). Cyanamid's new take on performance appraisal. *Harvard Business Review, 66*(3), 36–37, 40–41.

84. See note 14.

85. Bernardin, H. J., and Orban, J. A. (1990). Leniency effects as a function of rating format purpose for appraisal, and rater individual differences. *Journal of Business and Psychology, 5,* 197–211.

86. See note 80.

87. See note 15, Barrett and Kernan (1987). See also: Sulsky, L. M., and Balzer, W. K. (1988). Meaning and measurement of performance rating accuracy: Some methodological and theoretical concerns. *Journal of Applied Psychology, 73*(3), 497–506.

88. See note 30, Kane and Lawler (1979).

EXERCISE 10.1
THE DEVELOPMENT OF A
PERFORMANCE APPRAISAL SYSTEM
FOR INSTRUCTORS*

OVERVIEW

The purpose of this exercise is to explore the concept of performance. You will discover that multiple activities determine overall performance and that various criteria can be applied to these activities to create a set of performance dimensions. You will follow several steps to construct a performance appraisal form that could be used to assess your instructors. Finally, you will examine the variability of performance and include this in your assessment of performance.

LEARNING OBJECTIVES

After completing this exercise, you should be able to:

1. Have a better understanding of the multidimensionality of performance.
2. Know how to construct measurable performance dimensions.
3. Understand the steps involved in the development of an appraisal system.

PROCEDURE

Step 1. Prior to class, complete Parts A, B, and C, below.

Part A: The Multidimensionality of Performance Assessment

What leads you to believe that your instructors perform well or poorly in your courses? Do their lectures entirely determine your rating? Are there other outcomes that influence your rating? In other words, is performance multidimensional?

Which of the following activities would you consider to be relevant in rating an instructor's overall performance? To show how important each of these is, divide up 100 percentage points among these to show how much you think each one should be weighted (one or more may be given a weight of zero).

_____ Lecture organization
_____ Oral explanation
_____ Providing examples
_____ Conducting exercises
_____ Using audiovisual media
_____ Grading
_____ Course-related advising and feedback
_____ Classroom interaction
100% Total

Enter the activity weight in the space provided in Exhibit 10.1.1.

Part B: Determining Performance Criteria

The value of an instructor's performance in each of the above activities can be considered from several different perspectives. For example, we might consider performance on grading from the perspectives of its quality and timeliness. Each of these perspectives is called a "criterion." The examples that follow illustrate some of the criteria on which performance in these instructor activities can be evaluated. You are to decide which of these combinations of an activity and a criterion are appropriate to include.

For example, the cell "quality of grading" in Exhibit 10.1.1 refers to _how well_ or how accurately the instructor graded exams, assignments, etc. The cell "timeliness of grading" refers to _how quickly_ the exams or assignments were graded. These two aspects of grading determine how an instructor did in the grading category overall. Obviously, an instructor could have accurately graded the exams and achieved a perfect rating on quality of grading but not done so well on the timeliness of grading those exams. Conversely, another instructor may have graded the exams promptly but perhaps not graded the exams so that they accurately reflected students' achievement.

Another example is "interpersonal impact of course-related advising and feedback," which refers to whether the instructor gave you encouragement and confidence in overcoming your difficulties in the course as opposed to making you feel that further effort would get you nowhere. Another example might be "quantity of classroom interaction," which would refer to the number of times the instructor asked a question or invited comments during the class.

Your role is to select the cells of the matrix in Exhibit 10.1.1 which would be relevant to assessing an instructor's performance. Each of the categories to the left is referred to as an "instructor activity" and the criteria on which performance can be valued are listed across the top under the heading of "criteria." (Review the definitions of these four criteria in Figure 10.2.) Place an X in each cell you select as relevant for any activity given a weight greater than zero in Part A.

---

*Contributed by Jeffrey S. Kane and Kimberly F. Kane.

EXHIBIT 10.1.1
MATRIX OF INSTRUCTOR ACTIVITIES AND CRITERIA

Name_____ Group _____

INSTRUCTOR ACTIVITY	ACTIVITY WEIGHT*	CRITERIA			
		Quality	Quantity	Timeliness	Interpersonal Impact
Lecture organization _____		Wt: #1 Wt: #2	1 2	1 2	1 2
Oral explanation _____		Wt: #1 Wt: #2	1 2	1 2	1 2
Providing examples _____		Wt: #1 Wt: #2	1 2	1 2	1 2
Conducting exercises _____		Wt: #1 Wt: #2	1 2	1 2	1 2
Using audiovisual media _____		Wt: #1 Wt: #2	1 2	1 2	1 2
Grading _____		Wt: #1 Wt: #2	1 2	1 2	1 2
Course-related advising and feedback _____		Wt: #1 Wt: #2	1 2	1 2	1 2
Classroom interaction _____		Wt: #1 Wt: #2	1 2	1 2	1 2

* Must total 100%

Part C: Weighting of Performance Dimensions

The cells you have chosen are referred to as *performance dimensions*. Each performance dimension consists of the combination of a job activity and a criterion. Next, you will need to look at each row of the matrix and assign weights that reflect the relative importance of each of the relevant criteria in determining performance on the activity as a whole. Do this by distributing 100 points among the criteria you designated as relevant to each activity. For example, if the only two criteria for grading were quality and timeliness, perhaps the importance of these would be equally split, 50 and 50. If quality were seen as more important, perhaps the numbers would be 60 and 40. Enter these percentages in the space labelled Wt. #1 for the "grading" row.

Once you have assigned numbers to each of the *relevant* performance dimensions in the matrix, multiply each number by the numbers that were determined in Part A of this exercise (the activity weights). Let's say that you assigned "grading" a 30 in Part A, and further, you set the relative importance of "quality of grading" at 60 and "timeliness of grading" at 40. The weight of each of these performance dimensions in the matrix (as a percentage of the whole matrix) would be:

Quality of grading   = 30% × 60% = 18%
Timeliness of grading = 30% × 40% = 12%

Fill in the weights for the rest of the performance dimensions in the matrix in the space labelled Wt. #2. These percentages will add up to 100 percent.

Step 2. In small groups, students should compare their individual results from Parts A to C and develop a strategy for determining a group response. Once the group has developed a strategy, a response should be derived and assignments should be made for the derivation of descriptors in Part D.

Part D: Creation of PLDs

The next step is to create statements that exemplify the best and worst extremes of each of the performance dimensions the group chose as appropriate to rate. In order to determine how well or poorly the instructor performed on any of these performance dimensions, one must first identify what exemplifies good performance and what exemplifies poor performance. Only by having explicit anchors can a rater provide a meaningful rating.

Statements used as anchors at the ends and middle of a good-bad continuum must clearly state the behavior or result that constitutes each of these three scale points. These statements are referred to as *performance level descriptors* (PLDs). These PLDs would be placed at the 1, 3, and 5 points of a 1 to 5 scale.

Each group should create PLDs for the end and middle points of the scale for each of the performance dimensions assigned by the instructor. Write out the PLDs and put them at the appropriate points on a 1 to 5 scale. Exhibit 10.1.2 presents examples of PLDs for three performance dimensions.

Step 3. After the scales have been completed for each performance dimension, the instructor will present a sample of the scales for practice ratings. Part E should be completed by each student.

Part E: Performance as a Distribution

Think of the performance of an instructor whom you've had the opportunity to observe. Have you noticed that he or she doesn't *always* present organized lectures and may not *always* return your exams at the next class session, *always* provide a lot of examples in class, or *always* explain the subject matter in a clear and understandable manner?

The instructor's performance is likely to vary from day to day depending on his or her ability and the amount of effort exerted. Motivational state, physical health, amount of sleep, distractions in the environment, and other phenomena produce variations in behavior that determine your impression of the person's overall performance.

When you created the 1 to 5 scales in Part D, you may have realized that an instructor's performance didn't always fit at one level. If you had to rate someone on these scales and put a check mark at only one point along the scale, you'd do so with the realization that sometimes the instructor did better than that level and sometimes worse than that level. Further, instructors differ in how consistently they achieve their "typical" levels of performance.

In order to capture the full picture of a person's performance, it is necessary to show how the performance was distributed across the levels of outcomes described by a rating scale such as the scales you have created. This can be done by specifying the percentage of times that an instructor achieved each level of performance, out of all the times that the person was required to perform that activity. The result, called a *performance graph*, is illustrated in Exhibit 10.1.3.

Assume that this was the graph for timeliness of grading and that the outcome levels were defined as the number of class sessions that passed before the instructor returned the exams: 1, more than four class sessions; 2, four class sessions; 3, three class sessions; 4, two class sessions; and 5, the next class session. The graph would show that the person never delayed returning the exams more than four sessions, 10 percent of the time waited four sessions before returning the exams, 20 percent of the time waited three sessions before returning the exams, 40 percent of the time waited two sessions before returning the exams, and 30 percent of the time returned the exams at the next class session. These total to 100 percent.

For this part of the exercise, you are to make a performance graph out of the performance dimension scales that students created earlier, with the PLDs as anchors at either end of the scale and in the middle of the scale.

Now, think again of the instructor with whom you are familiar. What does the performance graph look like

EXHIBIT 10.1.2

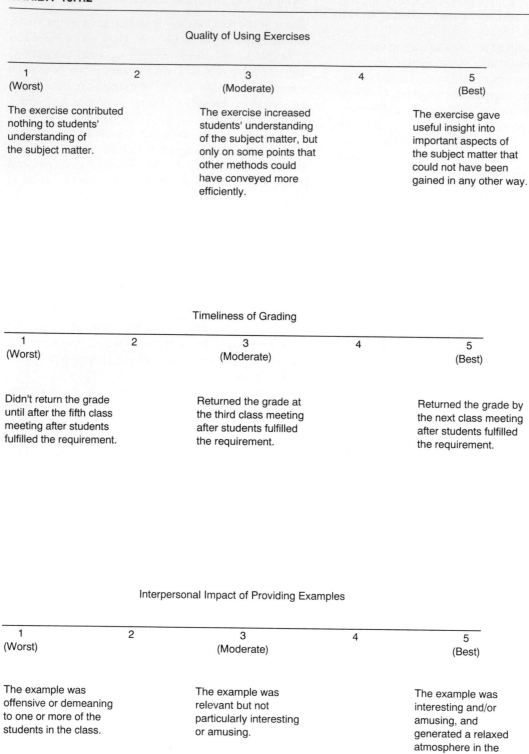

Quality of Using Exercises

1	2	3	4	5
(Worst)		(Moderate)		(Best)

The exercise contributed nothing to students' understanding of the subject matter.

The exercise increased students' understanding of the subject matter, but only on some points that other methods could have conveyed more efficiently.

The exercise gave useful insight into important aspects of the subject matter that could not have been gained in any other way.

Timeliness of Grading

1	2	3	4	5
(Worst)		(Moderate)		(Best)

Didn't return the grade until after the fifth class meeting after students fulfilled the requirement.

Returned the grade at the third class meeting after students fulfilled the requirement.

Returned the grade by the next class meeting after students fulfilled the requirement.

Interpersonal Impact of Providing Examples

1	2	3	4	5
(Worst)		(Moderate)		(Best)

The example was offensive or demeaning to one or more of the students in the class.

The example was relevant but not particularly interesting or amusing.

The example was interesting and/or amusing, and generated a relaxed atmosphere in the class.

EXHIBIT 10.1.3

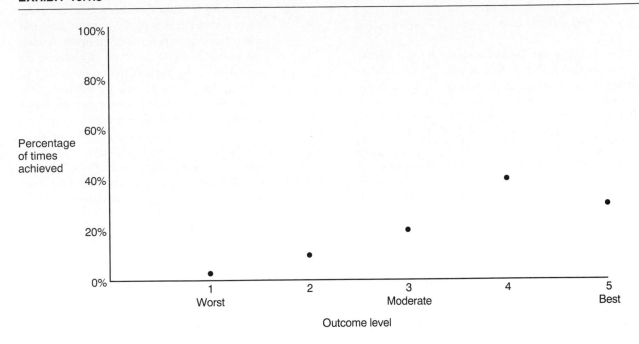

for each of the different performance dimensions for that person? Plot each performance graph independently of the other graphs, thinking only of the relevant anchors for that particular scale.

When you finish, look at the graphs as a group. Do you see any patterns emerging? Do you notice that the instructors are generally consistent in their behavior? Do some of the performance dimensions show more variation than others?

Look at particular groups of performance graphs—for example, all those relating to the same criterion. Are there patterns that show up when you look at all the "timeliness" graphs? (Is this person consistently late? Does he or she consistently procrastinate?) Do all the graphs having to do with "quality" show that the person does very high quality work? What about interpersonal impact? If so, what are the implications of this finding?

Part F: Calculating an Overall Mean Performance Score

Step 4. Next, an overall mean performance score will be calculated for the instructor. This calculation incorporates only the most basic parameter of performance, that of average (mean) performance. More sophisticated calculations of overall performance can take into consideration other relevant factors such as situ-

ational constraints on performance (things that prevented the instructor from performing as well as he or she could have done), as well as two additional parameters of performance: consistency of performance and avoidance of negative outcomes. The distributions depicted in the performance graphs are scored the same way that a grade point average is scored. Let's again use the example of the timeliness of grading. The distribution of the performance graph shown in Part E is as follows:

LEVEL	PERCENTAGE
1	0
2	10
3	20
4	40
5	30

Multiply the level times the percentage to get an average percentage for each performance dimension, as follows:

$$1 \times 0\% = 0.00$$
$$2 \times 10\% = 0.20$$
$$3 \times 20\% = 0.60$$
$$4 \times 40\% = 1.60$$
$$\underline{5 \times 30\% = 1.50}$$
$$3.90 \quad \text{total}$$

An average of 3.90 divided by a possible 5.0 is

$$3.90/5.00 = 0.78 \quad \text{or} \quad 78\%$$

Now, multiply the weight assigned to this performance dimension in Part C (which was 12 percent in the example) by the average of 78 percent which was just calculated:

$$12\% \times 78\% = 9.4\%$$

The instructor scores 9.4 percent for this dimension. Calculate all the other performance dimensions in exactly the same way. After making these calculations, add up the scores for all the performance dimensions to find the instructor's overall performance score.

Step 5. Group discussion should focus on the ability of students to make frequency judgments, the relative effectiveness of this type of appraisal relative to other types discussed in the chapter, the susceptibility of this type of performance appraisal to the various biases discussed in Chapter 10, and the criteria for evaluating the effectiveness of this performance appraisal system. Do the students feel that this approach to performance appraisal is superior to whatever form of appraisal they have used in the past to evaluate instructors? Would this be useful feedback for instructors? Finally, how would this approach work in industry?

EXERCISE 10.2
PRICE WATERHOUSE V. HOPKINS*

OVERVIEW

The purpose of this exercise is to familiarize students with an important U.S. Supreme Court case related to performance appraisal and to learn the implications of the case for appraisal system development, implementation, and administration.

LEARNING OBJECTIVES

After completing this exercise, you should be able to:

1. Understand the importance of performance appraisal for EEO litigation.
2. Suggest methods of performance appraisal which are legally defensible and which will result in the most valid results for the organization.
3. Understand how appraisal data may be used to make staffing (e.g., promotion) decisions.

*Contributed by Gregory Redmon.

PROCEDURE

Step 1. You have been retained as a consultant to advise Price Waterhouse on matters related to a lawsuit against the company and on methods which could be adopted to prevent further legal action against the company. Review the actual case summary in Exhibit 10.2.1.

Step 2. Prepare a report to the vice president of HR for Price Waterhouse, addressing the following issues: (1) Explain in detail whether you believe that Hopkins was a victim of illegal discrimination. (2) List the steps that can be taken in selecting partners to prevent a recurrence of this problem. Include a critique of the current system and specific recommendations for change. Be sure to include recommendations for evaluating partners' performance and for use of appraisal data in making promotion decisions. Complete the assessment questions on Form 10.2.1.

Step 3. In small groups, review the written recommendations of each group member and reach consensus on the specific recommendations you would propose for changing the system. Each group member should review the assessment responses as well. One group representative should present the findings to the class.

EXHIBIT 10.2.1
BACKGROUND CASE INFORMATION ON PRICE WATERHOUSE

At Price Waterhouse, a nationwide professional accounting partnership, a senior manager becomes a candidate for partnership when the partners in the local office submit his or her name as a candidate. All the other partners in the firm are then invited to submit written comments on each candidate—on either a "long" or a "short" form, depending on the partner's degree of knowledge about the candidate. Not every partner in the firm submits comments on every candidate. After reviewing the comments and interviewing the partners who submitted them, the firm's Admissions Committee makes a recommendation to the Policy Board. This recommendation will be that the firm either accept the candidate for partnership, put the application on hold, or deny the promotion outright. The Policy Board then decides whether to submit the candidate's name to the entire partnership for a vote, to hold the candidacy, or to reject the candidate. The recommendation of the Admissions Committee and the decision of the Policy Board are not controlled by fixed guidelines: a certain number of positive comments from partners will not guarantee a candidate's admission to the partnership, nor will a specific quantity of negative comments necessarily defeat the application. Price Waterhouse places no limit on the number of persons whom it will admit to the partnership in any given year.

Ann Hopkins had worked at Price Waterhouse's Office of Government Services in Washington, D.C., for 5 years when the partners in that office proposed her as a candidate for partnership. Of the 662 partners at the firm at that time, 7 were women. Of the 88 persons proposed for partnership that year, only 1—Hopkins—was a woman. Of the 88 candidates, 47 were admitted to the partnership, 21 were rejected, and 20—including Hopkins—were held for reconsideration the following year. Of the 32 partners who had submitted comments on Hopkins, 13 supported her bid for partnership, 3 recommended that her candidacy be placed on hold, 8 stated that they did not have an informed opinion about her, and 8 recommended that she be denied partnership.

In a jointly prepared statement supporting her candidacy, the partners in Hopkins' office showcased her successful 2-year effort to secure a $25 million contract with the Department of State, labeling it "an outstanding performance" and one that Hopkins carried out "virtually at the partner level." Despite Price Waterhouse's attempt at trial to minimize her contribution to this project, District Court Judge Gerhardt Gesell specifically found that Hopkins had "played a key role in Price Waterhouse's successful effort to win a multi-million dollar contract with the Department of State." Indeed, he went on, "none of the other partnership candidates at Price Waterhouse that year had a comparable record in terms of successfully securing major contracts for the partnership."

The partners in Hopkins' office praised her character as well as her accomplishments, describing her in their joint statement

EXHIBIT 10.2.1 *(Continued)*

as "an outstanding professional" who had a "deft touch" as well as a "strong character, independence and integrity." Clients appear to have agreed with these assessments. At trial, one official from the State Department described her as "extremely competent, intelligent, . . . strong and forthright, very productive, energetic and creative." Another high-ranking official praised Hopkins' decisiveness, broadmindedness, and "intellectual clarity"; she was, in his words, "a stimulating conversationalist." Evaluations such as these led Judge Gesell to conclude that Hopkins "had no difficulty dealing with clients and her clients appear to have been very pleased with her work" and that she "was generally viewed as a highly competent project leader who worked long hours, pushed vigorously to meet deadlines and demanded much from the multidisciplinary staffs with which she worked."

On too many occasions, however, Hopkins' aggressiveness apparently spilled over into abrasiveness. Staff members seem to have borne the brunt of Hopkins' brusqueness. Long before her bid for partnership, partners evaluating her work had counseled her to improve her relations with staff members. Although later evaluations indicated an improvement, Hopkins' perceived shortcomings in this important area eventually doomed her bid for partnership. Virtually all the partners' negative remarks about Hopkins—even those of partners supporting her—had to do with her "interpersonal skills." Both "supporters and opponents of her candidacy," stressed Judge Gesell, "indicated that she was sometimes overly aggressive, unduly harsh, difficult to work with and impatient with staff."

There were clear signs, though, that some of the partners reacted negatively to Hopkins' personality because she was a woman. One partner described her as "macho"; another suggested that she "overcompensated for being a woman"; a third advised her to take "a course at charm school." Several partners criticized her use of profanity; in response, one partner suggested that those partners objected to her swearing only "because it is a lady using foul language." Another supporter explained that Hopkins "had matured from a tough-talking somewhat masculine hard-nosed manager to an authoritative, formidable, but much more appealing lady partner candidate." As Judge Gesell found, the reason for the Policy Board's decision to place her candidacy on hold was to improve her chances for partnership. One partner advised that Hopkins should "walk more femininely, talk more femininely, dress more femininely, wear make-up, have her hair styled, and wear jewelry."

Dr. Susan Fiske, a social psychologist and associate professor of psychology at Carnegie-Mellon University, testified at the trial that the partnership selection process at Price Waterhouse was likely influenced by gender stereotyping. Her testimony fo-

cused not only on the overtly gender-based comments of partners but also on gender-neutral remarks, made by partners who knew Hopkins only slightly, that were intensely critical of her. One partner, for example, stated that Hopkins was "universally disliked" by staff, and another described her as "consistently annoying and irritating"; yet these people had very little direct contact with Hopkins. According to Fiske, Hopkins' uniqueness (as the only woman in the pool of candidates) and the subjectivity of the evaluations made it likely that sharply critical remarks such as these were the product of gender stereotyping—although Fiske admitted that she could not say with certainty whether any particular comment was the result of stereotyping. Fiske based her opinion on a review of the submitted comments, explaining that it was commonly accepted practice for social psychologists to reach this kind of conclusion without having met any of the people involved in the decision-making process.

In previous years, other female candidates for partnership also had been evaluated in gender-based terms. As a general matter, Judge Gesell concluded that female "candidates were viewed favorably if partners believed they maintained their femininity while becoming effective professional managers" and that, in this environment, "to be identified as a 'women's libber' was regarded as a negative comment." In fact, the judge found that in previous years "one partner repeatedly commented that he could not consider any woman seriously as a partnership candidate and believed that women were not even capable of functioning as senior managers—yet the firm took no action to discourage his comments and recorded his vote in the overall summary of the evaluations."

Judge Gesell found that Price Waterhouse legitimately emphasized interpersonal skills in its partnership decisions, and also found that the firm had not fabricated its complaints about Hopkins' interpersonal skills as a pretext for discrimination. Moreover, he concluded, the firm did not give decisive emphasis to such traits only because Hopkins was a woman, although there were male candidates who lacked these skills but were admitted to partnership. The judge found that the accepted male candidates had possessed other positive traits that Hopkins lacked. The judge went on to decide that some of the partners' remarks about Hopkins stemmed from their view of the "proper behavior of women" and that Price Waterhouse had done nothing to disavow reliance on such comments. In fact, Price Waterhouse had given credence and effect to partners' comments that resulted from gender stereotyping. Price Waterhouse presented testimony that even if they had not been "guilty" of gender stereotyping, they would have made the same decision regarding Hopkins.

Source: Price Waterhouse v. Hopkins, U.S. 99 S. Ct. 1775, 49 FEP Cases 954 (1989).

FORM 10.2.1

Name _____ Group _____

1. What legal statute applies to this case?

2. Is the Hopkins case a disparate treatment or a disparate impact case? Explain your answer.

3. What changes should Price Waterhouse make in the process of selecting partners? Be specific.

4. What steps would you take at Price Waterhouse to prevent a similar legal problem in the future?

5. Is gender stereotyping illegal? If so, does Hopkins prevail in this case?

EXERCISE 10.3
AN ASSESSMENT OF FACULTY
EVALUATION

OVERVIEW

The purpose of this exercise is to consider appraisal issues in the context of faculty evaluation. Each student should develop a user evaluation form and then interview at least two professors in order to determine faculty views on the appraisal process. The students should construct the interviews using the design components of an appraisal system, as discussed in Chapter 10 (e.g., who should do the rating, what type of rating instrument should be used, the content and uses of the rating instrument).

LEARNING OBJECTIVES

After completing this exercise, you should be able to:

1. Understand the key factors related to the perceived effectiveness and ineffectiveness of an appraisal system.
2. Note the variability in attitudes toward appraisal among individuals in similar jobs with regard to such issues as the purposes to be served by the data, the rating sources (e.g., students, peers, outside experts), and the weights placed on the criteria (e.g., teaching, research, service).

PROCEDURE

Part A: Individual Analysis

Step 1. Each student should interview at least two professors, preferably one of whom has yet to be granted tenure. Each interview should be of short duration (15 to 20 minutes) and should

address two general questions with regard to faculty appraisal: (1) How is faculty appraisal done? and (2) What improvements could be made in the system? Attempt to gather as much information as possible on all the critical design issues of appraisal. Note any recommendations which are made by the professors, as well as their views of the appraisal system's effectiveness. Try to get a copy of the actual appraisal form and any related documents.

Step 2. Prepare a report describing the appraisal system. On the basis of your own analysis, your reading of the chapter, and the recommendations of the professors, provide specific recommendations for either improving the current appraisal system or developing a new one.

Step 3. Individually, students should respond to the assessment questions on Form 10.3.1.

Part B: Group Analysis

Step 1. In small groups, review each other's reports. What variables appeared to have the most to do with the perceived effectiveness or ineffectiveness of the appraisal system(s)? Does there appear to be any consistent difference between the perspectives of tenured and untenured faculty?

Step 2. Keeping the design features discussed in the chapter in mind, each group should attempt to reach consensus on recommendations for an effective appraisal system. The recommendations should be made in the context of the purposes of the appraisal system. Students should justify any differences in appraisal system characteristics which they recommend for different appraisal purposes. One group member should present the recommendations to the rest of the class.

FORM 10.3.1

Name _____

1. What characteristics appear to have the most to do with perceived effectiveness of the appraisal system?

2. To what extent did you agree with the general view of the faculty members regarding the role of students in the appraisal process?

3. Given the way in which the appraisal system is described, do you think the institution could defend a lawsuit which in some way involved the appraisal system?

4. By order of priority, what three things would you change about the appraisal system to increase its effectiveness?

C H A P T E R

DIRECT AND INDIRECT COMPENSATION*

---

*Contributed by Lee P. Stepina and James R. Harris.

OVERVIEW

Few areas of human resource management (HRM) are more important to employees and employers than compensation. The compensation package, consisting of pay and benefits, is a major expense which critically affects the competitive position of the firm. Compensation levels determine employees' lifestyles, status, self-worth, and feelings toward the organization. In addition, compensation can have a profound impact on employee recruitment, motivation, productivity, and turnover.

Compensation is critical to people because pay and benefits can meet many needs. Most basic, of course, is the fact that money is necessary to buy food and shelter. Beyond the satisfaction of the most basic needs, pay and the things it buys are signs of achievement, prestige, power, and status in our society. Pay is also a sign of the worth of the individual to the organization and thus enhances the self-esteem of the well-paid employee.[1]

Since employee compensation is often the largest cost item to an organization (e.g., as much as 90 percent of costs in many service organizations), the effect of compensation programs on an organization's competitive position should be obvious. Organizations desire to motivate employees to engage in behaviors and to perform in a manner that sustains or improves the competitive advantage of the firm. Employees will perform to the extent that the performance itself or the organizational rewards fulfill important needs. For example, completing a difficult project may in and of itself provide the employee with an internal feeling of accomplishment. In addition, completion of the project may include an external reward provided by the organization, such as a bonus.

Although internal rewards play an important part in employee motivation, there is a basic problem with their use. Internal rewards can be given to employees only by the employees themselves. If you feel little or no satisfaction from completing a challenging task, there is little an organization can do about it. While organizations can and do try to structure conditions (and, as discussed in Chapter 5, select personnel based on the job-person "matching" model) in order to satisfy individuals' growth and achievement needs, there is no known way to make someone enjoy the intrinsic aspects of their work. Objective external rewards, on the other hand, are more within the control of an organization. An organization can decide whether or not to give a bonus or merit raise. If such an award is given, employees will be rewarded regardless of their internal needs states. Since pay amounts and methods of disbursement can be varied to an infinite degree, organizations can use pay to substantially affect employee behavior. The fact that organizations can manipulate the amounts and distribution of this reward makes pay a powerful means of achieving organizational effec-

tiveness.[2] Conversely, of course, mismanagement of pay can lead to dissatisfied employees and can seriously hinder the company's competitive position.

The purpose of this chapter is to review the influences of compensation on important outcomes for the organization and the employee. We will provide an overview of both direct and indirect compensation. Direct compensation is the basic wage and salary system, plus performance-based pay. Indirect compensation is the general category for employee benefits—mandated protection programs, health insurance, pay for time not worked, and various other employee benefits. We will also consider the influence of government and unions on compensation. Finally, a framework will be presented for managing pay to achieve both individual and organizational needs. Because of the strong movement in this country toward pay-for-performance systems, Chapter 12 will be devoted to a thorough treatment of this subject.

OBJECTIVES

After studying this chapter, you should be able to:

1. Understand how individuals perceive the value of pay.
2. Know the basic theories underlying pay systems.
3. Distinguish between internal and external equity.
4. Know the basic approaches to and advantages and disadvantages of job evaluation.
5. Identify the contemporary issues in indirect compensation.
6. Understand the government's role in compensation.
7. Discuss the role of labor markets in pay administration.
8. Understand the essential differences in executive compensation for international assignments.

When we read newspaper stories about Roberto Goizueta, the chairman of Coca-Cola Company, making in excess of $86 million in 1991, or Steven Ross of Time-Warner Inc. making almost $50 million in 1990, or Steven Wolf, United Airlines chief executive officer (CEO), getting more than $18 million, or Madonna earning over $10 million a year, or Ryne Sandberg of the Chicago Cubs receiving over $7 million per year, few of us have a neutral "So what?" reaction. On one hand, the numbers suggest to us that Goizueta, Ross, Wolf, Madonna, and Sandberg must be very good at what they do (though Time-Warner reported a loss in the same year and United Airlines profits fell 71 percent). We might also consider the very pleasant lifestyle that such large paychecks can buy.

In general, however, such salaries lead most of us to wonder whether it's fair for people to make so much money. When we think of fairness, we might compare the salaries cited above to how much we make or how much someone we know makes. Or we might consider the fact that the average schoolteacher makes only $25,000 while entertainment and sports figures earn millions. We might wonder what exactly CEOs do to justify exorbitant salaries. However we evaluate such salaries, two crucial factors emerge that influence everyone's perception of pay. First, our key concern is the fairness or equity of pay. Society teaches us from an early age to be fair, and we develop a need to be treated fairly. Unfairness makes us uncomfortable, and we strive to give others what they deserve and to have them do likewise to us. Second, the evaluation of fairness requires some standard for evaluation. We laugh at Native Americans who sold Manhattan Island for $24, but how did they know whether $24 was fair or not? If, for example, they found out that other Native Americans sold Long Island for $1000, they might feel cheated. But without a standard for comparison, the fairness of the deal could not be evaluated. Thus, whether we consider our own pay level or someone else's, it is necessary to look at that pay level relative to some other level to evaluate its fairness.

The above reasoning is the basis of equity theory. Equity theory begins with the assertion that fairness or equity is important to people. Inequity is uncomfortable to individuals and creates a need for them to restore equity. Whether one is being treated equitably or not is determined by comparing one's own situation with some other situation through the use of a "comparison other." The "comparison other" need not be another person (although it often is). Additional sources of comparison could be one's own pay in the past or future, or the expectations created by the organization.[3]

The actual comparison takes place by evaluating one's own inputs and outcomes relative to the "comparison other's" inputs and outcomes. In the case of pay, inputs could include the individual's education and experience, competency on the job, productivity, effort, and/or job requirements. Pay is, of course, the outcome we are concerned with, but other outcomes such as prestige, promotions, praise, interesting work, and pleasant coworkers could also be considered.

Equity theory can be summarized as follows:

$$\frac{\text{Inputs person}}{\text{Outcomes person}} = \frac{\text{"inputs other"}}{\text{"outcomes other"}}$$

Figure 11.1 incorporates the above formula into an expanded explanation of the components of equity. In evaluating the equity of one's pay, a number of possible comparisons exist. Three groups of comparisons in particular are relevant to the management of pay. In each case, inequity leads to specific undesirable employee reactions.[4] Concern with each of these three types of inequity has led to specific techniques to ensure that fairness is achieved.

The first area of comparison for pay is the evaluation of *external equity.* In making an external equity comparison, employees compare the pay they receive to pay in other organizations. The clearest type of external comparison is that made by a new college graduate faced with several job offers. The jobs may be very similar, but each company is offering a different compensation package.

Each employer sets starting salary offers based on their ability to pay and on their perceptions of the labor market for a given job. If there are many potential employees available, and demand for these employees is weak, employers will offer low salaries. If, on the other hand, supply is low and demand is high, higher salaries will be required to attract applicants. The central point is that attracting employees from the external market involves competition among employers.

A person who has worked for an extended period of time in an organization may find that other firms pay higher than the current employer. This person will feel that he or she is being inequitably paid relative to what other firms are paying. If such feelings are particularly strong and cannot be alleviated by other valued outcomes (e.g., job location, the work itself, benefits), the employee may seek employment elsewhere.

Decisions made by employers on issues of pay relative to other firms are called *pay-level decisions.* Although employers and their compensation specialists make individual pay-level decisions for each job, employers tend to have an overall pay-level strategy. Some employers choose to pay above the external market, hoping to attract the best applicants and keep current employees. Other employers choose to pay below the market rate for jobs, usually because they can afford no other strategy. Most commonly, employers choose a third strategy, paying at the market. These strategies and their implications are discussed in more detail later in this chapter.

Whatever strategy is chosen, the basic technique for ensuring external equity is the determination of market conditions. Market conditions are determined by surveying other employers who are competing for the same employees.[5] In addition, exit interviews with employees who have terminated and recruiting experiences provide information on the effectiveness of pay-level strategies.

The second type of comparison made by employees is *internal equity,* or equity within the organization. Employees evaluate the pay for their *job* relative to the pay for other *jobs* within their company. Thus, secretaries might evaluate their pay relative to maintenance workers, or first-level managers might compare their pay

FIGURE 11.1

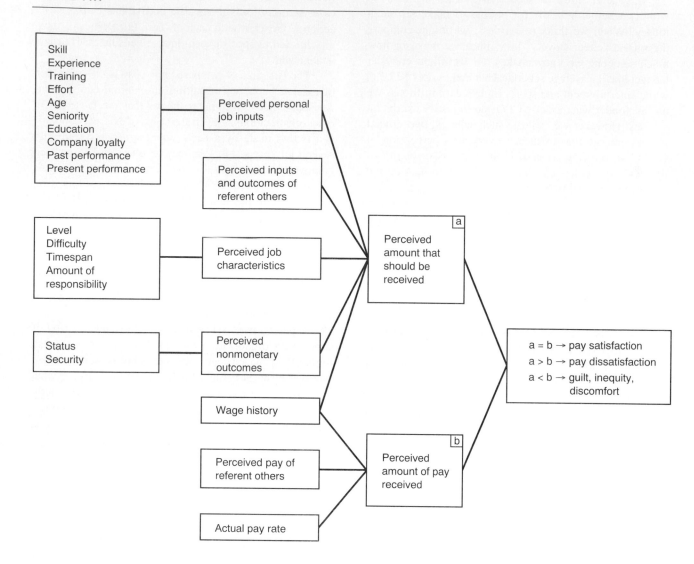

to that of middle managers. The focus of internal equity comparisons is on pay differentials and whether these differentials are proportional to differences in value and contribution of the jobs to the organization. The resulting set of internal pay rates with differentials is called the *pay structure.*

JOB EVALUATION*

The pay structure of an organization is determined by the process of job evaluation.[6] Job evaluation involves deciding on the value of the job to the organization through

*Contributed by Alan Cabelly.

ranking or rating systems. This process would be simple if each job's contribution to the organization's success could be quantified in terms of value added by the job. For most jobs, however, such assessment is difficult if not impossible. Instead, factors such as skills required, training, responsibility, educational requirements, and decision making are typically used as proxies for contribution. These proxies or compensable factors represent a policy statement by the organization about what it wants to pay for.

Job evaluation systems are commonly grouped into two major categories: quantitative and nonquantitative. The most commonly used nonquantitative methods are classification and ranking, while the most common quantitative methods are factor comparison and point factor. Figure 11.2 presents a summary of these four approaches.

FIGURE 11.2

METHOD	PROCEDURE	ADVANTAGES	DISADVANTAGES
Nonquantitative			
Ranking (paired comparison)	Rank-order whole jobs for worth or compare pairs of jobs.	Simplest method: inexpensive, easily understandable.	Only general rating of "worth"—not very reliable; doesn't measure differences between jobs.
Classification	Compare job descriptions to grade descriptions.	Simple, easy to use for large number of jobs; one rating scale.	Ambiguous, overlapping grade descriptions.
Quantitative			
Factor comparisons	Select benchmark jobs; use a fixed scale of compensable factors (e.g., mental, physical, working conditions); rank jobs on factors; assign values to factors.	Small number of factors and less overlap.	No degree definitions; difficult to evaluate new jobs.
Point-factor	Reduce general factors to subfactors; give each factor weights and points; use points to determine grades.	More specific and larger number of factors; off-the-shelf plans available (e.g., Hay Plan); more precise measurements.	Time-consuming process; more difficult to understand; greater opportunity to disagree.

The starting point for all job evaluation methods is a current job description and job specifications (recall the discussion in Chapter 4). Job descriptions should be reviewed for purposes of determining the extent to which they reflect the jobs as they are currently performed and the extent to which enough information is provided in the descriptions to enable job evaluators to evaluate the job. As discussed in Chapter 4, there are several methods which can be used to develop job descriptions with sufficient detail to enable job evaluators to make reliable judgments.[7] Job descriptions and specifications can also be rewritten to reflect a new competitive thrust or strategic plan for the organization. For example, one south Florida company paid a premium to employees who spoke Spanish or Portuguese because of a new Latin American thrust in its international marketing operation.

Nonquantitative Systems

Nonquantitative methods call for the evaluation of a whole job relative to other jobs or to general descriptions of jobs within an organization. For example, a job description of a customer service representative may be compared to the job description of a word processing specialist. The responsibility of the evaluator is to determine which of the jobs is more important or worth more to the organization. The major types of nonquantitative job evaluation procedures are *job classification* and *job ranking.*

CLASSIFICATION. Originally developed by the federal government for the civil service system, classification is used today in many large organizations and is still the most common method of evaluation in government. The classification system establishes a specific number of levels, or grades, within which all jobs must be placed. For example, the federal government has 18 levels. Each level has a set description of the types of tasks and responsibilities involved in a typical job at that grade. The salary range for each level is also set. When classifying a job, the job analyst reviews the job description for a particular job and chooses the grade which most closely matches the job description.

A major advantage of classification is its ease of use. The language is fairly easily understood, and workers can readily see how their jobs fit into the system. In addition, classification allows for comparisons of a large number of jobs and can facilitate transfers and promotions. It should be clear, for example, that a level 7 job requires somewhat more skill or responsibility than does a level 6 job, while a level 13 would entail significantly greater skill or responsibility than would a level 9. Figure 11.3 presents a part of the classification system used in the federal government.

Classification is not without its difficulties. Chief among these is the ambiguity of the grade descriptions which serve as the basis of the job classification. For example, grade descriptions might be said to have "moderate" degrees of responsibilities, "high" degrees of skill,

FIGURE 11.3
GRADE DESCRIPTIONS FOR FEDERAL JOB CLASSIFICATION SYSTEM—SERVING AS A YARDSTICK IN JOB RATING

Grade GS-1. Includes all classes of positions the duties of which are to perform, under immediate supervision, with little or no latitude for the exercise of independent judgment, the following: (1) the simplest routine work in office, business, or fiscal operations or (2) elementary work of a subordinate technical character in a professional, scientific, or technical field.

Grade GS-18. Includes all classes of positions the duties of which are: (1) To serve as the head of a bureau. This position, considering the kind and extent of the authorities and responsibilities vested in it, and the scope, complexity and degree of difficulty of the activities carried on, is exceptional and outstanding among the whole group of positions of heads of bureaus. (2) To plan and direct, or to plan and execute, new or innovative projects.

---

or "low" degrees of autonomy. This ambiguity fosters disagreements between management, supervisors, and job holders regarding the grade classification which is ultimately made for the job.

RANKING. Ranking is the simplest method of job evaluation and the most commonly used in small business. On the basis of an examination of job descriptions or sometimes just job titles, jobs are ranked or compared in terms of their worth or importance to the organization. Ranks may also be derived using paired comparisons, a method which requires comparisons between all possible pairs of jobs (i.e., the job judged to be more valuable or important than all other jobs is the most valuable, etc.). One problem with paired comparisons rests in the number of comparisons which must be made if all possible pairs of jobs are compared (i.e., $N(N - 1)/2$, where N is the number of jobs compared). Thus, in a company with only 8 jobs, only 28 comparisons are required; but where 20 jobs must be compared, 190 such comparisons must be done. Recall our discussion in Chapter 10. Rater fatigue can be a problem, and consistency of comparisons can be difficult. Procedures are available for sampling the population of all possible job pairs if a large number of jobs must be evaluated.

The major problem with the ranking method is the crudeness of the comparisons which are made and the lack of data on the differences between jobs (e.g., you know only that job A is more important than job B, but not by how much). Usually only a criterion such as the importance or worth of the job is used as the basis of the ranking or comparison. Such comparisons are often unreliable.

Quantitative Systems

Quantitative systems divide jobs into component parts and require absolute or relative value judgments about how much of a component part a particular job requires. The two most popular types of quantitative systems are the factor comparison and point-factor methods.

At the heart of both types of quantitative systems is the assumption that comparing whole jobs is at best difficult and at worst an impossible feat. Instead, the key question is the extent to which certain job factors (e.g., skill, effort, education, experience) provide more value to a company than others (e.g., physical effort, working conditions).

FACTOR COMPARISON METHOD. Factor comparison chooses key (benchmark) jobs for its initial comparisons. Benchmark jobs should be well known to the evaluators and should be jobs which the evaluators acknowledge to be compensated at the appropriate level. Most factor comparison systems call for ratings on a number of defined compensable factors such as mental requirements, skill requirements, physical requirements, responsibilities, and working conditions. Job descriptions for all jobs under study are reviewed in the context of the factor definitions. Job evaluators then rank each benchmark job on each factor. Dollar values, based on external-market rates for the benchmark jobs, are then assigned to each factor for each job.

After the benchmark jobs are rated, all jobs to be evaluated undergo a similar process, by comparing their components with the rankings for the benchmark jobs. Thus, the components of each job under study are ranked and given a dollar value. All values are then totaled to derive the compensation for the job.

POINT-FACTOR METHOD. The point-factor method does not rank jobs but rather establishes standards and assesses the degree to which a particular job fits a set standard for a factor. The point-factor method is the most frequently used method of job evaluation.[8] Numerous compensation consulting firms specialize in the installation, development, or adaptation of point-factor systems.

The components typically evaluated in point-factor methods are codified in the Equal Pay Act (EPA) of 1963. As discussed in Chapter 3, organizations are permitted to pay people based on assessments of their skill, mental requirements, effort, responsibility, and working conditions. Most point-factor systems include these factors, although the names of the factors may differ somewhat.

The point-factor system uses a job evaluation committee which studies a job or job description, divides the job into separate factors and subfactors, determines how much of the factor is required for each job, and assigns a point total to each factor. Point totals for the job are added together to arrive at a total value for each job. When each job has its point values, the job evaluation structure is complete.

The most popular point-factor method is the Hay plan, developed by Hay and Associates, an international consulting firm. The Hay plan calls for an evaluation of the "know-how," "problem solving," and "accountability" of each job under study. These three universal factors are further divided into eight subfactors. The Hay plan is used by over 5000 organizations in over 35 countries. Figure 11.4 presents a summary of the Hay plan factors and their definitions.

A crucial step in the point-factor method is the determination of the compensable factors which are to be rated. The selection of the factors and their definitions provide the operational definition of "worth" to the organization. Thus, the factors selected should emphasize the characteristics the organization considers to be most important for its effectiveness and its strategic plan. Precise definitions of the factors will enhance the reliability of the point ratings across committee members.[9]

Each factor can also be defined by degrees, with a separate definition for each degree. The degrees are then allocated different weights or points. Figure 11.5 presents an example of the degree definitions for one factor of a point-factor system.

Once the factors have been identified and defined, weights must be assigned to each degree of each factor, based on the relative importance of the factors to the organization. A common procedure allows for the distribution of 100 percent among the factors. Each factor is then given a percentage weight based on its importance, with the total weight equal to 100 percent.

Once the rating scales are developed and weights are derived, the job evaluation committee evaluates each job using the factors and degree definitions. The members typically rate each job individually, selecting that degree which is most compatible with the job description. Next, the committee meets for purposes of reaching consensus on the point ratings. The essential part of the process is that all evaluations must be based on the job descriptions and specifications.

The job's point values on all factors are tabulated. This total represents the job's "worth." Finally, this value is matched against the firm's compensation structure to determine the appropriate pay range.

Point-factor and factor comparison systems allow dissimilar jobs to be compared on components which can be reliably compared and which are thought to be critical to the organization's success. The results from these methods are generally easier to justify; however, the systems can be more difficult to explain to workers and there are more aspects of the process which can be challenged. The factor comparison and point-factor systems use similar methodology in choosing the factors to be rated. The distinction between these two methods lies in how individual evaluations are made. Factor comparison methods use comparative standards according to which job factors are compared across jobs, while point-factor methods employ absolute standards according to which jobs are compared to specific standards which translate into points.

What Is the Final Structure?

At the conclusion of the evaluation process, all the jobs within the organization will have received a total point value. This figure, by itself, tells nothing about how jobs relate to each other. The point-factor structure (or structures) is what will identify relative relationships between jobs.

The compensation decision makers must decide whether all jobs will be grouped together, or whether they will be sorted into "job families." If there is only one grouping, the next process is simple: rank-order the jobs according to point values.

FIGURE 11.4
COMPENSABLE FACTORS OF THE HAY PLAN

KNOW-HOW	PROBLEM-SOLVING	ACCOUNTABILITY
Sum total of every kind of skill, however acquired, required for acceptable job performance. Know-how has three subfactors: (1) Practical procedures, specialized techniques. (2) Ability to integrate and harmonize the diversified functions of management. (3) Interpersonal skills.	Original, "self-starting" thinking required by the job for analyzing, evaluating, creating, reasoning. Problem solving has two subfactors: (1) The thinking environment in which problems are solved. (2) The thinking challenge of the problem.	Answerability for action and for the consequences of the action; the measured effect of the job. Accountability has three subfactors: (1) Freedom to act (personal control). (2) The impact of the job on end results (direct, indirect). (3) Magnitude—general dollar size of areas most affected by the job.

**FIGURE 11.5
EXAMPLE OF DEGREE DEFINITION FOR
ONE FACTOR**

FACTOR: PHYSICAL REQUIREMENTS
This factor appraises the physical effort required by a job, including its intensity and degree of continuity. Analysis of this factor may be incorrect unless a sufficiently broad view of the work is considered.

DEGREE
1. Light work involving a minimum of physical effort. Requires only intermittent sitting, standing, and walking.
2. Repetitive work of a mechanical nature. Small amount of lifting and carrying. Occasional difficult working positions. Almost continuous sitting or considerable moving around.
3. Continuous standing or walking, or difficult working positions. Working with average-weight or heavy materials and supplies. Fast manipulative skill in almost continuous use of machine or office equipment on paced work.

A higher degree rating for a job translates into a greater number of job evaluation points.

Most organizations choose to group their jobs by families. A job family is any logical grouping in which all jobs have at least one common characteristic. Typical groupings include executive, managerial, technical, professional, clerical, skilled labor, and unskilled labor. Some firms group their positions simply by exempt (from wage and hour laws) and nonexempt jobs. Most important, the job families chosen should be meaningful for the particular organization.

The purpose of developing job families is to simplify the comparison process, making results more easily explained to workers. Lawyers, for example, are more comfortable seeing themselves compared with other professionals, as opposed to being compared with laborers. In addition, utilizing job families makes any labor market comparison process easier, because it allows inconsistencies within families to be more readily observed and fixed.

Utilizing job families is not without its problems. Chief among these is explaining to workers in different job families how their jobs, evaluated at the same number of points, are paid significantly different wages. This argument gets at the essence of the pay equity or comparable worth movement, which we will examine in the next section.

Job evaluation in general and the point-factor method in particular are not without critics. One expert on the subject states that job evaluation reinforces an outdated, bureaucratic management style in which workers are depersonalized by equating them with job duties rather than with what they are capable of doing.[10] He further states that job evaluation can create unnecessary "pecking orders" in organizations, as well as power relationships that create a preoccupation with internal equity while neglecting a focus on what the competition is up to.

One alternative to traditional compensation systems based on job evaluation is *skill-based*, or *knowledge-based*, *pay*. This pay structure links pay differences either to depth of knowledge for a job or to the number of different sets of tasks employees are certified to perform. Thus, employee pay is not based on the work actually performed but rather on the critical skills or knowledge an employee has. A small but growing number of companies have adopted skill-based pay structures for manufacturing facilities with team-based, participative assembly processes (e.g., some Ford and GM plants, Honeywell, and Rubbermaid).[11]

Pay Equity or Comparable Worth

One specific application of job evaluation systems is the policy of comparable worth or pay equity, which we introduced in Chapter 3. First enunciated by a United Nations subcommittee in 1934 and adopted as policy in 1951 by over 100 nations (not including the United States), comparable worth or pay equity requires a pay structure that is strictly based on an internal assessment of job worth. Pay equity assumes that the traditional method of achieving equity within, *but not between*, job families is inherently unfair. The theory of "within but not between" assumes, for example, that clerical jobs are compared to each other, that skilled trades jobs are compared to each other, and that professional jobs are compared to each other. The critical assumption of "within but not between" is that jobs in different families are *not* compared (and cannot be compared) with each other. Thus, a skilled trade job evaluated at 400 points on a point-factor system might be paid 20 percent higher than a clerical job receiving the same number of points. The external market is used to set rates within the various job families. Advocates of comparable worth maintain that the labor market undervalues the importance of jobs performed predominantly by women.

Traditionally, the lower-paid job families include many women's jobs. For a number of reasons, the job families with a large proportion of "female-dominated" jobs (defined in most comparable worth studies as jobs in which more than 70 percent of incumbents are women) have been compensated at a lower rate than have job families with many "male-dominated" jobs. In Washington State, for example, the average wages of women were 20 percent lower than those of men for jobs found to have the same number of job evaluation points. Thus, jobs such as those in the clerical families were found to have internally inequitably lower salaries when compared to predominantly male jobs such as skilled trades.

Pay equity proponents maintain that job evaluation can be used to derive an internally equitable pay system and that the external market (i.e., what other organizations are paying for specific jobs) should not be used because it is discriminatory. Comparable worth studies are designed to identify and alleviate problems of pay inequity. The focus of the study is on pay inequities between female-dominated and male-dominated jobs.

Most pay equity or comparable worth studies have been conducted in the public sector. One study found that 31 states were formally reviewing their pay systems for inequities and had already enacted some legislation.[11] Although there has been considerable political activity on the subject, there is no federal mandate for a comparable worth pay policy, although attempts have been made to adopt a pay equity policy for federal government pay. Many collective bargaining contracts have proposed comparable worth pay adjustments. The Equal Pay Act requires only that identical or highly similar jobs be paid equally; it does not require comparable pay for dissimilar jobs. However, in *Gunther v. County of Washington*, the Supreme Court held that claims of sex discrimination in compensation were not restricted to identical jobs under Title VII of the Civil Rights Act of 1964.[12] The courts have yet to decide a case in favor of comparable worth as a pay policy.

Washington State provided the biggest test of comparable worth when, in 1986, new pay rates were set for 62,000 state workers based on a comparable worth study. Many of the adjusted pay levels differed sharply from the external market rates. Wages for female-dominated jobs in Washington State have increased over twice as much as wages for male-dominated jobs, and the gap between the wages of men and women has been reduced to 5 percent. For example, based on the point method of job evaluation, secretaries, nurses, and teachers' aides were granted substantial comparable worth adjustments, while other jobs (e.g., prison guard, truck driver) were given no adjustment at all. Unfortunately, to defray the $400 million price tag for the comparable worth adjustments, the state has been forced to cut cost-of-living adjustments for many other state jobs, resulting in differences in excess of 30 percent between what the state and the private sector pay for some male-dominated jobs. The state has great difficulty filling these positions. Many of the concerns which have been expressed about the ramifications of a comparable worth policy are now being echoed in Ontario, Canada, where comparable worth is required for all jobs, public and private. Considerable disagreement has developed in the retail food industry over the points to be assigned to each of the point factors. Some organizations (e.g., Warner-Lambert, T. Eaton) report few difficulties in implementing the plan but lament over the cost of pay adjustments.

There can be little question that differences between male and female wages will be reduced under a comparable worth policy. Women in Sweden, for example, earn 92 percent of what men earn under a long-standing pay equity program. Other examples of reductions in the wage gap since the implementation of a pay equity program are found in the United Kingdom, Ireland, Switzerland, and Australia.

Internal versus External Equity

The debate over comparable worth underscores the problems of reconciling internal and external concepts of pay equity, probably the most difficult problem in compensation. On one hand, as evidenced by the problems in the state of Washington, if employers fail to meet market rates, they are unable to attract and retain employees. On the other hand, if market rates are met, incumbent employees in other occupations may feel that they have been treated inequitably. Unfortunately, there is no universal solution. Most employers compromise on a case-by-case basis, sometimes increasing rates for critical occupations while paying slightly below the market for other, less critical occupations. Some organizations have provisions for "special" increases which are requested through a procedure requiring detailed justification for the request.

Fortunately, the third type of equity can peacefully coexist with both internal and external equity concerns. Individual equity involves the pay of an individual employee relative to that of other employees performing the same or similar work. While external equity is concerned with the market value of a job and internal equity is concerned with the contribution of the job to the organization, individual equity focuses on the contributions of a single worker within a job classification for the organization. In this regard, organizations want to reward employees for remaining with the organization (seniority) and for their performance on the job (pay for performance or merit pay). By rewarding individuals for loyalty and performance, organizations encourage continued membership and higher levels of performance.

The mechanism for rewarding seniority is straightforward. Employees often receive an across-the-board raise each year to recognize the investment of another year of their life in the organization. Another approach is to reward employees for service over a longer period of time (e.g., 5 or 10 years). Pay for performance is a much more difficult proposition.[13] In jobs for which objective measures of performance exist, the process of linking pay to performance is fairly straightforward. Commissions for salespersons based on a percentage of sales are an example of using objective standards to make pay decisions. Unfortunately, objective performance data do not exist for many jobs. Instead, merit pay is determined by performance appraisals which are typically made by supervisors. As discussed in Chapter 10, the quality of such evaluations is the critical component in the perceived equity of individual pay. Pay-for-performance systems are discussed in detail in Chapter 12.

The primary result of inequity in individual pay is a reduction in motivation.[14] When employees feel that high effort and performance inputs are not rewarded, they cease (or reduce) such efforts. In addition, high turnover and unionization will also tend to occur in cases in which employees perceive individual pay inequity.

To summarize, employees consider external market equity, internal (job) equity, and individual equity. Failure to reward employees fairly leads to feelings of inequity and dissatisfaction with pay. The consequences of inequity and dissatisfaction for an organization are serious. Figure 11.6 summarizes these consequences.

Techniques have been developed to ensure fairness in all three aspects of pay. Wage surveys monitor external equity, job evaluation addresses internal equity, and performance appraisals lead to rewards for individual performance. Successful application of these techniques leads to satisfied and motivated employees.

Yet satisfied and motivated employees are only part of the picture from the employer's viewpoint. Certainly a pay system that employees like and that leads to high performance and low turnover is desirable. However, an additional concern for employers is cost control.

While an employer can envision a pay plan that can meet all the equity concerns, the cost of such a plan is a critical concern. Fortunately, a well-executed pay plan not only ensures fairness to employees but also ensures that the employer will not pay too much. Pay is an exchange relationship, and a well-designed pay plan ensures that both sides get a fair exchange. It should be noted that a good pay plan is not a guarantee of a successful HR function. A good pay plan does, however, create a climate of trust between employer and employees that contributes to high organizational performance.[15]

Figure 11.7 summarizes the impact of equity on compensation techniques and the outcomes of such techniques. In the next section we consider another goal of compensation systems: legal compliance.

GOVERNMENT'S ROLE IN DIRECT COMPENSATION

In the previous section our emphasis was on the importance of equity to employees and the reasons why employers attempt to set up practices that enhance the chances for equity. Unfortunately, some employers have failed to meet even minimum requirements of fairness—compen-

FIGURE 11.6
MODEL OF THE CONSEQUENCES OF PAY DISSATISFACTION

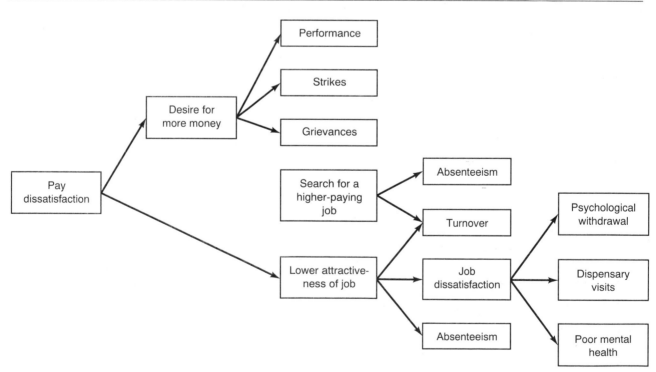

Source: E. E. Lawler III, *Pay and organization development.* Reading, MA: Addison-Wesley, 1981, p. 233. Reprinted with permission.

FIGURE 11.7
A PAY MODEL

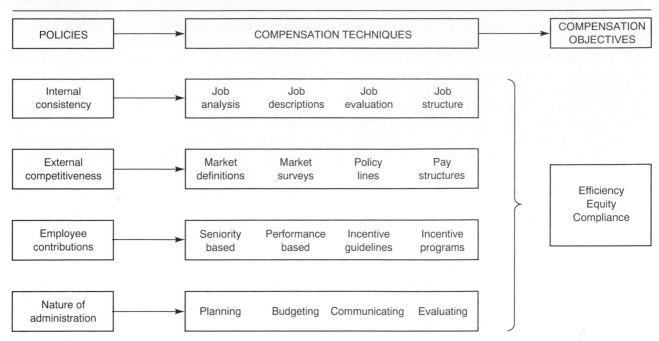

Source: G.T. Milkovich and J.M. Newman, *Compensation.* Plano, TX: Business Publications, 1990, p. 8. Reprinted with permission.

sating employees to some extent on the basis of sex or race, paying less than a "living" wage, not compensating employees for overtime, and following other unfair practices. Because of the importance of pay, Congress, state legislatures, and city councils have adopted laws which seek to guarantee employees fairness in certain aspects of compensation. The major provisions of these laws at the federal level are summarized in Figure 11.8 and are discussed below.

Fair Labor Standards Act

While all states have laws governing minimum wages and hours of work, the most far-reaching law concerning compensation is the Fair Labor Standards Act (FLSA) of 1938. The major provisions of the act cover hours of work, minimum wage, child labor, and equal pay. The FLSA covers about 50 million workers.

The FLSA requires that employees covered by the act receive their normal hourly rate plus a 50 percent premium (time and a half) for all hours worked over 40 per week. The purpose of this provision (passed during the Depression) was to create additional jobs through work sharing by assessing employers a penalty for using current workers beyond the normal work week. Today, however, given the high costs of benefits and the high skill levels of workers, it is often cheaper for employers to pay the 50 percent premium than to hire new employees.

FIGURE 11.8
SUMMARY OF FEDERAL LAWS AFFECTING COMPENSATION

PROVISIONS	LAW
Fair Labor Standards Act (FLSA) of 1938	Sets minimum wage ($4.25 per hour in 1991, overtime, child-labor conditions).
Equal Pay Act (EPA) of 1963	Equal pay for equal work (amended FLSA).
Davis-Bacon Act of 1931	Workers in construction industry must be paid at prevailing local rate for government contracts.
Walsh-Healey Act of 1936	Workers in goods must be paid at prevailing industry rates.
Services Contract Act of 1936	Workers in services must be paid at prevailing industry rates.

The FLSA also sets a minimum wage for hourly work. Originally $.25, the minimum wage as of 1991 was $4.25. A "training wage" ($3.60 per hour) is also possible during the first 3 months of employment. The overtime and minimum wage provisions do not apply to all workers in all industries. For example, professional, executive, and administrative workers are exempt from overtime provisions, while restaurant workers can be paid below the minimum wage. These exemptions have been amended a number of times, and their interpretation continues to be one of the most complicated areas of the law.

The type of work performed also makes a difference in the child-labor provisions of the FLSA. Children must be at least 18 years old to perform hazardous work; at least 16 to work in manufacturing, mining, and transportation; and at least 14 to work in most other jobs. Additional exceptions exist for each age group. A number of major corporations have been indicted recently for violation of child-labor laws.

Finally, the FLSA was amended in 1963 to include provisions referred to as the *Equal Pay Act*. Discussed in greater detail in Chapter 3, the EPA makes it illegal to discriminate in pay on the basis of sex when "employees perform equal work on jobs in the same establishment requiring equal skill, effort and responsibility performed under similar working conditions" [29 USC 206 (d)]. Executives, professionals and administrators, in addition to almost all other employees, are covered by the EPA.

As we suggested above, many have argued that the EPA should be applied to differentials in pay based on a comparable worth argument. This argument has been rejected by the courts but, as we discussed above, has been adopted in some form for certain employees under state and local laws.

The existence of the EPA and its coverage does not preclude a pay discrimination suit under Title VII of the Civil Rights Act of 1964. While the EPA covers only substantially equal jobs, the Civil Rights Act has no such limitations. Thus, as discussed in Chapter 3, plaintiffs who establish that they have been paid a lower rate because of sex, race, color, religion, or national origin are eligible for judicial relief regardless of the similarity of the work to other work.

Prevailing Wage Laws

In order to assure that workers employed on government projects receive fair wages relative to other, local workers, Congress has enacted three pieces of legislation requiring employers to meet prevailing wage levels when doing business with the federal government. These three acts—The Davis-Bacon Act of 1931, the Walsh-Healey Act of 1936, and the Services Contract Act of 1936— cover federal contracts for construction, goods, and services, respectively.

While prevailing wage levels have traditionally been equal to union wage levels, changes in the regulations require employers to pay an average wage or the wage paid to a majority of local employees for a given occupation. These regulations, in effect, create a higher minimum wage for federally funded projects and ensure that large projects awarded on competitive bids do not lower wage rates for a region.

Legal Compliance

In addition to the major pieces of federal legislation, many states and localities have laws that cover workers who are not under the federal laws, or cover areas of compensation that are not subject to federal regulation. Whatever the source of legislation, it is critical for employers to be aware of all regulations that apply to their workforce and to ensure compliance. Failure to comply with legal requirements can lead to costly back-pay settlements, fines, and substantial legal fees.

One method undertaken by employers to ensure compliance is the compliance audit. A compliance audit consists of an analysis of employee records and organizational policies to ensure that both the spirit and the letter of the law are being met. The complexity of the law continues to increase because of new legislation and shifting court interpretation of existing law. It is therefore essential that personnel professionals keep abreast of current developments through publications in the field, and that they seek competent legal opinions on questionable cases.

UNIONS

Since unions are covered at length in Chapters 14 and 15, only brief mention will be made of their critical role in compensation. The importance of unions is underestimated by many who cite declining membership figures. Although unions do not have the clout they once had, unions in many industries continue to set trends in wages which are followed by many companies desiring to remain nonunion. In addition, unions influence prevailing wages required by federal law.

Compensation rates, the most visible (and costly) clause in union-management agreements, are usually a major area of disagreement in negotiations. Union leaders, acting on behalf of the membership who elected them, keep a close watch on the expectations of members for certain wage levels. These expectations are influenced by how much other workers are making, the cost of living, and perceptions of the financial health of the firm. Thus, equity perceptions concerning external comparisons and the distribution of profits between the firm and workers play a critical role in determining union demands.

Recent years have seen management taking a more open approach in dealing with union leaders in order to bring workers' perceptions more in line with competitive realities. The employee involvement program at Ford Motor Company, negotiated between Ford and the United Auto Workers (UAW), is an example. The success of this approach has led to more realistic union expectations and fewer conflicts in negotiations. In some cases, such as the auto industry, management has negotiated contracts that tie compensation levels to profit levels in a pay-for-organizational-performance arrangement that recognizes realistic competitive influences on an organization's ability to pay. As we will discuss in Chapter 12, however, this is more the exception than the rule with regard to union contracts, and unions often attempt to change such arrangements if corporate profits sour.

EXTERNAL INFLUENCES: PAY LEVELS STRATEGY

As noted earlier, the relationship of organizational pay levels to those of other organizations has a number of very important impacts on the firm. Pay levels that are felt to be inequitable by employees can lead to lower productivity, higher turnover, and unionization and strikes, and can cause the organization to have difficulty in recruiting. On the other hand, pay levels that are too high can put a firm in a noncompetitive position relative to competitors.

These concerns form the basis for an organization's choice of pay-level strategy. You'll recall that organizations can pay above, below, or at market rates for their jobs.[16] Firms paying above the market rate tend to be those that must compete for scarce employees, are very large, have high profits, operate in product markets with few competitors, have a low ratio of labor cost to total cost, and/or have problems with employee unrest. Firms with above-market pay policies include International Business Machines (IBM), Digital Equipment Corporation, and General Electric Company (GE). Clearly, a high wage-level policy would provide benefits to almost all firms, and yet few operate under conditions that allow such a policy.

Most firms tend to meet the wage levels paid by competitors. This allows a company to keep prices competitive while effectively attracting and retaining employees. An organization that pays market rates seeks to recruit and keep employees through its attractiveness as a place to work (offering good supervision, interesting work, etc.), while matching the average of competitor's wages.

Many unions have applied this approach through *pattern bargaining,* in which they attempt to achieve identical wage rates across an industry in order to "take wages out of competition." This was the case for many years in the auto industry and resulted in wage increases being uniformly added to car prices across the three major auto companies. With wage costs equal, manufacturers competed through better management and product design.

Finally, as mentioned previously, some firms pay their employees below-market rates. Since such an approach guarantees little choice in applicants and higher turnover, few firms voluntarily choose such a strategy. Instead, firms operating in highly competitive product or service markets with a high ratio of labor costs to total costs have little choice but to pay below-market rates. This is typically the case in firms that must compete with companies which manufacture goods in the third world. For example, the textile industry competes with producers in Hong Kong, Taiwan, and South Korea. In these countries, wage rates are a fraction of the U.S. minimum wage and few benefits are provided, if any. U.S. manufacturers competing with goods from these countries have great difficulty in maintaining even a market-rate pay-level policy.

No matter which of the above policies is chosen and no matter what the reason for the choice, no real strategy can be chosen without an accurate assessment of what rates are being paid in the market. First, however, we must define what we mean by the term "labor market."

Labor Markets and Their Relevance to an Organization

A *labor market* is a hypothetical place in which all sellers of labor (employees) with certain characteristics (skills, education, experience) meet with the buyers of labor (employers) to make deals (to hire). The price paid by the buyer is determined by the number of sellers (representing supply) and the number of buyers (representing demand).

There are many such labor markets.[17] The problem for an employer trying to set wage levels relative to a market is to determine the nature and size of the appropriate market. It has already been mentioned that a critical defining factor of labor markets is the nature of the employees available in terms of occupation or skills. As a first pass in determining markets, employers can narrow their focus to the total number of people who can perform the job of concern. Using skills as a criterion also helps to focus an employer's search for information on other employers who hire employees requiring similar skills.

Not all workers who can perform a clerical job in the United States might be willing to move from, say, California to New York, since plenty of clerical jobs are available in California. On the other hand, a professor of philosophy might be perfectly willing to make such a move when few jobs are available out West. The point is that geography and the distance people are willing to move or commute further redefines the scope of a labor market. Generally, high-level jobs requiring much training and experience tend to have a national labor market pool, while low-level jobs tend to have regional or local labor markets.

Other employers who produce the same products or services also help to define labor markets. Since employers must compete on labor costs with these firms, their wage rates are important to consider. In some cases, firms in different industries pay substantially different amounts of money to employees with the same qualifications. An engineer, for example, is much more critical to the success of an engineering consulting firm than that same engineer would be to a firm in which he or she was in a strictly support position.

To summarize, the relevant market for an organization is defined by the skills needed, by employers competing for the same skills, by geography, and by employers producing the same or similar products. These factors form the basis for determining the going rate for a job. The method by which other employers are asked for information to determine the relevant market rate is called a "wage survey."

Wage Surveys

Determining the market rates for jobs requires planning by the personnel department.[18] The first decision involves determining what jobs are to be investigated. Rarely does a firm gather survey data on all its jobs. Instead, most firms choose key or benchmark jobs that are representative of all the jobs under consideration. By determining the market rates for key jobs, companies can then relate pay levels of other jobs to the key jobs by comparing the positions of the nonsampled jobs with those of the key jobs in the pay structure. The problem is to determine key jobs that are representative. The jobs chosen should have a known content, be stable, cover a large proportion of the workforce, and represent each unique occupational group in the organization.

Once the jobs to be considered are determined, the relevant labor market is determined by using the factors outlined earlier. Thus, a geographic area of concern for the benchmark jobs is determined, and competitors in products and in the labor market are identified.

At this point, the analyst is faced with a basic decision: Should the organization purchase data, hire consultants to conduct the survey, rely on surveys in the public domain, or conduct its own survey? There are numerous surveys available. Some, like those conducted by the federal Bureau of Labor Statistics (BLS), are free. Often industries or professional groups survey their membership and make the results available free of charge for members or participants in the study. In addition, many consulting firms conduct surveys and charge companies for the results, usually with a discount for companies that participated. Figure 11.9 shows the results of such a survey.

The advantages of buying a survey include lower costs relative to conducting a survey, immediate availability of data, and avoidance of tying up staff time in conducting the survey. There are, however, some major disadvantages. One disadvantage is that the data is often out of date. For example, BLS data is often several years old before it's published. Another disadvantage involves the adequacy of available data in meeting an employer's definition of the relevant labor market. National figures on salary are of limited use in determining wages in a local labor market in which wages may vary substantially from national averages. In addition, the jobs surveyed may not be equivalent to those in the organization. Sometimes two organizations will use the same job titles to describe different job duties. Thus, when using published survey data it is difficult to feel confident of the match between the job of concern and the surveyed job.

An alternative is to conduct your own survey.[19] Surveys are conducted through telephone or personal interviews and/or by questionnaires. Employers are free to choose the appropriate jobs, the relevant geographic market, and the competitors, based on an analysis of their own needs. Carefully conducted surveys ensure appropriate matching of key jobs to surveyed jobs.

Obviously, the validity of a survey is determined by the quality of the data collection. Well-designed questionnaires and trained interviewers ensure that only comparable jobs are included in the survey and that complete data is obtained. Generally, interviews provide the best data. The data collected should include not only information on the key jobs and their comparability to the surveyed organization's jobs but also information on benefits, bonuses, and other methods of compensation besides direct salary. Failure to include these factors would give a distorted picture of the total compensation package offered. It is also useful to collect information on the characteristics of the organization to determine how similar the organization is to the surveyed firm. Figure 11.10 presents an example of a salary survey.

Companies are generally willing to provide confidential salary and benefit data. Although some firms decline to participate, most are just as interested as the surveying company in the results of the survey and will participate in return for confidentiality about their rates and a copy of the final survey results.

Obviously, tailor-made surveys offer some definite advantages over purchased surveys. These advantages in accuracy and relevance must be weighed against the costs and time involved in developing an in-house survey. Conducting a survey through interviews often involves substantial staff time and travel costs. Even after the data are collected, analysis and computer time can be expensive.

Once data is obtained on key jobs in the external market, it is combined with data on internal value (job evaluation) to set pay ranges for jobs. These results are used for the benchmark jobs and form the basis of an equitable pay system for the organization.

FIGURE 11.9
EXAMPLE OF BLS WAGE SURVEY*

OCCUPATION AND LEVEL	NUMBER OF EMPLOYEES	MONTHLY SALARIES				ANNUAL SALARIES			
		MEAN	MEDIAN	MIDDLE RANGE		MEAN	MEDIAN	MIDDLE RANGE	
				FIRST QUARTILE	THIRD QUARTILE			FIRST QUARTILE	THIRD QUARTILE
Accountants									
I	15,209	$1,850	$1,860	$1,666	$2,024	$22,198	$22,320	$19,992	$24,290
II	33,353	2,258	2,209	2,020	2,450	27,093	26,508	24,242	29,.400
III	45,508	2,774	2,739	2,499	3,032	33,293	32,873	29,988	36,385
IV	23,190	3,512	3,449	3,149	3,795	42,140	41,383	37,785	45,540
V	7,506	4,454	4,390	3,998	4,807	53,453	52,679	47,981	57,685
VI	1,448	5,689	5,555	5,015	6,281	68,270	66,660	60,176	75,370
Auditors									
I	1,423	1,956	1,916	1,749	2,083	23,473	22,991	20,992	24,990
II	2,452	2,363	2,303	2,139	2,532	28,359	27,636	25,665	30,388
III	3,418	2,896	2,791	2,500	3,195	34,753	33,487	30,000	38,340
IV	1,869	3,536	3,466	3,082	3,910	42,434	41,592	36,985	46,920
Chief accountants									
I	940	3,391	3,458	3,175	3,466	40,691	41,496	38,100	41,597
II	1,028	4,443	4,233	4,034	4,831	53,316	50,800	48,414	57,977
III	500	5,776	5,733	5,255	6,206	69,316	68,800	63,064	74,466
IV	110	7,384	7,219	6,583	8,094	88,608	86,633	78,994	97,129
Attorneys									
I	1,310	2,839	2,654	2,499	3,110	34,073	31,851	29,988	37,320
II	3,432	3,545	3,499	3,064	3,774	42,539	41,983	36,765	45,289
III	4,625	4,613	4,540	4,082	5,081	55,362	54,478	48,980	60,976
IV	4,407	5,853	5,748	5,256	6,397	70,231	68,972	63,075	76,769
V	2,116	7,300	7,139	6,444	8,001	87,595	85,666	77,333	96,012
VI	676	9,180	8,871	8,112	10,249	110,162	106,457	97,347	122,988
Buyers									
I	8,421	1,848	1,772	1,625	2,005	22,170	21,266	19,499	24,064
II	23,555	2,333	2,290	2,050	2,556	27,999	27,480	24,600	30,668
III	17,656	3,007	2,961	2,696	3,280	36,088	35,532	32,351	39,360
IV	5,125	3,635	3,540	3,180	4,008	43,620	42,483	38,165	48,096
Computer programmers									
I	8,770	1,878	1,833	1,666	2,082	22,531	21,996	19,992	24,984
II	29,726	2,202	2,174	1,995	2,409	26,422	26,090	23,940	28,910
III	37,369	2,620	2,608	2,378	2,832	31,440	31,291	28,539	33,986
IV	17,593	3,116	3,090	2,876	3,335	37,396	37,080	34,507	40,020
V	6,986	3,795	3,790	3,560	4,030	45,536	45,480	42,720	48,360
Systems analysts									
I	20,895	2,615	2,581	2,380	2,812	31,380	30,972	28,560	33,744
II	42,898	3,154	3,124	2,883	3,400	37,848	37,485	34,596	40,800
III	26,377	3,684	3,657	3,374	3,974	44,214	43,882	40,484	47,688
IV	8,021	4,338	4,326	3,973	4,673	52,054	51,914	47,681	56,078
V	827	5,449	5,500	4,770	6,070	65,388	66,000	57,240	72,840
Systems analyst managers									
I	6,131	4,097	4,007	3,707	4,400	49,164	48,081	44,482	52,803
II	4,931	4,645	4,578	4,225	5,042	55,735	54,932	50,696	60,504
III	1,882	5,421	5,280	4,920	5,848	65,056	63,361	59,040	70,172
IV	228	6,298	6,312	5,914	6,697	75,579	75,744	70,972	80,360
Job analysts									
II	418	2,163	2,150	1,874	2,331	25,957	25,802	22,483	27,974
III	755	2,747	2,673	2,460	3,015	32,958	32,071	29,521	36,180
IV	495	3,492	3,399	3,125	3,766	41,904	40,784	37,500	45,192

FIGURE 11.9
EXAMPLE OF BLS WAGE SURVEY (CONTINUED)

OCCUPATION AND LEVEL	NUMBER OF EMPLOYEES	MONTHLY SALARIES		MIDDLE RANGE		ANNUAL SALARIES		MIDDLE RANGE	
		MEAN	MEDIAN	FIRST QUARTILE	THIRD QUARTILE	MEAN	MEDIAN	FIRST QUARTILE	THIRD QUARTILE
Directors of personnel									
I.........................	1,717	$3,508	$3,515	$3,165	$3,749	$42,091	$42,183	$37,985	$44,982
II.........................	2,421	4,216	4,165	3,800	4,635	50,589	49,980	45,600	55,620
III.........................	1,042	5,908	5,876	5,298	6,480	70,900	70,507	63,575	77,761
IV.........................	301	7,308	7,081	6,497	7,730	87,696	84,966	77,969	92,763
Chemists									
I.........................	2,304	2,218	2,189	2,045	2,333	26,161	26,268	24,542	27,996
II.........................	5,526	2,584	2,562	2,355	2,764	31,013	30,745	28,260	33,168
III.........................	7,775	3,176	3,165	2,857	3,475	38,113	37,985	34,286	41,699
IV.........................	8,033	3,818	3,823	3,540	4,082	45,812	45,876	42,483	48,980
V.........................	4,292	4,581	4,573	4,215	4,957	54,971	54,878	50,580	59,483
VI.........................	1,469	5,501	5,515	4,998	5,900	66,011	66,180	59,976	70,800
VII.........................	370	6,647	6,465	6,283	7,184	79,759	77,585	75,402	86,208
Engineers									
I.........................	29,607	2,466	2,474	2,332	2,600	29,592	29,688	27,989	31,200
II.........................	65,445	2,773	2,749	2,574	2,957	33,278	32,987	30,886	35,486
III.........................	121,166	3,196	3,165	2,916	3,456	38,353	37,985	34,986	41,472
IV.........................	134,682	3,815	3,793	3,475	4,115	45,777	45,522	41,700	49,380
V.........................	89,649	4,599	4,562	4,186	4,988	55,194	54,744	50,228	59,856
VI.........................	36,607	5,476	5,450	4,970	5,928	65,710	65,400	59,640	71,140
VII.........................	9,360	6,300	6,229	5,717	6,835	75,594	74,748	68,603	82,017
VIII.........................	1,542	7,326	7,196	6,565	7,958	87,914	86,355	78,780	95,493
Registered nurses									
I.........................	1,601	1,954	1,899	1,735	2,156	23,443	22,791	20,820	25,871
II.........................	4,220	2,379	2,341	2,119	2,617	28,545	28,090	25,428	31,404
III.........................	184	2,922	2,916	2,607	3,200	35,059	34,986	31,287	38,400
Licensed practical nurses									
II.........................	352	1,637	1,657	1,343	1,933	19,640	19,887	16,119	23,190
Engineering technicians									
I.........................	3,930	1,490	1,477	1,350	1,628	17,879	17,724	16,200	19,540
II.........................	13,496	1,776	1,764	1,595	1,939	21,317	21,169	19,135	23,268
III.........................	28,498	2,086	2,067	1,847	2,296	25,028	24,804	22,164	27,555
IV.........................	31,375	2,504	2,482	2,222	2,742	30,043	29,788	26,667	32,903
V.........................	17,341	2,895	2,855	2,632	3,128	34,742	34,263	31,584	37,533
Drafters									
II.........................	9,375	1,390	1,343	1,257	1,517	16,676	16,119	15,079	18,199
III.........................	16,971	1,779	1,733	1,560	1,931	21,345	20,798	18,720	23,169
IV.........................	15,097	2,211	2,167	1,969	2,417	26,535	25,998	23,628	29,004
V.........................	8,749	2,714	2,709	2,420	2,995	32,567	32,508	29,035	35,936
Computer operators									
I.........................	6,635	1,253	1,220	1,062	1,375	15,039	14,640	12,739	16,503
II.........................	30,874	1,538	1,499	1,333	1,720	18,452	17,993	15,994	20,638
III.........................	23,538	1,904	1,871	1,666	2,085	22,846	22,455	19,992	25,020
IV.........................	6,480	2,253	2,249	2,009	2,448	27,040	26,989	24,108	29,375
V.........................	1,001	2,575	2,587	2,300	2,780	30,900	31,042	27,600	33,360
Photographers									
II.........................	671	2,052	1,999	1,821	2,292	24,620	23,990	21,852	27,506
III.........................	664	2,430	2,452	2,200	2,632	29,164	29,430	26,400	31,582
IV.........................	358	2,820	2,890	2,515	3,070	33,844	34,681	30,184	36,840

Note: Employment and average salaries in private nonservice industries for selected professional, administrative, technical, and clerical occupations, United States, except Alaska and Hawaii, March 1988.

FIGURE 11.10
COMPENSATION SURVEY PACKAGE

1. Letter of Transmittal

Dear   :

   In accordance with our telephone conversation, I am enclosing a survey questionnaire with a self-addressed, stamped envelope. Thank you for agreeing to participate.

   The survey has three sections: Organization Policy, Employee Benefits, and Job Data. Answers to the *policy* section will assist us in relating compensation differences among the participating organizations. Because of their ever-expanding importance and cost, *employee benefits* have become increasingly important to many organizations. The *job data* section is the heart of the survey. If you have any doubt about the similarity of the job you match with the one we describe, please feel free to comment in the margin beside the matching job. Or, if you wish, send us a copy of your parallel job description and we will do the matching.

   To ensure anonymity of your response, we will not list organizations by name or make any grouping where it is possible to combine such data as number of organization, size of organization, or number of employees so that identification of a specific organization is possible. *We have coded each survey only to allow us to check with you concerning any missing data or where it appears that the data may have been incorrectly transcribed by transposing numbers or placing a number in the wrong column.

   After compilation and analysis of the surveys, each participating organization will receive a summary. If you need further information or clarification of summary data, please call me.

                                        Sincerely yours,

                                        Compensation Manager
                                        OLYMPIA, INC.

....

*A Bit of Information for the Surveyor:

   A National Labor Relations Board ruling required a company to provide the following information to its bargaining union:
            (1) Area wage rates,
            (2) Companies surveyed,
            (3) Identification of which rates came from a particular company.
However, the NLRB does not require an organization to disclose the identity of the companies if it is not furnished such information. In essence, this protects companies using survey data provided by outside parties. ("Total Disclosure of Wage Data," *Compensation Review*, Third Quarter 1971, pp. 5—6.)

FIGURE 11.10 *(Continued)*

2. The Survey
Organizational Policy

Staff and Hours

Number of employees? _____

How many hours per week do your employees normally work? _____

    How much time allotted for lunch? _____

    How many breaks? _____ How much time allotted for them? _____

Do you offer 4 day workweeks? YES _____ NO _____

Do any of your employees work on shifts? YES _____ NO _____

If YES, answer below:

Shift	*Shift Hours*	*% Premium Pay*
Evening (2nd)	_____	_____
Late Night (3rd)	_____	_____
Other	_____	_____

Do you have any form of Flextime (allowing employees to choose working hours)? YES _____ NO _____

If YES, please describe.

_____

_____

Salary Payment Policies

If your standard number of hours worked per week is less than 40, do you pay overtime for hours in excess of the normal workweek but less than 40? YES _____ NO _____

If certain groups within the organization have less than a 40-hour workweek, please list them.

Group	Hours
_____	_____
_____	_____
_____	_____

What is the overtime rate for individuals required to work on regularly scheduled holidays?
1 1/2 times normal pay _____ 2 times normal pay _____ Other _____

Have you paid a bonus or made a supplemental salary payment at any time within the past 12 months? YES _____ NO _____
If YES: Date of last one _____ Approximate % of salary _____

Please identify occupational groups receiving bonuses:

_____

_____

(Continued)

FIGURE 11.10 (Continued)

Have you granted any general across-the-board adjustments in salary within the past 24 months?   YES _____   NO _____   If YES:

Date	Approximate % Adjustment
1. _____	_____
2. _____	_____

Are they linked to the Bureau of Labor Statistics Consumer Price Index? YES _____   NO _____   If linked to any other price index, please indicate. _____

Starting Salaries—High School Graduates

What is your average starting salary for a high school graduate with *no* work experience who cannot type or take shorthand? $ _____

What is your average starting salary for a high school graduate with *no* work experience who can type 50—60 words per minute accurately? $ _____

What is your average starting salary for a high school graduate with *no* work experience who can type 50—60 words per minute and take shorthand 80—90 wpm? $ _____

Starting Salaries—Community College—Technical School Graduates

What is your average starting salary for a technical school graduate who has a usable technical skill? $ _____

What is your average starting salary for a community college graduate with an Associate Degree pursuing a *non-technical* occupation in your firm? $ _____

Starting Salaries—College Graduates

What is your average starting salary for a college graduate with a Bachelor's degree in Business Administration, Accounting, Finance, Economics, Management, etc., pursuing a *non-technical* occupation in your firm? $ _____

What is your average starting salary for a college graduate with a Bachelor's degree in Engineering, Mathematics, Statistics, etc., pursuing a *technical* occupation in your firm? $ _____

FIGURE 11.10 *(Continued)*

Employment Policies

Do you pay employment agency fees for non-college graduates?

YES _____   NO _____

If YES: Do you pay the fee at the time of employment?   YES _____   NO _____

If NO: When? _____

Employee Benefits

Paid Vacations

What paid vacations are allowed?

Years Service (inclusive)	Weeks of Vacations Allowed		
	Nonexempt	Exempt	Executive
0—1	_____	_____	_____
2—4	_____	_____	_____
5—9	_____	_____	_____
10—15	_____	_____	_____
Others	_____	_____	_____

Can unused vacation time be carried over to the following year?

YES _____   NO _____

If YES, *how many* days? _____

Paid Holidays

How many paid holidays do you grant? _____

Check all that apply:

Christmas Day	_____	Independence Day	_____
New Year's Day	_____	Labor Day	_____
Washington's Birthday	_____	Columbus Day	_____
Martin Luther King's Birthday	_____	Veteran's Day	_____
Good Friday	_____	Thanksgiving Day	_____
Memorial Day	_____	Employee's Birthday	_____

Sick Leave

Do you have an official sick leave plan?   YES _____   NO _____

How many days of sick leave do you grant per year? _____

Do you have a waiting period before an employee is eligible for sick leave?   YES _____   NO _____

FIGURE 11.10 (Continued)

Do you have a lifetime maximum number of sick leave days an employee can take?   YES _____   NO _____

Do you have a plan that permits the employee to convert sick leave to other employees?   YES _____   No _____

If YES, check the applicable conversion:

Cash_____   Carryover to future years _____
Vacation _____   Credit at retirement _____

Other Leaves

Do you grant leave with pay for any of the following reasons?

Reason	Number of Days	Reason	Number of Days
Jury Duty	_____	Death in Family	_____
Marriage	_____	Dental Appointment	_____
Graduation Exercises	_____	Maternity or Paternity	_____
Family Illness	_____	Other	_____

Thrift Plan

Do you have a thrift plan?   YES _____   NO _____

How much does the employer contribute per $1.00 of employee contribution? (Please circle appropriate amount)
$0.25, $0.50, $0.75, $1.00, other (if other list amount) _____

Credit Union

Do you offer a credit union?   YES _____   NO _____

What interest do you pay on savings? _____

What interest do you charge on loans? _____

Insurance Benefits

Do you have a group hospitalization and/or surgical plan?
YES _____   NO _____

If YES: What per cent is paid by employer? _____

What is monthly cost to employee?   Single Plan $_____
                                      Family Plan $_____

Is there a major medical addition to the regular insurance plan?
YES _____   NO _____

If YES, what is the one-time illness maximum? $_____

What is the lifetime illness maximum? $_____

At what amount of "out of pocket" employer cost per illness does the major medical plan assume full responsibility? $_____

FIGURE 11.10 *(Continued)*

Do you have a group dental plan?   YES _____   NO _____

If YES, what per cent is paid by employer? _____ %

Do you have a group life insurance plan?   YES _____   NO _____

If YES, is it contributory?   YES _____   NO _____

If YES, what percentage does the employer pay? _____ %

Is the amount of insurance that is made available a percentage of annual salary?   YES _____   NO _____

If YES, what amount of insurance is made available as a multiple of annual salary? (please circle the appropriate figure)
1.5,   2.5,   3.5,   other (if other, list) _____

Is there a base to your insurance plan?   YES _____   NO _____

If YES, what is the base? _____

Is there a cap to your insurance plan?   YES _____   NO _____

If YES, what is the cap? _____

Pension Plan

Do you have a pension plan?   YES _____   NO _____

Does it include all employees?   YES _____   NO _____

If NO: Which groups are excluded?   _____

_____   _____

Is it integrated with Social Security?   YES _____   NO _____

How do you determine the average salary for pension purposes? (Please circle your method)
Salary of final 3 yrs.,   5 yrs.,   10 yrs.,   career average, other (if other, please describe) _____

Is it a defined benefit plan?   YES _____   NO _____

If YES, what formula do you use for determining final pension benefits?

_____

Is it a defined contribution plan?   YES _____   NO _____

If YES, how do you determine contributions?

_____

Which ERISA vesting plan are you using?

_____

What is your normal retirement age? (Please circle appropriate number)
55,   60,   62,   65,   other (if other, please state) _____

FIGURE 11.10 *(Continued)*

Do you have an early retirement eligibility? YES _____ NO _____
If YES, how do you determine (please circle appropriate method)
Age, Service, Age and service, Other (if other, please describe)
_____

Have you provided a pension plan supplement for retirees in the past
five years? YES _____ NO _____

Do you provide death benefits for retirees? YES _____ NO _____

Do the retirees contribute to the death benefit premiums?
YES _____ NO _____

General

Do you provide a cafeteria service for your employees? YES _____ NO _____
If YES, do you subsidize the operation? YES _____ NO _____
If YES, % of subsidization _____

Do you provide parking for all employees or subsidize parking fees?
YES _____ NO _____
If subsidized, approximate cost per employee: $ _____

Do you have a labor union among your non-clerical employees?
YES _____ NO _____

Do you have a labor union among your clerical employees?
YES _____ NO _____

Do you have an educational reimbursement plan? YES _____ NO _____
If YES, for what programs (circle appropriate programs)
High School, Undergraduate, Graduate, Vocational
If YES, what percentage of tuition do you reimburse?
(circle appropriate amount)   50%,   75%,   100%,
other (if other please list) _____ %

Merit Review Plan

Do you have a merit rating plan for executives? YES _____ NO _____
Briefly describe: _____

Do you have a merit rating plan for non-executives?
YES _____ NO _____ Briefly describe: _____
_____

FIGURE 11.10 *(Continued)*

Job Data

Our Job Title _____   Other Possible Titles _____

Job Code   _____

Thumb-Nail Job Description:

Special Notes: This section of the form must be completed by the
                surveying organization prior to the printing of the
                form.(See text material on *Job Data* for example)

PLEASE COMPLETE THIS FORM FOR YOUR COMPARABLE JOB:

Job Title: _____   Degree of Fit

Job Code: _____

                                            1   2   3   4   5 [a]

Minimum Pay: _____
(or entry-level hiring rate)   (circle the appropriate number)

Maximum Pay: _____
(or maximum longevity rate)

Please indicate on each line the number of employees receiving the
particular rate of pay and indicate the rate under the applicable column.

Number of Employees	Dollars				Average Years On This Job
	Per Hour	Per Week	Per Month	Per Year	

[a] 1 = poor fit   3 = moderate fit   5 = identical fit
    2 = slight fit   4 = considerable fit

FIGURE 11.10 *(Continued)*

PAY SUMMARY SHEET FOR EACH JOB IN THE SURVEY

Job Title _____   Job Code _____

Job Summary:

Reporting Data

Number of firms   _____

Number of employees   _____

Average pay reported   _____

Actual Pay Data

Number of firms reporting   _____

Lowest reported pay rate   _____

First quartile pay rate   _____

Median pay rate   _____

Third quartile pay rate   _____

Highest reported pay rate   _____

Range Data Reported

Number of firms reporting   _____

Lowest reported pay range   _____

Median reported minimum range _____

Median reported of the median
  of the ranges   _____

Median reported maximum range _____

Highest reported pay range   _____

Ranking of Reported Pay

    Pay shown below is rank-ordered from low to high. If the first
value begins at "0," the list is in deciles. If the first value begins
at "1," the figures are actual pay. (Deciles were used when more than
25 individual pay rates were reported.)

0 _____				
1 _____	6 _____	11 _____	16 _____	21 _____
2 _____	7 _____	12 _____	17 _____	22 _____
3 _____	8 _____	13 _____	18 _____	23 _____
4 _____	9 _____	14 _____	19 _____	24 _____
5 _____	10 _____	15 _____	20 _____	25 _____

Source: R. I. Henderson, *Compensation management.* Reston, VA: Reston Publishing Co., 1985, pp. 366–370.
Reprinted with permission.

INDIRECT COMPENSATION

Employee benefits are indirect forms of compensation which are intended to improve or maintain the quality of life for employees. Three benefits programs are federally mandated: unemployment insurance, social security, and workers' compensation. Like direct compensation, the major objective for most organizational indirect compensation programs is to attract, retain, and motivate employees.

During World War II, the War Labor Board exempted employee benefits from wage stabilization controls; the reasoning was that since such benefits were "on the fringe of wages," increases in this area would not be inflationary. At that time, benefits were less than 5 percent of pay. According to the U.S. Chamber of Commerce, benefits add an average of $.38 for $1.00 of payroll, or about 28 percent of total compensation costs.[20] Indirect compensation in the form of health and life insurance, pension plans, vacation time, and social welfare programs is a critical (and expensive) component of an organization's compensation package.

According to the *Human Resources Yearbook,* the 1980s saw an "unrelenting succession of employee benefit legislative and regulatory changes."[21] There is every reason to believe that state and federal legislative interest in this area will continue into the 1990s. Given the federal deficit, employee benefits are likely to be a continuing target for extra tax revenue.

While employee benefit programs were at one time quite uniform, there is now considerable variance in the benefits which are offered by organizations beyond the core basic welfare and retirement programs. The diversity of benefit programs which are offered tend to vary as a consequence of the organization's HRM philosophy, its size, its location, and the type of business. For example, companies such as IBM, Procter & Gamble, Stride Rite, Arthur Andersen, and Johnson & Johnson have a strong pro-family orientation to their benefit package, with options such as family-care leave, child- and elder-care support, dependent-care accounts, adoption benefits, alternative work schedules, and on-site day care. In general, larger companies offer a wider array of benefits. Figure 11.11 presents a summary of the results of a recent Chamber of Commerce survey on trends in employee benefits.

Benefits as a percentage of payroll have risen 20 percent since 1950. There are several reasons for this dramatic increase.[22] First, the employer response to wage stabilization during the Korean war was to increase benefits in order to attract and retain employees. The increase in benefits was thus substantial in the early 1950s. Second, the Social Security Act, enacted in 1935 as a retirement program, was expanded to cover more employees

FIGURE 11.11
EMPLOYEE BENEFITS IN THE UNITED STATES

1. There is great variance in benefit programs which are offered by organizations. Fewer than 2 percent of respondents provide benefits which are less than 18 percent of payroll. Almost 5 percent of companies offer benefits which are 50 percent or more of payroll.
2. The average payment was 39 percent of payroll, or $5.13 per payroll hour and $10,708 per year per employee.
3. Industry payments vary greatly. The textile industry averaged 29 percent, while primary metals paid more than 50 percent.
4. Larger firms pay more benefits than smaller firms.
5. Health and life insurance programs are now almost universal.
6. Employee payroll deductions for benefits include 3 percent for pensions and various savings plans, 0.9 percent for medical insurance, and 0.8 percent for life insurance and other benefits.

Source: Survey of Employee Benefits. Washington: U.S. Chamber of Commerce, 1990.

with a variety of other benefits (e.g., survivor, disability, and health benefits). Third, the evolving federal tax policy favored the establishment of pension programs for both employees and employers. Fourth, labor unions put great emphasis on employee benefits in their negotiations subsequent to court rulings declaring benefits subject to collective bargaining.

In addition to social security, other federal legislation has significantly influenced benefits. For example, the Age Discrimination in Employment Act (ADEA) as amended in 1986 established several benefit protections for older workers. The Retirement Equity Act of 1984 made the legal coverage of previous legislation more comprehensive for the workforce. In general, this legislation made employees more aware of benefit programs and thus raised demand for certain types of programs. The final major reason for the dramatic increase in employee benefits is the emphasis placed on them by employers. While some programs reflect a concern for the needs of employees (e.g., long-term disability, child care), other programs were established based on a belief that some benefits can have a positive impact on the "bottom line." For example, companies which have adopted pro-family benefit packages firmly believe that family concerns often cause high employee turnover and can affect recruitment and retention of highly qualified personnel. Employee stock ownership programs (ESOPs), suggestion systems, and educational programs are other benefit programs which some experts link to increases in productivity, job satisfaction, and organizational effectiveness.

There has been a general leveling of benefits as a percentage of payroll since 1980 due to a greater attention to the costs of the programs by management and, particularly in the health insurance area, a variety of cost-containment measures. The cost of benefits, particularly health insurance, is thought by some experts to be a major competitive disadvantage for American companies. The percentage of U.S. gross national product (GNP) spent on health care is projected to be around 14 percent by 1995, contrasted with a projected percentage of less than 8 percent for major international competitors. U.S. companies now assume the bulk of this tab. According to one expert in labor costs, "the growing burden for corporate America is in non-wage items—particularly big jumps in health insurance premiums, imposed by the insurers, and higher social security taxes, imposed by the government."[23]

Research supports the importance of the benefits package in applicants' job selection process.[24] Recent research, for example, shows that women are particularly attracted to a company with a strong pro-family indirect compensation package. However, employees tend to grossly underestimate the cost of benefits to the organization. For example, one study found that current employees estimated the cost of benefits to the organization to be 12 percent, whereas the actual cost was 31 percent.[25] Another study found that 7 percent of employees surveyed estimated the cost to the employer to be zero.[26] Organizations are now working harder to explain the cost of the benefit package to employees so that, as one benefits manager put it, they can realize a better "bang for the buck."

The Importance of Benefits Planning

On account of their enormous costs and the financial commitment which is made for the future, benefits planning has become a critical component of HR planning processes. Because of federal and state laws on legal obligations to retirees regarding benefits, the long-term cost of benefits can be overwhelming. The American automotive industry, for example, maintains that benefits obligations, including those to retirees, are one of the primary reasons U.S. companies have so much difficulty in competing on price.

Benefits managers typically begin with a general policy statement and develop a 3- to 5-year strategic plan in the context of a number of internal and external factors. The most important of these factors are general business objectives for the future; cost factors; the compensation strategy which the organization is taking; employee preferences; collective bargaining effects; benefits programs of competitive employers; taxation, legal, and regulatory implications and changes; and the HRM philosophy of the organization. Experts agree that benefits programs should be closely coordinated with direct compensation in order for the entire compensation program to be most effective.

The Legal Implications of Indirect Compensation

The Pregnancy Discrimination Act of 1978, an amendment to Title VII of the Civil Rights Act of 1964 (discussed in Chapter 3), requires that pregnancy and pregnancy-related disabilities be treated the same as other disabilities. The Supreme Court extended this coverage to include spouses of employees. Employers who offer hospitalization, temporary disability plans, and sick leave are now legally required to include pregnancy as a covered condition. In addition, several states require that employers provide short paid leave time for pregnant employees (usually about 60 percent of base pay for 10 weeks).

Women tend to live longer than men. This fact obviously affects the number of payments in a pension program; women on the average receive retirement benefits longer than men. Organizations once responded to this fact either by requiring women to pay more into the pension or by providing a lower monthly payout to women after retirement. Both of these practices are now illegal.

Amendments to the ADEA now require employers to allow employees over the age of 65 to continue in a pension program. In addition, health and life insurance must be available to employees between the ages of 65 and 70 if the benefit is offered by the employer.

The Internal Revenue Service (IRS) will classify a pension plan as discriminatory if an employer's contribution for employees in lower pay classes is less than that which the employer contributes to higher-paid employee pensions. Many employers also offer a 401(k) plan, which is a tax shelter program enabling employees to reduce their tax liabilities. However, the IRS requires that such plans be made available to everyone in the organization if the organization makes it available to anyone.

Major Parts of Benefits Programs

According to the U.S. Chamber of Commerce, benefits can be classified into three general categories: health and security, payments for time not worked, and employee services. Within each of these broad categories there are numerous options. The sections to follow will review the most common of these options.

HEALTH AND SECURITY BENEFITS

The benefits of greatest concern to both employees and employers today are probably in the form of medical and health-care insurance. Other forms of benefits in this category are life insurance, workers' compensation, accidental death and disability coverage, unemployment insurance, sick leave, social security, and pension plans.

Health Insurance

The vast majority of employers in the United States provide health insurance for employees. Approximately 75 percent of private-sector and 80 percent of public-sector employees are provided with some form of health insurance. Most employers also provide insurance for dependents. These plans typically cover hospitalization (room, board, and services), surgery, and major medical expenses. For organizations with health insurance, there is typically a basic coverage for all employees, with additional coverage for salaried employees. Disability allowances are typically more generous for professional and managerial employees. The typical "comprehensive" model of health insurance requires employees to pay for the first $100 or $200 of expenses before they are eligible for group coverage. Health-care benefits are typically provided through private insurance companies, a Blue Cross/Blue Shield Association, or some form of self-funding arrangement.

As stated above, the cost of health insurance to employers skyrocketed in the 1980s, forcing organizations to institute a variety of cost-containment measures. The average yearly cost of health benefits per employee is now in excess of $2300.[27] Health insurance costs amounted to 24 percent of after-tax corporate profit in one survey year.[28] General Motors (GM) estimates that the cost of health insurance adds $370 to the cost of each automobile they produce while Chrysler puts the figure at $700. The Ford Motor Company estimated that it paid in excess of $15 million in unnecessary hospital bills in 1 year. According to market researchers, the high cost of providing health insurance to an aging workforce and to retirees is the biggest factor in making domestic vehicles more expensive to produce in this country. Unfortunately for the automakers, the 3-year contract negotiated with the United Auto Workers (UAW) makes virtually no changes in health care benefits.

Among the most common approaches to controlling costs are:[29] (1) increases in the deductible and the extent of employee contribution or copayment for medical care; (2) second opinions from physicians (one study found a savings of $2.63 for every $1 spent, when second opinions are used); (3) incentives for outpatient surgery, testing, and greater consumer awareness; and (4) the formation of business coalitions which oversee health-care activity and negotiate with health-care providers.[30] Recent research indicates that these approaches are effective. Other approaches include health maintenance organizations (HMOs) and preferred provider organizations (PPOs).

HMOs are organizations of health-care professionals who provide services on a prepaid basis. PPOs are usually hospitals which offer reduced rates based on a contractual arrangement with the organization. Many larger organizations have realized considerable savings since implementing HMO or PPO programs. GM, for example, experienced its first reduction in health insurance costs in over 25 years after it contracted for HMO and PPO services.[31] One survey found that 52 percent of corporate respondents indicated that HMOs saved them money.[32] A few big employers have made HMOs mandatory for new employees, thus restricting their options in the selection of medical services. Employees at GM's Saturn plant, the Lockheed Corporation, and Rockwell International, for example, are given health benefits only through HMOs. Lockheed's evaluation of this program found that employees were generally satisfied with this program. The most successful cost-containment programs have reduced allowances, imposed incentives to save, increased deductibles, and increased flexibility in coverage.

There has been an increase in coverage for other forms of health insurance in addition to the basic medical coverage. Dental care, mental health coverage, drug-abuse treatment, home health care, and vision care are the most common forms of the extended coverage. About 90 percent of employers now sponsor some form of dental coverage.[33]

In this age of corporate downsizing, one of the biggest fears of employees is to be suddenly left without health insurance. Congress has assuaged those fears somewhat with the passage of the Consolidated Omnibus Budget Reconciliation Act (COBRA) of 1986. As amended in 1988, COBRA requires employers with 20 or more employees to continue offering employees health-care benefits at 102 percent of the premium cost for as long as 18 months after the employee leaves. Divorced or surviving spouses are allowed up to 36 months of coverage. Employers pay stiff penalties for violations of this provision of COBRA. The law also imposes strict administrative requirements on benefits programs.

A 1990 study found that 84 percent of companies provide medical coverage to retirees. However, 53 percent of respondents also indicated that they have reduced the benefit in some way in the last 2 years.[34] Some organizations (e.g., Bank of America) have eliminated retiree health care coverage for new hires. The Retirees Health Benefits Bankruptcy Protection Act of 1988 is designed to protect retirees when an employer cuts retirement benefits after filing for bankruptcy.

Life Insurance

One of the oldest and most common forms of employee benefit is group life insurance. Group life insurance provides coverage to all employees of an organization, without physical examinations and with premiums typically based on the group's characteristics. The most common level of life insurance is twice the salary level of the employee. The majority of plans call for the employer to pay the entire premium, although about a third of organizations require the employee to pay a portion of the premium. Many companies now offer optional additional life insurance along with dependent term insurance and other survivor benefits.

Sickness and Disability Insurance

Workers' compensation mandates payments for permanent or temporary work-related disabilities, with the amount of the payments varying across the states. Workers' compensation is compulsory in all but two states (Texas and New Jersey). The average payment is about 60 percent of an employee's earnings. The law provides that workers must be paid a disability benefit which is based on a percentage of their wages, an amount which varies across the states. Each state also specifies the length of the payment period and a maximum amount which can be paid. There are also provisions for the payment of medical expenses.

Social security also provides coverage in the event of permanent, work-related illness or injury. In addition, some employers offer add-ons to the coverage offered through workers' compensation and social security. In general, the combined coverage sums to about 75 percent of the amount employees would earn if they were working.

Unemployment Insurance

Employees who are covered by the Social Security Act of 1935 and who are laid off are eligible for unemployment compensation for up to 26 weeks. A 1991 bill extended these benefits for up to an additional 20 weeks. Eligible employees must apply for the insurance through a state employment agency, which will attempt to locate suitable alternative employment. In order to be eligible for the insurance, the worker must have been employed previously in an occupation covered by the insurance (almost all occupations are), must have been dismissed by the organization but not for misconduct, must be available for work and actively seeking employment, and (in all states but Rhode Island and New York) must not be unemployed because of a labor dispute.

The amount of the benefit varies by state and is determined by the employee's previous wage level up to a maximum amount. The average is about $175 per week. The source of these funds is the federal payroll tax, which is based on the wages paid out, but the level varies by state. An unemployed worker's benefits are charged to the organization, with the insurance rates for companies varying as a function of the amount which is charged to each organization.

Supplemental unemployment insurance programs are also common in some industries (e.g., auto, steel, rubber). Typically negotiated through collective bargaining, these programs augment unemployment compensation and can provide weekly benefits in the event that employees' work weeks are reduced or they are permanently terminated. Through the efforts of the UAW, union employees who are laid off in the auto industry can receive over 90 percent of their after-tax pay through unemployment insurance and the negotiated supplemental programs.

Only about 8 percent of employees of medium to large firms are covered by some form of supplemental unemployment insurance (SUB), but many employees are covered by a form of severance pay in the event they are terminated for reasons other than cause. Professionals and managers are generally granted higher severance allowances because it usually takes longer for them to obtain comparable employment.

Pensions

There are three major sources of retirement income: social security benefits, individual savings, and pension plans. Employers play a major role in all three of these sources. They pay half of employees' social security taxes, provide for a variety of individual savings incentives through credit unions, and sponsor pension programs. A pension is a payment to a retired employee based on the extent and level of employment with the organization. There are now about half a million private employer pension plans which cover about 75 percent of nonfarm American workers. However, some industries (e.g., manufacturing, mining, construction, transportation) are more likely to offer pension plans than are others (e.g., retail, service). Larger organizations are also more likely to offer pensions than are smaller ones. Public employees are also typically covered by pension plans. Some pension plans require employees to pay into the pension (the amount is withdrawn from their paychecks), while others are entirely financed by the employer. The employer sets aside funds each year which are managed by trustees (usually insurance companies). Taxes on employer contributions are deferred, and retirees pay taxes on the pension as they receive it. Pension plans must conform to strict requirements established in the Internal Revenue Code.

Because of previous employer abuses and mismanagement, pension administration is now heavily regulated by state and federal government. The most significant piece of legislation is the Employment Retirement Income Security Act (ERISA) of 1974. ERISA requires that all persons participating in retirement plans be notified about the plans in writing and in understandable language.

The U.S. Department of Labor has provided guidelines on the preparation of such written material. ERISA also created the Pension Benefit Guaranty Corporation (PBGC), which acts as an insurance agency in the event that an organization cannot meet its pension obligations (the organization must forfeit 30 percent of its net worth if it fails to meet obligations to its retirees). The PBGC fully guarantees benefit programs which have been in effect for at least 5 years and guarantees payment up to $22,300 per year. The PBGC has been saddled with responsibility for over 1500 pension plans since it was established. ERISA does not require an organization to have a private pension plan. The law simply regulates those plans which exist.

There are other important provisions of ERISA. The employer must select one of three alternative vesting requirements (the most common is a 10-year service requirement). New standards are stipulated for fiduciary behavior (the fiduciary administers the pension fund). The employer must also provide detailed information to the Department of Labor on an annual basis regarding the status of the pension fund.

Most pension plans are defined-benefit plans which guarantee a specific payment based on a percentage of preretirement pay. The amount is based on years of service, average earnings during a specified period of time (e.g., the last 5 years), and age at time of retirement. When combined with social security benefits, retirement pay averages about 50 percent of final average pay. A small but growing percentage of pension plans (about 5 percent) are indexed to adjust pensions for inflation.

Defined-contribution plans have been growing in popularity in recent years because they can be linked to organizational performance. However, the Tax Reform Act of 1986 has removed some of the employee incentives to save by restricting the amount which can be contributed and imposing stiff penalties on withdrawal of funds. Stock bonuses, savings plans, profit sharing, and ESOPs are examples of defined-contribution plans. Future employee benefits depend on the growth of the benefit fund. If the organization prospers, the fund will be greater and the employee will have a better pension. Employers prefer this approach to benefits because they will never owe more than that which was contributed. Everything beyond this amount is a direct function of the investment of the money which was contributed. A growing number of organizations now offer a combination of defined-benefit and defined-contribution plans.

The Retirement Equity Act of 1984 mandates that all employees age 21 and older must be included in the plan and that employees may have breaks in service of up to 5 years before they lose credit for previous experience. Years for "vesting" (minimum number of years required to be eligible for benefits) must be counted starting at age 18. Also, a year of maternity or paternity leave can-

not be counted as 1 of the 5 years of break in service. This legislation is particularly beneficial to women, who are more likely to take extended leaves for child rearing. Under this law, pension benefits are now considered a joint asset in a divorce settlement, and employers must provide accrued benefits to surviving spouses of employees who were vested but died before becoming eligible.

The graying workforce is burdening some of the largest U.S. producers because of pension and benefit obligations to retirees. At GM, for example, the ratio of active to retired workers is about $2:1$. At Ford, the ratio is about $1.5:1$. At the Nissan plant in Tennessee, by contrast, only 1 of over 3000 workers was eligible to retire in 1990, and he opted to stay on because he liked the work. The plant had no other retirement obligations.

PAY FOR TIME NOT WORKED

The cost of paid time off is one of the highest benefit expenses for employers today. According to the U.S. Department of Labor, payments for time not worked average over 13 percent of payroll.[35] According to the same survey, over 3 percent of payroll is spent on paid rest periods such as lunch, coffee breaks, travel time, and clean-up time. The major types of days off for which employees are paid are vacations, holidays, sick leave, personal days, and days to perform civic responsibilities (e.g., jury duty, witness duty, military obligations). Vacation time usually depends on the employee's length of service. According to one survey, employees with 10 years of experience in medium-size to large firms average 16 days of vacation, while employees with 15 years of experience average 18.5 days of vacation. One survey found that 25 percent of organizations offer 5- and 6-week vacations for 25-year employees. In general, hourly employees must work a greater number of years than salaried employees in order to qualify for the same number of vacation days. The trend among union employees is toward longer time for vacations relative to those of nonunion employees.

Hourly and salaried employees average nine holidays per year, with the type of business having an effect on the holidays which are recognized. An increasing minority of organizations now offer two or more personal days off per year for a variety of personal reasons (e.g., death or illness in the family, legal matters, eye examinations, special events). A list of acceptable reasons is typically published, and employees then choose to use their allowed days at their own discretion.

The majority of organizations offer sick leave for their employees, with an average of about 10 days per year.[36] When sick leave is offered, employees can often accumulate unused days, in case of a prolonged illness or injury in the future. Some organizations maintain sick leave banks from which employees can borrow sick leave in an emergency. A small number of organizations offer "well pay"; employees get extra pay when they are not absent or tardy for a specified period of time.

EMPLOYEE SERVICES

A great variety of benefits fit under the third U.S. Chamber of Commerce category. Figure 11.12 presents a list of the possible services. The most common employee services are education programs, financial services such as credit unions, sports and health programs and facilities, employee assistance programs (EAPs) and mental health care, housing and relocation services, employee recognition programs, and child care. We will briefly discuss each of these below.

Education Programs

Many organizations have educational programs for their employees which range from tuition refunds for col-

FIGURE 11.12
EMPLOYEE SERVICES

- Educational assistance
- Financial assistance
- Food service
- Transportation programs
- Wellness programs
- Recreational programs
- Company car
- Legal assistance
- Employee assistance programs
- Child care
- Auto insurance
- Clothing allowance
- Relocation expenses
- Parking allowance
- Stock programs
- Merchandise reductions
- Elder care
- Adoption services
- Employee recognition programs
- Suggestion systems
- Prescription drugs
- Gift matching
- Charter flights
- Special purchasing agreements

lege to literacy training. Some companies are helping their workers cope with educating their children. Aluminum Co. of America, for example, hands out more than 200 scholarships a year to employees' children. According to the Bureau of Labor Statistics (BLS), 86 percent of full-time employees of medium-size to large U.S. firms are covered by some form of tuition-aid plan. While the principal objective of these programs is to keep employees up to date in their fields of expertise, some programs are designed to prepare employees for other opportunities within the organization. Surprisingly, despite the wide availability of educational assistance through American employers, only about 5 percent of employees take advantage of this benefit. This may be because most employers do a poor job of communicating the availability of the assistance and the connection between education and career mobility.

Financial Services

Through a variety of programs, some organizations provide assistance to employees on financial matters. Payroll savings plans, credit unions, and various thrift plans are three of the most common. Payroll savings plans often provide company matching funds for employee savings. Credit unions provide convenient savings options and often offer competitive loans to employees. There are over 17,000 credit unions active today, with assets in excess of $125 billion and over 52 million members.[37] Many employers also offer extensive financial counseling to executives.

Sports and Health Programs

Gaining popularity as benefits are organized sports, recreational, and health or "wellness" programs for employees. One survey found that 75 percent of organizations at least sponsored recreational programs.[38] Many companies offer facilities for these activities as well. Among the common wellness programs are weight control and exercise activities and antismoking assistance. Unfortunately, with a few exceptions, there has been little systematic research to justify this benefit or the various programs from a financial perspective.[39] However, reports from such companies as Kimberly-Clark, New York Telephone, and Prudential Life Insurance Company provide some evidence for the effectiveness of "wellness" programs.[40]

Employee Assistance Programs (EAPs) and Mental Health Care

EAPs typically provide counseling, diagnosis, and treatment for substance abuse, family and marital problems, depression, and financial and other personal difficulties.

EAPs are used by about 70 percent of Fortune 500 companies, with about one-third of U.S. employees having access to the programs. Other companies simply cover treatment for mental disorders. One survey found a 27 percent increase in costs associated with EAPs and other mental health care in a recent year. EAPs tend to be cheaper and more effective than simple reimbursement for outside counseling.[41] We will discuss wellness programs and EAPs in more detail in Chapter 16.

Housing and Relocation Services

It is estimated that U.S. companies spend over $14 billion annually to relocate employees. One survey found that the average cost of a domestic relocation is over $40,000. Of course, the cost of international relocation is substantially greater.[42] Most companies also offer assistance in selling homes because of relocation and to defray expenses for locating a new home. Special loan programs are sometimes available for purchasing new homes. Some companies provide spouse job placement services as well.

Employee Recognition Programs

A growing number of organizations offer awards to employees for extended service, work-related achievements, and suggestions for improving organizational effectiveness. For tax reasons, the awards are often in the form of gifts and travel rather than cash. Suggestion systems offer incentives to employees who submit ideas which result in greater efficiency or profitability for the company. According to the National Association of Suggestions Systems, employees were awarded almost $125 million for suggestions in 1991.

Child Care

There is evidence that company-sponsored child-care programs reduce employee absences, improve recruitment, and help to retain valuable employees.[43] Barnett Bank in Florida, for example, reported a substantial increase in job applications as a direct function of its child-care program. Dominion Bankshares in Roanoke, Virginia, reported decreased absences among its 950 employees after its on-site center was established. Over 4000 U.S. companies now offer some form of child-care support, including referrals or financing. A small but growing number of companies offer on-site centers. With a variety of government financial incentives now available, and considerable political activity on the subject, there is every reason to believe that child care will become quite common as an employee benefit in years to come. Child-care assistance is usually included in cafeteria-style benefit programs, which are discussed below.

There is a growing recognition that illness among employees' children can be costly to the company in terms of absenteeism, tardiness, and work stress. Transamerican Life, with a predominantly female staff of 3700, estimated that it was losing $180,000 per year due to employee absences caused by sick children. The company tackled the problem by setting up a subsidized sick child-care center. Other companies offer similar programs. American Telephone and Telegraph (AT&T) invested in sick bays through hospitals and child-care centers. Hoffman-LaRoche and Hughes Aircraft offer sick care to employees' children through convenient medical centers. The 3M Company covers up to 78 percent of the fees for home health care for children.

CAFETERIA-STYLE BENEFIT PLANS

About 23 percent of U.S. companies now offer flexible, or cafeteria-style, benefit plans.[44] Because of the increased diversity of the workforce, employees tend to prefer the flexible plans, and employers can realize cost savings through them. Cafeteria plans enable the employee to select a benefit package from a list of available options. The benefit program can thus provide a closer match between the individual employee's needs and the plan. Figure 11.13 presents a list of the benefit options which can be included in a cafeteria plan, based on federal tax regulations. Organizations typically assess employee preferences for various benefit options through a survey. Cafeteria plans are particularly advantageous to the two-earner family since all redundant coverage can be eliminated and savings can be realized.

The simplest and most common form of cafeteria plan is the reimbursement account which allows employees to pay for certain benefits through a tax-free account. The Educational Testing Service, for example, allocates either 3 or 6 percent of employees' salaries for the selection of the optional component of the benefit package, the difference depending on length of service. Other models prescribe either a core benefit package plus optional add-ons or a modular approach, which has a set number of plans from which the employee selects one.

The growth of cafeteria-style plans has been impeded by the reluctance of compensation managers who view them as "administrative nightmares" and too confusing for employees. These perceptions probably help to explain why fewer than 10 percent of white-collar workers and fewer than 5 percent of blue-collar workers have such plans despite substantial employee support for the approach. Another reason is undoubtedly the confusion over the employer tax and legal implications of such plans. Unions have also been reluctant to support the plans. With the increased adoption of sophisticated user-friendly computer software for maintenance data and for commu-

FIGURE 11.13
WHAT CAN BE INCLUDED IN A CAFETERIA PLAN?

NONTAXABLE BENEFITS
Accident and health insurance

Dependent life insurance (up to $2000)

Disability benefits

Group legal service

Group term life insurance (up to $50,000)

Noninsured tax-deductible medical expenses

Noninsured tax-deductible dependent-care expenses

TAXABLE BENEFITS
Cash

Dependent life insurance (over $2000)

Group term life insurance (over $50,000)

Vacation days

DEFERRED COMPENSATION
Elective employee deferrals under a 401(k) plan

SPECIFICALLY EXCLUDED FROM INCLUSION IN A CAFETERIA PLAN
Deferred compensation plans—other than 401(k) as above

Educational assistance benefits

No-additional-cost services

Qualified employee discounts

Qualified employer-provided transportation

Scholarships and fellowship grants

Working condition fringes

Source: R. M. McCaffery, *Employee benefit programs*. Boston: PWS-Kent, 1988, p. 173. Reprinted with permission.

nication of choice options to employees, there is likely to be a steady increase in the use of cafeteria-style benefit plans in the future. One variation of the cafeteria plan is a reimbursement account in which employees set aside an amount from their salary which is used to pay for child care, health insurance, and other benefits. The advantage of these accounts for employees is that the money is deducted from their paychecks before taxes. The disadvantage is that any money not spent reverts to the company.

COMMUNICATING THE BENEFIT PROGRAM

As stated at the outset, employees have little understanding of the costs involved in a benefit program.[45] According to one expert in the field, employee communication is the "keystone of the program . . . without effective com-

munication, a benefit program remains incomplete and the considerable effort and expense consumed in planning, designing, and administering plans becomes largely unproductive."[46] While distributing benefit summaries pursuant to the requirement of ERISA provides a cursory understanding of the major components of the benefit package, the effectiveness of the package is undermined unless employees gain an appreciation of the advantages and superiority of the program relative to competitors' programs. ERISA simply requires that "Summary Plan Descriptions" be "written in a manner calculated to be understood by the average plan participant." Employees must be aware of and understand the benefits which are available to them in order for the employer to fully realize the objectives for which the benefits were established.

The goal in benefit communication should be to present the worth of the benefit package to current and future employees. To that end, many employers now provide counseling for employees to enhance their understanding of the benefit program beyond that which is conveyed in written form. Among the other methods used to explain benefits are: paycheck inserts, employee publications, posters, and audio or video recorded messages. At Citicorp, for example, 56,000 employees are exposed to software, videos, seminars, and several other teaching tools which explain their new flexible benefit program. Each Citicorp employee receives a printout of benefits compared to the previous year, a computer disk, and a workbook that explains how to determine the tax and out-of-pocket implications of the benefit options.

Benefit programs which require some employee contribution to the cost are not only more efficient but tend to enhance employees' understanding of the benefit program and its cost to the employer. Also, the growth in cafeteria-style plans means the employees should be more informed about the costs of the various benefit options.

The trend in the United States continues to be an increase in the amount and types of benefits which are available to the American worker. However, because of the federal deficit, increased taxes on such benefits are probable. Employees tend to devalue the worth of benefits. Sophisticated communication programs which "sell" the benefit package are likely to be more widely used in the future. ERISA, the Retirement Equity Act, and the amendments to the ADEA regarding mandatory retirement have caused employers to assess their pension programs to make certain that they are in compliance. Most companies have instituted cost-containment programs for their health-care benefits, with generally positive results. Other important trends are the increase in cafeteria-style plans and the development and spread of new benefit programs such as child care and recreational and wellness programs.

INTERNATIONAL EXECUTIVE COMPENSATION*

As discussed in previous chapters, international business generates about one-third of U.S. corporate profits. As growth prospects for the U.S. market level off, and Eastern Europe and nations of the former Soviet Union become more stabilized, many American corporate leaders are concluding that international business must become the key to their companies' future growth potential. To transform that growth potential into a profitable reality, U.S. companies will need to staff their international operations with managers who are both technically competent and culturally proficient. We discussed the selection issue in Chapters 6 and 7 and the training issue in Chapter 8.

The type and amount of compensation necessary to attract technically and culturally qualified international executives vary widely according to the nationality category from which executives are chosen. Three executive nationality categories are commonly recognized in shaping international compensation policies:

1. **Parent-country nationals (PCNs).** PCNs are executives whose nationality is the same as that of the country in which the parent company is based. Thus, an American manager of a GM leasing subsidiary in the United Kingdom would be a PCN, as would an Italian manager of an Olivetti distribution facility in the United States.
2. **Third-country nationals (TCNs).** TCNs are executives whose nationality is neither that of the parent-company country nor that of the host country where the parent company's affiliate (and the TCN's job) is located. A German working for a Dow Chemical experimental laboratory in Mexico would be an example of a TCN.
3. **Host-country nationals (HCNs).** HCNs are nationals of the country in which the foreign affiliate is located. A Frenchman managing the French sales subsidiary of 3M Company and an American managing a Mitsubishi plant in Illinois would be classified as HCNs.

The compensation package structured for the expatriate (i.e., the PCN or TCN) is ordinarily more complex and expensive than that for the HCN. Because of that greater complexity and cost, we will discuss first, and in somewhat greater detail, the compensation issues affecting the expatriate executive. The more frequent, but less exacting and more easily affordable, situation of compensating HCN executives is addressed subsequently.

---

*This section was contributed by Thomas H. Becker.

Expatriate Compensation

The discussion here is oriented primarily toward designing a compensation program for U.S. PCNs (i.e., U.S. employees assigned abroad by U.S. companies). Many TCN compensation features vary markedly from those included in a PCN's package. However, because each is an expatriate and because it is the common non-host-country citizenship status that drives many of the important compensation features of both, the TCN is treated here as a special case of the PCN.

The salary and fringe benefits paid to a PCN are intended to ensure that U.S. executives do not suffer any material loss due to working abroad. By using a balance-sheet approach to compensation, U.S. companies attempt to keep overseas executives on at least a financial par with their domestic colleagues. "The balance-sheet approach to international compensation is a system designed to equalize the purchasing power of employees at comparable position levels living overseas and in the home country, and to provide incentives to offset qualitative differences between assignment locations."[47] Maintaining such purchasing-power equality typically proves to be very expensive. For example, it is reported that the total cost to the employer of maintaining an American manager in Ireland and in Tokyo is, respectively, three times and six times the cost of maintaining a manager in a comparable position at home.[48] The Civil Rights Act of 1991 also provides protection for Americans on overseas assignments who can show that their compensation has been affected by their race, color, national origin, religion, or sex.

The high cost of the compensation package required to induce a U.S. executive to move to, and perform well in, a foreign country is a function of three factors in the assignment profile: (1) the position, (2) the locale, and (3) the individual. The primary roles that these factors play in matching a compensation package to an assignment profile are shown in Figure 11.14. Some of the elements often found in an executive's overseas compensation package are described below.

POSITION FACTORS. The following are a few of the more common compensation elements designed to accommodate needs which are specific to a particular position.

- **Base salary.** A PCN's base salary must be competitive with the amount that an employee with similar responsibilities and duties would receive at home; it is *not* geared to what a similar job would pay in the host-country labor market. In the case of TCNs, a majority of U.S. companies "tie base salaries to [their TCNs'] home countries rather than to U.S. or host country salary structures."[49]

FIGURE 11.14
MATCHING A COMPENSATION PACKAGE TO AN ASSIGNMENT PROFILE

		THESE ASSIGNMENT VARIABLES	OCCASION THESE COMPENSATION NEEDS	
Assignment profile	Position factors	Responsibilities and duties	Base salary	Compensation package
		Operating performance	Incentive bonus	
		Assignment duration	Periodic salary adjustments	
		Status and prestige	Representation allowance	
		Travel requirements	Official travel allowance	
	Locale factors	Remoteness	Rest and relaxation	
		Physical or cultural adversity	Hardship and home leave	
		Sanitation	Medical care	
		Physical security	Hazardous duty or security allowance, ransom insurance	
		Housing cost	Housing allowance	
		Housing availability	Temporary quarters allowance	
		Transfer incidentals	Relocation allowance	
		School availability	Education allowance	
		Economic security	Retirement benefits	
		Income taxes	Tax equalization	
		Purchasing power	Currency of payment	
	Individual factors	Reluctance to move	Foreign service premium	
		Family income	Spousal employment	
		Asset exposure	Home and auto protection	
		Number of dependents	Dependent costs	

- **Incentive bonus.** Because of the influence of variables such as exchange-rate changes, transfer prices, and inflation over which a PCN manager may have little or no control, a majority of U.S. companies base PCNs' incentive bonuses on local-currency budget compared to actual operating performance.
- **Periodic salary adjustment.** According to a recent study, 56 percent of U.S.-based multinational companies (MNCs) said that a foreign assignment was either detrimental or immaterial to an executive's career.[50] This finding suggests the possibility that the longer PCNs remain in an overseas position, the greater the risk that their job skills will have obsolesced and their career prospects ebbed, upon eventual return to headquarters. To soften the effect of such an unwelcome contingency, and to compensate for normal seniority-based pay increments, periodic salary increases are often included in compensation negotiations.
- **Representation allowance.** Middle-level American managers working abroad may find that their duties entail dealing with high-level individuals such as CEOs of major local corporations or cabinet ministers of the host country. Because authority tends to be more visible in many countries than it is in the U.S., it is often essential for PCN executives to learn to display the accoutrements of rank. Such power signals may include club memberships, chauffeured vehicles, elaborate offices, and prestigious home addresses.
- **Travel allowances.** Foreign assignments often require more travel—both local and international—than domestic positions. It is common practice to compensate executives for official travel by reimbursing the transportation component against receipts, and the lodging, meals, and incidentals component on a per diem basis.

LOCALE FACTORS. Because the cost of living varies widely from locale to locale (even within the same country), cost-of-living allowances (COLAs) should be designed to enable the PCN or TCN to enjoy a standard of living abroad that is comparable to what she or he would enjoy at home. Some of the compensation elements often negotiated as COLAs are described below.

- **Rest and relaxation (R&R).** Living in a remote, culturally unfamiliar, or climatically harsh locale exacts a toll and may impair job performance if PCNs (and occasionally TCNs) are not allowed to "recharge their batteries" in more pleasant or comfortable surroundings. While R&R time is generally charged against the employee's vacation leave, the related travel and per diem expenses for the employee and accompanying dependents are reimbursed by the employer.
- **Hardship allowance and home leave.** Locales qualifying for R&R frequently also qualify the PCN or TCN for hardship payment granted as a percentage of base salary. In addition to this payment, the hardship allowance may include fees for family membership in a social or recreational club, as well as home leave. A typical home leave policy may grant the PCN executive, on a biannual basis, 1 month of salaried vacation in the United States, with round-trip transportation to the U.S. home of record and per diem expenses paid by the employer. Most companies discourage the taking of home leave in close conjunction either with the beginning or end of an overseas assignment or with R&R leave. It is common to take advantage of the PCN's presence in the United States by accompanying home leave with training and/or consultation at headquarters.
- **Medical care.** Sanitary and security conditions in some foreign locales may compel a company to provide its PCN executives with additional life, health, or dental insurance coverage. In some locales, the employee and dependents may need to travel to another country to receive care comparable to that given in the United States.
- **Hazardous duty allowance.** Terrorism, political instability, kidnapping, and criminal violence in places like Beirut, Bogota, and Lima expose PCNs and TCNs to a higher personal risk than they would experience at home. To compensate for the potential dangers, the employee may be provided with hazardous duty allowance (computed as a percentage of base salary), bodyguards, home and office security systems, training (frequently for the entire family) in self-defense and evasive driving techniques, and ransom insurance. Interestingly (and for obvious reasons), ransom insurance is one of the few employee benefits which the company does not boast of publicly—nor are employees briefed in detail on this form of insurance.
- **Housing allowance.** Duplicating the amenities of a typical American home in a foreign environment is often a tall order, and may entail substantial additional costs. The costs of leasing a home, round-trip shipment of the PCN's personal and household effects, and storage in the United States of other effects (e.g., boats, classic cars, valuable jewelry or collec-

tions, and artwork) should be included in calculating housing allowances.
- **Temporary quarters allowance.** Even where housing is expensive, accommodations closely equivalent to U.S. standards are not always readily available. As a consequence, the U.S. executive and his or her family may have to reside in a hotel or other interim furnished lodging until they can move into "permanent" housing. On one occasion, an American executive assigned to a South American country resided with his family in a hotel for 3 months while awaiting promised construction to be finished on the house he had agreed to lease. Losing patience, he opted to move into the house prematurely—and for the next 3 years was forced to enter and exit from his second-floor bedroom by an outside wooden ladder, and to use his not-too-nearby landlord's home for occasional hot-water showers.
- **Relocation allowance.** This allowance helps to ease the PCN's or TCN's transition to living abroad by compensating for related additional expenses such as clothing appropriate to severe climates, electric converters, and a local driver's license.
- **Education allowance.** Local public and private schooling for the expatriate's children may be inadequate or expensive. In some cases, children may have to attend a boarding school in the United States or a third country. Allowances for local or foreign education of PCN or TCN children may include transportation (typically one round trip per year if the school and job assignment locations are widely separated), room and board, tuition, books and supplies, and uniforms.
- **Retirement benefits.** HRM experts report that "U.S. PCNs typically remain under their home company's benefit program . . . [but that such] plans rarely cover TCNs." They further state that because "in some countries PCNs can not opt out of local social security programs . . . the MNC normally pays for these additional costs."[51]
- **Tax equalization.** Because a U.S. PCN must pay U.S. income tax as well as host-country income tax, most U.S. companies will make up the difference if the latter tax liability exceeds the former. It is important to note that the U.S. Tax Reform Act of 1986 allows a U.S. citizen to exempt the first $70,000 of qualifying foreign-earned income from federal income tax. This provision has the effect of significantly reducing a PCN's U.S. tax liability and, as a consequence, increasing the amount that the PCN's employer would have to pay to close the gap between the U.S. and host-country tax liabilities. For this reason, employers will often calculate the tax equalization payment as if the PCN were earning the taxable income in the United States.

- **Currency of payment.** The thrust of practice is to pay U.S. expatriate salaries partly in dollars and partly in host-country currency. Being paid in U.S. dollars may enable PCN executives to save in dollars (if host-country currency exchange controls are in effect), to forgo paying host-country income taxes on the dollar portion of income received, and to enjoy full local purchasing power (if host-country inflation is outpacing devaluation of its currency). U.S. companies, on the other hand, would often prefer to make all compensation payments in host-country currency to avoid saddling the local subsidiary with a hard-currency liability, a particularly onerous burden if exchange controls or remittance limits exist.

INDIVIDUAL FACTORS. We have seen that a variety of position- and locale-related factors play a central role in shaping a compensation package to fit a particular assignment profile. In the final analysis, however, the compensation package is designed to fit the individual executive who, after all, is the subject of the assignment. Some of the compensation elements designed to meet the widely variant responses of individual executives to a foreign job assignment are discussed below.

- **Foreign service premium.** Individuals respond differently to the prospect of a foreign assignment. Whereas leaving familiar surroundings, adjusting to a new culture and new job challenges, and exposing oneself to possible career-path disruptions upon repatriation may be an exciting adventure for some people, it may seem like a burdensome sentence for others. To ease the discomfort of adjustments, companies often negotiate a foreign service premium to induce reluctant executives to accept an overseas position.
- **Spousal employment.** A spouse's employment income may make an important contribution to the total income of the executive's family. Often the expatriate's working spouse is unable to find appropriate employment or to receive a work permit in the foreign country. All or a portion of the resulting relinquished income may have to be paid by the company.[52]
- **Home and automobile protection.** The ownership of a home and one or more cars by a U.S. expatriate being assigned abroad may occasion complicated questions about what to do with these possessions prior to transfer. If an executive is concerned about suffering monetary losses by being forced to rent or sell assets under adverse conditions, the company may have to be prepared to indemnify all or a portion of such losses.
- **Dependent costs.** As the number of the executive's dependents increases, so will the company's cost of covering many of the COLAs and perhaps even the foreign service premium. In the case of executives with many dependents, companies may find that the associated dependent-driven escalations in compensation expense simply make overseas assignments too costly.

HCN Compensation

Not long ago, it was traditional for U.S. affiliates to staff their overseas affiliates with U.S. executives. This practice stemmed partially from a lack of qualified HCN managerial candidates and partially from the conviction that only an experienced U.S. manager could represent the "company way" of doing business. These rationales for favoring the use of U.S. PCNs in key overseas positions have become increasingly difficult to defend in recent years. Indeed, there now is a heightened general awareness of the cost-effective contributions HCNs can make to subsidiary performance. As a result, U.S. companies today largely employ HCN managers in their subsidiaries abroad.

Because the compensation standard of expatriates is competitive with their home salaries and benefits, expatriate compensation will generally be at a higher level than that of local nationals. While such a gap between expatriate and HCN compensation does not go unnoticed in the subsidiary, it is generally accepted that the expatriate possesses special expertise—even if it is only nationality—that justifies the disparity in compensation levels. To eliminate the compensation gap between expatriates and HCNs by raising HCN compensation would only eliminate one compensation disparity while creating another—that between MNC HCNs and local company HCNs—and would set in motion a salary cost spiral that would benefit no one in the long run. To avoid that contingency, it is general practice to use "local compensation levels as guidelines when developing HCN compensation policies."[53]

When designing compensation policies for HCNs, it is essential to adjust for differences in compensation practices among different countries. The examples below illustrate some of the reasons why it is important to adapt HCN salaries and benefits to local practices:

- High severance pay in Latin America may induce a company to relegate aging but highly paid local executives to secondary management positions so that more dynamic younger managers may be promoted to very responsible positions.
- High personal income tax rates in the United Kingdom may argue in favor of keeping down taxable salaries for HCNs there and raising their non-taxable perquisites accordingly.
- Strong group cohesiveness in Japan may dictate against compensation policies that, in rewarding individual

performance, may broaden differences in intragroup salaries and benefits.

SUMMARY

Because of its importance, individuals are very concerned with the fairness of their pay relative to others both within and outside their organization. Organizations are also very concerned with pay, not only because of its importance as a cost of doing business but because it motivates important decisions of employees about taking a job, leaving a job, and working on the job.

Government attempts to ensure that discrimination does not exist in compensation and that certain minimum levels of fairness exist in compensation. A number of federal, state, and local laws regulate compensation.

Based on their financial state, their competitive strategy, and the nature of their business, companies set a pay policy relative to other firms. Once this policy is determined, organizations either buy or develop surveys that assess wage rates that other companies are paying. These results are combined with the results of a job evaluation which determine the value of the job to the organization. International compensation requires special considerations and often additional direct and indirect compensation.

Once ranges are developed for jobs, then the process of pay administration turns to the appropriate individuals within each pay range. Criteria for placement in a pay range include years of experience and performance levels. Individuals vary on these factors, and their pay ideally should be set based on experience and performance in order to reward employees for exemplary performance and commitment to the organization.

In the next chapter, we consider the methods used to reward employees for their individual contributions to the organization. As we shall see, these decisions are by no means easy, but when combined with appropriate pay ranges, they are the organization's best shot at motivating employees to continued organizational membership and higher levels of performance.

DISCUSSION QUESTIONS

1. Some experts argue that organizations need to focus more attention on external competitiveness and that the internal focus encourages employees to devote too much attention to other members of the company and not the competition. What do you think?

2. Do you think the United States should have a minimum wage? Explain your answer.

3. How would you go about determining the relevant labor market for any given job?

4. What are the pros and cons of the different approaches to gathering external pay data?

5. How should an organization integrate its competitive strategy into its compensation system? What specific steps would you follow?

6. Should the federal government mandate a family leave policy for employers?

7. What is comparable worth and how does it relate to a pay system? How is comparable worth (or pay equity) different from a pay system based on a point-factor job evaluation?

8. Do you support a national health care system for all United States citizens? Explain your position.

9. What are the major advantages and disadvantages of cafeteria-style benefit programs?

10. What does an employer's HRM philosophy have to do with its benefit program?

11. Given that employees undervalue the cost of benefits, why should a company not drop benefits and simply add more direct compensation?

12. Should an organization provide child-care benefits for its employees? Why?

NOTES

1. Rock, M. L., and Berger, L. A. (eds.) (1991). *The compensation handbook: A state-of-the-art guide to compensation strategy and design.* New York: McGraw-Hill. See also: Lawler, E. E. (1981). *Pay and organizational effectiveness.* Reading, MA: Addison-Wesley. Heneman, R. L., Greenberger, D. B., and Strasser, S. (1988). The relationship between pay for performance and pay satisfaction. *Personnel Psychology, 41,* 745–760. See also: Balkin, D. B., and Gomez-Mejia, L. R. (1987). Matching compensation and organizational strategies. *Strategic Management Journal, 11,* 153–169. Gerhart, B., and Milkovich, G. T. (1992). Employee compensation: Research and practice. In M. D. Dunnette and L. M. Hough (eds.), *Handbook of industrial and organizational psychology.* Palo Alto, CA: Consulting Psychologists Press, Inc. Gomez-Mejia, L. R., and Balkin, D. B. (1989). Effectiveness of individual and aggregate compensation strategies. *Industrial Relations, 28,* 431–445. Gomez-Mejia, L. R., and Balkin, D. B. (1992). *Compensation, organizational strategy, and firm performance.* Cincinnati, Ohio: South-Western Publishing. Gomez-Mejia, L. R., and Welbourne, T. M. (1988). Compensation strategy: An overview and future steps. *Human Resource Planning, 11,* 173–189. Milkovich, G. T. (1988). A strategic perspective on compensation management. *Research in Personnel and Human Resources Management, 6,* 263–288.

2. Gerhart, B., and Milkovich, G. T. (1990). Organizational differences in managerial compensation and financial performance. *Academy of Management Journal, 33,* 663–691. See also: Note 1, Milkovich, (1988). Gomez-Mejia, L. R., and Welbourne, T. M. (1988). Compensation strategy: An overview and future steps. *Human Resource Planning, 11,* 173–189. Abowd, J. M. (1990). Does performance-based managerial compensation affect corporate performance? *Industrial and Labor Relations Review, 43,* 52S–73S. Balkin, D. B., and Gomez-Mejia, L. R. (1987). Toward a contingent theory of compensation strategy. *Strategic Management Journal, 8,* 169–182.

3. Mowday, R. (1983). Equity predictors of behavior in organizations. In R. Steers and L. Porter (eds.), *Motivation and work behavior,* 3d ed. New York: McGraw-Hill, pp. 91–113. See also: Folger, R., and Konovsky, M. (1989). Effects of procedural and distributive justice on reactions to pay raise decisions. *Academy of Management Journal, 32,* 115–130. Bartol, K. M., and Martin, D. C. (1989). Effects of dependence, dependency threats, and pay secrecy on managerial pay allocations. *Journal of Applied Psychology, 74,* 105–113. Eisenhardt, K. M. (1990). Agency theory: An assessment and review. *Academy of Management Review, 14,* 57–74. Eisenhardt, K. M. (1988). Agency- and institutional-theory explanations: The case of retail sales compensation. *Academy of Management Journal, 31,* 488–511.

4. Meyer, H. H. (1987). How can we implement a pay for performance policy successfully? In D. Balkin and L. Gomez-Mejia (eds.), *New perspectives in compensation.* Englewood Cliffs, NJ: Prentice-Hall, pp. 179–186. See also: Kanter, R. (1987). From status to contribution: Some organizational implications of the changing basis for pay. *Personnel, 64*(1), 12–37.

5. Rynes, S. L., and Milkovich, G. T. (1986). Wage surveys: Dispelling some myths about the "market wage." *Personnel Psychology, 39,* 71–90. See also: Fay, C. H. (1989). External pay relationships. In L. R. Gomez-Mejia (ed.), *Compensation and benefits.* Washington, D.C.: Bureau of National Affairs. Gerhart, B. (1990). Gender differences in current and starting salaries: The role of performance, college major and job title. *Industrial and Labor Relations Review, 43,* 418–433. Gerhart, B., and El Cheikh, N. (1991). Earnings and percentage female: A longitudinal study. *Industrial Relations, 30,* 62–78. Gerhart, B., and Milkovich, G. T. (1989). Salaries, salary growth, and promotions of men and women in a large, private firm. In R. Michael, H. Hartmann, and B. O'Farrell (eds.), *Pay equity: Empirical Inquiries.* Washington, D.C.: National Academy Press. Rynes, S. L., Weber, C., and Milkovich, G. T. (1989). Effects of market survey rates, job evaluation and job gender on job pay. *Journal of Applied Psychology, 74,* 114–123.

6. Gomez-Mejia, L. R., Page, R. C., and Tornow, W. W. (1982). A comparison of the practical utility of traditional, statistical and hybrid job evaluation approaches. *Academy of Management Journal, 25,* 70–89. See also:

Kane, J. S. (ed.) (1991). Alternative perspectives on job evaluation. *Human Resource Management Review, 1,* 91–162. Davis, K. R., and Sauser, W. I. Jr. (1991). Effects of alternative weighting methods in a policy-capturing approach to job evaluation: A review and empirical investigation. *Personnel Psychology, 44,* 85–127. Doverspike, D., Carlisi, A. M., Barrett, G. V., and Alexander, R. A. (1983). Generalizability analysis of a point-method job evaluation instrument. *Journal of Applied Psychology, 68,* 476–483. Gupta, N., and Jenkins, G. D. (1991). Job evaluation: An overview. *Human Resources Management Review, 1,* 91–96. Barrett, G. (1991). Comparison of skill-based pay with traditional job evaluation techniques. *Human Resources Management Review, 1,* 97–106. Wittig, M. A., and Berman, S. L. (1991). A set of validity criteria for modeling job-based compensation systems. *Human Resources Management Review, 1,* 107–118. Weiner, N. J. (1991). Job evaluation systems: A critique. *Human Resources Management Review, 1,* 119–132. Gupta, N., and Jenkins, G. D. (1991). Practical problems in using job evaluation systems to determine compensation. *Human Resources Management Review, 1,* 133–144.

7. Arvey, R. (1986). Sex bias in the job evaluation process. *Personnel Psychology, 39*(2), 315–336. See also: Madigan, R. M., and Hoover, D. J. (1986). Effects of alternative job evaluation methods on decisions involving pay equity. *Academy of Management Journal, 29,* 84–100. Dufetel, L. (1991). Job evaluation: Still at the frontier. *Compensation and Benefit Review,* July–August, 53–67. Huber, V. L. (1991). Comparison of supervisor-incumbent and female-male multidimensional job evaluation ratings. *Journal of Applied Psychology, 76,* 115–121. Leonard, J. S. (1990). Executive pay and firm performance. *Industrial and Labor Relations Review, 43,* 13S–29S. Mount, M. K., and Ellis, R. A. (1987). Investigation of bias in job evaluation ratings of comparable worth participants. *Personnel Psychology, 40,* 85–96.

8. Barrett, G., and Doverspike, D. (1989). Another defense of point factor job evaluation. *Personnel, 66*(3), 33–37. See also: Lawler, E. E. (1986). What's wrong with point-factor job evaluation? *Compensation and Benefit Review, 18*(2), 20–28. Plachy, R. (1986). The case for effective point-factor job evaluation. *Personnel, 64*(4), 30–32. Lawler, E. E. (1991). Paying the person: A better approach to management. *Human Resources Management Review, 1,* 145–154. Mahoney, T. A. (1991). Job evaluation: Endangered species or anachronism? *Human Resources Management Review, 1,* 155–160.

9. Hahn, D. C., and Diploye, R. L. (1988). Effects of training and information on the accuracy and reliability of job evaluations. *Journal of Applied Psychology, 73*(2), 146–153.

10. See note 8, Lawler, 1986.

11. Ledford, G. (1991). Three cases of skill based pay: An overview. *Compensation and Benefits Review,* March–April, 11–23. Milkovich, G. T., and Broderick, R. F. (1991). Developing a compensation strategy. In M. Rock

and L. Berger (eds.), *Handbook of Compensation*. New York: McGraw-Hill.

12. Pfeffer, J., and Davis-Blake, A. (1987). Understanding organizational wage structures: A resource dependence approach. *Academy of Management Journal, 30,* 437–456. See also: Bielby, W.T., and Baron, J.N. (1984). A woman's place is with other women: Sex segregation and statistical discrimination. *American Journal of Sociology, 91,* 759–799. Smith, R.S. (1988). Comparable worth: Limited coverage and the exacerbation of inequality. *Industrial and Labor Relations Review, 61,* 227–239.

13. Pearce, J.L., Stevenson, W.B., and Perry, J.L. (1985). Managerial compensation based on organizational performance: A time series analysis of the effects of merit pay. *Academy of Management Journal, 28*(2), 261–278.

14. Jordan, P.C. (1986). Effects of extrinsic reward on intrinsic motivation: A field experiment. *Academy of Management Journal, 29*(2), 405–411.

15. Stovich, P. (1984). Performance measurement and reward systems: Critical to strategic management. *Organizational Dynamics, 12,* 45–57. See also: Gerhart, B., and Rynes, S. (1991). Determinants and consequences of salary negotiations by graduating male and female MBAs. *Journal of Applied Psychology, 76,* 256–262.

16. Henderson, R. (1989). *Compensation management.* Englewood Cliffs, NJ: Prentice-Hall, p. 253. See also: Wallace, M.J. Jr., and Fay, C.H. (1988). *Compensation theory and practice.* Boston: PWS-Kent. Wallace, M.J. Jr. (1990). Rewards and renewal: America's search for competitive advantage through alternative pay strategies. American Compensation Association: Scottsdale, AZ. Gomez-Mejia, L.R., Tosi, H., and Hinkin, T. (1987). Managerial control, performance, and executive compensation. *Academy of Management Journal, 30,* 51–70.

17. Marshall, F.R., King, A.G., and Briggs, V.M. (1980). *Labor economics: Wage employment and trade unions.* Homewood, IL: Richard D. Irwin. Weber, C., and Rynes, S. (1991). Effects of compensation strategy on job pay decisions. *Academy of Management Journal, 34,* 86–109.

18. See note 5.

19. Fielder, B.L. (December 1982). Conducting a wage and salary survey. *Personnel Journal,* (1), 879–880.

20. U.S. Chamber of Commerce (1991). *Employee benefits 1990,* Washington: U.S. Chamber of Commerce. See also: Hay Group (1991). *Annual Survey of Employee Benefits.* Philadelphia, PA: Hay Consulting Group.

21. McArdale, F.B. (1989). Personnel update. *Human resources yearbook 1989.* Englewood Cliffs, NJ: Prentice-Hall, p. 2.7.

22. McCafferty, R.M. (1988). Employee benefit programs: A total compensation perspective. Boston, MA: PWS-Kent.

23. Uchitelle, L. (June 4, 1990). Offsetting the price of labor costs. *The New York Times,* p. C2. See also: Holzer, H.J. (1990). Wages, employer costs, and employee performance in the firm. *Industrial and Labor Relations Review, 43,* 147S–164S.

24. See note 22. See also: Dreher, G.F., Ash, R.A., and Bretz, R.D. (1988). Benefit coverage and employee cost: Critical factors in explaining compensation satisfaction.

Personnel Psychology, 41, 237–254. Barber, A.E., Dunham, R.B., and Formisano, R.A. (1992). The impact of flexible benefits on employee satisfaction: A field study. *Personnel Psychology, 45,* 55–76.

25. Bernardin, H.J. (1989). *A survey of state employee attitudes toward benefits.* Unpublished report to the Florida legislature.

26. See note 22.

27. Labor Letter (Jan. 30, 1990). *The Wall Street Journal.*

28. Herzlinger, R.E., and Schwartz, J. (1985). How companies tackle health care costs: Part I. *Harvard Business Review,* p. 69.

29. Cascio, W. (1992). *Managing human resources.* New York: McGraw-Hill.

30. Reisler, M. (November/December 1986). Game plan for business coalitions on health care. *Harvard Business Review,* pp. 56–59.

31. Bureau of National Affairs (Apr. 3, 1986). *Bulletin of Management,* p. 115.

32. Labor Letter (Jan. 30, 1990). *The Wall Street Journal.*

33. Hewitt Associates (1987). Salaried employee benefits provided by major U.S. employers in 1986. Lincolnshire, IL: Hewitt Associates.

34. Solomon, J. (May 17, 1990). Retirees, companies head for showdown over moves to reduce health coverage. *The Wall Street Journal,* pp. B1, B10.

35. U.S. Department of Labor (1986). Employee benefits in medium to large firms. Washington, DC: Department of Labor, p. 3.

36. See note 35.

37. Credit Union National Association (March 1986). *Economic Report,* Madison, WI: Credit Union National Association.

38. Debats, K. (August 1981). Industrial recreation programs: A new look at an old benefit. *Personnel Journal,* pp. 620–627.

39. Wolfe, R.A., Ulrich, D.O., and Parker, D.F. (1987). Employee health maintenance programs: Review, critique and research agenda. *Journal of Management, 13,* 603–616.

40. Fottler, M.D., and Lanning, J.A. (Fall 1986). A comprehensive incentive approach to employee health care cost containment. *California Management Review, 29,* 75–93.

41. Winslow, R. (Dec. 13, 1989). Spending to cut mental health costs. *The Wall Street Journal.* p. B1.

42. Johnson, A.A. (April 1984). Relocation: Getting more for the dollars you spend. *Personnel Administrator,* pp. 29–35.

43. Densford, L.E. (May/June 1987). Make room for baby: The employer's role in solving the day care dilemma. *Employee Benefit News,* pp. 19–37.

44. Labor Letter (Mar. 27, 1990). *The Wall Street Journal,* p. 1.

45. Wilson, M., Northcraft, G.B., and Neale, M.A. (1985). The perceived value of fringe benefits. *Personnel Psychology, 38,* 309–320. See also: Mitchell, O.S. (1988). Worker knowledge of pension provisions. *Journal of Labor Economics, 6,* 21–37.

46. See note 22.

47. O'Reilly, M. (1988). Total remuneration: The international view. *Compensation and Benefits Review,* pp. 46–55. See also: Capdevielle, P. (June 1989). International comparisons of hourly compensation costs. *Monthly Labor Review, 112,* 10–12. Drucker, P. F. (March 16, 1988). Low wages no longer give competitive edge. *Wall Street Journal,* p. 32. Freeman, R. B., and Weitzman, M. L. (1987). Bonuses and employment in Japan. *Journal of the Japanese and International Economies, 1,* 168–194. Hashimoto, M. (1990). Employment and wage systems in Japan and their implications for productivity. In A. S. Blinder (ed.), *Paying for productivity,* pp. 245–294. Washington, D.C.: The Brookings Institution.

48. Shehzad, N. (1984). The American expatriate manager's role and future in today's world, *Human Resource Planning,* pp. 55–61.

49. Raymann, J., and Twinn, B. (1983). *Expatriate compensation and benefits: An employer's handbook,* London, England: Kogan Page. Cited in Dowling, P., and Schuler, R. (1990). *International dimensions of human resource management.* Boston: PWS-Kent, p. 121.

50. Moran, Stahl, and Boyer Inc. (1990). Reported in *The New York Times,* June 17, 1990, sec. 3, p. 1.

51. See note 49, Dowling and Schuler (1990).

52. Lublin, J. (Jan. 26, 1984). More spouses receive help in job searches when executives take positions overseas. *The Wall Street Journal,* p. 35.

53. Schuler, R. S., and Dowling, P. J. (1988). Survey of ASPA/I members. New York: Stern School of Business, New York University. Reported in Dowling and Schuler (1990), p. 120 (see note 49).

EXERCISE 11.1
PROBLEMS IN THE PAY SYSTEM*

OVERVIEW

Chapter 11 discusses the implications of perceptions of internal and external inequity for criteria such as employee performance and turnover. This exercise describes a situation in which an organization has already realized the effects of perceived inequities.

LEARNING OBJECTIVES

After completing this exercise, you should be able to:

1. Determine the critical variables which must be considered in assessing the fairness of a pay system.
2. Assess the weights to be given to data related to internal and external equity.
3. Develop a system which can more closely monitor the effects of pay on critical personnel data.

PROCEDURE

Part A: Individual Analysis

After reading Chapter 11 and prior to class, read the scenario below and Exhibits 11.1.1, 11.1.2, and 11.1.3. Then answer the questions in Form 11.1.1.

Part B: Group Analysis

In groups of about six, students should first review one another's 11.1.1 forms and then attempt to reach consensus on the questions. The group should prepare a concise, written response to each item in Form 11.1.1.

SCENARIO

Denise Nance is the director of the Computer Center/ User Assistance (CCUA) department of a large urban manufacturing company in the Southeast. Recently, a serious problem has developed in her division. A growing percentage of employees have terminated in the past year, with profound effects on unit productivity and costs.

*Contributed by James R. Harris and Lee P. Stepina.

While turnover in her department has always been a problem, it now appears to have gotten out of hand. Until recently, turnover ran about 20 percent per year for lower-division staff personnel and 15 percent per year for middle-division employees. In the last 3 months, however, CCUA has lost five Data Processing II employees (50 percent) and six Computer Analyst I employees (75 percent). Previously, Ms. Nance had no policy regarding exit interviews or turnover control, but informal discussions with the individuals who have left have led to the hypothesis that many employees terminate because they feel underpaid.

What further complicates matters is that Ms. Nance's superior, Julie Linquist, the vice president of technical services, is becoming increasingly concerned about the costs associated with the HR function at CCUA. Exhibit 11.1.1 presents a recent memo from Ms. Linquist to Ms. Nance concerning the problem.

Following the orders given by Ms. Linquist, Ms. Nance conducted phone interviews with 12 former employees (the only ones who were available) and distributed questionnaires to her current workforce.

The survey results indicated a number of interesting findings, which are summarized in Exhibit 11.1.2. The dominant reason for individuals leaving CCUA was pay. The current workforce also indicated strong dissatisfaction with current pay levels. Although the survey was not limited to Data Processing II and Computer Analyst I positions, both Ms. Nance and Ms. Linquist feel that these two positions are of particular concern. Responses from both current and past employees in these two job classifications were similar to those of the entire sample.

Data Processing IIs currently earn $8.10 to $8.68 per hour, or approximately $16,500 per year. The only financial benefit for these employees is 40 hours of paid leave for the first year, with an increase of 5 hours for every 1000 hours of service. Limited health insurance is provided by the company at a cost of $300 per year per employee. CCUA usually employs 10 Data Processing IIs, but the current level is only 7.

Computer Analyst Is are salaried employees who earn between $18,512 and $23,500. Their paid leave is 9 days for the first year of service, which increases by 2 days for every following year, with a limit of 21 days of paid leave. Full health insurance and other benefits currently cost the company $900 per year for each Computer Analyst I. There are usually 8 Computer Analyst Is on staff. Recruitment costs for each Data Processing II is $250; for each Computer Analyst II, it is $750.

Ms. Nance budgets $215,490 annually for Data Processing IIs and $243,984 for Computer Analyst Is. The company is in the sixth month of its fiscal year.

EXHIBIT 11.1.1

```
To:    Denise Nance, Director of CCUA
From:  Julie Linquist, Vice President of Technical Services
Re:    Personnel Problems
```

I don't know what's going on down there, but Jon Anderson of placement services just informed me that you requested another listing for a data processing person and another computer analyst. According to my records, that's the fifth data processing person and the sixth computer analyst you have lost this year! It costs a lot of money to hire new people. This is obviously not the pattern that I want to see from your department. I want you to investigate this immediately.

I want you to contact the individuals whom you lost and find out why they left. I also want you to talk to the employees who are still there and find out what, if anything, could potentially be causing the high turnover. Let's get this problem cleared up now.

EXHIBIT 11.1.2
SURVEY RESULTS

CURRENT EMPLOYEES	MEAN	SD
Supervision	2.1	.0
Working conditions	1.9	1.8
Task characteristics	3.0	2.1
Pay	4.2	0.5
Benefits	4.3	1.1
Work hours	3.1	.9
Physical conditions	1.4	1.5
General satisfaction	3.9	0.7

EMPLOYEE WHO LEFT		
Supervision	1.9	1.5
Working conditions	2.4	1.7
Task characteristics	3.7	2.0
Pay	4.8	1.1
Benefits	4.5	0.6
Work hours	3.0	2.0
Physical conditions	1.7	0.5
General satisfaction	4.2	1.2

REASONS FOR LEAVING	
Not enough money	83.3%
Spouse left area	8.3%
Child-care problems	8.3%

EXHIBIT 11.1.3
EXCERPT FROM DATAMATION

TITLE	AVERAGE WEIGHTED SALARY	MFG./ CONSUMER	MFG./ INDUSTRIAL	BANKING	OTHER FINANCIAL SERVICES	DP SERVICES	WHOLESALE DISTRIBUTION
IS MANAGEMENT							
CIO/VP	106,864	128,611	100,741	124,318	109,130	157,500	130,000
Manager/Supervisor	65,811	83,333	74,821	76,500	67,143	60,000	57,143
END-USER SUPPORT							
Manager End-User Computing	56,808	74,167	62,667	57,500	58,500	55,000	48,750
Information Center Manager	54,346	56,667	60,833	56,818	53,500	63,333	49,000
PC Specialist Support	38,058	40,000	48,077	39,211	36,250	37,000	38,636
LAN Manager	45,880	55,000	52,857	46,000	46,000	52,000	52,000
WP Supervisor	36,538	55,000	42,500	32,600	34,000	40,000	34,000
SYSTEMS ANALYSIS/PROGRAMMING							
Manager	65,357	83,182	63,913	68,611	64,286	66,364	72,000
Senior Systems Analyst and Programmer	50,345	50,714	53,333	52,143	51,471	56,250	52,000
Systems Analyst and Programmer	43,220	44,000	43,462	45,250	42,647	48,750	60,455
Intermediate Analyst and Programmer	37,517	40,000	38,571	37,750	38,000	38,125	40,000
Junior Analyst and Programmer	30,156	28,750	35,714	30,000	27,143	32,500	26,875
APPLICATION/OPERATING SYSTEMS PROGRAMMING							
Manager	64,481	79,000	67,667	68,529	71,765	68,750	66,667
Senior Applications/Operating Sys. Prog.	52,434	55,000	55,938	52,353	56,000	55,000	53,125
Applications/Operating Sys. Prog.	44,419	48,571	46,250	46,176	46,563	46,429	40,000
Intermediate Applications/Operating Sys. Prog.	37,150	42,500	40,000	35,000	38,636	35,000	37,500
Junior Applications/Operating Sys. Prog.	29,709	30,000	32,500	29,615	30,455	30,000	28,750
DATA COM/TELECOM/CONNECTIVITY							
Network Manager (LAN-WAN)	57,546	63,750	59,643	59,643	72,500	57,222	58,333
Telecommunications Manager	57,136	58,750	66,111	59,231	67,500	63,125	60,000
Communications Specialist	42,276	37,000	43,000	41,667	46,818	40,000	43,750
DATABASE							
Database Manager/Administrator	61,077	71,000	60,500	64,643	70,385	52,500	62,000
Database Analyst	48,194	52,000	55,000	46,000	51,250	42,500	47,500
Microcomputer/Workstation Manager	44,500	35,000	55,000	46,818	43,750	47,500	43,750
Data Processor	22,500	21,000	24,000	23,000	21,500	21,000	22,000

| | | | | | | AVERAGE SALARY BY COMPANY REVENUE ($ MILLION) | | | | |
GOVERNMENT	MEDICAL/ LEGAL	TRANS./ UTILITIES	EDUCATION	CONSTRUCTION/ MINING	OTHER	>$250	$250– $500	$500– $5,000	$5,000– $20,000	$20,000+
71,731	64,500	114,167	103,571	76,667	101,600	82,292	84,697	104,844	128,780	129,700
51,739	42,500	66,667	51,250	52,000	65,104	50,204	61,094	68,534	75,811	73,269
53,750	–	63,462	49,000	43,750	54,310	47,200	46,667	58,871	62,593	60,857
47,500	40,000	61,364	46,000	–	51,500	43,529	46,250	56,957	60,741	56,071
30,455	27,143	41,071	31,429	30,000	38,250	36,053	31,600	39,405	40,429	40,833
42,500	40,000	44,500	34,000	40,000	45,833	42,368	46,667	48,519	46,250	46,172
36,667	40,000	40,000	25,000	25,000	38,846	32,500	40,000	36,667	38,235	37,000
55,294	40,000	67,105	50,000	62,500	65,814	58,958	53,421	65,288	71,216	68,261
45,926	40,000	52,750	40,000	46,000	49,375	46,935	46,250	49,500	53,784	52,843
38,571	35,000	42,727	32,500	40,000	41,667	45,000	39,464	42,750	43,663	44,692
31,316	25,000	39,000	32,500	40,000	38,448	35,000	38,333	38,256	36,250	38,500
27,500	25,000	35,313	25,000	25,000	28,913	32,500	31,000	28,529	28,750	31,667
53,333	47,500	66,875	47,500	62,500	62,027	51,667	51,250	66,395	70,789	68,889
47,105	–	56,875	45,000	47,500	50,286	43,947	46,667	52,391	55,429	57,206
37,500	40,000	47,000	36,000	55,000	43,500	41,500	37,273	44,390	45,571	46,562
33,571	–	38,846	32,500	–	36,250	40,000	30,455	38,448	35,556	39,444
23,125	–	37,273	25,000	26,000	26,875	30,000	26,875	30,192	29,038	31,176
49,231	47,500	68,750	40,000	55,000	60,000	46,154	61,667	54,630	80,000	64,500
46,429	–	54,231	43,750	55,000	55,556	41,538	48,333	57,000	82,258	61,852
36,786	–	49,000	36,250	55,000	41,071	39,000	33,182	39,189	45,825	47,857
51,786	–	69,000	55,033	70,000	55,962	47,778	51,364	60,000	66,818	66,765
42,143	–	50,000	40,000	55,000	46,136	46,000	46,429	46,207	48,500	50,781
43,000	40,000	47,600	40,000	–	38,848	35,714	43,750	45,000	44,412	47,941
20,000	23,000	20,500	20,000	–	23,000	20,000	22,000	23,000	23,500	24,000

FORM 11.1.1

Name _____   Group _____

You have been retained as a consultant to evaluate the situation in the CCUA department and make recommendations for action. Ms. Nance wants your views on the following:

1. Are industry-type, geographical, or job-type adjustments in current salary levels required? Explain your answer.

2. If so, what adjustments are necessary? What adjustments are needed in Ms. Nance's current and future HR budgets?

3. What specific strategy should be used in the future so that turnover problems can be anticipated and (preferably) avoided.

EXERCISE 11.2
*SHOULD THE STATE ADOPT A PAY EQUITY POLICY?**

OVERVIEW

Chapter 11 discusses the controversial issue of pay equity, or comparable worth. Many U.S. state and municipal governments and more than 100 county governments have adopted some form of pay equity policy for government workers. Ontario, Canada, has mandated pay equity for all public and private employers. Many collective bargaining contracts now place great emphasis on pay equity adjustments, based on studies which find evidence of gender- or race-based inequities in pay systems. The purpose of this exercise is to examine the issues and implications of pay equity for public and private employers. Students will review a summary of a pay equity study.

LEARNING OBJECTIVES

After completing this exercise, you should be able to:

1. Understand the major components of a pay equity study.

---

*Contributed by Sue Dahmus.

2. Anticipate some of the advantages and disadvantages of a pay equity policy.
3. Discuss the implications of pay equity adjustments for market rates and private-sector employment.

PROCEDURE

Part A: Individual Analysis

Congratulations! You have been appointed to the State University Task Force on Compensation. Prior to class your assignment is to review the report (Exhibit 11.2.1) submitted by a consulting firm under contract to an ad hoc committee of the state legislature. After reviewing state compensation information and conducting a pay equity study, this highly credible consulting firm has made specific recommendations to the legislature. As a member of the Task Force, your job is to take a position on each recommendation. On Form 11.2.1, state your position and provide a justification in the space provided. Also, prior to class, complete the assessment questions for the exercise.

Part B: Group Analysis

In groups of about six, students should review one another's Form 11.2.1 and then attempt to reach consensus on the three recommendations. Each group should prepare concise justifications for its recommendations. Students should also review responses to the assessment questions.

EXHIBIT 11.2.1
EXECUTIVE SUMMARY OF PAY EQUITY STUDY

The underlying theory of pay equity is that the wages for female- and minority-dominated occupations are artificially depressed because of historical bias against the value of "women's work." The goal of pay equity studies is to use objectively measured criteria to examine the relative values of all jobs to an employer in an effort to correct for any gender- and race-based undervaluation.

Crucial to pay equity policy is the recognition that jobs that require equivalent or *comparable* skill, effort, responsibility, and working conditions should be compensated equally. Once implemented, pay equity policy assures that an employer's classification and compensation systems are administered and maintained objectively and fairly.

To accomplish the above objective, we examined a representative sample of 300 classes in the career service system. This served as the basis for our analysis in determining objectively what job content characteristics the state values when setting pay. The question which guided this study is as follows: In setting pay rates, does the state value work differently (and perhaps in a biased manner) in male-dominated jobs as compared to female- and minority-dominated jobs? In other words, is there a difference in monetary return for jobs with similar characteristics and requirements?

The state utilizes a position classification system whereby positions are consolidated into job families and these families are assigned to pay grades. This study was designed to provide a model of "equitable compensation" for the state that is largely based upon its current pay policy. Using this model, the analysis shows which position classes are underpaid because of the influence of female or minority dominance of the job. The recommendations, if adopted, will bring female- and minority-dominated position classes in line with equitable compensation.

The approach utilized for this study is called *policy capturing*. Through policy capturing, the relative worth to the state of all jobs in a system is evaluated. As a first step, a compensation model is developed in which specific job content features—such as the number of persons supervised, the level of education, the level of analytic reasoning, and the years of prerequisite experience—

are grouped into compensable factors. These factors are then weighted in such a way that they statistically "predict" the current wage structure. In other words, the weights for each compensable job content characteristic are derived from a statistical model that makes explicit what is currently valued on an implicit basis within an organization. The relationship between what people do and what they are paid thus becomes clear. Pay equity adjustments are indicated when this relationship is violated simply because the jobs are performed by females and minorities. This methodology was selected because it does not impose outside standards for fair compensation on the state. Rather, it looks at the current compensation policy and simply adjusts the existing system in instances in which its own standards are not met. Policy-capturing techniques thus allow the state to adjust its salary grades to eliminate any influence of gender or race bias without radically altering its basic philosophy of compensation.

FINDINGS

As a result of the above analyses, it was determined that there is substantial undervaluation of female- and minority-dominated position classes in the career service system. A model of equitable compensation has been developed to adjust for the resulting pay inequities.

Another objective of this study was to assess the cost of correcting gender- or race-based pay inequities for the purpose of budget planning by the legislature. The total cost to the state of making pay equity adjustments in the female- and minority-dominated position classes is estimated to be $75,552,000. An implementation model is recommended that suggests an appropriations schedule of $9,552,000 in the first year and $16,500,000 per year in the next 4 years.

The wage-setting process in the state is not structured in a way that facilitates the maintenance of internal equity. This is primarily because there is no quantitative job evaluation system tied to a unified wage structure that would keep future inequities from occurring. Women and minorities are also underrepresented in job classes at the upper end of the wage structure.

FORM 11.2.1

Name _____   Group _____

1. The state legislature should appropriate $75,552,000 to cover the costs of the pay equity adjustments indicated by this study.

Agree _____   Disagree _____

JUSTIFICATION:

2. To ensure a systematic and uniform job evaluation and wage setting system, the state should adopt a point-factor job evaluation system that is anchored to a uniform salary structure. The outside figure for full implementation of an equitable system is $140,000.

Agree _____   Disagree _____

JUSTIFICATION:

3. The state should establish an affirmative action policy with respect to practices for women and minorities because such groups are underrepresented in job classes at the upper end of the wage structure.

Agree _____   Disagree _____

JUSTIFICATION:

Name _____ Group _____

1. If the state follows the recommendations, what impact will the policy have upon private-sector compensation?

2. To create internal equity faster and more cheaply, the consultants could have recommended reducing the pay of "overvalued" jobs (all male-dominated). Please comment.

3. Some experts maintain that the imposition of the point-factor evaluation system emphasizes bureaucratic control, encourages workers to do only what the organization dictates in the job description, and makes the organization too internally focused. Please comment.

EXERCISE 11.3
EWING OIL SUPPLY COMPANY*

OVERVIEW

Chapter 11 discusses the various factors which figure into pay determination. While some companies have very strict guidelines on maintaining internal or external equity, other companies maintain flexibility to allow managers greater latitude in decision making. The purpose of this exercise is to have students consider factors related to pay determination and adopt a policy for a typical compensation situation.

LEARNING OBJECTIVES

After completing this exercise, you should be able to:

1. Understand the trade-offs involved in considerations of internal and external equity.
2. Know the advantages and disadvantages of fixed versus firm pay policies.

PROCEDURE

Part A: Individual Analysis

Prior to class, read the scenario below for Ewing Oil Supply Company and take a position on each issue presented in Form 11.3.1. Bring your completed Form 11.3.1 to class for discussion.

---

*Contributed by James A. Breaugh.

Part B: Group Analysis

In groups of about six, students should review all members' completed forms and then attempt to reach consensus on each question. Each student should be prepared to present a 3-minute rationale for the group's position. Class discussion will focus on the consistency of recommendations across groups and on the weights given the various factors.

SCENARIO

You are the Texas district manager of Ewing Oil, an oil equipment company. You have been in this job for the last 4 years. Five branch managers report directly to you. As part of your managerial duties, you annually evaluate the performance of these five individuals. You recently have done the evaluations but have not yet shared them with the respective individuals. First, you must decide upon salary increases for the next year. Your company gives you tremendous salary discretion in making decisions regarding raises. The salary range for branch managers is from $28,000 to $39,750. For next year, you have a salary increase "pool" of $10,000. To help you make sound salary increase decisions, you have compiled the information reported below. For company records, you must document both the factors that influenced your decisions and the information you plan on sharing with each of the employees. Thus, your task is to:

1. Determine the size of the raise you will give each branch manager.
2. Discuss the factors which influenced your decisions.
3. Outline the points you would raise in discussing his or her salary increase with each of the five branch managers.

**EXHIBIT 11.3.1
INFORMATION ON THE BRANCH MANAGERS**

1. **Ellen Panza—branch manager, Houston.** Fifteen months ago, Ellen completed her M.B.A. degree under somewhat unusual circumstances. She received a Ford Foundation fellowship which paid her tuition to Rice University as well as 50 percent of her salary. Under the Smith Foundation program, which grants fellowships to young minorities and women, a company is required to pay the fellowship recipient 50 percent of his or her current salary during the period of academic work. Thus, Ellen's second most recent performance review reflects only 3 months on the job. You believe that several companies (including one of your competitors) are interested in Ellen. You know she has gone on at least one job interview.
2. **David Green—branch manager, Dallas.** Of the five branch managers, you believe that David is the most dedicated to Ewing Oil. His father was a career Ewing employee and you believe that David may be also. He completed an M.B.A. from Southern Methodist University before he started to work for Ewing Oil. Money seems extremely important to David. He sees the size of his salary increase as an index of his competence. David is somewhat tied to Dallas because his wife works as an attorney for a local law firm.
3. **Larry Foster—branch manager, Lubbock.** Larry has complained to you about being taken for granted. He does not believe that he is being paid fairly, given his experience and past performance. He believes that the company is more concerned about fancy M.B.A.s who "job-hop" than about loyal, long-term employees. In addition, Larry feels that he should be given extra compensation for living in Lubbock rather than a more desirable location. Your perception is that, of the five branch managers, Larry works the fewest hours per week.
4. **Julio Perez—branch manager, San Antonio.** Julio is the first Hispanic branch manager Ewing has ever employed. He has shown remarkable improvement over the last 12 months. Given his background, you believe he could easily find an equivalent or better job if he chose to leave Ewing Oil. He has also asked about being nominated by Ewing as a candidate for a Smith Foundation fellowship. You believe that if Julio got an M.B.A., he would receive numerous offers from other companies at a considerably higher salary level.
5. **Frank Kemp—branch manager, Austin.** Prior to joining Ewing Oil, Frank was a quarterback in the National Football League for 16 years. Overall, you have been satisfied with his performance. However, you believe he could be an outstanding branch manager if he didn't spend so much time on outside speaking engagements. Frank has complained to you that he believes he is underpaid compared to newer employees. He has said that he would fully commit himself to his job if you'd increase his salary to a level commensurate with his age and experience.

	ELLEN PANZA	DAVID GREEN	LARRY FOSTER	JULIO PEREZ	FRANK KEMP
Age	28	34	51	31	48
Sex	female	male	male	male	male
Race	C	C	C	H	C
Years with Ewing	5	10	22	3	11
Years as branch manager	3	5	15	2	6
Education	MBA	MBA	BS-chem.	BE-ed.	BA-bus.
Married	no	no	yes	yes	yes
Children at home	no	no	1 (age 10, mentally disabled)	no	2 (ages 13, 16)
Current salary	$29,500	$33,500	$36,800	$31,200	$32,100
Salary prior to current one	$28,550	$32,250	$35,750	$30,200	$30,850
Most recent appraisal					
Past performance	6	7	6	5	5
Promotion potential	6	7	3	5	5
Second most recent appraisal					
Past performance	6	6	5	3	6
Promotion potential	5	6	4	4	5
Salary compared to market	30%	50%	65%	40%	45%

Note: "Past performance" is a summary rating which is made on a 7-point scale (1 = unsatisfactory standing, 7 = outstanding). "Promotion potential" is a summary rating which reflects a supervisor's judgment of potential (1 = little potential, 7 = outstanding potential). "Salary compared to market" is a figure that compares the current salary of a branch manager to those holding comparable jobs in Texas. 50% = the average salary for comparable jobs.

FORM 11.3.1

Name _____   Group _____

RECOMMENDATIONS	RAISE	JUSTIFICATION	ISSUES TO RAISE
1. Ellen Panza			
2. David Green			
3. Larry Foster			
4. Julio Perez			
5. Frank Kemp			

12

C H A P T E R

PAY FOR PERFORMANCE*

---

*Contributed by E. Brian Peach and M. Ronald Buckley.

OVERVIEW

As we discussed in Chapters 10 and 11, one of the strongest trends in compensation administration today is the installation of some form of incentive or pay-for-performance (PFP) system.[1] Controlling labor costs through the establishment of a clear linkage between pay and performance is considered to be a key human resource management (HRM) component for competitive advantage. In addition, increased concerns over productivity and meeting customer requirements have prompted renewed interest in methods designed to motivate employees. You may recall from our discussion of the Baldrige Award in Chapter 1 that Federal Express, a 1990 winner in service, was cited for the clear linkage it established between worker pay and customer satisfaction data.

Many other companies have also endeavored to establish a stronger connection between employee pay and critical criteria. Recent survey data indicates that between 50 and 96 percent of U.S. companies are now using some form of PFP system,[2] up from less than 10 percent in 1980. A recent survey of Fortune 1000 companies found that 31 percent of companies have PFP systems which cover all employees in the organization.[3] Even the federal government operates on a form of PFP compensation system. Among organizations which have recently implemented some form of PFP system for nonmanagerial employees are General Motors (GM), Continental Bank, Blockbuster Video, Burger King, United Parcel Service (UPS), Federal Express, Merrill Lynch, Grumman, and Reebok. GM put more than 26,000 workers on a merit pay system after abandoning across-the-board increases. PFP systems may be more common for executives. A 1990 survey found performance incentives add 29 percent to the pay of executives earning $100,000 or more, and a 1991 survey by Peat Marwick found that chief executive officers' (CEOs') pay is generally tracking corporate performance.[4] For example, pay for CEOs rose over 20 percent when their companies had more than a 20 percent increase in return on equity but fell 14 percent when return on equity declined.

PFP systems come in all shapes and sizes. One of the most important distinctions is the level-of-performance measurement. The most common approach is to tie pay to individual performance in a merit pay system, but a growing number of companies now tie pay to unit or group performance, and others tie pay to organizational or company performance. Within each of these three general categories, however, there are numerous approaches. As we discussed in Chapter 10, the accurate measurement of performance, at whatever level of aggregation, is perhaps the major stumbling block in PFP efforts.

Does PFP work? *The Wall Street Journal* described the research evidence as "skimpy,"[5] and a 1991 review

of the literature concluded that "the evidence is insufficient to determine conclusively whether merit pay can enhance individual performance."[6] Nonetheless, many firms are convinced that the approach works. Domino's Pizza claims an increase in sales in excess of 20 percent after implementing a complicated PFP system. International Business Machines (IBM) reported a 200 percent increase over 10 years in productivity in the manufacturing of typewriters—an increase that IBM attributes to its PFP system. Ford Motor Company credits its PFP system with "improved worker morale and quality of work."[7] One survey of companies using some form of PFP reported improved output from two out of three companies when incentives are provided for meeting specific performance targets.[8]

The purpose of this chapter is to review the major types of PFP systems and to discuss their relative advantages and disadvantages. The determinants of performance will be described first, followed by an exploration of questions of fairness and practicality regarding PFP. Next, the major problems associated with PFP will be reviewed. The second part of the chapter reviews the major types of PFP and the problems with measuring performance.

OBJECTIVES

After studying this chapter, you should be able to:

1. Understand the alternatives to PFP systems.
2. Identify the critical variables related to the selection of the most appropriate PFP system.
3. Review the evidence on the effectiveness of different PFP systems.
4. Determine the relative advantages and disadvantages of the various PFP systems.

As discussed in Chapter 11, although pay is regarded as a motivator, each organization is confronted with a unique set of issues and problems related to PFP and must develop a strategy to deal with them. The consideration of a PFP system should be made in the context of this strategy. The most important considerations are the measurement and determinants of performance. Figure 12.1 presents a summary of the possible determinants of performance.

Increases in pay for increases in performance must be valued by the specific employee or work unit for which the PFP plan is intended—and must be valued highly relative to other rewards. Occasionally group norms or cultural values deemphasize money or at least differential rewards for differential outputs. Unions, for example, have traditionally opposed pay systems based

FIGURE 12.1
DETERMINANTS OF PERFORMANCE

1. Worker values money.
2. Money is valued relative to other rewards.
3. Desired performance must be measurable.
4. Worker must be able to control rate of output.
5. Worker must be capable of increasing output.
6. Worker must believe that capability to increase exists.
7. Worker must believe that increased output will result in receiving a reward.
8. Size of reward must be sufficient to stimulate increased effort.

on individual or unit-level output, such as piece-rate incentive systems. Some unions [e.g., the United Auto Workers (UAW), the Communication Workers of America] have become more receptive to PFP systems in recent years. Ford's profit sharing plan resulted in each of the over 150,000 eligible Ford employees receiving an average of $3700 in 1988 alone. At GM's new Saturn plant, UAW members work for a salary (about $35,000 per year), with 20 percent of the amount fluctuating up or down since it is tied to assessments of car quality, productivity, and profits. These examples are certainly exceptions rather than the rule. In general, unions favor only organizationwide PFP systems and not individual PFP systems, which the unions maintain will inevitably pit worker against worker. When the state of Florida mandated an individual merit pay system for teachers, the American Federation of Teachers (AFT) worked diligently to promote regulations regarding the merit pay, which ultimately led to the demise of the system. Within 2 years, the state had rescinded the individual PFP program.

Some companies regard individual PFP systems as contrary to their team-oriented philosophy of management and organizational culture. United Technologies is an example of one company which espouses this view. Its PFP reward system uses only aggregated methods of rewards in which unit and companywide performance measures are the basis. Money also fails to motivate if the required level of extra effort results in unacceptable fatigue to the worker or prevents the worker from enjoying a valued social life.

The organization must also identify the measures of performance (e.g., outputs, products, services, behaviors, cost reductions) in which increases are desirable. For example, increased output may be desirable only in situations in which there is customer demand for more of the product. Needless to say, the organization should tie pay only to aspects of performance which are of value. Continental Bank, for example, sought a competitive advantage through improvements in its customer service. Its PFP system placed significant weight on the measure-

ment and rewarding of performance in this area. Perhaps encouraged by the Valdez oil spill in Alaska and Exxon's woeful response, Conoco made environmental issues a major strategic priority. Environmental criteria became a component of its incentive system for top managers. Xerox Corporation places great emphasis on customer service and now uses customer survey data as a criterion in its bonus system. According to Xerox's president, it is possible that an executive of a profitable unit would not get a bonus at all if the customer survey data indicated poor performance. The Aluminum Company of America now emphasizes improvements in safety records as a part of its managerial bonus system. Merrill Lynch was concerned about the loss of new brokers who had recently completed their expensive 17-week training program. The company installed a straight salary system with deferred commission contingent on 2 years of service. All commission was lost if the executives quit prior to 2 years. The new incentive system also included a $100,000 bonus for brokers who stayed with the company for 10 years. Workers at a Monsanto Corporation chemical plant in Louisiana can earn bonuses for meeting goals that include reducing injuries and preventing emissions from escaping into the environment.

All the determinants presented in Figure 12.1 are intimately related. For example, to determine the nature of a reward which should be offered for an increased level of effort, a firm must know the relative importance of money to the average worker, the increased value to the firm of any given performance increase, and the worker's perception of the increased effort required.

PROBLEMS WITH PAY FOR PERFORMANCE

There are many potential problems with PFP systems.[9] Figure 12.2 presents a summary of the problems judged by experts to be most responsible for the failure of such systems. First of all, PFP systems can be expensive to develop and maintain. In addition to the initial cost of establishing standards and rates, changes in procedures, equipment, and product may require revision of any existing standards and reward structures. In many cases a revision of the compensation system will be viewed with suspicion. Historically, some short-sighted firms have taken advantage of changes in the production process to reduce the amount of reward for any given level of effort. Such actions can have a long-term negative effect on worker responses to PFP systems.

One frequent problem is that workers do not feel that rewards are closely linked to performance. Employees may believe that the performance measure does not accurately assess performance. This is a common problem when performance is measured by ratings. Employees

FIGURE 12.2
REASONS FOR THE FAILURES OF PFP SYSTEMS

1. Poor perceived connection between performance and pay.
2. The level of performance-based pay is too low relative to base pay. The cost of more highly motivating programs may be prohibitive.
3. Lack of objective, countable results for most jobs, requiring the use of performance ratings.
4. Faulty performance appraisal systems, with poor cooperation from managers, leniency bias in the appraisals, and resistance to change.
5. Union resistance to such systems and to change in general.

often have inflated ideas about their performance levels, which translate into unrealistic expectations about rewards as well. One study found that the majority of workers rated slightly less than perfect (e.g., 8 on a 9-point scale) were more dissatisfied than satisfied with the rating.[10] Given these beliefs, a large portion of the workforce may receive performance ratings below their expectations, and rewards will likely fall short of expectations. As discussed in Chapter 10, there can be a perception of bias in the process even if such bias does not exist. Many problems can arise in a PFP system which relies on performance appraisals. To the extent that workers perceive that the performance measurement component of the PFP system is biased or invalid, the perceived connection between pay and performance will be undermined and the PFP system will be less effective. Some experts on PFP go so far as to say that if performance must be measured by ratings, PFP is not worth the trouble. One such expert concluded that when ratings must be used, "the approach is so flawed that it is hard to imagine a set of conditions which would make it effective."[11] While this conclusion may be overly pessimistic, there is no denying that PFP systems based on ratings of performance can be problematic.

Many PFP plans have failed because the performance measure which was rewarded was not related to the aggregated performance objectives of the organization as a whole and to those aspects of performance which were most important to the organization. For example, a PFP system may put inordinate emphasis on the quantity of output when the organizational emphasis is on quality improvement or cost effectiveness. As one expert in compensation put it, "Companies are terrified they will put the wrong weightings on things and encourage the wrong kind of behavior."[12] The organization must constantly ensure that the aspects of performance which are emphasized in the PFP system are the same ones which are the priority of the organization. Recall from our discussion of performance appraisal in Chapter 10 that it is possible to weight performance dimensions

(which are combinations of job functions with criteria: quantity, quality, timeliness, need for supervision, effects on constituents, and cost). This weighting process should reflect the strategic plan of the unit and the organization. Unfortunately, the measurement process for PFP systems is far more haphazard than this. In fact, one survey found that the majority of workers who were paid on a PFP system had little understanding of the criteria for performance measurement.[13]

The organization should also ensure that workers are capable of increasing their performance. You may recall the discussion in Chapter 10 regarding constraints on performance. An employee working on an assembly line or operating a machine with a preset speed may not have opportunity to increase the quantity of performance. For higher pay to result in higher performance, workers must believe in (and be capable of) higher levels of performance. When workers believe that performance standards exceed their capabilities, they will not expend extra effort.

One of the most common problems with PFP systems is that an insufficient amount of money is available for meritorious performance. For example, a 1990 survey of 459 firms found that the most effective workers received 8 percent increases, while lower-rated workers received around 5 percent. The most effective computer programmers received an additional $17 per month more than satisfactory workers on annual salaries of about $40,000. Says one expert on the subject, this difference is "hardly enough to push someone to excel."[14] While experts differ on the subject, the lowest level recommended is between 10 and 15 percent of base salary for the money to be considered significant and for the PFP system to be effective.[15] Digital Equipment Corporation has a range of 0 to 30 percent, and Westinghouse has a range of 0 to 19 percent, but most companies are at lower levels. At Continental Bank, for example, an employee earning $3000 per month received the very highest performance appraisal and was thus eligible for the highest PFP award—5 percent. The next year that individual was earning $3150 per month (before taxes). Most employees who were surveyed on the PFP system didn't think the amount of money involved in the PFP system was worth the extra effort.

TYPES OF PAY FOR PERFORMANCE

Selecting a PFP System

In designing a PFP system, four major questions should be asked: (1) Who should be included? (2) Whose performance will be measured? (3) How will performance be measured? (4) Which incentives will be used? The process for developing the characteristics of a performance appraisal system apply to the first three questions, all of which were discussed in Chapter 10.

A PFP system should be developed with a specific group in mind, such as production workers, middle management, salespeople, engineers, professionals, or senior executives and top management. Many companies use different PFP systems for different jobs. For example, McDonald's has eight different PFP systems for various classes of employees. IBM has six different systems. Many companies have different PFP systems as a function of the organizational and unit-level strategies, with some form of market share measurement for a start-up product or service and stock, or cost cutting for a more established product or service line. Some companies use a variety of different PFP systems for the same job families. For example, AMOCO has an individual merit pay system, a unit-level PFP measurement, and an employee stock ownership program (ESOP) for the same employees. Other companies have reward systems which are compatible with an egalitarian culture that attempts to minimize the distance between people at different levels in the organizational hierarchy. Digital, for example, has only one reward system for all employees.

While cash payments and other rewards such as vacations and prizes are more flexible and suited to short-run objectives, stock options are appropriate for long-run objectives. In general, stock options replace all or part of a raise for lower-level managers, while they are typically additions to upper-management pay. Over 90 percent of U.S. Fortune 500 companies offer some form of stock option for executives. Although there are several types of stock options, the most popular today are incentive options which give an executive the right to purchase stock at a specified price within a designated time period. This approach is especially appealing to executives and corporations because of its tax benefits relative to other stock options.

Another strong trend is a PFP system in which the performance-based pay is not permanently tied to an employee's base pay.[16] GM, for example, pays a lump sum based on corporate profits, and the lump sum does not increase an employee's base salary. As we mentioned above, the Saturn plant operates on a 20 percent rate of "risk" for all salaried workers, with no tie-in to the base salary. Champion International pays managers based on growth in earnings per share of stock relative to the stock of the 15 major competitors. The bonus awarded to the 12 senior managers is not tied to the managers' base pay. Federal Express managers have "small spot" awards of $100 which are available for unusual achievement.

The decision to use a group, unit, or individual PFP plan is obviously critical. As we discussed in Chapter 10, the major issues are the extent to which output is controlled at the group or individual level, whether the individual contribution can be measured, and the extent to which teamwork among unit members would be affected by the PFP system.

At Champion, for example, earnings are compared only to the company's major competitors so as to control for factors beyond the influence of the managers, such as inflation, interest rates, and general state of the economy. Managers perceive this relative comparison to be fairer than comparisons to absolute earnings, which are more susceptible to changes in the general state of the economy. Individual PFP systems are more effective when specific worker contributions can be clearly measured. If individual contributions cannot be measured reliably, then the smallest number of workers whose performance is determined to be important (e.g., related to strategic objectives) and of course measurable would constitute the incentive group.

An organization may choose to use a group plan even when it is possible to measure output on an individual basis. Individual PFP plans can increase competition between workers and may reduce cooperation and teamwork. Workers will be less likely to assist their coworkers if such an effort will adversely affect their own production rate or potential rewards. Where cooperation is considered essential, a group incentive program is preferred. For example, at the GM Saturn plant in Tennessee, while individual measurement was possible on a number of important outcome measures, an individual PFP system was thought to be contrary to the company's team-oriented approach to production. Thus, Saturn's UAW-endorsed PFP system is based strictly on unit-level and company-wide measures of performance. Of course, there are many examples of individually based PFP systems even where teamwork is critical. Michael Jordan would probably go elsewhere if the Chicago Bulls paid him the same as the other starters and paid everyone based on team performance. The critical issues regarding the level of aggregation of the performance measures (individual, group, organization) are identifying and measuring performance criteria which the organization seeks to increase or improve in its strategic plan and then linking pay to those measurements.

Individual PFP Plans

Individual PFP systems can be divided into merit pay systems and incentive systems tied to production rates. The most common and perhaps the most troublesome PFP system is an individual system, known most often as a *merit pay plan*, in which performance is measured through performance appraisal. *Incentive plans* rely on some countable result or results to be used as a basis for setting the PFP rate, and *sales incentive plans* have their own unique characteristics. Let us examine each of these methods next.

MERIT PAY. As you review the reasons for the failure in PFP systems in Figure 12.2, you will see that many of these reasons are unfortunately characteristic of merit pay systems. The most serious problem is the failure to create a clear linkage between employee performance and pay. The performance appraisal system and the evaluators of performance are mainly responsible for this problem. There are several factors related to the appraisal system which contribute to this breakdown in the linkage between pay and performance. The fundamental problem is with measuring performance, a problem compounded in service industries in which individual performance is more difficult to measure. Another cause of the measurement problem is the lack of skill of those who do the appraisals. As we discussed in Chapter 10, this lack of skill is often manifested in leniency bias in the ratings. Leniency causes ratings to be so bunched at the high end of the rating scale that very little distinction can be made between superior and other performances. The result is twofold: (1) a merit pay system in which the amount of the merit pay is relatively trivial because so many individuals are judged to be eligible and (2) a system in which the best performers perceive gross inequities in a system that is supposed to be based on merit.

Though we discussed leniency in Chapter 10, the discussion of methods designed to reduce leniency bias bears repeating, since leniency is so critical to the effectiveness of any merit pay system based on performance appraisal. One approach is to impose a forced-distribution rating or ranking system in which the number of people rated at the highest level is controlled (recall our discussion of IBM's new system in Chapter 10). Raters tend to dislike this approach. Another approach is to select and/ or train managers in an effort to avoid this common source of bias. Research indicates that the people who show leniency bias tend to show it across rating situations (e.g., no matter whom they are rating), thus indicating a need to identify and train those with a tendency to commit the error. Research also shows that those with a tendency to commit the error can be identified and that training can be used to reduce the extent of the problem.[17] The training consists of (1) role-playing exercises in conducting performance appraisal interviews and, in particular, in providing negative information; (2) learning methods for enhancing observational skills prior to the appraisal; and (3) learning procedures for the development of more clearly defined dimensions for appraisal.

Many quality improvement experts maintain that pay should not be linked to performance, particularly at the individual level. Deming, the most highly regarded of the quality gurus, believes that performance appraisal fosters competition among individual workers and diverts attention away from systems related to the quality of the product or service. We will discuss this issue more thoroughly in Chapter 13.

Despite Deming's comments, there can be no uncertainty that individuals prefer to be paid on the basis of some measure of individual performance. The problem is creating the linkage when the criteria are ambiguous. The merit pay principle is easy when criteria are available which are countable (e.g., not rated by supervisors) and important (linked to the strategic plan of the organization or unit or to specific customer requirements). Unfortunately, outside of sales, most jobs do not provide these criteria, and we are thus left with ratings. However, ratings by customers at the extent to which customer expectations are met is a preferable alternative to supervisory ratings. Federal Express conducts customer-related performance reviews every 6 months. In addition to the recommendations presented in Chapter 10 for sound performance appraisal systems, Figure 12.3 presents a set of recommendations for the use of individual merit pay systems.

INCENTIVE PAY. Incentive pay is based on units produced and provides the closest connection between individual effort or performance and individual pay. Nonetheless, this form of PFP has fallen into disfavor as the growing number of jobs in the service sector precludes the establishment of a clear standard for determining the rate of production and the piece rate. Even for companies in which incentive systems would seem to work, there is often trouble. The major problem with in-

FIGURE 12.3
RECOMMENDATIONS FOR MERIT PAY PLANS

1. Use a bonus system in which merit pay is not tied to the base salary.
2. Maintain a bonus range from 0 to 20 percent for lower pay levels and from 0 to 40 percent for higher levels.
3. Pay attention to the process issues of the merit pay plan. Involve workers in decision making and maintain an open communication policy.
4. Take performance appraisal seriously. Hold raters accountable for their appraisals, and provide training.
5. Focus on key organizational factors that affect the pay system. Information systems and job designs must be compatible with the performance measurement system.
6. Include group and team performance in evaluation. Evaluate team performance where appropriate, and base part of individual merit pay on the team evaluation.
7. Consider special awards separately from an annual merit allocation which recognizes major accomplishments.

Source: Adapted from E. E. Lawler, *Strategic pay.* San Francisco, CA: Jossey-Bass, 1990. Reprinted with permission.

centive systems is that an adversarial relationship usually develops between workers and management. Workers make every effort to maximize their financial gains by attempting to manipulate the system of setting rates, setting informal production norms, and filing grievances regarding rate adjustments.

There are numerous examples of worker attempts to sabotage piece-rate incentive systems. One expert on pay systems tells the story of how a sales force selling baby foods in south Florida kept secret their highly successful efforts at selling the food to senior citizens because they feared that their standard would be adjusted because of the more favorable market sector to which they were assigned.[18]

There are two types of individual incentive systems based on nonrated output: the piece-rate system and the standard hourly rate. Many variations of piece work have been used over the years, but most share common characteristics. A firm using the piece-rate system will determine an appropriate amount of work to be accomplished in a set period of time (e.g., an hour) and then define this as the standard. (Recall from our discussion in Chapter 4 that job analysis methods can be used to establish work standards.) Then, using either internal or external measures, a fair rate is set for this period of time. The piece rate is then calculated by dividing the base wage by the standard. Today, to comply with regulations such as the minimum wage, piece-rate plans include an hourly wage and a piece-rate incentive.

The basic piece rate is the oldest and most common wage incentive plan. The earliest approach, popular in textile and apparel mills, was called *straight piece work*. In this approach, a worker was paid per unit of production. Used in early American times, when work was done at home on the piece-rate system, this approach is still popular today. Data processing personnel, customer service representatives, and clerks, for example, are paid based on a specific formula tied to the finished product.

The basic piece rate provides a production incentive based on production beyond the standard. The approach may suffer from production variability which can disrupt the flow of the work product. Variability occurs because employees may be willing to forgo extra effort on some days when they are tired, bored, or ill, but then they work especially hard on days when they need some extra money. Frederick Taylor developed the *differential rate* as a response to the variation potential in piece-rate systems.[19] Taylor's differential rate had two outcomes related to pay: one for performing below standard and the other for meeting or exceeding the standard. One major advantage of piece-rate systems is that they are easy to understand. They are useful in labor-intensive industries such as textiles or agriculture, where production can be reliably measured. Migrant workers who harvest fruit and vegetables are often paid by unit of production.

Unfortunately, most jobs outside of sales and straight assembly work do not have a reliable measure of production or performance. Another problem is that adjustments in the standard are required whenever there is a significant change in the machinery or production methods. Finally, work group norms can develop which will restrict the productivity of any one individual. Employees may worry that high earnings under the PFP system will result in an adjustment of the standard. Also, some workers may worry that high productivity may ultimately translate into layoffs or terminations if inventories get too large.

Standard hourly rates differ in that the production standard is expressed in time units. Using job analysis, the standard time for a given task is established and the organization then sets a fair hourly wage rate. The standard rate for any task is the wage rate times the standard. For example, if the standard time for a task is 4 hours and the fair hourly wage is $10, the standard rate is $40. The worker receives the $40 standard rate of pay regardless of the length of time it takes to complete the task. A common example is auto body repair. A customer is given an estimate based on a standards book listing the time required to repair various parts of a car and the hourly wage rate. Insurance companies use a similar book to check the accuracy of the estimate.

In some standard hourly plans, the rate varies with output. For example, the Halsey plan,[20] developed in 1891 by Frederick Halsey, divided between employer and worker the savings realized from performing a task in less than the standard time. Halsey believed that sharing the rewards with management would reduce the likelihood that management would increase the standard as worker output increased. Although Halsey proposed a one-third worker and two-thirds organization split, today his plan is more commonly known as the "Halsey 50-50 plan," because savings are equally divided.

Incentive systems in their various forms tend to work better when the situation is repetitive, the pace is under the direct control of individual workers, there is little or no interaction or cooperation required between workers, and the results can be easily measured. Some banks have piece-rate systems for data entry jobs in which individuals entering check amounts have virtually no interaction with coworkers, workers can control the rate of data entry, and the computer tallies the rate of production. One bank reported a 30 percent increase in production after installing a piece-rate system for data entry personnel.[21] Many telephone reservationists, whose performance is closely monitored by computer, are also paid by piece rate. Many of the reservationist services have left the United States because lower rates can be set on foreign soil. When you call American Airlines, for example, you may be talking to an agent working on the island of Nassau in the Atlantic Ocean.

The adversarial relationship which quickly develops between workers and management can be reduced or eliminated if workers participate in the rate-setting process through task forces. Says one expert, "if they do not involve employees, there is a good chance that the employees will find a way to get involved—for example, by organizing a union."[22]

One of the most successful piece-ratio systems which has been in place for over 50 years can be found at Lincoln Electric in Cleveland, Ohio. Workers receive no hourly wage, no paid sick days, and no paid vacation. They are simply paid for what they produce and a percentage of company profits. Many workers earned in excess of $100,000 in 1990. Turnover is very low and workers and management are very satisfied with the system.

When managers are considering an incentive system, they must take into account the firm's organizational strategy, culture, and position in the marketplace. Incentive plans in manufacturing may be indicated if there are (1) high labor costs, (2) a high level of cost competition in the marketplace, (3) relatively slow advances in technology, and (4) a high level of trust and cooperation between labor and management.[23]

The loss of jobs conducive to individual incentive systems, particularly the manufacturing sector, combined with the trend toward more team-based work systems, indicates that the decline in individual incentive systems based on rates of production will continue.

SALES INCENTIVE PLANS. Sales incentive plans share many of the characteristics of individual incentive plans, but there are also unique requirements. The determinants of employee control over output and measurability both have added dimensions for sales. Because an output measure can be easily established as the level of sales, in dollars or units, a common assumption is that salespeople are paid strictly on the volume of product sold. In many cases, however, employers expect salespeople to perform duties beyond strictly sales. If duties such as customer training, product development, market surveys, and credit checks are required, then the PFP system should involve complex measures of performance which include these dimensions along with sales data. Thus, a critical first step for a sales incentive program, as for all other incentive programs, is to determine what aspects of performance are most important to the firm. The next step is to decide on the methods of measurement and the appropriate levels of compensation. As we discussed above, many companies now incorporate client- or customer-based survey results into their sales compensation systems to underscore the need for nurturing customer relations as well as selling products and services.

Approximately 75 percent of salespeople are on an incentive plan.[24] Commission plans pay the salesperson directly on sales data. Although simple in concept, commissions can become complex. Ordinarily, commissions are a percentage of the dollar value of sales. However, the percentage can increase, decrease, or be constant in relation to changes in sales volume, depending on the nature of the product and its market. Commissions should provide sufficient incentive to the salesperson without adding too much to product cost. Because commissions can be highly variable over time, some firms protect salespeople from low sales periods by using a draw-plus-commission system. At J. C. Penney, for example, a salesperson can draw against an account up to a predetermined limit during slack periods. During periods of higher commissions, the draw account is repaid from commissions in excess of the draw limit. A draw is essentially an interest-free loan to the salesperson, repayable when commissions exceed the draw limit. Another common sales incentive plan uses commissions in conjunction with a salary. The base salary serves as a guaranteed minimum wage, and the commissions are an incentive to sell. Inclusion of salary as part of compensation is useful when the firm requires the salesperson to perform activities other than sales.

Many variations of sales compensation exist. Bonuses for a specific product and bonuses for sales levels are common. In each case, the reward should be tied to a specific performance that is of value to the firm and that justifies the additional expense. Sales incentive programs may have equity problems that differ from a manufacturing situation. Operators of similar machines face the same workplace challenge, but salespeople with different territories may experience different levels of opportunity and challenge. These potential constraints on performance can not only affect the basic fairness and equity of the system but also cause legal problems. Herman Miller terminated a female employee for failure to meet a sales quota in a difficult territory. She argued that her opportunity to meet the quota was severely restricted by factors beyond her control, among them the lack of sample products which were made available to other sales personnel. Many companies manipulate the sales incentive system depending on the sales history of a particular territory. For example, Steelcase offers greater incentives for new business in low-volume territories. Many companies offer rewards other than money as recognition for sales performance. Trips and prizes, which can be purchased by the company at a price considerably less than the cost of cash-only incentive programs, are quite common as a form of sales commission today, particularly in insurance, real estate, and the tourism industry.

Group Incentive Plans

There has been a remarkable increase in the number of group incentive plans recently, with the majority of gain-sharing plans introduced in the United States in the past 10 years. Profit sharing plans have also increased in the last 5 years. Manufacturing organizations are more likely to adopt group plans than are service-oriented firms. Group plans are generally preferable to individual plans under the increasingly popular team-based approaches to production or service we discuss in Chapter 13.

Successful group incentive plans require the same determinants as individual plans. The measures differ in that a group plan must be based on a measure of group performance or productivity. The use of group plans is particularly effective when cooperation and teamwork are essential and when a goal of the system is to enhance the feeling of participation. Group plans are most useful when tasks are so interrelated that it is difficult (or impossible) to identify an individual output measure. The size of the "group" can range from two people to plant-wide or companywide. The smaller the group, the more a worker will identify individual effort as affecting group performance.

Group PFP plans require special considerations. First, there is potential for conflict when all group members receive the same reward regardless of individual input. Second, strong group norms that control output can inhibit group efforts. However, there is increasing evidence that group incentives increase productivity.[25]

PROFIT SHARING. Profit sharing is designed to motivate cost savings by allowing workers to share in benefits of increased profits. As we discussed in Chapter 11, retirement income for employees is frequently linked to a profit sharing plan. Rewards can be periodic cash disbursements or deposits to an employee account. Either a predetermined percentage of profit or a percentage above a certain threshold is allocated to a pool (e.g., 10 to 25 percent). This pool is disbursed to employees on the basis of some ratio, usually related to their wage. Most companies now have options from which the employee may select a particular profit sharing plan compatible with his or her long-range plans.[26] Profit sharing has been criticized as being remote and perceptually unrelated to individual performance, but research indicates that it produces generally positive results.[27] Many firms also use profit sharing as a tool to control employee turnover. At Johnson & Johnson, the allocation is distributed in equal increments over a period of years, and an employee sacrifices remaining distributions by leaving the firm before the period is up. Obviously, some of the incentive value of profit sharing for higher performance is lost when it is used in this fashion. In general, profit sharing works best as an incentive when the group size is small enough that employees believe they have some impact on group profitability.

While employees generally approve of profit sharing, they get testy when their base pay is affected in a negative way by profit sharing provisions. When Du Pont Corporation announced that there would be 4 percent cuts in the base pay of all its 20,000 employees due to poor sales in the fibers division, worker dissatisfaction was so high that the profit sharing plan was scrapped. If the company was profitable, workers would have earned an additional 12 percent above their base pay under the plan. The major reason for the dissatisfaction with the system was the lack of perceived connection between worker performance and company profits. UAW workers at Caterpillar struck the company in 1991 partially because they wanted an increase in base salary and a decrease in the risk of the profit sharing plan. The 1992 UAW contract for the 4700 Saturn workers scaled back the profit sharing component of the innovative wage accord. Poor sales at Saturn in 1991 had a great deal to do with the union's position.

GAIN SHARING. More gain-sharing plans were instituted in the mid-1980s than in the previous 50 years.[28] Gain-sharing plans either try to reduce the amount of labor required for a given level of output (cost saving) or increase the output for a given amount of labor (productivity increase). The method for determining the standard production rate and the incentive rate must be clearly defined. Gain-sharing plans generally are based on the assumption that better cooperation among workers and between workers and managers will result in greater effectiveness. Successful plans require an organizational climate characterized by trust across organizational levels, worker participation, and cooperative unions. An organized employee suggestion system is also characteristic of almost all gain-sharing plans. To maximize cost saving and productivity increases, there must be employee involvement in the plan development and execution. A successful gain-sharing plan requires workers and management to work toward a common goal. Gain sharing encounters difficulty when management downgrades employee input or unions adopt a strong adversarial position.

Gain-sharing plans are different from profit sharing in two major ways: (1) Gain sharing is based on a measure of productivity, not profit. (2) Gain-sharing rewards are given out frequently, whereas profit sharing is annual and often tied to a retirement plan as deferred payment.

There are three basic approaches to gain sharing, although there is considerable variation within these categories. The three approaches are the Scanlon, the Rucker, and the Improshare plans. The *Scanlon plan,* the most common gain-sharing plan, measures the relationship between the sales value of production and labor costs. However, all measures of productivity can be (and often are) adapted to particular situations. For example, one firm uses both the labor/sales ratio and the cost-of-quality/sales ratio as financial measures. Another firm uses savings on warranty costs as a measure for its engineers and designers. As one expert puts it, "The financial measures of performance have great educational value in spurring employee understanding of business fundamentals... financial measures tend to closely parallel overall firm performance."[29]

The Scanlon plan is the oldest form of gain sharing.[30] Developed by Joseph Scanlon, a steelworker, a union official, and later a professor at the Massachusetts Institute of Technology, the plan was originally devised to keep the La Pointe Steel Company from going bankrupt. The plan received wide public attention because of a *Life Magazine* article published in 1946. Its unique aspects were: (1) rewarding the group for suggestions by individuals in the group; (2) joint labor-management committees designed to propose and evaluate labor-saving suggestions; and (3) a worker reward share based on reduced costs, not increased profits. The Scanlon plan uses a formula to determine the employee's share of cost saving. The labor/production value ratio is the ratio of labor costs (total wage bill) to total value of production (TVOP) for a base year. Selection of the base year is critical to avoid basing the labor costs on a period of unusual conditions. In some cases, the base period is an average of several years. To compute savings, the labor/production value ratio is multiplied by the total production value for a selected current period (i.e., quarterly, semiannually, annually). If the current labor costs are less than the standard costs, savings are allocated to the workers, with a portion to the firm. Also, some portion is placed in a fund to protect against future labor costs exceeding the standard cost. Periodically, this fund is disbursed to the employees. Scanlon plans require a considerable commitment by workers and management to cooperate in the development and maintenance of the program.

The track record for Scanlon plans is mixed. There are some great success stories. One paint manufacturer in Texas reported a 78 percent increase in production over its 17-year history of using a Scanlon plan.[31]

The *Rucker plan* is another successful group incentive system. Instead of a labor/production value ratio as in Scanlon, the Rucker plan uses an economic productivity index called *labor contribution to value added* (LCVA). Somewhat more complex to calculate than the Scanlon ratio, this index assumes a constant ratio of labor costs/total value added by the firm in production. This plan defines the productivity ratio (PR) as the value added to production by labor divided by labor cost, which is the same as 1/LCVA. During any period, the productivity ratio is multiplied by labor cost to obtain an expected current value of production. The actual current value of production is subtracted from the expected value, and a positive difference is considered to be savings.

As in the Scanlon plan, a portion is paid to employees, and some is retained to be distributed at the end of the accounting period. The calculations used in the Rucker plan provide advantages and disadvantages. The advantages are the linkage of rewards to savings other than labor savings, plus greater flexibility. Concepts such as value added and the way it allows for inflation make the Rucker plan difficult to understand and explain.

The third category of gain sharing is *Improshare*, which stands for "improved productivity through sharing."[32] Improshare is similar to Scanlon except that the Improshare ratio uses standard hours rather than labor costs. Engineering studies or past performance data are used to specify the standard number of hours required to produce a base production level. Savings in hours result in reward allocation to workers.

All three types of gain-sharing plans use a productivity ratio to capture labor's contribution to value added. The differences among them lie in how labor's cost is calculated for the numerator and how organizational output is measured for the denominator.

In addition to the productivity ratio, other issues influence the selection of a gain-sharing plan. The most important aspect of a PFP system, strength of reinforcement, is roughly equal for the three methods. A summary of the issues to be considered in selecting a plan is provided in Figure 12.4.

Success of gain-sharing plans in general depends on significant involvement and support by high-level management, actual employee participation, and realistic employee and union expectations. Companies which are reluctant to involve unions in strategic planning will also have difficulty with gain-sharing programs.[33] One expert on the subject has recommended a feasibility assessment for the installation of a gain-sharing program. Figure 12.5 presents a summary of his recommendations.

EMPLOYEE STOCK OWNERSHIP PLANS. Whether it is to provide incentives for productivity reasons, to generate sources of cash, to ward off corporate raiders, or to reduce tax liability, *employee stock ownership plans* (ESOPs) are becoming more common. Like numerous European companies, many of our nation's largest companies have ESOPs (e.g., Anheuser-Busch, Lockheed, J. C. Penney, Texaco, Procter & Gamble, Avis, Polaroid). An estimated 200 public companies established ESOPs in 1988 and 1989.[34] Since Congress passed the first ESOP bills in the 1970s, over 10,000 companies with more than 10 million workers have established

FIGURE 12.4
A COMPARISON AMONG GAIN-SHARING PLANS

PLAN	STRENGTH OF REINFORCEMENT	SCOPE OF FORMULA	PERCEIVED FAIRNESS OF FORMULATION	EASE OF ADMINISTRATION	PRODUCTION VARIABILITY
		BEHAVIORIAL AND ORGANIZATIONAL ISSUES IN SELECTING A PLAN			
Scanlon	Reinforcement hindered because incentives tied to group performance.	Narrowly concerned with sales.	Simplicity of formula and broad base of cooperation yield perception of fairness.	Simplicity makes administration easy.	Rapid peaking of production cycles not easy to deal with.
Rucker	Reinforcement hindered because incentives tied to group performance.	Even more narrow than Scanlon in that sales value of production is corrected for inflation.	Complexity slightly reduces perceived fairness. Requires somewhat less cooperation than Scanlon.	Value-added concept and formula exclusions difficult to administer.	Formula for calculating value added specifically deals with changing economic conditions.
Improshare	Reinforcement hindered because incentives tied to group performance.	Narrow measures of labor hours saved.	Lack of employee involvement in development of plan may reduce perceived fairness.	Simplicity makes administration easy.	Management must closely monitor inventory to ensure that variability in economic conditions is reflected in production changes.

Source: G. Milkovich and J. Newman, *Compensation.* Homewood, IL: Richard D. Irwin, 1990, p. 349. Reprinted with permission.

ESOPs. In principle, ESOPs sound like a terrific idea: companies sell stock to workers in order to give them a financial stake in the company. Stock allocations are made to the employee's account based on relative base pay. Constant revision of the tax code has led to other names for ESOPs, such as TRASOPs from the Tax Revision Act of 1976 and PAYSOPs from the Economic Recovery Act of 1981. Indications are that such programs work in general, because profitability increases as the portion of employee ownership increases. However, they tend to work better when combined with extensive employee involvement and problem solving.[35] A popular method designed to replace fixed compensation costs with variable wages and benefits, ESOPs give the organization greater flexibility in response to a competitive environment. Santa Fe Railway reduced employee pay in

FIGURE 12.5
FACTORS TO CONSIDER IN DESIGNING A GAIN-SHARING PROGRAM

1. **Performance and financial measures.** The bonus formula must be perceived as reasonable, accurate, and equitable.
2. **Plant or facility size.** Plants with fewer than 500 employees are ideally suited to gain sharing, while plants with over 2000 employees are not.
3. **Types of production.** Plants with highly mixed types of production will find it difficult to introduce gain sharing because the measurement process is so complicated.
4. **Workforce interdependence.** Highly integrated work units are ideal for gain sharing.
5. **Workforce composition.** Some workforces are not motivated by financial incentives (e.g., secondary workers, older workers).
6. **Potential to absorb additional output.** Initial increase in productivity must be useful to the organization and must not entail negative consequences for the workforce (e.g., layoffs).
7. **Potential for employee efforts.** Can employee efforts actually affect productivity to a significant extent, or does automation (or other factors) impede worker effects?
8. **Present organizational climate.** An initial level of trust is required.
9. **Union-management relations.** Union should be an active partner in program development.
10. **Capital investment plans.** Don't install gain sharing if large capital investments are planned.

Source: Adapted from M. Schuster, Gainsharing: Do it right the first time. *Sloan Management Review,* Winter 1987, pp. 17–25.

1990 for the first time in the company's 122-year history. The pay cuts were replaced with stock options which resulted in bonus checks for all 2400 salaried employees in 1992. Some employees received checks in excess of $100,000. Needless to say, Santa Fe employees are now very happy with the new incentive system.

Managerial and Executive Incentives

Research supports the use of long-term reward systems for executives, which are directly tied to the long-term strategic goals of the firm. Incentives for managers and executives can have a significant impact upon the fortunes of an organization.[36] In general, executive incentive plans are linked to net income, some measure of return on investment, or total dividends paid. These incentives are paid in the form of bonuses not permanently tied to base pay. CEOs often receive almost 50 percent of their compensation from this type of plan. Recently, highly paid executives and their contributions to corporations have been challenged.[37] Incentive plans can raise total pay to astronomical levels. According to one 1991 survey, among the executives with the highest pay, including salary, bonuses, and long-term payouts, were Anthony O'Reilly of Heinz ($75 million) and Leon Hirsch of U.S. Surgical ($23 million). Coca-Cola's Roberto Goizueta took the prize in 1991 with a total pay package in excess of $86 million (considerably more than Steven Jobs received when he sold Apple Computer, the product and company he founded). Despite the fact that corporate profits slid by 4.2 percent in 1989, CEO compensation rose by 8 percent (median compensation was $1 million). The median annual compensation of big-company CEOs, including salary, options, and bonuses, was $1.3 million in 1991. Even during a recession, CEO pay rose significantly. Though they were already earning 160 times what average blue-collar employees received, U.S. CEOs still garnered 12 to 15 percent raises in 1990, a year in which corporate profits fell 12 percent. (They managed only 4.2 percent raises in 1991.) CEOs in Canada, Europe, and Japan earn less than half of what U.S. CEOs make. U.S. CEO pay seems to be primarily driven by what other U.S. CEOs make, no matter how absurd. There is a political movement to control the apparent runaway inflation of executive compensation. In 1991, a bill was introduced in the U.S. Senate to give stockholders more of a say in executive pay.[38]

A principal distinction between managerial and executive incentives is the time horizon of the performance measure which is the basis of the incentive. Lower-level managers typically have incentives based on short-term measures, whereas top executives have both short- and long-term performance incentives. Managers and executives have a wider area of discretion in making decisions that affect the firm. As a consequence, the PFP system is designed to reinforce a sense of commitment to the organization. Most managers receive bonuses related to profit. The amount is usually awarded as a percentage of their base pay, although there is a trend toward awarding lump sums not tied to the base pay. As higher profitability thresholds are attained, the manager receives bigger bonuses. The bonus structure for any given manager often depends on the relative contributions of all managers, with the assessment of relative contribution made at a higher level. This method suffers from the drawbacks discussed previously regarding profit sharing for individuals. Many managers might feel that they have a negligible impact on organization profits. As the link between performance and pay becomes weaker, the reward loses incentive value. The link can be strengthened by clearly defining performance standards, while basing the amount of the reward on corporate profitability.

Executives should be concerned with the long-term viability of the firm. There are many situations in which a decision option can have a conflicting impact on a firm's short- and long-run profitability. Investing in research and development (R&D) will depress short-term profit but should lead to maintenance of a long-run competitive position. Cutting back on services provided may add to short-run profits but damage market share in the long run.

Long-term rewards focus on future profitability. The most popular approach is based on appreciation of stock value using various stock purchase plans.[39] Almost 90 percent of the 500 largest industrials had stock option plans in 1985, up from 52 percent in 1974.[40] A stock option plan gives an executive the right to purchase a stock, over a specified period, at a fixed price. The theory is that if the executive is prudent and hard-working, the stock price will go up. If the stock price does increase, the executive can purchase it at the lower fixed price, effectively receiving as a bonus the difference between the fixed purchase price and the higher market price. Congress periodically revises legislation controlling the awarding of stock options. These limitations have typically affected only options exceeding $100,000 per year.

There are many variations on stock options. *Stock appreciation rights* (SARs), for example, do not involve buying stock. Having been awarded rights to a stock at a fixed price for a specified period, the executive can call the option and receive the difference between the fixed and market prices in cash. *Restricted stock plans* give shares as a bonus, but with restrictions.[41] The restrictions may be that the executive cannot leave the company or sell the stock for a specified time. *Performance share plans* award units based on both short- and long-term measures. These units are later translated into stock awards. Other incentive stock option plans are part of retirement packages. These may include profit sharing and stock bonus plans. In both cases, employers pay into a retirement fund based on corporate profits.

Recent evidence suggests that stock incentives may not be effective. In 1989, the average annual return on investment at 28 Fortune 500 companies offering these types of stock awards (including Sara Lee, Unisys, and Bristol-Myers) was 11 percent. Companies not offering these incentives realized a 16 percent return during the same period.[42]

Executive incentives of the future are likely to be tied to long-term corporate performance which may involve qualitative assessment of performance along with corporate financial performance. New products and service lines, environmental impact assessments, and new territorial penetration are some of the long-range measures which may be used to assess executive performance. For example, McDonald's and General Electric (GE) place considerable weight on their long-term growth in the European sector as a basis for compensating senior management. The trend in executive compensation is against heavy reliance on stock prices as a basis for compensating executives, since such reliance would promote short-term perspectives to the detriment of the long-term strategic plan of the organization.

Entrepreneurial and Special PFP Programs

Under the competitive pressures of the 1980s, many companies are attempting to retain entrepreneurial mavericks within the corporate umbrella.[43] For example, many high-tech firms are funding employee ventures by using innovative compensation schemes.[44] The basic principle is that the employee places a major portion of salary at risk, with the percentage of employee ownership of the venture determined by the portion of salary at risk. The potential for large returns replaces many of the standard perks expected by employees. Payoffs may have a variety of bases, from profits produced by the venture to increases in parent company stock value. Although such payoffs may be less than if the venture were truly independent, the risk for the venture employee is also more limited. In addition, there is the support and expertise available from the parent. American Telephone and Telegraph (AT&T), for example, wanted to increase the risk its people were willing to take in entrepreneurial efforts. Three venture approaches were offered, corresponding to the levels of risk the venture employee was willing to take.

Many companies have adopted special award programs for major accomplishments. IBM, Amoco, Xerox, and Digital, for example, have programs in which the awards can exceed $100,000 for R&D discoveries. American Express has $5000 awards for "exceptional performers." These special programs are independent of any other PFP systems within the company.

MANAGERIAL IMPLICATIONS

In general, a well-designed PFP system should lead to lower costs, higher profits, and a higher degree of individual or group motivation, which thus requires less supervision. Introduction of a well-designed PFP system can provide a more accurate estimate of labor costs as well as prompt workers to make more effective use of their time, supplies, and equipment.

Incentive systems have several potential drawbacks. Emphasizing one measure can lead to reduced performance levels in other measures. A strong focus on output can reduce quality, which will lead to increased costs in quality control. In addition, a focus on output can jeopardize safety. A second drawback is the overhead expense of installing and maintaining the PFP system. Unless the production process is very stable, maintenance costs can be substantial. A third drawback is the difficulty in setting standards that accurately reflect task requirements and are perceived as fair. This problem can be greater when a system adds new processes or equipment, as workers will be suspicious of new standards. A fourth drawback is that there will be resistance to change as a consequence of the PFP system. Unions have been born out of attempts to radically alter compensation systems, such as from a straight pay system to a PFP system. In addition to the typical fear of anything new, workers may oppose change to avoid being victimized by new rates and standards.

Management will resist change because of the expense of revising the system, the time required to do performance appraisals, and the difficulties which develop in defending PFP decisions. Finally, variations in pay due to performance differences may lead to conflict. When measures are explicit and objective, some conflict will occur. When methods are subjective or ambiguous, as with the typical performance appraisal system, significant reward differences may not be perceived as justified, resulting in even greater conflict.

SUMMARY

The PFP system must support the competitive strategy and values of the organization. If the strategy emphasizes entrepreneurial activity and independent effort, individual PFP systems become increasingly important and effective. Incentive systems must be compatible with organizational values. Closed, secretive cultures do not mix well with performance incentives. Openness and trust is necessary if employees are to accept the standards and believe in the equity of the rewards. Organizational design also affects the nature of incentives selected. Individual PFP plans are preferable when individual contributions on important criteria can be clearly measured and important teamwork is not seriously undermined by the process. Highly interdependent jobs or groups will dictate group or organizational PFP plans.

As one expert on the subject has put it, "Paying for performance will not solve all of the motivational problems associated with the new workforce and strong international competition. However, it can be an important part of a total management system that is designed to create a highly motivating work environment."[45] The bottom line remains that for any PFP system to work, rewards valued by the worker must be clearly linked to outcomes valued by the employer. Chapter 13 will turn to other organizational systems which can contribute to the productivity and the competitive advantage of the organization.

DISCUSSION QUESTIONS

1. Deming and other quality experts think PFP is a bad idea. What do you think?
2. Why is trust between an employer and employee important in establishing a successful PFP system?
3. When is a group PFP plan better than an individual plan?
4. What factors should an organization take into consideration before implementing a PFP system?
5. Should CEO pay be regulated by the federal government?
6. Some experts maintain that you shouldn't bother with PFP if you must rely on performance appraisals to get performance data. Do you agree or disagree? Please explain your position.
7. Describe the differences between short- and long-term incentives. When should long-term incentives be used?
8. How does entrepreneurial pay differ from other PFP systems?
9. Why are unions generally opposed to PFP systems? How does that make you feel about unions?
10. If PFP is such a good idea, why doesn't everyone use it?

NOTES

1. Heneman, R. (1992). *Merit pay.* Reading, MA: Addison-Wesley.

2. Lawler, E. E. (1990). *Strategic pay.* San Francisco, CA: Jossey-Bass.

3. Labor Letter (Dec. 12, 1989). *The Wall Street Journal,* p. 1.

4. Labor Letter (Sept. 24, 1991). *The Wall Street Journal,* p. 1. See also: The Conference Board (1990). *Variable pay: New performance rewards.* Research Bulletin No. 246. New York: The Conference Board.

5. See note 3.

6. Milkovich, G. T., and Wigdor, A. K. (1991). *Pay for performance.* Washington: National Academy Press, p. 4.

7. See note 3.

8. Labor Letter (Dec. 5, 1989). *The Wall Street Journal,* p. 1.

9. Geis, A. A. (January 1987). Making merit pay work. *Personnel,* pp. 52–60. See also: Heneman, R. L. (1990). Merit pay research. *Research in Personnel and Human Resource Management, 8,* 203–263. Heneman, R. L., Greenberger, D. B., and Strasser, S. (1988). The relationship between pay-for-performance perceptions and pay satisfaction. *Personnel Psychology, 41,* 745–759. Markham, S. E. (1988). Pay-for-performance dilemma revisited: Empirical example of the importance of group effects. *Journal of Applied Psychology, 73,* 172–180. Schwab, D. P., and Olson, C. A. (1990). Merit pay practices: Implications for pay-performance relationships. *Industrial and Labor Relations Review, 43,* 237–255. Scott, W. E. Jr., Farh, J., and Podsakoff, P. M. (1988). The effects of "intrinsic" and "extrinsic" reinforcement contingencies on task behavior. *Organization Behavior and Human Decision Processes, 41,* 405–425.

10. Bernardin, H. J., and Kane, J. S. (1993). Performance appraisal: A contingency approach to system development and evaluation. Boston: PWS-Kent.

11. Lawler, E. E. (1984). Pay for performance: A motivational analysis. University of Southern California Report, G84-9(57), p. 12. See also: Wagner, J. A. III, Rubin, P., and Callahan, T. J. (1988). Incentive payment and nonmanagerial productivity: An interrupted time series analysis of magnitude and trend. *Organizational Behavior and Human Decision Processes, 42,* 47–74.

12. Johnson, A. M. (May 20, 1990). *The New York Times,* p. 29.

13. Bernardin, H. J., and Villanova, P. J. (1986). Performance appraisal. In E. Locke (ed.), *Generalizing from laboratory to field research.* Boston, MA: D. C. Heath.

14. Kay, I. (Aug. 9, 1990). Quoted in Labor Letter, *The Wall Street Journal,* p. 1.

15. Kanter, R. M. (January 1987). From status to contribution: Some organizational implications of the changing basis for pay. *Personnel,* pp. 12–24. See also: Konrad, A. M., and Pfeffer, J. (1990). Do you get what you deserve? Factors affecting the relationship between productivity and pay. *Administrative Science Quarterly, 35,* 258–285.

16. See note 1. See also: Folger, R., and Konovsky, M. A. (1989). Effects of procedural and distributive justice on reactions to pay raise decisions. *Academy of Management Journal, 30,* 115–130.

17. See note 15.

18. See note 2.

19. Henderson, R. I. (1989). *Compensation management,* 5th ed. Englewood Cliffs, NJ: Prentice-Hall.

20. Halsey, F. A. (1891). The premium plan of paying for labor. *Transactions, American Society of Mechanical Engineers, 12,* 755–764.

21. See note 2.

22. See note 2.

23. Schwinger, P. (1975). *Wage incentive systems.* New York: Halsted.

24. See note 19.

25. Pritchard, R. D., Jones, S. D., Roth, P. L., Stuebing, K. K., and Ekeberg, S. E. (1988). Effects of group feedback, goal setting, and incentives on organizational productivity. *Journal of Applied Psychology, 73*(2), 337–358.

26. See note 25.

27. See note 2.

28. Welbourne, T. M., and Gomez-Mejia, L. R. (July-August 1988). Gainsharing revisited. *Compensation and Benefits Review,* pp. 19–28.

29. Schuster, M. (Winter 1987). Gainsharing: Do it right the first time. *Sloan Management Review,* p. 23. See also: Bullock, R. J., and Lawler, E. E. (1984). Gainsharing: A few questions, and fewer answers. *Human Resource Management, 23*(1), 23–40. Hatcher, L., and Ross, T. L. (1991). From individual incentives to an organization-wide gainsharing plan: Effects on teamwork and product quality. *Journal of Organizational Behavior, 12,* 169–183. Rollins, T. (May-June 1989). Productivity-based group incentive plans: Powerful, but use with caution. *Compensation and Benefits Review,* 39–50.

30. Lesieur, F. (1958). *The Scanlon plan: A frontier in labor management relations.* New York: John Wiley & Sons.

31. Graham-Moore, B. (1990). 17 years of experience with the Scanlon plan: Desota revisited. In B. Graham-Moore and T. L. Ross (eds.), *Gainsharing.* Washington: Bureau of National Affairs, pp. 139–173. See also: Graham-Moore, B., and Ross, T. L. (1990). *Gainsharing.* Washington, D.C.: Bureau of National Affairs.

32. Fein, M. (1980). *An alternative to traditional managing.* Hillsdale, NJ: Mitchell Fein.

33. See note 31.

34. Farrell, C., and Hoerr, J. (May 1989). ESOPS: Are they good for you? *Business Week,* pp. 116–123. See also: Chelius, J., and Smith, R. S. (1990). Profit sharing and employment stability. *Industrial and Labor Relations Review, 43,* 256–273. Cone, M. A., and Svejnar, J. (1990). The performance effects of employee ownership plans. In A. S. Blinder (ed.), *Paying for productivity,* pp. 245–294. Washington, D.C.: The Brookings Institution. Coates, E. M. III (April 1991). Profit sharing today: Plans and provisions. *Monthly Labor Review,* April 1991, pp. 19–25.

35. Blasi, J. (1985). *Employee ownership: Revolution not rip-off.* New York: John Wiley & Sons. See also: Florkowski,

G.W. (1991). Profit sharing and public policy: Insights for the United States. *Industrial Relations, 30,* 96–115. Florkowski, G.W. (1987). The organizational impact of profit sharing. *Academy of Management Review, 12,* 622–636. Hammer, T. H. (1988). New developments in profit sharing, gainsharing, and employee ownership. In J. P. Campbell, R. J. Campbell, and Associates (eds.), *Productivity in Organizations.* San Francisco: Jossey-Bass Publishers. Klein, K. J. (1987). Employee stock ownership and employee attitudes: A test of three models. *Journal of Applied Psychology* [monograph], *72,* 319–332. Kruse, D. L. (1991). Profit-sharing and employment variability: Microeconomic evidence on the Weitzman theory. *Industrial and Labor Relations Review, 44,* 437–453. Pierce, J. L., Rubenfeld, S., and Morgan, S. (1991). Employee ownership: A conceptual model of process and effects. *Academy of Management Review, 16,* 121–144.

36. Crystal, G. S. (1984). Pay for performance: It's not dead after all. *Compensation Review, 3,* 24–25.

37. Crystal, G. S. (1991). *In search of excess: The overcompensation of American executives.* New York: W.W. Norton.

38. Lublin, J. (June 4, 1991). Are chief executives paid too much? *The Wall Street Journal,* p. B1.

39. Thompson, J. H., Smith, L. M., and Murray, A. F. (September-October 1986). Management performance incentives: Three critical issues. *Compensation and Benefits Review,* pp. 41–47.

40. Goodson, J. R., McGee, G. W., and Ginter, P. M. (August 1988). Stock options. *Personnel Administrator,* pp. 71–75.

41. Edelstein, C. M. (1981). Long term incentives for management, Part 4: Restricted stock. *Compensation Review,* pp. 31–40. See also: Kerr, J., and Bettis, R. A. (1987). Board of directors, top management compensation, and shareholder returns. *Academy of Management Journal, 30,* 645–665.

42. Castro, J. (Apr. 15, 1991). CEOs: No pain, just gain. *Time,* pp. 40–41. See also: Puffer, S. M., and Weinrop, J. P. (1991). Corporate performance and CEO turnover: The role of performance expectations. *Administrative Science Quarterly, 36,* 1–19.

43. Balkin, D. B., and Logan, J. W. (January-February 1988). Reward policies that support entrepreneurship. *Compensation and Benefits Review,* pp. 19–32. See also: Kahn, L. M., and Sherer, P. D. (1990). Contingent pay and managerial performance. *Industrial and Labor Relations Review, 43,* 107–120.

44. See note 2. See also: Kerr, J., and Slocum, J.W. Jr. (1987). Managing corporate culture through reward systems. *Academy of Management Executive, 1*(2), 99–108. Lawler, E. E. III (1989). Pay for performance: A strategic analysis. In L. R. Gomez-Mejia (ed.), *Compensation and Benefits.* Washington, D.C.

45. See note 2.

EXERCISE 12.1
THE DESIGN OF A PFP SYSTEM FOR MEGA MANUFACTURING*

OVERVIEW

The purpose of this exercise is to evaluate the feasibility of different approaches to PFP given the strategic plan of the organization. As discussed in Chapter 12, the effectiveness of a PFP system is dependent upon a number of factors. This exercise will give students the opportunity to consider some of the factors involved in proposing a PFP system.

LEARNING OBJECTIVES

After completing this exercise, you should be able to:

1. Identify the key organizational variables which should be considered in the development and/or revision of a PFP system.
2. Understand the role of and importance of other HRM activities (e.g., job analysis, performance appraisal) in the development of a PFP system.

PROCEDURE

Part A: Individual Analysis

Prior to class, read the scenario and Exhibits 12.1.1 and 12.1.2. You have been retained as a consultant who must report to Ellen Lennett, Director of Incentive Program Development at Mega Manufacturing corporate headquarters. You must address the five issues raised in Form 12.1.1. Respond to each of the issues and recommend a specific program that supports both Mega's incentive policy and Kanto's situation. Your recommendation should consider *at least* the five points. Bring Form 12.1.1 to class. Also prior to class, complete the assessment questions.

Part B: Group Analysis

Step 1. Working in groups of about six people, each member should review the individual reports and take notes on the most important points. Each member should also devise his or her own strategy for identifying the best possible group response for each of the five questions in Form 12.1.1, plus any additional issues which the group considers relevant. The group should devise a list of key questions which must be answered by management before a firm position can be taken on the elements of the PFP system.

Step 2. One group member should be designated to make a 3-minute presentation of the group's position before the rest of the class. A class-wide discussion should then focus on the various recommended plans.

SCENARIO

Mega Manufacturing International is a large diversified company with corporate headquarters in Boston. It has manufacturing plants, R&D facilities, and distribution and marketing centers in the United States and around the world. Mega Manufacturing is pursuing a long-range strategy of producing high-technology products for three markets: military, industrial, and retail consumers. Because of the intense competitive pressures in its chosen arenas, Mega Manufacturing believes that it must obtain the maximum effort from its personnel. In support of this belief, Mega Manufacturing has adopted a policy of PFP. Typically, many of its divisions have incentives comprising a substantial portion of executive pay (40 to 150 percent of base pay in the various types of incentives possible) and a significant portion of supervisory and employee compensation (5 to 25 percent possible).

To expand its capabilities in the new electronic surface mount technology, Mega Manufacturing acquired GW Industries, which had several plants producing high-quality surface-mount electronic parts. The Kanto Assembly Plant is part of GW Industries; however, it was an old plant producing electronic parts for an industrial process that is rapidly approaching obsolescence. Although the products are produced on an assembly line, individual workers have relatively little contact with each other, and the skills required are relatively low. Kanto had been a profitable operation for GW, but Mega Manufacturing has to switch Kanto to a different product and process or close the plant.

Kanto has a reputation for paying average to below-market wages, but it is viewed as a dependable and stable employer with a good benefits package. As a consequence, Kanto has had a stable and loyal workforce. Because of the buyout of GW, however, and the consequent uncertainty surrounding Kanto's future, there has been talk of unionizing and some of the more skilled employees are known to be seeking other jobs.

---

*Contributed by E. Brian Peach and M. Ronald Buckley.

Mega has decided to offer Kanto the opportunity to manufacture an extremely complex switching device for a military contract. Although the total manufacturing process is complex, it can be broken down into steps, with each step consisting of individual skills which can be learned relatively quickly. Groups of individuals, each with a specific skill, will have to work closely together to achieve the required quality levels for each step in the switching device assembly. The nature of the process is such that each individual will have to take an active interest in the success of the assembly, or the device will be unsatisfactory.

The two memos in Exhibits 12.1.1 and 12.1.2 may be relevant to the recommendations you will make. Ellen Lennett has just received the following notes, one (Exhibit 12.1.1) from Don Walker, vice president, compensation and benefits, and the other (Exhibit 12.1.2) from Bill Idrey, a compensation specialist whom Ms. Lennett sent to help the Kanto personnel department.

EXHIBIT 12.1.1

```
To:       Ellen Lennett
Subject:  Kanto Incentive Program
From:     Don Walker
```

```
We need to give Kanto some more help on setting up its incentives to
adequately support the new switching assembly process. We cannot allow the
conversion process to delay us in completing switching assemblies, as there is
a large late delivery penalty. Also, Bids and Contracting apparently goofed
and bid too low on the contract to maintain our usual margins. It appears we
have to make up 3 percent somewhere.
```

EXHIBIT 12.1.2

To: Ellen Lennett
Subject: Kanto Incentive Program
From: Bill Idrey

Just a quick note to advise you of some early problems I'm encountering.

1. The employees are learning the new skills, but the supervisors are having trouble (resisting?) learning the necessary composite skills.

2. The parts we're getting from our Indonesian plant sometimes test okay individually but will not work in the final assembly. It is apparently not feasible to test the intermediate assembly steps.

3. Although the job analysis report indicates that the steps and tasks are essentially equal, two of the assembly steps are perceived as being more important and thus as having higher status by the workers.

4. Robert Horne, the plant manager, is complaining that the new final quality check supervisor, Beatrice Inggold, is too strict and will slow down production.

5. Engineers from Design and Fabrication come in and watch, occasionally making suggestions, but I'm darned if I can see what they are contributing.

FORM 12.1.1

Your name _____ Group _____

1. Would an incentive program be appropriate at Kanto? Explain your position.

2. If an incentive program would be appropriate, should there be one, two, or several plans?

3. Who should be included in the incentive program?

4. What should be the basis for incentive payments?

5. What kind of incentives should be included?

Exercise 12.1
Assessment Questions

Name _____   Group _____

1. What were the key variables you considered in your selection of an individual or a group-based PFP system for Kanto?

2. What changes in organizational characteristics would seriously affect your recommendations?

3. What circumstances would lead you to conclude that a PFP system would not be in the best interests of the organization?

EXERCISE 12.2
SPEEDY PIZZA'S INCENTIVE SYSTEM*

OVERVIEW

Chapter 12 describes some of the problems which can develop with PFP systems. The purpose of this exercise is to describe a situation in which the reward or punishment system in its present form may not be in the best interests of the organization. The student must decide how the reward system can be adjusted so that the results of the compensation system will be compatible with the strategic plan of the organization.

LEARNING OBJECTIVES

After completing this exercise, you should be able to:

1. Analyze a particular company's problems in relation to its personnel practices and reward system.
2. Explore ethical issues surrounding the company's reward policies.
3. Explore options regarding compensation and PFP and the organization's responsibility for its actions.

PROCEDURE

Part A: Individual Analysis

Prior to class, read the scenario. Prepare a written answer to each of the questions presented on Form 12.2.1. Also, answer the assessment questions.

Part B: Group Analysis

Working in groups of about six, review the individual written responses of all group members and develop a new compensation or reward system which will accomplish the goals of the organization. The group should take a position on whether a PFP system is appropriate for delivery personnel and (if so) what its major characteristics should be. Assume that Speedy Pizza's 25-minute policy cannot be changed.

SCENARIO

You are a management consultant who was contacted recently by Jack Rand, the vice president of a Chicago-

based firm, Speedy Pizza Company. Speedy Pizza has 50 stores in Chicago and in nearby suburbs and cities, and is well known for its fast and reliable delivery service. One marketing technique which the company has used successfully in the past 2 years is to promise customers a free pizza coupon if their pizza is not delivered within 25 minutes of the phone order. This technique has proved so successful that the company has been able to open more stores and is currently considering diversifying into the dine-in restaurant market.

During your initial meeting with Jack Rand, Jack tells you that the company is experiencing a serious problem with its pizza delivery personnel. In the last 1½ years, there have been an inordinate number of injuries and even one death among pizza drivers, because of driving accidents which occurred while the pizza drivers were delivering pizzas. These high accident rates have recently been receiving the attention of top management at Speedy Pizza because of the most recent accident, which occurred just 2 weeks ago. In this accident, both the Speedy Pizza driver and the passengers in another car were seriously hurt when the Speedy Pizza driver went through a stop sign in a residential neighborhood and collided with the other car. Fortunately, the Speedy Pizza driver and the passengers in the other car are no longer in critical condition; however, the Speedy Pizza driver's family as well as the family of the other involved accident victims have stated to the local press that they plan to sue Speedy Pizza for damages.

According to the Speedy Pizza driver's family, the Speedy Pizza driver ran the stop sign because of pressure from Speedy Pizza management to deliver the pizza within 25 minutes, and therefore Speedy Pizza is at fault for the accident. However, during your meeting with Jack Rand, he vehemently denied that Speedy Pizza pressures their drivers to speed, saying, "Let me tell you, we give new drivers a week-long training orientation session just to emphasize safety. Even our drivers' mottos are explicitly against speeding: 'Knead with Speed, Deliver with Safety' and 'Service without Speed, Safety Above All.' In other words, the speed that we use to get our pizzas to the customers in 25 minutes occurs *in* the store, not on the roads! We stress this over and over to our drivers. We even have safety signs up all over the store for them! Let me tell you what I think the problem is. I think the problem is with the HR Branch when they hire these pizza drivers. I think they're hiring poor drivers to begin with, and all the training in the world can't change them."

At the end of your meeting with Jack, you told him you planned to investigate the problem further, and get back to him with your findings within the next 2 weeks. Your first step in the investigation was to visit with the HR Branch to see what criteria are used to hire pizza drivers. In addition, you met with various pizza drivers to get a profile of the current pizza delivery personnel.

---

*Contributed by Ann M. Herd and Caroline C. Wilhelm.

You found that pizza drivers are hired on the basis of structured inverviews, references, and written application forms containing, among other things, driving records and grade point averages. You found that most pizza drivers are high school or college students with fairly good grades and excellent references, who are trying to earn money for school and extracurricular activities. They are attracted to the job because the hours are flexible and easily accommodate their class schedules. In addition, the company advertises itself as having enormous career opportunities for anyone who is willing to start at the bottom and work hard to get to the top.

You spoke with several pizza drivers about their jobs and safety concerns. Some of the drivers expressed concern about pay and safety. One driver said, "Oh sure, the company tells you they don't want you to speed, but the bottom line is that my store takes $2 out of your pay for every late pizza that is delivered. Lots of times they give you several pizzas to deliver at one time, and you know it's almost impossible to get them all delivered within the 25 minutes. So what can you do? Plus, they keep tabs on which driver in each store delivers the most late pizzas, and they put this in your record! Not only that, but they put a sign up each month announcing the driver who delivers the most late pizzas. Most of us drivers would like to move up in the company while we're here—*nobody* wants to get the "Late Driver of the Month" award. So what do you expect us to do?"

FORM 12.2.1

Name _____ Group _____

1. What sort of reinforcement system is used with the pizza drivers? Is this a PFP system?

2. Based on the information given, to what do you attribute Speedy Pizza's accident rate problems? What other information do you need to know about Speedy Pizza Company's situation?

3. Are there any ethical issues in this case? Should Speedy Pizza Company continue its current practices regarding payment, selection, and training of delivery personnel? In your opinion, does the company have any obligation to make changes?

4. What specific recommendations would you make to top management of the Speedy Pizza Company? Should a PFP system be implemented? If so, what steps should be followed to develop such a system? What are the key features of such a system? (Again, assume that the 25-minute policy *cannot* be changed.)

Name _____ Group _____

1. What do you regard as the trade-offs for PFP in the situation at Speedy Pizza?

2. What other components of an HRM system should be considered in revising the compensation system?

*EXERCISE 12.3 MANAGEMENT TRAINING FOR DEE'S PERSONALIZED BASKETS**

OVERVIEW

The purpose of this exercise is to provide an opportunity for students to develop a framework for a PFP system, training for the program, and the evaluation of the training. The problem is one with which many organizations are confronted today. As discussed in Chapter 12, while PFP is the preferred method of compensation for most jobs, there are many problems with such systems. One of the most important problems is the apparent inability of evaluators to be critical in their evaluations (i.e., the leniency bias). Many experts on PFP systems maintain that the leniency bias is the major problem with most PFP systems in operation today which use ratings as the basis for measurement. This exercise is designed to allow students to consider this problem and to suggest possible solutions through a formal training program and evaluation.

LEARNING OBJECTIVES

After completing this exercise, you should be able to:

1. Consider the various PFP options for a given situation.
2. Consider the training needed for a PFP system.
3. Evaluate the relative advantages and disadvantages of the different approaches to training program development and methodology.

---

*Contributed by Jarold Abbott.

4. Consider the various issues related to training development, including transfer, relapse, and cost.
5. Develop an evaluation design which can assess the effects of training.

PROCEDURE

Part A: Individual Analysis

Prior to class, read Chapter 12 thoroughly. Also, review the section in Chapter 8 on evaluating training programs. Then read the background material on Dee's Personalized Baskets presented in Exhibit 12.3.1. Complete the PASES in Exhibit 12.3.2, and answer the questions in Form 12.3.1 and the assessment questions for the exercise.

Part B: Group Analysis and Allocation of Duties

Step 1. Assume the role of a team of HR consultants to consider the installation of the PFP system. Specifically, you have been asked to develop a managerial training program for managers to prepare them for the new PFP system. You have also been asked to evaluate the effectiveness of the training program.

Step 2. Among the critical issues that your team should address are those listed in Form 12.3.1. Review each consultant's responses to Form 12.3.1. Discuss each response and prepare a plan to deal with each.

Step 3. Prepare a 3-minute presentation for the vice president which covers your team's ideas regarding the design and evaluation of the training program. Remember that management will weight heavily both your recommendations and your plan for implementation.

EXHIBIT 12.3.1
BACKGROUND MATERIAL FOR DEE'S PERSONALIZED BASKETS

Nancy Harrison, HRM vice president of Dee's Personalized Baskets in Orlando, Florida, is disturbed by lagging productivity figures and problems of product quality. She is intrigued by the results of a recent attitude survey of her employees. She has decided to experiment with an individualized PFP system of compensation. The company's current system of compensation pays straight hourly rates to non-supervisory personnel and straight salary to all supervisory and managerial personnel, with a year-end bonus which is a percentage of base pay as determined by the board. The attitude survey results indicated that employees felt that they would work harder if they perceived a stronger tie between their level of effort and their pay. Each of the 200 employees who would be part of the new pay system prepares individual baskets of perfumes, fancy soaps, fancy foods, wine, etc. These baskets are ordered by customers for presentation as gifts to clients and potential clients. Some employee discretion is involved in the preparation of the baskets, and the finished product can be evaluated for quality and cost effectiveness.

Few respondents to the survey felt that they were recognized in any significant way for working harder than others. The people most disturbed by the failure to recognize greater effort were also the ones who indicated that they were likely to seek other employment. The organization has a performance appraisal system but the ratings are generally very high. For the last performance appraisal period, the average rating of effectiveness made by the 20 supervisors was 7.5 on a 9-point rating scale (with 9 representing "highly effective" performance).

In an effort to assess managerial readiness for a PFP system, the Performance Appraisal Self-Efficacy Scale (PASES) was administered to all 20 supervisors. The form is shown in Exhibit 12.3.2. Previous research indicates that scores on the PASES have also been shown to be correlated with performance rating inflation (i.e., a higher score on the PASES is related to higher or more lenient ratings). Fair and objective performance ratings are of course critical for the successful maintenance of an individualized PFP system. The mean score on the PASES for the 20 supervisors was found to be below the mean for supervisors who had been identified in research to be fair and objective performance evaluators.

EXHIBIT 12.3.2
PERFORMANCE APPRAISAL SELF-EFFICACY SCALE (PASES)

Name_____ Group _____

Indicate the degree of discomfort you would feel in the following situations. Answer as candidly as possible by indicating what is true for you. Use the following scale to write in one number in the blank to the left of each item.

> 5 = High discomfort
> 4 = Some discomfort
> 3 = Undecided
> 2 = Very little discomfort
> 1 = No discomfort

_____ 1. Telling an employee who is also a friend that he or she must stop coming to work late.

_____ 2. Telling an employee that his or her work is only satisfactory, when you know that he or she expects an above-satisfactory rating.

_____ 3. Talking to an employee about his or her performance on the job.

_____ 4. Conducting a formal performance appraisal interview with an ineffective employee.

_____ 5. Asking an employee if he or she has any comments about your rating of his or her performance.

_____ 6. Telling an employee who has problems in dealing with other employees that he or she should do something about it (e.g., take a course, read a book).

_____ 7. Telling a male subordinate that his performance must improve.

_____ 8. Responding to an employee who is upset over your rating of his or her performance.

_____ 9. Having to terminate someone for poor performance.

_____ 10. Letting an employee give his or her point of view regarding a problem with performance.

_____ 11. Giving a satisfactory rating to an employee who has done a satisfactory (but not exceptional) job.

_____ 12. Letting a subordinate talk during an appraisal interview.

_____ 13. Being challenged to justify an evaluation in the middle of an appraisal interview.

_____ 14. Being accused of playing favorites in the rating of your staff.

_____ 15. Recommending that an employee be discharged.

_____ 16. Telling an employee that his or her performance can be improved.

_____ 17. Telling an employee that you will not tolerate his or her taking extended coffee breaks.

_____ 18. Warning an ineffective employee that unless performance improves, he or she will be discharged.

_____ 19. Telling a female subordinate that her performance must improve.

_____ 20. Encouraging an employee to evaluate his or her own performance.

FORM 12.3.1

Name _____ Group number _____

1. What types of training are required in order to prepare managers for the PFP system?

2. What methods of training (e.g., informational, experiential) do you recommend? Why?

3. What is your experimental design? Who should receive the training?

4. What specific criteria will you use to evaluate the results? (Provide some examples of criteria.)

5. What will be the basis of your final recommendation to the vice president of HR regarding companywide implementation of the training?

6. What role (if any) should the PASES score play in the training program? (In order to answer this question, the student should complete the PASES and evaluate its usefulness. The instructor will provide feedback on each student's score on the PASES relative to normative data.)

7. How will the training program you have devised protect the organization from leniency bias?

Exercise 12.3
Assessment Questions

Name_____ Group_____

1. Do you think the PASES is an accurate predictor of a supervisor's tendency to avoid confrontation and therefore rate more leniently? Explain your answer. Do you agree with the interpretation of your score?

2. How could accurate measurement be enhanced at Dee's Personalized Baskets?

3. What type of PFP system do you recommend for Dee's? Explain your answer.

13

C H A P T E R

STRATEGIES FOR IMPROVING QUALITY, PRODUCTIVITY, AND QUALITY OF WORK LIFE

OVERVIEW

As noted throughout this book, U.S. corporations have been struggling with a productivity growth crisis, particularly in the services sector, where the majority of new jobs and economic growth have developed in the last decade. We have discussed some of the theories behind the lackluster performance of the United States in productivity growth and product and service quality. A recurring theme of the book is that competitive advantage can be created and sustained by enhancing organizational capability in the form of more effective human resource management (HRM) programs. We have described the most effective approaches to human resource (HR) planning and job analysis, recruitment strategies, selection methods, training and development programs, performance management, and compensation systems which can create a competitive advantage when the focus is on customer requirements.

As we discussed in Chapter 1, employees now require an improved quality of work life (QWL) and seek greater involvement, challenge, and responsibility at work. Many firms have turned to new interventions designed to enhance product and service quality, productivity, and QWL, because they were faced with a growing body of research which supports the use of such interventions from a purely economic standpoint and with political demands to at least do something different. As we discussed in Chapter 12, pay for performance (PFP) is one such intervention for improving productivity and quality. Other quality and productivity programs are the focus of this chapter.

Over 210,000 companies requested applications for the government-sponsored Baldrige Awards in 1991 alone. This model of quality and productivity improvement has had a major impact upon the intervention and organizational change strategies of both large and small U.S. corporations. Even companies which have not formally applied for the award are implementing quality improvement programs based on the Baldrige criteria. As we discussed in Chapter 1, HRM activities are a critical component of the Baldrige criteria. We will explore these activities in this chapter, both in the context of the Baldrige criteria and as independent movements in quality and productivity improvement.

OBJECTIVES

After studying this chapter, you should be able to:

1. Understand the importance of strategies for enhancing U.S. productivity, quality, and QWL.

2. Describe ways to redesign the work environment to improve organizational capability and increase competitive advantage.

3. Describe several strategies for enhancing employee participation and involvement.

4. Explain what is involved in the total quality management (TQM) movement.

5. Describe the Baldrige criteria for quality and the relationship of these criteria to improvement programs.

6. Understand the relative effectiveness of various interventions for enhancing quality, productivity, and QWL.

DEFINING PRODUCTIVITY

As we discussed in Chapter 1, productivity can be defined in a variety of ways by an organization, depending on its goals (e.g., profits, customer satisfaction). The definitions also vary as a function of the type of firm and industry. Generally, productivity refers to a ratio of ouput to input. Inputs may include labor hours or costs, production costs, and equipment costs. Outputs may consist of sales, earnings, market share, and defects.[1] Many firms now assume or have shown that productivity is affected significantly by employees' knowledge, skills, abilities, attitudes, and behaviors. A variety of improvement programs start with this assumption and proceed with different intervention strategies.

DEFINING QUALITY

As we discussed in Chapter 10, quality can be assessed by looking at performance, reliability, conformance to standards, durability, and serviceability, and by complying with customers' requirements.[2] Three of the leading experts on quality, Philip Crosby, Joseph Juran, and W. Edwards Deming, offer their opinions on quality. Crosby defines *quality* as "conformance to the requirements . . . and doing what you said you were going to do." He also refers to quality as "freedom from waste, freedom from trouble, and freedom from failure." Juran says that *quality* involves "those features of what's being produced that respond to the customer's needs and that create the income." Deming defines *quality* as "meeting and exceeding the customer's needs and expectations— and then continuing to improve."[3]

Regardless of the specific definition, most experts agree that quality must be defined by the particular firm, with major input from internal and external customers. Quality cannot, however, simply refer to customer satisfaction. The customer must be satisfied, but at a low enough cost and expense to enable the organization to be competitive with other firms. Virtually anyone can achieve high quality if there is an infinite supply of money. The trick is to achieve high quality combined with the lowest possible cost. Recall our discussion in Chapter 10 identifying cost as one of the six criteria for performance assessment.

CRITERIA FOR ASSESSING PRODUCTIVITY AND QUALITY

Some of the more common measures and ratios used to assess productivity and quality include:

- Customer satisfaction
- Number of errors
- Market share
- Number of items sold
- Return on investment
- Net earnings per share
- Output per employee
- Customer complaints
- Rate of reworks
- Overtime worked
- Absenteeism
- Workmanship
- Defects or mistakes
- Dollar volume of sales
- Profit
- Response rate
- Labor costs per unit produced
- Accuracy
- Completion of projects
- Rate of breakage
- Employee job satisfaction
- Number of employee quits

ASSESSING THE NEEDS FOR QUALITY AND PRODUCTIVITY IMPROVEMENT

Since a variety of different measures can be used to estimate productivity and quality, each organization will need to determine its own measures based on its unique goals and objectives. For example, one firm may decide to focus its efforts on improving market share, while another may be more interested in decreasing its rate of defects. Certainly, multiple measures should be used to gauge organizational improvements. For example, at Northern Telecom, design engineering teams develop anywhere from three to seven performance ratios including re-

worked drawings as a percentage of total drawings, overdue drawings as a percentage of total drawings, and overtime hours as a percentage of total hours.[4]

Diagnosing the Problem(s)

To design programs to improve an organization's effectiveness, a firm must first determine whether poor productivity or quality actually exists. It may be that the firm is experiencing lower profits because the country is in a recession, or seasonal changes may be responsible. Reliable measurements of the key quality criteria are a necessary condition for measuring improvement. Productivity or quality interventions should not be initiated without reliable and valid measures of the key criteria. In fact, as we discussed in Chapters 1 and 2, clarity in customer requirements should be the driving force behind even the conceptualization of any intervention strategy. In Chapters 10 and 12, we discussed the need for valid measurements of individual or unit performance in the context of customer requirements in order to evaluate and reward exemplary performance.

A variety of factors could account for poor productivity or quality. We have discussed constraints on performance such as outdated equipment, unpredictable workloads, inefficient work flow, inappropriate job design, and poor or inadequate training as examples of HRM activities which can be very costly. Recall that we presented a list of 22 possible constraints on individual and group performance which were beyond the control of the worker or work unit, all variables which may account for low productivity or quality of work (see Figure 10.8). In addition to worker ability and motivation, some or all of these constraints may be changeable, given organizational circumstances. Intervention strategies should only be planned and implemented in the context of these possible constraints, the probability of changing them with some intervention strategy, and the extent to which the change is important in terms of customer requirements.

Most intervention strategies assume that the major causes of productivity or quality problems are employee abilities and motivation. However, leaders of the TQM movement suggest that at least 80 to 85 percent of the productivity and quality problems in firms are due to system factors, not people factors. TQM gurus such as Deming suggest that defective materials, poor product design, management errors, and outdated or poorly maintained equipment account for the vast majority of problems.[5] They contend that more emphasis should be given to improving these system factors and less to improving people factors. The TQM enthusiasts insist, however, that workers are a great source of information about these problems in terms of how to reduce or eliminate them.

Interestingly, these are the same factors that Japanese supervisors are likely to see as the causes of poor quality rather than workforce problems.[6]

The issue of how much poor productivity and quality are due to person and how much to system factors is currently under debate. Most experts would, however, agree that what is important is diagnosing the reasons for the performance problem prior to implementing any improvement strategies. All would agree that employees and, of course, customers are in great positions to identify problems and suggest improvements. You will recall that in Chapter 10 we proposed that performance raters be conceptualized as customers with the required products and services of internal customers linked to the requirements of external customers.

The strategies that are chosen to address the problems should be tailored to the specific problems. Today, many different approaches are being marketed as productivity- and quality-enhancing programs. For example, a plethora of consulting firms now use the Baldrige criteria as their intervention model. Organizations need to be careful to avoid the latest fad and to choose the program which will be best able to meet their specific needs in terms of customer requirements. The interventions they select may focus on changing the work environment or adopting a participative culture to enhance productivity or motivation. Some of the more popular programs are described in a later section.

DEFINING QUALITY OF WORK LIFE

Quality of work life refers to the level of satisfaction, motivation, involvement, and commitment individuals experience with respect to their lives at work. QWL is the degree to which individuals are able to satisfy their important personal needs (e.g., a need for independence) while employed by the firm. Companies interested in enhancing employees' QWL generally try to instill in employees the feelings of security, equity, pride, family democracy, ownership, autonomy, responsibility, and flexibility.[7] They try to treat employees in a fair and supportive manner, to open up communication channels at all levels, to offer employees opportunities to participate in decisions affecting them, and to empower them to carry through on assignments.

Characteristics of QWL Programs

Most QWL programs focus on some of the following features[8]:

- Employment conditions (safety, health, physical environment)

- Equity of pay, benefits, and other rewards
- Employment security
- Social interaction
- Self-esteem
- Democracy (participation in decision making)
- Worker satisfaction
- Income adequacy
- Voluntary participation by employees
- Training provided to employees, managers, and support staffs (e.g., HR professionals) on their new roles and responsibilities
- Availability of ongoing skills training
- Encouragement of multiskills development and job rotation
- Participation by the union, when relevant
- Team building

AWARDS FOR ORGANIZATIONAL IMPROVEMENTS

Deming Prize

One of the first awards established to recognize improvements in product or service quality was the Deming Prize, awarded in Japan. The Deming Price was established in 1950 by Union of Japanese Scientists and Engineers (JUSE), in honor of W. Edwards Deming. Deming is credited with assisting Japan to become a world leader since World War II. To Japanese firms, the Deming Prize is one of the most coveted awards. It is given to companies or divisions that excel in quality management. While many Japanese firms have received the award, the first U.S. firm to receive the award was Florida Power & Light, which is based in Miami. One joint U.S.-Japanese venture which won the award in 1982 was the company formed by Hewlett-Packard and Yokogawa Electric Corp.[9]

Malcolm Baldrige Award

The most significant award for quality in the United States is the Malcolm Baldrige National Quality Award, established by the U.S. Congress in 1987. Named for the late Commerce Secretary, the Baldrige is administered by the National Institute of Standards and Technology of the Department of Commerce. The President personally presents these prestigious awards in a ceremony in Washington.

As we have discussed in other chapters, the purpose of the Baldrige award is to promote national awareness of the importance of quality and to recognize U.S. firms for quality achievements. Seven categories are used to assess quality management and improvement. These are, in order of importance: customer service, HR utilization, quality results, quality assurance of products and services, leadership, strategic quality planning, and information and analysis. Figure 13.1 presents descriptions of each of these categories.

The Baldrige Award was modeled upon the Deming Prize, and both focus on quality improvements. The Baldrige Award allows any publicly or privately owned

FIGURE 13.1
MALCOLM BALDRIGE AWARD CRITERIA

A total of 1000 points is possible, in the following categories:

CUSTOMER SATISFACTION (300 POINTS)
This category considers the company's knowledge of the customer, overall customer service systems, responsiveness, and ability to meet requirements and expectations. It also examines current levels and trends in customer satisfaction.

HR UTILIZATION (150 POINTS)
This category examines the effectiveness of the company's efforts to develop and utilize the full potential of the workforce for quality, and to maintain an environment conducive to full participation, continuous improvement, and personal and organizational growth.

QUALITY RESULTS (150 POINTS)
This category considers quality levels and improvement based on objective measures. The measures are derived from analysis of customer requirements and expectations and analysis of business operations. In addition, the category's criteria compare a company's quality levels with those of competing firms.

QUALITY ASSURANCE OF PRODUCTS AND SERVICES (140 POINTS)
This category deals with the systematic approaches used by the company for total quality control of goods and services. It is based primarily on process design and control, including control of procured materials, parts, and services. It also examines the integration of quality control with continuous quality improvement.

LEADERSHIP (120 POINTS)
This category examines primarily how the senior executives create and sustain a clear and visible quality value system, along with a supporting management system. It also looks at the senior executives' and the company's leadership and support of quality developments, both inside and outside the company.

STRATEGIC QUALITY PLANNING (80 POINTS)
This category examines the company's planning process for retaining or achieving quality leadership, including the ways that a company integrates quality improvement planning into overall business planning. Also examined are the company's short- and long-term priorities in regard to achieving or sustaining a quality leadership position.

INFORMATION AND ANALYSIS (60 POINTS)
This category studies the scope, validity, use, and management of data and information that underlie the company's total quality system. Also examined is the adequacy of data and information to support a prevention-based approach to quality, using "management by fact."

business in the United States to apply, with the stipulation that only one division of a company can apply in a given year. Firms spend several years qualifying for the Deming Prize, using consultants from JUSE. Application for the Baldrige Award requires submission of up to 75 pages for a completed application form. The application for the Deming Prize may run up to 1000 pages.[10]

In 1990, Federal Express Corp. won the Baldrige Award for service industries; International Business Machines (IBM) in Rochester, New York, and Cadillac Motor Car Division won for manufacturing firms; and the Wallace Company won for small businesses. Winners must wait 5 years before reapplying for the award. The 1991 winners were all electronics manufacturing firms (Solectron, San Jose, California; Zytec, Eden Prairie, Minnesota; and Marlow Industries, Dallas, Texas). There were no winners in the services area.

The Baldrige award has spawned a consulting industry specializing in preparing companies for a Baldrige application and suggesting major interventions in the way the company does business and deals with its employees. Most U.S. companies that request the application materials simply use them to evaluate their own programs and make changes. Figure 13.2 presents details of the criteria in the HR utilization category. Many of the largest U.S. corporations have used the Baldrige criteria as a model for major organizational change processes. IBM and Ford are two notable examples.

The President's Award for Quality and Productivity Improvement

On November 2, 1989, President George Bush made the statement, "The improvement of quality in products and the improvement of quality in service—these are national priorities as never before."

The President's Award is given annually to an agency or major component of an agency in the federal government that has implemented TQM in an outstanding manner and is providing high-quality service to its customers. The criteria used to make the 1991 President's Award are based on a total of 200 points. They are allocated according to quality and productivity results (50 points), focus on the customer (40 points), quality assurance (30 points), top-management leadership and support (20 points), strategic planning (15 points), employee training and recognition (15 points), employee empowerment and teamwork (15 points), and measurement and analysis (15 points).

Other Quality Awards

In 1990, the Labor Investing for Tomorrow (LIFT) America Award was created to acknowledge successful

FIGURE 13.2
MALCOLM BALDRIGE CRITERIA FOR "HR UTILIZATION"

4.0 Human Resource Utilization (150 points)

4.1 Human Resource Management (20 points)

AREAS TO ADDRESS

a. How human resource plans are derived from the quality goals, strategies, and plans: (1) short term (1–2 years) and (2) longer term (3 years or more). Address major specific requirements such as training, development, hiring, involvement, empowerment, and recognition.

b. Key quality goals and improvement methods for human resource management practices such as hiring and career development.

c. How the company analyzes and uses its overall employee-related data to evaluate and improve the effectiveness of all categories and all types of employees.

Percent score _____

Notes:

(1) Human resource plans and improvement activities might include one or more of the following: mechanism for promoting cooperation such as internal customer/supplier techniques or other internal partnerships; initiatives to promote labor–management cooperation such as partnerships with unions; creation or modifications in recognition systems; mechanisms for increasing or broadening employee responsibilities; and education and training initiatives. They might also include developing partnerships with educational institutions to develop employees and to help ensure the future supply of well-prepared employees.

(2) "Types of employees" takes into account factors such as employment status, bargaining unit membership, and demographic makeup.

4.1 (+) Strengths and (–) Areas for Improvement

FIGURE 13.2 *(Continued)*

4.2 Employee Involvement (40 points)

Describe the means available for all employees to contribute effectively to meeting the company's quality objectives; summarize trends and current levels of involvement.

AREAS TO ADDRESS

a. Management practices and specific mechanisms, such as teams or suggestion systems, the company uses to promote employee contributions to quality objectives, individually and in groups. Summarize how and when the company gives feedback.

b. Company actions to increase employee authority to act (empowerment), responsibility, and innovation. Summarize principal goals for all categories of employees.

c. Key indicators the company uses to evaluate the extent and effectiveness of involvement by all categories and types of employees and how the indicators are used to improve employee involvement.

d. Trends and current levels of involvement by all categories of employees. Use the most important indicator(s) of effective employee involvement for each category of employee.

Percent score _____

Note:

Different involvement goals and indicators may be set for different categories of employees, depending upon company needs and upon the types of responsibilities of each employee category.

4.2 (+) Strengths and (–) Areas for Improvement

FIGURE 13.2 (Continued)

4.3 Quality Education and Training (40 points)

Describe how the company decides
what quality education and training
is needed by employees and how it
utilizes the knowledge and skills
acquired; summarize the types of
quality education and training
received by employees in all
employee categories

AREAS TO ADDRESS

a. (1) How the company assesses needs for
the types and amounts of quality education
and training received by all categories of
employees (describe how the needs assessment addresses work unit requirements to
include or have access to skills in problems
analysis and problem solving to meet their
quality objectives); (2) methods for the delivery
of quality education and training; and (3) how
the company ensures on-the-job reinforcement
of knowledge and skills.

b. Summary and trends in quality education and
training received by employees; (2) percent of
employees receiving quality education and
training in each employee category annually;
(3) average hours of quality education and
training annually per employee; (4) percent
of employees who have received quality
education and training; and (5) percent of
employees who have received education and
training in statistical and other quantitative
problem-solving methods.

c. Key methods and indicators the company uses
to evaluate and improve the effectiveness of its
quality education and training. Describe how
the indicators are used to improve the quality
education and training of all categories and
types of employees.

Note:

Quality education and training addresses the knowledge and skills employees need to meet the quality objectives associated with their
responsibilities. This may include basic quality awareness, problem solving, meeting customer requirements, and other quality-related
aspects of skills.

4.3 (+) Strengths and (–) Areas for Improvement

FIGURE 13.2 *(Continued)*

4.4 Employee Recognition and Performance Measurement (25 points)

AREAS TO ADDRESS

a. How recognition, reward, and performance measurement for individuals and groups, including managers, supports the company's quality objectives; (1) how quality relative to other business considerations such as schedules and financial results is reinforced; and (2) how employees are involved in the development and improvement of performance measurements.

b. Trends in recognition and reward of individuals and groups, by employee category, for contributions to quality.

c. Key indicators the company uses to evaluate and improve its recognition, reward, and performance measurement processes.

Percent score _____

4.4 (+) Strengths and (–) Areas for Improvement

FIGURE 13.2 *(Continued)*

4.5 Employee Well-Being and Morale (25 points)

Describe how the company maintains a work environment conducive to the well-being and growth of all employees; summarize trends and levels in key indicators of well-being and morale.

AREAS TO ADDRESS

a. How well-being and morale factors such as health, safety, satisfaction, and ergonomics are included in quality improvement activities. Summarize principal improvement goals, methods, and indicators for each factor relevant and important to the company's work environment. For accidents and work-related health problems, describe how root causes are determined and how adverse conditions are prevented.

b. Mobility, flexibility, and retraining in job assignments to support employee development and/or to accommodate changes in technology, improved productivity, changes in work processes, or company restructuring.

c. Special services, facilities, and opportunities the company makes available to employees. These might include one or more of the following: counseling, assistance, recreational or cultural, non-work-related education, and outplacement.

d. How and how often employee satisfaction is determined.

e. Trends in key indicators of well-being and morale. This should address, as appropriate: satisfaction, safety, absenteeism, turnover, attrition rate for customer-contact personnel, grievances, strikes, and worker compensation. Explain important adverse results, if any. For such adverse results, describe how root causes were determined and corrected, or give current status. Compare results on the most significant indicators with those of industry averages, industry leaders, and other key benchmarks.

Percent score _____

4.5 (+) Strengths and (−) Areas for Improvement

programs which improve the quality of the U.S. workforce. Sixteen awards are given in four categories: employee work life programs, employee training, school-to-work programs, and business-school partnerships. Recipients in 1990 included Monsanto, located in St. Louis, Missouri; Plumley Companies in Tennessee; American Telephone and Telegraph (AT&T) Communications; and the Thomas J. Lipton Company of Independence, Missouri. The impact of the LIFT America Award on American business and HRM is not yet known.

In addition to the national awards, many firms have established their own quality awards. For example, Westinghouse created the George Westinghouse Quality Award program as its own competition for quality. All divisions of the company are eligible for two awards, "most improved," and "best." The winners receive a trophy and a $200,000 check to spend any way they want within the firm's code of conduct.[11] Motorola, Xerox, International Business Machines (IBM), Domino's Pizza, and Mayflower Moving also have internal quality award programs.

PROGRAMS FOR ENHANCING QUALITY, PRODUCTIVITY, AND QWL

A variety of programs exist for improving quality, productivity, and the QWL experienced by employees. The following sections describe programs that emphasize redesigning work environments and programs that focus on enhancing employee participation. You will note that all fit within the Baldrige framework for quality improvement as well.

REDESIGNING WORK ENVIRONMENTS

As we discussed in Chapters 4 and 10 in particular, productivity and quality may be influenced by factors associated with the work environment. Unpredictable or excessive workloads, last-minute changes in the assigned work, lack of proper equipment, and inefficient work flow can severely inhibit the productivity of even the best employees. Thus, it is important to ensure that the work is designed to maximize productivity and quality. Several strategies exist for designing the work environment to meet an organization's goals for high quality and productivity. They include work site design, or ergonomics; robotics; computers and office automation; job design (e.g., job enrichment, job enlargement, job rotation); and alternative work arrangements (e.g., flexible work arrangements, permanent part-time work, job sharing, compressed workweek). All these interventions have implications for HRM activities.

Work Site Design or Ergonomics

DEFINING ERGONOMICS. *Ergonomics* is a science concerned with designing jobs and equipment to fit the physical abilities of individuals (e.g., their senses, movement patterns, physical limitations). The basis for redesigning the work site is research which illustrates that the physical aspects of the workplace influence employees' productivity and morale. For example, limited office privacy and work space have been shown to be related to lower employee job satisfaction.[12]

STRATEGIES FOR WORK REDESIGN. Some ways the work site can be redesigned are as follows[13]:

- Improve the work flow.
- Reduce repetitive physical motions (e.g., hand movements).
- Adjust the lighting.
- Allow employees to personalize the work area (e.g., with pictures, plants).
- Use pleasing colors in the office.
- Create private offices and work spaces.
- Supply lounges for rest breaks.
- Rearrange, adjust, or replace equipment, parts, and work spaces.
- Place team members close together so that they can interact easily.
- Provide adjustable office furniture to fit varying body physiques and particular work activities.

POPULARITY AND BENEFITS OF ERGONOMICS. For years, an ergonomic approach has been used to design jobs in such firms as Armco Steel, Inc.; Days Inn; Martin Marietta; and Hanes Corporation.[14] Recently, ergonomics has become even more popular as employees stay in the workforce longer and jobs are altered to meet their changing physical needs (e.g., better lighting for older workers). In addition, with the passage of the Americans with Disabilities Act (ADA) in 1990, the ergonomic approach has become increasingly popular to redesign jobs to accommodate individuals with disabilities (e.g., hearing impairments, loss of mobility).

Redesigning jobs according to principles of ergonomics is valuable since it helps individuals to accommodate to jobs, breaks down physical barriers, and makes jobs more accessible to individuals. For example, the hotel chain Days Inn has opened up opportunities for individuals who have physical handicaps that prevent them from using their hands to serve as reservationists. Such employees are able to type reservations by using special equipment built into head-and-chin sets.[15]

As noted in Chapter 3, the passage of the ADA mandates that organizations make reasonable accommodations in employment opportunities for individuals with disabilities. In many cases, this necessitates redesigning jobs to better accommodate individuals. While these efforts are costly in some cases, it is believed that the benefits will outweigh the costs in terms of enhanced organizational productivity and increases in the potential labor pool.

Robotics

U.S. firms have increasingly turned to robotics and other forms of automation to enhance organizational productivity and quality. Robots have become more prevalent in manufacturing industries such as General Motors (GM), Ford Motor Company, Whirlpool, and Chrysler.[16] One interesting trend is the way U.S. firms have shifted in their use of automation. In addition to adopting new technologies to reduce labor costs, companies are now implementing robotics to cut lead times, increase quality, and decrease inventories.[17]

ADVANTAGES OF ROBOTS. Robots are capable of performing a variety of tasks such as moving parts, tools, and equipment; cutting; welding; painting; detecting errors; sewing; sorting parts; testing products; and performing quality control. In addition, they can make and communicate decisions with minimal human supervision.[18] Relative to humans, robots are very cost-effective.[19] While an assembly line worker may cost a firm up to $24 an hour, including benefits, a robot can be operated for less than $6 an hour. Since one robot does the work of up to six employees, this can ultimately lead to tremendous cost savings.[20]

Robots work more efficiently than humans (i.e., their up time is 95 percent compared to 75 percent for blue-collar workers). They don't require benefits (e.g., sick leave, vacations, health insurance, retirement, pension, child care), and they don't have absenteeism problems. They can work multiple shifts; perform dirty, hazardous, or dangerous jobs; be exposed to toxic substances; detect defects; and perform operations to the same level of quality each time. Also, with robots, ethical counterproductivity problems (e.g., espionage, theft, discrimination) are not a concern.[21]

CAUTIONS WITH USING ROBOTS. There are some cautions associated with the use of robots in the workplace. First, of course, start-up costs may preclude their development or adaptation, especially in smaller firms. Second, organizations cannot just adopt the latest technologies as a quick fix. They need to be able to make compatible changes in management practices as well, and to show that the costs of automation are worth it to the firm. For example, GM committed 70 percent of its worldwide expenditures to modernization and auto-

mation of its domestic manufacturing base, yet had little to show for the expenses, at least in the short run.[22]

Plans to bring robots into the workplace may be met by employee concerns about job security, job changes, management attitudes toward workers, and the value of robots. Generally, lower-skilled employees fear losing their jobs or having to relearn their jobs. Higher-skilled employees, on the other hand, report more positive attitudes toward robots; they see robots as providing them with opportunities to expand their skills.[23] In part, employees' fears about job security are justified. Generally, each robot replaces several workers (from two to six). In fact, it is estimated that by the year 2000, robots will replace almost 3 million manufacturing employees, and that only 2 to 5 percent of the U.S. workforce will be employed in manufacturing. Not everyone, however, agrees that robots will displace large numbers of employees.[24]

Computers and Office Automation

Office automation and computers have been increasingly used by staff, managers, and professionals. In 1987 alone, U.S. companies added $17 billion of computers and process-control equipment.[25] Still, the United States lags behind many other countries in spending on automation through information systems.

Some of the equipment being used are word and image processors, audiovisual conferencing and graphics preparation machines, personal computers (PCs), electronic mail machines, and software specifically designed for HRM activities. Computers are now used routinely to analyze the quality of a product while it is still on the computer screen. For example, AT&T Bell Laboratories uses computers to remove potential problems from a product design. As we have mentioned throughout this book, more user-friendly HRM and managerial software becomes available every year, and more companies are adopting computer technology for HRM practices and quality improvement. HRM software is available for HR planning, equal employment opportunity (EEO) compliance, job analysis, personnel selection, and performance appraisal. Automated office tools and software could save American businesses up to $300 billion in the 1990s.[26]

With the increased automation of HRM and other managerial practices come some potential problems. Now that individuals communicate through fax machines and electronic mail, they may have fewer opportunities to refine their social and interpersonal skills. This could be detrimental in jobs where social skills are critical (e.g., sales, public relations). In addition, having information so readily accessible increases concerns about privacy, secrecy, and espionage. Also, employees may be resistant to using computers. They may be fearful of being unable to master the new technology or worried that they will be replaced once the computers are implemented.[27] In addition, they may be concerned (and justifiably so) that management will be able to better monitor their work output (e.g., by examining their computer usage). As we discussed in Chapter 10, performance monitoring via the computer is much more common today, and its control is the subject of pending federal legislation.

Dealing with Employee Concerns about Robots, Computers, and Automation

To reduce the resistance employees may have regarding robots and automation, several suggestions are offered:[28]

- Involve employees in the decision to automate or implement robots.
- Communicate implementation issues to all employees (i.e., when the robots or computers will be brought on, what jobs they will perform).
- Inform employees about the benefits of automation.
- Provide employees with training in use of the automated equipment, and evaluate the effects of the training.
- Allow employees time to practice and experiment with the new equipment.
- Get line management support for the new equipment.
- Address problems of displaced workers.
- Have a training staff on hand who can readily answer ongoing questions.
- Have a maintenance staff readily available to fix equipment failures.
- Upgrade the equipment in a timely fashion.

Job Design Approaches

JOB ENRICHMENT. In Chapter 4 we discussed job enrichment as one approach to enhancement of employees' motivation, satisfaction, and performance on the job. The Job Characteristics Model, developed by J. R. Hackman and G. R. Oldham in 1976, was presented as a popular enrichment model and process. As conceptualized in Figure 13.3, the job is redesigned by building in the five core job characteristics of skill variety, task identity, task significance, autonomy, and feedback. *Skill variety* refers to the degree to which tasks are performed that require different abilities and skills. *Task identity* means completing a whole and identifiable piece of work having a visible outcome, such as preparing a budget report or assembling a radio. *Task significance* refers to the degree to which the job has substantial importance or meaning. *Autonomy* refers to the degree of freedom and discretion allowed in scheduling work and work proce-

dures (e.g., scheduling breaks, time to work on projects). *Feedback* refers to the amount of direct information received from the job about performance effectiveness. As we discussed in Chapter 4, the extent to which a job is perceived to have these characteristics is measured by the Job Diagnostic Survey (JDS), sample items of which can be found in Figure 4.12. In many ways, the JDS is like an employee attitude survey which is used to assess workers' perspectives on major issues related to the workplace.

If the five core characteristics are built into the job, employees should experience several crucial psychological states, including finding the work *meaningful,* feeling *responsible* for work outcomes, and having *knowledge of the actual results* of work activities. The extent to which an employee experiences these psychological states should be related to important personal and work-related outcomes such as higher motivation, increased job satisfaction, and, to a lesser extent, lower absenteeism and turnover.[29]

Research results on the relationship between job redesign efforts and increased performance have been mixed.[30] Several variables may influence the degree to which the effects exist, including the employee's need for growth. According to the Job Characteristics Model, individuals with greater growth needs should respond more favorably to job redesign efforts, while employees with lower growth needs may be less positively influenced. At Monsanto, employees were allowed to redesign their work and to participate to a great extent in the decision-making process. This resulted in increased productivity, reduced costs, and improved customer service.[31]

JOB ROTATION. *Job rotation* is a job "redesign" technique only in the sense that individuals are given the opportunity to move from one job to another to learn and experience a variety of tasks. One of the benefits of job rotation is that it increases the variety of employees' skills and thus the number of employees who can perform any one type of job. This offers an employer more flexibility in staffing. Research on the effects of job rotation is not as impressive as that on job enrichment.[32]

USING JOB REDESIGN APPROACHES. Regardless of the job redesign approach used, employees' reactions will vary. Some are interested in receiving more challenge, autonomy, and responsibility on their jobs, and others prefer routine and predictable jobs. In addition, jobs vary in the degree to which they can easily be redesigned. Many employees and union representatives look at redesign efforts as an attempt to get more work out of them and, when the redesign is not combined with adjustments in compensation, as just another form of "exploitation."

FIGURE 13.3
JOB CHARACTERISTICS MODEL

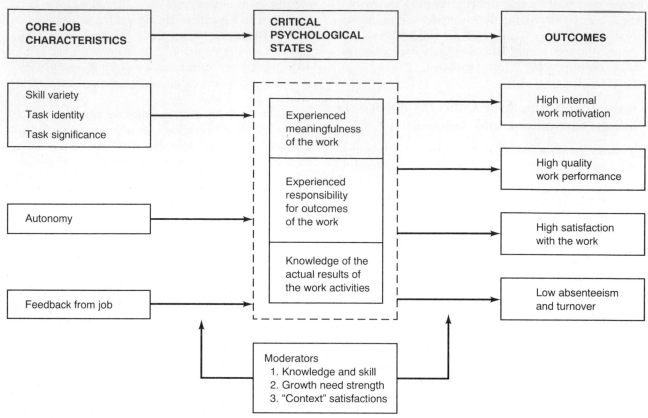

Source: J. R. Hackman and G. R. Oldham, *Work redesign.* Reading, MA: Addison-Wesley, 1980, p. 77. Reprinted with permission.

Alternative Work Arrangements

In recent years, many organizations have begun using a variety of new work arrangements. In fact, a recent survey of 521 of the nation's largest firms indicated that more than 90 percent offered alternative schedules ranging from flextime to job sharing to summers off.[33] These programs are designed to help employees to balance their work and nonwork lives (e.g., families, leisure, community activities).[34] Some of the more popular programs include flexible working arrangements (e.g., flextime, permanent part-time work, job sharing, and compressed work weeks). At US Sprint, all the programs mentioned here were established in 1990.[35]

FLEXIBLE WORKING ARRANGEMENTS. Nearly 30 percent of U.S. firms now offer some version of flextime. *Flextime* means that an employee has flexible starting and stopping hours. Generally, most employees are required to be at work during the middle (core) of the day (i.e., between ten a.m. and two p.m.). About 15 percent of employers make nine a.m. to three p.m. their core

period, while another 28 percent make nine a.m. to four p.m. their core period.

Flextime has been shown to be effective in relieving work-family conflicts among private-sector employees.[36] In addition, the federal government's survey of 325,000 employees who participated in a flextime program discovered that 90 percent of them believed the program was at least somewhat important in resolving their work-family problems.[37] Flextime has been related to less tardiness, less absenteeism, and less sick leave.[38] In fact, in a study of 13 firms using flextime, absenteeism was reduced by up to 50 percent. Flextime has also led to increased productivity and quality of work.[39]

One disadvantage associated with flextime is the difficulty in scheduling meetings and trying to locate employees. Also, it may require the use of time clocks, which are often perceived by employees as a managerial control mechanism. Flextime may not be appropriate for all jobs. Where tasks are highly interdependent (e.g., on an assembly line), it may be more difficult to administer.[40]

Today, some firms are expanding on the idea behind flextime. For instance, Barrios Technology offers flexible work hours and flexible workplaces (*flexplace*). Flexplace offers employees the option of working at home or in a satellite office close to home. At Pacific Bell, 70 percent of the employees working at home reported higher job satisfaction.[41] *Telecommuting* is another option which enables employees to work at home, using computers, video displays, and telephones to transmit letters and completed work back to the office. This program has become more popular for a variety of professional and technical jobs.[42] In other flexible arrangements, Continental Savings Bank in New Haven, Connecticut, allows some employees to leave work early during the school year and to take summer vacations without pay in order to spend more time with their children.[43]

PERMANENT PART-TIME WORK. A recent work arrangement is the use of permanent part-time work. While part-time work has always been available on a temporary basis for some jobs, it has only recently been applied on a permanent basis to professional jobs. Among the companies offering permanent part-time work are AT&T, Barrios Technology, Digital Equipment Corporation, Du Pont Corporation, Drake Business Schools, Arthur Anderson, and Herman Miller.[44] While little research is available on the effectiveness of these changes, research in some firms showed that part-timers were more productive than full-timers and had lower absenteeism.[45]

JOB SHARING. Job sharing refers to a situation in which two people divide the responsibilities of a regular, full-time job. For example, one person may work mornings, while the other person works afternoons. Job sharing has only recently gained in popularity as a viable work arrangement in U.S. firms. For example, Aetna Life & Casualty Insurance Company now has 125 job-sharing teams.[46] Job sharing is still not used, however, to a very large extent in U.S. firms.[47]

Job sharing provides the organization more staffing flexibility and enables the firm to attract and keep good employees. In addition, one study found that each member of a job-sharing team does close to 80 percent of the work of a full-time employee, rather than the expected 50 percent.[48] Employees favor job sharing because it allows them to reduce their work hours while keeping their professional skills up to date.[49]

COMPRESSED WORKWEEKS. One innovative arrangement allows employees to work fewer days during the week, with longer hours per day. For example, employees may work four 10-hour days instead of five 8-hour days. This type of work schedule has been an option for years for workers in some occupations, including firefighters, police officers, nurses, hair stylists, and technicians. Today, it is being used in other occupations and

firms, including tellers at Citibank and operators at US Sprint.[50] Using compressed workweeks has shown a number of benefits for employers. One benefit is that this arrangement allows employees to better accommodate their other life demands (e.g., parental roles), so that they are not forced to leave the firm. In addition, it allows an organization to make better use of its equipment and resources. Employee morale and productivity are higher, and tardiness and absenteeism are lower.[51] There are some drawbacks, however. Understaffing, scheduling meetings, and coordinating team projects are three common problems. Perhaps one of the most serious concerns is the increased employee fatigue brought on by working longer hours on a given day.[52]

PARTICIPATIVE INTERVENTIONS

Participative programs for enhancing QWL have been in existence for years. They have become even more popular in recent years due to the perceived importance of the Baldrige Award and the growing recognition that such programs work. The Wallace Company, for example, a Houston-based industrial pipe, valve, and fittings distributor, instituted a quality program at the recommendation of one of its major customers in order to improve on-time delivery and invoice accuracy, and thus to keep the customer's business. Numerous other companies have adopted participative employee involvement (EI) programs in recent years; among them are Bell South, First Union Bank, Procter & Gamble, and Upjohn.

Generally, it is believed that involving employees in decision-making processes will result in improved job attitudes and cooperation, and reduced turnover, absenteeism, and grievances. These effects are, however, contingent upon whether there is sufficient time to involve employees in decision making and upon whether employees have the ability to participate and an interest in participating.

Three approaches to EI have been identified: parallel suggestion involvement systems, job involvement systems, and high-involvement work systems.[53]

In *parallel suggestion involvement systems*, job design, organizational structures, and managerial roles are not altered. Employees are allowed to participate in problem identification, problem solving, and decision making through such vehicles as quality circles (QCs), task forces, opinion surveys, and suggestion systems. In these forms of involvement, participation is something that occurs outside employees' regular job assignments.

Job involvement systems may be individual (e.g., job enrichment) or group-based [e.g., autonomous work groups (AWGs) or self-managing teams]. In job enrichment, jobs are changed so that individual workers are allowed more variety, autonomy, feedback, and personal growth. In group-based strategies, work is organized around teams, and work groups are allowed to take over certain "management" functions. In job involvement systems, the job design is altered; however, the organizational structure and managerial roles are not changed.

High-involvement work systems combine job involvement and a team-oriented work design with changes in organizational structure and managerial roles. These systems typically have fewer layers of management than traditional work systems. Such systems can operate very efficiently and with high flexibility.

The three EI approaches can be useful in different situations. What is important is that the EI approach must match the current operating system and practices of the organization. Sometimes EI is implemented in direct contradiction of current organizational systems. When this happens, EI is more likely to fail than it is to change the organization.

Survey Systems*

A major component of the scoring system for the Malcolm Baldrige Award involves accounting for the state of the human organization through participative programs. In addition, a growing body of research shows that participative programs are effective in increasing productivity as well as product and service quality. As a result, greater attention is being paid to development of tools for analysis and control of both the HRM function and the human organization. These tools may be used for measuring the performance of the HR system, evaluating that performance, and initiating corrective action when needed to bring performance in line with organizational objectives. The measurements reflect the attitudes, motivations, and satisfaction levels which characterize the human organization. A number of leading firms—including IBM; Xerox; General Electric (GE); Texas Instruments, Inc.; and Motorola—have pioneered the development of survey systems which facilitate these measurements. On the basis of the winners of past Baldrige Awards, it is obvious that Baldrige judges place considerable weight on formal survey feedback systems.

Survey results reveal an organization's strengths and weaknesses, and provide a means for comparing results with norms established by data from other organizations as well as with internal norms established in other departments. An example of a typical employee survey and definitions of the factors which are assessed are shown in Figures 13.4 and 13.5.

---

*Contributed by Fred E. Schuster.

In addition to their measurement function, employee surveys may also be used to facilitate planned organization change and team building based on feedback and discussion of the survey data.[54] Companies often begin the review of survey data by comparing the organization's data to outside or internal norms, to establish an initial benchmark. If the same survey is repeated in subsequent years, what becomes especially valuable is the ability to compare data for a given year for the organization as a whole and for various subdivisions (such as departments or divisions) with the data from previous years. Analysis of the trend of data over several years is a particularly powerful tool for understanding what is going on in an organization.

Many organizations also find it useful to compare the data (and trends) for different units across the organization so as to pinpoint specific parts of the organization where particular issues or concerns may be arising. This approach facilitates the development of action strategies specific to individual parts of the organization as well as other action strategies relevant for the entire organization. Survey data also promote the early identification of difficulties and permit timely response before minor concerns become major issues.

Along with opinion surveys, a variety of participative interventions exist, ranging from informal suggestion systems to formalized TQM programs or AWGs. Some of the more popular programs are described in a later section.

The Relationship between Participative Programs and Unions

In designing participative interventions, employers must be sure that the programs are not directly related to union activities. Committees should not serve as a bargaining unit for employees nor be connected to a union-organizing drive. In addition, the committees should be composed primarily of volunteer employee representatives, more than management members. The U.S. Department of Labor estimates that at least one-third of all major companies have some form of employee participation program. Numerous cases are now before the National Labor Relations Board (NLRB) to test whether such programs are legal under federal labor law. Many labor attorneys maintain that QCs and self-directed teams interfere with a worker's right to form independent labor organizations. (We will discuss this issue at greater length in Chapter 14.)

The design and implementation of QWL programs should be done with the agreement or participation of the union. For example, when the Aluminum Company of America (ALCOA) plants located in Tennessee wanted to use more participative approaches and work teams, the

FIGURE 13.4
EXAMPLE OF AN EMPLOYEE OPINION SURVEY

Human Resources Index

The objective of this survey is to determine how members of this organization feel about the effectiveness with which the organization's human resources are managed. The survey provides you an opportunity to express your opinions in a way that is constructive. Your views will be valuable in assisting the organization to evaluate and improve its performance.

The survey is to be done anonymously. Please **do not put your name** on the response sheet or identify your response in any way. Responses can in no way be traced to any individual. The frank and free expression of your own opinions will be most helpful to the organization.

Listed below are a series of statements. After you have read each statement, please decide the extent to which the statement describes your own situation and your own feelings, using the following scale:

A) almost never
B) not often
C) sometimes (i.e., about half the time)
D) often
E) almost always

Then, using a No. 2 pencil darken the appropriate box on the response sheet. For example, if you believe that the statement is true "sometimes" darken block C on the answer sheet next to the number corresponding to the indicated statement.

Questions 65 and 66 should be answered in **pencil** on the back of the **response sheet.**

When you have completed the survey, please return the response sheet and this survey form in accordance with the directions in the cover letter.

IN THIS ORGANIZATION:

1. There is sufficient communication and sharing of information between groups.

2. The skills and abilities of employees are fully and effectively utilized.

3. Objectives of the total organization and my work unit are valid and challenging.

4. The activities of my job are satisfying and rewarding.

5. I have received the amount and kind of training which I need and desire to do my job well.

6. Leadership in this organization is achieved through ability.

7. Rewards are fairly and equitably distributed.

8. First-level supervision is of a high quality.

9. Management has a high concern for production and effectively communicates this concern.

10. My job provides ample opportunity for a sense of individual responsibility.

11. There is a sense of loyalty and belonging among members of this organization.

.
.
.

63. By and large, most members of this organization are sensitive, perceptive, and helpful to one another.

64. In general, complete and accurate information is available for making organizational decisions.

- -

65. The things I like best about this organization are: _____

66. The things I would most like to change are: _____

Source: Fred. E. Schuster, Professor of Management, Florida Atlantic University, Boca Raton, FL 33431. Copyright © 1977. Reprinted with permission.

FIGURE 13.5
FACTOR DEFINITIONS FROM AN EMPLOYEE ATTITUDE SURVEY

1. **Reward system (RWD):** Compensation, benefits, perquisites, and other (tangible and intangible) rewards.
2. **Communication (COM):** Flow of information downward, upward, and across the organization.
3. **Organization effectiveness (OE):** Level of confidence in the overall abilities and success of the organization; how well the organization achieves its objectives.
4. **Concern for people (CP):** The degree to which the organization is perceived as caring for the individuals who work for it.
5. **Organization objectives (OO):** The extent to which individuals perceive the organization to have objectives that they can understand, feel proud of, and identify with.
6. **Cooperation (COP):** The ability of people throughout the organization to work effectively together to achieve shared goals.
7. **Intrinsic satisfaction (IS):** Rewards that people receive from the work itself (sense of achievement, pride in a job well done, growth and development, feeling of competence).
8. **Structure (STC):** Rules and regulations, operating policies and procedures, management practices and systems, the formal organization structure, and reporting relationships.
9. **Relationships (REL):** Feelings which people have about others in the organization.
10. **Climate (CLM):** The atmosphere of the organization, the extent to which people see it as a comfortable, supportive, pleasant place to work.
11. **Participation (PAR):** Opportunity to contribute one's ideas, to be consulted, to be informed, and to play a part in decision making.
12. **Work group (WG):** Feelings about the immediate group of people with whom one works on a daily basis.
13. **Intergroup competence (ITG):** The ability of separate work groups to work smoothly and effectively together to accomplish shared objectives.
14. **First-level supervision (FLM):** Confidence which members of the organization have in the competence and integrity of first-line supervisors.
15. **Quality of management (QM):** Confidence which members of the organization have in the competence and integrity of middle and higher management.

Source: Fred E. Schuster, Professor of Management, Florida Atlantic University, Boca Raton, FL 33431. Copyright © 1979. Reprinted with permission.

company involved the unions in the discussions. Likewise, GM made sure it had union agreement for its QWL programs.[55] Cadillac used joint teams of union and management representatives at all plants to outline a training plan for quality improvement. Skilled hourly workers were given training in process modeling, statistical methods, health and safety, and leadership skills.[56] This program helped Cadillac to earn the Baldrige Award. Figure 13.6 illustrates the strategy adopted by Ford to enhance employee involvement in collaboration with the United Auto Workers (UAW).

The Excelling through Teamwork (ETT) program initiated by the Thomas J. Lipton Company was administered in partnership with Teamsters Local 838. This program used employee involvement in decision making and statistical process controls to improve quality and productivity. Similarly, employees of AT&T Communications receive training and career development assistance from the Alliance for Employee Growth and Development, a joint labor-management training program in Somerset, New Jersey. These two programs were among the first recipients of the LIFT America Award given in 1990.[57]

While the UAW has supported the use of participative programs, unions have generally opposed them because of concerns over losing their power in organizations. Most unions maintain that collective bargaining between management and a union may be necessary to reach agreement on the use of a participative program. Strategies for dealing with unions are described in more detail in Chapters 14 and 15.

Quality Circles

DEFINING QC. A *quality circle* is a small group of employees (usually 7 to 10) who volunteer to meet several hours each week to address productivity and quality problems. The members identify, analyze, and make recommendations about problems in their work area. Usually, the employees are members of a work unit from the same department. Often, their supervisor serves as the circle leader, while an HR staff member is a facilitator who helps to guide the circle through the problem-solving process. The primary topic of discussion of most circles is quality issues, although they do consider other topics. Figure 13.7 illustrates some of the more common issues for discussion. Generally, QC programs address the quality of the product, the quality of service, and QWL.[58]

DEVELOPING A QC PROGRAM. Most QC programs in U.S. firms are similarly developed, although there are some differences in how they are tailored to particular firms. Generally, a QC program involves six primary phases, as follows: (1) start-up, (2) initial problem solving, (3) presentation and approval of initial suggestions, (4) implementation of solutions, (5) expansion and continued problem solving, and (6) decline. Figure 13.8 describes the major activities which take place in each phase and the destructive forces which might exist.[59] Most QCs exist for several years, usually until the members run out of problems to address or lose interest in the activity.

FIGURE 13.6
FORD MOTOR COMPANY'S PARTICIPATIVE MANAGEMENT/EMPLOYEE INVOLVEMENT MODEL

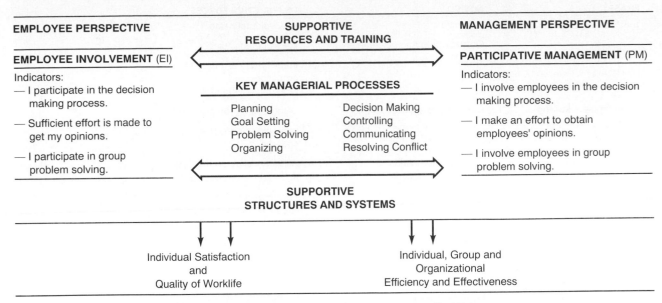

Source: P. A. Banas. The relationship between participative management and employee involvement at Ford Motor Company. In R. W. Beatty, H. J. Bernardin, and J. E. Nickel (eds.), *The productivity sourcebook.* Amherst, MA: Human Resource Development Press, 1987, p. 266. Reprinted with permission.

USING A QC PROGRAM.   QC programs can be used in a variety of ways, including (1) collecting ideas for work improvements from those closest to the work itself (i.e., the work group), (2) providing opportunities for problem solving, (3) dealing with special projects on a temporary basis, (4) enhancing personal and professional growth of QC members, (5) team building, and (6) help-

ing the organization make the transition to a more participative culture. Regarding the last use, some organizations start out implementing QC programs to get employees adjusted to the idea of being more involved. They have QC members work on identifying and solving problems. Following this, they change the voluntary circle meetings to on-the-job staff meetings, provide training for QC members, and then form semiautonomous work groups.[60]

A variety of suggestions have been given for ensuring that QCs are used effectively in organizations. They include:[61]

FIGURE 13.7
TOPICS FOR CONSIDERATION BY QUALITY CIRCLES

AREAS OF INTEREST	PERCENTAGE OF ACTIVITY
Quality	22
Efficiency	12
Cost	11
Equipment	10
Morale	10
Process control	9
Missed work (absenteeism)	8
Safety	4
Learning	3
Others	11

Source: A. S. Warren, Jr. The nature of quality circles. In J. E. Ross and W. C. Ross (eds.), *Japanese quality circles and productivity.* Reston, VA: Reston Publishing Co., 1982, p. 29. Reprinted with permission.

- Obtain managerial support and involvement for the program.
- Identify goals for the program and evaluation criteria.
- Do not expect the QC program to solve all problems in the organization.
- Make sure managers realize that any changes will take time.
- Inform all employees about the philosophy and goals of the program.
- Keep the program voluntary.
- Select group members based on their technical expertise and their support of the program's goals.
- Prepare individuals for their new roles in a participative culture.
- Provide ongoing training for participants in the techniques to be used.

FIGURE 13.8
DEVELOPMENTAL ASPECTS OF A QUALITY CIRCLE

PHASE	ACTIVITY	DESTRUCTIVE FORCES
Start-up	Publicize	Low volunteer rate
	Obtain funds and volunteers	Inadequate funding
	Train	Inability to learn group processes and problem-solving skills
Initial problem solving	Identify and solve problems	Disagreement on problems
		Lack of knowledge of operations
Approval of initial suggestions	Present and have initial suggestions accepted	Resistance by staff groups and middle management
		Poor presentation and suggestions because of limited knowledge
Implementation	Relevant groups act on suggestions	Prohibitive costs
		Resistance by groups that must implement
Expansion of problem solving	Form new groups	Member-nonmember conflict
	Old groups continue	Raised aspirations
		Lack of problems
		Expense of parallel organization
		Savings not realized
		Rewards wanted
Decline	Fewer groups meet	Cynicism about program
		Burnout

Source: Reprinted by permission of the *Harvard Business Review.* From Quality circles after the fad, by E. E. Lawler III and S. A. Burns, *63*(1). Copyright © 1985 by the President and Fellows of Harvard College; all rights reserved.

- Provide training for managers as coordinators.
- Provide training for support staff who will serve as facilitators. (For example, Polaroid trains its HR staff to be facilitators.)
- Start with a pilot test of the program in a supportive department.
- Implement the suggestions made by employees.
- Provide recognition for the employees' efforts.

POPULARITY AND EFFECTIVENESS OF QC PROGRAMS. The use of QC programs in the United States increased steadily in the last decade. One estimate is that over 90 percent of Fortune 500 companies now have QC programs.[62] Some of the firms using QCs are GE, IBM, GM, Honeywell, Bethlehem Steel, Ford Motor Company, Hughes Aircraft, Westinghouse, Honeywell, Digital Equipment, Control Data, Xerox, Procter & Gamble, Lockheed, Boeing, Martin Marietta, Radio Corporation of America (RCA), and TRW.[63]

One of the reasons why QC programs are popular in the U.S. today may be that they have been used so successfully by Japan. In the 1950s Japan began a full-scale effort to improve product quality. By the early 1980s, more than 10 million employees were QC members and had been responsible for annual savings up to $25 billion.[64] As is well known, Japan has become a world leader in productivity and has set quality standards in electronics, steel, automobiles, and photographic equipment. Most Japanese firms are highly committed to making continuous improvements through quality circles.[65]

QC programs have been shown to reduce costs and improve productivity and quality.[66] Research is mixed, however, with some studies indicating positive effects on productivity, quality, absenteeism, and job attitudes, and other studies indicating no changes or less positive results.[67]

Autonomous Work Groups or Self-Managing Teams

DEFINING AWGS OR SELF-MANAGING WORK TEAMS.

Autonomous work groups (also known as *self-managing work teams*) are employee groups with a high degree of decision-making responsibility and behavioral control for completing their work. Usually, the team is given "empowerment" or responsibility for producing the entire product or service. A team essentially replaces the boss by taking over responsibilities for scheduling, hiring, ordering, and firing. Digital Equipment Corporation, Rubbermaid, and Corning are examples of major manufacturing facilities with work teams, but the approach is also catching on in the services sector. At the team-based Chrysler plant in New Castle, Indiana, team members communicate with customers and do all hiring.[68] AWGs have some similarities to QCs since they are based on employee participation, and yet they also have some differences. Figure 13.9 compares the two interventions in several domains.

AWGs usually elect an internal leader who also serves as a full-time member. Management may appoint an external leader or coordinator. The external leader serves primarily as a facilitator rather than as a supervisor. He or she may assist the group in receiving feedback on the quality and quantity of their performance from the perspective of internal and external customers as well as make any structural changes in the work design. The coordinator is also responsible for helping the group acquire needed resources (e.g., equipment) and technical assistance.[69]

ACTIVITIES OF AWGS OR SELF-MANAGING WORK TEAMS.

AWGs or most self-managing work teams are involved in a number of different activities, including:[70]

- Recording quality control statistics
- Making scheduling assignments
- Solving technical problems
- Setting group or team goals
- Resolving internal conflicts
- Assessing group or team performance
- Making task assignments to group or team members
- Preparing a budget
- Training members
- Selecting new members
- Allocating pay raises for members

SUGGESTIONS FOR USING AWGS OR SELF-MANAGING WORK TEAMS.

For AWGs or self-managing work teams to be effective, several conditions are necessary. Training is necessary for group or team members in a variety of human relations skills (such as problem solving, group dynamics, conflict resolution, cooperation, and participation) and technical skills (such as statistical quality control and budget preparation). The

FIGURE 13.9
A COMPARISON OF QC PROGRAMS AND SELF-MANAGING TEAMS

CHARACTERISTIC	PARTICIPATION CONCEPT	
	QUALITY CIRCLES	SELF-MANAGING TEAMS
Implementation	Mostly in mature plants	Mostly in new, "green-field" sites
Ease of startup	Moderate in ease and speed	Much more difficult and lengthy
Participation	Usually totally voluntary	Usually not voluntary, but individual participation levels vary
Membership	Subset of work group	The entire work group
Leadership	Initial leader, frequently a supervisor, may be elected or appointed by management	Internal leader elected; external leader appointed by management
Type and frequency of problems	One at a time, usually a larger issue for a long period, selected from a wide range	Many small day-to-day issues, selected from a wider range
Implementation authority	Usually recommend; sometimes implement	Usually implement
Motivational impact	Moderate to strong	Stronger
Relationship to existing organization	An overlay	Largely replaces existing organization

Source: H. P. Sims, Jr., and J. W. Dean, Jr. Beyond quality circles: Self-managing teams. *Personnel, 62*(1), 1985, 25–32.
Reprinted by permission of publisher from *Personnel,* January 1985. © 1985 American Management Association, New York. All rights reserved.

training should be updated to keep individuals current and focused on the goals of the team. Training is also necessary for managers in their new roles as facilitators, especially since the new roles require them to have very different relationships with their subordinates. In addition to training, AWGs and teams need to receive current information and resources to carry out their work assignments, as well as time and space to engage in group or team activities.

POPULARITY AND EFFECTIVENESS OF AWGS OR SELF-MANAGING WORK TEAMS. By the mid 1980s, over 200 plants in the U.S. were reported to be using AWGs or self-managing work teams.[71] Some managers believe that self-managing teams or AWGs help to increase productivity anywhere from 20 to 50 percent and to reduce scrap, lost time, and poor-quality products. Chrysler, for example, reports reduced production costs, defects, and employee absenteeism. In other cases, results have been mixed regarding the effects on productivity.[72]

Employees report that team membership provides them with more autonomy, flexibility, skills variety, training opportunities, and, in some cases, financial benefits (e.g., group-based bonuses). It is not surprising, then, that firms have found that employees who are members of AWGs or self-managing teams experience higher job satisfaction and better morale.[73] One caution that should be noted is that it often takes up to 2 years for some of the positive effects of these programs to materialize. Managers need to be patient in their expectations of results, and they should guarantee job security in order to enable employees to feel comfortable enough to take risks and to be creative and innovative.

Total Quality Management

DEFINING TQM. *Total quality management* is a participative intervention involving every employee and manager in the organization. It involves a significant change in an organization's culture, including its goals, mission, philosophy, and procedures. The major emphasis of the TQM movement is to make every employee and every manager responsible for making continuous improvements in the quality of the company's services and products in order to satisfy customers' needs.[74] This is critical because it has been shown that U.S. manufacturing firms can spend up to 30 percent of their operating budgets on just detecting and correcting errors.[75]

A *customer,* in this context, is anyone who is the recipient of a product or service, whether he or she is inside or outside the firm. For example, a receptionist's customers could include a boss who gives the reception-

ist a report to be typed, employees in other departments who exchange files and information with the receptionist, and individuals who phone in their requests regarding the firm. At Federal Express and American Express, employees are responsible for developing formal contracts with their customers that outline what is expected of them. Performance criteria are defined by customers, not by supervisors.[76]

GUIDING PRINCIPLES OF TQM. Many of the major principles of TQM are based on the ideas of two Americans—W. Edwards Deming and Joseph M. Juran, who are experts on statistical process control and quality management. Their ideas have been embraced by Japan since the 1950s. It has only been in the last decade, however, that U.S. firms have paid much attention to issues of quality or to the recommendations of Deming and Juran.[77] Some of their ideas are described below.[78]

- Meet the customer's requirements on time, the first time, and 100 percent of the time. This involves identifying who the customers are and clarifying what their requirements or expectations are.
- Strive to have 0 percent defects and to do error-free work. For example, at Motorola, employees are focused on achieving a goal called "Six Sigma" by 1992, which means no more than 3.4 defects per million Motorola products and services.[79]
- Manage by prevention. Defects and errors can occur at any part of the process from design of a product to completion. Don't wait until after the product is completed to look for defects. Make sure that you do not build defects into any phase. Trace all errors to their sources and correct them.
- Use statistical process control (SPC) methods. SPC gauges the performance of the manufacturing process by monitoring changes in whatever is being produced. The intent is to detect potential problems before they lead to poor-quality products, to determine the reason for deviations, and to adjust the process to make it more stable.[80]
- Measure the cost of quality. Illustrate the difference in the costs incurred for preventing errors *before* products are produced versus detecting and correcting them *after* they have been produced.

DEMING'S 14 PRINCIPLES. Many organizations (e.g., Cadillac, American Express, Johnson & Johnson) have profited by seminars on Deming's philosophy of quality improvement. He argued for 14 points that should be followed.[81] These are:

1. Create constancy of purpose for improvement of product and service.

2. Adopt the new philosophy.
3. Cease dependence on mass inspection.
4. End the practice of awarding business on the basis of price tag alone. Instead, minimize total cost by working with fewer suppliers.
5. Improve constantly and forever every process for planning, production, and service.
6. Institute modern methods of training, using statistics.
7. Adopt and institute leadership. Focus supervision on helping people to do a better job.
8. Drive out fear. Encourage two-way communication.
9. Break down barriers between staff areas. Encourage problem solving through teamwork.
10. Eliminate slogans, exhortations, and targets for the workforce.
11. Eliminate numerical quotas for the workforce and numerical goals for people in management.
12. Remove barriers that rob people of pride of workmanship.
13. Encourage education and self-improvement for everyone.
14. Take action to accomplish the transformation.

SUGGESTIONS FOR TQM PROGRAMS. Once a TQM program is designed and ready to be implemented, there are a variety of suggestions for enhancing the TQM experience.[82] These are:

- Make the program organizationwide.
- Obtain the support of managers at all levels.
- Prioritize problem areas, and start work on only a few critical problems.
- Provide ongoing training for employees in the importance of quality, statistical control methods, analytical skills, and strategies for solving quality problems. Allow employees opportunities to use their new skills on the job.
- Encourage and facilitate collaboration between divisions in the firm (i.e., across cross-functional boundaries).
- Provide training in TQM to suppliers and don't accept poor quality from them. At Motorola, for example, suppliers who do not state intentions for applying for the Baldrige Award are dropped.[83]
- Use reward systems to support the participative culture. Make rewards congruent with the work design (i.e., use group-based rewards if the intent is to foster a collaborative environment).
- Have supervisors provide recognition to employees.
- Use natural work units for the teams.
- Recognize that the focus is on *continuous* improvements (i.e., that improvements are never completed).

- Give employees the tools and resources they will need to analyze and solve problems.
- Follow up on the suggestions made by employees.
- Keep quality improvements cost-effective.

POPULARITY OF TQM. In the past decade, TQM programs have become extremely popular in a variety of private- and public-sector organizations, including manufacturing firms, service industries, and government agencies. Because they have suffered severe market share losses due to poor quality, the textile, steel, automobile, and major appliance industries have become committed to TQM principles. Some of the organizations that have implemented TQM include AT&T, Du Pont, Hewlett-Packard, Kodak, Cadillac, Federal Express, L. L. Bean, Toyota, Xerox, Motorola, Baxter Health Care, Corning Glass Works, IBM, GM, McCormick Spice, Westinghouse, Tennessee Valley Authority (TVA), Wallace Company, M&M Mars, Florida Power & Light, Procter & Gamble, Alcoa, and Ford Motor Company.[84] One reason for the popularity of TQM is its effectiveness in Japan and other leading countries. For example, TQM programs have been credited with a large role in making the Japanese world leaders in quality.[85] Many TQM efforts have been specifically developed and implemented in the context of the Baldrige Awards. For example, Figure 13.10 presents a TQM model developed in the context of the seven Baldrige categories.

EFFECTIVENESS OF TQM. Although few empirical studies have been conducted, both Juran and Deming have reported numerous case examples to illustrate that TQM is a cost-effective strategy. Juran stated that in a typical firm with $1 billion in revenues, the average savings per TQM project exceeds $100,000 a year. With training costs ranging from $5000 to 20,000, Juran maintains that the average firm will see a 5 to 20 times payback in the first year, with improved productivity, market share, and profitability over the long term.[86] Other evidence suggests that TQM programs are effective at improving quality and reducing the costs of rework, as well as improving job satisfaction, internal communications, and work procedures.[87]

In many firms using TQM, the numbers speak for themselves. At Toyota, production became more efficient (i.e., fewer workers were needed to produce the same number of cars), and fewer defects due to quality problems were found.[88] At IBM, revenue per employee increased 35 percent from 1986 to 1989, and the time to develop a new mid-range computer was reduced in half. Cadillac, a 1990 Baldrige Award winner, applied Deming's process model for quality improvement, and has achieved reductions of up to 71 percent in reliability problems since

FIGURE 13.10
MODEL OF TQM IN THE CONTEXT OF THE BALDRIGE AWARD CRITERIA

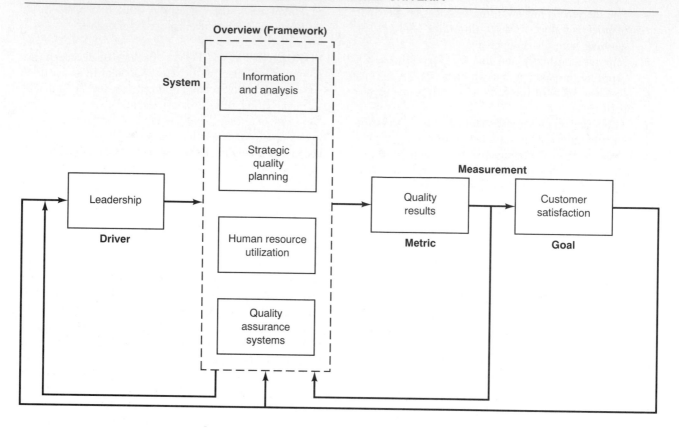

1986. Cadillac also found a 16 percent increase in customer satisfaction from 1985 to 1989. At Wallace Company, between 1987 and 1990, sales increased 69 percent, and operating profits increased 7.4 times.[89] A joint venture of the United States and Japan, formed by Hewlett-Packard and Yokogawa Electric Corp., utilized statistical process control techniques. From 1975 to 1985, the company's manufacturing costs decreased 42 percent and product defects declined 79 percent. Market share increased 193 percent, profits rose 244 percent, and revenues per employee increased 120 percent.[90] From 1985 to 1988, employee suggestions increased fivefold and resulted in more than 2300 quality improvements in manufacturing and administration.[91]

Most of the reports of the positive effects of TQM and statistical process control emanate from manufacturing and not from service. Virtually all of Deming's writing and experience are also derived from consultation in manufacturing. Thus, the extent to which TQM's methods and effects generalize to service is still unknown. Particularly in the context of the Baldrige Awards, there can be little doubt that much greater attention is being given to quality management in U.S. corporations.

THE ROLE OF THE HR DEPARTMENT IN ORGANIZATIONAL IMPROVEMENTS

According to the criteria for the Baldrige Award, HR utilization is considered one of the most important issues for companies to emphasize. This includes specific training programs in quality, general training and development programs, communication systems, suggestions systems, customer-focused performance appraisal systems, and opinion surveys.[92]

In most firms, HR professionals are in the best position to address these issues. They understand the organization's mission and can develop improvement programs to be consistent with the firm's goals. In addition, they are familiar with the various personnel systems in the organization (e.g., training, appraisal, compensation, motivation) and can make sure than any new programs implemented are designed to fit with the existing systems. Also, HR professionals generally have more training than managers and employees in human relations skills, and can train others in management participation and employee involvement techniques.

While the HR department should take an active role in organizational efforts to improve productivity and quality, this often does not occur. Even in progressive companies, HR professionals are so busy with "putting out fires" that they have difficulty in finding the time for new programs. Sometimes HR professionals do not feel comfortable in assuming responsibility for productivity improvement programs. In other cases, the industrial engineering staff takes on the responsibility.[93]

There are, however, cases in which the HR staff is actively involved in designing, implementing, and evaluating improvement interventions that are to be used. For example, one survey indicated that HR professionals were responsible for developing or implementing productivity improvement programs in 40 percent of firms surveyed.[94] In other companies, HRM professionals worked closely with top executives to develop improvement programs.[95] In the Tennessee Valley Authority, for instance, some of the HR staff have been reassigned to work closely with top managers in an organizationwide TQM initiative. At IBM, all TQM training was developed, implemented, and evaluated through the HR function, working closely with line management.

Roles in Designing Programs

HR professionals need to involve employees, managers, customers, and the union in the design of improvement programs. This can be done by establishing a task force composed of representatives from every group, who work together to define the problems and offer recommendations. This level of teamwork and joint planning is necessary to ensure that the final programs will be accepted and used by all organizational members. It is especially important to solicit the ideas and suggestions of middle-level managers and supervisors, since these individuals are in a position to greatly influence how others view the new interventions. Their opinions can be collected by interviews or survey methods, or by less formal means.

When they are designing improvement programs, HR professionals often conduct needs assessments to determine which systems are working well and which are not. They may gather data by conducting individual or group interviews, observing work practices, administering surveys, or leading employee focus groups. *Focus groups* consist of employees and customers, usually serving on a volunteer basis, who meet to try to identify and discuss organizational concerns related to productivity or quality.

After conducting a needs assessment, the HR professional must be able to work with the organizational representatives to establish priorities for initiating improvements. The HR professional should keep everyone

informed and be prepared to make revisions in the design. Changes may be necessary to fine-tune the new program or to adjust it to new philosophies articulated by top managers. As we discussed in Chapter 12, the HR staff should review the reward system to be sure that the new programs are compatible with the compensation and incentive systems. For example, the programs at IBM, Procter & Gamble, Intel, and Johnson & Johnson have been designed so that employees are rewarded for efforts in line with the organizations' new goals.[96]

Roles in Implementing and Evaluating Programs

When programs are being implemented, HR professionals are usually responsible for training managers and employees in the new systems. They are also often responsible for convincing others in the organization of the importance of the new programs. Thus, they may have to deal with potential resistance to change and sell individuals on the benefits of the proposed programs. While some members of the organization may be supportive of the new programs, others (e.g., managers) may be concerned about costs, loss of supervisory power, time off from work for employee participation, and the potential usefulness of the interventions. HR professionals should try to gain managerial participation early in the process, so as to build support and to lessen later resistance. Use of pilot projects may aid in checking out the program and fostering positive attitudes about the intervention. Training programs should be evaluated using control groups and more than reactive criteria (see Chapter 8).

To evaluate the programs, HR professionals should provide a baseline for measuring and tracking results.[97] They should also be prepared to describe the potential cost effectiveness of the proposed programs and collect data to show actual dollar value (see Appendix A).

THE EFFECTIVENESS OF IMPROVEMENT PROGRAMS

Organizational improvement programs are generally effective in improving employee quality, productivity, and QWL. In a review of 207 published studies, the 11 different interventions examined increased employee productivity in 87 percent of studies. The programs that were most effective included financial compensation, training, goal setting, participative supervision, and sociotechnical systems (e.g., AWGs, alternative working arrangements). Also, favorable attitudes toward work resulted from the programs, indicating that productivity and QWL could be improved at the same time.[98] In addition, a survey of

3000 firms by the Strategic Planning Institute indicated that as quality increases, productivity, profitability, market share, and return on investment also increase.[99]

Criteria and Designs for Measuring Effectiveness

As noted throughout this chapter, interventions may be implemented to meet a variety of different purposes. The primary purposes are to enhance productivity, quality of services and products, and QWL. To assess whether programs are working, the firm needs to examine changes in the relevant criteria described earlier in this chapter.

Research designs should be utilized so that the organization will be in a position to assess changes as a result of the new programs. The reader is referred to Chapter 8 to review these designs. Measurements on the important criteria should be taken both before and after the program is implemented to determine whether the programs had an effect on the criteria of interest (e.g., performance productivity, absenteeism). Reactions to the programs can also be collected after implementation to see whether employees have favorable opinions about the program. Longitudinal designs should be used since organization-wide improvement programs often take years to show any effects. For example, with TQM, firms must realize that it takes anywhere from 1 to 10 years just to fully implement the system.[100]

Factors Affecting the Effectiveness of Programs

COMMITMENT. In the United States, quality programs are not typically tied to the rest of the organizational systems (e.g., appraisal, rewards). Quality teams work on company time by taking individuals out of their normal work activities, and team members report their findings and recommendations back to the organization. In addition, most U.S. manufacturing firms do not determine defect rates by statistical methods, although these approaches are gaining in popularity.[101]

According to a survey conducted by the American Society for Quality Control, 20 percent of respondents said their companies do not have quality improvement programs. In firms having quality programs, few employees actually participate. A variety of reasons have been given, including: they weren't given opportunities to participate in the process, they didn't believe that quality programs have any effect, or they were too busy. Employees also stated that their firms talked about quality but really did not seem committed to it. In other words, firms rarely followed through on the action plans devel-

oped. Twenty-five percent of respondents expressed dissatisfaction with their firms' rate of quality improvement, although an equal number were highly satisfied.[102]

It appears that if improvement programs are to be effective in the United States, employees and managers will need to increase their level of commitment to the enhancement of quality and productivity. As Juran noted, Americans have the tendency to focus on short-term goals (i.e., "Take the money and run") rather than to be concerned about meeting customers' long-term needs and requirements.[103] Top management will need to illustrate that they are serious about improvements. Lower-level managers will need to give employees greater opportunities to participate in the process, as well as giving them the autonomy to implement their ideas.[104] Creating a stronger connection between quality improvements and the reward system is certainly a constructive step. For example, excellence in manufacturing is not even stated by managers as a top priority in many U.S. manufacturing firms.

TRAINING. Training will have to become an integral part of any improvement program. This has been true for firms which have won the prestigious Baldrige Award. For example, at Federal Express, all employees are required to complete two formal training programs. "The Quality Advantage" (TQA) teaches employees how to write contracts with their customers, while "Quality Action Teams" (QAT) emphasizes development of problem-solving skills. Likewise, at Wallace Company, all employees are required to attend quality awareness classes which focus on developing team-building and problem-solving skills and understanding statistical process control. At IBM, training focuses on general quality information and processes and on specific, job-related training (e.g., defect reduction). Since 1985, Cadillac has required training of its executive staff and engineering teams in Deming's quality improvement philosophy.[105] Saturn requires several hours of training for all employees in order to facilitate their continuous improvement efforts.

Not only is it important to provide training for employees, but they must also be given the opportunities to use the new skills. In addition, evaluations of the effectiveness of the programs are becoming increasingly more important. In fact, conducting evaluations of quality improvement programs is one area which clearly distinguishes the Baldrige Award winners from the applicants.[106]

COMPATIBILITY WITH OTHER SYSTEMS. It is critical that improvement programs be developed to be compatible with other systems in the firm. For example, employees need to be thoroughly trained in the skills they will need, and should be appraised on and rewarded for using those skills. Figure 13.11 illustrates how

FIGURE 13.11
RELATIONSHIPS OF QWL AND PRODUCTIVITY PROGRAMS TO OTHER ORGANIZATIONAL SYSTEMS

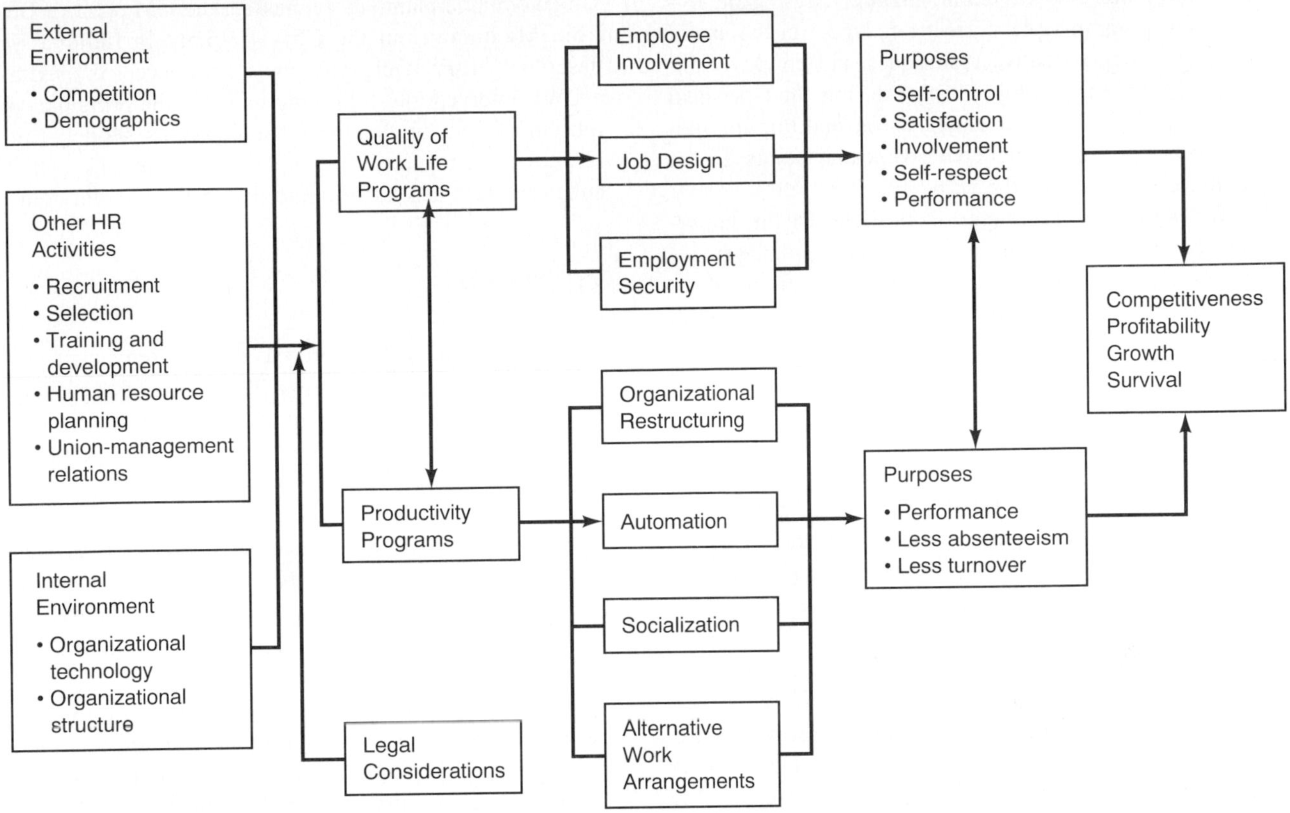

Source: R. S. Schuler and V. L. Huber, *Personnel and human resource management,* p. 408. Reprinted by permission.

improvement efforts can be interrelated with other organizational systems.

Relative Effectiveness of Programs

One review found that participative interventions and job enrichment increased productivity (i.e., there were reported productivity gains of 0.5 and 17 percent, respectively). These gains were, however, lower than those acquired through the use of financial incentives and goal-setting techniques (gains of 30 and 16 percent, respectively).[107]

Another study found that job enrichment, sociotechnical approaches (e.g., AWGs), and alternative work arrangements (e.g., flextime) were related to increased productivity, but not to the same degree as the gains from financial incentives and training programs. Interestingly, work rescheduling methods were related to less employee turnover, while other programs showed no such relationship. The effects of improvement programs varied as a function of organization size, organization type, and type of worker. The impact of intervention programs was greater in small firms and government agencies, and with managerial, professional, and sales employees. Finally, it was suggested that firms should use multiple, well-integrated interventions to improve productivity.[108]

In general, more studies are needed to assess the relative effectiveness of organizational improvement programs. This is especially true for the newer, more participative approaches such as TQM, robotics, and QCs.

INTERNATIONAL IMPROVEMENT PROGRAMS

Japan

As stated earlier, improvement programs have been used successfully in other countries, particularly Japan. Many of these strategies, which have come to embody "Japanese management style," have their origin in American management thought.[109] This may explain why quality programs in the United States and Japan are similar in many ways. They are also different, however. In Japan, improvement programs place greater reliance on the use of statistical process-control techniques and employee involvement. Often, employees meet during their personal free time, place a greater emphasis on making continuous improvements, and receive a financial bonus for the overall performance of the firm.

Japanese and U.S. supervisors differ in the importance they attach to quality issues. In Japan, managers always believe they are in a crisis, which motivates them to continually work harder. U.S. supervisors often do not view quality as a high priority, nor do they think their production workers are greatly concerned with quality.[110] In some cases, U.S. supervisors have not even seen a formal quality statement written by their firm. They do not attach as much importance to objectives such as meeting specific customer requirements, producing defect-free products, improving workers' productivity, or achieving low-cost production, although they do emphasize the meeting of production schedules to a greater extent than do their Japanese peers.[111]

Japanese employees and supervisors receive much more quality training than their U.S. counterparts. For example, a higher percentage of Japanese supervisors are taught how to identify problems in work designs and equipment, even outside their immediate work area.[112] The greater emphasis Japan places on training ranges from orientation programs to training in statistical quality control. In one survey, it was reported that over 80 percent of Japanese business firms provide job training for employees at the firm. The training often goes beyond job skills preparation and involves the broader education of the employee. While U.S. firms are lagging behind in the amount of training they provide employees, one firm, Plumley Companies, was recently recognized for the comprehensive training it offers to its employees. In addition to skills training, the firm provides G.E.D. preparation and home-study courses for employees and their families on a voluntary basis.[113]

Employees in Japanese firms are expected to be multiskilled within 5 years after joining the firm.[114] Job rotation is necessary to develop a variety of skills. This strengthens the flexibility of Japan's workforce, and may partially explain why Japanese firms are better able to quickly adapt to changes in the market than are U.S. firms.

Sweden

Sweden is another country that uses progressive improvement interventions. Perhaps the best-known example is the Volvo plant which redesigned jobs in the early 1970s from an assembly-line structure to use of work teams with job rotation. Today, this approach is used in some U.S. firms, including the Saturn and Nissan automobile plants in Tennessee, the GM plant in Detroit, Michigan, and the Chrysler plant in Indiana we described earlier. Generally, the team concept is used as a QWL intervention, following many of the principles of job enrichment or the Job Characteristics Model. Employees work together to complete an entire task, which enhances their task identity, skill variety, and autonomy.

SUMMARY

Many U.S. organizations are faced with significant productivity and quality problems. The status of the United States as a world leader in productivity has been questioned, as other countries (e.g., Japan, France, Germany) have outpaced the United States in both productivity growth and quality. Many U.S. firms now realize the extent of the crisis, but only recently have they made serious attempts to rectify the situation. On the other hand, Japan adopted the quality principles espoused by American quality experts (e.g., Deming and Juran) during the 1950s.

Quality, productivity, and QWL may be popular buzzwords, but the basic concerns are here to stay. Many experts argue that these are critical issues, as American firms continue to lose market share in major industries such as computers, motor vehicles, metals, electronics, and aerospace.[115] U.S. organizations must integrate into their entire firms the basic tenets of quality and productivity improvement with a focus on meeting or exceeding customer requirements. In addition, continuous improvements in all domains are needed if U.S. firms are going to move back to the top and remain there. The criteria available for the Baldrige Award are an excellent model for organizational change in this area.

Fortunately, a number of interventions exist which offer U.S. firms the opportunity to improve employees' QWL and regain the competitive edge. Improvement programs include interventions to redesign the work environment and participative approaches. *Work redesign* interventions include the use of ergonomics, robotics, computers and office automation, job design (e.g., job enrichment, job rotation), and alternative work arrangements (e.g., flexible work arrangements, part-time work, job sharing, compressed workweeks). *Participative* programs include QCs, opinion surveys, AWG or self-managing work teams, and TQM.

Some U.S. firms have already started using many of these programs, with positive results. By making investments in people, product design, and process improvement, they have improved quality, productivity, and

QWL for their employees.[116] HR professionals should be well-informed about these various programs so that they will be in a good position to guide U.S. firms in their future improvement efforts.

Unions have been more receptive recently to the productivity programs we describe here and the pay-for-performance systems discussed in Chapter 12. For example, the highly successful team-based Chrysler assembly plant in Indiana was conceptualized and developed with full cooperation from the United Auto Workers. Rubbermaid's Wooster, Ohio, plant is team-based, a manufacturing process endorsed by the union. There are numerous other examples where unions have cooperated in improvement programs. Managers must be fully aware of issues related to labor relations as they contemplate such programs. We will examine labor relations and collective bargaining in the next two chapters.

DISCUSSION QUESTIONS

1. How can HRM activities be coordinated with the Baldrige Award criteria?
2. Do you agree that variability in individual or group performance is primarily due to factors beyond the individual or group's control (e.g., poor resources, inadequate training, weak management, inefficient work flow)? Explain your response.
3. Could you use AWGs or self-managing work teams in the classroom? Explain your answer.
4. Describe a situation in which redesigning the work environment could enhance productivity or quality.
5. Describe the steps you would take to change an organization from an autocratic management style to one in which there is a high degree of employee involvement and participation.
6. What impact has the TQM movement had on enhancing organizational effectiveness (i.e., quality and productivity)?
7. Offer some suggestions for how various HR systems in organizations (e.g., performance appraisal, job analysis, training, career development) can be designed to reflect the basic tenets of TQM.
8. Which organizational improvement strategies are most likely to encounter the greatest employee resistance? Why? What recommendations would you offer to management to manage the resistance?
9. How would you convince workers or unions that productivity improvement is not simply an attempt to get more work for the same money?
10. Could you use TQM at a university? How would you do it?
11. Should TQM be combined with pay-for-performance? How? Explain your answer.

NOTES

1. Chew, W. B. (1988). No-nonsense guide to measuring productivity. *Harvard Business Review, 66*(1), 110–118. See also: Beatty, R. W., Bernardin, H. J., and Nickel, J. E. (1987). *The productivity sourcebook.* Amherst, MA: Human Resource Development Press.
2. Garvin, D. A. (1987). Competing on the eight dimensions of quality. *Harvard Business Review, 65*(6), 101–109.
3. Schaaf, D. (1991). Beating the drum for quality. *Training, 28*(3), 5–12. See also: Forker, L. B. (1991). Quality: American, Japanese, and Soviet perspectives. *Academy of Management Executive, 5*(4), 63–74.
4. See note 1.
5. Bluestone, M. (June 8, 1987). The push for quality. *Business Week,* pp. 130–135. See also: Garvin, D. A. (1988). Quality problems, policies, and attitudes in the United States and Japan: An exploratory study. *Academy of Management Journal, 29*(4), 653–673.
6. See note 5, Garvin (1988).
7. Rosow, J. (1981). Quality of work life issues for the 1980's. *Training and Development Journal, 35*(3), 33–52.
8. Davis, L. E., and Cherns, A. B. (eds.) (1975). *The quality of working life: Vol. I. Problems, prospects, and the state of the art.* New York: The Free Press. See also: Tuttle, T. C. (1983). Organizational productivity: A challenge for psychologists. *American Psychologist, 38*(4), 479–486.
9. See note 5, Bluestone (June 8, 1987).
10. Segalla, E. (1989). All for quality and quality for all. *Training and Development Journal, 43*(9), 36–45. See also: Hill, R. C., and Freedman, S. M. (1992). Managing the quality process: Lessons from a Baldrige Award winner: A conversation with CEO John W. Wallace. *Academy of Management Executive, 6*(1), 76–88.
11. See note 10.
12. Oldham, G. R., and Fried, Y. (1987). Employee reactions to work space. *Journal of Applied Psychology, 72*(1), 75–80.
13. Crawmer, R. (March 1987). Flexibility for interiors. *Nation's Business, 75,* 38–42, 44. See also: Padgett, T. C. (1987). Getting supervisory help in improving productivity. *Training and Development Journal, 41*(1), 48–50. Schuler, R. S., and Huber, V. L. (1990). *Personnel and human resource management,* 4th ed. Saint Paul, MN: West Publishing.
14. Staff (1984). Ergonomics training eases man-machine interface. *Management Review, 73*(10), 55.
15. See note 13, Schuler and Huber (1990).
16. Crocker, O. L., and Guelker, R. (1988). The effects of robotics on the workplace. *Personnel, 65*(9), 26–36.
17. Pennar, K. (June 6, 1988). The productivity paradox. *Business Week,* 100–102.
18. See note 16. See also: Mitchell, R., Brandt, R., Schiller, Z., and Ellis, J. (Dec. 22, 1986). Boldly going where no robot has gone before. *Business Week,* p. 45.

19. Rohan, T. M. (Feb. 23, 1987). Bosses—Who needs 'em? *Industry Week*, pp. 15–16.

20. See note 16.

21. See note 16. See also: Fisher, C. D., Schoenfeldt, L. F., and Shaw, J. B. (1991). *Human resource management*. Boston, MA: Houghton Mifflin.

22. See note 16.

23. Chao, G. T., and Kozlowski, S. W. (1986). Employee perceptions on the implementation of robotic manufacturing technology. *Journal of Applied Psychology, 71*(1), 70–76.

24. See note 16. See also: Shenkar, O. (1988). Robotics: A challenge for occupational psychology. *Journal of Occupational Psychology, 61*(1), 103–112.

25. See note 17.

26. Staff (1981). Want to boost managerial productivity and cut costs? Try automation! *Personnel, 58*(2), 39–40. See also: Parthasarthy, R., and Sethi, S. P. (1992). The impact of flexible automation on business strategy and organizational structure. *Academy of Management Review, 17*, 86–111.

27. Quible, Z., and Hammer, J. N. (1984). Office automation's impact on personnel. *Personnel Administrator, 29*(9), 25–32.

28. See note 16. See also: note 27.

29. Hackman, J. R., and Oldham, G. R. (1980). *Work redesign*. Reading, MA: Addison-Wesley.

30. Fried, Y., and Ferris, G. R. (1987). The validity of the Job Characteristics Model: A review and meta-analysis. *Personnel Psychology, 40*, 287–322. See also: Dean, J. W., and Snell, S. A. (1991). Integrated manufacturing and job design: Moderating effects of organization inertia. *Academy of Management Journal, 34*(4), 776–804.

31. Staff (1991). Quality gets a lift. *Personnel, 68*(1), p. 16. See also: Griffin, R. W. (1991). Effects of work redesign on employee perceptions, attitudes, and behaviors: A long-term investigation. *Academy of Management Journal, 34*(2), 425–435.

32. See note 29. See also: Hazzard, L., Mautz, J., and Wrightsman, D. (1992). Job rotation cuts cumulative trauma cases. *Personnel Journal, 71*, 29–33.

33. Holcomb, B. (July 1991). Time off: The benefit of the hour. *Working Mother*, pp. 31–35.

34. Russell, J. E. A. (1991). Career development interventions in organizations. *Journal of Vocational Behavior, 38*, 237–287. See also: Loscocco, K. A., and Roschelle, A. R. (1991). Influences on the quality of work and nonwork life: Two decades in review. *Journal of Vocational Behavior, 39*, 182–225.

35. See note 33.

36. Greenhaus, J. H., and Beutell, N. J. (1985). Sources of conflict between work and family roles. *Academy of Management Review, 10*, 76–88.

37. Fernandez, J. P. (1986). *Child care and corporate productivity: Resolving family/work conflicts*. Lexington, MA: D. C. Heath.

38. Peterson, D. (1980). Flexitime in the United States: The lessons of experience. *Personnel, 57*, 21–37.

39. See note 33. See also: Nollen, S. (1977). Does flexitime improve productivity? *Harvard Business Review, 56* (9/10), 12–22.

40. Dessler, G. (1991). *Personnel/human resource management*, 5th ed. Englewood Cliffs, NJ: Prentice-Hall.

41. See note 33.

42. Atchison, S. D. (Oct. 27, 1986). These top executives work where they play. *Business Week*, p. 132.

43. See note 37. See also: Zeitz, B., and Dusky, L. (1988). *The best companies for women*. New York: Simon & Schuster.

44. See note 33. See also: note 43, Zeitz and Dusky (1988).

45. See note 37. See also: note 34.

46. See note 33.

47. Betz, N. E., and Fitzgerald, L. F. (1987). *The career psychology of women*. Orlando, FL: Academic Press.

48. Closson, M. (October 1976). Company couples flourish. *Business Week, 25*, 112.

49. See note 37. See also: note 33.

50. See note 33.

51. See note 33.

52. *1987 AMS flexible work survey*. (1987). Willow Grove, PA: Administrative Management Society.

53. Lawler, E. E. (1986). *High-involvement management: Participative strategies for improving organizational performance*. San Francisco: Jossey-Bass. See also: Atchison, T. (1991). The employment relationship: Untied or re-tied? *Academy of Management Executive, 5*(4), 52–62. Magjuka, R. J., and Baldwin, T. T. (1991). Team-based employee involvement programs: Effects of design and administration. *Personnel Psychology, 44*(4), 793–812.

54. Schuster, F. E. (1986). *The Schuster report: The proven connection between people and profits*. New York: John Wiley & Sons. See also: Staff (1991). The Red Cross learns to listen and earns employee commitment. *Personnel, 68*(4), 12.

55. French, W. L. (1990). *Human resources management*, 2d ed. Boston, MA: Houghton Mifflin.

56. See note 55.

57. See note 32.

58. Warren, A. S., Jr. (1982). The nature of quality circles. In J. E. Ross and W. C. Ross (eds.), *Japanese quality circles and productivity*. Reston, VA: Reston Publishing, pp. 24–41.

59. Lawler, E. E., III, and Mohrman, S. A. (1985). Quality circles after the fad. *Harvard Business Review, 63*(1), 64–71.

60. See note 59.

61. See note 55. See also: Griffin, R. W. (1988). Consequences of quality circles in an industrial setting: A longitudinal assessment. *Academy of Management Journal, 31*(2), 338–358. Ingle, S. (1982). How to avoid quality circle failure in your company. *Training and Development Journal, 36*(6), 54–59. Lawler, E. E., III, and Mohrman, S. A. (1987). Quality circles: After the honeymoon. *Organizational Dynamics, 15*(4), 42–54.

62. See note 59.
63. Burns, J. E. (May/June 1982). Honeywell quality circle boom: Part of growing American trend. *Industrial Management*. See also: note 21, Fisher, Schoenfeldt, and Shaw (1991); note 59.
64. See note 61, Ingle (1982).
65. Cole, R. E. (1983). Improving product quality through continuous feedback. *Management Review, 72*(10), 8–12.
66. See note 58. See also: Adam, E. E. (1991). Quality circle performance. *Journal of Management, 17*(1), 25–39.
67. Barrick, M. R., and Alexander, R. A. (1987). A review of quality circle efficacy and the existence of positive-findings bias. *Personnel Psychology, 40*(3), 579–592.
68. Sims, H. P., and Dean, J. W., Jr. (1985). Beyond quality circles: Self-managing teams. *Personnel, 62*(1), 25–32. See also: Lublin, J. S. (February 13, 1992). Trying to increase worker productivity, more employers alter management style. *The Wall Street Journal,* B1, B3.
69. Rohan, T. M. (Jan. 20, 1986). Putting exotic technology to work. *Industry Week,* pp. 37–42.
70. See note 61, Lawler and Mohrman (1987). See also: Note 68.
71. See note 68. See also: Bettenhausen, K. L. (1991). Five years of groups research: What we've learned and what needs to be addressed. *Journal of Management, 17*(2), 345–382.
72. Goodman, P. S., Devadas, R., and Griffith Hughson, T. L. (1988). Groups and productivity: Analyzing the effectiveness of self-managing teams. In J. P. Campbell, R. J. Campbell, and Associates (eds.), *Productivity in organizations: New perspectives from industrial and organizational psychology.* San Francisco, CA: Jossey-Bass, pp. 295–327.
73. See note 68. See also: Schilder, J. (1992). Work teams boost productivity. *Personnel Journal, 71,* 67–86. Cordery, J. L., Mueller, W. S., and Smith, L. M. (1991). Attitudinal and behavioral effects of autonomous group working: A longitudinal field study. *Academy of Management Journal, 34*(2), 464–476.
74. Walton, M. (1990). *Deming management at work.* New York: G. P. Putnam's Sons.
75. See note 5, Bluestone (June 8, 1987).
76. Bernardin, H. J. (1992). An 'analytic' framework for customer-based performance content development and appraisal. *Human Resource Management Review, 2,* 81–102.
77. See note 5, Bluestone (June 8, 1987).
78. Wagel, W. H. (1987). Corning zeroes in on total quality. *Personnel, 64*(7), 4–9.
79. See note 10.
80. See note 5, Bluestone (June 8, 1987).
81. Deming, W. E. (1986). *Out of the crisis.* Cambridge: Massachusetts Institute of Technology, Center for Advanced Engineering Study.
82. See note 40.
83. See note 10.
84. See note 5, Bluestone (June 8, 1987).
85. Nemoto, M. (1987). *Total quality control for management.* Englewood Cliffs, NJ: Prentice-Hall.
86. Cocheu, T. (1989). Training for quality improvement. *Training and Development Journal, 43*(1), 56–62.
87. See note 21, Fisher, Schoenfeldt, and Shaw (1991). See also: Staff (1991). Quality is as quality does. *Personnel, 68*(1), 16.
88. See note 13, Schuler and Huber (1990).
89. See note 56.
90. See note 5, Bluestone (June 8, 1987).
91. See note 10.
92. See note 10.
93. Layton, W. G., and Johnson, E. J. (1987). Break the mold: Strategies for productivity. *Personnel Journal, 66*(5), 75–78.
94. Bureau of National Affairs (September 1984). Productivity improvement programs. In *Personnel Policies Forum 138,* Washington: Bureau of National Affairs, p. 3.
95. See note 94.
96. See note 93.
97. See note 93.
98. Katzell, R. A., and Guzzo, R. A. (1983). Psychological approaches to productivity improvement. *American Psychologist, 38*(4), 468–472.
99. See note 86.
100. See note 10.
101. Rohan, T. M. (1983). Quality or junk? Facing up to the problem. *Industry Week, 219*(6), 72–79.
102. See note 87, Staff (1991).
103. Dumas, R. A., Cushing, N., and Laughlin, C. (1987). Making quality control theories workable. *Training and Development Journal, 41*(2), 30–33.
104. See note 87, Staff (1991).
105. See note 56.
106. See note 10.
107. Locke, E. A., Feren, D. B., McCaleb, V. M., Shaw, K. N., and Denny, A. T. (1980). The relative effectiveness of four methods of motivating employee performance. In K. D. Duncan and M. M. Wallis (eds.), *Changes in working life.* New York: John Wiley & Sons.
108. Guzzo, R. A., Jette, R. D., and Katzell, R. A. (1985). The effects of psychologically based intervention programs on worker productivity: A meta-analysis. *Personnel Psychology, 38*(2), 275–291.
109. Hummel, R. P. (1987). Behind quality management: What workers and a few philosophers have always known and how it adds up to excellence in production. *Organizational Dynamics, 16*(1), 71–78. See also: Schuster, F. E. (1988). Reviving productivity in America. *Personnel Administrator, 33*(7), 65–68.
110. Schaaf, D. (1991). Beating the drum for quality. *Training, 28*(3), 5–12.
111. See note 5, Garvin (1988).
112. See note 5, Garvin (1988). See also: Juran, J. M. (1981). Product quality: A prescription for the West; Part I:

Training and improvement programs. *Management Review, 70*(6), 9–14.

113. See note 32.
114. See note 13, Schuler and Huber (1990).
115. Leonard, F. S., and Sasser, W. E. (1982). The incline of quality. *Harvard Business Review, 60*(5), 163–171. See also: note 3.

116. See note 115, Leonard and Sasser (1982). See also: Ganster, D. C., and Schaubroeck, J. (1991). Work stress and employee health. *Journal of Management, 17*(2), 235–271.

EXERCISE 13.1
JOB ENRICHMENT AT THE HERDHELM HOTEL*

OVERVIEW

As described in Chapter 13, Hackman and Oldham's Job Characteristics Model is a popular approach to redesigning and enriching jobs. The emphasis is on building into jobs the critical psychological states of experienced meaningfulness, responsibility, and knowledge of results. This is done to improve employees' motivation, satisfaction, and quality of work life, and to lower their absenteeism and turnover. The purpose of this exercise is to employ the Job Characteristics Model to understand the nature of the job of housekeeper at the Herdhelm Hotel.

LEARNING OBJECTIVES

After completing this exercise, you should be able to:

1. Apply the principles of job enrichment presented in Hackman and Oldham's Job Characteristics Model to a work situation.
2. Identify benefits and constraints associated with job redesign efforts.
3. Evaluate the Hackman and Oldham approach relative to alternative methods of productivity and quality-of-work-life improvements.

PROCEDURE

Part A: Individual Analysis

Prior to class, read the scenario for the housekeeping department at the Herdhelm Hotel, and also read Exhibit 13.1.1. Answer the questions in Form 13.1.1.

Part B: Group Analysis

Working in groups of about six, each member should read all the other students' 13.1.1 forms. Together, the group should then attempt to reach consensus on the questions in Form 13.1.1. Prepare a 4-minute presentation of the consensus plan and alternative approaches. A group spokesperson will be designated by the instructor.

*Contributed by Ann M. Herd and Caroline C. Wilhelm.

Part C: Class Discussion and Assessment

Step 1. Discuss the feasibility of each group's plan. In particular, consider how the recommendations might require changes in the way housekeepers are selected and rewarded, and how the suggestions might necessitate changes in other jobs at the Herdhelm Hotel. The issues of cost and alternative plans should be addressed.

Step 2. Following group discussion, students should complete the assessment questions for this exercise.

SCENARIO: BACKGROUND ON THE HERDHELM HOTEL HOUSEKEEPING DEPARTMENT

Overlooking the downtown area of a southeastern city, the Herdhelm Hotel is a mid-sized establishment featuring luxury accommodations and a staff of nearly 200 employees. The hotel competes with the finest hotels in the area and focuses on luxury and customer satisfaction in its marketing. The housekeeping department consists of 34 women under the supervision of an executive housekeeper. The staff is responsible for cleaning the hotel's 225 rooms and suites. Throughout the hotel's 7-year history, high rates of absenteeism and turnover have plagued the housekeeping department. Recently, however, complaints from unsatisfied guests concerning the cleanliness of the rooms have prompted management to take action. Hoping to bring about improvements in the situation, management hired Dr. Laura Hagerty, a local consultant, to investigate the problem and make recommendations. In order to gain familiarity with the work of the housekeeping staff, Dr. Hagerty obtained job descriptions from the HR department. These are provided in Exhibit 13.1.1. After reviewing the job descriptions, Dr. Hagerty conducted extensive interviews with members of the housekeeping department and identified the problem areas described below.

High on the housekeepers' list of complaints was the quality of supervision they received. Many comments focused on the executive housekeeper and how she administered performance feedback. "She doesn't tell us if we've done a good job," said Terry, a 28-year-old employee. In general, housekeepers perceived a lack of performance feedback from the executive housekeeper. However, a more perplexing problem concerned the checkers, a select group of housekeepers whose responsibility it was to inspect the rooms after they were cleaned. Checkers were viewed as applying room cleanliness standards arbitrarily. "I can clean two rooms the same way and get

EXHIBIT 13.1.1
JOB DESCRIPTIONS FOR HOUSEKEEPING DEPARTMENT

Job title: Executive Housekeeper

Department: Housekeeping

Immediate supervisor: Assistant Hotel Manager

Job Summary

Delegates housekeeping duties to employees and sees that they are carried out.
Responsible for overall cleanliness of hotel rooms.

Tasks and Duties

1. Obtains numbers and locations of occupied rooms each day, and assigns rooms
   to housekeepers for cleaning.

2. Plans employees' work schedules on a monthly basis.

3. Examines time cards daily and records number of hours worked by each
   employee on a payroll sheet.

4. Orders cleaning supplies and other housekeeping items as needed.

5. Takes periodic inventory of linens.

6. Inspects a random sample of rooms to ensure that they have been properly
   cleaned and that all items (e.g., soap) are in the correct places.

7. Notifies housekeepers of substandard work.

8. Holds monthly meeting with housekeepers to discuss work problems and
   make announcements.

9. Trains new employees to perform housekeeping duties.

10. Performs housekeeping duties as needed.

Working Conditions

Indoor environment.

Works at least 60 hours per week, including nights and weekends.

Dress Requirements

Uniform required.

Minimum Qualifications

Supervisory and motivation skills.

Communication skills.

Organizational skills.

EXHIBIT 13.1.1 *(Continued)*

Job title: Housekeeper

Department: Housekeeping

Immediate supervisor: Executive Housekeeper

Job Summary

Responsible for cleaning hotel rooms and for delivering room linens to laundry.

Tasks and Duties

1. Obtains numbers and locations of occupied rooms from executive housekeeper each morning.

2. Examines cart to ensure that it is adequately supplied with cleaning agents, linens, and toiletries (e.g., soap, shampoo). Obtains needed supplies from Housekeeping Department.

3. Strips linens from bed and removes towels from bathroom.

4. Cleans shower, sink, and toilet. Sweeps and mops bathroom floor. Cleans mirrors and counters.

5. Replaces tissue paper, soap, and toiletries in bathroom.

6. Places clean towels in bathrooms.

7. Vacuums carpet.

8. Dusts furniture.

9. Makes bed with clean linens.

10. Empties trash cans.

11. Supplies room with matches and notepaper if necessary.

12. Notifies maintenance department of any needed repairs (e.g., lights).

13. Places linens in laundry chute and empties trash bag from cart.

Working Conditions

Indoor environment.

Works at least 40 hours per week, including nights and weekends.

Dress Requirements

Uniform required.

Minimum Qualifications

Ability to operate vacuum cleaner.

EXHIBIT 13.1.1 *(Continued)*

Job title: Checker/Housekeeper

Department: Housekeeping

Immediate supervisor: Executive Housekeeper

Job Summary

Carries out the requests of the executive housekeeper. Examines the quality of housekeepers' work.

Tasks and Duties

1. Assists housekeepers in obtaining supplies for carts.

2. Checks to see that housekeepers have linens and vacuum cleaners.

3. Evaluates the cleanliness of rooms according to established criteria and marks each item inspected on a checklist.

4. Notifies housekeepers if work is substandard.

5. Assists executive housekeeper in planning employees' work schedules and in recording hours worked on time sheets.

6. Performs housekeeping duties as needed.

Working Conditions

Indoor environment.

Works at least 50 hours per week, including nights and weekends.

Dress Requirement

Uniform required.

Minimum Qualifications

Inspection skills.

Communication and interpersonal skills.

Organizational skills.

different marks on them from different checkers," reported Sylvia, a hotel employee for 4 years. Lack of consistent standards meant that housekeepers received inconsistent feedback on numerous occasions and created a sense of confusion within the department.

A second pervasive problem was the perception among housekeepers that their work was not as highly valued as that of other hotel employees. Many housekeepers reported being treated as "second-class citizens" by other employees such as cashiers, bellhops, and managers. "They never smile or speak to us. They don't even say hello. Most times they pretend we're not even here," said Rose, one of the hotel's most tenured employees. Not only did housekeepers feel that they lacked respect from hotel employees, but they also perceived condescension from guests. "Customers are snobbish toward us and act like it's an inconvenience for us to clean their rooms," reported Luanne, who works part-time as a housekeeper. In addition to their esteem concerns, many housekeepers felt alienated from other hotel employees. "We don't know anything about what goes on in the rest of the hotel," said Wanda, whose mother and sister are also housekeepers. Several women said they felt purposely excluded from hotelwide employee meetings, which they were seldom able to attend due to work schedule conflicts. Such exclusion, they believed, was merely another sign that housekeepers were considered less important than other hotel employees.

Finally, the nature of the work itself was a frequent source of complaints. "Let's face it, making beds all day can get pretty boring," said Terry. Boredom, however, was a small frustration compared to the exasperation felt by housekeepers when checkers interfered with their work. "They lord over us, watching us like hawks. They tell us what to do and how to do it, as if we don't know anything about our jobs," Terry continued. Some housekeepers said they would have preferred to conduct their own quality inspections, but management had resisted the idea. Any effort among housekeepers to gain control over their work was doomed, they said, and there was no finer example than the 24-minute time allowance for cleaning each room. Housekeepers had fought bitterly for more time, arguing that their work pace was controlled in such a way that it was impossible to do a good job. "I always feel rushed and worn out trying to meet the deadline, and I end up cutting corners just to get everything done. There's no way I can do this job the way I'd like," said Hazel, one of the hotel's newest hires. The consequence for spending more than the allotted time on rooms was a warning slip from the executive housekeeper. Hoping to avoid such a reprimand, many housekeepers reported that they worked through the 15-minute break allowed each day in order to make up lost time.

Dr. Hagerty reflected on the employees' concerns. Consistent with the interview responses, a recent survey of housekeepers had revealed low levels of satisfaction with the present situation. Management was anxious to address the problems, as the job performance of housekeepers was critical to customer satisfaction and, therefore, to hotel business. With only 2 days left before she met with management, Dr. Hagerty began to prepare her recommendations.

FORM 13.1.1

Name_____ Group_____

1. Evaluate the job of a housekeeper as it is presently designed, using the five core job dimensions from the Job Characteristics Model. To what extent is the job enriched?

2. How amenable to job enrichment is the housekeeper's job? What characteristics of the employees should you consider to determine their readiness for job enrichment?

3. Propose a specific chronological plan to enrich the housekeeper's job.

4. As an alternative to changes based on Hackman and Oldham's model, what other productivity and QWL programs might you consider for this job? Would a pay-for-performance system work? If so, what would it look like?

Exercise 13.1
Assessment Questions

Name _____ Group _____

1. What effects do you expect a redesign of the housekeeper job to have on the core job dimensions?

2. How do you expect the housekeepers to respond to changes in the core job dimensions?

3. What are the most important features of the Job Characteristics Model for the housekeeper's jobs?

4. How would you set up an experiment in order to assess the effects of your new job redesign program for the housekeeper's job? What criteria would you use to assess effects?

EXERCISE 13.2
THE USE OF EMPLOYEE
OPINION SURVEYS AT JOHNSON
*APPLIANCES, INC.**

OVERVIEW

Chapter 13 discussed some of the most popular and effective worker participation programs. The use of employee opinion surveys is one such program. Many of our largest and most successful corporations use employee surveys as part of the strategic and HR planning process. The purpose of this exercise is to give students an opportunity to consider the use and value of survey data in an organization.

LEARNING OBJECTIVES

After completing this exercise, you should be able to:

1. Have a better understanding of how employee survey data can be used within an organization.
2. Know the issues related to survey data processes which must be considered in the interpretation of the data and the recommendations based on the data.

PROCEDURE

Part A: Individual Analysis

Prior to class, read the scenario on Johnson Appliances and read Exhibit 13.2.1. You are a member of the task force at Johnson with the objective of interpreting the survey results and (if necessary) recommending action to be taken based on these results. Your instructor may assign you to play a specific role. Complete Form 13.2.1 prior to coming to class. You may want to review Figure 13.5 regarding the dimensions surveyed.

Part B: Group Analysis

Student groups of about six should review all their individual 13.2.1 forms and then attempt to reach consensus

---

*Contributed by Fred E. Schuster.

on the specific actions to be taken, based on the survey results. Also, each group should take a specific position on whether Johnson Appliances should use an outside agent for the feedback sessions.

SCENARIO

Johnson Appliances, Inc., is a retail chain consisting of 28 outlets located in two states. The outlets sell a wide variety of consumer appliances and electronic products. Johnson has been financially successful since its second year of operation, making a profit in each of the last 20 years while growing steadily at the rate of 1 or 2 outlets per year. Top management believes that one of the firm's assets has been a stable, loyal, and motivated workforce; turnover has generally been much lower than average for competing firms in their industry.

Three years ago the company began annual use of a standardized survey feedback instrument in order to better control the HRM function, to obtain early warning of any developing problems in the human organization, and to facilitate team building and organization development.

In general, top management had been quite pleased with the overall results of the survey process; they felt confident that the information had been useful in formulating plans for HRM, tracking accomplishments, and initiating team-building efforts. Elliott Johnson, the president of Johnson Appliances, recently received the report in Exhibit 13.2.1 from the consulting firm which had been contracted to administer the climate survey annually.

As Elliott Johnson examined the executive summary and the data from the most recent survey (see Exhibits 13.2.2 and 13.2.3), he felt that they were quite helpful to management in assessing the overall condition of the firm's human organization. He recognized, however, that there were some major differences in the results from one division to another. He was particularly puzzled by the responses from the Warehouse Division (see Exhibit 13.2.4). Although he was unsure exactly what action was called for, he was convinced that the matter required urgent attention.

EXHIBIT 13.2.1
EXECUTIVE SUMMARY, HR INDEX—JOHNSON APPLIANCES, INC.

The rate of participation in the survey was 73 percent, which is a very satisfactory response rate. This response rate is sufficient to justify the assumption that those responding are a representative sample of the total population of Johnson Appliances. We should strive for an even higher rate of response in the future. Few sheets were returned incorrectly marked, and the quality of the response sheets was quite high; those responsible for administration are to be congratulated.

The overall index data for the total organization surveyed continues to exceed the norms for the Human Resources Index (HRI), as it has each year that the survey has been conducted. The index did drop again, however, between this year and last year, as it has the last 2 years. Each of the groups within the company, except Service, experienced the drop in the overall index. Because the number of people in this group participating in the survey dropped sharply this year, it is impossible to say whether the increase in the index reflects a change in conditions or merely a change in survey participants. Interestingly, Service is the group that last year had the lowest index, suggesting the *possibility* that some remedial action may have been successful.

As would be expected, there is substantial variation among the different groups within the company, with Administration, Data Processing, and Accounting having the highest indexes, followed by Sales Staff and Service. The group with the lowest index by far was the department heads, with Warehouse and Showroom/Warehouse being the next lowest. It is surprising that the lowest factor for the department heads is "participation," followed by "organizational climate." The mean for the department heads on "participation" is 2.04, which is 1.03 below the mean for the company as a whole.

For the total organization surveyed, the highest factors (again, as last year) were "supporting structure" (STC), "first-level supervision" (FLM), and "relationships" (REL). The lowest factors were "participation" (PAR), "intrinsic satisfaction" (IS), and "reward system" (RWD).

Among the individual items, some of the most noteworthy are:

Much Higher than Average for the Company

5. I have received the amount and kind of training which I need and desire to do my job well.
9. Management has a high concern for production and effectively communicates this concern.
10. My job provides ample opportunity for a sense of individual responsibility.
35. Rules and regulations are reasonable, and they aid in achieving organizational objectives.
36. This is a socially responsible organization in every way (its products, waste disposal, marketing techniques, employment practices, etc.).
53. The physical environment at work is comfortable, safe, and conducive to effective performance.
60. Employees feel free to discuss things about the job with their immediate boss.
61. This is an ethical organization in every respect.

Much Lower than Average for the Company

12. People can participate in and influence decisions which affect them.
20. My job provides ample opportunity for advancement.

43. People can participate in and influence decisions which are fundamental to the organization as a whole.
56. Decision making is widespread throughout the organization, rather than being concentrated at the top.

Further insight into the meaning of these especially significant individual items is provided by the written responses to items 65 and 66. Employees provided a number of *constructive* suggestions for improvement; this indicates that people generally have confidence in the ability of the organization to grow and to improve, and they are willing to actively participate in the process. Employees continue to have many positive feelings about the organization and remain proud of the company they work for. Responses to item 65 ("the things I like best about the organization") indicated several perceived strengths that can be built upon:

- Like working for Johnson Appliances; a good company to work for.
- Warm and comfortable atmosphere.
- Company image.
- Appreciate educational opportunities, training programs, and other benefits provided.
- Great products/values; focus on customer satisfaction.
- Management is fair, caring, and has concern for employees.
- Dynamic company—seeking growth but willing to change and adapt to changing conditions.
- Great people to work with at all levels.

On the other hand, the conditions that employees stated most often they would like to change (item 66) were:

- Goals are set too high.
- Overstaffed showrooms—leads to cutthroat competition.
- Need compensation changes: pay raises; bonus/commission system needs to be restructured.
- Management should be salaried.
- Store managers should not be allowed to sell; managers now compete with sales staff for sales.
- Problems with finance company; change finance company (they make too many mistakes that cost sales).
- Too much politics in promotions; more minorities are needed in management.
- Better insurance package needed for employees (health insurance).
- Concern for employees not as high as in the past; management is not listening.
- Need for more and better communication.
- Hours too long; need to reschedule holiday hours; more flexibility needed in work schedules.
- Sales staff should not do merchandising, inventory, etc.
- Need to improve management skills.

As was true last year, a number of open-ended responses seemed to relate to a core issue of goal setting and showroom management.

CONCLUSION

Morale and commitment of the human organization across the company continue to be satisfactory; there are, however, still significant opportunities for improvement. While the image of the organization and its practices remains generally positive, there is a perception that the climate has continued to deteriorate somewhat over the past year. An effort to raise the overall index for the total organization and for each unit within it to the 4.0 level over a period of 2 to 3 years through a program of planned organization change remains a challenging but worthwhile goal. The responses obtained this year are not incompatible with an objective of attaining the 4.0 level in some areas of the organization over the next 12- to 24-month period while showing improvement throughout the company.

We recommend that the data from the HRI be reported to groups of employees at all levels of the organization as a means of widening communication and implementing organizational improvement. These employees could then be involved in proposing and discussing changes which would address the concerns uncovered by the survey. This process has proved effective in a number of organizations in providing opportunities for increased information sharing and participation. Moreover, this recommendation seems especially appropriate in view of the many written comments expressing the desire for more communication and expanded opportunities for participation.

You may wish to consider the advantages of having a change agent external to the organization serve as a facilitator in these discussions. This may be particularly appropriate with regard to further discussion of the data and its implications by the department heads. This process would in itself be a direct means of improving opportunities for information sharing and participation, a key need cited by employees throughout the organization.

EXHIBIT 13.2.2

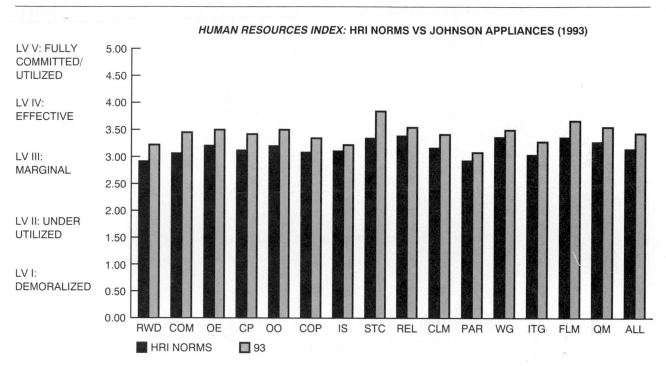

HUMAN RESOURCES INDEX: HRI NORMS VS JOHNSON APPLIANCES (1993)

EXHIBIT 13.2.3

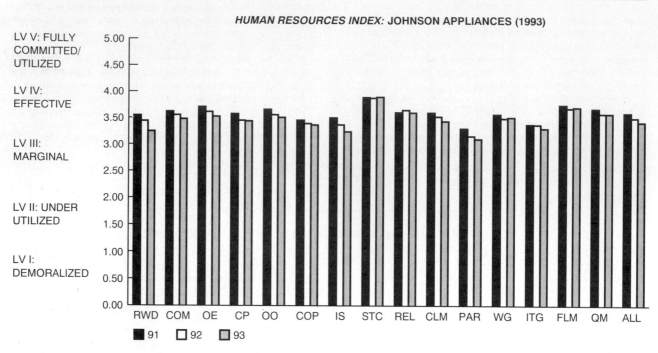

HUMAN RESOURCES INDEX: JOHNSON APPLIANCES (1993)

copyright © 1979 Fred E. Schuster

EXHIBIT 13.2.4

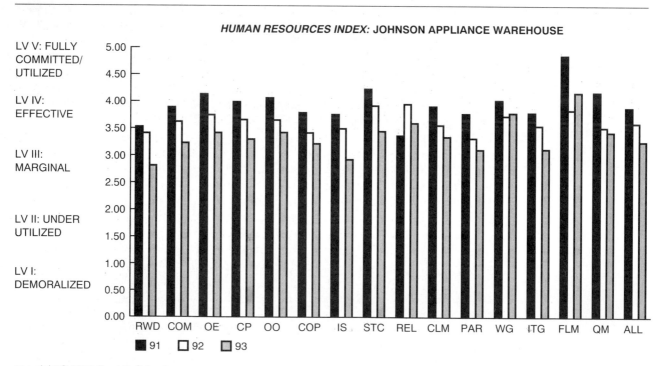

HUMAN RESOURCES INDEX: JOHNSON APPLIANCE WAREHOUSE

copyright © 1979 Fred E. Schuster

FORM 13.2.1

Name _____ Group _____

1. What is your general reaction to the survey results and how they should be interpreted?

2. What do you regard as the three most significant problems revealed by the survey data?
   a.

   b.

   c.

3. To what extent should management be held responsible for the survey results? What (if any) other data should you review prior to recommending specific action?

4. What is your priority of specific actions to take based on the data? (by order of importance)
   a.

   b.

   c.

5. Do you recommend that an outside change agent help with the feedback process? Why or why not?

6. To what extent does the process described here subscribe to the Baldrige criteria? What else needs to be done?

EXERCISE 13.3
EMPLOYEE INVOLVEMENT FOR
COMPETITIVE ADVANTAGE*

OVERVIEW

As discussed in Chapter 13, in response to increased competitive pressures and to worker demands, many employers are implementing EI processes. EI is viewed as a necessary part of an overall organizational effectiveness strategy and a TQM system. Involvement is seen as a way to tap into the creative potential of the workforce to increase both productivity and job satisfaction. The focus of this exercise will be on determining an appropriate EI strategy for meeting an organization's needs to become more competitive.

LEARNING OBJECTIVES

After completing this exercise, you should be able to:

1. Understand a three-level model of employee involvement.
2. Use several diagnostic scales to select an involvement strategy compatible with the current operating systems of an organization.
3. Develop recommendations for increasing the degree and effectiveness of employee involvement in organizations.

PROCEDURE

Part A: Individual Analysis

Prior to class, read Chapter 13 and the background information and scenario on the Galaxy Corporation. Using the three diagnostic scales provided in Form 13.3.1, rate the Galaxy Corporation on each dimension. As an employee involvement expert, your charge is to develop a set of recommendations to present to Galaxy Corporation executives. These recommendations should cover (1) the current state of Galaxy Corporation on each of the diagnostic dimensions, (2) the appropriate employee involvement strategy for Galaxy, given its current state, and (3) a list of issues that must be addressed if EI is to be successful at Galaxy. Answer all the questions in Form 13.3.1.

*Contributed by Larry A. Pace.

Part B: Group Analysis and Consensus

Working in groups of about six, students should review one another's 13.3.1 forms. The group should then discuss the individuals' ratings of and recommendations for Galaxy Corporation's current state, and develop a group consensus on the rating for each scale and a set of recommendations for Galaxy. Each group should prepare a 5-minute presentation on the group's recommendations.

Part C: Group Presentation and Class Discussion

After group presentations, the class should discuss the similarities and differences among the groups' conclusions and recommendations.

SCENARIO: THE GALAXY CORPORATION

Galaxy Corporation has a total of 5000 employees in 10 plants around the country. Galaxy's main product is a line of packaging and sealing materials used by a variety of customers including automotive, office product, and military organizations. Most of Galaxy's production workers are members of an international union. Galaxy's workforce has recently been cut by 10 percent through layoffs driven by increased competition and excessive overhead costs.

Galaxy specializes in materials used by its customers to package and wrap products for internal and external distribution. Galaxy also manufactures and sells a line of equipment that automatically wraps and seals customer packages using Galaxy's and other manufacturers' packaging materials. Galaxy has a large and, until recently, growing share of its primary market packaging materials. Sales and profits in the automated packaging equipment line have been disappointing at best, and the deepest personnel cuts have occurred in the Packaging Equipment Department (PED).

Galaxy has experienced recent demands from customers for increasingly rigid quality standards. In addition, customers have begun to complain that Galaxy's prices are too high. Galaxy recently lost a large government contract to another bidder. A chief reason for the loss of the contract was that Galaxy's equipment broke down repeatedly during a demonstration for officers at the military installation.

The president of Galaxy Corporation, I. M. Astor, is convinced that Galaxy's problems with quality and cost cannot be solved unless Galaxy's production employees become more involved in problem solving and decision making at the shop floor level. Astor has asked his vice president of HR, Deborah B. Green, to look at various approaches to employee involvement. He told her, "Find me an approach that will work and get it operational quickly." Because of the quality problems Galaxy has experienced, and also because of the embarrassment associated with the breakdowns at the product demonstration, Mr. Astor wants the EI process to be implemented in the production operation responsible for manufacturing the automated packaging equipment, the PED.

Mr. Astor has told Ms. Green that his biggest concern about EI is that he doesn't want to raise expectations in the workforce to an unnecessarily high level. He has also stated that he doesn't believe that PED's managers can be trusted, and that the HRM department should be in charge of EI.

Although Galaxy's production operators are unionized, Astor has said that he doesn't want the union involved in the initial discussions of EI. In his words, "We'll tell them what we're going to do after we've decided. Then we'll ask them to get behind us to save the jobs of their members."

Ms. Green's analysis of Galaxy's current climate and operating systems has revealed the following:

- Galaxy is a traditionally organized company with a functional organizational structure. Its departments are Production, Sales and Marketing, Product Development, Quality Control, Finance and Planning, PED, and HR.
- There are nine layers of management between Mr. Astor and the typical production operator in the PED.
- The production operations of the PED are organized around a traditional assembly line. Work design and job standards have been developed for each individual work station and are highly specific. Most production jobs are highly routine and fractionated. Workers have highly detailed job descriptions.
- The majority of the line supervisors in PED rose through the ranks of hourly workers and do not have formal education beyond high school. The prevailing opinion among the supervisors concerning the production workers is that they are not really trying as hard as they could to improve quality and reduce costs.
- The reward system at Galaxy has historically stressed quantity of production. This is especially true in PED.
- There has been an emphasis on keeping production lines running at virtually any cost. Further, there is an assumption that any problems with quality will be found and fixed by the Quality Control Department.
- The average PED production worker is a white male, 45 years of age, with a high school education.
- Worker satisfaction is at an all-time low in PED, according to a recent employee survey. Last year 70 percent of Galaxy's PED production operators said that they were satisfied or very satisfied with their jobs; this year's percentage was 54.
- Galaxy has recently invested heavily in new production technologies that were supposed to streamline the manufacturing process in PED. These technologies have not, however, lived up to their promise. Galaxy has actually seen costs and rework go *up* after institution of these systems.
- PED supervisors were given a brief introduction to the new systems by the vendor who sold them to Galaxy. Supervisors were then told to train their workers on the new systems. Supervisors were also told, however, that they would receive no relief on production targets during training and that the training should be as brief as possible.

FORM 13.3.1

Name _____ Group _____

The survey forms presented below are designed to measure both the congruence in organizational systems and the readiness of an organization for different types of EI. Use of these forms can help managers and HRM professionals to diagnose the current state of the organization and to plan the appropriate EI intervention. Congruence may be said to exist if the scores on all the scales are similar. If the scores are not similar, the action plan must include efforts to achieve organizational system congruence in addition to or even in preparation for an EI intervention.

For each item below, circle the number that best describes your own assessment of Galaxy Corporation, based on the information provided. Remember that if the three forms produce conflicting results, the organization demonstrates a lack of congruence.

I. <u>Worker Characteristics</u>

Need to be told just what to do and how to do it. Otherwise, they will do nothing.	1 2 3 4 5 6	Willing to assume responsibility for what needs to be done and then do it.
Willing to let others make most of the decisions affecting their work.	1 2 3 4 5 6	Will protest if they are not consulted on matters affecting their work.
Capable of handling a limited number of tasks.	1 2 3 4 5 6	Cable of doing jobs involving a variety of tasks.
Can tolerate boring work.	1 2 3 4 5 6	Demand interesting work.
Have a relatively low level of skill or knowledge.	1 2 3 4 5 6	Have a relatively high level of skill or knowledge.
Work best if someone else controls the pace of their own work.	1 2 3 4 5 6	Work best if they control the pace of their own work.

Total: _____

<u>Diagnosis:</u> If the total of the ratings in this section is 15 or less, the employees may need training before EI is started, and a parallel suggestion involvement is indicated. If the total is between 16 and 26, the workers would likely respond to a job involvement strategy. For a total of 27 or higher, the indicated involvement approach is a high-involvement work system.

FORM 13.3.1 *(Continued)*

II. Current Structure of Jobs and Work

Jobs are clearly defined, structured, and stable.	1 2 3 4 5 6	Jobs are flexible and permit group problem solving.
There is a clear hierarchy of authority.	1 2 3 4 5 6	There is delegation of authority to those who do the job.
The most important motivators are financial (e.g., earnings, profits).	1 2 3 4 5 6	The most important motivators are nonfinancial (e.g., challenge, teamwork).
Job methods are defined by specialists.	1 2 3 4 5 6	Job methods are left up to the individual or the group.
Production targets are set by management.	1 2 3 4 5 6	Production targets are left up to the employees.
People are given only the specific information they need to do the job.	1 2 3 4 5 6	People have easy access to all the information they deem relevant.
There is close supervision, tight control, and well-maintained discipline.	1 2 3 4 5 6	There is democratic supervision, little external control, and self-discipline.

Total: _____

Diagnosis: If the total of the ratings in this section is 17 or less, the job and work design are highly fractionated, and the appropriate form of involvement is a parallel suggestion system. Scores between 18 and 31 indicate that a job involvement system could be implemented. Totals of 32 or higher would argue for the introduction of a high-involvement work system.

FORM 13.3.1 *(Continued)*

III. Organizational Diagnosis

Decision making occurs at the top of the organization.	1 2 3 4 5 6	Decision making occurs at all levels of the organization.
The control mechanisms of the organization focus on fixing the accountability for errors.	1 2 3 4 5 6	The control mechanisms of the organization focus on self-control and problem solving.
Managers make little effort to develop the HRs of the company.	1 2 3 4 5 6	Managers fully support the necessity of developing the HRs of the company.
Attitudes toward the organization are predominately unfavorable.	1 2 3 4 5 6	Attitudes toward the organization are predominately favorable.
There is little trust between supervisors and subordinates.	1 2 3 4 5 6	There is high trust between supervisors and subordinates.
Supervisors do not solicit the ideas and opinions of their subordinates.	1 2 3 4 5 6	Supervisors solicit the ideas and opinions of their subordinates.

Total: _____

Diagnosis: If the total of the ratings in this section is 15 or less, the organizational system is control-oriented and will not tolerate direct changes to job design, organizational structure, or worker and managerial roles. Therefore, the appropriate form of involvement is parallel suggestion involvement. A total of 16 to 26 indicates that job involvement could be increased through job enrichment or a work team strategy. A total of 27 or higher indicates that the organization's system is commitment-oriented, and the appropriate form of involvement is a high-involvement work system.

IV. <u>Questions Regarding the EI Intervention.</u>

1. If you were vice president of HR, what concerns would you express to Mr. Astor regarding his directives?

2. What EI strategy do you recommend? Explain your answer. What (if any) additional information do you require?

3. What issues should Galaxy address before implementing any EI program?

4. Are there any other HR interventions which would be helpful for this situation?

14

C H A P T E R

LABOR RELATIONS*

*Contributed by Nancy Brown Johnson.

OVERVIEW

Management students today often learn the "ideal" way to manage firms' human resources (HR), making it difficult for them to comprehend the adverse working environments that often led to unionization. People in the early part of the century often worked under conditions many of us cannot fathom—"dark, satanic mills," with workweeks of at least 60 hours and with no provisions for safety, illness, vacations, or retirement.[1] Thus, the union's role in improving these conditions was clear. While the goal of unions today is still to improve working conditions and increase workers' economic status, the need and effects are far more subtle than they were during the early years of unions in America.

As discussed in Chapters 3 and 11, the United States has legislation governing wages and hours, equal employment opportunity (EEO), pensions, mergers, social security, and health and safety. Research shows that there is little to be gained from worker exploitation in this country. Further, the relatively clean service industry, not the harsh factories, provide for a substantial proportion of present-day employment. Today's workers face mental rather than physical strains, which makes the need for union intervention less clear-cut.

Though union membership in the United States dropped substantially in the 1980s to less than 17 percent of the nonfarm U.S. workforce, unions are nonetheless an important influence upon workers and firms—both union and nonunion. Union influence is much greater outside of the U.S., particularly in Europe. There are still over 70,000 local unions and 173 national unions. Of these, 110 belong to the influential AFL-CIO, which represents about 80 percent of all unionized employees in the United States. Obviously, union firms are more constrained because many HR decisions, such as compensation, promotion, demotion, and termination, require union involvement. In general, management must handle personnel matters with the union rather than with each individual employee. As we discussed in Chapters 11 and 12, unions have a great influence over pay structure and the compensation system in general. Nonunion firms also concern themselves with union activities because they usually desire to maintain their nonunion status. To do so, these firms must be aware of unions and their history, their goals, the legal constraints, and their influences upon firms. Obviously, the working conditions, wages, and terms of employment of unionized firms have an effect upon the way in which nonunion employers manage their HR in order to maintain nonunion status. For example, the Nissan automobile plant in Smryna, Tennessee, has provided favorable benefits to its employees to date, and despite considerable effort on the part of union organizers, the employees have voted to stay nonunionized. As we

discussed in Chapter 13, unions are also very much involved in productivity improvement programs.

This chapter will begin with a brief history of the labor movement in the United States. We will review the major legislation affecting the labor movement and management today. We then discuss the contemporary labor movement and the future. The factors and procedures related to union organizing will also be covered, along with an overview of labor relations in other countries. Chapter 15 will explore the collective bargaining process.

OBJECTIVES

After studying this chapter you should:

1. Be familiar with the development and effects of labor unions.
2. Understand the basic elements of labor law.
3. Understand the correlates of union organizing and why people join unions.
4. Be able to describe current trends and issues in labor relations.
5. Understand the basic differences between labor relations in the United States and in other countries.

Today, many business students hold a negative view of the American labor movement. Many see unions as antimanagement, striving to control or even reduce productivity while demanding higher wages and ironclad protection for workers regardless of their performance. This extreme view may derive to some extent from a lack of historical perspective on labor relations in this country. Let us begin this chapter by providing this perspective.

THE LIFE CYCLE OF THE AMERICAN LABOR MOVEMENT

Most organizations go through relatively uniform and progressive life cycles that are not easily reversed.[2] The labor movement is no exception. Labor unions in the United States have developed in a predictable pattern, evolving from the unique circumstances facing labor. This life-cycle approach yields a useful framework for exploring and interpreting the historical development of the U.S. labor movement. Figure 14.1 presents a summary of the life cycle of the U.S. labor movement.

Entrepreneurial Stage: Colonial Times to 1885

In the entrepreneurial stage, organizations experiment with alternative philosophies and structures before settling on

FIGURE 14.1
LIFE CYCLE OF THE U.S. LABOR MOVEMENT

STAGE	PERIOD	CHARACTERISTICS
Entreprenurial	Colonial–1885	Experimentation; anticapitalist; Knights of Labor; *Philadelphia Cordwainers* case; mixed assemblies
Collectivity	1886–1930	Rise of AFL—basic structure for U.S. labor; AFL accepted capitalism; exclusive jurisdiction; skilled trades only; temporary injunction; yellow-dog contracts; open shop movement
Formalization, control, and eiaboration	1931–1954	CIO formed; NLRA passed (1935); decentralization of movement; changing legal environment; *yellow-dog contracts* unenforceable
Decline	1955–1979	AFL-CIO merger membership down; increased management opposition; Landrum-Griffin Act (1959)
Late decline	1980–present	Significant drop in membership; increasing international competition; deregulation of labor movement

the form they will eventually take. Little planning and coordination occur within these organizations. Yet, at the same time, they attempt to develop a niche. Early labor movements that ended in failure in the 1800s experimented with various ideas and beliefs, providing useful lessons for the founders of the existing labor movement. Early labor endeavors included the workingmen's parties that used the political system to elect candidates and obtain legislation. Further, they believed in bringing the means of production under the direct control of the workers through direct action such as strikes. These movements served as early experiments in dealing with the adverse conditions facing the workers of the 1800s and the early 1900s. All these movements advocated dramatic reform in the existing capitalistic system, which was a major factor in their downfall. In contrast, a few successful skilled trade unions, arising during the Civil War period, accepted capitalism and focused on basic economic issues such as raising wages and improving working conditions. Several of these unions still exist today. In general, however, the early 1800s served as a time of trial and error for labor movements.

The Knights of Labor provided particularly salient lessons for the founders of today's labor movement. The Knights took a peaceful, reformist approach, supporting education and workers' cooperatives for improving workers' societal positions. The leadership did not advocate the use of the strike, although the members did strike against Jay Gould, a well-known railroad financier. This strike brought them notoriety and additional members, yet also illustrated the inconsistencies between beliefs and actions which contributed to their later down-

fall. In addition, their structure, known as "mixed assemblies," allowed virtually all workers to become members. Because these workers had little in common, limited attachment to the Knights resulted.[3] In particular, frustration developed among the craft workers. They held more bargaining power than unskilled workers due to the difficulty in replacing them during a strike; therefore, they felt that they supported the entire organization. The strikes' success and the mixed assemblies' failure supplied lessons for the American Federation of Labor (AFL).

During the entrepreneurial stage, management also experimented with legal weapons to fight labor unions. No legislation governed unions at this time; therefore, common-law principles took precedence. The 1794 *Philadelphia Cordwainers* case originated the criminal conspiracy doctrine. The court found the cordwainers (shoemakers) guilty of a conspiracy because of restraint of trade across state lines. In 1842, *Commonwealth v. Hunt* overturned the criminal conspiracy doctrine by stating that actions designed to convince nonmembers of the Boston Journeymen Bootmakers' Society to join were no longer seen as criminal. This case established the ends-means test, in which a strike's legality depended upon the legality of the end sought and the means used. The courts judged the legality of the ends and means, and they tended to sympathize with business.

Collectivity Stage: The Rise of the AFL

In the collectivity stage, the basic organizational model is formed. Informal structures, high commitment, and a sense of mission characterize this stage—and the AFL's early days. In 1984, Samuel Gompers, founder and long-term president of the AFL, stated, "It was the crusading spirit that sustained many of us in those early days. We placed the cause of labor before everything else—personal advancement, family, comfort, or anything."[4] The AFL formed the basic structure and principles for the U.S. labor movement.

In contrast to earlier movements, the AFL accepted capitalism. Pragmatically oriented and working within the existing economic system, the AFL established a primary goal of improving workers' economic position by advocating the avoidance of long-run reformist goals, collective bargaining buttressed by the strike, and no government intervention. In addition, it restricted membership to skilled trades because of the bargaining power of these trades. It also advocated "exclusive jurisdiction," in which a group of employees could be represented by only one union. The existing U.S. labor movement differs little in principle from the model formally established in 1886.[5]

With labor's growing successes, management began to develop new legal tactics for resisting labor unions. The *temporary injunction,* one of these tactics, is a court order that was originally intended to prevent irreversible financial or property damage by barring labor's actions (e.g., strikes) until the court ruled formally on the actions' legality. In the case of strikes, the courts issued frequent injunctions which served as effective strike breakers. The *yellow-dog contract* is an agreement stating that joining a union will result in termination. This tactic effectively thwarted unions since employers required workers to sign such contracts as a condition of employment. Although workers could be fired "at will" anyway, the yellow-dog contract remained a useful strategy for obtaining court injunctions to defeat union organizing attempts.

The turn of the century brought relatively steady growth in labor union membership. Union membership, as a percentage of the total labor force, climbed steadily from about 6.5 percent in 1900 to 17.6 percent of the nonagricultural labor force in 1920. The government, for the first time, recognized the labor movement's viability and partially contributed to this growth. To reduce strikes during World War I, the government created the tripartite National War Labor Board, with members from labor, management, and the public. In exchange for the right to strike, employers agreed to recognize labor's right to organize and bargain collectively.

This growth trend reversed as the 1920s brought declining union membership. With the advent of the human relations school of management, employers themselves began to provide workers with better wages and working conditions. Thus, workers had less reason to unionize. Further, some firms established company unions, which were controlled by the company and served to deter legitimate unions. Employers also joined forces to frustrate unions through the open shop movement and the American Plan. For example, the Chamber of Commerce created the open shop movement, advocating union-free shops by mounting an antiunion publicity campaign. In contrast to the Chamber's openness, employers secretly established the American Plan to associate the labor movement with foreign subversives. These factors, combined with relative prosperity during the 1920s, contributed to the decline of unions.[6]

Formalization, Control, and Elaboration of Structure: The Statutory Period

In the formalization and control stage, organizations relied heavily on rules, maintenance, and efficiency. Procedures became institutionalized and leadership became conservative, and so organizations resisted change. The AFL leadership actively opposed change in the 1930s by resisting industrial unionists and strictly adhering to craft unionism. By the 1930s, major industries such as automobiles, steel, and rubber had expanded. Yet, the AFL believed that organizing the "unskilled" workers of these industries would weaken the labor movement because they lacked bargaining power. The issue came to a head at the 1935 AFL convention when the industrial unionists formed the Committee for Industrial Organization against the craft unionists' will. The committee's explicit purpose was to organize industrial workers. The committee was expelled by the AFL and renamed itself the Congress of Industrial Organization (CIO). Domain expansion, adaptation, renewal, and decentralization also characterize organizations in this stage. Consistent with domain expansion, the CIO began an extensive drive to organize industries such as steel, rubber, meatpacking, and automobiles in the late 1930s and early 1940s. The AFL began adapting to CIO competition by a renewed organization effort. These endeavors contributed to tremendous membership gains for the entire labor movement, despite the movement's decentralization into two separate entities. Figure 14.2 illustrates trends in union membership beginning in 1930.

The changing legal environment also fostered a growth in union membership during the 1930s. Figure 14.3 highlights the provisions of some of the key legislation affecting the labor movement. In 1926, the *Railway Labor Act,* the first significant piece of labor legislation, encouraged collective bargaining for handling railroad disputes. Labors' large legal inroads, nonetheless, occurred during the Depression. During this time, sympathies began changing from supporting big business to backing labor. Many believed that labor unions provided a "countervailing power" to aid in controlling business interests. Thus, in 1932 Congress passed the *Norris-LaGuardia Act,* which severely restricted the use of the injunction and made yellow-dog contracts unenforceable.

FIGURE 14.2
TRENDS IN THE U.S. LABOR MOVEMENT

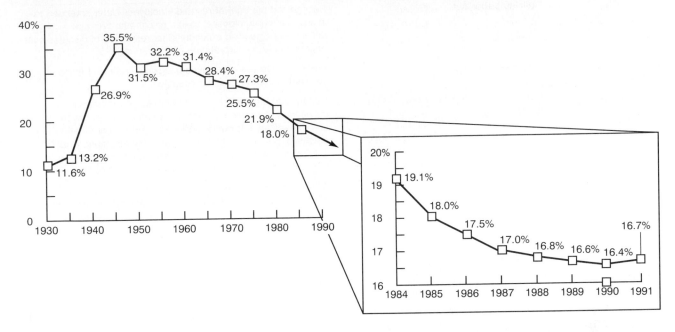

Source: *Unemployment & Earnings*, January 1992.

Considered to be neutral, the act was intended to restore a balance of power between labor and management.

Congress enacted the 1935 *National Labor Relations Act* (NLRA) as a pro-labor bill; it is also known as the *Wagner Act*. The NLRA formally recognized workers' right to organize and bargain collectively with representatives of their own choosing. To enforce that right, the bill described what constituted unfair labor practices by employers. Prohibited activities for employers included: (1) interfering with employee representation and collective bargaining rights; (2) dominating or interfering with the affairs of unions; (3) discriminating in regard to hiring, retention, or any employment condition against workers who engage in union activity or who file unfair labor practice charges; and (4) not bargaining in good faith with employee representatives. Further, the bill established the National Labor Relations Board (NLRB) to enforce the *Wagner Act* and to conduct representation elections. Essentially, the goal of the NLRA was to regulate the *processes* of organizing and collective bargaining, not necessarily the *outcomes*.

World War II inspired the creation of another board, this one called the "War Labor Board," which requested no-strike pledges and wage-price controls from labor. At the end of the war, the strike rate skyrocketed because of labor's attempts to regain wages foregone during the war. Public sentiment quickly turned against the labor movement and ultimately led to the passage of the 1947 *Taft-Hartley Act*. Taft-Hartley drafters intended to restore a

balance between labor and management by regulating labor activities. Labor, however, called it the "slave labor bill." The bill amended the NLRA by describing what constituted unfair labor practices by unions, including: (1) restricting the usage of the strike, including granting the president of the United States the power to issue an injunction against a strike; (2) restricting unions from interfering with workers' right to organize; and (3) prohibiting union discrimination against workers who did not want to participate in union activities, including strikes. In addition, the Taft-Hartley Act provided states with the option of enacting right-to-work legislation. Right-to-work laws declare that union security agreements which require membership as a condition of employment are illegal. Twenty-one states have enacted right-to-work laws. To aid in the peaceful settlement of contractual disputes, Congress created the *Federal Mediation and Conciliation Service* (FMCS) and provided emergency dispute provisions for the settlement of strikes affecting national health and safety. Thus, the Taft-Hartley Act further restricted union activity. Unfair labor practices by management were also reaffirmed under the Taft-Hartley Act. Figure 14.4 presents a summary of the major implications of the NLRA and the Taft-Hartley Act.

Decline: 1955–1980

A glance at Figure 14.2 illustrates that union membership peaked in 1955 and has been declining ever since.

FIGURE 14.3
SUMMARY OF MAJOR U.S. LABOR LEGISLATION

YEAR ENACTED	LEGISLATION	KEY PROVISIONS
1926	Railway Labor Act	Recognized the right of railroad employees (later amended to include airline employees) to join unions and bargain collectively. Specified procedures for resolution of disputes over negotiation and interpretation of the contract.
1932	Norris-LaGuardia Act	Restricted the use of injunctions against labor and made yellow-dog contracts unenforceable.
1935	National Labor Relations Act (NLRA) (Wagner Act)	Recognized employees' rights to organize and bargain collectively, described employer unfair labor practices to enforce employee's rights, provided for union certification elections, and created the National Labor Relations Board (NLRB) to conduct elections and investigate unfair labor practices.
1947	Labor-Management Relations Act (Taft-Hartley Act)	Described union unfair labor practices, including secondary boycotts, established the Federal Mediation and Conciliation Service (FMCS) to aid in dispute resolution, provided for emergency procedures, and enabled states to pass right-to-work laws.
1959	Labor-Management Reporting and Disclosure Act (Landrum-Griffin Act)	Established employee "bill of rights," required unions to file annual financial reports, and regulated trusteeships. Union members have the right to: (1) nominate candidates for union office, (2) vote in union elections, and (3) attend union meetings.
1978	Civil Service Reform Act	Established right of federal employees to have union representation. Created the Federal Labor Relations Authority to monitor federal labor relations. Forbade wage negotiations and prohibited strikes.

In particular, union density dropped significantly in the 1980s, with only 16.7 percent of the U.S. workforce unionized as of 1991. Conflict, bureaucracy, rigidity, and conservatism differentiate organizational decline. Similar criticism has been leveled against organized labor and may partially account for the drop in membership. Targets of criticism include a lack of effective leadership, more time spent on worker representation than on organization, and membership apathy. Yet organizational decline need not be inevitable, and the elaboration of the structure stage can lead to organizational renewal. Nonetheless, since the mid-1950s the labor movement has decreased for several reasons.[7] The structural hypothesis contends that unions have had less success in organizing *growing* sectors of the economy as compared to *declining* economic sectors. For example, the labor movement experiences more success in organizing goods-producing industries than service industries, and northern industries rather than southern industries.

New technology represents another force which affects industrial relations. At Caterpillar, plant modernization precipitated the prolonged strike which swept the company in late 1991 and 1992. The company demanded concessions in the form of reduced job classifications and less strict work rules to increase workforce flexibility to adapt to changes in manufacturing processes.

A second hypothesis for union membership decline suggests that management opposition has increased and has become more sophisticated. For example, many consulting firms today specialize in "union prevention." In addition, management can indirectly oppose unions through "positive personnel policies" that offer nonunion workers wages and benefits comparable to those of union workers. These policies may make unions relatively less attractive for the 1990s. Further, management can directly oppose unions by fighting them through legal or illegal organizing campaigns.

Another reason given for union membership decline is that public policy changes, such as right-to-work laws, have imperiled union growth. In addition, recent protective labor legislation (e.g., *The Civil Rights Act* of 1991, antitakeover laws, plant-closing legislation, state restrictions on employment-at-will, and pension reform) provides protection which are comparable to union representation, reducing the attractiveness of union representation. Finally, some people believe that unions have shifted their emphasis from organizing new workers to representing existing workers, thus naturally leading to lower levels of unionization. This argument, however, is under debate.[8]

The decline of unions has also been partially attributed to the fact that Congress has not supported fa-

FIGURE 14.4
MAJOR IMPLICATIONS OF NLRA AND TAFT-HARTLEY ACT

BY MANAGEMENT (WAGNER ACT)	BY UNION (TAFT-HARTLEY ACT)
Interfere with, restrain, or coerce employees in the exercise of their rights to organize, bargain collectively, and engage in other activities for their mutual aid or protection (e.g.,. threaten employees with the loss of a job if they vote for the union).	Restrain or coerce employees in the exercise of their right to join or not join a union.
Dominate or interfere with the formation or administration of any labor organization or contribute financial or other support to it.	Restrain or coerce an employer in the selection of his or her bargaining or grievance representative.
Encourage or discourage membership in any labor organization by discrimination with regard to hiring or tenure or conditions of employment, subject to an exception for valid union-security agreements.	Cause or attempt to cause an employer to discriminate against an employee due to membership or nonmembership in a union, subject to an exception for valid union-shop agreements.
Discharge or otherwise discriminate against an employee because he or she has filed charges or given testimony under the Wagner Act.	Refuse to bargain collectively (in good faith) with an employer if the union has been designated as a bargaining agent by a majority of the employees.
Refuse to bargain collectively with representatives of the employees; that is, bargain in good faith.	Induce or encourage employees to stop work in order to force an employer or self-employed person to join a union or to force an employer or other person to stop doing business with any other person (secondary boycott).
	Induce or encourage employees to stop work in order to force an employer to recognize and bargain with the union where another union has been certified as a bargaining agent (strike against a certification).
	Induce or encourage employees to stop work in order to force an employer to assign particular work to members of the union instead of to members of another union (jurisdictional strike).
	Charge an excessive or discriminatory membership fee as a condition to becoming a member of the union.
	Cause or attempt to cause an employer to pay for services that are not performed or not to be performed (featherbedding).

Source: Adapted with permission from J. J. Kenny and L. G. Kahn, *Primer of labor relations.* Washington: Bureau of National Affairs, 1989, pp. 1–3.

vorable labor legislation. In the late 1950s, the U.S. Senate held hearings investigating and exposing union corruption that ultimately resulted in the 1959 *Landrum-Griffin Act.* Designed to protect workers from their unions, the act provided for the employee "bill of rights," union filing of annual financial statements with the Department of Labor, and the requirement that unions hold national and local officer elections every 5 years and 3 years, respectively. Some unions had been using trusteeships to control dissident local unions, by placing the local unions under the national's control. The *Landrum-Griffin Act* began regulating trusteeships in order to ensure that they were used for legitimate purposes. After the act was passed, the labor unions made two failed attempts to pass favorable private-sector labor legislation in the 1970s. Unions have, however, successfully supported an extension of unemployment benefits and general social legislation, including the 1990 Americans with Disabilities Act (ADA) and the 1991 Civil Rights Act (see Chapter 3). At the state level, the labor movement has also been successful in supporting family leave laws and merger and acquisition regulation. All this legislation may, however, lead to the decline of union membership

as individual workers perceive enough protection being offered from organizations.

Late Decline: 1980s

Between 1980 and 1990, union membership declined by 8 percent.[9] Over 2 million manufacturing jobs were lost in that decade, due primarily to plant closings, mergers, and layoffs. Some have argued that this dramatic drop in membership has come about because of growing environmental pressures and that it reflects a significant transformation in industrial relations.[10] For example, increased international competition and deregulation affect union membership rates. International competition in industries such as automobiles, rubber, and steel has greatly affected industrial relations issues for these industries. In the late 1960s, for instance, the United Auto Workers (UAW) organized unions in the "big three" automakers which accounted for virtually all the U.S. market. This level of organization was combined with pattern bargaining (in which a settlement reached with the first company serves as a model for all the remaining negotiations and settlements), which meant that all automakers had comparable labor costs that could be passed on to the consumer. With the Japanese entry into the U.S. automotive market, U.S. consumers could choose between Japanese and American cars. This led to U.S. autoworkers' wages being brought back into competition with Japanese workers' wages, since industry survival depends partially on wage, benefit, and work-rule concessions. The 3-year agreement signed in 1990 between the UAW and the big three U.S. automakers built in significant reductions in the workforce through attrition and buyouts of older workers, in exchange for greater job security. However, even as early as December 1990, GM announced 60,000 further reductions in employment over a 3-year period. With Big Three financial losses of $7.5 billion in 1991 and a UAW strike fund in excess of $850 million, the 1993 negotiations should be very interesting.

Deregulation of industries such as airlines and trucking has played a critical role in shaping the 1980s industrial relations environment. In the late 1970s, Congress legislatively deregulated airlines and trucking. This has profoundly affected these industries and their industrial relations. One regulatory effect apparently caused wages to be above competitive levels. This wage effect resulted from regulators' setting prices based upon costs (of which wages were a portion) and from regulators' creating entry barriers to prevent nonunion competitors from entering the industry and competing on the basis of wages. Deregulation introduced new competitive pressures in both industries. In trucking because of nonunion industry entrants, unionization declined from about 63 percent in 1973 to less than 30 percent in 1985.[11] In airlines, financial barriers to industry entry restricted the number of new entrants, so that concession bargaining became the norm. In 1986, 70 percent of airline collective bargaining agreements had two-tier wage scales, in which new employees' wages were set below those of existing workers on the same job.[12] For example, the two-tier pay system negotiated with American Airlines in 1983 resulted in new pilots getting up to 50 percent less pay than current employees. However, deregulation has apparently not led to lower wages for employees.[13]

PUBLIC-SECTOR UNION MEMBERSHIP

While private-sector union membership had dropped to 16.7 percent of wage and salary earners by 1991, the public sector maintained a ratio of 43 percent.[14] Despite the currently high level of representation rates for government workers, public-sector unions appear to be following the same growth and development stages as private-sector unions—albeit at a lagged pace.[15] Public-sector growth and development can be characterized in three phases: little organization (before 1960), rapid increase in bargaining and membership (between 1960 and 1975), and slow growth (from 1975 to the present). Several reasons are offered for this trend. Limited union organization occurred before 1960 partly because private-sector labor legislation did not cover public-sector employees and public-sector laws did not begin emerging until after 1960. Second, public-sector employment remained relatively stable compared to that of the private sector, giving public-sector workers a sense of security. Finally, the public-sector strike prohibition combined with no protective labor legislation left unions with little bargaining power. These factors combined to give public-sector workers before 1960 little reason to organize.

After 1960, however, environmental changes created more incentives for public-sector unionization. Factors such as relatively low wages eroded by inflation provided some impetus for public-sector workers to organize. Further, many government workers, such as teachers, were already members of organizations that could, and did, become bargaining agents. The relative lack of sophistication of public-sector employers in organizing antiunion campaigns also fostered unionization efforts. This lack of sophistication often meant that employers did not strongly resist unionization. The first state legislation and federal executive orders providing for public-sector collective bargaining were also enacted during this period. While prohibiting strikes, the 1978 Civil Service Reform Act established the right of federal employees to have union representation. Now federal regulations make it easier for unions to try to organize the 3 million nonunion employees of public hospitals. These factors have all contributed to the rise in public-sector labor union growth. However, public-sector structural changes such as the tax reform movement of the 1980s, along with increased management resistance, may have led to a flattening of public-sector unionization growth in the most recent years.[16]

REASONS WORKERS JOIN UNIONS

Research indicates that there are three general reasons why workers join unions. These include: (1) perceptions of the work environment, (2) desires to participate in or influence employment conditions, and (3) employee beliefs about the effects of unions. Figure 14.5 presents a model of these determinants.

Workers' dissatisfaction with their jobs, and in particular their dissatisfaction with their wages, benefits, and supervision, are most related to the tendency to vote for a union.[17] For example, one study of over 87,000 workers in retail found that attitudes toward supervision, wages, and benefits measured 3 to 15 months prior to a formal

FIGURE 14.5
DETERMINANTS OF PROPENSITY TO JOIN UNIONS

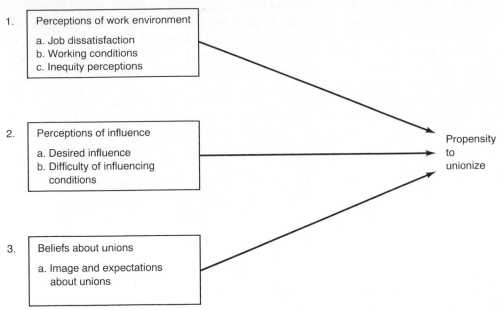

1. Perceptions of work environment
   a. Job dissatisfaction
   b. Working conditions
   c. Inequity perceptions

2. Perceptions of influence
   a. Desired influence
   b. Difficulty of influencing conditions

3. Beliefs about unions
   a. Image and expectations about unions

Propensity to unionize

Source: T. Kochan, *Collective bargaining and industrial relations.* Homewood, IL: Richard D. Irwin, 1980, p. 144. Reprinted with permission.

union organizing effort were strong predictors of the subsequent vote for unionization. For example, a 1989 study within the Federal Aviation Administration (FAA) found similar results prior to a certification vote to reunionize air traffic controllers. The union vote varied across regions of the FAA and correlated significantly with attitudes toward supervision, pay, and perceived work stress. One surprising finding from the research on why people vote for unions is that the work itself does not seem to be strongly related to union voting. The best predictors in several studies are attitudes toward pay and working conditions, rather than the work itself.

A second general reason for joining unions is a belief that there are no other options for either gaining more influence at the workplace or finding employment elsewhere. In general, to the extent that management has mechanisms enabling employees to voice their concerns about HRM policy, there is less tendency to favor unionization. A formal grievance procedure, for example, which has been used successfully by employees, would deter union activity since workers perceive that there are alternatives to unions as an approach to correcting problems at work.

The third critical reason for joining unions is that employees believe unions can actually improve conditions and, in particular, can have an impact at their own workplace.[18] Companies really work on influencing em-

ployees' beliefs in this regard. Campaign tactics by management include written communications, meetings, threats, and actions against union supporters. These can negatively affect workers' votes for unionization. Japanese firms with U.S. operations have been particularly adept at launching antiunion campaigns and quite successful in winning certification elections. Companies often use consultants who specialize in refuting the claims of union organizers and presenting horrendous scenarios that would develop if the union should prevail. It is estimated that there are over 1000 such firms and an additional 1500 private consultants in the union prevention or "busting" business.[19]

While many Americans believe unions can improve things at work, many are generally hostile to unions. They think unions protect ineffective workers, abuse their power through strikes, are corrupt, and impede productivity improvement programs. One study found that knowing an employee's general opinion about unions in these areas was a strong predictor of how the employee would vote for union representation.[20]

THE EFFECTS OF UNIONS

Workers join unions to improve their wages, working conditions, and job security. This section presents results regarding whether or not unions actually do provide these improvements and what these effects mean for firm performance. Two perspectives dominate the literature on the effects of labor unions: monopoly and collective voice.[21] Economists traditionally believe that labor unions behave as labor market monopolies. They see unions as primarily raising wages, which results in economic inefficiencies and ultimately adverse effects for workers and firms. The collective voice perspective views unions more positively by concentrating on their beneficial economic and political aspects. These two perspectives are described below.

Monopoly Effects

The monopoly view of unions starts with the premise that unions raise wages above competitive levels. How much unions raise wages varies across labor markets, industries, occupations, and demographic groups, as well as data and estimation procedures. Overall, estimates of union and nonunion wage differentials are around 15 percent higher for union employees.[22] Unions also apparently have a significant positive effect on fringe benefits. These estimates, however, vary by demographic group. This variation partially results from a union philosophy that workers doing the same job should receive the same pay. Thus, those who are usually paid the least tend to benefit the most from unionization. Studies show that younger workers, nonwhites, people living in the South and the West, and blue-collar workers seem to gain the most from unionization. Interestingly, little apparent difference exists between the wage gains from unionization for males and females. Research on public-sector unions shows a +5 percent pay differential for public-sector employees represented by unions versus public-sector employees not represented.[23]

Variations in union wage effects across industries partly occur due to the union's ability to take "wages out of competition." If unions raise wages too much in a competitive market, they threaten the firm's and their own survival. Wages can be taken out of competition in several ways. First, labor demand may be relatively insensitive to wage changes (inelastic). That is, consumers will absorb the increased labor costs without offsetting employment effects. Factors which contribute to labor demand inelasticity include labor costs being a small proportion of total costs; insensitivity of product demand to changes in prices; and an inability to substitute labor for capital, either through technology or through markets.[24]

The extent of union organization in a particular market can also affect union monopoly power. More unionized markets have greater union/nonunion wage differentials because of less nonunion wage competition. The extent of bargaining coverage further augments this effect. This coverage can take several forms. For example, one union may bargain for the entire market—so that all union firms in the industry have virtually identical contracts. In the auto industry, the UAW bargains with one of the big three automakers and then uses this contract as a pattern for the remaining settlements. A union negotiating simultaneously with numerous employers, as in steel and coal, provides another example of extensive industry coverage. A union that bargains at the plant level has much less monopoly power than those that negotiate on a broader basis.

Some economists condemn unions because they believe the union wage effect leads to inefficient firm responses such as substituting labor for capital. They argue that society suffers due to resource misallocation between the union and the nonunion sectors. However, unions strongly believe in equal pay for equal work. This union policy reduces the amount of wage dispersion within firms, within the union sector, and between blue-collar and white-collar workers. These equalizing effects, estimates show, outweigh the inequality produced by the union/nonunion wage differential by almost 3 percent, although the interpretation of these findings are somewhat controversial.[25] Further, many American workers prefer pay-for-performance (PFP) systems over straight pay, and unions generally favor pay systems based strictly on seniority, with little or no distinction made between individual workers based on their performance. For example, unions representing college professors usually lobby state legislatures to provide only across-the-board raises rather than discretionary money that would enable administrators to base pay on meritorious performance. Union negotiators at Du Pont Corporation and at the General Motors (GM) Saturn plant worked hard in 1991 to dismantle elements of the PFP systems negotiated in the 1980s. Workers at Saturn were dissatisfied in 1991 because 20 percent of their annual pay was tied to profit measures which were not realized since the car was introduced. The 1991 contract proposal was much more traditional in terms of base pay and benefits.

Collective Voice Effects

Workers have several choices when they feel dissatisfied with their jobs: they can do nothing, they can quit their job, or they can complain and try to improve the conditions around them (i.e., voice their concerns). In work settings, the voice of one employee is rarely effective at bringing about change. In addition, many workers fear termination for revealing their true feelings to management. Most workers find it easier to fight for work improvements through a union. Banding together and creating a "collective voice" offers protection from the fear of raising concerns to management. Union advocates maintain that the collective voice reduces worker quit rates, thereby leading to retention of experienced workers, lowering a firm's training costs, and raising its productivity. Another side benefit is that management is forced to become more efficient when faced with the necessity of providing higher wages to unionized employees.

Union Effects on Firm Performance: Productivity, Profits, and Stock Price

The collective voice mechanism suggests that unions may actually have positive effects on management. If so, why does management strenuously resist unions? Are they behaving rationally? Or do they resist unions only because unions threaten their decision-making autonomy? Recent empirical evidence regarding union productivity, profitability, and stock price effects suggests that management may behave rationally in resisting unions.

Two theories exist regarding unions' effects upon firms' productivity.[26] On one hand, productivity is predicted to decrease in unionized firms because unions create resource misallocation and demand restrictive work rules. In contrast, the collective voice view predicts that productivity gains may occur because the union wage effect causes firms to manage better, employ better-quality labor, substitute capital for labor, and reduce voluntary turnover, leading to the development of a more experienced and better-trained labor force. Others attribute any productivity gains more to organizational survival than to collective voice effects.[27] To remain competitive, management *must* improve productivity.

The evidence is mixed regarding the effects of unions on organizational productivity.[28] Different studies have shown that unions have positive, negative, and no influences upon productivity. Positive productivity effects generally tend to be found in competitive industries with higher union wage effects (i.e., where firm survival apparently depends upon offsetting the higher wage costs with increased productivity). One review of the research concluded that, in general, productivity remains higher in union establishments than in nonunion establishments. This conclusion is controversial and the subject of much debate.[29] The researchers concluded that when unions and management are working for a "bigger pie" as well as fighting over their relative shares, the result is higher productivity. Under conditions of poor labor-management relations, where the focus is on taking a bigger share of the same size pie, the result is usually lower productivity.

If unions do improve productivity, how can management behave rationally by resisting unions? Apparently union productivity effects do not sufficiently outweigh the negative impact of unions on accounting profits and stock prices. Studies show that unionization negatively affects accounting profits and shareholder wealth. For example, shareholder wealth decreases during union organizing campaigns and strikes, and increases during concession bargaining.[30] In addition, unions do not seem to change the overall firm value, but they do redistribute the firm's economic profits from the stockholders to the workers.

Unions and Quality of Work Life Issues

As we discussed in Chapter 13, quality-of-work-life (QWL) issues came to the forefront in the 1980s and continue to play an important role in the labor-management relationship. Some QWL programs such as job redesign efforts, upward communication, team-based work configurations, and quality circles (QCs) have elicited a variety of union responses.[31] Overt hostility and resistance characterize some unions' reactions to QWL programs. A significant faction of the UAW membership at the Saturn plant, for example, opposes the negotiated worker involvement programs. These members fear that management intends to use these programs to circumvent the union and the collective bargaining relationship. Other members cautiously indicate that they prefer the collective bargaining process to QWL programs but will support QWL programs if there is no attempt to bust the union or interfere with the collective bargaining process. Many have argued that union support remains critical for successful implementation of QWL programs. One study cited management neglect in terms of not inviting union participation early enough, or not inviting it at all, as a contributing factor to many failures of QWL programs.[32] Generally, in union settings the management are seen to be more careful in evaluating the decision to implement a QWL program than in firms where a union is not present.[33]

There is limited research on the effects of QWL efforts in union settings. Two studies found that QWL programs did not have any effect upon a firm's economic performance.[34] However, recall the positive results reported in Chapter 13 at Chrysler's New Castle, Indiana, assembly plant. The UAW-endorsed, workteam approach has reduced car defects and decreased absenteeism and grievances. Other research has shown that QWL programs can improve a firm's labor relations.[35] In addition, nonunion companies which encourage communication and participation programs also have been successful in maintaining nonunion status.[36] Research on QWL programs is relatively new and these findings are preliminary; however, they suggest that QWL programs may have an important influence upon the labor-management environment.

Union Effects on Worker Satisfaction

Added voice benefits and better wages and working conditions would seem to predict that union workers would be more satisfied than nonunion workers. Interestingly, evidence strongly points to the contrary. Supervision, coworkers, and job content create more dissatisfaction for union workers than for nonunion workers. Only pay provides more union satisfaction.[37] The exit/voice hypothesis suggests that this results from unions' encouraging members to voice their dissatisfaction rather than to quit. Voluntary turnover rates are substantially lower under unions. Alternatively, union workers may feel compelled to stay because of the "golden handcuffs" of better wages, health insurance, and working conditions: they may feel that they cannot afford to quit when they are dissatisfied.

THE FUTURE OF UNIONS IN THE UNITED STATES

Union Membership

The future of unions in the United States is unclear. Some predict, by extrapolating the downward union membership trend, that we will become a country without unions. Another group of experts predicts that the decline in unionization will level off, and that a minimum level of unionization will keep nonunion employers from slipping back into past abuses of employees (1991 data supports this view). Other experts predict that the union movement will resume its growth.[38] This group believes that more workers will desire unionization as workers in the white-collar and service sector become increasingly frustrated. In addition, women and minorities tend to favor unionization, and the rate of women and minorities entering the workforce is higher than the rate of white males. In fact, the one bright spot for unions in the 1980s was the great increase in the number of women who belong to unions.

The 1980s have been called "a decade of despair" for the labor movement. The 1980s began with President Ronald Reagan's crushing of the Professional Air Traffic Controllers Organization (PATCO) and ended with the Eastern Airlines, Pittston Coal, and Greyhound strikes, and the failure of the UAW to gain certification of the Nissan plant in Tennessee and the Honda plant in Ohio. Due to the growing public acceptance of "replacement" workers (striking unionists call them "scabs"), strikes are losing their effectiveness. The 5-month strike by UAW workers at Caterpillar ended abruptly in 1992 when the company began the process of hiring workers to replace the 12,000 strikers. The number of strikes decreased through the 1980s, along with the number of workdays lost to labor activity.[39] The NLRB decision which allows employers to hire temporary workers during a union-endorsed work slowdown was also a major blow.[40] A report by the Economic Policy Institute, a liberal research

group, concluded that walkouts lasted almost a year longer when permanent employee substitutes were hired, almost six times the average duration of a strike when temporary or no replacements are used. Unions want Congress to ban "permanent replacements" because some employers are now provoking a strike in order to replace union members with low-wage, low-benefit workers. In 1990, replacements were used in 59 of 425 work stoppages. NLRB cases in this area have increased in recent years.

The failure to organize the Nissan plant illustrates some of the fundamental obstacles to the labor movement today. The UAW spent 18 months recruiting the 2400 workers of the Tennessee plant, only to lose the election by over a 2:1 margin. Nissan's antiunionization effort was very sophisticated, using strategies by outside consultants, videotapes, and closed-circuit television (CCTV) programs about the problems with unions. Communications focused on the cost of union dues, strike possibilities, and the loss of employee control to national union leadership. It was an uphill battle for the union. The company even selected the plant site in Tennessee and the individual workers based on their dispositions toward collective bargaining. Further, the company used a number of legal maneuvers to delay the certification vote.

Today, in most firms, employers are resisting unionization efforts with greater skill, and the results have been successful. As we discussed in Chapter 13, many companies use annual employee opinion surveys to assess the attitudinal pulse of the workforce. Significant changes in attitudes toward pay, benefits, supervision, work hours, or workload are red flags signaling potential trouble. The Tenneco Corporation, for example, will use a labor relations specialist to intervene in any region of the United States, on the basis of changes in employee attitudes as reflected on the nationwide survey. This quick response technique has been highly successful in deterring organizing efforts.

Some labor leaders have called for a more militant position and greater solidarity across unions. As stated by Lane Kirkland, president of the AFL-CIO, "There's a new spirit of solidarity that's emerging. I think it augurs well for the labor movement."[41] There are major disagreements on strategy even within major unions. Within the UAW, for example, some factions strongly oppose the "jointness" agreements between the automotive industry and the UAW. *Jointness* refers to the Japanese style of labor-management cooperation within the plant. Militants maintain that this cooperative spirit amounts to nothing more than a sellout to management at the time of major concessions by the union.

Some unions are challenging major components of Japanese management practices as violations of NLRA. For example, the union at Du Pont's largest chemical plant has charged that the company's Quality Circles (QCs) constituted an employer-dominated labor organization and thus violated NLRA. Of course, QCs and other worker involvement programs are lawful if the union endorses them in a collective bargaining agreement. These are now 250 Japanese-owned automotive supply plants in the United States with a combined total of 75,000 workers. While the UAW represents very few of these plants as of 1991, organizing them is a priority, since the union has lost over 500,000 members since 1979.

A 1989 report by the AFL-CIO recommended a strategy for the 1990s.[42] Along with the call for "associate" or partial memberships, the report recommends a focus on the growing service sector of the labor force. The most sophisticated (and successful) of the service-sector unions is the American Federation of State, County, and Municipal Employees (AFSME), which emphasizes workplace dignity and safety, pay equity programs (comparable worth), resistance to performance monitoring, and career development. AFSME claimed an additional 100,000 workers in 1988 and 1989 alone. Most experts predict that if union representation is to increase in the 1990s, the focus of organizing must be on clerical workers, data processors, salespersons, nurses, auditors, financial services, computer technicians, and other major occupations of the service sector. In many of these jobs, women represent the majority of workers. Interestingly, while the total of union membership declined in the 1980s, the number of women who belong to unions increased in 1990 relative to 1980 (women now represent 25 percent of the total number of union members). By 1988, in the private services and financial industries, fewer than 8 percent of employees belonged to unions. Only 28 banks out of 14,000 had collective bargaining agreements. From the perspective of union organizers, there is considerable room for improvement and expansion.

Mergers and Acquisitions

A common occurrence in the 1980s was for a new company to buy a failing (or failed) business. What then are the legal obligations of the new company with regard to active collective bargaining agreements? Federal labor law addresses the duties of the new employer to recognize and bargain with the predecessor's union. In the 1987 *Fall River Dying v. the NLRB,* the U.S. Supreme Court established that when (1) a successor employer shows "substantial continuity" in business operations, (2) the bargaining unit is appropriate (performing essentially the same jobs under the same working conditions, and (3) the predecessor employed a majority of the new employer's workers, then the successor employer is required to recognize and bargain with the predecessor union.[43] However, there is no duty imposed on the successor employer to hire the predecessor's workers unless the failure to hire them is based upon their union status.

Also, the successor is not legally required to adopt an old collective bargaining agreement that was made with the predecessor.

As we discussed in Chapter 5, the *Worker's Adjustment Retraining Notification Act* (WARN) of 1988 poses some legal and financial concerns for successor employers. This act requires that workers be given at least 60 days' notice of layoffs of 50 or more employees that compose over one-third of the employer's workforce. The penalty for failing to give advance notice is a day's back pay for every employee for every day less than 60 days that the employer fails to give notice. Successor employers who plan to lay off workers need to be cognizant of the time restrictions imposed upon them by this legislation.

Union lobbyists have been successful in passing legislation regulating mergers and acquisitions. According to the Investor Responsibility Research Center, 39 states now have some form of antitakeover statute. This legislation typically requires a lengthy waiting period for completion of a takeover or for approval by the corporation's board of directors. Legislation enacted in Massachusetts is considered the most favorable for unions. Hostile takeovers in Massachusetts require approval by the board of directors, and a long waiting period is stipulated for the takeover. Workers laid off within 2 years of the takeover get severance pay, and new management must recognize all existing collective bargaining agreements.

Retraining Provisions

Mergers and acquisitions, downsizing, and deregulation have all posed great threats to job security, particularly for union workers. One of the key ways that unions have begun to deal with this threat is through retraining provisions in collective bargaining agreements. For example, job security has become a prime concern of unions in the deregulated and technologically changing telephone industry. The Communication Workers of America (CWA) responded to this security threat in 1992 by negotiating an elaborate system of job posting and retraining provisions which help to prepare workers through education to move into new positions as the old ones are phased out. The agreement is proving invaluable for AT&T workers as the company is eliminating 6,000 human operators with computerized voice recognition systems. The contracts negotiated between the UAW and the big three U.S. automakers in 1990 also include several job security provisions. The Saturn contract offered by the UAW in 1992 enables workers to earn bonus money if they undergo additional training.

Other Negotiating Issues

Many unions intend to focus on changing the two-tier pay scales negotiated in the 1980s. According to one study, only 6 percent of 962 labor contracts negotiated in 1989 included two-tier plans, down from a peak of 11 percent in 1985.[44] Employees hired under two-tier systems are now flexing their collective muscles with their unions to eliminate separate wage scales.

There are other signs of turmoil for collective bargaining in the 1990s. The auto industry is pushing for greater productivity, while labor continues to ponder the concessions of the 1980s. GM and Chrysler are pushing for three-shift auto plants to boost productivity, while the UAW staunchly opposes the plan because it reduces the number of workers needed. UAW workers at the Japanese-owned Mazda plant in Michigan have been at odds with management over a number of major issues. Japanese executives have pledged to resist collective bargaining in future plants. The 4700 workers at GM's Saturn plant approved a new labor contract in 1992 scaling back many of the innovative provisions of the original agreement for the new plant.

Employee Benefits

With declining membership and the need to attract women, unions have emphasized health insurance and family-oriented benefits in recent years.[45] In 1983, the AFL-CIO called for national and international unions to emphasize family-oriented issues, such as child care and leave, in collective bargaining. Generally, women represent a majority of the membership in most of the unions that are taking an active role in child care and family leave. For example, unions such as the American Federation of Teachers (AFT), the Amalgamated Clothing and Textile Workers Union, the International Ladies Garment Workers Union, the Communication Workers of America, and the National Union of Hospital and Health Care Employees have taken active roles in child-care and family leave issues. In some cases a union lobbies for child-care funds from the state legislature, and in others a union is directly involved in supporting child-care centers. The UAW and Ford jointly operate child-care resource and referral centers in 26 locations.[46] Currently, unions are also lobbying for a federal law on child care and family leave and have had a major role in the passage of family leave laws in several states.

INTERNATIONAL LABOR RELATIONS*

There are several unique characteristics of the U.S. labor relations system relative to systems in most other coun-

tries.[47] Among the most significant are the following: (1) In the United States, unions have exclusive representation (i.e., there is representation by only one union for any given job in the United States). In Europe, more than one union, often with religious and political affiliations, may represent the same workers. (2) In the United States, the government plays a passive role in labor relations and dispute resolution, characterized by regulating the process, not the outcomes. In Western and Eastern European countries, Australia, Canada, and Latin America, the role of the government is much more active. (3) In the United States, there is generally an adversarial relationship between the union and management, while in most other countries the relationship is much more conciliatory and cooperative. (4) Collective bargaining in the United States is more decentralized (i.e., agreements are negotiated primarily at the local level). Unions in Europe, Japan, and Canada rely primarily on industry-wide negotiation.

In several countries, trade unions influence firm economic and financial decisions by including worker representatives as members on the supervisory boards. Codetermination is usually associated with Germany because, there, a full-parity system was established in the steel and coal industry. Labor and management are equally represented on the supervisory boards of these companies. Some form of codetermination can also be found in other industries in Germany. Since 1976, German law has required companies with over 2000 employees to have the same numbers of management and worker representatives on the supervisory board (which is usually composed of 11 members including the chair, who is chosen by the other 10 members). The decisive vote is cast by the "neutral" chair in tie situations. AEG-Telefunken, a German appliance and machinery company, provides a good example of the codetermination principle: AEG (today a division of Daimler-Benz) was in deep financial trouble in the early 1980s. Surprisingly, the chair cast the deciding vote in favor of the labor representatives' proposal to persuade the government to provide more aid.[48]

A lack of understanding of union structure and the underlying social dimension is often cited as a major cause of difficulties for expatriate American managers of multinational corporations. While American managers tend to have an antiunion orientation in their management style, unions carry considerably more clout in other countries. This attitude can often result in serious (and quick) trouble. For example, Johnson & Johnson's new joint venture with a German pharmaceutical company ran into difficulties from the start because Johnson & Johnson managers apparently did not recognize the importance of the work councils at German plants and the practical implications of "codetermination" for the manufacturing process. Codetermination also stipulates that a labor director must be treated as a manager who is charged

---

*Contributed by Marion Schubinski.

with attending to worker concerns. Labor directors have great influence in Germany and often participate in corporate strategic planning. The management board is elected by the supervisory board and must include a labor director who is approved by labor representatives. Johnson & Johnson's expatriate managers did not recognize the significance of the labor director in the daily operation of the joint venture plants. Consequently, the firm experienced problems from the start on matters related to work rules, productivity measures, and job responsibilities.

Similar cases of difficulties for expatriate managers have been noted in Japan, where joint consultation systems are very common and very alien to American managers. Over 75 percent of Japan's largest employers have a joint consultation system in which employee groups meet monthly with management to discuss policy, production, personnel issues, and even financial matters. Although not as common as in large companies, consultation systems and participative management systems are becoming more common in small and medium-sized Japanese companies as well. Japan has *enterprise unions* in which most firms have a single union with virtually all job families in the same union. There is no clear distinction between labor and management. Bargaining is done by the central organization during the "spring offensive" with details then negotiated at the individual company.

Union membership is lower in the U.S. (16.7 percent) than in any of the other western world countries. Sweden (83 percent), Denmark (73 percent), Belgium (53 percent), Ireland (52 percent), Great Britain (41 percent), Italy (40 percent), and West Germany (38 percent) have the highest union membership rates. About 38 percent of Canada's workers belong to unions. While many Central and South American countries have a higher percentage of workforce union membership (e.g., Mexico, Argentina, Brazil), there is no guaranteed right to collective bargaining. Unions in Central and South American are generally very political.

Union membership is decreasing in many European countries. In Great Britain, for example, membership has dropped about 15 percent in the last 15 years. Unions there are closely tied to the Labour Party and are quite militant. Wildcat strikes, for example, which are illegal in the United States, have replaced the grievance process as the means of labor protest.

Labor unions influence multinational corporation (MNC) decisions in several ways[49]: (1) by manipulating wage levels to the point where cost structures may become noncompetitive, (2) by restricting the ability to vary employment levels at will, and (3) by objecting to global integration of MNC operations. Perhaps the most serious labor relations difficulty for MNCs in other countries is the inability to vary employment levels at will, which is so common in the United States. For example, when Ford's sales plummeted during the 1991 Gulf war, several U.S. plants were closed almost immediately to control inventory. Ford plants in Germany, however, could only be closed after an extended period of consultation with affected parties. Many European countries impose stiff fines for terminating or laying off employees, even if the layoffs are temporary. Dismissals are usually the last resort, because of the large social impact of firing.

There are two types of agreements that are usually made between companies and employees on the subject of dismissal.[50] The first is made in advance and states the conditions for layoffs, if and when warranted. The second type of agreement stipulates the treatment of employees after termination. Reactions to both of these agreements vary. In the United Kingdom, for example, advance provisions for dismissal tend to be viewed by both employers and trade unions with some objections. Employers perceive reduced options and a lack of flexibility. Trade unions feel that agreements in advance imply acceptance of dismissals, which contradicts union policy. French unions view prior agreements as opportunities to organize the opposition, while French employers think that prior agreements provide a framework that keeps them from being forced into posttermination concessions under stress. In Germany, advance agreements on dismissals are not mandatory, and some companies prefer to avoid them. Experience has shown that the work councils use the framework agreement only as a basis for negotiation of better financial compensation due to job losses.

Another problem for MNCs is the inability to integrate optimal manufacturing operations across borders because powerful labor unions exert strong political pressure. The result of this suboptimization is higher manufacturing costs. The influence of the German Metal Workers' union on GM operations is often cited as a case in point.

The instability within the countries which comprised the Soviet Union makes it almost impossible to predict how labor unions will emerge in future relations between workers, management, and the government. Obviously, as these countries move to a free market, substantial changes in the area of labor relations may be expected. If the countries continue to follow the trend toward democracy, trade union power will probably rise, as it has in Poland through the Solidarity union.

The pro-labor Organization for Economic Cooperation and Development in Paris has issued "Guidelines for MNCs" which attempt to guarantee the same basic social and labor relations rights for all workers. However, union attempts to develop uniform standards for MNCs have not proven very fruitful to date.

What should be clear from this brief discussion of international labor relations is that we can make very few generalizations about labor relations across borders. The role of government, social agendas, religious affiliation, and underlying political and economic issues must be understood before one can thoroughly understand the diversity of international labor relations. Of particular interest should be the effects of the proposed European Community (E.C.) on labor relations in those and other countries which do business in the European sector. Some members of the proposed European Community, led by France, are calling for collective bargaining at the European level. Questions regarding the vast differences in the right to participate in company decisions, health-care coverage, work schedules, benefits, training guarantees, and wages across the E.C. countries will have to be addressed in a cooperative spirit. Whether the various constituents of this negotiation can actually reach agreement will be very interesting to determine.

SUMMARY

The history of the labor movement has evolved according to the life-cycle theory of general organizational development. Decline, however, is not inevitable. Organizations can undergo revitalization and adapt to the changing environment, or they can become obsolete and go the direction of the buggy whip. The direction unions will take is not clear. Evidence indicates that not all employers will respond generously and benevolently when they are not faced with collective action. In addition, workers still express dissatisfaction about their jobs and job security. The question remains whether or not unions can address employee dissatisfactions and whether employees believe unions can do something about the dissatisfaction. Certainly, unions continue to address workers' economic concerns; however, the future of unions remains uncertain. There can be no doubt that international competition has had the greatest effect upon the industries which were the most heavily unionized. The free trade agreement with Canada and the negotiations for free trade with Mexico are an additional burden for union organizers in manufacturing. The public perception is that unions were to some extent responsible for the troubles of the auto and steel industries. Unions will have to deal with this perception as they endeavor to rebound from their troubles in the 1980s. They will also have to recruit new members from among workers who may have a negative view about unions or who may feel that, after PATCO, Eastern Airlines, and Greyhound, unions are ineffective in improving working conditions, job security, or wages.

The turmoil with unions comes at a time when increasing competitive pressure demands that organizations be much more flexible in their operations. Long-term labor relations agreements which restrict an employer's ability to adjust workforce strength, hours to be worked, part-time employment, work rules, plant closings, and other downsizing options may be problematic. Unions must realize that managers need more moderate and flexible collective bargaining agreements when the market for products and services is so dynamic.[51] Labor leaders must promote the long-term interests of members and the organization. Management must be able to alter its course as the economic situation dictates. Management must also realize that employees are a critical constituency and have great power to effect the success of the organization. As the Massachusetts Institute of Technology (MIT) study on industrial productivity concluded, management must accept labor representatives as "legitimate and valued partners in the innovation process."[52] Collective bargaining agreements in the 1990s will surely build in more flexibility than agreements made in the 1980s and will (it is hoped) promote a less adversarial, more cooperative relationship between labor and management.

Currently, labor relations across the world are in turmoil due to the dynamic political changes of the last few years. Within the proposed European Community, major unions—from every country and representing their own political, religious, and economic constituents and basic self-interests—are endeavoring to reach agreement on the "social dimension" of the new European order. International labor relations will be a very interesting area to follow in the next few years.

Chapter 15 will explore the process of collective bargaining and some of the major features of a collective bargaining agreement. The strategies being pursued by unions in the 1990s will also be emphasized.

DISCUSSION QUESTIONS

1. Compensation packages negotiated through collective bargaining agreements are a major cause of our inability to compete in many sectors of the international market. Do you agree or disagree? Explain your answer.
2. Should public employees be allowed to strike?
3. What are the major effects of unions on wages? What other effects do unions have upon management and the organization?
4. What do you believe the future of unions will be? Why?
5. If unions are to survive, what do you think they will have to do to attract and maintain members?
6. Should companies be allowed to hire workers based on their attitudes toward unions?
7. Should companies be allowed to hire permanent replacement workers after a strike? Explain your answer.

NOTES

1. Schrank, R. (1979). Are unions an anachronism? *Harvard Business Review, 57,* 107–115.

2. Quinn, R. E., and Cameron, K. (1983). Organizational life cycles and shifting criteria of effectiveness: Some preliminary evidence. *Management Science, 29,* 33–51.

3. Perlman, S. (1929). *History of trade unionism in the United States.* New York: Macmillan.

4. Gompers, S. (1984). *Seventy years of life and labor.* Ithaca, NY: Institute for Labor Relations.

5. Strauss, G. (1988). Australian labor relations through American eyes. *Industrial Relations, 27,* 131–148.

6. Cameron, K. S., Kim, M. U., and Whetten, D. (1987). Organizational effects on decline and turbulence. *Administrative Science Quarterly, 32,* 222–240.

7. Moore, W. J., and Newman, R. J. (1988). A cross-section analysis of the postwar decline in American trade union membership. *Journal of Labor Research, 9,* 111–112.

8. Voos, P. (1984). Trends in union organizing expenditures. *Industrial and Labor Relations Review, 38,* 52–63.

9. Freeman, R. B., and Medoff, J. L. (1984). *What do unions do?* New York: Basic Books.

10. Kochan, T. A., Katz, H. C., and McKersie, M. (1986). *The transformation of American industrial relations.* New York: Basic Books. See also: Holley, W. H., and Jennings, K. M. (1991). *The labor relations process.* Hillsdale, IL: Dryden. Strauss, G., Gallagher, D. G., and Fiorito, J. (1991). *The state of the unions.* Madison, WI: Industrial Relations Research Association, University of Wisconsin.

11. Rose, N. L. (1987). Labor rent sharing and regulation: Evidence from the trucking industry. *Journal of Political Economy, 95,* 1146–1178.

12. Thomas, S. L. (1988). *Some observations on the impact of two-tier collective bargaining on firm performance.* Working paper 87-23. Macomb, IL: Western Illinois University, Center for Business and Economic Research.

13. Johnson, N. B. (1991). Airline workers' earning and union expenditures under regulation. *Industrial and Labor Relations Review, 45,* 154–165.

14. Gifford, C. D. (ed.). (1986). *Directory of U.S. labor organizations, 1986–87.* Washington: Bureau of National Affairs.

15. Burton, J. F., and Thomason, T. (1988). The extent of collective bargaining in the public sector. In B. Aaron, J. M. Najita, and J. L. Stern (eds.), *Public sector bargaining.* Madison, WI: Industrial Relations Research Association, pp. 1–51.

16. Coleman, C. J. (1989). Federal sector labor relations: A reevaluation of the policies. *Journal of Collective Negotiations in the public sector, 16,* 121–124.

17. Feared, J., and Greyer, C. R. (1982). Determinants of U.S. unionism: Past research and future needs. *Industrial Relations, 21,* 1–32. See also: Heneman, H. G., III, and Sandver, M. H. (1983). Predicting the outcome of union certification elections: A review of the literature. *Industrial and Labor Relations Review, 36,* 537–560.

Curme, M. A., Hirsch, B. T., and Macpherson, D. M. (1990). Union membership and contract coverage in the United States, 1983–1988. *Industrial and Labor Relations Review, 44,* 5–33. Newton, L. A., and Shore, L. M. (1992). A model of union membership: Instrumentality, commitment, and opposition. *Academy of Management Review, 17,* 275–298.

18. Deshpande, S. P., and Fiorito, J. (1989). Specific and general beliefs in union voting models. *Academy of Management Journal, 32,* 883–897. See also: Feared, J., Lowman, C., and Nelson, F. D. (1987). The impact of human resource policies on union organizing. *Industrial Relations, 26,* 113–126. Newton, L. A., and Shore, L. M. (1992). A model of union membership: Instrumentality, commitment, and opposition. *Academy of Management Review, 17,* 275–298.

19. Getman, J. G., Goldberg, S. B., and Herman, J. B. (1976). *Union representation elections: Law and reality.* New York: Russell Sage Foundation. See also: Ivancevich, J. M. (1992). *Human resource management.* Homewood, IL: Irwin.

20. Brett, J. M. (1980). Why employees want unions. *Organizational dynamics, 8,* 47–59.

21. See note 9.

22. See note 9.

23. See note 9.

24. Marshall, A. (1929). *Principles of Economics.* New York: Macmillan.

25. See note 9.

26. See note 9.

27. Hirsch, B. T., and Addison, J. T. (1986). *The economic analysis of unions: New approaches and evidence.* Boston, MA: Allen & Unwin.

28. Bemmels, B. (1987). How unions affect productivity in manufacturing plants. *Industrial and Labor Relations Review, 40,* 241–253.

29. Burton, J. F. (ed.). (1985). Review symposium: What do unions do? *Industrial and Labor Relations Review, 38,* 244–263.

30. Becker, B. E., and Olsen, C. A. (1987). Labor relations and firm performance. In M. M. Kleiner, R. N. Block, M. Roomkin, and S. W. Salsburg (eds.), *Human resources and performance of the firm.* Madison, WI: Industrial Relations Research Association, pp. 43–86. See also: Cutcher-Gershenfeld, J. (1991). The impact on economic performance of a transformation in workplace relations. *Industrial and Labor Relations Review, 44,* 241–260.

31. Gershenfeld, W. J. (1987). Employee participation in firm decisions. In M. M. Kleiner, R. N. Block, M. Roomkin, and S. W. Salsburg (eds.), *Human resources and performance of the firm.* Madison, WI: Industrial Relations Research Association, pp. 123–158. See also: Ferman, L. A., Hoyman, M., Cutcher-Gershenfeld, J., and Savoie, E. J. (eds.). (1991). *Joint training programs: A union-management approach to preparing workers for the future.* Ithaca, NY: ILR Press, School of Industrial and Labor Relations, Cornell University. Hammer, T. H., Currall, S. C., and Stern, R. N. (1991). Worker

representation on boards of directors: A study of competing roles. *Industrial and Labor Relations Review, 44,* 661–680.

32. Gold, C. (1986). *Labor management committees: Confrontation, cooptation, or cooperation?* Ithaca, NY: ILR Press.

33. Goll, I., and Hochner, A. (1987). Labor-management practices as a function of environmental pressures and corporate idealogy in union and nonunion settings. *Proceedings of the Fortieth Annual Meeting of the Industrial Relations Research Association,* 516–524.

34. Katz, H. C., Kochan, T. A., and Gobeille, K. R. (1984). Industrial relations performance, economic performance, and QWL programs: An interplant analysis. *Industrial and Labor Relations Review, 37,* 3–17. See also: Katz, H. C., Kochan, T. A., and Weber, M. C. (1985). Assessing the effects of industrial relations systems and efforts to improve the quality of working life on organizational effectiveness. *Academy of Management Review, 28,* 509–526.

35. Steel, R. P., Jennings, K. R., Mento, A. J., and Hendrix, W. H. (1988). *Effects of institutional employee participation on industrial labor relations.* Paper presented at the meeting of the Academy of Management, Anaheim, CA.

36. Feared, J., Lowman, C., and Nelson, F. D. (1987). The impact of human resource policies on union organizing. *Industrial Relations, 26,* 113–126.

37. Schwochau, S. (1987). Union effects on job attitudes. *Industrial and Labor Relations Review, 40,* 219–220.

38. Heckschier, C. S. (1988). *The new unionism.* New York: Basic Books.

39. Capelli, P. (1990). Collective bargaining. In J. A. Fossum (ed.), *Employee and labor relations.* Washington: Bureau of National Affairs, pp. 4-180 to 4-217. See also: Kotlowitz, A. (Aug. 28, 1987). Labor's turn. *The Wall Street Journal,* pp. 1, 14.

40. Kotlowitz, A. (April 12, 1987). Labor's shift: Finding strikes harder to win, more unions turn to slowdowns. *The Wall Street Journal,* pp. 1, 7.

41. Kirkland, L. (Nov. 19, 1989). A call for solidarity. Speech to the AFL-CIO.

42. Brown, C., and Reich, M. (1989). When does union-management cooperation work? A look at NUMMI and GM—Van Nuys. *California Management Review, 31,* 26–41. See also: Cooke, W. N. (1990). Factors influencing the effect of joint union-management programs on employee-supervisor relations. *Industrial and Labor Relations Review, 43,* 587–603.

43. Mace, R. F. (1921). The Supreme Court's labor law successorship doctrine after *Fall River Dyeing. Labor Law Journal, 39,* 102–109.

44. Tomsho, R. (Apr. 20, 1990). Employers and unions feeling pressure to eliminate two-tier labor contracts. *The Wall Street Journal,* pp. B1, B5.

45. Auerbach, J. D. (1988). *In the business of child care.* New York: Praeger.

46. Huth, S. P. (1989). Ford, UAW to expand joint child care referral program. *Employee Benefit Plan Review, 44,* p. 54.

47. Dunlop, J. T. (May 1988). Have the 1980's changed U.S. industrial relations? *Monthly Labor Review,* pp. 29–34.

48. A Business International Research Report. (1982). *Managing Manpower in Europe.* New York: Business International Corporation.

49. Dowling, P. J., and Schuler, R. S. (1990). *International dimensions of human resource management.* Boston, MA: PWS-Kent. See also: Sasaki, N. (1990). *Management and industrial structure in Japan.* Oxford: Pergamon Press. Adams, R. J. (1989). North American industrial relations: Divergent trends in Canada and the U.S. *International Labour Review, 128,* 47–64. Okubayashi, K. (1989). The Japanese industrial relations system. *Journal of General Management, 14,* 67–88.

50. See note 48.

51. Hirsch, B. T. (1992). Firm investment behavior and collective bargaining strategy. *Industrial Relations, 31,* 95–121.

52. Dertouzos, M. L., Lester, R. K., and Solow, R. M. (1989). *Made in America: Regaining the competitive edge.* Cambridge, MA: MIT Press. Arthur, J. B., and Dworkin, J. B. (1991). Current issues in industrial and labor relations research and practice. *Journal of Management, 17*(3), 515–552.

EXERCISE 14.1
ORGANIZING A UNION*

OVERVIEW

Research shows that management often neither anticipates nor understands the motivation of employees to organize into unions. The purpose of this exercise is to explore an organizing effort from the perspectives of labor and of management.

LEARNING OBJECTIVES

After completing this exercise, you should be able to:

1. Understand the process of starting a union organizing effort.
2. Know the steps involved in the certification process.
3. Be able to consider employee and employer reactions to a union organizing effort.
4. Know the laws and regulations that govern the process of union organizing both from labor's perspective and from management's perspective.

PROCEDURE

Part A: Individual Analysis

Step 1. Prior to class, read the scenario below and follow the directions of the assignment.
Step 2. Each student will be assigned to either the "union organizer" role or the "general manager" role. Each role requires you to write a letter to be used in your arguments. These roles are described in Exhibit 14.1.1.

Part B: Group Analysis

Step 1. Form small groups in which members are grouped by like assignment (i.e., all union organizers together and all general managers together). The members should first review one another's letters and outlines. One letter should be selected as the most effective, then edited,

and submitted as the group response. Each group should also derive a chronology of steps to be taken by the union organizer or Mr. Cameron.
Step 2. A representative from each group should write the chronological steps on a blackboard or flip chart so that comparisons across groups can be made. The writer of the most effective letter from each group should then read the letter to the class. Discussion should center on the most important elements for each side and the legal implications of various strategies proposed.

SCENARIO

You are a customer service representative for American Rental Car (ARC), a national rental car company. Recently, the employees at the three installations in the southeastern United States which are managed by the general manager, Scott Cameron, have experienced dissatisfaction. No raises have been given in over a year, employee benefits are sparse, employees' preferences have not been considered in the assignment of work schedules or installations, and an automated employee monitoring system has been implemented. Many of the 100 full-time employees have been talking about unionization, although many have yet to be convinced that unionization provides the best answer. The average age of the 100 employees is 29; there are 58 females and 41 minorities. Some employees strongly believe that a union can address some of the workers' concerns. Consequently, they have contacted the Customer Service Reps of America (CSRA) for help in organizing the southeastern region of ARC. Despite numerous attempts, the CSRA has been successful in organizing only three other ARC installations nationwide, because the firm engages in a very tough (and often questionably legal) campaign to stop any union organizing efforts. Before the CSRA will send an organizer to your location, it wants to be persuaded that enough employees back the union to merit the expense. Thus, it has suggested that as a first step someone write a letter to the workers to convince them of the benefits of unionization and enlist their support.

---

*Contributed by Nancy Brown Johnson.

EXHIBIT 14.1.1

UNION ORGANIZER ROLE

Write a letter to your coworkers about the factors involved in the case. You remember from the chapter why people join unions and the benefits of membership, and you want to be sure to include these factors in your letter. Yet you know that your fellow workers will still wonder why the possible costs of unionization (e.g., union dues, getting fired, being permanently assigned to the midnight shift, and being harassed by their supervisor) are worth the benefits. From your speech class you know the importance of providing answers to counterarguments if you wish to effectively convince your coworkers to support the union.

Prepare a chronological outline for the union organizing effort, covering what steps or procedures are to be followed, what data you should gather, what to look for in management's reaction, and what to do if management does not respond fairly. Also, prepare a chronological outline of what you anticipate to be management's reaction to the union organizing effort (i.e., the steps that management will take during the course of the organizing effort).

GENERAL MANAGER ROLE

Assume the role of Scott Cameron and draft a letter to your three supervisors and six assistant supervisors stipulating what can and cannot be done regarding the union organizing effort. For example, you were just informed that one of the supervisors, Meredith Sterrett, has already begun to establish a "paper trail" on one of the union sympathizers so that he can be terminated for poor performance if "things get out of hand." She also told an employee that if a CSRA representative showed up at her installation, she would "call the cops and have him arrested for trespassing." She recently refused to hire a black female applicant because both of the applicant's parents were members of a union. You will need to respond to Ms. Sterrett's actions. You should also prepare an outline of a meeting to be held regarding the union organizing effort and what the firm should do regarding worker concerns.

Also, prepare a chronology of steps which management should take in response to the organizing effort.

EXERCISE 14.2
ATTITUDES TOWARD UNIONS

OVERVIEW

Research indicates that general attitudes toward unions are strongly correlated with a number of workplace behaviors. These attitudes, sometimes based on limited facts about unions and their actual effects, can have a profound effect on a number of reactions in the workplace. Research also shows that expectancies regarding union behavior and activities can affect subsequent negotiations and managerial behaviors toward union activity. From the workers' perspective, attitudes can also affect reactions to union organizing efforts, perceptions of the extent to which unions can affect workers' pay and working conditions, and job attractiveness.

The purpose of this exercise is to assess attitudes toward unions in general and the extent to which these attitudes are grounded in fact. Discussion will center on the implications of the attitudes for union-management relations.

LEARNING OBJECTIVES

After completing this exercise, you should be able to:

1. Understand the implications of preconceived attitudes toward union-management relations and managerial behavior.

2. Know some of the myths and truths about unions and the effects of unions.

3. Adopt a more objective perspective on the subject of unions.

PROCEDURE

Part A: Individual Analysis

Prior to reading Chapter 14 and prior to class, complete the questionnaire in Form 14.2.1.

Part B: Group Analysis

In class, the instructor will group you according to your scores on Form 14.2.1 and present norms for the data. Group discussion should focus first on the bases for students' responses (i.e., the basis of opinions expressed in Form 14.2.1). Each group should then attempt to reach consensus on item 1 of Form 14.2.1. Each group should organize a 3-minute presentation addressing the consensus point of view on item 1. Support your group's position with specific information.

FORM 14.2.1

Name _____ Group _____

With regard to unions in the United States today, use the following scale to indicate your opinion about each statement:

> 5 = Strongly agree
> 4 = Agree
> 3 = Undecided
> 2 = Disagree
> 1 = Strongly disagree

1. U.S. productivity would be much higher if it weren't for unions.

2. Unions protect incompetent workers so long as they belong to the union.

3. Unions interfere with management attempts to increase productivity.

4. Unions are corrupt.

5. Unions (and not management) are responsible for the adversarial relationship which exists between unions and management.

6. Union wages are not competitive in a global economy.

7. Union rule making and regulations stifle attempts to improve the quality of our products or services.

8. Unions should be outlawed.

9. Unions are violent during strikes.

10. More protection is needed for replacement workers who are threatened and harassed by striking unionists.

11. Workers and management would get along fine if it weren't for unions.

12. The United States could be more competitive if we could get rid of unions.

13. Unions are needed to control management.

14. Unions are by nature adversarial and uncooperative with management.

15. Unions tend to resist quality improvement programs.

16. Big labor has excessive political power in Washington.

17. Unions are undemocratic in their organizational structure.

18. Union workers are less satisfied with their wages and benefits than are nonunion workers.

19. Unions tend to oppose pay-for-performance (PFP) systems.

20. Companies should be allowed to screen people based on their general attitudes toward unions.

21. Union wages have outpaced nonunion wages over the last 10 years.

22. Management should be allowed to hire replacement workers immediately after a strike action.

23. Union membership should be mandatory if the union represents the other employees at the company.

15

C H A P T E R

COLLECTIVE BARGAINING*

*Contributed by Roger L. Cole.

OVERVIEW

Collective bargaining occurs when representatives of a labor union meet with management representatives to determine employees' wages and benefits, to create or revise work rules, and to resolve disputes or violations of the labor contract. As noted in Chapter 14, union membership has been declining over the past few decades. Despite this fact, for more than 17 million workers, collective bargaining still represents the primary process for determining their wages, benefits, and working conditions. During the past 200 years, the strength of unions has varied, often as a result of the prevailing economic conditions. It is unlikely that unions or collective bargaining will disappear. To survive, though, the faces of labor relations and of unions themselves will have to change during the coming years. Unions must successfully attract white-collar workers, women, and minorities as these groups continue to increase in the labor force.

For those in the field of human resource management (HRM), a knowledge of labor relations and collective bargaining is important. In fact, it is often difficult to separate labor relations as a human resource (HR) function from the many other HR functions. For example, labor relations is closely tied to HR planning since the labor contract generally stipulates policies and procedures related to promotions, transfers, job security, and layoffs. Recruiting and selection are also tied to the labor contract, since, in a union shop, those hired must eventually join the union. Finally, the area of HR in which a knowledge of collective bargaining is probably most critical is compensation and benefits, since almost all aspects of wages and benefits are subject to negotiation.

Collective bargaining should be viewed by both union and management as a two-way street. This means that the basic interests of management must be protected as well as the rights of employees. The two sides have a responsibility to each other. For example, unions should not expect management to concede on issues which would ultimately impair the company's ability to stay in business. Likewise, management must recognize the rights of employees to form unions and to argue for improved wages and working conditions.

OBJECTIVES

After studying this chapter, you should be able to:

1. Define collective bargaining and discuss its importance in the field of HRM.
2. Describe a typical labor contract, the legal requirements governing collective bargaining, and various bargaining structures.
3. Understand the steps involved in preparing and conducting contract negotiations.
4. Identify ways to resolve bargaining deadlocks or impasses, and the bases for the union's and management's power at the bargaining table.
5. Identify the issues in collective bargaining related to wages and supplementary economic benefits.
6. Explain how to administer a labor contract.
7. Discuss the purposes of the grievance procedure and the arbitration process, and describe the steps involved in both.
8. Describe current trends in collective bargaining.

THE LABOR CONTRACT

A labor contract is a formal agreement between a union and management which specifies the conditions of employment and the union-management relationship over a mutually agreed upon period of time (usually 2 to 3 years). The labor contract specifies what the two parties have agreed upon regarding issues such as wages, benefits, and working conditions. The process involved in reaching this agreement is a complex and difficult job requiring both sides to be willing to reconcile their differences and compromise their interests.

Legal Requirements

The Taft-Hartley Act of 1947 (section 8d) states: "to bargain collectively is [to recognize]...the mutual obligation of the employer and representative of the employees to meet at reasonable times and confer in good faith with respect to wages, hours, and other terms and conditions of employment,... or the negotiation of an agreement, or any question arising thereunder, and the execution of a written contract incorporating any agreement reached if requested by either party,... such obligation does not compel either party to agree to a proposal or require the making of a concession."[1] Thus, the law requires that the employer negotiate with the union once the union has been recognized as the employees' representative. Good-faith bargaining has the following characteristics:

• Meetings for purposes of negotiating the contract are scheduled and conducted at reasonable times and places.
• Realistic proposals are submitted.
• Reasonable counterproposals are offered.
• Each party signs the agreement once it has been completed.

Good-faith bargaining does not mean that either party is required to agree to a final proposal or to make concessions.

The National Labor Relations Board (NLRB) further defines the "duty to bargain" as covering bargaining on all matters concerning rates of pay, wages, hours of employment, and other conditions of employment.[2] Examples of some of the subjects of bargaining are listed in Figure 15.1. "Mandatory" issues for bargaining include wages, benefits, and job security, while "permissive" or "nonmandatory" issues have no direct relationship to wages, hours, or working conditions. Permissive issues can be introduced into the discussion by either party; however, the other party is not obligated to discuss them or include them in the labor contract.

BARGAINING STRUCTURES

Bargaining does not necessarily take place between a single union and a single employer. In fact, bargaining can be structured to take many forms, depending upon the relations among the union's negotiating units (i.e., industrywide, national, regional) and the type of employer negotiating unit (i.e., multiemployer, companywide, plant).[3] The parties involved may decide that a larger negotiating unit would be advantageous. Space does not allow a detailed discussion of all the various collective bargaining structures; therefore, two of the more common structures will be discussed here.

FIGURE 15.1
EXAMPLES OF MANDATORY AND PERMISSIVE COLLECTIVE BARGAINING ISSUES

MANDATORY ISSUES
1. Wage clauses, including overtime
2. Labor-grade job classifications
3. Wage rate ranges
4. Pay steps within labor grades
5. Wage differentials for undesirable types of work
6. Pay guarantees for employees who are asked to report to work when no work is available
7. Extensions of premium pay for work on undesirable shifts, holidays, and weekends
8. Remuneration for hours worked in excess of a "standard" workday or workweek
9. Employee benefits such as paid vacations and pension plans
10. Job security, including income-security devices
11. Profit sharing plans

PERMISSIVE ISSUES
1. Seniority rights
2. Discipline
3. Rest periods
4. Work-crew size
5. Workload size

Coordinated or Coalition Bargaining

This type of structure involves the banding together of unions for contract negotiation purposes.[4] Together, presenting a united front, they make common union demands. Coalition bargaining has been used at such companies as General Electric Company (GE), Westinghouse Electric Corp., Union Carbide, and General Telephone and Electronics (GTE).[5] This type of bargaining is advantageous to unions for avoiding management pressures to concede. For example, when an employer is bargaining with a single union, especially a weak union, if the employer obtains a "favorable" contract, it may use the favorable contract as leverage to obtain concessions from other stronger unions. With coalition bargaining, this is less likely. While coalition bargaining is no panacea, unions have been encouraged by the results they have achieved in using it. The Communications Workers of America and the International Brotherhood of Electrical Workers used the coalition strategy in their 1992 negotiations with AT&T. The negotiations set the pattern for later negotiations with the six regional "Baby Bells."

Multiemployer Bargaining

This type of bargaining involves a number of employers who come together to negotiate a contract with a national union.[6] A "master agreement" is the end result. Multiemployer bargaining can be conducted in a specific geographic region or labor market, or it can cover an entire industry. This type of bargaining is common among industries which comprise a large number of relatively small employers, such as the garment industry, retail and wholesale trade, and professional sports. When multiemployer bargaining units are used, one set of negotiators speaks for all employers and any agreement is applied to all members of the bargaining association.

CONDUCTING LABOR CONTRACT NEGOTIATIONS

Preparing for Negotiations

Because of the complexity of the issues and the broad range of topics discussed during negotiating sessions, a substantial amount of preparation time is required.[7] Effective bargaining means presenting an orderly and factual case for each side. Today, this requires much more skill and sophistication than it did in earlier days, when shouting and expression of strong emotions in smoke-filled rooms were frequently the keys of getting one's proposals accepted. Now, to prepare for negotiations, one must have a detailed planning strategy. Negotiating teams typically begin data gathering for the next negotiation session immediately after a contract is signed. Preparation includes reviewing and diagnosing the mistakes and weaknesses of previous negotiations and gathering information on recent contract settlements in the local area and industrywide (e.g., comparative industry and occupational wage rates and fringe benefits). Preparation also includes gathering data on economic conditions, studying consumer price indices, determining cost-of-living trends, and looking at projections regarding the short- and long-term financial outlook. Internal to the firm, data such as minimum and maximum pay by job classification, shift work data, cost and duration of breaks, an analysis of grievances, and overtime data are almost always of interest to both sides. Often unions and large corporations have research departments which collect necessary data for negotiations. Computers make this assignment much less burdensome. Management is likely to come armed with data regarding grievances and arbitration, disciplinary actions, transfers, promotions, layoffs, overtime worked, individual performance measures, and wage payments.

During the preparation phase of contract negotiations, an employer develops a written plan covering its bargaining strategy. The plan takes into account what the employer considers the union's goals to be and the degree to which it is willing to concede on various issues. Such a plan is useful to the negotiators because it helps them to identify the relative importance of each issue in the proposal.

When preparing for negotiations, both sides must become familiar with other contract agreements in similar industries and in the same region. Also, they must determine what patterns have been established which relate to wages, benefits, and working conditions. Obviously, the unions want to obtain wage and benefit increases which are at least equal to those provided in other agreements in their industry or region, while employers will attempt to minimize increases by citing employers in the area who offer lower wages and fewer benefits.

Both the union and management send their negotiating teams to the bargaining table. The union's negotiating team generally consists of local union officials, union stewards, and one or more specialists from the national union staff. Management's negotiating team usually consists of one or more production or operations managers, a labor lawyer, a compensation specialist, a benefits specialist, and a chief labor relations specialist, who heads the team.

The success of contract negotiations relies heavily on the skills and knowledge of the members of the negotiating teams.[8] Effective negotiators should have a working knowledge of trade union principles, operations, economics, psychology, statistics, and labor law. Also, they should have strong research skills. From a psycho-

logical standpoint, not only must negotiators be good judges of human nature but they also must have effective human relations skills. A good understanding of human nature is invaluable, particularly when a negotiator must decide whether to bluff or to gamble. Negotiators must know when to listen, when to speak, when to stand their ground, when to concede, when to horse-trade, and when to make counterproposals. Timing is everything. Effective speaking and debating skills are essential.

Early Meetings in Contract Negotiations

One of the most important objectives of early bargaining meetings is to establish a climate for negotiations.[9] In other words, it must be determined whether the tone of the negotiations is going to be one of mutual trust with "nothing up our sleeves," one of suspicion with a lot of distortion and misrepresentation, or one of hostility with a lot of name calling and accusations. Also, early meetings are used to establish the bargaining authority of each party and to determine rules and procedures which will be used throughout the negotiation process. Both parties try to avoid disclosing the relative importance they attach to each proposal so that they will not have to pay a higher price than is necessary to have the proposal accepted. Generally, each side tries to determine how far the other side is willing to go in terms of concessions, and the minimum levels each is willing to accept. It is best not to establish a position which is too extreme, nor one which is too inflexible. For instance, "take it or leave it" proposals are typically ineffective. One of the best examples of a "take it or leave it" philosophy of bargaining was found at GE from the 1940s to the 1970s. During this period, GE's policy was that management initially brought to the bargaining table its final proposal. The unions obviously viewed this as unethical and illegal (lack of good-faith bargaining). After a U.S. Supreme Court ruling found the company guilty of bad-faith bargaining, GE eventually relinquished this policy.[10]

Successful negotiations are contingent upon each side's remaining flexible. It is hoped that the end result will be a "package" representing the maximum and minimum levels acceptable to each of the parties. The bargaining zone, which is illustrated in Figure 15.2, is the area bounded by the limits which the union and employer are willing to concede. If neither the union nor management is willing to change its demands enough to bring them within the inside boundaries of the bargaining zone, or if neither is willing to extend the limits to accommodate the other's demands, then negotiations reach a deadlock.

The union team is first to present its initial proposals. Usually, the original union proposal demands more than it expects to end up with (i.e., it makes exces-

FIGURE 15.2
DESIRES, EXPECTATIONS, AND TOLERANCE
LIMITS THAT DETERMINE THE BARGAINING ZONE

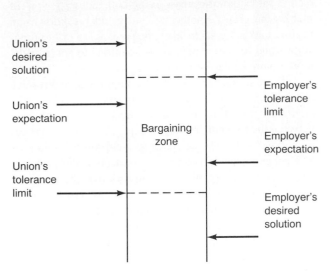

Source: R. Stagner and H. Rosen, *Psychology of union-management relations.* Belmont, CA: Wadsworth, 1965, p. 96. Reprinted by permission of the publisher, Brooks/Cole Publishing Company, Monterey, California.

sive demands in terms of changes in, additions to, and deletions from the previous contract), which will allow leverage for trading off for management concessions. The management negotiating team then states the management case, often presenting unrealistic counterproposals and data supporting the view that union workers are treated well. For example, in the 1992 negotiations between the National Hockey League (NHL) and the NHL Players Association, the president of the NHL asked early on why the union would "reject an offer when $9.00 out of every $10.00 a fan spends on a game ticket goes to NHL players, and the proposed system would raise wages to an average of at least $420,000?" Of course, the union countered with average salary data from the National Basketball Association and Major League Baseball. The early meetings are often characterized by the two parties' remaining far apart on the issues; however, as negotiations proceed, there is generally movement toward a pattern of agreement. As topics are discussed and considered, mutual concessions are offered, counterproposals are made, and eventually a tentative agreement is reached.

When a tentative agreement is reached, in most cases, the union members vote on the contract. If it is approved, the contract is ratified; if it is voted down, more negotiating takes place. The next step involves the actual drafting of a formal document, attempting to keep it in simple, clear, and concise terms. In fact, however, most contracts are difficult to read and some sections are virtually incomprehensible for the rank and file (e.g., most often sections on seniority and grievance procedures).

Many labor agreements are over 100 pages long. The last step is the actual signing of the agreement by the representatives of the union and management. The typical labor agreement defines the responsibilities and authority of unions and management and stipulates what management activities are not subject to union authority (e.g., purchasing and hiring).

Bargaining Techniques

The objective of each party during contract negotiations is to be able to leave the negotiations with its interests upheld in the contract. To reach this objective, each negotiating team uses a variety of bargaining techniques.[11] Two commonly used techniques include the trading point procedure and the use of counterproposals. When using the *trading point procedure,* management evaluates the demands of the union to determine which of them the union is most interested in obtaining. For example, management may determine that a wage increase of $1.44 per hour is the demand the union is most anxious to secure. Once this is determined, management may agree to the wage increase. In return for this concession, however, management may insist that the union accept only a fraction of another of its demands (e.g., job security). *Counterproposals* are another frequently used bargaining tool. For example, management might respond to the union's demand for a $1.44 increase in hourly wages by offering a counterproposal of a $0.95 increase. The union might then propose an increase of $1.30, which might be followed by management's offer of $1.05. Such counterproposals may continue until a compromise is reached.

Variables Affecting the Likelihood of Reaching Agreement

Many factors affect the ability of a union and management to reach an agreement. A few of these will be discussed below.

CURRENT HEALTH OF THE ECONOMY AND THE INDUSTRY. When economic conditions are good, unions generally make more significant contract gains during negotiations. This is because management's resistance to union demands tends to be weaker in prosperous times. Conversely, when economic conditions are poor, unions tend to lose ground. A good example of this occurred during the recessions of the early 1980s and the early 1990s. Large economic concessions were made by unions. Due to the loss of many jobs and the extremely hard economic times which accompanied the recession, job security became the most pressing issue for the unions. For example, in labor negotiations between General Motors (GM) and the United Auto Workers (UAW) in 1990, job security was one of the most important issues.[12] Job security was the major issue in the 1992 negotiations between AT&T and the Communications Workers of America (CWA).[13]

TECHNOLOGICAL INNOVATIONS. Because improved technology (e.g., automation, robotics) may lead to job losses and job insecurity, bargaining agreements may be affected. For example, the Communications Workers of America union has resisted AT&T's modernization efforts and, in particular, the company's goal of replacing one-third of its 18,000 operators with computers that recognize voice commands.[14] In some cases, a stalemate in bargaining or a strike may result when significant technological advances are evident in the industry.

BARGAINING HISTORY BETWEEN THE PARTIES. The success or failure of past bargaining sessions between the parties tends to influence future sessions. If, for example, past negotiations were bitter and hostile, there may be some carryover to current negotiations. This happened at Eastern Airlines, where past troubles led to continued difficult negotiations which contributed to the demise of the airline.[15]

LAWS AND ADMINISTRATIVE RULINGS. Since the Wagner Act of 1935, the government has become increasingly involved in the regulation of labor relations in the United States (e.g., the Taft-Hartley Act of 1947, the Landrum-Griffin Act of 1959, the Civil Service Reform Act of 1978).[16] As a result, additional rulings and laws may influence the degree to which bargaining agreements are reached.

PUBLIC OPINION. Whom the public is siding with at a given time often brings pressure to bear upon one side or the other. During the strike at the *New York Daily News,* many readers sided with the striking workers and thus boycotted the paper until the strikers were rehired.[17] This explains why both sides often try to gain the public's sympathy.

Resolving Bargaining Deadlocks and Impasse Resolution

As discussed earlier, successful negotiations are dependent upon both parties' remaining flexible and willing to concede. If neither is willing to do so, negotiations reach a deadlock or impasse, which can eventually result in a strike on the part of the union or a lockout on the part of management. So, how can breakdowns in negotiations be avoided? One way is to delay consideration of the more

difficult issues until the later stages of bargaining and, for the time being, to simply agree to disagree on the tougher decisions. The easier questions can be considered in the beginning, thus giving both sides a feeling of making progress. Another way to avoid breakdowns in negotiations is for each side to be prepared to offer propositions and to accept alternative solutions to some of the more controversial issues.

If two parties are unable to compromise and resolve a deadlock, then they have the option of calling in a *mediator,* a neutral third party who reviews the dispute between the two parties and attempts to open up communication channels by suggesting compromise solutions and concessions. Mediation is based upon the principle of voluntary acceptance. This means that the mediator has no conclusive power or authority to impose his or her recommendations on either party. In fact, either party may accept or reject the mediator's recommendations. The Federal Mediation and Conciliation Service (FMCS) was established by the Taft-Hartley Act. Over 300 mediators perform their services for free and mediate about 15,000 labor disagreements per year.[18]

Sometimes government intervention is necessary to resolve deadlocks. This occurs generally in cases in which a work stoppage would threaten the national security or the public welfare. For example, one of the provisions of the Taft-Hartley Act is a national emergency strike provision which gives the President of the United States the power to stop a strike if it imperils national health or safety.[19] In most cases the government will call upon the services of the FMCS to resolve such bargaining deadlocks.

POWER IN COLLECTIVE BARGAINING

The Union's Economic Power in Collective Bargaining

The basis for the union's power in collective bargaining is economic and generally takes one of three forms: striking the employer, picketing the employer, or boycotting the employer.

STRIKING THE EMPLOYER. One tool a labor union can use to motivate an employer to reach an agreement is to call a strike. A *strike* is simply a refusal on the part of employees to perform their jobs.[20] Strikes typically occur when a union is unable to obtain an offer from management that is acceptable to its members. About 10 to 15 percent of contract negotiations end in a strike. Several illustrations of strikes are evident in recent labor contract negotiations. For example, in 1989, the Writers' Guild of America staged a strike against television producers which resulted in a delay of the new television season.[21] In the same year, in the Pittston coal mines, a strike was called and escalated to the point of involving various labor organizations.[22]

While strikes tend to receive a lot of attention from the media, in fact, lost workdays to strikes represent less than 1 percent of total workdays. Time lost to strikes was at an all-time low in 1988 but increased considerably in 1989 through 1991. Before a union goes on strike, it must first assess the consequences of a strike and its members' willingness to make the sacrifices and endure the hardships (e.g., lost pay) that are part of striking. Part of this assessment also involves determining whether or not the employer can continue operating by using supervisory and nonstriking employees. Automated firms like AT&T and the Baby Bells have fully developed strike plans which enable the companies to operate at near 100 percent capacity. There are a number of risks attached to striking. For one, replacement employees can vote the union out in an NLRB-conducted decertification election. Also, a strike can result in a loss of union members, and the public may withdraw its support.

The power of strikes to pressure management has been seriously diminished during the past decades. Automation, recent court rulings, and a growing number of unemployed workers willing to serve as replacements have helped management. After Congress passed the Wagner Act in 1935, workers' rights to organize and to strike were guaranteed. However, in 1938 a court decision weakened this right by permitting the permanent replacement of economic strikers by management.[23] The use of replacement workers seriously undermines the economic pressure which strikes once had. Even though this court decision was made in 1938, it was not until the 1980s that the ruling was frequently applied. For example, the 1992 strike by the UAW against Caterpillar ended abruptly when Caterpillar began their plan to hire replacement workers. This was the first time an industrial giant (Caterpillar is the world's largest manufacturer of construction equipment) tried to replace thousands of union workers. Many workers who went on strike in the last decade have found that their jobs were not waiting for them when the strike ended. In *TWA v. Independent Federation of Flight Attendants,* the Supreme Court in 1989 ruled that the airline did not violate the Railway Labor Act by refusing to displace "crossover" employees to allow union strikers to reclaim their jobs.[24] Another setback was a 1981 law which declared striking workers and their families ineligible for food stamps.

Sometimes unions will call for a strike vote simply as a vote of confidence to strengthen the union position. In other words, the union does not want to strike, nor does it intend to strike. Rather, it uses the strike vote as a bargaining ploy to gain concessions. A strike deadline is established, which often coincides with the end of the "old" contract. This deadline forces both sides to reexamine their "final" positions and frequently increases their willingness to compromise. For example, the NHLPA called for a strike only a few weeks before the start of the 1992 NHL playoffs, a most lucrative time for some NHL owners. The strategy worked as the union was able to negotiate a favorable settlement.

PICKETING THE EMPLOYER. Another basis for union power is the picket. The picket is used by employees on strike to advertise their dispute with management and to discourage others from entering or leaving the premises. Picketing usually takes place at the plant or company entrances. It can result in severe financial losses for a firm and can eventually lead to a shutdown of the plant if enough employees refuse to cross the picket line. For example, the machinists of Eastern Airlines picketed the company in 1989. When pilots and flight attendants honored the picket lines of the machinists, the airline faced severe difficulty with operations.[25] Picket lines can become very emotional at times, especially when employees or replacements attempt to cross them. These people may become the target of verbal insults and sometimes even physical violence. You may recall, in the late 1980s, the media coverage of pickets by professional football players and the abuse given to players and replacements who crossed the picket lines. Companies now hire security firms to protect nonstriking and replacement workers. For example, Dannon, the yogurt maker, maintained operations during a strike with the Teamsters Union with replacement workers and 100 guards who escorted Dannon trucks. All the guards were "armed" with video cameras. In some cases, unions that are not directly involved in a strike may not cross the striking union's picket line, thus preventing supplies or equipment from entering the plant.

BOYCOTTING THE EMPLOYER. Boycotting involves refusing to patronize an employer—in other words, refusing to buy or use the employer's products or services. As an incentive to employees to honor the boycott, heavy fines may be levied against union members if they are caught patronizing an employer who is the subject of a union boycott. The union hopes that the general public will also join the boycott to put additional pressure on the employer. For example, you may be familiar with recent requests from farm workers for consumers to stop buying fruits and vegetables. Another example was the previously mentioned strike at the *New York Daily News,* when some readers boycotted the paper until the striking employees were rehired.[26]

Generally, there are two types of boycotts: the primary boycott and the secondary boycott. The primary boycott involves the refusal of the union to allow members to patronize a business where there is a labor dispute. In most cases, these types of boycotts are legal. A secondary boycott refers to the union trying to induce third parties, such as suppliers and customers, to refrain from any business dealings with an employer with whom it has a dispute. This type of boycott, as provided for under the Taft-Hartley Act, is illegal.

Employer's Power in Collective Bargaining

Employers may come to the bargaining table with their own base of power. Foremost is their ability to determine how to use capital within the organization. This enables them to decide whether and when to close down the company, the plant, or certain operations within the plant; to transfer operations to another location, or to subcontract out certain jobs. All these decisions must be made in accordance with the law. This means that management must be sure that its actions are not interpreted by the NLRB as attempts to avoid bargaining with the union.[27] What if you were fired because you refused an employer's order to commit an unfair labor practice? If you were a supervisor, would you be protected? The NLRB and the courts say that you are, under Taft-Hartley.

If an employer is confronted with a strike by one or more of its unions, then the firm must weigh the costs associated with enduring the strike against the costs of agreeing to the union's demands. There are a number of considerations the employer must take into account: (1) how the employer's actions will affect future negotiations with the union, (2) how long the firm and the union can endure a strike, and (3) whether business can continue during the strike.[28]

Today, employers are better able to endure strikes than they were in the past. This is because the hiring of replacements has greatly weakened the power of the strike. The NFL used mainly replacement players during the 1987 strike with the player's union. The owners realized higher profits during the strike although attendance was down. The players had no strike fund and negotiated a settlement to management's liking in only 3 weeks. In general, union members are now less willing to support a strike, and without strike unity, the power of the strike is negligible. Also, technological advances have increased some employers' ability to operate during a strike with a substantially reduced staff. Strikes in the public sector are illegal in 41 states, although walkouts have occurred in some states where strikes are illegal. Federal employees cannot strike pursuant to the 1978 Civil Service Reform Act.

Mutual aid pacts have also helped individual companies to hold out against strikes. Strike funds and strike insurance have allowed companies to be reimbursed for business lost because of a strike.[29] A good example of how a mutual aid pact was used by an employer occurred in 1981 when major league baseball players went on strike. The club owners had purchased $50 million worth of strike insurance, which they were able to collect during the work stoppage.[30]

The lockout is another source of power for the employer. A *lockout* is basically a shutting down of operations, usually as a reaction to a strike. The lockout can also be used to fight union slowdowns, damage to property, or violence within the plants. For example, owners of major league baseball teams used the lockout in 1990 as a response to the strike of the players.[31] Generally, lockouts are not used very often because they lead to revenue losses for the firm. Many states allow employees who are locked out to draw unemployment benefits, thus weakening the power of the lockout.

COLLECTIVE BARGAINING ISSUES

The major issues discussed in collective bargaining fall under the following four categories:[32]

1. **Wage-related issues.** These include such topics as how basic wage rates are determined, cost-of-living adjustments (COLAs), wage differentials, overtime rates, wage adjustments, and two-tier wage systems.
2. **Supplementary economic benefits.** These include such issues as pension plans, paid vacations, paid holidays, health insurance plans, dismissal pay, reporting pay, and supplementary unemployment benefits (SUBs).
3. **Institutional issues.** These consist of the rights and duties of employers, employees, and unions, including union security (i.e., union membership as a condition of employment), check-off procedures (i.e., when the employer collects dues by deducting them from employees' paychecks), employee stock ownership plans (ESOPs), and quality of work life (QWL) programs.
4. **Administrative issues.** These include such issues as seniority, employee discipline and discharge procedures, employee health and safety, technological changes, work rules, job security, and training.

While the last two categories contain important issues, the wage and benefit issues are the ones which typically receive the greatest amount of attention at the bargaining table. While most of these issues were discussed in Chapter 11, let us list the most significant of them here.

WAGE ISSUES

Wage issues are the No. 1 collective bargaining issue. They are the issues which most often lead to stalemates and deadlocks, and are the leading cause of strikes. During the late 1970s and 1980s, wage issues accounted for over 40 percent of work stoppages. According to the Bureau of Labor Statistics (BLS), 96 percent of all major private-sector contracts negotiated in 1991 raised wages. These increases averaged about 3 percent for the first year and 2.1 percent over the full term of the contract.[33]

Methods for Determining Wage Rates

Various methods or standards are used for determining basic wage rates. We will discuss three standards which are used to reach a settlement on fair and equitable wages.[34]

COMPARATIVE NORM. This standard is one of the most widely used for determining wage rates. It looks at other employer-union relationships to ensure that wage conditions are uniform throughout the community and/or industry. As we discussed in Chapter 11, this is based upon comprehensive wage and salary surveys of the community and industry wage structure, which are conducted before negotiations begin. For example, the NHLPA presented data during its 1992 negotiation with the NHL that showed average hockey players to be below the averages of NFL, NBA, and major league baseball players. The wage rates in the community are compared with the ones which currently exist in the company or plant. If the company or plant rates are below community or industry rates, the union will most likely argue for a wage increase. Conversely, if the rates in the company are higher than the comparable community rates, the employer may argue for holding rates steady. Comparative norms are used to determine wage rates in many industries, including the steel industry and trucking industry, where the respective unions are careful to ensure that wages are comparable across various firms.[35] In the 1988 negotiations between Chrysler and the UAW, the two parties agreed to return to "contract parity" with GM and Ford.[36] In other words, Chrysler would adopt wage, benefit, and job security levels similar to those at the other two car manufacturers.[37] There are many factors to be considered in utilizing the comparative norm principle as a standard for wage settlements. These include the company's ability to meet the economic demands placed upon it (i.e., determining whether it has available financial resources), ensuring that comparisons are made with appropriate companies, and taking into account different systems of wages and benefits used by different companies (e.g., one firm may pay lower basic wages but give more holidays).[38]

ABILITY TO PAY. A second wage-determining standard is the company's ability to pay a wage increase. Many factors go into determining whether a company is able to pay. These include the firm's level of profits, the ratio of labor costs to total costs, how much is spent on fringe benefits, and the ease with which the company can pass the costs of wage increases on to the consumer in the form of higher prices. For example, the NHL countered the NHLPA's comparative data on average salaries by presenting comparative television revenue data showing hockey lagging far behind baseball, football, and basketball. At the *New York Post* in 1990, unions agreed to pay cuts and job cuts because the newspaper was facing severe financial problems which were threatening publication. International competition in all major industries now makes it much more difficult for U.S. companies to simply pass added costs on to the consumer. One study of the steel, rail, trucking, and meat packing industries concluded that the philosophy of essentially passing labor increases on to the consumer had resulted in the competitive destruction of the industries.[39]

STANDARD OF LIVING. The question which must be addressed here is what constitutes a decent standard of living. One way of answering this question is by referring to a U.S. Department of Labor report, "City Worker's Family Budget." This report describes what a "modest but adequate standard of living" is for a family of four living in a large city or suburbs. The amounts vary from city to city.[40]

Cost-of-Living Adjustments

The changing cost of living is another determinant in wage negotiations. Thus, COLAs are part of many labor contracts. They are strongly favored by unions, because they provide for the adjustment of wages during the contract period rather than waiting for the contract to expire. On the other hand, management is usually against COLA clauses, since the adjustments become a part of employees' basic wage rates. The BLS indicates that the proportion of workers under contracts covered by COLA protection is declining (from 60 percent between 1976 and 1984 to 40 percent in 1989).[41] Nevertheless, during 1989, 61 percent of worker's income losses to inflation, on the average, were recovered through negotiated COLAs.[42] There are two methods for determining COLA during the labor agreement period: escalator clauses and wage reopener clauses.

ESCALATOR CLAUSES. Also known as "COLA provisions," *escalator clauses* state that workers' wages should rise and fall automatically with fluctuations in the cost of living. Most escalator clauses use the Consumer Price Index (CPI) as the standard for measuring changes in real income. The Department of Labor uses 1967 as the base year for purposes of calculating the CPI.

According to most escalator clauses, wage changes are automatically adjusted in accordance with changes in the CPI during the life of the labor contract. The contract will specify how frequently the CPI will be reviewed for wage adjustment purposes. Generally, it is reviewed quarterly. For example, the 1991 contract between General Dynamics and the machinists' union has a COLA clause which provides for quarterly adjustments of 1 cent for every 3-point increase in the CPI.[43] Most escalator clauses include a "floor" and a "cap," to provide some boundaries for the rise and fall of wages.

WAGE REOPENERS. This type of adjustment allows either the company or the union to reopen the labor contract for purposes of negotiating a new wage structure at specified intervals (e.g., annually for 3-year contracts). The electronic workers at a Ford Motor Company Refrigeration Products plant reopened their contract in 1988, which subsequently resulted in a pay raise.[44] Whichever party wants the wage change offers the other party written notice (generally 60 days ahead) of its intention to reopen wage negotiations. Usually the reason for reopening wage negotiations is changes in the cost of living.

Wage Differentials

Wage differentials refer to different rates of pay for different employees performing the same kind of work in the same type of job. These different rates of pay are provided for in the contract. One of the more common forms of wage differentials is premium pay for working undesirable shifts such as late afternoon, evening, night, and early morning. For example, a contract might call for the second shift to receive 10 percent more pay than the first shift and the third shift to receive 10 percent more pay than the second shift. Premium pay may also go to those who perform supervisory or instructional duties, or hazardous, dirty, or undesirable work.

Wage differentials are lawful except if they are used to discriminate against employees. As noted in Chapter 3, the Equal Pay Act of 1963 and Title VII of the Civil Rights Act of 1964 made it illegal to discriminate on the basis of race, sex, or national origin with regard to compensation. The 1990 ADA makes it illegal to discriminate against persons with disabilities. For example, a company cannot pay a person with a disability less money because the company had to make a "reasonable accommodation."

Overtime and Flextime

OVERTIME. Most contracts call for the standard 8-hour day and 40-hour week. Anyone working more than the standard 40-hour week must be paid at overtime rates (usually time and a half, sometimes double) for hours beyond 40. The Fair Labor Standards Act (FLSA) of 1938 provides nonexempt employees with the basic 40-hour workweek. A shorter workweek can, however, be negotiated. In some cases, a labor agreement may give an employer the right to force employees to work overtime. These provisions also, however, generally require the employer to give advance notice and to be willing to accept reasonable excuses from employees for not being able to work overtime (e.g., medical reasons). Boeing Company and the International Association of Machinists and Aerospace Workers signed a contract limiting mandatory overtime, requiring double-time pay after a specific amount of overtime, and pledging no reprisals for employees who reject voluntary overtime.[45] Other provisions related to overtime specify that overtime work must be shared equally among various employee classifications. Not doing so can be the grounds for a grievance. If a union can prove that an employer failed to offer certain employees an opportunity to work overtime, then the employer may have to pay those employees the amount which they would have earned if they had been given the opportunity.

FLEXTIME. This type of work scheduling allows employees to select, within certain limits, the hours they want to work each day. Employees still work 8 hours per day; however, they have greater flexibility in choosing their starting and quitting times. In almost all flextime provisions, there is a core time (e.g., ten a.m. to three p.m.) during which all employees must work. While unions are not overly enthusiastic about flextime schedules, tending to see them as another way for management to reduce overtime payments, some unions have supported them in the hope of attracting more women (e.g., AFSME).

Two-Tier Wage Systems

Two-tier wage systems are pay systems designed to protect the wage structure for current employees, while at the same time providing new employees with lower pay rates. Rubbermaid negotiated such a system in 1982 as a condition of keeping its Wooster, Ohio, plant open. Two-tiered pay systems have been used frequently in the airline industry with pilots. For example, American Airlines' newly hired pilots were paid at a rate 50 percent less than pilots who were already working for the airline when the agreement took effect in 1983.[46]

As we discussed in Chapter 14, the use of two-tier wage systems has been declining since 1986. Unions strongly oppose the pay systems, and there are a number of problems inherent in them. These problems exist not only for the new hires but the higher-tier employees too. For new hires, there is a sense of unfairness; they are doing the exact same job for significantly less money. For the higher-tier employees, there is a sense of fear; many believe that management is going to try to get rid of them or cut their hours since they are costing the company more than the new hires.

ISSUES RELATED TO INDIRECT COMPENSATION

As we discussed in Chapter 11, since the 1940s, indirect compensation or "fringe benefits" have risen at a rate of approximately 1 percent per year. Recently, these benefits, which include pension plans, paid vacations and holidays, health insurance, and unemployment benefits, have accounted for close to 40 percent of payroll or over $500 billion each year.[47] Unions can take much of the credit for this phenomenal increase in benefits since they have achieved the additions through their negotiating efforts. As illustrated in Figure 15.3, in many cases unions have argued for receiving increases in a variety of forms rather than just in wage increases. In this section, some of the economic benefits will be discussed.

Pension Plans

Private pension plans have been around since the 1940s. As Americans continued to live longer, it became apparent that the social security system could not provide all the financial resources that retirees needed.[48] Also, management began to realize that it had a responsibility to its employees after they retired, so it began to provide pension plans. Today, pension plans are accepted by most employers as a part of business expenses. The 1990 contract between Nabisco Brands and the Bakery, Confectionery, and Tobacco Workers union, for example, increased employer contributions to pensions and increased the maximum monthly pension rate for employees aged 65 with 25 years of service.[49]

The financing of pension plans is often a topic of discussion at the bargaining table. As discussed in Chapter 11, there are two methods for financing pension plans: noncontributory and contributory. About 75 percent of contracts are noncontributory, meaning that employers finance the entire cost of the retirement benefits. Needless to say, these plans are favored by the unions. In contributory financing, employees pay some percentage of the cost of the plan.

Vacations with Pay

Today, vacations with pay are a standard provision of all labor contracts. That was not always the case; prior to World War II, very few union employees received pay during their vacations. While paid vacations have come to be an expected part of the job, management views them as among the most expensive benefits since they involve the payment of wages for time not worked. A 3-week vacation is fairly common for employees with 10 or more years of service. Most contracts require that the employee must have worked a specified number of days or months prior to taking a vacation. In most contracts, management has the final word in scheduling vacation periods. Generally, scheduling takes into consideration seniority as well as employees' preferences.[50]

FIGURE 15.3
UNION PREFERENCES FOR WAGE FORMS

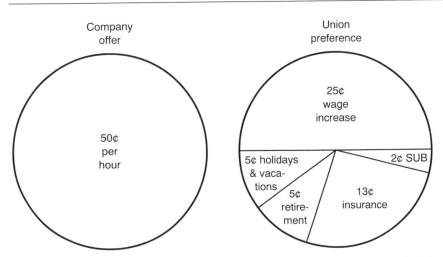

Source: J. A. Fossum, *Labor relations: Development, structure, process,* 4th ed. Homewood, IL: Richard D. Irwin, 1989, p. 189. Reprinted with permission.

Holidays with Pay

Paid holidays have not always been a standard part of the labor agreement. Today, however, almost all contracts provide for a certain number of paid holidays. The average number in union contracts is 10, one more than the average for all American workers. Generally, most contracts require employees to work the last scheduled day before and the first scheduled day after a holiday, except in cases of illness, family death, etc. This is not always the case. For example, the UAW at Deere & Company in Iowa and Illinois recently added another day to the July 4 weekend to ensure a 4-day holiday.[51] If an employee chooses to work on a holiday, most agreements provide for double-time pay for this workday.[52]

Health and Welfare Insurance Plans

With the escalating costs of health care, one of the more common features of labor contracts is health insurance. Health benefits may cover life insurance or death benefits; accidental death and dismemberment benefits; accident and sickness benefits; hospital, surgical, maternity, and medical care benefits; dental care benefits: psychiatric treatment benefits; and in some cases, maternity or paternity leave.

As we discussed in Chapter 11, there have been attempts by employers to reduce the rising costs of health care. Two ways of doing so have been by starting health maintenance organizations (HMOs), which provide specified services for a predetermined amount, and by using preferred provider organizations (PPOs), which offer discounts on services.[54]

Over the past several years, unions have resisted efforts by firms to raise deductibles on health coverage, to cut services, and to shift all or part of the premiums to workers. This resistance at times has led to some very serious labor-management disputes such as the United Mine Workers (UMW) strike against Pittston coal in 1989.[54]

Dismissal or Severance Pay

About 40 percent of contracts have provisions for dismissal or severance pay to be provided to employees who are laid off.[55] These types of provisions are frequently found in contracts with steelworkers and autoworkers. The contract stipulates that, to receive payment, employees must have lost their jobs for acceptable reasons. Usually, these reasons include such things as technological change, plant mergers, permanent curtailment of operations, and permanent employee disability. Reasons not acceptable for receiving severance pay include involuntary employee turnover for just cause (e.g., employee theft, poor performance) and voluntary turnover.

The amount of severance pay an employee receives depends upon his or her length of service. One rule of thumb sometimes stipulated in contracts is 1 week's wages for each year of service prior to dismissal. In 1990, GM and the UAW signed a contract which provided unemployment benefits of nearly 85 percent of regular pay for up to 3 years, an unprecedented agreement.[56] A 1988 contract between GE and a coalition of unions offered a $7500 retirement payment to employees terminated due to a discontinued product line, work transfers, or automation.[57] Generally, most contracts require that if a dismissed employee is rehired, the severance pay received to date must be paid back either in lump sum or in payroll deductions.

Reporting Pay

Reporting pay provisions are included in most contracts and guarantee a certain amount of compensation for a day in which the employee is scheduled to work. Reporting pay usually ranges from a 1-hour guarantee to a full-day guarantee; most provide for 4 hours pay per day.[58] Also, most contracts provide for a release of obligation on the part of the employer. That is, the employer is relieved of any obligation to guarantee work or make cash payments if management notifies employees in advance not to report for work or if the firm is unable to provide work because of "floods, fires, strikes, power failures, or acts of God."

Income Security Programs

Supplementary unemployment benefit (SUB) plans, as the name suggests, are designed to supplement unemployment benefits provided by state unemployment insurance systems. These benefits provide income to unemployed workers even after the state's benefits have run out. SUB plans are designed to cope with short-term plant closings and recessions. About half of all manufacturing workers in the United States have some kind of SUB plan.[59] Employees must have a certain amount of service with the company before they become eligible for these benefits. The system works by having eligible employees acquire credit units at a specified rate per week. After a stipulated period of time (usually 1 to 5 years), they are credited with the units and can then trade off for SUB pay if they become unemployed. SUBs usually have a maximum unemployment duration of 52 weeks. During that period, employees are allowed to draw benefits only up to the amount of credits they have accumulated. The amount they can receive is usually around 60 to 65 percent of their take-home pay (including both SUB and any state system payments). At GM, the electronic workers contract provides laid-off employees with up to 36 weeks supplemental unemployment benefits equal to 95 percent of their take-home pay.[60]

The SUB system is funded by requiring the employer to contribute a certain amount of money per work hour (e.g., 10 cents per hour). When the amount in the fund reaches a specified size, the employer may stop making payments to it. When fund finances fall below that stipulated amount, however, the employer must resume payments.

ADMINISTRATION OF THE LABOR CONTRACT

As discussed earlier in this chapter, the labor contract establishes the general framework for labor relations by spelling out the rights and benefits of employees and the obligations and rights of management. The labor contract is designed to protect the rights of employees, employers, and unions. Of course, along with those rights come a number of responsibilities.

The earlier part of this chapter dealt with the negotiation of the labor contract. In this part of the chapter, we will address the application and interpretation of the labor agreement. Despite the incredible amount of time and effort that go into negotiating and carefully writing the contract, most are written in such broad, ambiguous terms that a great deal of interpretation is required in order to put the contract to work. As we said earlier, most rank-in-file union workers do not clearly understand the labor contract.

Most of the problems associated with the interpretation or application of the labor contract are resolved bilaterally at the lower levels of the *grievance* procedure (i.e., between the supervisor and the employee). Grievance procedures and the time limits associated with them are generally spelled out in the contract for the purpose of reaching quick, fair, and equitable solutions to contract problems. Unresolved grievances proceed progressively to higher and higher levels of management and union representation. If the grievance procedure fails (i.e., if the grievance reaches a deadlock or stalemate), most contracts stipulate that the final step will be binding *arbitration*. Arbitration involves bringing in a third party, an impartial outsider mutually agreed upon by the two parties, to decide the controversy. In the following section, both the grievance procedure and the arbitration process will be reviewed. Figure 15.4 illustrates what these processes look like.

Grievance Procedure

When an employee believes that the labor agreement has been violated, the employee files a grievance. A grievance is a formal complaint regarding the event, action, or practice which violated the contract. The grievance procedure serves a number of purposes.[61] The primary purpose is to determine whether the labor contract has been violated. Also, the grievance procedure is designed to settle alleged contract violations in as friendly and orderly a fashion as possible, before they become major issues. Other purposes of the grievance procedure include preventing future grievances from arising, improving communication and cooperation between labor and management, and helping to obtain a better climate of labor relations. Most contracts provide a multistep, formal, orderly process for filing a grievance. The grievance procedure is designed to help clarify what often is not clear in the contract (e.g., defining lawful or unlawful conduct). Much of the interpretation of the contract which takes place during a grievance proceeding must take into account extenuating circumstances, including both the current human and economic factors.

Grievance procedures generally establish the following: (1) how the grievance will be initiated, (2) the number of steps in the process, (3) who will represent each party, and (4) the specified number of working days within which the grievance must be taken to the next step in the hearing. Failure to comply with time limits may result in forfeiture of the grievance.[62]

INITIATING THE FORMAL GRIEVANCE. In most cases the labor contract stipulates that the employee's grievance must be expressed orally or in writing to the employee's immediate supervisor. One advantage of expressing the grievance in written form is that it reduces the chance that differing versions of the grievance will be circulated. It also forces the employee to approach the grievance in a comparatively rational manner, thus helping to eliminate or reduce the likelihood of trivial complaints or feelings of hostility. In some cases, a grievance may be taken directly to the union steward, who will then discuss it with the employee's supervisor.

Most contract violations resulting in grievances are not committed consciously or with willful intent. They tend to be the result of an oversight or misunderstanding. Since this is often the case, such oversights or misunderstandings can be resolved at the lower levels if the supervisor is willing to take the time and effort to listen to the employee's concerns.

To make progress toward resolution of the grievance, a number of obstacles must be overcome. These include dealing with personality conflicts and prejudices that might exist between the supervisor and employee. In addition, differences of opinion regarding the interpretation or application of the contract must be resolved. Also, since grievances may give rise to the expression of strong emotions or feelings, these too must be acknowledged and dealt with.

RESOLUTION OF GRIEVANCES. Most grievances are settled early in the process. Settlement generally

**FIGURE 15.4
A GRIEVANCE PROCEDURE**

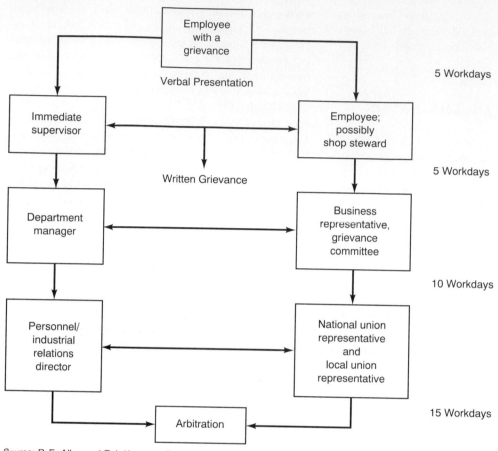

Source: R. E. Allen and T. J. Keaveny, *Contemporary labor relations*, 2d ed. Reading, MA: Addison-Wesley, 1988, p. 530. Reprinted with permission.

occurs after an employee has either presented his or her grievance in writing to the supervisor or appealed to the next higher level. An early settlement is contingent, however, upon each side's being willing to listen to the other side and discuss the problem in a rational and objective manner. Settlement can be hampered if one or both sides enter the procedure with an attitude of "win-lose" as opposed to "win-win."

When a grievance does not get settled in the first or second step, it goes to a higher level, often to company representatives (e.g., a general superintendent) and union representatives (e.g., a grievance committee). These representatives meet to further discuss the grievance and try to reach a solution agreeable to all. In most cases, the burden of proof in a grievance proceeding is on the union.

Sometimes a mediator will be brought in to help resolve the grievance. The mediator's role in a grievance resolution is much the same as in contract mediation (i.e., to get the two parties to communicate, and to offer compromise solutions). The mediator's role is not to es-

tablish which side is right or wrong. His or her recommendations and suggestions can be accepted or rejected by either party. The role of the mediator, as will be seen later, is much different from that played by the arbitrator, whose decisions are final and binding.[63]

NONUNION GRIEVANCE PROCEDURES. Grievance procedures are found not only in companies in which a labor contract exists but also in nonunion companies. In fact, almost two-thirds of nonunion firms have developed some form of formal grievance system.[64] Like union grievance procedures, the immediate supervisor plays a key role. Often, a "round table" is established which consists of employee and management representatives. This group generally meets on a regular basis for the purpose of resolving grievances.

In order for nonunion grievance procedures to be successful, all employees should be educated in terms of how the process works. Also, there should exist an atmosphere of trust, so that employees will feel free to use the process without fear of reprisal by management. Finally, employees must see the process as one that management takes seriously and handles quickly, fairly, and thoroughly.

Arbitration Process

While there is no law which forces parties to include arbitration in their labor agreements (either party can refuse to incorporate any arbitration provisions), approximately 96 percent of all labor agreements in the United States do provide for arbitration as the final step in the grievance procedure.[65] In the majority of grievances filed, arbitration is not necessary since resolutions are usually made during lower-level discussions. In fact, arbitration should be the last resort after all other options in the grievance process have failed. Arbitration involves bringing in an impartial third party (referred to as the "arbitrator" or "adjudicator"), who is mutually agreed upon by both parties to break the deadlock between the union and management. Unlike the mediator's role of providing *recommended* solutions, the arbitrator's role is to make a ruling which is "final and binding upon both parties."

Major League Baseball is one organization which uses binding arbitration in salary determination. In this form of negotiation, the player and the team each put in an offer for what they consider to be an acceptable salary. If no agreement is reached, the arbitrator hears arguments from both sides and chooses one of the figures. This decision then becomes binding to both the player and the team.

Arbitration is generally not used as a method of breaking a deadlock in negotiating a new labor contract. This is because both labor and management would prefer to make their own decisions regarding conditions of employment rather than have these decisions made by a third party (i.e., the arbitrator).

THE DECISION TO ARBITRATE.   The decision about whether or not to take a grievance to arbitration depends upon a number of factors and circumstances. At least two things might happen before arbitration becomes necessary: (1) the union could withdraw the grievance, or (2) the employer could give in. If neither of these happens, both sides must weigh the costs of arbitration. Both sides must take into account whether or not the case is important enough to justify the costs in terms of time, money, and effort. They should also determine what the chances are for a favorable ruling. Unions must give consideration to the recent trends related to favorable awards to unions. For example, in 1986, a study by the American Arbitration Association (AAA) found that unions won only 32 percent of the grievance cases submitted to binding arbitration.[66]

According to the fair representation doctrine, unions cannot ignore their legal obligation to provide assistance to their members who are pursuing a grievance. Even if a union knows that an employee's case is weak, it often pursues the case to demonstrate its commitment to its members. In addition, management cannot refuse to arbitrate unresolved grievances if the labor contract contains an arbitration clause. This was established in a 1957 U.S. Supreme Court ruling.[67]

SELECTION OF THE ARBITRATOR.   Most labor agreements state that union and management will select an arbitrator from a panel of names submitted by either the FMCS or the AAA.[68] Neither party is, however, obligated to use either service. One of these organizations will provide the two parties with a list of names (usually seven) from its roster of arbitrators. The two parties will then agree upon an arbitrator through a process of elimination or some other mutually acceptable procedure.

Most of the arbitrators listed with the above organizations are lawyers or college professors, though such a background is not a prerequisite. In choosing an arbitrator, what would the two parties look for? In terms of personal characteristics, they would desire an individual who is incorruptible; free of bias; aware of the principles of arbitration; and patient, sympathetic, and understanding. Also, the arbitrator should be willing to listen to the evidence, witnesses, documents, and arguments presented by both sides; able to keep the meeting moving; and able to conduct a fair, orderly, thorough, and speedy hearing. Further, the arbitrator should treat witnesses fairly, keep control of the process, and have a sound understanding of labor relations. Given this extensive list of characteristics, it is not surprising that union and management have difficulty in selecting and agreeing on an arbitrator.

Many labor contracts stipulate a procedure for appointing an arbitrator. In some cases, a *permanent* arbitrator may be appointed under the terms of the labor agreement. The advantages of using a permanent arbitrator are that it saves time in the selection process, the arbitrator is already familiar with the contract and the current state of labor relations in the company, and there is a greater likelihood of uniformity in decisions because there tends to be more consistency in the interpretation of the contract. The other option for selecting an arbitrator is what is known as the "ad hoc method," which simply calls for a different arbitrator for each case. Despite the fact that the selection process takes longer, the ad hoc method is more popular precisely because the parties are not stuck with the same arbitrator for every case.

THE ARBITRATION PROCESS.   While arbitration hearings are considered quasi-judicial, they are less formal than court proceedings. The arbitration hearing begins with a submission agreement, either oral or written, which describes the issues to be resolved through arbitration. Once the issues are presented, it is up to each of the parties to educate the arbitrator about relevant issues, facts, evidence, and arguments. The arbitrator does not play the role of fact finder; however, he or she does have the right to question witnesses or to request additional facts.

Arbitrators are not bound by formal rules of evidence like those used in a court of law. For example, hearsay evidence may be introduced as long as it is identified as such. In addition, throughout the arbitration proceedings, a court recorder may be present to prepare a transcript of the hearing.

BASIS FOR THE ARBITRATOR'S DECISION AND AWARD.

After hearing all the evidence, the arbitrator writes his or her opinion supporting the decision and award. This includes providing a written rationale for the decision (i.e., an explanation of why the decision was made the way it was). The written opinion of the arbitrator presents the basic issues of the case, the pertinent facts, the position and arguments of each party, the merits of each position, and the reasons for the decision (i.e., an explanation to the "losing" side). As a rule of thumb, the arbitrator is given 30 days in which to consider the evidence and to prepare a decision.

A fair decision and award must be based strictly upon the facts, evidence, and arguments presented in the case. Also, they should be based upon an accurate assessment and interpretation of the contractual clauses of the labor agreement. The contract is the final authority. That is why the contract language is so important; it should be as clear-cut and precise as possible. Unfortunately, contractual language usually is unclear and ambiguous and has many different meanings.

In reaching a decision, an arbitrator must decide whether the employee was accorded due process. That is, it is the right of each employee to be informed of any unsatisfactory performance and to have the opportunity to defend himself or herself against such charges. The arbitrator must also determine whether the employer had just cause for any actions taken against the complainant. One final consideration for the arbitrator is to make sure that his or her decision is not based upon precedents established in previous cases, but rather on the facts of the current case. Emotional appeals and horse trading have no place in arbitration proceedings. The arbitrator's awards should be clear and to the point. If the union receives the award, the arbitrator should state explicitly what actions the employer must take to comply with the provisions of the contract.

CRITICISMS OF ARBITRATION PROCESS.

Probably the criticisms heard most often about arbitra-

tion relate to costs and delays. Arbitration can be both expensive and time-consuming. However, supporters of arbitration will counter that argument with the fact that the costs associated with strikes and lockouts are even greater. The average fee for an arbitrator now typically exceeds $2000 per day, plus expenses. These costs include all the arbitrator's expenses such as hotel, travel, and meals; his or her time to analyze and write up the case and opinion; and other miscellaneous costs such as those associated with lawyers and stenographers.

A few strategies have been found to reduce the costs of arbitration. These include developing a system to ensure that only grievances of high importance to the union and employer end up in arbitration, using arbitrators from the local area, consolidating grievances into one hearing, and having the arbitrator issue an award without providing a detailed written opinion.

The arbitration process is frequently criticized for being too time-consuming. Cases often become backlogged due to arbitrators' busy schedules. Also, the actual hearings get drawn out because of the need to read lengthy transcripts or briefs. Finally, the writing of the opinion is very time-consuming. A study done in 1983 found that on the average, 228 days elapsed from the time both parties requested a panel of arbitrators to the day the actual award was issued.[69] Several things can be done to cut down on this excessive time. These include using new arbitrators with smaller caseloads, creating a permanent panel of arbitrators from which to choose, and cutting out transcripts and posthearing briefs (i.e., having the arbitrator take his or her own notes).

Some employers try to reduce arbitration time and costs by using a form of expedited arbitration sometimes referred to as *miniarbitration*. Miniarbitration requires that a hearing be held within 10 days after an appeal is made. Also, arbitration hearings are completed in 1 day, the arbitrator's decision must be made within 48 hours after the close of the hearing, there are no transcripts or briefs, and the fee is paid for only the hearing day. Miniarbitration is not always appropriate, but it generally works well with simple, routine cases. Another alternative is a process called *grievance mediation*, which combines aspects of mediation and arbitration. It is much less formal than arbitrations, with no briefs or cross-examinations of witnesses.

LEGAL SUPPORT FOR ARBITRATION.

The U.S. Supreme Court has made several rulings regarding arbitration during the past 30 years. Most of these decisions have supported and strengthened the arbitration process and defined more clearly the relationship between arbitration and the courts. Three important cases influencing the arbitration process were decided in 1960. Known as the "Steelworker's Trilogy," they are *United Steelworkers of America v. Warrior & Gulf Navigation Company,*

United Steelworkers of America v. Enterprise Wheel & Car Corporation, and *United Steelworkers of America v. America Manufacturing Company.*[70] The courts may direct arbitration but cannot determine the merits of a dispute. In fact, on several occasions, the Supreme Court has reversed decisions by a lower court regarding the power of federal courts to evaluate the merits of a dispute. Other cases brought before the Supreme Court have also resulted in reversals of lower court rulings. One such case demonstrated that neither the union nor management may use the courts to set aside an arbitrator's award.

In several recent cases, the Supreme Court has taken a favorable view of arbitration. In *Gilmer v. Interstate/ Johnson Lane Corporation,* the Court in 1991 recognized the legality of a compulsory arbitration agreement as a condition of employment. Robert Gilmer signed the agreement as a part of his application to the New York Stock Exchange. When he was terminated at age 62, he tried to bring suit under ADEA. The Court said the compulsory arbitration agreement ruled out such a suit. The decision, however, did *not* stipulate that employees could be forced to accept arbitration as an alternative to lawsuits under ADA, ADEA, the Civil Rights Act, etc. This critical issue has not been resolved by the courts. The 1991 Civil Rights Act and the ADA endorse alternative dispute resolution techniques.[71]

There is one circumstance in which an arbitrator's decision could be subject to reversal by a federal court. This is when it is determined that the union did not provide fair representation to the employee or employees involved in the arbitration.

CURRENT TRENDS IN COLLECTIVE BARGAINING

What does the future hold for collective bargaining? As we move closer to the twenty-first century, will we continue to use our current methods of bargaining to reach a contract settlement? Some critics of conventional collective bargaining say that the current system cannot survive because it is inefficient, ineffective, excessively time-consuming, and characterized by exaggerated opening demands and inflated counterproposals.

During the 1980s, a number of changes took place in the labor relations environment. The massive layoffs caused by recessions and foreign competition caused both union and management to reexamine their bargaining goals and tactics. Unions had always believed that they had the right to challenge the way management ran the business. While they still expect this to some degree, there has been a movement away from the adversarial bargaining relationship beset by conflict, toward a relationship characterized more by accommodation. For example, cooperation and collaboration were evident in the labor negotiations between the National Basketball Association (NBA) and the players' association, when the union agreed to keep an unwanted "salary cap," with a schedule of minimum annual increases.[72] U.S. Steel managers and union officials now have regular meetings to discuss quality, customer service, retraining, and health-care costs. Ten years ago, management and the union discussed such issues only at the bargaining table. As Thomas Usher, the president of U.S. Steel, put it, "there is a growing realization that we are not going to make it without the union and the union is not going to make it without us."[73]

The days of table pounding, yelling, and threatening may be over. Contract negotiations today are more orderly and rational, and less emotional and deceitful. However, as we discussed in Chapter 14, there is also a growing faction of more "militant" unionists who believe labor has offered too many concessions.

"Cooperation" and "collaboration" are the words being used to describe contract negotiations today. This collaboration can take many forms. For example, management can create committees on which employees are represented [e.g., shop committees, department committees, quality circles (QCs)]. Also, there has been a movement toward greater cooperation in handling disciplinary problems and resolving grievances.

Concessionary Bargaining

Concessionary bargaining involves a union's giving back to management some of what it has gained in previous bargaining. Why would labor be willing to give back what it worked so hard to obtain? Usually such a move is prompted by labor leaders who recognize the need to assist employers in reducing operating costs in order to prevent layoffs and plant closings. Thus, it is often economic adversity that motivates concessionary bargaining. A good example is the 1992 agreement between GM and the International Union of Electronic Workers which granted GM around-the-clock operations, wage and benefit concessions for new hires, and a 2-week mass vacation. The concessions were made to save over 3000 jobs at a plant in Ohio. The UAW has accused GM of "whipsawing," pitting plant against plant to gain concessions. In some cases, despite a financial crisis, the union may not be willing to concede. This may be because the union does not view management's arguments as credible. Thus, the degree of trust and credibility between management and the union may influence the extent to which concessionary bargaining occurs.

What kinds of concessions are sought by employers? Often they relate to wages; for example, putting a cap on increases in compensation. As discussed in Chapter 12, management has emphasized various forms of pay-for-performance systems in lieu of standard base-pay increases. For example, in return for wage concessions, the union may receive a gain-sharing plan that links compensation with performance data, or some form of profit sharing or stock ownership. Many unions focused on job security issues in the late 1980s and early 1990s. For example, the CWA emphasized job security in its 1992 negotiations with AT&T and the "Baby Bells." Their focus was on finding new jobs for operators who were replaced by automated systems. In 1990, GM agreed to a lifetime employment experiment covering 80 percent of its workforce at four plants. Furthermore, they agreed to a "guaranteed income stream" to protect high-seniority workers threatened by layoffs. Other demands made by unions in return for concessions include restrictions on work rules, transfers of work, subcontracting, and plant closures; getting advance notice of shutdowns and severance pay; and transfer rights for displaced employees. GM closed their Willow Run, Michigan, plant because the local UAW representatives refused to bend on work rules while the Arlington, Texas, plant stayed open because the UAW locals agreed to change long-established work rules and reduce the number of job classifications.[74] Other union concessions are expected in 1992 negotiations. The local union at Rubbermaid's Wooster, Ohio, plant made numerous concessions in 1992 when Rubbermaid threatened to close the plant and move the operation overseas.

U.S.-Based Multinationals*

One reality that unions are going to be faced with more and more in the future is that of multinational corporations. As noted in Chapter 14, unions may become tremendously frustrated as corporations establish operations in other countries which are not under the jurisdiction of U.S. labor law. Currently, there are no international collective bargaining laws.[75] Many union jobs have been exported to other countries where companies receive tax concessions and lower labor costs. Clearly, future discussions will continue to focus on determining viable collective bargaining procedures for the increasing number of multinational corporations.

As we stated in Chapter 14, comparisons of labor relations issues across countries is very difficult since there are many other social, legal, historical, political, and religious differences across borders as well. For example, the definition and process of collective bargaining are very different in Europe than in the United States. The 1992 public-sector strike in Germany clearly illustrated the relatively greater power of unions in many European countries than in the United States. The strike virtually shut commerce down for several weeks. In the

United States, *collective bargaining* refers to negotiations between a local union and the employer.[76] In most European countries and Japan, negotiations occur at the industry level between an employer's association and the national trade union. Even in companies where trade union representation is low, the collective bargaining process has an impact, since it is highly concentrated in the largest, most visible companies, which build a well-publicized wage standard for other industries. Europeans also perceive collective bargaining as a form of class struggle tied to the political process. For example, a high percentage of labor activists in other countries are socialists who work within the system to make changes in capitalist economic systems. In the United States, the major labor unions embrace the capitalist system and negotiate primarily in economic areas.

In general, the structure of labor unions tends to reflect the historical perspective with significant diversity in labor relations and union structure across countries. Transnational collective bargaining has not yet been accomplished by unions despite active political negotiations to achieve that end. Europe is dominated by industry-wide bargaining but not across borders. Some experts view the social dimension related to labor relations as one of the major obstacles to the success of the proposed European Community.[77] While the social dimension charter for the European Community stresses the role of national laws and collective bargaining, a goal of the association is to achieve a common labor perspective and to have cross-border consultative bodies. Several large European companies are now pursuing such relationships on their own. With the political upheaval in the Eastern bloc nations and the transition to the 1992 European Community, international collective bargaining is in a tumultuous state. As we discussed in Chapter 14, multinational U.S. corporations should have a clear understanding of labor relations issues and collective bargaining policy prior to embarking upon any international venture.

SUMMARY

As a result of the changes taking place in the size and composition of the workforce, the advances in technology, and the increased competition from foreign businesses, the future of unions and the collective bargaining system is uncertain. Some have predicted that the days of unions are over unless they incorporate these changes into their collective bargaining strategies. There is little doubt that unions must be willing to be flexible and to adapt to the changes taking place.[78] What worked in the 1800s and even through the 1950s will not work in the 1990s and beyond. Unions must find a way to attract the new entrants into the labor force—such as women, minorities, and

---

*Contributed by Marion Schubinski.

immigrants—if they are to survive. Unions and collective bargaining will continue to play an important role in the lives of American workers as long as they are able to help workers overcome dissatisfaction with management and to meet their economic needs. Greater cooperation between labor and management is needed to make organizations more effective and competitive. In some industries, that cooperation may be necessary in order to survive.

DISCUSSION QUESTIONS

1. How would a union benefit from using coalition or multiemployer bargaining structures?
2. Describe how union and management might prepare for labor negotiations. How are their preparations similar and different?
3. Why is it advantageous for both union and management to be flexible regarding bargaining issues?
4. Describe the sources of power brought to the bargaining table by union and management.
5. Describe the major collective bargaining issues of today. What do you foresee as the major issues of the future? Explain your response.
6. Explain how the grievance procedure and the arbitration process differ. What are the relative advantages and disadvantages of each in settling labor-management disputes?
7. Employers should be allowed to require applicants to sign binding arbitration agreements and forgo the right to a judicial forum for certain laws. Explain your position.

NOTES

1. Lawyer, J. E. (1947). The United States Labor-Management Relations Act of 1947. *International Labor Review, 56*(2), 125–166.
2. McCulloch, F. W., and Bornstein, T. (1974). *The National Labor Relations Board.* New York: Praeger.
3. Morse, B. (1974). *How to negotiate the labor agreement.* Detroit, MI: Trands.
4. Sloane, A. A., and Witney, F. (1988). *Labor relations.* Englewood Cliffs, NJ: Prentice-Hall. See also: Holley, W. H., and Jennings, K. M. (1991). *The labor relations process.* Chicago: Dryden Press.
5. See note 4.
6. Fisher, C. D., Schoenfeldt, L. F., and Shaw, J. B. (1990). *Human resource management.* Boston, MA: Houghton-Mifflin.
7. See note 4.
8. Loughran, C. S. (1984). *Negotiating a labor contract: A management handbook.* Washington: Bureau of National Affairs.
9. See note 4.
10. Northrop, H. R. (1966). Boulwarism vs. coalitionism: The 1966 GE negotiations. *Management of Personnel Quarterly, 5*(2), 8.
11. See note 3.
12. Swoboda, F. (Sept. 14, 1990). GM, UAW closer to contract; job security remains an issue. *The Washington Post,* p. G3.
13. Ramirez, A. (March 31, 1992). AT&T and 2 unions hold talks. *The New York Times,* p. C3.
14. Quimp, M. G. (Aug. 16, 1990). Operators angered over automation. *The Washington Post,* pp. C1, C4. See also: Note 13.
15. Kuttner, R. (1985). Sharing power at Eastern Air Lines. *Harvard Business Review, 63,* 91–101.
16. Bellace, J. R., Berkowitz, A., and Van Dusen, B. D. (1979). *The Landrum-Griffin Act.* Philadelphia: University of Pennsylvania. See also: Note 1.
17. Gonzalez, D. (Nov. 4, 1990). *News'* loyal readers are split on strike, too. *The New York Times,* p. 38.
18. Dilts, D. A., and Karim, A. (1990). The effect of mediators' qualities and strategies on mediation outcomes. *Industrial Relations, 45,* 22–37. See also: Hamilton, M. M., and Swoboda, F. (July 10, 1990). Mediators declare impasse between Eastern and pilots: Action sets stage for contract showdown. *The Washington Post,* p. D3. Labor Letter, Federal mediators renew bid to avert Pan Am strike (Feb. 4, 1988). *The Wall Street Journal,* p. 1.
19. See note 3.
20. Imberman, W. (1983). Who strikes—and why? *Harvard Business Review, 61,* 18–28.
21. Gerard, J. (Jan. 16, 1989). A season the networks would rather not repeat. *The New York Times,* p. D8.
22. Brown, F. (Oct. 2, 1989). Opposing sides in Pittston coal strike digging in for the long haul. *Knoxville News-Sentinel,* pp. A1–A2.
23. AFL-CIO Committee for Workplace Fairness (1990). Washington, DC: AFL-CIO.
24. Hicks, J. P. (Apr. 15, 1992). Union declares end to a strike at Caterpillar. *The New York Times, 1,* p. A8. See also: Bulletin to Management (Apr. 13, 1989). *The Bureau of National Affairs,* p. 113.
25. Associated Press (Mar. 6, 1989). Eastern pleads with its pilots, plan to picket railroads dropped. *Knoxville News-Sentinel,* p. A1.
26. See note 18.
27. Sherman, A. W., Jr., Bohlander, G. W., and Chruden, H. J. (1988). *Managing human resources,* 8th ed. Cincinnati, OH: South-Western.
28. See note 27.
29. See note 4.
30. Doane, D. P. (June 29, 1981). Impact of the baseball strike. *U.S. News & World Report,* pp. 64–65.
31. Chass, M. (Mar. 15, 1990). Negotiators led to water but don't drink. *The New York Times,* p. B12.
32. Schuler, R. S., and Huber, V. L. (1990). *Personnel and human resource management,* 4th ed. St. Paul, MN: West Publishing.

33. Gehan, S. (1992). *Bargaining '91*. Washington, DC: AFL-CIO.

34. See note 4, Holley and Jennings (1991).

35. Ansberry, C. (July 17, 1989). Steelworkers ratify accords with 2 firms; National Steel vote avoids strike; Inland approval avoids possible lockout. *The Wall Street Journal*, p. A4. See also: Karr, A. R., and Machalaba, D. (Mar. 15, 1991). Trucking firms, Teamsters forge 3-year accord. *The Wall Street Journal*, p. A2.

36. Bureau of Labor Statistics (1988). U.S. Dept. of Labor.

37. See note 36.

38. See note 4.

39. Fruhan, W. (1985). Management, labor, and the golden goose. *Harvard Business Review, 63*, 131–141.

40. Bureau of Labor Statistics (1990). City worker's family budget. Washington: U.S. Department of Labor.

41. See note 40.

42. Davis, W. M. (1989). *Labor-management relations*, 4th ed. New York: McGraw-Hill.

43. Bureau of Labor Statistics (1991). U.S. Dept. of Labor.

44. See note 36.

45. Bureau of Labor Statistics (1989). U.S. Dept. of Labor.

46. Flax, S. (Jan. 9, 1984). Pay cuts before the job even starts. *Fortune*, p. 75.

47. See note 4.

48. Freeman,. R. B. (1983). Unions, pensions, and union pension funds. *Working paper series*. Cambridge, MA: National Bureau of Economic Research.

49. See note 39.

50. See note 4, Holley and Jennings (1991).

51. See note 33.

52. See note 4, Holley and Jennings (1991).

53. Allen, R. E., and Keaveny, T. J. (1988). *Contemporary labor relations*, 2d ed. Reading, MA: Addison-Wesley.

54. See note 22.

55. See note 4.

56. Patterson, G. (Jan. 29, 1991). Blue-collar boon; auto workers now on layoff have a sturdy safety net. *The Wall Street Journal*, pp. A1, A12.

57. See note 36.

58. See note 53.

59. See note 34.

60. See note 43.

61. Dastmalchian, A., and Ng, I. (1990). Industrial relations climate and grievance outcomes. *Industrial Relations*, 45, 311–324. See also: Salipante, P. F., and Bouwen, R. (1990). Behavioral analysis of grievances: Conflict sources, complexity and transformation. *Employee Relations, 12*, 17–22.

62. See note 27.

63. See note 61.

64. Diaz, E. D., Minton, J.W., and Saunders, D. M. (April 1987). A fair nonunion grievance procedure. *Personnel Journal*, 13–18.

65. See note 4.

66. See note 41.

67. See note 4.

68. See note 53.

69. *Daily Labor Report* (May 14, 1983). Labor arbitration seen in need of improvement, p. 1.

70. See note 61.

71. Nager, G. D., and Jenab, D. B. (Apr. 26, 1992). Keep workplace disputes out of court. *The New York Times*, p. 13.

72. NBA and union in accord (Apr. 27, 1988). *The New York Times*, p. B17.

73. Hicks, J. P. (Apr. 3, 1992). The steel man with kid gloves. *The New York Times*, pp. C1, C3.

74. Ingrassia, P., and White, J. B. (Feb. 25, 1992). GM posts record '91 loss of $4.45 billion, sends tough message to UAW on closings. *The Wall Street Journal*, A3, A6.

75. Spyropoulos, G. (1990). Labour law and labour relations in tomorrow's social Europe. *International Labour Review, 129*, 733–750. See also: Northrup, H. R., Campbell, D. C., and Slowinski, B. J. (1988). Multinational union-management consultation in Europe: Resurgence in the 1980s? *International Labour Review, 5*, 525–543.

76. Dowling, P. J., and Schuler, R. S. (1990). *International dimensions of human resource management*. Boston, MA: PWS-Kent

77. Lee, B. (August 1991). Preparing for Europe 1992: U.S. multinationals and the social charter. Paper presented at the annual meeting of the Academy of Management, San Francisco.

78. Rosenbaum, M. (1989). Partners in productivity: An emerging consensus in labor-management relations. *Productivity Review, 8*, 357–364. See also: Drucker, P. J. (1990). Peter Drucker asks: Will unions ever again be useful organs of society? *Industry Week, 238*, 16–22.

EXERCISE 15.1
ARBITRATION CASES*

OVERVIEW

Chapter 15 discussed the role of arbitration in unionized environments and the proliferation of formal grievance procedures in nonunion companies. The purpose of this assignment is to give you an opportunity to experience how a professional arbitrator handles cases through the application and interpretation of contractual language and evaluation of evidence. The basic question for you is: As the arbitrator, what is your decision and why? After completion of your evaluation, consider the arbitration process itself and its implications for HR effectiveness. Also, ask yourself whether a grievance and arbitration system should be adopted in a nonunion setting in the interests of fairness and the prevention of union organizing.

LEARNING OBJECTIVES

After completing this exercise, you should be able to:

1. Understand the steps involved in most arbitration processes.
2. Discuss the implications of the grievance arbitration process for employees and employers.

PROCEDURE

Part A: Individual Assignment

Two arbitration cases are presented in Exhibits 15.1.2 and 15.1.4. Prior to class, your assignment is to review

the cases and reach a decision on each. The cases are real; however, names have been changed as well as some identifying details. Be sure that you read the section in your text on the grievance procedure and the arbitration process before you begin work on the exercise.

Your decision should be based on the background presented and should be accompanied by a defense of that decision. A model of a decision write-up is included here as a guide (Exhibit 15.1.1). Subscribe to this model in doing your write-up. We are not interested in whether or not you agree with the actual opinion of the arbitrator, but rather whether you can demonstrate sound and logical reasoning in your conclusions. Your instructor will provide you with the arbitrator's final decision so that you can find out whether you did agree. Bring your two write-ups to class.

Part B: Group Analysis

Step 1. Working in small groups, students should review their individual reports and critique the rationales for their positions. Each group should attempt to reach consensus on the final decisions. Two group members should be designated to present to the class the consensus decisions for the two cases.

Step 2. After reaching its decisions, each group should take a position on whether an arbitration process should be adopted in a nonunion environment to handle employee grievances. A third student should be prepared to present this position to the class and the steps of the grievance/arbitration process.

---

*Contributed by Roger L. Cole.

EXHIBIT 15.1.1
MODEL FOR WRITE-UP OF DECISION: ARBITRATION OPINION

Name of employer: Acme Chemicals, Inc.
Name of union: United Chemical Workers of America
Name of grievant: Bob Lewis
Name of arbitrator: [Your name]

ISSUE
Was there just cause, under the agreement between the parties, for the discharge of Bob Lewis, the grievant, for failure to satisfy training requirements of his position? If no, what would be the remedy?

ANALYSIS AND CONCLUSIONS
The basic dispute in this case centers on the termination of the grievant, Bob Lewis, because he did not satisfy well-defined training standards. This case does not involve any issue about whether the training standards were too high or the training period was too short. The union, United Chemical Workers of America, asserts that without good reason, Acme Chemicals, Inc., denied Bob Lewis an extension of time to complete the training. I conclude, however, that there is no substantial basis for that claim, and the grievance must be denied.

Bob Lewis lacked three of the required 10 sign-offs for completion of the mandatory training. Despite the fact that he listed several factors that impeded his performance during the training (his father was ill, he had car trouble, etc.), I conclude that these reasons are not sufficient to support a request for an extension of time.

The union's argument that an automatic extension should have been granted, I believe, must be rejected. The training plan does not provide for an automatic extension for any trainee who cannot meet the 6-month deadline.

I conclude, in summary, that this grievance cannot be granted because of the grievant's failure to satisfy the remaining training requirements or to demonstrate some basis for an extension.

AWARD
This grievance is denied.

Arbitrator's [your] signature

Date

EXHIBIT 15.1.2
CASE OF THE UNAPPROVED ABSENCE AND DISCIPLINARY SUSPENSION

Company: Cumberland Power and Light Company, Melonville
Union: Mechanical Engineers International Union
Grievant: Alice Smith

BACKGROUND INFORMATION

Cumberland Power and Light Company (CP&L) is a public utility with corporate headquarters located in Melonville. CP&L generates and distributes electric power for a 20-county region utilizing fossil and hydro plants.

The grievant in this case, Alice Smith, is a mechanical engineer for CP&L. In April a year ago, Ms. Smith received a memorandum from Nathan Rogers, the Melonville area manager, entitled "Notice of Unapproved Absence and Disciplinary Suspension." In the memo, Rogers stated, "On March 22, you were expected to report to work at eight a.m. as regularly scheduled. At one p.m. you were expected to report to our corporate offices located in downtown Melonville for a conference on several grievances that you had filed. You did not report to work as scheduled; instead, you reported to the downtown office at ten a.m. and attended a grievance conference held for another employee, Mr. Sam Billings. When questioned about your leave status for the morning, you stated that you had received approval to be absent from Jill Thompson, your supervisor. Ms. Thompson told me that you did not request approval to be absent. Therefore, your absence from work from eight a.m. to twelve noon has been recorded as unapproved. Because you were absent without approval and you misrepresented this to me, I am suspending you from work and pay status for 3 calendar days."

Subsequently, Ms. Smith filed a grievance which went through the appropriate steps as outlined in the labor agreement. Ultimately, it was sent to arbitration, which is where you, the selected arbitrator, come into the picture. The basic question presented to you is whether or not the company violated the contract agreement when it suspended the grievant for 3 days without pay and charged her 4 hours AWOL. If so, what is the appropriate remedy?

POSITION OF THE UNION

The union stated that the company must have been aware of the scheduled grievance conferences at ten a.m. for Mr. Billings and at one p.m. for the grievant on the date in question. They contend that both Ms. Smith and Mr. Billings notified their supervisor, Ms. Thompson, that they were meeting with their union representative at eight a.m. the next day to prepare for their grievance conferences. According to testimony presented, Ms. Smith was on the phone in a room in which Ms. Thompson was present. Ms. Smith turned to Ms. Thompson and said that the union representative wanted them (Smith and Billings) at the corporate office at eight a.m. to discuss the grievance. There was no verbal response from Ms. Thompson.

Both Smith and Billings reported to the downtown corporate offices and met with their union representative as scheduled. Further they contend that Ms. Smith was not treated evenhandedly since no action was taken against Mr. Billings. The company also did not follow a progressive discipline procedure as stipulated in the labor agreement. The union contends that the grievant did not have any previous warnings from her supervisor in this particular area. The progressive discipline policy calls for the following sequence in discipline: oral warning, written warning, suspension, and discharge. Employees must be forewarned as to what to expect for certain kinds of violations.

POSITION OF THE COMPANY

Despite the language referenced in Article II of the agreement (see Exhibit 15.1.3), the company contends that the grievant was aware that she had the responsibility for requesting and arranging the approved absence. However, the grievant did not make such arrangements and was not authorized to attend the other employee's conference, nor did she have any interest or part in that conference. Their supervisor, Ms. Thompson, testified that neither Smith nor Billings talked to her about their upcoming absences. Not only that, but when questioned about her absence, Smith told the area manager, Nathan Rogers, that she had received permission. The grievant knew the consequences of her not being at her work station. The company agrees that Smith had permission to attend her conference at one p.m. but not an eight a.m. meeting or a ten a.m. meeting. The company contends that there was no reason for her to be at the ten a.m. meeting with Mr. Billings. Therefore, the action taken by management was not discriminatory, unfair, or arbitrary.

YOUR ANALYSIS, CONCLUSIONS, AND AWARD

Now that you have the background and the evidence presented by the company and the union, it is time for you to weigh the evidence, draw your conclusions, and make your award (i.e., deny the grievance or sustain it). use the format in Exhibit 15.1.1 to write up your report. Remember that it is not important whether or not you agree with the official decision of the arbitrator; what is important is that you show evidence of taking into account all the facts presented.

EXHIBIT 15.1.3
RELATED EXCERPTS FROM THE CONTRACT

ARTICLE II—EXCUSE FROM WORK TO PARTICIPATE IN GRIEVANCE PROCEEDINGS

An aggrieved employee and any other employee or employees who represent him or her or act as witnesses for him or her and whose participation in grievance proceedings is jointly determined by Cumberland and the union to be necessary are excused from work for the time required to permit such participation without loss of pay.

EXHIBIT 15.1.4
CASE OF THE TERMINATION OF JUAN PEREZ

Company: Steinberg's Fertilizer Company, Columbus
Union: Security Guard International Association, Local
           No. 2598
Grievant: Juan Perez

BACKGROUND INFORMATION

Steinberg's Fertilizer Company, headquartered in Columbus, is a leading producer of organic fertilizers with five plants scattered throughout the state. Four months ago, Juan Perez, a security guard at the Columbus plant, filed a grievance against the company for wrongful termination. The grievance went through the normal channels but was not resolved. Therefore, the union and company have turned to arbitration and have selected you as arbitrator.

The grievant, Juan Perez, has been employed at Steinberg's as a security guard since 1980. He has been transferred several times and at one time or another has worked at each of the five plants operated by Steinberg's. There is little in his employment history since 1980 to draw any special attention to him until his recent reassignment to the Columbus plant. It should be noted that he had been assigned 6 years ago to this plant but had been transferred out. He was also employed at the Columbus plant at the time of his discharge.

Six months ago, Perez was sent a termination notice which advised him that he was being dismissed for: (1) carrying a personal firearm in an unauthorized area and (2) violations of company policy related to protection of property, personal conduct, and alertness while on duty. Specifically, it was alleged that Perez had an unauthorized (i.e., personal) firearm on the plant site and used it on the company's property (i.e., at the firing range). The second charge was that Perez failed to lock three gates at the end of his shift. On the basis of these violations, plus his prior violation of leaving the premises in a company vehicle without authorization, Perez was terminated.

POSITION OF THE UNION

In regard to the first charge, the union argued in Perez's defense that the grievant's immediate supervisor, Sam Cofer, was biased against him due to a prior investigation which had occurred during Perez's first assignment at the Columbus plant. The union pointed out that it is not unusual for guards to bring personal weapons onto company premises for use on the firing range and for storage and that there has been implicit consent to allow shooting of predatory animals on site. The union contended that Mike Morrison, the supervisor who made the decision to terminate Perez, had no personal direct knowledge of the occurrences in question; instead, he relied on information in Perez's personnel file and information furnished to him by other officers on the plant site. In regard to firing the weapon on the premises in an unauthorized area, there were no eyewitnesses to this shooting.

According to records presented by the union, during previous assignments, Perez's performance evaluations had been mostly adequate or above. There had been, however, a 1-year period approximately 6 years ago during which Perez had received several disciplinary write-ups. The supervisor at the time was Sam Cofer, the same supervisor who recently turned him in for the violations which led to his termination. In fact, the only unfavorable evaluations Perez has received while employed at Steinberg's have been received when Sam Cofer was his immediate supervisor. In regard to the second charge outlined in his termination notice (his not locking the gates), Perez did admit to having been confused about this specific responsibility.

POSITION OF THE COMPANY

The company argued that the seriousness of the more recent violations plus Perez's record of prior violations justified his termination. In addition, the company pointed out that Perez had received a final warning several years before and therefore had been placed on notice that his job was in jeopardy.

The company presented documented evidence of twelve disciplinary write-ups given to Perez during an 18-month period 6 years earlier. These occurred while Perez was at the Columbus plant under the supervision of Sam Cofer. They also presented copies of Perez's performance evaluations while he was at the Columbus plant, all of which were unfavorable.

In addressing the second charge against Perez (related to property security), the company stated that this charge was based primarily on a report filed by a fellow officer, Chrystal Ford. Ms. Ford's report stated that upon reporting to work she had found that the guard on the previous shift (Perez) had not locked the gates as required and had not performed the necessary paperwork.

YOUR ANALYSIS, CONCLUSIONS, AND AWARD

Now that you have the background and the perspectives of the company and the union, it is time for you to weigh the evidence, draw your conclusions, and make your award (deny the grievance or sustain it). Use the format presented earlier to write up your report. Remember that it is not important whether or not you agree with the official decision of the arbitrator; what is important is that you show evidence of taking into account all the facts presented.

C H A P T E R

EMPLOYEE HEALTH
AND SAFETY*

---

*Contributed by H. John Bernardin and Harriette S. McCaul.

OVERVIEW

Employers, unions, and employees have a great and growing interest in health and safety issues related to the workplace. Some facts explain this concern. In any given year, 1 employee out of every 10 is killed or injured at work. Based on the most current data available for one year, there were 6.8 million incidents of occupational injury or illness. Approximately 25 percent of Americans with disabilities have those disabilities because of a work-related accident or illness. About 400,000 people per year contract diseases or illnesses judged to be related to their occupations. There are over 4000 occupational deaths per year and almost 5 million reported accidents (studies indicate that reported accidents represent about half of all accidents).[1]

The cost to employers can be immense in financial terms as well. One of the largest meatpackers, John Morrell and Co. of Sioux Falls, South Dakota, was cited by the Occupational Safety and Health Administration (OSHA) in 1988 and assessed a $4.33 million fine for safety violations. According to the federal agency, more than 800 of the 2000 employees at the plant sustained "serious and sometimes disabling injuries." The rate of injuries at the plant was 652 times the rate of injuries for businesses in general. USX, the giant steel company, was fined $7.3 million for numerous violations of safety, health, and record keeping, including 58 "willful" hazards. Criminal charges (and convictions) against management for willful neglect of worker health and safety are now quite common. Fines are now being levied against companies which violate the 1991 government regulation mandating the protection of workers against acquired immune deficiency syndrome (AIDS) and other viruses.

This chapter will review the costs of employee deaths, injuries, illnesses, and the regulatory environment which seeks to improve work safety and health. Considerable attention will be given to the role of the Occupational Safety and Health Administration Act (OSHA) of 1970 and the federal regulations which have been issued pursuant to this law. OSHA is without question one of the greatest legislative accomplishments of organized labor. We will also review the research on the effectiveness of this legislation. The final portion of the chapter will cover some of the contemporary issues related to employee health and safety and discuss some of the controversial steps organizations are taking to improve their employee health, safety, and performance records (e.g., drug testing, antismoking policies, employee assistance programs).

OBJECTIVES

After studying this chapter, you should be able to:

1. Describe the extent of and costs of employee accidents, illnesses, and deaths on the job.
2. Discuss the role of workers' compensation programs for job-related injuries and illnesses.
3. Explain the functions of the OSHA and review research on the effectiveness of the OSHA Act and related regulation.
4. Discuss recent approaches which have been used to improve workplace safety and health.
5. Review contemporary issues and programs which seek to improve worker health and safety.

There is a growing awareness of management failures to pay enough attention to the health and safety of their employees. This awareness has translated into criminal charges and financial devastation for some companies. Indeed, many deaths, injuries, and illnesses occur because of safety violations, poor equipment design, or negligence. The Union Carbide accident in Bhopal, India, for example, which killed over 3000 people in 1984, was considered by most experts to be a result of equipment design flaws which could have been avoided. Over 40 lawsuits worth billions of dollars were filed against the company. Philips Petroleum was recently fined $5.7 million for willful safety breaches after 23 workers were killed in an explosion at a Texas petrochemical plant. Two USX plants reported 17 deaths related to employer safety violations. Another meatpacker, the Iowa Beef Packers, agreed to redesign its jobs to curtail crippling muscle and nerve ailments after a horrible record of injuries. Three managers of Film Recovery Systems in Illinois received 25-year sentences for recklessly exposing their employees to cyanide fumes. This is not an isolated occurrence. In several cases over the last few years, state prosecutors have argued successfully for criminal prosecution of managers who caused injury or illness of employees.

The death and accident figures presented above vary substantially as a function of industry and occupation. Among the most dangerous jobs are miner, heavy construction worker, firefighter, flour mill employee, sheet metal worker, lumber and forestry employee, and blue-collar employee in manufacturing or petrochemicals. The automotive industry showed the highest increase in accidents in 1989. According to OSHA, the most hazardous major industry in the United States is meatpacking, in which employees have 4 times as many injuries as the national average.

While the current statistics are disturbing, they do not compare to the early days of industrial growth in the United States. The industrial revolution was born with little concern for employee health or safety. Working conditions were often so unbearable that employees began to demand that management implement safeguards. Union activity placed great emphasis on improving working conditions. Many older Americans suffer today because of conditions to which they were exposed at work. For example, 49 workers from a foundry in Michigan got tuberculosis because of their exposure to silica at the foundry in the 1940s (silica is a glassy material found in sand). Of course, there are thousands of other examples. U.S. health and safety standards are also superior to those in many parts of the world. In most other countries which maintain reliable data on the subject, injury and illness figures are even more alarming than those in the United States.

Without question, the American workplace is safer today than it was 40 years ago, but there is still considerable room for improvement. There are over 50,000 different chemicals in regular use today. Most have never been tested for toxicity, and no regulatory restraints affect their use. New materials, composed of exotic combinations of plastics, carbons, and other substances, are introduced into the workplace at an alarming rate, with little knowledge of their interactive effects on worker health. Another growing problem is *repetitive trauma disorder,* the so-called disease of the nineties. The Labor Department reported in 1990 that this disorder accounted for 60 percent of the 6.8 million job-related injuries. Workers today also suffer more subtle forms of health problems at work. One 1991 study concluded that workplace stress, for example, has reached epidemic proportions due to company restructuring, increased work demands, layoffs, downsizing, conflicts with family obligations, etc.[2]

In addition to the obvious effects of pain, suffering, and quality of life, the impact of injuries and illnesses on productivity is enormous. Over 47 million workdays were lost to work-related illness or injury in 1989 (the last year for which data are available), an increase of 3 percent from the previous year. The average direct cost to organizations in disability payments through workers' compensation is 1 percent of payroll. The indirect costs for replacing employees, wages paid out while the worker is disabled, damage to company equipment or property, and time and expense for investigating the accident are estimated to be 5 percent of payroll.[3] The bottom-line cost is in excess of $33 billion per year in lost wages, health insurance costs, and various other indirect costs. Given these statistics, the interest in health and safety issues by employees, employers, and government agencies is certainly understandable.

There are many laws designed to protect workers from illness and injury. The foundry referred to earlier now must abide by strict OSHA standards regarding silica emissions. As evidenced by the fine against John Morrell discussed above, penalties are imposed on employers for violations of these laws and regulations. OSHA levied fines against companies in excess of $5 million in 1990 alone. Among the companies cited were General Dynamics, General Motors (GM), Lockheed, and Du Pont. The Chrysler Corporation has been cited frequently for safety abuses and, in particular, for failure to notify workers that they may be exposed to harmful chemicals. Under OSHA rules, employees now have a "right to know" about hazards to which they may be exposed at work. Companies are now required to issue a "hazard communication" to their workers when they may be exposed to certain hazardous chemicals. (We will discuss this and other OSHA regulations below.) In some states, if a fatality occurs from a willful violation of safety rules, company officials can serve time in prison and pay substantial fines. In addition, as one state attorney general puts it, "the workplace offers no refuge from criminal laws."[4] Prosecutors are now charging employers and supervisory personnel with involuntary manslaughter for negligence regarding workplace safety. This type of criminal prosecution can involve much heavier penalties.

In addition to this legal pressure, many employers seek to provide a safe working environment because they wish to foster a high quality of work life (QWL) for their employees. Other employers recognize the costliness of accidents, illnesses, and injuries and endeavor to reduce costs as much as possible through a variety of health and safety programs.

We will first review the major legislation related to health and safety, the steps which organizations have taken to reduce accidents and injuries, and the major contemporary issues which affect employee health and safety. We will cover the major controversies of the day, such as drug testing, antismoking positions, and AIDS policies.

LEGAL ISSUES RELATED TO HEALTH AND SAFETY

Workers' Compensation

As we discussed in Chapter 11, workers' compensation is a federally mandated insurance program based on the concept of "liability without fault," which provides that workers who are victims of work-related injury or illness are granted benefits regardless of who is responsible for the accident, injury, or illness. This means that if an organization participates in the workers' compensation system, a worker may not sue the employer for negligence, even if the injury was clearly the employer's fault. On the other hand, even careless or accident-prone workers are generally covered by workers' compensation, and injuries that are the result of coworkers' negligence are also covered. Some state laws, however, deny benefits if the worker was under the influence of alcohol or controlled substances (illegal drugs) when the injury occurred.

The policy and provisions of workers' compensation vary across states, and not all jobs are covered. Workers' compensation provides for death, medical, and wage benefits derived from premiums paid by employers. In an effort to encourage safety, the size of the premium paid by an employer is partially determined by the health and safety record of the particular industry and the particular employer (i.e., there are lower premiums for industries with better safety records). There is great variability in payouts for injuries, however. Even today, body parts are worth different amounts in different states. If you lose an eye in Massachusetts, you get $16,458, but lose it in North Dakota and you get $8000. You get $12,000 if you lose a foot in Massachusetts but twice as much in Mississippi.

When a worker is injured on the job (or develops a disabling occupational disease), the worker must file a claim, either with the company or its insurance carrier (or in some states, with a state agency) to request workers' compensation benefits. In most states, benefits begin after a short (2- to 5-day) waiting period, and include a wage replacement payment (a percentage of the worker's salary) and reimbursement of medical costs. The employer (or its insurance carrier) may require the injured worker to be treated by a doctor selected by the company.

Employers may contest a workers' compensation claim if they believe that (1) the injury (or illness) is not a result of the work; (2) the employee is capable of performing the job despite the injury or illness; or (3) the employee has made a fraudulent claim. Other issues that may involve a challenge to a workers' compensation claim include heart attacks, strokes, or other stress-related problems. In some states, the law places the burden on the employee to prove that the disabling condition was a result of work effort or work-related stress and would not have occurred otherwise.

Some employees are challenging the no-fault assumptions of the workers' compensation system, arguing that an employer who knowingly exposes workers to hazardous substances or dangerous working conditions should not be protected from negligence lawsuits. In most instances, the courts have ruled that all employer conduct short of an "intentional wrong" will fall under the rubric of workers' compensation. But one state court ruled that workers who alleged a corporate conspiracy to withhold from employees the fact that they were developing a serious occupational disease could sue the company for negligence and fraud.[5]

The fact that a company may have violated an OSHA standard (discussed in the next section of this chapter) will not necessarily remove the protection of workers' compensation. The no-fault provisions of the system (with the above-noted exception) make irrelevant the issue of whether the employer or the worker was to blame. The worker gets medical treatment and a portion of his or her wages; the employer is insulated from litigation in return for paying the workers' compensation benefits.

If a worker becomes disabled due to a job-related accident or illness, the employer is then obligated under the Americans with Disabilities Act to provide "reasonable accommodation" for that worker. This might include job restructuring or reassignment. An ethical issue for management to consider is what is the company's responsibility to retrain workers who become disabled due to job-related injuries or illnesses to enable them to qualify for other jobs.

While provisions of workers' compensation laws such as the premium imposed encouraged employers' efforts to improve their health and safety records, the effects of such provisions were not very impressive. Many states took matters into their own hands in an effort to do more in this area, creating a myriad of rules and regulations. The result was a lack of uniformity in policies and regulations across the states, a situation which prompted political pressure from numerous constituencies, particularly unions, for a federal law aimed primarily at the reduction and prevention of occupational fatalities, injuries, and illnesses. The result of the pressure was the passage of the OSHA Act. The next section will cover this critical piece of legislation.

The Occupational Safety and Health Administration Act

The Occupational Safety and Health Administration was created in 1970 within the U.S. Department of Labor. The purpose of OSHA is to:

1. Encourage employers and employees to reduce workplace hazards and to implement new or improve existing safety and health programs.
2. Provide for research in occupational safety and health to develop innovative ways of dealing with occupational safety and health problems.
3. Establish "separate but dependent responsibilities and rights" for employers and employees for the achievement of better safety and health conditions.
4. Maintain a reporting and record-keeping system to monitor job-related injuries and illnesses.
5. Establish training programs to increase the number and competence of occupational safety and health personnel.

6. Develop mandatory job safety and health standards and enforce them effectively.
7. Provide for the development, analysis, evaluation, and approval of state occupational safety and health programs.

Coverage of the OSHA Act of 1970, which extends to virtually all employers and their employees in the United States, is provided either directly by federal OSHA or through an OSHA-approved state program (21 states have their own programs).

STANDARDS. OSHA is responsible for developing enforceable safety standards. It is the employers' responsibility to become familiar with the standards applicable to their establishments and to ensure that employees have and use personal protective gear and equipment when required for safety. Where OSHA has not promulgated specific standards, employers are responsible for following the act's general duty clause.

The general duty clause states that each employer "shall furnish...a place of employment which is free from recognized hazards that are causing or are likely to cause death or serious physical harm to his [or her] employees." This means that if a workplace situation involves foreseeable danger of potential injury, the employer is required to eliminate or reduce that danger through redesign or new equipment, or by training workers about safety.

In 1989, OSHA greatly expanded its role in protecting workers from hazardous materials. Maximum exposure limits were set for 164 substances for the first time, and limits were tightened for 212 others. The limits cover the maximum amount a worker can be exposed to during an 8-hour workday. Among the substances regulated for the first time were wood dust, grain dust, gasoline, acrylic acid, tungsten, and welding fumes. OSHA also cut maximum exposure limits for, among other substances, carbon monoxide, chloroform, and hydrogen.

RECORD KEEPING AND REPORTING. Before OSHA became effective, no centralized and systematic method existed for monitoring occupational safety and health problems. Statistics on job injuries and illnesses were collected by some states and by some private organizations. With OSHA came the first basis for consistent, nationwide procedures—a vital requirement for gauging safety problems and solving them.

Employers with 11 or more employees must maintain records of occupational injuries and illnesses as they occur. The purposes of keeping records are to permit the Bureau of Labor Statistics (BLS) to compile data, to help define high-hazard industries, and to inform employees of the status of their employers' records.

What is considered to be an occupational injury or illness? An *occupational injury* is any injury, such as a cut, fracture, sprain, or amputation, which results from a work-related accident or from exposure involving a single incident in the work environment. An *occupational illness* is any abnormal condition or disorder, other than one resulting from an occupational injury, caused by exposure to environmental factors associated with employment. Included are acute and chronic illnesses or diseases which may be caused by inhalation, absorption, or ingestion of or direct contact with toxic substances or harmful agents. Alcoholism has even been considered an occupational illness in a case involving an employee who developed an alcohol-related problem as a result of the socializing responsibilities associated with his job.

All occupational illnesses must be recorded, regardless of severity. All occupational injuries must be recorded if they result in:

- Death (must be recorded regardless of the length of time between the injury and death)
- One or more lost workdays
- Restriction of work or motion
- Loss of consciousness
- Transfer to another job
- Medical treatment (other than first aid)

RECORD-KEEPING FORMS. Record-keeping forms must be maintained for 5 years at the establishment and must be available for inspection by representatives of OSHA. Only two forms are needed for record keeping. Figures 16.1 and 16.2 present copies of OSHA forms 200 and 101.

Workplace Inspection

AUTHORITY TO INSPECT. To enforce its standards, OSHA is authorized under the act to conduct workplace inspections. Every establishment covered by the act is subject to inspection by OSHA compliance safety and health officers (COSHOs), who are chosen for their knowledge and experience in the occupational safety and health field, and who are trained in OSHA standards and in recognition of safety and health hazards.

Under the act, "upon presenting appropriate credentials to the owner, operator or agent in charge," a COSHO is authorized to:

- "Enter without delay and at reasonable times any factory, plant, establishment, construction site or other areas, workplace, or environment where work is performed by an employee of an employer."

FIGURE 16.1
OSHA FORM 200

Bureau of Labor Statistics
Log and Summary of Occupational
Injuries and Illnesses

NOTE: This form is required by Public Law 91-596 and must be kept in the establishment for 5 years. Failure to maintain and post can result in the issuance of citations and assessment of penalties.

RECORDABLE CASES: You are required to record information about every occupational death; every nonfatal occupational illness; and those nonfatal occupational injuries which involve one or more of the following: loss of consciousness, restriction of work or motion, transfer to another job, or medical treatment (other than first aid).

U.S. Department of Labor

For Calendar Year 19 ___   Page ___ of ___

Form Approved
O.M.B. No. 1220-0029

Company Name
Establishment Name
Establishment Address

Case or File Number	Date of Injury or Onset of Illness	Employee's Name	Occupation	Department	Description of Injury or Illness	Extent of and Outcome of INJURY						Type, Extent of, and Outcome of ILLNESS										
						Fatalities	Nonfatal Injuries					Type of Illness							Fatalities	Nonfatal Illnesses	
						Injury Related	Injuries With Lost Workdays				Injuries Without Lost Workdays	CHECK Only One Column for Each Illness							Illness Related	Illnesses With Lost Workdays		Illnesses Without Lost Workdays
Enter a nonduplicating number which will facilitate comparisons with supplementary records.	Enter Mo./day.	Enter first name or initial, middle initial, last name.	Enter regular job title, not activity employee was performing when injured or at onset of illness. In the absence of a formal title, enter a brief description of the employee's duties.	Enter department in which the employee is regularly employed or a description of normal workplace to which employee is assigned, even though temporarily working in another department at the time of injury or illness.	Enter a brief description of the injury or illness and indicate the part or parts of body affected. Typical entries for this column might be: Amputation of 1st joint right forefinger; Strain of lower back; Contact dermatitis on both hands; Electrocution–body.	Enter DATE of death. Mo./day/yr.	Enter a CHECK if injury involves days away from work, or days of restricted work activity, or both.	Enter a CHECK if injury involves days away from work.	Enter number of DAYS away from work.	Enter number of DAYS of restricted work activity	Enter a CHECK if no entry was made in columns 1 or 2 but the injury is recordable as defined above.	Occupational skin diseases or disorders	Dust diseases of the lungs.	Respiratory conditions due to toxic agents	Poisoning (systemic effects of toxic materials)	Disorders due to physical agents	Disorders associated with repeated trauma	All other occupational illnesses	Enter DATE of death. Mo./day/yr.	Enter a CHECK if illness involves days away from work, or days of restricted work activity, or both.	Enter a CHECK if illness involves days away from work.	Enter number of DAYS away from work.	Enter number of DAYS of restricted work activity	Enter a CHECK if no entry was made in columns 8 or 9.
(A)	(B)	(C)	(D)	(E)	(F)	(1)	(2)	(3)	(4)	(5)	(6)	(a)	(b)	(c)	(d)	(e)	(f)	(g)	(8)	(9)	(10)	(11)	(12)	(13)

PREVIOUS PAGE TOTALS

INJURIES

ILLNESSES

TOTALS (Instructions on other side of form.)

Certification of Annual Summary Totals By ___   Title ___   Date ___

POST ONLY THIS PORTION OF THE LAST PAGE NO LATER THAN FEBRUARY 1.

OSHA No. 200

FOLD

FIGURE 16.2
OSHA FORM 101

U.S. Department of Labor

Bureau of Labor Statistics
Supplementary Record of
Occupational Injuries and Illnesses

This form is required by Public Law 91-596 and must be kept in the establishment for *5 years*. Failure to maintain can result in the issuance of citations and assessment of penalties.	Case or File No.	Form Approved O.M.B. No. 1220-0029

Employer

1. Name

2. Mail address (*No. and street, city or town, State, and zip code*)

3. Location, if different from mail address

Injured or Ill Employee

4. Name (*First, middle, and last*)   Social Security No.

5. Home address (*No. and street, city or town, State, and zip code*)

6. Age   7. Sex: (*Check one*)   Male ☐   Female ☐

8. Occupation (*Enter regular job title*, not *the specific activity he was performing at time of injury.*)

9. Department (*Enter name of department or division in which the injured person is regularly employed, even though he may have been temporarily working in another department at the time of injury.*)

The Accident or Exposure to Occupational Illness

If accident or exposure occurred on employer's premises, give address of plant or establishment in which it occurred. Do not indicate department or division within the plant or establishment. If accident occurred outside employer's premises at an identifiable address, give that address. If it occurred on a public highway or at any other place which cannot be identified by number and street, please provide place references locating the place of injury as accurately as possible.

10. Place of accident or exposure (*No. and street, city or town, State, and zip code*)

11. Was place of accident or exposure on employer's premises?   Yes ☐   No ☐

12. What was the employee doing when injured? (*Be specific. If he was using tools or equipment or handling material, name them and tell what he was doing with them.*)

13. How did the accident occur? (*Describe fully the events which resulted in the injury or occupational illness. Tell what happened and how it happened. Name any objects or substances involved and tell how they were involved. Give full details on all factors which led or contributed to the accident. Use separate sheet for additional space.*)

Occupational Injury or Occupational Illness

14. Describe the injury or illness in detail and indicate the part of body affected. (*E.g., amputation of right index finger at second joint; fracture of ribs; lead poisoning; dermatitis of left hand, etc.*)

15. Name the object or substance which directly injured the employee. (*For example, the machine or thing he struck against or which struck him; the vapor or poison he inhaled or swallowed; the chemical or radiation which irritated his skin; or in cases of strains, hernias, etc., the thing he was lifting, pulling, etc.*)

16. Date of injury or initial diagnosis of occupational illness   17. Did employee die? (*Check one*)   Yes ☐   No ☐

Other

18. Name and address of physician

19. If hospitalized, name and address of hospital

Date of report	Prepared by	Official position

OSHA No. 101 (Feb. 1981)

- "Inspect and investigate during regular working hours, and at other reasonable times, and within reasonable limits and in a reasonable manner, any such place of employment and all pertinent conditions, structures, machines, apparatus, devices, equipment and materials therein, and to question privately any such employer, owner, operator, agent or employee."

With very few exceptions, inspections are conducted without advance notice. In fact, alerting an employer in advance of an OSHA inspection can bring a fine of up to $1000 and/or a 6-month jail term.

If an employer refuses to admit the COSHO, or if an employer attempts to interfere with the inspection, the act permits appropriate legal action.

Based on a 1978 U.S. Supreme Court ruling in *Marshall v. Barlow's Inc.,*[6] OSHA may not conduct warrantless inspections without an employer's consent. It may, however, inspect after acquiring a judicially authorized search warrant based upon administrative probable cause or upon evidence of a violation.

If employees are represented by a recognized bargaining representative, the union ordinarily will designate an employee representative to accompany the compliance officer. Similarly, if there is a plant safety committee, the employee members of that committee will designate the employee representative.

INSPECTION TOUR. After an opening conference, the COSHO and accompanying representatives proceed through the establishment, inspecting work areas for compliance with OSHA standards. The route and duration of the inspection are determined by the compliance officer. While talking with employees, the compliance officer makes every effort to minimize work interruptions. The compliance officer observes conditions, consults with employees, may take photos (for record-keeping purposes), takes instrument readings, and examines records.

Employees are consulted during the inspection tour. The compliance officer may stop and question workers, in private if necessary, about safety and health conditions and practices in their workplaces. Each employee is protected, under the act, from discrimination for exercising his or her safety and health rights.

Posting and record keeping are checked. The compliance officer will inspect records of deaths, injuries, and illnesses which the employer is required to keep. He or she will check to see that a copy of the totals from the last page of OSHA form 200 has been posted.

CLOSING CONFERENCE. After the inspection tour, a closing conference is held between the compliance officer and the employer or the employer's representative.

It is a time for free discussion of problems and needs—a time for frank questions and answers.

The compliance officer discusses with the employer all unsafe or unhealthful conditions observed on the inspection and indicates all apparent violations for which a citation may be issued or recommended. The employer is told of appeal rights.

The compliance officer explains that OSHA area offices are full-service resource centers that provide a number of services, such as speakers, handout packages of materials which can be distributed to interested persons, and training and technical materials on safety and health matters. The compliance officer also explains the requirements of the *Hazard Communications Standard,* according to which employers must establish a written, comprehensive hazard communication program which includes provisions for container labeling, material safety data sheets, and an employee training program. (Employers have been cited for over 50,000 violations of the Hazard Communication Standard since 1985.)

Services Available

CONSULTATION ASSISTANCE. Free consultation assistance is available to employers who want help in establishing and maintaining a safe and healthful workplace. Largely funded by OSHA, the service is provided at no cost to the employer.

Besides helping employers to identify and correct specific hazards, consultation can include assistance in developing and implementing effective workplace safety and health programs with emphasis on the prevention of worker injuries and illnesses. Training and education services are also provided.

VOLUNTARY PROTECTION PROGRAMS. The Voluntary Protection Programs (VPPs) represent one component of OSHA's effort to extend worker protection beyond the minimum required by OSHA standards. These programs, along with others such as expanded on-site consultation services and full-service area offices, are cooperative approaches which, when coupled with an effective enforcement program, expand worker protection to help meet the goals of OSHA.

Two VPPs—Star and Merit—are designed to:

- Recognize outstanding achievement of firms that have successfully incorporated comprehensive safety and health programs into their total management systems.
- Motivate other companies to achieve excellent safety and health results in the same outstanding way.
- Establish a relationship between employers, employees, and OSHA that is based on cooperation rather than coercion.

The Star program is the most demanding and the most prestigious. It is open to an employer in any industry who has successfully managed a comprehensive safety and health program to reduce injury rates below the national average for the industry. Specific requirements for the program include systems for management commitment and responsibility; hazard assessment and control; and safety planning, rules, work procedures, and training which are in place and operating effectively. Among the 1992 "Stars" are IBM in Austin, Texas; Occidental Chemical in Louisiana; Mobil Mining and Minerals; Motorola in Texas; and Texaco USA, Exploration Division.

The Merit program, also open to any industry, is primarily a steppingstone to Star program participation. An employer with a basic safety and health program which is committed to improving the company's program and which has the resources to do so within a specified period of time may work with OSHA to meet Star qualifications. Among the 1992 Merit winners were Georgia-Pacific in Louisiana, Rohm-Haas of Philadelphia, and Midas International in Ohio.

TRAINING AND EDUCATION. OSHA's 72 area offices are full-service centers offering a variety of informational services such as speakers, publications, audio-visual aids on workplace hazards, and technical advice. The OSHA Training Institute in Des Plaines, Illinois, provides basic and advanced training and education in safety and health for federal and state compliance officers; state consultants; other federal agency personnel; and private-sector employers, employees, and their representatives. Institute courses cover areas such as electrical hazards, machine guarding, ventilation, and ergonomics.

RESPONSIBILITIES UNDER OSHA. As an employer, you must:

- Meet your general duty responsibility to provide a workplace free of recognized hazards that are causing or are likely to cause death or serious physical harm to employees, and to comply with standards, rules, and regulations issued under the act.
- Be familiar with mandatory OSHA standards and make copies available to employees for review upon request.
- Inform all employees about OSHA.
- Examine workplace conditions to make sure they conform to applicable standards.
- Minimize or reduce hazards.
- Make sure employees have and use safe tools and equipment (including appropriate personal protective equipment), and that such equipment is properly maintained.

- Use color codes, posters, labels, or signs when needed, to warn employees of potential hazards.
- Establish or update operating procedures and communicate them so that employees will follow safety and health requirements.
- Provide medical examinations when required by OSHA standards.
- Report to the nearest OSHA office within 48 hours any accident that is fatal or that results in the hospitalization of five or more employees.
- Keep OSHA-required records of work-related injuries and illnesses, and post a copy of the totals from the last page of OSHA form 200 during the entire month of February each year.
- Post, at a prominent location within the workplace, the OSHA poster (OSHA 2203) informing employees of their rights and responsibilities.
- Provide employees, former employees, and their representatives with access to the Log and Summary of Occupational Injuries and Illnesses (OSHA form 200) at a reasonable time and in a reasonable manner.
- Cooperate with the OSHA compliance officer by furnishing names of authorized employee representatives who may be asked to accompany the compliance officer during an inspection.
- Not discriminate against employees who properly exercise their rights under the act.
- Post OSHA citations at or near the worksite involved. Each citation, or a copy thereof, must remain posted until the violation has been abated or for 3 working days, whichever is longer.

Although OSHA does not cite employees for violations of their responsibilities, each employee "shall comply with all occupational safety and health standards and rules, regulations, and orders issued under the Act" that are applicable.

RIGHTS FOR EMPLOYEES: PROTECTION FOR USING RIGHTS. Employees have a right to seek safety and health on the job without fear of punishment. That right is spelled out in Section 11(c) of the act.

The law says employers shall not punish or discriminate against workers for exercising rights such as:

- Complaining to an employer, union, OSHA, or any other government agency about job safety and health hazards
- Filing safety or health grievances
- Participating in a workplace safety and health committee or in union activities concerning job safety and health
- Participating in OSHA inspections, conferences, or hearings, or other OSHA-related activities

If an employee is exercising these or other OSHA rights, the employer is not allowed to discriminate against that worker in any way, such as through firing, demotion, taking away seniority or other earned benefits, transferring the worker to an undesirable job or shift, or threatening or harassing the worker.

In *Whirlpool v. Marshall*, the U.S. Supreme Court ruled in 1981 that although there is no specific language in the law about walking off a job, employees who have a reasonable apprehension of death or serious injury may refuse to work until that safety hazard is corrected. The employer may not discipline or discharge a worker who exercises this right, although the employer need not pay the worker for the hours not worked.[7]

Workers who believe that they have been punished for exercising safety and health rights must contact the nearest OSHA office within 30 days of the time they learn of the alleged discrimination. A union representative can file the complaint for the worker. The worker does not have to complete any form. Any OSHA staff member will complete the forms, asking what happened and who was involved.

Following a complaint, OSHA investigates. If an employee has been illegally punished for exercising safety and health rights, OSHA asks the employer to restore that worker's job earnings and benefits. If necessary, and if it can prove discrimination, OSHA takes the employer to court. In such cases the worker does not pay any legal fees. If a state agency has an OSHA-approved state program, employees may file their complaint with either the federal OSHA or the state agency under its laws.

OTHER RIGHTS. As an employee, you have the right to:

- Review copies of appropriate OSHA standards, rules, regulations, and requirements that the employer should have available at the workplace.
- Request information from your employer on safety and health hazards in the area, on precautions that may be taken, and on procedures to be followed if an employee is involved in an accident or is exposed to toxic substances.
- Request the OSHA area director to conduct an inspection if you believe that hazardous conditions or violations of standards exist in your workplace.
- Have your name withheld from your employer, upon request to OSHA, if you file a written and signed complaint.
- Be advised of OSHA actions regarding your complaint and have an informal review, if requested, of any decision not to inspect or to issue a citation.
- Have your authorized employee representative accompany the OSHA compliance officer during the inspection tour.

- Respond to questions from the OSHA compliance officer, particularly if there is no authorized employee representative accompanying the compliance officer.
- Observe any monitoring or measuring of hazardous materials and have the right to see these records, as specified under the act.
- Have your authorized representative, or yourself, review the Log and Summary of Occupational Injuries and Illnesses (OSHA form 200) at a reasonable time and in a reasonable manner.
- Request a closing discussion with the compliance officer following an inspection.
- Submit a written request to the National Institute for Occupational Safety and Health (NIOSH) for information on whether any substance in your workplace has potentially toxic effects in the concentration being used, and have your name withheld from your employer if you so request.
- Be notified by your employer if he or she applies for a variance from an OSHA standard, testify at a variance hearing, and appeal the final decision.
- Submit information or comment to OSHA on the issuance, modification, or revocation of OSHA standards and request a public hearing.

The Effects of OSHA

There is no question but that OSHA has had a profound impact on employer actions regarding health and safety issues. The establishment of formal safety committees, improved equipment and machinery, improved medical facilities and staff, and, in general, greater emphasis on safety and prevention are among the major changes that are the direct result of OSHA. Of course, many employers consider some of the standards to be unacceptable, arbitrary, trivial, and unattainable, and many of the regulations to be excessively detailed and costly (see Figure 16.3). One study puts the figure at $25 billion over the first 10 years of the law.[8] OSHA has come under fire from safety experts for imposing trivial fines—at times, only in the hundreds of dollars. Two months before the horrendous Philips Petroleum explosion in 1989, OSHA neglected to do a complete inspection of the plant after an accident killed one worker. OSHA does have some power to ask the Justice Department to prosecute employers who intentionally or negligently injure their employees, but critics of OSHA have maintained that state prosecutions are necessary because few employers have been charged under federal law. In fact, a 1988 congressional study found that only 14 people had been prosecuted under OSHA for risking their employees' health or safety and none had been sentenced to prison. State prosecutions are more common.

There is renewed vigor at OSHA, however. Enforcement and fines have increased sharply since Ronald

FIGURE 16.3
THE COWBOY AFTER OSHA

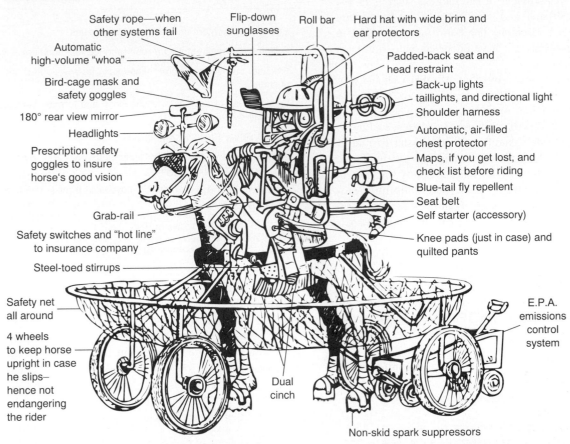

Safety rope—when other systems fail

Flip-down sunglasses

Roll bar

Hard hat with wide brim and ear protectors

Automatic high-volume "whoa"

Bird-cage mask and safety goggles

180° rear view mirror

Headlights

Prescription safety goggles to insure horse's good vision

Grab-rail

Safety switches and "hot line" to insurance company

Steel-toed stirrups

Safety net all around

4 wheels to keep horse upright in case he slips— hence not endangering the rider

Padded-back seat and head restraint

Back-up lights taillights, and directional light

Shoulder harness

Automatic, air-filled chest protector

Maps, if you get lost, and check list before riding

Blue-tail fly repellent

Seat belt

Self starter (accessory)

Knee pads (just in case) and quilted pants

E.P.A. emissions control system

Dual cinch

Non-skid spark suppressors

Source: Copyright © 1972 by Devin. Reprinted with permission.

Reagan cut back OSHA activity during his first presidential term. Fines for health and safety violations exceeded $50 million in 1991 alone, and OSHA has requested an increase in fine limits and criminal penalties for willful violations. OSHA is now using its subpoena powers to have employees testify under oath about safety violations. Business executives now face jail terms for their behavior and policies regarding the health and safety of their workers. State Supreme Courts in New York, Illinois, and Michigan have already ruled that employers can face criminal charges and prison, and other cases are pending. As stated by the New York's Chief Judge, Sol Wachtler, "federal law on workplace safety does not preempt state prosecutions of employers whose criminal activity happens to be centered in the workplace or directed at employees." The renewed zeal has created a fearful perspective among employers. As one expert put it, "for the first time, the cost of ignoring OSHA has become greater than the cost of complying."[9]

The key question, however, is whether OSHA has reduced deaths, accidents, or injuries. The data on this question are mixed. One early congressional investiga-

tion found no significant reduction in work-related deaths, illnesses, or injuries since the law took effect.[10] In fact, there has been an increase in injuries and illnesses since 1984, which some people attribute to the loosening of standards and regulations imposed by a pro-business administration. The Labor Department recently reported that workplace injuries caused by repetitive motion have increased sharply.[11] The report also said that 4 percent of full-time workers suffered from some form of illness or injury on the job in 1988, the highest rate since 1980.

OSHA is focused almost exclusively on unsafe working conditions and managerial responsibility. Virtually no attention is given to employee behavior and responsibility. Because of this lack of attention, most experts agree that the impact of OSHA on accident rates will be fairly small (one study predicts a 25 percent reduction in accidents at a maximum).[12] GM, for example, reported that in 1976 it was spending $15 per car to comply with OSHA regulations but that there had been no positive impact on accident rates as a function of the regulations.[13]

Other experts maintain that the long-term impact of OSHA will be overwhelmingly positive because of the increased knowledge of hazardous substances discovered through OSHA activities. For example, critical information about a great number of carcinogens such as PCBs, cotton dust, asbestos, and vinyl chloride can be directly linked to OSHA research. The banning of asbestos in 1989 would probably not have occurred had it not been for OSHA research.

The right-to-know provisions of OSHA should also have a positive impact on company health and safety records. These provisions specify the employees' right to know if they are working with unsafe substances, how to work with them safely, and how to administer first aid if workers come in contact with toxic chemicals. These provisions also require that a "Material Safety Data Sheet" be provided with each chemical used. This form provides all necessary information about the substance, what precautions to take, and how to treat any injury associated with its use.

Unions take a much more positive position on the effects of OSHA. One study, for example, reports a 10 percent drop in fatalities and a 15 percent drop in total injuries since the implementation of OSHA.[14] Unions have been at the forefront in utilizing many of the preventative provisions of OSHA. For example, over 20,000 workers are trained annually in the recognition and control of work hazards. Still, unions favor more aggressive enforcement which is more uniform across the country and a faster process for the development of new standards.

PROGRAMS TO REDUCE ACCIDENTS AT WORK

Organizations have tried a variety of different strategies directed at reducing or eliminating unsafe behaviors at work. These programs can be classified into four general areas: personnel selection, employee training, incentive programs, and safety rules and regulations. Figure 16.4 presents a summary of the characteristics of the safety programs that have proved successful. Research indicates that high management commitment and involvement in plant safety matters appears to be highly correlated with low accident rates.[15]

Personnel Selection

We have all used the expression "accident-prone" to describe an acquaintance who inadvertently destroyed something. Is it possible to predict accident proneness and thus make personnel decisions accordingly? Organizations such as Domino's Pizza, Greyhound, and every police department in the nation would love to be able to avoid employing individuals with a knack for traffic mishaps. Unfortunately, while there have been numerous attempts

FIGURE 16.4
CORRELATES OF SUCCESSFUL SAFETY PROGRAMS

Strong management concern for safety issues

Full-time safety director who reports to top management

Frequent use of safety promotions such as newsletters and posters

Frequent use of accident investigations and formal accident reporting systems

Formal safety training for employees and supervisors

Frequent positive contacts between employees and supervisors regarding safety matters

Stable workforce (i.e., older employees with more years of company service)

Source: M. J. Smith, H. H. Cohen, A. Cohen, and R. J. Cleveland, Characteristics of successful safety programs. *Journal of Safety Research, 1,* 5–15, 1978. Reprinted with permission.

to identify careless, accident-prone people, the evidence really boils down to only two general findings: (1) older employees are safer than younger ones (regardless of job tenure), and (2) physical characteristics, such as hearing and vision, are related to accident rates when they are critical aspects of a job. Chapter 6 described the Safety Locus of Control (SLC) test, which appears to have potential for the prediction (and prevention) of employee accidents. Further research is certainly needed in this area.

Safety Training

Training programs are typical in industries with serious accident problems. Training programs generally focus on hazards at work, safety rules and regulations, and safe and unsafe work behaviors. For example, one study describes a bakery which developed a detailed behavior observation code of safe and unsafe behaviors.[16] Participants in the safety program were shown slides of the safe and unsafe behaviors. Goals were set for increasing the percentage of safe behaviors, and a feedback chart was set up for monitoring group performance. Supervisors were also trained in giving positive reinforcement for safe work behaviors. The training and monitoring increased the percentage of safe behaviors more than 20 percent.

Many manufacturers use a peer review process to improve safety records. The objective is to shape behavior with immediate and constant feedback and positive reinforcement. At Aluminum Company of America, all workers must submit safety suggestions, and they are rewarded for good ones. Production-line workers can stop the line at any time if they spot a safety problem. Other companies employ industrial psychologists and engineers to study the worker-machine interface. At Du Pont Corporation, engineers observe workers and then redesign valves and install key locks to reduce accidents. At Monsanto's Pensacola, Florida, plant psychologists used the critical incident technique (CIT) of job analysis to study the causes of accidents. Experts drew "cause trees" to identify the root causes of the less than obvious problems. If a worker slipped on oil, for example, the root cause would not be oil but the failure of maintenance to attend to an oil leak. A safety score card was also prepared, and workers review processes to check for "short cuts and deviations" which ultimately predict trouble. Safe workers win recognition at weekly safety meetings. Free lunches and promotions are tied to safety records. As a result of this comprehensive approach to safety, Monsanto's record has improved from 6.5 to 1.6 lost-time injuries per hundred workers in the 5 years of the program.

One survey indicated that most manufacturing plants have only informal employee training procedures for safety. Typically, a new employee is given a brief orientation to company policy, including safety issues; spends a day or two with a first-line supervisor or lead person; and is then expected to work safely at a reasonable level of productivity. Research indicates that a formal system of safety training is more effective. One study supported the use of accident simulations as a training method.[17]

OSHA has issued "voluntary training guidelines" for employers, which provide a framework for the development, administration, and evaluation of training programs. These guidelines are especially helpful for organizations which have no expertise in formal training development and evaluation.

Incentive Systems

As we discussed in Chapter 12, many employers have safety contests in which company units compete with one another for cash or prizes. Other contests are set up so that each unit competes with its own safety record. If a lower number of accidents occurs, an award is given. At Du Pont, directors give safety awards and workers with cash prizes if their units remain accident-free for 6 months. At Kodak, volunteer observers take turns supervising peers and providing token awards (e.g., free Cokes). There has been little systematic research on incentive systems for accident reduction. When awards are substantial, failure to report accidents is certainly a possibility.

Safety Rules

Most companies now publish employee handbooks with formal rules and regulations which stipulate what employees can and cannot do in the workplace. Unfortunately, many of these rules and regulations are too general

to be effective. The most effective employee safety handbooks are those which carefully describe the steps to be taken on the job to ensure maximum safety. For each step, potential dangers are identified to alert the worker. In addition to specificity in the rules, it is also critical to get workers to read and comprehend safety handbooks. Some companies require that employees pass a test about safety-related issues before they begin work.

No matter how thorough the training, safety rules will be meaningless if they are not enforced. There are, unfortunately, numerous cases in which a worker ignored a safety rule and was injured, or a supervisor ordered workers to ignore a safety rule. Consistent enforcement of safety rules, with discipline for infractions, will benefit management in several ways. First, it will send a clear message to employees that the company takes safety seriously. Second, it should reduce injuries. Third, a company may be able to avoid an OSHA citation if it can demonstrate that it complied with relevant OSHA standards (or the general duty clause), that it trained its workers properly, and that the injury was the result of a worker's deliberate flouting of a known work rule. Documentation of consistent discipline for work rule violations would be necessary in order for a company to avoid OSHA liability.

CONTEMPORARY ISSUES RELATED TO HEALTH AND SAFETY

AIDS and the Workplace

The nation was shocked to learn in 1991 that basketball legend Magic Johnson had tested positive for the AIDS virus. AIDS is now the leading cause of death for persons between the ages of 25 and 44. According to the Center for Disease Control (CDC), by the end of 1993, 275,000 Americans will have died of the disease. Needless to say, AIDS has become a critical health-care issue for employers and employees alike. The costs of treating AIDS are expected to exceed $2 billion by 1995. The estimated losses in productivity are over $65 billion for 1993.

AIDS victims are now protected by a variety of state and local laws which prohibit discrimination against persons with disabilities. As we discussed in Chapter 3, AIDS has typically been defined legally as a disability under the Rehabilitation Act of 1973, which prohibits discrimination against the disabled by federal contractors, and is also covered by the 1990 Americans with Disabilities Act (ADA). There has been a flood of recent lawsuits related to AIDS, and the disease has been interpreted as a disability in most courts. For example the Florida Commission of Human Relations ruled that a teacher who was dismissed from his job because he had

AIDS was a victim of disability discrimination. The teacher was awarded almost $200,000.

OSHA issued new standards regarding AIDS and other viruses in 1991. Employers must provide gloves, masks, mouth guards, and smocks for workers who might come in contact with blood. Employers must also write an "exposure control plan," identify workers who might be at risk, and train them on how to protect themselves. Employers who violate the regulations are subject to OSHA penalties. Employers must also offer voluntary hepatitis B vaccinations to all employees who might be exposed to the virus.

Most major companies have developed specific policies to deal with AIDS-related issues at work. The usual position is that AIDS-afflicted employees should be treated the same as other employees as long as they are able to do their jobs. The Bank of America allows co-workers to transfer from departments where there are AIDS victims, but there has not been a single request. This is undoubtedly due to the fact that the bank has provided a great deal of information about the disease to its employees and, in particular, about the very low risk of transmission in the workplace (through 1990, the CDC had not found a single case of AIDS transmission based on casual contact at work). The CDC takes the position that AIDS-afflicted employees do not have to be isolated or restricted from any work area, although there is sharp debate about disclosure and possible restrictions in hospitals, food service, and dental settings. Caution is suggested for health-care workers and of course for patients or clients who may be exposed to blood, mucous membranes, or lesions. The new ADA requires that employers make "reasonable accommodation" for persons with disabilities so that they may join (and stay in) the workforce. Thus, if symptoms related to AIDS prevent an employee from performing the "essential functions" of one job, "reasonable accommodation" may entail finding that person another job within the organization that he or she can perform.

Levi Straus and IBM have been at the forefront in the development of a comprehensive AIDS-awareness program. The educational component of the Levi Straus program includes informative brochures, a manager's guide to treating AIDS-afflicted employees, a policy manual, and a guidebook for policymakers. The company also provides an opportunity for employees to meet with medical professionals to discuss the issues in more detail.[18] Levi Straus is very satisfied with its program because it has had no lawsuits, no employees refusing to work with AIDS-afflicted employees, and no request for reassignments. IBM sent out a brochure on AIDS (developed by the CDC) to all 240,000 of its employees. The IBM policy is to encourage AIDS-afflicted employees to work as long as they are capable and to ensure their privacy.

Figure 16.5 presents a risk assessment questionnaire which workers (and students) can use to assess their risk of acquiring or transmitting any sexually transmitted disease, including the virus that causes AIDS.

Drugs in the Workplace

It is not necessary to remind students that the abuse of controlled substances is a serious social problem—one that plagues employers as well as law enforcement agencies. It has been estimated that drug abuse costs the U.S. economy as much as $60 billion annually in lost productivity, accidents, absenteeism, medical claims, and thefts.[19] As we discussed in Chapter 6, many companies have responded to this crisis with a drug testing program. The Drug-Free Workplace Act of 1988 requires federal contractors to provide a drug-free workplace. Organizations must have specific policies on substance abuse, establish awareness programs, and notify employees and applicants that a drug-free state is a condition of employment.

A 1992 survey found that 75 percent of all companies test at least some employees and applicants for drug use. Over 25 percent of companies now conduct random drug testing of current employees. Motorola, for example, recently ordered all 100,000 of its U.S. employees to undergo random drug testing at least once every 3 years.[20]

Before a company initiates a drug testing policy or program, the following questions should be addressed: Why do we want this program? Do we have a problem with drugs in our company? What will we do with the results of drug tests? Can our current discipline policy handle violations of this policy? How much will the program cost? Can we afford it? Will it affect morale? Should it be a punitive or rehabilitative program? Only after these questions are answered satisfactorily should a company consider the implementation of a drug testing program.

Companies use five different approaches to drug testing: preemployment screening, random testing of current employees, "reasonable cause" testing in response to performance problems, return-to-duty testing after drug treatment or suspension, and postaccident testing. Science makes it possible to ascertain whether a person has ingested a controlled substance, and more and more companies are joining the ranks of those who at least test applicants for the presence of drugs. Surprisingly, workers are quite tolerant of testing. A 1989 Gallup poll found that 60 percent of those questioned even supported random drug testing of current employees with no probable cause.[21]

Two questions that science has not yet been able to answer, however, are exactly how much of a controlled substance an individual must ingest in order to be impaired and just what "impaired" means. For example,

FIGURE 16.5
RISK ASSESSMENT FORM FOR SEXUALLY TRANSMITTED DISEASES

This form is confidential— it is not a permanent part of your medical record.

Many factors must be considered in assessing your health and fitness. Among these are: (1) your risk of acquiring or transmitting any sexually transmitted disease (STD) and (2) your use of psychoactive chemicals in connection with sexual activity, a practice that can increase your risk of acquiring an STD. STDs considered here include, but are not limited to: gonorrhea; syphilis; genital herpes; genital warts; chlamydia; hepatitis B; giardiasis; infection with HIV, the virus that causes AIDS.

Please be honest in responding to the questions—we assure you that this document will be handled with the utmost confidentiality by you and your health care provider only. Please feel free to discuss the results with your provider. You may retain the survey for your own reference. *In any event, it will not be placed in your medical record.*

There are 11 questions listed below. Please check the one single answer that best describes your preferences or activities.

1. How many sexual partners have you had *per month* in the last year?
   3 _____ 5 or more
   2 _____ 2–4
   1 _____ 0–1

2. How many partners did you have *per month* in the year previous?
   3 _____ 5 or more
   2 _____ 2–4
   1 _____ 0–1

3. The kinds of sexual contacts I have are:
   3 _____ one-time or anonymous "tricks," "one night stands," groups, or prostitutes
   2 _____ multiple times with two or more partners
   1 _____ exclusively with one partner

4. I have sexual encounters or contacts most frequently
   3 _____ in baths, bookstores, parties, "massage parlors," "spas," public restrooms, autos
   1 _____ in my or my partner's home

5. The frequency with which I use drugs or alcohol to enhance my sexual encounters:
   3 _____ frequently
   2 _____ occasionally
   1 _____ rarely/never

6. I have injected myself with one or more recreational drugs in the past 5 years.
   4 _____ yes
   1 _____ no

7. I have sexual encounters most frequently in:
   3 _____ New York, Los Angeles, San Francisco, Miami, Washington, Dallas, Houston, Newark, Atlanta
   2 _____ other large urban areas (Boston, Philadelphia, St. Louis, Seattle, San Diego, etc.)
   1 _____ small cities, towns, rural areas

8. Those kinds of sexual activities I practice most frequently are (please circle specific activities):
   4 _____ vaginal or anal intercourse without a condom
   3 _____ "protected" vaginal or anal intercourse (use of condoms and spermicides)
   2 _____ oral-genital contact
   1 _____ masturbation, massage, body rubbing, kissing

9. My current sexual partner and I have discussed our previous sexual behavior and experiences with each other.
   4 _____ no
   1 _____ yes

FIGURE 16.5 *(Continued)*

10.   I negotiate with sexual partners for safer sexual practices.
      4 _____ no
      2 _____ sometimes
      1 _____ yes

11.   I ask potential sexual partners about their use of drugs and steroids, especially their use of needles.
      4 _____ no
      2 _____ sometimes
      1 _____ yes

Add up the numbers from each question (1–11) and see the key below to determine your level of risk.

My score is _____ .

If you answered "1" (the last option) for question 8, deduct 3 points.

Total adjusted score _____ .

KEY:

17 or more: You appear to be at high risk for developing STDs, including HIV infection, and for possibly developing dependence on psychoactive substances. You should visit your health care provider immediately to discuss your risk of these dangers.

12–16 points: You appear to be at moderate risk for developing either an STD or chemical dependence and are encouraged to lower your overall risk by altering the behaviors that resulted in high scores on some of the questions. See your health care provider for any questions or concerns you may have regarding your risk.

11: You are at low risk for problems and are encouraged to continue your healthy behavior. Please feel free to contact your health care provider at any time for updated information regarding safer sex, AIDS, or any other issues.

   This scoring system was designed to: (1) increase your awareness of STDs and the risk factors associated with acquiring or transmitting STDs, (2) stimulate self-evaluation of your health and your sexual lifestyle, and (3) encourage your taking responsibility for your health and the health of your sexual contacts. **This questionnaire is yours to keep and review. It will not go into your medical records even if you bring it to your health care provider.**

Source: American College Health Association, Rockville, MD, 1989. Reprinted with permission.

most states have set a 0.10 percent blood alcohol level to establish impairment by alcohol; a similar standard does not exist for controlled substances. While some employers declare that a drug test result showing *any* amount of a controlled substance will be grounds for rejecting an applicant or discharging a worker, other employers have set some level as the threshold for an assumption that the employee is impaired. Computerized tests are now available to help employers determine whether workers in safety-related jobs are impaired. One test operates like a video game and takes less than a minute to determine eye-hand coordination and reaction time. Old Town Trolley Tours of San Diego, California, uses the test to assess drivers.

   Because of the lack of a standard for impairment, combined with the manner in which the presence of drugs is usually ascertained (generally, a urine test), many employment decisions made on the basis of positive drug test results have been legally challenged. Some experts maintain that hair analysis, a reliable but more costly alternative to urinalysis, is a less invasive technique which may not be as legally troublesome. Although there are no federal laws regulating drug testing, drug testing programs have been challenged using a number of legal theories. Although private-sector employers have generally been able to successfully defend their drug testing programs in court, there are exceptions. In California, for example, the court ruled that Southern Pacific wrongfully fired a computer programmer when she refused to provide a random-test urine specimen. Another California court ruled that Kerr-McGee Chemical Corporation violated a worker's privacy by requiring her to submit to a drug test. However, other California decisions have supported drug testing. Lower courts in Michigan and Texas have recently sided with employers on random urinalysis, while a court in New Jersey found for the plaintiff. In the words of one labor attorney, the employee drug testing is a "legal minefield...a quagmire of legal problems."[22] Utah is the only state which clearly permits drug testing of employees and applicants, and authorizes firing employees who refuse to be tested. Maine explicitly allows testing for "probable cause," but limits random testing to safety-sensitive jobs.

Although public employers are bound by the Fourth Amendment of the U.S. Constitution (which forbids "unreasonable" searches and seizures), even characterizing a urine test as either a search (of the urine) or a seizure (of body fluids) has not led irrevocably to judicial declarations that drug testing by public employers is unconstitutional. Recent U.S. Supreme Court decisions have permitted public employers to use drug testing for employees engaged in jobs in which public safety is an issue, such as railroad engineers, U.S. Customs agents, and nuclear power plant workers. Private-sector employers, however, are not bound by the Fourth Amendment, and challenges must be based on contract claims or "public policy" grounds.

This does not mean, however, that a company may establish a drug testing program without concern for potential legal consequences. Unionized employers must bargain with the union about the procedures to be used, according to the National Labor Relations Board (NLRB). Nonunionized employers must consider that not all positive results may indicate that the employee is presently impaired, or has even ingested a controlled substance, as the ingestion of innocuous substances (poppy seeds, quinine water) may result in a positive test result. At a minimum, the company should make sure that its program includes the following:

- Notice to employees (or applicants) that drug testing will be conducted, and the procedures to be used
- An opportunity for the individual to disclose which prescription or over-the-counter drugs he or she is currently taking, as well as other information that might skew the test results

- A careful chain of custody to ensure that samples are not lost, mixed up, or switched
- A dignified but secure method of collecting samples
- Confirmation of all positive results with more sensitive tests
- The opportunity for the individual to have the sample retested at his or her own expense
- Confidentiality of test results

In developing a drug testing policy, a company must determine what, if any, substances are permissible (e.g., will a positive reading for marijuana be treated the same way as a positive reading for heroin?). It must also determine whether, if testing is done on current employees, testing will be done only "for cause" (for example, after an accident or if a supervisor determines that an employee appears impaired) or randomly, without cause.

Potential legal claims in regard to drug testing in the public sector include Fourth Amendment challenges to the testing (if there was no reasonable cause to conclude that the employee had ingested controlled substances) or a violation of an employee's constitutional due process rights (if the employee is discharged without being given an opportunity to challenge the test results). All employers may face charges of defamation (if test results become known to anyone but those who need the information), contract claims (for currently employed workers), and, perhaps, claims of discrimination against workers with disabilities (for example, if the employee is a recovering drug abuser).

Human resource (HR) managers are well advised to consult with legal counsel before beginning to develop a drug testing program. Model programs that have withstood litigation are available, and an attorney can advise managers of any state laws that may affect the way the program is designed or administered.

Smoking in the Workplace

One of the most volatile issues for human resource management (HRM) people today is the company position on smoking. Growing evidence that health care costs more for smokers than for nonsmokers is prompting some companies to levy additional charges on smokers. A 1990 Environmental Protection Agency (EPA) report also concludes that secondhand smoke is causing 3800 lung cancer deaths per year. The American Heart Association has stated that passive smoking is the third-greatest preventable cause of death in the United States. The Wisconsin Labor and Industry Review Commission awarded an employee $23,400 in worker's compensation benefits due to exposure to secondhand smoke over an 8-year period, which caused a permanent disability. The California

Compensation Insurance fund paid $85,000 in damages to an employee who suffered a heart attack directly related to exposure to smoke at work.

The EPA "Guide to Workplace Smoking Policies" recommends that employers create separately ventilated smoking lounges. While the majority of organizations still allow smoking in most areas with very few constraints, a growing number have developed restrictive policies which range from the use of designated smoking areas to the banning of all smoking at the workplace and nonsmoking as a condition of employment.

OSHA will almost certainly issue regulations regarding smoking in the workplace. Section 654(a) of OSHA states that the "general duty" of employers is to provide places of employment "free of recognized hazards that are causing or likely to cause death or serious physical harm to his employee." In 1992, OSHA took the initial steps in considering tobacco smoke as a workplace hazard. Given that the Surgeon General's report now documents the effects of sidestream smoke and the Environmental Protection Agency places tobacco smoke in the top tier of known carcinogens, the OSHA obligation seems obvious.

It is the consensus of legal opinion that companies can ban smoking in the workplace, except where smoking is expressly allowed as part of a union contract or where legislation exists which protect smokers. A New Jersey state law, for example, prohibits discrimination in hiring, pay, and working conditions against smokers "unless the employer has a rational basis for doing so." Unfortunately, it is now up to employers to determine what constitutes a "rational basis." (Is higher health-care cost a rational basis?) At least eight other states have laws protecting smokers from discrimination, and several states now have pending legislation.[23] There are no laws which either prohibit employers from banning smoking at work or from taking action against employees who violate such bans.

Provident Indemnity Life Insurance Co. offers nonsmokers 33 percent discounts on health and life insurance. At Mahoning Culvert in Youngstown, Ohio, smokers who are attempting to quit contribute 50 cents a day to a pool which accumulates for 1 year. To that pool of $182.50, the company adds $817.50 to reward each smoker who managed to quit for a year. An additional $500 is given the second year. Other companies have drawings for prizes and other incentives to encourage employees to quit smoking. Some companies have taken the punitive route. Lutheran Health Systems, a Fargo, North Dakota, hospital and nursing home chain, charges smokers a 10 percent premium on their health insurance. U-Haul International deducts $5 every other week from the paychecks of employees who smoke.

Several fire departments have imposed deadlines by which smoking firefighters must quit or be terminated. Particularly in hazardous work environments where the risks of cancer are great, even without the added risk of tobacco, companies are likely to impose no-smoking rules. While insurance premiums and unnecessary health-care costs are major reasons for employers' increased interest in issues related to smoking, pressure by nonsmokers for a smoke-free work environment has also certainly contributed to the development of formal smoking policies at many organizations today.

A seven-step plan has been proposed for the development of a smoking policy:[24] (1) Top management should make a commitment to development of a smoking policy. (2) Pertinent state and local laws should be reviewed. (3) Unions should be involved (if applicable). (4) The smoking policy should be tailored to particular work situations or stations. (5) A committee of smokers and nonsmokers from a cross section of the workforce should be formed. (6) The workforce should be surveyed to determine attitudes toward smoking and toward possible smoking policies. (7) A proposed policy should be circulated throughout the workplace. Consistent enforcement of policy violations will encourage compliance. Following implementation of a policy developed in this manner plus enforcement of violations on a consistent basis should facilitate employee acceptance and compliance.

Video Display Terminals

Over 30 million Americans now work with video display terminals (VDTs). Many workers who spend considerable time in front of them complain of eyestrain, various muscular and wrist problems, and complicated or failed pregnancies. While one California study found that pregnant women who worked at VDTs for 20 hours or more a week had twice as high a risk of miscarriage as other clerical workers, a larger, more recent study sponsored by the federal government found no relationship between long exposure to VDTs and miscarriage.[25] Unions such as the American Federation of State and Municipal Employees (AFSME) are now demanding that pregnant women be allowed to switch to jobs not involving VDTs. There is no denying that electrical and magnetic fields can influence biological processes. The critical question related to VDTs is the extent to which exposure at that level is harmful. More research is urgently needed.

Several states and municipalities have issued guidelines regarding work with VDTs in order to reduce repetitive trauma disorder. New Jersey, for example, requires 15-minute breaks every 2 hours and eye exams every 5 years for all state employees who work with VDTs. The city of San Francisco has strict guidelines regarding chair, terminal, and screen flexibility, plus required breaks for employees who work with VDTs. The World Health Organization (WHO) has adopted a standard that says workers should sit at least 3 feet away from the back of a terminal (where the radiation is generated). While the evidence on the effects of VDTs is questionable, the psychological stress related to work with VDTs is now well documented, since workers are now more aware of the possibility that VDTs could affect their health or that of their offspring. The next section will examine the general area of occupational stress.

Occupational Stress

According to a 1991 survey conducted by the Northwestern National Life Insurance Company, workplace stress is truly epidemic.[26] The stress is making workers sick and affecting productivity and accident rates. Job stress is also a frequently cited problem in workers' compensation claims, many of which are considered by experts to be fraudulent.

Job stress has been defined as a "situation wherein job-related factors interact with a worker to change his or her psychological and/or physiological condition such that the person is forced to deviate from normal functioning."[27] Stress is considered to be a major problem for workers in today's highly competitive environment, with its emphasis on cost control, reduced labor expense, and higher productivity. *Stress* should be distinguished from a *stressor,* which is an object or event that causes the stress. For example, the speculation that work with VDTs may be hazardous could be considered a stressor which may cause stress in some employees. Exposure to secondhand smoke all day, which may cause cancer, now serves as a stressor for many nonsmoking workers. Figure 16.6 presents a model of the antecedents, outcomes, and consequences of stress. Stressors can be found in the physical environment due, for example, to lighting or noise problems, temperature, or bad air. We know that these potential stressors can have an interactive effect such that, for example, temperature combined with a noisy environment may cause even greater stress than the two sources independently.

Prolonged exposure to certain job demands has been linked to several measures of mental and physical stress as well as productivity problems and absenteeism. *Job demands* have been defined as psychological stressors such as working too hard or too fast, having too much to do, or having conflicting demands. An individual may perceive role conflict when pressures from two or more sources are exerted such that complying with one source creates greater problems regarding another source (e.g., workers trying to maintain a high quality standard while simultaneously trying to meet a very difficult quantity standard, or managers attempting to hit a quota for production while reducing labor costs). Another source of stress is role ambiguity, in which workers simply do not understand what is expected on the job, or in which what is expected is contrary to what they think should be done. An example of role ambiguity occurs when your boss is vague about your responsibilities or the timeframe in which you have to complete specific tasks. Research on role ambiguity and conflict is plentiful. As in other areas related to stress, the reactions to stressors tend to vary widely depending on individuals' characteristics. For example, people with type A personalities suffer more stress and experience a greater number of health problems than do type B people. Type A people tend to do just about everything fast (walk, talk, eat) and to have little tolerance for people who go at a more moderate pace.[28]

Other sources of individual stress include conflicts between job obligations and family obligations. Women in particular tend to experience this conflict. "Family responsibilities can place tremendous pressure on women. When both husband and wife have careers, the wife is often expected to keep her housekeeping role in addition to her work role.... More and more superwoman is now questioning her multiple roles. And with this uncertainty comes more conflict and stress."[29] As we discussed in Chapter 9, many corporations are aware of this extra burden on women and are providing employment options designed to reduce this source of stress. Companies such as Du Pont, Merck, and General Mills offer family leave, flexible work schedules, and on-site day care, for example. A 1991 Conference Board review of 80 studies found reduced turnover and absenteeism and increased productivity in companies which help employees balance work with family obligations.[30]

The work group, unit, or organization can be a stressor as well, aside from the issues of role ambiguity and conflict. Particularly in this era of downsizing or "rightsizing," many U.S. corporations are feeling the competitive crunch by making hard decisions to reduce overhead costs. Supervisors and managers are being asked to make hard personnel decisions regarding employee cutbacks. Employees worry more now that their jobs may be on the line. Survey data from IBM since 1988, for example, reflect the downturn in the company's fortunes and the pressures being brought to bear on managers as they make substantial labor cutbacks through unfavorable reassignments and terminations for poor performance. Jobs affected by recent major changes are generally stressful. If a company has been purchased, gone through a layoff or downsizing, imposed mandatory overtime, or undergone a major reorganization, the employees, regardless of rank, are likely to have high levels of stress.

FIGURE 16.6
A MODEL FOR ORGANIZATIONAL STRESS RESEARCH

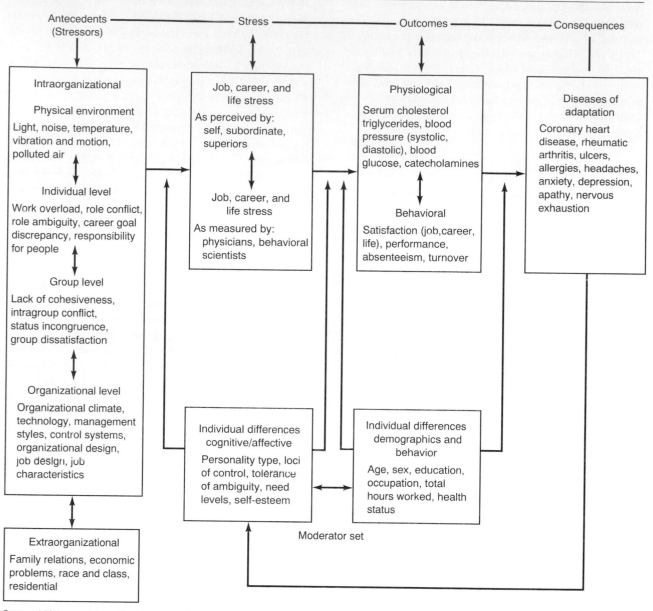

Source: J. M. Ivancevich and M.T. Matteson, Stress and work: A managerial perspective. Glenview, IL: Scott, Foresman, 1980. Reprinted with permission.

Some jobs are more likely to cause stress than others. Air traffic controllers, for example, report higher than average rates of ulcers, chest pain, and headaches, but only after 3 years of work. Police work is also very stressful. While high-level executives lament their highly stressful responsibilities, in fact the evidence regarding stress-related illnesses does not support the belief that higher-level management jobs are more stressful than other jobs. In fact, one large-scale study found that rates of coronary heart disease were greater at lower manage-

ment levels.[31] The relatively low rate of stress for executives may be related to job decision latitude. Researchers in occupational stress hypothesize that stress is a function of high job demands in combination with low control at work. That is, when an individual has little authority to make decisions in a highly demanding job, the most negative aspects of stress should be expected.[32]

A relatively new term for one type of stress is "burnout," which reflects an emotional reaction in people who work in human services and work closely with people.

Burnout is common among police officers, teachers, social workers, and nurses. People experiencing burnout develop cynical attitudes toward their jobs and clients and typically feel emotional exhaustion, depersonalization, and a sense of low personal accomplishment or control.[33] Is burnout inevitable in these jobs? Apparently not. A stress reduction program for public school teachers found that the effects of burnout could be reduced by using positive feedback about teacher competencies.[34] Figure 16.7 presents a sample of questions from a well-known survey on worker burnout.

As noted in Figure 16.6, there are psychological, physiological, and behavioral consequences of stress. However, reactions to the same stressors vary greatly with the individual. Although individual reactions are difficult to predict, it is known that some people can handle tremendous amounts of stressors without any manifest stressful reactions. Other people fall apart. Some turn to drugs or alcohol. The VDT example provided above may cause psychological stress, as manifested in anxiety, depression, irritability, and hostility. Psychological stress may also have physiological consequences such as high blood pressure, numbness, and heart problems. Of course, stress may also affect work performance, work attendance, and accident rates. These consequences can have profound (and costly) organizational consequences, including effects on union organizing, workers' compensation claims, poor work products, and legal problems. In 1991, for example, McDonald's Corporation was held liable in a fatal crash caused by a 19-year-old who had worked a double shift.

Stress management and reduction programs are common in industry today. At Motorola, for example, programs emphasize exercise, nutrition, relaxation techniques, time management, and self-awareness. Other organizations have attempted to reduce physical stressors by redesigning the workplace. Role ambiguity and role conflict can often be reduced by interventions following a job analysis and survey research. Studies point to immediate supervisors as a primary source of stress among workers. Survey data may help to pinpoint unit-level problems before they result in serious organizational difficulties such as termination, absences, and disabilities.

Many organizations incorporate their stress reduction programs into comprehensive employment assistance programs (EAPs). We will examine these programs next.

Employee Assistance Programs

As we discussed in Chapter 11, EAPs are a growing form of employee benefit, providing help to over 26 million U.S. employees for a variety of problems. There are over 10,000 organizations with formal EAPs treating job stress, alcoholism and other forms of drug abuse, marital and emotional difficulties, and financial problems. The number of EAPs has increased recently because the thousands of companies with federal contracts must adopt formal antidrug policies under the provisions of the 1988 Drug-Free Workplace Act. Many EAPs are also equipped to handle problems related to AIDS. The general goal of an EAP is to provide treatment for employees who are having problems so that they can return to normal, productive functioning on the job. While the vast majority of these organizations are large, even small businesses are getting involved with EAPs through the formation of consortiums with other small businesses.

Most EAP referrals are based on assessments of job performance by supervisors. Employees can also volunteer for such programs. EAP staff often provide training for managers and supervisors on making "constructive confrontations" with their employees regarding work-related deficiencies. Supervisors are thus exempted from trying to diagnose the causes of a problem. Getting at the cause of the performance problem is left to professionals (e.g., people with graduate degrees in psychology and social work), who are trained to make such diagnoses and treat employees accordingly. Most EAPs are based on the principle of voluntary participation.

An EAP is typically run by an outside health service organization, with an average cost of about $35 per employee per year. The limited data on the effects of EAPs are quite positive. One study reported savings of $2.74 for every $1.00 spent on the EAP. AT&T reported savings of almost $600,000 as a result of its EAP activities. In one study of 110 employees, 85 percent of poor performers were judged to be no longer poor after the EAP program. The rate of improvement for all participants was 86 percent. There was a significant decrease in the number of accidents in which these individuals were involved. Absenteeism also went down, as did visits to the medical department. In short, at least for this sample of AT&T workers, the EAP was a smashing success.[35] United

---

FIGURE 16.7
SAMPLE QUESTIONS FROM THE
MASLACH-JACKSON BURNOUT INVENTORY

I feel emotionally drained from my work.

I feel used up at the end of the day.

I feel like I'm at the end of my rope.

I worry that this job is hardening me emotionally.

I've become more callous toward people since I took this job.

Source: C. Maslach and S.E. Jackson, The measurement of experienced burnout. *Journal of Occupational Behavior, 2,* 99–113, 1981. Reprinted with permission.

Airlines estimates that for every $1.00 spent for its EAP, it realizes savings of $16.35 through reduction in employee absences.[36] Labor unions generally support drug counseling and EAPs but oppose coercion to participate in such programs as a condition of employment, as well as opposing drug testing of any kind.

GM reports that about 10 percent of its 600,000-employee workforce are experiencing alcohol or other drug-related problems. There is thus little wonder that GM emphasizes substance abuse in its EAP programs. As we stated earlier, many other organizations have responded to problems of substance abuse by implementing drug testing programs, which may involve entry-level screening for drug usage as well as random drug testing of current employees. Such policies are controversial but, in most circumstances, legal. Under the doctrine of employment at will, employers may dismiss employees for any reason other than those covered by statute (e.g., race, sex, religion, age). Firing an employee who flunks a drug test is not only legal but has been done thousands of times. However, most HRM experts take the position that termination should be a last resort after an attempt at intervention through an EAP, which should be prompted by unacceptable performance.

Wellness Programs

Due to the skyrocketing health insurance costs we described in Chapter 11, many companies have set up "wellness" or health management programs for employees. *Wellness* is defined as a "freely chosen lifestyle aimed at achieving and maintaining an individual's good health."[37] Companies have discovered that the best way to reduce health insurance costs is to keep employees healthy. In general, healthy employees are more productive than unhealthy ones. The Association for Fitness in Business (AFB) reports that over 700 organizations now offer formal wellness programs involving health assessment, exercise planning, counseling or support groups, stress management, weight control, and smoking cessation.

Some insurance companies offer reduced rates for organizations with organized wellness programs. Wellness programs are often integrated into the EAP of the company.[38]

At New York Telephone, the wellness program focuses on the following major areas of health: smoking cessation, cholesterol reduction, alcohol abuse control, fitness training, stress management, and cancer screening. New York Telephone reported savings of almost $3 million because of reduced absences and medical treatment as a consequence of its wellness program. Kimberly-Clark offers a variety of health-related programs, including an exercise routine available at the fit-

ness center on the premises, weight control consultation, blood pressure analysis and treatment, and nutritional advice. These programs are available to the company's entire workforce, and 88 percent of employees are enrolled in one or more of the programs. While the cost is high (about $435 per employee, per year), the director of the program is certain the bottom line will support its effectiveness. There are many other success stories. IBM, Johnson & Johnson, Tenneco, Campbell Soup, and Xerox all report success with their "wellness" programs. One Xerox work location provides a soccer field, an Olympic-size pool, two gyms, tennis courts, a weight room, and over 2000 acres of running space. Johnson & Johnson reports savings of $378 per employee as a result of its comprehensive wellness program, which it now also administers for 60 other companies. The goals of the program are rather basic: stop smoking, eat fruit and fewer fatty foods, get some exercise, and buckle up. A 1983 Health Research Institute (HRI) study of the nation's 1500 largest companies found that companies with formal wellness programs paid $1061 per employee per year for health-related costs while companies without such programs paid $1,456.[39]

SUMMARY

Top management is taking a more active role in improving the health and safety of workers. Figure 16.8 presents a summary of managerial steps for improving the work environment, as recommended by one expert.[40]

The first step (affirming management commitment) means that management must make resources available for health and safety issues. Research shows that plants with superior health and safety records spend more money on health and safety. The second step for improving the

FIGURE 16.8
EIGHT ESSENTIAL STEPS IN IMPROVING THE WORK ENVIRONMENT

1. Affirm management's commitment to a safe and healthy environment.
2. Review current safety objectives and policies.
3. Conduct periodic evaluations and inspections of the workplace.
4. Identify potential and existing work hazards, in the areas of safety and health.
5. Identify the employees at risk.
6. Make the necessary improvements in the workplace.
7. Prepare and conduct preventive programs.
8. Monitor the feedback results and evaluate costs.

Source: S. Greenfeld, *Management's safety and health imperative: Eight essential steps to improving the work environment.* Minerva Occasional Paper Series (2.9). Cincinnati, OH: Xavier University, 1989.

work environment calls for a clearly established policy and results-oriented set of objectives for health and safety. Third, managers should perform planned and unplanned inspections of work sites to assess compliance. Fourth, as the safety manager at Du Pont put it, "When plant managers begin to audit people and their actions, dramatic changes occur.... Audits foster fewer unsafe acts." Managers should also establish an atmosphere in which employees feel comfortable about reporting unsafe working conditions, so that all potential hazards can be identified. The fifth step is to identify particular employees at risk, so that appropriate training and policies can be developed. The development of an employee data base or the use of a comprehensive personnel inventory (see Chapter 5) could assist with this effort. The sixth step for enhancing managerial attention is to make corrections in the work environment based on the research and employee data analysis. This may include a number of preventive measures. With the proliferation of complaints regarding tunnel carpal syndrome and related stress symptoms, this step may include ergonomics, or workstation redesign. Where the job situation contributes to an unsafe environment, management should take the appropriate action. The seventh step calls upon management to prepare and conduct preventive programs. Aggressive antidrug policies, EAPs, and wellness programs are examples. The final step is for managers to evaluate what they are doing and feed the results back to employees. An assessment of the monetary value of health and safety programs is one necessary component of this step. (Appendix A presents some useful methods for making such an assessment.) Many companies report considerable savings from such programs. Gillette, for example, saved over $1,200,000 from its health and safety programs. Procter & Gamble reported direct cost savings in excess of $1.5 million.

A more aggressive OSHA, new regulations, the threat of heavy fines and possible criminal prosecution, staggering health insurance costs, and research which shows that healthy employees are more productive employees have all contributed to the renewed attention to health and safety issues. More companies are developing formal health and safety policies, and management is now more likely to be held accountable for accident rates and other health-related measures. The 1990s are likely to see even greater interest in the subject and, in particular, more programs that focus on employee behavior. Drug testing and antismoking programs, EAPs, and wellness programs hold promise as methods which can contribute to the goal of a more productive and healthier workforce.

Managers are now being held accountable for the health and safety of their employees. In the present legal environment, managers are generally responsible for the actions of their employees. Prevention and training on health and safety issues should be major organizational concerns.

DISCUSSION QUESTIONS

1. Why are accident rates reliably higher for younger workers even after controlling for years on the job? In other words, why is a 20-year-old with 3 years of experience more likely to be involved in an accident than a 30-year-old with 3 years of experience? After you develop your theory for this fact, explain how companies can intervene to reduce (or wipe out) the effect.
2. How could you as a manager develop a strategy for increasing employees' motivation to work more safely?
3. Devise a training program and a policy directed at increasing the physical fitness of your employees. Take a position on smoking and other health-related matters, and state whether you would make the programs mandatory.
4. Do you think that managers should be held criminally liable for health and safety violations? Should they go to jail for such violations? If so, under what conditions? If not, why not?
5. Do you support a policy of random drug testing for all employees? Explain.
6. Should a company be allowed to prohibit smoking on or off the job for its employees? Explain your answer.
7. Given the accumulated evidence on the effects of smoking, why hasn't OSHA taken any steps to regulate smoking in the workplace?

NOTES

1. Bureau of Labor Statistics (1990). *Statistics-occupational injuries and illnesses.* Washington: Department of Labor. See also: DeWitt, K. (May 7, 1992). Senate panel hears of human toll in workplace. *The New York Times,* p. C20.
2. Bureau of Labor Statistics (1991). *Survey of work-related health.* Washington: Department of Labor.
3. Labor Letter (June 13, 1991). *The Wall Street Journal,* p. 1. See also: Karr, A. R. (May 2, 1990). White House backs raising penalties levied by OSHA. *The Wall Street Journal,* p. A8.
4. Vlasic, B. (July 23, 1989). Death in the workplace. *The Detroit News,* p. 1.
5. Verespej, M. A. (May 21, 1990). OSHA goes to court. *Industry Week,* 91–92. See also: Redeker, J. R., and Tang, D. J. (April 1988). Criminal accountability for work place safety. *Management Review,* 32–36. Glaberson, W. (Oct. 17, 1990). Court upholds prosecution of employer for job hazard. *The New York Times,* p. A16.

6. *Marshall v. Barlow's Inc.* (1978). 1978 OSH D, Sn. 22, 735. Chicago: Commerce Clearing House.

7. *Whirlpool Corp. v. Marshall* (Feb. 26, 1981). *Daily Labor Report,* Washington: Bureau of National Affairs.

8. Accident Facts (1983). Chicago, IL: National Safety Council.

9. See note 5, Verespej (1990). See also: Brooks, J. (1977). Failure to meet commitments in the Occupational Safety and Health Act. Washington: U.S. Congress, Committee on Government Operations.

10. Kilborn, P. (Nov. 6, 1989). Rise in worker injuries is laid to computer. *The New York Times,* p. B1. See also: Swoboda, F. (Jan. 12, 1990). OSHA targets repetitive motion injuries. *Washington Post,* p. A10.

11. See note 1.

12. Cook, W. N., and Gautschi, F. H. (1981). OSHA plant safety programs and injury reduction. *Industrial Relations, 20,* 245–257.

13. Ashford, N. A. (1977). *Crisis in the workplace: Occupational disease and injury.* A Report to the Ford Foundation. Cambridge, MA: MIT Press.

14. Kirkland, L. (July 1980). OSHA: A ten year success story. *AFL-CIO American Federationist,* pp. 1–4.

15. Smith, M. J., Cohen, H. H., Cohen, A., and Cleveland, R. J. (1978). Characteristics of successful safety programs. *Journal of Safety Research, 1,* 5–15.

16. Komaki, J., Barwick, K. D., and Scott, L. R. (1978). A behavioral approach to occupational safety: Pinpointing and reinforcing safe performance in a food manufacturing plant. *Journal of Applied Psychology, 63,* 434–445.

17. Dunbar, R. (June 1975). Manager's influence on subordinate's thinking about safety. *Academy of Management Journal, 18,* 364–369.

18. Feuer, D. (June 1987). AIDS at work: Fighting the fear. *Training,* 61–71. See also: Elliott, R. H., and Wilson, T. M. (Fall 1987). AIDS in the workplace: Public personnel management and the law. *Public Personnel Management,* 209–219. Breuer, N. L. (January 1992). AIDS issues haven't gone away. *Personnel Journal, 71,* 47–49. Elkiss, H. (1991). Reasonable accommodation and unreasonable fears: An AIDS policy guide for human resource personnel. *Human Resource Planning, 14,* 183–190. Brown, D. R., and Gray, G. R. (Summer 1991). Designing an appropriate AIDS policy. *Employment Relations Today, 18,* 149–155.

19. Labaton, S. (Dec. 5, 1989). The cost of drug abuse: $60 billion a year. *The New York Times,* B1, B30. See also: Matin, D. K. (1986). Privacy rights and drug testing. *Employment Relations Today, 13,* 253–268. Mendelson, S. R., and Libbin, A. E. (1988). The right to privacy at the workplace. *Personnel, 65,* 65–72. Like, S. K. (Winter 1990–1991). Employee drug testing. *Small Business Reports, 16*(3), 347–358. Lehman, W. E., and Simpson, D. D. (1992). Employee substance use and on-the-job behaviors. *Journal of Applied Psychology, 77,* 309–321.

20. American Management Association (1992). *The AMA handbook for developing employee assistance and counseling programs.* Washington, D.C.: AMA.

21. See note 19.

22. Green, W. (Nov. 21, 1984). Drug-testing becomes corporate mine field. *The Wall Street Journal,* p. B1.

23. Winslow, R. (Mar. 6, 1990). Will firms shift costs to smokers? *The Wall Street Journal,* pp. B1, B4. See also: Rundle, R. L. (Jan. 14, 1990). U-Haul puts high price on vices of its workers. *The Wall Street Journal,* pp. 1, B10. Coil, J. H. 3d, and Rice, C. M. (Autumn 1991). Smoker protection statutes: Fifteen states now protect smokers from discrimination based on their off-the-job tobacco use. *Employment Relations Today, 18,* 383–390.

24. Schein, D. D. (1987). Should employers restrict smoking in the workplace? *Labor Law Journal, 38,* 173–178. See also: Karr, A. R., and Gutfeld, R. (Jan. 16, 1992). OSHA inches toward limiting smoking. *The Wall Street Journal,* pp. B1, B7.

25. Stevens, W. K. (March 14, 1991). Study backs safety of video terminals. *The New York Times,* p. C21. See also: Sullivan, J. F. (Nov. 29, 1989). New Jersey acts on video terminals. *The New York Times,* p. Y13. Gettings, L., and Maddox, E. N. (1989). Overview: When health means wealth. *The Human Resources Yearbook,* Englewood Cliffs, NJ: Prentice-Hall, pp. 6.1–6.4. Author (June 1991). Group criticizes NIOSH VDT study [found no link between occupational use of video display terminals and miscarriage]. *Occupational Health and Safety, 60,* 10.

26. See note 3.

27. Beehr, T. A., and Newman, J. E. (1990). Job stress, employee health, and organizational effectiveness: A facet analysis, model and literature review. *Personnel Psychology, 31,* 665–699. See also: Ivancevich, J. M., and Ganster, D. C. (1987). *Job stress: From theory to suggestion.* New York: Haworth. Schaubroeck, J., Ganster, D. C., and Fox, M. L. (1992). Dispositional affect and work-related stress. *Journal of Applied Psychology, 77,* 322–335.

28. Matteson, M. T., Ivancevich, J. M., and Smith, S. V. (1984). Relation of type A behavior to performance and satisfaction among sales personnel. *Journal of Vocational Behavior, 25,* 203–214.

29. Chusmir, L., and Durand, D. (May 1987). Stress and the working woman. *Personnel,* pp. 38–43; see especially p. 41. See also: Author (May 1991). Survey pinpoints stress among working women. *Risk Management, 38,* 12.

30. Conference Board (1991). *Work schedules and productivity.* Atlanta: The Conference Board.

31. Modic, S. (Feb. 20, 1989). Surviving burnout: The malady of our age. *Industry Week,* pp. 28–34. See also: Ganster, D. C., and Schaubroeck, J. (1991). Work stress and employee health. *Journal of Management, 17,* 235–271.

32. Ganster, D. C., and Fusilier, M. R. (1989). Control in the workplace. In C. L. Cooper and I. T. Robertson (eds.), *International review of industrial and organizational psychology.* Chichester, England: Wiley, pp. 235–280.

33. Maslach, C., and Jackson, S. (1981). The measurement of experienced burnout. *Journal of Occupational Behavior, 2,* 99–113.

34. Russell, D. W., Altmaier, E., and Velzen, D. V. (1987). Job-related stress, social support, and burnout among

classroom teachers. *Journal of Applied Psychology, 72,* 269–274. See also: Cherniss, C. (1992). Long-term consequences of burnout: An exploratory study. *Journal of Organizational Behavior, 13,* 1–11.

35. Gaeta, E., Lynn, R., and Grey, L. (May–June 1982). AT&T looks at program evaluation. *EAP Digest,* pp. 22–31. See also: Freudenheim, M. (Nov. 13, 1989). More aid for addicts on the job. *The New York Times,* pp. 27, 39.

36. See note 25.

37. Health Insurance Association of America (1983). *Your guide to wellness at the worksite.* Washington, D.C.: Health Insurance Association of America, p. 3.

38. Wolfe, R. A., Ulrich, D. O., and Parker, D. F. (1987). Employee health management programs: Review, critique, and research agenda. *Journal of Management, 13,* 603–615. See also: Erfurt, J. C., Foote, A., and Heirich, M. A. (1992). The cost effectiveness of worksite wellness programs for hypertension control, weight loss, smoking cessation, and exercise. *Personnel Psychology, 45,* 5–27. Moore, T. L. (1991). Build wellness from an EAP base. *Personnel Journal, 70,* 104.

39. Hartman, S., and Cozzetto, J. (August 1984). Wellness in the workplace. *Personnel Administrator,* 117–125. See also: Erfurt, A. E., Dunham, R. B., and Heirich, M. A. (1992). The cost effectiveness of worksite wellness programs for hypertension control, weight loss, smoking cessation, and exercise. *Personnel Psychology, 45,* 5–28.

40. Greenfeld, S. (July 1989). *Management's safety and health imperative: Eight essential steps to improving the work environment.* Occasional Paper 2.9. Cincinnati, OH: Xavier University, Minerva Education Institute.

EXERCISE 16.1
THE DEVELOPMENT OF A COMPANY SMOKING POLICY

OVERVIEW

One of the most controversial health issues is smoking in the workplace. Smoking has been taken for granted in most work settings. Little consideration has been given to either (1) the effects of smoking on the health of both smokers and nonsmokers or (2) the potential cost to the organization. This is so even though smoking is a known cause of cancer, heart disease, and generally bad health. As discussed in Chapter 16, many states now have legislation mandating smoke-free work environments, while some states have taken steps to protect smokers' rights.

LEARNING OBJECTIVES

After completing this exercise, you should be able to:

1. Understand the interpersonal dynamics of policy development, particularly policy which significantly affects (and changes) the work environment.
2. Use negotiating skills in relation to your positions on a controversial matter which has no "correct answer."
3. Use your writing skills in attempting to assuage readers who may not be easily persuaded to agree with your positions.

PROCEDURE

Part A: Individual Analysis

Prior to class time: Read the scenario and respond as directed.

Part B: Group Analysis

In class: Assemble in groups and compare your developmental strategies. Attempt to reach consensus on the correct approach to take in the formulation of the policy. List all the variables which should be taken into consideration and all questions of clarification which must be answered. Either students will be paired off or each student should review all the other group members' reports and provide constructive suggestions for improving them. (The critiques should focus on the drafts rather than starting from scratch.) The feedback from the students should then be used in the preparation of a second letter. Each student group should select one edited letter which they consider to be the best.

The consensus-derived strategy should then be presented to the rest of the class and the selected letter should be read. Subsequent discussion should focus on the likely reactions of the major constituencies of the law firm and the overall impact of the new policy.

SCENARIO

You have been appointed to a committee charged with the development of a smoking policy for the clerical staff of a law firm. There are no laws or regulations which require the imposition of such a policy and there is currently no such policy in existence. However, several of the younger secretaries and some attorneys have complained about smoke in the work area, which is a large room (2000 square feet with average ventilation) housing 30 secretaries. Many of the law partners prefer to hire only nonsmokers in the future, and some take the position that current employees who smoke should be told that they must quit within 6 months or they will be terminated. Ten of the secretaries smoke, seven of whom have worked for the firm for over 10 years. Two of the seven have disabilities and have some difficulty getting around. Up to now, all employees have been free to smoke any time and any place they chose.

You have been asked to develop a strategy for the development of a policy and to recommend a policy as you see the situation. What steps should you follow in formulating a policy? Review your options, which range from taking no action whatsoever to imposing a strict ban on smoking for all employees either on or off the job. You have also been asked to take a position on a possible policy which specifies that new employees be nonsmokers and that current employees must stop smoking within 6 months. Assume that you have followed the steps of the developmental plan and are ready to draft a policy. Draft a short letter which explains the policy to the secretaries. What procedures should be followed to establish a firm policy? What action should be taken for those who choose to violate the policy? What (if any) additional data do you need in order to make a specific recommendation?

EXERCISE 16.2
THE DEVELOPMENT OF AN
ANTIDRUG POLICY*

OVERVIEW

As a result of the Drug-Free Workplace Act, which went into effect in 1989, all federal contractors are required to provide their employees with a drug-free workplace. The Drug-Free Workplace Act includes the following guidelines.

1. Furnish a policy statement prohibiting controlled substances in the workplace.
2. Notify employees (regular and contract) of the prohibition and the expected penalties of violating the policy.
3. Establish a drug-free awareness program.
4. Notify employees that conformance to the drug-free policy is a condition of employment.
5. Employees must notify the employer within 5 days if they are convicted of violating a criminal drug statute while in the workplace.
6. Contractor must notify the contracting agency of any such convictions.
7. For all employees convicted, the contractor must impose a sanction or require the completion of a substance-abuse treatment program.
8. Continue to make a good-faith effort to maintain a drug-free workplace.

LEARNING OBJECTIVES

After completing this exercise, you should be able to:

1. Consider implications of different policies regarding drug testing.
2. Understand the options available for deterrence of drug use and enforcement of an antidrug policy.

PROCEDURE

Part A: Individual Analysis

Prior to class, read the scenario and respond as directed.

*Contributed by Marilyn Perkins.

Part B: Group Analysis

In groups, each member should review the memos of all other members. Each group should attempt to reach consensus on a recommendation to the board. The recommendation must deal with all the issues raised above. Take a definitive position on random testing for all employees and on what specific steps should be taken if an employee tests positive.

SCENARIO

You are the manager of the HR department of a major federal contractor. One of your responsibilities includes implementing the drug-free workplace program mandated by the federal government. Your organization is responsible for conducting costly and sensitive research. The machinery used in the research is complex and could be dangerous if not used properly. Some of the experiments being conducted are risky and could pose a hazard to the environment or a threat to national security. However, not all employees work with the dangerous machinery or on the sensitive experiments.

As part of the drug-free workplace program, the position of the security department includes the following:

- Any employee with a substance-abuse problem should be reported to the security department, regardless of whether the substance abuse was detected by management or self-reported.
- Drug testing should be conducted for all individuals filling sensitive positions and randomly for the entire organization.
- All positive test results should be reported to the security department.
- All employees testing positive should be terminated.
- Any job applicant with a history of drug or alcohol abuse should not be hired.

The EAP representatives have reviewed the security department's position and disagree strongly with the proposed sanctions. In the EAP, 70 percent of the employees referred to employee counseling are self-referred. If the EAP is required to report the self-referrals to the security department, the EAP representatives argue, employees will not seek help from the EAP and will ultimately go untreated. The EAP representatives also contend that the termination sanction proposed by the security department is inhumane and may be in violation of the Rehabilitation Act of 1973, the ADA, or inalienable rights of privacy. One board member has stated that mass drug testing as proposed "makes a mockery of the presumption of innocence and strongly implies that someone who refuses to submit to a test is guilty. . . . the level of expectations of privacy is diminishing and we are slowly surrendering our dignity."

The board of directors has requested that you, as a task force member, develop a response to both the security department and the EAP representatives. Take into consideration the health and safety of the company as well as the rights of the employees. Consider the following: the Drug-Free Workplace Act, employees' right to privacy, the confidentiality of the drug-testing program, and access to the EAP. Prepare a 3-page memo to the board of directors in which you take a position on the matter. Be prepared to defend your position in group discussion.

EXERCISE 16.3
THE DEVELOPMENT OF A HEALTH
AND SAFETY POLICY

OVERVIEW

Chapter 16 discusses the renewed vigor with which OSHA is pursuing violations of the 1970 OSHA Act. The purpose of this exercise is to have you consider the implications of health and safety regulation for managerial activities.

LEARNING OBJECTIVES

After completing this exercise, you should be able to:

1. Understand the steps which should be taken pursuant to OSHA regulation.
2. Know the rights of employers and employees with regard to OSHA regulation.

PROCEDURE

Part A: Individual Analysis

Read the following scenario prior to class. You have been retained as a consultant to implement compliance with OSHA. As consultant, how would you approach the problem and what kind of advice and help would you give? Complete Form 16.3.1 and bring it to class.

Part B: Group Analysis

In class, groups should review the completed 16.3.1 forms of individual members and attempt to reach con-

sensus on all three aspects of the report. One group member should report the consensus recommendations to the rest of the class.

SCENARIO

Dynamic Duo, Inc., opened its manufacturing plant several months ago. Dynamic Duo, Inc., is owned and operated by two enterprising business students from Poedunk University in Poedunk, U.S.A. The company has 50 employees, most of whom work on the floor of the plant, handling the heavy equipment needed to manufacture widgets. One supervisor is in charge. Dynamic Duo, Inc., is concerned about safety, but the owners know nothing about OSHA.

Before you have a chance to advise Dynamic Duo, the plant is visited by a compliance officer who simply enters the plant and conducts a tour, unaccompanied by either management or employees. At the end of the tour, the compliance officer presents Dynamic Duo with a citation and a penalty. The Dynamic Duo owners call you in as consultant and ask you what they should do next.

Unfortunately for Dynamic Duo, Inc., soon after the compliance officer's visit, five employees are injured or become ill, all on the same day. One is seriously injured, having caught his hand in a conveyor. Another has become mysteriously ill, and three others have suffered minor cuts. The owners call you in again and ask you whether they need to inform anybody of the accidents and the illness, or to record them somehow.

FORM 16.3.1

Name _____ Group _____

1. What questions would you ask Dynamic Duo's owners?

2. What legal steps would you recommend that Dynamic Duo take?

3. What advice would you give the owners concerning the company's obligations under OSHA to record accidents?

MEASUREMENT ISSUES IN HUMAN RESOURCE MANAGEMENT*

*Contributed by Marcia J. Avedon.

OVERVIEW

A great deal of human resource management (HRM) describes the characteristics of people and the work they do. Managers are trying to measure attributes of different people, jobs, and organizations. In previous chapters, we have argued that better measurement makes for better HRM decisions and can contribute to competitive advantage. As we discussed in Chapters 2 and 3, better measurement can serve to increase organizational capability and to avoid (or prevail in) costly equal employment opportunity (EEO) litigation. With the passage of the 1991 Civil Rights Act and the 1990 Americans with Disabilities Act (ADA), the need for more precise measurement becomes all the more urgent.

The purpose of measurement is to derive quantitative data on people or work attributes. These data can then be used to make important decisions related to staffing, training, employee development, compensation, and other HRM decisions or programs. The use of better measurement in HRM parallels the need for precise measurement of other components of business such as finance, marketing, and operations management.

To create an effective measurement instrument, we must be clear on what we want to measure. If we administer a psychological test to job applicants, we want to be able to say that a specific applicant possesses more or less of some important attribute. For example, if I am trying to hire a salesperson, I might want to know whether an applicant possesses sufficient "aggressiveness" to be able to handle reluctant potential clients who may not be interested at first in purchasing electric belly button cleaners. I need a measuring device of some sort to measure "aggressiveness." I could select a published test which purports to measure the trait. I could ask questions in an employment interview which I feel would help me to assess aggressiveness. I could ask each applicant's former employers how aggressive he or she is. Thus, this discussion of measurement issues related to staffing does not apply just to paper-and-pencil tests. The purposes of measurement in HRM are the same regardless of the method used to collect the information. In addition to personnel selection applications, the measurement issues we explore in this appendix are relevant for other types of assessments of individual differences such as performance appraisals, attitude surveys, or management development assessments and training effects.

Issues regarding measurement do not apply only to the characteristics of people. We are also interested in measuring the characteristics of work itself, of the work output or performance of organizations, and of groups or units within organizations. Questions such as how valuable certain jobs are for an organization or how important certain tasks or activities are for productivity can be of major interest to HRM specialists. The measurement

of such variables through job analysis or job evaluation is vital for the usefulness of such information. As discussed in Chapter 11, a compensation system may be based on the results of a job analysis which rates the importance of various work tasks or activities, or a job evaluation which develops judgments on the relative worth of jobs. Several states and municipalities now set pay rates based on pay equity studies which attempt to determine the relative worth of jobs for organizational effectiveness. How relative worth is assessed is obviously a measurement issue.

The purpose of this appendix is to explore the major issues related to the measurement of HRM activities and to discuss their implications for improving HRM effectiveness. We will focus our attention on the reliability, validity, and utility of HRM measurement activities.

OBJECTIVES

After studying this appendix, you should be able to:

1. Understand the criteria for effective measurement.
2. Know the meaning of and relationships between reliability, validity, and utility.
3. Understand the procedures to be followed in the determination of each.

The management of Delmarva Power and Light Company, an electric utility in eastern Maryland, Delaware, and Virginia, recognized that technological changes and heightened competition required increased competency in their personnel. Therefore, management renegotiated with the unions for testing job applicants and for "progression" testing at specific intervals of employees' career paths. The agreement was that the progression tests were to be tied to pay increases according to length of service. For example, substation technicians after 2 years, 4 years, and 6 years of service needed to pass tests demonstrating their increased competence in order to receive pay increases. Also, the personnel were to participate in on-the-job and classroom training to develop the new competencies necessary for the jobs. After the union agreements were established to make it possible to increase the competence of personnel at Delmarva through training and testing, the programs had to be developed. This presented a series of important measurement tasks.

First, the competencies (i.e., the knowledges, skills, and abilities) that were critical to performing the jobs at each level in the career path had to be accurately described. Thus, the job analysis process was the first measurement task. The next measurement task was to construct job-relevant entry and progression tests. Next, the tests were to be validated to demonstrate that they actually predicted job performance or competence. Also, the new training and testing programs had to be evaluated for their effectiveness. The evaluation also involved measurement tasks.

The test batteries developed to select new hires were composed of both published and new written tests. The applicants for the substation technician job had to take a test battery that included tests of mechanical ability, ability to follow oral directions, reading comprehension, teamwork or cooperation, and basic math. The progression test batteries were all new tests of specific job knowledge and skills. The progression tests incuded both written and performance tests. For example, the substation technicians had to answer questions on the functions of circuit breakers, switches, and transformers and also to demonstrate their ability to detect live voltage on a piece of equipment, using the appropriate tools and safety precautions.

The tests resulted in scores that served to measure individuals' job competence. The scores are quantitative descriptions of peoples' strengths and weaknesses. How did Delmarva management know that the progression test scores really depicted substation technicians' competence to perform the job? The validation process provided this evidence. The test validation began when the tests were constructed according to the job analysis results. Then, evidence was collected by comparing employees' test scores to performance appraisal ratings by supervisors. This relationship between test scores and job performance for the entry-level test was an indication that the test predicted job performance.

The last aspect of the project was evaluation. After the new competency program had been in place for 18 months, the supervisors of the staff in the program completed surveys that measured the perceived effectiveness of the training and testing and identified needs for improving the program. Also, other measurements were collected for evaluation purposes, such as measures of agreement between examiners for the performance tests. These measures were very important to ensure that appropriate personnel decisions would be made. In this situation, one objective of the measurement strategy was that no matter who the examiner was, the substation technician performing the task of detecting whether there was live voltage would always get the same (or nearly the same) score.

THE PURPOSES OF MEASUREMENT IN HRM

Measurement has four general purposes in HRM:

1. **Description.** Measurement can be used to describe the characteristics or properties of a job, person, or organizational unit (i.e., to determine "what is happen-

ing"). For example, job analysis is used to describe the tasks, knowledge, skills, and other requirements of a job through various measurement techniques. As discussed in Chapter 4, job analysis data often serves as the foundation for HRM programs.

2. **Evaluation.** Measurement can be used to evaluate the outcome of an HRM program (i.e., to determine "what has happened"). For example, to evaluate the success of a new training program, I might want to measure trainees' satisfaction with the training or changes in their job performance as a result of training.

3. **Needs assessment.** Measurement can be used to assess HRM needs in an organization (i.e., to determine "what should happen"). For example, an employee opinion survey might be constructed to collect data on how to improve employees' satisfaction with aspects of their jobs and the organization.

4. **Prediction.** Measurement can be used to gather data to predict future outcomes. For example, applicants for jobs are often given employment tests, and the scores are used to predict the applicants' future job performance (as at Delmarva). The test data is used to measure attributes determined to be relevant for job success.

These four general purposes of measurement are not mutually exclusive in HRM programs. Actually, we often obtain measurements for several of these purposes. For instance, the employee opinion survey may be used to *describe* employees' current perceptions and levels of satisfaction, *evaluate* new programs, and *assess future* organizational *needs*. The competency program at Delmarva is an example that incorporated all four of these measurement purposes.

To accomplish any of these purposes, HRM measurement systems must possess certain characteristics. The most important of these characteristics are reliability, validity, and utility. One purpose of this appendix is to provide a primer on these critical measurement characteristics. We will discuss the relationships between reliability, validity, and utility, as well as methods available for their assessment. Let's start out with some working definitions.

Validity has to do with whether the scores on a measuring device truly represent what you intended them to represent. For example, were you truly measuring "aggressiveness" with a 20-item personality test you used? Were you truly measuring "job worth" with your job evaluation system? Is your instructor truly measuring your knowledge of the subject matter by virtue of the exams used in this class? Are you really measuring job performance with your performance appraisal system? Another useful definition of *validity* is the extent to which a measuring device achieves the aims of the user.

For example, validity may have to do with whether a personality test can predict on-the-job sales performance. For the job evaluation system, validity is the extent to which the system measures the job factors that are valued in the particular organization. The measurement system may have little validity for explaining and guiding compensation decisions in another organization. As one scholar put it, "One validates not a test, but an interpretation of data arising from a specified procedure.... Because every interpretation has its own degree of validity, one can never reach the simple conclusion that a particular test is valid."[1]

Reliability has to do with the consistency or reproducibility of what it is you are measuring.[2] Reliability is a necessary but insufficient condition for validity (i.e., a measuring device cannot be valid unless it is reliable). The opposite does not hold true. If I asked you to take a ruler and measure the space between your eyes and then divide this number by your shoe size, you could probably obtain almost the same result every time you performed the calculation (the score would be consistent or reliable). If I claimed, however, that this score was a measure of your intelligence, I would have entered the more important domain of validity. I would have to produce considerable evidence that my measuring technique was actually measuring intelligence. Validity is obviously a lot harder to demonstrate or establish than is reliability. It is harder to show that a measure "truly" represents what I said it represents or that it actually accomplishes what I want it to accomplish. Reliability and validity are distinctly different but nonetheless related. Remember, you cannot have a valid measuring device unless it is reliable.

Utility has to do with the extent to which a particular HRM program (e.g., selection or promotion tests, recruitment practice, training, compensation) is beneficial to an organization in terms of productivity and dollar value.[3] Obviously, for our personality test to improve sales productivity, it must be valid. However, there are other factors which affect the utility of a HRM program. For selection programs, the selection ratio (the number of people hired relative to the number who apply) becomes important. If every person who takes the test must be hired to be a salesperson, regardless of his or her test score (a selection ratio of 1.0), the test has no utility even if it has high validity and reliability. Another important factor in determining the utility of a HRM program is the cost of developing, implementing, and maintaining the program. This must be weighed against the benefits of the program versus its alternatives. We will discuss the relationships between validity, utility, cost, and the other factors associated with utility later in this appendix. Before exploring the interrelationships among these measurement characteristics, let's examine each of these concepts in more detail. We will begin with reliability since adequate reliability is the necessary condition—the one that must exist before we can achieve validity or utility.

RELIABILITY

Most of you are familiar with the Scholastic Aptitude Test (SAT) or the American College Test (ACT). Scores on one of these tests may have had something to do with your attendance at your college or university. You probably know people who claim that the score they obtained was much lower than their true level of ability or aptitude. (Have you ever had anyone tell you he or she scored higher than deserved?) You have undoubtedly heard stories of wild parties the night before the exam, or that the examination room was too hot (or cold), or that the student had a horrible cold the day the test was taken. While some of these explanations may be fabrications or rationalizations for scores which sound more like bowling averages, some are legitimate descriptions of the circumstances under which the test was taken. These circumstances are directly related to the reliability of a measurement procedure. To the extent that scores on some measuring devices vary widely as a consequence of such circumstances, it can be said that the procedure is unreliable. For the record, research shows that the SAT and ACT tests are highly reliable tests which reveal scores that do not generally fluctuate a great deal. (This does not mean, by the way, that different individuals' scores cannot vary widely—only that, in general, scores on the tests when taken twice by the same individual will not vary greatly.)

Remember that the purpose of measurement is to provide a numerical description in terms of the extent to which people (or jobs/organizations) possess some characteristic of interest. For example, universities are interested in the extent to which you possess the characteristics required for success as a student. However, one of the realities of measurement is that if the same test or procedure is administered to the same individual several times, that individual will not score the same each time. Of course, the score may change in some systematic fashion, as, for example, when you improve your skill or knowledge between administrations of the test. There are also random, unsystematic fluctuations. In general, scores on the better tests [like the SAT or the General Mental Ability Test (GMAT)] are less susceptible to this type of fluctuation.

When a measuring device is susceptible to random, unsystematic fluctuations, we have less faith in the interpretation of any one score on the device. When a measuring device is susceptible to random, unsystematic variation, that device is unreliable. Reliability, then, is the extent to which a measuring device is free of unsystematic, error variance. While there will always be some unreliability in a HRM measuring procedure, one of the critical goals in measurement is to obtain the highest level of reliability possible. Of course, this means the highest reliability possible within practical constraints. For example, longer tests are in general more reliable than shorter tests. [This, by the way, is why the SAT, the GRE, the GMAT, the LSAT, and most important tests are so long.] However, the administration and scoring of a 500-item test may be impractical. Instead, the test developer might use a 100-item test which can be completed in 1 hour. While the test developer knows that the decision to use a shorter test will probably lower the reliability of the scores somewhat, the time constraints for test administration dictate the shorter test. The goal in measurement should be to maximize reliability within the practical constraints of the situation.

A high correlation coefficient (.80 or higher) indicates strong agreement between two sets of scores. For example, if 200 people took the verbal part of the SAT twice, the two sets of scores could be correlated. To the extent that the people who scored high on the test the first time also scored high on the test the second time and the people who scored poorly on the test the first time also scored poorly the second time, the SAT would be considered reliable. (In actual studies of this nature, the reliability of the SAT exceeds .90, indicating strong agreement in the scores across two administrations.)

Perfect reliability is defined as a correlation of 1.0. Reliability will drop if, as in the examples presented above, there are random, uncorrelated errors in measurement. *Random* errors occur when people have bad days or when they skip a response on the computer scanning device, thereby rendering all of their subsequent answers incorrect. *Uncorrelated* means that the random factors which affected the scores by people on one administration did not also affect the scores by people on the second administration. For example, if a person is ill both times that he or she takes the test, the reliability of the test will not be affected (scores will be lower because of the illness, but the scores will be lower on both tests). The same argument applies if the circumstances of the test administration do not change. For example, if it were 22°C (72°F) in the room when you took the test the first time and 22°C (72°F) when you took it the second time, reliability would not be affected.

Reliability is important for HRM measurement because we are often trying to predict something with the measuring device. Just as the major purpose of the SAT is to predict success in college, employment tests are often used to predict who is going to be successful on the job. For example, the aggressiveness test was proposed because we thought it could predict who would sell the most electric belly button cleaners. If our measuring de-

vice cannot even yield a score which is reliable in the first place, what chance do we have of predicting anything with it? If scores by the same individual vary widely on two administrations of the "aggressiveness" test, what chance do we have to predict actual sales success by using the test? The test scores don't even correlate with themselves! Thus, the accuracy of our prediction from any measuring device is limited by the extent of reliability in the device. The principle is that reliability is a necessary but insufficient condition for validity.

Estimates of Reliability

There are several methods used for estimating reliability. Each of these methods considers different conditions which might result in changes in scores on a measuring device. The type of estimate to use depends on the particular circumstances in which the device is being used. Reliability will vary with the different estimates which are used. Ideally, however, a good measuring device should have high reliability regardless of the estimate of reliability which is used. There are three major types of reliability estimates: the test-retest method, equivalent or parallel forms, and internal consistency. Two other measures related to the concept of reliability are interrater reliability and the standard error of measurement (SEM). We will now discuss these important concepts.

TEST-RETEST RELIABILITY. The simplest method for estimating reliability is the test-retest method. With test-retest, reliability is obtained by administering the same form of the test to the same people on two different occasions. A test-retest estimate yields a *coefficient of stability*. The time interval between the two administrations of the device will affect the reliability estimate (in general, the longer the interval, the lower the reliability). Any circumstances or factors which affect performance on the test in one administration and not in the other can affect test reliability. For example, if the conditions for test administration vary, reliability can be affected. If, between test administrations, some of the test takers were exposed to training, experience, or learning which was relevant to the content of the test, its reliability would be lowered. Test-retest reliability is most appropriate when you are measuring the reliabilty of job performance ratings, personality tests, physical attributes (e.g., the 40-yard dash in football tryouts), and job knowledge tests in which the entire domain of knowledge is on the test. The appropriate time interval between measurements depends on the type of measurement. In general, the interval should be long enough so that the test taker cannot remember his or her responses on the first administration but short enough so that experience between administrations could not seriously affect the scores.

As with most estimates of reliability, the Pearson product-moment correlation is used to compute test-retest reliability, using the following formula:

$$r = \frac{N \sum XY - (\sum X)(\sum Y)}{\sqrt{[N \sum X^2 - (\sum X)^2][N \sum Y^2 - (\sum Y)^2]}}$$

where X are the scores on test 1 and Y are the scores on test 2.

In words, the formula asks you to perform the following operations on the data in order to compute the *numerator* portion of the formula: (1) Multiply each X score by its corresponding Y score. (2) Sum each of these products; then set this number aside and perform steps 3 to 5. (3) Sum each of the raw scores for both X and Y separately. (4) Multiply these two sums. (5) Divide the product by the number of paired observations N. (6) Subtract this quotient from the sum you computed in steps 1 and 2 above.

To compute the *denominator,* do the following: (7) Square each X value. (8) Sum these squared X values and set this number aside before performing steps 9 to 13. (9) Sum each of the X values. (10) Square this sum. (11) Divide this squared sum by the number of paired observations (N). (12) Subtract this quotient from the sum of squares you computed in steps 7 and 8. (13) Take the square root of this difference. Finally, perform the same operations (steps 7 to 13) for the Y values. Once you have done this, (14) multiply this value by the value you obtained for the X scores.

The final operation (15) requires you to divide the value you estimated for the numerator by the value you estimated for the denominator.

PARALLEL OR EQUIVALENT FORMS. Sometimes two different measuring devices are available which purport to measure the same thing. For example, I may have two different vocabulary tests which I constructed to be equivalent with respect to difficulty level and content. Using the same correlational analysis as with test-retest, I can calculate a *coefficient of equivalence.* A low correlation can be interpreted as an indication that the two measuring devices do not measure the same thing. For example, if I administered my two vocabulary tests to the same people and found a correlation of .40 between the two sets of scores, I could conclude that one (or both) of my tests was not doing a very good job of measuring vocabulary. As another example, two different multiple-choice exams could be written for this appendix and administered to the same group of students

two weeks apart. A low correlation between the two sets of scores might indicate that one of the exams was not representative of the possible questions I could have asked on the exam.

INTERNAL CONSISTENCY. The most common method for assessing reliability today yields a *coefficient of internal consistency.* The underlying theory of internal consistency is that a measuring device should be measuring consistently throughout the length of the instrument. For example, the first 10 items on an exam should measure the same attribute as the last 10 items. The basic rationale behind internal consistency is that you can subdivide the test and correlate scores on the various portions. If the correlations are high, your test is said to have good internal consistency. Thus, a person who got most of the answers correct on one part of the exam will also get most of the answers correct on other parts. Responses on the various items are thus intercorrelated.

One general rule with regard to reliability is: The longer the test, the more reliable the score. Since you have subdivided a test to derive a coefficient of internal consistency, a correction must be made because you "shortened" the test when you calculated the reliabilty.

The Spearman-Brown correction formula is available for making the correction to derive the estimate of reliability if it were calculated using the whole test. The Spearman-Brown formula is as follows:

$$rxx' = 2r_{xx/1 + r_{xx}}$$

(This version of the formula is used especially for split-half reliabilty estimates, where $rxx' = $ reliability for the total test and $rxx = $ the correlation between the scores on the two halves of the test.)

The most widely used methods for calculating internal consistency are the Kuder-Richardson reliability coefficient and the coefficient alpha. The Kuder-Richardson is used when there are correct answers on the test, as, for example, a job knowledge test. The coefficient alpha is used when there are no correct answers, as on an attitude survey. Both of these methods are now almost always calculated by a computer as part of an item analysis program used to evaluate the qualities of a measuring instrument. Both methods correlate responses on all possible pairs of items on the instrument.

INTERRATER RELIABILITY. A very common and important measure of reliability focuses on the evaluator rather than on the measuring device itself. For measurement systems which involve people in the evaluation or rating process, this estimate is critical. Interrater reliability is particularly important when you are using job evaluation ratings, performance appraisal data, or interview assessments. Of course, the ideal is consistent measurement across raters. In other words, when applicants are being interviewed for a job, it shouldn't matter by whom particular applicants are interviewed. The evaluation of an applicant's job potential should not vary with the evaluator. Unfortunately, as discussed in Chapter 7, it often does.

Interrater reliability is a measure of the extent to which scorers agree in their evaluations of the same people. An estimate can be derived by having a sample of ratees rated by two raters and then correlating the sets of scores. A low reliability estimate may indicate that one rater is evaluating people very differently than other evaluators. One way of increasing the reliability of a set of scores is to use a number of evaluators to make independent evaluations. A rating averaged across more than one evaluator tends to be more reliable than a rating from one evaluator. We discussed these issues at greater length in Chapters 7 and 10.

Our interpretation of the various estimates of reliability really depends on the purposes to be served by the scores. In general, more reliable measurement instruments are superior, but there is no minimum level of reliability which is acceptable. The most important principle with regard to the use of the scores is that reliability places a ceiling or lower bound on the validity of the device. Thus, if the reliability of a device is low, it is questionable whether the device will be valid for any important administrative purpose. In general, to the extent that scores have substantial administrative significance, reliability should be as high as possible. Critical decisions require highly reliable data. For example, methods used to promote people into or hire people for important positions within an organization should have high reliability (greater than .80). Unfortunately, personnel decisions are often based on unreliable data. While methods with lower reliability may still be useful, more errors in decision making will be made when the measuring device has lower reliability.

STANDARD ERROR OF MEASUREMENT. Reliability is also related to the faith we can place in any one score for a particular individual. Using the standard error of measurement, we can estimate the range of scores that could be expected from a person if there were repeated administrations of the same instrument. The *standard error of measurement,* which is indirectly related to the reliability of a device, can help to determine whether the differences in scores between two or more people are important. In general, the higher the reliability of a device, the more weight we can place on small differences in scores between individuals. The formula for the SEM is as follows:

$$SEM = \sigma_x \sqrt{1 - r_{xx}}$$

where σ_x is the standard deviation of the scores and r_{xx} is reliability. For example, let's say the reliability of a test on the material in this appendix was .80 and the standard deviation of the test scores was 4. The SEM for the test would thus be 1.79. If you had a score of 50 and another student had a score of 44, we could conclude that the difference in the two scores was important, reliable, and meaningful. If the other student's score was 48, a conclusion that your score was meaningfully different from the other student's would be much more questionable. (At least two SEMs between scores would provide more confidence in interpretation.)

VALIDITY

It is possible to develop measuring devices which approach perfect reliability. With perfect reliability, a test would give the same score for a test taker from one test administration to the next, day in and day out. While there are no actual HRM instruments which report reliabilities of 1.0, there are many instruments which report reliabilities of .90 and higher. However, what do measurements with this level of reliability really mean? Earlier we said that high reliability is very important and is a necessary but insufficient condition for validity. But we really don't known much about the validity of an instrument just because we know it has high reliability. Reliability only says that we have measured "something" consistently. It does not say that we have measured what we wanted to measure. This is the province of validity. The only thing we can know for sure with regard to reliability is that low reliability guarantees little or no validity.

As stated above, validity has to do with the inferences we draw from scores on some measuring device. Like reliability, more than one study or analysis can be conducted to determine the validity of an instrument. These analyses are part of the validation process. Three major strategies for validation are criterion-related, construct-related, and content-related analyses.[4] There are several methods within each of these strategies. However, underlying all of them are two investigative questions: (1) What do scores on the measuring device actually measure? (2) What do scores on the measuring device predict? Validity always concerns the extent to which the evidence we have accumulated supports the inferences that are made regarding scores on the device. It is the inferences which are validated. The same measuring device can thus have different validities depending on the purposes which the scores may serve. Getting back to our SAT example, the SAT Quantitative score has shown high validity in the prediction of college grade-point averages (GPAs) in engineering and scientific curricula. However, its validity in predicting GPAs in other majors is lower. The SAT Quantitative score has little validity if we are attempting to predict success in sales. Thus, the magnitude of the validity of the test or any other measuring device depends on the inferences we wish to make. These inferences are related to the variables or criteria we are attempting to predict. (The same argument applies to the verbal component of the SAT and numerous other subscales on these types of tests.) Validity must be considered in the context for which the data are collected. Let us now examine the three general strategies for validation.

Criterion-Related Validity

As with the SAT example, if we elect to pursue a criterion-related approach to validation, the obtained validity and the significance of the measurement device will differ as a consequence of the criteria selected. Criterion-related validation is the process by which we actually correlate scores on some measuring device or "predictor" (e.g., the SAT, our aggressiveness personality scale, an interview) with some criterion measure (e.g., college GPA, sales performance, supervisory ratings). The Pearson product-moment correlation coefficient is used to compute criterion-related validity—the same formula as presented above, with X as the predictor score and Y as the criterion score. In an employment setting, the most common criterion-related validation study involves a correlation between scores on an employment test and performance ratings by supervisors. A less common type of study relates scores on some measuring device to other important criteria such as sales, accidents, absenteeism, or employee turnover. All these approaches are criterion-related validation studies. Figure A.1 presents a list of the most common criteria of interest to HRM specialists.

Remember that validity is not an absolute but depends on the context or purpose for which the device is used and the inferences we wish to make. With criterion-related validation, we are testing the inference that our measuring device can predict some important criterion (e.g., one of those listed in Figure A.1). Thus, our main concern is with the relationship between scores on our measuring device and scores on some important criterion, not the content of the measuring device itself. The measuring device is valid to the extent that it can successfully predict or correlate with the criterion. The importance of the measuring device and its relative validity is directly relevant to the importance the organization attaches to the particular criteria under study. (See Chapters 10 and 13 for related discussions.)

The correlation coefficient can be used to reflect the relationship between some predictive device and some criterion. As with reliability, the higher the correlation,

FIGURE A.1
APPRAISALS OF ON-THE-JOB PERFORMANCE

Training performance. Either judgments by trainers or training test scores.

Objective performance data. Countable results such as numbers of customer complaints, objects produced, dollar value of sales, number of publications, home runs, etc.

Personnel data. Records of absenteeism, tardiness, accidents, salary or promotion history, special awards, tenure or turnover, employee theft.

Work samples. A specimen or sample of the job is developed to serve as a criterion for a validation study. The work sample may also be a part of the training program.

the stronger the relationship between the predictor and the criterion. In order to calculate criterion-related validity, scores are needed on both the predictor and the criterion for a large sample of people (at least 100 sets of scores for criterion-related validation). The sample of study participants should be representative of the population of people who will be assessed in the actual testing situation. In other words, if we were attempting to validate the aggressiveness measure we discussed earlier, we would need to correlate about 100 sets of scores on the aggressiveness test with a criterion measure such as sales volume. While such research can be done with fewer than 100 people, our faith in the conclusions we draw from the results is a direct function of the number of people in the sample. In general, studies involving smaller samples are more likely to obtain results with erroneous conclusions

The two different types of criterion-related validation studies are *predictive* and *concurrent*. The major distinctions between the two approaches are the sample of participants and the time the data are collected. With predictive validation, job applicants are measured on some device at one point in time and criterion data are collected at a later time. After time has passed, during which the study participants perform on the job (or in school), the criterion or performance data are collected. Scores on the measuring device are then correlated with the criterion measure. With concurrent validation, data are collected at approximately the same time the measurement is made. For example, a new test could be developed and administered to current employees. Scores on this test could then be correlated with performance data collected at the same time. With predictive validation, scores on some predictor are obtained from a sample of job applicants. Typically, some other method is used to make hiring decisions about the applicants. Ideally, scores on the device under study should not be known to anyone in the organization who is either making hiring decisions or providing the criterion data. Persons selected based on the other methods should then perform on the job for a period of time long enough to yield reliable criterion scores (e.g., performance appraisals, sales records, employee absences, turnover). The predictor data are then retrieved and the scores are correlated with the criterion measure. The strength of the relationship indicates the validity of the device for predicting the criterion.

An obvious question is why use predictive validation when concurrent validation can be completed with no time interval. The answer has to do with the objectives for the measuring device. If our intention with the device is to predict performance at some later point in time, predictive validation is the ideal strategy. If our measuring device is intended to describe a person's current state of knowledge or achievement rather than to predict subsequent performance, concurrent validation is an appropriate strategy. Thus, the difference can be illustrated with two questions: (1) *Concurrent design:* Can the person perform the job now? (2) *Predictive design:* Is the person capable of performing the job at a later date?

In addition to the need for large sample sizes in performing criterion-related validation, there are two other important considerations. First, the sample of study participants should be representative of the population of persons for whom the device is to be used. Thus, the sample should be composed of people who are approximately the same age; have the same socioeconomic background; and have the same level of verbal skills, education, and training. Second, the sample participants should have the same level of motivation as the future job applicants who may be taking the test. The ideal is to involve actual job applicants, who are asked to complete the device as if the scores were to be used in the actual personnel decision (e.g., whether they're hired or not). This condition is especially important when we are trying to validate devices on which there is an opportunity to distort or fake responses. For example, our aggressiveness personality scale may be transparent to the extent that a real job applicant could figure out how to respond in order to get a good score. If this test is validated on a sample of people who have no motivation to distort their responses (e.g., they already have the job), our validation results may say little or nothing about the ability of the instrument to predict some criterion when it is actually used to make decisions about people. Thus, for measuring devices which have the potential for being faked by people who are particularly motivated to obtain employment (or a promotion), it is critical that the validation study be conducted with a sample of employees who are similarly motivated. Thus, predictive validation is the best strategy whenever you are attempting to validate instruments which can be faked (e.g., personality tests, interest inventories, or attitudinal instruments). Research supports the use of a concurrent validity design when validating tests which cannot be faked, providing you can get study participants to perform as well as they possibly can. Cognitive ability tests, discussed in Chapter 6, such as the Wonderlic and the WAIS can thus be validated using a concurrent design.

Concurrent and predictive validity designs are not interchangeable. The selection of the appropriate design must be made in the context of the purposes for which the instrument is to be used, the type of instrument, whether job experience has a significant impact on instrument scores, and the similarity of study participants to the population of people for whom the instrument is being considered in the first place.

Several factors can affect the obtained validity coefficient in either type of criterion-related design. The characteristics of the criterion measure used and range restriction are two of the most important. Whether the criterion is performance appraisals, sales volume, employee tenure or turnover, absenteeism, or accident rates, assurances must be made that the measures derived are important and valid measures of effectiveness on the job and that the resultant scores are reliable assessments of the criterion. For example, it would be a mistake to use sales for a 1-week period as a criterion in a validation study since such a record of sales is probably not a reliable measure of sales volume (recall our discussion regarding the relationship between test length and reliability). The same principle holds here. We need a reliable measure of sales success, so we should increase the "test length" by collecting more sales data over a longer period of time. Similar arguments can be made for any of the other criteria which are used in these validations. In validating the SAT, for example, it would be preferable to use a GPA which is compiled over several semesters (or all 4 years) rather than just one semester. If we are relying on performance appraisal data as the criteria, it is preferable to use more than one rater and to collect ratings at more than one point in time (recall our discussion of interrater reliability). Sometimes we may want to know what the computed validity would be if we had a perfectly reliable set of criterion scores. The following formula is used to correct the validity coefficient for criteria unreliability:

$$r_{xy'} = \frac{r_{xy}}{\sqrt{r_{xy}}}$$

where $r_{xy'}$ is the estimate of true validity after correcting for unreliability, r_{xy} is the obtained validity, and r_{yy} is the estimate of reliability of the criterion measure. The corrected validity coefficient is often referred to as the "true validity" of the measurement device.

Range restriction has to do with the variability or distribution of scores on both the predictor and the criterion. Figure A.2 presents a scatterplot of test scores and criterion scores, with no restriction in the range of scores on either the predictor or the criterion.

FIGURE A.2
EFFECTS OF RANGE RESTRICTION
ON CORRELATION

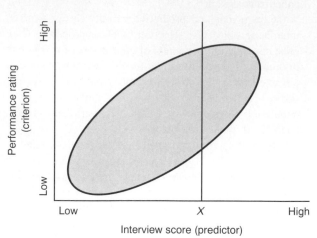

Source: W. F. Cascio. *Applied Psychology in personnel management.* 1991, p. 160. Reprinted by permission of Prentice-Hall, Englewood Cliffs, NJ.

Note that the relationship appears to be strong. But look at what would happen if we were to remove the portion of the scatterplot that is to the left of the line drawn perpendicular to the predictor line. If all the scores to the left of this line were eliminated from the validation study and only the scores to the right of the line were used in the validation, the correlation would be lower. This is range restriction. Range restriction can occur when the predictor you are trying to validate is actually used to make hiring decisions before you attempt to validate. Thus, people with the lower scores might not have criterion data because they were not hired. Range restriction can also occur on the criterion side whenever people are not included in the study because their performance on the criterion was so good or so bad that the organization took some action. For example, if the good performers are promoted and the poor performers are fired, the range of remaining performers will be restricted if there is no way that the data on the good and bad performers can be retrieved for the study.

Range restriction can be a big problem in concurrent validity designs. Fortunately, there are statistical corrections available for range restriction if certain data are available on the applicant population. Thus, the obtained validity coefficient can be corrected for range restriction to reveal a better estimate of the true validity of the measuring instrument.

Construct-Related Validity

The focus of a construct-related validation process is on the measuring instrument itself, that is, on the construct the instrument is actually measuring. The basic objective of construct validity is understanding rather than prediction. With construct validation, the meaning of the construct is defined and the manner in which the construct is related to other constructs is researched.[5] Construct validation involves a series of diverse studies, which should include criterion-related validation research. These studies test hypotheses about the construct which is proposed. Among the types of research done are: (1) a variety of reliability indexes, including internal consistency, (2) expert judgment regarding the content of the test, (3) correlations of the new device with other instruments hypothesized to be related (our new measure of "aggressiveness" should be related to other personality measures which purport to measure "dominance" or "aggressiveness"), (4) the ability of the instrument scores to predict actual behavior or behavior in an experimental context (e.g., people who score high on the aggressiveness measure are more likely to take control of a discussion group required to solve a problem), and (5) a variety of multivariate statistical analysis. Obviously, establishing construct validity cannot be accomplished in one study.

Construct validity is strengthened by the accrual of evidence (i.e., no single study is sufficient). The process of construct validation is often left to test developers who present the evidence in the test manual. The HRM specialist adopts the test for use based on the arguments presented for the construct validity of the device and also, often, on a job analysis which found this construct to be important for job performance. Tests which have been around a long time and subjected to numerous studies are best supported with this approach to validation rather than with a single criterion-related validity study, the results of which may have been affected by a number of factors unrelated to the true validity of the device. For example, as discussed in Chapter 6, the most popular personality tests such as the Minnesota Multiphasic Personality Instrument (MMPI) and the Sixteen Personality Factors Test (16PF) are supported by numerous studies which illustrate their construct validity. The responsibility of the HRM specialist is to develop a rationale to justify the use of the instrument in a particular setting.

There may be times when the HRM specialist would need to collect validity evidence for a measurement instrument based on a construct validation approach. For example, if a new job evaluation system were developed, I might want to examine the relationship between scores on the new system and other job evaluation systems from similar organizations to see if the "job worth" construct was statistically related using the various instruments. As another example, if a HRM specialist developed a job knowledge test for entry into accounting jobs, construct validity evidence might include the correlation between applicants' test scores, their GPAs in accounting courses, and their years of relevant experience in accounting. The HRM specialist would be trying to demonstrate that the new test related to other measures of knowledge of accounting, the construct of interest.

Content-Related Validity

Content-related validity is the most common type of validation invoked when an organization ends up in court and the validity or job relatedness of some selection or promotional device is contested. Content validity concerns the extent to which the content of a measurement device includes a representative sample of the population of content or situations the device is attempting to measure. Content validity exists when the content of the measuring device is representative of the content in the actual job. The focus is on the adequacy of the sampling of the contents of the device. The judgment of adequacy can be based on a systematic assessment of the contents of the device. Content validity is used in achievement testing when a population of potential areas for testing is defined and a strategy for sampling from this population is presented. Subject matter experts (SMEs) are often used in a content validation strategy. The SMEs may be asked to judge the extent to which a particular content area, or even a particular test item, is related to successful job performance. For example, SMEs for the job of firefighter may be asked to indicate to what extent knowledge of various chemical reactions to fire is related to success as a firefighter. If enough SMEs indicate that such knowledge is critical for successful job performance, then the relevant test questions are said to be content-valid. A quantitative job analysis can be very helpful in the establishment of content validity for a measuring device (see Chapter 4).

As an example, assume we are interested in developing a test to be used to select a HRM specialist. We conduct a job analysis and determine that the major requirements of the job are as follows:

1. Ability to develop employee opinion surveys (critically important)
2. Ability to administer and score employee opinion surveys (critically important)
3. Ability to direct testing and validation studies (critically important)
4. Ability to develop methods for psychological assessments of managerial personnel (important)

If we wanted to develop a content-valid measuring device to be used in the hiring of this person, we would write test items which would assess knowledge in these critical areas of responsibility. To the extent that the test-item content could be linked to the results of the job analysis in terms of importance, knowledge, skills, and abilities, the argument for the content validity of the test would be stronger.

The appropriateness of a content-validity approach to validation depends mainly upon the job content being assessed. Providing that the job involves very specific tasks (e.g., typing, developing tests) or knowledge, and providing that there is general agreement on how to score performance on the tasks or the test items, there will be little argument with the opinion of the experts in their assessment. When job performance involves more abstract constructs such as leadership or aggressiveness, the appropriateness of the content validity approach to validation can be seriously questioned.

Validity Generalization

Criterion-related validity was long believed to be "situation-specific." That is, if a test was developed and validated in one setting, its validity did not generalize to another seemingly similar setting for the same job. For example, if a test was developed and validated for the selection of police officers in one city using a criterion-related validation strategy, the obtained validity coefficient did not apply to police officer selection in other cities. The validity was said to be *situation-specific.* Differences in obtained validity coefficients for what appeared to be similar types of jobs and settings were thought to be due to subtle differences in the specific tasks or behaviors to be performed in these various settings. Considerable recent research disputes the notion of situation specificity.[6] It is now clear that a great many of the fluctuations obtained across studies were simply a consequence of the way the studies were conducted and, in particular, the small sample sizes used in most of the studies. Recall that it was recommended that at least 100 subjects be used in a criterion-related validity study. In fact, most of the older validity studies involved fewer than 50 participants. Sampling error alone accounted for most of the fluctuations in the obtained validity coefficients. When the criterion-related validities which were compiled across settings are corrected for sampling error, the corrected validities do not differ substantially. Thus, validities tend to generalize across settings. Since there have been thousands of validity studies, it is possible to derive an estimate of validity in a particular setting without conducting another criterion-related validity study. This is a critical and controversial conclusion, particularly with respect to the potential legal ramifications for the use of testing to make personnel decisions.

UTILITY

We mentioned earlier that the utility of any measuring device is dependent on the validity of that device. But utility depends on other factors as well. Recall that utility is the extent to which a measuring device or HRM program improves the quality of the workforce in a cost-effective manner. Utility addresses the critical issue of "productivity improvement," using estimates of the dollars to be saved or gained if the measuring device or HRM program were to be used.[7] If we define *utility* as increase in productivity in dollar terms,[8] utility generally is a function of quantity (i.e., the number of people involved and the length of time they are affected, quality (i.e., the validity or effect size, the variability in performance, and the average score of those selected in a hiring situation), and cost. So, utility = quality × quantity − cost. Utility formulas can be used to estimate the dollar value of selection instruments and other HRM interventions.

The formulas are slightly different for selection and nonselection programs, but they both indicate the net result, or "payoff." Let's go over the components of each of the two formulas. For selection programs, the general utility formula is:

Utility = quantity × quality − cost

$$\text{Utility} = [(N)(T)] \times [(r_{xy/\text{true}})(\text{SD}_y)(Z)] - N(C)$$

where N = the number of employees selected per year, T = the average tenure of employees, rxy/true = the corrected validity coefficient, SD_y = the standard deviation of job performance in dollar terms, Z = the average standardized score on the test for those selected, C = the cost of testing one employee, and N = the total number of persons tested. Notice that the validity coefficient is included in our utility estimate and that, since it is "true" validity, reliability is also considered.

Research has demonstrated that the standard deviation of job performance (SD_y) can be conservatively estimated at 40 percent of the annual salary for a job.[9] This is a major research finding because it allows HRM specialists to speak to business managers and executives in terms of financial data. This finding permits HRM programs to be compared to other business initiatives (e.g., marketing efforts), in which costs and benefits are easily quantified in dollar terms.

For other types of HRM programs aimed at productivity improvement (e.g., reward or incentive programs, training, recruiting efforts) the general utility formula is:

Utility = quantity × quality − cost

$$\text{Utility} = [(N)(T)] \times [(d_{\text{true}})(\text{SD}_y)] - N(C)$$

where the symbols have the same meanings as above and (d_{true}) = the true effect size or difference in performance between the group in the program and a matched group not in the program after correction for criterion unreliability.

Another useful formula indicates the minimum benefits required over the length of time the program has an effect. For a selection program, the length of time is the average tenure of the employees. This formula tells us the minimum utility needed for the program to be cost-effective. Therefore, in planning HRM programs, the expected utility or payoff can be compared to this minimum or break-even value. The formula is:

$$B \geq C_T(1 + R)^T$$

where B = benefits, C_T = total cost of the program (cost per employee × number of employees involved), R = cost of capital, and T = length of effect or average tenure. Thus, this formula can be used to justify a new HRM program by indicating how much the program will "pay back" in benefits.

When the utility formula was first applied to a valid test used to select computer programmers, the researchers found an average gain of $6679 in productivity per year for each new programmer hired with the test.[10] Assuming that the average programmer works almost 10 years, this is a gain of over $64,000 per programmer. Obviously, valid selection devices and other HRM programs can have great utility to an organization. In order to maximize utility for personnel selection, organizations have to be selective in their hiring decisions. They must also be capable of hiring those people who scored the best on the test. Thus, while valid tests are certainly necessary, the organization must attract and hire people who have the greatest potential for high performance on the job. Organizations should strive to use the most valid tests while at the same time recruiting as many potentially eligible job candidates as possible.

SUMMARY

Organizations spend a great deal of time measuring people and work attributes. Through myriad devices and methods, they measure aptitudes, abilities, knowledge, personality, interests, attitudes, preferences, suitability or promotability, job importance or worth, task importance and frequency, job performance, absences, employee behaviors, and a number of other important variables. Reliability, validity, and utility are critical for all these measurements. HRM specialists and practicing managers should strive to ensure a maximally feasible level of reliability and validity for all its methods. Also, utility estimates should be used to evaluate and justify personnel measurement instruments and other types of HRM programs. The more reliable and valid the measurement devices or HRM programs, the more useful they are for organizational decision making. The selection of appropriate type or types of reliability, validity, and utility to use depends on the particular circumstances and the purposes for which the measurement device or program has been developed.

DISCUSSION QUESTIONS

1. If you were the director of staffing for a major corporation and you were reviewing published tests to be used in the selection of entry-level professionals in your organization, what questions would you ask about the tests and why? What data or evidence would you want to examine?
2. What is the interrelationship between validity and reliability? Can you have validity without reliability, or vice versa?
3. How are validity and reliability related to utility? Can you have utility without validity? Can you have utility without reliability?
4. What are the different strategies for validation? When would each be best utilized?
5. How would you evaluate a validation or utility study in the context of an ultimate criterion related to customer requirements?

NOTES

1. Cronbach, L. J. (1971). Test validation. In F. L. Thorndike (ed.), *Educational Measurement*. Washington, DC: American Council on Education, p. 445. See also: Ghiselli, E. E., Campbell, J. P., and Zedeck, S. (1981). *Measurement theory for the behavioral sciences*. San Francisco: W. H. Freeman. Green, B. F. (1981). A primer of testing. *American Psychologist, 16*, 1001–1011. Stine, W. W. (1989). Meaningful inference: The role of measurement in statistics. *Psychological Bulletin, 105*, 147–155. Cronbach, L. J. (1989). Construct validation after thirty years. In R. Linn (ed.), *Intelligence*. Urbana, IL: University of Illinois Press, pp. 147–171.
2. Feldt, L. S., and Brennan, R. L. (1989). Reliability. In R. L. Linn (ed.), *Educational measurement*. New York: Macmillan, pp. 105–146.
3. Becker, B. E. (1989). The influence of labor markets on human resource utility estimates. *Personnel Psychology, 42*, 531–546. Bobko, P., Karren, R., and Kerkar, S. P. (1987). Systematic research needs for understanding supervisory-based estimates of SD_y in utility analysis. *Organizational Behavior and Human Decision Processes, 40*, 69–95. Raju, N. S., Burke, M. J., and Normand, J. (1990). A new approach for utility analysis. *Journal of Applied Psychology, 75*, 3–12. Rich, J. R., and Boudreau, J. W. (1987). The effects of variability and risk in selection utility analysis: An empirical comparison. *Personnel Psychology, 40*, 55–84.
4. American Educational Research Association, American Psychological Association, and National Council on Measurement in Education (1985). *Standards for education and psychological testing*. Washington, DC: American Psychological Association. See also: Binning, J. F., and Barrett, C. V. (1989). Validity of personnel decisions: A conceptual analysis of the inferential and evidential bases. *Journal of Applied Psychology, 76*, 478–494. Gatewood, R. D., and Feild, H. S. (1990). *Human Resource Selection*. Chicago, IL: Dryden Press. Sussman, M., and Robertson, D. U. (1986). The validity of validity: An analysis of validation study designs. *Journal of Applied Psychology, 71*, 461–468. Wainer, H., and Braun, H. I. (eds.) (1988). *Test validity*. Hillsdale, NJ: Lawrence Erlbaum.
5. Bollen, K., and Lennox, R. (1991). Conventional wisdom as measurement: A structural equation perspective. *Psychological Bulletin, 110*, 305–314. See also: Austin, J. T., Villanova, P., Kane, J. S., and Bernardin, H. J. (1991). Construct validation of performance measures: Issues, development, and evaluators of indicators. In G. R. Ferris and K. M. Rowland (eds.), *Research in personnel and human resources management*. Greenwich, CT: JAI Press, pp. 159–233.
6. Burke, M. J. (1984). Validity generalization: A review and critique of the correlation model. *Personnel Psychology, 37*, 93–113. James, L. R., Demaree, R. G., and Mulaik, S. A. (1986). A note on validity generalization procedures. *Journal of Applied Psychology, 71*, 440–450. Schmidt, F. L., Hunter, J. E., and Raju, N. S. (1988). Validity generalization and situational specificity: A second look at the 75% rule and Fisher's z transformation. *Journal of Applied Psychology, 73*, 665–672. Osburn, H. G., and Callender, J. (1992). A note on the sampling variance of the mean uncorrected correlation in meta-analysis and validity generalization. *Journal of Applied Psychology, 77*, 115–122.
7. Cascio, W. F. (1991). *Costing human resources*. Boston, MA: Kent-PWS.
8. Steffy, B. D., and Maurer, S. D. (1988). Conceptualizing and measuring the economic effectiveness of human resource activities. *Academy of Management Review, 13*, 271–286. Vance, R. J., and Colella, A. (1990). The utility of utility analysis. *Human Performance, 3*, 123–139.
9. Hunter, J. E., and Schmidt, F. L. (1982). Fitting people to jobs: The impact of personnel selection on national productivity. In M. D. Dunnette and E. A. Fleishman (eds.), *Human performance and productivity*, vol. 2: *Human capability assessment*. Hillsdale, NJ: Lawrence Erlbaum. See also: Schmidt, F. L. (1988). The problem of group differences in ability test scores in employment selection. *Journal of Vocational Behavior, 33*, 272–292. Becker, B. E., and Huselid, M. A. (1992). Direct estimates of SD_y and the implications for utility analysis. *Journal of Applied Psychology, 77*, 227–233. Judiesch, M. K., Schmidt, F. L., and Mount, M. (1992). Estimates of the dollar value of employee output in utility analysis: An empirical test of two theories. *Journal of Applied Psychology, 77*, 234–250.
10. Schmidt, F. L., Hunter, J. E., McKenzie, R., and Muldrow, T. (1979). The impact of valid selection procedures on workforce productivity. *Journal of Applied Psychology, 64*, 609–626. See also: Guion, R. M., and Gibson, W. M. (1988). Personnel selection and placement. *Annual Review of Psychology, 39*, 349–374.

EXERCISE A.1
THE CALCULATION AND INTERPRETATION OF RELIABILITY AND VALIDITY ESTIMATES*

OVERVIEW

A variety of tests are used by organizations to facilitate personnel decisions. Interviews and performance ratings as well as the more traditional paper-and-pencil selection tests are used by organizations, with varying degrees of success. Recall from Chapter 6 that the process of test validation has less to do with the test itself than with the inferences drawn on the basis of the test scores. That is, in use of test results to make personnel decisions, what is at issue is the proper use of tests in relation to decisions to hire, promote, provide training for, or terminate employees.

The purpose of this exercise is to increase students' awareness of measurement issues in the area of personnel management by providing them with a scenario of test-based decision making in a hypothetical organization. The exercise asks you to play the role of consultant to a large company that has had limited experience in using tests for personnel decision making. Aware of the potential for misuse of test results, the company has asked you, as an outside consultant, to troubleshoot its personnel testing and performance appraisal programs in order to reduce the likelihood of culpability should the company face litigation over its hiring practices.

LEARNING OBJECTIVES

After completing this exercise, you should be able to:

1. Employ the major concepts related to effective measurement.
2. Derive estimates of test reliability and validity, and to demonstrate competence in understanding the procedures to be followed in the determination of both.
3. Demonstrate mastery of legal and technical issues involved in test-based personnel decisions.

PROCEDURE

Part A: Individual Analysis

Prior to class, review the scenario presented below and answer the questions on Form A.1.1. Bring all your statistical work to class along with Form A.1.1.

*Contributed by T. R. Biddle and Peter Villanova.

Part B: Group Analysis

In groups of about six, all members should review one another's responses and reach consensus on the correct answers. Each group should prepare a 3-minute presentation summarizing its position on item 8 of Form A.1.1. The instructor will appoint the presenter for each group.

SCENARIO

For over 40 years, ABC Manufacturing had been a small regional provider of letter-shaped noodles to canned soup makers. All this changed about 5 years ago when the ABC board of directors decided to expand the variety of noodle shapes it would produce and market. Once limited to shaping noodles into small stars and the first three letters of the alphabet, the company now produces noodles to represent the entire alphabet and a large number of other shapes and symbols (e.g., ampersands, question marks, and Greek letters).

Because of a recent agreement with a large canned soup maker to produce alphabet-shaped noodles for its alphabet soup, ABC needed to hire 50 new employees to operate the noodle-pressing machines. At ABC, each of these workers would possess the job title of "noodle-press operator." Noodle-press operators use noodle-pressing machines to cut large, thin slabs of soft pasta into specified shapes. As each slab of pasta arrives at a workstation, a noodle-press operator carefully aligns and levels the slab so that it lies flat and centered on the noodle-press board. The noodle-press operator then selects and mounts the noodle-press stencil that conforms to the customer's specifications (e.g., the stencil determines noodle shape, thickness, and size). Then the noodle-press operator pulls a handle that lowers the noodle-press stencil onto the soft pasta slab. Once the slab is cut, the noodle-press operator carefully lifts up the slab at one end, thus freeing the cut noodle shapes from the pasta slab. The cut noodle shapes are placed on a conveyor and transported to the drying and packaging area. The remaining portion of the slab is placed in a bin to be reprocessed. The job requires good eye-hand coordination, the ability to follow precise work orders to ensure that the pasta is handled hygienically, and the ability to operate the noodle press in such a manner that as little as possible of the pasta slab is returned for reprocessing.

Mr. Ydobon, ABC's personnel officer, had been conducting interviews and administering the Wonderlic Personnel Test (see Chapter 6) to applicants for a month and was about to begin hiring. Mr. Redael, company president, was pleased with the progress Mr. Ydobon was making, since it was important that the new employees be hired in a timely manner in order to meet production deadlines.

Unfortunately, Mr. Ydobon left the company suddenly after he administered the Wonderlic and interviewed the job applicants. As a consequence, Mr. Redael was faced with the responsibility for making the hiring decisions. Compounding this problem was the fact that neither the records of Mr. Ydobon's interviews nor the test results could be found. Mr. Redael decided to call all the applicants in for a "second interview." It later occurred to Mr. Redael that he knew little about fair employment practices and was not sure how wise it would be for him to select workers on the basis of the ratings he made during the second interview. Therefore, he felt the safest thing to do was hire the first 50 people who applied for the job. He was confident that this would ensure legal protection for his employment practice, and besides, he needed 50 workers immediately to fulfill the orders of the new customer.

Several months later, and shortly after the second performance appraisal for the new employees, the records of the test scores and original interviews were found in an unmarked box in the stockroom. Because he is unfamiliar with the Wonderlic and the entire personnel selection process, Mr. Redael has called you in as an outside consultant to ABC's personnel department. You have compiled the raw data summary shown in Exhibit A.1.1. You decide to do a validity study with the available data.

EXHIBIT A.1.1
RAW DATA FROM THE FILES OF ABC MANUFACTURING

S	R	Y	r	W	A	B		S	R	Y	r	W	A	B		S	R	Y	r	W	A	B		S	R	Y	r	W	A	B
1	2	4	6	28	6	6		0	1	5	3	31	5	4		1	1	3	6	29	5	5		0	1	3	4	29	4	5
0	1	4	6	33	6	5		1	1	5	6	34	6	6		0	1	4	6	30	5	6		0	2	3	5	23	4	4
0	2	3	4	27	5	5		0	1	3	5	35	5	6		1	1	5	5	33	7	7		0	2	3	3	28	6	4
1	2	5	5	30	5	6		1	1	5	7	31	5	7		0	1	5	5	27	4	4		1	1	6	6	26	5	5
0	2	6	4	21	4	6		1	1	5	5	25	6	6		1	2	6	6	24	6	4		1	1	6	5	28	5	5
1	1	5	5	31	5	7		1	1	4	4	29	5	5		0	1	3	4	28	4	4		0	1	6	2	33	5	5
1	2	5	6	22	7	6		1	2	3	5	28	5	6		1	1	2	7	26	6	5		1	2	4	4	28	5	5
1	2	4	4	32	5	5		1	1	4	5	31	6	7		1	1	5	5	33	7	7		1	2	3	4	32	5	4
1	1	5	6	31	6	6		1	1	3	7	33	4	5		1	1	5	6	34	6	7		0	1	6	4	30	5	5
0	2	2	6	23	4	5		0	1	6	3	31	4	3		0	2	2	4	25	5	4		0	1	6	5	35	6	6
1	2	3	7	30	5	5		0	2	4	4	29	6	6		1	2	4	6	28	6	6		0	2	5	5	30	3	3
0	1	6	3	30	5	4		1	1	3	4	31	7	5		0	1	2	5	27	4	4		1	1	3	7	28	5	5
1	1	3	6	30	5	5		1	1	5	4	33	6	7																

S = sex, 0 = female, and 1 = male; R = race, 1 = white, and 2 = nonwhite;
Y = Ydobon's interview rating; r = Redael's interview rating (interview ratings are judgments of potentiality on a scale from 1 to 7 with "7" indicating "the highest potential");
W = score on the Wonderlic; A = the first performance appraisal rating; B = the second performance appraisal rating (ratings on a 1 to 7 scale with "7" indicating "highly effective" performance).

FORM A.1.1

Name _____ Group _____

1. What is the validity of the interview ratings? What data did you use to determine validity?

2. What is the validity of the Wonderlic? What was used in your analysis?

3. Would you suggest averaging the ratings of more than one interviewer? Explain why or why not. Then compute, using the formula given in Appendix A, the correlation between the average of the two interview ratings and the averaged performance ratings to determine whether your contention is supported by the data.

4. Mr. Redael wants to know the level of reliability for the Wonderlic. You inform him of the .76 correlation you have computed between the odd- and even-numbered items on the test, and add that with statistical correction, the reliability will be even higher. Compute the corrected reliability estimate and write a brief explanation of why the correction should be applied.

5. Often the criteria organizations employ to evaluate the work performance of employees are characterized by relatively low reliability. Explain how unreliability among performance ratings adversely affects the observed validity of a predictor. Also, compute the correlation between the two performance ratings. What type of reliability or validity does such a calculation represent?

Name_____ Group _____

6. Using the correction formula, estimate the validity of the Wonderlic, assuming a perfectly reliable set of performance ratings.

7. Based on an analysis of the information you have on the noodle-press operator job, what predictors should be used in the future for hiring purposes?

8. Should ABC continue use of the Wonderlic for employee selection? What arguments can be made for and against such use in the context of the Civil Rights Act of 1991 and the ADA?

9. Given that any test used to select employees is likely to result in some decision errors (i.e., some employees who would be predicted to fail actually succeed, and vice versa), is it fair to applicants to use a fallible predictor to make such decisions? That is, should we do away with all employment tests that do not have perfect predictive accuracy? What is the fairest solution to this dilemma for both applicants and employers?

10. What specific changes would you make to the validation study to increase your confidence in the results?

11. What information do you need to assess the relative utility of the Wonderlic versus the interview?

EXERCISE A.2
HUMAN RESOURCE DECISION-MAKING EXERCISE*

OVERVIEW

Organizational decision makers often require justification and a rationale for HRM programs. HR managers must be able to explain and defend how their programs fit into the overall organizational strategy and goals. Also, the bottom-line impact of such programs on important organizational outcomes must be projected and demonstrated. Measurement methods provide information to justify the value of HRM programs and to assist in organizational decision making.

The purpose of this exercise is to provide you with a scenario that requires you first to compare the attributes of three HRM programs and then to recommend a decision based on measurement information. The exercise requires you to play the role of director of HR for a large company and to analyze data to justify your recommendations to the chief executive officer (CEO) and the board of directors.

LEARNING OBJECTIVES

After completing this exercise, you should be able to:

1. Evaluate empirical data on various types of HRM programs.
2. Compute estimates of true effect size or true validity of HRM programs and demonstrate understanding of these concepts.
3. Apply the major concepts and basic formulas in utility analysis.
4. Make HRM decisions based on various attributes and analyses of programs.

PROCEDURE

A: Individual Analysis

Prior to class, read the scenario below and answer all questions on Form A.2.1. Bring all your statistical work to class, along with the completed Form A.2.1.

---

*Contributed by Marcia J. Avedon.

B: Group Analysis

Working in groups of about six people, members should compare their answers and derive a group response to each question on Form A.2.1. Your instructor will provide you with a group response sheet.

SCENARIO

BuyWise Groceries has been a major national grocery chain for 25 years. For most of the last 20 years, BuyWise was the leader in the Northeast, Middle Atlantic, and Southeast regions of the United States. In the rest of the nation, the company's position in the market fluctuated within the top five major grocery chains. However, during the last 3 years, the company's stronghold in the eastern United States has declined to second in the industry and another competitor has been gaining some of the BuyWise market share.

The BuyWise board of directors decided 1 year ago that a major factor associated with this decline in market share was the performance of the store managers, particularly in the eastern regions. The board of directors and the CEO, Pat Williams, directed you, the BuyWise director of HR, to hire a consultant to:

1. Conduct a job analysis of the store manager positions.
2. Propose three HRM programs designed to improve the store managers' performance.
3. Conduct a pilot test of the three programs.

The consultant's study was to take 1 year. On the basis of the results of the study and knowing what you did about measurement information in HRM decision making, you were instructed to provide recommendations to the board and to Pat Williams regarding three new programs for improving store managers' performance.

You knew the consultant must have empirical results demonstrating the validity, reliability, and cost effectiveness of the programs. Also, you wanted to be sure that other practical considerations were addressed. After careful review of various consultants' proposals, you selected the Effectiveness Inc. consulting firm to conduct the study.

In brief, the methodology utilized by Effectiveness Inc. included:

1. **Conducting a job analysis of the BuyWise store manager positions across the country.**
2. **Developing a criterion measure for assessing the performance of the store managers.** This was a

composite measure of performance ratings and quantitative financial measures (e.g., sales and profit).

3. **Proposing three new HR interventions:**
   a. A test, the Management Ability Indicator (MAI), designed and validated for BuyWise with a con-current criterion-related design for selecting new store managers by predicting performance
   b. An incentive compensation system that more di-rectly links store managers' salary to their stores' financial performance
   c. A management training program focused on merchandising, financial management, and per-sonnel management

4. **Pilot testing each of the three programs.** A sample of 300 current store managers took the MAI for the pilot test. The incentive compensation pro-gram and the management training program were each pilot-tested in five stores. The stores were matched on a number of key characteristics such as tenure of the manager, financial history of the store, and region. Also, comparison stores were selected and matched to the other stores in order to see how the new compensation and training programs compared to the existing programs at BuyWise. Performance information was collected on all store managers in the pilot test.

5. **Presenting a report with the results of the study, including the measured effects of the new pro-grams on the store managers' performance.**

Exhibit A.2.1 summarizes the results of the study by Ef fectiveness Inc.

For each of the three proposed programs, Effective-ness Inc. computed the *effect size or validity*. For the incentive compensation and management training pro-grams, the effect size was computed to demonstrate the average difference in job performance between store managers who were in the program and the matched group of store managers who were not in the program. The Ef-fectiveness Inc. consultants correlated the test scores of the store managers on the MAI with the job performance measures (i.e., the criteria) in order to get the validity co-efficient r_{xy}.

Effectiveness Inc. computed the *reliability of the criterion*—that is, the estimate of the accuracy of the performance measurement, or how much error there is in the estimates. The computed reliability was .90. The symbol for reliability is r_{yy}.

Also, as part of the study, the average *cost per em-ployee* was computed for each of the programs. This es-timate included both the one-time costs of development and the per-administration costs (e.g., printing and scor-ing the MAI, printing training materials, etc.). The *num-ber of employees* who could reasonably be included in each program per year was estimated. For the MAI this was the number of new store managers to be hired, in-cluding new hires and promotions from lower levels. All 500 store managers could be included in the incentive compensation program, but it was projected that only 200 of these managers could be trained in 1 year.

Other data, such as the *average annual salaries* of new and existing store managers, the estimated *length of the effect* of the program, the *corporate interest rate,* and the average MAI score (i.e., the *standardized test score*), were also gathered.

EXHIBIT A.2.1
RESULTS OF THE BUYWISE PILOT TEST

ATTRIBUTE	MANAGEMENT ABILITY INDICATOR	INCENTIVE COMPENSATION PROGRAM	MANAGEMENT TRAINING PROGRAM
Observed effect size (*d*) or validity (r_{xy})	$r = .40$	$d = .80$	$d = .70$
Reliability of performance criterion (r_{yy})	.90	.90	.90
Cost per employee (*C*)	$25.00	$500.00	$300.00
Number of employees involved in program per year (*N*)	50 new store managers	500 store managers	200 store managers
Average annual salary of employees in program	$35,000.00 (new)	$45,000.00 (all)	$45,000.00 (all)
Length of effect/average tenure (*T*)	3 years (tenure)	4 years (length of effect)	4 years (length of effect)
Corporate interest rate (cost of capital) (*R*)	0.25	0.25	0.25
Average standardized test score (*Z*)	1.40	N/A	N/A

FORM A.2.1

Name_____ Group_____

1. What is the true effect size or validity for each of the three programs (since you know that the criterion measure is not perfectly reliable)? Explain the meaning of these results.

2. Since you have no empirical evidence of either the average dollar value of job performance of a store manager in BuyWise or the standard deviation of job performance (SD_y) in dollar terms, you need to make an estimate. You know this estimate is important to determine the utility of the programs. Based on the data in Exhibit A.2.1 and research knowledge to date, what is your best estimate of SD_y for the three programs? Explain what this figure represents.

3. What are the minimum required benefits during the length of time each program has an effect (or during the average tenure on the job for the MAI)?

FORM A.2.1 *(Continued)*

4. Given that you now know the minimum utility needed for each of the programs to be beneficial or cost-effective, compute the expected actual payoff or utility of each of the three programs. Refer to Exhibit A.2.1 for the values, except for true r_{xy} and true d, which you computed in question 1, and SD_y, which you computed in question 2.

5. Based on the results, which of the three programs would you recommend to Pat Williams and the board of directors? Why? Would you recommend more than one program? Justify your answer.

6. What additional information (if available) would you want to help you in further defending or justifying selection of one of these programs? Consider additional practical, legal, or financial issues.

ASSESSMENT GUIDELINES AND ASSESSMENT FORMS FOR SELF, PEER, AND DESIGNATED ASSESSORS

Appendix B presents the material necessary for assessments of your performance in the individual and group exercises. Your instructor has elected to use either (1) the "certified assessor" approach, in which certain students are designated to serve as assessors for specific exercises, or (2) the self/peer assessments, which are completed by group members at the conclusion of an exercise.

The "certification" process usually entails the designated assessors' being examined on the written responses to the exercise prior to the day on which the exercise is to be done in class. Assessors should receive specific feedback on their written responses and have a clear understanding of appropriate responses to the exercises.

Your instructor may elect to use the self/peer approach to assessment in addition to or as an alternative to the "certified assessor" approach. Regardless of the approach your instructor uses, students should get familiar with the competencies which are identified and defined in Exhibit B.1.1. Research has identified these competencies as critical for success in management. The exercises in this book are designed to enhance these competencies as you learn, integrate, and apply the HRM content of each chapter.

ASSESSMENT BY A DESIGNATED ASSESSOR

Prior to Observation

1. Review the materials of the assigned chapter and the exercise to which you are assigned. Complete the exercise and make sure your responses are reviewed by the instructor prior to class.
2. Ten critical competencies are listed below, and their definitions are given in Exhibit B.1.1. Study the definitions of the relevant competencies before you begin your observation or make any assessments. The 10 critical competencies are:
   a. Analytical thinking
   b. Behavioral flexibility
   c. Decision making
   d. Leadership
   e. Oral communication; presentation
   f. Perception of threshold cues
   g. Personal impact
   h. Planning and organizing
   i. Self-objectivity
   j. Written communication

Observation

3. After you are assigned to a group in class, review the exercise and the competencies. Before discussion begins, take a seat outside the circle of participants and do not discuss the exercise with group members. (You are strictly an observer/assessor.) Before discussion, quickly review each group member's individual exercise response. Make a note of the name of any member who has not prepared a written response. Return the exercises to the members.
4. Once discussion begins, observe the behavior of each discussant, keeping the competencies in mind as a frame of reference.
5. Record your observations on a plain sheet of paper, being careful to note who said what during discussion. Avoid any kind of evaluation at this point. (Do not use a complete-sentence format.) Be as precise and complete as possible in recording your observations. Do not try to translate your observations into competencies until the observation period is over. Your attention should only be directed toward making accurate observations and keeping good notes.
6. At the conclusion of the discussion, collect all written responses. *As soon after class as possible,* review your observation notes, assign a positive or negative (+ or −) value to each observation, and determine what competency each observation illustrates. Next to each observation, enter the letter of the relevant competency next to the + or − value.
7. Carefully review and critique each member's written responses, noting *and correcting* any misspellings, poor grammar, incomprehensible sentences, etc.

Rating on Competencies

8. Enter your name ("Observer"), the participant's name, and the exercise number in the spaces provided on the Self/Peer Assessment form. Review the written responses from each participant and your notes on the discussion, paying careful attention to your classification of each of the observations into the competencies and the positive or negative value you assigned to each observation. Also, keep in mind that the way in which the participant completed the written portion of the assignment applies to other competencies in addition to "Written Communication." For example, the written part of the exercise often reflects outstanding or unsatisfactory "Analytic Thinking" or "Decision Making." Make sure you consider the written response of each participant along with his or her group performance. Make a rating of each participant on one competency. For example, start with "Analytic Thinking" and rate each participant on this competency. Then move on to the next competency. Use the rating scale presented below to make your assessments.

Overall Assessment

9. After making your assessments on all relevant competencies, make a summary rating of the level of effectiveness of each participant in the completion of the exercise. Include in this assessment your overall evaluation of the participant's written response and contribution to the group.

Feedback

10. After rating all participants on all relevant competencies and the summary rating, use the reverse side of the form to summarize your observations and assessments for feedback to each participant. The feedback should be constructive and should ideally include both positive and negative comments. Focus on the way in which each student completed the written response and participated in the group analysis. Concentrate your feedback more on the way the exercise was completed and the way in which the student participated than on specific comments about the correctness of the answer (the instructor will provide this information to the whole class).

Rating Scale

Use the following rating scale to make your assessments:

    7 = Outstanding
    6 = Very good
    5 = Above average
    4 = Satisfactory
    3 = Below satisfactory
    2 = Well below satisfactory
    1 = Poor
    NO = Not observed

A very small percentage of students should be rated 7. This rating is reserved for only the very best performance for a competency. Most ratings should be at or near the 4 level. Usually, however, when you are observing a group of about six people, close to the full range of performance levels should be observed and therefore rated. Be sure to rate all participants on one competency and then proceed to the next competency.

What if a Group Member Doesn't Participate?

How do you rate someone who says virtually nothing during the group discussion? The answer to this question depends on the particular competency. Inactivity in the group would constitute a *low score* for the following competencies: behavioral flexibility, leadership, and planning and organizing. Inactivity would probably require a rating of "NO" (Not observed) for the other competencies. Failure to do the written part of an assignment should be rated a "1" poor.

AFTER COMPLETING STEPS 1–10, TURN IN *ALL MATERIALS* (INCLUDING OBSERVATION NOTES) TO THE INSTRUCTOR.

SELF-ASSESSMENT WITH DESIGNATED ASSESSORS

Students who participated in a group exercise which was observed by a "certified assessor" should do a self-assessment of his or her performance on the competencies. Self-assessments should be made *before receiving* assessment results and feedback from the assessor. After reviewing the competencies, record your self-assessments in the assessment log and enter the exercise number in Appendix C. Make ratings as instructed.

SELF/PEER ASSESSMENT

If you are asked to make a self/peer assessment of the group performance, review the competencies and take notes as you review each group member's written response. As soon as possible after group discussion, make assessments of yourself and each group member on a separate self/peer assessment form and provide feedback for peers on the reverse side. Follow the procedure described above using the same scale for rating.

ASSESSMENT LOG

Students should maintain an assessment log (Appendix C, Exhibits C.1.1 and C.1.2) made up of self-assessments and peer and/or assessor ratings. Enter your self-assessments in the Student Assessment Log (C.1.1). If you get feedback from peers or more than one designated assessor on an exercise, derive an average rating for each competency and enter the averages in C.1.2. Make certain self-assessments are completed on an exercise prior to receiving feedback on that exercise from assessors or peers. Logs are provided for ratings in Appendix C. If peer assessments are made, self-assessments should be made on a Self/Peer Assessment form and then entered in the log. If designated assessors are used, self-assessments should be made directly in the log (C.1.1, page 709).

1. **Analytic thinking:** Identifying the fundamental ideas, concepts, themes, or issues that help to integrate, interpret, and/or explain underlying patterns in a set of information or data.

    Did the student apply the appropriate material from the book or class discussion in order to solve the problem? Did he or she consider both sides of the issue in reaching a solution? Was the appropriate case or study cited? Did he or she correctly perceive the relative importance of the information being considered?

2. **Behavioral flexibility:** Modifying behavior to reach a goal; adapting one's behavior to respond functionally to changes in the situation or environment.

    Did the student bend on an issue in group discussion after it was clear that her or his position was not convincing? Did the student assist in getting the group to a consensus position or was the student adamant about a position without justifying it? Were different strategies attempted to reach consensus? Did the student attempt to integrate the opinions of others? Did she or he remain calm when others disagreed?

3. **Decision making:** Choosing among alternative courses of action that are based on logical assumptions and available factual information. This includes a basic willingness to form judgments, make decisions, take action, and/or commit oneself in complex situations.

    Did the student arrive at the appropriate solution to the problem? Was he or she willing to take a stand on a controversial issue? Did he or she understand and consider the ramifications of the decision? Did the student present logical, data-based positions? Was he or she willing to take a stand?

4. **Leadership:** Utilization of appropriate interpersonal styles to stimulate and guide individuals or groups toward goal and/or task accomplishment.

    Did the student help to structure the assignment to assist in reaching consensus in the time allotted? Did the student attempt to get all group members involved? Did the student listen carefully to the opinions of others?

5. **Oral communication; presentation:** Effective expression of ideas or viewpoints to others in individual or group situations (includes gestures, nonverbal communications, and the use of visual aids).

    Did the student speak concisely (to the point) and stick to the problem? Were there any nervous habits such as "ahs" or "you knows"? Did other group members seem to grasp what the student was saying? Were distracting mannerisms avoided, such as finger pointing or pencil tapping? Did the student speak to the whole group or just one or two people? Was the appropriate language used with no slang, etc.? Was the appropriate eye contact used?

6. **Perception of threshold cues:** Perception of minimal cues in the behavior of others, which includes social sensitivity, sensing reactions of others, and ability to read nonverbal cues.

    Did the student deal with sensitive information in a diplomatic manner? Did the student follow up on non-verbal cues which seemed to indicate disagreement? Did the student recognize key points by others?

7. **Personal impact:** Creating and commanding a good early impression, commanding attention and respect, and showing an air of confidence through verbal and nonverbal presentation.

    Did the student get the group off to a strong start by suggesting strategies in a manner that showed confidence? Was his or her presentation convincing?

8. **Planning and organizing:** Establishing a course of action to enable self and/or others to accomplish specific goals; planning proper assignments of personnel and appropriate allocations of resources.

    Was the student instrumental in defining the problem and the strategy for reaching consensus? Did she or he help to clarify the goals of the presentation and/or the group report? Was the student instrumental in getting the assignment done on time?

9. **Self-objectivity:** Realistic evaluation of one's own assets and liabilities; this includes insight into personal motives, skills, and abilities as applied to the job or task.

    Did the student have a clear understanding of the extent to which he or she had based a position on knowledge, research, logic, etc?

10. **Written communication:** Clear, appropriate, and grammatical expression of ideas in writing.

    Did the student use the appropriate grammar, sentence structure, and spelling? Did she or he write clearly, concisely, and legibly? Was the appropriate vocabulary used? Was slang avoided?

Source: Adapted from a study by the American Assembly of Collegiate Schools of Business, 1985.

SELF/PEER ASSESSMENT FORM

Directions: First, *rate* each individual using the scale (1 = poor, 2 = well below satisfactory, 3 = below satisfactory, 4 = satisfactory, 5 = above average, 6 = very good, 7 = outstanding; NO = not observed).

	Analytic Thinking	Behavioral Flexibility	Decision Making	Leadership	Oral Communication; Presentation	Perception of Threshold Cues	Personal Impact	Planning and Organizing	Self-Objectivity	Written Communication	Overall Assessment
Observer _____ Participant _____ Exercise Number _____											
Observer _____ Participant _____ Exercise Number _____											
Observer _____ Participant _____ Exercise Number _____											
Observer _____ Participant _____ Exercise Number _____											
Observer _____ Participant _____ Exercise Number _____											
Observer _____ Participant _____ Exercise Number _____											

ASSESSOR'S NAME _____

ASSESSEE'S NAME _____

ASSESSOR'S NAME _____

ASSESSEE'S NAME _____

ASSESSOR'S NAME _____

ASSESSEE'S NAME _____

ASSESSOR'S NAME _____

ASSESSEE'S NAME _____

ASSESSOR'S NAME _____

ASSESSEE'S NAME _____

ASSESSOR'S NAME _____

ASSESSEE'S NAME _____

SELF/PEER ASSESSMENT FORM

Directions: First, *rate* each individual using the scale (1 = poor, 2 = well below satisfactory, 3 = below satisfactory, 4 = satisfactory, 5 = above average, 6 = very good, 7 = outstanding; NO = not observed).

	Analytic Thinking	Behavioral Flexibility	Decision Making	Leadership	Oral Communication; Presentation	Perception of Threshold Cues	Personal Impact	Planning and Organizing	Self-Objectivity	Written Communication	Overall Assessment
Observer											
Participant											
Exercise Number											
Observer											
Participant											
Exercise Number											
Observer											
Participant											
Exercise Number											
Observer											
Participant											
Exercise Number											
Observer											
Participant											
Exercise Number											
Observer											
Participant											
Exercise Number											

ASSESSOR'S NAME _____

ASSESSEE'S NAME _____

ASSESSOR'S NAME _____

ASSESSEE'S NAME _____

ASSESSOR'S NAME _____

ASSESSEE'S NAME _____

ASSESSOR'S NAME _____

ASSESSEE'S NAME _____

ASSESSOR'S NAME _____

ASSESSEE'S NAME _____

ASSESSOR'S NAME _____

ASSESSEE'S NAME _____

SELF/PEER ASSESSMENT FORM

Directions: First, *rate* each individual using the scale (1 = poor, 2 = well below satisfactory, 3 = below satisfactory, 4 = satisfactory, 5 = above average, 6 = very good, 7 = outstanding; NO = not observed).

	Analytic Thinking	Behavioral Flexibility	Decision Making	Leadership	Oral Communication; Presentation	Perception of Threshold Cues	Personal Impact	Planning and Organizing	Self-Objectivity	Written Communication	Overall Assessment
Observer											
Participant											
Exercise Number											
Observer											
Participant											
Exercise Number											
Observer											
Participant											
Exercise Number											
Observer											
Participant											
Exercise Number											
Observer											
Participant											
Exercise Number											
Observer											
Participant											
Exercise Number											

ASSESSOR'S NAME _____

ASSESSEE'S NAME _____

ASSESSOR'S NAME _____

ASSESSEE'S NAME _____

ASSESSOR'S NAME _____

ASSESSEE'S NAME _____

ASSESSOR'S NAME _____

ASSESSEE'S NAME _____

ASSESSOR'S NAME _____

ASSESSEE'S NAME _____

ASSESSOR'S NAME _____

ASSESSEE'S NAME _____

SELF/PEER ASSESSMENT FORM Directions: First, *rate* each individual using the scale (1 = poor, 2 = well below satisfactory, 3 = below satisfactory, 4 = satisfactory, 5 = above average, 6 = very good, 7 = outstanding; NO = not observed).

Observer / Participant / Exercise Number	Analytic Thinking	Behavioral Flexibility	Decision Making	Leadership	Oral Communication; Presentation	Perception of Threshold Cues	Personal Impact	Planning and Organizing	Self-Objectivity	Written Communication	Overall Assessment
Observer											
Participant											
Exercise Number											

Observer / Participant / Exercise Number	Analytic Thinking	Behavioral Flexibility	Decision Making	Leadership	Oral Communication; Presentation	Perception of Threshold Cues	Personal Impact	Planning and Organizing	Self-Objectivity	Written Communication	Overall Assessment
Observer											
Participant											
Exercise Number											

Observer / Participant / Exercise Number	Analytic Thinking	Behavioral Flexibility	Decision Making	Leadership	Oral Communication; Presentation	Perception of Threshold Cues	Personal Impact	Planning and Organizing	Self-Objectivity	Written Communication	Overall Assessment
Observer											
Participant											
Exercise Number											

Observer / Participant / Exercise Number	Analytic Thinking	Behavioral Flexibility	Decision Making	Leadership	Oral Communication; Presentation	Perception of Threshold Cues	Personal Impact	Planning and Organizing	Self-Objectivity	Written Communication	Overall Assessment
Observer											
Participant											
Exercise Number											

Observer / Participant / Exercise Number	Analytic Thinking	Behavioral Flexibility	Decision Making	Leadership	Oral Communication; Presentation	Perception of Threshold Cues	Personal Impact	Planning and Organizing	Self-Objectivity	Written Communication	Overall Assessment
Observer											
Participant											
Exercise Number											

Observer / Participant / Exercise Number	Analytic Thinking	Behavioral Flexibility	Decision Making	Leadership	Oral Communication; Presentation	Perception of Threshold Cues	Personal Impact	Planning and Organizing	Self-Objectivity	Written Communication	Overall Assessment
Observer											
Participant											
Exercise Number											

ASSESSOR'S NAME _____

ASSESSEE'S NAME _____

ASSESSOR'S NAME _____

ASSESSEE'S NAME _____

ASSESSOR'S NAME _____

ASSESSEE'S NAME _____

ASSESSOR'S NAME _____

ASSESSEE'S NAME _____

ASSESSOR'S NAME _____

ASSESSEE'S NAME _____

ASSESSOR'S NAME _____

ASSESSEE'S NAME _____

SELF/PEER ASSESSMENT FORM

Directions: First, *rate* each individual using the scale (1 = poor, 2 = well below satisfactory, 3 = below satisfactory, 4 = satisfactory, 5 = above average, 6 = very good, 7 = outstanding; NO = not observed).

	Analytic Thinking	Behavioral Flexibility	Decision Making	Leadership	Oral Communication; Presentation	Perception of Threshold Cues	Personal Impact	Planning and Organizing	Self-Objectivity	Written Communication	Overall Assessment
Observer											
Participant											
Exercise Number											

	Analytic Thinking	Behavioral Flexibility	Decision Making	Leadership	Oral Communication; Presentation	Perception of Threshold Cues	Personal Impact	Planning and Organizing	Self-Objectivity	Written Communication	Overall Assessment
Observer											
Participant											
Exercise Number											

	Analytic Thinking	Behavioral Flexibility	Decision Making	Leadership	Oral Communication; Presentation	Perception of Threshold Cues	Personal Impact	Planning and Organizing	Self-Objectivity	Written Communication	Overall Assessment
Observer											
Participant											
Exercise Number											

	Analytic Thinking	Behavioral Flexibility	Decision Making	Leadership	Oral Communication; Presentation	Perception of Threshold Cues	Personal Impact	Planning and Organizing	Self-Objectivity	Written Communication	Overall Assessment
Observer											
Participant											
Exercise Number											

	Analytic Thinking	Behavioral Flexibility	Decision Making	Leadership	Oral Communication; Presentation	Perception of Threshold Cues	Personal Impact	Planning and Organizing	Self-Objectivity	Written Communication	Overall Assessment
Observer											
Participant											
Exercise Number											

	Analytic Thinking	Behavioral Flexibility	Decision Making	Leadership	Oral Communication; Presentation	Perception of Threshold Cues	Personal Impact	Planning and Organizing	Self-Objectivity	Written Communication	Overall Assessment
Observer											
Participant											
Exercise Number											

ASSESSOR'S NAME _____

ASSESSEE'S NAME _____

ASSESSOR'S NAME _____

ASSESSEE'S NAME _____

ASSESSOR'S NAME _____

ASSESSEE'S NAME _____

ASSESSOR'S NAME _____

ASSESSEE'S NAME _____

ASSESSOR'S NAME _____

ASSESSEE'S NAME _____

ASSESSOR'S NAME _____

ASSESSEE'S NAME _____

SELF/PEER ASSESSMENT FORM

Directions: First, *rate* each individual using the scale (1 = poor, 2 = well below satisfactory, 3 = below satisfactory, 4 = satisfactory, 5 = above average, 6 = very good, 7 = outstanding; NO = not observed).

	Analytic Thinking	Behavioral Flexibility	Decision Making	Leadership	Oral Communication; Presentation	Perception of Threshold Cues	Personal Impact	Planning and Organizing	Self-Objectivity	Written Communication	Overall Assessment
Observer											
Participant											
Exercise Number											
Observer											
Participant											
Exercise Number											
Observer											
Participant											
Exercise Number											
Observer											
Participant											
Exercise Number											
Observer											
Participant											
Exercise Number											
Observer											
Participant											
Exercise Number											

ASSESSOR'S NAME _____

ASSESSEE'S NAME _____

ASSESSOR'S NAME _____

ASSESSEE'S NAME _____

ASSESSOR'S NAME _____

ASSESSEE'S NAME _____

ASSESSOR'S NAME _____

ASSESSEE'S NAME _____

ASSESSOR'S NAME _____

ASSESSEE'S NAME _____

ASSESSOR'S NAME _____

ASSESSEE'S NAME _____

SELF/PEER ASSESSMENT FORM

Directions: First, *rate* each individual using the scale (1 = poor, 2 = well below satisfactory, 3 = below satisfactory, 4 = satisfactory, 5 = above average, 6 = very good, 7 = outstanding; NO = not observed).

	Analytic Thinking	Behavioral Flexibility	Decision Making	Leadership	Oral Communication; Presentation	Perception of Threshold Cues	Personal Impact	Planning and Organizing	Self-Objectivity	Written Communication	Overall Assessment
Observer											
Participant											
Exercise Number											
Observer											
Participant											
Exercise Number											
Observer											
Participant											
Exercise Number											
Observer											
Participant											
Exercise Number											
Observer											
Participant											
Exercise Number											
Observer											
Participant											
Exercise Number											

ASSESSOR'S NAME _____

ASSESSEE'S NAME _____

ASSESSOR'S NAME _____

ASSESSEE'S NAME _____

ASSESSOR'S NAME _____

ASSESSEE'S NAME _____

ASSESSOR'S NAME _____

ASSESSEE'S NAME _____

ASSESSOR'S NAME _____

ASSESSEE'S NAME _____

ASSESSOR'S NAME _____

ASSESSEE'S NAME _____

SELF/PEER ASSESSMENT FORM

Directions: First, *rate* each individual using the scale (1 = poor, 2 = well below satisfactory, 3 = below satisfactory, 4 = satisfactory, 5 = above average, 6 = very good, 7 = outstanding; NO = not observed).

(Block 1)

Observer _____
Participant _____
Exercise Number _____

Analytic Thinking	Behavioral Flexibility	Decision Making	Leadership	Oral Communication; Presentation	Perception of Threshold Cues	Personal Impact	Planning and Organizing	Self-Objectivity	Written Communication	Overall Assessment

(Block 2)

Observer _____
Participant _____
Exercise Number _____

Analytic Thinking	Behavioral Flexibility	Decision Making	Leadership	Oral Communication; Presentation	Perception of Threshold Cues	Personal Impact	Planning and Organizing	Self-Objectivity	Written Communication	Overall Assessment

(Block 3)

Observer _____
Participant _____
Exercise Number _____

Analytic Thinking	Behavioral Flexibility	Decision Making	Leadership	Oral Communication; Presentation	Perception of Threshold Cues	Personal Impact	Planning and Organizing	Self-Objectivity	Written Communication	Overall Assessment

(Block 4)

Observer _____
Participant _____
Exercise Number _____

Analytic Thinking	Behavioral Flexibility	Decision Making	Leadership	Oral Communication; Presentation	Perception of Threshold Cues	Personal Impact	Planning and Organizing	Self-Objectivity	Written Communication	Overall Assessment

(Block 5)

Observer _____
Participant _____
Exercise Number _____

Analytic Thinking	Behavioral Flexibility	Decision Making	Leadership	Oral Communication; Presentation	Perception of Threshold Cues	Personal Impact	Planning and Organizing	Self-Objectivity	Written Communication	Overall Assessment

(Block 6)

Observer _____
Participant _____
Exercise Number _____

Analytic Thinking	Behavioral Flexibility	Decision Making	Leadership	Oral Communication; Presentation	Perception of Threshold Cues	Personal Impact	Planning and Organizing	Self-Objectivity	Written Communication	Overall Assessment

ASSESSOR'S NAME _____

ASSESSEE'S NAME _____

ASSESSOR'S NAME _____

ASSESSEE'S NAME _____

ASSESSOR'S NAME _____

ASSESSEE'S NAME _____

ASSESSOR'S NAME _____

ASSESSEE'S NAME _____

ASSESSOR'S NAME _____

ASSESSEE'S NAME _____

ASSESSOR'S NAME _____

ASSESSEE'S NAME _____

SELF/PEER ASSESSMENT FORM

Directions: First, *rate* each individual using the scale (1 = poor, 2 = well below satisfactory, 3 = below satisfactory, 4 = satisfactory, 5 = above average, 6 = very good, 7 = outstanding; NO = not observed).

	Analytic Thinking	Behavioral Flexibility	Decision Making	Leadership	Oral Communication; Presentation	Perception of Threshold Cues	Personal Impact	Planning and Organizing	Self-Objectivity	Written Communication	Overall Assessment
Observer											
Participant											
Exercise Number											
Observer											
Participant											
Exercise Number											
Observer											
Participant											
Exercise Number											
Observer											
Participant											
Exercise Number											
Observer											
Participant											
Exercise Number											
Observer											
Participant											
Exercise Number											

ASSESSOR'S NAME

ASSESSOR'S NAME

ASSESSOR'S NAME

ASSESSOR'S NAME

ASSESSOR'S NAME

ASSESSOR'S NAME

ASSESSEE'S NAME

ASSESSEE'S NAME

ASSESSEE'S NAME

ASSESSEE'S NAME

ASSESSEE'S NAME

ASSESSEE'S NAME

SELF/PEER ASSESSMENT FORM

Directions: First, *rate* each individual using the scale (1 = poor, 2 = well below satisfactory, 3 = below satisfactory, 4 = satisfactory, 5 = above average, 6 = very good, 7 = outstanding; NO = not observed).

Observer	Analytic Thinking	Behavioral Flexibility	Decision Making	Leadership	Oral Communication; Presentation	Perception of Threshold Cues	Personal Impact	Planning and Organizing	Self-Objectivity	Written Communication	Overall Assessment
Participant											
Exercise Number											

Observer	Analytic Thinking	Behavioral Flexibility	Decision Making	Leadership	Oral Communication; Presentation	Perception of Threshold Cues	Personal Impact	Planning and Organizing	Self-Objectivity	Written Communication	Overall Assessment
Participant											
Exercise Number											

Observer	Analytic Thinking	Behavioral Flexibility	Decision Making	Leadership	Oral Communication; Presentation	Perception of Threshold Cues	Personal Impact	Planning and Organizing	Self-Objectivity	Written Communication	Overall Assessment
Participant											
Exercise Number											

Observer	Analytic Thinking	Behavioral Flexibility	Decision Making	Leadership	Oral Communication; Presentation	Perception of Threshold Cues	Personal Impact	Planning and Organizing	Self-Objectivity	Written Communication	Overall Assessment
Participant											
Exercise Number											

Observer	Analytic Thinking	Behavioral Flexibility	Decision Making	Leadership	Oral Communication; Presentation	Perception of Threshold Cues	Personal Impact	Planning and Organizing	Self-Objectivity	Written Communication	Overall Assessment
Participant											
Exercise Number											

Observer	Analytic Thinking	Behavioral Flexibility	Decision Making	Leadership	Oral Communication; Presentation	Perception of Threshold Cues	Personal Impact	Planning and Organizing	Self-Objectivity	Written Communication	Overall Assessment
Participant											
Exercise Number											

ASSESSOR'S NAME _____

ASSESSEE'S NAME _____

ASSESSOR'S NAME _____

ASSESSEE'S NAME _____

ASSESSOR'S NAME _____

ASSESSEE'S NAME _____

ASSESSOR'S NAME _____

ASSESSEE'S NAME _____

ASSESSOR'S NAME _____

ASSESSEE'S NAME _____

ASSESSOR'S NAME _____

ASSESSEE'S NAME _____

SELF/PEER ASSESSMENT FORM

Directions: First, *rate* each individual using the scale (1 = poor, 2 = well below satisfactory, 3 = below satisfactory, 4 = satisfactory, 5 = above average, 6 = very good, 7 = outstanding; NO = not observed).

	Analytic Thinking	Behavioral Flexibility	Decision Making	Leadership	Oral Commu- nication; Presentation	Perception of Threshold Cues	Personal Impact	Planning and Organizing	Self- Objectivty	Written Communication	Overall Assessment
Observer											
Participant											
Exercise Number											
Observer											
Participant											
Exercise Number											
Observer											
Participant											
Exercise Number											
Observer											
Participant											
Exercise Number											
Observer											
Participant											
Exercise Number											
Observer											
Participant											
Exercise Number											

ASSESSOR'S NAME _____

ASSESSOR'S NAME _____

ASSESSOR'S NAME _____

ASSESSOR'S NAME _____

ASSESSOR'S NAME _____

ASSESSOR'S NAME _____

ASSESSEE'S NAME _____

ASSESSEE'S NAME _____

ASSESSEE'S NAME _____

ASSESSEE'S NAME _____

ASSESSEE'S NAME _____

ASSESSEE'S NAME _____

SELF/PEER ASSESSMENT FORM

Directions: First, *rate* each individual using the scale (1 = poor, 2 = well below satisfactory, 3 = below satisfactory, 4 = satisfactory, 5 = above average, 6 = very good, 7 = outstanding; NO = not observed).

	Analytic Thinking	Behavioral Flexibility	Decision Making	Leadership	Oral Communication; Presentation	Perception of Threshold Cues	Personal Impact	Planning and Organizing	Self-Objectivity	Written Communication	Overall Assessment
Observer											
Participant											
Exercise Number											
Observer											
Participant											
Exercise Number											
Observer											
Participant											
Exercise Number											
Observer											
Participant											
Exercise Number											
Observer											
Participant											
Exercise Number											
Observer											
Participant											
Exercise Number											

ASSESSOR'S NAME _____

ASSESSEE'S NAME _____

ASSESSOR'S NAME _____

ASSESSEE'S NAME _____

ASSESSOR'S NAME _____

ASSESSEE'S NAME _____

ASSESSOR'S NAME _____

ASSESSEE'S NAME _____

ASSESSOR'S NAME _____

ASSESSEE'S NAME _____

ASSESSOR'S NAME _____

ASSESSEE'S NAME _____

SELF/PEER ASSESSMENT FORM

Directions: First, *rate* each individual using the scale (1 = poor, 2 = well below satisfactory, 3 = below satisfactory, 4 = satisfactory, 5 = above average, 6 = very good, 7 = outstanding; NO = not observed).

Block 1

	Analytic Thinking	Behavioral Flexibility	Decision Making	Leadership	Oral Communication; Presentation	Perception of Threshold Cues	Personal Impact	Planning and Organizing	Self-Objectivity	Written Communication	Overall Assessment
Observer											
Participant											
Exercise Number											

Block 2

	Analytic Thinking	Behavioral Flexibility	Decision Making	Leadership	Oral Communication; Presentation	Perception of Threshold Cues	Personal Impact	Planning and Organizing	Self-Objectivity	Written Communication	Overall Assessment
Observer											
Participant											
Exercise Number											

Block 3

	Analytic Thinking	Behavioral Flexibility	Decision Making	Leadership	Oral Communication; Presentation	Perception of Threshold Cues	Personal Impact	Planning and Organizing	Self-Objectivity	Written Communication	Overall Assessment
Observer											
Participant											
Exercise Number											

Block 4

	Analytic Thinking	Behavioral Flexibility	Decision Making	Leadership	Oral Communication; Presentation	Perception of Threshold Cues	Personal Impact	Planning and Organizing	Self-Objectivity	Written Communication	Overall Assessment
Observer											
Participant											
Exercise Number											

Block 5

	Analytic Thinking	Behavioral Flexibility	Decision Making	Leadership	Oral Communication; Presentation	Perception of Threshold Cues	Personal Impact	Planning and Organizing	Self-Objectivity	Written Communication	Overall Assessment
Observer											
Participant											
Exercise Number											

Block 6

	Analytic Thinking	Behavioral Flexibility	Decision Making	Leadership	Oral Communication; Presentation	Perception of Threshold Cues	Personal Impact	Planning and Organizing	Self-Objectivity	Written Communication	Overall Assessment
Observer											
Participant											
Exercise Number											

ASSESSOR'S NAME _____

ASSESSEE'S NAME _____

ASSESSOR'S NAME _____

ASSESSEE'S NAME _____

ASSESSOR'S NAME _____

ASSESSEE'S NAME _____

ASSESSOR'S NAME _____

ASSESSEE'S NAME _____

ASSESSOR'S NAME _____

ASSESSEE'S NAME _____

ASSESSOR'S NAME _____

ASSESSEE'S NAME _____

SELF/PEER ASSESSMENT FORM

Directions: First, *rate* each individual using the scale (1 = poor, 2 = well below satisfactory, 3 = below satisfactory, 4 = satisfactory, 5 = above average, 6 = very good, 7 = outstanding; NO = not observed).

	Analytic Thinking	Behavioral Flexibility	Decision Making	Leadership	Oral Communication; Presentation	Perception of Threshold Cues	Personal Impact	Planning and Organizing	Self-Objectivity	Written Communication	Overall Assessment
Observer											
Participant											
Exercise Number											

	Analytic Thinking	Behavioral Flexibility	Decision Making	Leadership	Oral Communication; Presentation	Perception of Threshold Cues	Personal Impact	Planning and Organizing	Self-Objectivity	Written Communication	Overall Assessment
Observer											
Participant											
Exercise Number											

	Analytic Thinking	Behavioral Flexibility	Decision Making	Leadership	Oral Communication; Presentation	Perception of Threshold Cues	Personal Impact	Planning and Organizing	Self-Objectivity	Written Communication	Overall Assessment
Observer											
Participant											
Exercise Number											

	Analytic Thinking	Behavioral Flexibility	Decision Making	Leadership	Oral Communication; Presentation	Perception of Threshold Cues	Personal Impact	Planning and Organizing	Self-Objectivity	Written Communication	Overall Assessment
Observer											
Participant											
Exercise Number											

	Analytic Thinking	Behavioral Flexibility	Decision Making	Leadership	Oral Communication; Presentation	Perception of Threshold Cues	Personal Impact	Planning and Organizing	Self-Objectivity	Written Communication	Overall Assessment
Observer											
Participant											
Exercise Number											

	Analytic Thinking	Behavioral Flexibility	Decision Making	Leadership	Oral Communication; Presentation	Perception of Threshold Cues	Personal Impact	Planning and Organizing	Self-Objectivity	Written Communication	Overall Assessment
Observer											
Participant											
Exercise Number											

ASSESSOR'S NAME _____

ASSESSEE'S NAME _____

ASSESSOR'S NAME _____

ASSESSEE'S NAME _____

ASSESSOR'S NAME _____

ASSESSEE'S NAME _____

ASSESSOR'S NAME _____

ASSESSEE'S NAME _____

ASSESSOR'S NAME _____

ASSESSEE'S NAME _____

ASSESSOR'S NAME _____

ASSESSEE'S NAME _____

SELF/PEER ASSESSMENT FORM Directions: First, *rate* each individual using the scale (1 = poor, 2 = well below satisfactory, 3 = below satisfactory, 4 = satisfactory, 5 = above average, 6 = very good, 7 = outstanding; NO = not observed).

Observer / Participant / Exercise Number	Analytic Thinking	Behavioral Flexibility	Decision Making	Leadership	Oral Communication; Presentation	Perception of Threshold Cues	Personal Impact	Planning and Organizing	Self-Objectivity	Written Communication	Overall Assessment
Observer											
Participant											
Exercise Number											

Observer / Participant / Exercise Number	Analytic Thinking	Behavioral Flexibility	Decision Making	Leadership	Oral Communication; Presentation	Perception of Threshold Cues	Personal Impact	Planning and Organizing	Self-Objectivity	Written Communication	Overall Assessment
Observer											
Participant											
Exercise Number											

Observer / Participant / Exercise Number	Analytic Thinking	Behavioral Flexibility	Decision Making	Leadership	Oral Communication; Presentation	Perception of Threshold Cues	Personal Impact	Planning and Organizing	Self-Objectivity	Written Communication	Overall Assessment
Observer											
Participant											
Exercise Number											

Observer / Participant / Exercise Number	Analytic Thinking	Behavioral Flexibility	Decision Making	Leadership	Oral Communication; Presentation	Perception of Threshold Cues	Personal Impact	Planning and Organizing	Self-Objectivity	Written Communication	Overall Assessment
Observer											
Participant											
Exercise Number											

Observer / Participant / Exercise Number	Analytic Thinking	Behavioral Flexibility	Decision Making	Leadership	Oral Communication; Presentation	Perception of Threshold Cues	Personal Impact	Planning and Organizing	Self-Objectivity	Written Communication	Overall Assessment
Observer											
Participant											
Exercise Number											

Observer / Participant / Exercise Number	Analytic Thinking	Behavioral Flexibility	Decision Making	Leadership	Oral Communication; Presentation	Perception of Threshold Cues	Personal Impact	Planning and Organizing	Self-Objectivity	Written Communication	Overall Assessment
Observer											
Participant											
Exercise Number											

ASSESSOR'S NAME _____

ASSESSOR'S NAME _____

ASSESSOR'S NAME _____

ASSESSOR'S NAME _____

ASSESSOR'S NAME _____

ASSESSOR'S NAME _____

ASSESSEE'S NAME _____

ASSESSEE'S NAME _____

ASSESSEE'S NAME _____

ASSESSEE'S NAME _____

ASSESSEE'S NAME _____

ASSESSEE'S NAME _____

A P P E N D I X

STUDENT
ASSESSMENT LOG

Each student should maintain a log of his or her assessments. Forms are provided for ratings by the assessors or peers and your own self-assessments. Entries should be made in chronological order so that performance trends can be evaluated. Space is also provided for deriving an average. Make sure self-ratings are made *before* you receive ratings from peers or assessors. If you received peer assessments on an exercise, calculate and enter the average rating in the appropriate assessment log. Competencies which are rated as "no" should *not* be included in deriving the average.

EXHIBIT C.1.1

STUDENT SELF-ASSESSMENT LOG—RATINGS

NAME _____

Exer. #	Analytical Thinking	Behavioral Flexibility	Decision Making	Leadership	Oral Communication; Presentation	Perception of Threshold Cues	Personal Impact	Planning & Organizing	Self-Objectivity	Written Communication	Overall Assessment
AVERAGE											

Use the following rating scale to make your self-assessment: 7 = outstanding; 6 = very good; 5 = above average; 4 = satisfactory; 3 = below satisfactory; 2 = well below satisfactory; 1 = poor.

EXHIBIT C.1.2

STUDENT ASSESSMENT LOG—RATINGS BY PEERS/ASSESSORS

NAME _____

Exer. #	Analytical Thinking	Behavioral Flexibility	Decision Making	Leadership	Oral Communication; Presentation	Perception of Threshold Cues	Personal Impact	Planning & Organizing	Self-Objectivity	Written Communication	Overall Assessment
AVERAGE											

INDEX

Dougherty, T.W., 359
Douglas, J. A., 233
Doverspike, D., 457
Dowd, J. J., 361
Dowling, P. J., 190, 235, 323, 459, 588, 614
Dreher, G. F., 359, 458
Driver, M. J., 359, 362
Drucker, P., 8, 16, 459, 614
Dudding, R. C., 188
Dufetel, L., 457
Dumas, R. A., 547
Dunbar, R., 642
Duncan, K. D., 547
Dunette, M. D., 131, 234
Dunham, R. B., 458, 643
Dunlop, J. T., 588
Dunnette, M. D., 189, 322, 456, 663
Durand, D., 642
Dusky, L., 362, 546
Dutton, P., 301, 321
Dworkin, J. B., 588
Dyer, L, 43, 187, 188
D'Aunno, T., 188

Earley, P. C., 228, 403
Eaton, N. K., 234
Eaton, R., 186
Edelstein, C. M., 493
Eder, R. W., 274, 275
Edwards, M. R., 403
Eisenhardt, K. M., 457
Ekeberg, S. E., 493
Elcheikh, N., 457
Elkiss, H., 642
Elliott, R. H., 642
Ellis, H. C., 322
Ellis, J., 545
Ellis, R. A., 457
Embley, K., 402
Endicott, F. S., 189
Erfurt, A. E., 643
Erfurt, J. C., 643
Erwin, F. W., 234
Ettlie, J. E., 188

Facteau, J. D., 404
Faley, R. H., 234
Farh, J., 403, 492
Farr, J., 402, 403
Farrell, C., 493
Farren, C., 346, 348, 359, 360, 362
Faux, V. A., 360
Fay, C. H., 458
Fear, R. D., 275
Feared, J., 587, 588
Feild, H. S., Jr., 189, 233, 663
Feimer, N., 233
Fein, M., 493
Feld, D. E., 233
Feldman, D. C., 322, 343, 359–362

Feldman, J. M., 402
Feldt, L. S., 663
Fenton, J.W., 234
Fenwick-Magrath, J. A., 361
Feren, D. B., 547
Ferman, L. A., 587
Fernandez, J. P., 546
Ferris, G., 16, 81, 132, 188, 235, 274, 275, 323, 546, 663
Fcuer, D., 642
Fielder, B. L., 458
Fine, S. A., 126, 132
Finney, M. I., 3, 16
Fiol, C. M., 43
Fiorito, J., 587
Fisher, C. D., 322, 404, 546, 547, 613
Fisher, T. D., 360
Fiske, C., 16
Fiske, D. W., 403
Fiske, E. B., 321
Fiske, S. T., 403
Fitzgerald, L. F., 234, 359, 546
Flanagan, J. C., 132
Flax, S., 614
Fleishman, E. A., 233, 663
Fletcher, W. L., 360
Florkowski, G. W., 493
Fogli, L., 402
Folger, R., 457, 492
Fombrun, C., 187, 359, 401
Foote, A., 643
Forker, L. B., 545
Formisano, R. A., 458
Forward, G. E., 321
Fossum, J. A., 588, 605
Fottler, M. D., 458
Fowler, E. M., 189
Fox, M. L., 642
Fox, S., 403
Francis, G. J., 188
Freedman, S. M., 16, 545
Freeman, R. B., 459, 587, 614
Freeman, S. J., 16, 176, 188
French, W., 323, 546
Freudenheim, M., 643
Fried, Y., 132, 545, 546
Friedman, L., 132
Friedman, S. D., 361
Fruhan, W., 614
Fuchsberg, G., 17
Fulmer, R. M., 323
Fusilier, M. R., 642

Gabor, A., 403
Gael, S., 114, 119, 120, 126, 131, 132
Gaertner, K. N., 361
Gaeta, E., 643
Gallagher, D. G., 587
Gannon, M. J., 188, 189
Ganster, D. C., 548, 642
Garcia, M. F., 274
Garvin, D. A., 545, 547

Gatewood, R. D., 233, 663
Gaugler, B. B., 234, 235
Gautschi, F. H., 642
Gehan, S., 614
Geidt, T., 234
Geis, A. A., 492
Gellerman, S. W., 404
Gerard, J., 613
Gerhard, B., 189
Gerhart, B., 275, 456–458
Gershenfeld, W. J., 587
Getman, J. G., 587
Gettings, L., 642
Ghiselli, E. E., 233, 663
Ghorpade, J.V., 402
Gibson, W. M., 663
Gier, J. A., 273
Gifford, C. D., 587
Giles, W. F., 189
Gilliam, P., 321
Ginter, P. M., 493
Gioia, D. A., 402
Gist, M. E., 322
Glaberson, W., 641
Glaser, R., 233
Gobeille, K. R., 588
Goddard, R.W., 16
Godkewitsch, M., 321
Goizueta, R., 420, 490
Gold, C., 588
Goldberg, R. T., 234
Goldberg, S. B., 587
Golden, K. A., 188
Goldstein, I. L., 320, 321, 323
Goldstein, M. A., 274
Goll, I., 588
Gomez-Mejia, L. R., 402, 456–458, 493
Gompers, S., 574, 587
Gonzalez, D., 613
Goodale, J. G., 16, 188, 359, 360
Gooding, G. J., 359
Goodman, P. S., 547
Goodson, J. R., 323, 493
Gordon, J., 298, 321, 322
Gottschalk, E. C., Jr., 360
Gould, R., 275
Graham-Moore, B., 493
Granrose, C. S., 359
Graves, L. M., 274
Gray, D. A., 321
Gray, G. R., 642
Grayson, C. J., 4, 6, 16
Green, B. F., 401, 663
Green, W., 642
Greenberger, D. B., 456, 492
Greenfeld, S., 640, 643
Greenhaus, J. H., 359–362, 546
Greenlaw, P. S., 188
Gregersen, H. B., 362
Grenig, J., 402
Grey, L., 643
Greyer, C. R., 587
Griffeth, R. W., 275
Griffin, R. W., 546
Griffith Hughson, T. L., 547

SUBJECT INDEX